PHILIP'S

WORLD ATLAS

TWELFTH EDITION

IN ASSOCIATION WITH

THE ROYAL GEOGRAPHICAL SOCIETY

WITH THE INSTITUTE OF BRITISH GEOGRAPHERS

Contents

World Statistics

The World in Focus

World Cities

World Maps

Europe

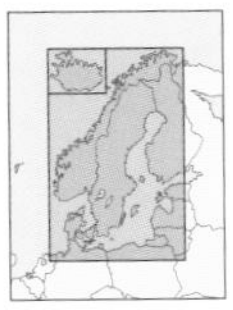

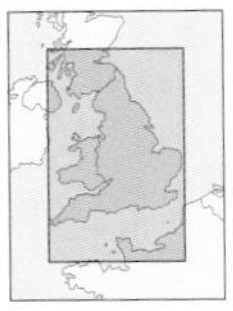

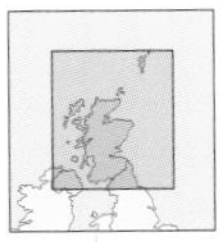

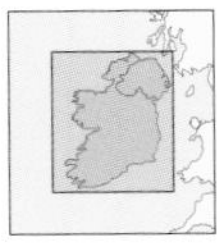

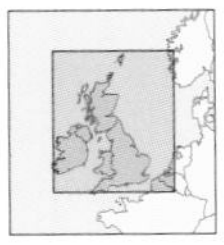

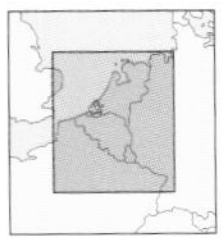

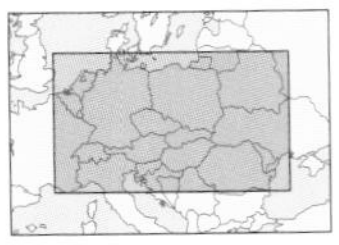

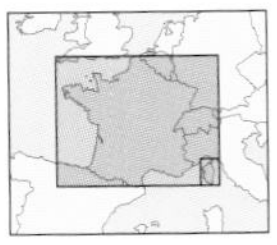

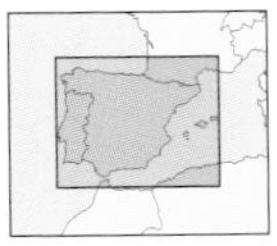

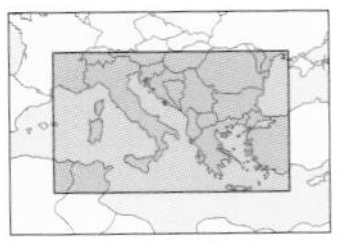

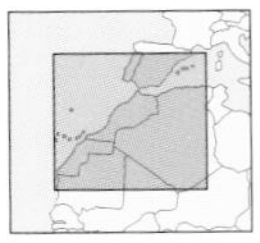

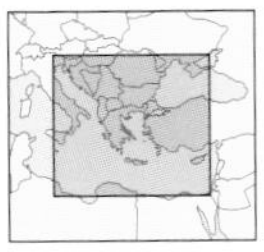

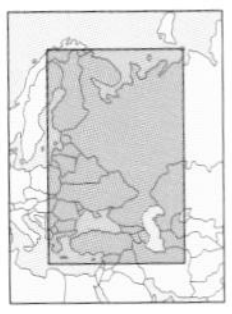

Asia

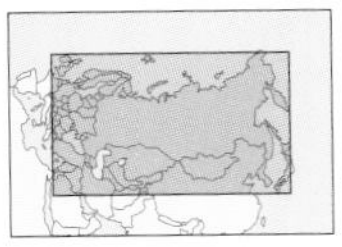

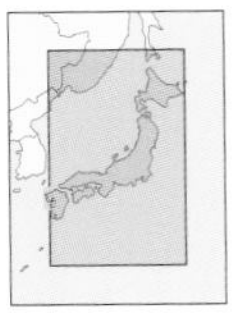

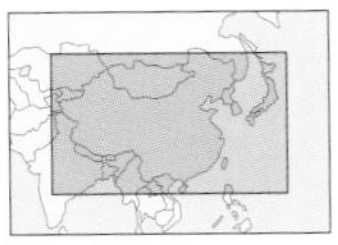

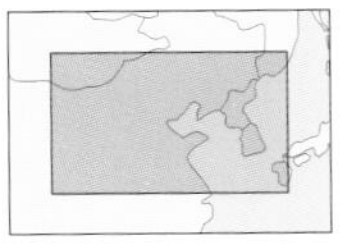

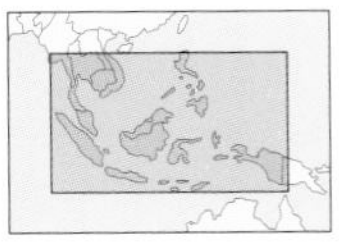

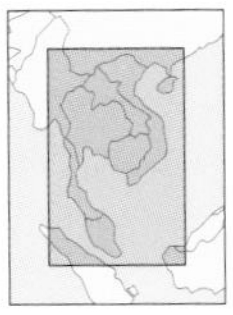

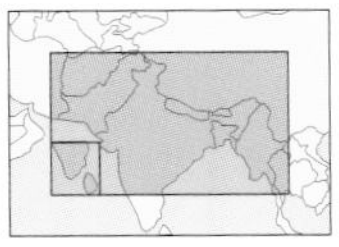

The Indo-Gangetic Plain
1:6 000 000

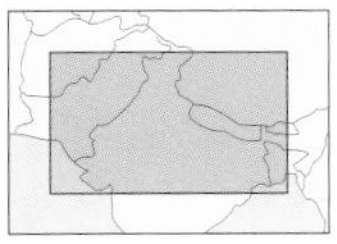

42–43

The Middle East
1:7 000 000

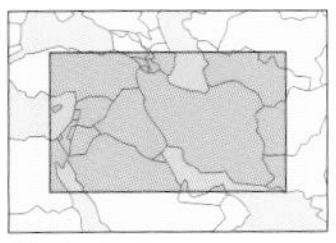

44–45

Arabia and the Horn of Africa 1:15 000 000

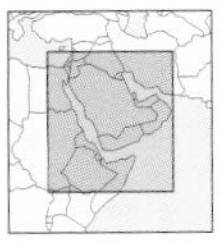

46

The Near East 1:2 500 000

47

Africa

Africa: Physical
1:42 000 000 48

Africa: Political
1:42 000 000 49

Northern Africa
1:15 000 000

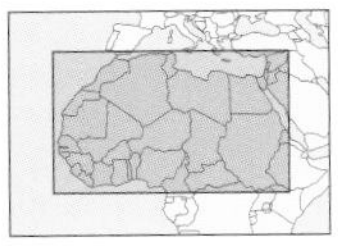

50–51

Central and Southern Africa
1:15 000 000

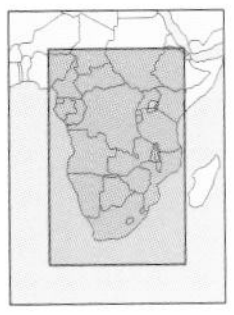

52–53

East Africa 1:8 000 000

54–55

Southern Africa
1:8 000 000
Madagascar 1:8 000 000

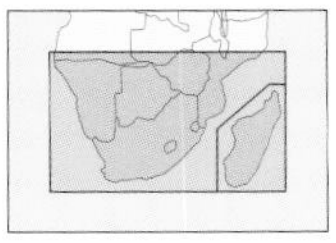

56–57

Australia and Oceania

Australia and Oceania: Physical and Political
1:50 000 000 58

New Zealand 1:6 000 000

59

Western Australia
1:8 000 000

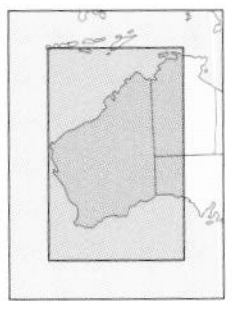

60–61

Eastern Australia
1:8 000 000

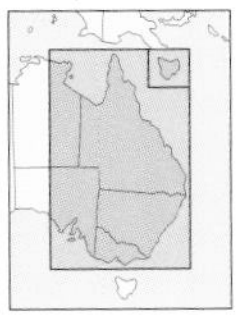

62–63

Pacific Ocean
1:54 000 000 64–65

North America

North America: Physical
1:35 000 000 66

North America: Political
1:35 000 000 67

Canada
1:15 000 000
Alaska 1:30 000 000

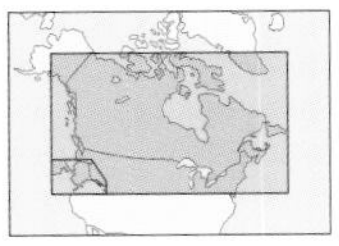

68–69

Eastern Canada
1:7 000 000

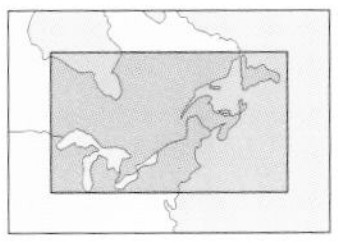

70–71

Western Canada
1:7 000 000

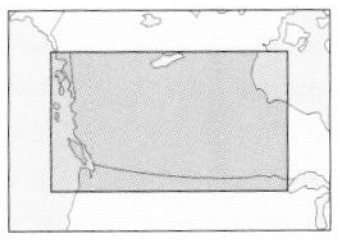

72–73

United States
1:12 000 000
Hawaii 1:10 000 000

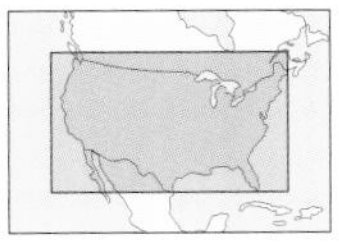

74–75

Eastern United States
1:6 000 000

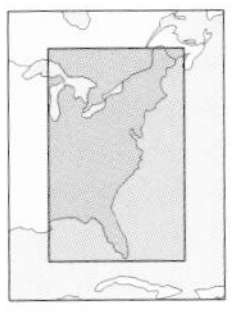

76–77

North-eastern United States
1:2 500 000

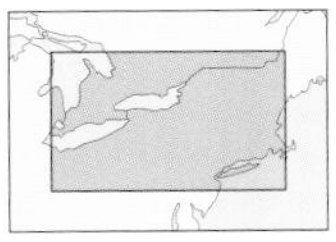

78–79

Middle United States
1:6 000 000

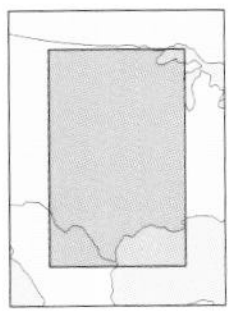

80–81

Western United States
1:6 000 000

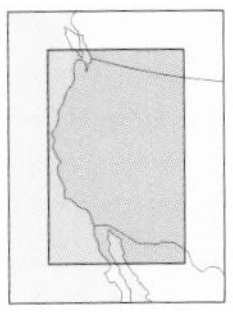

82–83

Central and Southern California and Washington
1:2 500 000

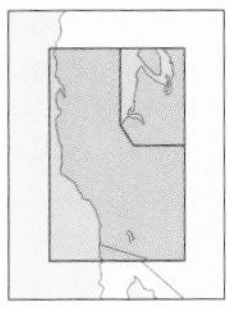

84–85

Mexico 1:8 000 000

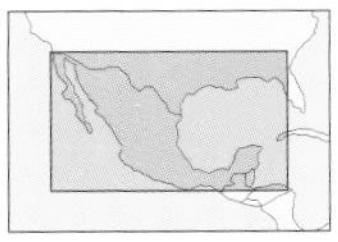

86–87

Central America and the West Indies 1:8 000 000

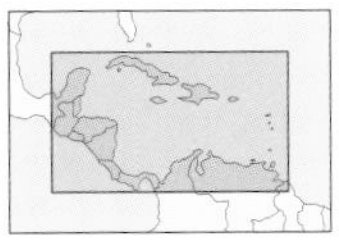

88–89

South America

South America: Physical
1:35 000 000 90

South America: Political
1:35 000 000 91

South America – North
1:16 000 000

92–93

Central South America
1:8 000 000

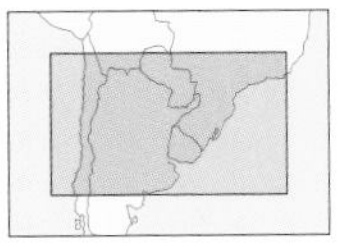

94–95

South America – South
1:16 000 000

96

Index to World Maps
97–176

World: Regions in the News 177

World Statistics: Countries

This alphabetical list includes all the countries and territories of the world. If a territory is not completely independent, the country it is associated with is named. The area figures give the total area of land, inland water and ice. The population figures are 2001 estimates. The annual income is the Gross Domestic Product per capita† in US dollars. The figures are the latest available, usually 2000 estimates.

Country/Territory	Area km² Thousands	Area miles² Thousands	Population Thousands	Capital	Annual Income US $
Afghanistan	652	252	26,813	Kabul	800
Albania	28.8	11.1	3,510	Tirana	3,000
Algeria	2,382	920	31,736	Algiers	5,500
American Samoa (US)	0.2	0.08	67	Pago Pago	8,000
Andorra	0.45	0.17	68	Andorra La Vella	18,000
Angola	1,247	481	10,366	Luanda	1,000
Anguilla (UK)	0.1	0.04	12	The Valley	8,200
Antigua & Barbuda	0.44	0.17	67	St John's	8,200
Argentina	2,767	1,068	37,385	Buenos Aires	12,900
Armenia	29.8	11.5	3,336	Yerevan	3,000
Aruba (Netherlands)	0.19	0.07	70	Oranjestad	28,000
Australia	7,687	2,968	19,358	Canberra	23,200
Austria	83.9	32.4	8,151	Vienna	25,000
Azerbaijan	86.6	33.4	7,771	Baku	3,000
Azores (Portugal)	2.2	0.87	243	Ponta Delgada	11,040
Bahamas	13.9	5.4	298	Nassau	15,000
Bahrain	0.68	0.26	645	Manama	15,900
Bangladesh	144	56	131,270	Dhaka	1,570
Barbados	0.43	0.17	275	Bridgetown	14,500
Belarus	207.6	80.1	10,350	Minsk	7,500
Belgium	30.5	11.8	10,259	Brussels	25,300
Belize	23	8.9	256	Belmopan	3,200
Benin	113	43	6,591	Porto-Novo	1,030
Bermuda (UK)	0.05	0.02	64	Hamilton	33,000
Bhutan	47	18.1	2,049	Thimphu	1,100
Bolivia	1,099	424	8,300	La Paz/Sucre	2,600
Bosnia-Herzegovina	51	20	3,922	Sarajevo	1,700
Botswana	582	225	1,586	Gaborone	6,600
Brazil	8,512	3,286	174,469	Brasília	6,500
Brunei	5.8	2.2	344	Bandar Seri Begawan	17,600
Bulgaria	111	43	7,707	Sofia	6,200
Burkina Faso	274	106	12,272	Ouagadougou	1,000
Burma (= Myanmar)	677	261	41,995	Rangoon	1,500
Burundi	27.8	10.7	6,224	Bujumbura	720
Cambodia	181	70	12,492	Phnom Penh	1,300
Cameroon	475	184	15,803	Yaoundé	1,700
Canada	9,976	3,852	31,593	Ottawa	24,800
Canary Is. (Spain)	7.3	2.8	1,577	Las Palmas/Santa Cruz	17,100
Cape Verde Is.	4	1.6	405	Praia	1,700
Cayman Is. (UK)	0.26	0.1	36	George Town	24,500
Central African Republic	623	241	3,577	Bangui	1,700
Chad	1,284	496	8,707	Ndjaména	1,000
Chile	757	292	15,328	Santiago	10,100
China	9,597	3,705	1,273,111	Beijing	3,600
Colombia	1,139	440	40,349	Bogotá	6,200
Comoros	2.2	0.86	596	Moroni	720
Congo	342	132	2,894	Brazzaville	1,100
Congo (Dem. Rep. of the)	2,345	905	53,625	Kinshasa	600
Cook Is. (NZ)	0.24	0.09	21	Avarua	5,000
Costa Rica	51.1	19.7	3,773	San José	6,700
Croatia	56.5	21.8	4,334	Zagreb	5,800
Cuba	111	43	11,184	Havana	1,700
Cyprus	9.3	3.6	763	Nicosia	13,800
Czech Republic	78.9	30.4	10,264	Prague	12,900
Denmark	43.1	16.6	5,353	Copenhagen	25,500
Djibouti	23.2	9	461	Djibouti	1,300
Dominica	0.75	0.29	71	Roseau	4,000
Dominican Republic	48.7	18.8	8,581	Santo Domingo	5,700
East Timor	14.9	5.7	737	Dili	N/A
Ecuador	284	109	13,184	Quito	2,900
Egypt	1,001	387	69,537	Cairo	3,600
El Salvador	21	8.1	6,238	San Salvador	4,000
Equatorial Guinea	28.1	10.8	486	Malabo	2,000
Eritrea	94	36	4,298	Asmara	710
Estonia	44.7	17.3	1,423	Tallinn	10,000
Ethiopia	1,128	436	65,892	Addis Ababa	600
Faroe Is. (Denmark)	1.4	0.54	46	Tórshavn	20,000
Fiji	18.3	7.1	844	Suva	7,300
Finland	338	131	5,176	Helsinki	22,900
France	552	213	59,551	Paris	24,400
French Guiana (France)	90	34.7	178	Cayenne	6,000
French Polynesia (France)	4	1.5	254	Papeete	10,800
Gabon	268	103	1,221	Libreville	6,300
Gambia, The	11.3	4.4	1,411	Banjul	1,100
Gaza Strip (OPT)*	0.36	0.14	1,178	–	1,000
Georgia	69.7	26.9	4,989	Tbilisi	4,600
Germany	357	138	83,030	Berlin	23,400
Ghana	239	92	19,894	Accra	1,900
Gibraltar (UK)	0.007	0.003	28	Gibraltar Town	17,500
Greece	132	51	10,624	Athens	17,200
Greenland (Denmark)	2,176	840	56	Nuuk (Godthåb)	20,000
Grenada	0.34	0.13	89	St George's	4,400
Guadeloupe (France)	1.7	0.66	431	Basse-Terre	9,000
Guam (US)	0.55	0.21	158	Agana	21,000
Guatemala	109	42	12,974	Guatemala City	3,700
Guinea	246	95	7,614	Conakry	1,300
Guinea-Bissau	36.1	13.9	1,316	Bissau	850
Guyana	215	83	697	Georgetown	4,800
Haiti	27.8	10.7	6,965	Port-au-Prince	1,800
Honduras	112	43	6,406	Tegucigalpa	2,700
Hong Kong (China)	1.1	0.4	7,211	–	25,400
Hungary	93	35.9	10,106	Budapest	11,200
Iceland	103	40	278	Reykjavik	24,800
India	3,288	1,269	1,029,991	New Delhi	2,200
Indonesia	1,890	730	227,701	Jakarta	2,900
Iran	1,648	636	66,129	Tehran	6,300
Iraq	438	169	23,332	Baghdad	2,500
Ireland	70.3	27.1	3,841	Dublin	21,600
Israel	20.6	7.96	5,938	Jerusalem	18,900
Italy	301	116	57,680	Rome	22,100
Ivory Coast (= Cote d'Ivoire)	322	125	16,393	Yamoussoukro	1,600
Jamaica	11	4.2	2,666	Kingston	3,700
Japan	378	146	126,772	Tokyo	24,900
Jordan	89.2	34.4	5,153	Amman	3,500
Kazakstan	2,717	1,049	16,731	Astana	5,000
Kenya	580	224	30,766	Nairobi	1,500
Kiribati	0.72	0.28	94	Tarawa	850
Korea, North	121	47	21,968	Pyŏngyang	1,000
Korea, South	99	38.2	47,904	Seoul	16,100
Kuwait	17.8	6.9	2,042	Kuwait City	15,000
Kyrgyzstan	198.5	76.6	4,753	Bishkek	2,700
Laos	237	91	5,636	Vientiane	1,700
Latvia	65	25	2,385	Riga	7,200
Lebanon	10.4	4	3,628	Beirut	5,000
Lesotho	30.4	11.7	2,177	Maseru	2,400
Liberia	111	43	3,226	Monrovia	1,100
Libya	1,760	679	5,241	Tripoli	8,900
Liechtenstein	0.16	0.06	33	Vaduz	23,000
Lithuania	65.2	25.2	3,611	Vilnius	7,300
Luxembourg	2.6	1	443	Luxembourg	36,400
Macau (China)	0.02	0.006	454	–	17,500
Macedonia (FYROM)	25.7	9.9	2,046	Skopje	4,400
Madagascar	587	227	15,983	Antananarivo	800
Madeira (Portugal)	0.81	0.31	259	Funchal	12,120
Malawi	118	46	10,548	Lilongwe	900
Malaysia	330	127	22,229	Kuala Lumpur	10,300
Maldives	0.3	0.12	311	Malé	2,000
Mali	1,240	479	11,009	Bamako	850
Malta	0.32	0.12	395	Valletta	14,300
Marshall Is.	0.18	0.07	71	Dalap-Uliga-Darrit	1,670
Martinique (France)	1.1	0.42	418	Fort-de-France	11,000
Mauritania	1,030	398	2,747	Nouakchott	2,000
Mauritius	2	0.72	1,190	Port Louis	10,400
Mayotte (France)	0.37	0.14	163	Mamoundzou	600
Mexico	1,958	756	101,879	Mexico City	9,100
Micronesia, Fed. States of	0.7	0.27	135	Palikir	2,000
Moldova	33.7	13	4,432	Chişinău	2,500
Monaco	0.002	0.001	32	Monaco	27,000
Mongolia	1,567	605	2,655	Ulan Bator	1,780
Montserrat (UK)	0.1	0.04	8	Plymouth	5,000
Morocco	447	172	30,645	Rabat	3,500
Mozambique	802	309	19,371	Maputo	1,000
Namibia	825	318	1,798	Windhoek	4,300
Nauru	0.02	0.008	12	Yaren District	5,000
Nepal	141	54	25,284	Katmandu	1,360
Netherlands	41.5	16	15,981	Amsterdam/The Hague	24,400
Netherlands Antilles (Neths)	0.99	0.38	212	Willemstad	11,400
New Caledonia (France)	18.6	7.2	205	Nouméa	15,000
New Zealand	269	104	3,864	Wellington	17,700
Nicaragua	130	50	4,918	Managua	2,700
Niger	1,267	489	10,355	Niamey	1,000
Nigeria	924	357	126,636	Abuja	950
Northern Mariana Is. (US)	0.48	0.18	75	Saipan	12,500
Norway	324	125	4,503	Oslo	27,700
Oman	212	82	2,622	Muscat	7,700
Pakistan	796	307	144,617	Islamabad	2,000
Palau	0.46	0.18	19	Koror	7,100
Panama	77.1	29.8	2,846	Panamá	6,000
Papua New Guinea	463	179	5,049	Port Moresby	2,500
Paraguay	407	157	5,734	Asunción	4,750
Peru	1,285	496	27,484	Lima	4,550
Philippines	300	116	82,842	Manila	3,800
Poland	313	121	38,634	Warsaw	8,500
Portugal	92.4	35.7	9,444	Lisbon	15,800
Puerto Rico (US)	9	3.5	3,939	San Juan	10,000
Qatar	11	4.2	769	Doha	20,300
Réunion (France)	2.5	0.97	733	St-Denis	4,800
Romania	238	92	22,364	Bucharest	5,900
Russia	17,075	6,592	145,470	Moscow	7,700
Rwanda	26.3	10.2	7,313	Kigali	900
St Kitts & Nevis	0.36	0.14	39	Basseterre	7,000
St Lucia	0.62	0.24	158	Castries	4,500
St Vincent & Grenadines	0.39	0.15	116	Kingstown	2,800
Samoa	2.8	1.1	179	Apia	3,200
San Marino	0.06	0.02	27	San Marino	32,000
São Tomé & Príncipe	0.96	0.37	165	São Tomé	1,100
Saudi Arabia	2,150	830	22,757	Riyadh	10,500
Senegal	197	76	10,285	Dakar	1,600
Seychelles	0.46	0.18	80	Victoria	7,700
Sierra Leone	71.7	27.7	5,427	Freetown	510
Singapore	0.62	0.24	4,300	Singapore	26,500
Slovak Republic	49	18.9	5,415	Bratislava	10,200
Slovenia	20.3	7.8	1,930	Ljubljana	12,000
Solomon Is.	28.9	11.2	480	Honiara	2,000
Somalia	638	246	7,489	Mogadishu	600
South Africa	1,220	471	43,586	C. Town/Pretoria/Bloem.	8,500
Spain	505	195	38,432	Madrid	18,000
Sri Lanka	65.6	25.3	19,409	Colombo	3,250
Sudan	2,506	967	36,080	Khartoum	1,000
Surinam	163	63	434	Paramaribo	3,400
Swaziland	17.4	6.7	1,104	Mbabane	4,000
Sweden	450	174	8,875	Stockholm	22,200
Switzerland	41.3	15.9	7,283	Bern	28,600
Syria	185	71	16,729	Damascus	3,100
Taiwan	36	13.9	22,370	Taipei	17,400
Tajikistan	143.1	55.2	6,579	Dushanbe	1,140
Tanzania	945	365	36,232	Dodoma	710
Thailand	513	198	61,798	Bangkok	6,700
Togo	56.8	21.9	5,153	Lomé	1,500
Tonga	0.75	0.29	104	Nuku'alofa	2,200
Trinidad & Tobago	5.1	2	1,170	Port of Spain	9,500
Tunisia	164	63	9,705	Tunis	6,500
Turkey	779	301	66,494	Ankara	6,800
Turkmenistan	488.1	188.5	4,603	Ashkhabad	4,300
Turks & Caicos Is. (UK)	0.43	0.17	18	Cockburn Town	7,300
Tuvalu	0.03	0.01	11	Fongafale	1,100
Uganda	236	91	23,986	Kampala	1,100
Ukraine	603.7	233.1	48,760	Kiev	3,850
United Arab Emirates	83.6	32.3	2,407	Abu Dhabi	22,800
United Kingdom	243.3	94	59,648	London	22,800
United States of America	9,373	3,619	278,059	Washington, DC	36,200
Uruguay	177	68	3,360	Montevideo	9,300
Uzbekistan	447.4	172.7	25,155	Tashkent	2,400
Vanuatu	12.2	4.7	193	Port-Vila	1,300
Vatican City	0.0004	0.0002	0.89	Vatican City	N/A
Venezuela	912	352	23,917	Caracas	6,200
Vietnam	332	127	79,939	Hanoi	1,950
Virgin Is. (UK)	0.15	0.06	21	Road Town	16,000
Virgin Is. (US)	0.34	0.13	122	Charlotte Amalie	15,000
Wallis & Futuna Is. (France)	0.2	0.08	15	Mata-Utu	2,000
West Bank (OPT)*	5.86	2.26	2,091	–	1,500
Western Sahara	266	103	251	El Aaiún	N/A
Yemen	528	204	18,078	Sana	820
Yugoslavia (Serbia & Montenegro)	102.3	39.5	10,677	Belgrade	2,300
Zambia	753	291	9,770	Lusaka	880
Zimbabwe	391	151	11,365	Harare	2,500

*OPT = Occupied Palestinian Territory   N/A = Not Available

† Gross Domestic Product per capita has been measured using the purchasing power parity method. This enables comparisons to be made between countries through their purchasing power (in US dollars), showing real price levels of goods and services rather than using currency exchange rates.

World Statistics: Physical Dimensions

Each topic list is divided into continents and within a continent the items are listed in order of size. The bottom part of many of the lists is selective in order to give examples from as many different countries as possible. The order of the continents is the same as in the atlas, beginning with Europe and ending with South America. The figures are rounded as appropriate.

World, Continents, Oceans

	km²	miles²	%
The World	509,450,000	196,672,000	–
Land	149,450,000	57,688,000	29.3
Water	360,000,000	138,984,000	70.7
Asia	44,500,000	17,177,000	29.8
Africa	30,302,000	11,697,000	20.3
North America	24,241,000	9,357,000	16.2
South America	17,793,000	6,868,000	11.9
Antarctica	14,100,000	5,443,000	9.4
Europe	9,957,000	3,843,000	6.7
Australia & Oceania	8,557,000	3,303,000	5.7
Pacific Ocean	179,679,000	69,356,000	49.9
Atlantic Ocean	92,373,000	35,657,000	25.7
Indian Ocean	73,917,000	28,532,000	20.5
Arctic Ocean	14,090,000	5,439,000	3.9

Ocean Depths

Atlantic Ocean	m	ft
Puerto Rico (Milwaukee) Deep	9,220	30,249
Cayman Trench	7,680	25,197
Gulf of Mexico	5,203	17,070
Mediterranean Sea	5,121	16,801
Black Sea	2,211	7,254
North Sea	660	2,165
Indian Ocean	**m**	**ft**
Java Trench	7,450	24,442
Red Sea	2,635	8,454
Pacific Ocean	**m**	**ft**
Mariana Trench	11,022	36,161
Tonga Trench	10,882	35,702
Japan Trench	10,554	34,626
Kuril Trench	10,542	34,587
Arctic Ocean	**m**	**ft**
Molloy Deep	5,608	18,399

Mountains

Europe		m	ft
Elbrus	*Russia*	5,642	18,510
Mont Blanc	*France/Italy*	4,807	15,771
Monte Rosa	*Italy/Switzerland*	4,634	15,203
Dom	*Switzerland*	4,545	14,911
Liskamm	*Switzerland*	4,527	14,852
Weisshorn	*Switzerland*	4,505	14,780
Taschorn	*Switzerland*	4,490	14,730
Matterhorn/Cervino	*Italy/Switzerland*	4,478	14,691
Mont Maudit	*France/Italy*	4,465	14,649
Dent Blanche	*Switzerland*	4,356	14,291
Nadelhorn	*Switzerland*	4,327	14,196
Grandes Jorasses	*France/Italy*	4,208	13,806
Jungfrau	*Switzerland*	4,158	13,642
Grossglockner	*Austria*	3,797	12,457
Mulhacén	*Spain*	3,478	11,411
Zugspitze	*Germany*	2,962	9,718
Olympus	*Greece*	2,917	9,570
Triglav	*Slovenia*	2,863	9,393
Gerlachovka	*Slovak Republic*	2,655	8,711
Galdhöpiggen	*Norway*	2,468	8,100
Kebnekaise	*Sweden*	2,117	6,946
Ben Nevis	*UK*	1,343	4,406
Asia		**m**	**ft**
Everest	*China/Nepal*	8,850	29,035
K2 (Godwin Austen)	*China/Kashmir*	8,611	28,251
Kanchenjunga	*India/Nepal*	8,598	28,208
Lhotse	*China/Nepal*	8,516	27,939
Makalu	*China/Nepal*	8,481	27,824
Cho Oyu	*China/Nepal*	8,201	26,906
Dhaulagiri	*Nepal*	8,172	26,811
Manaslu	*Nepal*	8,156	26,758
Nanga Parbat	*Kashmir*	8,126	26,660
Annapurna	*Nepal*	8,078	26,502
Gasherbrum	*China/Kashmir*	8,068	26,469
Broad Peak	*China/Kashmir*	8,051	26,414
Xixabangma	*China*	8,012	26,286
Kangbachen	*India/Nepal*	7,902	25,925
Trivor	*Pakistan*	7,720	25,328
Pik Kommunizma	*Tajikistan*	7,495	24,590
Demavend	*Iran*	5,604	18,386
Ararat	*Turkey*	5,165	16,945
Gunong Kinabalu	*Malaysia (Borneo)*	4,101	13,455
Fuji-San	*Japan*	3,776	12,388
Africa		**m**	**ft**
Kilimanjaro	*Tanzania*	5,895	19,340
Mt Kenya	*Kenya*	5,199	17,057
Ruwenzori (Margherita)	*Ug./Congo (D.R.)*	5,109	16,762
Ras Dashan	*Ethiopia*	4,620	15,157
Meru	*Tanzania*	4,565	14,977
Karisimbi	*Rwanda/Congo (D.R.)*	4,507	14,787
Mt Elgon	*Kenya/Uganda*	4,321	14,176
Batu	*Ethiopia*	4,307	14,130
Toubkal	*Morocco*	4,165	13,665
Mt Cameroon	*Cameroon*	4,070	13,353
Oceania		**m**	**ft**
Puncak Jaya	*Indonesia*	5,029	16,499
Puncak Trikora	*Indonesia*	4,750	15,584
Puncak Mandala	*Indonesia*	4,702	15,427
Mt Wilhelm	*Papua New Guinea*	4,508	14,790
Mauna Kea	*USA (Hawaii)*	4,205	13,796
Mauna Loa	*USA (Hawaii)*	4,169	13,681
Mt Cook (Aoraki)	*New Zealand*	3,753	12,313
Mt Kosciuszko	*Australia*	2,237	7,339
North America		**m**	**ft**
Mt McKinley (Denali)	*USA (Alaska)*	6,194	20,321
Mt Logan	*Canada*	5,959	19,551
Citlaltepetl	*Mexico*	5,700	18,701
Mt St Elias	*USA/Canada*	5,489	18,008
Popocatepetl	*Mexico*	5,452	17,887
Mt Foraker	*USA (Alaska)*	5,304	17,401
Ixtaccihuatl	*Mexico*	5,286	17,342
Lucania	*Canada*	5,227	17,149
Mt Steele	*Canada*	5,073	16,644
Mt Bona	*USA (Alaska)*	5,005	16,420
Mt Whitney	*USA*	4,418	14,495
Tajumulco	*Guatemala*	4,220	13,845
Chirripó Grande	*Costa Rica*	3,837	12,589
Pico Duarte	*Dominican Rep.*	3,175	10,417
South America		**m**	**ft**
Aconcagua	*Argentina*	6,960	22,834
Bonete	*Argentina*	6,872	22,546
Ojos del Salado	*Argentina/Chile*	6,863	22,516
Pissis	*Argentina*	6,779	22,241
Mercedario	*Argentina/Chile*	6,770	22,211
Huascaran	*Peru*	6,768	22,204
Llullaillaco	*Argentina/Chile*	6,723	22,057
Nudo de Cachi	*Argentina*	6,720	22,047
Yerupaja	*Peru*	6,632	21,758
Sajama	*Bolivia*	6,542	21,463
Chimborazo	*Ecuador*	6,267	20,561
Pico Colon	*Colombia*	5,800	19,029
Pico Bolivar	*Venezuela*	5,007	16,427
Antarctica		**m**	**ft**
Vinson Massif		4,897	16,066
Mt Kirkpatrick		4,528	14,855

Rivers

Europe		km	miles
Volga	*Caspian Sea*	3,700	2,300
Danube	*Black Sea*	2,850	1,770
Ural	*Caspian Sea*	2,535	1,575
Dnepr (Dnipro)	*Black Sea*	2,285	1,420
Kama	*Volga*	2,030	1,260
Don	*Black Sea*	1,990	1,240
Petchora	*Arctic Ocean*	1,790	1,110
Oka	*Volga*	1,480	920
Dnister (Dniester)	*Black Sea*	1,400	870
Vyatka	*Kama*	1,370	850
Rhine	*North Sea*	1,320	820
N. Dvina	*Arctic Ocean*	1,290	800
Elbe	*North Sea*	1,145	710
Asia		**km**	**miles**
Yangtze	*Pacific Ocean*	6,380	3,960
Yenisey–Angara	*Arctic Ocean*	5,550	3,445
Huang He	*Pacific Ocean*	5,464	3,395
Ob–Irtysh	*Arctic Ocean*	5,410	3,360
Mekong	*Pacific Ocean*	4,500	2,795
Amur	*Pacific Ocean*	4,400	2,730
Lena	*Arctic Ocean*	4,400	2,730
Irtysh	*Ob*	4,250	2,640
Yenisey	*Arctic Ocean*	4,090	2,540
Ob	*Arctic Ocean*	3,680	2,285
Indus	*Indian Ocean*	3,100	1,925
Brahmaputra	*Indian Ocean*	2,900	1,800
Syrdarya	*Aral Sea*	2,860	1,775
Salween	*Indian Ocean*	2,800	1,740
Euphrates	*Indian Ocean*	2,700	1,675
Amudarya	*Aral Sea*	2,540	1,575
Africa		**km**	**miles**
Nile	*Mediterranean*	6,670	4,140
Congo	*Atlantic Ocean*	4,670	2,900
Niger	*Atlantic Ocean*	4,180	2,595
Zambezi	*Indian Ocean*	3,540	2,200
Oubangi/Uele	*Congo (D.R.)*	2,250	1,400
Kasai	*Congo (D.R.)*	1,950	1,210
Shaballe	*Indian Ocean*	1,930	1,200
Orange	*Atlantic Ocean*	1,860	1,155
Cubango	*Okavango Swamps*	1,800	1,120
Limpopo	*Indian Ocean*	1,600	995
Senegal	*Atlantic Ocean*	1,600	995
Australia		**km**	**miles**
Murray–Darling	*Indian Ocean*	3,750	2,330
Darling	*Murray*	3,070	1,905
Murray	*Indian Ocean*	2,575	1,600
Murrumbidgee	*Murray*	1,690	1,050
North America		**km**	**miles**
Mississippi–Missouri	*Gulf of Mexico*	6,020	3,740
Mackenzie	*Arctic Ocean*	4,240	2,630
Mississippi	*Gulf of Mexico*	3,780	2,350
Missouri	*Mississippi*	3,780	2,350
Yukon	*Pacific Ocean*	3,185	1,980
Rio Grande	*Gulf of Mexico*	3,030	1,880
Arkansas	*Mississippi*	2,340	1,450
Colorado	*Pacific Ocean*	2,330	1,445
Red	*Mississippi*	2,040	1,270
Columbia	*Pacific Ocean*	1,950	1,210
Saskatchewan	*Lake Winnipeg*	1,940	1,205
South America		**km**	**miles**
Amazon	*Atlantic Ocean*	6,450	4,010
Paraná–Plate	*Atlantic Ocean*	4,500	2,800
Purus	*Amazon*	3,350	2,080
Madeira	*Amazon*	3,200	1,990
São Francisco	*Atlantic Ocean*	2,900	1,800
Paraná	*Plate*	2,800	1,740
Tocantins	*Atlantic Ocean*	2,750	1,710
Paraguay	*Paraná*	2,550	1,580
Orinoco	*Atlantic Ocean*	2,500	1,550
Pilcomayo	*Paraná*	2,500	1,550
Araguaia	*Tocantins*	2,250	1,400

Lakes

Europe		km²	miles²
Lake Ladoga	*Russia*	17,700	6,800
Lake Onega	*Russia*	9,700	3,700
Saimaa system	*Finland*	8,000	3,100
Vänern	*Sweden*	5,500	2,100
Asia		**km²**	**miles²**
Caspian Sea	*Asia*	371,800	143,550
Lake Baykal	*Russia*	30,500	11,780
Aral Sea	*Kazakstan/Uzbekistan*	28,687	11,086
Tonlé Sap	*Cambodia*	20,000	7,700
Lake Balqash	*Kazakstan*	18,500	7,100
Africa		**km²**	**miles²**
Lake Victoria	*East Africa*	68,000	26,000
Lake Tanganyika	*Central Africa*	33,000	13,000
Lake Malawi/Nyasa	*East Africa*	29,600	11,430
Lake Chad	*Central Africa*	25,000	9,700
Lake Turkana	*Ethiopia/Kenya*	8,500	3,300
Lake Volta	*Ghana*	8,500	3,300
Australia		**km²**	**miles²**
Lake Eyre	*Australia*	8,900	3,400
Lake Torrens	*Australia*	5,800	2,200
Lake Gairdner	*Australia*	4,800	1,900
North America		**km²**	**miles²**
Lake Superior	*Canada/USA*	82,350	31,800
Lake Huron	*Canada/USA*	59,600	23,010
Lake Michigan	*USA*	58,000	22,400
Great Bear Lake	*Canada*	31,800	12,280
Great Slave Lake	*Canada*	28,500	11,000
Lake Erie	*Canada/USA*	25,700	9,900
Lake Winnipeg	*Canada*	24,400	9,400
Lake Ontario	*Canada/USA*	19,500	7,500
Lake Nicaragua	*Nicaragua*	8,200	3,200
South America		**km²**	**miles²**
Lake Titicaca	*Bolivia/Peru*	8,300	3,200
Lake Poopo	*Bolivia*	2,800	1,100

Islands

Europe		km²	miles²
Great Britain	*UK*	229,880	88,700
Iceland	*Atlantic Ocean*	103,000	39,800
Ireland	*Ireland/UK*	84,400	32,600
Novaya Zemlya (N.)	*Russia*	48,200	18,600
Sicily	*Italy*	25,500	9,800
Corsica	*France*	8,700	3,400
Asia		**km²**	**miles²**
Borneo	*South-east Asia*	744,360	287,400
Sumatra	*Indonesia*	473,600	182,860
Honshu	*Japan*	230,500	88,980
Sulawesi (Celebes)	*Indonesia*	189,000	73,000
Java	*Indonesia*	126,700	48,900
Luzon	*Philippines*	104,700	40,400
Hokkaido	*Japan*	78,400	30,300
Africa		**km²**	**miles²**
Madagascar	*Indian Ocean*	587,040	226,660
Socotra	*Indian Ocean*	3,600	1,400
Réunion	*Indian Ocean*	2,500	965
Oceania		**km²**	**miles²**
New Guinea	*Indonesia/Papua NG*	821,030	317,000
New Zealand (S.)	*Pacific Ocean*	150,500	58,100
New Zealand (N.)	*Pacific Ocean*	114,700	44,300
Tasmania	*Australia*	67,800	26,200
Hawaii	*Pacific Ocean*	10,450	4,000
North America		**km²**	**miles²**
Greenland	*Atlantic Ocean*	2,175,600	839,800
Baffin Is.	*Canada*	508,000	196,100
Victoria Is.	*Canada*	212,200	81,900
Ellesmere Is.	*Canada*	212,000	81,800
Cuba	*Caribbean Sea*	110,860	42,800
Hispaniola	*Dominican Rep./Haiti*	76,200	29,400
Jamaica	*Caribbean Sea*	11,400	4,400
Puerto Rico	*Atlantic Ocean*	8,900	3,400
South America		**km²**	**miles²**
Tierra del Fuego	*Argentina/Chile*	47,000	18,100
Falkland Is. (E.)	*Atlantic Ocean*	6,800	2,600

Philip's World Maps

The reference maps which form the main body of this atlas have been prepared in accordance with the highest standards of international cartography to provide an accurate and detailed representation of the Earth. The scales and projections used have been carefully chosen to give balanced coverage of the world, while emphasizing the most densely populated and economically significant regions. A hallmark of Philip's mapping is the use of hill shading and relief colouring to create a graphic impression of landforms: this makes the maps exceptionally easy to read. However, knowledge of the key features employed in the construction and presentation of the maps will enable the reader to derive the fullest benefit from the atlas.

Map sequence

The atlas covers the Earth continent by continent: first Europe; then its land neighbour Asia (mapped north before south, in a clockwise sequence), then Africa, Australia and Oceania, North America and South America. This is the classic arrangement adopted by most cartographers since the 16th century. For each continent, there are maps at a variety of scales. First, physical relief and political maps of the whole continent; then a series of larger-scale maps of the regions within the continent, each followed, where required, by still larger-scale maps of the most important or densely populated areas. The governing principle is that by turning the pages of the atlas, the reader moves steadily from north to south through each continent, with each map overlapping its neighbours.

Map presentation

With very few exceptions (e.g. for the Arctic and Antarctica), the maps are drawn with north at the top, regardless of whether they are presented upright or sideways on the page. In the borders will be found the map title; a locator diagram showing the area covered and the page numbers for maps of adjacent areas; the scale; the projection used; the degrees of latitude and longitude; and the letters and figures used in the index for locating place names and geographical features. Physical relief maps also have a height reference panel identifying the colours used for each layer of contouring.

Map symbols

Each map contains a vast amount of detail which can only be conveyed clearly and accurately by the use of symbols. Points and circles of varying sizes locate and identify the relative importance of towns and cities; different styles of type are employed for administrative, geographical and regional place names. A variety of pictorial symbols denote features such as glaciers and marshes, as well as man-made structures including roads, railways, airports and canals.

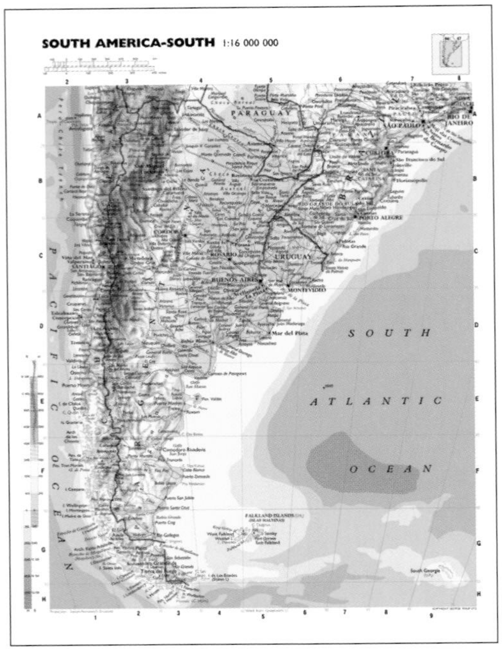

International borders are shown by red lines. Where neighbouring countries are in dispute, for example in the Middle East, the maps show the *de facto* boundary between nations, regardless of the legal or historical situation. The symbols are explained on the first page of the *World Maps* section of the atlas.

Map scales

The scale of each map is given in the numerical form known as the 'representative fraction'. The first figure is always one, signifying one unit of distance on the map; the second figure, usually in millions, is the number by which the map unit must be multiplied to give the equivalent distance on the Earth's surface. Calculations can easily be made in centimetres and kilometres, by dividing the Earth units figure by 100 000 (i.e. deleting the last five 0s). Thus 1:1 000 000 means 1 cm = 10 km. The calculation for inches and miles is more laborious, but 1 000 000 divided by 63 360 (the number of inches in a mile) shows that the ratio 1:1 000 000 means approximately 1 inch = 16 miles. The table below provides distance equivalents for scales down to 1:50 000 000.

LARGE SCALE

1:1 000 000	1 cm = 10 km	1 inch = 16 miles
1:2 500 000	1 cm = 25 km	1 inch = 39.5 miles
1:5 000 000	1 cm = 50 km	1 inch = 79 miles
1:6 000 000	1 cm = 60 km	1 inch = 95 miles
1:8 000 000	1 cm = 80 km	1 inch = 126 miles
1:10 000 000	1 cm = 100 km	1 inch = 158 miles
1:15 000 000	1 cm = 150 km	1 inch = 237 miles
1:20 000 000	1 cm = 200 km	1 inch = 316 miles
1:50 000 000	1 cm = 500 km	1 inch = 790 miles

SMALL SCALE

Measuring distances

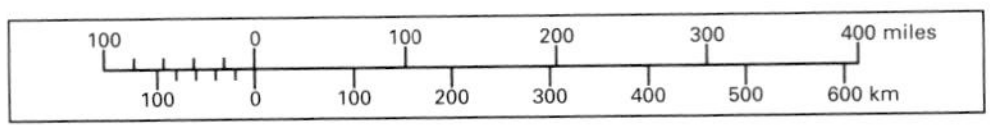

Although each map is accompanied by a scale bar, distances cannot always be measured with confidence because of the distortions involved in portraying the curved surface of the Earth on a flat page. As a general rule, the larger the map scale (i.e. the lower the number of Earth units in the representative fraction), the more accurate and reliable will be the distance measured. On small-scale maps such as those of the world and of entire continents, measurement may only be accurate along the 'standard parallels', or central axes, and should not be attempted without considering the map projection.

Latitude and longitude

Accurate positioning of individual points on the Earth's surface is made possible by reference to the geometrical system of latitude and longitude. Latitude *parallels* are drawn west–east around the Earth and numbered by degrees north and south of the Equator, which is designated 0° of latitude. Longitude *meridians* are drawn north–south and numbered by degrees east and west of the *prime meridian*, 0° of longitude, which passes through Greenwich in England. By referring to these co-ordinates and their subdivisions of minutes (1/60th of a degree) and seconds (1/60th of a minute), any place on Earth can be located to within a few hundred metres. Latitude and longitude are indicated by blue lines on the maps; they are straight or curved according to the projection employed. Reference to these lines is the easiest way of determining the relative positions of places on different maps, and for plotting compass directions.

Name forms

For ease of reference, both English and local name forms appear in the atlas. Oceans, seas and countries are shown in English throughout the atlas; country names may be abbreviated to their commonly accepted form (e.g. Germany, not The Federal Republic of Germany). Conventional English forms are also used for place names on the smaller-scale maps of the continents. However, local name forms are used on all large-scale and regional maps, with the English form given in brackets only for important cities – the large-scale map of Russia and Central Asia thus shows Moskva (Moscow). For countries which do not use a Roman script, place names have been transcribed according to the systems adopted by the British and US Geographic Names Authorities. For China, the Pin Yin system has been used, with some more widely known forms appearing in brackets, as with Beijing (Peking). Both English and local names appear in the index, the English form being cross-referenced to the local form.

THE WORLD IN FOCUS

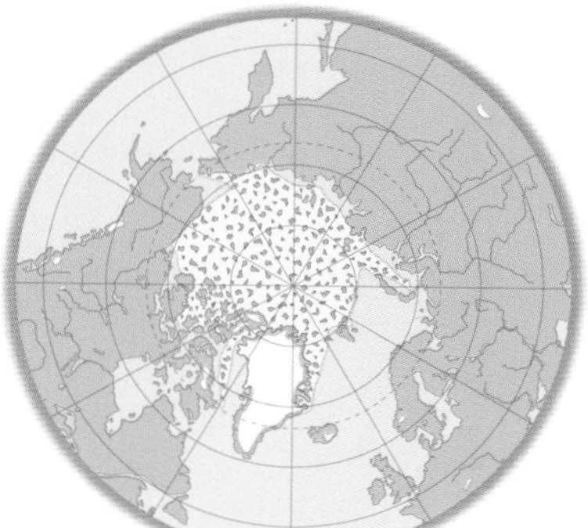

Planet Earth

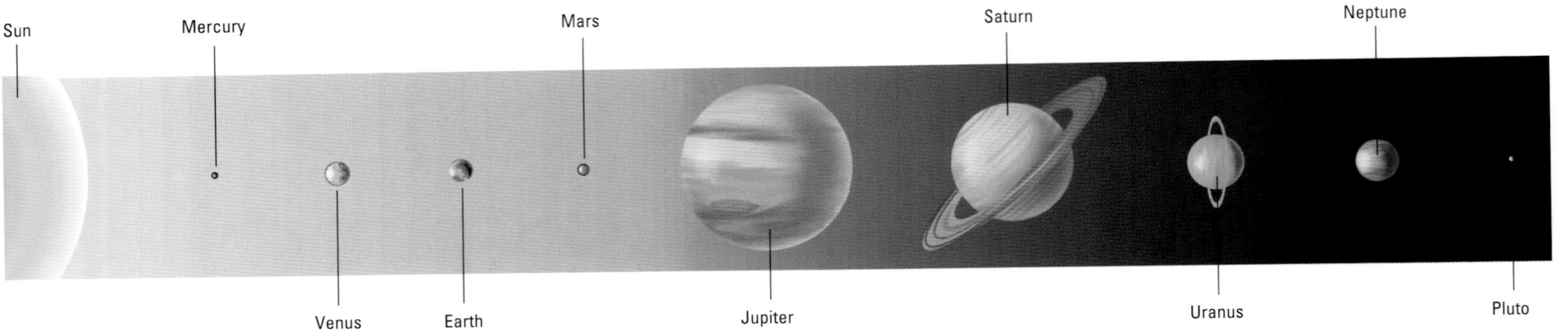

Sun
Mercury
Mars
Saturn
Neptune
Venus
Earth
Jupiter
Uranus
Pluto

The Solar System

A minute part of one of the billions of galaxies (collections of stars) that comprises the Universe, the Solar System lies some 27,000 light-years from the centre of our own galaxy, the 'Milky Way'. Thought to be about 4,600 million years old, it consists of a central sun with nine planets and their moons revolving around it, attracted by its gravitational pull. The planets orbit the Sun in the same direction – anti-clockwise when viewed from the Northern Heavens – and almost in the same plane. Their orbital paths, however, vary enormously.

The Sun's diameter is 109 times that of Earth, and the temperature at its core – caused by continuous thermonuclear fusions of hydrogen into helium – is estimated to be 15 million degrees Celsius. It is the Solar System's only source of light and heat.

Profile of the Planets

	Mean distance from Sun (million km)	Mass (Earth = 1)	Period of orbit (Earth years)	Period of rotation (Earth days)	Equatorial diameter (km)	Number of known satellites
Mercury	57.9	0.055	0.24 years	58.67	4,878	0
Venus	108.2	0.815	0.62 years	243.00	12,104	0
Earth	149.6	1.0	1.00 years	1.00	12,756	1
Mars	227.9	0.107	1.88 years	1.03	6,787	2
Jupiter	778.3	317.8	11.86 years	0.41	142,800	27
Saturn	1,427	95.2	29.46 years	0.43	120,000	30
Uranus	2,871	14.5	84.01 years	0.75	51,118	21
Neptune	4,497	17.1	164.80 years	0.80	49,528	8
Pluto	5,914	0.002	248.50 years	6.39	2,320	1

All planetary orbits are elliptical in form, but only Pluto and Mercury follow paths that deviate noticeably from a circular one. Near perihelion – its closest approach to the Sun – Pluto actually passes inside the orbit of Neptune, an event that last occurred in 1983. Pluto did not regain its station as outermost planet until February 1999.

The Seasons

Seasons occur because the Earth's axis is tilted at a constant angle of 23½°. When the northern hemisphere is tilted to a maximum extent towards the Sun, on 21 June, the Sun is overhead at the Tropic of Cancer (latitude 23½° North). This is midsummer, or the summer solstice, in the northern hemisphere.

On 22 or 23 September, the Sun is overhead at the Equator, and day and night are of equal length throughout the world. This is the autumn equinox in the northern hemisphere. On 21 or 22 December, the Sun is overhead at the Tropic of Capricorn (23½° South), the winter solstice in the northern hemisphere. The overhead Sun then tracks north until, on 21 March, it is overhead at the Equator. This is the spring (vernal) equinox in the northern hemisphere.

In the southern hemisphere, the seasons are the reverse of those in the north.

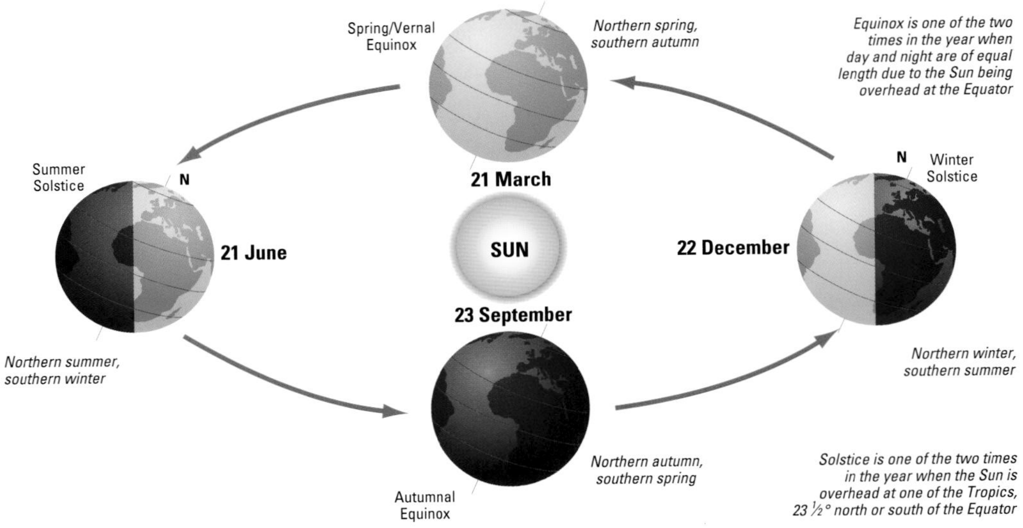

Spring/Vernal Equinox
Northern spring, southern autumn
Equinox is one of the two times in the year when day and night are of equal length due to the Sun being overhead at the Equator
Summer Solstice
N
21 March
N
Winter Solstice
21 June
SUN
22 December
23 September
Northern summer, southern winter
Northern winter, southern summer
Northern autumn, southern spring
Solstice is one of the two times in the year when the Sun is overhead at one of the Tropics, 23 ½° north or south of the Equator
Autumnal Equinox

Day and Night

The Sun appears to rise in the east, reach its highest point at noon, and then set in the west, to be followed by night. In reality, it is not the Sun that is moving but the Earth rotating from west to east. The moment when the Sun's upper limb first appears above the horizon is termed sunrise; the moment when the Sun's upper limb disappears below the horizon is sunset.

At the summer solstice in the northern hemisphere (21 June), the Arctic has total daylight and the Antarctic total darkness. The opposite occurs at the winter solstice (21 or 22 December). At the Equator, the length of day and night are almost equal all year.

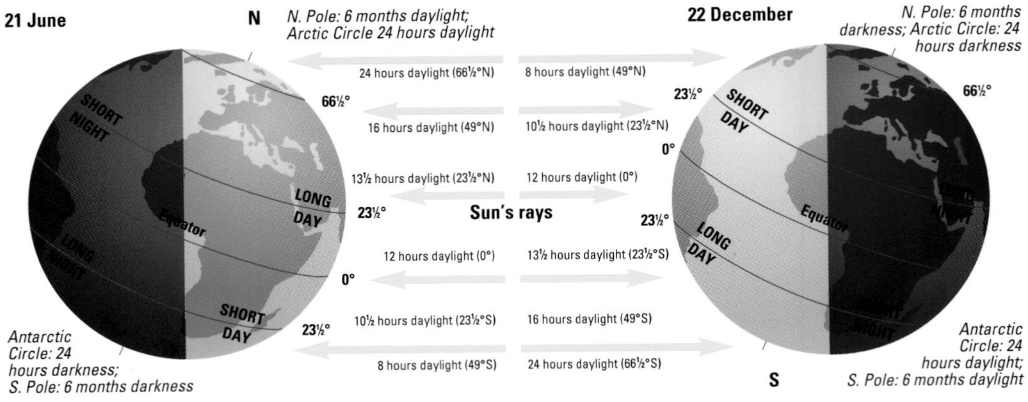

21 June
N
N. Pole: 6 months daylight; Arctic Circle 24 hours daylight
22 December
N. Pole: 6 months darkness; Arctic Circle: 24 hours darkness
24 hours daylight (66½°N)
8 hours daylight (49°N)
SHORT NIGHT
66½°
23½°
SHORT DAY
66½°
16 hours daylight (49°N)
10½ hours daylight (23½°N)
0°
13½ hours daylight (23½°N)
12 hours daylight (0°)
LONG DAY
23½°
Sun's rays
Equator
23½°
Equator
LONG DAY
LONG NIGHT
12 hours daylight (0°)
13½ hours daylight (23½°S)
0°
SHORT DAY
23½°
10½ hours daylight (23½°S)
16 hours daylight (49°S)
Antarctic Circle: 24 hours darkness; S. Pole: 6 months darkness
8 hours daylight (49°S)
24 hours daylight (66½°S)
S
Antarctic Circle: 24 hours daylight; S. Pole: 6 months daylight

Time

Year: The time taken by the Earth to revolve around the Sun, or 365.24 days.

Leap Year: A calendar year of 366 days, 29 February being the additional day. It offsets the difference between the calendar and the solar year.

Month: The approximate time taken by the Moon to revolve around the Earth. The 12 months of the year in fact vary from 28 (29 in a Leap Year) to 31 days.

Week: An artificial period of 7 days, not based on astronomical time.

Day: The time taken by the Earth to complete one rotation on its axis.

Hour: 24 hours make one day. Usually the day is divided into hours AM (ante meridiem or before noon) and PM (post meridiem or after noon), although most timetables now use the 24-hour system, from midnight to midnight.

Sunrise

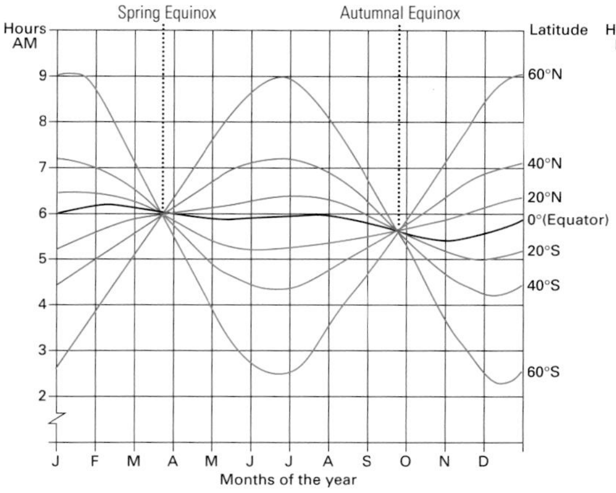
Spring Equinox
Autumnal Equinox
Hours AM
Latitude
9
8
7
6
5
4
3
2
60°N
40°N
20°N
0°(Equator)
20°S
40°S
60°S
J F M A M J J A S O N D
Months of the year

Sunset

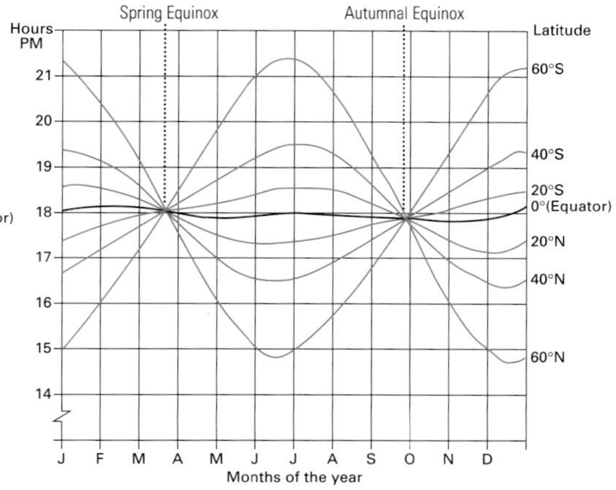
Spring Equinox
Autumnal Equinox
Hours PM
Latitude
21
20
19
18
17
16
15
14
60°S
40°S
20°S
0°(Equator)
20°N
40°N
60°N
J F M A M J J A S O N D
Months of the year

The Moon

Phases of the Moon

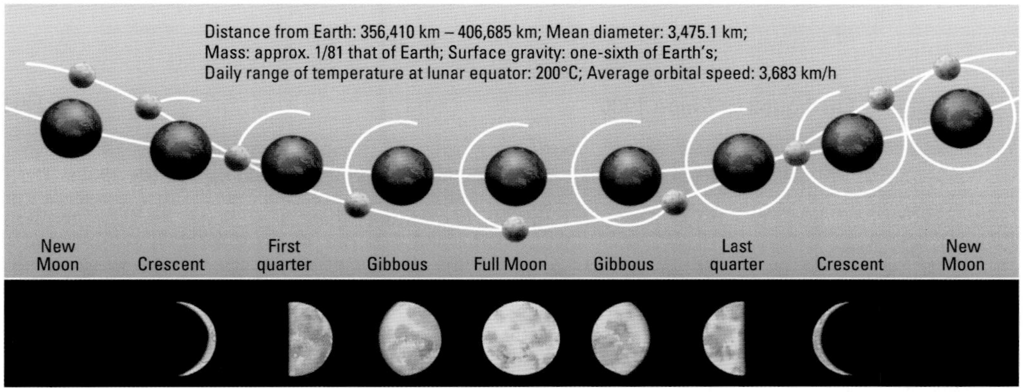
Distance from Earth: 356,410 km – 406,685 km; Mean diameter: 3,475.1 km;
Mass: approx. 1/81 that of Earth; Surface gravity: one-sixth of Earth's;
Daily range of temperature at lunar equator: 200°C; Average orbital speed: 3,683 km/h
New Moon
Crescent
First quarter
Gibbous
Full Moon
Gibbous
Last quarter
Crescent
New Moon

The Moon rotates more slowly than the Earth, making one complete turn on its axis in just over 27 days. Since this corresponds to its period of revolution around the Earth, the Moon always presents the same hemisphere or face to us, and we never see 'the dark side'. The interval between one full Moon and the next (and between new Moons) is about 29½ days – a lunar month. The apparent changes in the shape of the Moon are caused by its changing position in relation to the Earth; like the planets, it produces no light of its own and shines only by reflecting the rays of the Sun.

Eclipses

When the Moon passes between the Sun and the Earth it causes a partial eclipse of the Sun (1) if the Earth passes through the Moon's outer shadow (P), or a total eclipse (2) if the inner cone shadow crosses the Earth's surface. In a lunar eclipse, the Earth's shadow crosses the Moon and, again, provides either a partial or total eclipse.

Eclipses of the Sun and the Moon do not occur every month because of the 5° difference between the plane of the Moon's orbit and the plane in which the Earth moves. In the 1990s only 14 lunar eclipses were possible, for example, seven partial and seven total; each was visible only from certain, and variable, parts of the world. The same period witnessed 13 solar eclipses – six partial (or annular) and seven total.

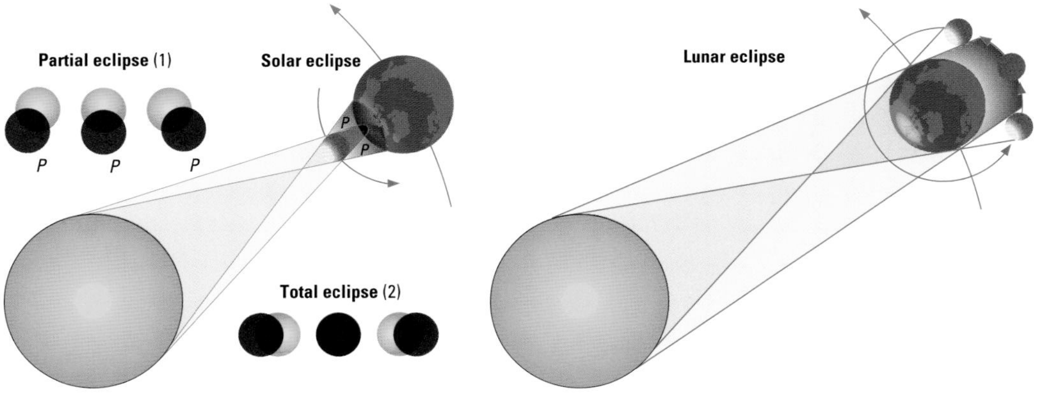
Partial eclipse (1)
P
P
P
Solar eclipse
P
P
Total eclipse (2)
Lunar eclipse

Tides

The daily rise and fall of the ocean's tides are the result of the gravitational pull of the Moon and that of the Sun, though the effect of the latter is only 46.6% as strong as that of the Moon. This effect is greatest on the hemisphere facing the Moon and causes a tidal 'bulge'. When the Sun, Earth and Moon are in line, tide-raising forces are at a maximum and Spring tides occur: high tide reaches the highest values, and low tide falls to low levels. When lunar and solar forces are least coincidental with the Sun and Moon at an angle (near the Moon's first and third quarters), Neap tides occur, which have a small tidal range.

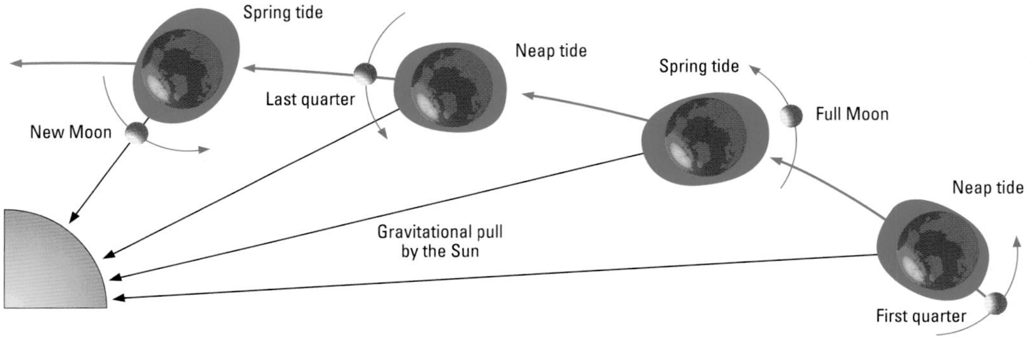
Spring tide
Neap tide
Spring tide
Last quarter
Full Moon
New Moon
Neap tide
Gravitational pull by the Sun
First quarter

Restless Earth

The Earth's Structure

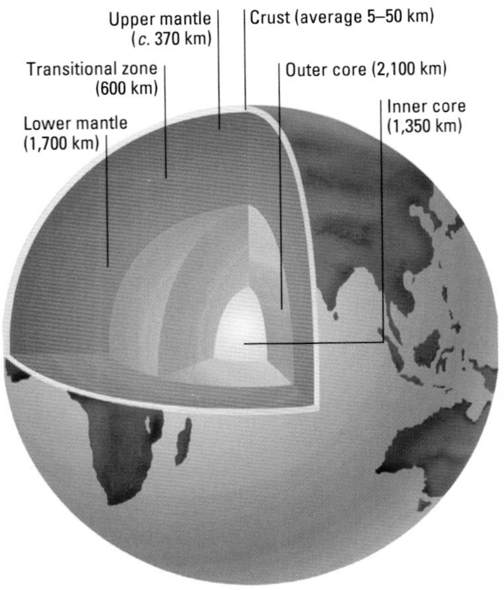

Continental Drift

About 200 million years ago the original Pangaea landmass began to split into two continental groups, which further separated over time to produce the present-day configuration.

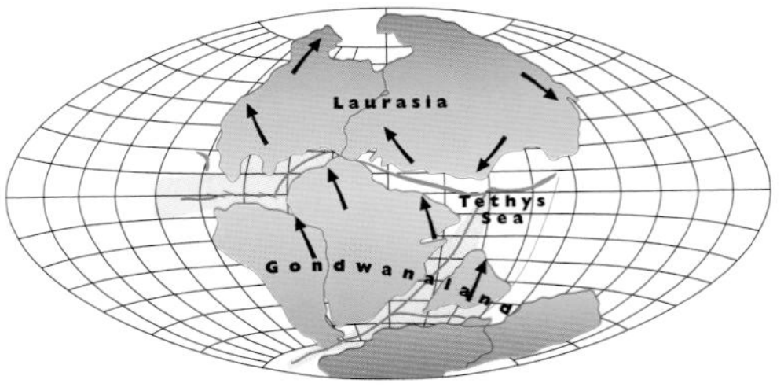

180 million years ago

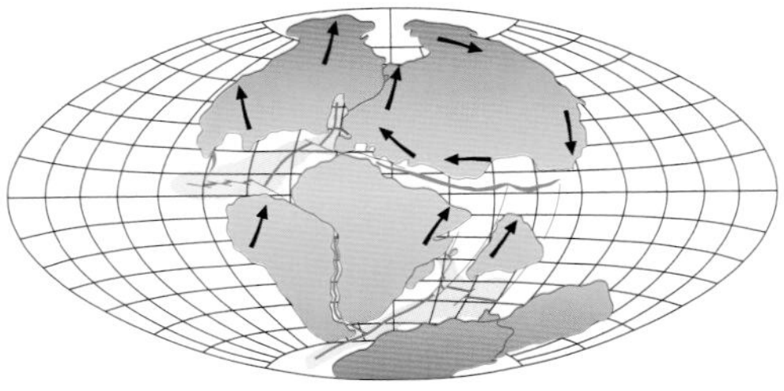

135 million years ago

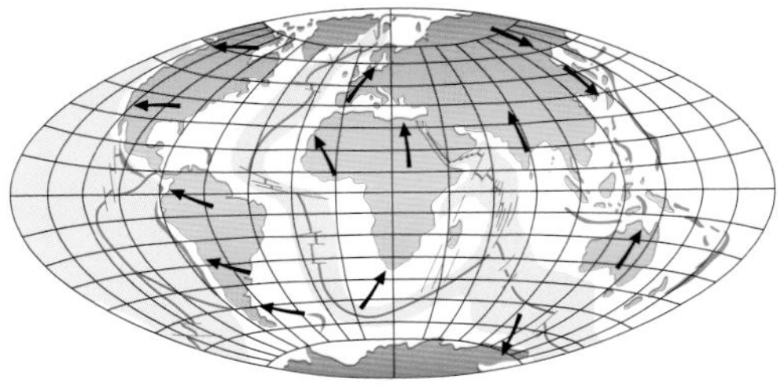

Present day

Trench
Rift
New ocean floor
Zones of slippage

Notable Earthquakes Since 1900

Year	Location	Richter Scale	Deaths
1906	San Francisco, USA	8.3	503
1906	Valparaiso, Chile	8.6	22,000
1906	San Francisco, USA	7.7	3,000
1906	Valparaiso, Chile	8.6	22,000
1908	Messina, Italy	7.5	83,000
1915	Avezzano, Italy	7.5	30,000
1920	Gansu (Kansu), China	8.6	180,000
1923	Yokohama, Japan	8.3	143,000
1927	Nan Shan, China	8.3	200,000
1932	Gansu (Kansu), China	7.6	70,000
1933	Sanriku, Japan	8.9	2,990
1934	Bihar, India/Nepal	8.4	10,700
1935	Quetta, India (*now* Pakistan)	7.5	60,000
1939	Chillan, Chile	8.3	28,000
1939	Erzincan, Turkey	7.9	30,000
1960	S. W. Chile	9.5	2,200
1960	Agadir, Morocco	5.8	12,000
1962	Khorasan, Iran	7.1	12,230
1964	Anchorage, USA	9.2	125
1968	N. E. Iran	7.4	12,000
1970	N. Peru	7.7	66,794
1972	Managua, Nicaragua	6.2	5,000
1974	N. Pakistan	6.3	5,200
1976	Guatemala	7.5	22,778
1976	Tangshan, China	8.2	255,000
1978	Tabas, Iran	7.7	25,000
1980	El Asnam, Algeria	7.3	20,000
1980	S. Italy	7.2	4,800
1985	Mexico City, Mexico	8.1	4,200
1988	N.W. Armenia	6.8	55,000
1990	N. Iran	7.7	36,000
1992	Flores, Indonesia	6.8	1,895
1993	Maharashtra, India	6.4	30,000
1994	Los Angeles, USA	6.6	51
1995	Kobe, Japan	7.2	5,000
1995	Sakhalin Is., Russia	7.5	2,000
1996	Yunnan, China	7.0	240
1997	N. E. Iran	7.1	2,400
1998	Takhar, Afghanistan	6.1	4,200
1998	Rostaq, Afghanistan	7.0	5,000
1999	Izmit, Turkey	7.4	15,000
1999	Taipei, Taiwan	7.6	1,700
2001	Gujarat, India	7.7	14,000
2002	Afyon, Turkey	6.5	44
2002	Baghlan, Afghanistan	6.1	1,000

Earthquakes

Earthquake magnitude is usually rated according to either the Richter or the Modified Mercalli scale, both devised by seismologists in the 1930s. The Richter scale measures absolute earthquake power with mathematical precision: each step upwards represents a tenfold increase in shockwave amplitude. Theoretically, there is no upper limit, but the largest earthquakes measured have been rated at between 8.8 and 8.9. The 12-point Mercalli scale, based on observed effects, is often more meaningful, ranging from I (earthquakes noticed only by seismographs) to XII (total destruction); intermediate points include V (people awakened at night; unstable objects overturned), VII (collapse of ordinary buildings; chimneys and monuments fall) and IX (conspicuous cracks in ground; serious damage to reservoirs).

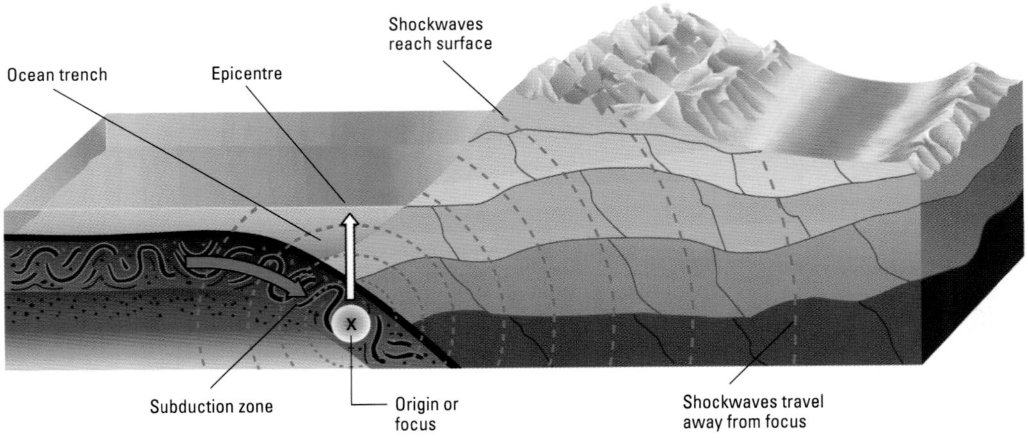

Structure and Earthquakes

Mobile land areas

Submarine zones of mobile land areas

Stable land platforms

Submarine extensions of stable land platforms

Mid-oceanic volcanic ridges

Oceanic platforms

1976○ Principal earthquakes and dates (since 1900)

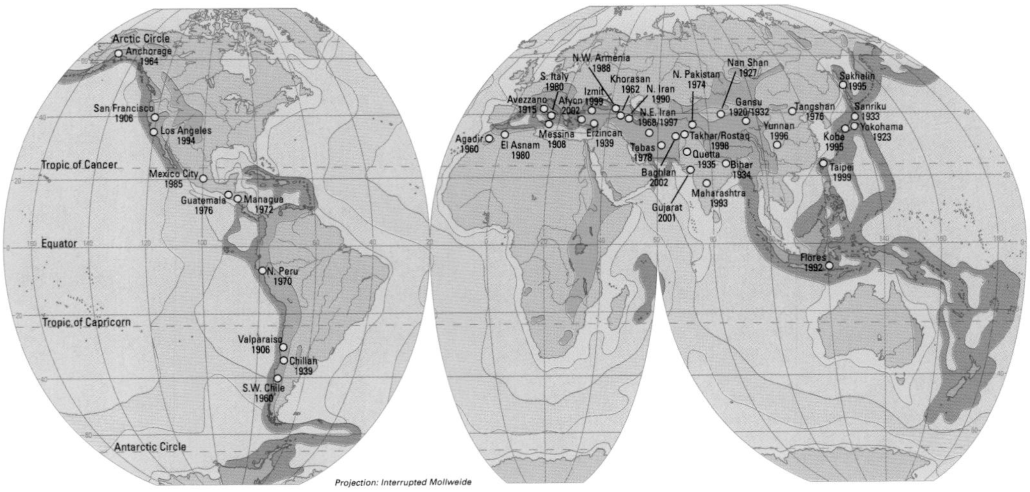

Earthquakes are a series of rapid vibrations originating from the slipping or faulting of parts of the Earth's crust when stresses within build up to breaking point. They usually happen at depths varying from 8 km to 30 km. Severe earthquakes cause extensive damage when they take place in populated areas, destroying structures and severing communications. Most initial loss of life occurs due to secondary causes such as falling masonry, fires and flooding.

Plate Tectonics

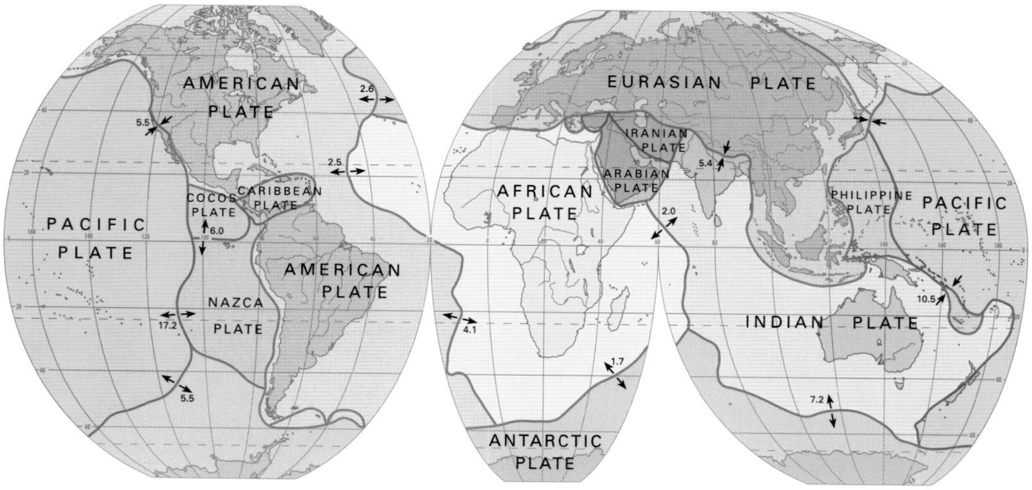
AMERICAN PLATE
5.5
2.6
2.5
COCOS PLATE
CARIBBEAN PLATE
6.0
PACIFIC PLATE
NAZCA PLATE
17.2
AMERICAN PLATE
5.5
EURASIAN PLATE
IRANIAN PLATE
ARABIAN PLATE
5.4
AFRICAN PLATE
2.0
4.1
1.7
PHILIPPINE PLATE
PACIFIC PLATE
10.5
INDIAN PLATE
7.2
ANTARCTIC PLATE

— Plate boundaries

PACIFIC Major plates

→ Direction of plate movements and rate of movement (cm/year)

The drifting of the continents is a feature that is unique to Planet Earth. The complementary, almost jigsaw-puzzle fit of the coastlines on each side of the Atlantic Ocean inspired Alfred Wegener's theory of continental drift in 1915. The theory suggested that the ancient super-continent, which Wegener named Pangaea, incorporated all of the Earth's landmasses and gradually split up to form today's continents.

The original debate about continental drift was a prelude to a more radical idea: plate tectonics. The basic theory is that the Earth's crust is made up of a series of rigid plates which float on a soft layer of the mantle and are moved about by continental convection currents within the Earth's interior. These plates diverge and converge along margins marked by seismic activity. Plates diverge from mid-ocean ridges where molten lava pushes upwards and forces the plates apart at rates of up to 40 mm [1.6 in] a year.

The three diagrams, left, give some examples of plate boundaries from around the world. Diagram (a) shows sea-floor spreading at the Mid-Atlantic Ridge as the American and African plates slowly diverge. The same thing is happening in (b) where sea-floor spreading at the Mid-Indian Ocean Ridge is forcing the Indian plate to collide into the Eurasian plate. In (c) oceanic crust (sima) is being subducted beneath lighter continental crust (sial).

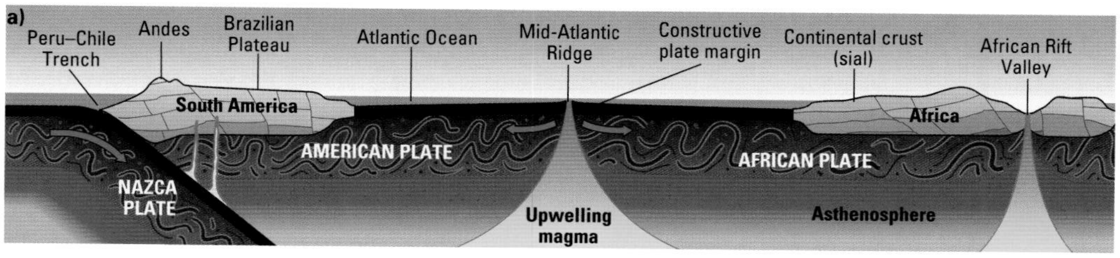
a)
Peru–Chile Trench
Andes
Brazilian Plateau
Atlantic Ocean
Mid-Atlantic Ridge
Constructive plate margin
Continental crust (sial)
African Rift Valley
South America
Africa
AMERICAN PLATE
AFRICAN PLATE
NAZCA PLATE
Upwelling magma
Asthenosphere

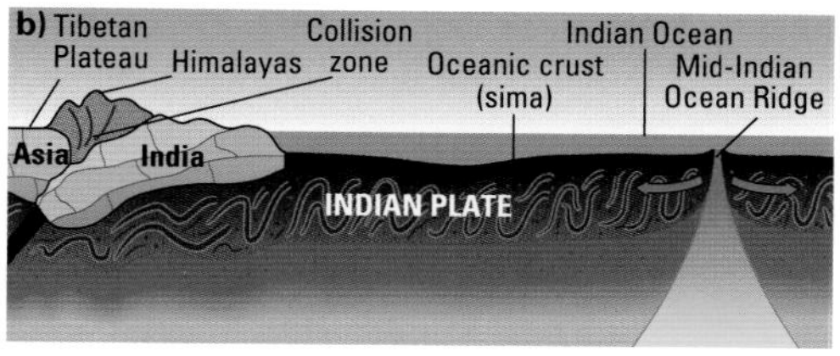
b) Tibetan Plateau
Himalayas
Collision zone
Indian Ocean
Oceanic crust (sima)
Mid-Indian Ocean Ridge
Asia
India
INDIAN PLATE

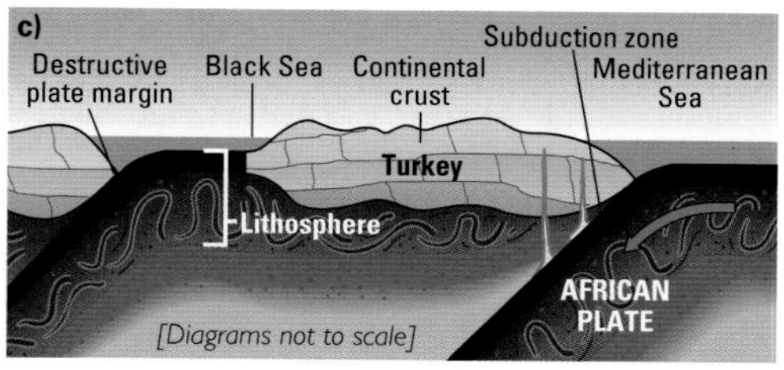
c)
Destructive plate margin
Black Sea
Continental crust
Subduction zone
Mediterranean Sea
Turkey
Lithosphere
AFRICAN PLATE
[Diagrams not to scale]

Volcanoes

Volcanoes occur when hot liquefied rock beneath the Earth's crust is pushed up by pressure to the surface as molten lava. Some volcanoes erupt in an explosive way, throwing out rocks and ash, whilst others are effusive and lava flows out of the vent. There are volcanoes which are both, such as Mount Fuji. An accumulation of lava and cinders creates cones of variable size and shape. As a result of many eruptions over centuries, Mount Etna in Sicily has a circumference of more than 120 km [75 miles].

Climatologists believe that volcanic ash, if ejected high into the atmosphere, can influence temperature and weather for several years afterwards. The 1991 eruption of Mount Pinatubo in the Philippines ejected more than 20 million tonnes of dust and ash 32 km [20 miles] into the atmosphere and is believed to have accelerated ozone depletion over a large part of the globe.

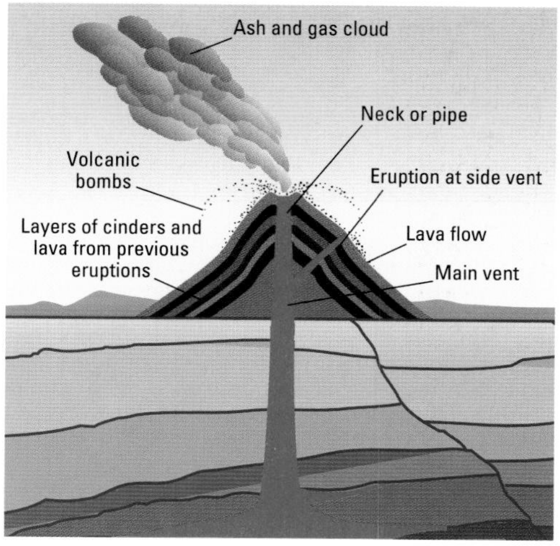
Ash and gas cloud
Neck or pipe
Volcanic bombs
Eruption at side vent
Layers of cinders and lava from previous eruptions
Lava flow
Main vent

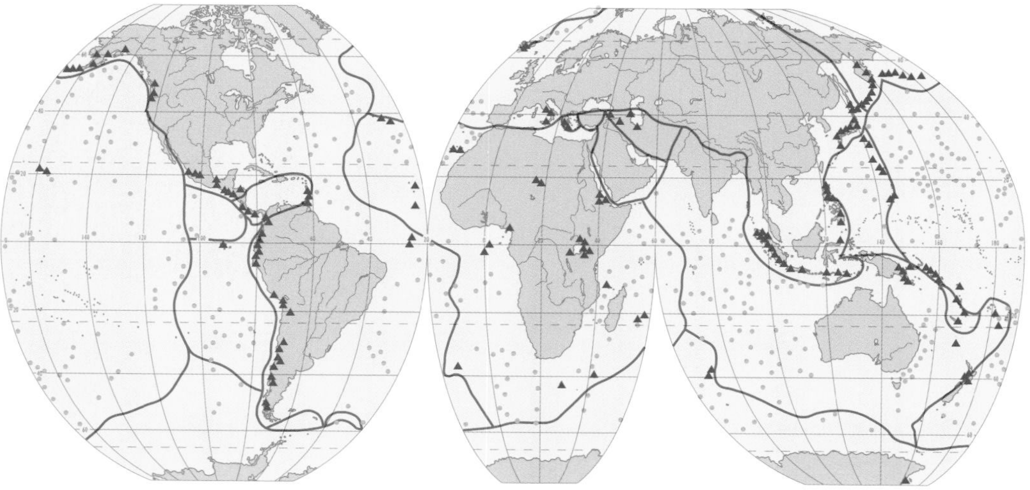

Distribution of Volcanoes

Volcanoes today may be the subject of considerable scientific study but they remain both dramatic and unpredictable: in 1991 Mount Pinatubo, 100 km [62 miles] north of the Philippines capital Manila, suddenly burst into life after lying dormant for more than six centuries. Most of the world's active volcanoes occur in a belt around the Pacific Ocean, on the edge of the Pacific plate, called the 'ring of fire'. Indonesia has the greatest concentration with 90 volcanoes, 12 of which are active. The most famous, Krakatoa, erupted in 1883 with such force that the resulting tidal wave killed 36,000 people and tremors were felt as far away as Australia.

● Submarine volcanoes

▲ Land volcanoes active since 1700

— Boundaries of tectonic plates

Landforms

The Rock Cycle

James Hutton first proposed the rock cycle in the late 1700s after he observed the slow but steady effects of erosion.

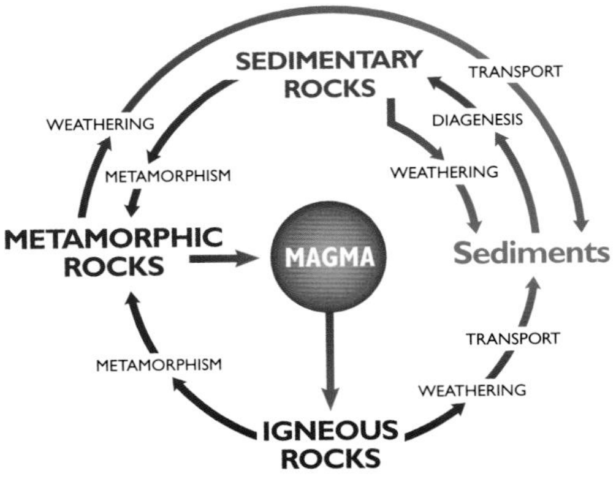

Above and below the surface of the oceans, the features of the Earth's crust are constantly changing. The phenomenal forces generated by convection currents in the molten core of our planet carry the vast segments or 'plates' of the crust across the globe in an endless cycle of creation and destruction. A continent may travel little more than 25 mm [1 in] per year, yet in the vast span of geological time this process throws up giant mountain ranges and creates new land.

Destruction of the landscape, however, begins as soon as it is formed. Wind, water, ice and sea, the main agents of erosion, mount a constant assault that even the most resistant rocks cannot withstand. Mountain peaks may dwindle by as little as a few millimetres each year, but if they are not uplifted by further movements of the crust they will eventually be reduced to rubble and transported away.

Water is the most powerful agent of erosion – it has been estimated that 100 billion tonnes of sediment are washed into the oceans every year. Three Asian rivers account for 20% of this total, the Huang He, in China, and the Brahmaputra and Ganges in Bangladesh.

Rivers and glaciers, like the sea itself, generate much of their effect through abrasion – pounding the land with the debris they carry with them. But as well as destroying they also create new landforms, many of them spectacular: vast deltas like those of the Mississippi and the Nile, or the deep fjords cut by glaciers in British Columbia, Norway and New Zealand.

Geologists once considered that landscapes evolved from 'young', newly uplifted mountainous areas, through a 'mature' hilly stage, to an 'old age' stage when the land was reduced to an almost flat plain, or peneplain. This theory, called the 'cycle of erosion', fell into disuse when it became evident that so many factors, including the effects of plate tectonics and climatic change, constantly interrupt the cycle, which takes no account of the highly complex interactions that shape the surface of our planet.

Mountain Building

Mountains are formed when pressures on the Earth's crust caused by continental drift become so intense that the surface buckles or cracks. This happens where oceanic crust is subducted by continental crust or, more dramatically, where two tectonic plates collide: the Rockies, Andes, Alps, Urals and Himalayas resulted from such impacts. These are all known as fold mountains because they were formed by the compression of the rocks, forcing the surface to bend and fold like a crumpled rug. The Himalayas are formed from the folded former sediments of the Tethys Sea which was trapped in the collision zone between the Indian and Eurasian plates.

The other main mountain-building process occurs when the crust fractures to create faults, allowing rock to be forced upwards in large blocks; or when the pressure of magma within the crust forces the surface to bulge into a dome, or erupts to form a volcano. Large mountain ranges may reveal a combination of those features; the Alps, for example, have been compressed so violently that the folds are fragmented by numerous faults and intrusions of molten igneous rock.

Over millions of years, even the greatest mountain ranges can be reduced by the agents of erosion (most notably rivers) to a low rugged landscape known as a peneplain.

Types of faults: Faults occur where the crust is being stretched or compressed so violently that the rock strata break in a horizontal or vertical movement. They are classified by the direction in which the blocks of rock have moved. A normal fault results when a vertical movement causes the surface to break apart; compression causes a reverse fault. Horizontal movement causes shearing, known as a strike-slip fault. When the rock breaks in two places, the central block may be pushed up in a horst fault, or sink (creating a rift valley) in a graben fault.

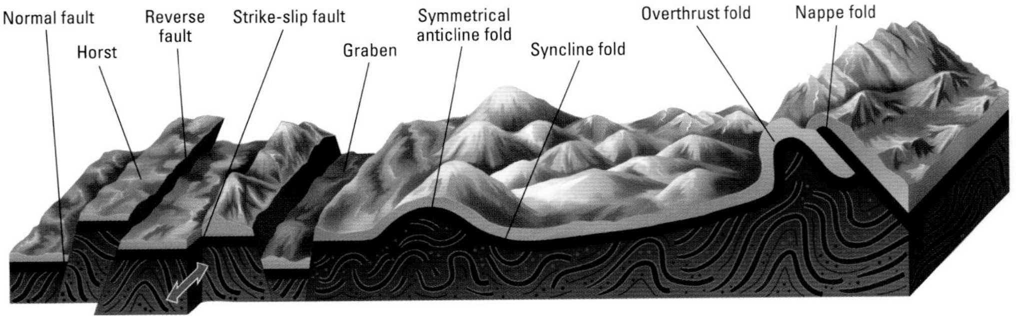

Types of fold: Folds occur when rock strata are squeezed and compressed. They are common therefore at destructive plate margins and where plates have collided, forcing the rocks to buckle into mountain ranges. Geographers give different names to the degrees of fold that result from continuing pressure on the rock. A simple fold may be symmetric, with even slopes on either side, but as the pressure builds up, one slope becomes steeper and the fold becomes asymmetric. Later, the ridge or 'anticline' at the top of the fold may slide over the lower ground or 'syncline' to form a recumbent fold. Eventually, the rock strata may break under the pressure to form an overthrust and finally a nappe fold.

Continental Glaciation

Ice sheets were at their greatest extent about 200,000 years ago. The maximum advance of the last Ice Age was about 18,000 years ago, when ice covered virtually all of Canada and reached as far south as the Bristol Channel in Britain.

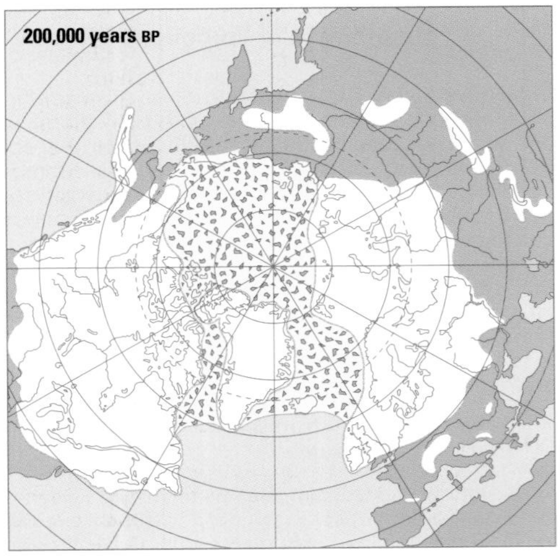

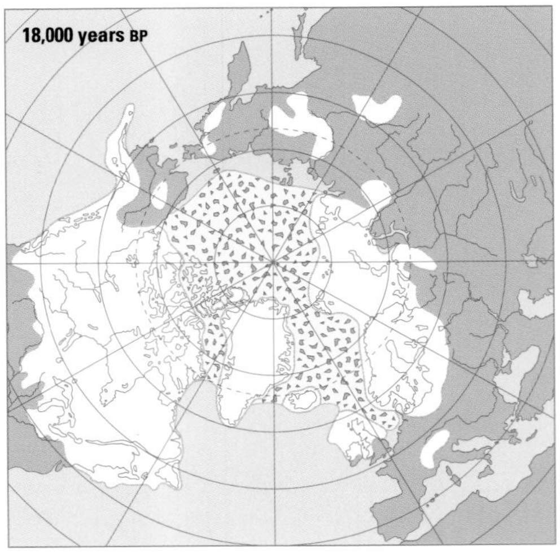

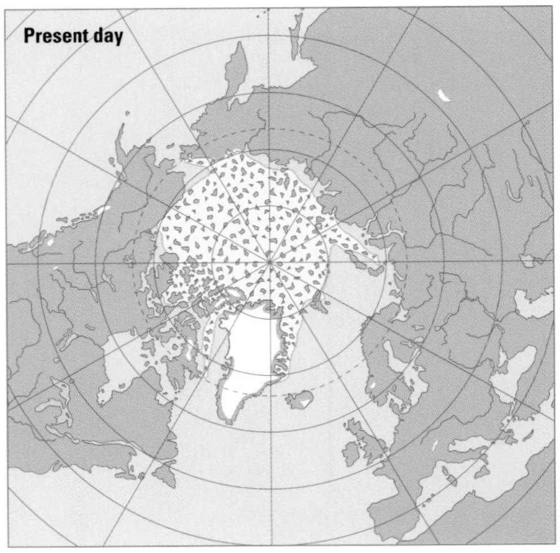

Natural Landforms

A stylized diagram to show a selection of landforms found in the mid-latitudes.

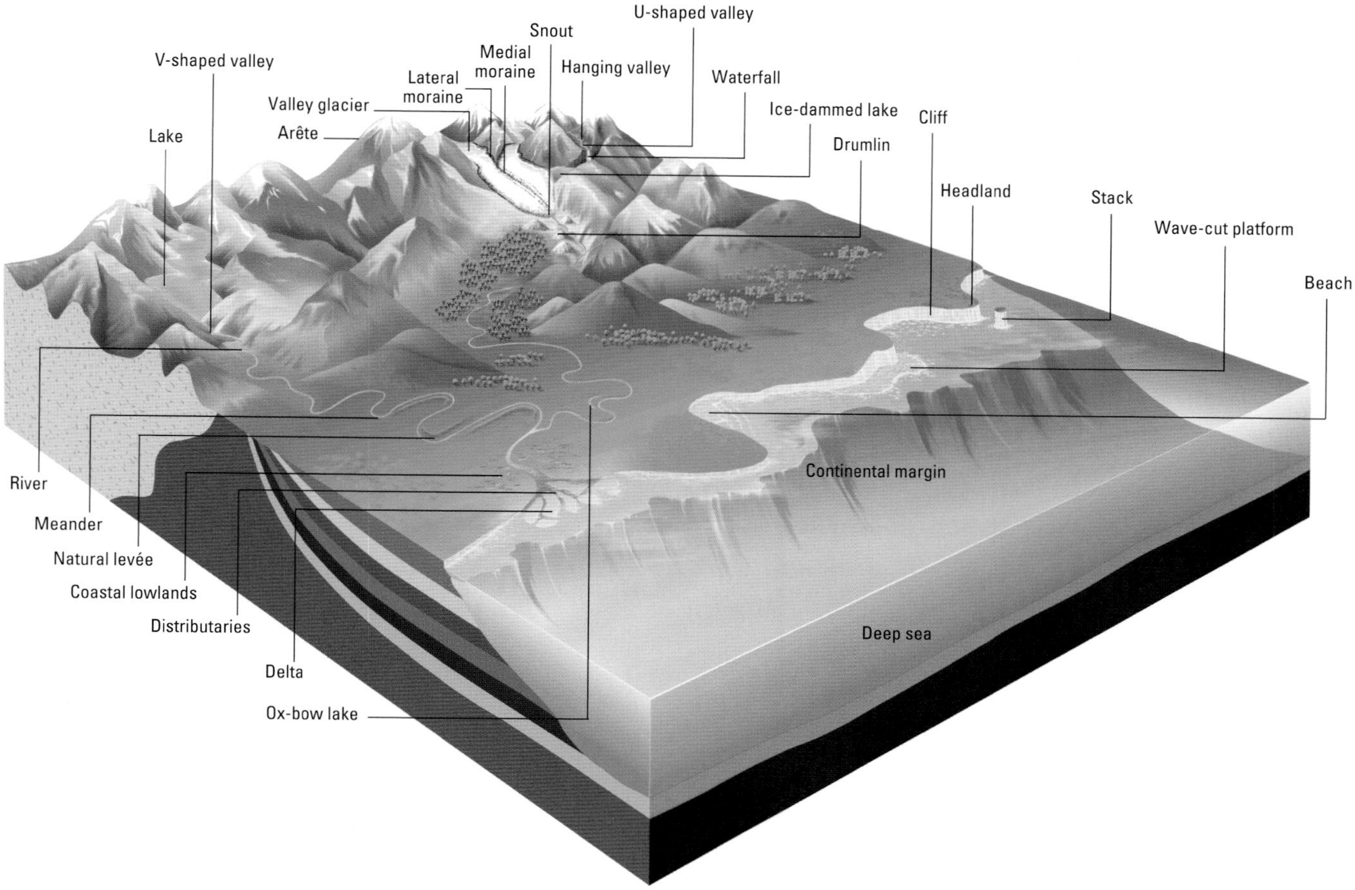

Desert Landscapes

The popular image that deserts are all huge expanses of sand is wrong. Despite harsh conditions, deserts contain some of the most varied and interesting landscapes in the world. They are also one of the most extensive environments – the hot and cold deserts together cover almost 40% of the Earth's surface.

The three types of hot desert are known by their Arabic names: sand desert, called *erg*, covers only about one-fifth of the world's desert; the rest is divided between *hammada* (areas of bare rock) and *reg* (broad plains covered by loose gravel or pebbles).

In areas of *erg*, such as the Namib Desert, the shape of the dunes reflects the character of local winds. Where winds are constant in direction, crescent-shaped *barchan* dunes form. In areas of bare rock, wind-blown sand is a major agent of erosion. The erosion is mainly confined to within 2 m [6.5 ft] of the surface, producing characteristic, mushroom-shaped rocks.

Surface Processes

Catastrophic changes to natural landforms are periodically caused by such phenomena as avalanches, landslides and volcanic eruptions, but most of the processes that shape the Earth's surface operate extremely slowly in human terms. One estimate, based on a study in the United States, suggested that 1 m [3 ft] of land was removed from the entire surface of the country, on average, every 29,500 years. However, the time-scale varies from 1,300 years to 154,200 years depending on the terrain and climate.

In hot, dry climates, mechanical weathering, a result of rapid temperature changes, causes the outer layers of rock to peel away, while in cold mountainous regions, boulders are prised apart when water freezes in cracks in rocks. Chemical weathering, at its greatest in warm, humid regions, is responsible for hollowing out limestone caves and decomposing granites.

The erosion of soil and rock is greatest on sloping land and the steeper the slope, the greater the tendency for mass wasting – the movement of soil and rock downhill under the influence of gravity. The mechanisms of mass wasting (ranging from very slow to very rapid) vary with the type of material, but the presence of water as a lubricant is usually an important factor.

Running water is the world's leading agent of erosion and transportation. The energy of a river depends on several factors, including its velocity and volume, and its erosive power is at its peak when it is in full flood. Sea waves also exert tremendous erosive power during storms when they hurl pebbles against the shore, undercutting cliffs and hollowing out caves.

Glacier ice forms in mountain hollows and spills out to form valley glaciers, which transport rocks shattered by frost action. As glaciers move, rocks embedded into the ice erode steep-sided, U-shaped valleys. Evidence of glaciation in mountain regions includes cirques, knife-edged ridges, or arêtes, and pyramidal peaks.

Oceans

The Great Oceans

Relative sizes of the world's oceans

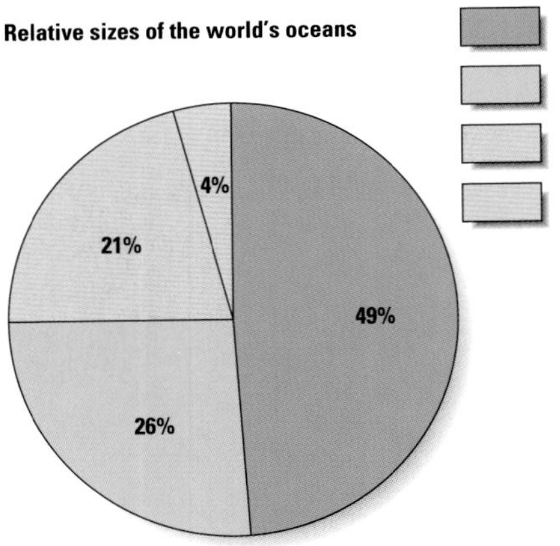

In a strict geographical sense there are only three true oceans – the Atlantic, Indian and Pacific. The legendary 'Seven Seas' would require these to be divided at the Equator and the addition of the Arctic Ocean – which accounts for less than 4% of the total sea area. The International Hydrographic Bureau does not recognize the Antarctic Ocean (even less the 'Southern Ocean') as a separate entity.

The Earth is a watery planet: more than 70% of its surface – over 360,000,000 sq km [140,000,000 sq miles] – is covered by the oceans and seas. The mighty Pacific alone accounts for nearly 36% of the total, and 49% of the sea area. Gravity holds in around 1,400 million cu. km [320 million cu. miles] of water, of which over 97% is saline.

The vast underwater world starts in the shallows of the seaside and plunges to depths of more than 11,000 m [36,000 ft]. The continental shelf, part of the landmass, drops gently to around 200 m [650 ft]; here the seabed falls away suddenly at an angle of 3° to 6° – the continental slope. The third stage, called the continental rise, is more gradual with gradients varying from 1 in 100 to 1 in 700. At an average depth of 5,000 m [16,500 ft] there begins the aptly-named abyssal plain – massive submarine depths where sunlight fails to penetrate and few creatures can survive.

From these plains rise volcanoes which, taken from base to top, rival and even surpass the tallest continental mountains in height. Mount Kea, on Hawaii, reaches a total of 10,203 m [33,400 ft], some 1,355 m [4,500 ft] more than Mount Everest, though scarcely 40% is visible above sea level.

In addition, there are underwater mountain chains up to 1,000 km [600 miles] across, whose peaks sometimes appear above sea level as islands such as Iceland and Tristan da Cunha.

The Ocean Depths

Average and maximum depths of the world's great oceans, in metres

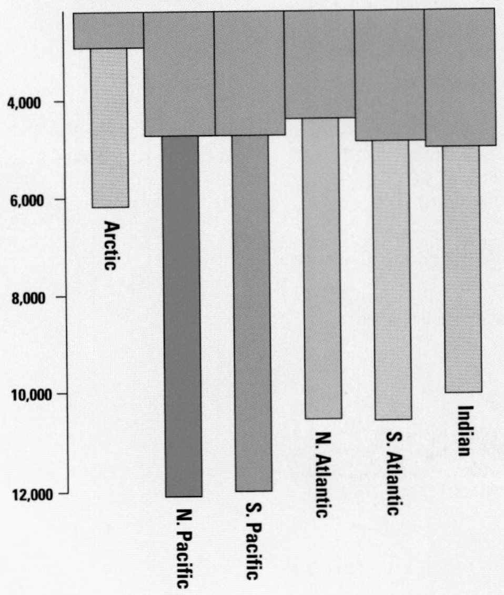

Ocean Currents

January temperatures and ocean currents

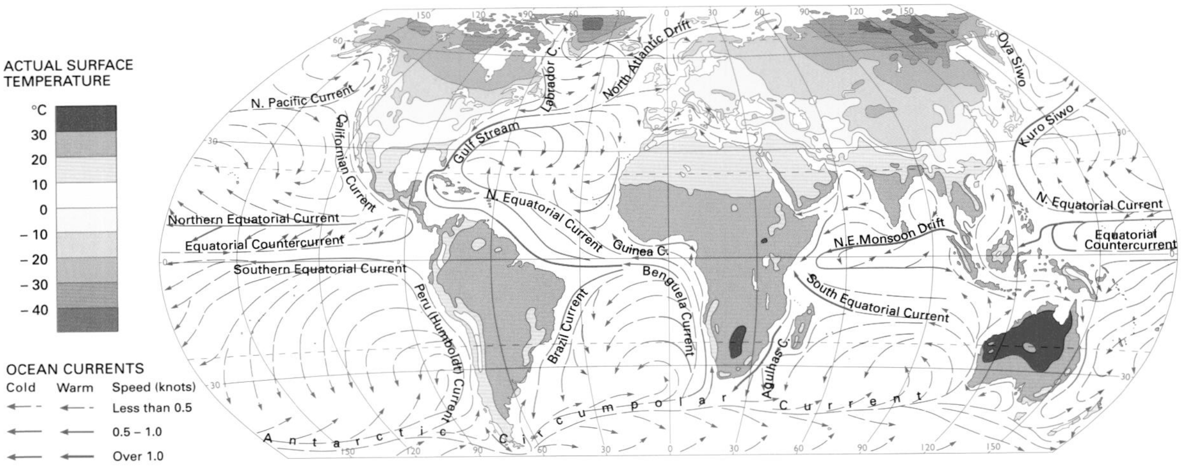

July temperatures and ocean currents

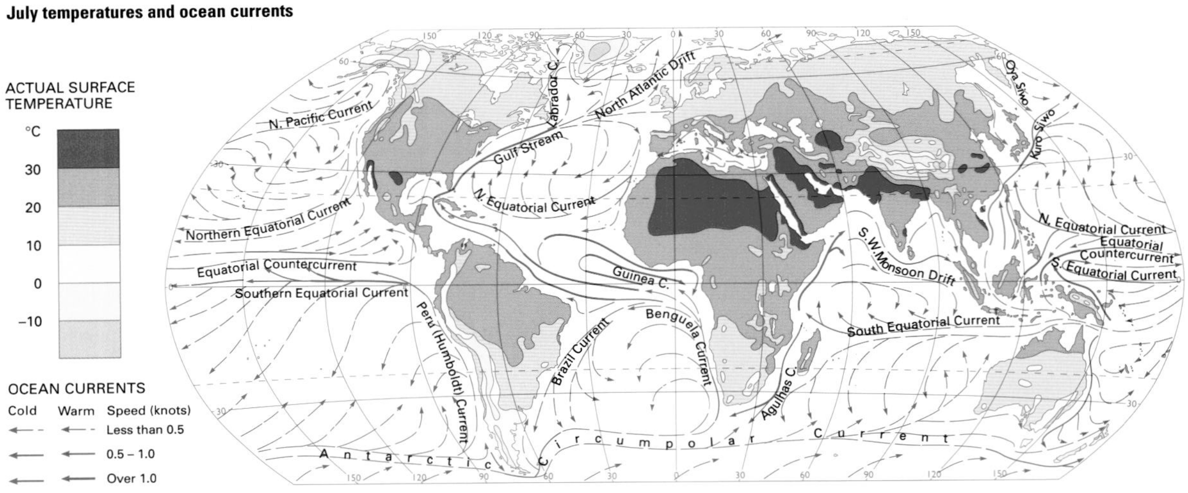

Moving immense quantities of energy as well as billions of tonnes of water every hour, the ocean currents are a vital part of the great heat engine that drives the Earth's climate. They themselves are produced by a twofold mechanism. At the surface, winds push huge masses of water before them; in the deep ocean, below an abrupt temperature gradient that separates the churning surface waters from the still depths, density variations cause slow vertical movements.

The pattern of circulation of the great surface currents is determined by the displacement known as the Coriolis effect. As the Earth turns beneath a moving object – whether it is a tennis ball or a vast mass of water – it appears to be deflected to one side. The deflection is most obvious near the Equator, where the Earth's surface is spinning eastwards at 1,700 km/h [1,050 mph]; currents moving polewards are curved clockwise in the northern hemisphere and anti-clockwise in the southern.

The result is a system of spinning circles known as gyres. The Coriolis effect piles up water on the left of each gyre, creating a narrow, fast-moving stream that is matched by a slower, broader returning current on the right. North and south of the Equator, the fastest currents are located in the west and in the east respectively. In each case, warm water moves from the Equator and cold water returns to it. Cold currents often bring an upwelling of nutrients with them, supporting the world's most economically important fisheries.

Depending on the prevailing winds, some currents on or near the Equator may reverse their direction in the course of the year – a seasonal variation on which Asian monsoon rains depend, and whose occasional failure can bring disaster to millions.

World Fishing Areas

Main commercial fishing areas (numbered FAO regions)

Catch by top marine fishing areas, thousand tonnes (1997)

1. Pacific, NW	[61]	26,785	28.7%
2. Pacific, SE	[87]	15,717	16.8%
3. Atlantic, NE	[27]	12,721	13.6%
4. Pacific, WC	[71]	9,753	10.5%
5. Indian, W	[51]	4,461	4.8%
6. Indian, E	[57]	4,228	4.5%
7. Atlantic, EC	[34]	3,873	4.2%
8. Pacific, NE	[67]	3,042	3.3%

Principal fishing areas

27
67
61
34
71
51
57
87

Leading fishing nations

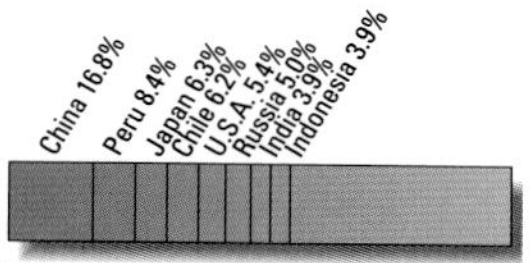

China 16.8%
Peru 8.4%
Japan 6.3%
Chile 6.2%
U.S.A. 5.4%
Russia 5.0%
India 3.9%
Indonesia 3.9%

World total catch (1997): 93,329,200 tonnes
(Marine catch 91.7% Inland catch 8.3%)

Marine Pollution

Sources of marine oil pollution (latest available year)

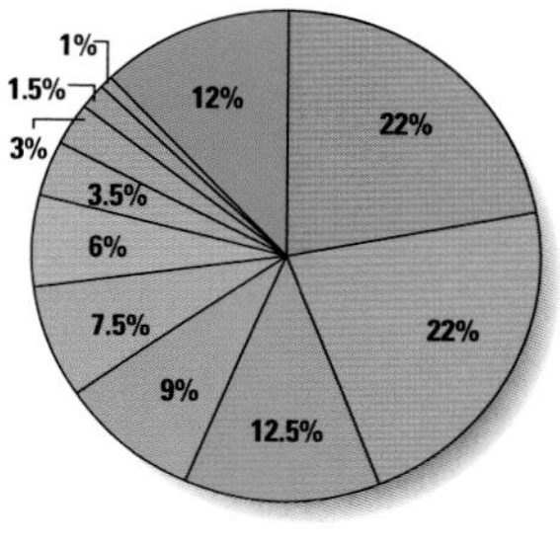

1%
1.5%
3%
12%
22%
3.5%
6%
7.5%
22%
9%
12.5%

- Tanker operations
- Municipal wastes
- Tanker accidents
- Bilge and fuel oils
- Natural seeps
- Industrial waste
- Urban runoff
- Coastal oil refining
- Offshore oil rigs
- River runoffs
- Other

Oil Spills

Major oil spills from tankers and combined carriers

Year	Vessel	Location	Spill (barrels)**	Cause
1979	Atlantic Empress	West Indies	1,890,000	collision
1983	Castillo De Bellver	South Africa	1,760,000	fire
1978	Amoco Cadiz	France	1,628,000	grounding
1991	Haven	Italy	1,029,000	explosion
1988	Odyssey	Canada	1,000,000	fire
1967	Torrey Canyon	UK	909,000	grounding
1972	Sea Star	Gulf of Oman	902,250	collision
1977	Hawaiian Patriot	Hawaiian Is.	742,500	fire
1979	Independenta	Turkey	696,350	collision
1993	Braer	UK	625,000	grounding
1996	Sea Empress	UK	515,000	grounding
Other sources of major oil spills				
1983	Nowruz oilfield	The Gulf	4,250,000†	war
1979	Ixtoc 1 oilwell	Gulf of Mexico	4,200,000	blow-out
1991	Kuwait	The Gulf	2,500,000†	war

** 1 barrel = 0.136 tonnes/159 lit./35 Imperial gal./42 US gal. † estimated

River Pollution

Sources of river pollution, USA (latest available year)

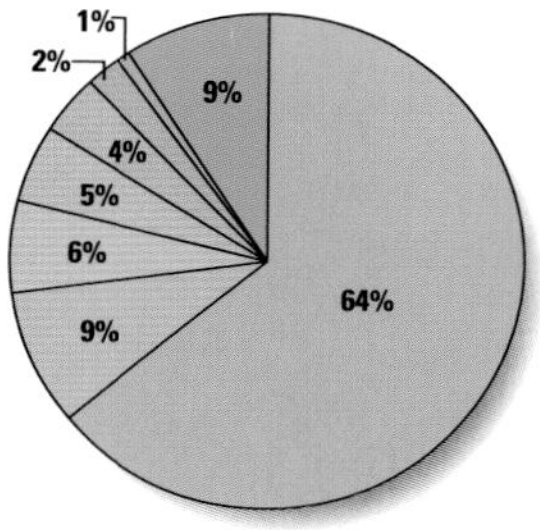

1%
2%
9%
4%
5%
6%
64%
9%

- Agriculture
- Mining
- Forestry
- Urban runoff
- Hydro-engineering
- Construction
- Land disposal
- Other

Water Pollution

- Severely polluted sea areas and lakes
- Polluted sea areas and lakes
- Areas of frequent oil pollution by shipping
- ◣ Major oil tanker spills
- ▲ Major oil rig blow-outs
- ▼ Offshore dumpsites for industrial and municipal waste
- — Severely polluted rivers and estuaries

The most notorious tanker spillage of the 1980s occurred when the *Exxon Valdez* ran aground in Prince William Sound, Alaska, in 1989, spilling 267,000 barrels of crude oil close to shore in a sensitive ecological area. This rates as the world's 28th worst spill in terms of volume.

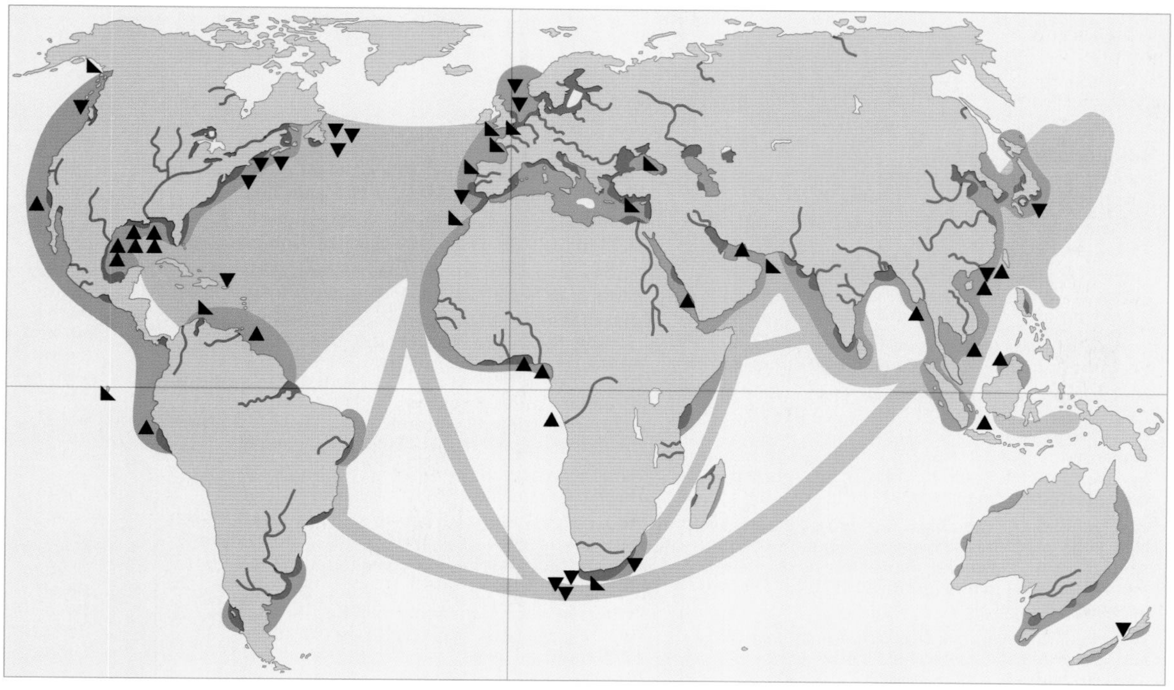

Climate

Climatic Regions

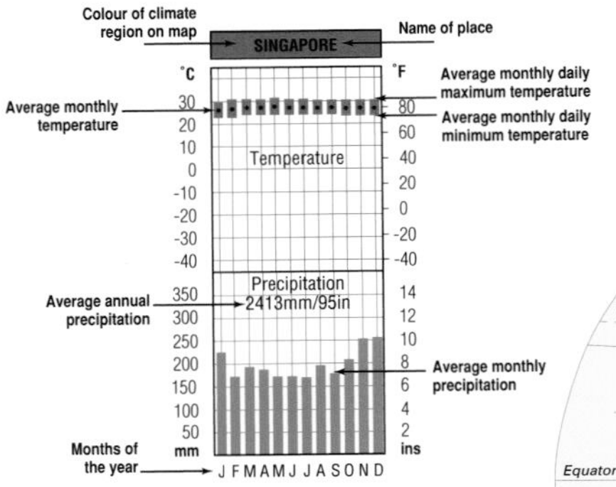

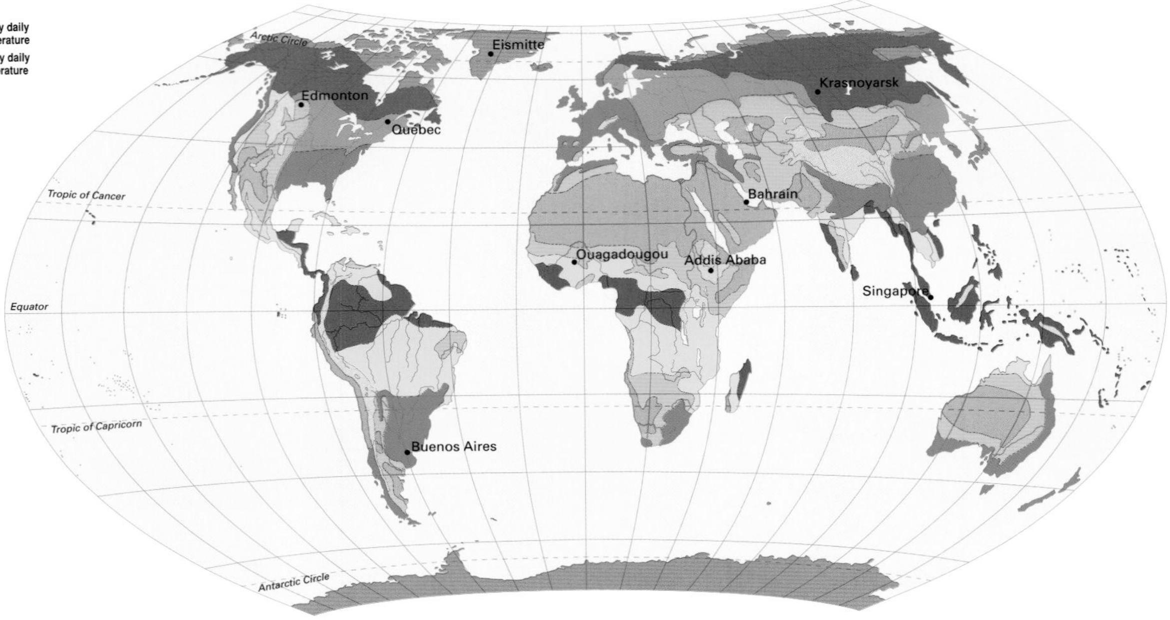

- Tropical climate (hot with rain all year)
- Desert climate (hot and very dry)
- Savanna climate (hot with dry season)
- Steppe climate (warm and dry)
- Mild climate (warm and wet)
- Continental climate (wet with cold winter)
- Subarctic climate (very cold winter)
- Polar climate (very cold and dry)
- Mountainous climate (altitude affects climate)

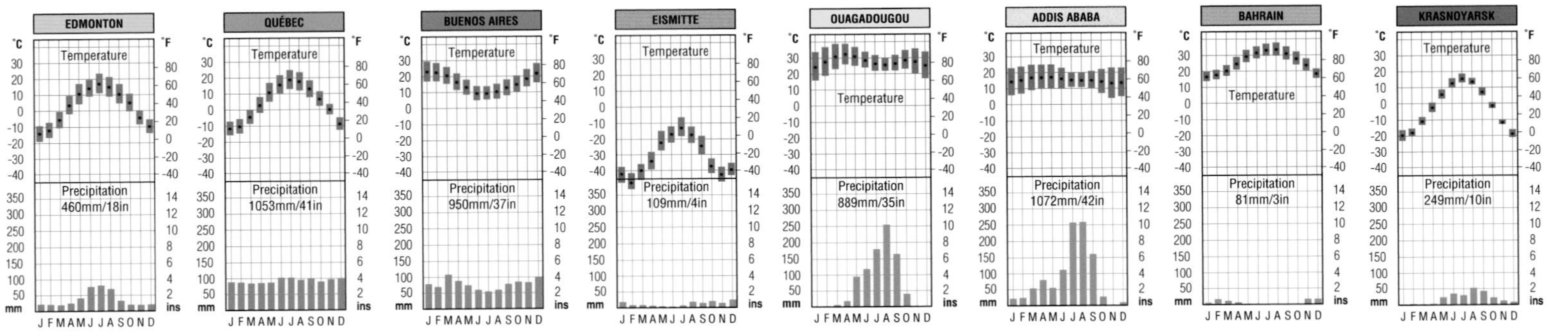

Climate Records

Temperature

Highest recorded shade temperature: Al Aziziyah, Libya, 58°C [136.4°F], 13 September 1922.

Highest mean annual temperature: Dallol, Ethiopia, 34.4°C [94°F], 1960–66.

Longest heatwave: Marble Bar, W. Australia, 162 days over 38°C [100°F], 23 October 1923 to 7 April 1924.

Lowest recorded temperature (outside poles): Verkhoyansk, Siberia, –68°C [–90°F], 6 February 1933.

Lowest mean annual temperature: Plateau Station, Antarctica, –56.6°C [–72.0°F]

Pressure

Longest drought: Calama, N. Chile, no recorded rainfall in 400 years to 1971.

Wettest place (12 months): Cherrapunji, Meghalaya, N. E. India, 26,470 mm [1,040 in], August 1860 to August 1861. Cherrapunji also holds the record for the most rainfall in one month: 2,930 mm [115 in], July 1861.

Wettest place (average): Mawsynram, India, mean annual rainfall 11,873 mm [467.4 in].

Wettest place (24 hours): Cilaos, Réunion, Indian Ocean, 1,870 mm [73.6 in], 15–16 March 1952.

Heaviest hailstones: Gopalganj, Bangladesh, up to 1.02 kg [2.25 lb], 14 April 1986 (killed 92 people).

Heaviest snowfall (continuous): Bessans, Savoie, France, 1,730 mm [68 in] in 19 hours, 5–6 April 1969.

Heaviest snowfall (season/year): Paradise Ranger Station, Mt Rainier, Washington, USA, 31,102 mm [1,224.5 in], 19 February 1971 to 18 February 1972.

Pressure and winds

Highest barometric pressure: Agata, Siberia (at 262 m [862 ft] altitude), 1,083.8 mb, 31 December 1968.

Lowest barometric pressure: Typhoon Tip, Guam, Pacific Ocean, 870 mb, 12 October 1979.

Highest recorded wind speed: Mt Washington, New Hampshire, USA, 371 km/h [231 mph], 12 April 1934. This is three times as strong as hurricane force on the Beaufort Scale.

Windiest place: Commonwealth Bay, Antarctica, where gales frequently reach over 320 km/h [200 mph].

Climate

Climate is weather in the long term: the seasonal pattern of hot and cold, wet and dry, averaged over time (usually 30 years). At the simplest level, it is caused by the uneven heating of the Earth. Surplus heat at the Equator passes towards the poles, levelling out the energy differential. Its passage is marked by a ceaseless churning of the atmosphere and the oceans, further agitated by the Earth's diurnal spin and the motion it imparts to moving air and water. The heat's means of transport – by winds and ocean currents, by the continual evaporation and recondensation of water molecules – is the weather itself. There are four basic types of climate, each of which can be further subdivided: tropical, desert (dry), temperate and polar.

Composition of Dry Air

Nitrogen	78.09%	Sulphur dioxide	trace
Oxygen	20.95%	Nitrogen oxide	trace
Argon	0.93%	Methane	trace
Water vapour	0.2–4.0%	Dust	trace
Carbon dioxide	0.03%	Helium	trace
Ozone	0.00006%	Neon	trace

El Niño

In a normal year, south-easterly trade winds drive surface waters westwards off the coast of South America, drawing cold, nutrient-rich water up from below. In an El Niño year (which occurs every 2–7 years), warm water from the west Pacific suppresses up-welling in the east, depriving the region of nutrients. The water is warmed by as much as 7°C [12°F], disturbing the tropical atmospheric circulation. During an intense El Niño, the south-east trade winds change direction and become equatorial westerlies, resulting in climatic extremes in many regions of the world, such as drought in parts of Australia and India, and heavy rainfall in south-eastern USA. An intense El Niño occurred in 1997–8, with resultant freak weather conditions across the entire Pacific region.

Normal year

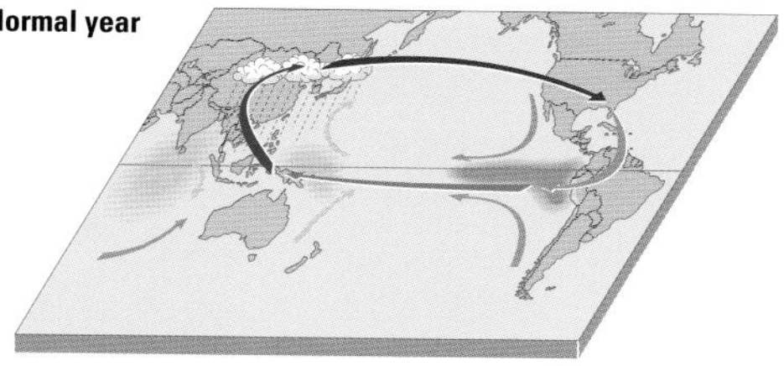

El Niño event

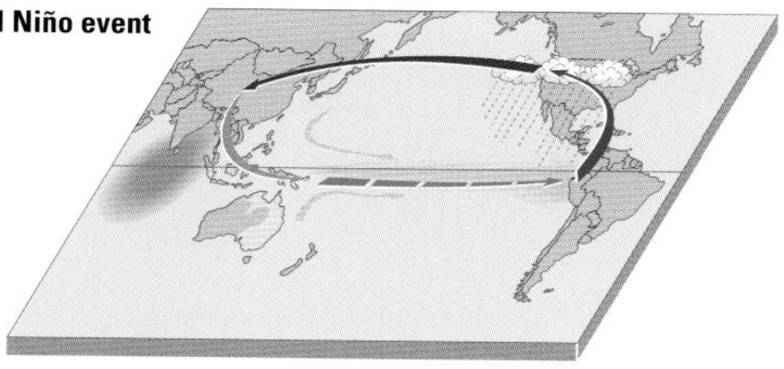

Beaufort Wind Scale

Named after the 19th-century British naval officer who devised it, the Beaufort Scale assesses wind speed according to its effects. It was originally designed as an aid for sailors, but has since been adapted for use on the land.

Scale	Wind speed km/h	mph	Effect
0	0–1	0–1	**Calm** Smoke rises vertically
1	1–5	1–3	**Light air** Wind direction shown only by smoke drift
2	6–11	4–7	**Light breeze** Wind felt on face; leaves rustle; vanes moved by wind
3	12–19	8–12	**Gentle breeze** Leaves and small twigs in constant motion; wind extends small flag
4	20–28	13–18	**Moderate** Raises dust and loose paper; small branches move
5	29–38	19–24	**Fresh** Small trees in leaf sway; wavelets on inland waters
6	39–49	25–31	**Strong** Large branches move; difficult to use umbrellas
7	50–61	32–38	**Near gale** Whole trees in motion; difficult to walk against wind
8	62–74	39–46	**Gale** Twigs break from trees; walking very difficult
9	75–88	47–54	**Strong gale** Slight structural damage
10	89–102	55–63	**Storm** Trees uprooted; serious structural damage
11	103–117	64–72	**Violent storm** Widespread damage
12	118+	73+	**Hurricane**

Conversions

°C = (°F − 32) × 5/9; °F = (°C × 9/5) + 32; 0°C = 32°F

1 in = 25.4 mm; 1 mm = 0.0394 in; 100 mm = 3.94 in

Temperature

Average temperature in January

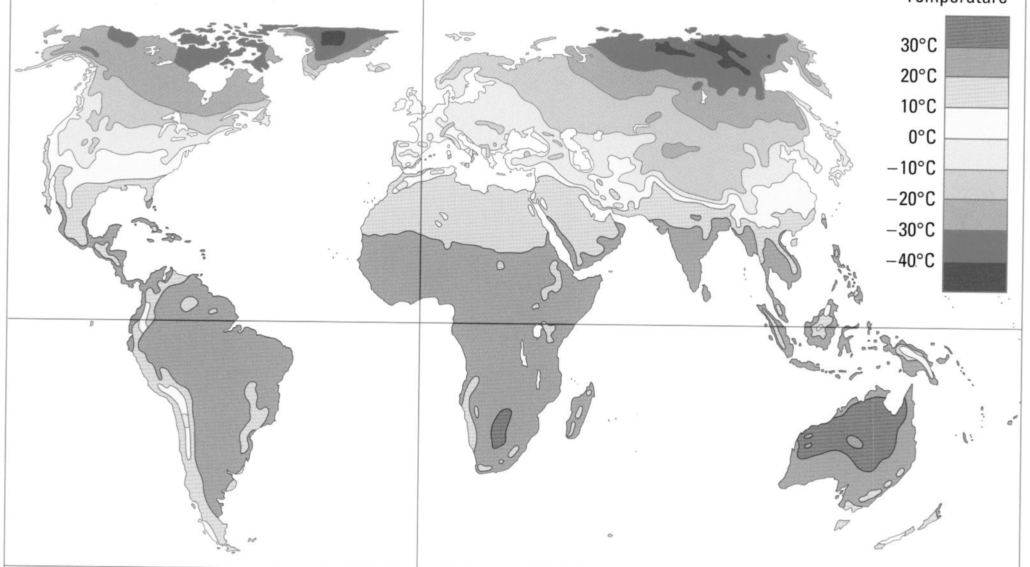
Temperature
30°C
20°C
10°C
0°C
−10°C
−20°C
−30°C
−40°C

Average temperature in July

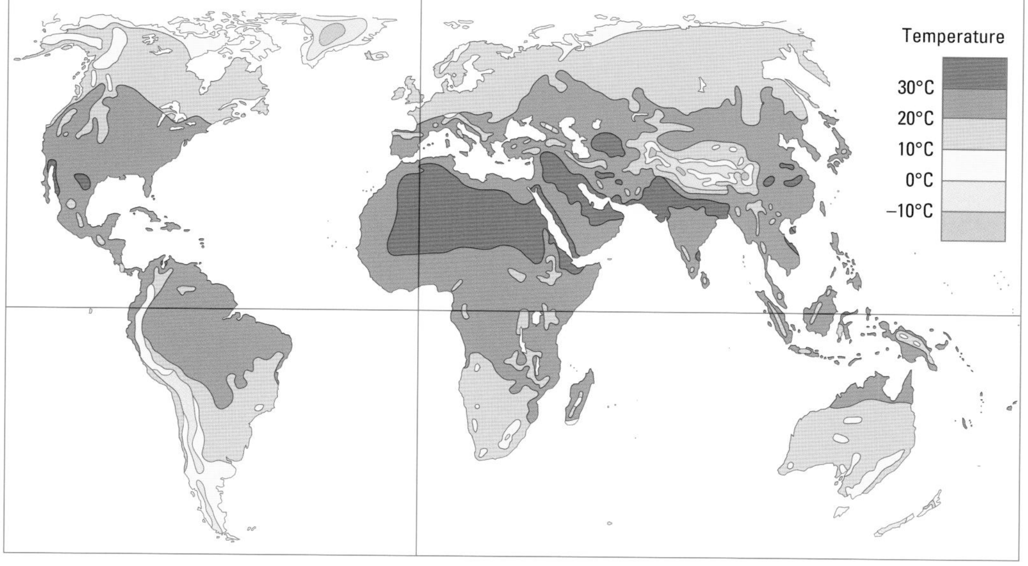
Temperature
30°C
20°C
10°C
0°C
−10°C

Precipitation

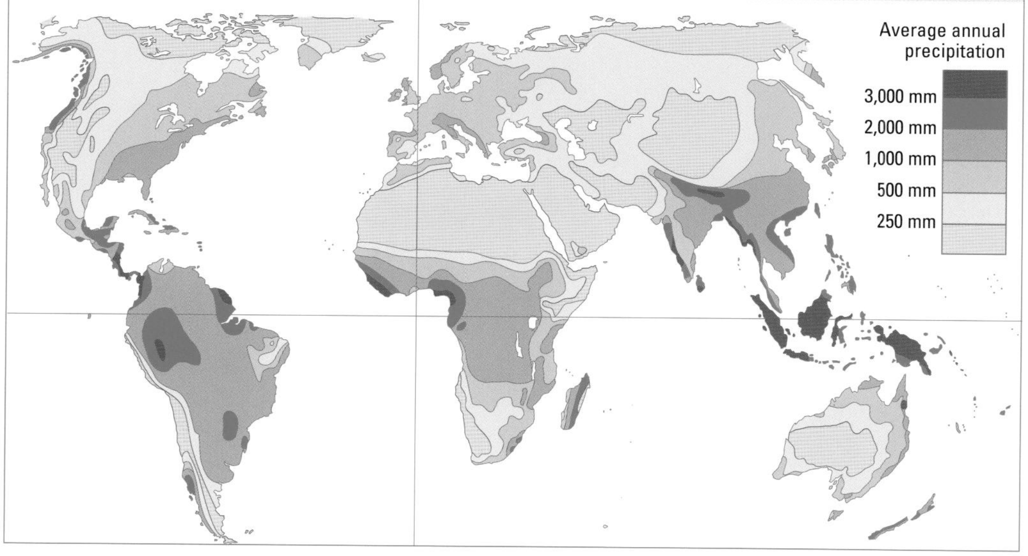
Average annual precipitation
3,000 mm
2,000 mm
1,000 mm
500 mm
250 mm

Water and Vegetation

The Hydrological Cycle

The world's water balance is regulated by the constant recycling of water between the oceans, atmosphere and land. The movement of water between these three reservoirs is known as the hydrological cycle. The oceans play a vital role in the hydrological cycle: 74% of the total precipitation falls over the oceans and 84% of the total evaporation comes from the oceans.

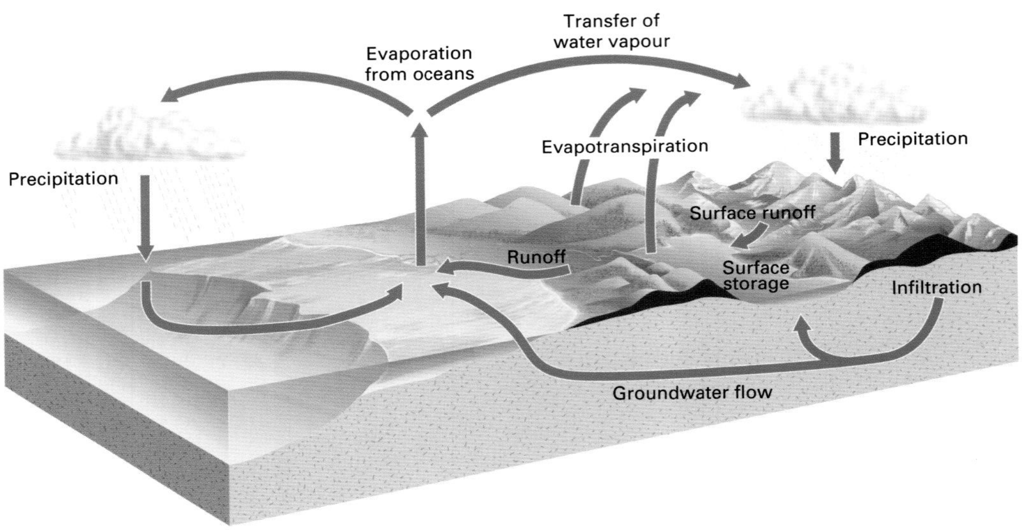

Water Distribution

The distribution of planetary water, by percentage. Oceans and ice caps together account for more than 99% of the total; the breakdown of the remainder is estimated.

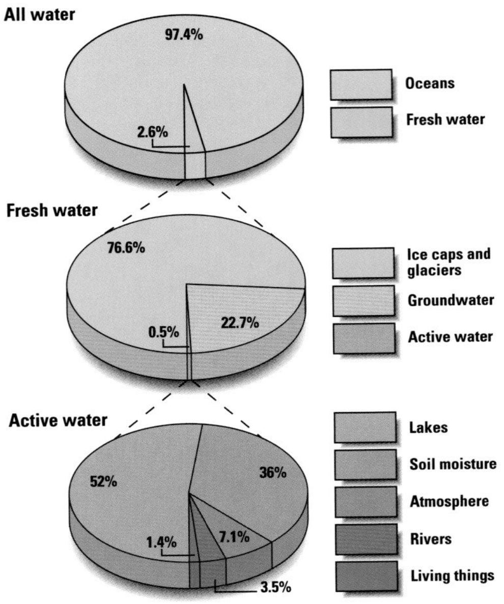

Water Utilization

Domestic | Industrial | Agriculture

The percentage breakdown of water usage by sector, selected countries (1996)

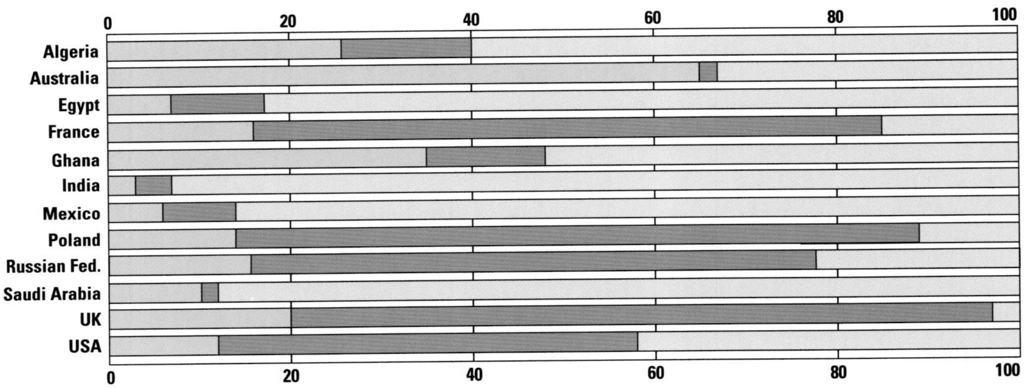

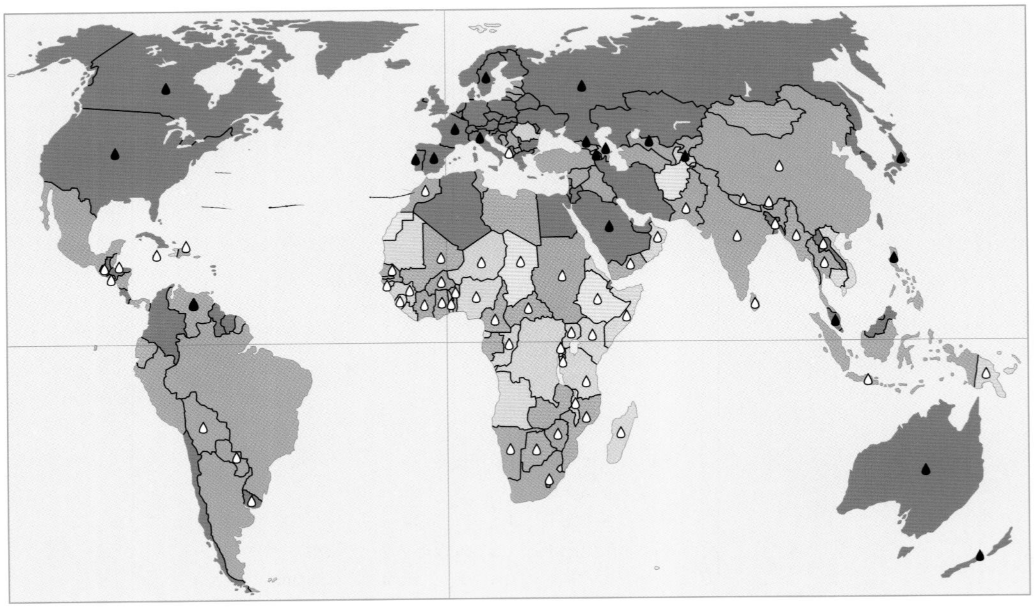

Water Usage

Almost all the world's water is 3,000 million years old, and all of it cycles endlessly through the hydrosphere, though at different rates. Water vapour circulates over days, even hours, deep ocean water circulates over millennia, and ice-cap water remains solid for millions of years.

Fresh water is essential to all terrestrial life. Humans cannot survive more than a few days without it, and even the hardiest desert plants and animals could not exist without some water. Agriculture requires huge quantities of fresh water: without large-scale irrigation most of the world's people would starve. In the USA, agriculture uses 42% and industry 45% of all water withdrawals.

The United States is one of the heaviest users of water in the world. According to the latest figures the average American uses 380 litres a day and the average household uses 415,000 litres a year. This is two to four times more than in Western Europe.

Water Supply

Percentage of total population with access to safe drinking water (2000)

- Over 90% with safe water
- 75 – 90% with safe water
- 60 – 75% with safe water
- 45 – 60% with safe water
- 30 – 45% with safe water
- Under 30% with safe water
- Under 80 litres per person per day domestic water consumption
- Over 320 litres per person per day domestic water consumption

NB: 80 litres of water a day is considered necessary for a reasonable quality of life.

Least well-provided countries

Afghanistan	13%	Sierra Leone	28%
Ethiopia	24%	Cambodia	30%
Chad	27%	Mauritania	37%

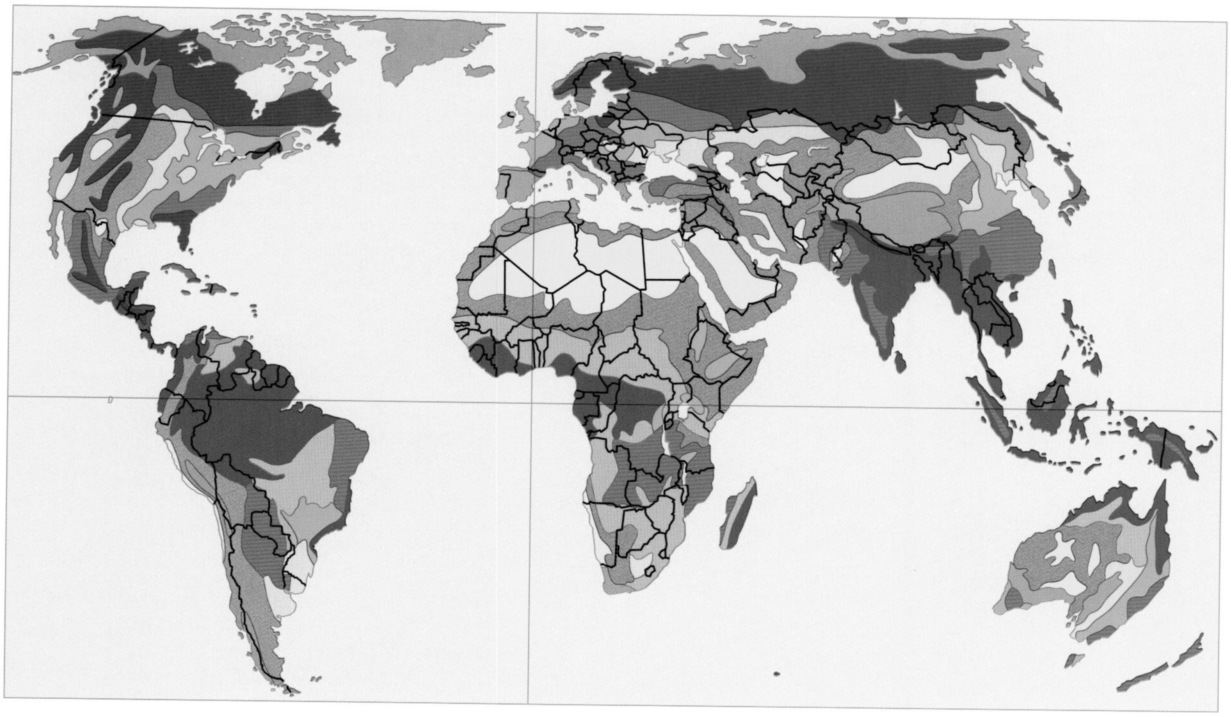

Natural Vegetation

Regional variation in vegetation

- Tundra and mountain vegetation
- Needleleaf evergreen forest
- Mixed needleleaf evergreen & broadleaf deciduous trees
- Broadleaf deciduous woodland
- Mid-latitude grassland
- Evergreen broadleaf and deciduous trees & shrubs
- Semi-desert scrub
- Desert
- Tropical grassland (savanna)
- Tropical broadleaf rainforest and monsoon forest
- Subtropical broadleaf and needleleaf forest

The map shows the natural 'climax vegetation' of regions, as dictated by climate and topography. In most cases, however, agricultural activity has drastically altered the vegetation pattern. Western Europe, for example, lost most of its broadleaf forest many centuries ago, while irrigation has turned some natural semi-desert into productive land.

Land Use by Continent

- Forest
- Permanent pasture and rough grazing
- Permanent crops and plantations
- Arable
- Non-productive

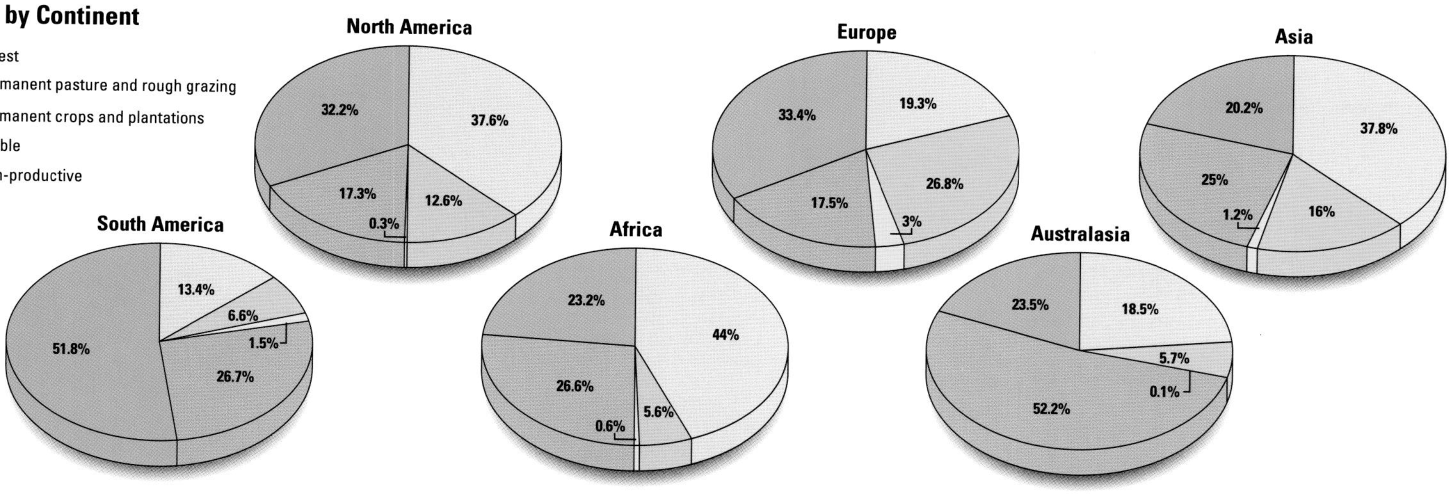

North America
32.2%
37.6%
17.3%
12.6%
0.3%
Europe
33.4%
19.3%
26.8%
17.5%
3%
Asia
20.2%
37.8%
25%
1.2%
16%
South America
13.4%
6.6%
1.5%
51.8%
26.7%
Africa
23.2%
44%
26.6%
0.6%
5.6%
Australasia
23.5%
18.5%
5.7%
0.1%
52.2%

Forestry: Production

	Forest and woodland (million hectares)	Annual production (1996, million cubic metres) Fuelwood and charcoal	Industrial roundwood*
World	***3,987.9***	***1,864.8***	***1,489.5***
S. America	829.3	193.0	129.9
N. & C. America	709.8	155.4	600.4
Africa	684.6	519.9	67.9
Asia	131.8	905.2	280.2
Europe	157.3	82.4	369.7
Australasia	157.2	8.7	41.5

Paper and Board

Top producers (1996)**		Top exporters (1996)**	
USA	85,173	Canada	13,393
China	30,253	USA	9,113
Japan	30,014	Finland	8,529
Canada	18,414	Sweden	7,483
Germany	14,733	Germany	6,319

* roundwood is timber as it is felled
** in thousand tonnes

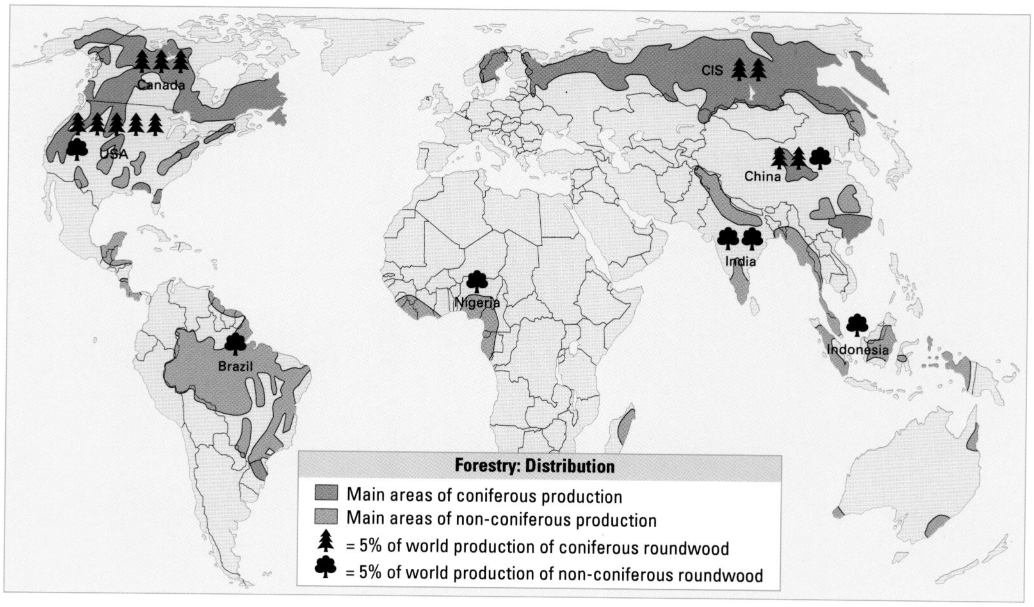

Canada
CIS
USA
China
India
Nigeria
Indonesia
Brazil
Forestry: Distribution
Main areas of coniferous production
Main areas of non-coniferous production
= 5% of world production of coniferous roundwood
= 5% of world production of non-coniferous roundwood

Environment

Humans have always had a dramatic effect on their environment, at least since the development of agriculture almost 10,000 years ago. Generally, the Earth has accepted human interference without obvious ill effects: the complex systems that regulate the global environment have been able to absorb substantial damage while maintaining a stable and comfortable home for the planet's trillions of lifeforms. But advancing human technology and the rapidly-expanding populations it supports are now threatening to overwhelm the Earth's ability to compensate.

Industrial wastes, acid rainfall, desertification and large-scale deforestation all combine to create environmental change at a rate far faster than the great slow cycles of planetary evolution can accommodate. As a result of overcultivation, overgrazing and overcutting of groundcover for firewood, desertification is affecting as much as 60% of the world's croplands. In addition, with fire and chain-saws, humans are destroying more forest in a day than their ancestors could have done in a century, upsetting the balance between plant and animal, carbon dioxide and oxygen, on which all life ultimately depends.

The fossil fuels that power industrial civilization have pumped enough carbon dioxide and other so-called greenhouse gases into the atmosphere to make climatic change a near-certainty. As a result of the combination of these factors, the Earth's average temperature has risen by approximately 0.5°C [1°F] since the beginning of the 20th century, and it is still rising.

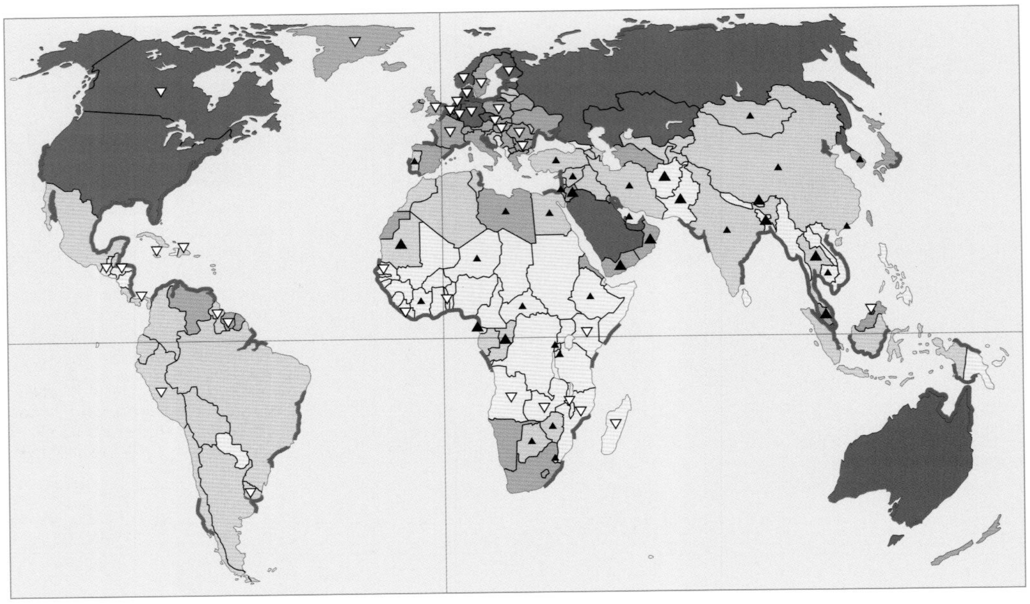

Global Warming

Carbon dioxide emissions in tonnes per person per year (latest available year)

- Over 10 tonnes of CO_2
- 5 – 10 tonnes of CO_2
- 1 – 5 tonnes of CO_2
- Under 1 tonne of CO_2
- No data available

Changes in CO_2 emissions 1980–90

- ▲ Over 100% increase in emissions
- ▲ 50–100% increase in emissions
- ▽ Reduction in emissions
- Coastal areas in danger of flooding from rising sea levels caused by global warming

High atmospheric concentrations of heat-absorbing gases appear to be causing a rise in average temperatures worldwide – up to 1.5°C [3°F] by the year 2020, according to some estimates. Global warming is likely to bring about a rise in sea levels that may flood some of the world's densely populated coastal areas.

Greenhouse Power

Relative contributions to the Greenhouse Effect by the major heat-absorbing gases in the atmosphere.

The chart combines greenhouse potency and volume. Carbon dioxide has a greenhouse potential of only 1, but its concentration of 350 parts per million makes it predominate. CFC 12, with 25,000 times the absorption capacity of CO_2, is present only as 0.00044 ppm.

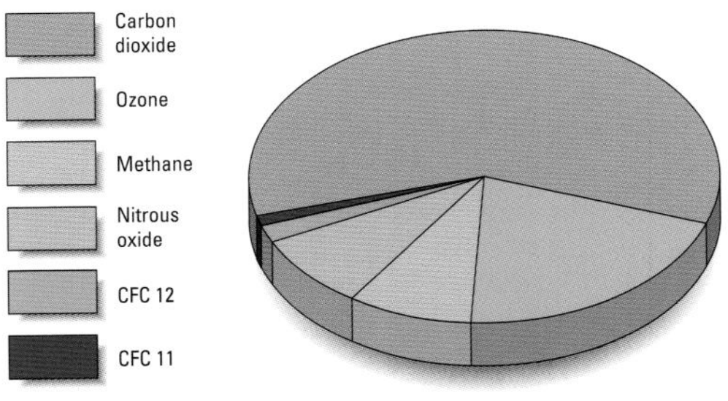

Carbon dioxide
Ozone
Methane
Nitrous oxide
CFC 12
CFC 11

Ozone Layer

The ozone 'hole' over the northern hemisphere on 12 March 1995.

The colours represent Dobson Units (DU). The ozone 'hole' is seen as the dark blue and purple patch in the centre, where ozone values are around 120 DU or lower. Normal levels are around 280 DU. The ozone 'hole' over Antarctica is much larger.

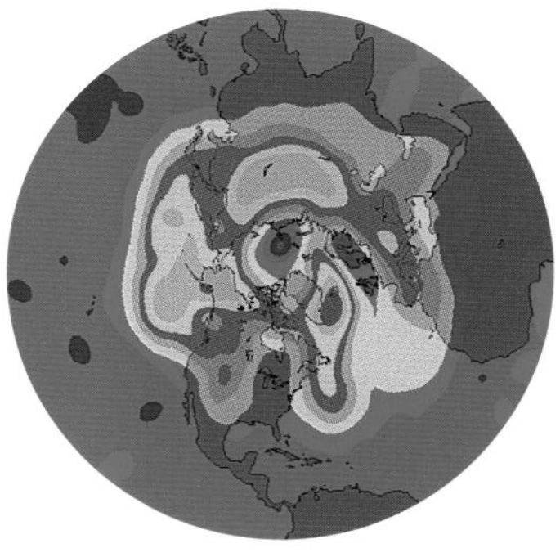

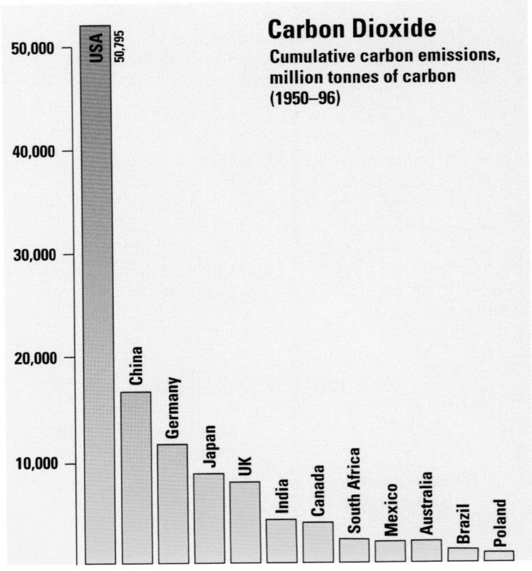

Carbon Dioxide
Cumulative carbon emissions, million tonnes of carbon (1950–96)
50,000
40,000
30,000
20,000
10,000
USA
50,795
China
Germany
Japan
UK
India
Canada
South Africa
Mexico
Australia
Brazil
Poland

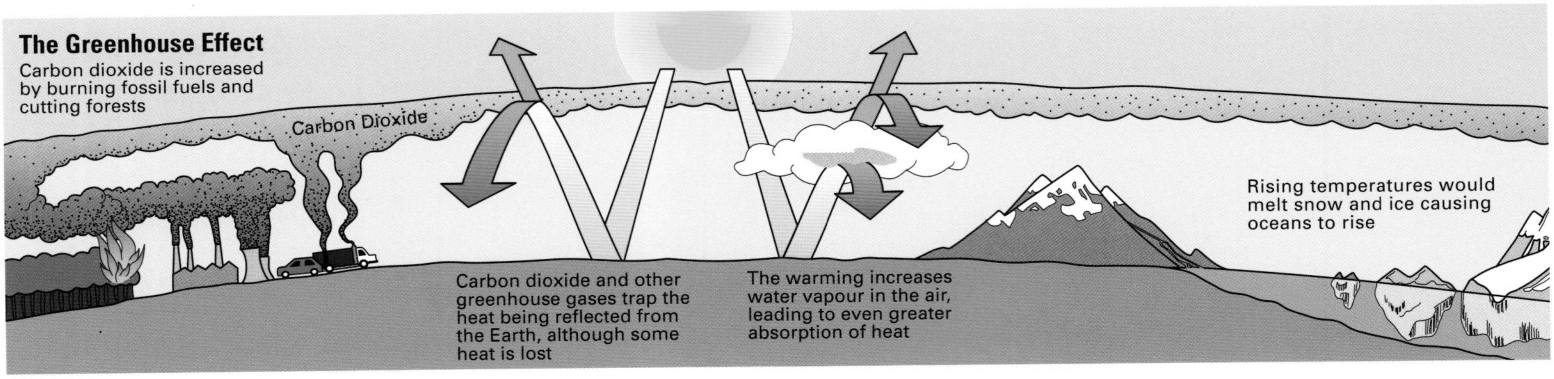

The Greenhouse Effect
Carbon dioxide is increased by burning fossil fuels and cutting forests
Carbon Dioxide
Carbon dioxide and other greenhouse gases trap the heat being reflected from the Earth, although some heat is lost
The warming increases water vapour in the air, leading to even greater absorption of heat
Rising temperatures would melt snow and ice causing oceans to rise

Desertification

- Existing deserts
- Areas with a high risk of desertification
- Areas with a moderate risk of desertification
- Former areas of rainforest
- Existing rainforest

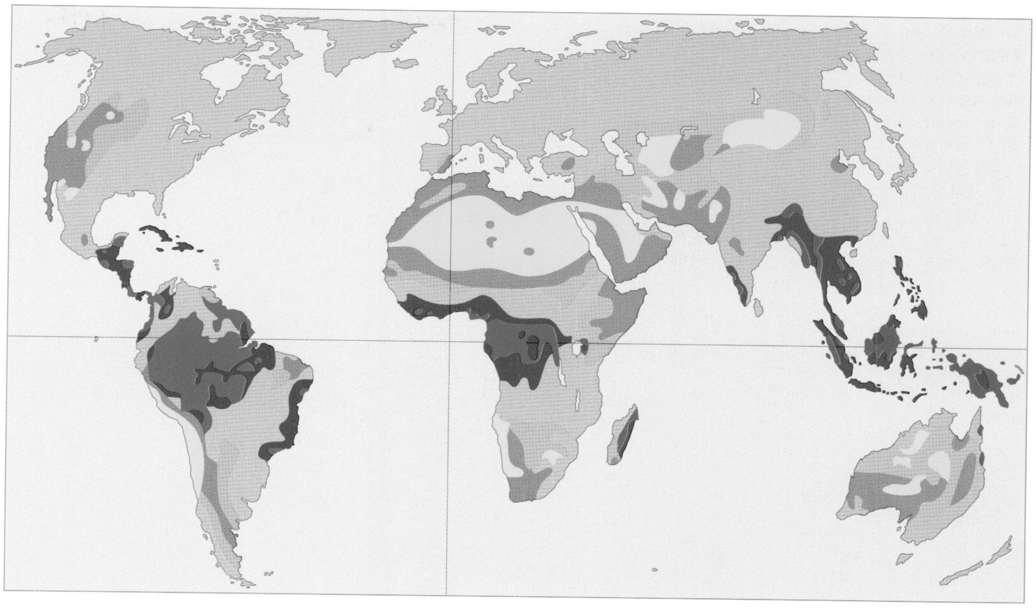

Forest Clearance

Thousands of hectares of forest cleared annually, tropical countries surveyed 1981–85, 1987–90 and 1990–5. Loss as a percentage of remaining stocks is shown in figures on each column.

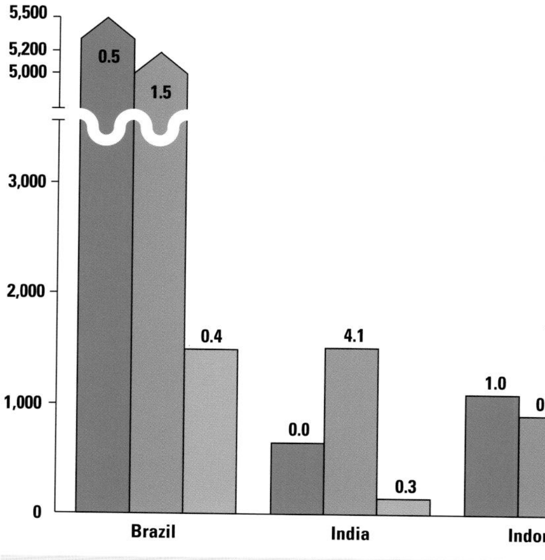

Deforestation

The Earth's remaining forests are under attack from three directions: expanding agriculture, logging, and growing consumption of fuelwood, often in combination. Sometimes deforestation is the direct result of government policy, as in the efforts made to resettle the urban poor in some parts of Brazil; just as often, it comes about despite state attempts at conservation. Loggers, licensed or unlicensed, blaze a trail into virgin forest, often destroying twice as many trees as they harvest. Landless farmers follow, burning away most of what remains to plant their crops, completing the destruction.

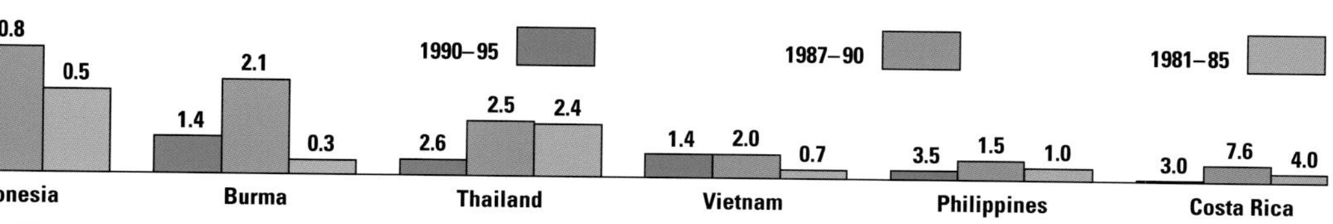

Ozone Depletion

The ozone layer, 25–30 km [15–18 miles] above sea level, acts as a barrier to most of the Sun's harmful ultra-violet radiation, protecting us from the ionizing radiation that can cause skin cancer and cataracts. In recent years, however, two holes in the ozone layer have been observed during winter: one over the Arctic and the other, the size of the USA, over Antarctica. By 1996, ozone had been reduced to around a half of its 1970 amount. The ozone (O_3) is broken down by chlorine released into the atmosphere as CFCs (chlorofluorocarbons) – chemicals used in refrigerators, packaging and aerosols.

Air Pollution

Sulphur dioxide is the main pollutant associated with industrial cities. According to the World Health Organization, at least 600 million people live in urban areas where sulphur dioxide concentrations regularly reach damaging levels. One of the world's most dangerously polluted urban areas is Mexico City, due to a combination of its enclosed valley location, 3 million cars and 60,000 factories. In May 1998, this lethal cocktail was added to by nearby forest fires and the resultant air pollution led to over 20% of the population (3 million people) complaining of respiratory problems.

Acid Rain

Killing trees, poisoning lakes and rivers and eating away buildings, acid rain is mostly produced by sulphur dioxide emissions from industry and volcanic eruptions. By the mid 1990s, acid rain had sterilized 4,000 or more of Sweden's lakes and left 45% of Switzerland's alpine conifers dead or dying, while the monuments of Greece were dissolving in Athens' smog. Prevailing wind patterns mean that the acids often fall many hundred kilometres from where the original pollutants were discharged. In parts of Europe acid deposition has slightly decreased, following reductions in emissions, but not by enough.

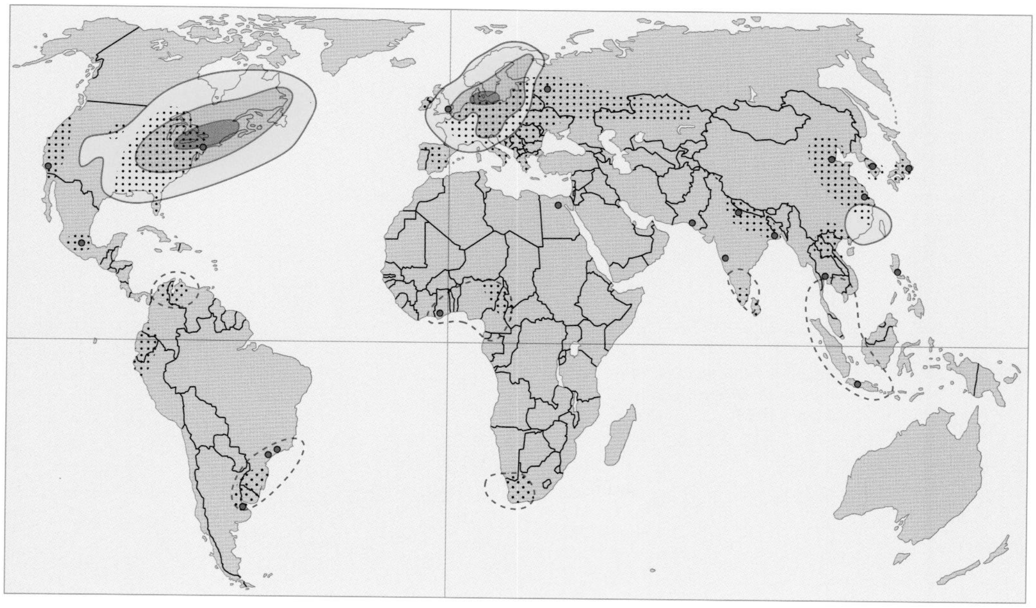

World Pollution

Acid rain and sources of acidic emissions (latest available year)

Acid rain is caused by high levels of sulphur and nitrogen in the atmosphere. They combine with water vapour and oxygen to form acids (H_2SO_4 and HNO_3) which fall as precipitation.

- Regions where sulphur and nitrogen oxides are released in high concentrations, mainly from fossil fuel combustion
- Major cities with high levels of air pollution (including nitrogen and sulphur emissions)

Areas of heavy acid deposition

pH numbers indicate acidity, decreasing from a neutral 7. Normal rain, slightly acid from dissolved carbon dioxide, never exceeds a pH of 5.6.

- pH less than 4.0 (most acidic)
- pH 4.0 to 4.5
- pH 4.5 to 5.0
- Areas where acid rain is a potential problem

CARTOGRAPHY BY PHILIP'S. COPYRIGHT PHILIP'S

Population

Demographic Profiles

Developed nations such as the UK have populations evenly spread across the age groups and, usually, a growing proportion of elderly people. The great majority of the people in developing nations, however, are in the younger age groups, about to enter their most fertile years. In time, these population profiles should resemble the world profile (even Kenya has made recent progress with reducing its birth rate), but the transition will come about only after a few more generations of rapid population growth.

World

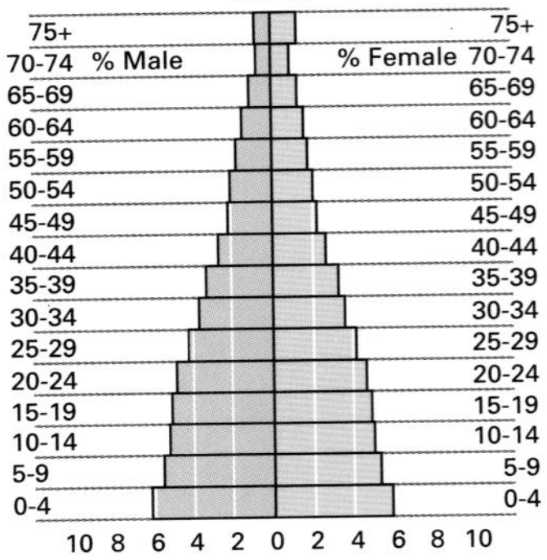

UK

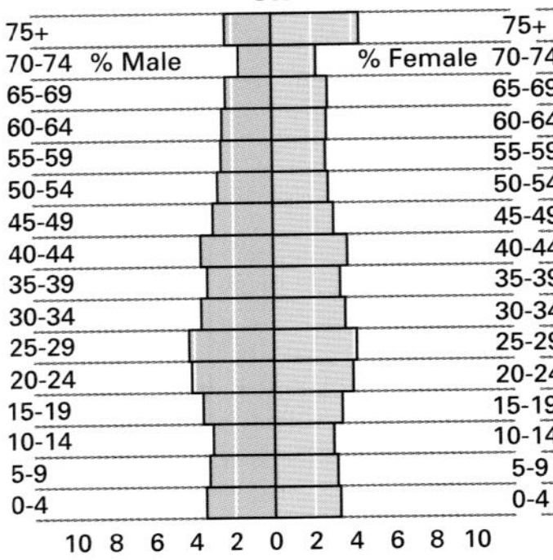

Kenya

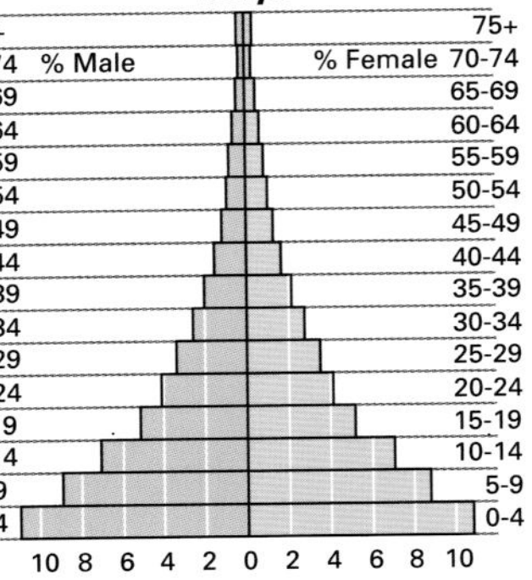

India

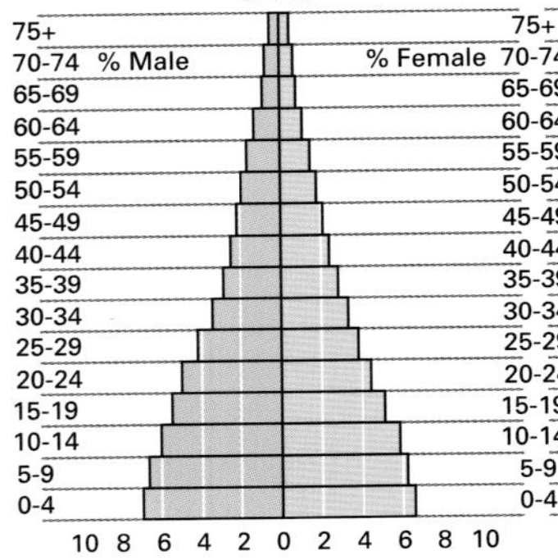

Saudi Arabia

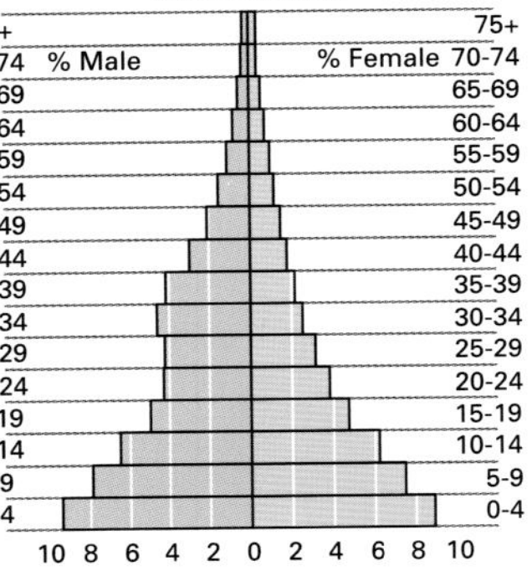

USA

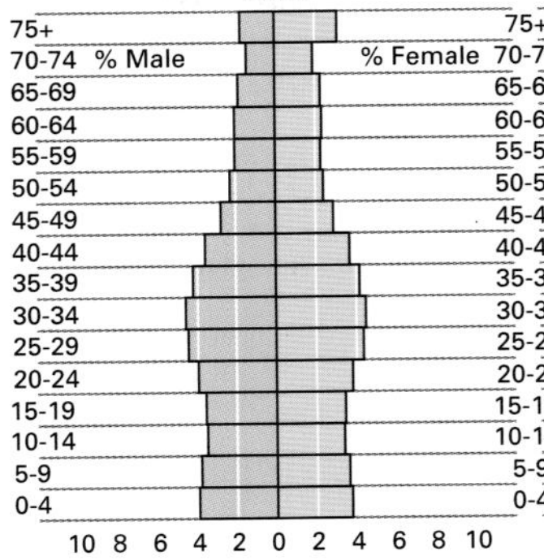

China

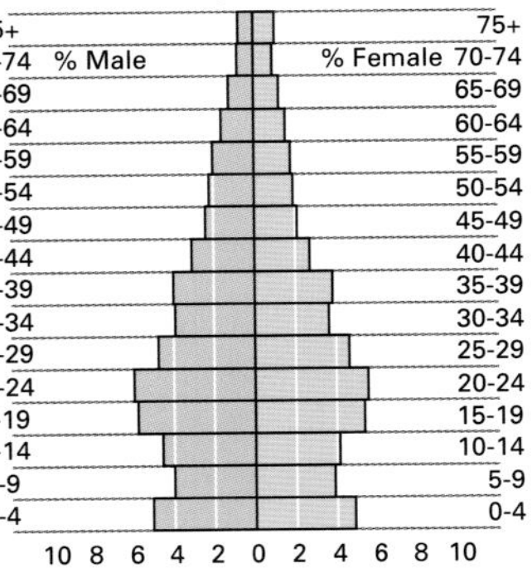

Most Populous Nations [in millions (2001 estimates)]

1. China	1,273	9. Japan	127	17. Iran	66
2. India	1,003	10. Nigeria	127	18. Ethiopia	66
3. USA	278	11. Mexico	102	19. Thailand	62
4. Indonesia	228	12. Germany	83	20. UK	60
5. Brazil	174	13. Philippines	83	21. France	60
6. Russia	145	14. Vietnam	80	22. Italy	58
7. Pakistan	145	15. Egypt	70	23. Congo (Dem. Rep.)	54
8. Bangladesh	131	16. Turkey	66	24. Ukraine	49

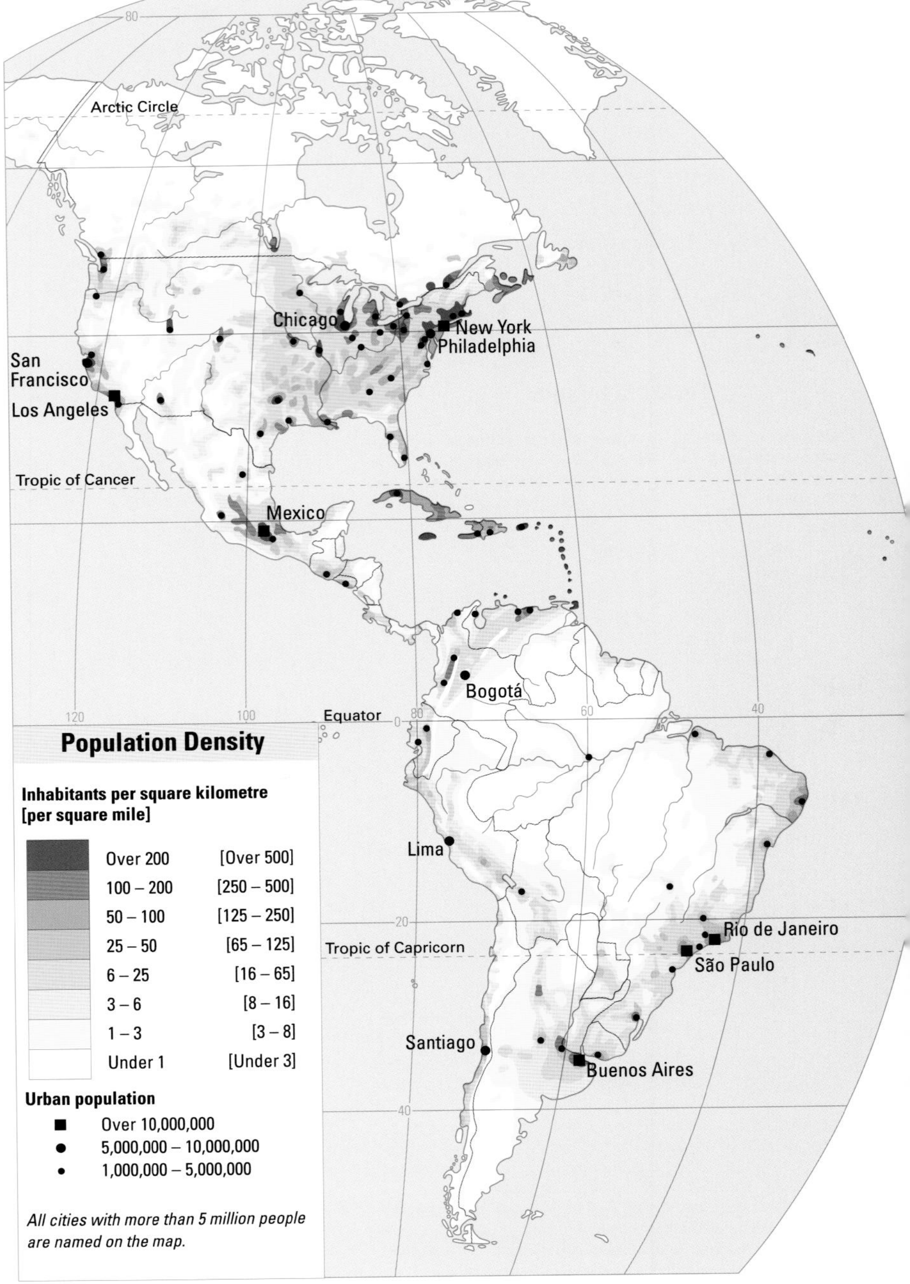

Continental Comparisons

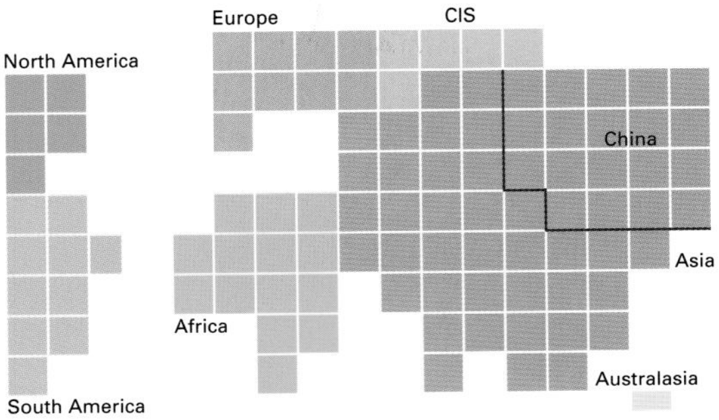

Each square in the diagram above represents 1% of the total world population (1995).

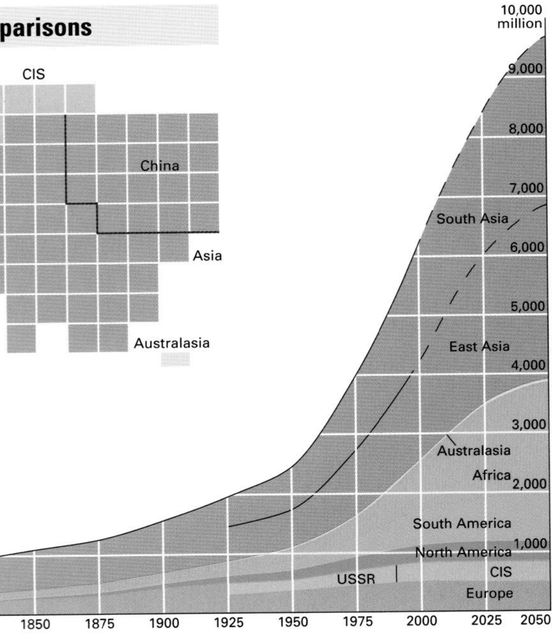

CARTOGRAPHY BY PHILIP'S. COPYRIGHT PHILIP'S

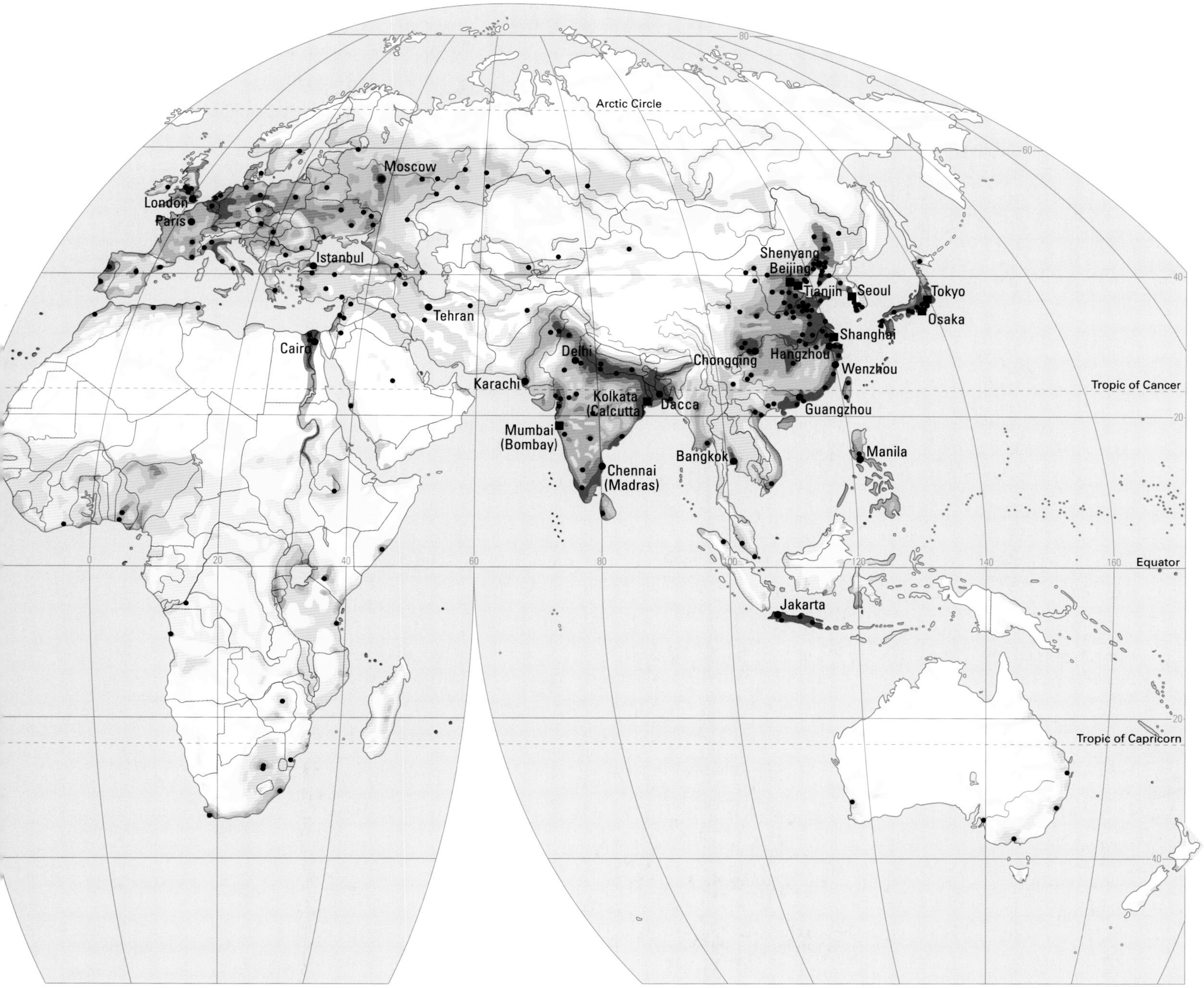

Arctic Circle
Moscow
London
Paris
Istanbul
Tehran
Cairo
Karachi
Delhi
Kolkata (Calcutta)
Dacca
Mumbai (Bombay)
Chennai (Madras)
Bangkok
Chongqing
Hangzhou
Shanghai
Wenzhou
Guangzhou
Shenyang
Beijing
Tianjin
Seoul
Tokyo
Osaka
Manila
Jakarta
Tropic of Cancer
Equator
Tropic of Capricorn

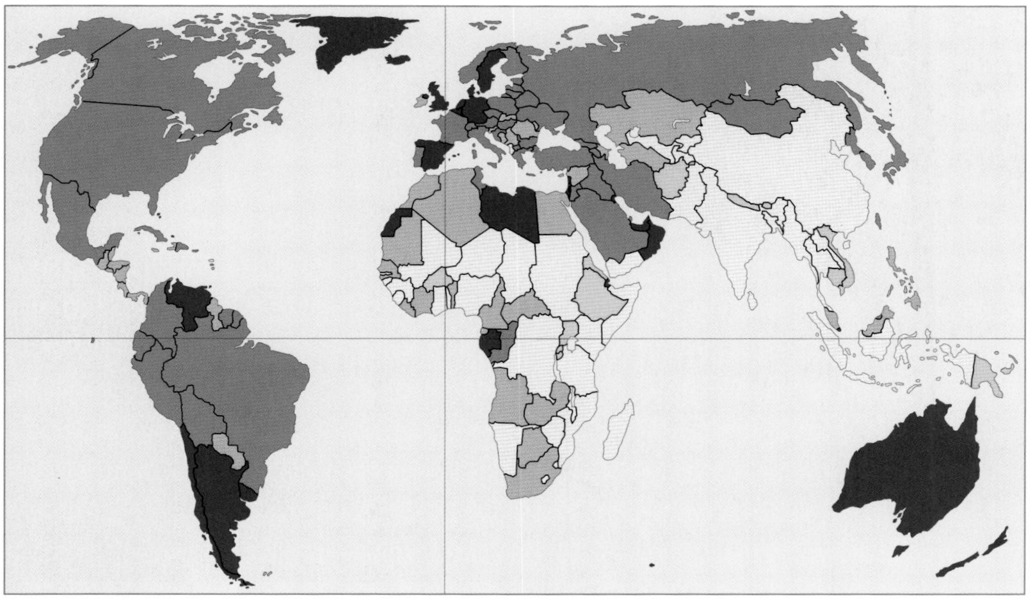

Urban Population

Percentage of total population living in towns and cities (2000)

- Over 80%
- 60 – 80%
- 40 – 60%
- 20 – 40%
- Under 20%

Most urbanized

Belgium	97%
W. Sahara	96%
Singapore	93%
UAE	93%
Iceland	93%

[UK 89%]

Least urbanized

Rwanda	6%
Bhutan	7%
East Timor	7%
Burunda	9%
Nepal	11%

CARTOGRAPHY BY PHILIP'S. COPYRIGHT PHILIP'S

The Human Family

Predominant Languages

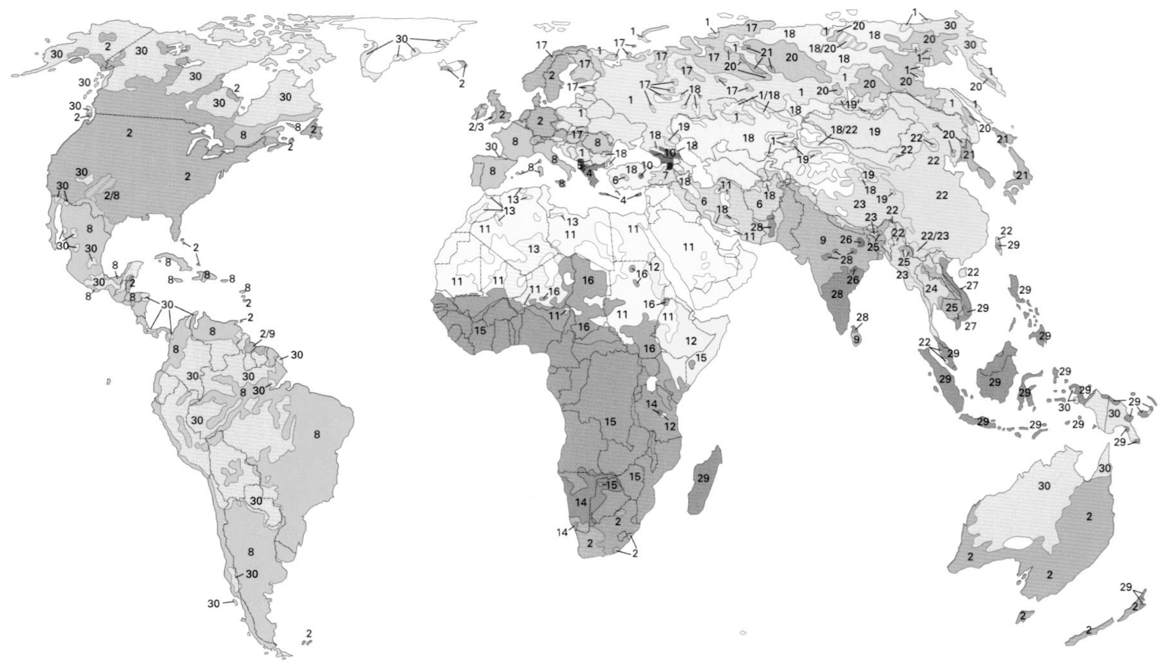

INDO-EUROPEAN FAMILY

- 1 Balto-Slavic group (incl. Russian, Ukrainian)
- 2 Germanic group (incl. English, German)
- 3 Celtic group
- 4 Greek
- 5 Albanian
- 6 Iranian group
- 7 Armenian
- 8 Romance group (incl. Spanish, Portuguese, French, Italian)
- 9 Indo-Aryan group (incl. Hindi, Bengali, Urdu, Punjabi, Marathi)

10 CAUCASIAN FAMILY

AFRO-ASIATIC FAMILY

- 11 Semitic group (incl. Arabic)
- 12 Kushitic group
- 13 Berber group

14 KHOISAN FAMILY

15 NIGER-CONGO FAMILY

16 NILO-SAHARAN FAMILY

17 URALIC FAMILY

ALTAIC FAMILY

- 18 Turkic group (incl. Turkish)
- 19 Mongolian group
- 20 Tungus-Manchu group
- 21 Japanese and Korean

SINO-TIBETAN FAMILY

- 22 Sinitic (Chinese) languages (incl. Mandarin, Wu, Yue)
- 23 Tibetic-Burmic languages

24 TAI FAMILY

AUSTRO-ASIATIC FAMILY

- 25 Mon-Khmer group
- 26 Munda group
- 27 Vietnamese

28 DRAVIDIAN FAMILY (incl. Telugu, Tamil)

29 AUSTRONESIAN FAMILY (incl. Malay-Indonesian, Javanese)

30 OTHER LANGUAGES

Languages of the World

Language can be classified by ancestry and structure. For example, the Romance and Germanic groups are both derived from an Indo-European language believed to have been spoken 5,000 years ago.

First-language speakers, 1999 (in millions)
Mandarin Chinese 885, Spanish 332, English 322, Bengali 189, Hindi 182, Portuguese 170, Russian 170, Japanese 125, German 98, Wu Chinese 77, Javanese 76, Korean 75, French 72, Vietnamese 68, Yue Chinese 66, Marathi 65, Tamil 63, Turkish 59, Urdu 58.

Official languages (% of total population)
English 27%, Chinese 19%, Hindi 13.5%, Spanish 5.4%, Russian 5.2%, French 4.2%, Arabic 3.3%, Portuguese 3%, Malay 3%, Bengali 2.9%, Japanese 2.3%.

Predominant Religions

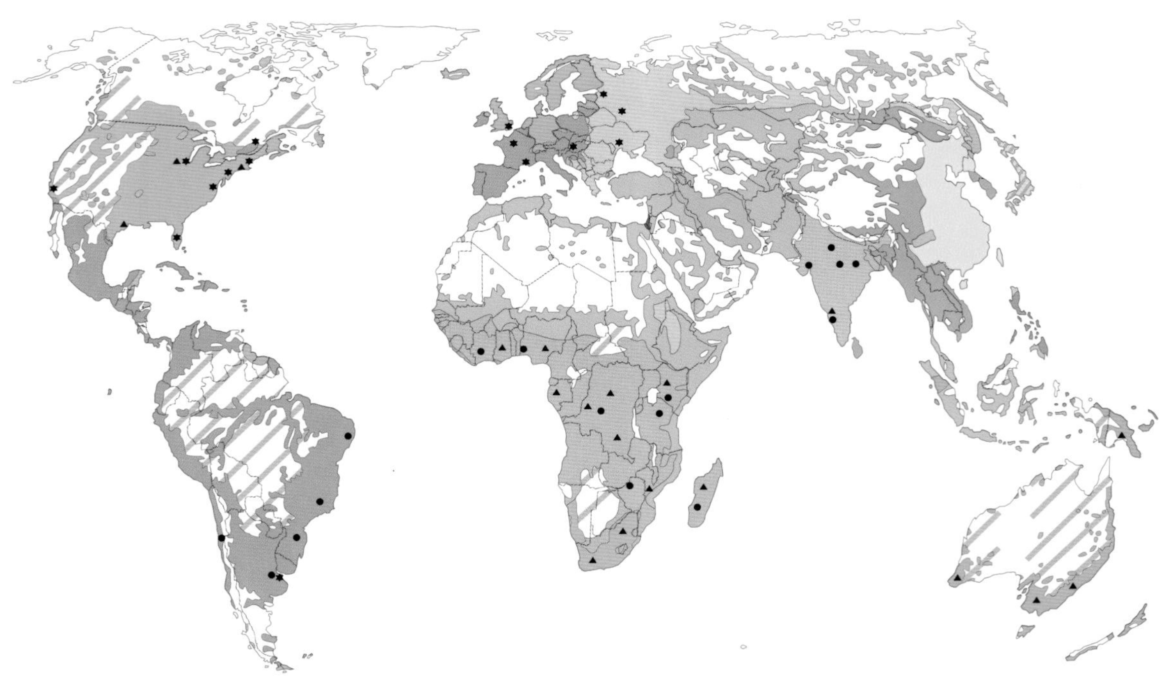

- Roman Catholicism
- Orthodox and other Eastern Churches
- Protestantism
- Sunni Islam
- Shiite Islam
- Buddhism
- Hinduism
- Confucianism
- Judaism
- Shintoism
- Tribal Religions

Religious Adherents

Religious adherents in millions (1998)

Christianity	1,980	Buddhist	360
Roman Catholic	*1,300*	Chinese Trad.	225
Orthodox	*240*	Indigenous	190
African sects	*110*	Sikh	23
Pentecostal	*105*	Yoruba	20
Others	*225*	Juche	19
Islam	1,300	Spiritism	14
Sunni	*940*	Judaism	14
Shiite	*120*	Baha'i	6
Others	*240*	Jainism	4
Hindu	900	Shinto	4
Secular	850		

United Nations

Created in 1945 to promote peace and co-operation and based in New York, the United Nations is the world's largest international organization, with 188 members and an annual budget of US $1.3 billion (2002). Each member of the General Assembly has one vote, while the five permanent members of the 15-nation Security Council – China, France, Russia, UK and USA – hold a veto. The Secretariat is the UN's principal administrative arm. The 54 members of the Economic and Social Council are responsible for economic, social, cultural, educational, health and related matters. The UN has 16 specialized agencies – based in Canada, France, Switzerland and Italy, as well as the USA – which help members in fields such as education (UNESCO), agriculture (FAO), medicine (WHO) and finance (IFC). By the end of 1994, all the original 11 trust territories of the Trusteeship Council had become independent.

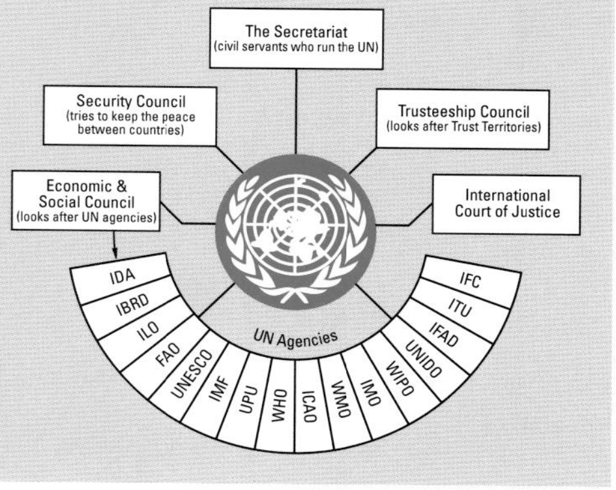

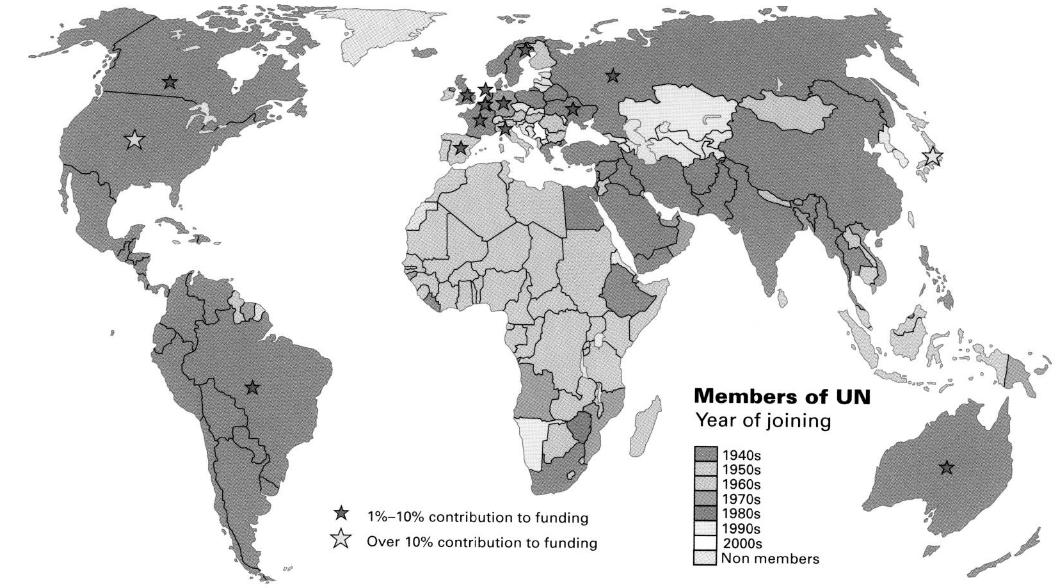

MEMBERSHIP OF THE UN In 1945 there were 51 members; by 2000 membership had increased to 188 following the admission of Kiribati, Nauru and Tonga. There are 3 independent states which are not members of the UN – Switzerland, Taiwan and the Vatican City. All the successor states of the former USSR had joined by the end of 1992. The official languages of the UN are Chinese, English, French, Russian, Spanish and Arabic.

FUNDING The UN regular budget for 2000 was US $1.3 billion. Contributions are assessed by the members' ability to pay, with the maximum 22% of the total (USA's share), the minimum 0.01%. The 15-country European Union pays over 37% of the budget.

PEACEKEEPING The UN has been involved in 54 peacekeeping operations worldwide since 1948.

International Organizations

ACP African-Caribbean-Pacific (formed in 1963). Members have economic ties with the EU.
ARAB LEAGUE (formed in 1945). The League's aim is to promote economic, social, political and military co-operation. There are 21 member nations.
ASEAN Association of South-east Asian Nations (formed in 1967). Cambodia joined in 1999.
CIS The Commonwealth of Independent States (formed in 1991) comprises the countries of the former Soviet Union except for Estonia, Latvia and Lithuania.
COLOMBO PLAN (formed in 1951). Its 26 members aim to promote economic and social development in Asia and the Pacific.
COMMONWEALTH The Commonwealth of Nations evolved from the British Empire; it comprises 16 Queen's realms, 32 republics and 5 indigenous monarchies, giving a total of 53. Nigeria was suspended in 1995, but reinstated in 1999.
EFTA European Free Trade Association (formed in 1960). Portugal left the original 'Seven' in 1989 to join what was then the EC, followed by Austria, Finland and Sweden in 1995. Only 4 members remain: Norway, Iceland, Switzerland and Liechtenstein.
EU European Union (evolved from the European Community in 1993). The 15 members – Austria, Belgium, Denmark, Finland, France, Germany, Greece, Ireland, Italy, Luxembourg, Netherlands, Portugal, Spain, Sweden and the UK – aim to integrate economies, co-ordinate social developments and bring about political union. These members, of what is now the world's biggest market, share agricultural and industrial policies and tariffs on trade. The original body, the European Coal and Steel Community (ECSC), was created in 1951 following the signing of the Treaty of Paris.
LAIA Latin American Integration Association (1980). Its aim is to promote freer regional trade.
NATO North Atlantic Treaty Organization (formed in 1949). It continues after 1991 despite the winding up of the Warsaw Pact. The Czech Republic, Hungary and Poland were the latest members to join in 1999.
OAS Organization of American States (formed in 1948). It aims to promote social and economic co-operation between developed countries of North America and developing nations of Latin America.
OAU Organization of African Unity (formed in 1963). Its 53 members represent over 94% of Africa's population. Arabic, French, Portuguese and English are recognized as working languages.

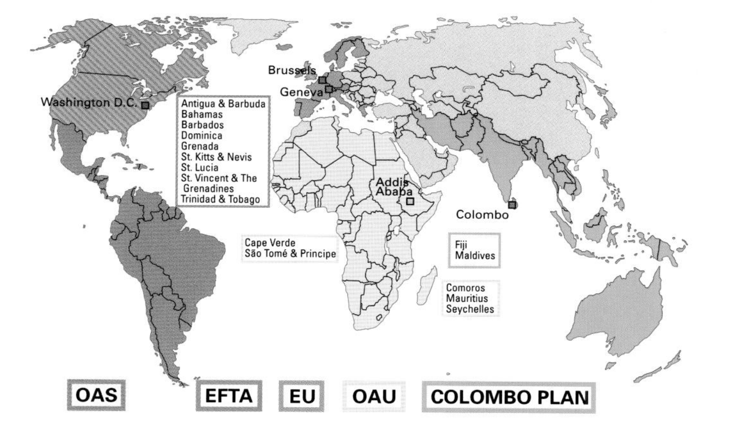

OECD Organization for Economic Co-operation and Development (formed in 1961). It comprises 29 major free-market economies. Poland, Hungary and South Korea joined in 1996. 'G8' is its 'inner group' of leading industrial nations, comprising Canada, France, Germany, Italy, Japan, Russia, UK andUSA.
OPEC Organization of Petroleum Exporting Countries (formed in 1960). It controls about three-quarters of the world's oil supply. Gabon left the organization in 1996.

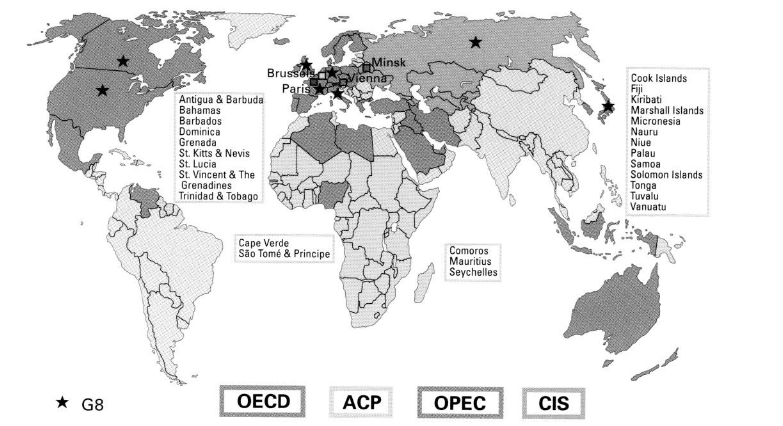

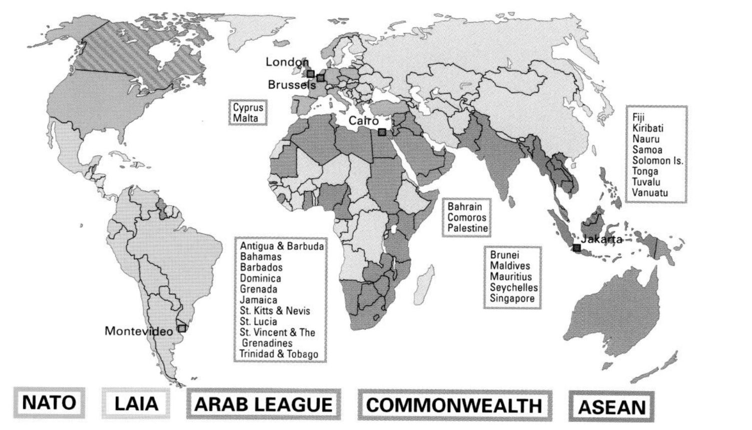

Wealth

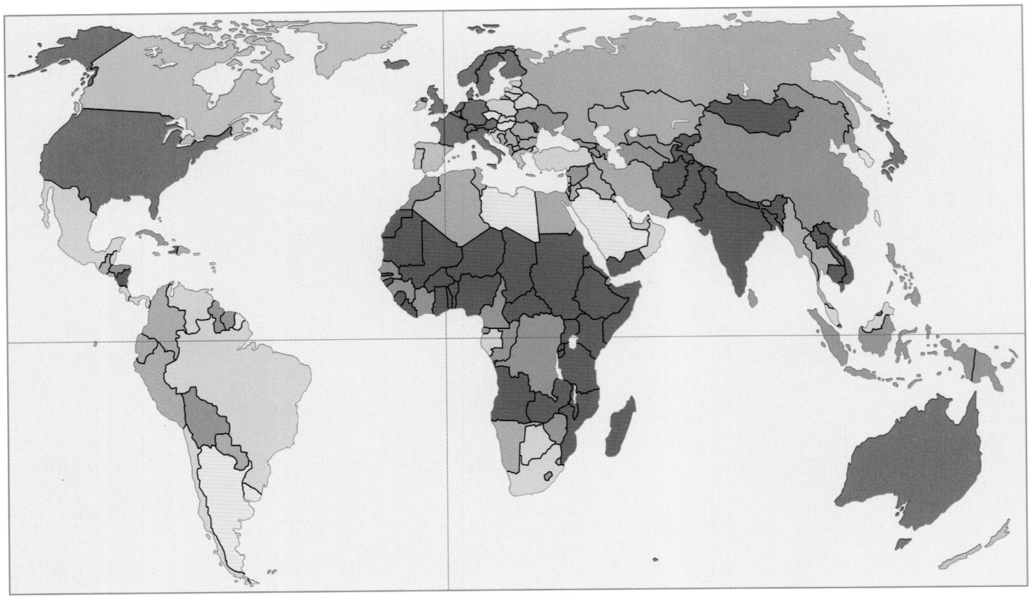

Levels of Income

Gross National Product per capita: the value of total production divided by the population (1999)

- Over 400% of world average
- 200 – 400% of world average
- 100 – 200% of world average

[World average wealth per person US $4,890]

- 50 – 100% of world average
- 25 – 50% of world average
- 10 – 25% of world average
- Under 10% of world average

Top 5 countries

Luxembourg	$44,640
Switzerland	$38,350
Bermuda	$35,590
Norway	$32,880
Japan	$32,230

Bottom 5 countries

Ethiopia	$100
Burundi	$120
Sierra Leone	$130
Guinea-Bissau	$160
Niger	$190

Wealth Creation

The Gross National Product (GNP) of the world's largest economies, US $ million (1998)

1.	USA	7,922,651	23.	Saudi Arabia	186,000
2.	Japan	4,089,910	24.	Denmark	176,374
3.	Germany	2,122,673	25.	Hong Kong	158,286
4.	Italy	1,666,178	26.	Norway	152,082
5.	France	1,466,014	27.	Poland	150,798
6.	UK	1,263,777	28.	Indonesia	138,501
7.	China	928,950	29.	Thailand	134,433
8.	Brazil	758,043	30.	Finland	124,293
9.	Canada	612,332	31.	Greece	122,880
10.	Spain	553,690	32.	South Africa	119,001
11.	India	421,259	33.	Iran	109,645
12.	Netherlands	388,682	34.	Portugal	106,376
13.	Mexico	380,917	35.	Colombia	106,090
14.	Australia	380,625	36.	Israel	95,179
15.	South Korea	369,890	37.	Singapore	95,095
16.	Russia	337,914	38.	Venezuela	81,347
17.	Argentina	324,084	39.	Malaysia	79,848
18.	Switzerland	284,808	40.	Egypt	79,208
19.	Belgium	259,045	41.	Philippines	78,896
20.	Sweden	226,861	42.	Chile	71,294
21.	Austria	217,163	43.	Ireland	67,491
22.	Turkey	200,505	44.	Pakistan	63,159

The Wealth Gap

The world's richest and poorest countries, by Gross National Product per capita in US $ (1999 estimates)

1.	Liechtenstein	50,000	1.	Ethiopia	100
2.	Luxembourg	44,640	2.	Congo (D. Rep.)	110
3.	Switzerland	38,350	3.	Burundi	120
4.	Bermuda	35,590	4.	Sierra Leone	130
5.	Norway	32,880	5.	Guinea-Bissau	160
6.	Japan	32,230	6.	Niger	190
7.	Denmark	32,030	7.	Malawi	190
8.	USA	30,600	8.	Eritrea	200
9.	Singapore	29,610	9.	Chad	200
10.	Iceland	29,280	10.	Nepal	220
11.	Austria	25,970	11.	Angola	220
12.	Germany	25,350	12.	Mozambique	230
13.	Sweden	25,040	13.	Tanzania	240
14.	Monaco	25,000	14.	Burkina Faso	240
15.	Belgium	24,510	15.	Mali	240
16.	Brunei	24,630	16.	Rwanda	250
17.	Netherlands	24,320	17.	Madagascar	250
18.	Finland	23,780	18.	Cambodia	260
19.	Hong Kong	23,520	19.	São Tomé & Príncipe	270
20.	France	23,480	20.	Laos	280

GNP per capita is calculated by dividing a country's Gross National Product by its total population.

Continental Shares

Shares of population and of wealth (GNP) by continent

Population

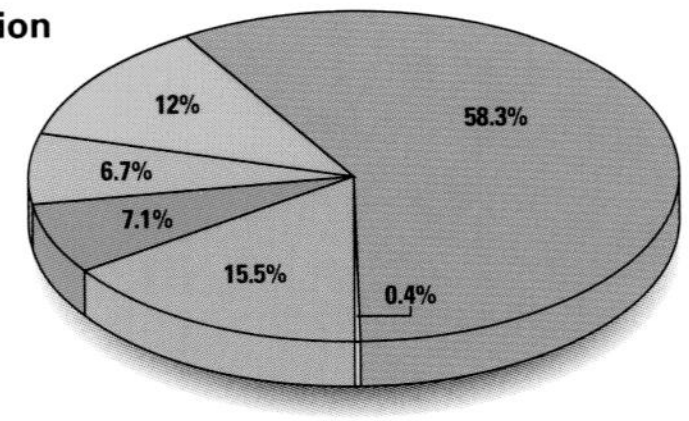

GNP

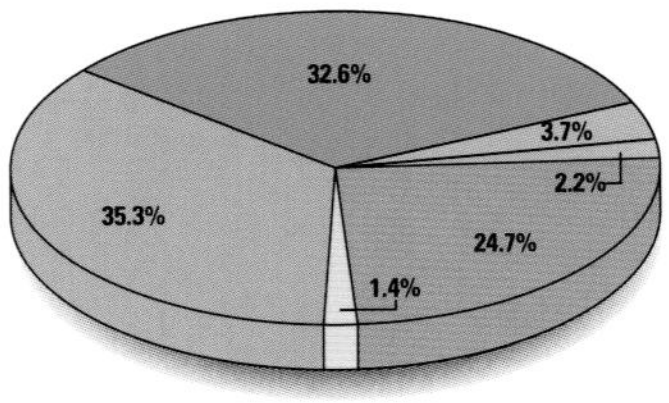

- Europe
- Asia
- South America
- Australia
- Africa
- North America

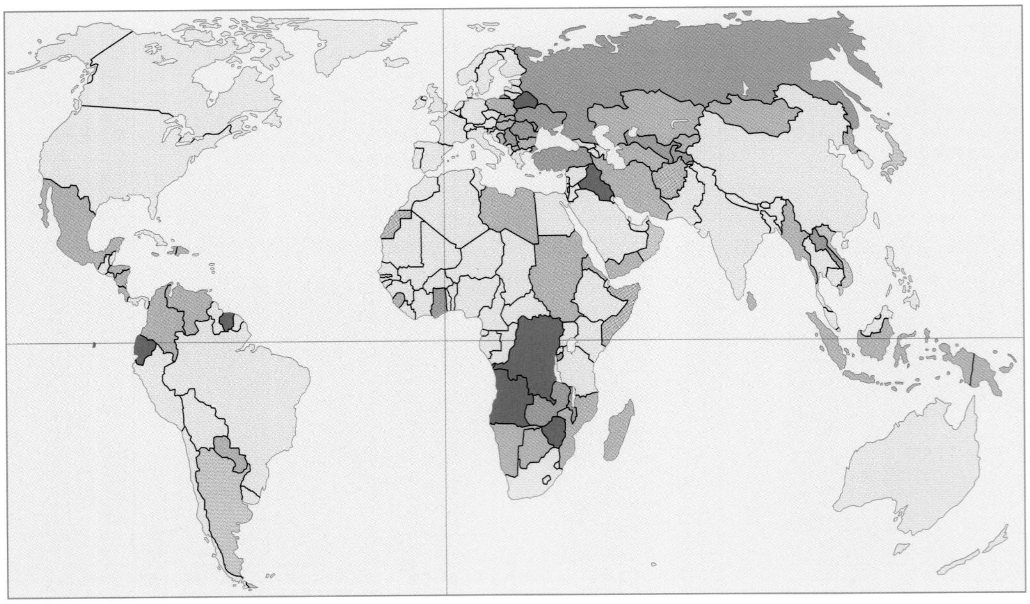

Inflation

Average annual rate of inflation (2000 est.)

- Over 50%
- 20 – 50%
- 7.5 – 20%
- 1 – 7.5%
- Negative inflation
- No data available

Highest average inflation

Congo (Dem. Rep.)	540%
Angola	325%
Belarus	200%
Iraq	100%
Ecuador	96%

Lowest average inflation

Nauru	–3.6%
Macau (China)	–1.8%
Argentina*	–0.9%
Oman	–0.8%
Japan	–0.7%

* During 2002, Argentina experienced a sharp rise in inflation which is not reflected on this map.

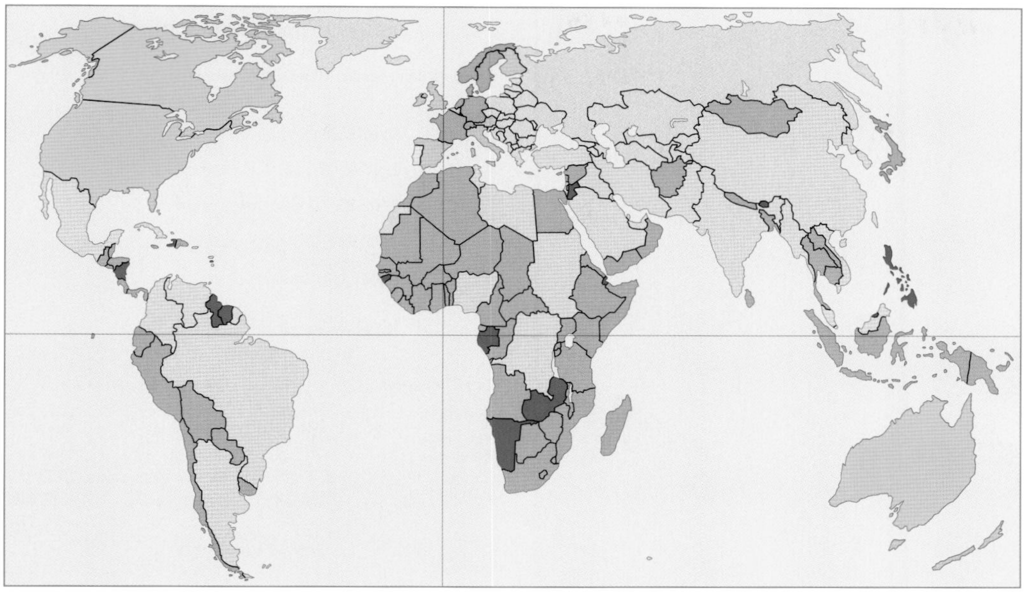

International Aid

Aid provided or received, divided by the total population, in US $ (1995)

Top 5 providers per capita (1994)	
France	$279
Denmark	$260
Norway	$247
Sweden	$201
Germany	$166

Top 5 receivers per capita (1994)	
São Tomé & P.	$378
Cape Verde	$314
Djibouti	$235
Surinam	$198
Mauritania	$153

Debt and Aid

International debtors and the aid they receive (1996)

Although aid grants make a vital contribution to many of the world's poorer countries, they are usually dwarfed by the burden of debt that the developing economies are expected to repay. In 1992, they had to pay US $160,000 million in debt service charges alone – more than two and a half times the amount of Official Development Assistance (ODA) the developing countries were receiving, and US $60,000 million more than total private flows of aid in the same year. In 1990, the debts of Mozambique, one of the world's poorest countries, were estimated to be 75 times its entire earnings from exports.

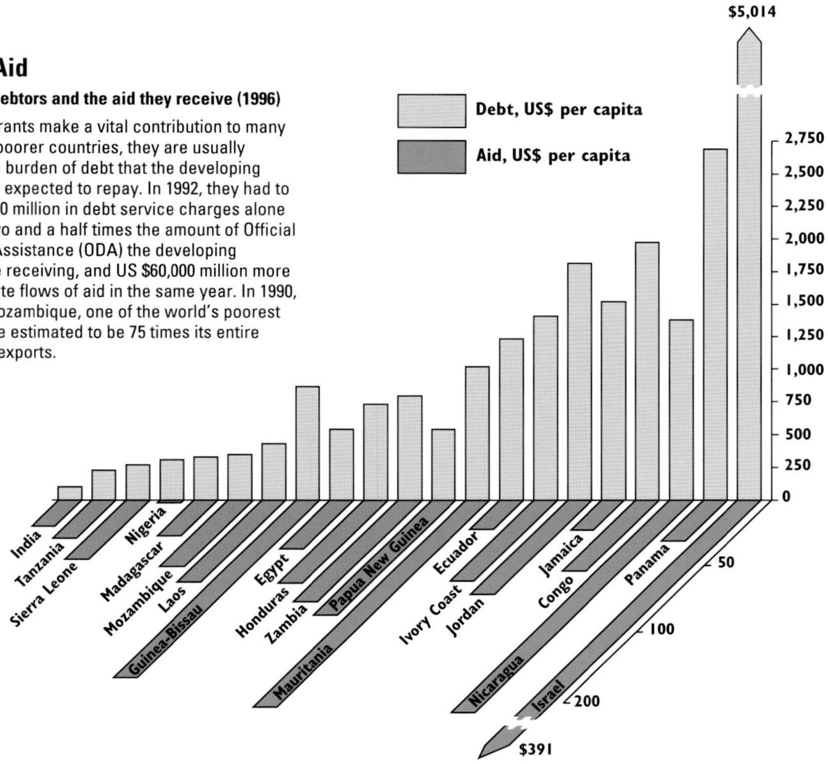

Distribution of Spending

Percentage share of household spending, selected countries

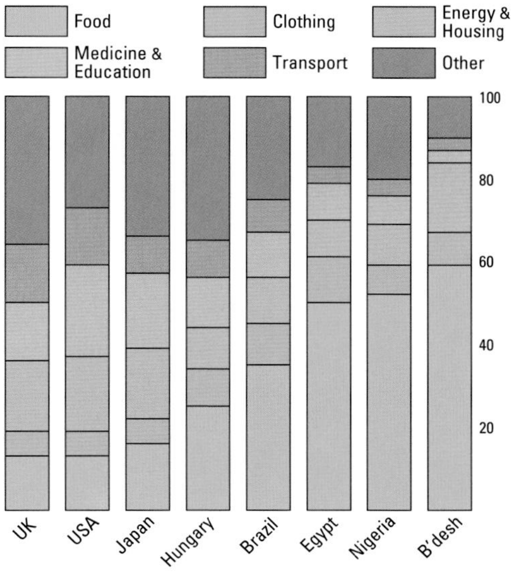

High Income

Number of radios, televisions and mobile 'phones for each 10,000 people, selected high income countries (1996)

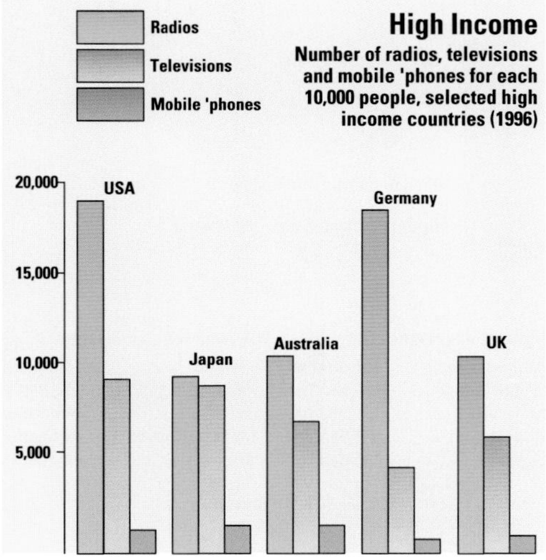

Middle Income

Number of radios, televisions and mobile 'phones for each 10,000 people, selected middle income countries (1996)

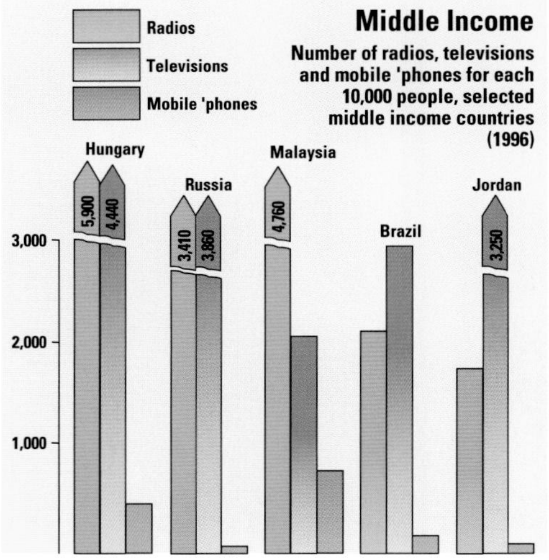

Low Income

Number of radios, televisions and mobile 'phones for each 10,000 people, selected low income countries (1996)

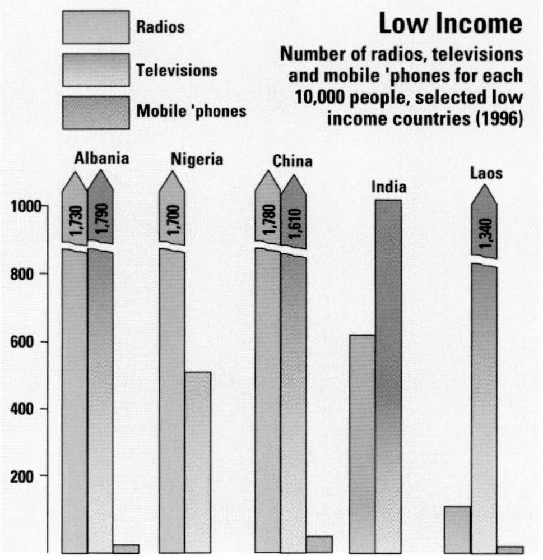

Quality of Life

Daily Food Consumption

Average daily food intake in calories per person (1997)

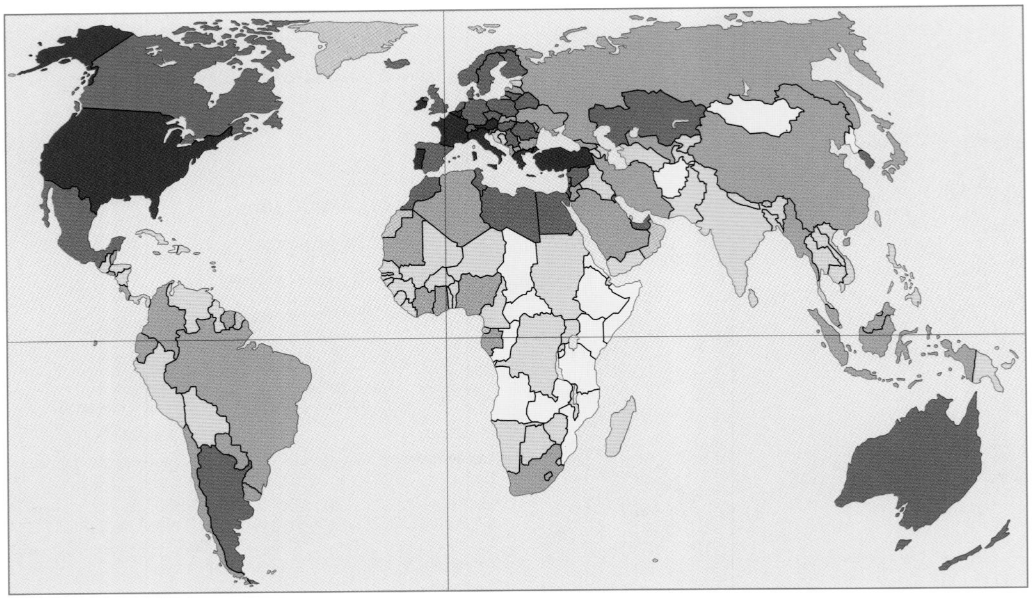

- Over 3,500 calories per person
- 3,000 – 3,500 calories per person
- 2,500 – 3,000 calories per person
- 2,000 – 2,500 calories per person
- Under 2,000 calories per person
- No available data

Top 5 countries		Bottom 5 countries	
Portugal	3,654 cal.	Somalia	1,573 cal.
Greece	3,617 cal.	Eritrea	1,627 cal.
Belgium	3,602 cal.	Burundi	1,687 cal.
Ireland	3,557 cal.	Afghanistan	1,732 cal.
Austria	3,555 cal.	Mozambique	1,782 cal.

[UK 3,211 calories]

Hospital Capacity

Hospital beds available for each 1,000 people (1996)

Highest capacity		Lowest capacity	
Switzerland	20.8	Benin	0.2
Japan	16.2	Nepal	0.2
Tajikistan	16.0	Afghanistan	0.3
Norway	13.5	Bangladesh	0.3
Belarus	12.4	Ethiopia	0.3
Kazakstan	12.2	Mali	0.4
Moldova	12.2	Burkina Faso	0.5
Ukraine	12.2	Niger	0.5
Latvia	11.9	Guinea	0.6
Russia	11.8	India	0.6

[UK 4.9] [USA 4.2]

Although the ratio of people to hospital beds gives a good approximation of a country's health provision, it is not an absolute indicator. Raw numbers may mask inefficiency and other weaknesses: the high availability of beds in Kazakstan, for example, has not prevented infant mortality rates over three times as high as in the United Kingdom and the United States.

Life Expectancy

Years of life expectancy at birth, selected countries (1997)

The chart shows combined data for both sexes. On average, women live longer than men worldwide, even in developing countries with high maternal mortality rates. Overall, life expectancy is steadily rising, though the difference between rich and poor nations remains dramatic.

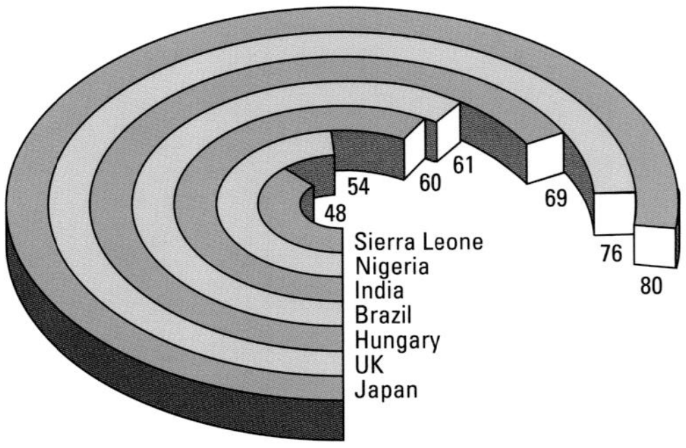

48
54
60
61
69
76
80
Sierra Leone
Nigeria
India
Brazil
Hungary
UK
Japan

Causes of Death

Causes of death for selected countries by percentage

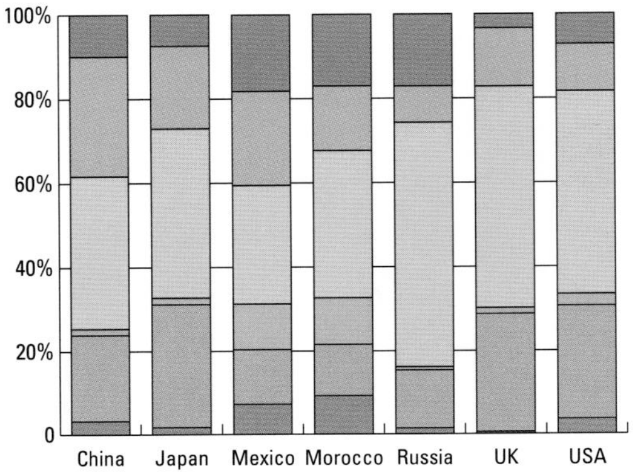

100%
80%
60%
40%
20%
0
China
Japan
Mexico
Morocco
Russia
UK
USA

- Accidents, poisoning & violence
- Respiratory & digestive diseases
- Nervous & circulatory diseases
- Metabolic disorders
- Cancers
- Infectious & parasitic diseases

Infant Mortality

Number of babies who died under the age of one, per 1,000 births (2000)

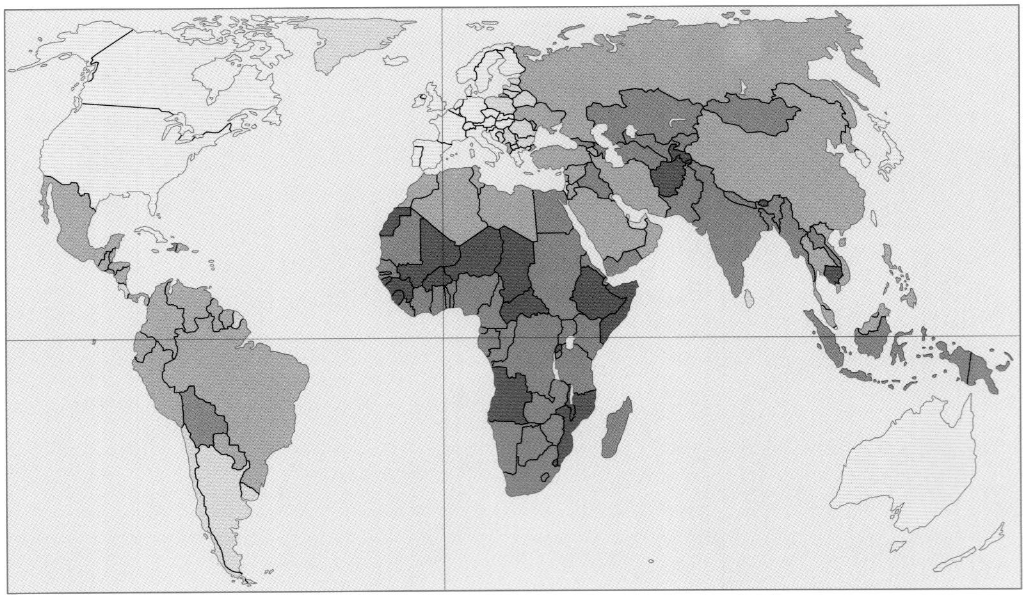

- Over 100 deaths per 1,000 births
- 50 – 100 deaths per 1,000 births
- 20 – 50 deaths per 1,000 births
- 10 – 20 deaths per 1,000 births
- Under 10 deaths per 1,000 births

Highest infant mortality		Lowest infant mortality	
Afghanistan	137 deaths	Iceland	5 deaths
W. Sahara	134 deaths	Finland	4 deaths
Malawi	131 deaths	Japan	4 deaths
Angola	126 deaths	Macau (China)	4 deaths
Somalia	126 deaths	Andorra	4 deaths

[UK 6 deaths]

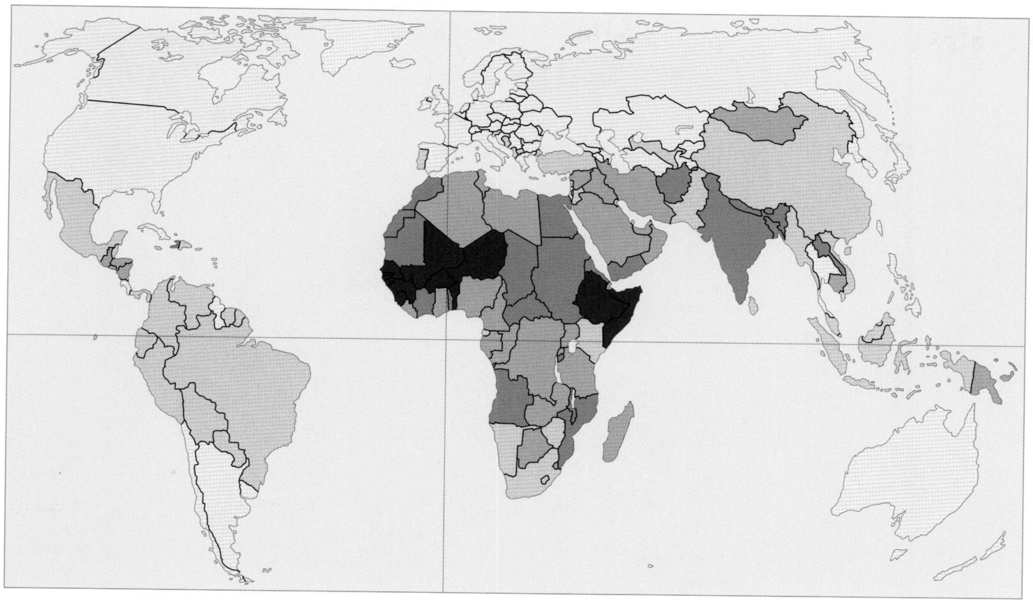

Illiteracy

Percentage of the total population unable to read or write (1999)

- Over 60% of population illiterate
- 40 – 60% of population illiterate
- 20 – 40% of population illiterate
- 5 – 20% of population illiterate
- Under 5% of population illiterate

Educational expenditure per person (latest available year)

Top 5 countries		Bottom 5 countries	
Sweden	$997	Chad	$2
Qatar	$989	Bangladesh	$3
Canada	$983	Ethiopia	$3
Norway	$971	Nepal	$4
Switzerland	$796	Somalia	$4

[UK $447]

Fertility and Education

Fertility rates compared with female education, selected countries (1992–95)

- Percentage of females aged 12–17 in secondary education
- Fertility rate: average number of children borne per woman

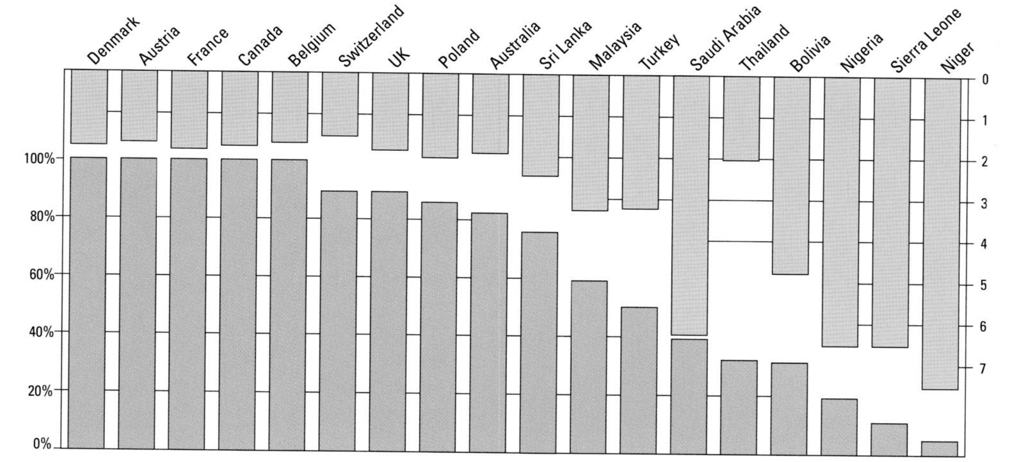

Living Standards

At first sight, most international contrasts in living standards are swamped by differences in wealth. The rich not only have more money, they have more of everything, including years of life. Those with only a little money are obliged to spend most of it on food and clothing, the basic maintenance costs of their existence; air travel and tourism are unlikely to feature on their expenditure lists. However, poverty and wealth are both relative: slum dwellers living on social security payments in an affluent industrial country have far more resources at their disposal than an average African peasant, but feel their own poverty nonetheless. A middle-class Indian lawyer cannot command a fraction of the earnings of a counterpart living in New York, London or Rome; nevertheless, he rightly sees himself as prosperous.

The rich not only live longer, on average, than the poor, they also die from different causes. Infectious and parasitic diseases, all but eliminated in the developed world, remain a scourge in the developing nations. On the other hand, more than two-thirds of the populations of OECD nations eventually succumb to cancer or circulatory disease.

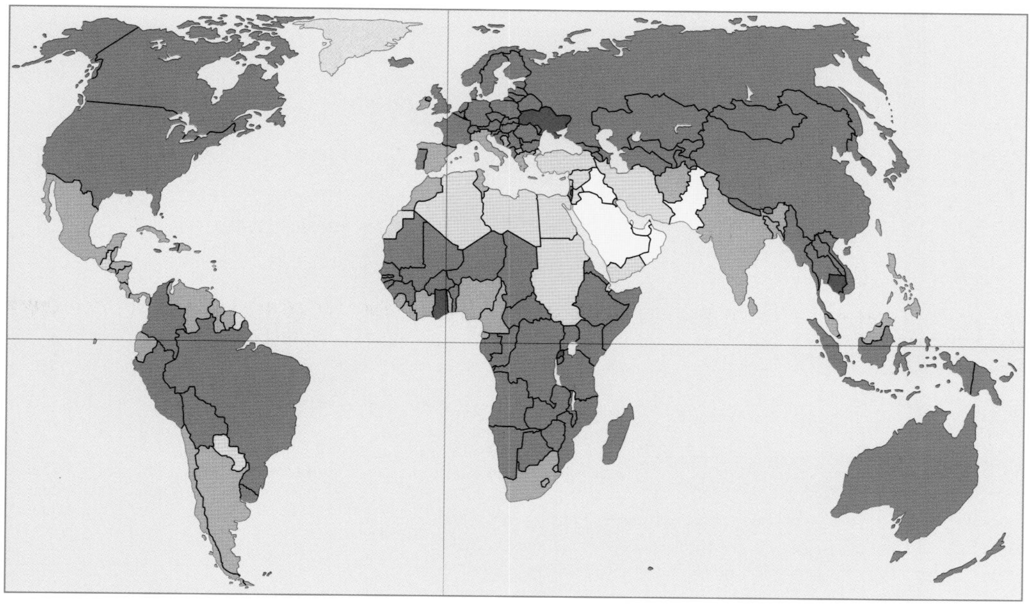

Women in the Workforce

Women in paid employment as a percentage of the total workforce (1997)

- Over 50% are women
- 40 – 50% are women
- 30 – 40% are women
- 20 – 30% are women
- 10 – 20% are women
- No available data

Most women in the workforce		Fewest women in the workforce	
Rwanda	56%	Oman	14%
Cambodia	53%	Saudi Arabia	13%
Ghana	51%	UAE	13%
Ukraine	50%	Qatar	13%
Vietnam	49%	Pakistan	13%

[USA 45%] [UK 44%]

Energy

Production

[Each square represents 1% of world energy production]

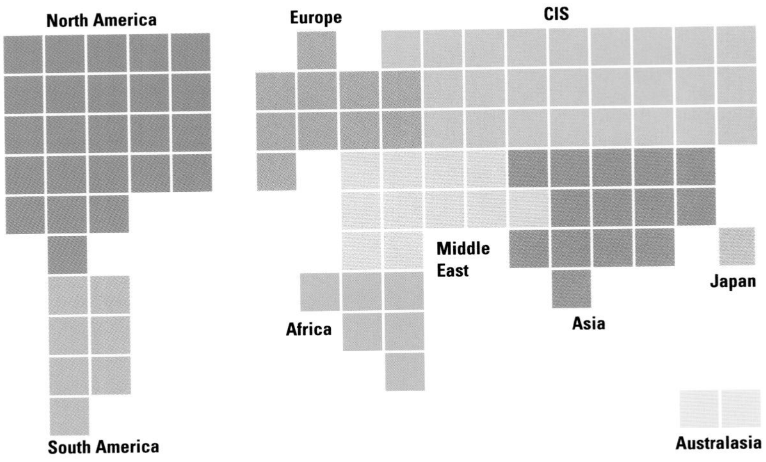

North America
Europe
CIS
Middle East
Japan
Africa
Asia
South America
Australasia

Consumption

[Each square represents 1% of world energy consumption]

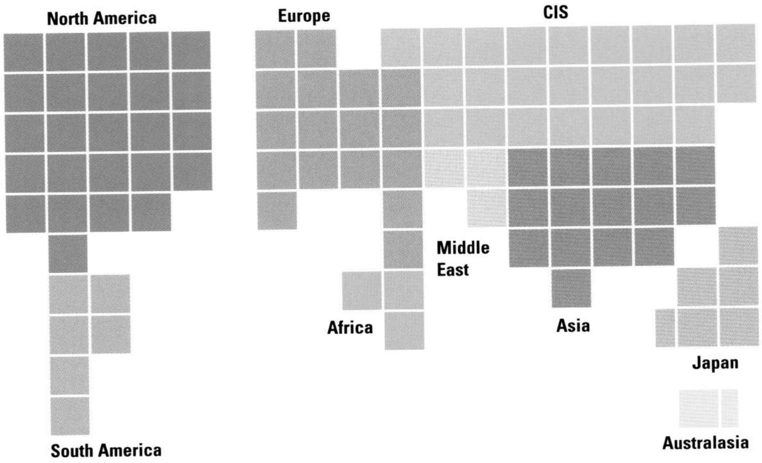

North America
Europe
CIS
Middle East
Africa
Asia
Japan
South America
Australasia

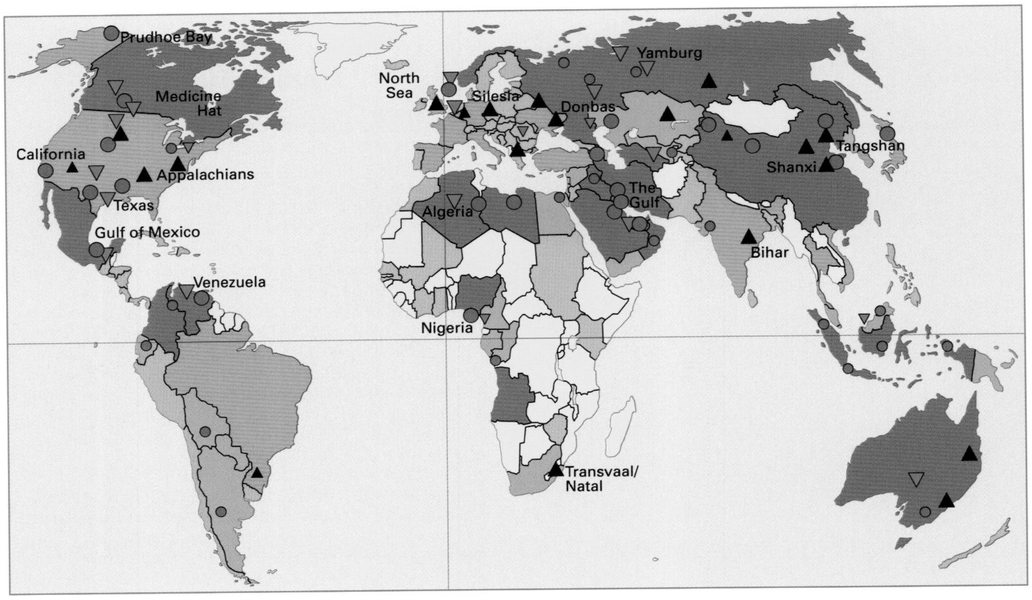

Prudhoe Bay
Medicine Hat
California
Appalachians
Texas
Gulf of Mexico
Venezuela
North Sea
Silesia
Donbas
Yamburg
Algeria
The Gulf
Nigeria
Tangshan
Shanxi
Bihar
Transvaal/ Natal

Energy Balance

Difference between energy production and consumption in millions of tonnes of oil equivalent (MtOe) (1997)

Energy deficit ↑

Over 35 MtOe

1 – 35 MtOe

Approx. balance

1 – 35 MtOe

Over 35 MtOe

Energy surplus ↓

Principal oilfields
Principal gasfields
Principal coalfields

Secondary oilfields
Secondary gasfields
Secondary coalfields

World Energy Consumption

Energy consumed by world regions, measured in million tonnes of oil equivalent in 1997. Total world consumption was 8,509 MtOe. Only energy from oil, gas, coal, nuclear and hydroelectric sources are included. Excluded are fuels such as wood, peat, animal waste, wind, solar and geothermal which, though important in some countries, are unreliably documented in terms of consumption statistics.

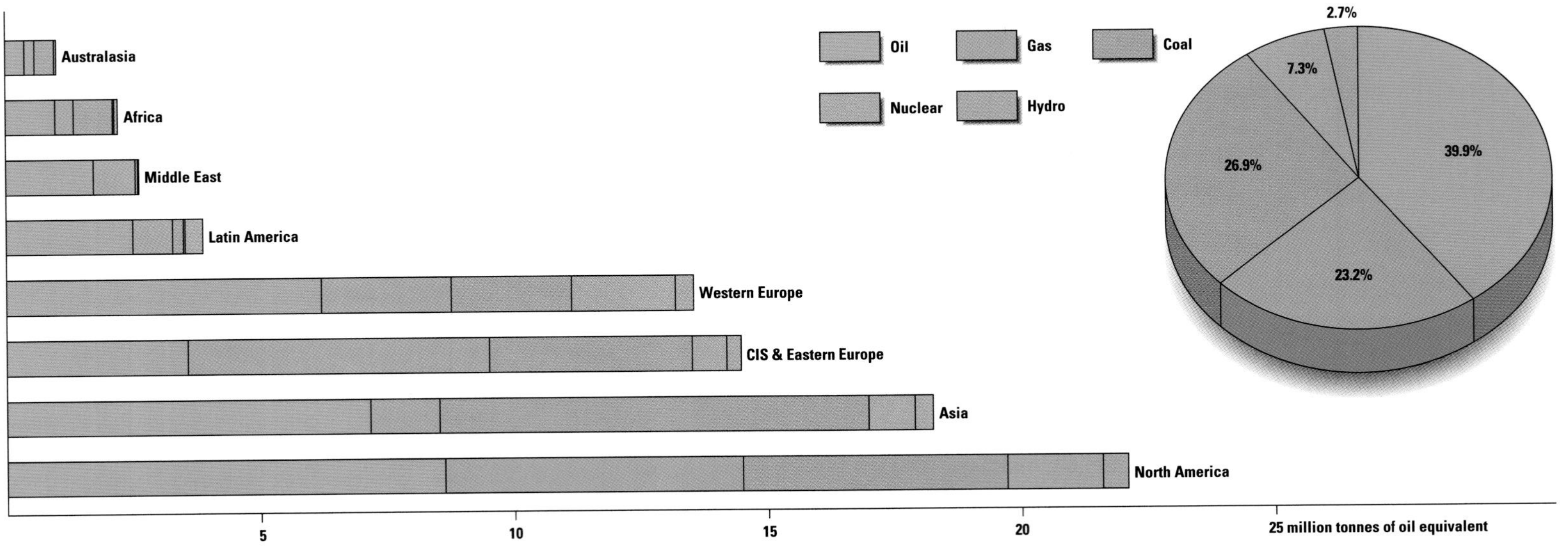

Australasia
Africa
Middle East
Latin America
Western Europe
CIS & Eastern Europe
Asia
North America
5
10
15
20
25 million tonnes of oil equivalent
Oil
Gas
Coal
Nuclear
Hydro
2.7%
7.3%
39.9%
26.9%
23.2%

Energy

Energy is used to keep us warm or cool, fuel our industries and our transport systems, and even feed us; high-intensity agriculture, with its use of fertilizers, pesticides and machinery, is heavily energy-dependent. Although we live in a high-energy society, there are vast discrepancies between rich and poor; for example, a North American consumes 13 times as much energy as a Chinese person. But even developing nations have more power at their disposal than was imaginable a century ago.

The distribution of energy supplies, most importantly fossil fuels (coal, oil and natural gas), is very uneven. In addition, the diagrams and map opposite show that the largest producers of energy are not necessarily the largest consumers. The movement of energy supplies around the world is therefore an important component of international trade. In 1999, total world movements in oil amounted to 2,025 million tonnes.

As the finite reserves of fossil fuels are depleted, renewable energy sources, such as solar, hydrothermal, wind, tidal and biomass, will become increasingly important around the world.

Nuclear Power

Major producers by percentage of world total and by percentage of domestic electricity generation (1998)

Country	*% of world total production*	*Country*	*% of nuclear as proportion of domestic electricity*
1. USA	29.2%	1. France	77%
2. France	15.9%	2. Sweden	47%
3. Japan	13.6%	3. Ukraine	44%
4. Germany	6.6%	4. South Korea	38%
5. Russia	4.3%	5. Japan	32%
6. UK	4.1%	6. Germany	29%
7. South Korea	3.7%	7. UK	28%
8. Ukraine	3.1%	8. USA	19%
9. Sweden	3.0%	9. Canada	13%
10. Canada	2.9%	10. Russia	13%

Although the 1980s were a bad time for the nuclear power industry (major projects ran over budget and fears of long-term environmental damage were heavily reinforced by the 1986 disaster at Chernobyl), the industry picked up in the early 1990s. Whilst the number of reactors is still increasing, however, orders for new plants have shrunk. In 1997, the Swedish government began to decommission the country's 12 nuclear power plants.

Hydroelectricity

Major producers by percentage of world total and by percentage of domestic electricity generation (1998)

Country	*% of world total production*	*Country*	*% of hydroelectric as proportion of domestic electricity*
1. Canada	12.6%	1. Norway	99.4%
2. USA	12.2%	2. Brazil	90.6%
3. Brazil	11.0%	3. Canada	59.1%
4. China	7.9%	4. Sweden	47.0%
5. Russia	6.0%	5. Russia	19.3%
6. Norway	4.4%	6. China	17.4%
7. Japan	3.9%	7. India	16.8%
8. India	3.1%	8. France	12.9%
9. Sweden	2.8%	9. Japan	9.8%
10. France	2.5%	10. USA	8.4%

Countries heavily reliant on hydroelectricity are usually small and non-industrial: a high proportion of hydroelectric power more often reflects a modest energy budget than vast hydroelectric resources. The USA, for instance, produces only 8% of power requirements from hydroelectricity; yet that 8% amounts to more than three times the hydropower generated by the whole of Africa.

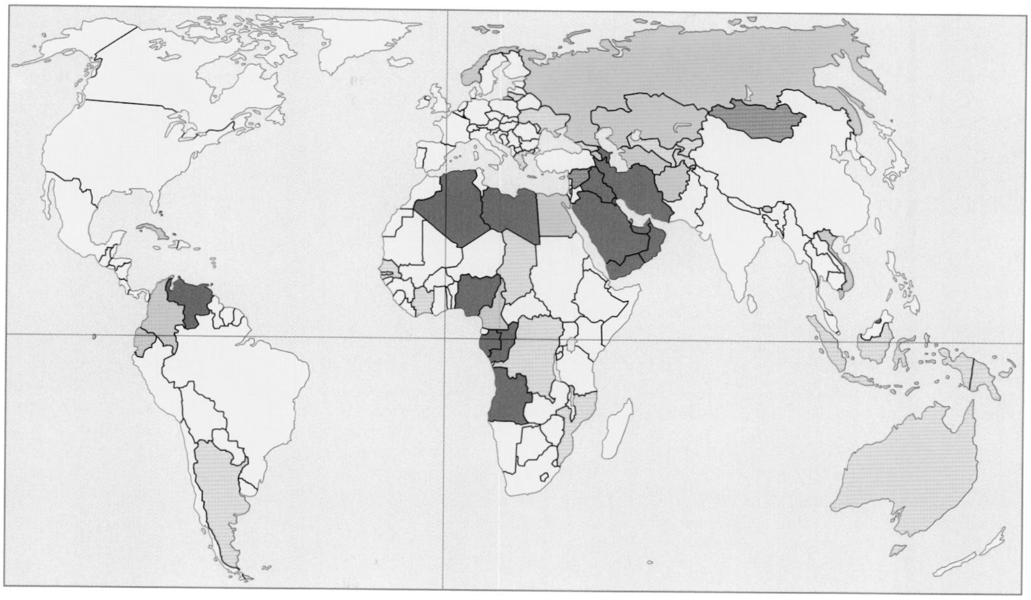

Fuel Exports

Fuels as a percentage of total value of exports (1999)

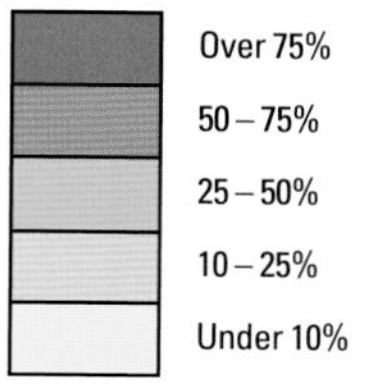
Over 75%
50 – 75%
25 – 50%
10 – 25%
Under 10%

In the 1970s, oil exports became a political issue when OPEC sought to increase the influence of developing countries in world affairs by raising oil prices and restricting production. But its power was short-lived, following a fall in demand for oil in the 1980s, due to an increase in energy efficiency and development of alternative resources.

Measurements

For historical reasons, oil is traded in 'barrels'. The weight and volume equivalents (shown right) are all based on average-density 'Arabian light' crude oil.

The energy equivalents given for a tonne of oil are also somewhat imprecise: oil and coal of different qualities will have varying energy contents, a fact usually reflected in their price on world markets.

Conversion Rates

1 barrel = 0.136 tonnes or 159 litres or 35 Imperial gallons or 42 US gallons

1 tonne = 7.33 barrels or 1,185 litres or 256 Imperial gallons or 261 US gallons

1 tonne oil = 1.5 tonnes hard coal or 3.0 tonnes lignite or 12,000 kWh

1 Imperial gallon = 1.201 US gallons or 4.546 litres or 277.4 cubic inches

World Coal Reserves

Proved coal reserves in place by region and country, thousand million tonnes (1999)

World Total = 984,211 million tonnes

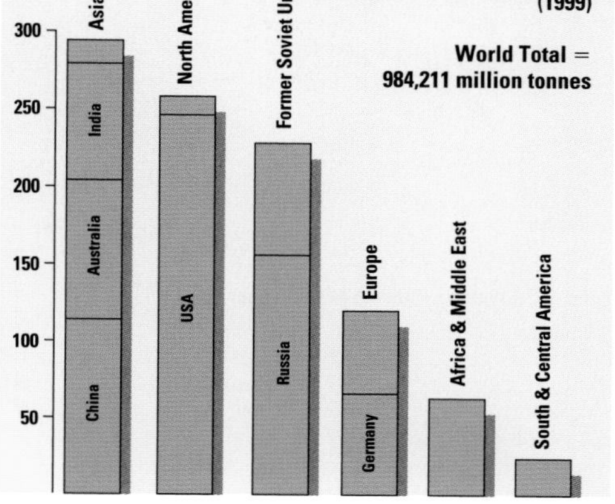
300
250
200
150
100
50
Asia Pacific
China
Australia
India
North America
USA
Former Soviet Union
Russia
Europe
Germany
Africa & Middle East
South & Central America

World Gas Reserves

Proved recoverable natural gas reserves by region and country, trillion cubic metres (1999)

World Total = 146 trillion cubic metres

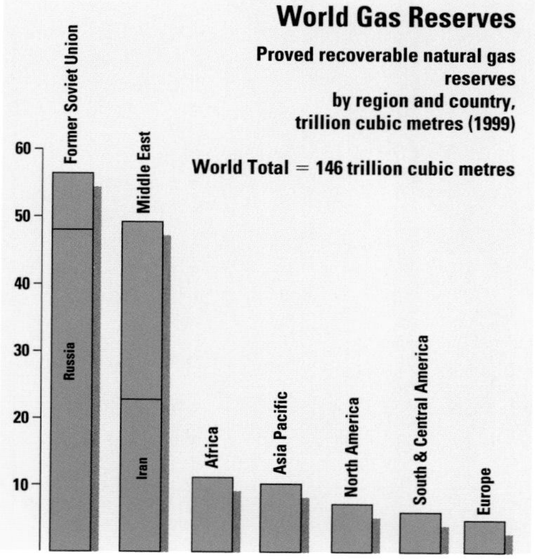
60
50
40
30
20
10
Former Soviet Union
Russia
Middle East
Iran
Africa
Asia Pacific
North America
South & Central America
Europe

World Oil Reserves

Crude oil reserves by region and country, thousand million tonnes (1999)

World Total = 140,400 million tonnes

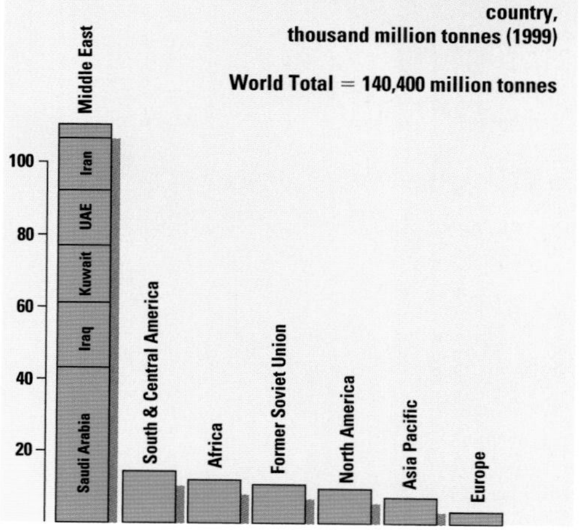
100
80
60
40
20
Middle East
Saudi Arabia
Iraq
Kuwait
UAE
Iran
South & Central America
Africa
Former Soviet Union
North America
Asia Pacific
Europe

Production

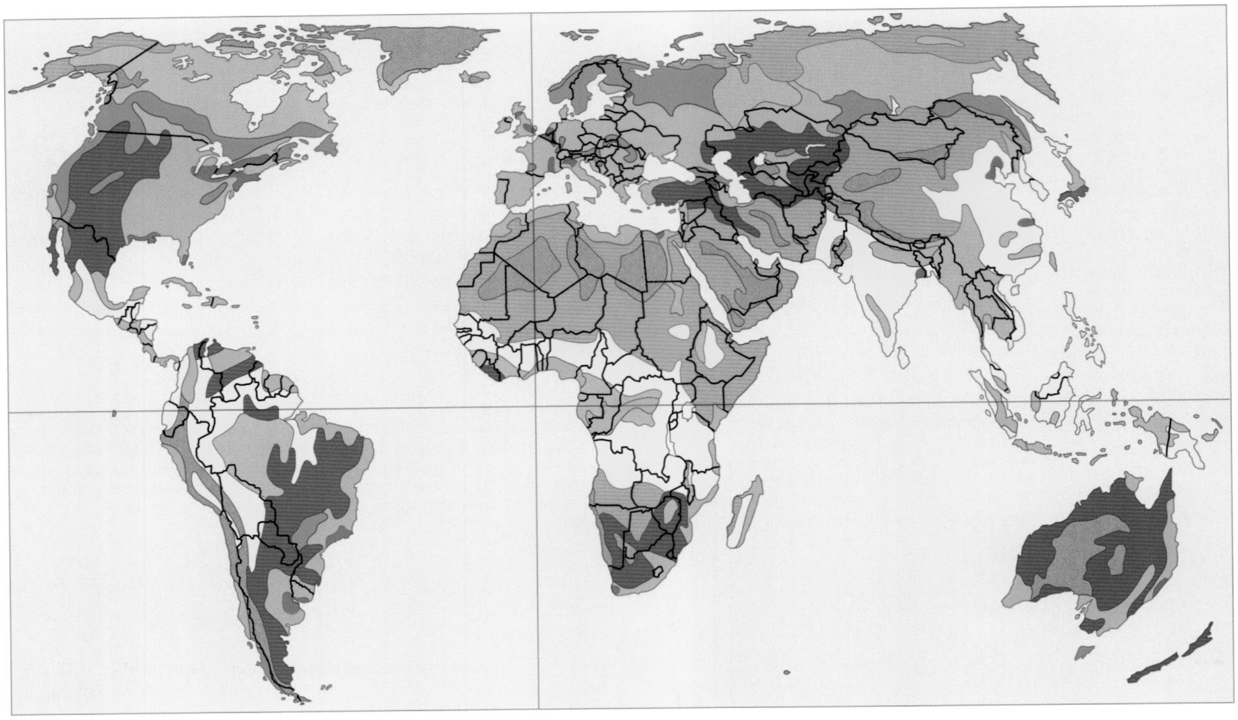

Agriculture

Predominant type of farming or land use.

- Nomadic herding
- Hunting, fishing and gathering
- Subsistence agriculture
- Commercial ranching
- Commercial livestock and grain farming
- Urban areas
- Forestry
- Unproductive land

The development of agriculture has transformed human existence more than any other. The whole business of farming is constantly developing: due mainly to the new varieties of rice and wheat, world grain production has increased by over 70% since 1965. New machinery and modern agricultural techniques enable relatively few farmers to produce enough food for the world's 6 billion or so people.

Staple Crops

Wheat

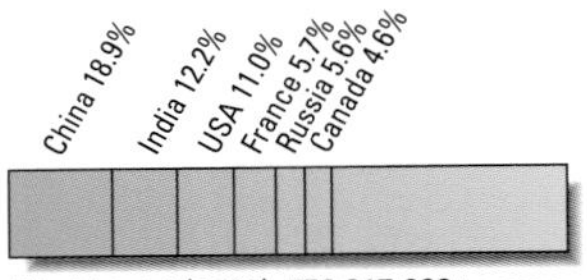
China 18.9%
India 12.2%
USA 11.0%
France 5.7%
Russia 5.6%
Canada 4.6%

World total (2000): 576,317,000 tonnes

Maize

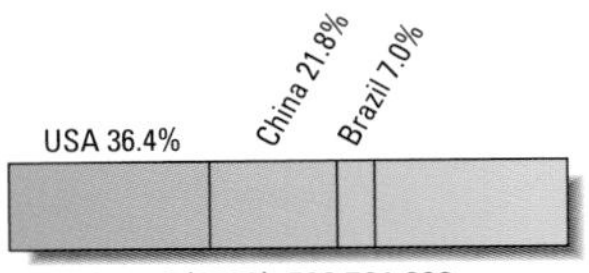
USA 36.4%
China 21.8%
Brazil 7.0%

World total (2000): 590,791,000 tonnes

Oats

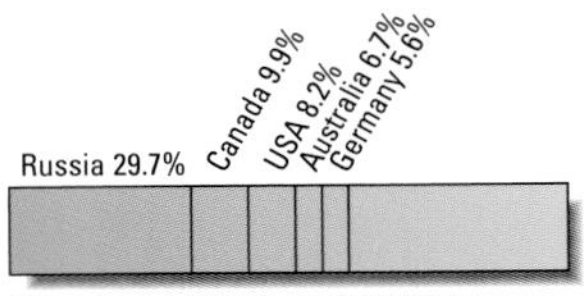
Russia 29.7%
Canada 9.9%
USA 8.2%
Australia 6.7%
Germany 5.6%

World total (2000): 25,953,000 tonnes

Millet

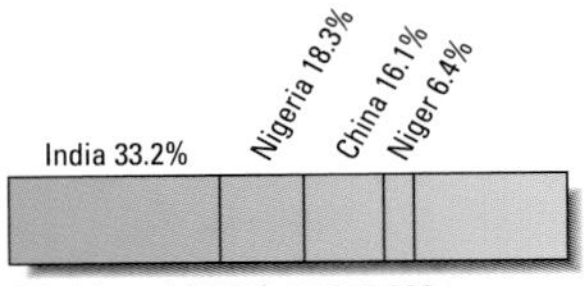
India 33.2%
Nigeria 18.3%
China 16.1%
Niger 6.4%

World total (2000): 27,255,000 tonnes

Rice

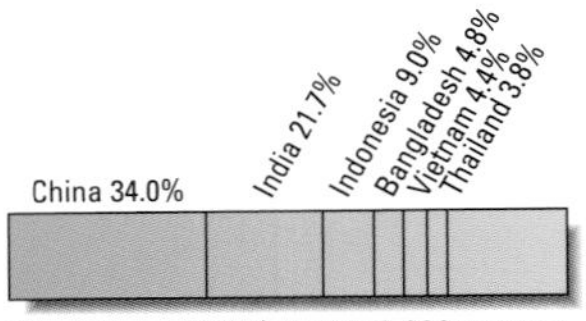
China 34.0%
India 21.7%
Indonesia 9.0%
Bangladesh 4.8%
Vietnam 4.4%
Thailand 3.8%

World total (2000): 598,852,000 tonnes

Potatoes

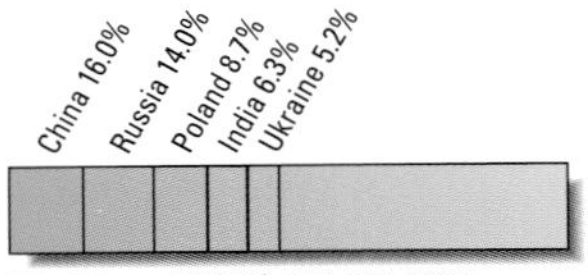
China 16.0%
Russia 14.0%
Poland 8.7%
India 6.3%
Ukraine 5.2%

World total (2000): 311,288,000 tonnes

Soya

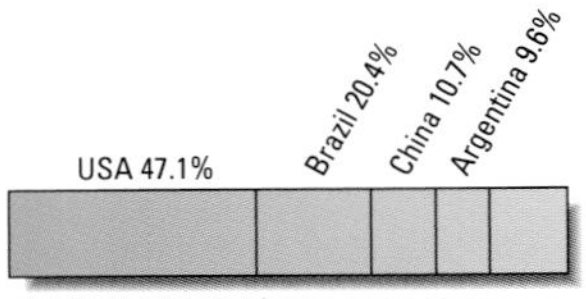
USA 47.1%
Brazil 20.4%
China 10.7%
Argentina 9.6%

World total (2000): 161,993,000 tonnes

Cassava

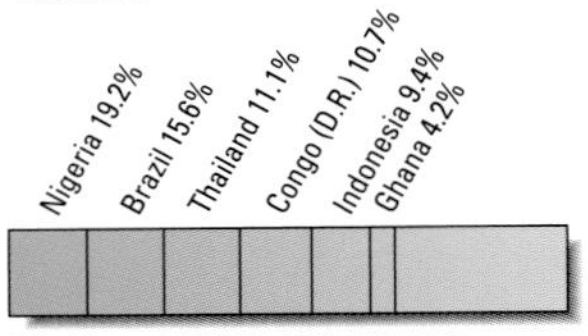
Nigeria 19.2%
Brazil 15.6%
Thailand 11.1%
Congo (D.R.) 10.7%
Indonesia 9.4%
Ghana 4.2%

World total (2000): 172,737,000 tonnes

Sugars

Sugar cane

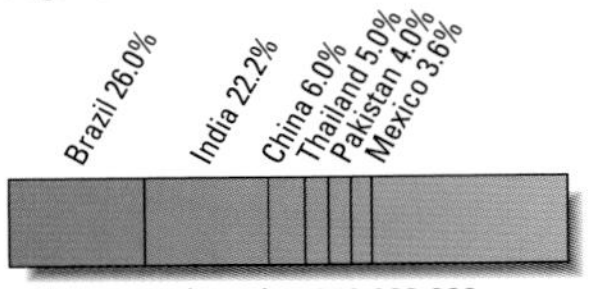
Brazil 26.0%
India 22.2%
China 6.0%
Thailand 5.0%
Pakistan 4.0%
Mexico 3.6%

World total (2000): 1,278,093,000 tonnes

Sugar beet

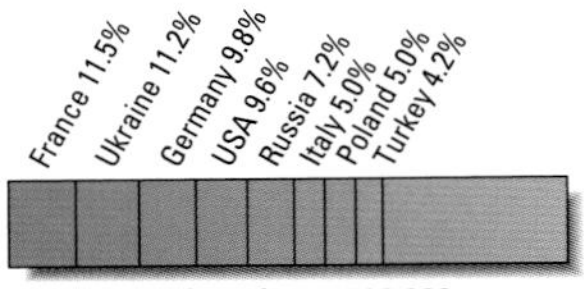
France 11.5%
Ukraine 11.2%
Germany 9.8%
USA 9.6%
Russia 7.2%
Italy 5.0%
Poland 5.0%
Turkey 4.2%

World total (2000): 244,780,000 tonnes

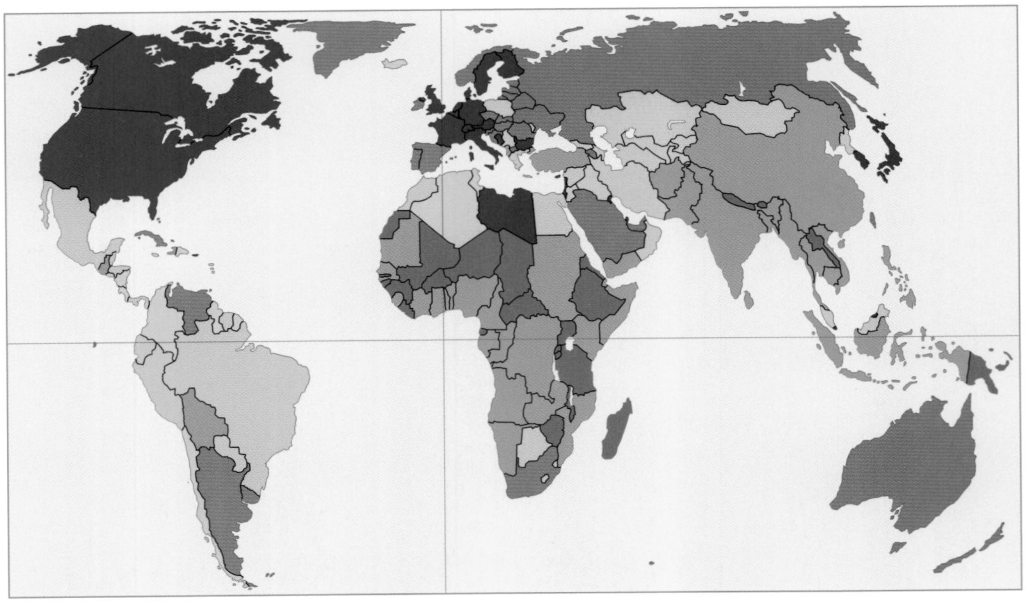

Employment

The number of workers employed in manufacturing for every 100 workers engaged in agriculture (1997)

Mainly agricultural countries:
- Under 10
- 10 – 50
- 50 – 100

Mainly industrial countries:
- 100 – 200
- 200 – 500
- Over 500

Selected countries (latest available year)

Singapore	8,860	Germany	800
Hong Kong	3,532	Kuwait	767
UK	1,270	Bahrain	660
Belgium	820	USA	657
Yugoslavia	809	Israel	633

CARTOGRAPHY BY PHILIP'S. COPYRIGHT PHILIP'S

Mineral Production

***Figures for aluminium are for refined metal; all other figures refer to ore production.**

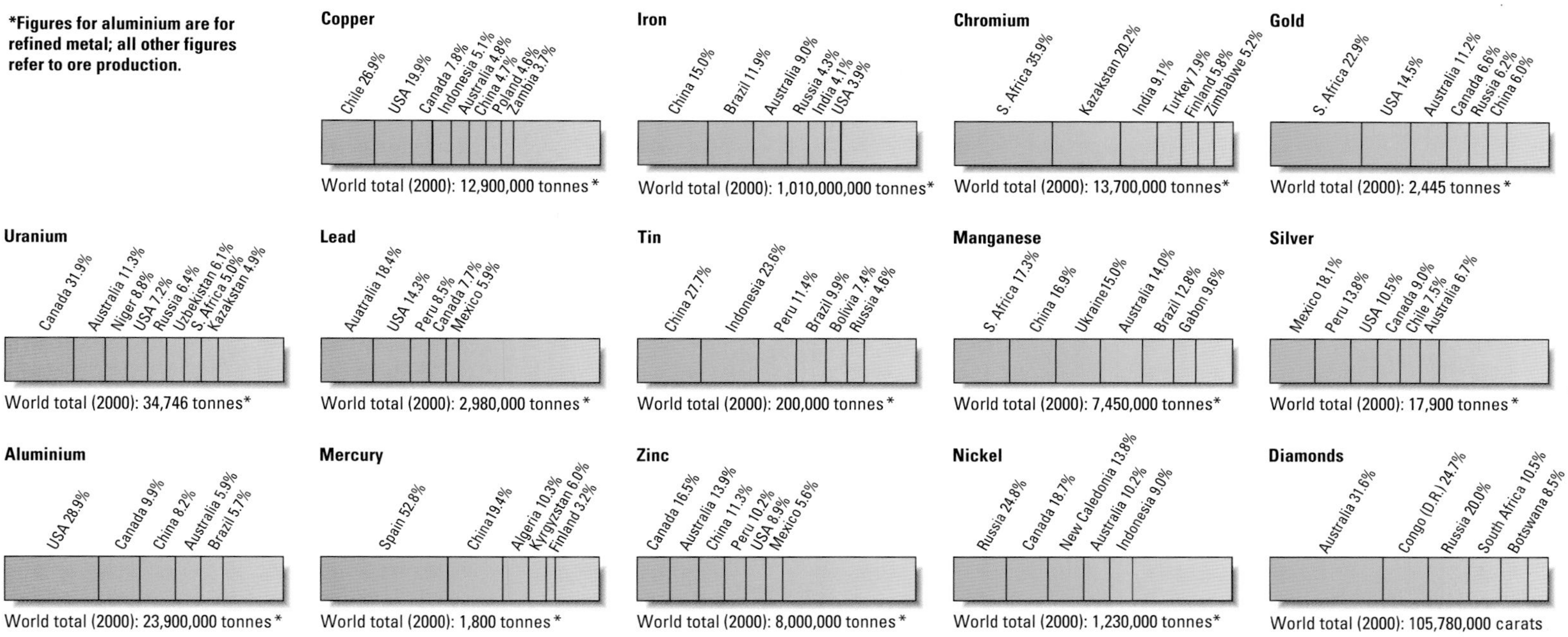
Copper
Chile 26.9% USA 19.9% Canada 7.8% Indonesia 5.1% Australia 4.8% China 4.7% Poland 4.6% Zambia 3.7%
World total (2000): 12,900,000 tonnes*
Iron
China 15.0% Brazil 11.9% Australia 9.0% Russia 4.3% India 4.1% USA 3.9%
World total (2000): 1,010,000,000 tonnes*
Chromium
S. Africa 35.9% Kazakstan 20.2% India 9.1% Turkey 7.9% Finland 5.8% Zimbabwe 5.2%
World total (2000): 13,700,000 tonnes*
Gold
S. Africa 22.9% USA 14.5% Australia 11.2% Canada 6.6% Russia 6.2% China 6.0%
World total (2000): 2,445 tonnes*
Uranium
Canada 31.9% Australia 11.3% Niger 8.8% USA 7.2% Russia 6.4% Uzbekistan 6.1% S. Africa 5.0% Kazakstan 4.9%
World total (2000): 34,746 tonnes*
Lead
Auatralia 18.4% USA 14.3% Peru 8.5% Canada 7.7% Mexico 5.9%
World total (2000): 2,980,000 tonnes*
Tin
China 27.7% Indonesia 23.6% Peru 11.4% Brazil 9.9% Bolivia 7.4% Russia 4.6%
World total (2000): 200,000 tonnes*
Manganese
S. Africa 17.3% China 16.9% Ukraine15.0% Australia 14.0% Brazil 12.8% Gabon 9.6%
World total (2000): 7,450,000 tonnes*
Silver
Mexico 18.1% Peru 13.8% USA 10.5% Canada 9.0% Chile 7.5% Australia 6.7%
World total (2000): 17,900 tonnes*
Aluminium
USA 28.9% Canada 9.9% China 8.2% Australia 5.9% Brazil 5.7%
World total (2000): 23,900,000 tonnes*
Mercury
Spain 52.8% China19.4% Algeria 10.3% Kyrgyzstan 6.0% Finland 3.2%
World total (2000): 1,800 tonnes*
Zinc
Canada 16.5% Australia 13.9% China 11.3% Peru 10.2% USA 8.9% Mexico 5.6%
World total (2000): 8,000,000 tonnes*
Nickel
Russia 24.8% Canada 18.7% New Caledonia 13.8% Australia 10.2% Indonesia 9.0%
World total (2000): 1,230,000 tonnes*
Diamonds
Australia 31.6% Congo (D.R.) 24.7% Russia 20.0% South Africa 10.5% Botswana 8.5%
World total (2000): 105,780,000 carats

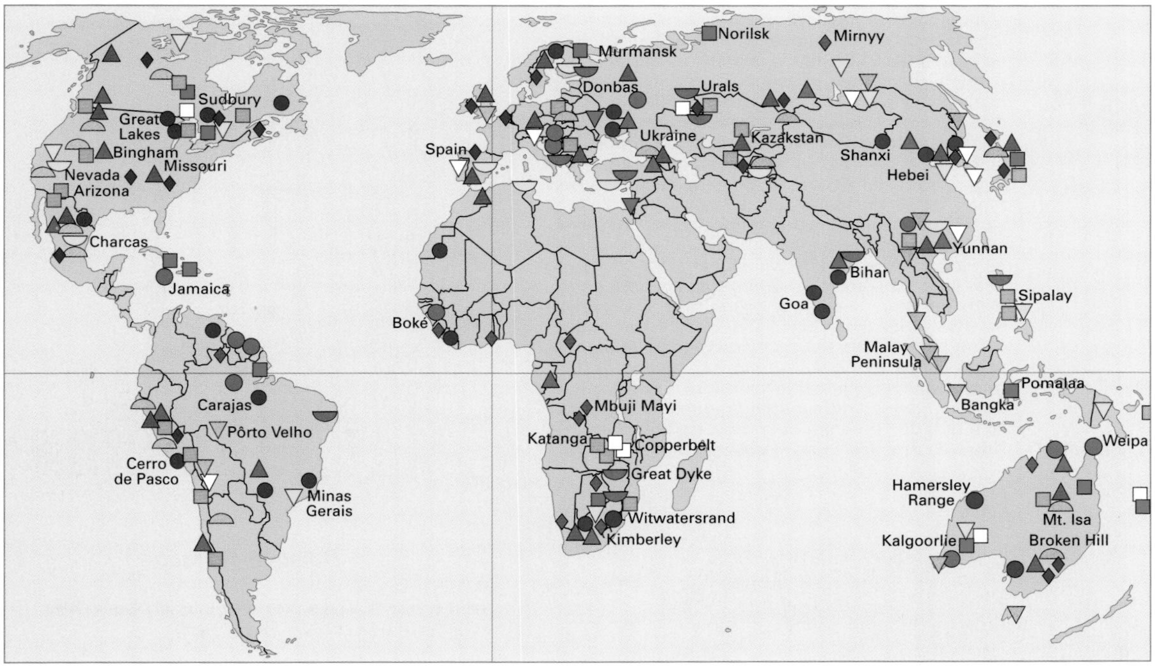
Norilsk
Mirnyy
Murmansk
Sudbury
Great Lakes
Bingham
Nevada
Arizona
Missouri
Charcas
Jamaica
Spain
Donbas
Urals
Ukraine
Kazakstan
Shanxi
Hebei
Yunnan
Bihar
Goa
Sipalay
Boke
Malay Peninsula
Pomalaa
Bangka
Mbuji Mayi
Katanga
Copperbelt
Great Dyke
Witwatersrand
Kimberley
Carajas
Pôrto Velho
Cerro de Pasco
Minas Gerais
Hamersley Range
Weipa
Mt. Isa
Broken Hill
Kalgoorlie

Mineral Distribution

The map shows the richest sources of the most important minerals. Major mineral locations are named.

- Gold
- Silver
- Diamonds
- Tungsten
- Iron Ore
- Nickel
- Chrome
- Manganese
- Cobalt
- Molybdenum
- Copper
- Lead
- Bauxite
- Tin
- Zinc
- Mercury

The map does not show undersea deposits, most of which are considered inaccessible.

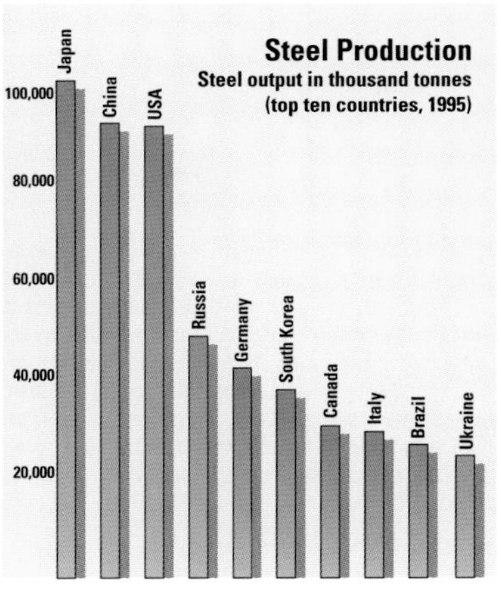
Steel Production
Steel output in thousand tonnes (top ten countries, 1995)
100,000
80,000
60,000
40,000
20,000
Japan
China
USA
Russia
Germany
South Korea
Canada
Italy
Brazil
Ukraine

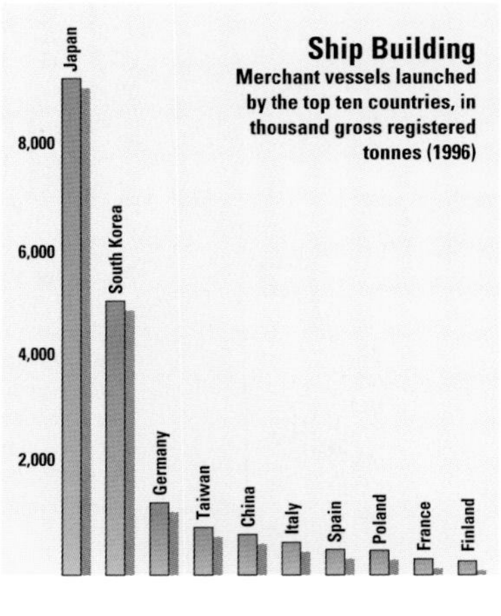
Ship Building
Merchant vessels launched by the top ten countries, in thousand gross registered tonnes (1996)
8,000
6,000
4,000
2,000
Japan
South Korea
Germany
Taiwan
China
Italy
Spain
Poland
France
Finland

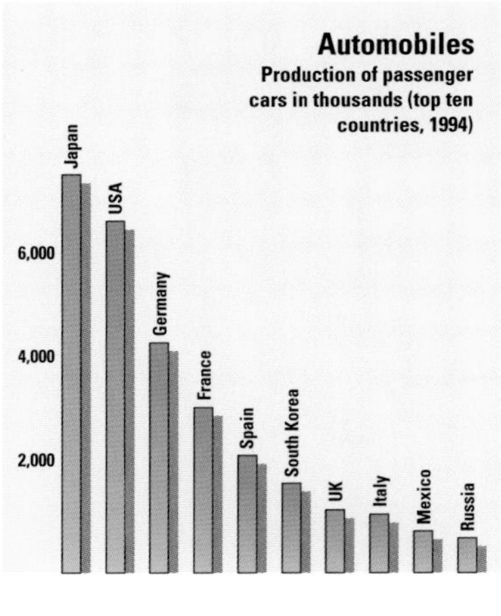
Automobiles
Production of passenger cars in thousands (top ten countries, 1994)
6,000
4,000
2,000
Japan
USA
Germany
France
Spain
South Korea
UK
Italy
Mexico
Russia

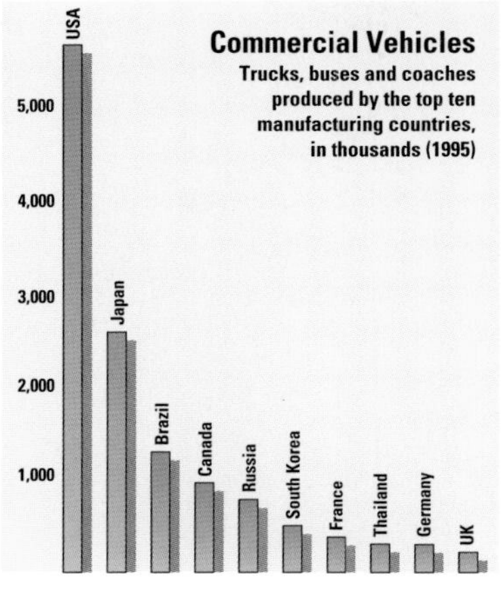
Commercial Vehicles
Trucks, buses and coaches produced by the top ten manufacturing countries, in thousands (1995)
5,000
4,000
3,000
2,000
1,000
USA
Japan
Brazil
Canada
Russia
South Korea
France
Thailand
Germany
UK

CARTOGRAPHY BY PHILIP'S. COPYRIGHT PHILIP'S

Trade

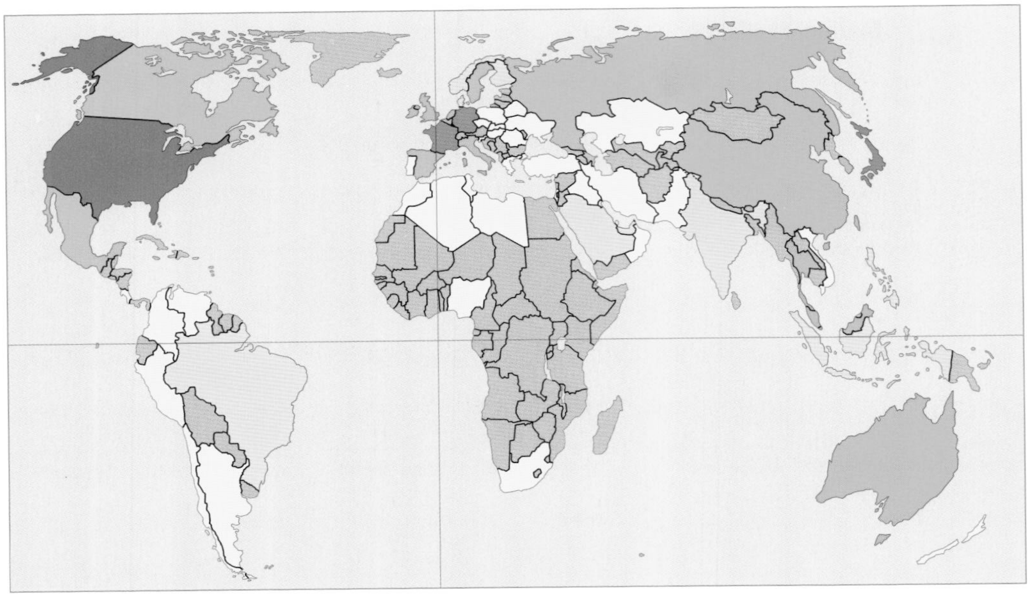

Share of World Trade

Percentage share of total world exports by value (1999)

- Over 10% of world trade
- 5 – 10% of world trade
- 1 – 5% of world trade
- 0.5 – 1% of world trade
- 0.1 – 0.5% of world trade
- Under 0.1% of world trade

International trade is dominated by a handful of powerful maritime nations. The members of 'G8', the inner circle of OECD (see page 19), and the top seven countries listed in the diagram below, account for more than half the total. The majority of nations – including all but four in Africa – contribute less than one quarter of 1% to the worldwide total of exports; the EU countries account for 40%, the Pacific Rim nations over 35%.

The Main Trading Nations

The imports and exports of the top ten trading nations as a percentage of world trade (1999). Each country's trade in manufactured goods is shown in dark blue.

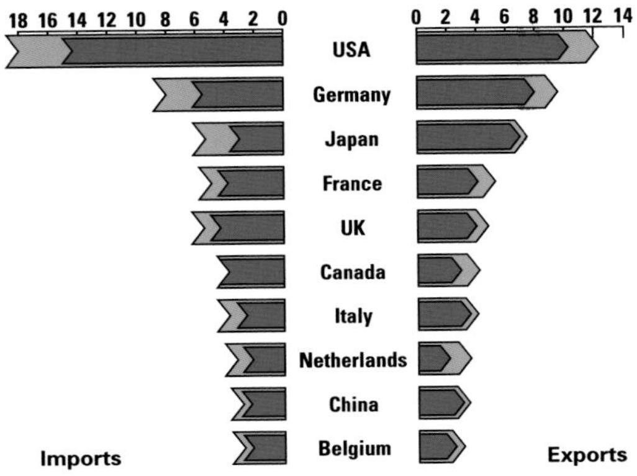
18 16 14 12 10 8 6 4 2 0
0 2 4 6 8 10 12 14
USA
Germany
Japan
France
UK
Canada
Italy
Netherlands
China
Belgium
Imports
Exports

Patterns of Trade

Thriving international trade is the outward sign of a healthy world economy, the obvious indicator that some countries have goods to sell and others the means to buy them. Global exports expanded to an estimated US $3.92 trillion in 1994, an increase due partly to economic recovery in industrial nations but also to export-led growth strategies in many developing nations and lowered regional trade barriers. International trade remains dominated, however, by the rich, industrialized countries of the Organization for Economic Development: between them, OECD members account for almost 75% of world imports and exports in most years. However, continued rapid economic growth in some developing countries is altering global trade patterns. The 'tiger economies' of South-east Asia are particularly vibrant, averaging more than 8% growth between 1992 and 1994. The size of the largest trading economies means that imports and exports usually represent only a small percentage of their total wealth. In export-concious Japan, for example, trade in goods and services amounts to less than 18% of GDP. In poorer countries, trade – often in a single commodity – may amount to 50% of GDP.

Traded Products

World merchandise exports by product grouping (1999). Values expressed as a percentage of world total

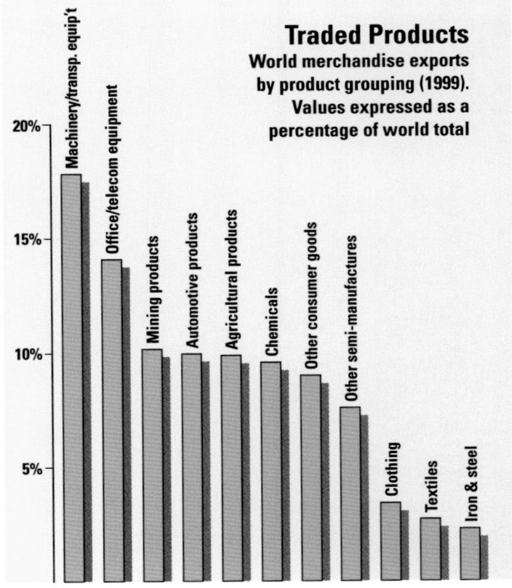
20%
15%
10%
5%
Machinery/transp. equip't
Office/telecom equipment
Mining products
Automotive products
Agricultural products
Chemicals
Other consumer goods
Other semi-manufactures
Clothing
Textiles
Iron & steel

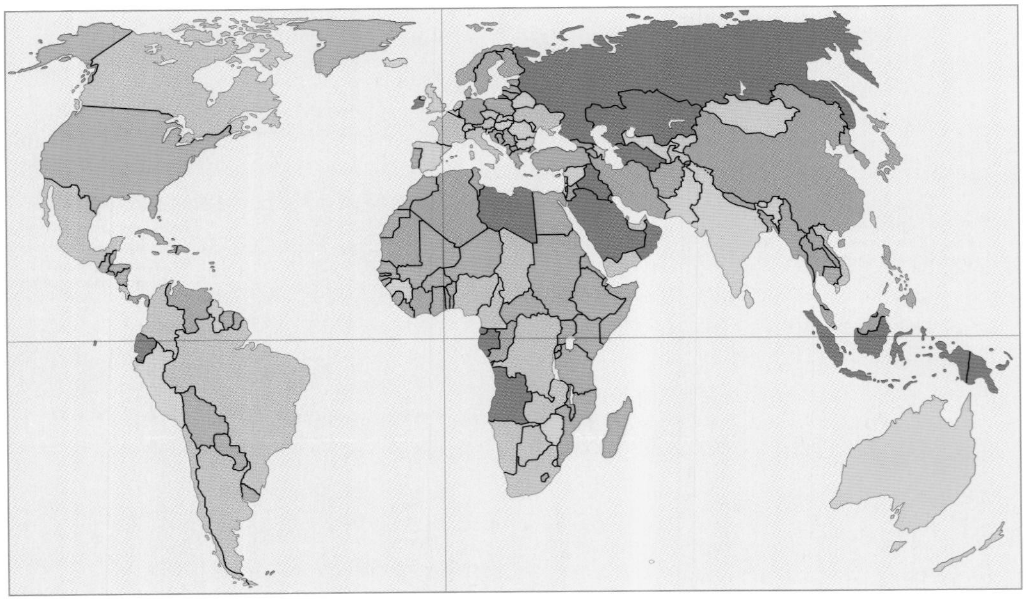

Balance of Trade

Value of exports in proportion to the value of imports (1999)

Exports exceed imports by:
- More than 40%
- 10 – 40%

- 10% either side

Imports exceed exports by:
- 10 – 40%
- More than 40%

The total world trade balance should amount to zero, since exports must equal imports on a global scale. In practice, at least $100 billion in exports go unrecorded, leaving the world with an apparent deficit and many countries in a better position than public accounting reveals. However, a favourable trade balance is not necessarily a sign of prosperity: many poorer countries must maintain a high surplus in order to service debts, and do so by restricting imports below the levels needed to sustain successful economies.

CARTOGRAPHY BY PHILIP'S. COPYRIGHT PHILIP'S

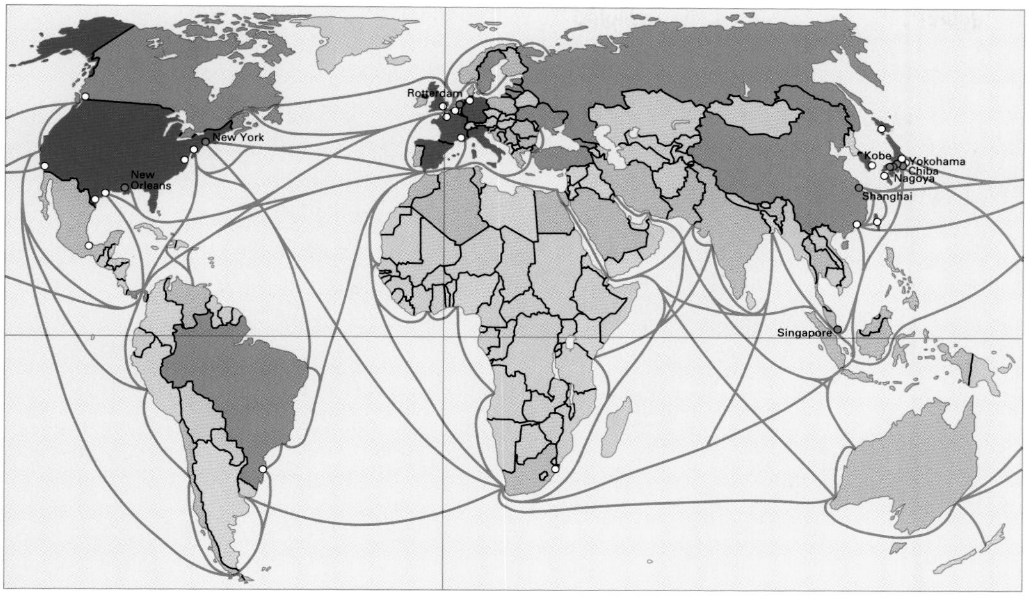

Rotterdam
New York
New Orleans
Kobe
Yokohama
Chiba
Nagoya
Shanghai
Singapore

Seaborne Freight

Freight unloaded in millions of tonnes (latest available year)

- Over 100
- 50 – 100
- 10 – 50
- 5 – 10
- Under 5
- Landlocked countries

Major seaports

- Over 100 million tonnes per year
- 50–100 million tonnes per year
- Major shipping routes

Cargoes

Type of seaborne freight

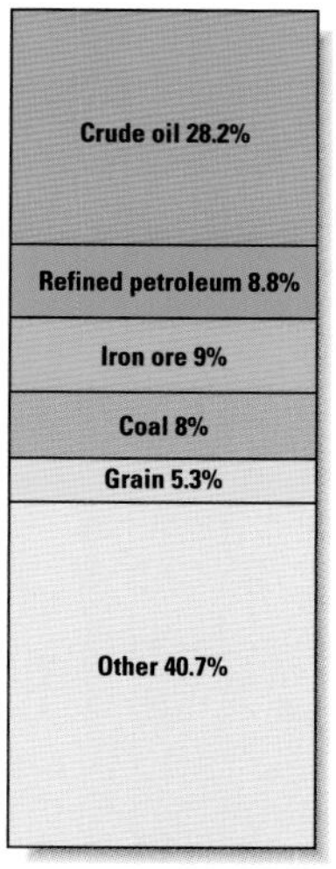

Crude oil 28.2%
Refined petroleum 8.8%
Iron ore 9%
Coal 8%
Grain 5.3%
Other 40.7%

Merchant Fleets

Merchant fleets in thousand gross tonnage (1999). A large number of vessels are registered in Liberia and Panama but they are not part of the national fleet.

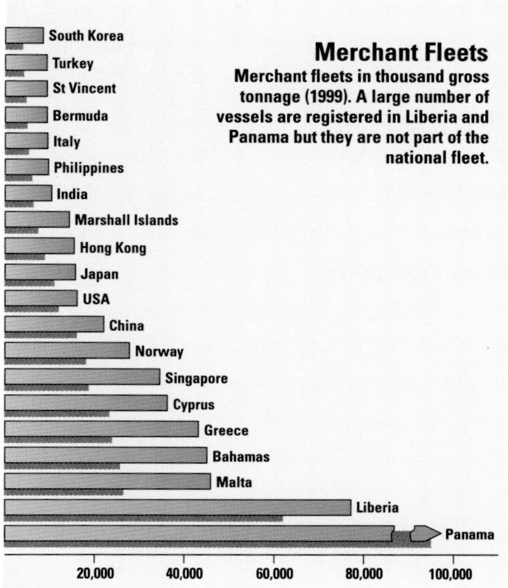

South Korea
Turkey
St Vincent
Bermuda
Italy
Philippines
India
Marshall Islands
Hong Kong
Japan
USA
China
Norway
Singapore
Cyprus
Greece
Bahamas
Malta
Liberia
Panama
20,000
40,000
60,000
80,000
100,000

The Great Ports

Total cargo traffic, in thousand tonnes (latest available year)

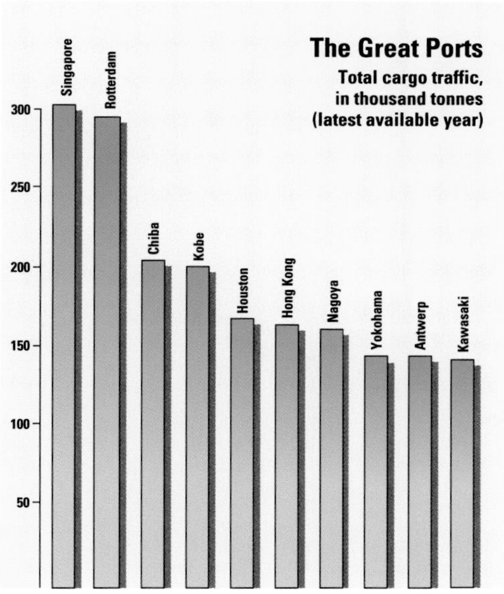

300
250
200
150
100
50
Singapore
Rotterdam
Chiba
Kobe
Houston
Hong Kong
Nagoya
Yokohama
Antwerp
Kawasaki

World Shipping

World merchant fleet by type of vessel and deadweight tonnage (latest available year)

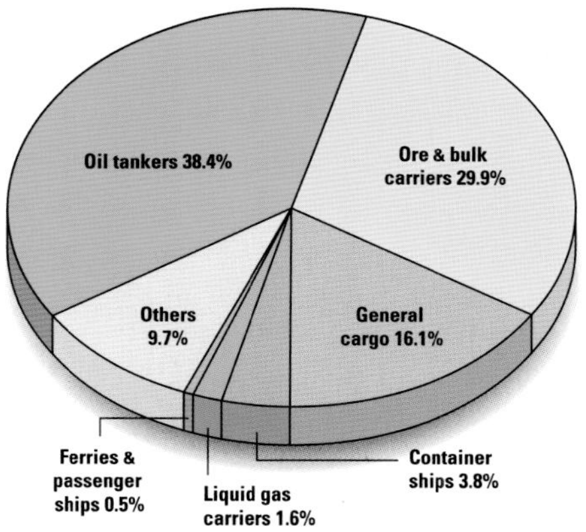

Oil tankers 38.4%
Ore & bulk carriers 29.9%
Others 9.7%
General cargo 16.1%
Ferries & passenger ships 0.5%
Liquid gas carriers 1.6%
Container ships 3.8%

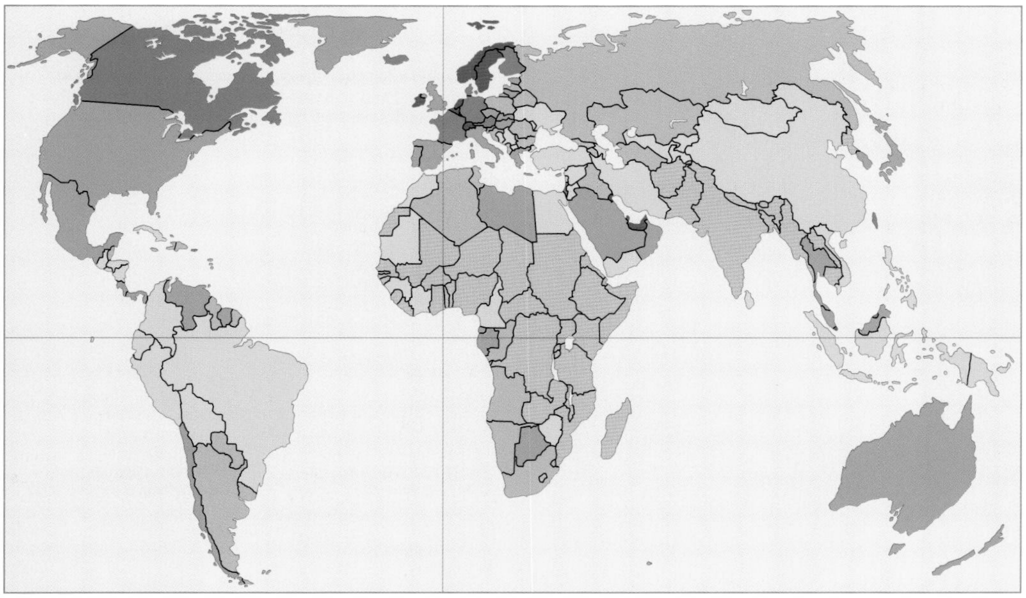

Exports Per Capita

Value of exports in US $, divided by total population (2000)

- Over 10,000
- 5,000 – 10,000
- 1,000 – 5,000
- 500 – 1,000
- 100 – 500
- Under 100

[UK 4,728] [USA 2,791]

Highest per capita

Kuwait	113,614
Liechtenstein	78,848
Singapore	31,860
Aruba (Neths)	31,429
Hong Kong (China)	28,290
Ireland	19,136

Travel and Tourism

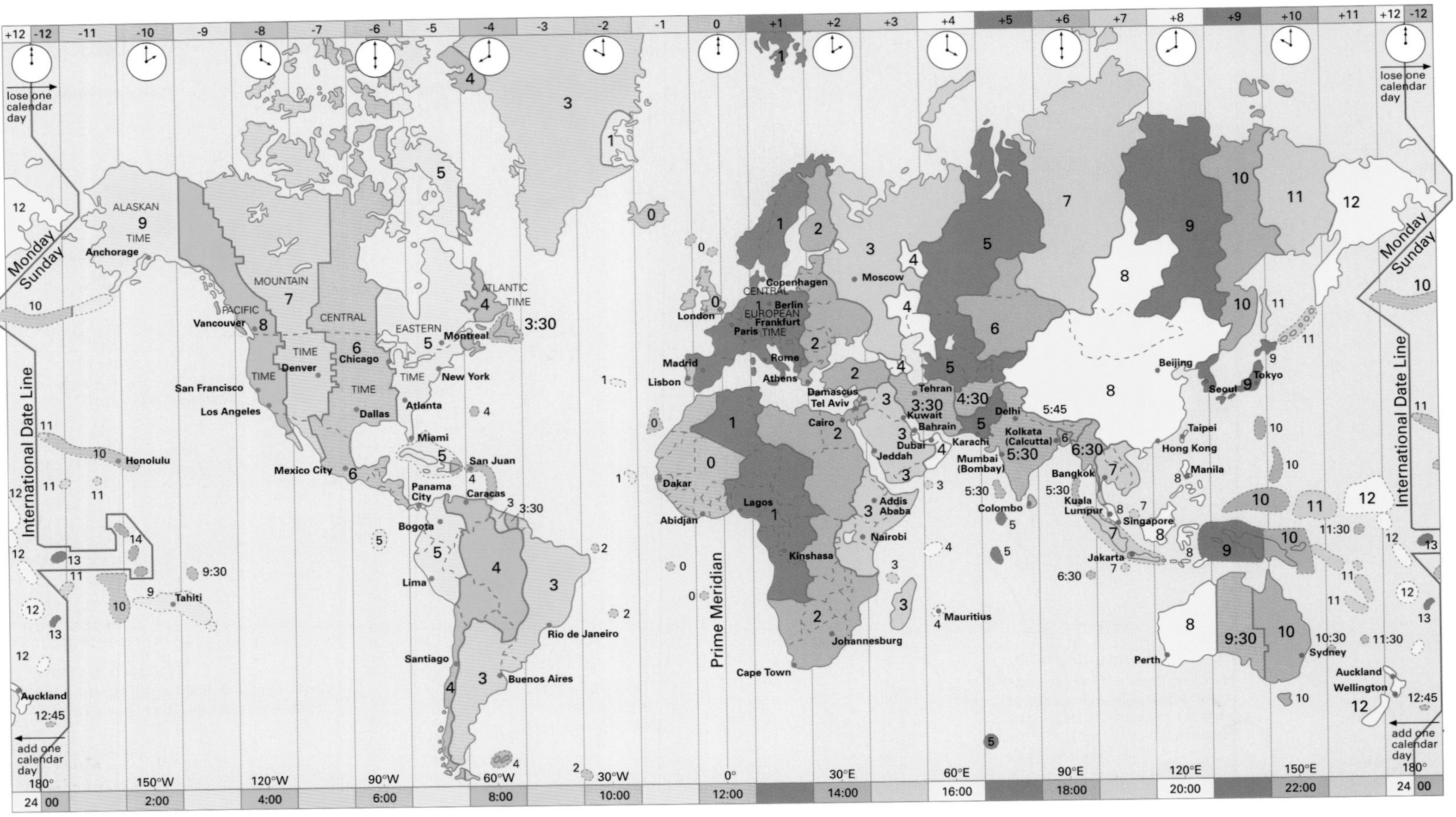

Projection: Mercator

Time Zones

- Zones using UT (GMT)
- Zones slow of UT (GMT)
- International boundaries
- 10 — Hours slow or fast of UT or Co-ordinated Universal Time
- Zones fast of UT (GMT)
- Half-hour zones
- Time zone boundaries
- International Date Line

Certain time zones are affected by the incidence of 'Summer Time' in countries where it is adopted.

Actual Solar Time, when it is noon at Greenwich, is shown along the top of the map.

The world is divided into 24 time zones, each centred on meridians at 15° intervals, which is the longitudinal distance the sun travels every hour. The meridian running through Greenwich, London, passes through the middle of the first zone.

Rail and Road: The Leading Nations

	Total rail network ('000 km) (1995)		Passenger km per head per year		Total road network ('000 km)		Vehicle km per head per year		Number of vehicles per km of roads	
1.	USA	235.7	Japan	2,017	USA	6,277.9	USA	12,505	Hong Kong	284
2.	Russia	87.4	Belarus	1,880	India	2,962.5	Luxembourg	7,989	Taiwan	211
3.	India	62.7	Russia	1,826	Brazil	1,824.4	Kuwait	7,251	Singapore	152
4.	China	54.6	Switzerland	1,769	Japan	1,130.9	France	7,142	Kuwait	140
5.	Germany	41.7	Ukraine	1,456	China	1,041.1	Sweden	6,991	Brunei	96
6.	Australia	35.8	Austria	1,168	Russia	884.0	Germany	6,806	Italy	91
7.	Argentina	34.2	France	1,011	Canada	849.4	Denmark	6,764	Israel	87
8.	France	31.9	Netherlands	994	France	811.6	Austria	6,518	Thailand	73
9.	Mexico	26.5	Latvia	918	Australia	810.3	Netherlands	5,984	Ukraine	73
10.	South Africa	26.3	Denmark	884	Germany	636.3	UK	5,738	UK	67
11.	Poland	24.9	Slovak Rep.	862	Romania	461.9	Canada	5,493	Netherlands	66
12.	Ukraine	22.6	Romania	851	Turkey	388.1	Italy	4,852	Germany	62

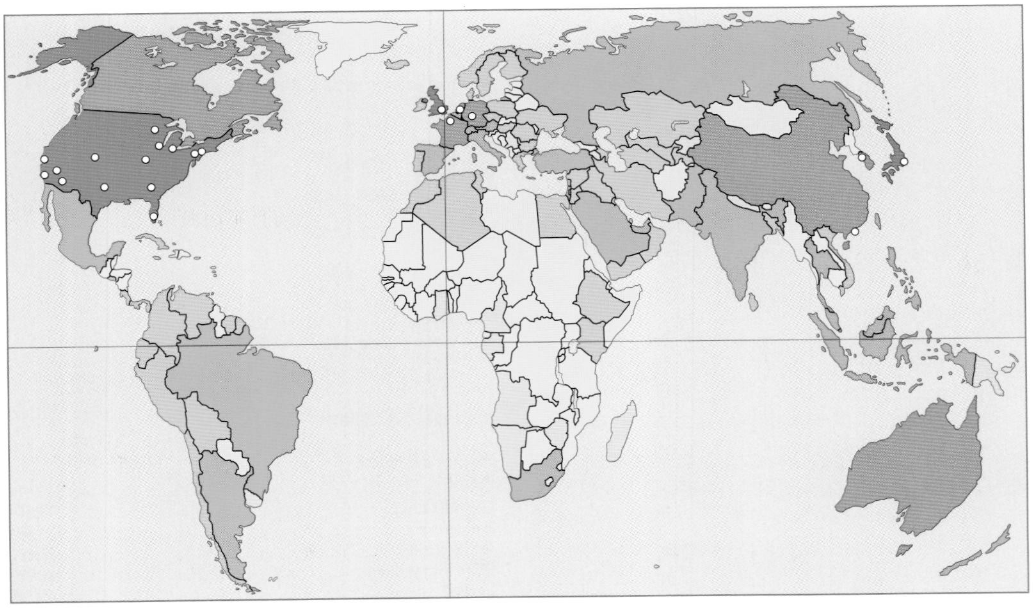

Air Travel

Passenger kilometres flown (the number of passengers – international and domestic – multiplied by the distance flown by each passenger from the airport of origin) (1997)

- Over 100,000 million
- 50,000 – 100,000 million
- 10,000 – 50,000 million
- 1,000 – 10,000 million
- 500 – 1,000 million
- Under 500 million
- ○ Major airports (handling over 25 million passengers in 2000)

World's busiest airports (total passengers)

1. Atlanta (Hartsfield)
2. Chicago (O'Hare)
3. Los Angeles (Intern'l)
4. London (Heathrow)
5. Dallas (Dallas/Ft Worth)

World's busiest airports (international passengers)

1. London (Heathrow)
2. Tokyo (Haneda)
3. Frankfurt (International)
4. Paris (De Gaulle)
5. Amsterdam (Schipol)

Destinations

- Cultural and historical centres
- Coastal resorts
- Ski resorts
- Centres of entertainment
- Places of pilgrimage
- Places of great natural beauty
- Popular holiday cruise routes

Visitors to the USA

Overseas travellers to the USA, thousands (1997 estimates)

1. Canada 13,900
2. Mexico 12,370
3. Japan 4,640
4. UK 3,350
5. Germany 1,990
6. France 1,030
7. Taiwan 885
8. Venezuela 860
9. South Korea 800
10. Brazil 785

In 1996, the USA earned the most from tourism, with receipts of more than US $75 billion.

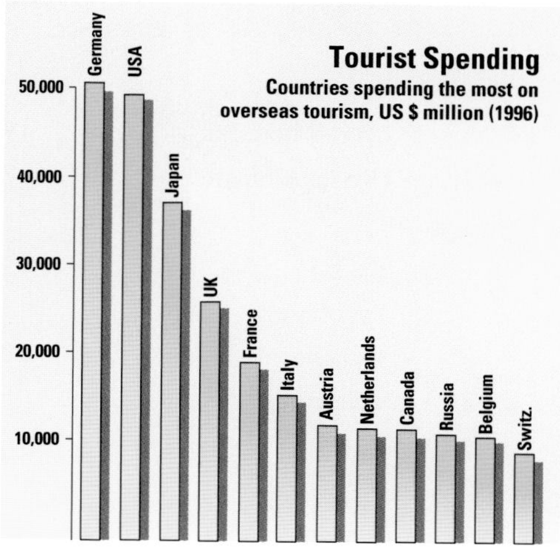

Importance of Tourism

	Arrivals from abroad (1996)	% of world total (1996)
1. France	66,800,000	10.2%
2. USA	49,038,000	7.5%
3. Spain	43,403,000	6.6%
4. Italy	34,087,000	5.2%
5. UK	25,960,000	3.9%
6. China	23,770,000	3.6%
7. Poland	19,514,000	3.0%
8. Mexico	18,667,000	2.9%
9. Canada	17,610,000	2.7%
10. Czech Republic	17,400,000	2.7%
11. Hungary	17,248,000	2.6%
12. Austria	16,642,000	2.5%

In 1996, there was a 4.6% rise, to 593 million, in the total number of people travelling abroad. Small economies in attractive areas are often completely dominated by tourism: in some West Indian islands, for example, tourist spending provides over 90% of total income.

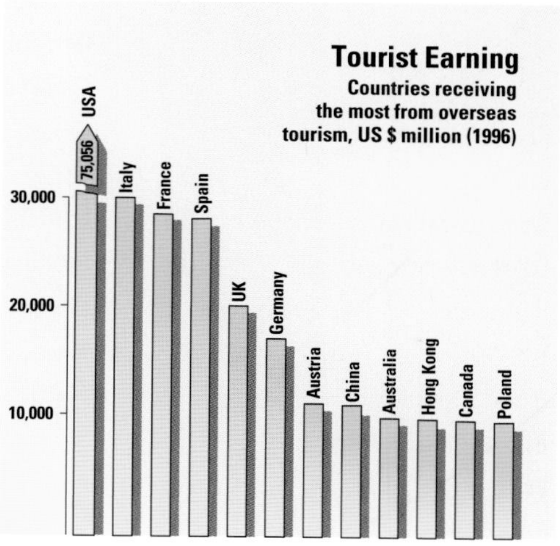

Tourism

Tourism receipts as a percentage of Gross National Product (1996)

- Over 10% of GNP from tourism
- 5 – 10% of GNP from tourism
- 2.5 – 5% of GNP from tourism
- 1 – 2.5% of GNP from tourism
- 0.5 – 1% of GNP from tourism
- Under 0.5% of GNP from tourism

Countries spending the most on promoting tourism, millions of US $ (1996)

Germany	51
USA	49
Japan	37
UK	25
France	18

Countries with largest tourism receipts, millions of US $ (1996)

USA	75
Italy	30
France	28
Spain	27
UK	21

The World In Focus: **Index**

WORLD CITIES

CITY MAPS

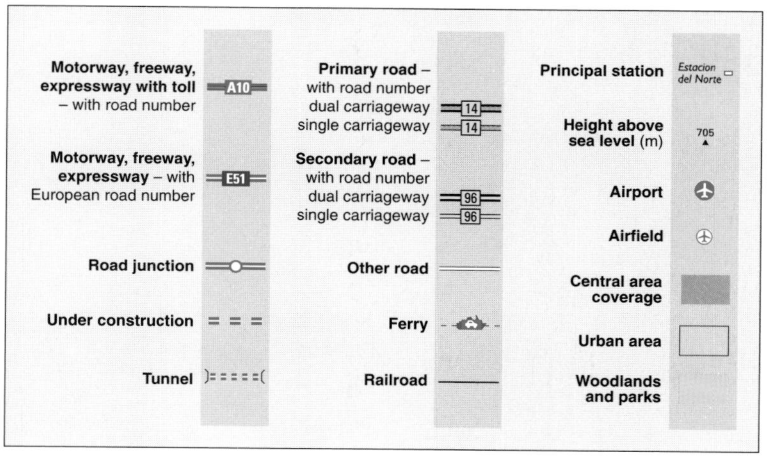

CENTRAL AREA MAPS

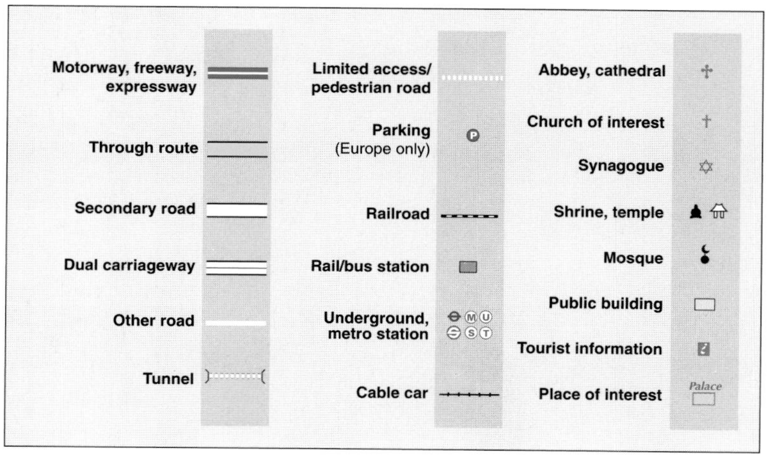

AMSTERDAM

0 km 5
0 miles 3

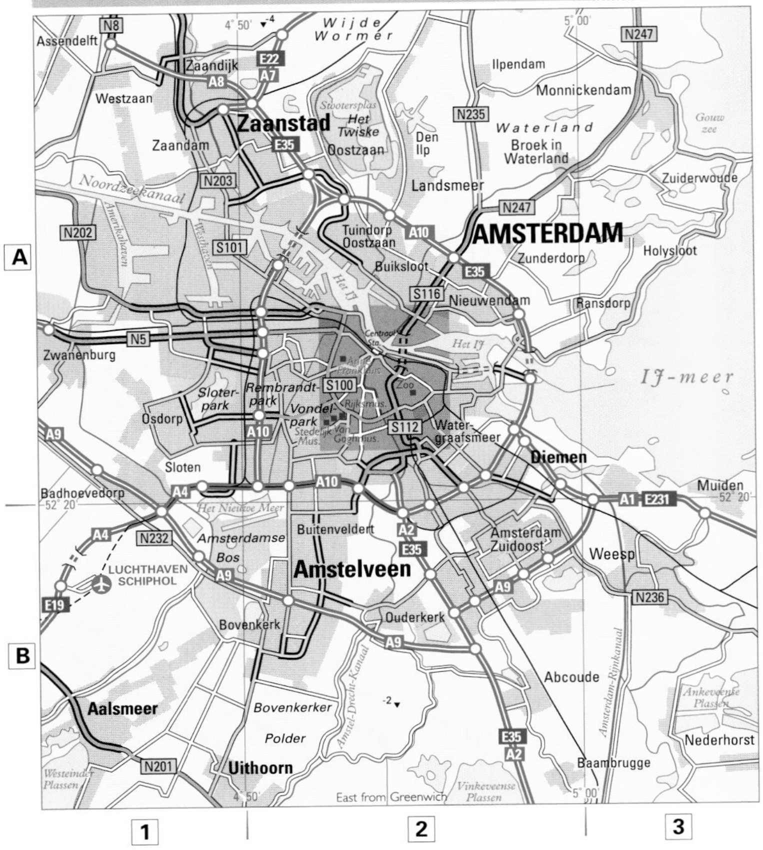

CENTRAL AMSTERDAM

0 km 1
0 miles 0.5

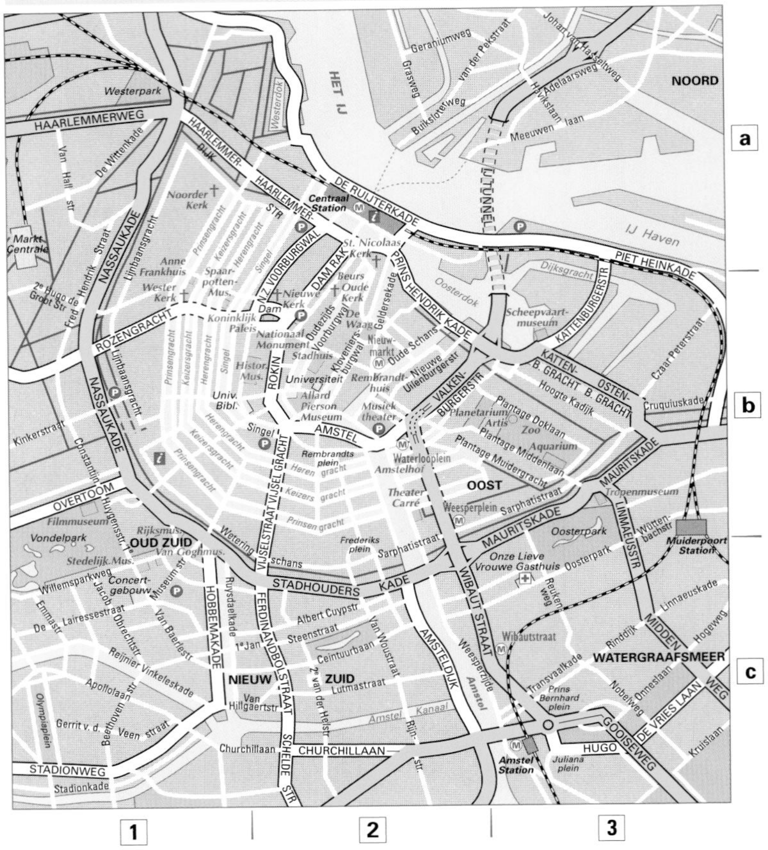

ATHENS

0 km 5
0 miles 3

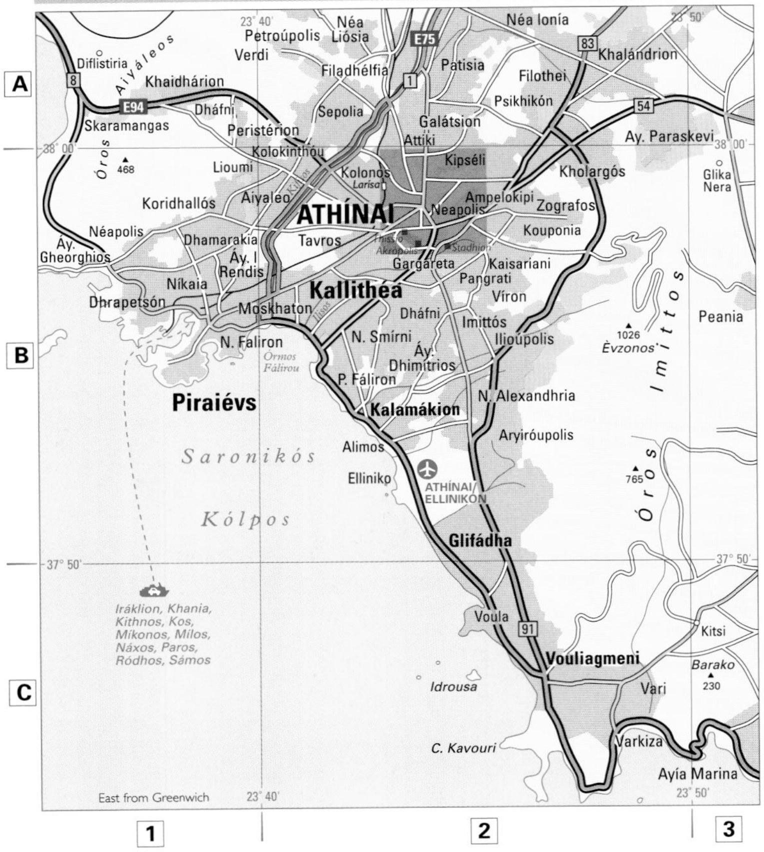

CENTRAL ATHENS

0 km 1
0 miles 0.5

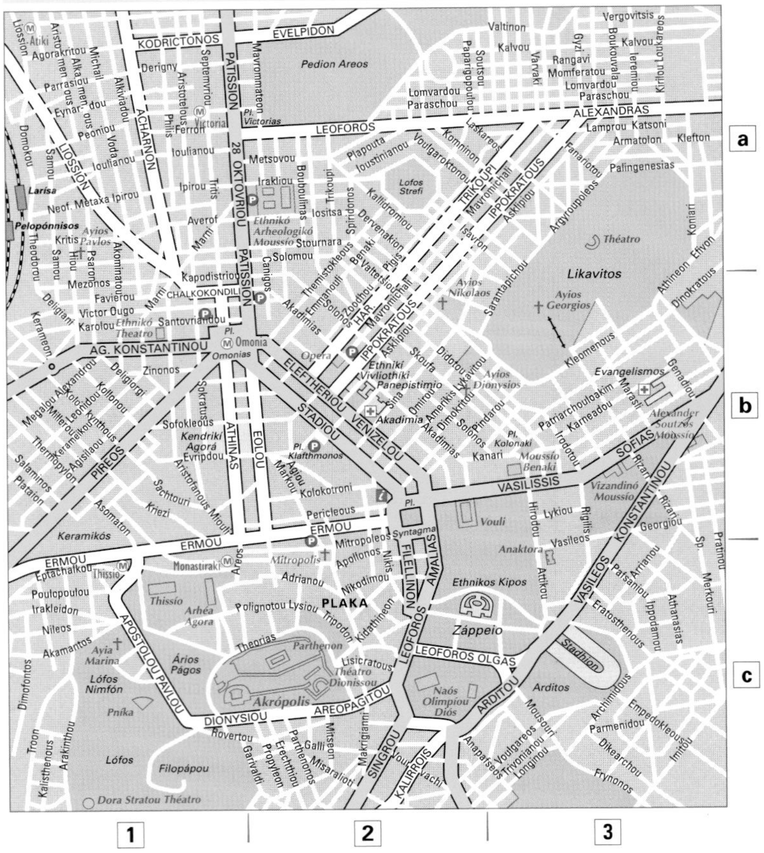

ATLANTA

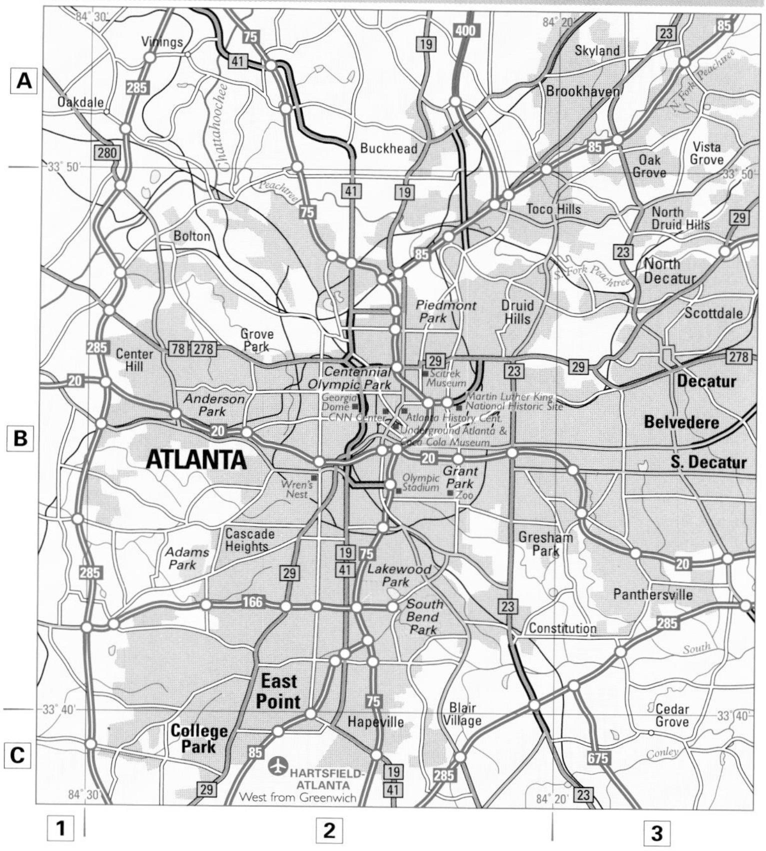
0 km 5
0 miles 3
Vinings
Oakdale
Skyland
Brookhaven
Buckhead
Chattahoochee
Peachtree
Oak Grove
Vista Grove
Toco Hills
North Druid Hills
Bolton
North Decatur
Piedmont Park
Druid Hills
Scottdale
Grove Park
Center Hill
Centennial Olympic Park
Sotrek Museum
Martin Luther King National Historic Site
Anderson Park
Georgia Dome
CNN Center
Atlanta History Cent.
Underground Atlanta & Coca Cola Museum
Decatur
Belvedere
ATLANTA
Wren's Nest
Grant Park
Zoo
Olympic Stadium
S. Decatur
Cascade Heights
Adams Park
Gresham Park
Lakewood Park
Panthersville
South Bend Park
Constitution
East Point
College Park
Hapeville
Blair Village
Cedar Grove
HARTSFIELD-ATLANTA
West from Greenwich
84° 30'
84° 20'
33° 50'
33° 40'
A
B
C
1
2
3

BAGHDAD

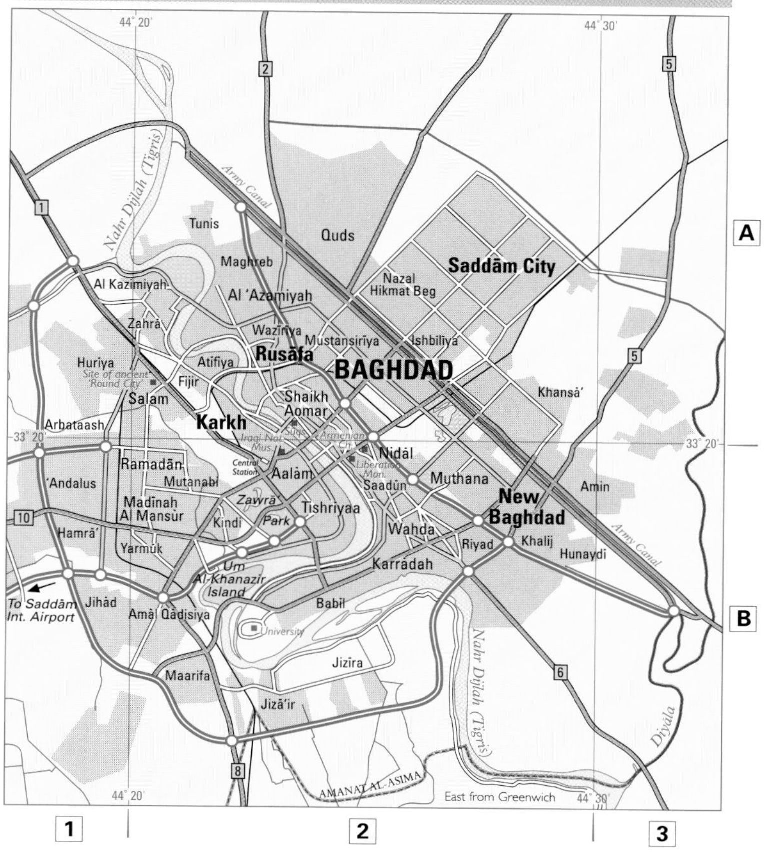
0 km 5
0 miles 3
44° 20'
44° 30'
Army Canal
Nahr Dijlah (Tigris)
Tunis
Quds
Maghreb
Al Kazimiyah
Al 'Azamiyah
Nazal Hikmat Beg
Saddām City
Zahrā
Waziriya
Mustansiriya
Ishbiliya
Huriya
Site of ancient 'Round City'
Atifiya
Fijir
Rusāfa
BAGHDAD
Salam
Shaikh Aomar
Khansā'
Arbataash
Karkh
Nidāl
'Andalus
Ramadān
Mutanabi
Aalām
Saadūn
Muthana
Amin
Central Station
Madīnah Al Mansūr
Zawrā
Park
Tishriyaa
New Baghdad
Hamrā'
Yarmūk
Kindi
Wahda
Riyad
Khalij
Hunaydi
Um Al-Khanazir Island
Karrādah
To Saddām Int. Airport
Jihād
Amāl Qādisiya
Babil
University
Jizira
Maarifa
Jizā'ir
Diyala
AMANAT AL-ASIMA
East from Greenwich
A
B
1
2
3

BANGKOK

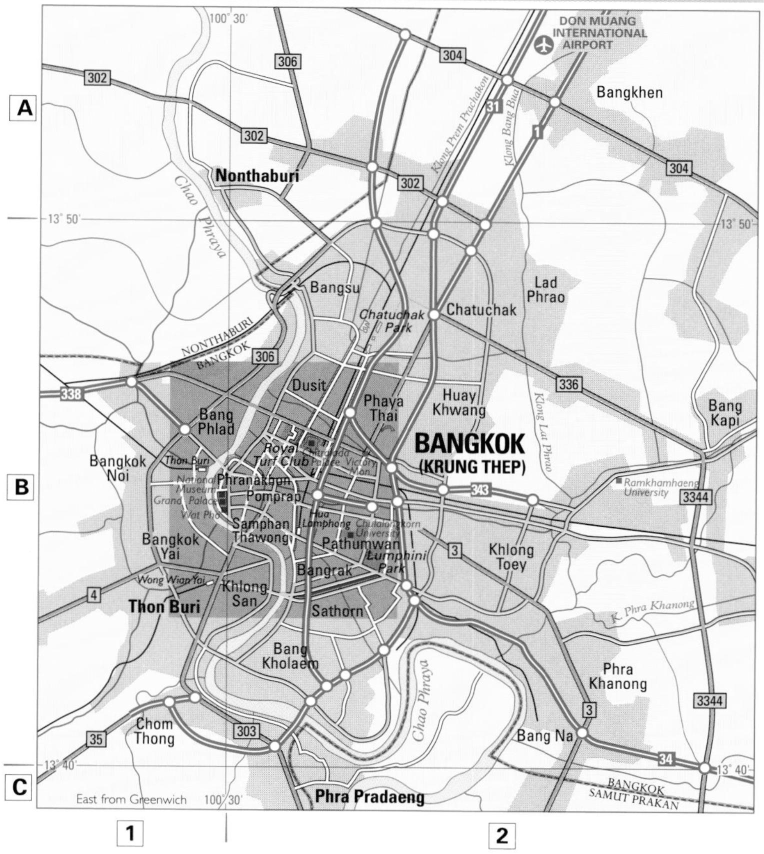
0 km 5
0 miles 3
100° 30'
DON MUANG INTERNATIONAL AIRPORT
Bangkhen
Klong Prem Prachakorn
Klong Bang Bua
Nonthaburi
13° 50'
Chao Phraya
Bangsu
Lad Phrao
Chatuchak Park
Chatuchak
NONTHABURI
BANGKOK
Dusit
Phaya Thai
Huay Khwang
Bang Kapi
Bang Phlad
BANGKOK (KRUNG THEP)
Klong Lat Phrao
Bangkok Noi
Royal Turf Club
Phranakhon
Pomprap
Ramkhamhaeng University
Samphan Thawong
Hua Lamphong
Chulalongkorn University
Pathumwan
Lumphini Park
Khlong Toey
Bangkok Yai
Wong Wian Yai
Khlong San
Bangrak
Thon Buri
Sathorn
K. Phra Khanong
Bang Kholaem
Phra Khanong
Chom Thong
Bang Na
Phra Pradaeng
13° 40'
East from Greenwich
BANGKOK
SAMUT PRAKAN
A
B
C
1
2

CENTRAL BANGKOK

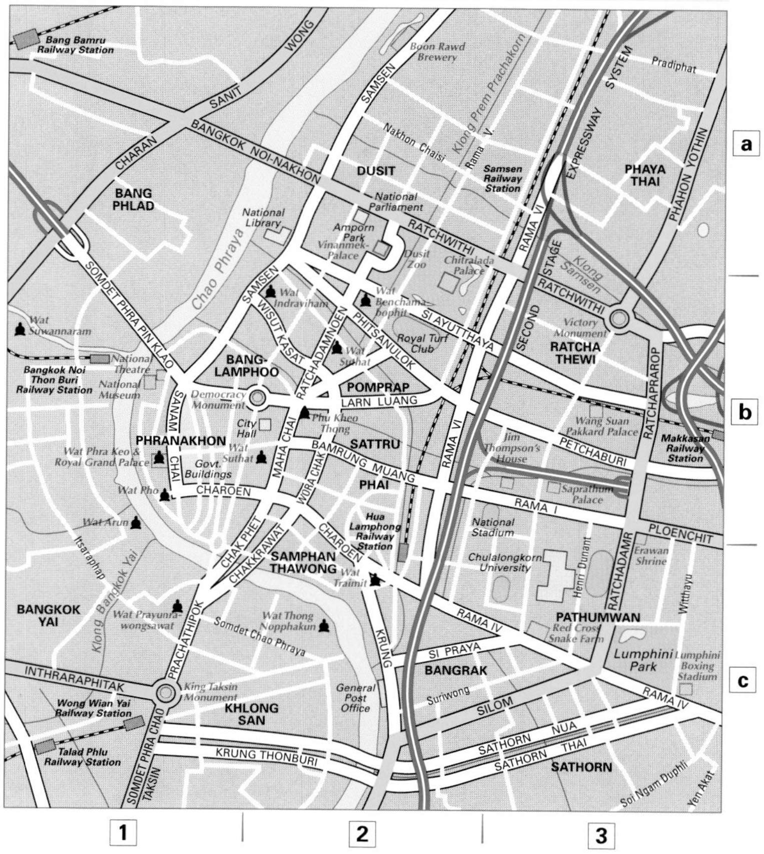
0 km 2
0 miles 1
Bang Bamru Railway Station
SANIT WONG
SAMSEN
Boon Rawd Brewery
Klong Prem Prachakorn
EXPRESSWAY SYSTEM
Pradiphat
CHARAN
BANGKOK NOI-NAKHON
Nakhon Chaisi
RAMA V
Samsen Railway Station
PHAYA THAI
PHAHON YOTHIN
DUSIT
BANG PHLAD
National Parliament
National Library
Ampom Park
Vimanmek Palace
RATCHWITHI
Dusit Zoo
Chitralada Palace
STAGE
Klong Samsen
SOMDET PHRA PIN KLAO
Chao Phraya
Wat Indraviharn
Wat Benchamabophit
SI AYUTTHAYA
SECOND
Victory Monument
Wat Suwannaram
WISUT KASAT
PHITSANULOK
Royal Turf Club
RATCHA THEWI
National Theatre
BANG-LAMPHOO
RATCHADAMNOEN
Wat Sothat
POMPRAP
Bangkok Noi Thon Buri Railway Station
National Museum
Democracy Monument
LARN LUANG
RATCHAPRAROP
Phu Khao Thong
Wang Suan Pakkard Palace
City Hall
Jim Thompson's House
PETCHABURI
Makkasan Railway Station
PHRANAKHON
SANAM CHAI
SATTRU
Wat Phra Keo & Royal Grand Palace
Govt. Buildings
Wat Suthat
BAMRUNG MUANG
PHAI
MAHA CHAI
Saprathum Palace
Wat Pho
CHAROEN
RAMA I
Wat Arun
National Stadium
PLOENCHIT
YOWARAT
Hua Lamphong Railway Station
Chulalongkorn University
Erawan Shrine
Henri Dunant
RATCHADAMRI
Witthayu
Itsaraphap
CHAK PHET
CHAKRAWAT
SAMPHAN THAWONG
Wat Traimit
BANGKOK YAI
Klong Bangkok Yai
Wat Prayunrawongsawat
Wat Thong Nopphakun
PATHUMWAN
Red Cross Snake Farm
RAMA IV
Lumphini Park
Lumphini Boxing Stadium
Somdet Chao Phraya
KRUNG
SI PRAYA
BANGRAK
INTHRARAPHITAK
PRACHATHIPOK
King Taksin Monument
General Post Office
Suriwong
Wong Wian Yai Railway Station
KHLONG SAN
SILOM
SATHORN NUA
Talad Phlu Railway Station
KRUNG THONBURI
SATHORN THAI
SOMDET PHRA CHAO TAKSIN
SATHORN
Soi Ngam Duphli
Yen Akat
a
b
c
1
2
3

BARCELONA

CENTRAL BARCELONA

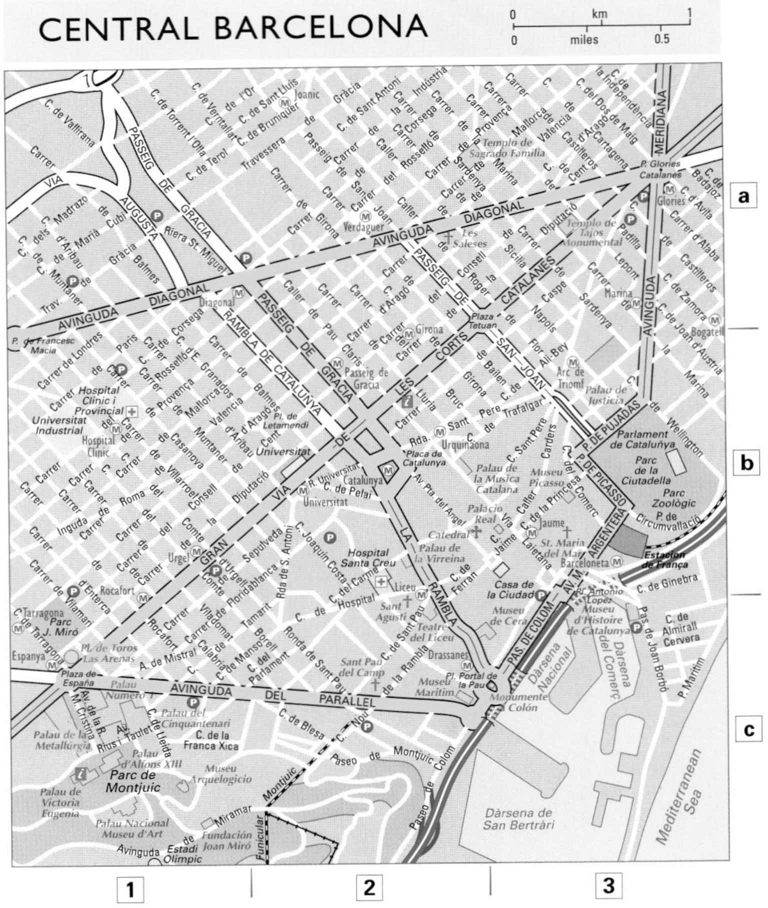

BEIJING

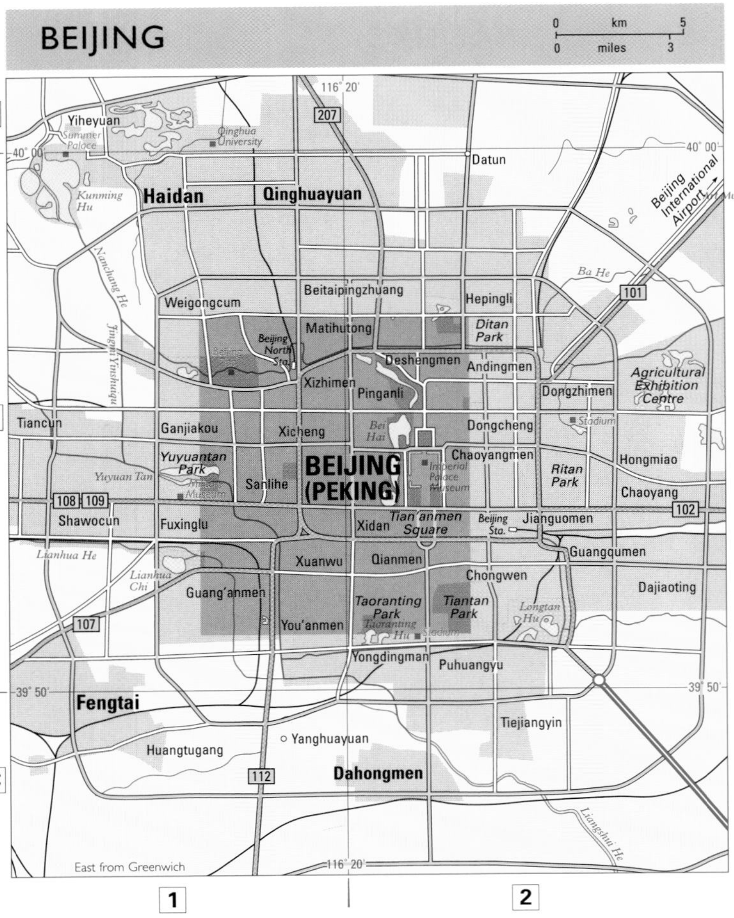

CENTRAL BEIJING

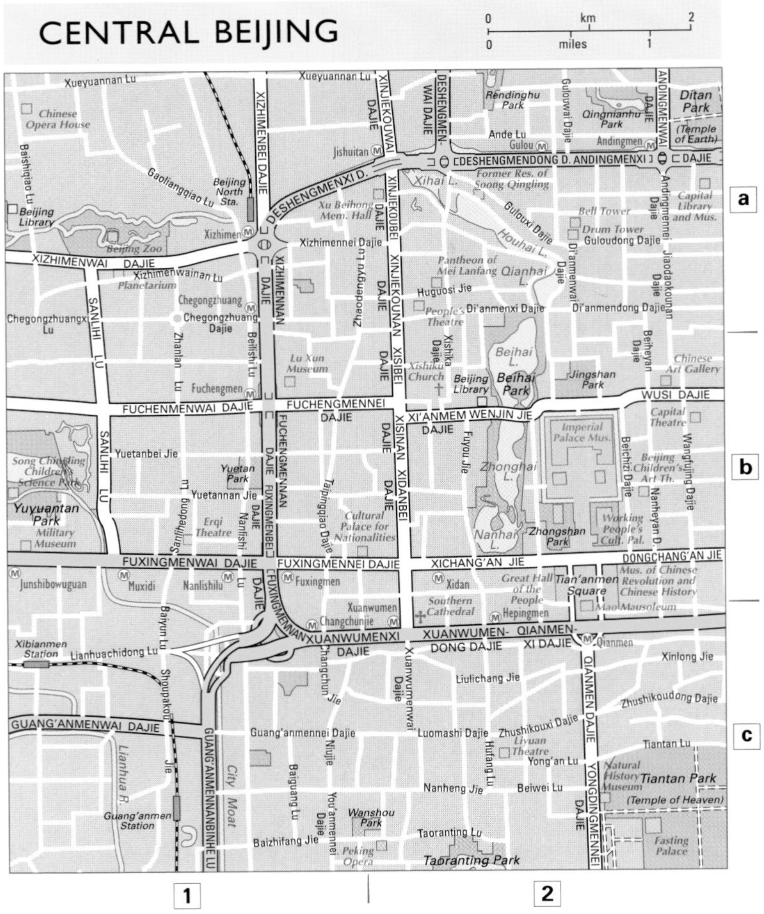

BERLIN

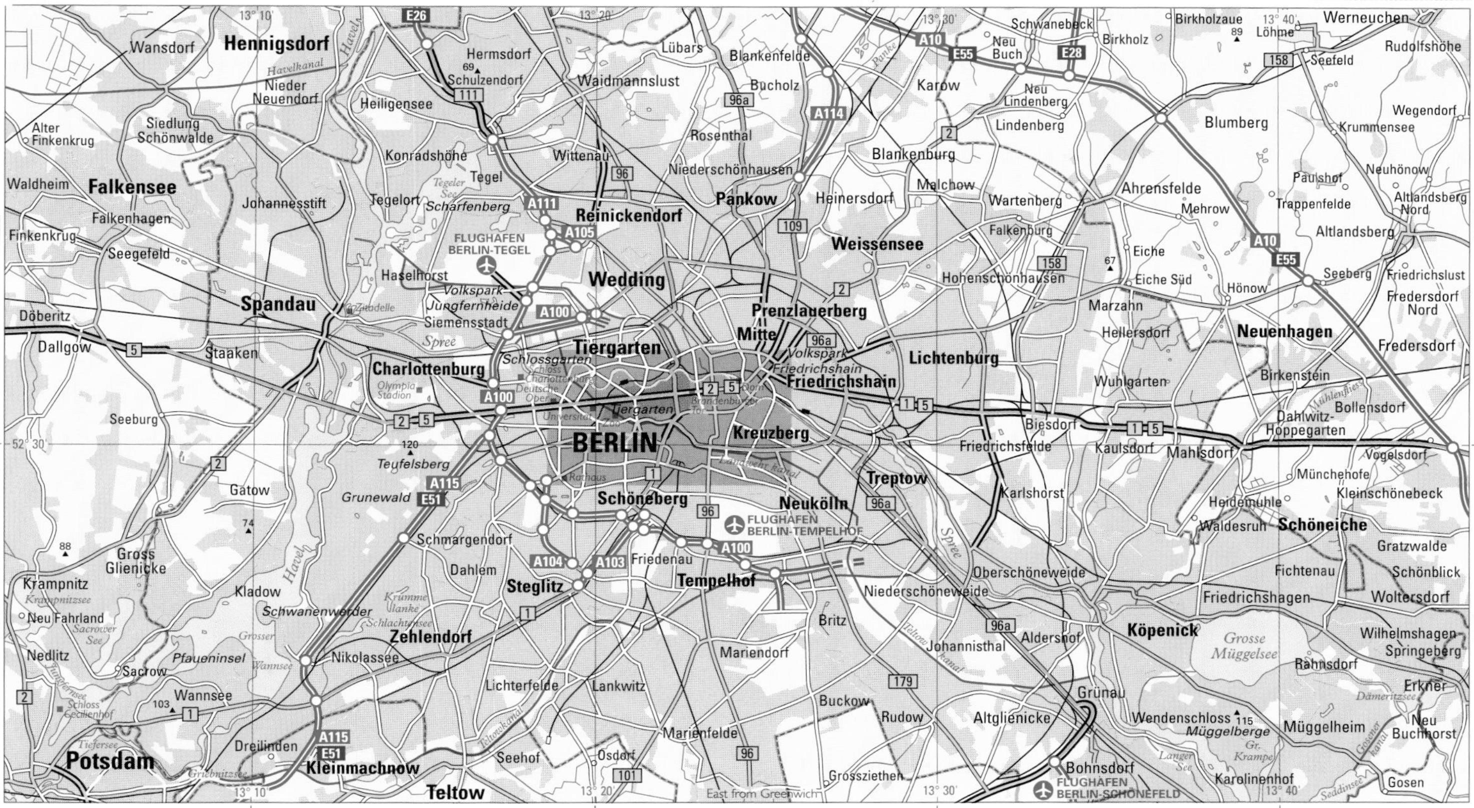

CENTRAL BERLIN

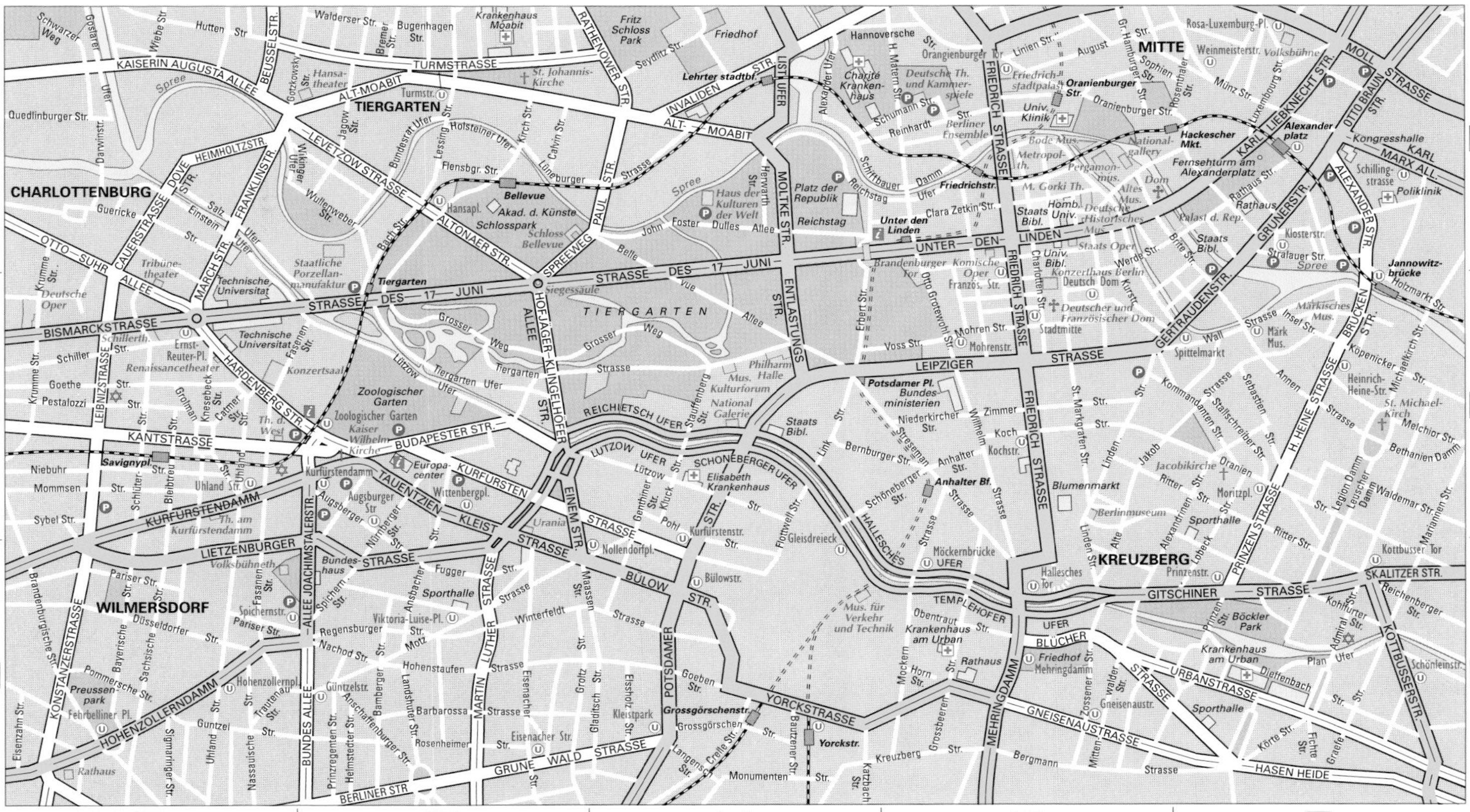

BOSTON

0 km 5
0 miles 3

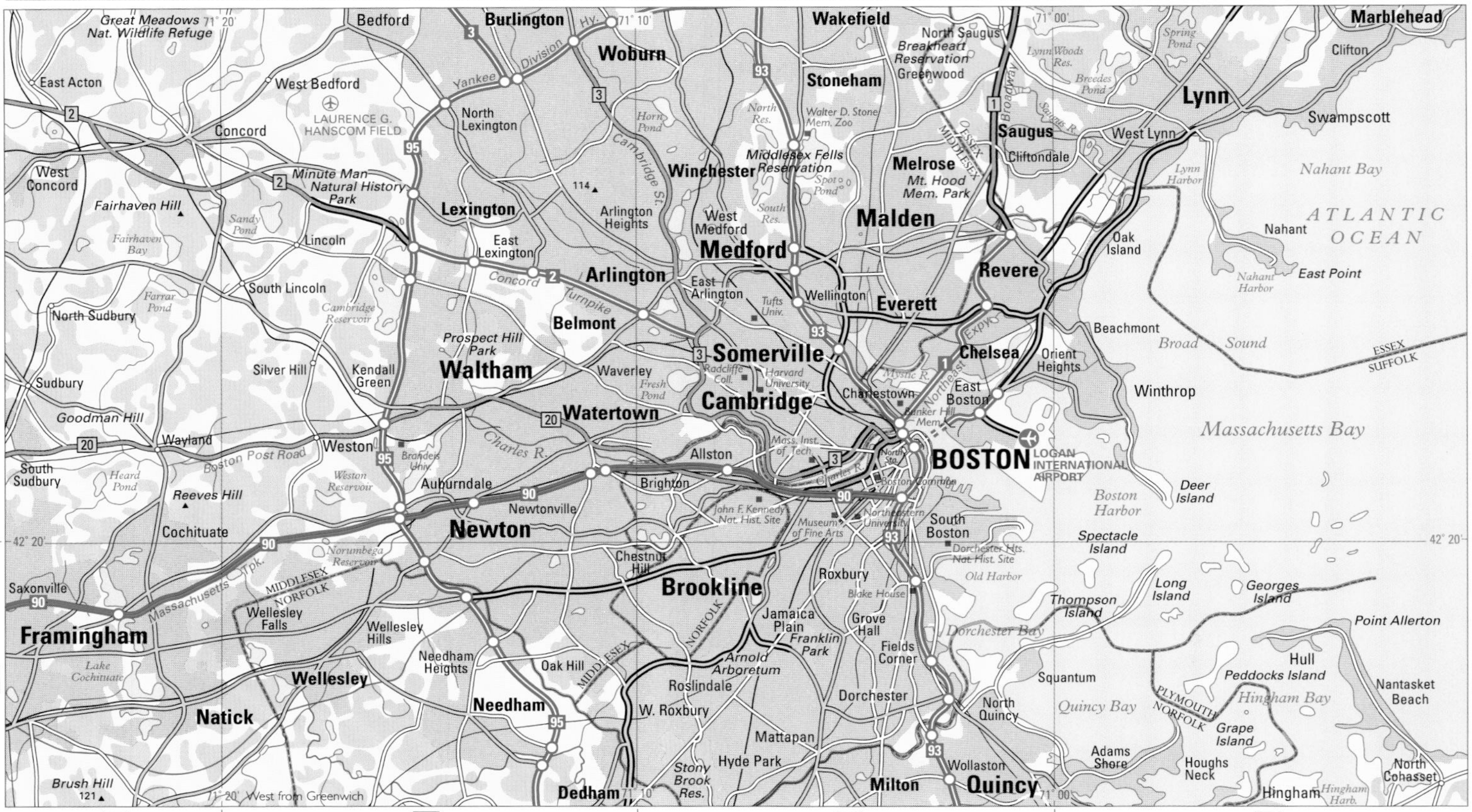

BRUSSELS

0 km 5
0 miles 3

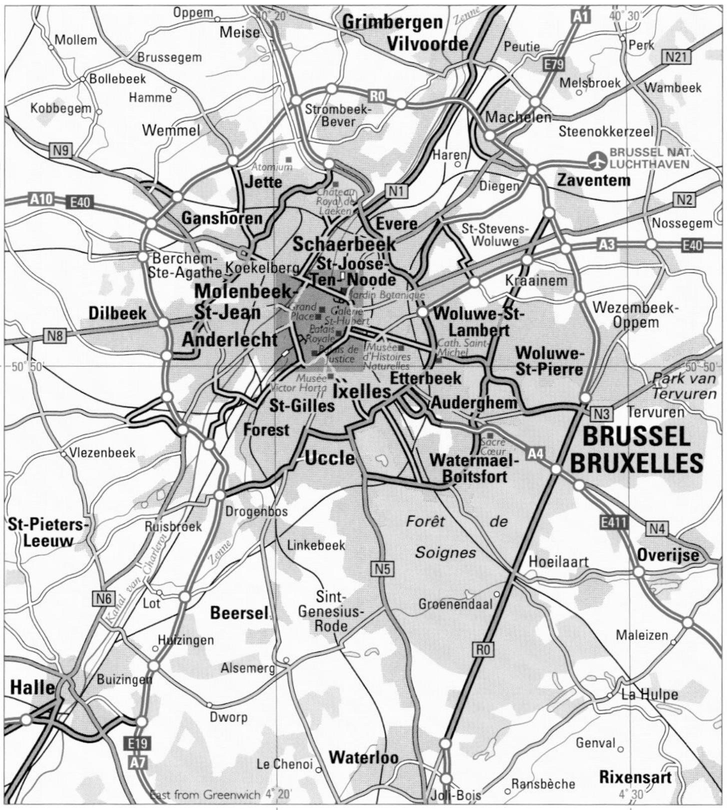

CENTRAL BRUSSELS

0 km 1
0 miles 0.5

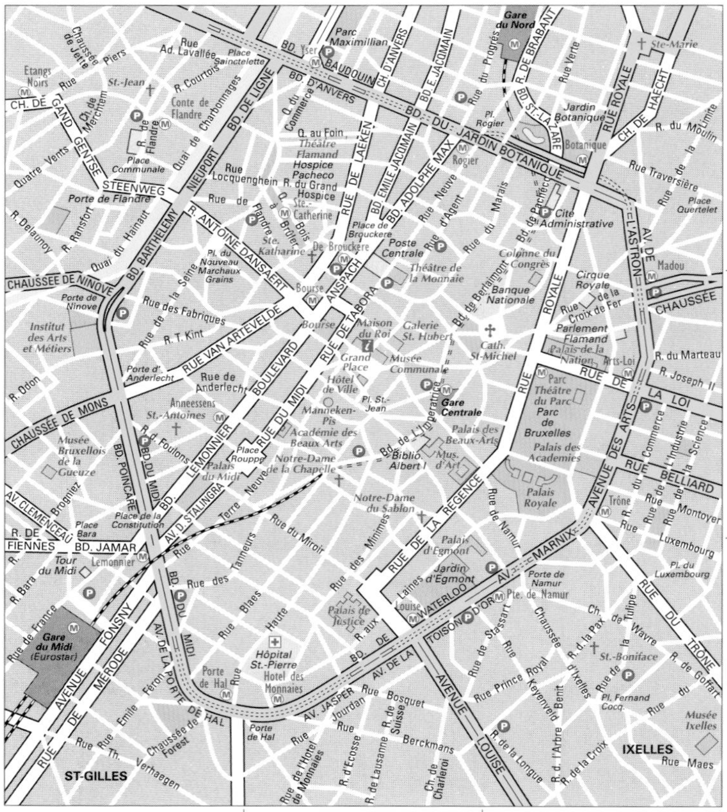

BUDAPEST

0 km 5 / 0 miles 3

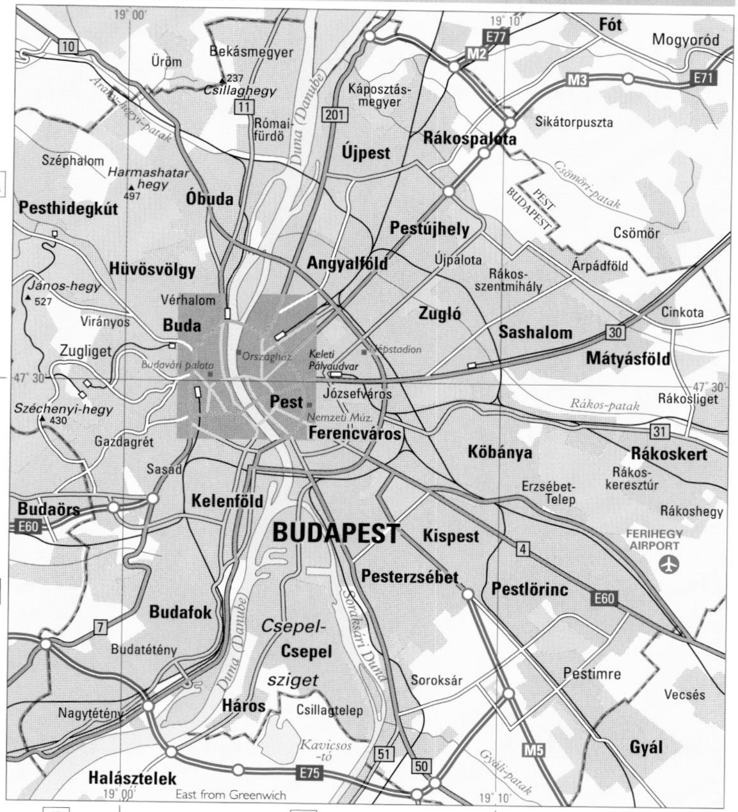

CENTRAL BUDAPEST

0 km 1 / 0 miles 0.5

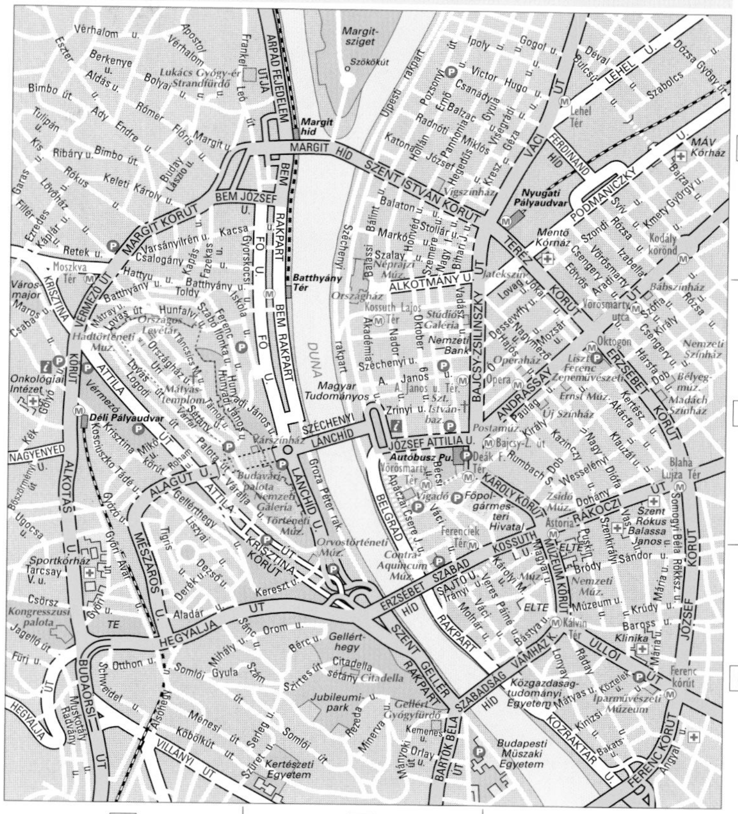

BUENOS AIRES

0 km 5 / 0 miles 3

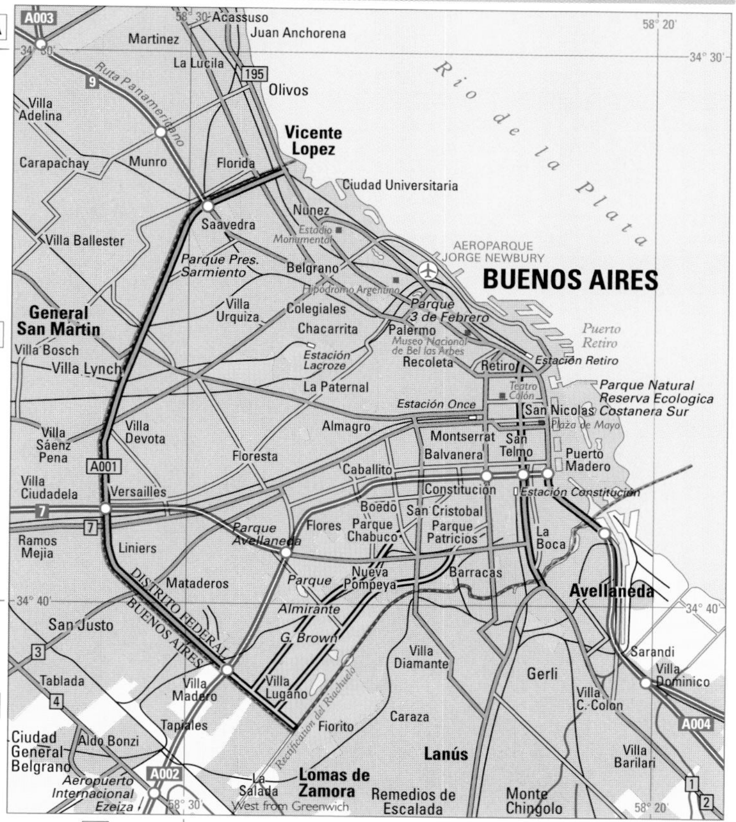

CAIRO

0 km 5 / 0 miles 3

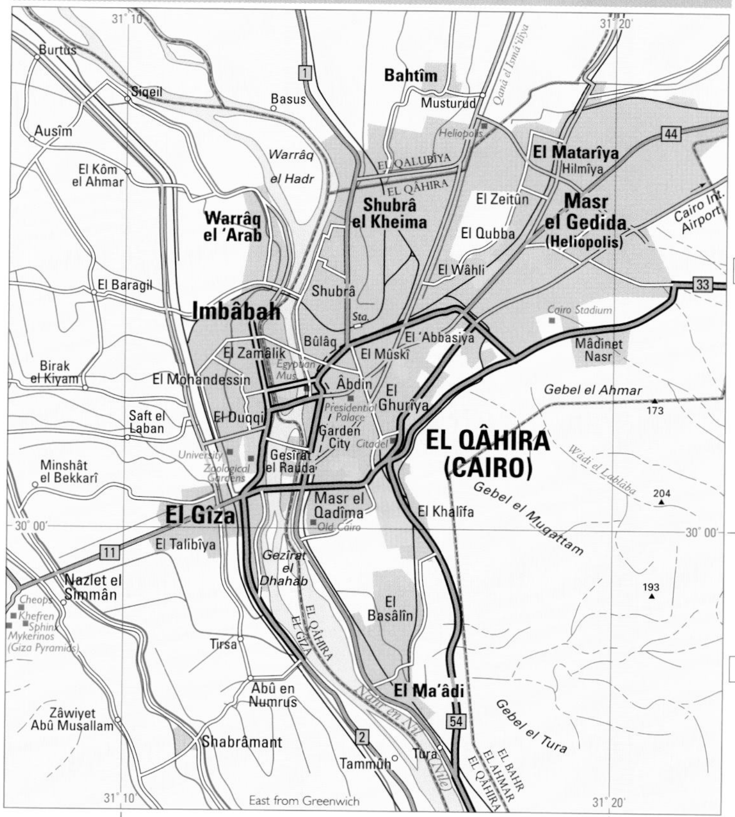

CALCUTTA

0 km 5
0 miles 3

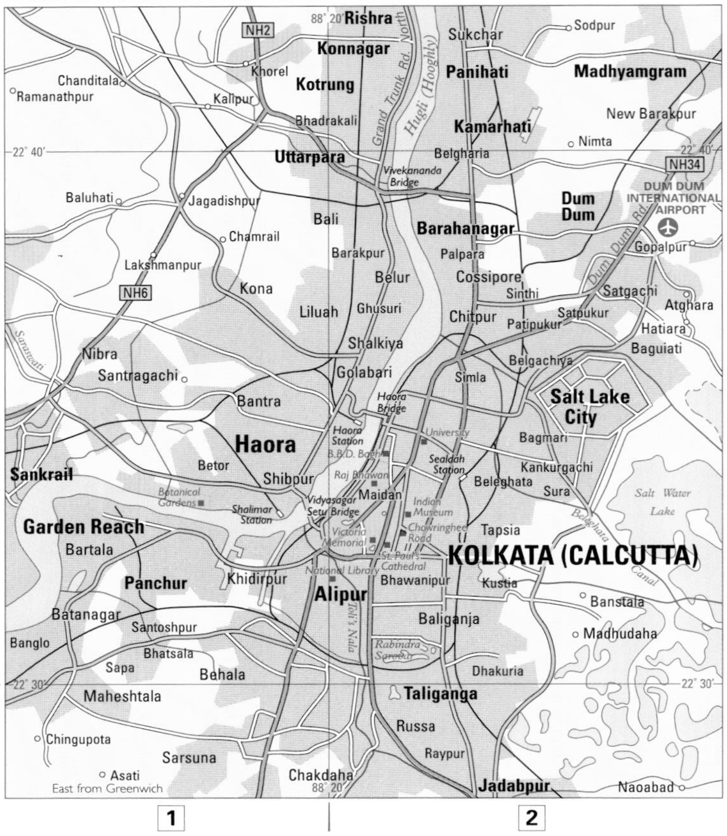

CANTON

0 km 5
0 miles 3

CAPE TOWN

0 km 5
0 miles 3

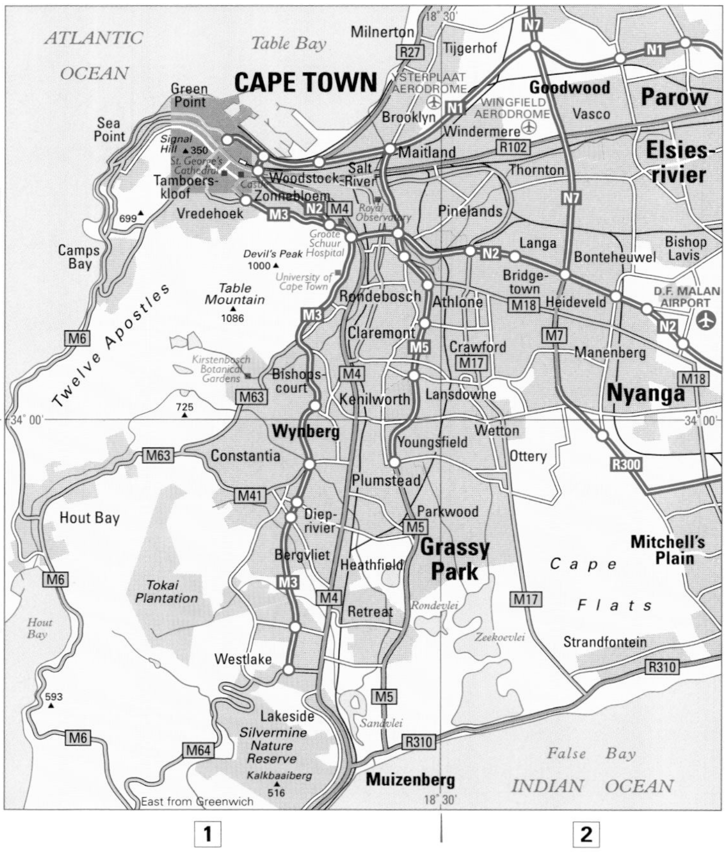

CENTRAL CAPE TOWN

0 km 0.5
0 miles 0.25

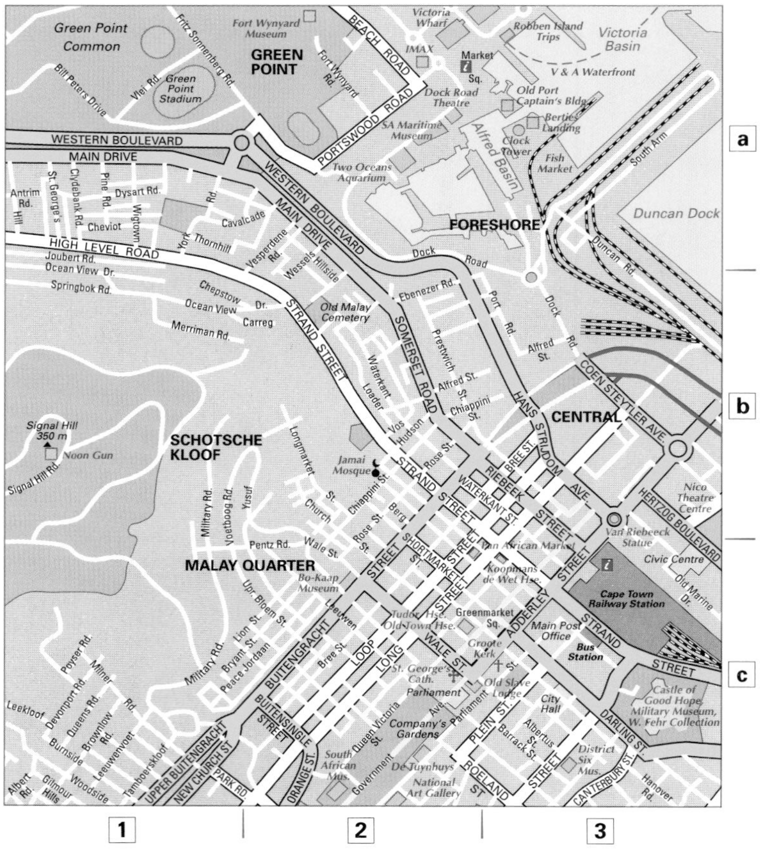

CHICAGO

0 km 5
0 miles 3

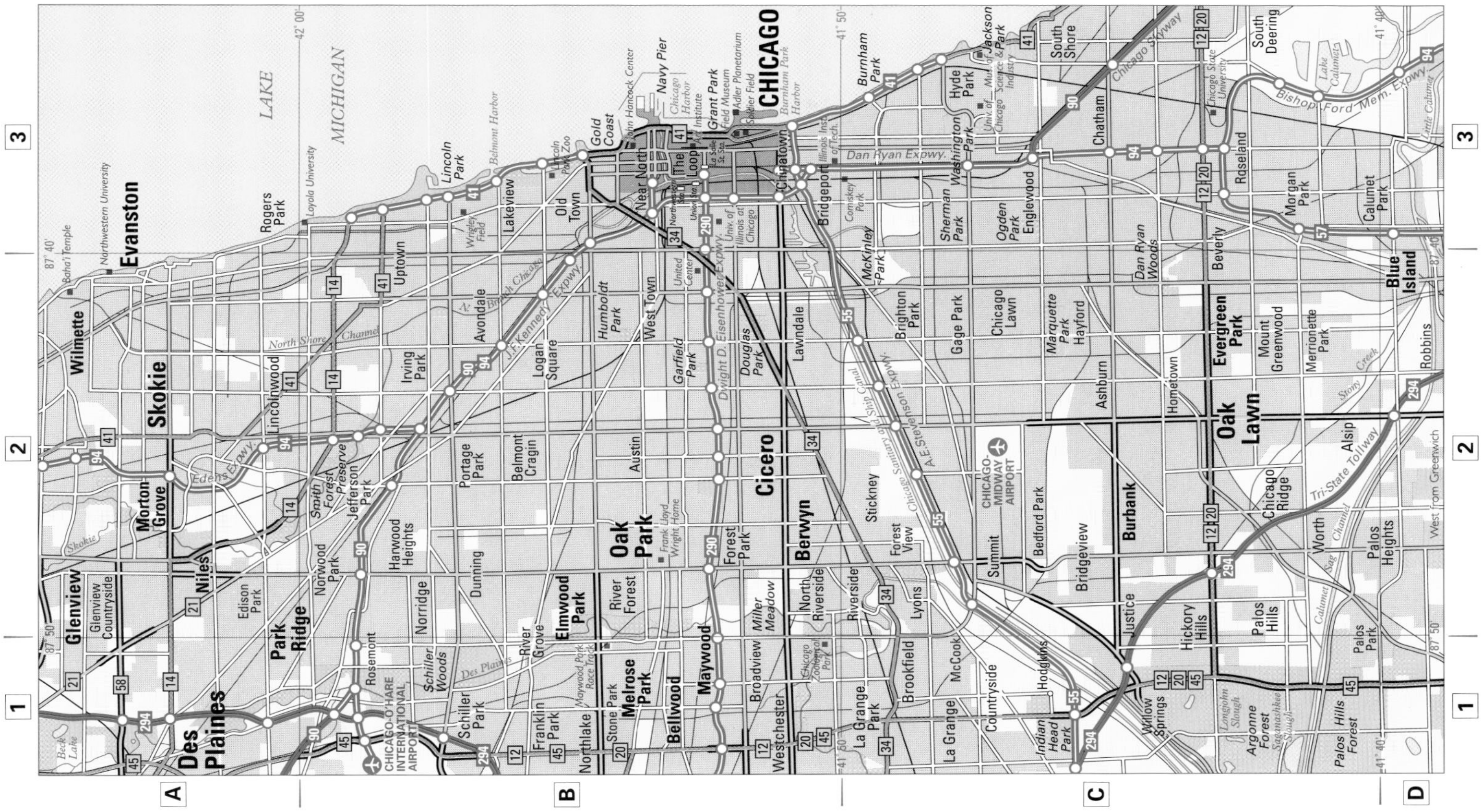

CENTRAL CHICAGO

0 km 1
0 miles 0.5

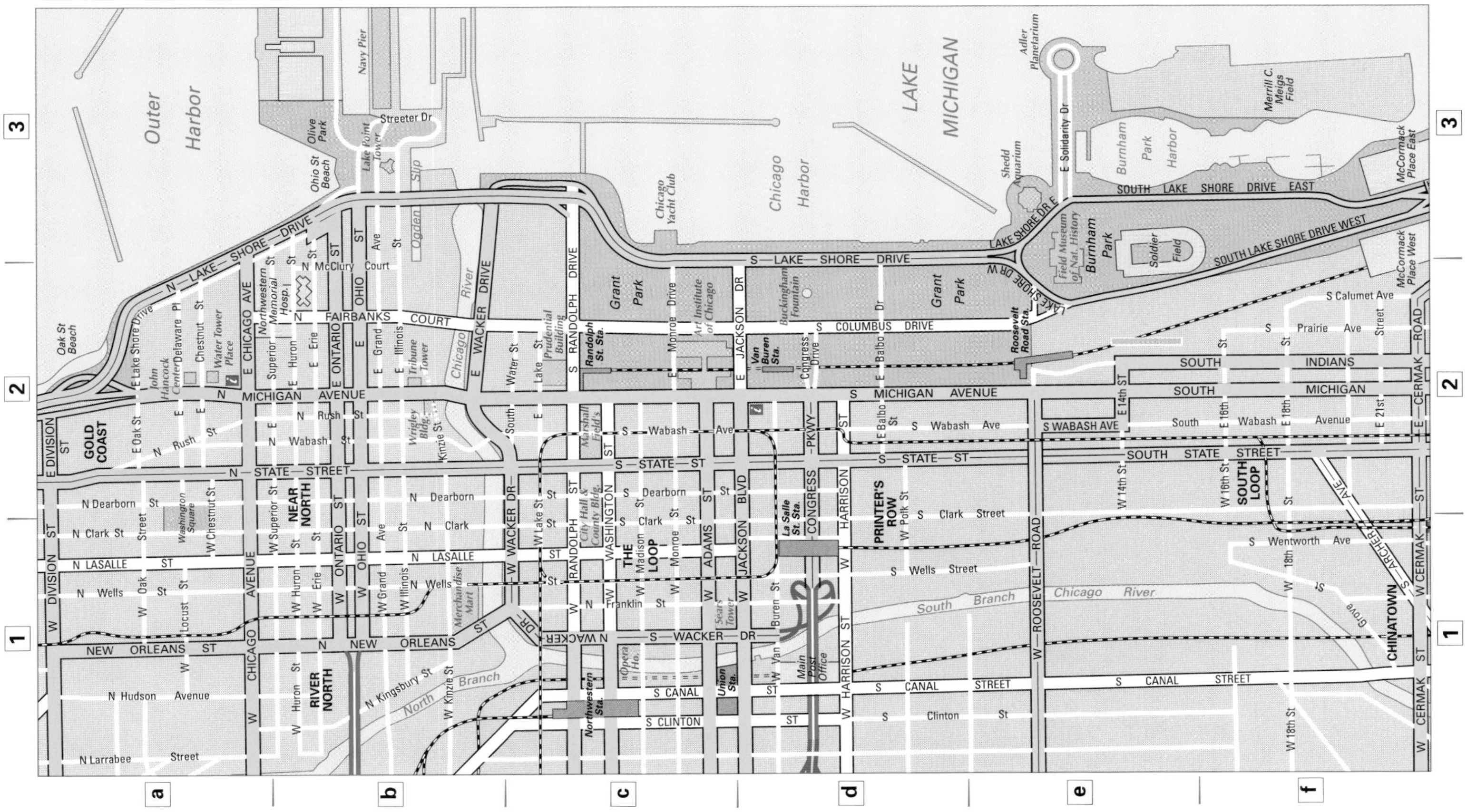

COPENHAGEN

0 km 5
0 miles 3

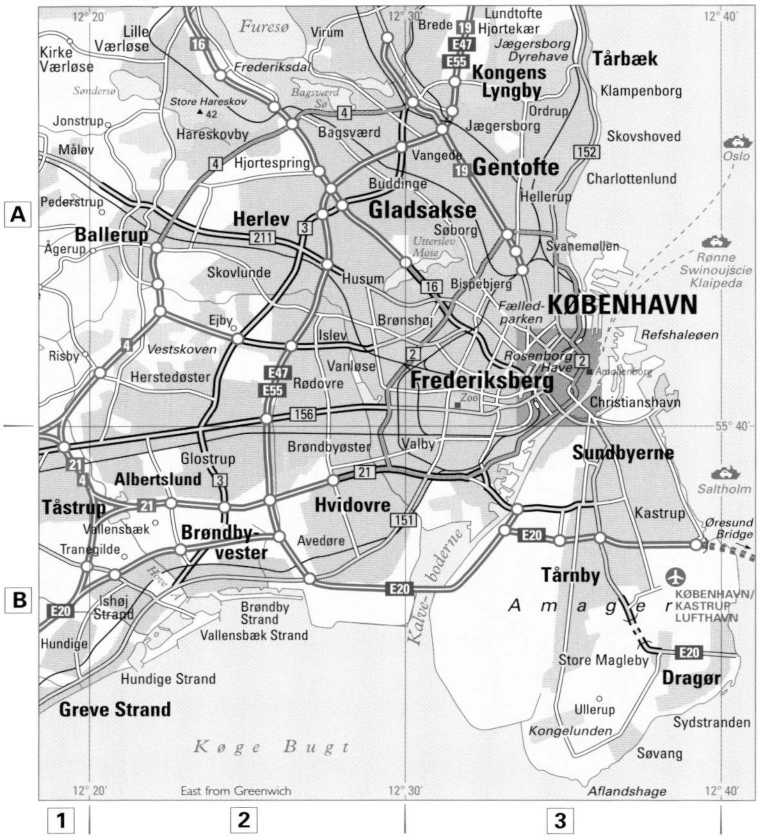

CENTRAL COPENHAGEN

0 km 0.5
0 miles 0.25

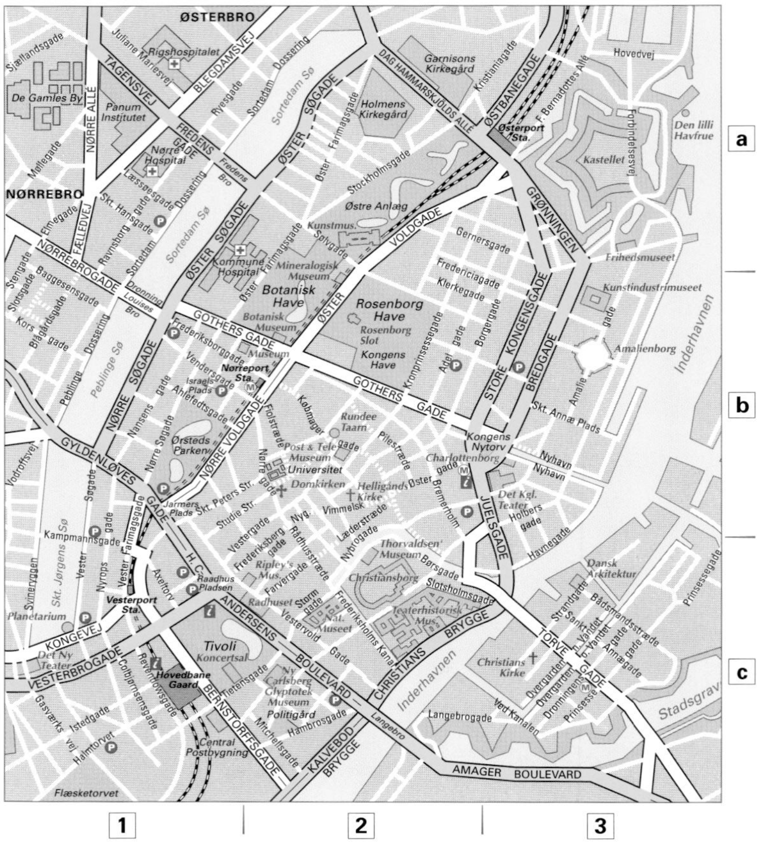

DELHI

0 km 5
0 miles 3

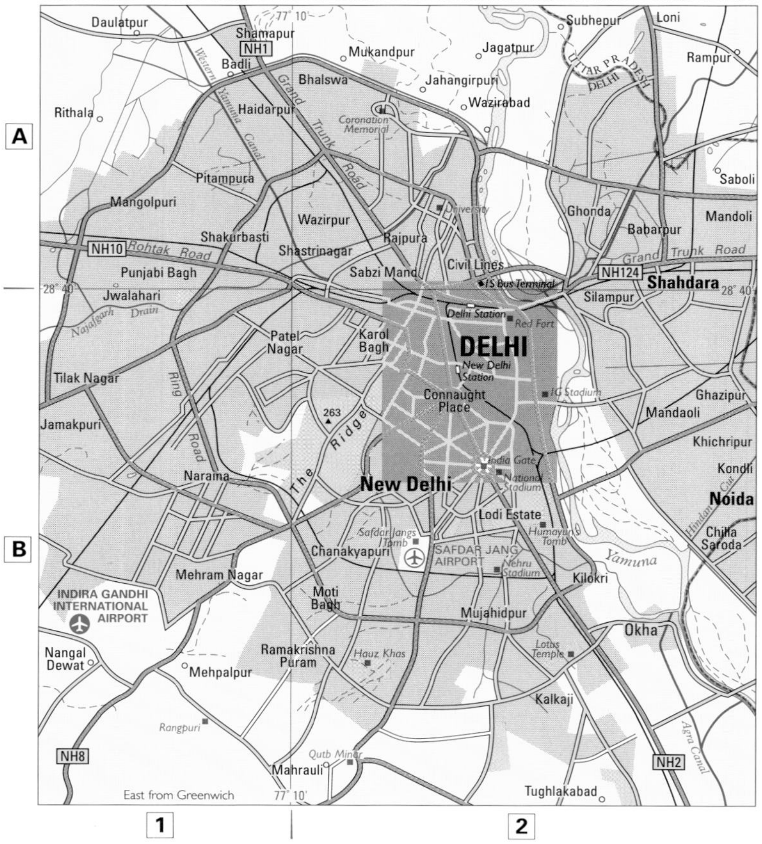

CENTRAL DELHI

0 km 2
0 miles 1

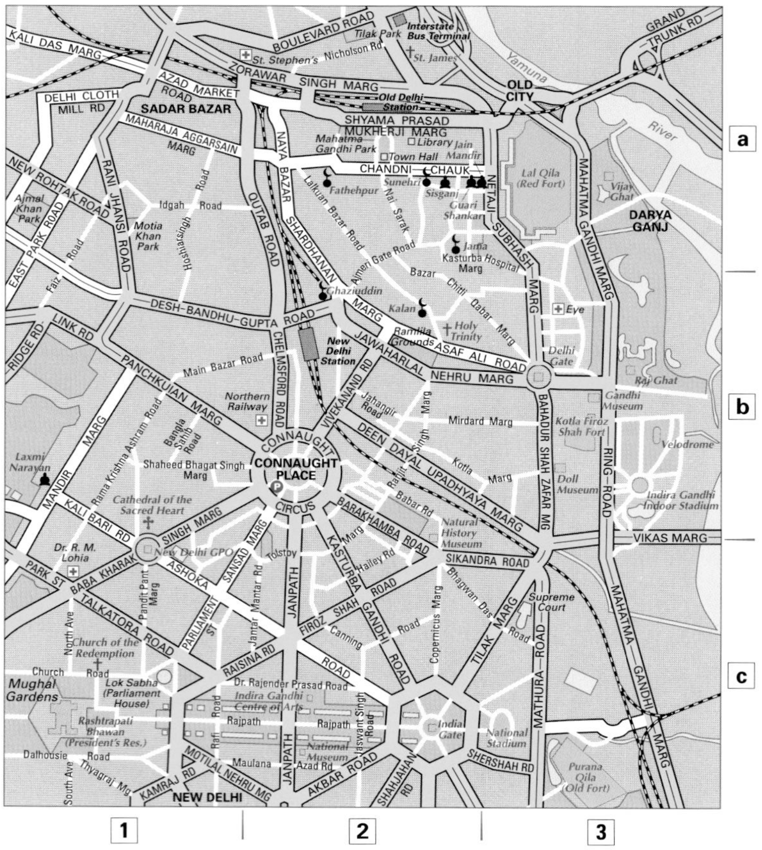

COPYRIGHT GEORGE PHILIP LTD

DUBLIN

0 km 5
0 miles 3

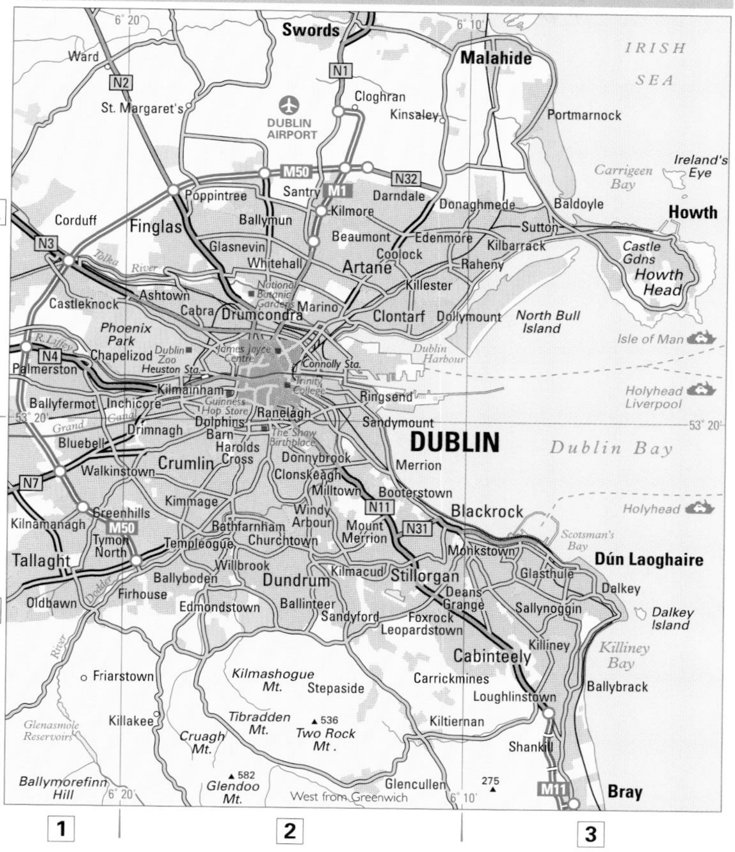

Swords
Ward
Malahide
IRISH SEA
St. Margaret's
Cloghran
Kinsaley
DUBLIN AIRPORT
Portmarnock
Ireland's Eye
Carrigeen Bay
Poppintree
Santry
Kilmore
Darndale
Donaghmede
Baldoyle
Howth
Corduff
Finglas
Ballymun
Glasnevin
Whitehall
Beaumont
Coolock
Edenmore
Kilbarrack
Sutton
Artane
Raheny
Castle Gdns
Howth Head
Ashtown
Cabra
Drumcondra
Marino
Killester
Clontarf
Dollymount
North Bull Island
Castleknock
Phoenix Park
Chapelizod
Palmerston
Isle of Man
Ballyfermot
Inchicore
Kilmainham
Ringsend
Holyhead Liverpool
Drimnagh
Ranelagh
Sandymount
Bluebell
Dolphins Barn
Harolds Cross
DUBLIN
Dublin Bay
Walkinstown
Crumlin
Donnybrook
Merrion
Clonskeagh
Milltown
Booterstown
Kimmage
Greenhills
Kilnamanagh
Rathfarnham
Windy Arbour
Blackrock
Holyhead
Tymon North
Templeogue
Churchtown
Mount Merrion
Monkstown
Tallaght
Willbrook
Dundrum
Kilmacud
Stillorgan
Glasthule
Dún Laoghaire
Ballyboden
Firhouse
Oldbawn
Edmondstown
Ballinteer
Sandyford
Deans Grange
Foxrock
Leopardstown
Sallynoggin
Dalkey
Dalkey Island
Cabinteely
Killiney
Killiney Bay
Friarstown
Kilmashogue Mt.
Stepaside
Carrickmines
Ballybrack
Loughlinstown
Glenasmole Reservoirs
Killakee
Tibradden Mt.
536
Two Rock Mt.
Cruagh Mt.
Kiltiernan
Shankill
Ballymorefinn Hill
582
Glendoo Mt.
West from Greenwich
Glencullen
275
Bray
M50
M1
M11
N1
N2
N3
N4
N7
N11
N31
N32
6° 20'
6° 10'
53° 20'
A
B
1
2
3

CENTRAL DUBLIN

0 km 0.5
0 miles 0.25

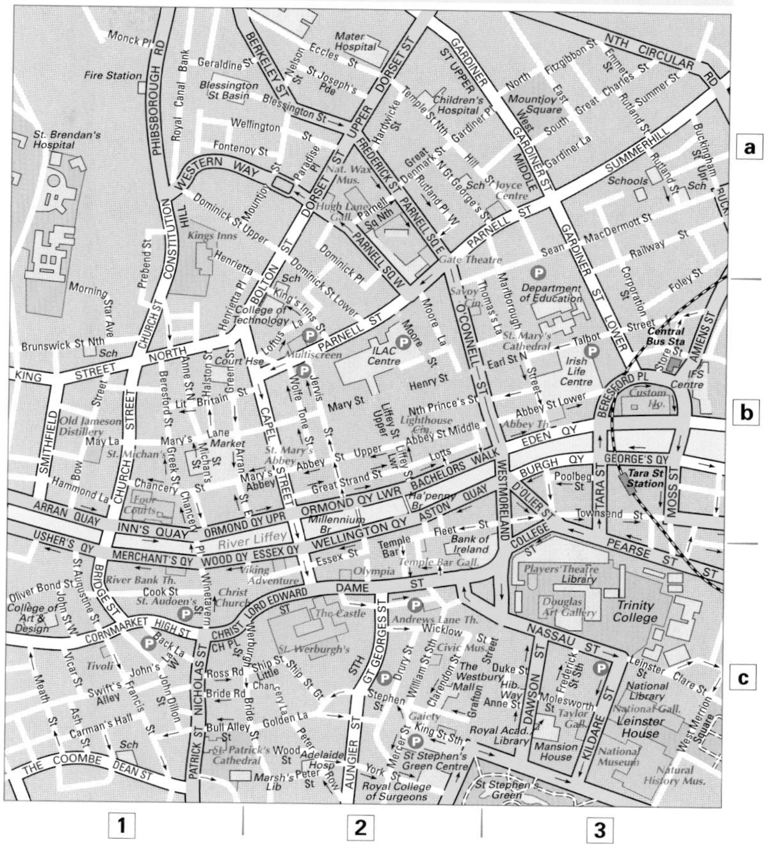

Moncks Pl
Fire Station
Geraldine St
Mater Hospital
Blessington St Basin
Blessington St
Children's Hospital
Mountjoy Square
St. Brendan's Hospital
Wellington St
Fontenoy St
Western Way
Nat. Wax Mus.
Hugh Lane Gall.
Parnell Sq
Joyce Centre
Schools
Summerhill
Kings Inns
Gate Theatre
Department of Education
College of Technology
Multiscreen
LAC Centre
St. Mary's Cathedral
Central Bus Sta
Brunswick St Nth
Irish Life Centre
IFS Centre
King Street
North
Smithfield
Old Jameson Distillery
Henry St
Abbey St Lower
Custom Ho.
Lighthouse Cin.
Abbey Th.
Eden Qy
St. Michan's
Bachelors Walk
Burgh Qy
George's Qy
Tara St Station
Four Courts
Chancery
Ormond Qy Lwr
Ormond Qy Upr
Arran Quay
Usher's Qy
Inn's Quay
River Liffey
Wellington Qy
Aston Quay
Millennium Br
Ha'penny Br
Merchant's Qy
Wood Qy
Essex Qy
Viking Adventure
Temple Bar
Temple Bar Gall.
Olympia
Bank of Ireland
Pearse St
College St
Players' Theatre
Library
Douglas Hyde Art Gallery
Trinity College
Oliver Bond St
River Bank Th.
Christ Church
Dame St
Lord Edward
The Castle
Andrews Lane Th.
College of Art & Design
Cornmarket
High St
St. Audoen's
Christ Ch Pl
St. Werburgh's
Civic Mus.
Westbury
Nassau St
Tivoli
Swift's Alley
Ross Rd
Bride Rd
Stephen St
Molesworth St
National Library
National Gall.
Leinster House
Mansion House
Royal Acad. Library
Carman's Hall
Bull Alley
St. Patrick's Cathedral
Golden La
St. Stephen's Green Centre
National Museum
Natural History Mus.
The Coombe
Dean St
Marsh's Lib
Adelaide Hosp
Royal College of Surgeons
St Stephen's Green
Merrion Square
a
b
c
1
2
3

EDINBURGH

0 km 5
0 miles 3

Dunfermline
Kinghorn
Burntisland
Pettycur
Aberdour Castle
Aberdour
M90
A921
Hillend
Dalgety Bay
Inchkeith
Rosyth
Inverkeithing
Inchcolm
Firth of Forth
North Queensferry
Forth Road Bridge
Forth Rail Bridge
Inchmickery
Queensferry
Cramond I.
Dalmeny House
Dalmeny
A904
A90
Cramond
Granton
Newhaven
Leith
Davidson's Mains
Pilton
Trinity
EDINBURGH
M9
Cramond Bridge
Braepark
Drylaw
Royal Botanic Garden
Warriston
Kirkliston
Turnhouse
Clermiston
Ravelston
New Town
Portobello
Joppa
EDINBURGH AIRPORT
Ingliston
North Gyle
Murrayfield
Old Town
Duddingston
Arthur's Seat 251
Gogar
Haymarket
A8
Ratho Station
A720
Corstorphine
Newington
Craigmillar
Newcraighall
M8
Sighthill
Gorgie
Morningside
Niddrie
Ratho
Union Canal
Wester Hailes
Craiglockhart
Braid
Royal Observatory
A7
A701
Danderhall
Millerhill
Bonnington
Hermiston
Colinton
A702
Fairmilehead
Gilmerton
Wilkieston
A71
Burnwynd
Juniper Green
Oxgangs
Kaimes
Liberton
Currie
Dalkeith
Eskbank
Kirknewton
Balerno
493
Allermuir Hill
Straiton
Loanhead
Newbattle
A70
Water of Leith
Malleny Mills
Harlaw Reservoir
Woodhouselee
Bilston
Polton
Bonnyrigg and Lasswade
Easter Howgate
Roslin
Newtongrange
Pentland Hills
Threipmuir Reservoir
499
Glencorse Res.
Milton Bridge
North Esk
Rosewell
Harperrig Reservoir
579
Scald Law
A701
Auchendinny
Silverburn
Penicuik
Kirkhill
Carrington
West from Greenwich
3° 20'
3° 10'
55° 40'
56°
A
B
1
2
3

CENTRAL EDINBURGH

0 km 0.5
0 miles 0.25

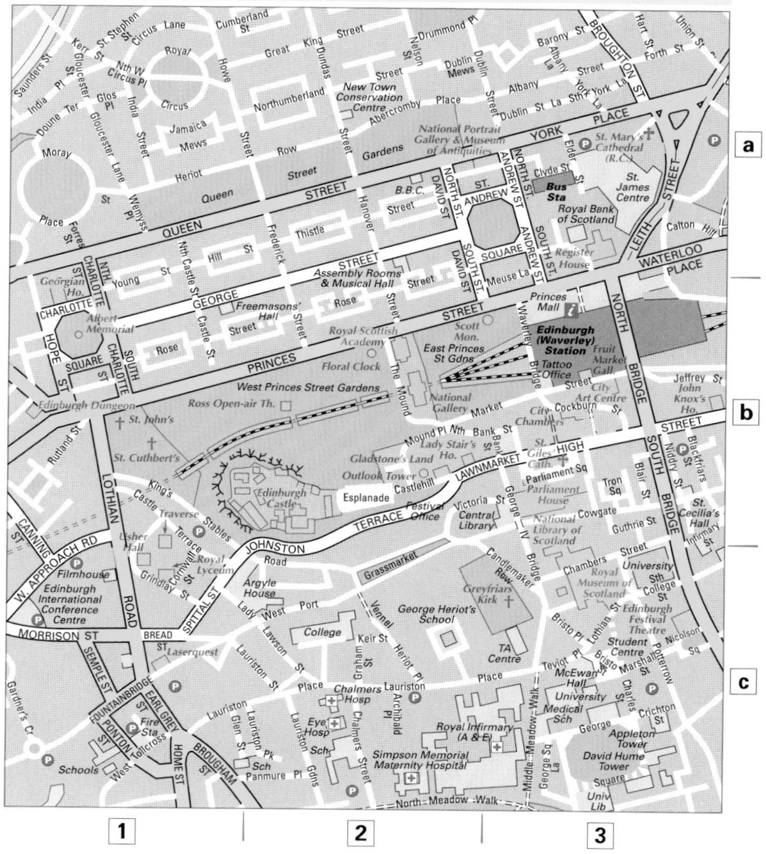

Circus Lane
Cumberland St
Drummond Pl
Royal Circus
Great King Street
Dublin Mews
Barony St
India Pl
Nth W Circus Pl
Circus Pl
New Town Conservation Centre
Albany St
Dublin St La Sth
York La
Northumberland
Abercromby Place
National Portrait Gallery & Museum of Antiquities
York Place
St. Mary's Cathedral (R.C.)
Jamaica Mews
Moray Place
Heriot Row
Queen Street Gardens
Bus Sta
St. James Centre
Queen Street
B.B.C.
Royal Bank of Scotland
Calton Hill
Thistle
St Andrew Square
Register House
Waterloo Place
Young St
Hill St
Assembly Rooms & Musical Hall
Rose Street
George Street
Freemasons' Hall
Charlotte Square
Georgian Ho.
Albert Memorial
Princes Mall
Royal Scottish Academy
Scott Mon.
Edinburgh (Waverley) Station
East Princes St Gdns
Tattoo Office
Fruit Market Gall.
Princes Street
Floral Clock
City Art Centre
West Princes Street Gardens
Ross Open-air Th.
National Gallery
Market St
Cockburn St
North Bridge
Jeffrey St
John Knox's Ho.
Edinburgh Dungeon
St. John's
St. Cuthbert's
Lady Stair's Ho.
Gladstone's Land
High St
St. Giles Cath.
Outlook Tower
Esplanade
Castlehill
Lawnmarket
Parliament Sq
Parliament House
Tron Sq
Edinburgh Castle
Festival Office
Victoria St
Central Library
National Library of Scotland
Cowgate
South Bridge
King's Stables Rd
Castle Terrace
Johnston Terrace
St. Cecilia's Hall
Lothian Road
Usher Hall
Royal Lyceum
Grassmarket
Chambers Street
University Coll.
Royal Museum of Scotland
Filmhouse
Edinburgh International Conference Centre
Argyle House
Greyfriars Kirk
George Heriot's School
Edinburgh Festival Theatre
Morrison St
Bread St
Laserquest
College
TA Centre
Student Centre
McEwan Hall
University Medical Sch
Lauriston Place
Chalmers Hosp
Eye Hosp
Royal Infirmary (A & E)
Fire Sta
George Sq
Appleton Tower
David Hume Tower
Simpson Memorial Maternity Hospital
Schools
Middle Meadow Walk
North Meadow Walk
Univ Lib
Fountainbridge
a
b
c
1
2
3

COPYRIGHT GEORGE PHILIP LTD

HELSINKI

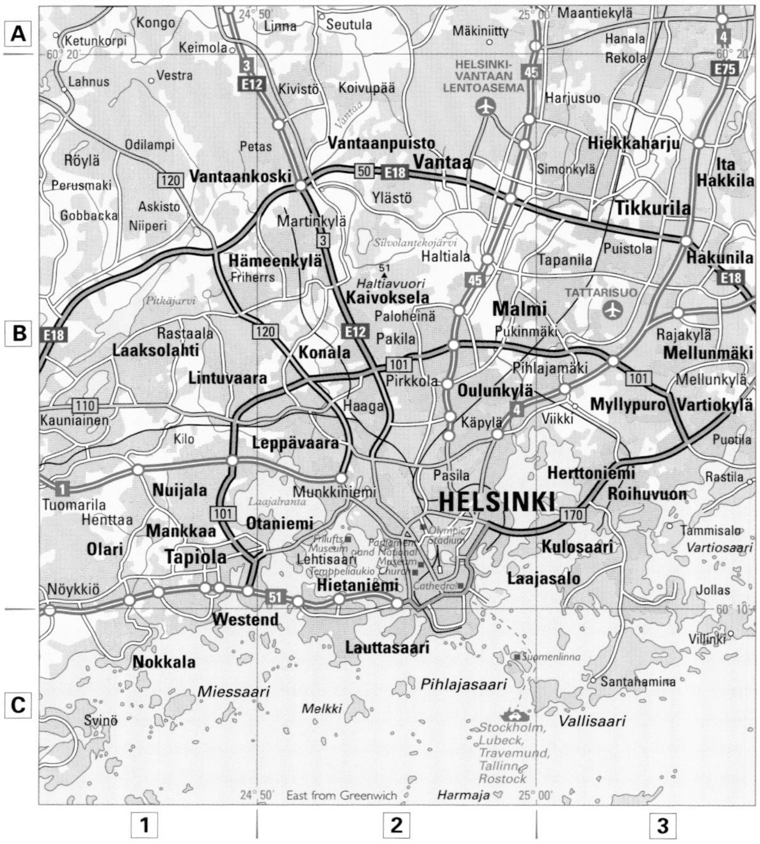

ISTANBUL

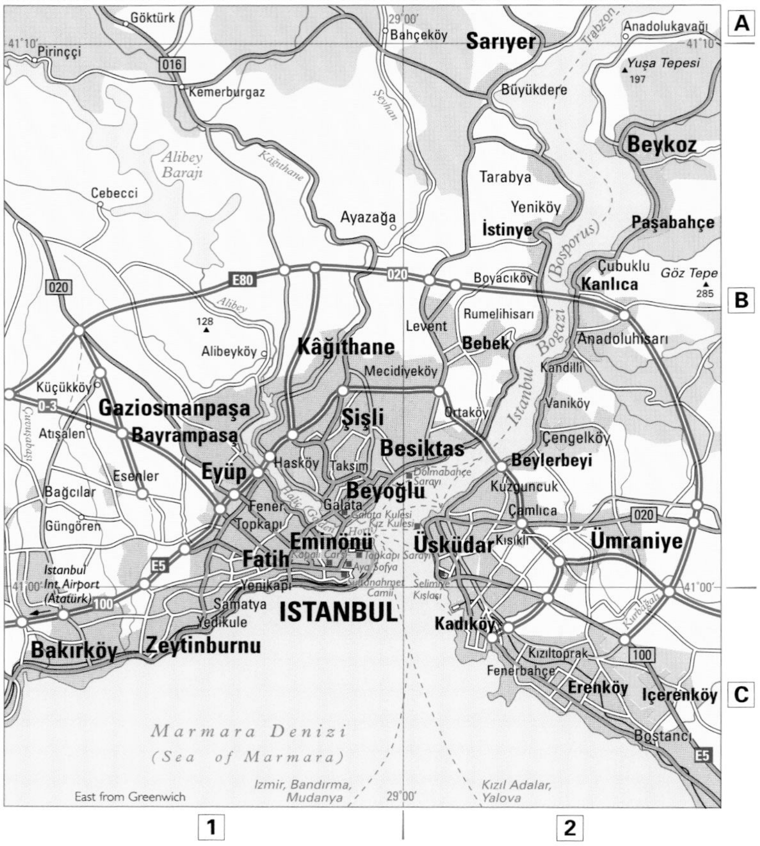

HONG KONG

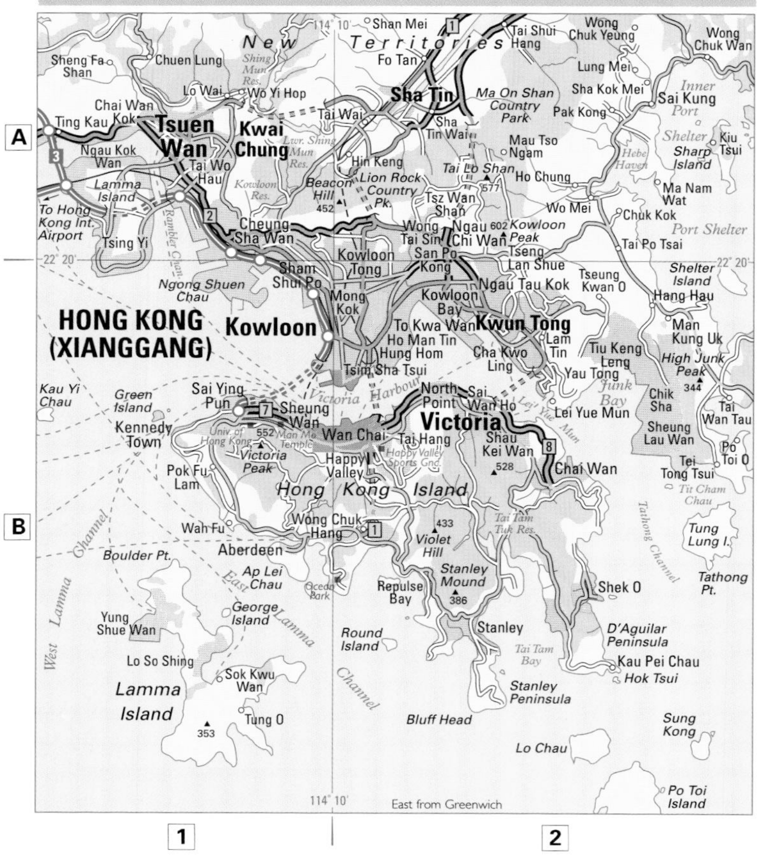

CENTRAL HONG KONG

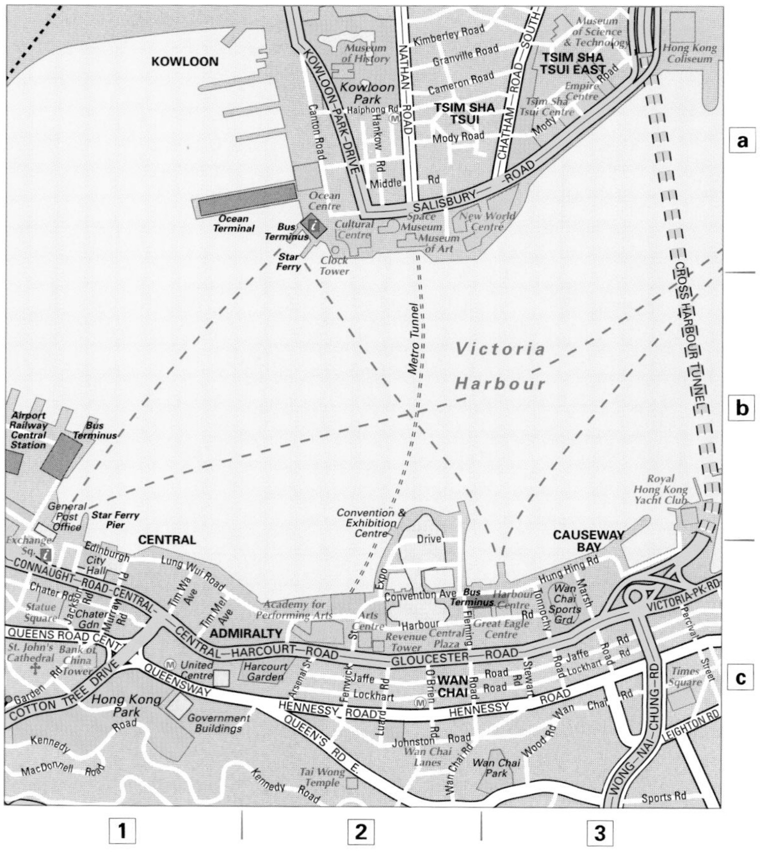

JERUSALEM

0 km 5
0 miles 3

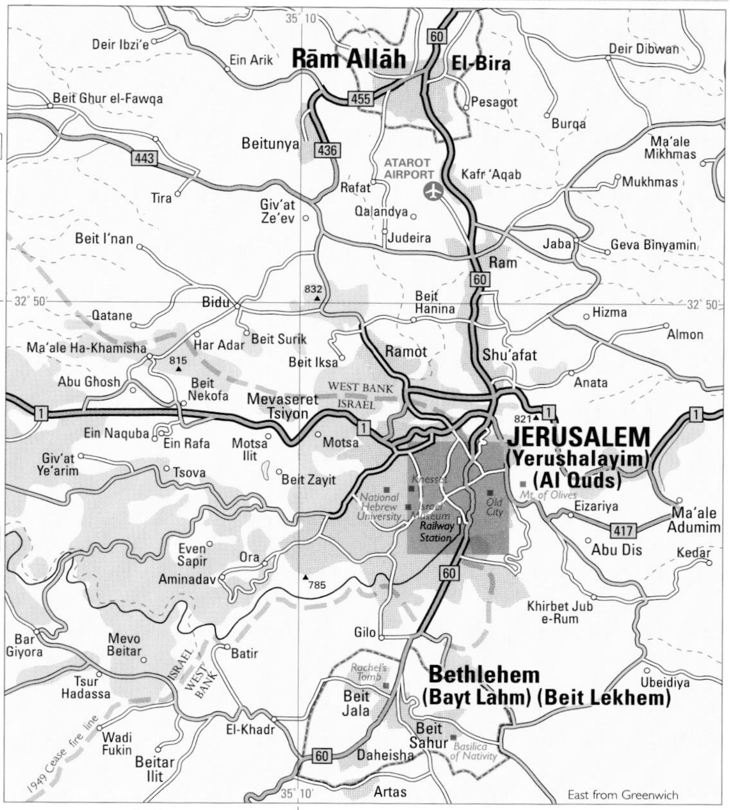
Deir Ibzi'e
Ein Arik
Rām Allāh
El-Bira
Deir Dibwan
Beit Ghur el-Fawqa
Pesagot
Burqa
Beitunya
Ma'ale Mikhmas
ATAROT AIRPORT
Kafr 'Aqab
Rafat
Mukhmas
Tira
Giv'at Ze'ev
Qalandya
Judeira
Beit I'nan
Jaba
Geva Binyamin
Ram
Bidu
Beit Hanina
Hizma
Qatane
Almon
Ma'ale Ha-Khamisha
Har Adar
Beit Surik
Ramot
Shu'afat
Beit Iksa
Abu Ghosh
Beit Nekofa
WEST BANK
ISRAEL
Anata
Mevaseret Tsiyon
Ein Naquba
Ein Rafa
Motsa Ilit
Motsa
JERUSALEM
(Yerushalayim)
(Al Quds)
Giv'at Ye'arim
Tsova
Beit Zayit
Knesset
National Hebrew University
Israel Museum
Railway Station
Old City
Mt. of Olives
Eizariya
Ma'ale Adumim
Abu Dis
Kedar
Even Sapir
Ora
Aminadav
Khirbet Jub e-Rum
Bar Giyora
Mevo Beitar
Gilo
Batir
Bethlehem
(Bayt Lahm) (Beit Lekhem)
Tsur Hadassa
Rachel's Tomb
Beit Jala
Ubeidiya
El-Khadr
Wadi Fukin
Beitar Ilit
Beit Sahur
Basilica of Nativity
Daheisha
Artas
1949 Cease fire line
East from Greenwich
A
B
1
2

CENTRAL JERUSALEM

0 km 1
0 miles 0.5

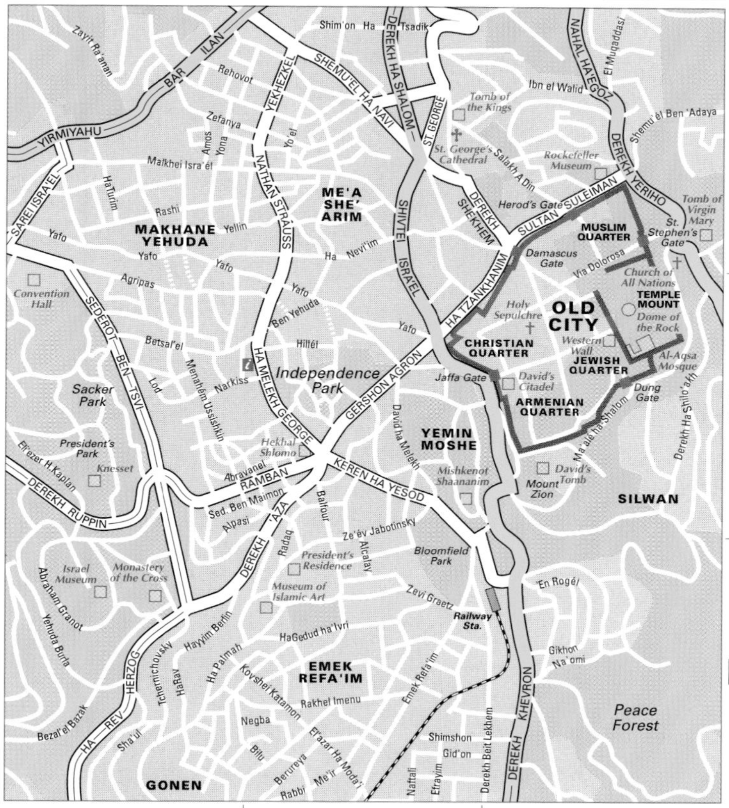
Shim'on Ha Tsadik
BAR ILAN
YIRMIYAHU
SHEMU'EL HA NAVI
Rehovot
YEKHEZKEL
Tomb of the Kings
Ibn el Walid
Shemu'el Ben 'Adaya
St. George's Cathedral
Rockefeller Museum
Malkhei Isra'el
NATHAN STRAUSS
ME'A SHE' ARIM
Herod's Gate
SULTAN SULEIMAN
DEREKH YERIHO
Tomb of Virgin Mary
St. Stephen's Gate
MAKHANE YEHUDA
MUSLIM QUARTER
Damascus Gate
Via Dolorosa
Church of All Nations
Convention Hall
Agripas
HA TZANKHANIM
Holy Sepulchre
OLD CITY
TEMPLE MOUNT
Dome of the Rock
CHRISTIAN QUARTER
Western Wall
Al-Aqsa Mosque
JEWISH QUARTER
Independence Park
Sacker Park
Jaffa Gate
David's Citadel
ARMENIAN QUARTER
Dung Gate
YEMIN MOSHE
President's Park
Knesset
Mishkenot Sha'ananim
David's Tomb
Mount Zion
SILWAN
DEREKH RUPPIN
RAMBAN
KEREN HA YESOD
Ze'ev Jabotinsky
Bloomfield Park
Israel Museum
Monastery of the Cross
President's Residence
Museum of Islamic Art
'En Rogel
Railway Sta.
EMEK REFA'IM
Gikhon Na'omi
Peace Forest
DEREKH KHEVRON
Derekh Beit Lekhem
GONEN
a
b
c
1
2
3

JAKARTA

0 km 5
0 miles 3

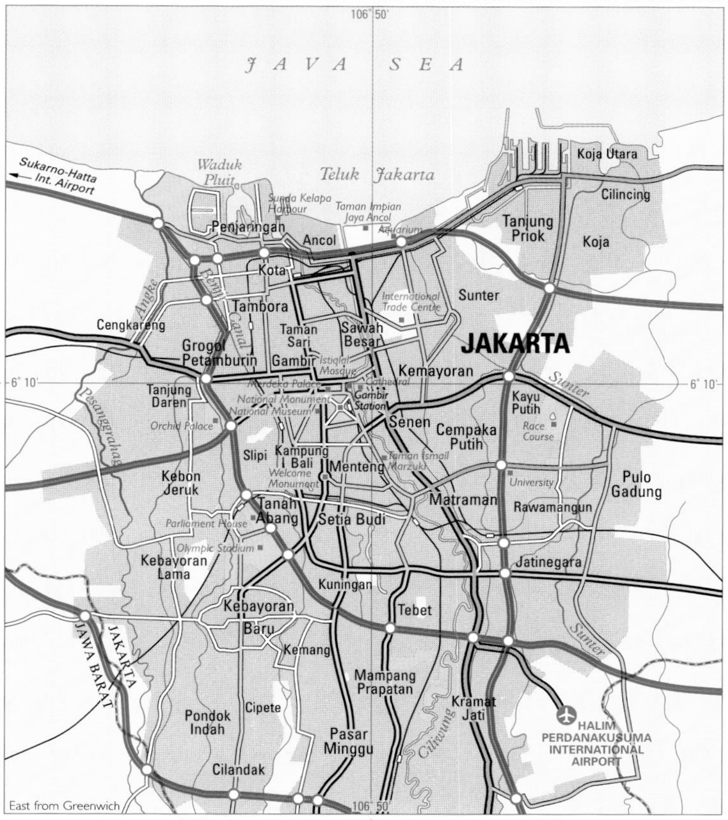
J A V A S E A
106° 50'
Koja Utara
Sukarno-Hatta Int. Airport
Waduk Pluit
Teluk Jakarta
Cilincing
Sunda Kelapa Harbour
Taman Impian Jaya Ancol
Aquarium
Tanjung Priok
Penjaringan
Ancol
Koja
Kota
International Trade Centre
Sunter
Cengkareng
Tambora
Taman Sari
Sawah Besar
JAKARTA
Grogol Petamburan
Gambir
Istiqlal Mosque
Kemayoran
Tanjung Duren
National Monument
National Museum
Gambir Station
Kayu Putih
Orchid Palace
Senen
Cempaka Putih
Race Course
Slipi
Kampung Bali
Welcome Monument
Menteng
Taman Ismail Marzuki
Kebon Jeruk
University
Pulo Gadung
Tanah Abang
Setia Budi
Matraman
Rawamangun
Parliament House
Olympic Stadium
Kebayoran Lama
Kuningan
Jatinegara
Kebayoran Baru
Tebet
Kemang
Mampang Prapatan
JAKARTA
JAWA BARAT
Pondok Indah
Cipete
Kramat Jati
HALIM PERDANAKUSUMA INTERNATIONAL AIRPORT
Pasar Minggu
Cilandak
Ciliwung
East from Greenwich
A
B
1
2

JOHANNESBURG

0 km 5
0 miles 3

28° 00'
Bryanston
Randpark Ridge
Randburg
Morningside
Sandton
Kelvin
Modderfontein
Parkmore
Linbropark
Ferndale
Sandown
Alexandra
Lakeside
Weltevreden Park
Fontainebleau
Blairgowrie
Hyde Park
Lombardy East
Florence Bloom Bird Sanctuary
Craighall Park
Windsor
Atholl
Bramley
Fairland
Parkhurst
Waverley
Edenvale
Linden
Parktown North
Highlands North
Northcliff
Herman Eckstein Park
Parkwood
Dunvegan
Quellerina
Emmarentia
Norwood
Sydenham
Jan Smuts Airport
Parkview
Houghton
West Park
Linksfield
Florida
Newlands
Westdene
The Wilds
Observatory
Bezuidenhout Park
Bedfordview
Westcliff
Parktown
Bosmont
J.G. Strijdom Post Office Tower
JOHANNESBURG
Auckland Park
Industria
Crosby
Univ. of Witwatersrand
Doornfontein
Kensington
Primrose
Mayfair
Central Sta.
Ellis Park
Museum Africa and Market Theatre
Malvern
New Canada Dam
Riverlea
New Canada
Selby
Germiston
Crown Mine
Noordgesig
Ophirton
Wemmer Pan
Rosherville Dam
Simmer and Jack Mines
Victoria Lake
Soweto
Soccer Stadium
Race Course
Rand Afrikaans University
National Exhibition Centre
Gold Reef City
RAND AIRPORT
Orlando East
Diepkloof
Turffontein
Regents Park
South Hills
Orlando Dam
Robertsham
Rosettenville
Alberton
Linmeyer
Mondeor
Florentia
Meredale
1818
Randhart
Glenvista
Alrode
Kliprivierspruit
Kibler Park
Klipriviersberg Nature Reserve
Mulbarton
Meyersdal
East from Greenwich
A
B
1
2

KARACHI

0 km 5
0 miles 3

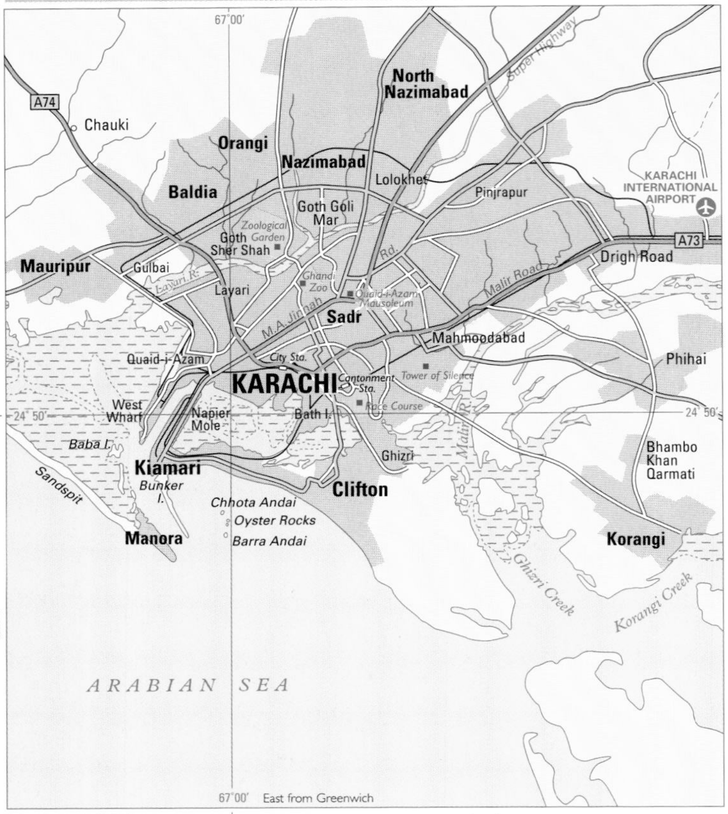

A B 1 2

LAGOS

0 km 5
0 miles 3

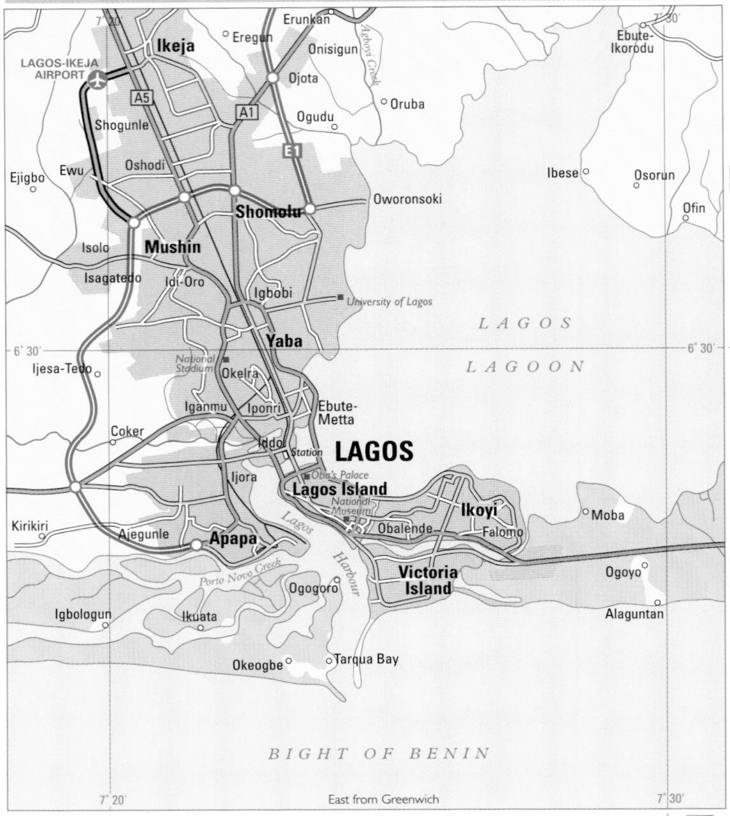

A B 1 2 3

LISBON

0 km 5
0 miles 3

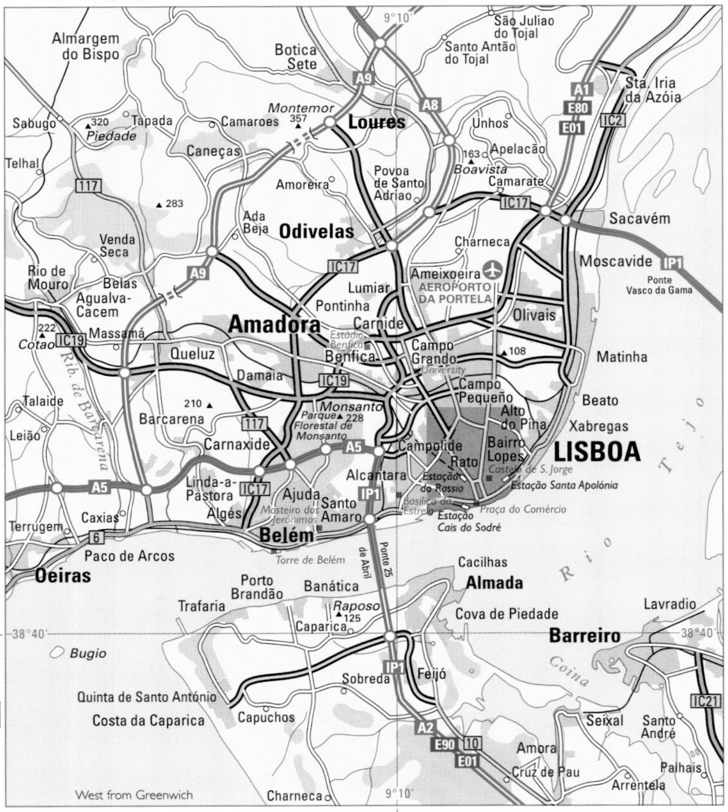

A B 1 2

CENTRAL LISBON

0 km 1
0 miles 0.5

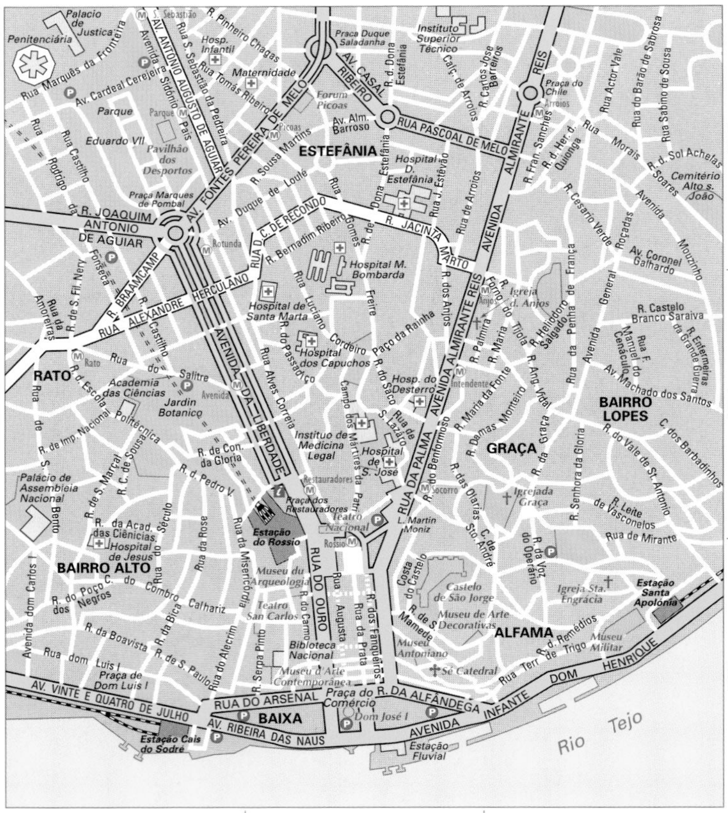

a b c 1 2 3

LONDON

0 km 5
0 miles 3

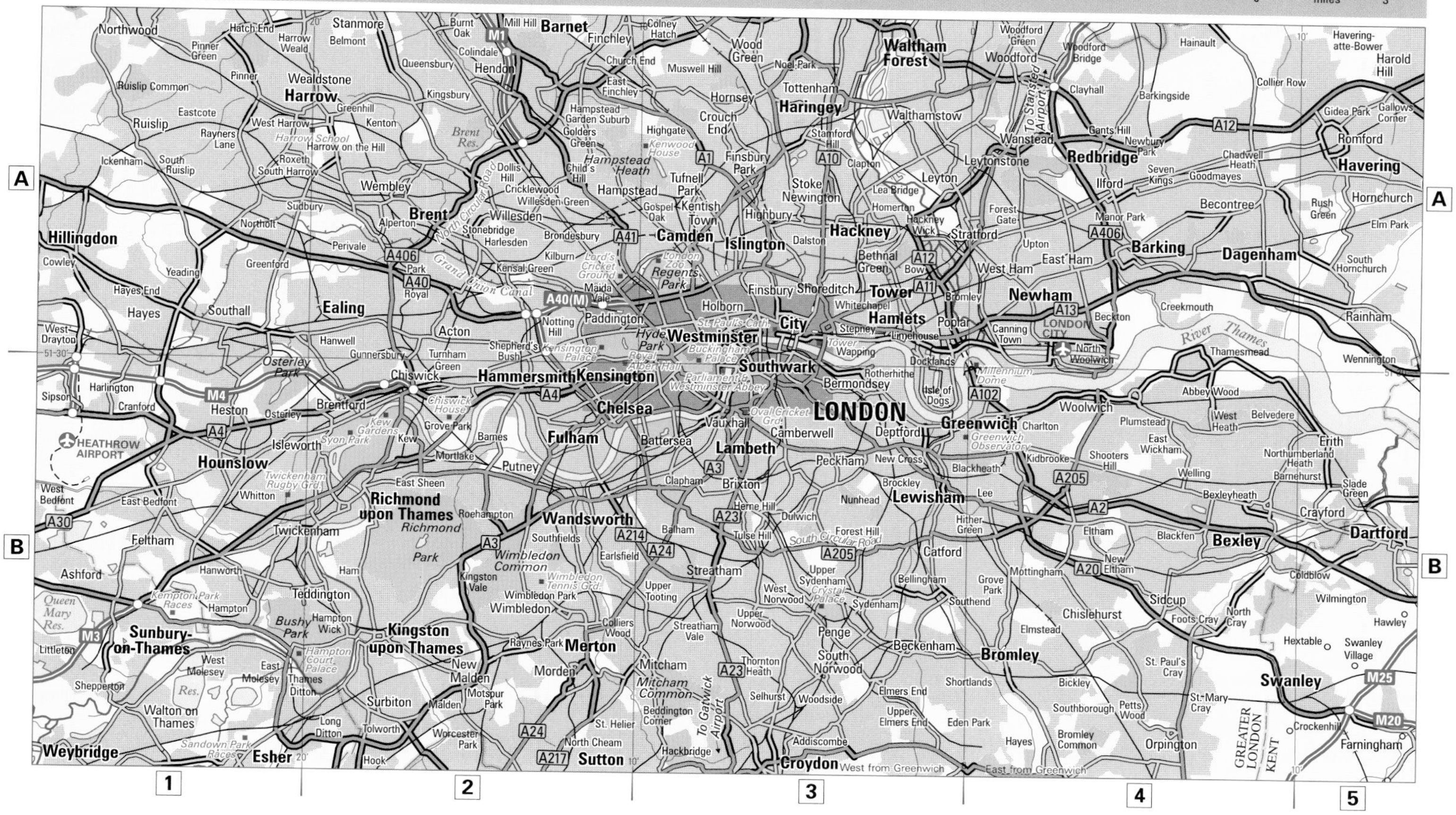

CENTRAL LONDON

0 km 2
0 miles 1

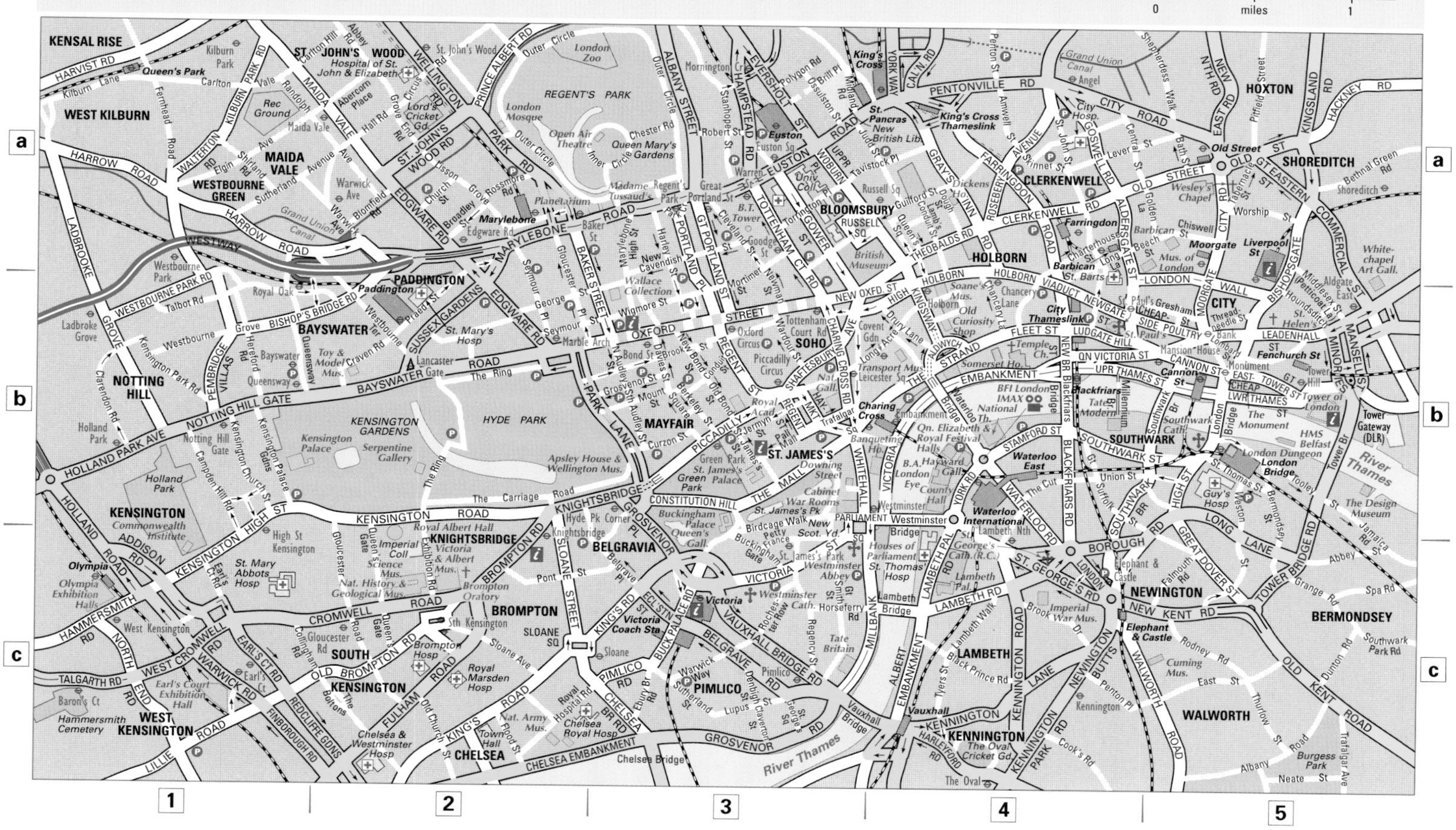

LOS ANGELES

0 km 5
0 miles 3

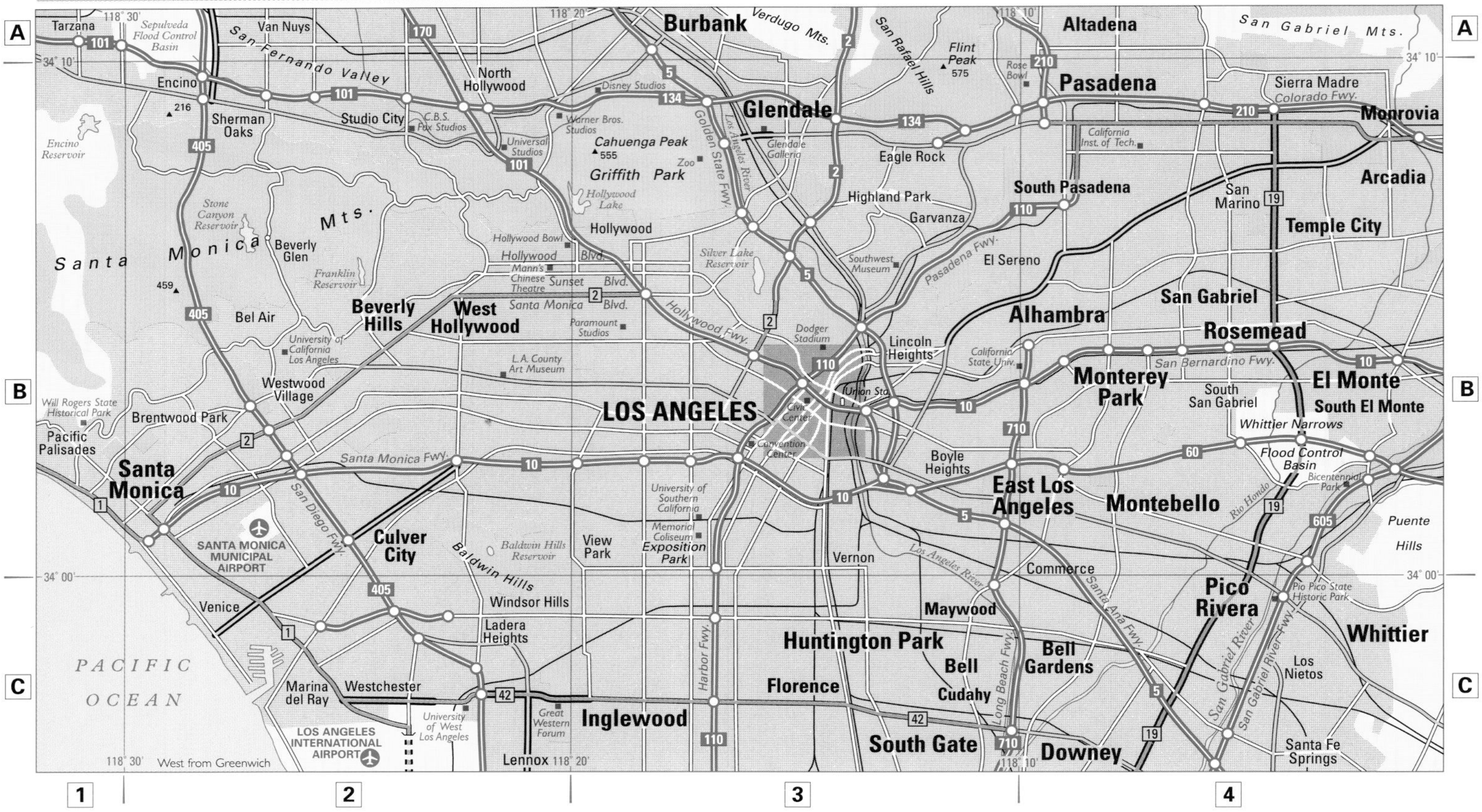

LIMA

0 km 5
0 miles 3

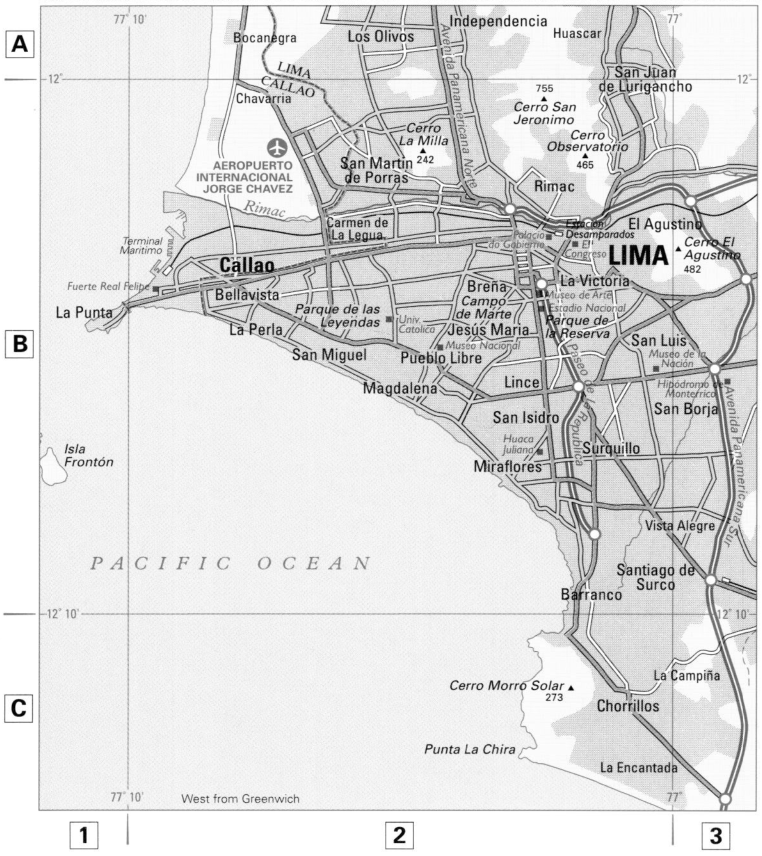

CENTRAL LOS ANGELES

0 km 1
0 miles 0.5

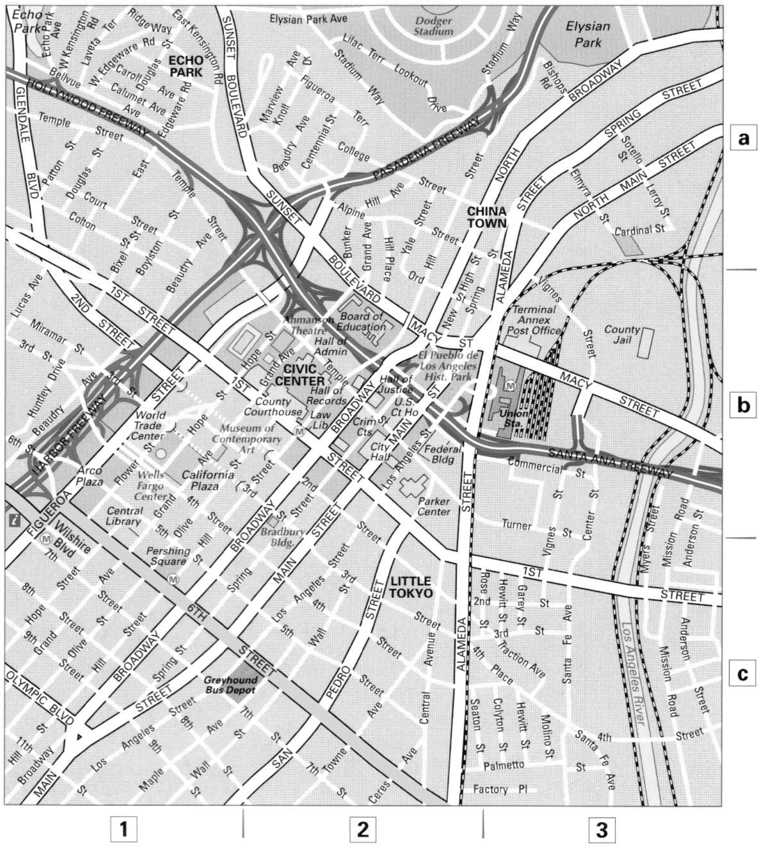

MADRID

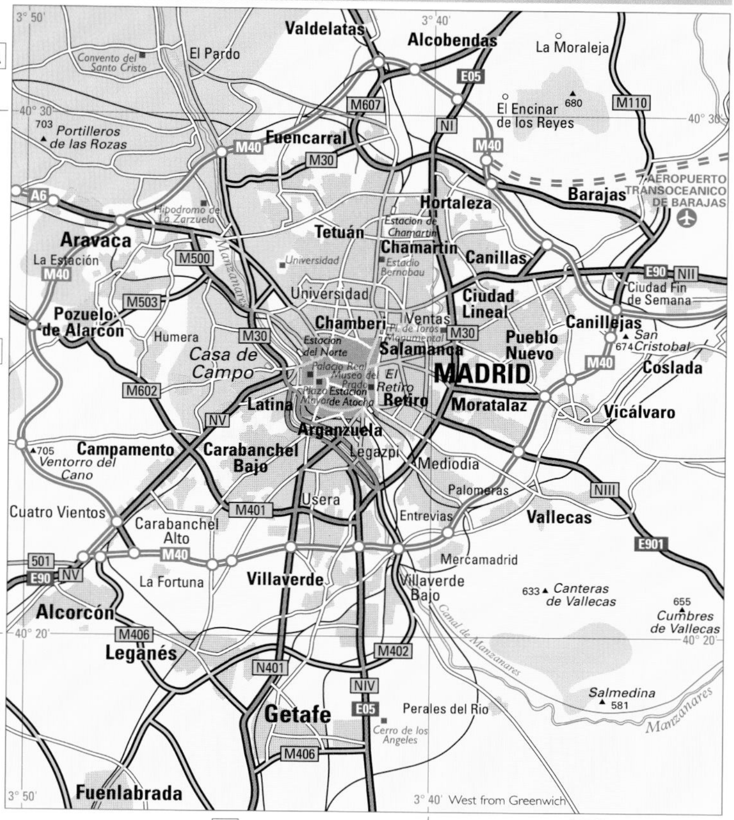
0 km 5
0 miles 3
Valdelatas
Alcobendas
La Moraleja
El Pardo
Convento del Santo Cristo
El Encinar de los Reyes
680
703 Portilleros de las Rozas
Fuencarral
AEROPUERTO TRANSOCEANICO DE BARAJAS
Barajas
Hortaleza
Aravaca
La Estación
Tetuán
Chamartin
Canillas
Universidad
Ciudad Lineal
Ciudad Fin de Semana
Pozuelo de Alarcón
Humera
Chamberi
Ventas
Canillejas
Casa de Campo
Salamanca
Pueblo Nuevo
San Cristobal
Coslada
MADRID
Latina
Retiro
Moratalaz
Vicálvaro
Arganzuela
Campamento
Carabanchel Bajo
Legazpi
Mediodia
705 Ventorro del Cano
Usera
Palomeras
Cuatro Vientos
Carabanchel Alto
Entrevias
Vallecas
La Fortuna
Villaverde
Mercamadrid
Villaverde Bajo
633 Canteras de Vallecas
655 Cumbres de Vallecas
Alcorcón
Leganés
Canal de Manzanares
Salmedina 581
Getafe
Perales del Rio
Cerro de los Angeles
Manzanares
Fuenlabrada
3° 50′
3° 40′
40° 30′
40° 20′
3° 40′ West from Greenwich
A6 M40 M500 M503 M30 M602 NV M401 M406 N401 M402 NIV E05 E90 NII NIII E901 M607 NI M110 501

A B C 1 2

CENTRAL MADRID

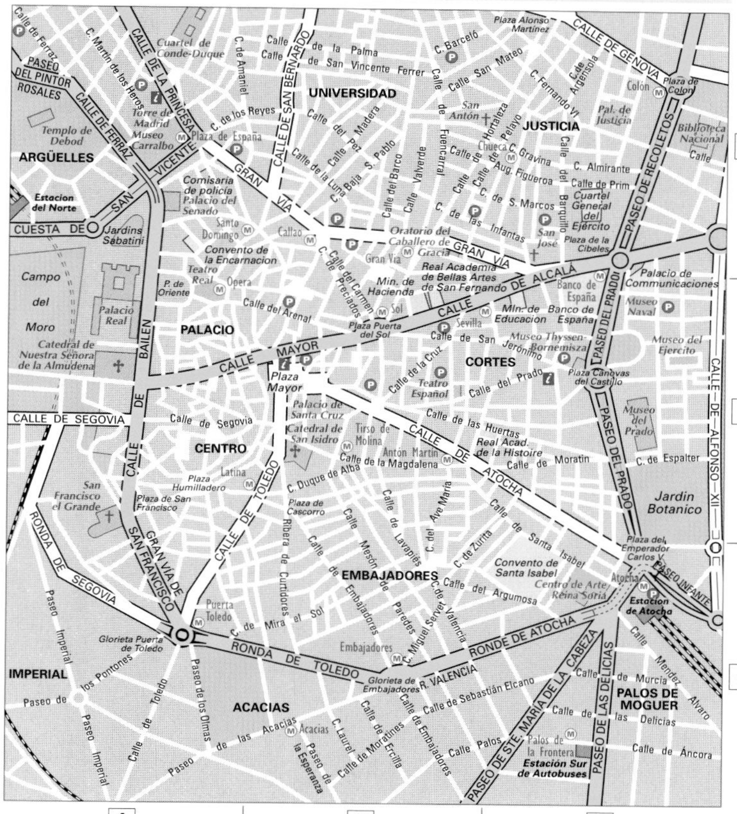
0 km 1
0 miles 0.5
PASEO DEL PINTOR ROSALES
CALLE DE LA PRINCESA
CALLE DE SAN BERNARDO
UNIVERSIDAD
JUSTICIA
CALLE DE GENOVA
PASEO DE RECOLETOS
Templo de Debod
ARGÜELLES
Plaza de España
GRAN VIA
Estacion del Norte
CUESTA DE SAN VICENTE
Jardins Sabatini
Campo del Moro
Palacio Real
P. de Oriente
Opera
PALACIO
CALLE DE ALCALA
Puerta del Sol
CALLE MAYOR
Plaza Mayor
CORTES
Museo del Prado
PASEO DEL PRADO
CALLE DE ALFONSO XII
CALLE DE SEGOVIA
CALLE DE BAILEN
Catedral de Nuestra Señora de la Almudena
CENTRO
CALLE DE ATOCHA
Jardin Botanico
San Francisco el Grande
GRAN VIA DE SAN FRANCISCO
CALLE DE TOLEDO
EMBAJADORES
Estación de Atocha
RONDA DE SEGOVIA
RONDA DE TOLEDO
RONDA DE ATOCHA
Glorieta Puerta de Toledo
IMPERIAL
ACACIAS
PALOS DE MOGUER
Estación Sur de Autobuses
PASEO DE LAS DELICIAS
PASEO DE STA MARIA DE LA CABEZA

a b c 1 2 3

MANILA

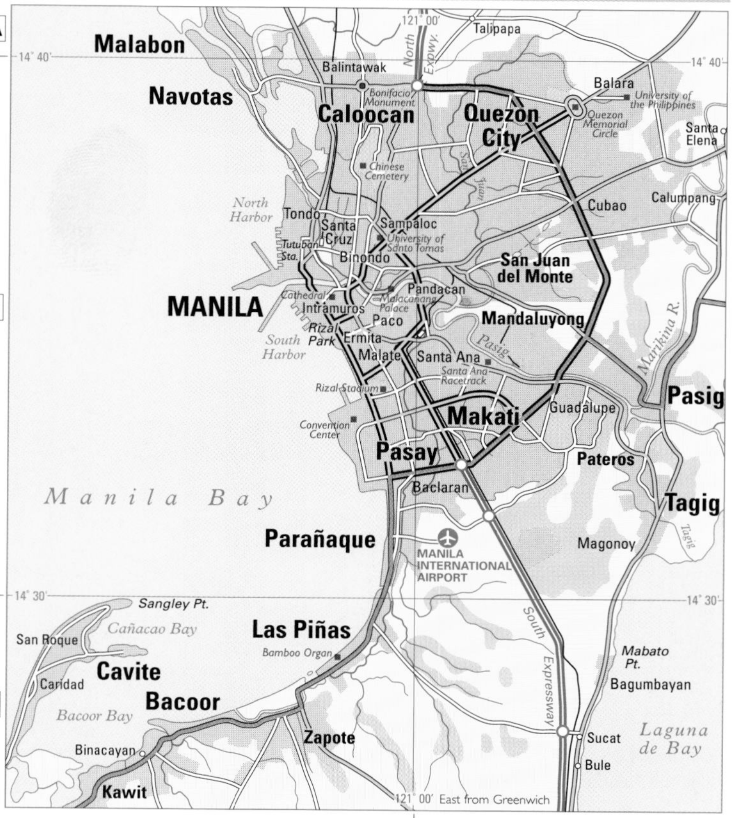
0 km 5
0 miles 3
121° 00′
14° 40′
14° 30′
Malabon
Talipapa
Balintawak
Bonifacio Monument
Navotas
Caloocan
Quezon City
Balara
University of the Philippines
Quezon Memorial Circle
Santa Elena
Chinese Cemetery
Cubao
Calumpang
North Harbor
Tondo
Santa Cruz
Sampaloc
University of Santo Tomas
Binondo
San Juan del Monte
MANILA
Intramuros
Pandacan
Malacanang Palace
Paco
Mandaluyong
Marikina R.
Rizal Park
Ermita
South Harbor
Malate
Santa Ana
Santa Ana Racetrack
Pasig
Rizal Stadium
Convention Center
Makati
Guadalupe
Pasay
Pateros
Manila Bay
Baclaran
Tagig
Parañaque
Magonoy
MANILA INTERNATIONAL AIRPORT
Sangley Pt.
Cañacao Bay
San Roque
Las Piñas
Bamboo Organ
Caridad
Cavite
Bacoor
Bacoor Bay
Mabato Pt.
Bagumbayan
South Expressway
Zapote
Binacayan
Sucat
Laguna de Bay
Bule
Kawit
121° 00′ East from Greenwich

A B C 1 2

MELBOURNE

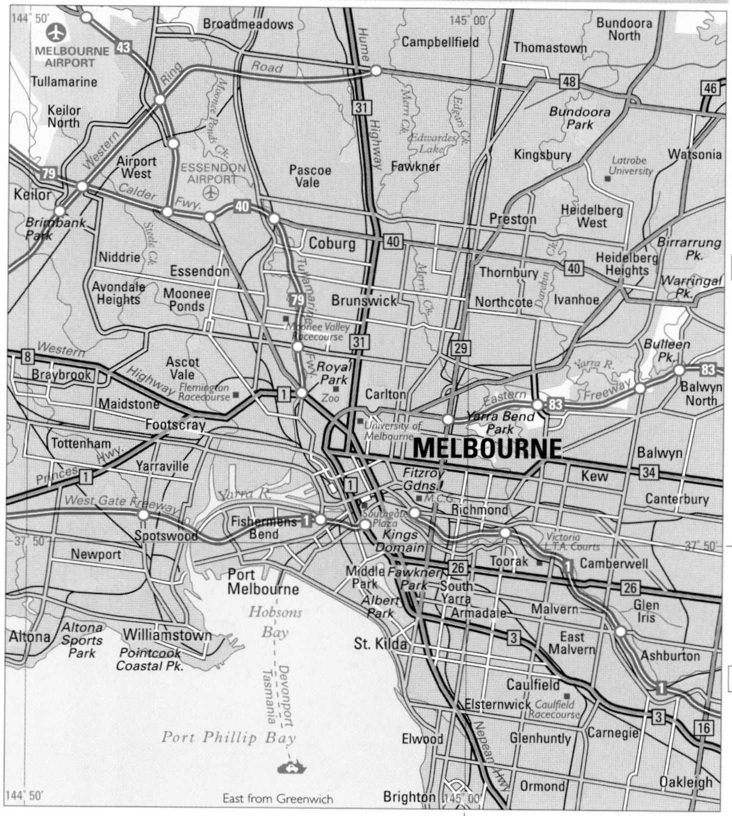
0 km 5
0 miles 3
144° 50′
145° 00′
37° 50′
Broadmeadows
Campbellfield
Thomastown
Bundoora North
MELBOURNE AIRPORT
Tullamarine
Keilor North
Bundoora Park
Kingsbury
Watsonia
Latrobe University
Airport West
ESSENDON AIRPORT
Pascoe Vale
Fawkner
Keilor
Calder Fwy.
Brimbank Park
Coburg
Preston
Heidelberg West
Niddrie
Essendon
Heidelberg Heights
Birrarrung Pk.
Warringal Pk.
Avondale Heights
Moonee Ponds
Brunswick
Thornbury
Northcote
Ivanhoe
Moonee Valley Racecourse
Braybrook
Ascot Vale
Flemington Racecourse
Royal Park
Zoo
Carlton
Bulleen Pk.
Balwyn North
Maidstone
Footscray
University of Melbourne
Yarra Bend Park
Tottenham
MELBOURNE
Balwyn
Yarraville
Fitzroy Gdns.
Kew
Canterbury
West Gate Freeway
Richmond
Spotswood
Fishermens Bend
Kings Domain
Newport
Port Melbourne
Middle Park
Fawkner Park
Toorak
Camberwell
South Yarra
Armadale
Malvern
Glen Iris
Hobsons Bay
Albert Park
Altona
Altona Sports Park
Williamstown
Pointcook Coastal Pk.
St. Kilda
East Malvern
Ashburton
Caulfield
Elsternwick
Caulfield Racecourse
Port Phillip Bay
Elwood
Glenhuntly
Carnegie
Brighton
Ormond
Oakleigh
Devonport Tasmania
East from Greenwich

A B 1 2

MEXICO CITY

0 km 5
0 miles 3

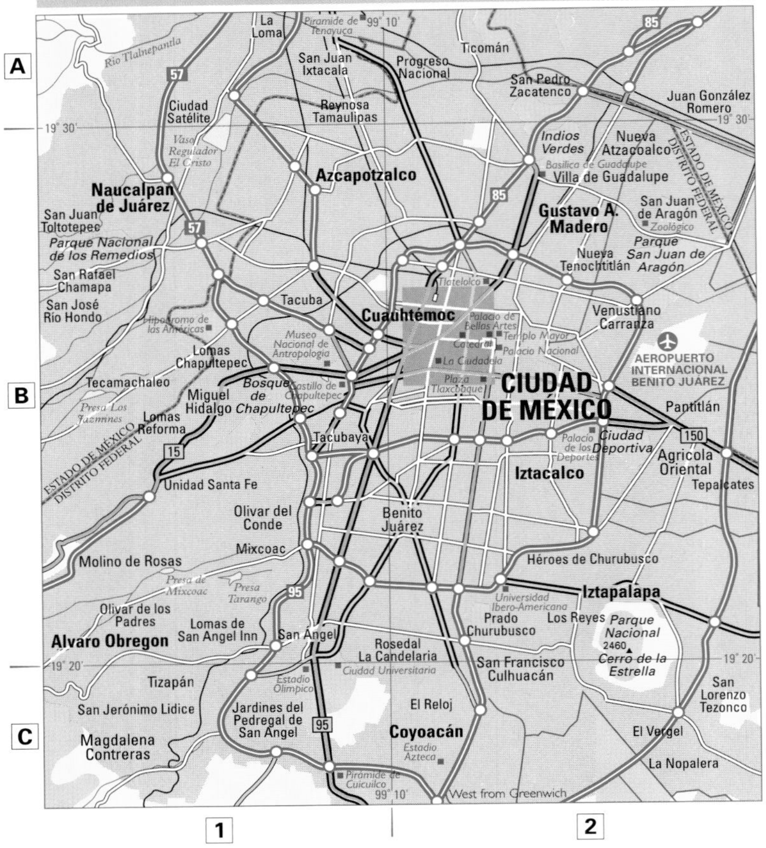

CENTRAL MEXICO CITY

0 km 1
0 miles 0.5

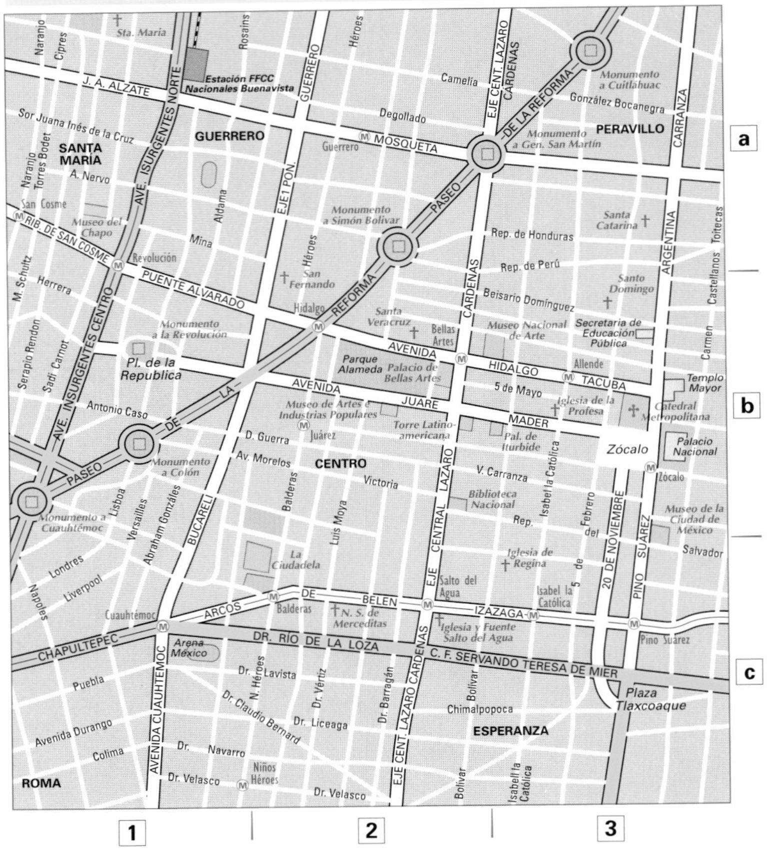

MIAMI

0 km 5
0 miles 3

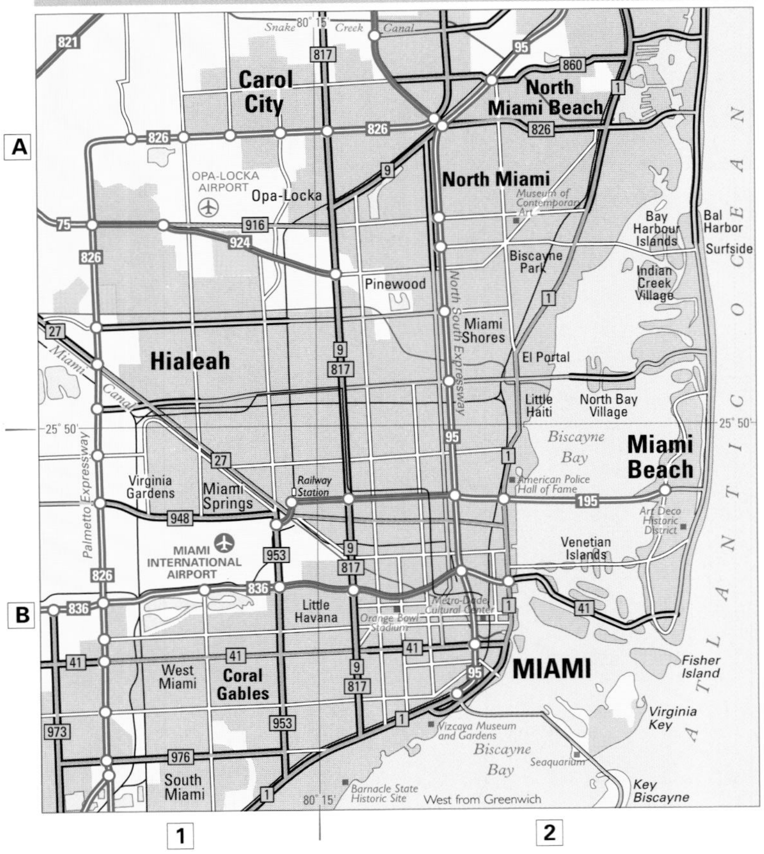

MILAN

0 km 5
0 miles 3

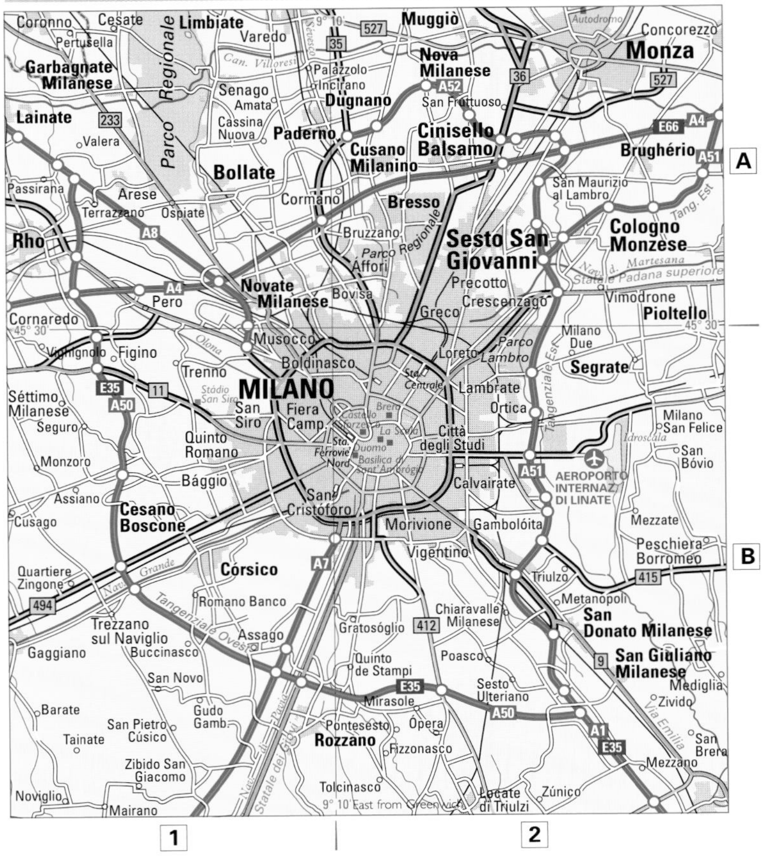

MOSCOW

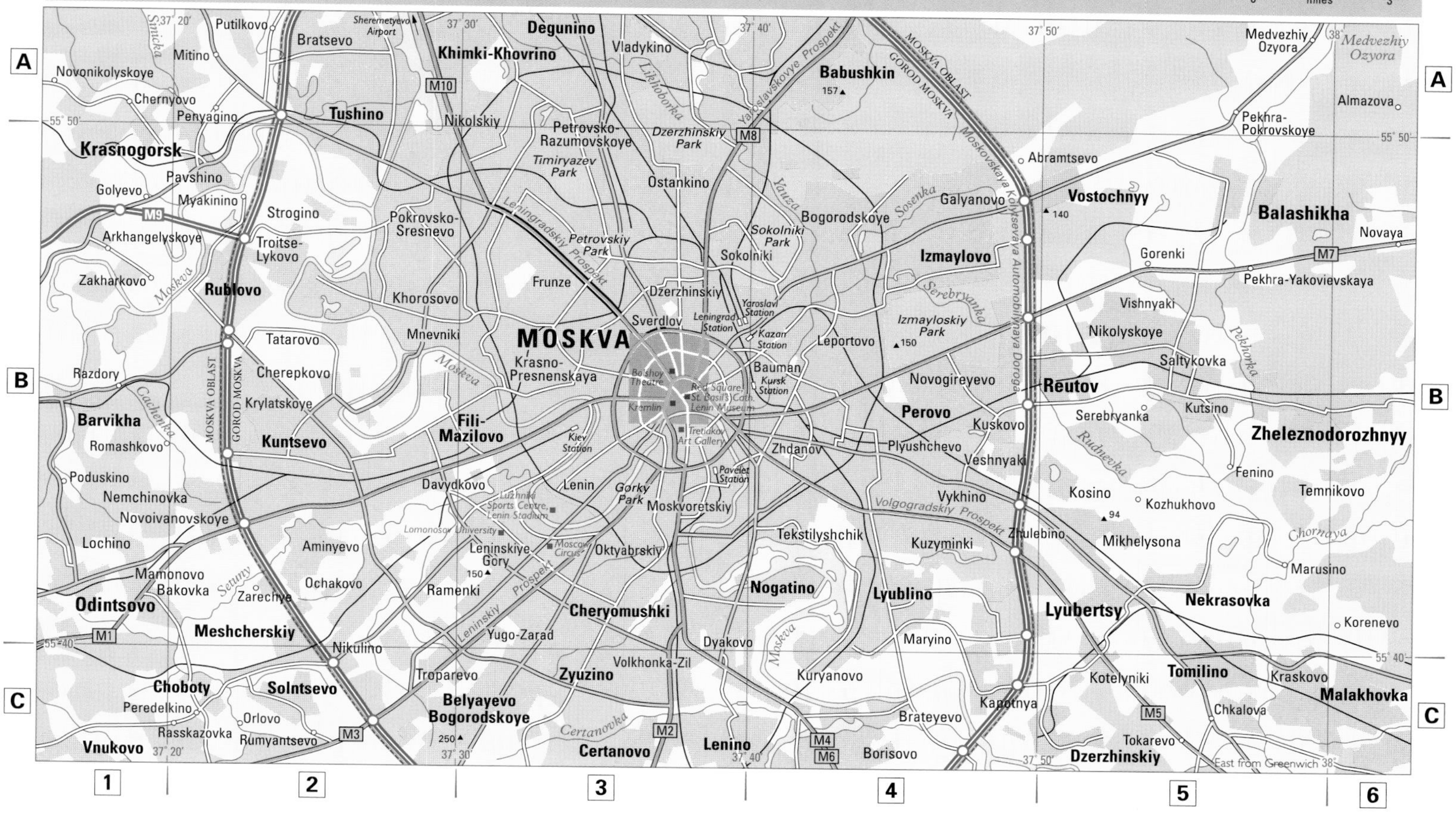

MONTRÉAL

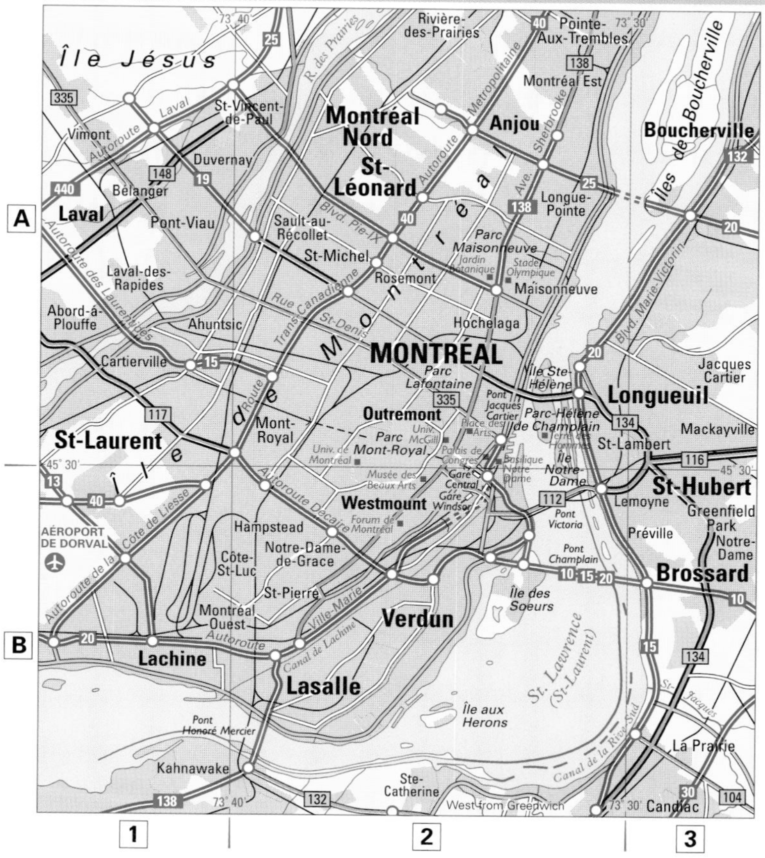

CENTRAL MOSCOW

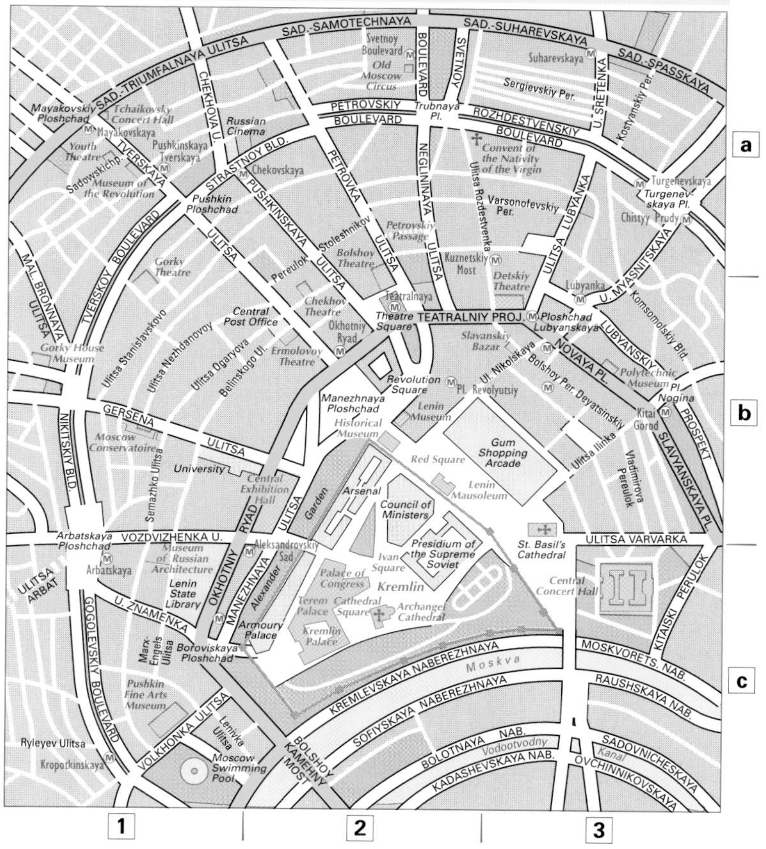

MUMBAI

0 km 5
0 miles 3

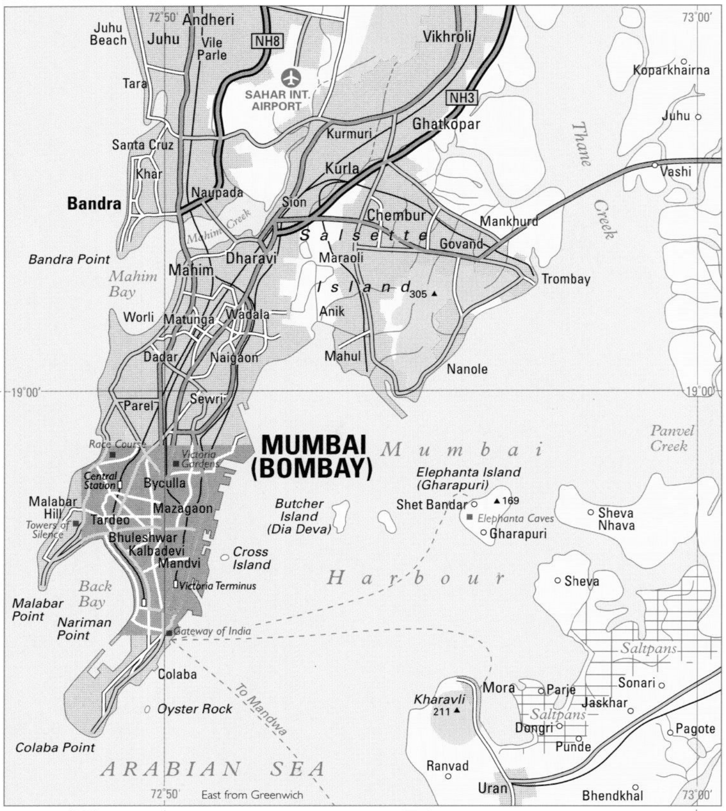

CENTRAL MUMBAI

0 km 2
0 miles 1

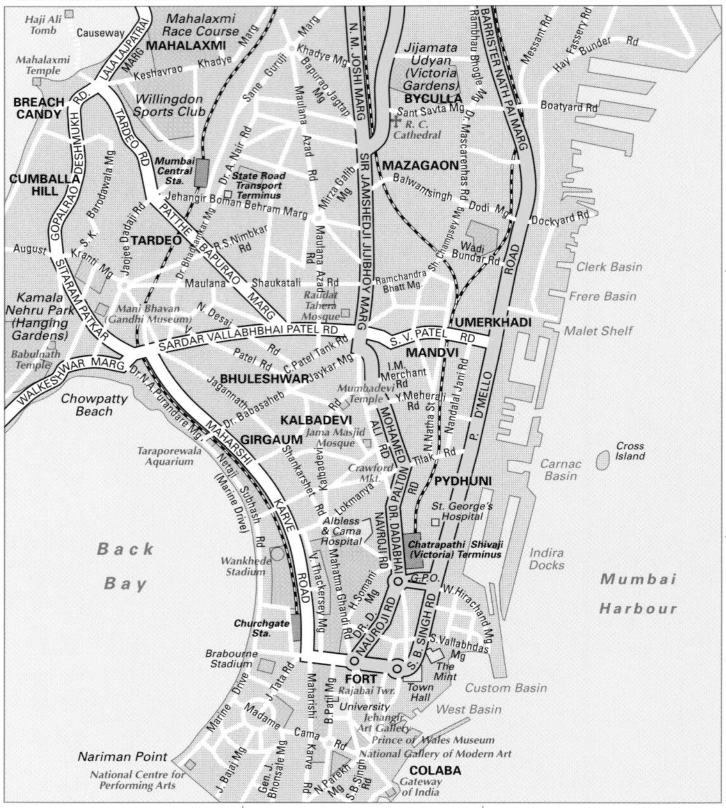

MUNICH

0 km 5
0 miles 3

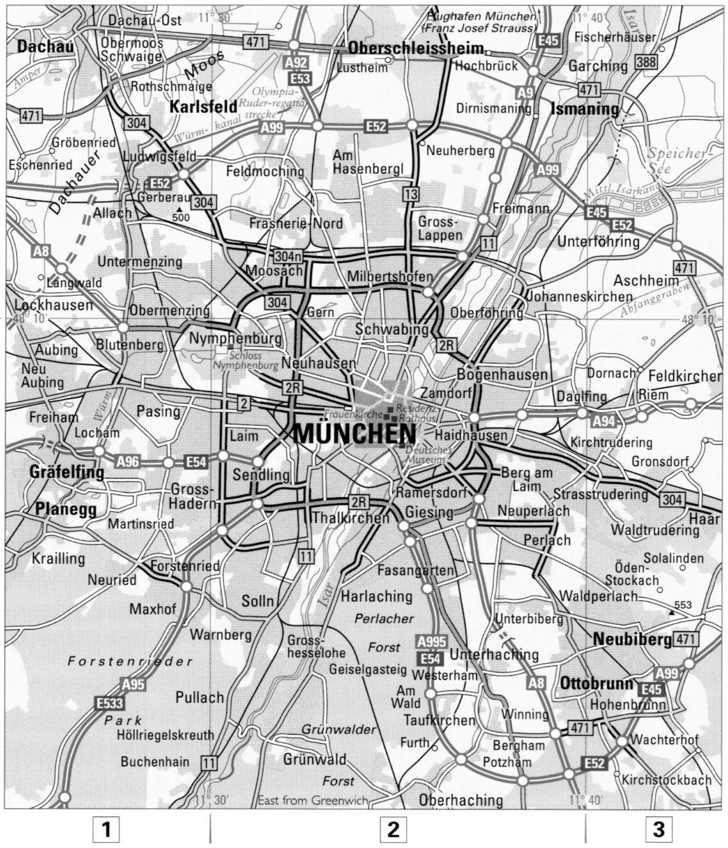

CENTRAL MUNICH

0 km 1
0 miles 0.5

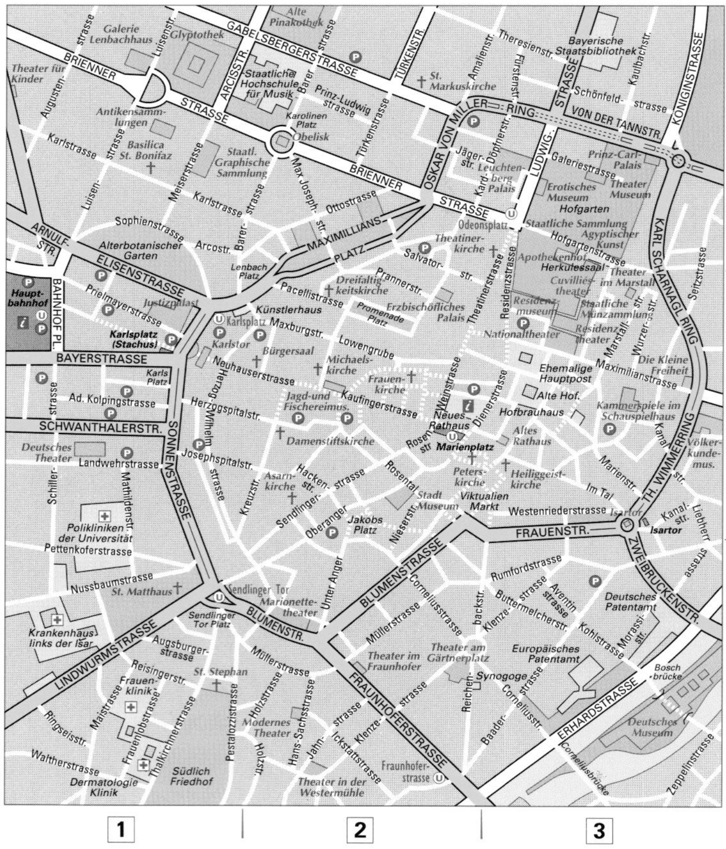

NEW YORK

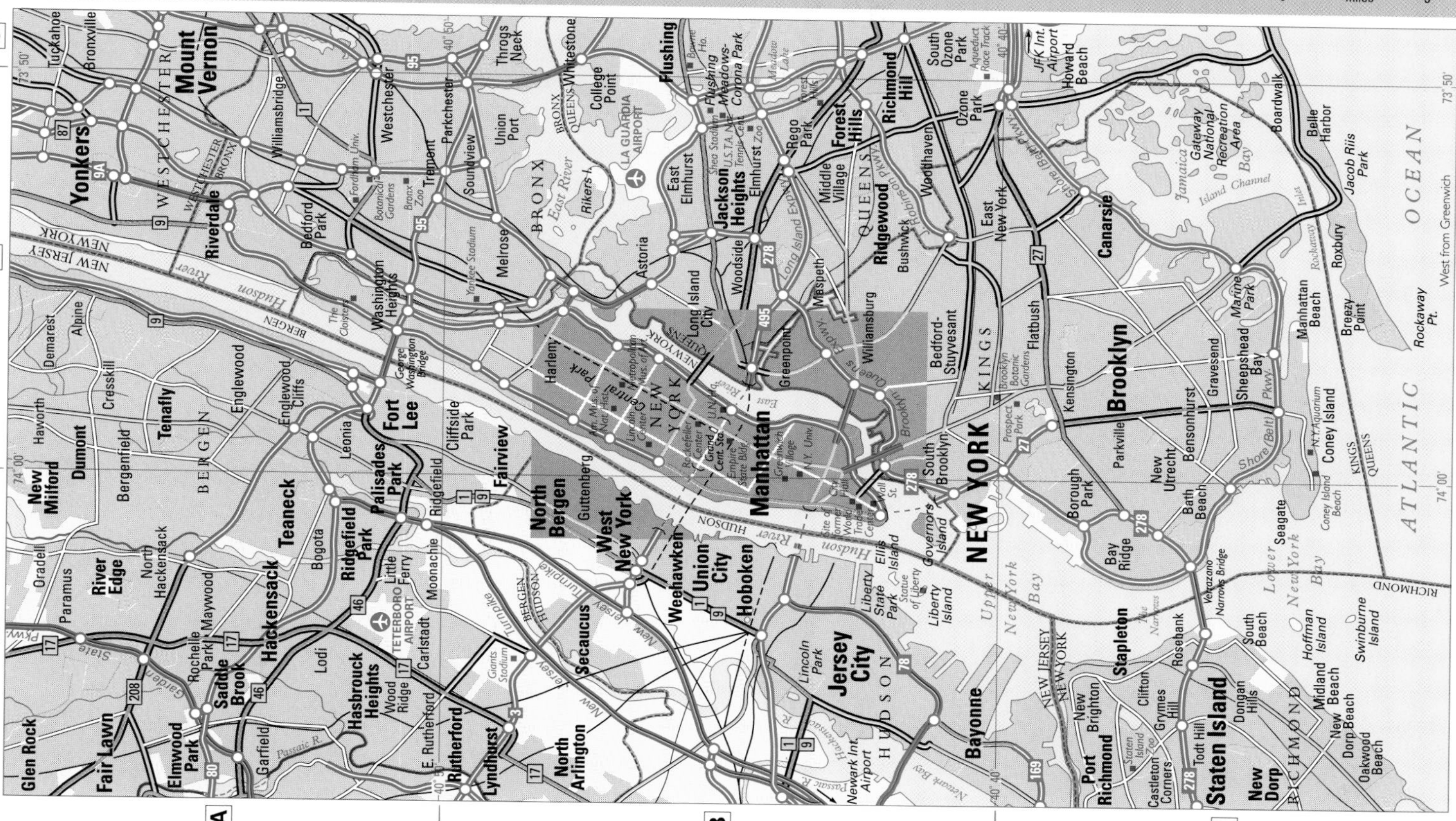

CENTRAL NEW YORK

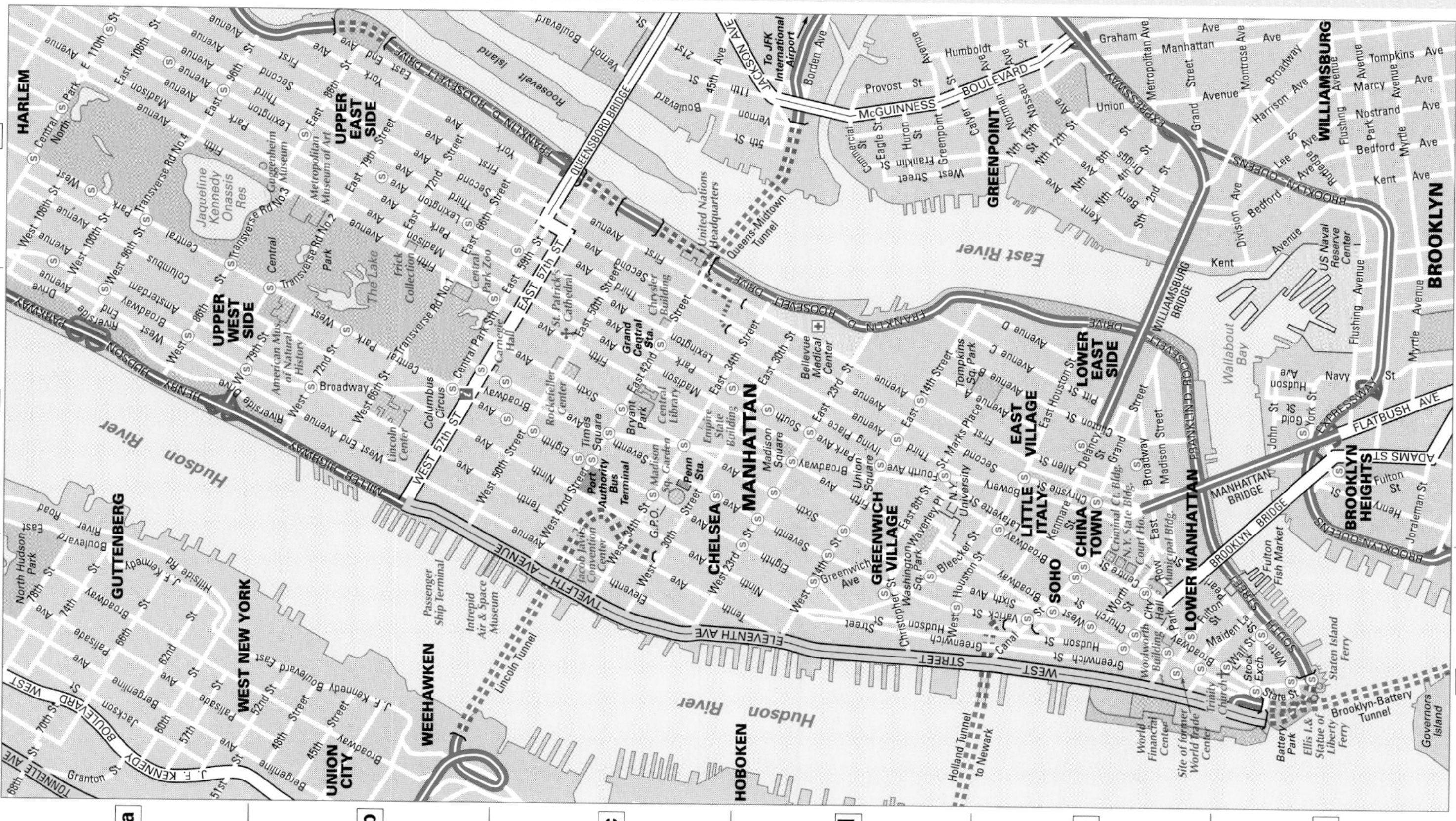

OSAKA

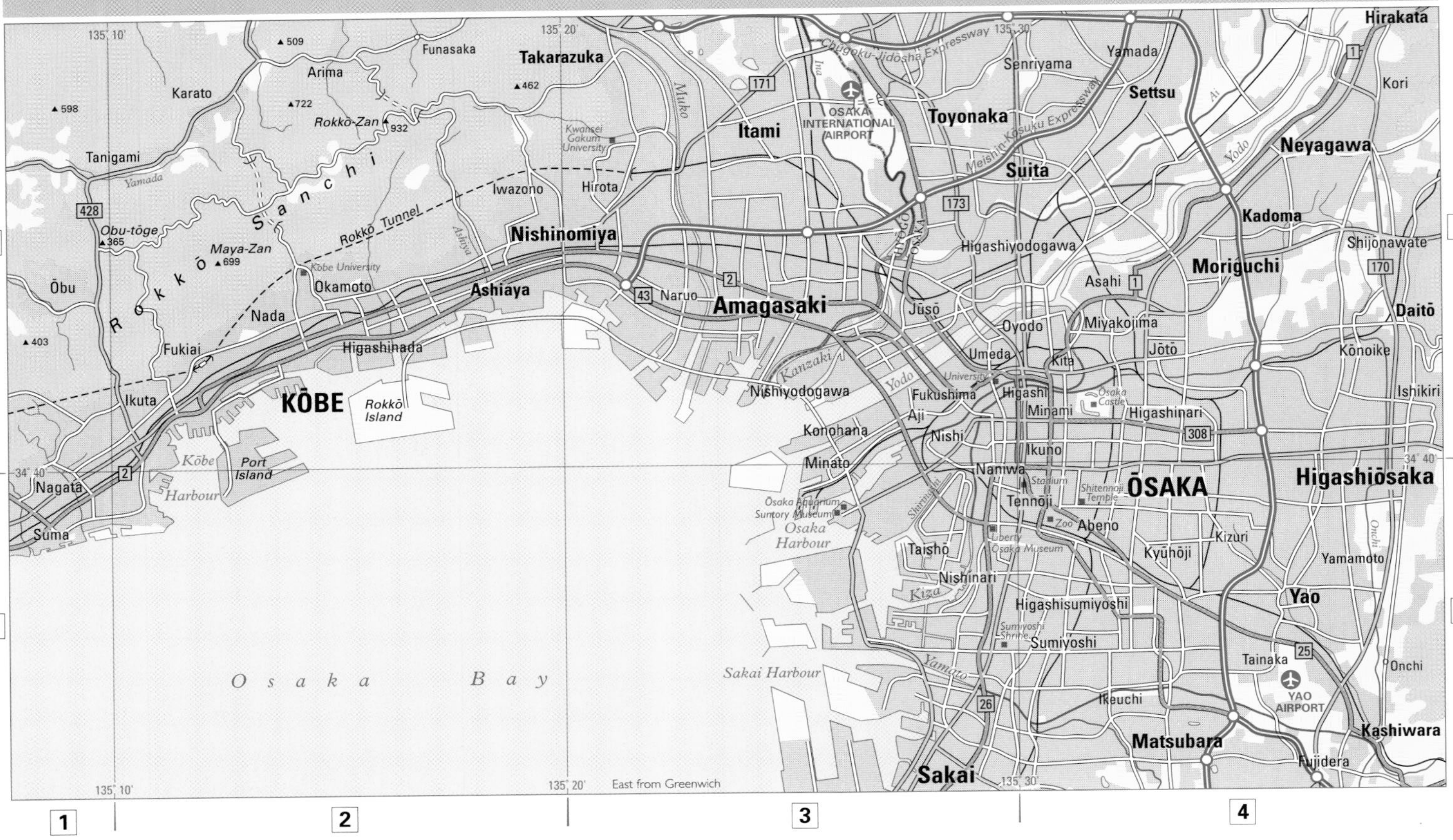
0 km 5
0 miles 3
Hirakata
Funasaka
Takarazuka
Arima
Karato
Rokkō-Zan 932
Senriyama
Yamada
Settsu
Kori
Itami
OSAKA INTERNATIONAL AIRPORT
Toyonaka
Tanigami
Kwansei Gakuin University
Suita
Neyagawa
Iwazono
Hirota
Rokkō Sanchi
Rokkō Tunnel
Obu-tōge
Maya-Zan 699
Nishinomiya
Kadoma
Higashiyodogawa
Shijonawate
Ōbu
Kobe University
Okamoto
Ashiya
Moriguchi
Asahi
Naruo
Amagasaki
Daitō
Nada
Jūsō
Oyodo
Miyakojima
Fukiai
Higashinada
Umeda
Kita
Jōtō
Kōnoike
Nishiyodogawa
Fukushima
Higashi
Osaka Castle
Ishikiri
Ikuta
KŌBE
Rokkō Island
Minami
Higashinari
Aji
Konohana
Nishi
Ikuno
Minato
Naniwa
Higashiōsaka
Nagata
Kōbe Harbour
Port Island
Stadium
Shitennoji Temple
ŌSAKA
Tennōji
Osaka Aquarium
Suntory Museum
Osaka Harbour
Zoo
Abeno
Suma
Liberty Osaka Museum
Kizuri
Taishō
Kyūhōji
Yamamoto
Nishinari
Yao
Higashisumiyoshi
Sumiyoshi Shrine
Sumiyoshi
Tainaka
YAO AIRPORT
Onchi
Osaka Bay
Sakai Harbour
Ikeuchi
Kashiwara
Matsubara
Fujidera
Sakai
East from Greenwich
135° 10'
135° 20'
135° 30'
34° 40'
A
B
1
2
3
4

OSLO

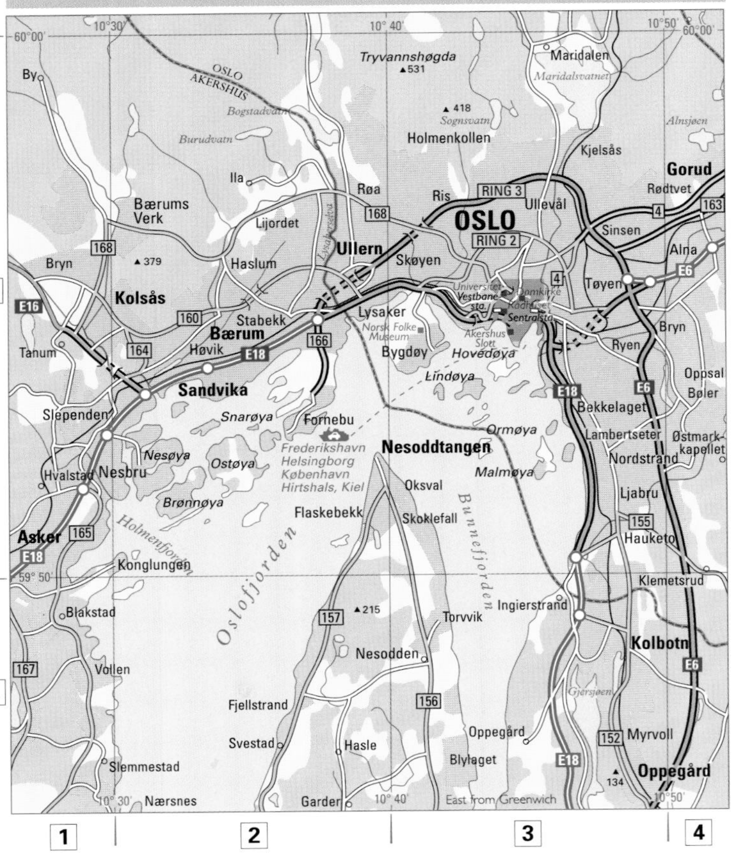
0 km 5
0 miles 3
60° 00'
10° 30'
10° 40'
10° 50'
By
OSLO AKERSHUS
Tryvannshøgda 531
Maridalen
Maridalsvatnet
Bogstadvatn
Sognsvatn
Burudvatn
Holmenkollen
Alnsjøen
Kjelsås
Gorud
Ila
Røa
Ris
RING 3
Rødtvet
Bærums Verk
Lijordet
OSLO
Ullevål
Sinsen
RING 2
Alna
Bryn
Haslum
Ullern
Skøyen
Tøyen
Kolsås
Stabekk
Vestbane
Lysaker
Universitet
Akershus Slott
Sentralstasjon
Bryn
Bærum
Norsk Folke Museum
Tanum
Høvik
Bygdøy
Hovedøya
Ryen
Sandvika
Lindøya
Oppsal
Slependen
Snarøya
Fornebu
Bekkelaget
Bøler
Ormøya
Lambertseter
Østmarkkapellet
Hvalstad
Nesbru
Nesøya
Frederikshavn Helsingborg København Hirtshals, Kiel
Nesoddtangen
Nordstrand
Østøya
Malmøya
Brønnøya
Oksval
Ljabru
Asker
Holmenfjorden
Flaskebekk
Skoklefall
Bunnefjorden
Hauketo
Konglungen
Oslofjorden
Klemetsrud
59° 50'
Blakstad
215
Torvvik
Ingierstrand
Kolbotn
Nesodden
Vollen
Gjersjøen
Fjellstrand
Oppegård
Myrvoll
Svestad
Hasle
Blylaget
Slemmestad
134
Oppegård
Nærsnes
Garder
East from Greenwich
E6
E16
E18
A
B
1
2
3
4

CENTRAL OSLO

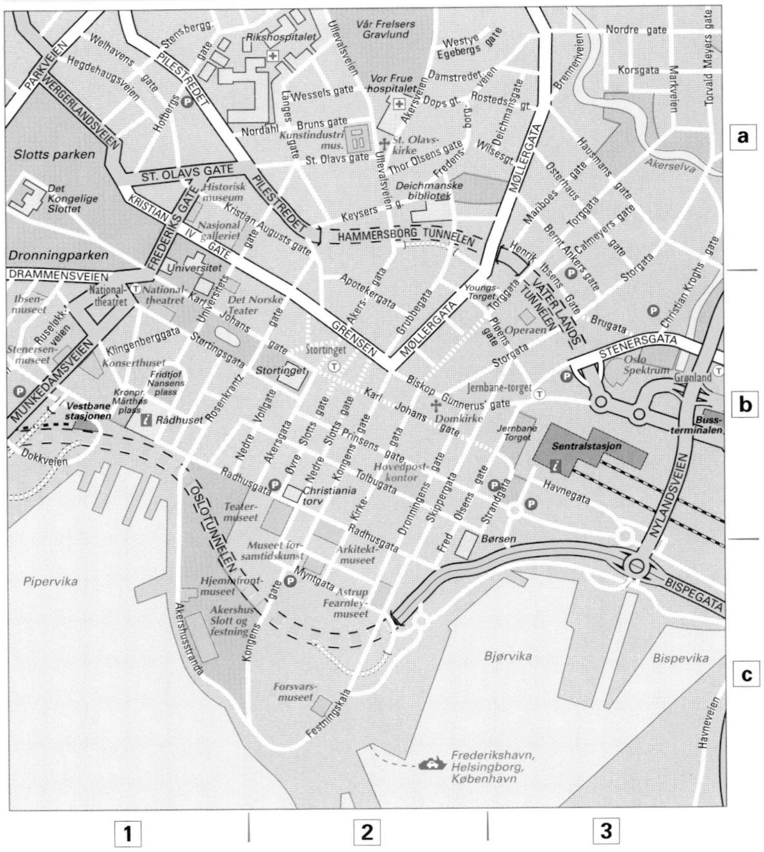
0 km 0,5
0 miles 0.25
Vår Frelsers Gravlund
Rikshospitalet
Stensberggata
Ullevålsveien
Westye Egebergs gate
Nordre gate
Korsgata
Welhavens gate
Hegdehaugsveien
PARKVEIEN
WERGELANDSVEIEN
PILESTREDET
Wessels gate
Vor Frue hospitalet
Damstredet
Dops gt.
Hostedsgate
Markveien
Torvald Meyers gate
Slotts parken
Nordahl Bruns gate
Kunstindustri mus.
St. Olavs gate
St. Olavs kirke
Thor Olsens gate
Akerselva
Det Kongelige Slottet
ST. OLAVS GATE
Historisk museum
Deichmanske bibliotek
MØLLERGATA
KRISTIAN IV GATE
Nasjonal galleriet
Kristian Augusts gate
Keysers gate
HAMMERSBORG TUNNELEN
Dronningparken
FREDERIKS GATE
Universitet
DRAMMENSVEIEN
Ibsen-museet
National-theatret
Det Norske Teater
Aporekergata
Youngs-Torget
VATERLANDS TUNNELEN
Operaen
Brugata
Stortingsgata
Stortinget
GRENSEN
Stenersen-museet
Konserthuset
Fridtjof Nansens plass
STENERSGATA
Oslo Spektrum
Grønland
Kronprinsesse Märthas plass
Rådhuset
Karl Johans gate
Domkirke
Jernbane-torget
Busstterminalen
MUNKEDAMSVEIEN
Vestbane stasjonen
Jernbane Torget
Sentralstasjon
Dokkveien
Christiania torv
Hovedpost-kontor
Havnegata
Rådhusgata
Teater-museet
Arkitekt-museet
Museet for samtidskunst
Børsen
NYLANDSVEIEN
OSLOTUNNELEN
Pipervika
Hjemmefront-museet
Astrup Fearnley-museet
BISPEGATA
Akershus Slott og festning
Bjørvika
Bispevika
Forsvars-museet
Festningsgata
Havneveien
Frederikshavn, Helsingborg, København
a
b
c
1
2
3

PARIS

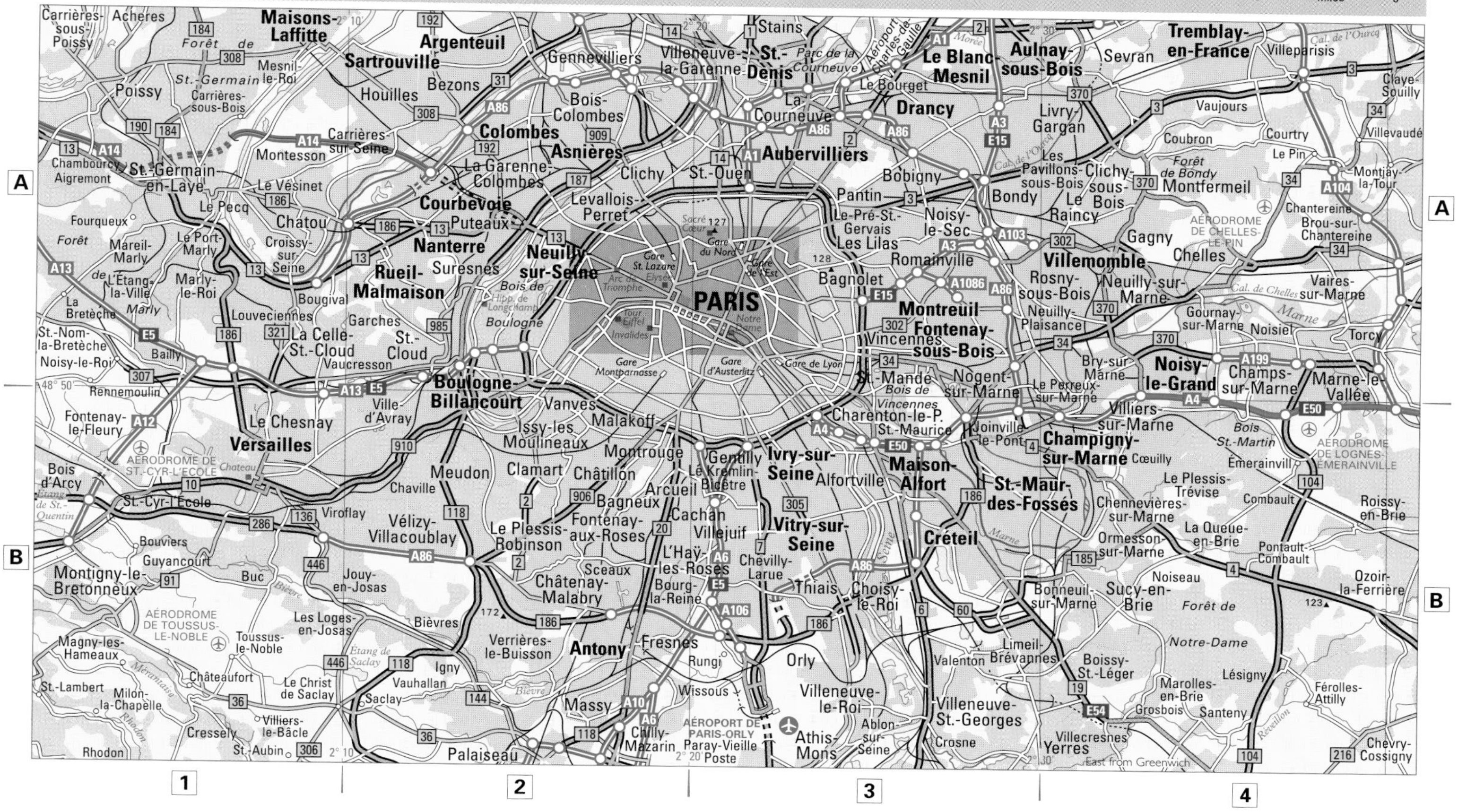

CENTRAL PARIS

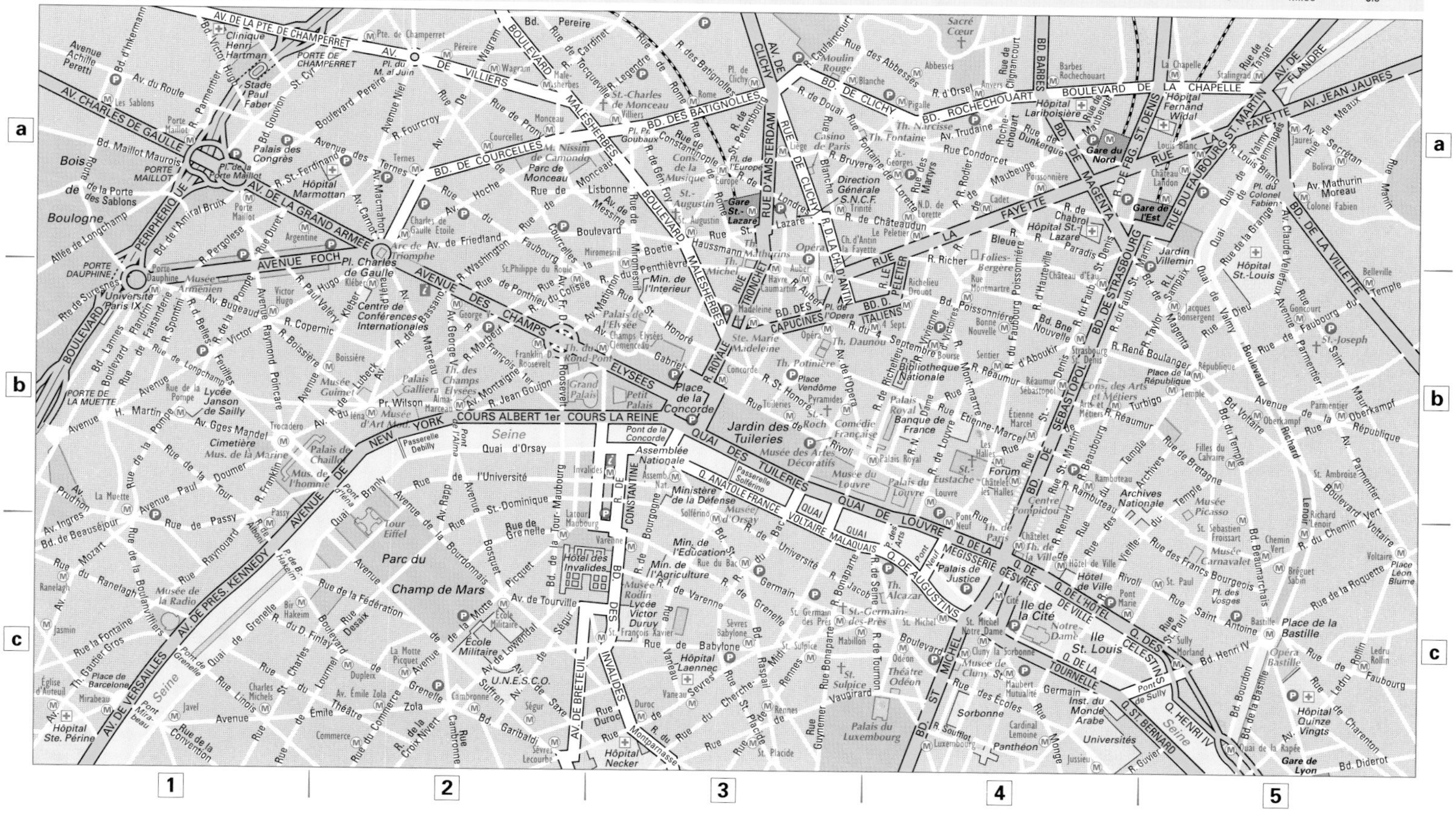

PRAGUE

0 km 5
0 miles 3

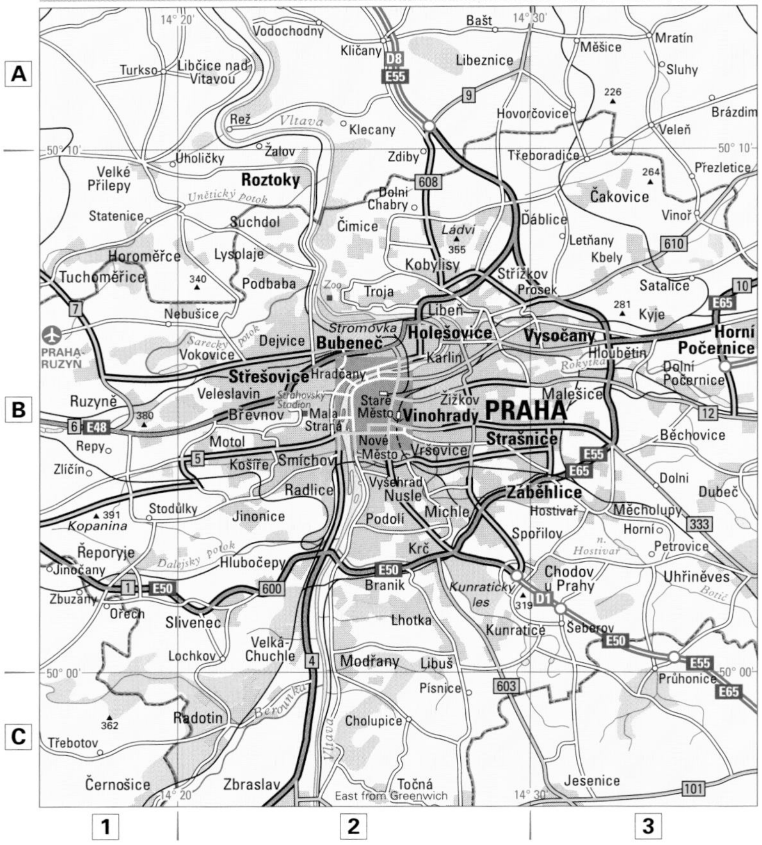

CENTRAL PRAGUE

0 km 1
0 miles 0.5

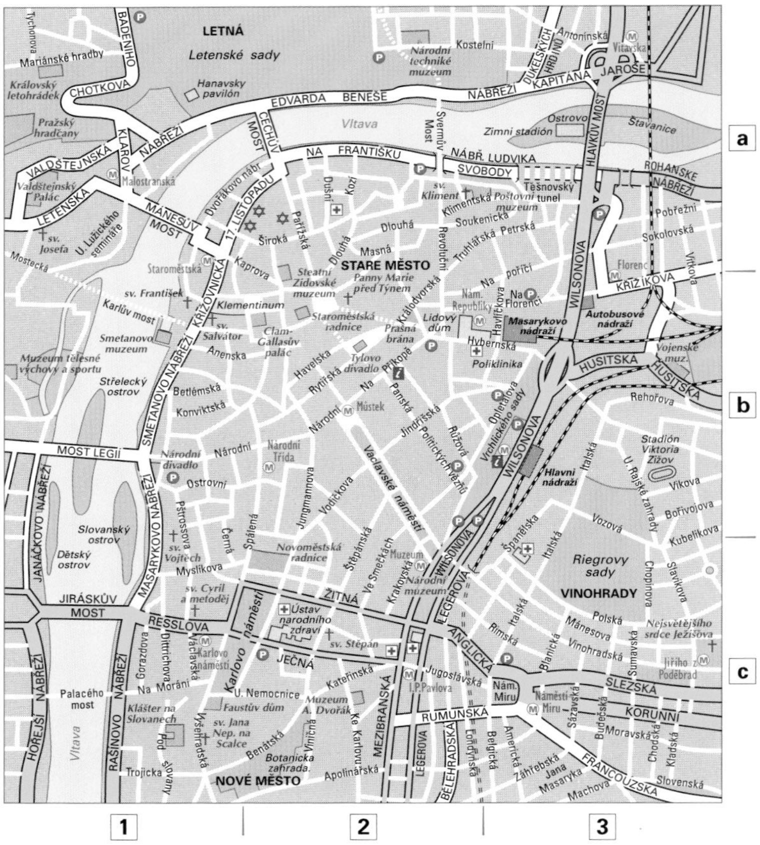

RIO DE JANEIRO

0 km 5
0 miles 3

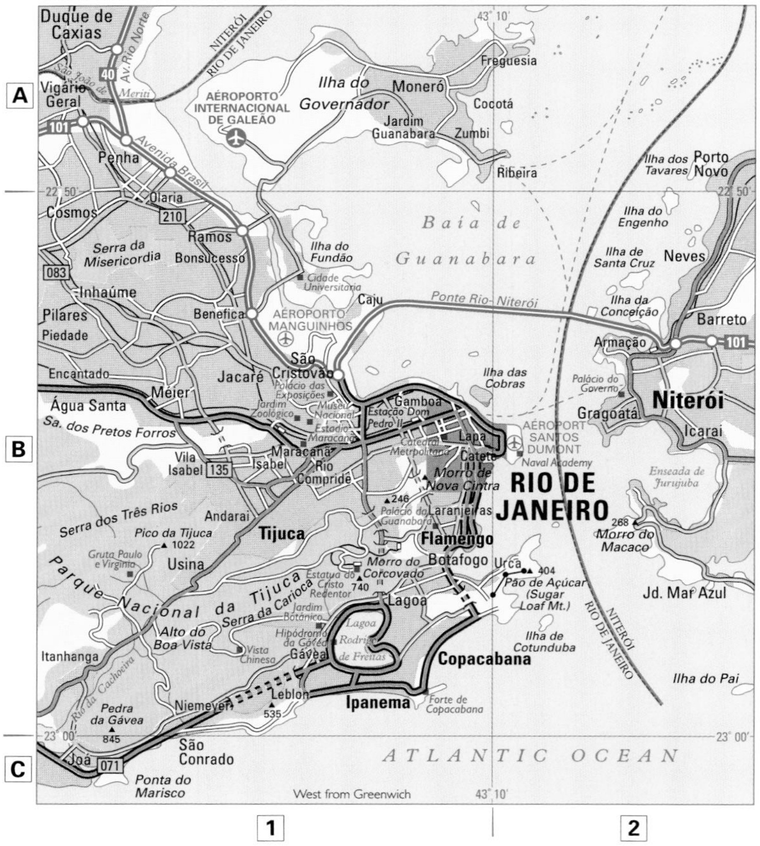

CENTRAL RIO DE JANEIRO

0 km 0.5
0 miles 0.25

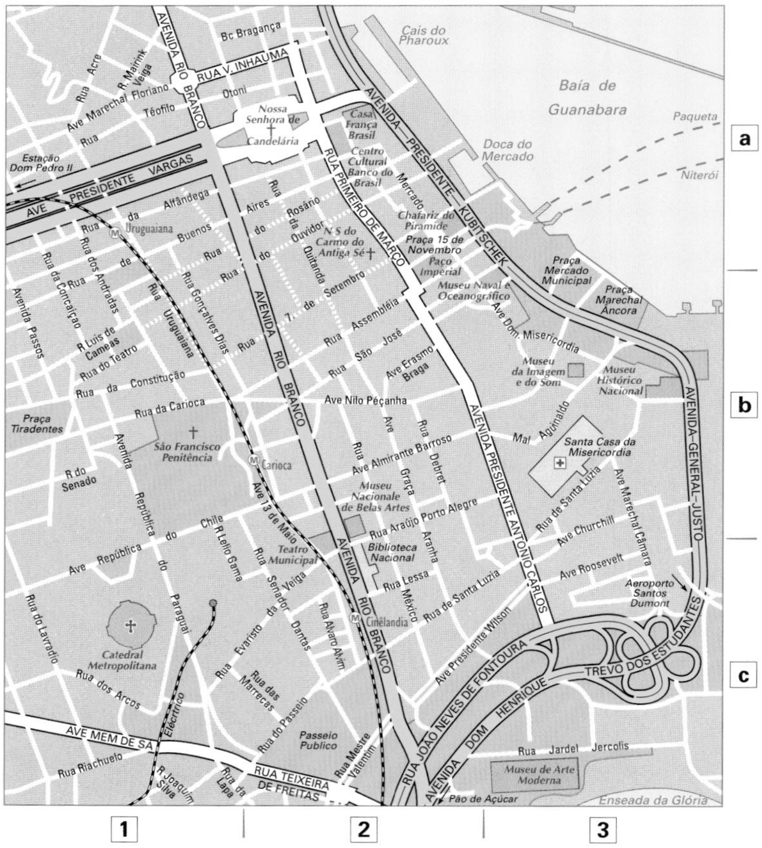

ROME

0 km 5
0 miles 3

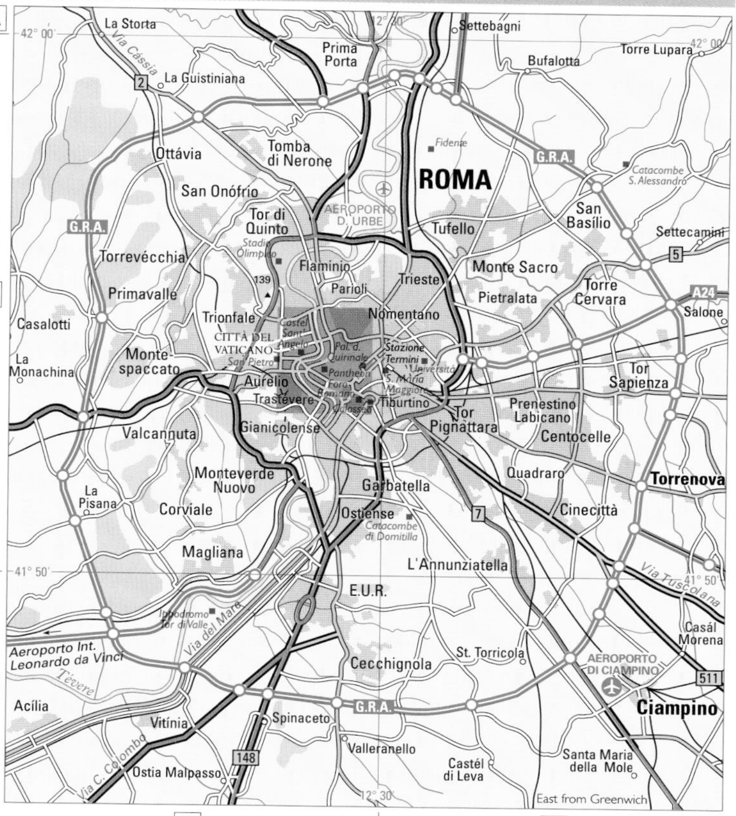

CENTRAL ROME

0 km 1
0 miles 0.5

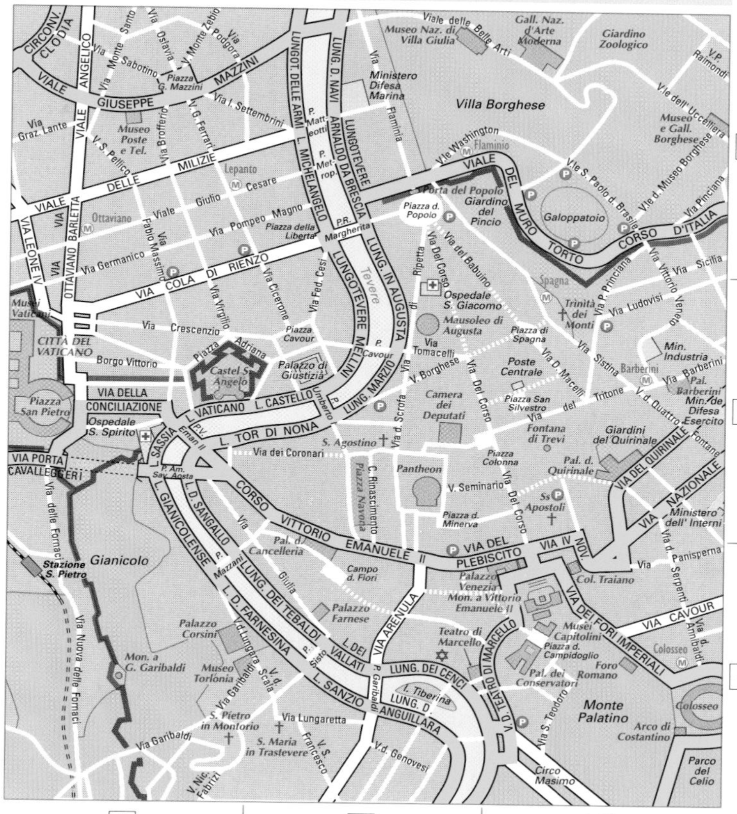

SAN FRANCISCO

0 km 5
0 miles 3

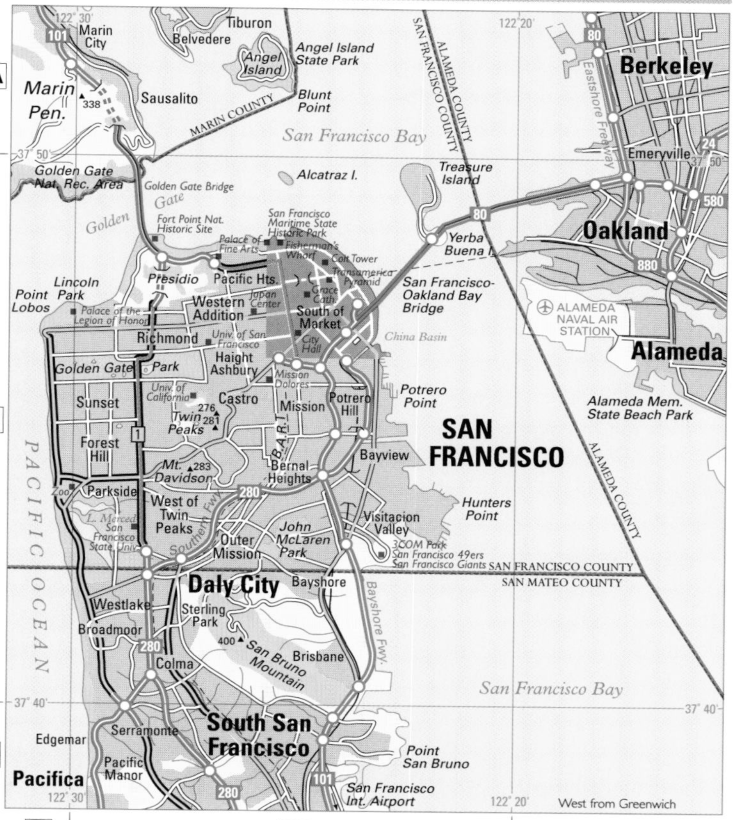

CENTRAL SAN FRANCISCO

0 km 0.25
0 miles 0.125

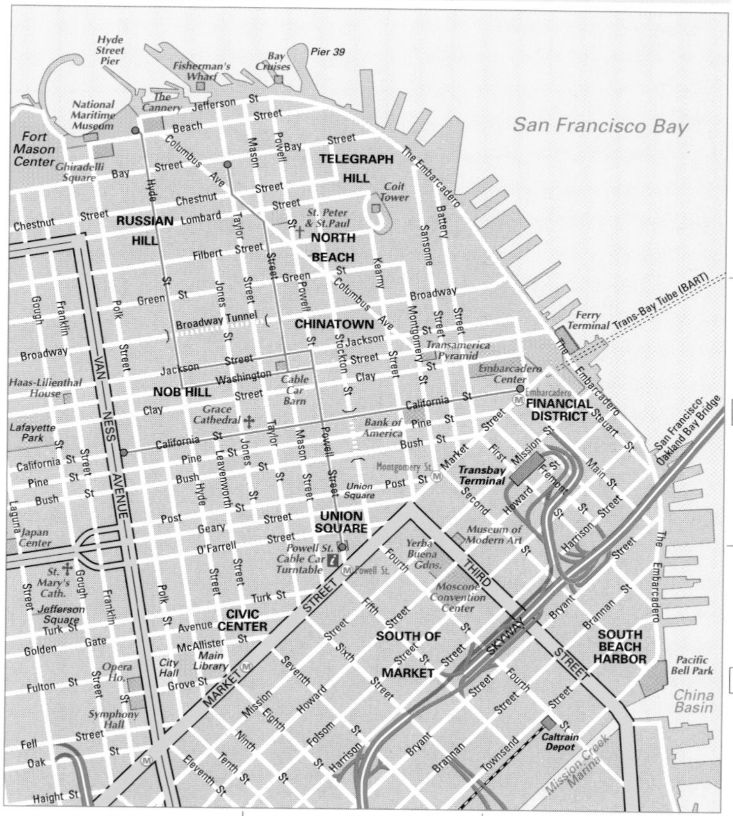

ST. PETERSBURG

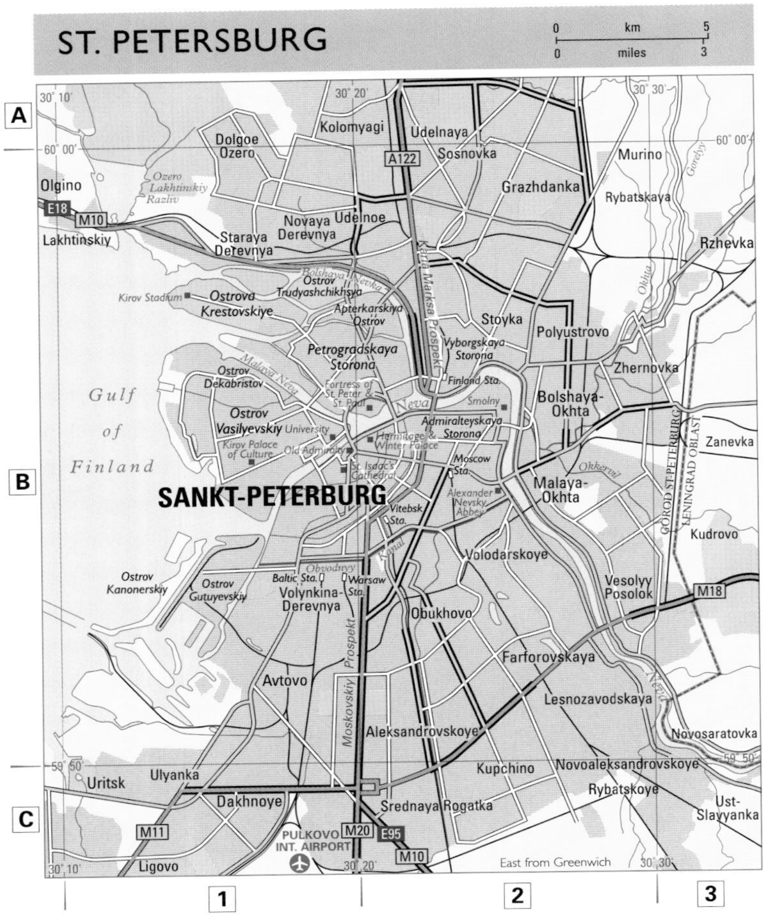

SANTIAGO

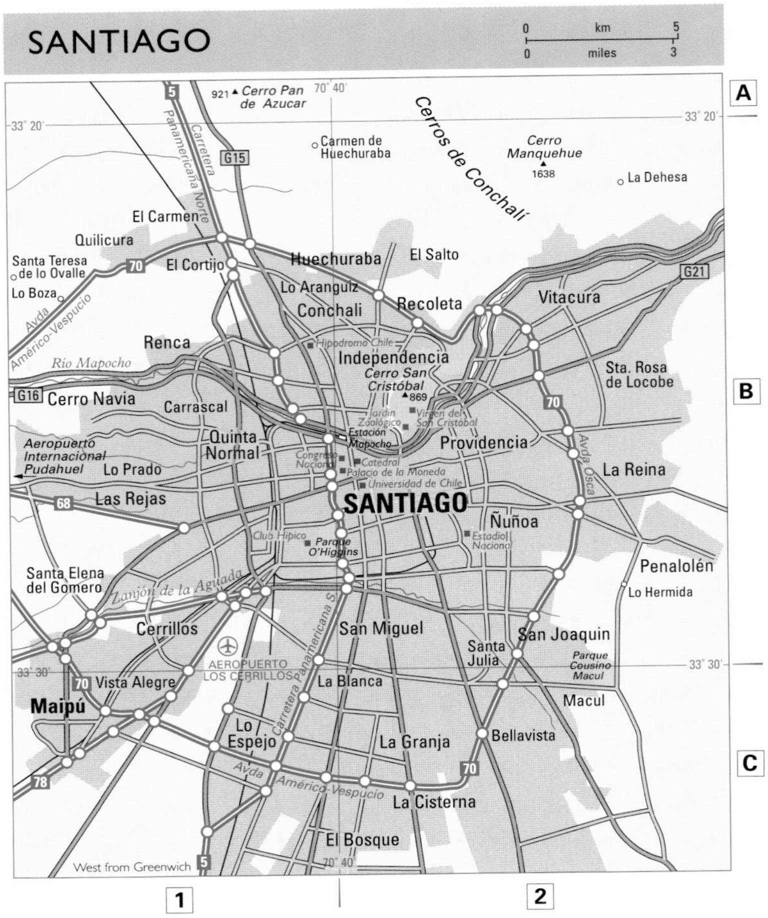

SÃO PAULO

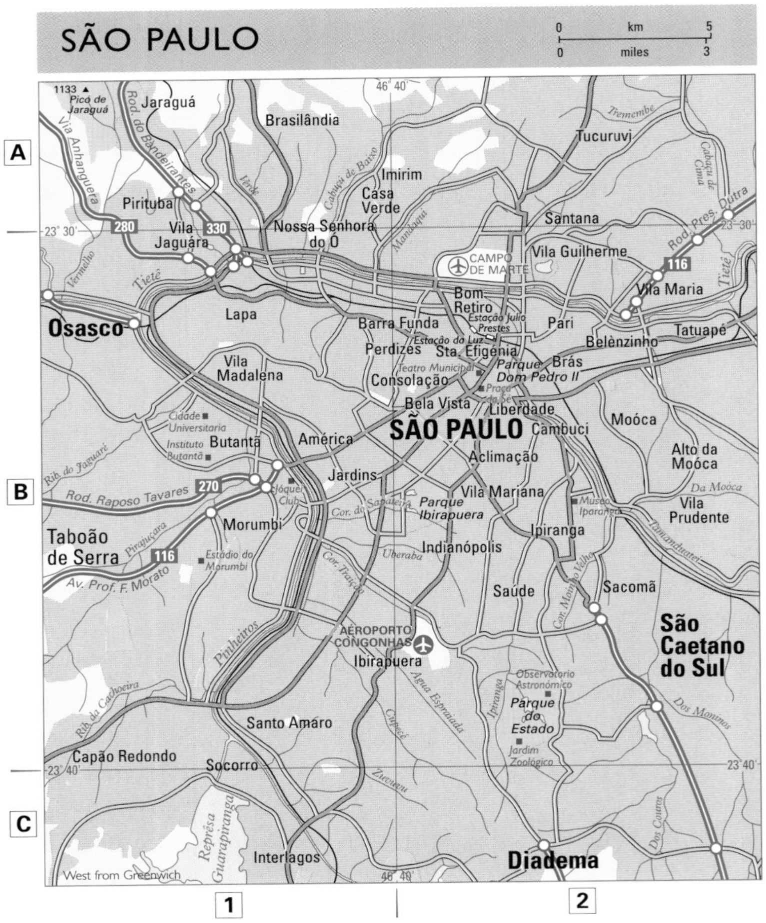

SEOUL

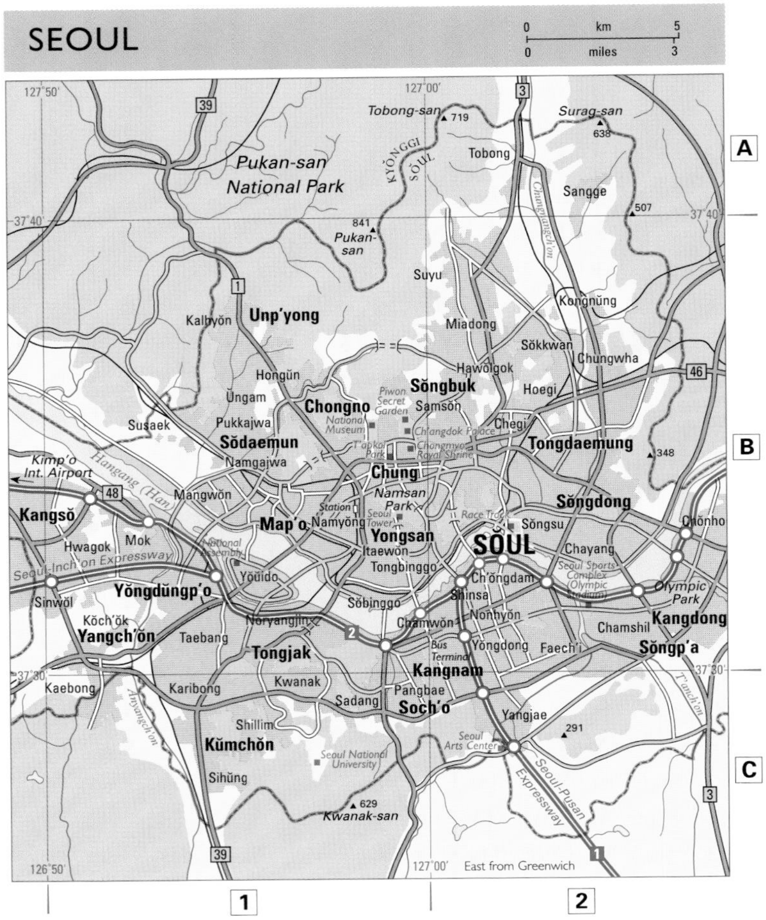

SHANGHAI

0 km 5
0 miles 3

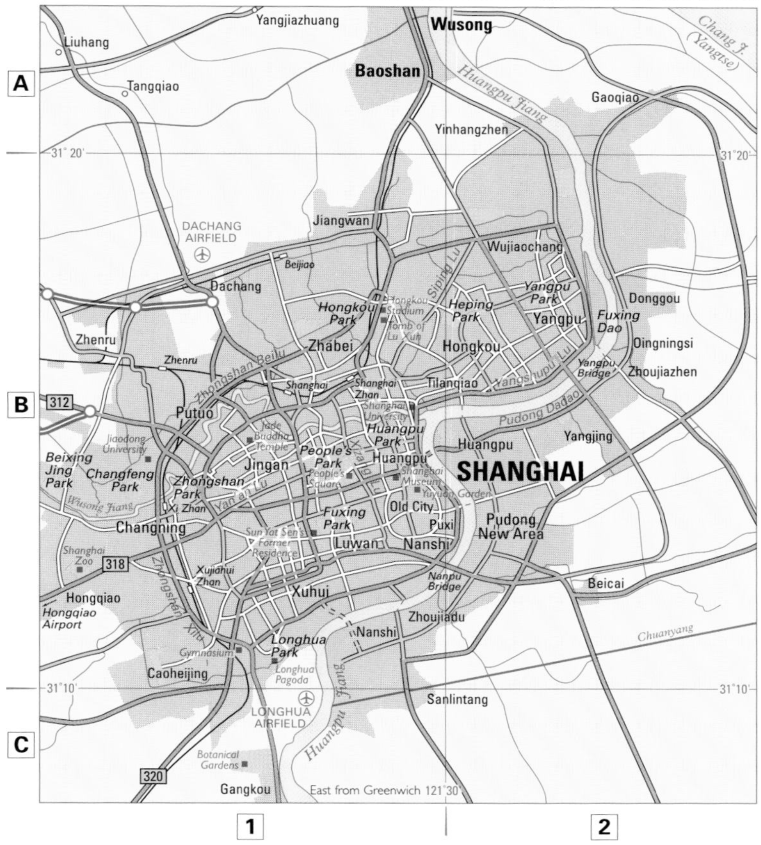
Yangjiazhuang
Wusong
Chang Jiang (Yangtse)
Liuhang
Tangqiao
Baoshan
Huangpu Jiang
Gaoqiao
Yinhangzhen
31°20'
Jiangwan
DACHANG AIRFIELD
Wujiaochang
Dachang
Beijiao
Hongkou Park
Hongkou Stadium
Tomb of Lu Xun
Heping Park
Yangpu Park
Yangpu
Fuxing Dao
Donggou
Zhenru
Zhabei
Hongkou
Qingningsi
Zhoujiazhen
Yangpu Bridge
Shanghai Zhan
Tilanqiao
Pudong Dadao
312
Putuo
Jade Buddha Temple
Shanghai University
Huangpu Park
Huangpu
Yangjing
Beixing Jing Park
Jiaodong University
Changfeng Park
Jingan
People's Park
People's Square
Shanghai Museum
Yuyuan Garden
SHANGHAI
Zhongshan Park
Xi Zhan
Old City
Puxi
Pudong New Area
Changning
Fuxing Park
Sun Yat Sen's Former Residence
Luwan
Nanshi
Shanghai Zoo
318
Xujiahui Zhan
Nanpu Bridge
Beicai
Hongqiao
Hongqiao Airport
Xuhui
Zhoujiadu
Longhua Park
Nanshi
Chuanyang
Gymnasium
Caoheijing
Longhua Pagoda
31°10'
LONGHUA AIRFIELD
Sanlintang
Botanical Gardens
320
Gangkou
East from Greenwich 121°30'
A
B
C
1
2

CENTRAL SINGAPORE

0 km 1
0 miles 0.5

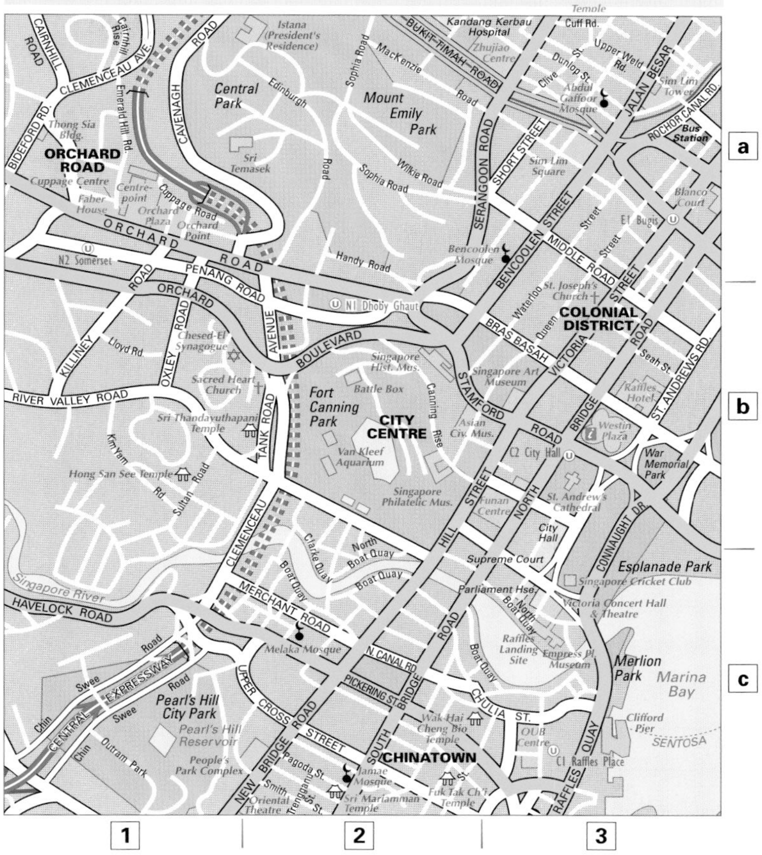
CAIRNHILL ROAD
Cairnhill Rise
Istana (President's Residence)
Kandang Kerbau Hospital
Cuff Rd.
BUKIT TIMAH ROAD
Zhujiao Centre
CLEMENCEAU AVE.
CAVENAGH ROAD
Central Park
Mount Emily Park
Upper Weld Rd
Abdul Gaffoor Mosque
JALAN BESAR
Sim Lim Tower
ROCHOR CANAL RD
Bus Station
BIDEFORD RD.
Thong Sia Bldg.
ORCHARD ROAD
Sri Temasek
SERANGOON ROAD
SHORT STREET
Sim Lim Square
Cuppage Centre
Centrepoint
Orchard Plaza
Orchard Point
Faber House
Sophia Road
Wilkie Road
Blanco Court
ORCHARD ROAD
Handy Road
Bencoolen Mosque
BENCOOLEN STREET
MIDDLE ROAD
N2 Somerset
PENANG ROAD
N1 Dhoby Ghaut
St. Joseph's Church
COLONIAL DISTRICT
ORCHARD ROAD
BOULEVARD
BRAS BASAH
VICTORIA
Chesed-El Synagogue
Singapore Hist. Mus.
Singapore Art Museum
KILLINEY ROAD
OXLEY ROAD
Lloyd Rd
Sacred Heart Church
Battle Box
Raffles Hotel
RIVER VALLEY ROAD
Fort Canning Park
CITY CENTRE
STAMFORD
Sri Thandavuthapani Temple
Asian Civ. Mus.
Westin Plaza
War Memorial Park
C2 City Hall
Van Kleef Aquarium
Hong San See Temple
Singapore Philatelic Mus.
Funan Centre
St. Andrew's Cathedral
TANK ROAD
City Hall
Supreme Court
Esplanade Park
HILL STREET
CONNAUGHT DR
CLEMENCEAU
Clarke Quay
North Boat Quay
Parliament Hse.
Singapore Cricket Club
Singapore River
Boat Quay
Victoria Concert Hall & Theatre
HAVELOCK ROAD
MERCHANT ROAD
Raffles Landing Site
Empress Pl. Museum
Melaka Mosque
Merlion Park
Marina Bay
CENTRAL EXPRESSWAY
N CANAL RD
Pearl's Hill City Park
PICKERING ST
Chulia St.
Pearl's Hill Reservoir
Wak Hai Cheng Bio Temple
OUB Centre
Clifford Pier
SENTOSA
People's Park Complex
Outram Park
UPPER CROSS STREET
SOUTH BRIDGE
CHINATOWN
C1 Raffles Place
NEW BRIDGE
Jamae Mosque
Sri Mariamman Temple
Fuk Tak Ch'i Temple
Oriental Theatre
RAFFLES QUAY
a
b
c
1
2
3

SINGAPORE

0 km 10
0 miles 6

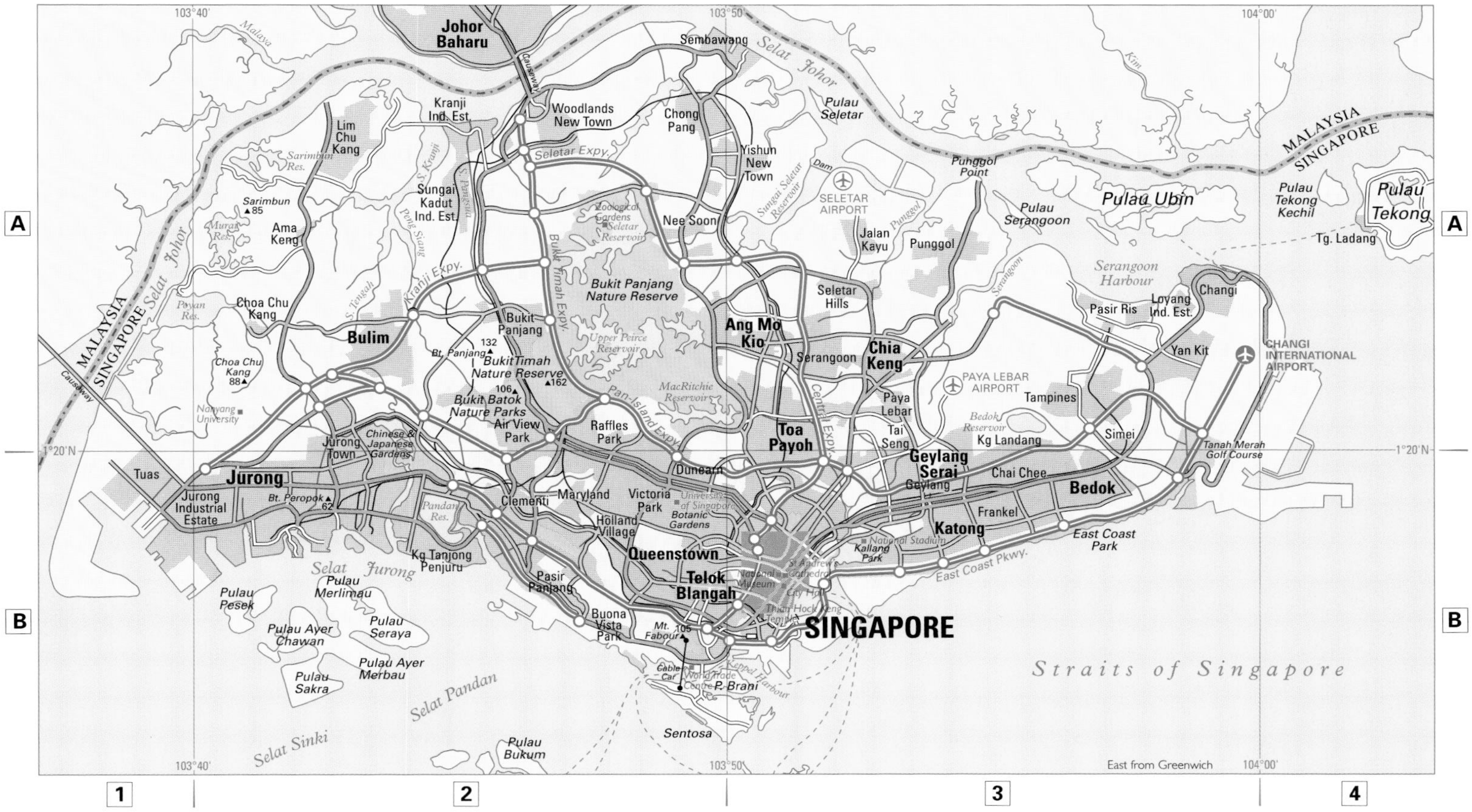
103°40'
103°50'
104°00'
Johor Baharu
Sembawang
Selat Johor
Causeway
Kranji Ind. Est.
Woodlands New Town
Chong Pang
Pulau Seletar
Lim Chu Kang
Sarimbun Res.
Seletar Expy.
Yishun New Town
Punggol Point
MALAYSIA SINGAPORE
Sarimbun 85
Sungai Kadut Ind. Est.
Zoological Gardens
Seletar Reservoir
Nee Soon
SELETAR AIRPORT
Pulau Ubin
Pulau Serangoon
Pulau Tekong Kechil
Pulau Tekong
Ama Keng
Murai Res.
Jalan Kayu
Punggol
Tg. Ladang
Bukit Timah Expy.
Kranji Expy.
Bukit Panjang Nature Reserve
Serangoon Harbour
Seletar Hills
Pasir Ris
Loyang Ind. Est.
Changi
Poyan Res.
Choa Chu Kang
Bukit Panjang
Upper Peirce Reservoir
Ang Mo Kio
Serangoon
Chia Keng
Yan Kit
CHANGI INTERNATIONAL AIRPORT
Bulim
132
Bt. Panjang
Bukit Timah Nature Reserve
162
Choa Chu Kang 88
106
Bukit Batok Nature Parks
MacRitchie Reservoir
PAYA LEBAR AIRPORT
Paya Lebar
Tampines
Nanyang University
Air View Park
Pan-Island Expy.
Raffles Park
Toa Payoh
Bedok Reservoir
Kg Landang
Simei
Jurong Town
Chinese & Japanese Gardens
Tai Seng
Tanah Merah Golf Course
1°20'N
Tuas
Jurong
Dunearn
Geylang Serai
Geylang
Chai Chee
Bedok
Jurong Industrial Estate
Bt. Peropok 62
Clementi
Maryland
Victoria Park
University of Singapore
Botanic Gardens
Frankel
Pandan Res.
Holland Village
Katong
East Coast Park
National Stadium
Kallang Park
Kg Tanjong Penjuru
Queenstown
Selat Jurong
Pasir Panjang
Telok Blangah
East Coast Pkwy.
Pulau Pesek
Pulau Merlimau
National Museum
St. Andrew's Cathedral
City Hall
Thian Hock Keng Temple
Pulau Ayer Chawan
Pulau Seraya
Buona Vista Park
Mt. Faber 105
SINGAPORE
Pulau Ayer Merbau
Straits of Singapore
Pulau Sakra
Cable Car
World Trade Centre
P. Brani
Keppel Harbour
Selat Pandan
Sentosa
Selat Sinki
Pulau Bukum
East from Greenwich
A
B
1
2
3
4

STOCKHOLM

0 km 5
0 miles 3

CENTRAL STOCKHOLM

0 km 0.5
0 miles 0.25

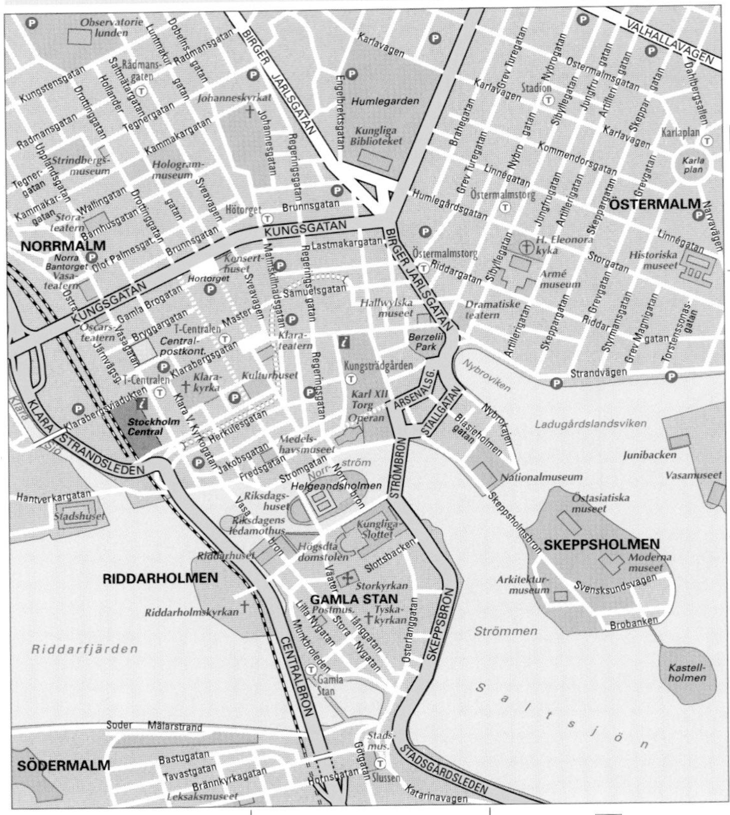

SYDNEY

0 km 5
0 miles 3

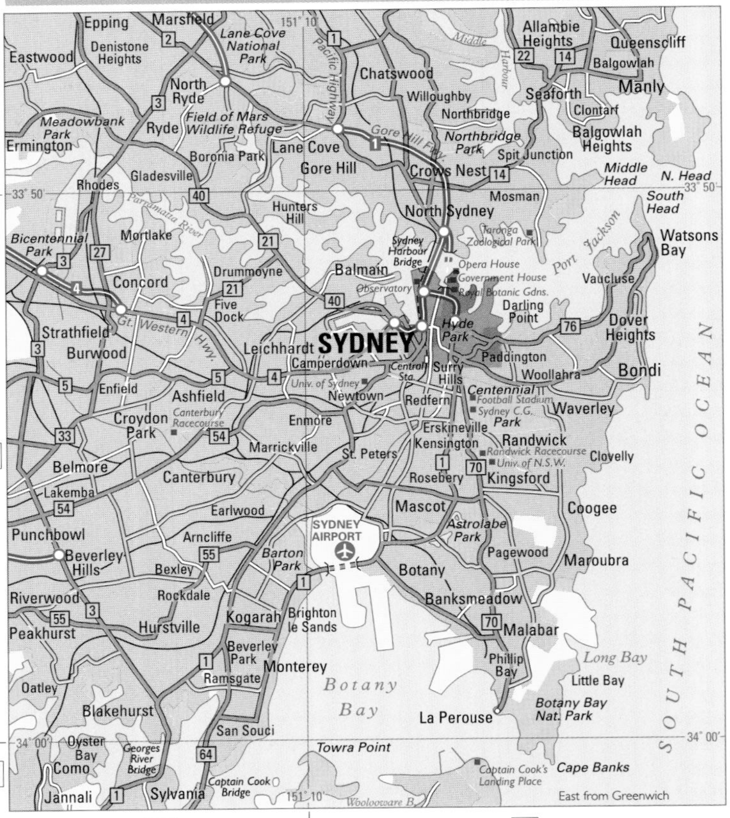

CENTRAL SYDNEY

0 km 2
0 miles 1

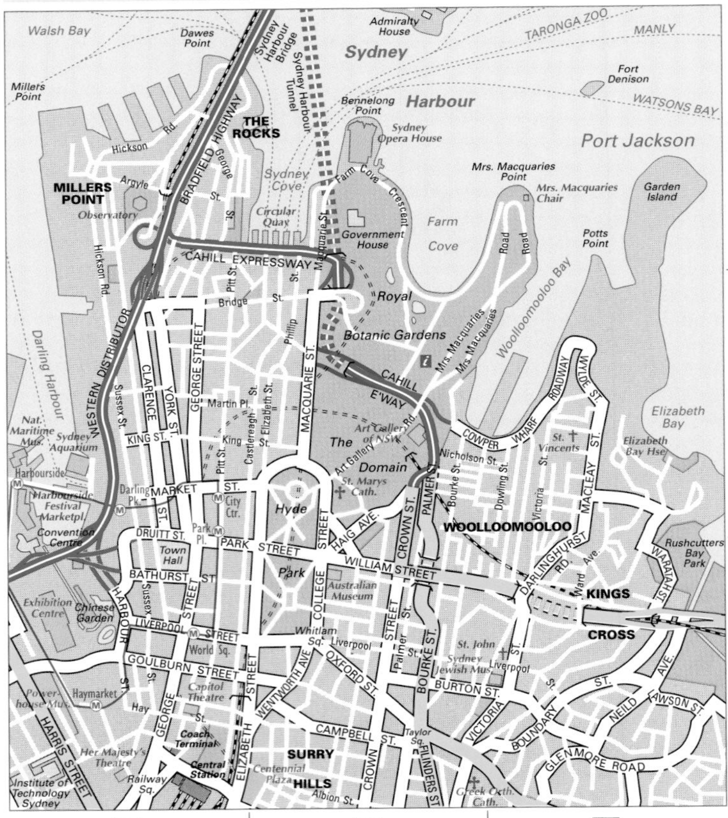

COPYRIGHT GEORGE PHILIP LTD

TOKYO

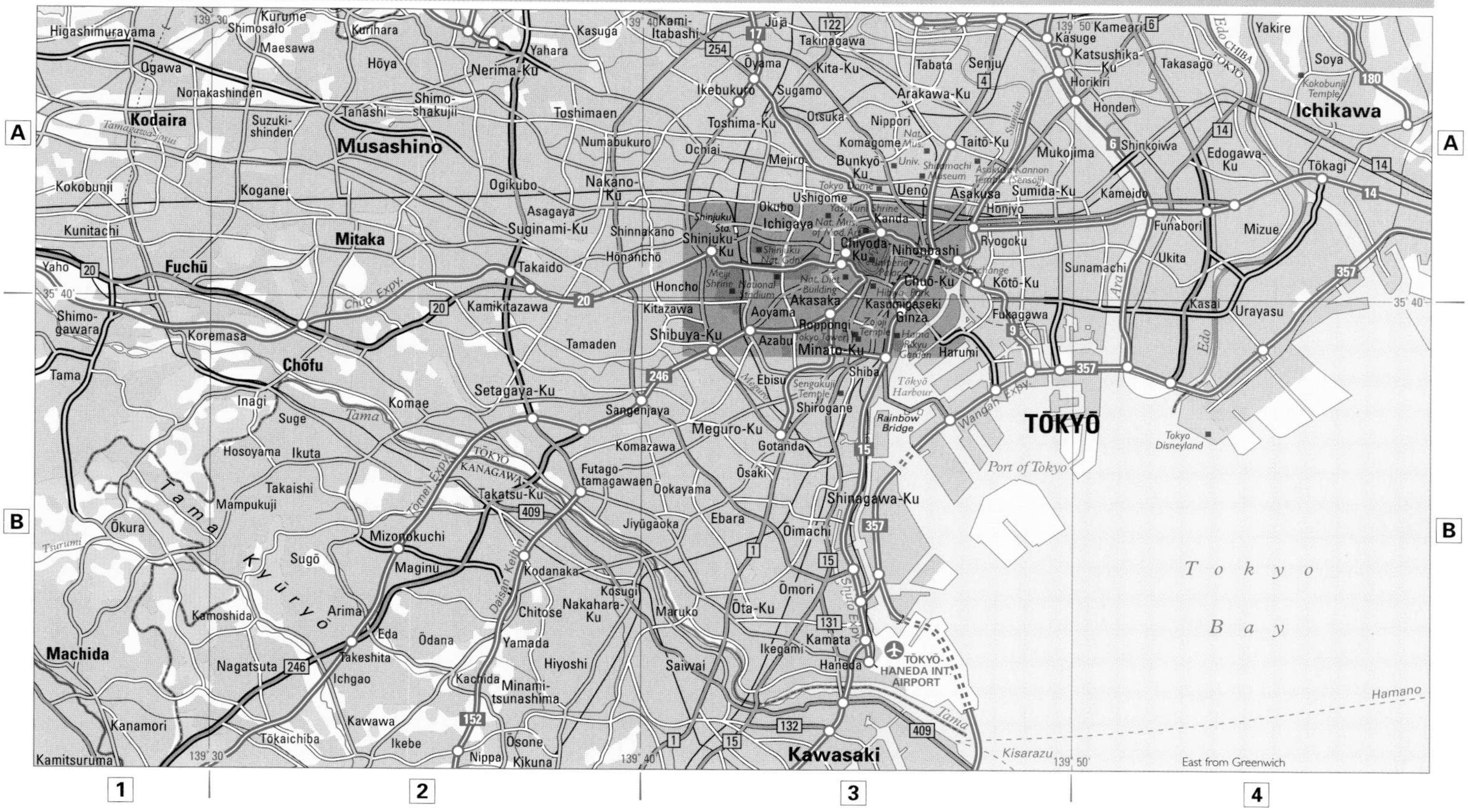

CENTRAL TOKYO

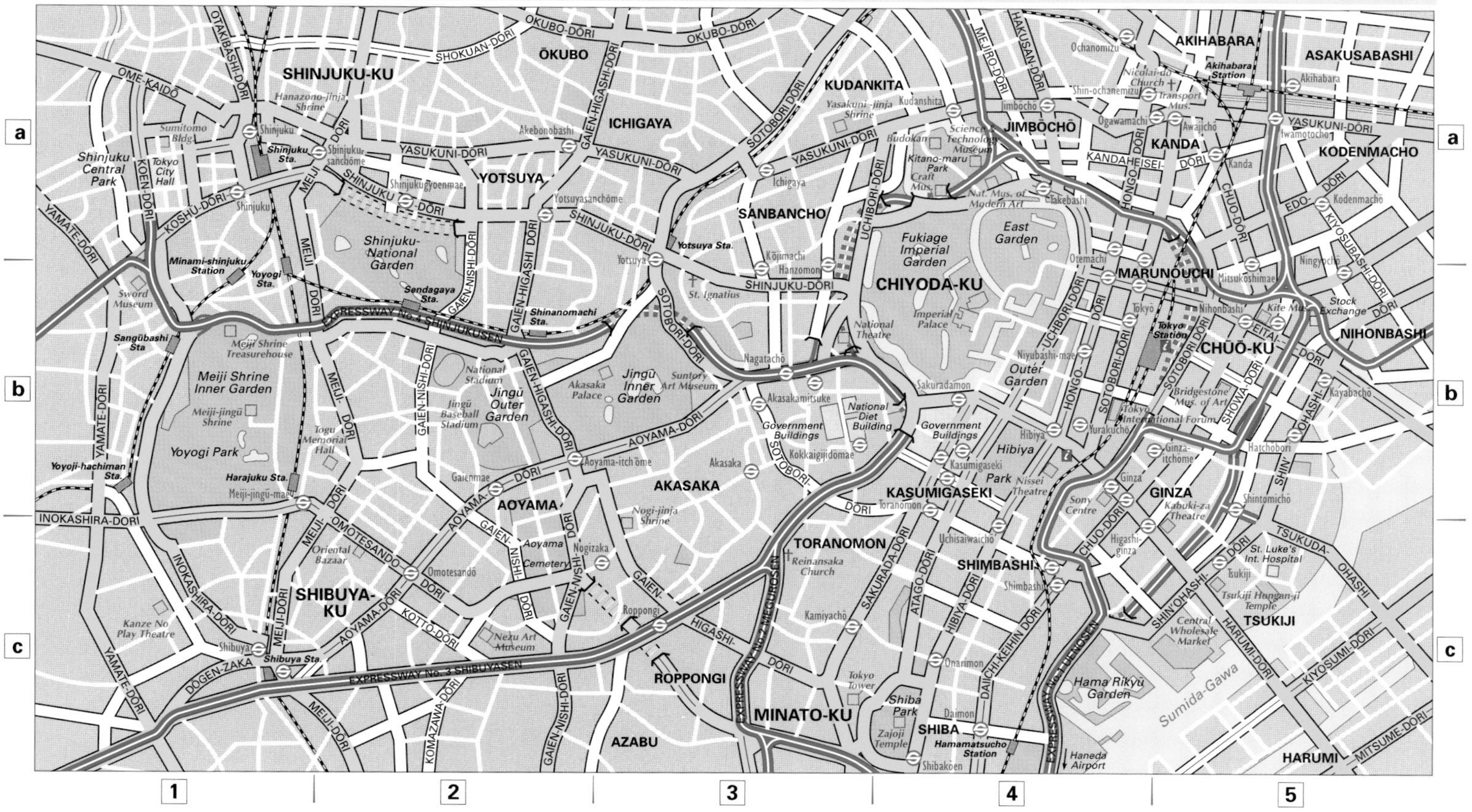

COPYRIGHT GEORGE PHILIP LTD

TEHRAN

0 km 5
0 miles 3

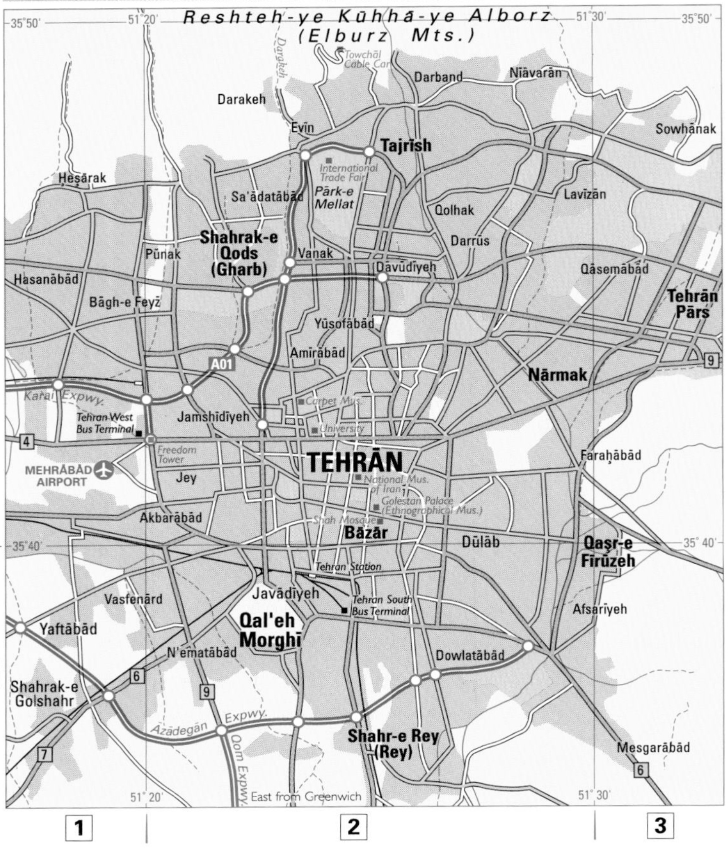

TIANJIN

0 km 5
0 miles 3

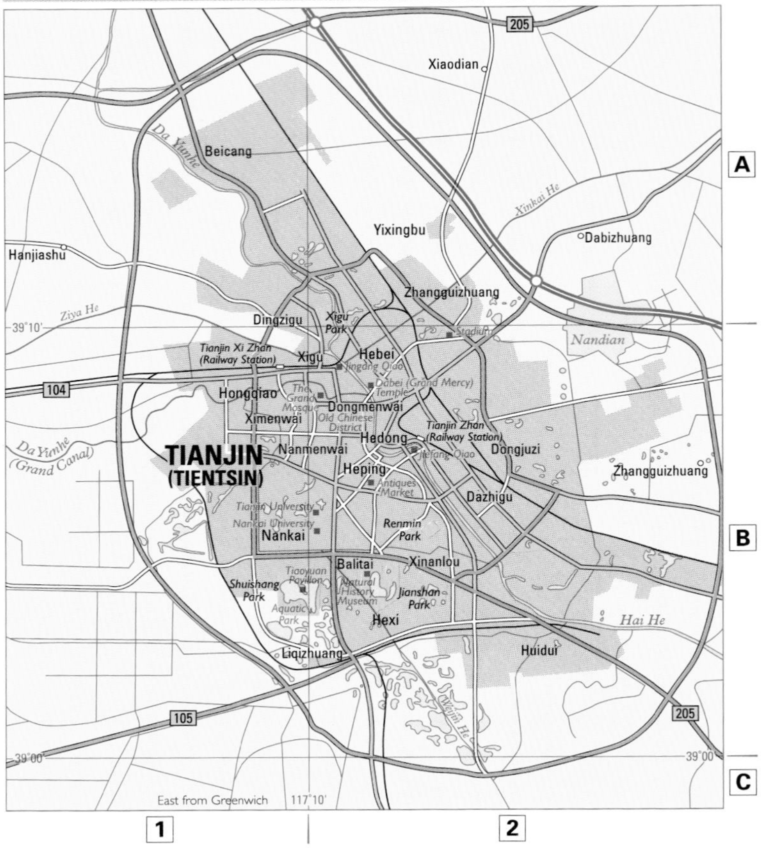

TORONTO

0 km 5
0 miles 3

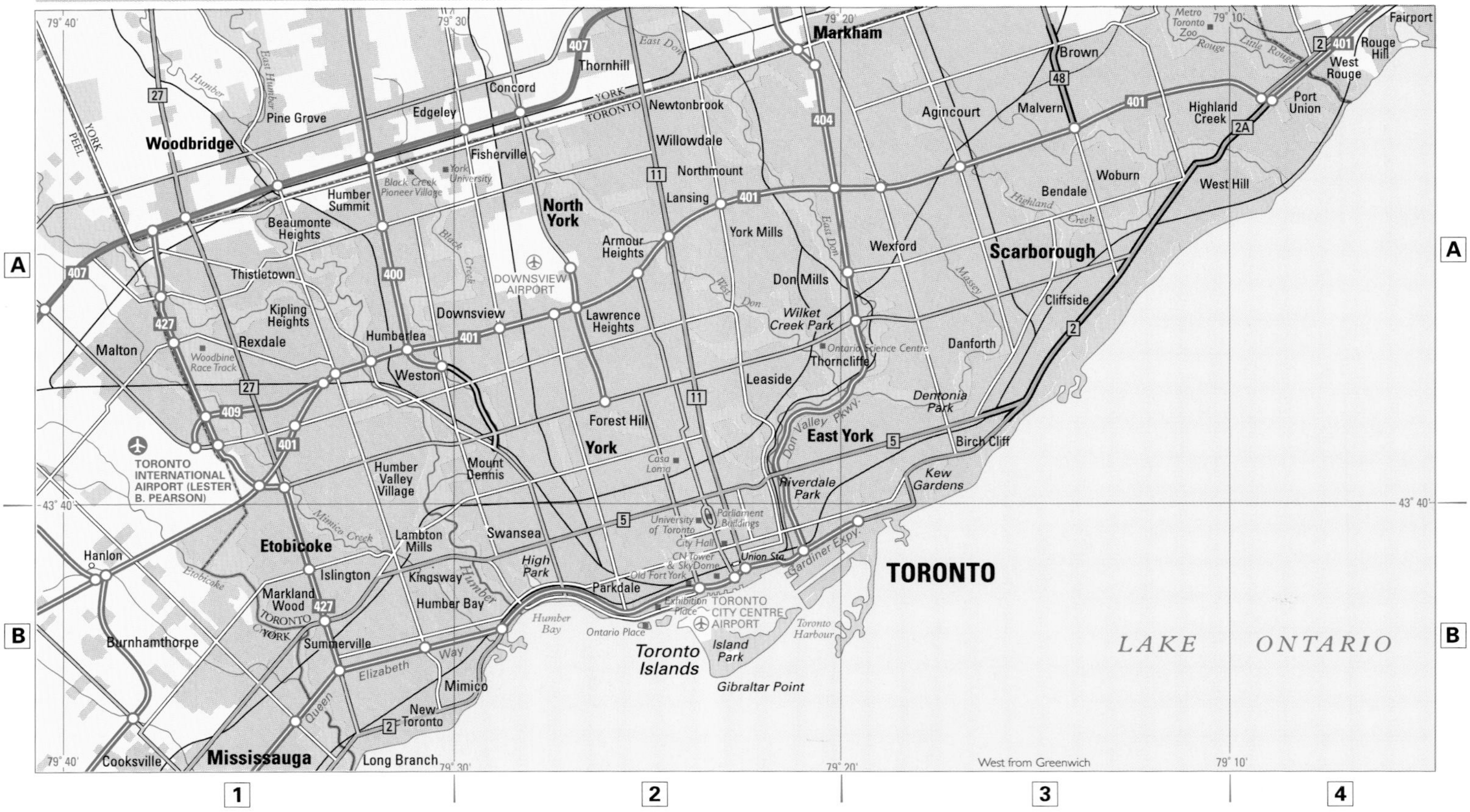

VIENNA

0 km 5
0 miles 3

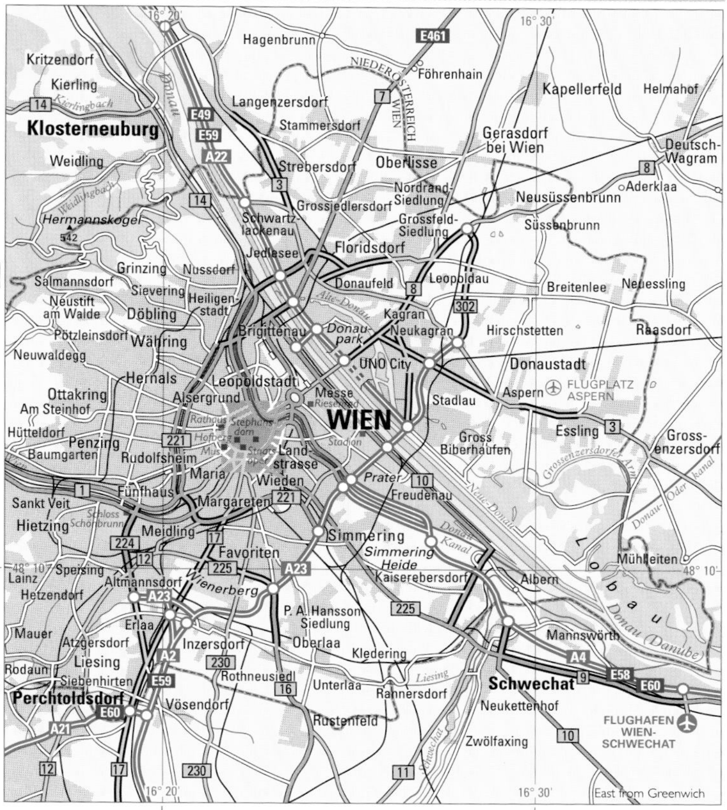

CENTRAL VIENNA

0 km 0.5
0 miles 0.25

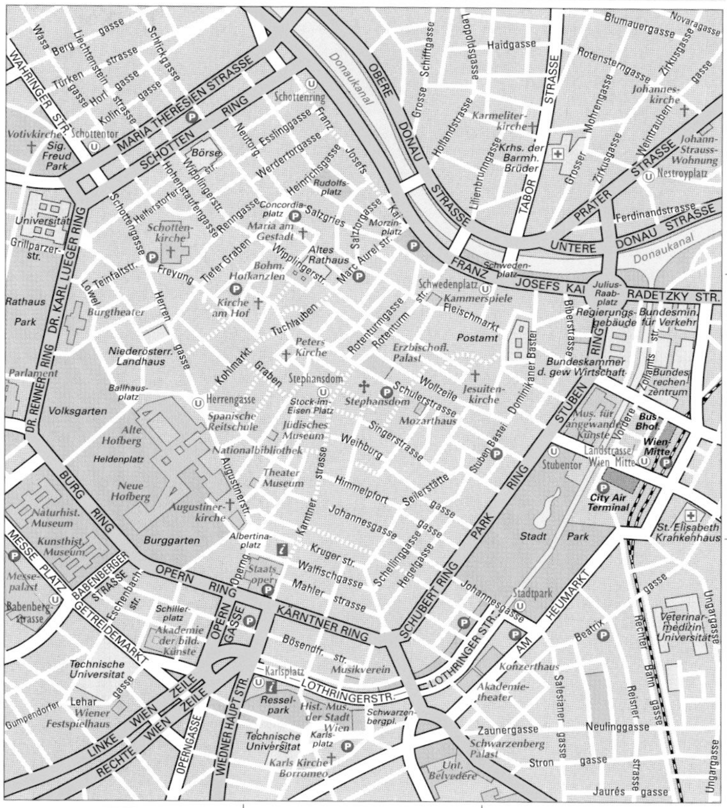

WARSAW

0 km 5
0 miles 3

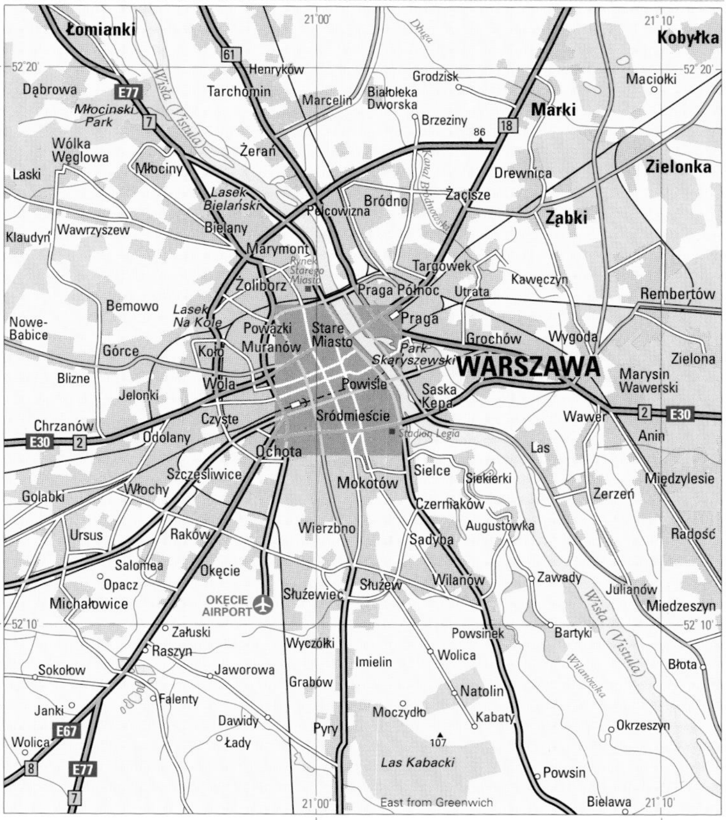

CENTRAL WARSAW

0 km 2
0 miles 1

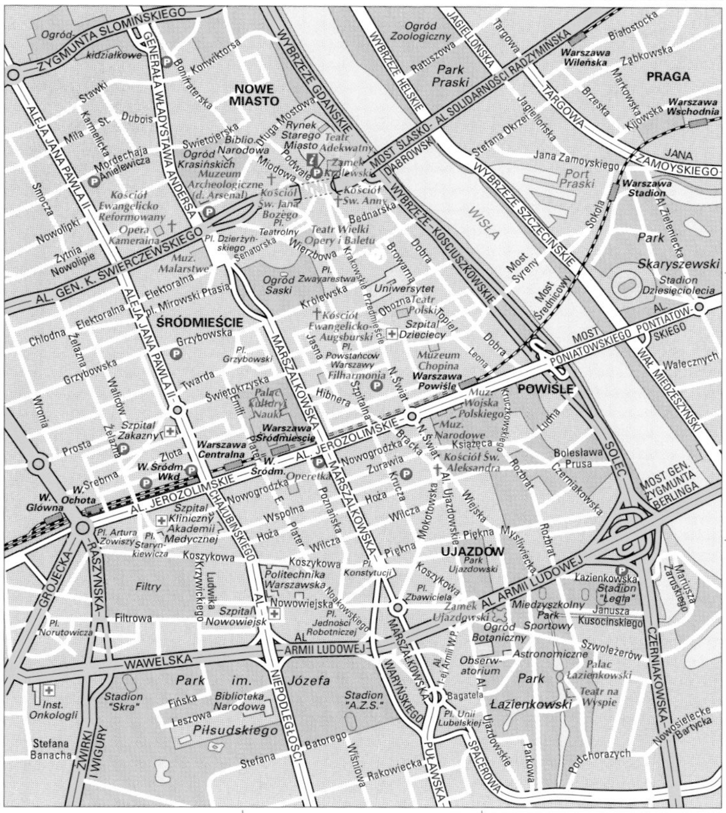

WASHINGTON

0 km 5
0 miles 3

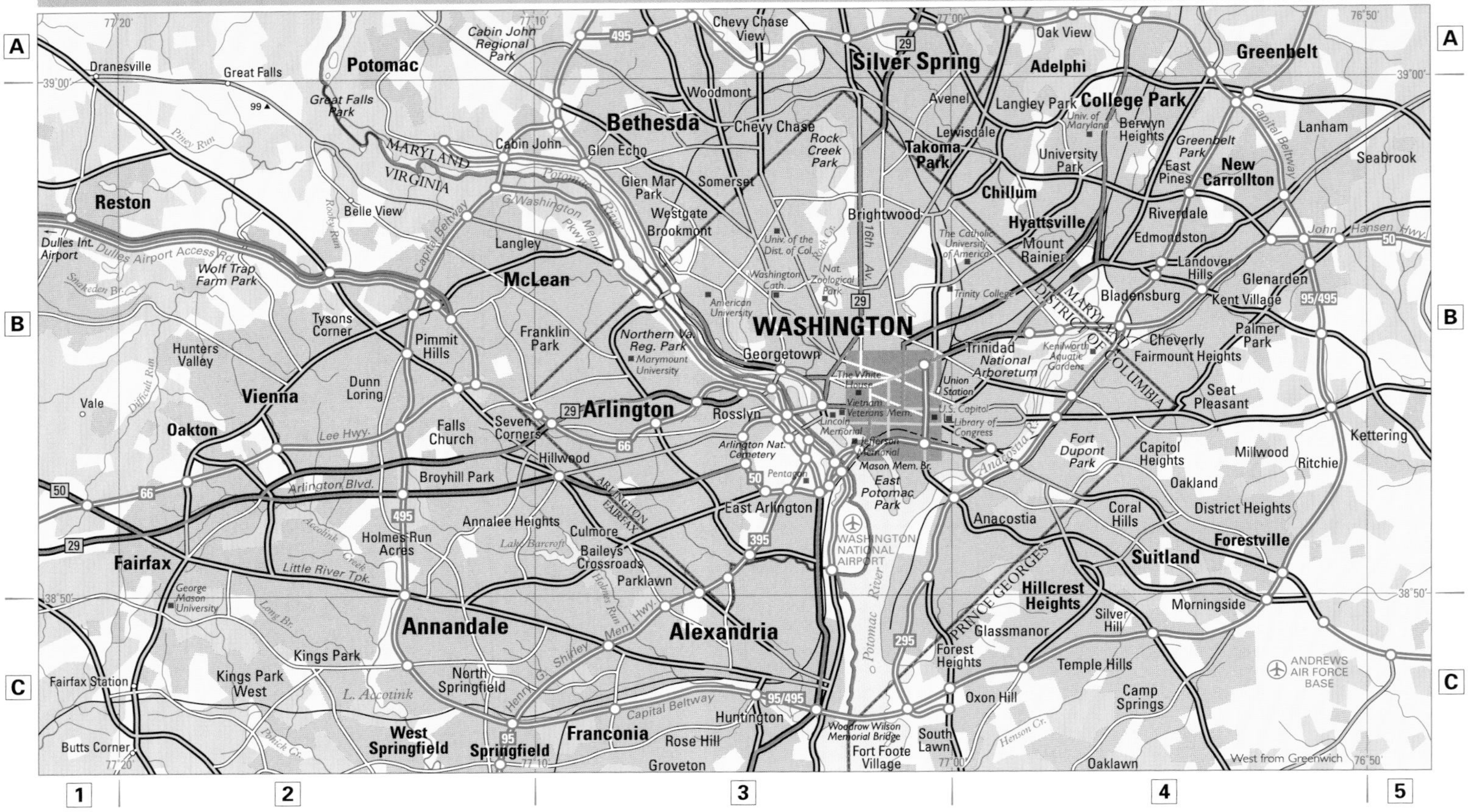

CENTRAL WASHINGTON

0 km 1
0 miles 0.5

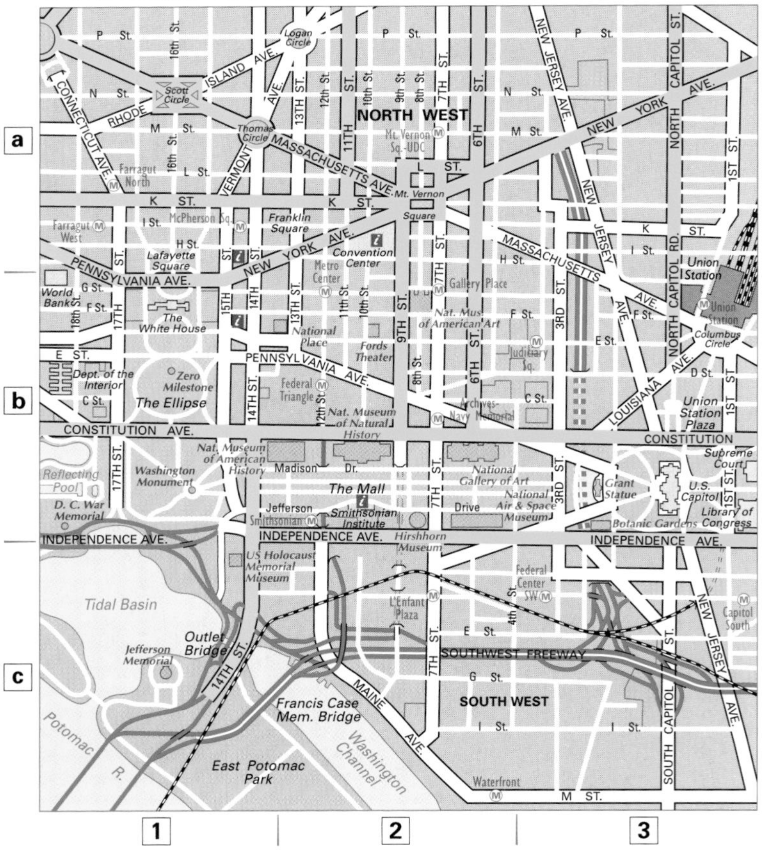

WELLINGTON

0 km 5
0 miles 3

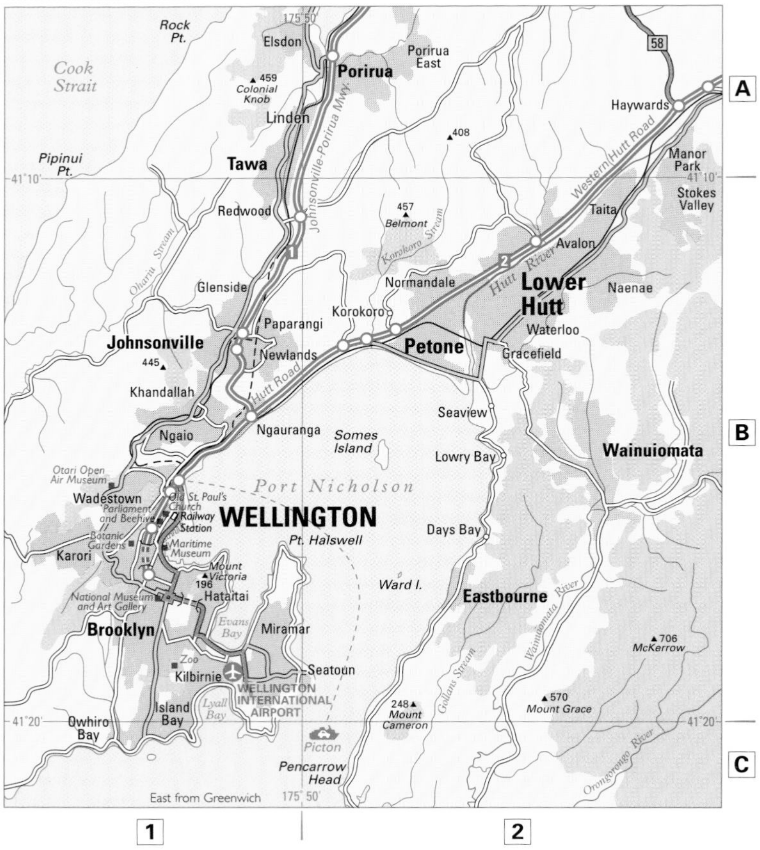

INDEX TO CITY MAPS

The index contains the names of all the principal places and features shown on the City Maps. Each name is followed by an additional entry in italics giving the name of the City Map within which it is located.

The number in bold type which follows each name refers to the number of the City Map page where that feature or place will be found.

The letter and figure which are immediately after the page number give the grid square on the map within which the feature or place is situated. The letter represents the latitude and the figure the longitude. Upper case letters refer to the City Maps, lower case letters to the Central Area Maps. The full geographic reference is provided in the border of the City Maps.

The location given is the centre of the city, suburb or feature and is not necessarily the name. Rivers, canals and roads are indexed to their name. Rivers carry the symbol → after their name.

An explanation of the alphabetical order rules and a list of the abbreviations used are to be found at the beginning of the World Map Index.

A

Aalām, *Baghdad* **3** B2
Aalsmeer, *Amsterdam* **2** B1
Abbey Wood, *London* **15** B4
Abcoude, *Amsterdam* **2** B2
Âbdin, *Cairo* **7** A2
Abeno, *Osaka* **22** B4
Aberdeen, *Hong Kong* **12** B2
Aberdour, *Edinburgh* **11** A2
Aberdour Castle, *Edinburgh* **11** A2
Abfanggraben →, *Munich* **20** A3
Ablon-sur-Seine, *Paris* **23** B3
Abord-à-Plouffe, *Montreal* **19** A1
Abramtsevo, *Moscow* **19** B4
Abu Dis, *Jerusalem* **13** B2
Abû en Numrus, *Cairo* **7** B2
Abu Ghosh, *Jerusalem* **13** B1
Acacias, *Madrid* **17** c2
Acassuso, *Buenos Aires* **7** A1
Accotink Cr. →, *Washington* **32** B2
Acheres, *Paris* **23** A1
Acília, *Rome* **25** C1
Aclimação, *São Paulo* **26** B2
Acton, *London* **15** A2
Açúcar, Pão de, *Rio de Janeiro* **24** B2
Ada Beja, *Lisbon* **14** A1
Adams Park, *Atlanta* **3** B2
Adams Shore, *Boston* **6** B4
Addiscombe, *London* **15** B3
Adelphi, *Washington* **32** A4
Aderklaa, *Vienna* **31** A3
Admiralteyskaya Storona, *St. Petersburg* **26** B2
Áffori, *Milan* **18** A2
Aflandshage, *Copenhagen* **10** B3
Afsarīyeh, *Tehran* **30** B2
Agboyi Cr. →, *Lagos* **14** A2
Ågerup, *Copenhagen* **10** A1
Ågesta, *Stockholm* **28** B2
Agincourt, *Toronto* **30** A3
Agora, Arhéa, *Athens* **2** c1
Agra Canal, *Delhi* **10** B2
Agricola Oriental, *Mexico City* **18** B2
Agua Espraiada →, *São Paulo* **26** B2
Agualva-Cacem, *Lisbon* **14** A1
Agustino, Cerro El, *Lima* **16** B2
Ahrensfelde, *Berlin* **5** A4
Ahuntsic, *Montreal* **19** A1
Ai →, *Osaka* **22** A4
Aigremont, *Paris* **23** A1
Air View Park, *Singapore* **27** A2
Airport West, *Melbourne* **17** A1
Aiyaleo, *Athens* **2** B2
Aiyáleos, Óros, *Athens* **2** B1
Ajegunle, *Lagos* **14** B2
Aji, *Osaka* **22** A3
Ajuda, *Lisbon* **14** A1
Akalla, *Stockholm* **28** A1
Akasaka, *Tokyo* **29** b3
Akbarābād, *Tehran* **30** A2
Akershus Slott, *Oslo* **22** A3
Akihabara, *Tokyo* **29** a5
Akrópolis, *Athens* **2** c2
Al 'Azamiyah, *Baghdad* **3** A2
Al Quds = Jerusalem, *Jerusalem* **13** B2
Alaguntan, *Lagos* **14** B2
Alameda, *San Francisco* **25** B3
Alameda, Parque, *Mexico City* **18** b2
Alameda Memorial State Beach Park, *San Francisco* **25** B3
Albern, *Vienna* **31** B2
Albert Park, *Melbourne* **17** B1
Alberton, *Johannesburg* **13** B2
Albertslund, *Copenhagen* **10** B2
Albysjön, *Stockholm* **28** B1
Alcantara, *Lisbon* **14** A1
Alcatraz I., *San Francisco* **25** B2
Alcobendas, *Madrid* **17** A2
Alcorcón, *Madrid* **17** B1
Aldershof, *Berlin* **5** B4
Aldo Bonzi, *Buenos Aires* **7** C1
Aleksandrovskoye, *St. Petersburg* **26** B2
Alexander Nevsky Abbey, *St. Petersburg* **26** B2
Alexander Soutzos Moussío, *Athens* **2** b3
Alexandra, *Johannesburg* **13** A2
Alexandra, *Singapore* **27** B2
Alexandria, *Washington* **32** C3
Alfama, *Lisbon* **14** c3
Alfortville, *Paris* **23** B3
Algés, *Lisbon* **14** A1
Alhambra, *Los Angeles* **16** B4
Alibey →, *Istanbul* **12** B1
Alibey Barajı, *Istanbul* **12** B1
Alibeyköy, *Istanbul* **12** B1
Alimos, *Athens* **2** B2
Alipur, *Calcutta* **8** B1
Allach, *Munich* **20** A1
Allambie Heights, *Sydney* **28** A2
Allard Pierson Museum, *Amsterdam* **2** b2
Allermuir Hill, *Edinburgh* **11** B2
Allerton, Pt., *Boston* **6** B4
Allston, *Boston* **6** A3
Almada, *Lisbon* **14** A2
Almagro, *Buenos Aires* **7** B2
Almargem do Bispo, *Lisbon* **14** A1
Almazovo, *Moscow* **19** A6
Almirante G. Brown, Parque, *Buenos Aires* **7** C2
Almon, *Jerusalem* **13** B2
Almond →, *Edinburgh* **11** B2
Alnabru, *Oslo* **22** A4
Alnsjøen, *Oslo* **22** A4
Alperton, *London* **15** A2
Alpine, *New York* **21** A2
Alrode, *Johannesburg* **13** B2
Alsemerg, *Brussels* **6** B1
Alsergrund, *Vienna* **31** A2
Alsip, *Chicago* **9** C2
Ålsten, *Stockholm* **28** B1
Älta, *Stockholm* **28** B3
Altadena, *Los Angeles* **16** A4
Alte-Donau →, *Vienna* **31** A2
Alte Hofburg, *Vienna* **31** b1
Alter Finkenkrug, *Berlin* **5** A1
Altes Rathaus, *Munich* **20** b3
Altglienicke, *Berlin* **5** B4
Altlandsberg, *Berlin* **5** A5
Altlandsberg Nord, *Berlin* **5** A5
Altmannsdorf, *Vienna* **31** B1
Alto da Moóca, *São Paulo* **26** B2
Alto do Pina, *Lisbon* **14** A2
Altona, *Melbourne* **17** B1
Alvaro Obregon, *Mexico City* **18** B1
Alvik, *Stockholm* **28** B1
Älvsjo, *Stockholm* **28** B2
Älvvik, *Stockholm* **28** A3
Am Hasenbergl, *Munich* **20** A2
Am Steinhof, *Vienna* **31** A1
Am Wald, *Munich* **20** B2
Ama Keng, *Singapore* **27** A2
Amadora, *Lisbon* **14** A1
Amagasaki, *Osaka* **22** A3
Amager, *Copenhagen* **10** B3
Amāl Qādisiya, *Baghdad* **3** B2
Amalienborg, *Copenhagen* **10** b3
Amata, *Milan* **18** A1
Ameixoeira, *Lisbon* **14** A2
América, *São Paulo* **26** B1
Amin, *Baghdad* **3** B2
Aminadov, *Jerusalem* **13** B1
Aminyevo, *Moscow* **19** B2
Amīrābād, *Tehran* **30** A2
Amora, *Lisbon* **14** B2
Amoreira, *Lisbon* **14** A1
Ampelokipi, *Athens* **2** B2
Amper →, *Munich* **20** A1
Amstel, *Amsterdam* **2** b2
Amstel →, *Amsterdam* **2** c2
Amstel-Drecht-Kanaal, *Amsterdam* **2** B2
Amstel Station, *Amsterdam* **2** c3
Amstelhof, *Amsterdam* **2** b2
Amstelveen, *Amsterdam* **2** B2
Amsterdam, *Amsterdam* **2** A2
Amsterdam-Rijnkanaal, *Amsterdam* **2** B3
Amsterdam Zoo, *Amsterdam* **2** b3
Amsterdam Zuidoost, *Amsterdam* **2** B2
Amsterdamse Bos, *Amsterdam* **2** B1
Anacostia, *Washington* **32** B4
Anadoluhisarı, *Istanbul* **12** B2
Anadolukavağı, *Istanbul* **12** A2
Anata, *Jerusalem* **13** B2
Ancol, *Jakarta* **13** A1
'Andalus, *Baghdad* **3** B1
Andarai, *Rio de Janeiro* **24** B1
Anderlecht, *Brussels* **6** A1
Anderson Park, *Atlanta* **3** B2
Andingmen, *Beijing* **4** B2
Andrews Air Force Base, *Washington* **32** C4
Ang Mo Kio, *Singapore* **27** A3
Ängby, *Stockholm* **28** A1
Angel I., *San Francisco* **25** A2
Angel Island State Park, *San Francisco* **25** A2
Angke, Kali →, *Jakarta* **13** A1
Angyalföld, *Budapest* **7** A2
Anik, *Mumbai* **20** A2
Anin, *Warsaw* **31** B2
Anjou, *Montreal* **19** A2
Annalee Heights, *Washington* **32** B2
Annandale, *Washington* **32** C2
Anne Frankhuis, *Amsterdam* **2** a1
Antony, *Paris* **23** B2
Anyangch'on, *Seoul* **26** C1
Aoyama, *Tokyo* **29** b2
Ap Lei Chau, *Hong Kong* **12** B1
Apapa, *Lagos* **14** B2
Apelacão, *Lisbon* **14** A2
Apterkarskiy Ostrov, *St. Petersburg* **26** B2
Ar Kazimiyah, *Baghdad* **3** B1
Ara →, *Tokyo* **29** A4
Arakawa-Ku, *Tokyo* **29** A3
Arany-hegyi-patak →, *Budapest* **7** A2
Aravaca, *Madrid* **17** B1
Arbataash, *Baghdad* **3** A1
Arc de Triomphe, *Paris* **23** a2
Arcadia, *Los Angeles* **16** B4
Arceuil, *Paris* **23** B2
Arco Plaza, *Los Angeles* **16** b1
Arese, *Milan* **18** A1
Arganzuela, *Madrid* **17** B1
Argenteuil, *Paris* **23** A2
Argonne Forest, *Chicago* **9** C1
Argüelles, *Madrid* **17** a1
Arima, *Osaka* **22** A2
Arima, *Tokyo* **29** B2
Ários Págos, *Athens* **2** c1
Arkhangelyskoye, *Moscow* **19** B1
Arlington, *Boston* **6** A2
Arlington, *Washington* **32** B3
Arlington Heights, *Boston* **6** A2
Arlington Nat. Cemetery, *Washington* **32** B3
Armação, *Rio de Janeiro* **24** B2
Armadale, *Melbourne* **17** B2
Armenian Quarter, *Jerusalem* **13** b3
Armour Heights, *Toronto* **30** A2
Arncliffe, *Sydney* **28** B1
Arnold Arboretum, *Boston* **6** B3
Árpádföld, *Budapest* **7** A3
Arrentela, *Lisbon* **14** B2
Årsta, *Stockholm* **28** B2
Art Institute, *Chicago* **9** c2
Artane, *Dublin* **11** A2
Artas, *Jerusalem* **13** B2
Arthur's Seat, *Edinburgh* **11** B3
Aryiróupolis, *Athens* **2** B2
Asagaya, *Tokyo* **29** A2
Asahi, *Osaka* **22** A4
Asakusa, *Tokyo* **29** A3
Asakusabashi, *Tokyo* **29** a5
Asati, *Calcutta* **8** C1
Aschheim, *Munich* **20** A3
Ascot Vale, *Melbourne* **17** A1
Ashburn, *Chicago* **9** C2
Ashburton, *Melbourne* **17** B2
Ashfield, *Sydney* **28** B1
Ashford, *London* **15** B1
Ashiya, *Osaka* **22** A2
Ashiya →, *Osaka* **22** A2
Ashtown, *Dublin* **11** A2
Askisto, *Helsinki* **12** B1
Askrikefjärden, *Stockholm* **28** A3
Asnières, *Paris* **23** A2
Aspern, *Vienna* **31** A2
Aspern, Flugplatz, *Vienna* **31** A3
Assago, *Milan* **18** B1
Assemblée Nationale, *Paris* **23** b3
Assendelft, *Amsterdam* **2** A1
Assiano, *Milan* **18** B1
Astoria, *New York* **21** B2
Astrolabe Park, *Sydney* **28** B2
Atarot Airport, *Jerusalem* **13** A2
Atghara, *Calcutta* **8** B2
Athens = Athínai, *Athens* **2** B2
Athínai, *Athens* **2** B2
Athinai-Ellinikón Airport, *Athens* **2** B2
Athis-Mons, *Paris* **23** B3
Athlone, *Cape Town* **8** A2
Atholl, *Johannesburg* **13** A2
Atīfīya, *Baghdad* **3** A2
Atişalen, *Istanbul* **12** B1
Atlanta, *Atlanta* **3** B2
Atlanta History Center, *Atlanta* **3** B2
Atomium, *Brussels* **6** A2
Attiki, *Athens* **2** A2
Atzgersdorf, *Vienna* **31** B1
Aubervilliers, *Paris* **23** A3
Aubing, *Munich* **20** B1
Auburndale, *Boston* **6** A2
Aucherdinny, *Edinburgh* **11** B2
Auckland Park, *Johannesburg* **13** B2
Auderghem, *Brussels* **6** B2
Augusta, Mausoleo di, *Rome* **25** b2
Augustówka, *Warsaw* **31** B2
Aulnay-sous-Bois, *Paris* **23** A3
Aurelio, *Rome* **25** B1
Ausîm, *Cairo* **7** A1
Austerlitz, Gare d', *Paris* **23** A3
Austin, *Chicago* **9** B2
Avalon, *Wellington* **32** B2
Avedøre, *Copenhagen* **10** B2
Avellaneda, *Buenos Aires* **7** C2
Avenel, *Washington* **32** B4
Avondale, *Chicago* **9** B2
Avondale Heights, *Melbourne* **17** A1
Avtovo, *St. Petersburg* **26** B1
Ayazağa, *Istanbul* **12** B1
Ayer Chawan, P., *Singapore* **27** B2
Ayer Merbau, P., *Singapore* **27** B2
Ayía Marina, *Athens* **2** C3
Ayía Paraskevi, *Athens* **2** A2
Áyios Dhimitrios, *Athens* **2** B2
Áyios Ioánnis Rendis, *Athens* **2** B1
Azabu, *Tokyo* **29** c3
Azcapotzalco, *Mexico City* **18** B1
Azteca, Estadia, *Mexico City* **18** C2
Azucar, Cerro Pan de, *Santiago* **26** A1

B

Baambrugge, *Amsterdam* **2** B2
Baba I., *Karachi* **14** B1
Babarpur, *Delhi* **10** A2
Babushkin, *Moscow* **19** A4
Back B., *Mumbai* **20** B1
Baclaran, *Manila* **17** B2
Bacoor, *Manila* **17** C1
Bacoor B., *Manila* **17** C1
Badalona, *Barcelona* **4** A2
Badhoevedorp, *Amsterdam* **2** A1
Badli, *Delhi* **10** A1
Bærum, *Oslo* **22** A2
Bağcılar, *Istanbul* **12** B1
Bággio, *Milan* **18** B1
Bāgh-e-Feyz, *Tehran* **30** A1
Baghdād, *Baghdad* **3** A2
Bagmari, *Calcutta* **8** B2
Bagneux, *Paris* **23** B2
Bagnolet, *Paris* **23** A3
Bagsværd, *Copenhagen* **10** A2
Bagsværd Sø, *Copenhagen* **10** A2
Baguiati, *Calcutta* **8** B2
Bagumbayan, *Manila* **17** C2
Bahçeköy, *Istanbul* **12** A1
Bahtîm, *Cairo* **7** A2
Baileys Crossroads, *Washington* **32** B3
Bailly, *Paris* **23** A1
Bairro Alto, *Lisbon* **14** c1
Bairro Lopes, *Lisbon* **14** b3
Baisha, *Canton* **8** B2
Baisha →, *Canton* **8** B2
Baixa, *Lisbon* **14** c2
Baiyun Airport, *Canton* **8** A2
Baiyun Hill Scenic Spot, *Canton* **8** B2
Bakırköy, *Istanbul* **12** C1
Bakovka, *Moscow* **19** B2
Bal Harbor, *Miami* **18** A2
Balara, *Manila* **17** B2
Balashikha, *Moscow* **19** B5
Baldia, *Karachi* **14** A1
Baldoyle, *Dublin* **11** A3
Baldwin Hills, *Los Angeles* **16** B2
Baldwin Hills Res., *Los Angeles* **16** B2
Balgowlah, *Sydney* **28** A2
Balgowlah Heights, *Sydney* **28** A2
Balham, *London* **15** B3
Bali, *Calcutta* **8** B1
Baliganja, *Calcutta* **8** B2
Balingsnäs, *Stockholm* **28** B2
Balingsta, *Stockholm* **28** B2
Balintawak, *Manila* **17** B1
Balitai, *Tianjin* **30** B2
Ballerup, *Copenhagen* **10** A2
Ballinteer, *Dublin* **11** B2
Ballyboden, *Dublin* **11** B2
Ballybrack, *Dublin* **11** B3
Ballyfermot, *Dublin* **11** A1
Ballymorefinn Hill, *Dublin* **11** B1
Ballymun, *Dublin* **11** A2
Balmain, *Sydney* **28** B2
Baluhati, *Calcutta* **8** B1
Balvanera, *Buenos Aires* **7** B2
Balwyn, *Melbourne* **17** A2
Balwyn North, *Melbourne* **17** A2
Banática, *Lisbon* **14** A1
Banco do Brasil, Centro Cultural, *Rio de Janeiro* **24** a2
Bandra, *Mumbai* **20** A1
Bandra Pt., *Mumbai* **20** A1
Bang Kapi, *Bangkok* **3** B2
Bang Kholaem, *Bangkok* **3** A2
Bang Na, *Bangkok* **3** B2
Bang Phlad, *Bangkok* **3** a1
Bangkhen, *Bangkok* **3** A2
Bangkok = Krung Thep, *Bangkok* **3** B2
Bangkok Noi, *Bangkok* **3** B1
Bangkok Yai, *Bangkok* **3** B1
Banglamphoo, *Bangkok* **3** b2
Banglo, *Calcutta* **8** B1
Bangrak, *Bangkok* **3** B2
Bangsu, *Bangkok* **3** B2
Bank, *London* **15** b5
Bank of America, *San Francisco* **25** b2
Bank of China Tower, *Hong Kong* **12** c1
Banks, C., *Sydney* **28** C2
Banksmeadow, *Sydney* **28** B2
Banstala, *Calcutta* **8** B2
Bantra, *Calcutta* **8** B1
Baoshan, *Shanghai* **27** A1
Bar Giyora, *Jerusalem* **13** B1
Barahanagar, *Calcutta* **8** B2
Barajas, *Madrid* **17** B2
Barajas, Aeropuerto Transoceanico de, *Madrid* **17** B2
Barakpur, *Calcutta* **8** A2
Barberini, Palazzo, *Rome* **25** b3
Barbican, *London* **15** a4
Barcarena, *Lisbon* **14** A1
Barcarena, Rib. de →, *Lisbon* **14** A1
Barcelona, *Barcelona* **4** A2
Barcelona-Prat, Aeropuerta de, *Barcelona* **4** B1
Barceloneta, *Barcelona* **4** A2
Barking, *London* **15** A4
Barkingside, *London* **15** A4
Barnes, *London* **15** B2
Barnet, *London* **15** A2
Barra Andai, *Karachi* **14** B2
Barra Funda, *São Paulo* **26** B2
Barracas, *Buenos Aires* **7** B2
Barranco, *Lima* **16** B2
Barreiro, *Lisbon* **14** B2
Barreto, *Rio de Janeiro* **24** B2
Bartala, *Calcutta* **8** B1
Barton Park, *Sydney* **28** B1
Bartyki, *Warsaw* **31** C2
Barvikha, *Moscow* **19** B1
Bastille, Place de la, *Paris* **23** c5
Basus, *Cairo* **7** A2
Batanagar, *Calcutta* **8** B1
Bath Beach, *New York* **21** C1
Bath I., *Karachi* **14** B2
Batir, *Jerusalem* **13** B1
Batok, Bukit, *Singapore* **27** A2
Battersea, *London* **15** B3
Battery Park, *New York* **21** f1
Bauman, *Moscow* **19** B4
Baumgarten, *Vienna* **31** A1
Bay Harbour Islands, *Miami* **18** A2
Bay Ridge, *New York* **21** C1
Bayonne, *New York* **21** B1
Bayshore, *San Francisco* **25** B3
Bayswater, *London* **15** b2
Bayt Lahm = Bethlehem, *Jerusalem* **13** B2
Bayview, *San Francisco* **25** B2
Bāzār, *Tehran* **30** A2
Beachmont, *Boston* **6** A4
Beacon Hill, *Hong Kong* **12** A2
Beato, *Lisbon* **14** A2
Beaumont, *Dublin* **11** A2
Beaumonte Heights, *Toronto* **30** A1
Bebek, *Istanbul* **12** B2
Běchovice, *Prague* **24** B3
Beck L., *Chicago* **9** A1
Beckenham, *London* **15** B3
Beckton, *London* **15** A4
Becontree, *London* **15** A4
Beddington Corner, *London* **15** B3
Bedford, *Boston* **6** A2
Bedford Park, *Chicago* **9** C2
Bedford Park, *New York* **21** A2
Bedford Stuyvesant, *New York* **21** B2
Bedford View, *Johannesburg* **13** B2
Bedok, *Singapore* **27** B3
Bedok, Res., *Singapore* **27** A3
Beersel, *Brussels* **6** B1
Behala, *Calcutta* **8** B1
Bei Hai, *Beijing* **4** B2
Beicai, *Shanghai* **27** B2
Beicang, *Tianjin* **30** A1
Beihai Park, *Beijing* **4** b2
Beijing, *Beijing* **4** B1
Beit Ghur el-Fawqa, *Jerusalem* **13** A1
Beit Hanina, *Jerusalem* **13** B2
Beit Iksa, *Jerusalem* **13** B2
Beit I'nan, *Jerusalem* **13** A1
Beit Jala, *Jerusalem* **13** B2
Beit Lekhem = Bethlehem, *Jerusalem* **13** B2
Beit Nekofa, *Jerusalem* **13** B1
Beit Sahur, *Jerusalem* **13** B2
Beit Surik, *Jerusalem* **13** B1
Beit Zayit, *Jerusalem* **13** B1
Beitaipingzhuan, *Beijing* **4** B1
Beitar Ilit, *Jerusalem* **13** B1
Beitsun, *Canton* **8** B2
Beitunya, *Jerusalem* **13** A2
Beixing Jing Park, *Shanghai* **27** B1
Békásmegyer, *Budapest* **7** A2
Bekkelaget, *Oslo* **22** A3
Bel Air, *Los Angeles* **16** B2
Bela Vista, *São Paulo* **26** B2
Bélanger, *Montreal* **19** A1
Belas, *Lisbon* **14** A1
Belas Artes, Museu Nacionale de, *Rio de Janeiro* **24** b2
Beleghata, *Calcutta* **8** B2
Belém, *Lisbon* **14** A1
Belém, Torre de, *Lisbon* **14** A1
Belènzinho, *São Paulo* **26** B2
Belgachiya, *Calcutta* **8** B2
Belgharia, *Calcutta* **8** B2
Belgrano, *Buenos Aires* **7** B2
Belgravia, *London* **15** c3
Bell, *Los Angeles* **16** C3
Bell Gardens, *Los Angeles* **16** C4
Bell Tower, *Beijing* **4** a2
Bellavista, *Lima* **16** B2
Bellavista, *Santiago* **26** C2
Belle Harbor, *New York* **21** C2
Belle View, *Washington* **32** B2
Bellevue, Schloss, *Berlin* **5** a2
Bellingham, *London* **15** B3
Bellwood, *Chicago* **9** B1
Belmont, *Boston* **6** A2
Belmont, *London* **15** A2
Belmont, *Wellington* **32** B2
Belmont Harbor, *Chicago* **9** B3
Belmore, *Sydney* **28** B1
Belur, *Calcutta* **8** B2
Belvedere, *Atlanta* **3** B3
Belvedere, *London* **15** B4
Belvedere, *San Francisco* **25** A2
Belyayevo Bogorodskoye, *Moscow* **19** C3
Bemowo, *Warsaw* **31** B1
Benaki, Moussío, *Athens* **2** b3
Bendale, *Toronto* **30** A3
Bendkhal, *Mumbai* **20** B2
Benefica, *Rio de Janeiro* **24** B1
Benfica, *Lisbon* **14** A1
Benito Juárez, *Mexico City* **18** B2
Benito Juárez, Aeropuerto Int., *Mexico City* **18** B2
Bensonhurst, *New York* **21** C2
Berchem-Sainte-Agathe, *Brussels* **6** A1
Berg am Laim, *Munich* **20** B2
Bergenfield, *New York* **21** A2
Bergham, *Munich* **20** B2
Bergvliet, *Cape Town* **8** B1
Beri, *Barcelona* **4** A1
Berkeley, *San Francisco* **25** A3
Berlin, *Berlin* **5** A3
Bermondsey, *London* **15** B3
Bernabeu, Estadio, *Madrid* **17** B1
Bernal Heights, *San Francisco* **25** B2
Berwyn, *Chicago* **9** B2
Berwyn Heights, *Washington* **32** B4
Besiktas, *Istanbul* **12** B2
Besós →, *Barcelona* **4** A2
Bethesda, *Washington* **32** B3
Bethlehem, *Jerusalem* **13** B2
Bethnal Green, *London* **15** A3
Betor, *Calcutta* **8** B1
Beurs, *Amsterdam* **2** b2
Beverley Hills, *Sydney* **28** B1
Beverley Park, *Sydney* **28** B1
Beverly, *Chicago* **9** C3
Beverly Glen, *Los Angeles* **16** B2
Beverly Hills, *Los Angeles* **16** B2
Bexley, *London* **15** B4
Bexley, *Sydney* **28** B1
Bexleyheath, *London* **15** B4
Beykoz, *Istanbul* **12** B2
Beylerbeyi, *Istanbul* **12** B2
Beyoğlu, *Istanbul* **12** B1
Bezons, *Paris* **23** A2
Bezuidenhout Park, *Johannesburg* **13** B2
Bhadrakali, *Calcutta* **8** A2
Bhalswa, *Delhi* **10** A2
Bhambo Khan Qarmati, *Karachi* **14** B2
Bhatsala, *Calcutta* **8** B1
Bhawanipur, *Calcutta* **8** B2
Bhuleshwar, *Mumbai* **20** b2
Białołeka Dworska, *Warsaw* **31** B2
Biblioteca Nacional, *Rio de Janeiro* **24** c2
Bicentennial Park, *Sydney* **28** B1
Bickley, *London* **15** B4
Bidu, *Jerusalem* **13** B1
Bielany, *Warsaw* **31** B1
Bielawa, *Warsaw* **31** C2
Biesdorf, *Berlin* **5** A4
Bièvre →, *Paris* **23** B1
Bièvres, *Paris* **23** B2
Bilston, *Edinburgh* **11** B2
Binacayan, *Manila* **17** C1
Binondo, *Manila* **17** B1
Birak el Kiyam, *Cairo* **7** A1
Birch Cliff, *Toronto* **30** A3
Birkenstein, *Berlin* **5** A5
Birkholz, *Berlin* **5** A4
Birkholzaue, *Berlin* **5** A4
Birrarrung Park, *Melbourne* **17** A2
Biscayne Bay, *Miami* **18** B2
Biscayne Park, *Miami* **18** A2
Bishop Lavis, *Cape Town* **8** A2
Bishopscourt, *Cape Town* **8** A1
Bispebjerg, *Copenhagen* **10** A3
Biwon Secret Garden, *Seoul* **26** B1
Björknas, *Stockholm* **28** B3
Black Cr. →, *Toronto* **30** A2
Blackfen, *London* **15** B4
Blackheath, *London* **15** B4
Blackrock, *Dublin* **11** B2
Bladensburg, *Washington* **32** B4
Blair Village, *Atlanta* **3** C2
Blairgowrie, *Johannesburg* **13** A2
Blakehurst, *Sydney* **28** B1
Blakstad, *Oslo* **22** B1
Blankenburg, *Berlin* **5** A3
Blankenfelde, *Berlin* **5** A3
Blizne, *Warsaw* **31** B1
Bloomsbury, *London* **15** a3
Błota, *Warsaw* **31** C3
Blue Island, *Chicago* **9** C2
Bluebell, *Dublin* **11** B1
Bluff Hd., *Hong Kong* **12** B2
Blumberg, *Berlin* **5** A4
Blunt Pt., *San Francisco* **25** A2
Blutenberg, *Munich* **20** B1
Blylaget, *Oslo* **22** B3
Bo-Kaap Museum, *Cape Town* **8** c2
Boa Vista, Alto do, *Rio de Janeiro* **24** B1
Boardwalk, *New York* **21** C3
Boavista, *Lisbon* **14** A2
Bobigny, *Paris* **23** A3
Bocanegra, *Lima* **16** A2
Boedo, *Buenos Aires* **7** B2
Bogenhausen, *Munich* **20** B2
Bogorodskoye, *Moscow* **19** B4
Bogota, *New York* **21** A1
Bogstadvatnet, *Oslo* **22** A2
Bohnsdorf, *Berlin* **5** B4
Bois-Colombes, *Paris* **23** A2
Bois-d'Arcy, *Paris* **23** B1
Boissy-St.-Léger, *Paris* **23** B4
Boldinasco, *Milan* **18** B1
Bøler, *Oslo* **22** A4
Bollate, *Milan* **18** A1
Bollebeek, *Brussels* **6** A1
Bollensdorf, *Berlin* **5** A5
Bollmora, *Stockholm* **28** B3
Bolshaya-Okhta, *St. Petersburg* **26** B2
Bolton, *Atlanta* **3** B2
Bom Retiro, *São Paulo* **26** B2
Bombay = Mumbai, *Mumbai* **20** B2
Bondi, *Sydney* **28** B2
Bondy, *Paris* **23** A3
Bondy, Forêt de, *Paris* **23** A4
Bonifacio Monument, *Manila* **17** B1
Bonneuil-sur-Marne, *Paris* **23** B4
Bonnington, *Edinburgh* **11** B1
Bonnyrig and Lasswade, *Edinburgh* **11** B3
Bonsucesso, *Rio de Janeiro* **24** B1
Bonteheuwel, *Cape Town* **8** A2
Boo, *Stockholm* **28** A3
Booterstown, *Dublin* **11** B2
Borisovo, *Moscow* **19** C4
Borle, *Mumbai* **20** A2
Boronia Park, *Sydney* **28** A1
Borough Park, *New York* **21** C2
Bosmont, *Johannesburg* **13** B1
Bosön, *Stockholm* **28** A3
Bosporus = Istanbul Boğazi, *Istanbul* **12** B2
Bostancı, *Istanbul* **12** C2
Boston Harbor, *Boston* **6** A4
Botafogo, *Rio de Janeiro* **24** B1
Botanisk Have, *Copenhagen* **10** b2
Botany, *Sydney* **28** B2
Botany B., *Sydney* **28** B2
Botany Bay Nat. Park, *Sydney* **28** B2
Botič →, *Prague* **24** B3
Botica Sete, *Lisbon* **14** A1
Boucherville, *Montreal* **19** A3
Boucherville, Îs. de, *Montreal* **19** A3
Bougival, *Paris* **23** A1
Boulder Pt., *Hong Kong* **12** B1
Boulogne, Bois de, *Paris* **23** A2
Boulogne-Billancourt, *Paris* **23** A2
Bourg-la-Reine, *Paris* **23** B2
Bouviers, *Paris* **23** B1
Bovenkerk, *Amsterdam* **2** B2
Bovenkerker Polder, *Amsterdam* **2** B2
Bovisa, *Milan* **18** A2
Bow, *London* **15** A3
Bowery, *New York* **21** e2
Boyacıköy, *Istanbul* **12** B2
Boyle Heights, *Los Angeles* **16** B3
Bradbury Building, *Los Angeles* **16** b2
Braepark, *Edinburgh* **11** B2
Braid, *Edinburgh* **11** B2
Bramley, *Johannesburg* **13** A2
Brandenburger Tor, *Berlin* **5** A3
Brani, P., *Singapore* **27** B3
Branik, *Prague* **24** B2
Brännkyrka, *Stockholm* **28** B2
Brás, *São Paulo* **26** B2
Brasilândia, *São Paulo* **26** A1
Brateyevo, *Moscow* **19** C4
Bratsevo, *Moscow* **19** A2
Bray, *Dublin* **11** B3
Braybrook, *Melbourne* **17** A1
Brázdim, *Prague* **24** A3
Breach Candy, *Mumbai* **20** a1
Breakheart Reservation, *Boston* **6** A3
Brede, *Copenhagen* **10** A3
Breeds Pond, *Boston* **6** A4
Breezy Point, *New York* **21** C2
Breitenlee, *Vienna* **31** A3
Breña, *Lima* **16** B2
Brent, *London* **15** A2
Brent Res., *London* **15** A2
Brentford, *London* **15** B2
Brentwood Park, *Los Angeles* **16** B2
Brera, *Milan* **18** B2
Bresso, *Milan* **18** A2
Brevik, *Stockholm* **28** A3
Břevnov, *Prague* **24** B2
Bridgeport, *Chicago* **9** B3
Bridgetown, *Cape Town* **8** A2
Bridgeview, *Chicago* **9** C2
Brighton, *Boston* **6** A3
Brighton, *Melbourne* **17** B1
Brighton le Sands, *Sydney* **28** B1
Brighton Park, *Chicago* **9** C2
Brightwood, *Washington* **32** B3
Brigittenau, *Vienna* **31** A2
Brimbank Park, *Melbourne* **17** A1
Brisbane, *San Francisco* **25** B2
British Museum, *London* **15** a3
Britz, *Berlin* **5** B3
Brixton, *London* **15** B3
Broad Sd., *Boston* **6** A4
Broadmeadows, *Melbourne* **17** A1
Broadmoor, *San Francisco* **25** B2
Broadview, *Chicago* **9** B1
Broadway, *New York* **21** e1
Brockley, *London* **15** B3
Bródno, *Warsaw* **31** B2
Bródnowski, Kanal, *Warsaw* **31** B2
Broek in Waterland, *Amsterdam* **2** A2
Bromley, *London* **15** B4
Bromley Common, *London* **15** B4
Bromma, *Stockholm* **28** A1
Bromma flygplats, *Stockholm* **28** A1
Brompton, *London* **15** c2
Brøndby Strand, *Copenhagen* **10** B2
Brøndbyøster, *Copenhagen* **10** B2
Brøndbyvester, *Copenhagen* **10** B2
Brondesbury, *London* **15** A2
Brønnøya, *Oslo* **22** A2
Brønshøj, *Copenhagen* **10** A2

C

D

E

F

G

H

I

J

K

L

M

S

T

Tacuba, *Mexico City* 18 B1
Tacubaya, *Mexico City* 18 B1
Taebang, *Seoul* 26 B1
Tagig, *Manila* 17 B2
Tagig →, *Manila* 17 B2
Tai Hang, *Hong Kong* 12 B2
Tai Lo Shan, *Hong Kong* 12 A2
Tai Po Tsai, *Hong Kong* 12 A2
Tai Seng, *Singapore* 27 A3
Tai Shui Hang, *Hong Kong* 12 A2
Tai Tam B., *Hong Kong* 12 B2
Tai Tam Tuk Res., *Hong Kong* 12 B2
Tai Wai, *Hong Kong* 12 A1
Tai Wan Tau, *Hong Kong* 12 B2
Tai Wo Hau, *Hong Kong* 12 A1
Tainaka, *Osaka* 22 B4
Taishō, *Osaka* 22 B3
Taita, *Wellington* 32 B2
Tajrīsh, *Tehran* 30 A2
Takaido, *Tokyo* 29 A2
Takaishi, *Tokyo* 29 B2
Takarazuka, *Osaka* 22 A2
Takasago, *Tokyo* 29 A4
Takatsu-Ku, *Tokyo* 29 B2
Takeshita, *Tokyo* 29 B2
Takinegawa, *Tokyo* 29 A3
Takoma Park, *Washington* 32 B3
Taksim, *Istanbul* 12 B1
Talaide, *Lisbon* 14 A1
Taliganga, *Calcutta* 8 B2
Talipapa, *Manila* 17 A2
Tallaght, *Dublin* 11 B1
Tallkrogen, *Stockholm* 28 B2
Tama, *Tokyo* 29 B1
Tama →, *Tokyo* 29 B2
Tama Kyūryō, *Tokyo* 29 B2
Tamaden, *Tokyo* 29 B2
Tamagawa-josui →, *Tokyo* 29 A1
Taman Sari, *Jakarta* 13 A1
Tamanduateí →, *São Paulo* 26 B2
Tamboerskloof, *Cape Town* 8 A1
Tambora, *Jakarta* 13 A1
Tammisalo, *Helsinki* 12 B3
Tammûh, *Cairo* 7 B2
Tampines, *Singapore* 27 A3
Tanah Abang, *Jakarta* 13 B1
Tanigami, *Osaka* 22 A2
Tanjung Duren, *Jakarta* 13 B1
Tanjung Priok, *Jakarta* 13 A2
Tanum, *Oslo* 22 A1
Taoranting Park, *Beijing* 4 c2
Tapada, *Lisbon* 14 A1
Tapanila, *Helsinki* 12 B3
Tapiales, *Buenos Aires* 7 C1
Tapiola, *Helsinki* 12 B1
Tapsia, *Calcutta* 8 B2
Tara, *Mumbai* 20 A1
Tarabya, *Istanbul* 12 B2
Tarango, Presa, *Mexico City* 18 B1
Tårbæk, *Copenhagen* 10 A3
Tarchomin, *Warsaw* 31 B1
Tardeo, *Mumbai* 20 B1
Targówek, *Warsaw* 31 B2
Tårnby, *Copenhagen* 10 B3
Tarqua Bay, *Lagos* 14 B2
Tåstrup, *Copenhagen* 10 B1
Tatarovo, *Moscow* 19 B2
Tathong Channel, *Hong Kong* 12 B2
Tathong Pt., *Hong Kong* 12 B2
Tatuapé, *São Paulo* 26 B2
Taufkirchen, *Munich* 20 B2
Tavares, I. dos, *Rio de Janeiro* 24 A2
Távros, *Athens* 2 B2
Tawa, *Wellington* 32 A1
Teaneck, *New York* 21 A1
Teatro Municipal, *Rio de Janeiro* 24 c2
Tebet, *Jakarta* 13 B2
Tecamachaleo, *Mexico City* 18 B1
Teddington, *London* 15 B1
Tegel, *Berlin* 5 A2
Tegel, Flughafen, *Berlin* 5 A2
Tegeler See, *Berlin* 5 A2
Tegelort, *Berlin* 5 A2
Tehrān, *Tehran* 30 A2
Tehrān Pārs, *Tehran* 30 A3
Tei Tong Tsui, *Hong Kong* 12 B2
Tejo, Rio →, *Lisbon* 14 A2
Tekstilyshchik, *Moscow* 19 B4
Telegraph hill, *San Francisco* 25 a2
Telhal, *Lisbon* 14 A1
Telok Blangah, *Singapore* 27 B2
Teltow, *Berlin* 5 B2
Teltow kanal, *Berlin* 5 B3
Temnikovo, *Moscow* 19 B6
Tempelhof, *Berlin* 5 B3
Tempelhof, Flughafen, *Berlin* 5 B3
Temple City, *Los Angeles* 16 B4
Temple Hills Park, *Washington* 32 C4
Temple Mount, *Jerusalem* 13 b3
Templeogue, *Dublin* 11 B2
Templo Mayor, *Mexico City* 18 b3
Tenafly, *New York* 21 A2
Tenayuca, Piramide de, *Mexico City* 18 A1
Tengah →, *Singapore* 27 A2
Tennoji, *Osaka* 22 B4
Tepalcates, *Mexico City* 18 B2
Terrazzano, *Milan* 18 A1
Terrugem, *Lisbon* 14 A1
Tervuren, *Brussels* 6 B3
Tervuren, Park van, *Brussels* 6 B3
Tetuán, *Madrid* 17 B1
Teufelsberg, *Berlin* 5 B2
Tévere →, *Rome* 25 B1
Thalkirchen, *Munich* 20 B2
Thames →, *London* 15 A4
Thames Ditton, *London* 15 B1
Thamesmead, *London* 15 A4
Thana Cr. →, *Mumbai* 20 A2
The Loop, *Chicago* 9 B3
The Ridge, *Delhi* 10 B2
The Wilds, *Johannesburg* 13 B2
Theater Carré, *Amsterdam* 2 b2
Théatro Dionissou, *Athens* 2 c2
Thiais, *Paris* 23 B3
Thissío, *Athens* 2 c1
Thistletown, *Toronto* 30 A1
Thomastown, *Melbourne* 17 A2
Thompson I., *Boston* 6 B4
Thon Buri, *Bangkok* 3 B1
Thornbury, *Melbourne* 17 A2
Thorncliffe, *Toronto* 30 A2
Thornhill, *Toronto* 30 A2
Thornton, *Cape Town* 8 A2
Thornton Heath, *London* 15 B3
Threipmuir Res., *Edinburgh* 11 B2
Throgs Neck, *New York* 21 B3
Thyssen Bornemisza, Museo, *Madrid* 17 b3
Tian'anmen Square, *Beijing* 4 B2
Tiancun, *Beijing* 4 B1
Tianjin, *Tianjin* 30 B1
Tiantan Park, *Beijing* 4 c2
Tibidabo, *Barcelona* 4 A1
Tibradden Mt., *Dublin* 11 B2
Tiburon, *San Francisco* 25 A2
Tiburtino, *Rome* 25 B2
Ticomán, *Mexico City* 18 A2
Tiefersee, *Berlin* 5 B1
Tiejiangyin, *Beijing* 4 C2
Tientsin = Tianjin, *Tianjin* 30 B1
Tiergarten, *Berlin* 5 A3
Tietê →, *São Paulo* 26 B2
Tigerhof, *Cape Town* 8 A2
Tigris = Nahr Dijlah →, *Baghdad* 3 B2
Tijuca, *Rio de Janeiro* 24 B1
Tijuca, Parque Nacional da, *Rio de Janeiro* 24 B1
Tijuca, Pico da, *Rio de Janeiro* 24 B1
Tikkurila, *Helsinki* 12 B3
Tilak Nagar, *Delhi* 10 B1
Tilanqiao, *Shanghai* 27 B1
Timah, Bukit, *Singapore* 27 A2
Times Square, *New York* 21 c2
Timiryazev Park, *Moscow* 19 B3
Ting Kau, *Hong Kong* 12 A1
Tira, *Jerusalem* 13 A1
Tirsa, *Cairo* 7 B2
Tishrīyaa, *Baghdad* 3 B2
Tiu Keng Leng, *Hong Kong* 12 B2
Tivoli, *Copenhagen* 10 a3
Tizapán, *Mexico City* 18 C1
Tlalnepantla →, *Mexico City* 18 A1
To Kwai Wan, *Hong Kong* 12 B2
Toa Payoh, *Singapore* 27 A3
Tobong, *Seoul* 26 B2
Tobong-san, *Seoul* 26 A2
Točná, *Prague* 24 C2
Toco Hills, *Atlanta* 3 B2
Todt Hill, *New York* 21 C1
Tōkagi, *Tokyo* 29 A4
Tokai Plantation, *Cape Town* 8 B1
Tōkaichiba, *Tokyo* 29 B2
Tokarevo, *Moscow* 19 C5
Tōkyō, *Tokyo* 29 B3
Tokyo B., *Tokyo* 29 B4
Tokyo-Haneda Int. Airport, *Tokyo* 29 B3
Tokyo Harbour, *Tokyo* 29 B3
Tolka R. →, *Dublin* 11 A1
Tolworth, *London* 15 B2
Tomb of Lu Xun, *Shanghai* 27 B1
Tomb of the Kings, *Jerusalem* 13 a2
Tomba di Nerone, *Rome* 25 B1
Tomilino, *Moscow* 19 C5
Tondo, *Manila* 17 B1
Tongbinggo, *Seoul* 26 B1
Tongjak, *Seoul* 26 B1
Tongmaemung, *Seoul* 26 B2
Tongqiao, *Shanghai* 27 A1
Toorak, *Melbourne* 17 B2
Topkapı, *Istanbul* 12 B1
Tor di Quinto, *Rome* 25 B1
Tor Pignattara, *Rome* 25 B2
Tor Sapienza, *Rome* 25 B2
Toranomon, *Tokyo* 29 c3
Torcy, *Paris* 23 A4
Toronto, *Toronto* 30 B3
Toronto, Univ. of, *Toronto* 30 B2
Toronto Harbour, *Toronto* 30 B2
Toronto I., *Toronto* 30 B2
Toronto Int. Airport, *Toronto* 30 A1
Toros Las Arenas, Pl. de, *Barcelona* 4 c1
Toros Monumental, Templo de, *Barcelona* 4 a3
Torre Latino-americana, *Mexico City* 18 b2
Torre Lupara, *Rome* 25 B2
Torre Nova, *Rome* 25 B2
Torrellas →, *Barcelona* 4 A1
Torrevécchia, *Rome* 25 B1
Toshima-Ku, *Tokyo* 29 A3
Toshimaen, *Tokyo* 29 A2
Tottenham, *London* 15 A3
Tottenham, *Melbourne* 17 A1
Tour Eiffel, *Paris* 23 c2
Toussus-le-Noble, *Paris* 23 B1
Toussus-le-Noble, Aérodrome de, *Paris* 23 B1
Tower Bridge, *London* 15 b5
Tower Hamlets, *London* 15 A3
Tower of London, *London* 15 A3
Towra Pt., *Sydney* 28 C2
Tøyen, *Oslo* 22 A3
Toyonaka, *Osaka* 22 A3
Trafalgar Square, *London* 15 b3
Trafaria, *Lisbon* 14 A1
Traição, Cor. →, *São Paulo* 26 B2
Tranegilde, *Copenhagen* 10 B2
Trångsund, *Stockholm* 28 B2
Transamerica Pyramid, *San Francisco* 25 b2
Transbay Terminal, *San Francisco* 25 b3
Trappenfelde, *Berlin* 5 A4
Trastévere, *Rome* 25 B1
Treasure I., *San Francisco* 25 B2
Třeboradice, *Prague* 24 B3
Třebotov, *Prague* 24 C1
Tremblay-en-France, *Paris* 23 A4
Tremembe →, *São Paulo* 26 A2
Tremont, *New York* 21 A2
Trenno, *Milan* 18 B1
Treptow, *Berlin* 5 B3
Trés Rios, Sa. dos, *Rio de Janeiro* 24 B1
Trevi, Fontana di, *Rome* 25 b3
Trezzano sul Navíglio, *Milan* 18 B1
Tribune Tower, *Chicago* 9 b2
Trieste, *Rome* 25 B2
Trinidad, *Washington* 32 B4
Trinity, *Edinburgh* 11 B2
Trinity College, *Dublin* 11 c3
Trionfale, *Rome* 25 B1
Triulzo, *Milan* 18 B2
Trocadero, *Paris* 23 b1
Troitse-Lykovo, *Moscow* 19 B2
Troja, *Prague* 24 B2
Trollbäcken, *Stockholm* 28 B3
Trombay, *Mumbai* 20 A2
Troparevo, *Moscow* 19 C2
Tropenmuseum, *Amsterdam* 2 b3
Trudyashchikhsya, Ostrov, *St. Petersburg* 26 B1
Tryvasshøgda, *Oslo* 22 A3
Tseng Lan Shue, *Hong Kong* 12 A2
Tsim Sha Tsui, *Hong Kong* 12 a2
Tsing Yi, *Hong Kong* 12 A1
Tsova, *Jerusalem* 13 B1
Tsuen Wan, *Hong Kong* 12 A1
Tsukiji, *Tokyo* 29 c5
Tsur Hadassa, *Jerusalem* 13 B1
Tsurumi →, *Tokyo* 29 B3
Tsz Wan Shan, *Hong Kong* 12 A2
Tuas, *Singapore* 27 B1
Tuchoměřice, *Prague* 24 B1
Tuckahoe, *New York* 21 A3
Tucuruvi, *São Paulo* 26 A2
Tufello, *Rome* 25 B2
Tufnell Park, *London* 15 A3
Tughlakabad, *Delhi* 10 B2
Tuileries, Jardin des, *Paris* 23 b3
Tuindorp Oostzaan, *Amsterdam* 2 A2
Tullamarine, *Melbourne* 17 A1
Tulse Hill, *London* 15 B3
Tung Lung I., *Hong Kong* 12 B2
Tung O, *Hong Kong* 12 B1
Tunis, *Baghdad* 3 A2
Tuomarila, *Helsinki* 12 B1
Tureberg, *Stockholm* 28 A1
Turffontein, *Johannesburg* 13 B2
Turkso, *Prague* 24 A1
Turnham Green, *London* 15 B2
Turnhouse, *Edinburgh* 11 B1
Tuscolana, Via, *Rome* 25 B2
Tushino, *Moscow* 19 A2
Twelve Apostles, *Cape Town* 8 A1
Twickenham, *London* 15 B1
Twickenham Rugby Ground, *London* 15 B1
Twin Peaks, *San Francisco* 25 B2
Two Rock Mt., *Dublin* 11 B2
Tymon North, *Dublin* 11 B1
Tysons Corner, *Washington* 32 B2

U

U.S. Capitol, *Washington* 32 b3
Ubeidiya, *Jerusalem* 13 B2
Uberaba →, *São Paulo* 26 B2
Ubin, P., *Singapore* 27 A3
Uccle, *Brussels* 6 B2
Udelnaya, *St. Petersburg* 26 A2
Udelnoe, *St. Petersburg* 26 B1
Udlding, *Munich* 20 A1
Ueno, *Tokyo* 29 A3
Úholičky, *Prague* 24 B1
Uhříněves, *Prague* 24 B3
Uithoorn, *Amsterdam* 2 B1
Újpalota, *Budapest* 7 A2
Újpest, *Budapest* 7 A2
Ukita, *Tokyo* 29 A4
Ullerup, *Copenhagen* 10 B3
Ullevål, *Oslo* 22 A3
Ulriksdal, *Stockholm* 28 A1
Ulyanka, *St. Petersburg* 26 B1
Um Al-Khanazir Island, *Baghdad* 3 B2
Umeda, *Osaka* 22 A3
Umerkhadi, *Mumbai* 20 b2
Ümraniye, *Istanbul* 12 B2
Underground Atlanta, *Atlanta* 3 B2
Unětický potok →, *Prague* 24 B2
Ŭngam, *Seoul* 26 B1
Unhos, *Lisbon* 14 A2
Unidad Santa Fe, *Mexico City* 18 B1
Union City, *New York* 21 B1
Union Port, *New York* 21 B2
Union Square, *New York* 21 d2
Union Square, *San Francisco* 25 b2
Union Station, *Washington* 32 b3
United Nations H.Q., *New York* 21 c3
Universidad, *Madrid* 17 B1
Universidad de Chile, *Santiago* 26 B2
University Park, *Washington* 32 B4
Unp'yong, *Seoul* 26 B1
Unter den Linden, *Berlin* 5 a4
Unterbiberg, *Munich* 20 B2
Unterföhring, *Munich* 20 A3
Unterhaching, *Munich* 20 B2
Unterlaa, *Vienna* 31 B2
Untermenzing, *Munich* 20 A1
Upper East Side, *New York* 21 b3
Upper Elmers End, *London* 15 B3
Upper New York B., *New York* 21 C1
Upper Norwood, *London* 15 B3
Upper Peirce Res., *Singapore* 27 A2
Upper Sydenham, *London* 15 B3
Upper Tooting, *London* 15 B3
Upper West Side, *New York* 21 a2
Upton, *London* 15 A4
Uptown, *Chicago* 9 B2
Uran, *Mumbai* 20 B2
Urayasu, *Tokyo* 29 B4
Urbe, Aeroporto d', *Rome* 25 B2
Urca, *Rio de Janeiro* 24 B2
Uritsk, *St. Petersburg* 26 C1
Üröm, *Budapest* 7 A2
Ursus, *Warsaw* 31 B1
Ursvik, *Stockholm* 28 A1
Usera, *Madrid* 17 B1
Ushigome, *Tokyo* 29 A3
Usina, *Rio de Janeiro* 24 B1
Üsküdar, *Istanbul* 12 B2
Ust-Slavyanka, *St. Petersburg* 26 C3
Uteke, *Stockholm* 28 A3
Utrata, *Warsaw* 31 B2
Uttarpara, *Calcutta* 8 B1
Utterslev Mose, *Copenhagen* 10 A2

V

Vadaul, *Mumbai* 20 A2
Vaires-sur-Marne, *Paris* 23 A4
Valby, *Copenhagen* 10 B2
Valcannuta, *Rome* 25 B1
Valdelatas, *Madrid* 17 A1
Vale, *Washington* 32 B1
Valenton, *Paris* 23 B3
Valera, *Milan* 18 A1
Vallcarca, *Barcelona* 4 A1
Valldoreix, *Barcelona* 4 A1
Vallecas, *Madrid* 17 B2
Vallensbæk, *Copenhagen* 10 B2
Vallensbæk Strand, *Copenhagen* 10 B2
Vallentunasjön, *Stockholm* 28 A2
Valleranello, *Rome* 25 C1
Vallisaari, *Helsinki* 12 C3
Vallvidrera, *Barcelona* 4 A1
Valvidrera →, *Barcelona* 4 A1
Van Goghmuseum, *Amsterdam* 2 c1
Vanak, *Tehran* 30 A2
Vangede, *Copenhagen* 10 A3
Vaniköy, *Istanbul* 12 B2
Vanløse, *Copenhagen* 10 A2
Vantaa, *Helsinki* 12 B2
Vantaa →, *Helsinki* 12 B2
Vantaankoski, *Helsinki* 12 B2
Vantaanpuisto, *Helsinki* 12 B2
Vanves, *Paris* 23 B2
Varedo, *Milan* 18 A1
Varkiza, *Athens* 2 C2
Varszínház, *Budapest* 7 b2
Vartiokylä, *Helsinki* 12 B3
Vartiosaari, *Helsinki* 12 B3
Vasamuseet, *Stockholm* 28 b3
Vasco, *Cape Town* 8 A2
Vasfanārd, *Tehran* 30 B2
Vashi, *Mumbai* 20 A2
Vasilyevskiy, Ostrov, *St. Petersburg* 26 B1
Vaso Regulador El Cristo, *Mexico City* 18 B1
Vaucluse, *Sydney* 28 B2
Vaucresson, *Paris* 23 A1
Vauhallan, *Paris* 23 B2
Vaujours, *Paris* 23 A4
Vauxhall, *London* 15 c4
Vecsés, *Budapest* 7 B3
Veleň, *Prague* 24 A3
Veleslavin, *Prague* 24 B2
Vélizy-Villacoublay, *Paris* 23 B2
Velka-Chuchle, *Prague* 24 B2
Velké Přilepy, *Prague* 24 B1
Venda Seca, *Lisbon* 14 A1
Venetian Islands, *Miami* 18 B2
Venezia, Palazzo, *Rome* 25 c2
Venice, *Los Angeles* 16 C2
Ventas, *Madrid* 17 B1
Ventorro del Cano, *Madrid* 17 B1
Venustiano Carranza, *Mexico City* 18 B2
Verde →, *São Paulo* 26 A1
Verdi, *Athens* 2 A2
Verdun, *Montreal* 19 B2
Vérhalom, *Budapest* 7 A2
Vermelho →, *São Paulo* 26 B1
Vernon, *Los Angeles* 16 B3
Verrières-le-Buisson, *Paris* 23 B2
Versailles, *Buenos Aires* 7 B1
Versailles, *Paris* 23 B1
Veshnyaki, *Moscow* 19 B4
Vesolyy Posolok, *St. Petersburg* 26 B2
Vestra, *Helsinki* 12 B1
Vestskoven, *Copenhagen* 10 A2
Vicálvaro, *Madrid* 17 B2
Vicente Lopez, *Buenos Aires* 7 B2
Victoria, *Hong Kong* 12 B2
Victoria, *London* 15 c3
Victoria, Mt., *Wellington* 32 B1
Victoria, Pont, *Montreal* 19 B2
Victoria and Albert Waterfront, *Cape Town* 8 a1
Victoria Gardens, *Mumbai* 20 B2
Victoria Harbour, *Hong Kong* 12 B1
Victoria Island, *Lagos* 14 B2
Victoria L., *Johannesburg* 13 B2
Victoria Lawn Tennis Courts, *Melbourne* 17 B2
Victoria Park, *Singapore* 27 B2
Victoria Peak, *Hong Kong* 12 B1
Victoria Wharf, *Cape Town* 8 a2
Vienna = Wien, *Vienna* 31 A2
Vienna, *Washington* 32 B2
View Park, *Los Angeles* 16 B3
Vigário Geral, *Rio de Janeiro* 24 A1
Vigentino, *Milan* 18 B2
Viggbyholm, *Stockholm* 28 A2
Vighignolo, *Milan* 18 B1
Viikki, *Helsinki* 12 B3
Vikhroli, *Mumbai* 20 A2
Vila Guilherme, *São Paulo* 26 B2
Vila Isabel, *Rio de Janeiro* 24 B1
Vila Jaguára, *São Paulo* 26 B1
Vila Madalena, *São Paulo* 26 B1
Vila Maria, *São Paulo* 26 B2
Vila Mariana, *São Paulo* 26 B2
Vila Prudente, *São Paulo* 26 B2
Viladecans, *Barcelona* 4 B1
Vile Parle, *Mumbai* 20 A2
Villa Adelina, *Buenos Aires* 7 B1
Villa Ballester, *Buenos Aires* 7 B1
Villa Barilari, *Buenos Aires* 7 C2
Villa Borghese, *Rome* 25 a3
Villa Bosch, *Buenos Aires* 7 B1
Villa C. Colon, *Buenos Aires* 7 C2
Villa Ciudadela, *Buenos Aires* 7 B1
Villa de Guadalupe, *Mexico City* 18 B2
Villa Devoto, *Buenos Aires* 7 B1
Villa Diamante, *Buenos Aires* 7 C2
Villa Dominico, *Buenos Aires* 7 C3
Villa Lugano, *Buenos Aires* 7 C2
Villa Lynch, *Buenos Aires* 7 B1
Villa Madero, *Buenos Aires* 7 C1
Villa Sáenz Pena, *Buenos Aires* 7 B1
Villa Urquiza, *Buenos Aires* 7 B2
Villaverde, *Madrid* 17 B1
Villaverde Bajo, *Madrid* 17 B1
Ville-d'Avray, *Paris* 23 B2
Villecresnes, *Paris* 23 B4
Villejuif, *Paris* 23 B3
Villemomble, *Paris* 23 A4
Villeneuve-la-Garenne, *Paris* 23 A2
Villeneuve-le-Roi, *Paris* 23 B3
Villeneuve-St.-Georges, *Paris* 23 B3
Villeparisis, *Paris* 23 A4
Villevaudé, *Paris* 23 A4
Villiers-le-Bâcle, *Paris* 23 B1
Villiers-sur-Marne, *Paris* 23 B4
Villinki, *Helsinki* 12 C3
Villoresi, Canale, *Milan* 18 A1
Vilvoorde, *Brussels* 6 A2
Vimodrone, *Milan* 18 A2
Vimont, *Montreal* 19 A1
Vinanmek Palace, *Bangkok* 3 a2
Vincennes, *Paris* 23 A3
Vincennes, Bois de, *Paris* 23 B3
Vinings, *Atlanta* 3 A2
Vinohrady, *Prague* 24 c3
Vinoř, *Prague* 24 B3
Violet Hill, *Hong Kong* 12 B2
Virányos, *Budapest* 7 A1
Virgen del San Cristóbal, *Santiago* 26 B2
Virginia Gardens, *Miami* 18 B1
Virginia Key, *Miami* 18 B2
Viroflay, *Paris* 23 B2
Víron, *Athens* 2 B2
Virum, *Copenhagen* 10 A2
Vishnyaki, *Moscow* 19 B5
Visitacion Valley, *San Francisco* 25 B2
Vista Alegre, *Lima* 16 B3
Vista Alegre, *Santiago* 26 C1
Vista Grove, *Atlanta* 3 A3
Vitacura, *Santiago* 26 B2
Vitinia, *Rome* 25 C1
Vitry-sur-Seine, *Paris* 23 B3
Vizandinó, Moussío, *Athens* 2 b3
Vladykino, *Moscow* 19 A3
Vlezenbeek, *Brussels* 6 B1
Vltava →, *Prague* 24 A2
Vnukovo, *Moscow* 19 C1
Vokovice, *Prague* 24 B2
Volgelsdorf, *Berlin* 5 B5
Volkhonka-Zil, *Moscow* 19 C3
Vollen, *Oslo* 22 B1
Volodarskoye, *St. Petersburg* 26 B2
Volynkina-Derevnya, *St. Petersburg* 26 B1
Vondelpark, *Amsterdam* 2 A2
Vösendorf, *Vienna* 31 B2
Vostochnyy, *Moscow* 19 B5
Voula, *Athens* 2 C2
Vouliagmeni, *Athens* 2 C2
Vredehoek, *Cape Town* 8 A1
Vršovice, *Prague* 24 B2
Vyborgskaya Storona, *St. Petersburg* 26 B2
Vykhino, *Moscow* 19 B4
Vyšehrad, *Prague* 24 B2

W

Wachterhof, *Munich* 20 B3
Wadala, *Mumbai* 20 A2
Wadestown, *Wellington* 32 B1
Wadi Fukin, *Jerusalem* 13 B1
Wah Fu, *Hong Kong* 12 B1
Wahda, *Baghdad* 3 B2
Währing, *Vienna* 31 A2
Waidmannslust, *Berlin* 5 A3
Wainuiomata, *Wellington* 32 B2
Wainuiomata R. →, *Wellington* 32 B2
Wakefield, *Boston* 6 A3
Waldesruh, *Berlin* 5 B4
Waldperlach, *Munich* 20 B3
Waldtrudering, *Munich* 20 B3
Walkinstown, *Dublin* 11 B1
Wall Street, *New York* 21 f1
Waltham, *Boston* 6 A2
Waltham Forest, *London* 15 A3
Walthamstow, *London* 15 A3
Walton on Thames, *London* 15 B1
Wambeek, *Brussels* 6 A3
Wan Chai, *Hong Kong* 12 B2
Wan Chai Lanes, *Hong Kong* 12 c2
Wandsworth, *London* 15 B2
Wankhede Stadium, *Mumbai* 20 c2
Wannsee, *Berlin* 5 B1
Wansdorf, *Berlin* 5 A1
Wanstead, *London* 15 A4
Wapping, *London* 15 A3
Ward, *Dublin* 11 A1
Ward I., *Wellington* 32 B2
Warnberg, *Munich* 20 B2
Warrâq el 'Arab, *Cairo* 7 A2
Warrâq el Hadr, *Cairo* 7 A2
Warringen Park, *Melbourne* 17 A2
Warriston, *Edinburgh* 11 B2
Warsaw = Warszawa, *Warsaw* 31 B2
Warszawa, *Warsaw* 31 B2
Wartenberg, *Berlin* 5 A4
Washington, *Washington* 32 B3
Washington Heights, *New York* 21 A2
Washington Monument, *Washington* 32 b1
Washington Nat. Airport, *Washington* 32 B3
Washington Park, *Chicago* 9 C3
Wat Arun, *Bangkok* 3 b1
Wat Pho, *Bangkok* 3 b1
Wat Phra Keo, *Bangkok* 3 b1
Wat Traimit, *Bangkok* 3 c2
Water of Leith, *Edinburgh* 11 B1
Water Tower Place, *Chicago* 9 a2
Watergraafsmeer, *Amsterdam* 2 A2
Waterland, *Amsterdam* 2 A2
Waterloo, *Brussels* 6 B2
Waterloo, *Wellington* 32 B2
Waterloo International, *London* 15 b4
Watermael-Boitsfort, *Brussels* 6 B2
Watertown, *Boston* 6 A2
Watsonia, *Melbourne* 17 A2
Waverley, *Boston* 6 A2
Waverley, *Johannesburg* 13 A2
Waverley, *Sydney* 28 B2
Waverley Station, *Edinburgh* 11 b3
Wawer, *Warsaw* 31 B2
Wawrzyszew, *Warsaw* 31 B1
Wayland, *Boston* 6 A1
Wazirabad, *Delhi* 10 A2
Wazīrīya, *Baghdad* 3 A2
Wazirpur, *Delhi* 10 A2
Wealdstone, *London* 15 A1
Wedding, *Berlin* 5 A3
Weehawken, *New York* 21 B1
Weesp, *Amsterdam* 2 B3
Weidling, *Vienna* 31 A1
Weidlingbach, *Vienna* 31 A1
Weigongcum, *Beijing* 4 B1
Weijin He →, *Tianjin* 30 B2
Weissensee, *Berlin* 5 A3
Wellesley, *Boston* 6 B2
Wellesley Falls, *Boston* 6 B2
Wellesley Hills, *Boston* 6 B2
Welling, *London* 15 B4
Wellington, *Boston* 6 A3
Wellington, *Wellington* 32 B1
Wells Fargo Center, *Los Angeles* 16 b1
Weltevreden Park, *Johannesburg* 13 A1
Wembley, *London* 15 A2
Wemmel, *Brussels* 6 A1
Wemmer Pan, *Johannesburg* 13 B2
Wenceslas Square, *Prague* 24 b2
Wendenschloss, *Berlin* 5 B4
Wenhuagong, *Tianjin* 30 B2
Wennington, *London* 15 A5
Werneuchen, *Berlin* 5 A5
West Bedford, *Boston* 6 A2
West Concord, *Boston* 6 A1
West Don →, *Toronto* 30 A2
West Drayton, *London* 15 A1
West Ham, *London* 15 A4
West Harrow, *London* 15 A1
West Heath, *London* 15 B4
West Hill, *Toronto* 30 A3
West Hollywood, *Los Angeles* 16 B2
West Kensington, *London* 15 c1
West Kilburn, *London* 15 a1
West Lamma Channel, *Hong Kong* 12 B1
West Lynn, *Boston* 6 A4
West Medford, *Boston* 6 A3
West Miami, *Miami* 18 B1
West Molesey, *London* 15 B1
West New York, *New York* 21 B1
West of Twin Peaks, *San Francisco* 25 B2
West Park, *Johannesburg* 13 A1
West Rouge, *Toronto* 30 A4
West Roxbury, *Boston* 6 B3
West Springfield, *Washington* 32 C2
West Town, *Chicago* 9 B2
West Wharf, *Karachi* 14 B1
Westbourne Green, *London* 15 a1
Westchester, *Chicago* 9 B1
Westchester, *Los Angeles* 16 C2
Westchester, *New York* 21 A2
Westcliff, *Johannesburg* 13 B2
Westdene, *Johannesburg* 13 B1
Westend, *Helsinki* 12 C1
Wester Hailes, *Edinburgh* 11 B2
Westerham, *Munich* 20 B2
Western Addition, *San Francisco* 25 B2
Western Wall, *Jerusalem* 13 b3
Westgate, *Washington* 32 B3
Westlake, *Cape Town* 8 B1
Westlake, *San Francisco* 25 B2
Westminster, *London* 15 A3
Westmount, *Montreal* 19 B2
Weston, *Boston* 6 A2
Weston, *Toronto* 30 A1
Weston Res., *Boston* 6 A2
Westwood Village, *Los Angeles* 16 B2
Westzaan, *Amsterdam* 2 A1
Wetton, *Cape Town* 8 B2
Wexford, *Toronto* 30 A3
Weybridge, *London* 15 B1
Wezembeek-Oppem, *Brussels* 6 A2
White House, The, *Washington* 32 b1
Whitechapel, *London* 15 A3
Whitehall, *Dublin* 11 A2
Whitehall, *London* 15 b3
Whittier, *Los Angeles* 16 C4
Whitton, *London* 15 B1
Wieden, *Vienna* 31 A2
Wien, *Vienna* 31 A2
Wien-Schwechat, Flughafen, *Vienna* 31 B3
Wienerberg, *Vienna* 31 B2
Wierzbno, *Warsaw* 31 B2
Wijde Wormer, *Amsterdam* 2 A2
Wilanów, *Warsaw* 31 B2
Wilanówka →, *Warsaw* 31 C2
Wilhelmshagen, *Berlin* 5 B5
Wilket Creek Park, *Toronto* 30 A2
Wilkieston, *Edinburgh* 11 B1
Willbrook, *Dublin* 11 B2
Willesden, *London* 15 A2
Willesden Green, *London* 15 A2
Williamsbridge, *New York* 21 A2
Williamsburg, *New York* 21 B2
Williamstown, *Melbourne* 17 B1
Willoughby, *Sydney* 28 A2
Willow Springs, *Chicago* 9 C1
Willowdale, *Toronto* 30 A2
Wilmersdorf, *Berlin* 5 c1
Wilmette, *Chicago* 9 A2
Wilmington, *London* 15 B5
Wilshire Boulevard, *Los Angeles* 16 c1
Wimbledon, *London* 15 B2
Wimbledon Common, *London* 15 B2
Wimbledon Park, *London* 15 B2
Wimbledon Tennis Ground, *London* 15 B2
Winchester, *Boston* 6 A3
Windermere, *Cape Town* 8 A2
Windsor, *Johannesburg* 13 A1
Windsor Hills, *Los Angeles* 16 C2
Windy Arbour, *Dublin* 11 B2
Winning, *Munich* 20 B2
Winthrop, *Boston* 6 A4
Wissous, *Paris* 23 B2
Wittenau, *Berlin* 5 A2
Witwatersrand, Univ. of, *Johannesburg* 13 B2
Włochy, *Warsaw* 31 B1
Wo Mei, *Hong Kong* 12 A2
Wo Yi Hop, *Hong Kong* 12 A1
Woburn, *Boston* 6 A3
Woburn, *Toronto* 30 A3
Woduk Pluit, *Jakarta* 13 A1
Wola, *Warsaw* 31 B1
Wolf Trap Farm Park, *Washington* 32 B2
Wolica, *Warsaw* 31 C2
Wolica, *Warsaw* 31 C1
Wólka Węglowa, *Warsaw* 31 B1
Wollaston, *Boston* 6 B3
Woltersdorf, *Berlin* 5 B5
Woluwe-Saint-Lambert, *Brussels* 6 A2
Woluwe-Saint-Pierre, *Brussels* 6 A2
Wong Chuk Hang, *Hong Kong* 12 B2
Wong Chuk Wan, *Hong Kong* 12 A2
Wong Chuk Yeung, *Hong Kong* 12 A2
Wong Tai Sin, *Hong Kong* 12 A2
Wood Green, *London* 15 A3
Wood Ridge, *New York* 21 A1
Woodbridge, *Toronto* 30 A1
Woodford, *London* 15 A4
Woodford Bridge, *London* 15 A4
Woodford Green, *London* 15 A4
Woodhaven, *New York* 21 B2
Woodhouselee, *Edinburgh* 11 B2
Woodlands New Town, *Singapore* 27 A2
Woodmont, *Washington* 32 B3
Woodside, *London* 15 B3
Woodside, *New York* 21 B2
Woodstock, *Cape Town* 8 A1
Woollahra, *Sydney* 28 B2
Woolloomooloo, *Sydney* 28 b2
Woolooware B., *Sydney* 28 C1
Woolwich, *London* 15 B4
Woolworth Building, *New York* 21 e1
Worli, *Mumbai* 20 A1
Worth, *Chicago* 9 C2
Wren's Nest, *Atlanta* 3 B2
Wrigley Building, *Chicago* 9 b2
Wuhlgarten, *Berlin* 5 A4
Wujiaochang, *Shanghai* 27 B2
Würm →, *Munich* 20 B1
Würm-kanal, *Munich* 20 A1
Wusong, *Shanghai* 27 A1
Wyczółki, *Warsaw* 31 C1
Wygoda, *Warsaw* 31 B2
Wynberg, *Cape Town* 8 B1

X

Xabregas, *Lisbon* 14 A2
Xianggang = Hong Kong, *Hong Kong* 12 B1
Xiaodian, *Tianjin* 30 A2
Xiaogang Park, *Canton* 8 B2
Xiaoping, *Canton* 8 A2
Xiasha chong, *Canton* 8 B1
Xichang, *Canton* 8 B2
Xicheng, *Beijing* 4 B1
Xidan, *Beijing* 4 B2
Xigu Park, *Tianjin* 30 A2
Xigucun, *Tianjin* 30 A1
Ximenwai, *Tianjin* 30 B1
Xinanlou, *Tianjin* 30 B2
Xinkai He →, *Tianjin* 30 A2
Xizhimen, *Beijing* 4 B1
Xu Beihong Mem. Hall, *Beijing* 4 a1
Xuanwu, *Beijing* 4 B1
Xuhui, *Shanghai* 27 B1

Y

Yaba, *Lagos* 14 A2
Yaftābād, *Tehran* 30 B1
Yahara, *Tokyo* 29 A2
Yaho, *Tokyo* 29 A1
Yakire, *Tokyo* 29 A4
Yamada, *Osaka* 22 A4
Yamada, *Tokyo* 29 B2
Yamamoto, *Osaka* 22 B4
Yamato →, *Osaka* 22 B3
Yamuna →, *Delhi* 10 B2
Yan Kit, *Singapore* 27 A3
Yanbu, *Canton* 8 B1
Yangch'ŏn, *Seoul* 26 B1
Yanghuayuan, *Beijing* 4 C1
Yangjae, *Seoul* 26 C2
Yangjiazhuang, *Shanghai* 27 A1
Yangpu, *Shanghai* 27 B2
Yangpu Park, *Shanghai* 27 B2
Yao, *Osaka* 22 B4
Yao Airport, *Osaka* 22 B4
Yarmūk, *Baghdad* 3 B1
Yarra →, *Melbourne* 17 A1
Yarra Bend Park, *Melbourne* 17 A2
Yarraville, *Melbourne* 17 A1
Yau Tong, *Hong Kong* 12 B2
Yauza →, *Moscow* 19 A4
Yeading, *London* 15 A1
Yedikule, *Istanbul* 12 C1
Yemin Moshe, *Jerusalem* 13 b2
Yenikapı, *Istanbul* 12 B1
Yeniköy, *Istanbul* 12 B2
Yerba Buena Gardens, *San Francisco* 25 c2
Yerba Buena I., *San Francisco* 25 B2
Yerres, *Paris* 23 B4
Yerushalayim = Jerusalem, *Jerusalem* 13 B2
Yiheyuan, *Beijing* 4 A1
Yinhangzhen, *Shanghai* 27 A2
Yishun New Town, *Singapore* 27 A3
Yixingbu, *Tianjin* 30 A2
Ylästö, *Helsinki* 12 B2
Yodo →, *Osaka* 22 A4
Yongdingman, *Beijing* 4 B2
Yŏngdong, *Seoul* 26 B2
Yŏngdŭngp'o, *Seoul* 26 B1
Yongfucun, *Canton* 8 B2
Yongjing, *Shanghai* 27 B2
Yongsan, *Seoul* 26 B1
Yonkers, *New York* 21 A2
York, *Toronto* 30 A2
York Mills, *Toronto* 30 A2
Yotsuya, *Tokyo* 29 a2
You'anmen, *Beijing* 4 B1
Yŏŭido, *Seoul* 26 B1
Youndsfield, *Cape Town* 8 B1
Yuanxiatian, *Canton* 8 A2
Yugo-Zarad, *Moscow* 19 B3
Yung Shue Wan, *Hong Kong* 12 B1
Yūsofābād, *Tehran* 30 A2
Yuyuantan Park, *Beijing* 4 b2

Z

Zaandam, *Amsterdam* 2 A1
Zaandijk, *Amsterdam* 2 A1
Zaanstad, *Amsterdam* 2 A1
Záběhlice, *Prague* 24 B2
Ząbki, *Warsaw* 31 B2
Żacisze, *Warsaw* 31 B2
Zahrā, *Baghdad* 3 A1
Zakharkovo, *Moscow* 19 B1
Žalov, *Prague* 24 A2
Załuski, *Warsaw* 31 C1
Zamdorf, *Munich* 20 B2
Zamek Królewski, *Warsaw* 31 a2
Zamek Ujazdowski, *Warsaw* 31 c3
Zanevka, *St. Petersburg* 26 B3
Zapote, *Manila* 17 C1
Záppeio, *Athens* 2 c2
Zarechye, *Moscow* 19 B2
Zaventem, *Brussels* 6 A2
Zawady, *Warsaw* 31 B2
Zâwiyet Abû Musallam, *Cairo* 7 B1
Zawrā' Park, *Baghdad* 3 B2
Zbraslav, *Prague* 24 C2
Zbuzany, *Prague* 24 B1
Zdiby, *Prague* 24 B2
Zeekoevlei, *Cape Town* 8 B2
Zehlendorf, *Berlin* 5 B2
Zenne →, *Brussels* 6 B1
Żerań, *Warsaw* 31 B1
Zerzeń, *Warsaw* 31 B2
Zeytinburnu, *Istanbul* 12 C1
Zhabei, *Shanghai* 27 B1
Zhangguizhuang, *Tianjin* 30 B2
Zhdanov, *Moscow* 19 B4
Zheleznodorozhnyy, *Moscow* 19 B6
Zhenru, *Shanghai* 27 B1
Zhernovka, *St. Petersburg* 26 B2
Zhicun, *Canton* 8 B2
Zhongshan Park, *Beijing* 4 b2
Zhongshan Park, *Shanghai* 27 B1
Zhoucun, *Canton* 8 A2
Zhoujiadu, *Shanghai* 27 B1
Zhoujiazhen, *Shanghai* 27 B2
Zhu Jiang →, *Canton* 8 B3
Zhulebino, *Moscow* 19 B5
Zhushadi, *Canton* 8 A3
Zielona, *Warsaw* 31 B3
Zielonka, *Warsaw* 31 B2
Ziya He →, *Tianjin* 30 A1
Žižkov, *Prague* 24 B2
Zličin, *Prague* 24 B1
Zócalo, *Mexico City* 18 b3
Zografos, *Athens* 2 B2
Żoliborz, *Warsaw* 31 B1
Zonnenbloem, *Cape Town* 8 A1
Zoo, *Beijing* 4 a1
Zugliget, *Budapest* 7 B1
Zugló, *Budapest* 7 A2
Zuiderwoude, *Amsterdam* 2 A3
Zumbi, *Rio de Janeiro* 24 A1
Zunderdorp, *Amsterdam* 2 A2
Zuvuvu →, *São Paulo* 26 C1
Zwanenburg, *Amsterdam* 2 A1
Zwölfaxing, *Vienna* 31 B2
Zyuzino, *Moscow* 19 C3

40 Cape Town, South Africa

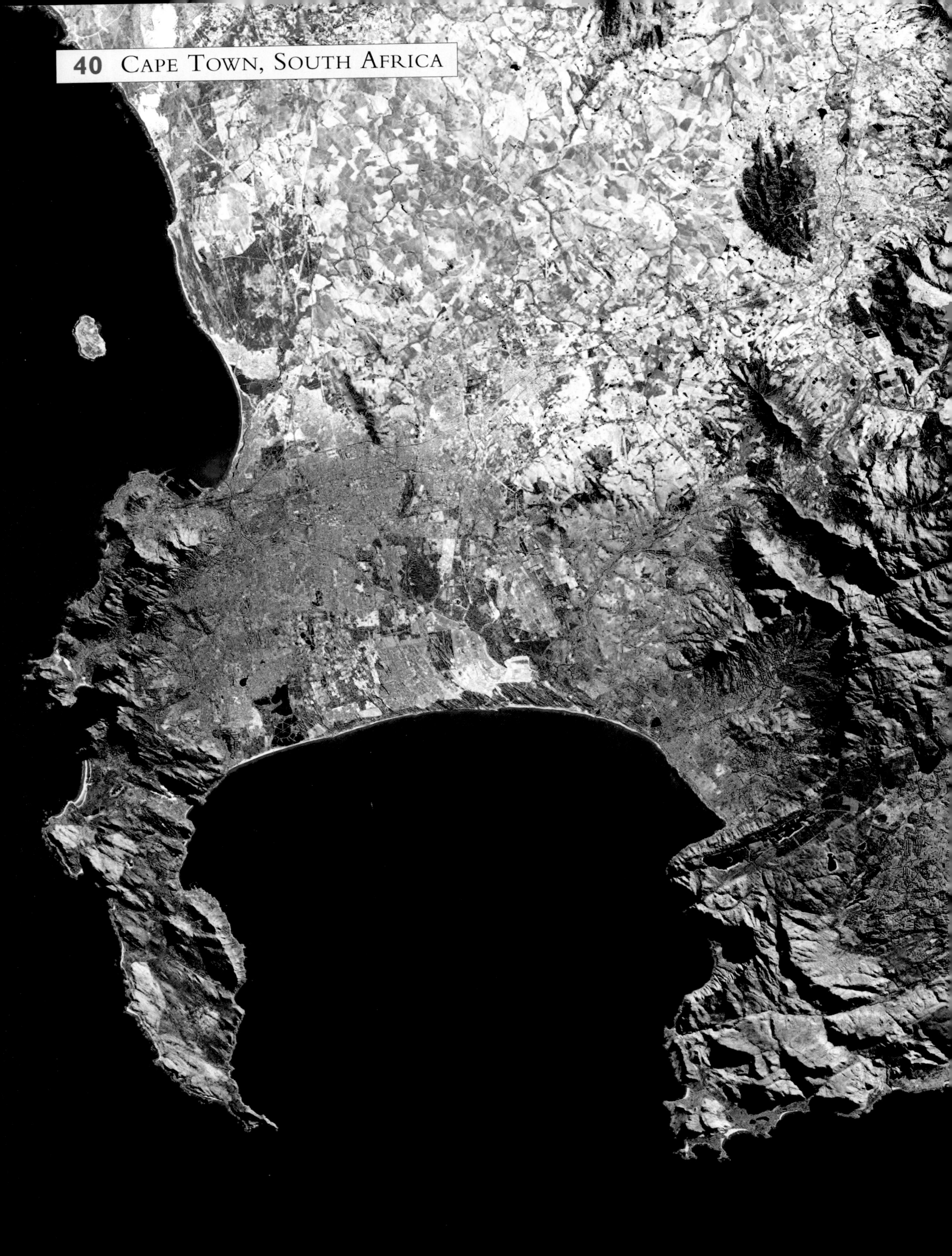

42 Karachi, Pakistan

44 NEW YORK, NY, USA

46 SANTIAGO, CHILE

48 Tokyo, Japan

WORLD MAPS

SETTLEMENTS

▣ PARIS ▪ Berne ⊙ Livorno ⊙ Brugge ⊚ Algeciras ○ *Frejus* ○ *Oberammergau* ○ *Thira*

Settlement symbols and type styles vary according to the scale of each map and indicate the importance of towns on the map rather than specific population figures

∴ Ruins or Archæological Sites

Wells in Desert

ADMINISTRATION

International Boundaries

International Boundaries (Undefined or Disputed)

Internal Boundaries

National Parks

Country Names

NICARAGUA

Administrative Area Names

KENT

CALABRIA

International boundaries show the *de facto* situation where there are rival claims to territory

COMMUNICATIONS

Principal Roads

Other Roads

Road Tunnels

Passes

Airfields

Principal Railways

Railways Under Construction

Other Railways

Railway Tunnels

Principal Canals

PHYSICAL FEATURES

Perrenial Streams

Intermittent Streams

Perennial Lakes

Intermittent Lakes

Swamps and Marshes

Permanent Ice and Glaciers

▲ 8848 Elevations in metres

▼ 8500 Sea Depths in metres

1134 Height of Lake Surface Above Sea Level in metres

ELEVATION AND DEPTH TINTS

Height of Land above Sea Level

Land Below Sea Level

Depth of Sea

in feet: 6000 4000 3000 2000 1500 1000 400 200 0

in metres: 18 000 12 000 9000 6000 4500 3000 1200 600

6000 12 000 15 000 18 000 24 000 in feet

0 200 2000 4000 5000 6000 8000 in metres

Some of the maps have different contours to highlight and clarify the principal relief features

THE WORLD : Political

Projection: *Hammer Equal Area*

10 11 12 13 14 15 16 17 18
A R C T I C O C E A N
Svalbard (Norw.)
Barents Sea
Novaya Zemlya
Kara Sea
Severnaya Zemlya
Laptev Sea
New Siberian Is.
East Siberian Sea
Wrangel I.
Arctic Circle
A
Murmansk
Norilsk
Verkhoyansk
Arkhangelsk
Salekhard
R U S S I A
Yakutsk
Okhotsk
Magadan
Sea of Okhotsk
Bering Sea
Petropavlovsk-Kamchatskiy
B
International Date Line
NORWAY
Oslo
SWEDEN
FINLAND
Helsinki
ST.PETERSBURG
Stockholm
EST.
LATVIA
LITH.
Copenhagen
DENMARK
Hamburg
Amsterdam
NETH.
Berlin
POLAND
Warsaw
BELARUS
Minsk
Brussels
BELG.
GERMANY
Prague
CZECH REP.
SLOVAK REP.
LUX.
Vienna
AUSTRIA
PARIS
Lyons
SW.
Kiev
UKRAINE
Odessa
Budapest
HUNG.
SLOV.
CROATIA
ROMANIA
Belgrade
YUG.
Bucharest
BULGARIA
Sofia
MAC.
ALB.
Marseilles
Milan
ITALY
Rome
Barcelona
Naples
Sardinia
Sicily
MALTA
Algiers
Tunis
TUNISIA
Tripoli
Benghazi
GREECE
Athens
Crete
ISTANBUL
Ankara
TURKEY
Izmir
Mediterranean Sea
Black Sea
MOSCOW
Perm
Yekaterinburg
Kazan
Samara
Saratov
Chelyabinsk
Volga
Volgograd
Astrakhan
Omsk
Tomsk
Novosibirsk
Krasnoyarsk
Barnaul
Astana
Qaraghandy
Irtysh
KAZAKSTAN
L. Balkhash
L. Baikal
Irkutsk
Ulan Ude
Ulan Bator
MONGOLIA
Amur
Sakhalin
Komsomolsk
Khabarovsk
Kuril Is.
Vladivostok
Sapporo
Harbin
Changchun
SHENYANG
NORTH KOREA
P'yongyang
SEOUL
SOUTH KOREA
BEIJING
TIANJIN
Dalian
JAPAN
TŌKYŌ
Ōsaka
Kitakyūshū
PACIFIC OCEAN
C
Ürümqi
CHINA
Taiyuan
Lanzhou
Xi'an
Nanjing
SHANGHAI
East China Sea
Wuhan
Chengdu
CHONGQING
Lhasa
TIBET
Fuzhou
Taipei
TAIWAN
Ryukyu Is.
Kunming
GUANGZHOU
HONG KONG
GEORGIA
Tbilisi
Yerevan
ARM.
Baku
AZER.
Caspian Sea
Aral Sea
UZBEKISTAN
KYRGYZSTAN
Bishkek
Almaty
Tashkent
Samarkand
Dushanbe
TAJIKISTAN
TURKMENISTAN
Ashkhabad
Tabriz
TEHRAN
Mashhad
CYPRUS
SYRIA
LEB.
Beirut
Damascus
Jerusalem
ISR.
Ammān
JORDAN
Baghdād
IRAQ
Esfahān
IRAN
Shīrāz
Kābul
AFGHANISTAN
Islamabad
JAMMU & KASHMIR
Lahore
PAKISTAN
Indus
DELHI
New Delhi
NEPAL
Katmandu
BHU.
Ganges
BANGLA-DESH
DACCA
Kanpur
INDIA
KARACHI
KOLKATA (Calcutta)
Nagpur
Ahmadabad
MUMBAI (Bombay)
Arabian Sea
Bay of Bengal
Hyderabad
CHENNAI (Madras)
Bangalore
Lakshadweep Is. (India)
Andaman Is. (India)
SRI LANKA
Colombo
Nicobar Is. (India)
MALDIVES
BURMA (MYANMAR)
Rangoon
Hanoi
Hainan
LAOS
Vientiane
VIET-NAM
THAILAND
BANGKOK
CAMBODIA
Phnom Penh
Ho Chi Minh City
South China Sea
MANILA
PHILIPPINES
Alexandria
CAIRO
Nile
EGYPT
Aswân
LIBYA
KUWAIT
BAHRAIN
QATAR
The Gulf
Riyadh
SAUDI ARABIA
Mecca
Abu Dhabi
U.A.E.
Muscat
OMAN
Red Sea
GERIA
NIGER
CHAD
L. Chad
Niamey
Kano
Ndjamena
NIGERIA
Abuja
Ibadan
Lagos
BENIN
TOGO
SUDAN
Omdurmân
Khartoum
Blue Nile
White Nile
Asmara
ERITREA
DJIBOUTI
Sana
YEMEN
Aden
G. of Aden
Socotra (Yemen)
Addis Ababa
ETHIOPIA
SOMALI REP.
CAMEROON
Douala
Yaoundé
CENTRAL AFRICAN REP.
Bangui
EQUATORIAL GUINEA
SÃO TOMÉ & PRINCIPE
Libreville
GABON
CONGO
Zaire
Kisangani
CONGO DEM.REP.OF THE
UGANDA
Kampala
L. Turkana
KENYA
Mogadishu
L. Victoria
Kigali
RWANDA
BURUNDI
Bujumbura
Nairobi
Brazzaville
Kinshasa
Kasai
Kananga
CABINDA (Angola)
Mombasa
Zanzibar
Dodoma
L. Tanganyika
TANZANIA
Dar es Salaam
Luanda
ANGOLA
Benguela
Lubumbashi
ZAMBIA
Lusaka
L. Malawi
Lilongwe
MALAWI
Harare
ZIMBABWE
MOZAMBIQUE
Bulawayo
NAMIBIA
Windhoek
BOTSWANA
Gaborone
Pretoria
Johannesburg
Maputo
SWAZILAND
SOUTH AFRICA
LESOTHO
Durban
Cape Town
C. of Good Hope
Port Elizabeth
Mozambique Channel
COMOROS
Mayotte (Fr.)
MADAGASCAR
Antananarivo
RÉUNION (Fr.)
Rodriguez
MAURITIUS
Cargados Carajos
Agalega Is.
Aldabra Is.
SEYCHELLES
Amirante Is.
Equator
INDIAN OCEAN
Diego Garcia
Chagos Arch. (U.K.)
Cocos Is. (Austral.)
Christmas I. (Austral.)
Tropic of Capricorn
Tropic of Cancer
MALAYSIA
Medan
Kuala Lumpur
PEN. MALAYSIA
SINGAPORE
Sumatra
SABAH
BRUNEI
SARAWAK
Borneo
Palembang
Banjarmasin
INDONESIA
JAKARTA
Bandung
Java
Surabaya
Ujung Pandang
IRIAN JAYA
EAST TIMOR
Timor
Arafura Sea
PAPUA NEW GUINEA
Port Moresby
C. York
New Ireland
New Britain
SOLOMON IS.
Darwin
Cairns
Townsville
Port Hedland
Alice Springs
AUSTRALIA
Rockhampton
Geraldton
Brisbane
Perth
Fremantle
Kalgoorlie-Boulder
Great Australian Bight
Adelaide
Darling
Newcastle
Sydney
Canberra
Melbourne
Tasmania
Hobart
Tasman Sea
Lord Howe I. (Austral.)
Norfolk I. (Austral.)
Auckland
North I.
NEW ZEALAND
Wellington
Christchurch
South I.
Dunedin
Stewart I.
Bounty Is. (N.Z.)
Antipodes Is.
Auckland Is. (N.Z.)
Campbell I. (N.Z.)
Macquarie Is. (Austral.)
Bonin Is. (Japan)
Volcano Is. (Japan)
Marcus I. (Japan)
NORTHERN MARIANAS (U.S.A.)
Wake I. (U.S.A.)
GUAM (U.S.A.)
Yap
PALAU
FEDERATED STATES OF MICRONESIA
Truk
Pohnpei
Caroline Is.
MARSHALL IS.
Gilbert Is.
NAURU
KIRIBATI
TUVALU
Santa Cruz I.
VANUATU
NEW CALEDONIA (Fr.)
FIJI
Suva
D
E
F
G
H
Amsterdam I. (Fr.)
St.Paul (Fr.)
Prince Edward Is. (S.Africa)
Crozet Is. (Fr.)
Kerguelen (Fr.)
McDonald Is. (Austral.)
Heard I. (Austral.)
Bouvet I. (Norw.)
SOUTHERN OCEAN
Antarctic Circle
Antarctica
Ross Sea
East from Greenwich

Hanoi ● Capital Cities

COPYRIGHT GEORGE PHILIP LTD.

ARCTIC OCEAN 1:35 000 000

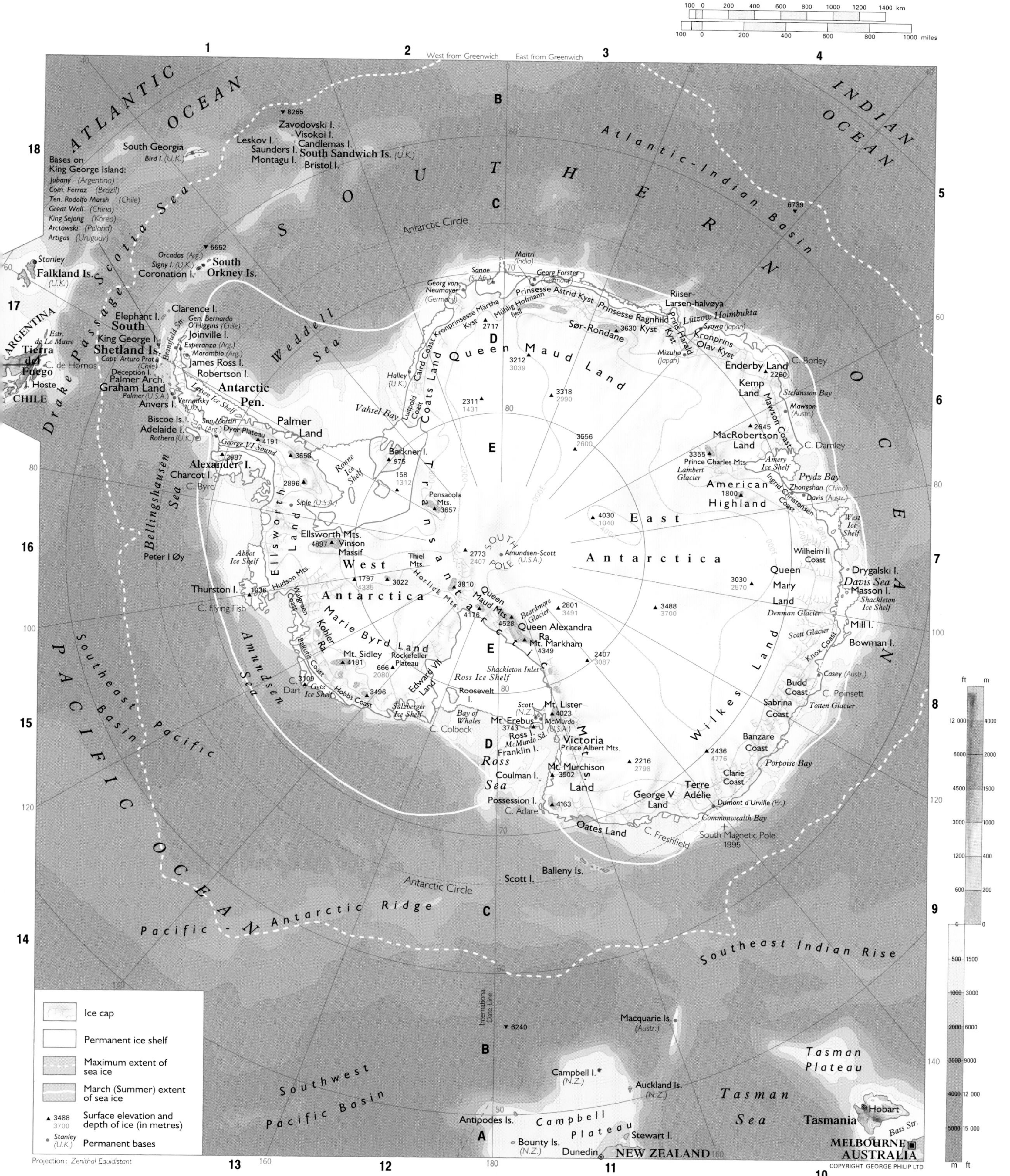
100 0 200 400 600 800 1000 1200 1400 km
100 0 200 400 600 800 1000 miles
West from Greenwich
East from Greenwich
ATLANTIC OCEAN
INDIAN OCEAN
PACIFIC OCEAN
SOUTHERN OCEAN
Atlantic-Indian Basin
Antarctic Circle
South Georgia
Bird I. (U.K.)
Zavodovski I.
Visokoi I.
Leskov I.
Candlemas I.
Saunders I.
Montagu I.
South Sandwich Is. (U.K.)
Bristol I.
8265
Bases on King George Island:
Jubany (Argentina)
Com. Ferraz (Brazil)
Ten. Rodolfo Marsh (Chile)
Great Wall (China)
King Sejong (Korea)
Arctowski (Poland)
Artigas (Uruguay)
Scotia Sea
Drake Passage
Stanley
Falkland Is. (U.K.)
ARGENTINA
Tierra del Fuego
C. de Hornos
I. Hoste
CHILE
Estr. de Le Maire
Orcadas (Arg.)
Signy I. (U.K.)
Coronation I.
South Orkney Is.
5552
Clarence I.
Elephant I.
South Shetland Is.
King George I.
Gen. Bernardo O'Higgins (Chile)
Joinville I.
Esperanza (Arg.)
Marambio (Arg.)
Capt. Arturo Prat (Chile)
James Ross I.
Deception I.
Robertson I.
Palmer Arch.
Graham Land
Palmer (U.S.A.)
Anvers I.
Vernadsky (U.K.)
Antarctic Pen.
Larsen Ice Shelf
Biscoe Is.
Adelaide I.
Rothera (U.K.)
San Martin (Arg.)
Dyer Plateau
George VI Sound
Palmer Land
4191
2987
3658
Alexander I.
Charcot I.
C. Byrd
Bellingshausen Sea
Weddell Sea
Vahsel Bay
Ronne Ice Shelf
Berkner I.
975
158
1312
Pensacola Mts.
3657
2896
Siple (U.S.A.)
Ellsworth Land
Ellsworth Mts.
4897 Vinson Massif
Abbot Ice Shelf
Peter I Øy
Thurston I.
3036
Hudson Mts.
Walgreen Coast
C. Flying Fish
West Antarctica
1797
4335
3022
Thiel Mts.
Horlick Mts.
3810
Marie Byrd Land
Kohler Ra.
Mt. Sidley
4181
Rockefeller Plateau
666
2080
Edward VII Land
Bakutis Coast
3109
C. Dart
Getz Ice Shelf
Hobbs Coast
3496
Sulzberger Ice Shelf
Amundsen Sea
Southeast Pacific Basin
Ross Ice Shelf
Roosevelt I.
Bay of Whales
C. Colbeck
Shackleton Inlet
Ross Sea
Mt. Erebus
3743
Ross I.
McMurdo Sd.
Franklin I.
Scott (N.Z.)
McMurdo (U.S.A.)
Mt. Lister
4023
Victoria Land
Prince Albert Mts.
Mt. Murchison
3502
Coulman I.
Possession I.
C. Adare
4163
Oates Land
C. Freshfield
Balleny Is.
Scott I.
Transantarctic Mts.
Queen Maud Mts.
4176
4528
Beardmore Glacier
Queen Alexandra Ra.
Mt. Markham
4349
2801
3491
2407
3087
2773
2407
SOUTH POLE
Amundsen-Scott (U.S.A.)
Halley (U.K.)
Luitpold Coast
Caird Coast
Coats Land
Kronprinsesse Martha Kyst
2717
Georg von Neumayer (Germany)
Sanae (S. Afr.)
Maitri (India)
Georg Forster (Germany)
Prinsesse Astrid Kyst
Mühlig Hofmann fjell
Queen Maud Land
Sør-Rondane
3630
Prinsesse Ragnhild Kyst
Prins Harald Kyst
Riiser-Larsen-halvøya
Lützow Holmbukta
Syowa (Japan)
Mizuho (Japan)
Kronprins Olav Kyst
3212
3039
3318
2990
2311
1431
3656
2600
Enderby Land
2260
C. Borley
Kemp Land
Stefansson Bay
Mawson (Austr.)
Mawson Coast
2645
MacRobertson Land
C. Darnley
3355
Prince Charles Mts.
Lambert Glacier
Amery Ice Shelf
Prydz Bay
Zhongshan (China)
Davis (Austr.)
Ingrid Christensen Coast
American Highland
1800
4030
1040
East Antarctica
West Ice Shelf
Wilhelm II Coast
Queen Mary Land
3030
2570
3488
3700
Drygalski I.
Davis Sea
Masson I.
Shackleton Ice Shelf
Denman Glacier
Mill I.
Scott Glacier
Knox Coast
Bowman I.
Casey (Austr.)
Budd Coast
C. Poinsett
Sabrina Coast
Totten Glacier
Wilkes Land
Banzare Coast
2436
4776
Porpoise Bay
2216
2798
Clarie Coast
Terre Adélie
George V Land
Dumont d'Urville (Fr.)
Commonwealth Bay
South Magnetic Pole 1995
6739
Pacific-Antarctic Ridge
Southeast Indian Rise
International Date Line
6240
Macquarie Is. (Austr.)
Tasman Plateau
Campbell I. (N.Z.)
Auckland Is. (N.Z.)
Tasman Sea
Southwest Pacific Basin
Campbell Plateau
Antipodes Is.
Bounty Is. (N.Z.)
Stewart I.
Dunedin
NEW ZEALAND
Tasmania
Hobart
Bass Str.
MELBOURNE
AUSTRALIA
ft m
12 000 4000
6000 2000
4500 1500
3000 1000
1200 400
600 200
0 0
500 1500
1000 3000
2000 6000
3000 9000
4000 12 000
5000 15 000
m ft
Ice cap
Permanent ice shelf
Maximum extent of sea ice
March (Summer) extent of sea ice
3488 3700 Surface elevation and depth of ice (in metres)
Stanley (U.K.) Permanent bases
Projection: Zenithal Equidistant
COPYRIGHT GEORGE PHILIP LTD

The Antarctic Treaty was signed in Washington in 1959 so that scientific and technical research could continue unhampered by international politics.

All territorial claims covering land areas south of latitude 60°S have been suspended. Those claims were:

Norwegian claim	45°E - 20°W	French claim	136°E - 142°E	British claim	80°W - 20°W
Australian claims	45°E - 136°E	New Zealand claim	160°E - 150°W	Argentine claim	74°W - 53°W
	142°E - 160°E	Chilean claim	90°W - 53°W		

EUROPE : Physical 1:20 000 000

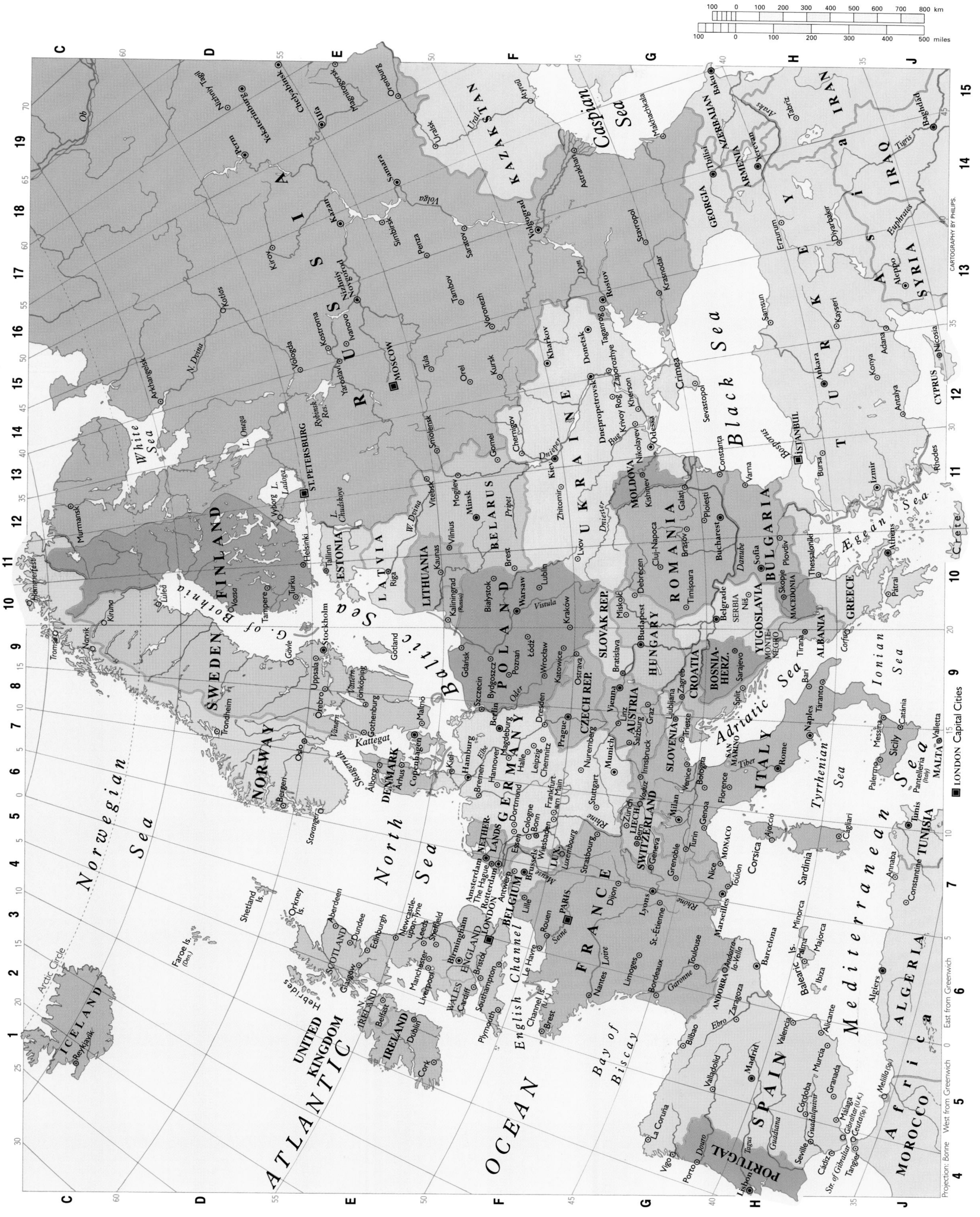
100 0 100 200 300 400 500 600 700 800 km
100 0 100 200 300 400 500 miles
ICELAND
Reykjavík
NORWAY
SWEDEN
FINLAND
DENMARK
UNITED KINGDOM
IRELAND
NETHERLANDS
BELGIUM
LUX.
GERMANY
FRANCE
SWITZERLAND
LIECH.
AUSTRIA
CZECH REP.
SLOVAK REP.
POLAND
HUNGARY
SLOVENIA
CROATIA
BOSNIA-HERZ.
YUGOSLAVIA
SERBIA
MONTENEGRO
MACEDONIA
ALBANIA
GREECE
BULGARIA
ROMANIA
MOLDOVA
UKRAINE
BELARUS
LITHUANIA
LATVIA
ESTONIA
RUSSIA
KAZAKSTAN
GEORGIA
ARMENIA
AZERBAIJAN
TURKEY
SYRIA
IRAQ
IRAN
CYPRUS
ITALY
SAN MARINO
MALTA
SPAIN
PORTUGAL
ANDORRA
MONACO
MOROCCO
ALGERIA
TUNISIA
Africa
Norwegian Sea
North Sea
ATLANTIC OCEAN
Bay of Biscay
English Channel
Baltic Sea
G. of Bothnia
White Sea
Black Sea
Caspian Sea
Mediterranean Sea
Adriatic Sea
Tyrrhenian Sea
Ionian Sea
Ægean Sea
Arctic Circle
■ LONDON Capital Cities
Projection: Bonne
West from Greenwich
East from Greenwich
CARTOGRAPHY BY PHILIPS

SCANDINAVIA 1:5 000 000

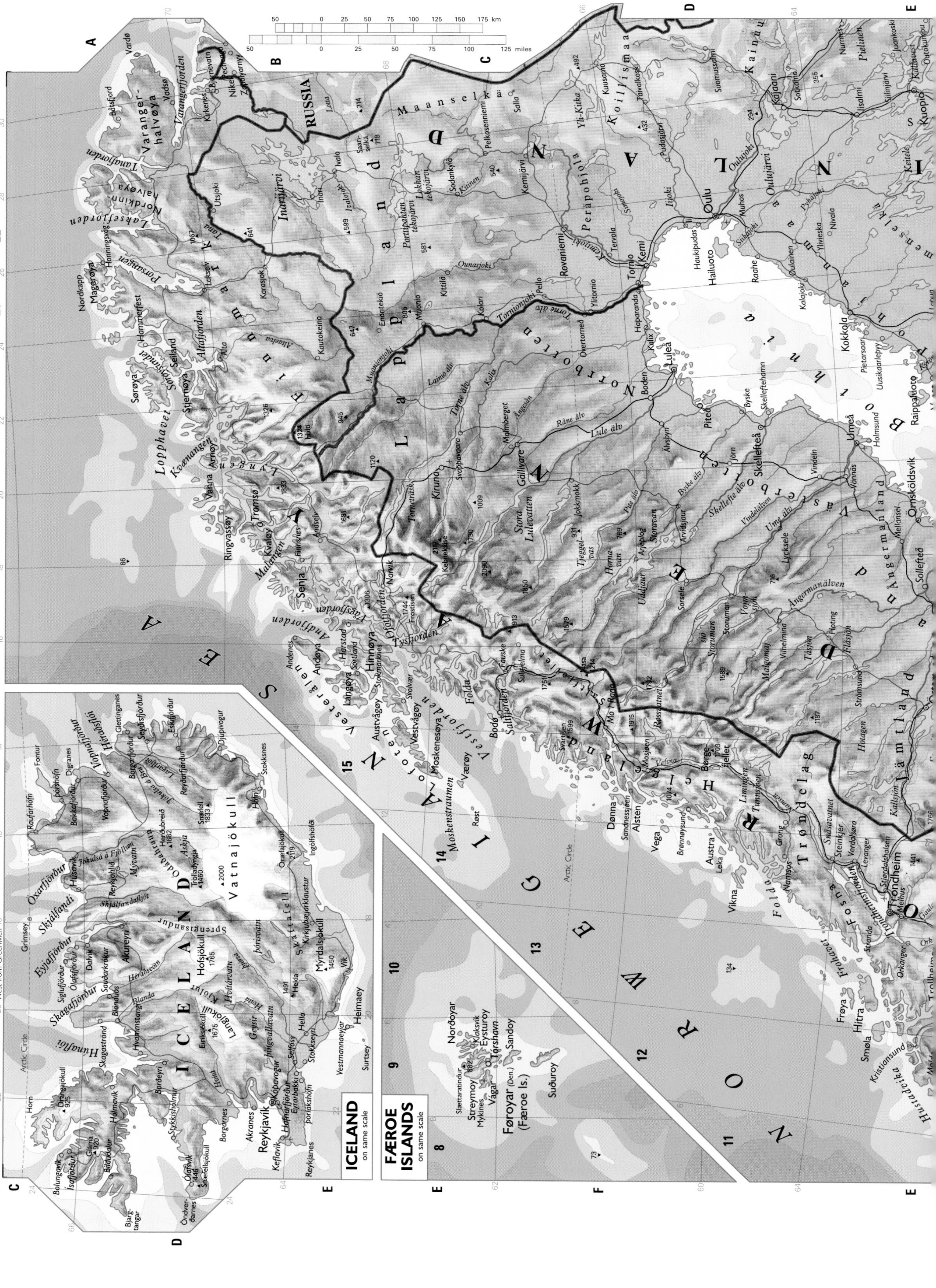

NORWAY
SWEDEN
FINLAND
ESTONIA
LATVIA
LITHUANIA
BELARUS
POLAND
GERMANY
DENMARK
BALTIC SEA
Gulf of Bothnia
Gulf of Finland
Gulf of Riga
Ålands hav
Skagerrak
Kattegat
STOCKHOLM
Oslo
Helsinki (Helsingfors)
Tallinn
Riga
Vilnius
KØBENHAVN (Copenhagen)
Göteborg (Gothenburg)
Bergen
Stavanger
Kristiansand
Turku (Åbo)
Tampere
Tartu
Kaunas
Klaipėda
Kaliningrad (Russia)
Gdańsk
Gdynia
Malmö
Gotland
Öland
Bornholm
Åland (Ahvenanmaa)
Hiiumaa (Dagö)
Saaremaa (Ösel)
Sjælland
Fyn
Lolland
Rügen
Vänern
Vättern
Mälaren
Svealand
Götaland
Jutland
Hardangervidda
Jotunheimen
Telemark
Värmland
Dalarna
Småland
Skåne
Zatoka Gdańska
Kurshskiy Zaliv
Chudskoye Ozero
Daugava
Neman
Nordfriesische Inseln
Mecklenburger Bucht
Kieler Bucht
Fehmarn Bælt
Store Bælt
Lille Bælt
Projection: Conical with two standard parallels
East from Greenwich
COPYRIGHT GEORGE PHILIP LTD.

ENGLAND AND WALES 1:2 000 000

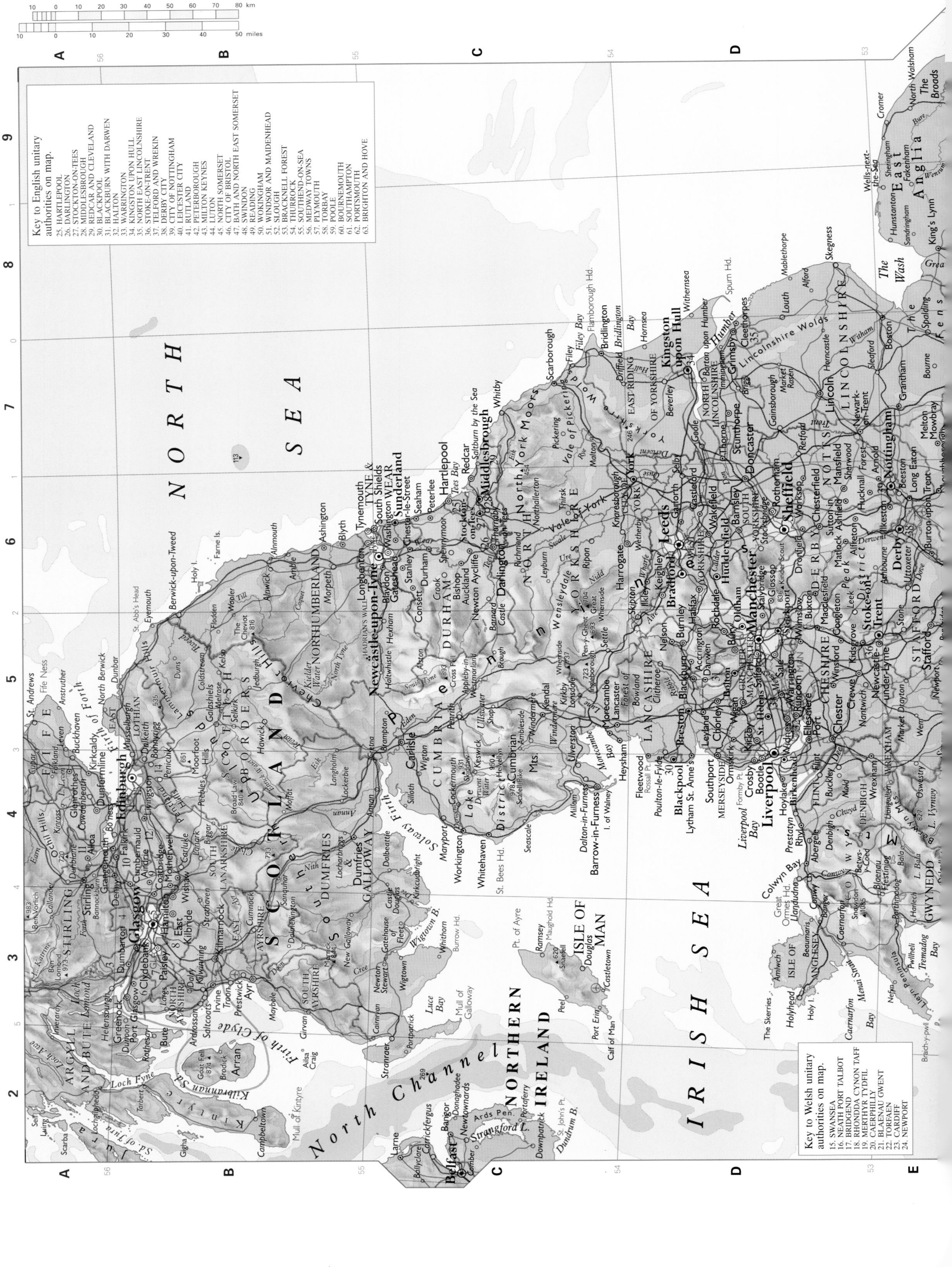

ENGLISH CHANNEL
Bristol Channel
WALES
ENGLAND
FRANCE
CHANNEL ISLANDS (U.K.)
Isles of Scilly
On same scale
Strait of Dover
Thames Estuary
Cardigan Bay
Lyme Bay
Baie de la Seine
Baie de la Somme
LONDON
BIRMINGHAM
Bristol
Cardiff
Southampton
Portsmouth
Brighton
Bournemouth
Plymouth
Exeter
Swansea
Newport
Oxford
Reading
Northampton
Coventry
Wolverhampton
Peterborough
Cambridge
Ipswich
Colchester
Chelmsford
Southend-on-Sea
Canterbury
Dover
Folkestone
Hastings
Eastbourne
Gloucester
Cheltenham
Swindon
Salisbury
Weymouth
Torquay
Penzance
Truro
Guernsey
Jersey
Alderney
Sark
Herm
Cherbourg
Le Havre
Rouen
Caen
Dieppe
Calais
Boulogne-sur-Mer
CORNWALL
DEVON
DORSET
SOMERSET
WILTSHIRE
HANTS
SURREY
KENT
EAST SUSSEX
WEST SUSSEX
ESSEX
SUFFOLK
NORFOLK
HERTS
BUCKS
OXFORD
BERKSHIRE
GLOUCS
HEREFORD
WORCESTER
WARWICK
NORTHAMPTON
CAMBRIDGE
BEDFORD
PEMBROKESHIRE
CARMARTHENSHIRE
CEREDIGION
POWYS
SHROPSHIRE
MANCHE
CALVADOS
SEINE-MARITIME
HAUTE-NORMANDIE
ft m
3000 1000
1500 500
600 200
300 100
0 0
50 150
100 300
200 600
m ft
Projection : Lambert's Conformal Conic
West from Greenwich
East from Greenwich
COPYRIGHT GEORGE PHILIP LTD.

Key to Scottish unitary authorities on map
1. CITY OF ABERDEEN
2. DUNDEE CITY
3. WEST DUNBARTONSHIRE
4. EAST DUNBARTONSHIRE
5. CITY OF GLASGOW
6. INVERCLYDE
7. RENFREWSHIRE
8. EAST RENFREWSHIRE
9. NORTH LANARKSHIRE
10. FALKIRK
11. CLACKMANNANSHIRE
12. WEST LOTHIAN
13. CITY OF EDINBURGH
14. MIDLOTHIAN
ORKNEY IS.
On same scale
SHETLAND IS.
On same scale
SCOTLAND
ATLANTIC OCEAN
NORTH SEA
ENGLAND
NORTHERN IRELAND
North Channel
Pentland Firth
Moray Firth
Firth of Forth
Firth of Clyde
Firth of Lorn
Solway Firth
Outer Hebrides
Inner Hebrides
North Minch
Little Minch
North West Highlands
Grampian Mountains
Cairngorm Mts.
Monadhliath Mts.
Southern Uplands
Lewis
Harris
North Uist
South Uist
Skye
Mull
Islay
Jura
Arran
Stornoway
Inverness
Aberdeen
Dundee
Perth
Stirling
Glasgow
Edinburgh
Fort William
Oban
Thurso
Wick
Elgin
Ben Nevis 1342
Dumfries
Carlisle
Newcastle-upon-Tyne
Belfast
Projection : Lambert's Conformal Conic
West from Greenwich

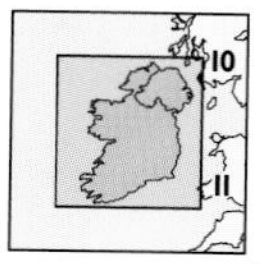
10
11

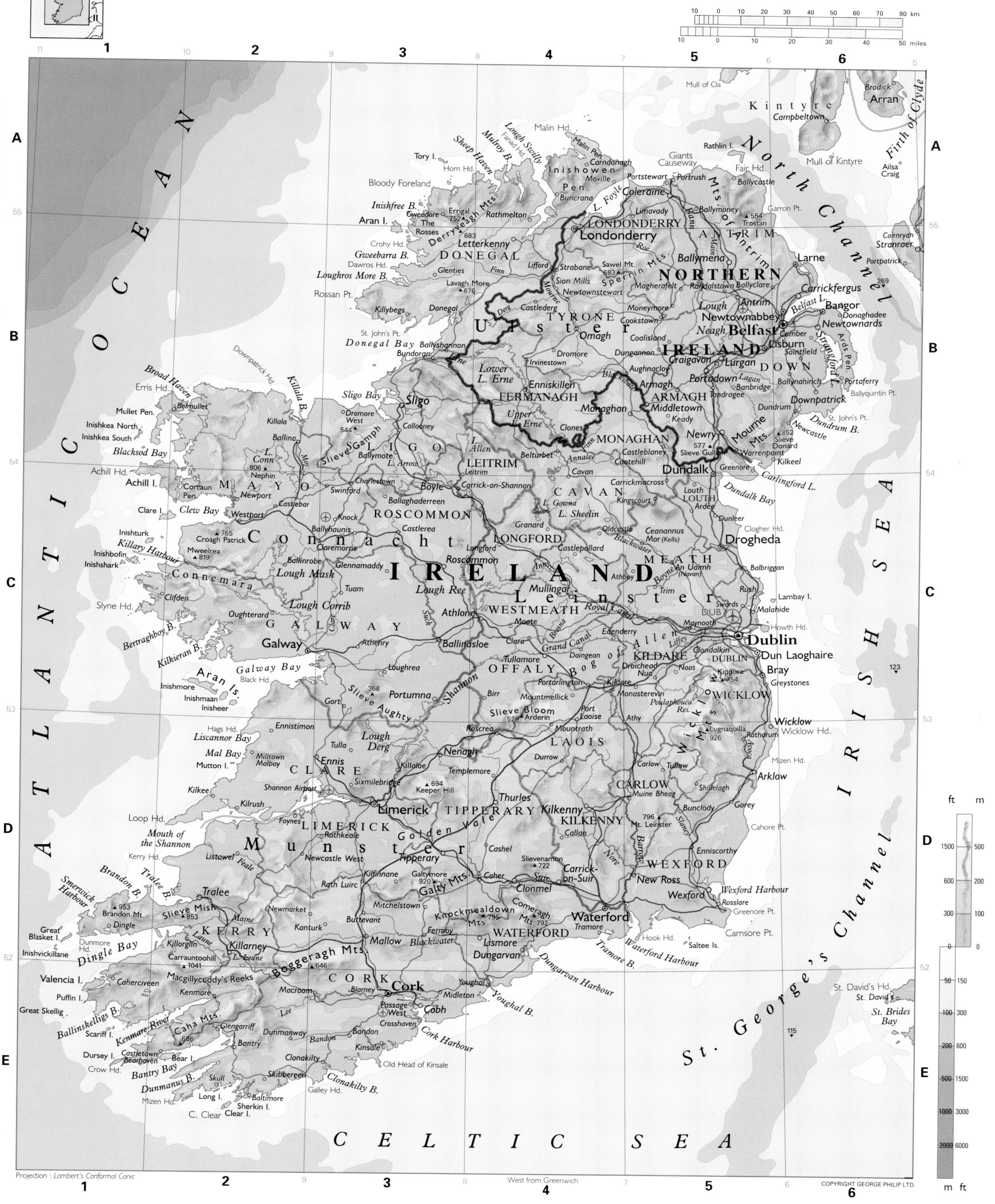
0 10 20 30 40 50 60 70 80 km
0 10 20 30 40 50 miles
ATLANTIC OCEAN
NORTH CHANNEL
IRISH SEA
St. George's Channel
CELTIC SEA
Kintyre
Campbeltown
Mull of Oa
Mull of Kintyre
Arran
Brodick
Firth of Clyde
Ailsa Craig
Cairnryan
Stranraer
Portpatrick
Rathlin I.
Fair Hd.
Giants Causeway
Malin Hd.
Malin Pen.
Inishowen Pen.
Carndonagh
Moville
Buncrana
Lough Swilly
Fanad Hd.
Mulroy B.
Sheep Haven
Horn Hd.
Tory I.
Bloody Foreland
Inishfree B.
Aran I.
Gweedore
Errigal 752
The Rosses
Derryveagh Mts.
683
Rathmelton
Letterkenny
Crohy Hd.
Gweebarra B.
Dawros Hd.
DONEGAL
Glenties
Finn
Loughros More B.
Lavagh More 676
Rossan Pt.
Killybegs
Donegal
St. John's Pt.
Donegal Bay
Ballyshannon
Bundoran
Erne
Lough Foyle
Portstewart
Portrush
Coleraine
Limavady
Bann
LONDONDERRY
Londonderry
Roe
Ballymoney
Mts. of Antrim
554 Trostan
Garron Pt.
ANTRIM
Ballymena
Larne
Strabane
Lifford
Sion Mills
Sawel Mt. 683
Sperrin Mts.
NORTHERN
IRELAND
Magherafelt
Randalstown
Ballyclare
Carrickfergus
Newtownstewart
Mourne
Derg
Castlederg
TYRONE
Moneymore
Cookstown
Antrim
Lough Neagh
Newtownabbey
Belfast L.
Bangor
Donaghadee
Newtownards
Belfast
Comber
Lisburn
Ulster
Omagh
Coalisland
Dungannon
Craigavon
Lurgan
Saintfield
Strangford L.
Ards Pen.
Portaferry
Ballyquintin Pt.
DOWN
Dromore
Irvinestown
Lower L. Erne
Enniskillen
FERMANAGH
Aughnacloy
Blackwater
Armagh
ARMAGH
Portadown
Lagan
Banbridge
Tandragee
Ballynahinch
Downpatrick
Middletown
Keady
Dundrum
St. John's Pt.
Dundrum B.
Monaghan
Upper L. Erne
Clones
MONAGHAN
Newry
Mourne Mts.
852 Slieve Donard
Newcastle
577 Slieve Gullion
Warrenpoint
Kilkeel
Carlingford L.
Greenore
Dundalk
Dundalk Bay
Louth
LOUTH
Ardee
Dunleer
Clogher Hd.
Drogheda
Downpatrick Hd.
Killala B.
Broad Haven
Erris Hd.
Belmullet
Mullet Pen.
Inishkea North
Inishkea South
Killala
Ballina
Moy
Blacksod Bay
L. Conn
806 Nephin
Achill Hd.
Achill I.
Corraun Pen.
MAYO
Newport
Clare I.
Clew Bay
Westport
Castlebar
Sligo Bay
Sligo
Dromore West
544
Ox Mts.
Slieve Gamph
SLIGO
Collooney
Ballymote
L. Arrow
L. Allen
LEITRIM
Leitrim
Belturbet
Annalee
Castleblaney
Cootehill
Carrickmacross
Charlestown
Swinford
Knock
Boyle
Carrick-on-Shannon
Ballaghaderreen
ROSCOMMON
CAVAN
Cavan
L. Gowna
L. Sheelin
Kingscourt
Inishturk
Croagh Patrick 765
Killary Harbour
Inishbofin
Inishshark
Mweelrea 819
Ballyhaunis
Castlerea
Claremorris
Connacht
Granard
LONGFORD
Longford
Castlepollard
Oldcastle
Ceanannus Mor (Kells)
Blackwater
MEATH
Ballinrobe
Glennamaddy
Roscommon
Inny
An Uaimh (Navan)
Boyne
Balbriggan
Connemara
Lough Mask
Tuam
IRELAND
Athboy
Trim
Rush
Lambay I.
Clifden
Lough Ree
Mullingar
Leinster
Swords
Malahide
Slyne Hd.
Lough Corrib
Suck
Athlone
WESTMEATH
Royal Canal
Maynooth
DUB
Howth Hd.
Oughterard
Clare
GALWAY
Moate
Brosna
Edenderry
Bog of Allen
Liffey
Dublin
Bertraghboy B.
Galway
Athenry
Ballinasloe
Clara
Grand Canal
KILDARE
Clondalkin
Dun Laoghaire
DUBLIN
Kilkieran B.
Tullamore
Daingean
Bray
Galway Bay
Black Hd.
Loughrea
OFFALY
Droichead Nua
Naas
Kippure 754
Greystones
123
Aran Is.
Inishmore
Inishmaan
Inisheer
368
Portumna
Shannon
Portarlington
Kildare
Monasterevin
Poulaphouca Res.
WICKLOW
Gort
Slieve Aughty
Birr
Mountmellick
Slieve Bloom 528 Arderin
Port Laoise
Athy
Wicklow Mts.
Wicklow
Wicklow Hd.
Hags Hd.
Ennistimon
Liscannor Bay
Lough Derg
Tulla
Roscrea
Mountrath
LAOIS
Lugnaquilla 926
Rathdrum
Avoca
Mal Bay
Milltown Malbay
Mutton I.
Ennis
CLARE
Killaloe
Nenagh
Durrow
Templemore
Carlow
Tullow
Mizen Hd.
Arklow
Shillelagh
Kilkee
Shannon Airport
Sixmilebridge
694 Keeper Hill
Thurles
CARLOW
Muine Bheag
Bunclody
Gorey
Loop Hd.
Kilrush
Limerick
TIPPERARY
Kilkenny
KILKENNY
796 Mt. Leinster
Slaney
Mouth of the Shannon
Foynes
LIMERICK
Rathkeale
Golden Vale
Callan
Cahore Pt.
Kerry Hd.
Listowel
Feale
Munster
Newcastle West
Tipperary
Cashel
Barrow
Nore
Enniscorthy
WEXFORD
Brandon B.
Tralee B.
Smerwick Harbour
Kilfinnane
Galtymore 920
Galty Mts.
Caher
Slievenamon 722
Suir
Carrick-on-Suir
New Ross
Wexford
Wexford Harbour
Tralee
953
Brandon Mt.
Slieve Mish
853
Maine
Rath Luirc
Clonmel
Rosslare
Greenore Pt.
Dingle
Newmarket
Mitchelstown
Knockmealdown Mts.
795
Comeragh Mts. 792
Waterford
Tramore
Great Blasket I.
KERRY
Kanturk
Buttevant
Fermoy
WATERFORD
Carnsore Pt.
Dunmore Hd.
Dingle Bay
Killorglin
Laune
Killarney
L. Leane
Mallow
Blackwater
Lismore
Hook Hd.
Saltee Is.
Inishvickillane
Carrauntoohill 1041
Boggeragh Mts.
646
Dungarvan
Tramore B.
Waterford Harbour
Dungarvan Harbour
Valencia I.
Caherciveen
Macgillycuddy's Reeks
CORK
Cork
Youghal
St. David's Hd.
St. David's
Puffin I.
Kenmare
Macroom
Blarney
Midleton
Youghal B.
Great Skellig
Ballinskelligs B.
Lee
Passage West
Cobh
St. Brides Bay
Kenmare River
Caha Mts.
686
Glengarriff
Dunmanway
Crosshaven
Scariff I.
Bandon
Cork Harbour
Dursey I.
Castletown Bearhaven
Bear I.
Bantry
Kinsale
115
Crow Hd.
Bantry Bay
Clonakilty
Old Head of Kinsale
Dunmanus B.
Skull
Skibbereen
Clonakilty B.
Mizen Hd.
Long I.
Baltimore
Sherkin I.
Galley Hd.
C. Clear
Clear I.
ft m
1500 500
600 200
300 100
0 0
50 150
100 300
200 600
500 1500
1000 3000
2000 6000
m ft
Projection : Lambert's Conformal Conic
West from Greenwich
COPYRIGHT GEORGE PHILIP LTD.

BRITISH ISLES 1:5 000 000

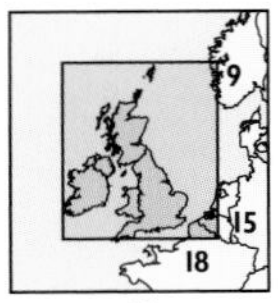

ATLANTIC OCEAN
NORTH SEA
CELTIC SEA
IRISH SEA
English Channel
Bristol Channel
St. George's Channel
North Channel
Pentland Firth
Moray Firth
Firth of Clyde
North Minch
Str. of Dover
UNITED KINGDOM
SCOTLAND
ENGLAND
WALES
NORTHERN IRELAND
IRELAND
FRANCE
NETHERLANDS
BELGIUM
NORWAY
Shetland Is.
Orkney Is.
Outer Hebrides
Inner Hebrides
Channel Is. (U.K.)
Isles of Scilly
I. of Man
Anglesey
Isle of Wight
Grampian Mts.
North West Highlands
Southern Uplands
Pennines
Cheviot Hills
Cumbrian Mts.
Cambrian Mts.
Cotswold Hills
Wicklow Mts.
Ben Nevis 1342
Lerwick
Kirkwall
Stornoway
Inverness
Aberdeen
Dundee
Perth
Stirling
Edinburgh
Glasgow
Newcastle-upon-Tyne
Sunderland
Middlesbrough
Carlisle
York
Leeds
Bradford
Kingston upon Hull
Blackpool
Preston
Manchester
Liverpool
Sheffield
Nottingham
Derby
Leicester
Birmingham
Wolverhampton
Coventry
Norwich
Cambridge
Oxford
LONDON
Southampton
Portsmouth
Brighton
Bristol
Cardiff
Swansea
Plymouth
Exeter
Bournemouth
Land's End
Penzance
Belfast
Londonderry
Dublin
Cork
Limerick
Galway
Waterford
Wexford
Bergen
Stavanger
Rotterdam
Antwerpen
Brussel (Bruxelles)
Calais
Dunkerque
Lille
Le Havre
Rouen
Cherbourg
Caen
Amiens
Projection: Conical with two standard parallels
West from Greenwich
East from Greenwich
COPYRIGHT GEORGE PHILIP LTD.

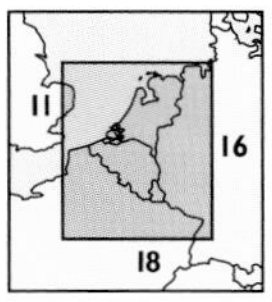

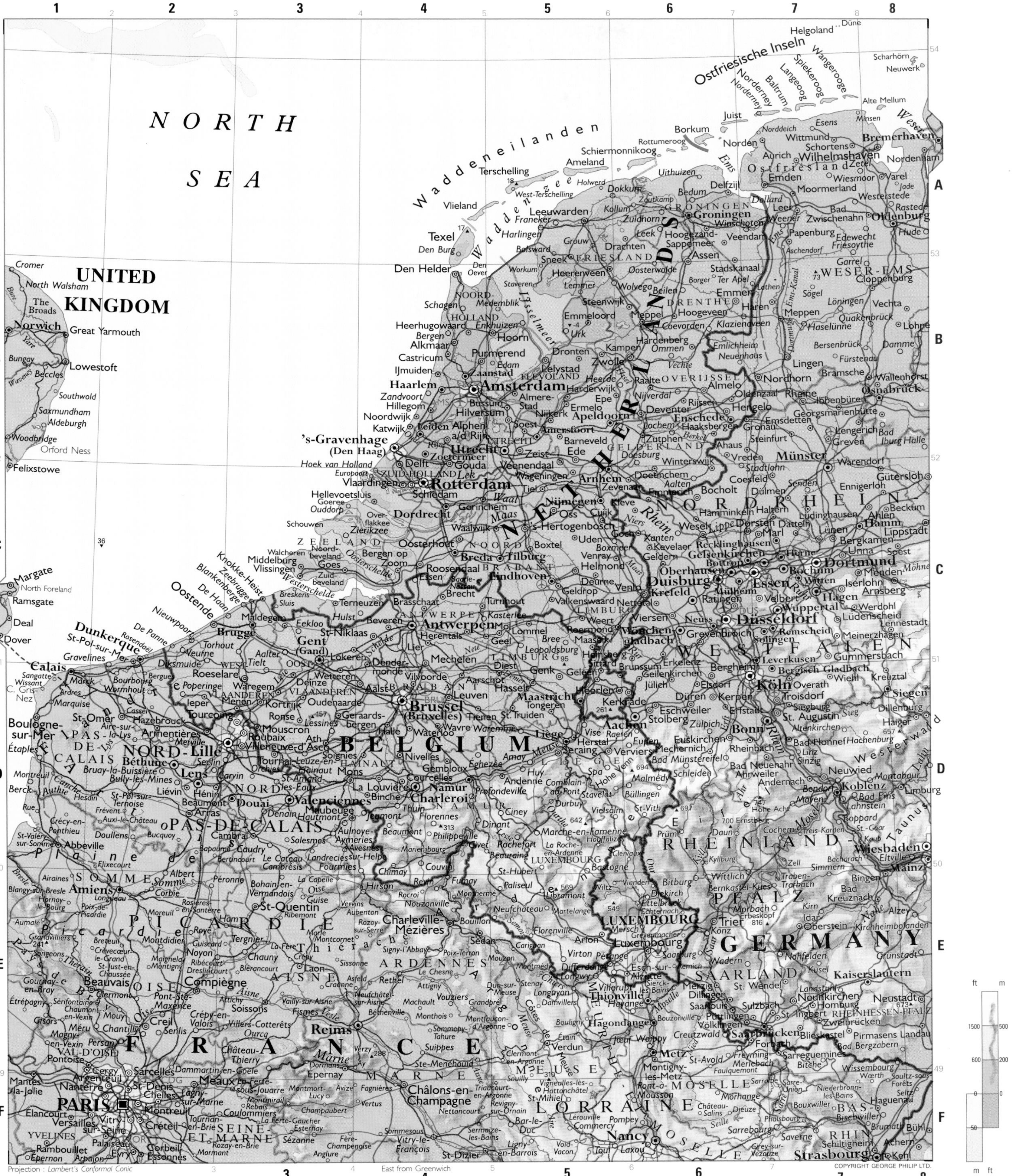

Underlined towns give their name to the administrative area in which they stand.

MIDDLE EUROPE 1:5 000 000

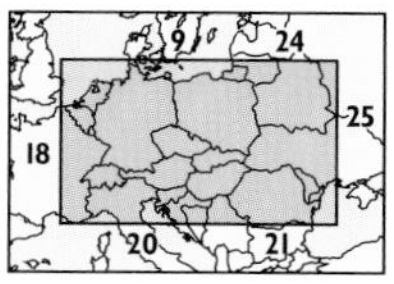

LITHUANIA
BELARUS
POLAND
UKRAINE
SLOVAK REP.
HUNGARY
ROMANIA
MOLDOVA
YUGOSLAVIA
BOSNIA-HERZEGOVINA
BULGARIA
Kaliningrad (Russia)
Zatoka Gdańska
Zalew Wiślany
Gdańsk
Gdynia
Elbląg
Olsztyn
Pojezierze Mazurskie
Bydgoszcz
Toruń
Włocławek
Płock
Poznań
WARSZAWA (Warsaw)
Łódź
Radom
Lublin
Białystok
Kielce
Częstochowa
Katowice
Kraków
Wrocław
Opole
Tarnów
Rzeszów
Przemyśl
Vilnius
Hrodna
MINSK
Baranavichy
Babruysk
Mahilyow
Homyel
Brest
Pinsk
Mazyr
Pripet Marshes
Kyyiv (Kiev)
Zhytomyr
Rivne
Lutsk
Lviv (Lvov)
Ternopil
Khmelnytskyy
Vinnytsya
Ivano-Frankivsk
Chernivtsi
Uzhhorod
Bila Tserkva
Podilska Vysochyna
Karpaty
Chişinău
Tiraspol
Tighina
Bălţi
Iaşi
Suceava
Botoşani
Bacău
Cluj-Napoca
Oradea
Satu Mare
Baia Mare
Târgu Mureş
Sibiu
Braşov
Timişoara
Arad
Craiova
Piteşti
Ploieşti
Galaţi
Brăila
Constanţa
BUCUREŞTI (Bucharest)
Transilvania
Carpaţii Meridionali
Dobruja
Bratislava
Košice
Žilina
Banská Bystrica
Ostrava
BUDAPEST
Miskolc
Debrecen
Szeged
Pécs
Győr
Balaton
BEOGRAD (Belgrade)
Novi Sad
Subotica
Vojvodina
Sarajevo
Tuzla
Ruse
Varna
Dunav
Dunărea (Danube)
Dnister
Vistula
East from Greenwich
COPYRIGHT GEORGE PHILIP LTD.

FRANCE 1:5 000 000

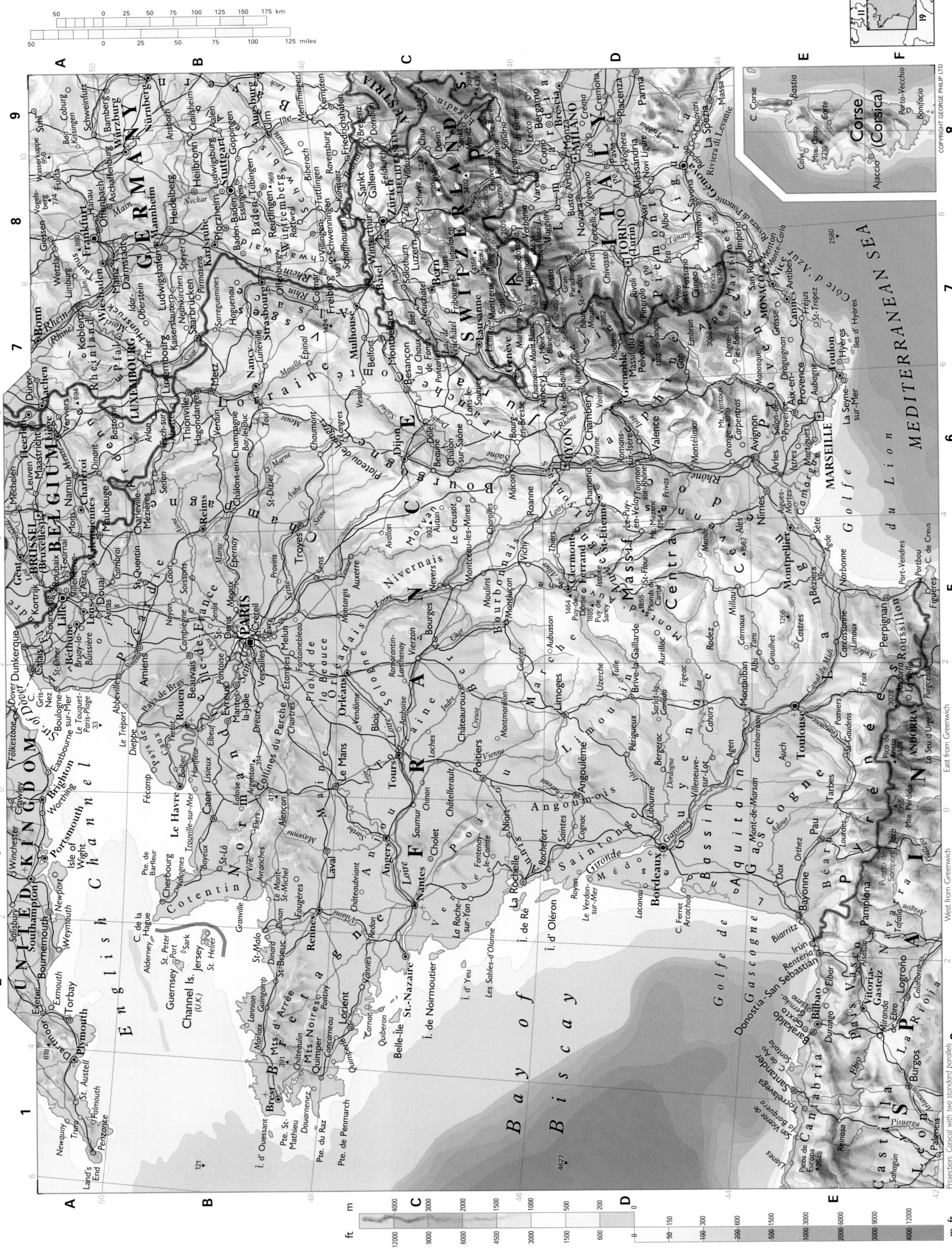

50 0 25 50 75 100 125 150 175 km
50 0 25 50 75 100 125 miles
FRANCE
UNITED KINGDOM
GERMANY
BELGIUM
LUXEMBOURG
SWITZERLAND
ITALY
SPAIN
ANDORRA
MONACO
LIECHTENSTEIN
AUSTRIA
English Channel
Bay of Biscay
Golfe de Gascogne
Golfe du Lion
MEDITERRANEAN SEA
Corse (Corsica)
PARIS
LYON
MARSEILLE
Bordeaux
Toulouse
Nantes
Strasbourg
Lille
Nice
Massif Central
Pyrénées
Alpes
Jura
Vosges
Bretagne
Normandie
Aquitaine
Provence
Bourgogne
Champagne
Lorraine
Picardie
Channel Is. (U.K.)
Projection: Conical with two standard parallels
West from Greenwich
East from Greenwich
COPYRIGHT GEORGE PHILIP LTD
m ft

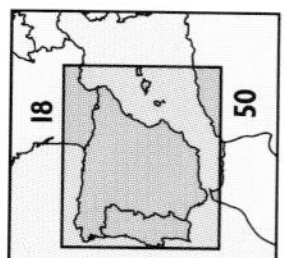
18
50

50 0 25 50 75 100 125 150 175 km
50 0 25 50 75 100 125 miles
SPAIN
PORTUGAL
FRANCE
ALGERIA
MOROCCO
ANDORRA
MADRID
LISBOA
BARCELONA
Valencia
Zaragoza
Sevilla
Málaga
Bilbao
Porto
Valladolid
Murcia
Córdoba
Granada
Alicante
Palma de Mallorca
Mallorca
Menorca
Eivissa (Ibiza)
Formentera
Toulouse
Montpellier
Perpignan
ALGER
Oran
Tanger
Tetouan
Ceuta (Sp.)
Melilla (Sp.)
Gibraltar (U.K.)
Str. of Gibraltar
Bay of Biscay
Golfe du Lion
Golfo de Valencia
G. de Cádiz
ATLANTIC OCEAN
MEDITERRANEAN SEA
Islas Baleares
Pyrénées
Cordillera Cantábrica
Sierra Nevada
Sierra Morena
Sierra de Gredos
Sierra de Guadarrama
La Mancha
Castilla y León
Costa Brava
Costa del Sol
Costa Blanca
Algarve
Projection: Conical with two standard parallels
COPYRIGHT GEORGE PHILIP LTD
West from Greenwich
East from Greenwich
m ft
4000 12000
3000 9000
2000 6000
1000 3000
500 1500
200 600
100 300
50 150
0
200 600
500 1500
1000 3000
1500 4500
2000 6000

ITALY AND THE BALKAN STATES 1:5 000 000

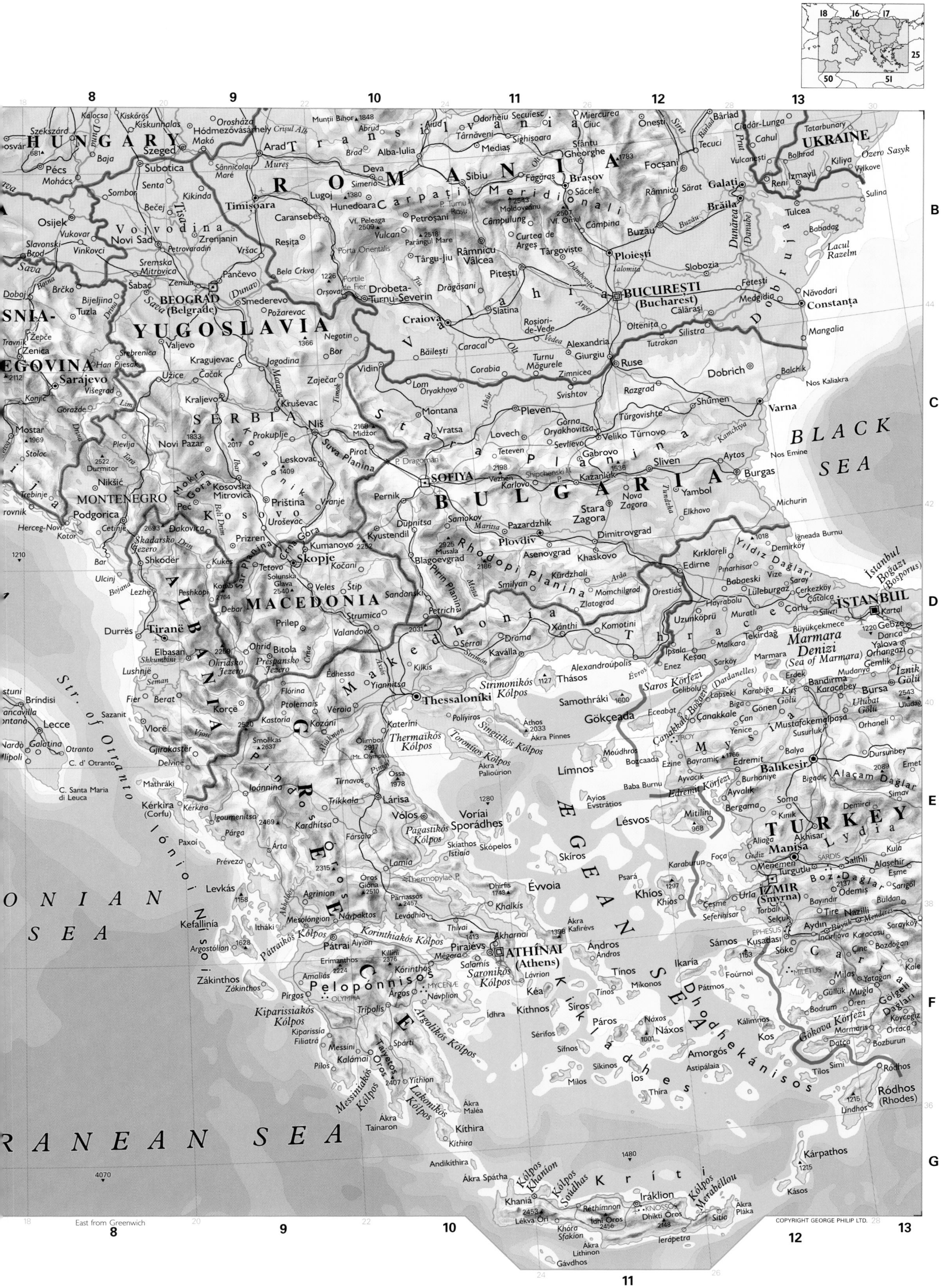
HUNGARY
ROMANIA
UKRAINE
YUGOSLAVIA
BOSNIA-
HERZEGOVINA
MONTENEGRO
SERBIA
BULGARIA
MACEDONIA
ALBANIA
GREECE
TURKEY
BLACK SEA
IONIAN SEA
MEDITERRANEAN SEA
AEGEAN SEA
Marmara Denizi (Sea of Marmara)
Str. of Otranto
Transilvania
Carpaţii Meridionali
Vojvodina
Walachia
Dobrogea
Stara Planina
Rhodopi Planina
Makedhonía
Thrace
Mysia
Lydia
Caria
Kikládhes
Dhodhekánisos
Pindhos
Pelopónnisos
Kríti
Kosovo
BUCUREŞTI (Bucharest)
BEOGRAD (Belgrade)
SOFIYA
ATHÍNAI (Athens)
İSTANBUL
Skopje
Tiranë
Sarajevo
Podgorica
Thessaloníki
İZMIR (Smyrna)
Constanţa
Varna
Burgas
Plovdiv
Craiova
Timişoara
Novi Sad
Niš
Pristina
Brăila
Galaţi
Ploieşti
Bursa
Balıkesir
Manisa
Edirne
Pátrai
Iráklion
Ródhos (Rhodes)
Kérkira (Corfu)
Lésvos
Khíos
Sámos
Límnos
Évvoia
Thermaïkós Kólpos
Saros Körfezi
Edremit Körfezi
Gökova Körfezi
Saronikós Kólpos
Korinthiakós Kólpos
Argolikós Kólpos
Lakonikós Kólpos
Messiniakós Kólpos
Kiparissiakós Kólpos
Pagastikós Kólpos
Dunărea (Danube)
Dunav
East from Greenwich
COPYRIGHT GEORGE PHILIP LTD.

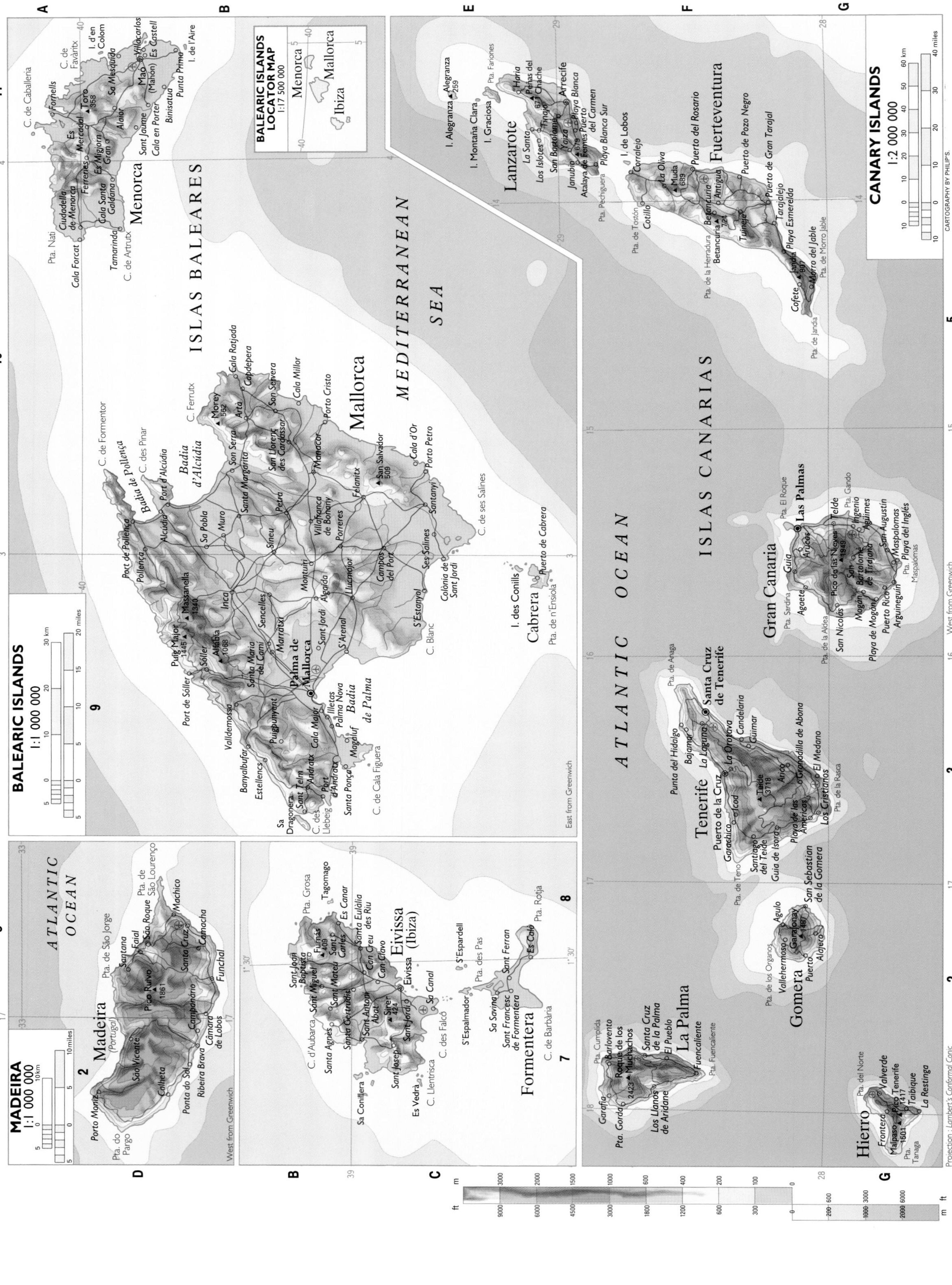
BALEARIC ISLANDS
1:1 000 000
BALEARIC ISLANDS LOCATOR MAP
1:17 500 000
Menorca
Mallorca
Ibiza
ISLAS BALEARES
MEDITERRANEAN SEA
Mallorca
Palma de Mallorca
Badia de Palma
Badia d'Alcúdia
Badia de Pollença
C. de Formentor
Pollença
Port de Pollença
Alcúdia
Inca
Sóller
Port de Sóller
Valldemossa
Andratx
Manacor
Felanitx
Campos del Port
Llucmajor
Santanyí
Artà
Capdepera
Cala Ratjada
Porto Cristo
Cala Millor
Puig Major
Cabrera
Menorca
Ciutadella de Menorca
Maó (Mahón)
Es Mercadal
Alaior
Fornells
Eivissa (Ibiza)
Sant Antoni Abat
Santa Eulàlia des Riu
Formentera
MADEIRA
1:1 000 000
ATLANTIC OCEAN
Madeira (Portugal)
Funchal
Santana
Machico
Pico Ruivo
Porto Moniz
São Vicente
Calheta
Ponta do Sol
Câmara de Lobos
CANARY ISLANDS
1:2 000 000
ISLAS CANARIAS
ATLANTIC OCEAN
Lanzarote
Arrecife
Fuerteventura
Puerto del Rosario
Gran Canaria
Las Palmas
Tenerife
Santa Cruz de Tenerife
Pico de Teide 3718
Puerto de la Cruz
La Palma
Santa Cruz de la Palma
Gomera
San Sebastian de la Gomera
Hierro
Valverde
West from Greenwich
East from Greenwich
Projection : Lambert's Conformal Conic
CARTOGRAPHY BY PHILIP'S.

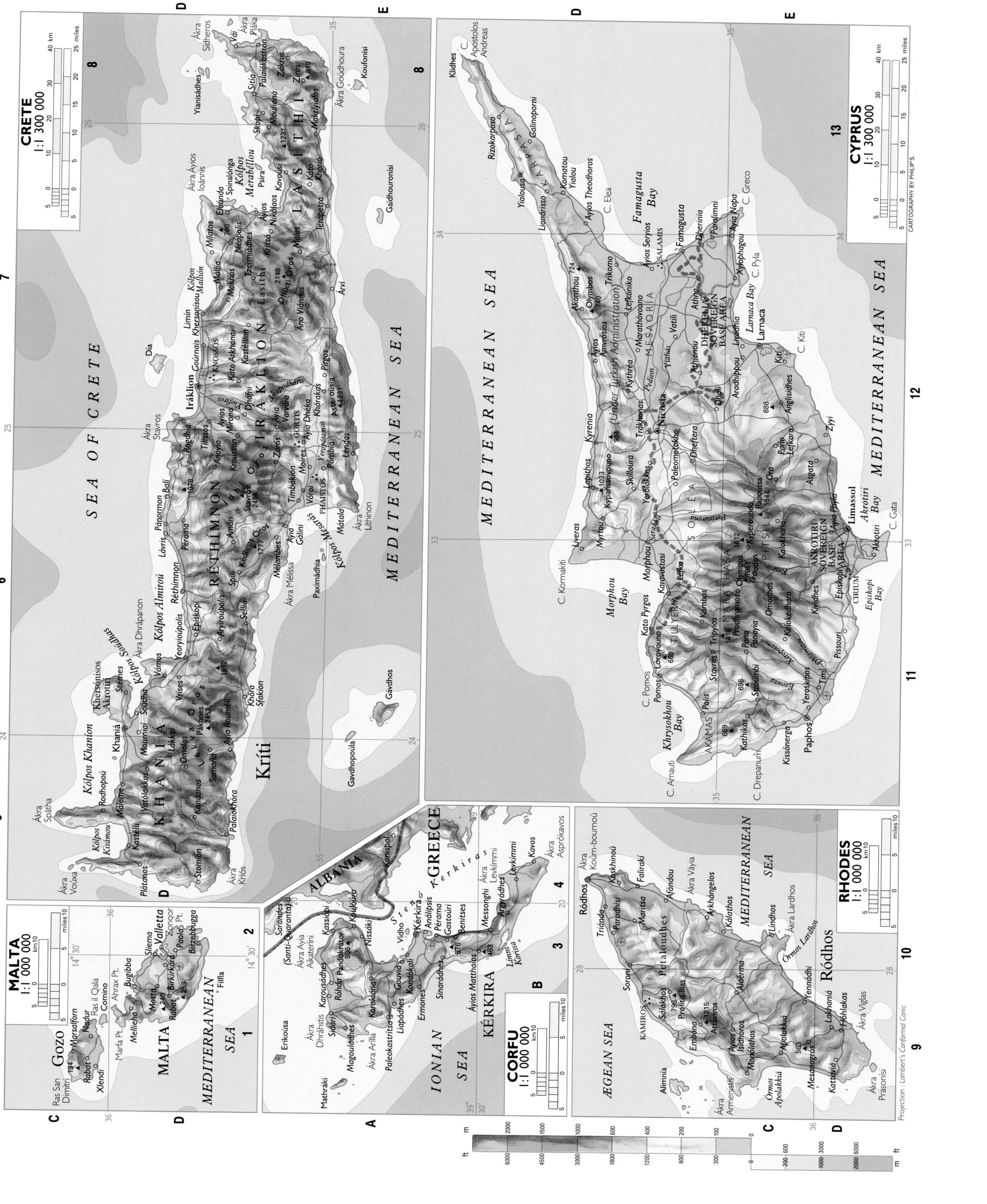
CRETE
1:1 300 000
CYPRUS
1:1 300 000
MALTA
1:1 000 000
CORFU
1:1 000 000
RHODES
1:1 000 000
SEA OF CRETE
MEDITERRANEAN SEA
IONIAN SEA
ÆGEAN SEA
Kríti
KÉRKIRA
Ródhos
GREECE
ALBANIA
CARTOGRAPHY BY PHILIP'S.
Projection : Lambert's Conformal Conic

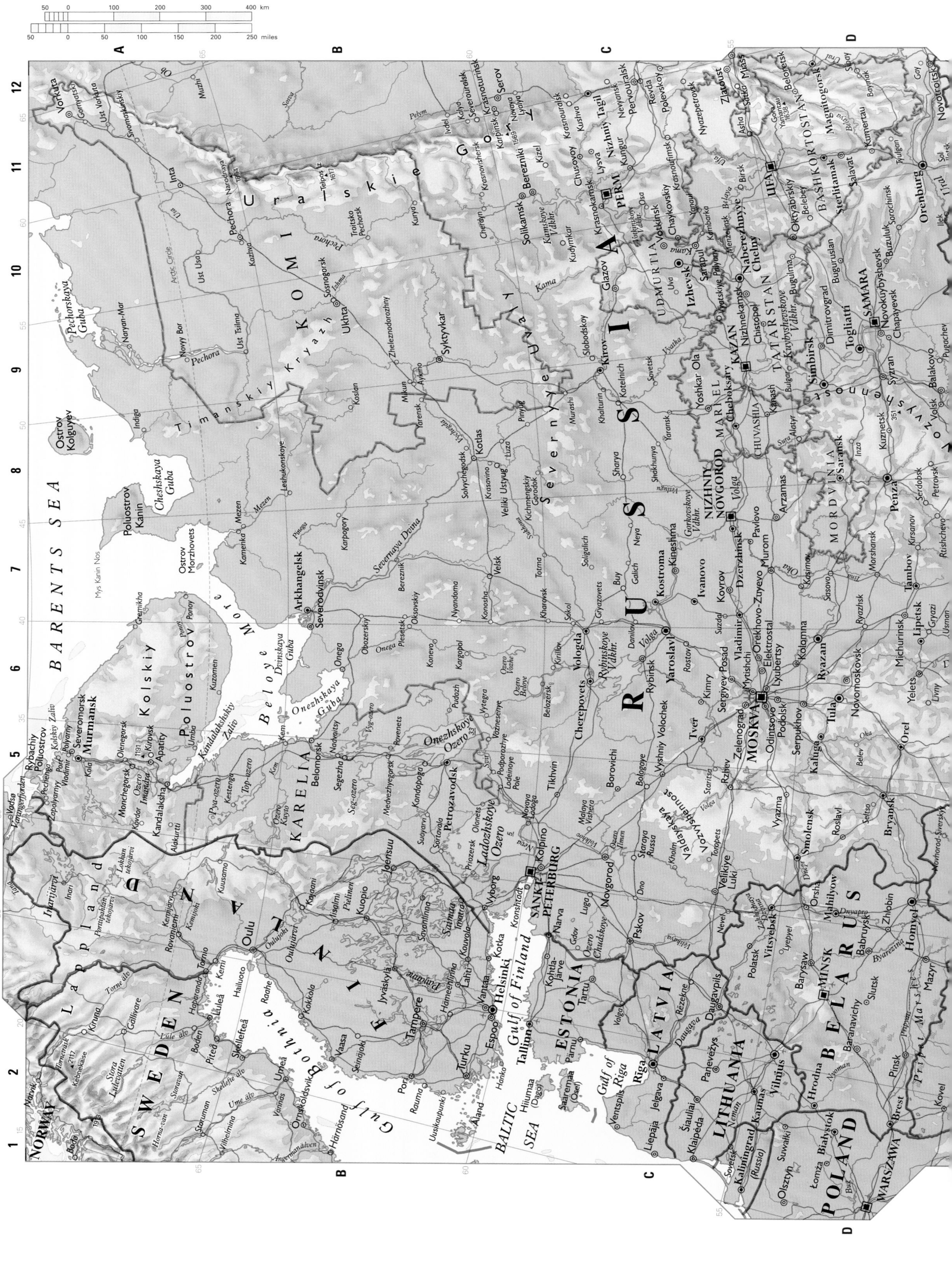
50 0 100 200 300 400 km
50 0 50 100 150 200 250 miles
BARENTS SEA
Beloye More
Gulf of Bothnia
Gulf of Finland
Gulf of Riga
BALTIC SEA
NORWAY
SWEDEN
FINLAND
ESTONIA
LATVIA
LITHUANIA
BELARUS
POLAND
RUSSIA
KOMI
KARELIA
UDMURTIA
TATARSTAN
BASHKORTOSTAN
CHUVASHIA
MARI EL
MORDVINIA
Lappland
Kolskiy Poluostrov
Timanskiy Kryazh
Severnyye Uvaly
Uralskie Gory
Ostrov Kolguyev
Poluostrov Kanin
Pechorskaya Guba
Cheshskaya Guba
Onezhskaya Guba
Dvinskaya Guba
Ladozhskoye Ozero
Onezhskoye Ozero
MOSKVA
SANKT-PETERBURG
Helsinki
Tallinn
Riga
Vilnius
MINSK
WARSZAWA
Murmansk
Arkhangelsk
Severodvinsk
Petrozavodsk
Vologda
Yaroslavl
Kostroma
Ivanovo
Nizhniy Novgorod
Kazan
Izhevsk
Perm
Ufa
Samara
Tolyatti
Penza
Syktyvkar
Ukhta
Vorkuta
Kirov
Oulu
Tampere
Turku
Kaliningrad (Russia)
Kaunas
Hrodna
Homyel
Bryansk
Smolensk
Tula
Ryazan
Orenburg
Magnitogorsk
Chelyabinsk

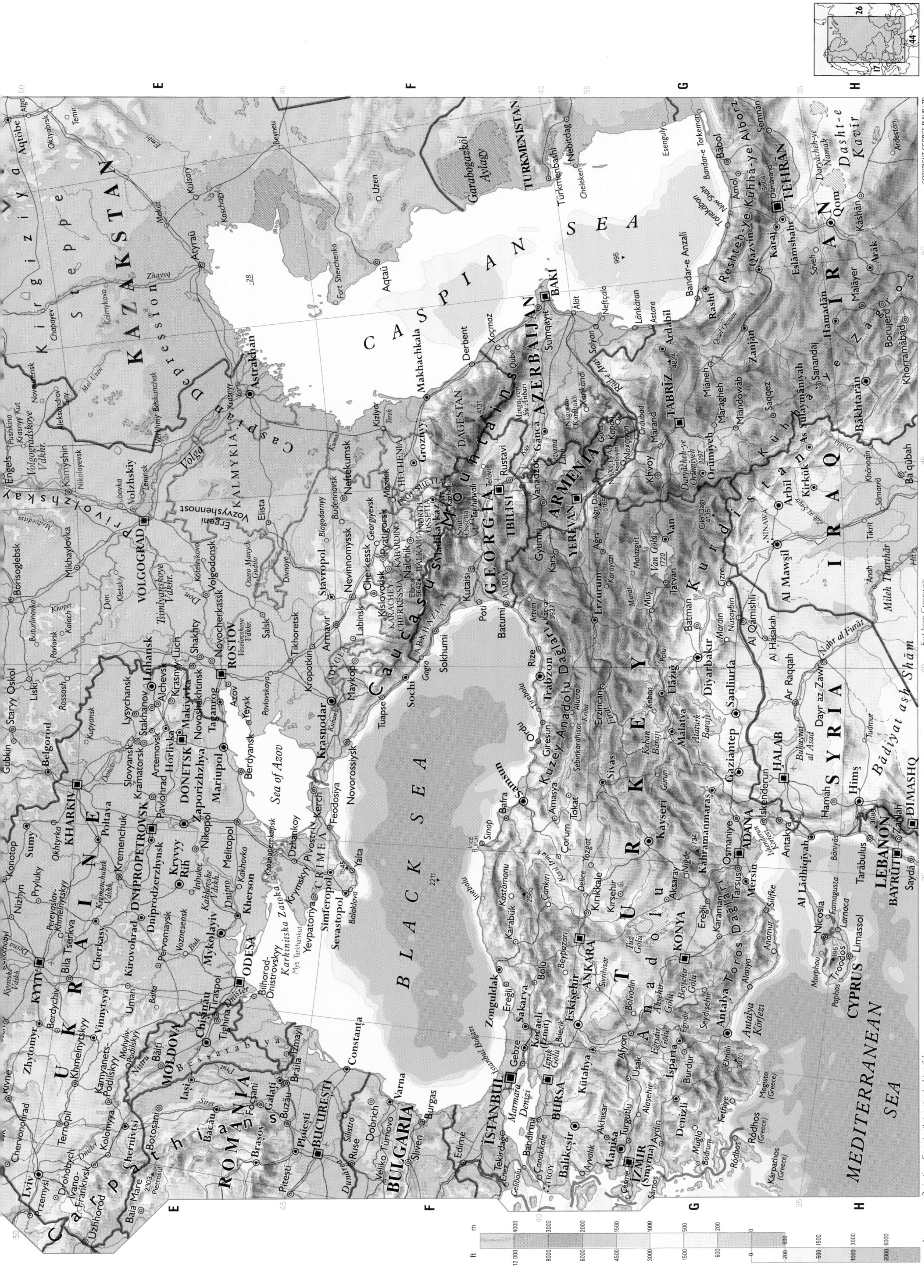
KAZAKSTAN
UKRAINE
ROMANIA
MOLDOVA
BULGARIA
GEORGIA
ARMENIA
AZERBAIJAN
TURKMENISTAN
TURKEY
SYRIA
IRAQ
IRAN
CYPRUS
LEBANON
BLACK SEA
CASPIAN SEA
MEDITERRANEAN SEA
Sea of Azov
Caucasus Mountains
Caspian Depression
CRIMEA
KALMYKIA
DAGESTAN
CHECHENIA
ABKHAZIA
Anadolu
Kurdistan
Zagros
ISTANBUL
ANKARA
BUCUREŞTI
KYYIV
KHARKIV
DNIPROPETROVSK
DONETSK
ODESA
VOLGOGRAD
ROSTOV
TBILISI
YEREVAN
BAKI
TEHRĀN
DIMASHQ
BAYRŪT
HALAB
Astrakhan
Atyraū
Makhachkala
Grozny
Krasnodar
Sevastopol
Simferopol
Samsun
Trabzon
Erzurum
Konya
Adana
İzmir
Bursa
Tabrīz
Al Mawşil
Projection: Conical with two standard parallels
East from Greenwich
COPYRIGHT GEORGE PHILIP LTD.

RUSSIA AND CENTRAL ASIA 1:20 000 000

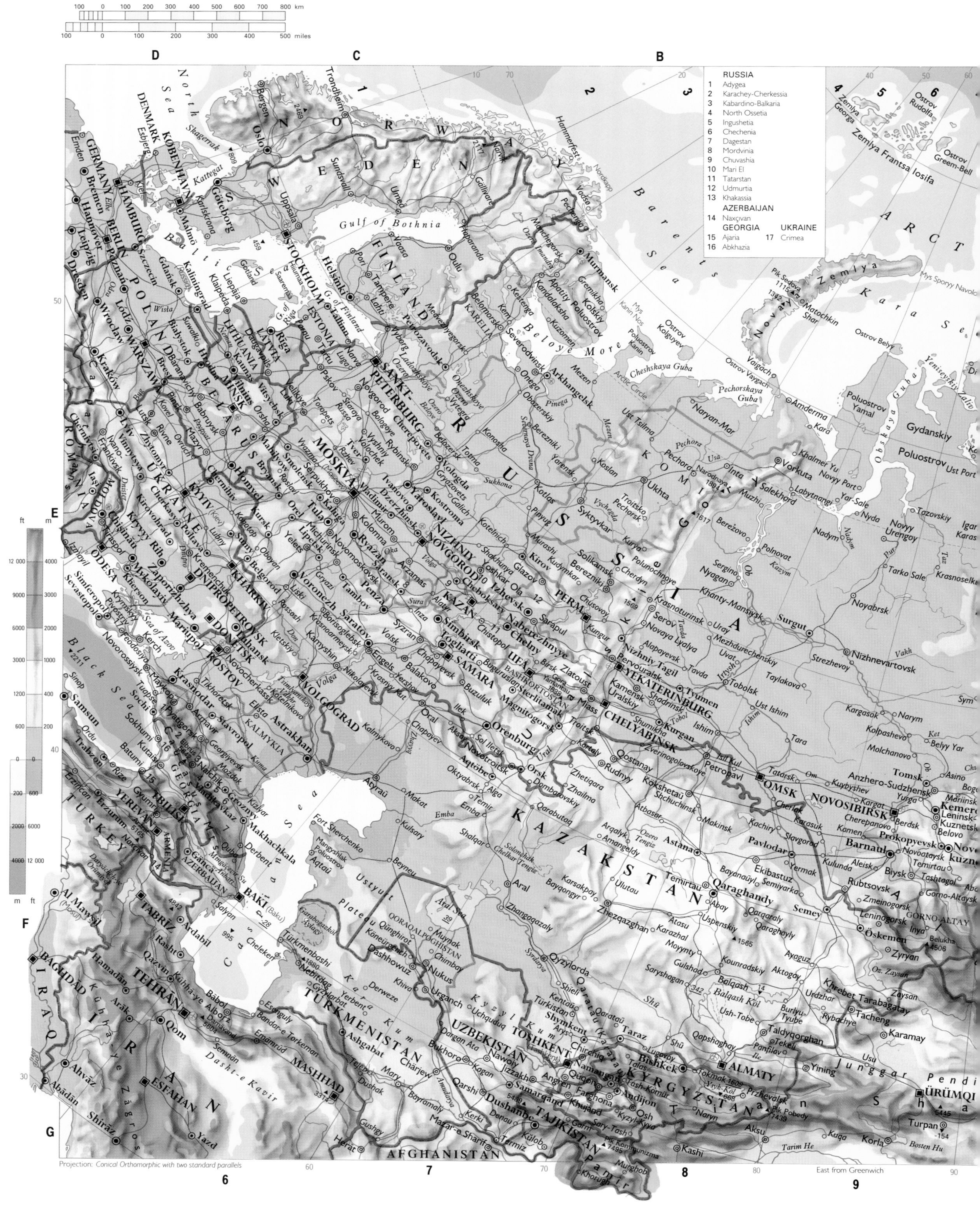

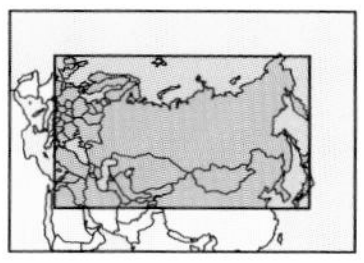

A
B
C
D
E
F
8 9 10 11 12 13 14 15 16 17 18 19
O C E A N
Laptev Sea
East Siberian Sea
Chukchi Sea
Bering Sea
Sea of Okhotsk
Sea of Japan
Severnaya Zemlya
Ostrov Shmidta
Ostrov Komsomolets
Ostrov Oktyabrskoy Revolyutsii
Ostrov Pioner
Ostrov Bolshevik
Mys Arkticheskiy
Mys Chelyuskin
Proliv Vilkitskogo
Poluostrov Taymyr
Gory Byrranga
Oz. Taymyr
Ostrov Bolshoy Begichev
Novosibirskiye Ostrova
Ostrov Kotelnyy
Ostrov Belkovskiy
Ostrov Stolbovoy
Ostrov Faddeyevskiy
Ostrov Novaya Sibir
Ostrova Delonga
Ostrov Bennetta
Ostrov Genriyetty
Ostrov Zhannetty
Ostrov Zhokhova
Lyakhovskiye Ostrova
Proliv Dmitriya Lapteva
Ostrov Vrangelya
Ostrova Medvezhi
Ostrov Ayon
Mys Buorkhaya
Mys Dezhneva (East C.)
St. Lawrence I. (U.S.A.)
Chukotskoye Nagorye
Anadyrskiy Zaliv
Koryakskoye Nagorye
Kolymskoye Nagorye
Sredinnyy Khrebet
Poluostrov Kamchatka
Penzhinskaya Guba
Gizhiginskaya Guba
Zaliv Shelikhova
Ostrov Karaginskiy
Komandorskiye Ostrova
Verkhoyanskiy Khrebet
Khrebet Cherskogo
Khrebet Dzhugdzhur
Stanovoy Khrebet
Yablonovyy Khrebet
Vostochnyy Sayan
Zapadnyy Sayan
Sikhote Alin
Da Hinggan Ling
Hangayn Nuruu
Hentiyn Nuruu
Gobi
R U S S I A
M O N G O L I A
C H I N A
Dongbei
NORTH KOREA
SOUTH KOREA
JAPAN
Sakhalin
Kurilskiye Ostrova
Hokkaido
Honshū
Arctic Circle
Norilsk
Khatanga
Nordvik
Tiksi
Verkhoyansk
Yakutsk
Magadan
Okhotsk
Ayan
Petropavlovsk-Kamchatskiy
Anadyr
Pevek
Uelen
Chersky
Srednekolymsk
Zhigansk
Olenek
Vilyuysk
Mirnyy
Lensk
Olekminsk
Aldan
Neryungri
Tynda
Bratsk
Krasnoyarsk
Kansk
Irkutsk
Angarsk
Ulan Ude
Chita
Blagoveshchensk
Khabarovsk
Komsomolsk
Vladivostok
Nakhodka
Yuzhno-Sakhalinsk
Okha
Nikolayevsk-na-Amur
Ulaanbaatar
Darhan
Choybalsan
Hailar
Manzhouli
QIQIHAR
HARBIN
Jiamusi
Mudanjiang
JILIN
CHANGCHUN
SHENYANG
FUSHUN
ANSHAN
DALIAN
Chifeng
Zhangjiakou
BEIJING
Hohhot
Baotou
Erenhot
Xilinhot
Hami
P'YONGYANG
Chŏngjin
Wŏnsan
SOUL
INCH'ON
TAEJON
TAEGU
PUSAN
SAPPORO
Hakodate
Aomori
Akita
Niigata
Kanazawa
OSAKA
Fuji-San 3776
Lena
Amur
Kolyma
Indigirka
Yana
Olenek
Vilyuy
Aldan
Angara
Yenisey
Nizhnyaya Tunguska
Podkamennaya Tunguska
Khatanga
Anabar
Omolon
Oloy
Maya
Zeya
Bureya
Ussuri
Argun
Nen Jiang
Songhua Jiang
Hulun Nur
Hövsgöl Nuur
Uvs Nuur
Gaxun Nur
Oz. Baykal
BURYATIYA
80 90 100 110 120 130 140 150 160 170
60
50
40
10 11 12 13 14
COPYRIGHT GEORGE PHILIP LTD.

ASIA : Physical 1:50 000 000

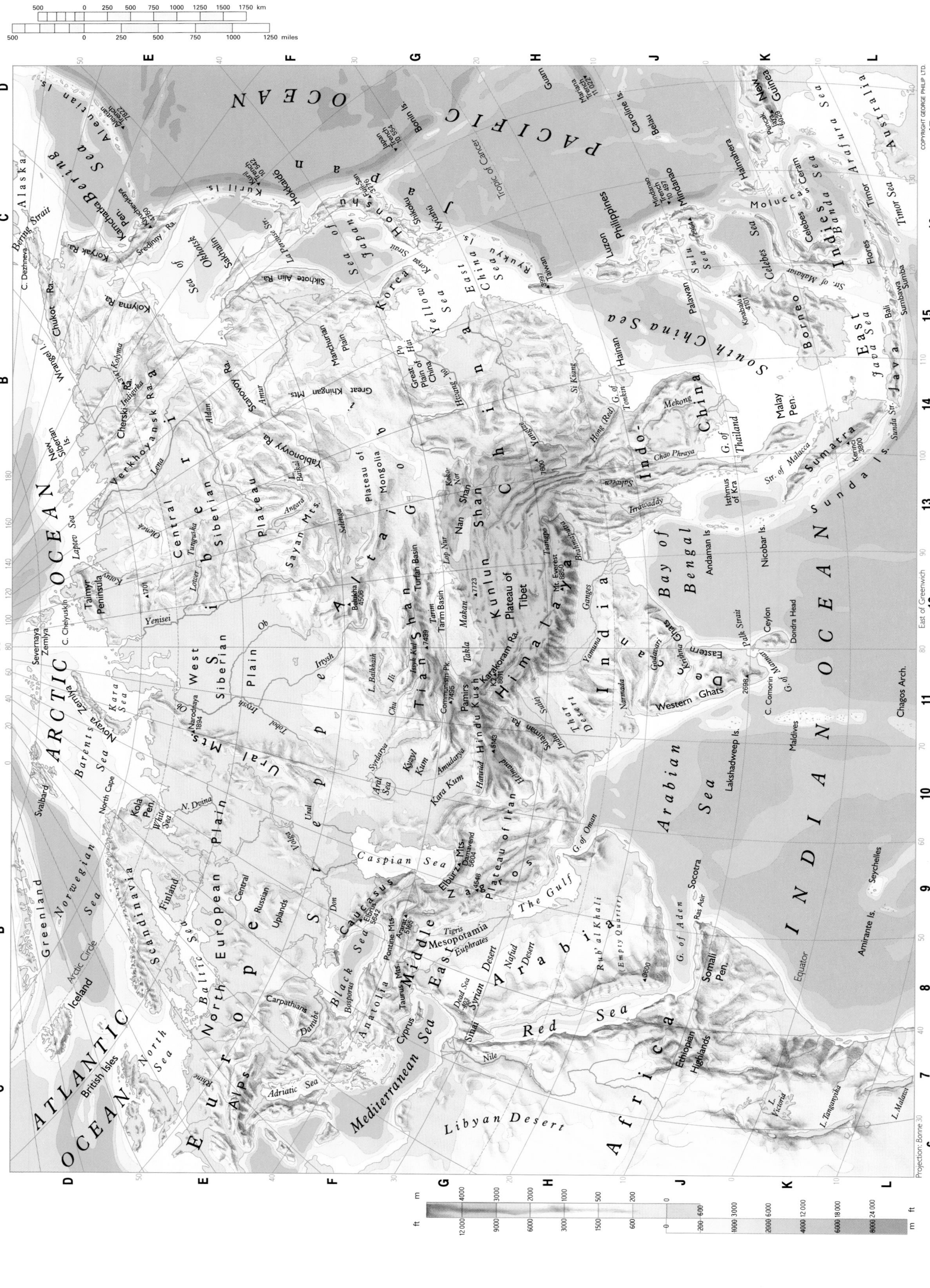

500 0 250 500 750 1000 1250 1500 1750 km
500 0 250 500 750 1000 1250 miles
ARCTIC OCEAN
PACIFIC OCEAN
INDIAN OCEAN
ATLANTIC OCEAN
RUSSIA
CHINA
MONGOLIA
KAZAKSTAN
UZBEKISTAN
TURKMENISTAN
KYRGYZSTAN
TAJIKISTAN
AFGHANISTAN
PAKISTAN
INDIA
NEPAL
BHUTAN
BANGLADESH
BURMA (MYANMAR)
THAILAND
LAOS
VIETNAM
CAMBODIA
MALAYSIA
SINGAPORE
INDONESIA
PHILIPPINES
TAIWAN
JAPAN
NORTH KOREA
SOUTH KOREA
IRAN
IRAQ
SYRIA
TURKEY
JORDAN
ISRAEL
LEBANON
CYPRUS
SAUDI ARABIA
YEMEN
OMAN
UNITED ARAB EMIRATES
QATAR
BAHRAIN
KUWAIT
GEORGIA
ARMENIA
AZERBAIJAN
SRI LANKA
MALDIVES
BRUNEI
EGYPT
SUDAN
ETHIOPIA
ERITREA
DJIBOUTI
SOMALI REP.
KENYA
UGANDA
TANZANIA
LIBYA
Europe
Africa
Caspian Sea
Black Sea
Red Sea
Mediterranean Sea
Arabian Sea
Bay of Bengal
South China Sea
East China Sea
Sea of Japan
Sea of Okhotsk
Bering Sea
Yellow Sea
Laptev Sea
Kara Sea
Barents Sea
Java Sea
Arafura Sea
Timor Sea
Banda Sea
Celebes Sea
Sulu Sea
TOKYO
BEIJING
MOSCOW
ST. PETERSBURG
TEHRAN
KARACHI
MUMBAI (Bombay)
KOLKATA (Calcutta)
CHENNAI (Madras)
SHANGHAI
HONG KONG
BANGKOK
JAKARTA
MANILA
ISTANBUL
CAIRO
Tropic of Cancer
Equator
Arctic Circle
Hanoi ● Capital Cities
Projection: Bonne 30
COPYRIGHT GEORGE PHILIP LTD.
East from Greenwich

JAPAN 1:5 000 000

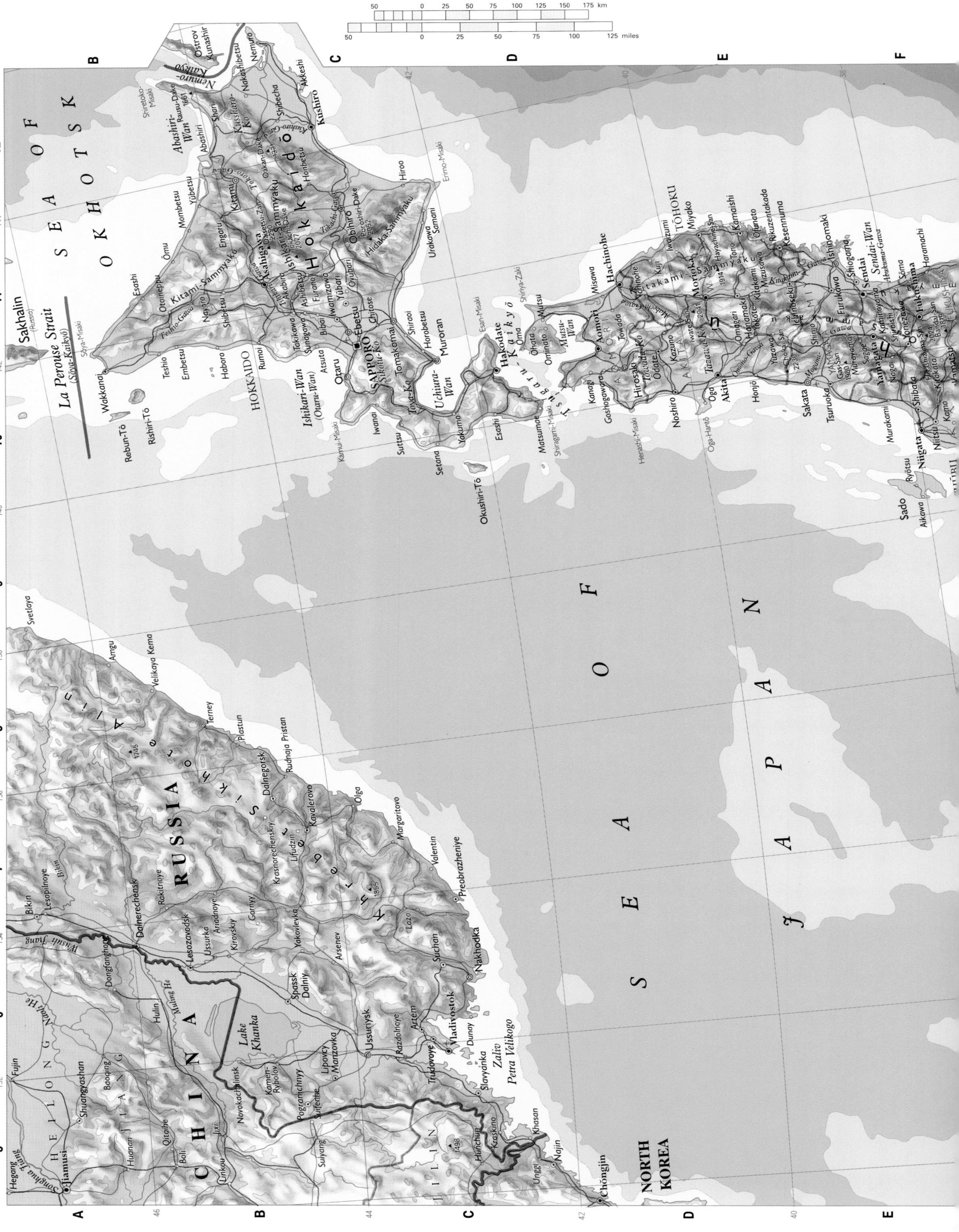

SOUTH KOREA
JAPAN
Korea Strait
PACIFIC OCEAN
Tsushima
Ullŭng-do (S. Korea)
Tok-do
Pohang
Yŏngdŏk
Oki-Shotō
CHŪGOKU
SHIKOKU
KINKI
KANTŌ
KYŪSHŪ
TOKYO
YOKOHAMA
KAWASAKI
NAGOYA
KYŌTO
ŌSAKA
KOBE
HIROSHIMA
KITAKYŪSHŪ
FUKUOKA
Higashiōsaka
Amagasaki
Sakai
Okayama
Kurashiki
Fukuyama
Himeji
Takamatsu
Tokushima
Matsuyama
Kōchi
Kumamoto
Kagoshima
Nagasaki
Ōita
Miyazaki
Shimonoseki
Kanazawa
Toyama
Nagano
Fukui
Gifu
Shizuoka
Hamamatsu
Chiba
Utsunomiya
Mito
Hitachi
Chōshi
Izu-Shotō
Hachijō-Jima
Ōsumi-Shotō
Yaku-Shima
Tane-ga-Shima
Tokara-Rettō
Satsunan-Shotō
Gotō-Rettō
Tosa-Wan
Kii-Suidō
Bungo-Suidō
Ise-Wan
Suruga-Wan
Toyama-Wan
Wakasa-Wan
RYUKYU ISLANDS
on same scale
EAST CHINA SEA
PACIFIC OCEAN
Nansei-Shotō (Ryukyu Is.)
Amami-Guntō
Okinawa-Guntō
Sakashima-Guntō
Miyako-Rettō
Yaeyama-Rettō
Senkaku-Shotō
Amami-Ō-Shima
Tokuno-Shima
Okinawa-Jima
Naha
Koza
Ishigaki-Shima
Iriomote-Jima
Miyako-Jima
Yonaguni-Jima
m ft
Projection: Conical with two standard parallels
East from Greenwich
COPYRIGHT GEORGE PHILIP LTD.

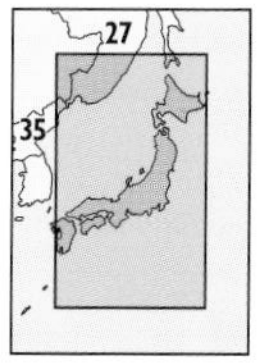
27
35

CHINA AND KOREA 1:15 000 000

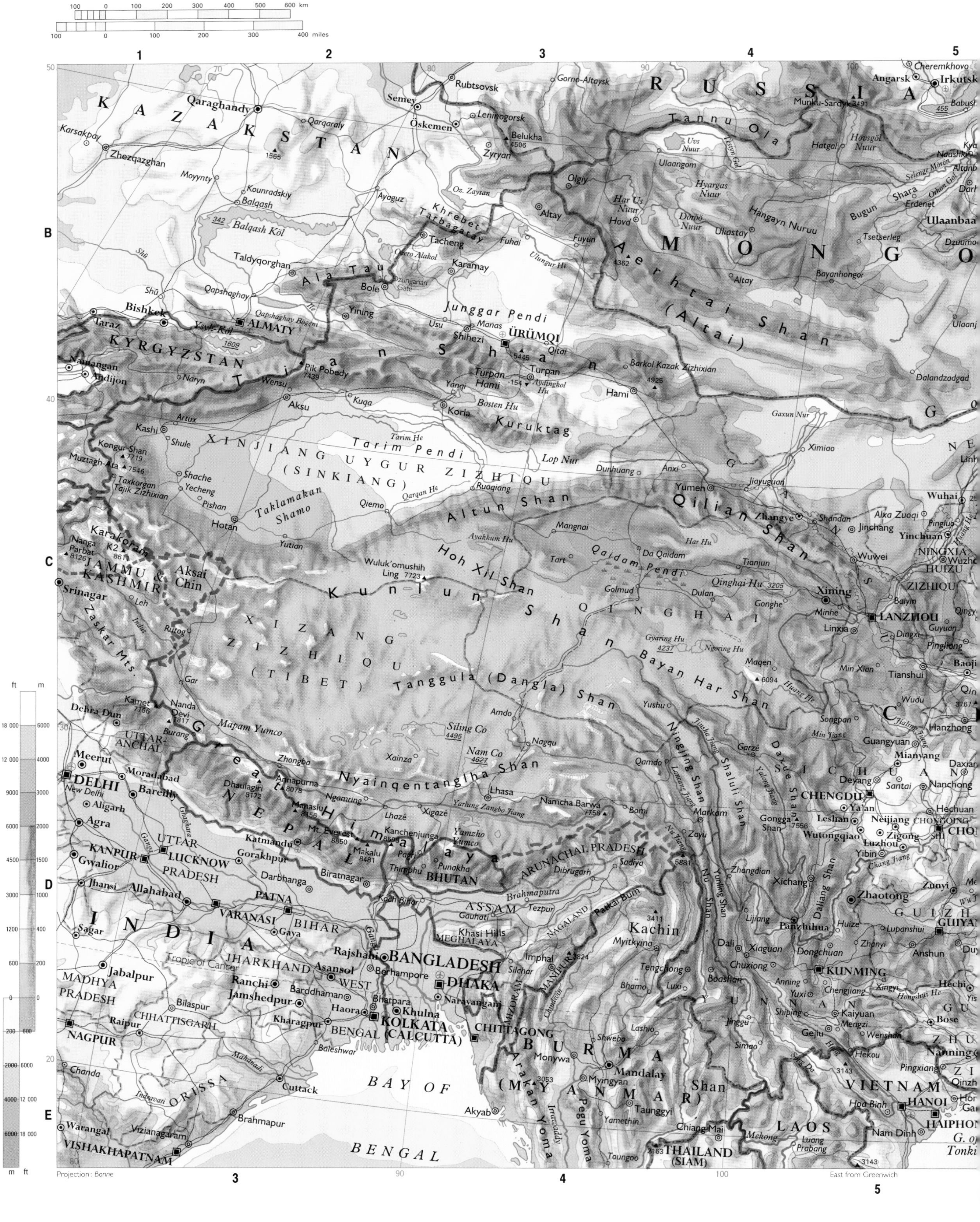

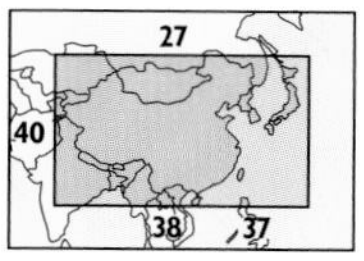

27
40
38
37

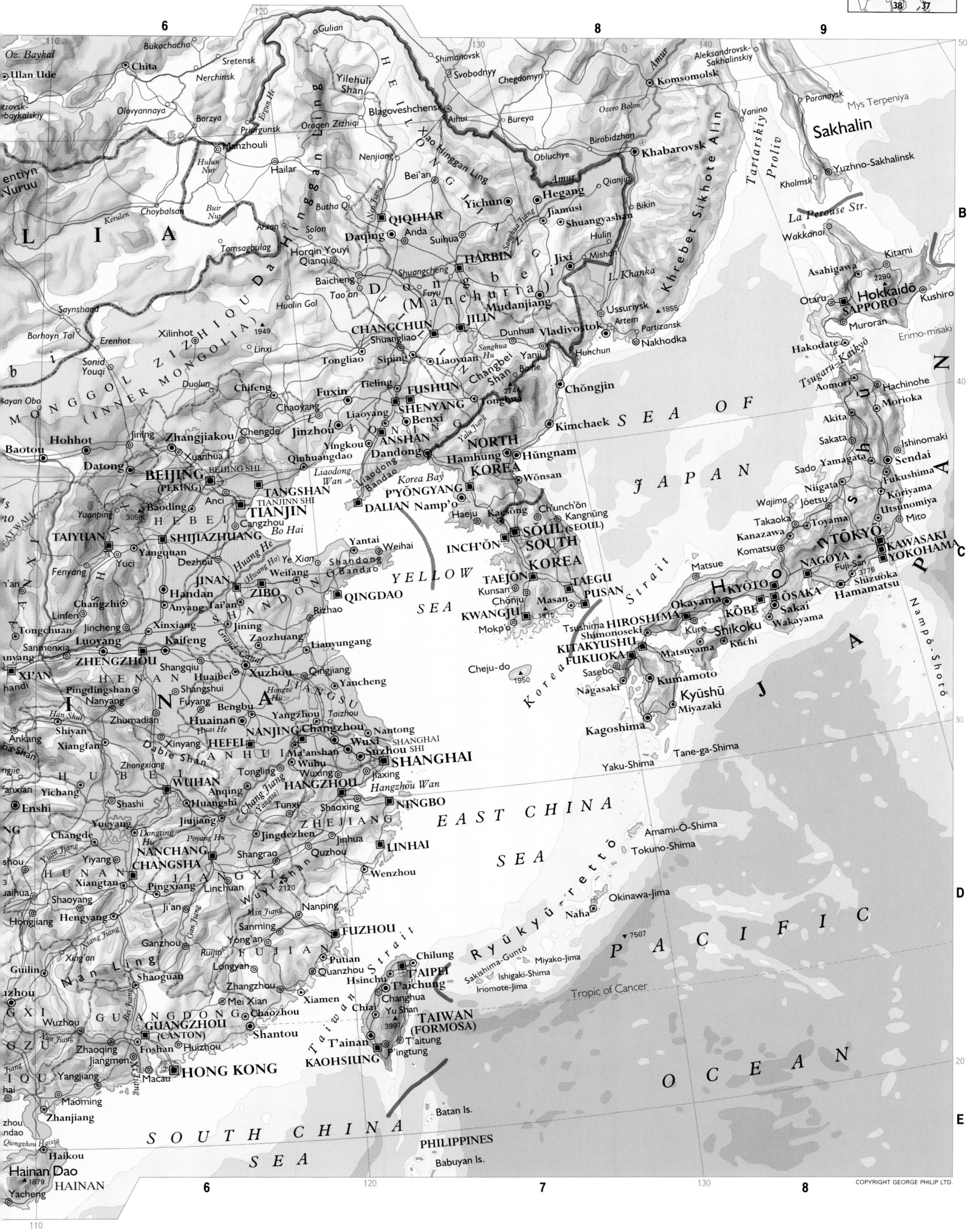

6
7
8
9
B
C
D
E
Oz. Baykal
Ulan Ude
Chita
Bukachacha
Sretensk
Nerchinsk
Olovyannaya
Borzya
Priargunsk
Manzhouli
Hulun Nur
Hailar
Choybalsan
Buir Nur
Kerulen
Arxan
Solon
Tamsagbulag
Saynshand
Erenhot
Borhoyn Tal
Sonid Youqi
Xilinhot
Linxi
Duolun
Chifeng
Baotou
Hohhot
Jining
Zhangjiakou
Xuanhua
Datong
Chengde
BEIJING
(PEKING)
BEIJING SHI
TANGSHAN
TIANJIN SHI
TIANJIN
Anci
Baoding
Qinhuangdao
Yuanping
3058
TAIYUAN
SHIJIAZHUANG
Yangquan
Yuci
Fenyang
Changzhi
Linfen
Handan
Anyang
JINAN
ZIBO
Tai'an
Dezhou
Cangzhou
Bo Hai
Ye Xian
Weifang
Yantai
Weihai
Shandong Bandao
QINGDAO
Rizhao
Jining
Zaozhuang
Lianyungang
Xinxiang
Kaifeng
Jincheng
Luoyang
Sanmenxia
Tongchuan
ZHENGZHOU
XI'AN
Shangqiu
Huaibei
Xuzhou
Qingjiang
Yancheng
Pingdingshan
Nanyang
Shangshui
Fuyang
Bengbu
Huainan
Zhumadian
Yangzhou
Taizhou
Hongze Hu
Huai He
Ankang
Shiyan
Xiangfan
Han Shui
Xinyang
HEFEI
NANJING
Changzhou
Nantong
Wuxi
Suzhou
SHANGHAI SHI
SHANGHAI
Ma'anshan
Wuhu
Wuxing
Tongling
Jiaxing
Hangzhou Wan
HANGZHOU
Zhongxiang
Dabie Shan
Yichang
WUHAN
Anqing
Shashi
Huangshi
Enshi
Chang Jiang (Yangtse)
Tunxi
Shaoxing
NINGBO
Yueyang
Jiujiang
Dongting Hu
Poyang Hu
Changde
Jingdezhen
Jinhua
LINHAI
NANCHANG
Yiyang
CHANGSHA
Shangrao
Quzhou
Xiangtan
Pingxiang
Linchuan
Wenzhou
Yuan Jiang
Wuyi Shan
2120
Shaoyang
Ji'an
Hengyang
Hongjiang
Min Jiang
Nanping
Gan Jiang
Sanming
FUZHOU
Ganzhou
Yong'an
Xiang Jiang
Xing'an
Ruijin
Longyan
Putian
Quanzhou
Guilin
Nan Ling
Shaoguan
Zhangzhou
Xiamen
Mei Xian
Chaozhou
Shantou
Wuzhou
GUANGZHOU
(CANTON)
Bei Jiang
Xi Jiang
Zhaoqing
Jiangmen
Foshan
Huizhou
Yangjiang
Macau
HONG KONG
Maoming
Zhanjiang
Haikou
Qiongzhou Haixia
Hainan Dao
1879
Yacheng
HAINAN
SOUTH CHINA SEA
Gulian
Shimanovsk
Svobodnyy
Chegdomyn
Yilehuli Shan
Blagoveshchensk
Aihui
Bureya
Orogen Zizhiqi
Nenjiang
Bei'an
Xiao Hinggan Ling
Da Hinggan Ling
Ergun He
Nen Jiang
Butha Qi
QIQIHAR
Anda
Daqing
Suihua
HEILONGJIANG
Horqin Youyi Qianqi
Baicheng
Tao'an
Shuangcheng
HARBIN
Songhua Jiang
Fuyu
Huolin Gol
1949
Dongbei (Manchuria)
NEI MONGGOL ZIZHIQU (INNER MONGOLIA)
CHANGCHUN
Shuangliao
JILIN
Tongliao
Siping
Liaoyuan
Songhua Hu
Mudanjiang
Dunhua
FUXIN
Tieling
FUSHUN
SHENYANG
Liaoyang
Benxi
Chaoyang
Jinzhou
ANSHAN
Yingkou
Dandong
LIAONING
Liaodong Wan
Liaodong Bandao
Korea Bay
DALIAN
Changbai Shan
2744
Tonghua
Yanji
Baihe
Yalu Jiang
Yichun
Hegang
Jiamusi
Shuangyashan
Qianjin
Bikin
Hulin
Jixi
Mishan
L. Khanka
Komsomolsk
Amur
Ozero Bolon
Birobidzhan
Obluchye
Khabarovsk
Khrebet Sikhote Alin
Ussuriysk
1855
Artem
Partizansk
Vladivostok
Nakhodka
Hunchun
Chŏngjin
Kimchaek
NORTH KOREA
Hamhung
Hŭngnam
Wŏnsan
P'YŎNGYANG
Namp'o
Haeju
Kaesŏng
Ch'unch'ŏn
Kangnŭng
SŎUL (SEOUL)
INCH'ŎN
SOUTH KOREA
TAEJŎN
TAEGU
PUSAN
Kunsan
Chŏnju
KWANGJU
Masan
1915
Mokp'o
Cheju-do
1950
Korea Strait
Tsushima
YELLOW SEA
SEA OF JAPAN
EAST CHINA SEA
Aleksandrovsk-Sakhalinskiy
Vanino
Poronaysk
Mys Terpeniya
Sakhalin
Tartarskiy Proliv
Yuzhno-Sakhalinsk
Kholmsk
La Perouse Str.
Wakkanai
Kitami
Asahigawa
2290
Hokkaidō
Otaru
SAPPORO
Kushiro
Muroran
Erimo-misaki
Hakodate
Tsugaru-Kaikyō
Aomori
Hachinohe
Morioka
Akita
Sakata
Ishinomaki
Sado
Yamagata
Sendai
Niigata
Fukushima
Kōriyama
Wajima
Jōetsu
Utsunomiya
Mito
Takaoka
Toyama
Kanazawa
Komatsu
TŌKYŌ
KAWASAKI
YOKOHAMA
Fuji-San
3776
Shizuoka
Hamamatsu
NAGOYA
Matsue
KYŌTO
ŌSAKA
Sakai
Wakayama
KŌBE
Okayama
HIROSHIMA
Kure
Shikoku
Kōchi
Shimonoseki
KITAKYUSHU
FUKUOKA
Matsuyama
Sasebo
Nagasaki
Kumamoto
Kyūshū
Miyazaki
Kagoshima
Honshu
JAPAN
Nampō-Shotō
Tane-ga-Shima
Yaku-Shima
Amami-Ō-Shima
Tokuno-Shima
Okinawa-Jima
Naha
Ryūkyū-rettō
7507
Sakishima-Guntō
Miyako-Jima
Ishigaki-Shima
Iriomote-Jima
Tropic of Cancer
Chilung
T'AIPEI
Hsinchu
T'aichung
Changhua
Chiai
Yu Shan
3997
TAIWAN (FORMOSA)
T'ainan
T'aitung
P'ingtung
KAOHSIUNG
Taiwan Strait
Batan Is.
PHILIPPINES
Babuyan Is.
PACIFIC OCEAN
110
120
130
140
50
40
30
20

COPYRIGHT GEORGE PHILIP LTD.

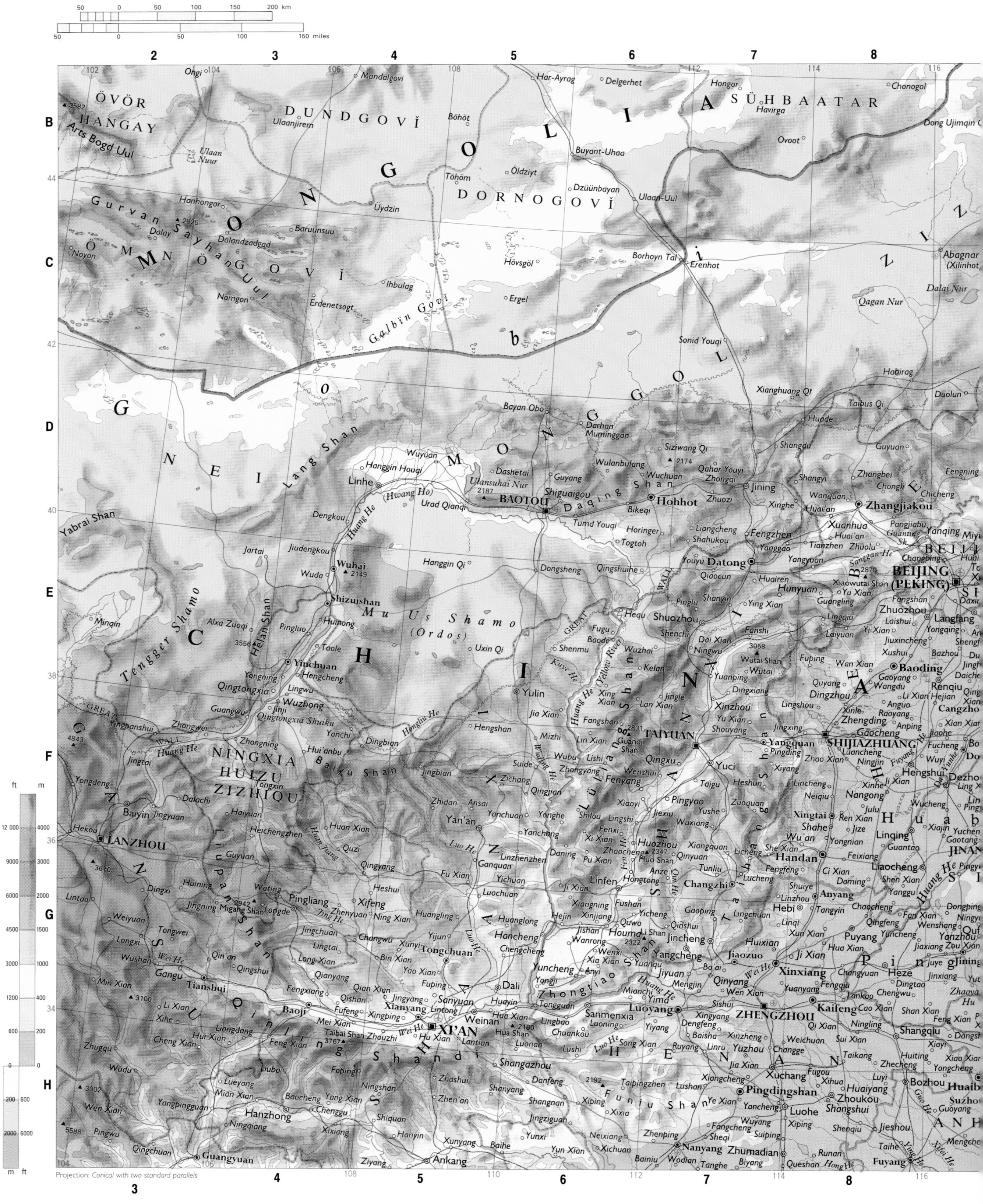

50 0 50 100 150 200 km
50 0 50 100 150 miles
2 3 4 5 6 7 8
B C D E F G H
ÖVÖR HANGAY
Arts Bogd Uul
DUNDGOVĬ
Ulaanjirem
Mandalgovi
Ongi
Ulaan Nuur
Böhöt
MONGOLIA
Har-Ayrag
Delgerhet
Hongor
SÜHBAATAR
Havirga
Chonogol
Dong Ujimqin Qi
Ovoot
Buyant-Uhaa
Öldziyt
Töhöm
Dzüünbayan
DORNOGOVĬ
Ulaan-Uul
Hanhongor
Üydzin
Gurvan Sayhan Uul
Dalay
Dalandzadgad
Baruunsuu
ÖMNÖGOVĬ
Noyon
Ihbulag
Nomgon
Erdenetsogt
Galbin Govi
Hövsgöl
Ergel
Borhoyn Tal
Erenhot
Abagnar Qi (Xilinhot)
Dalai Nur
Qagan Nur
Sonid Youqi
Gobi
Habirag
Xianghuang Qi
Duolun
Taibus Qi
NEI MONGGOL
Bayan Obo
Darhan Muminggan
Huade
Shangdu
Guyuan
Siziwang Qi
Lang Shan
Wuyuan
Hanggin Houqi
Linhe
Dashetai
Wulanbulang
Qahar Youyi Zhongqi
Wuchuan
Ulansuhai Nur
Guyang
Shiguaigou
BAOTOU
Daqing Shan
Hohhot
Zhuozi
Jining
Xinghe
Shangyi
Zhangbei
Chongli
Chicheng
Fengning
Wanquan
Huai'an
Zhangjiakou
Yabrai Shan
Dengkou
Huang He (Hwang Ho)
Urad Qianqi
Tumd Youqi
Bikeqi
Horinger
Togtoh
Liangcheng
Shahukou
Fengzhen
Yanggao
Tianzhen
Xuanhua
Huai'an
Zhuolu
Pangjiabu
Guanting Sk.
Yanqing
Jartai
Jiudengkou
Wuhai
Wuda
Hanggin Qi
Dongsheng
Qingshuihe
Youyu
Datong
Qiaocun
Huairen
Yangyuan
Sanggan He
Changping
BEIJING (PEKING)
Xiaowutai Shan
Yu Xian
Guangling
Fangshan
Zhuozhou
Hunyuan
Shizuishan
Huinong
Mu Us Shamo (Ordos)
Tengger Shamo
Helan Shan
Minqin
Alxa Zuoqi
Pingluo
Taole
Uxin Qi
GREAT WALL
Hequ
Pinglu
Shanyin
Ying Xian
Shuozhou
Shenchi
Fugu
Baode
Shenmu
Wuzhai
Kelan
Dai Xian
Ningwu
Fanshi
Wutai Shan
Wutai
Fuping
Wan Xian
Baoding
Lingqiu
Laiyuan
Yi Xian
Langfang
Laishui
Yongqing
Jiuxincheng
Xushui
Bazhou
Yinchuan
Hengcheng
CHINA
Yulin
Kuye He
Huang He (Yellow River)
Yongning
Qingtongxia
Lingwu
Wuzhong
Jinji
Qingtongxia Shuiku
Guangwu
Jia Xian
Xing Xian
Lan Xian
Jingle
Yuanping
Dingxiang
Xinzhou
Yu Xian
Shouyang
Quyang
Dingzhou
Gaoyang
Wangdu
Renqiu
Li Xian
Hejian
Cangzhou
Anguo
Raoyang
Xinle
Zhengding
Gaocheng
Jingxing
Lingshou
Anping
Yangquan
Pingding
SHIJIAZHUANG
Luancheng
Ningjin
Fucheng
Wuyi
Zhongwei
Yangpanshui
Zhongning
Yanchi
Dingbian
Hengshan
Honglu He
Fangshan
Guandi Shan
TAIYUAN
Mizhi
Lin Xian
Qingxu
Yuci
Zhao Xian
Xiyang
Hengshui
Dezhou
Jingtai
Yongdeng
NINGXIA HUIZU ZIZHIQU
Tongxin
Hui'anbu
Baiyu Shan
Jingbian
Suide
Wuding He
Wubu
Lishi
Zhongyang
Fenyang
Wenshui
Taigu
Heshun
Lincheng
Neiqiu
Nangong
Xinhe
Ji Xian
Zichang
Qingjian
Lüliang Shan
Xiaoyi
Pingyao
Jiexiu
Zuoquan
Yushe
Wuxiang
Xingtai
Ren Xian
Jize
Linqing
Wucheng
Julu
Baiyin
Jingyuan
Dalachi
Haiyuan
Zhidan
Ansai
Yan'an
Yanchuan
Yonghe
Shilou
Lingshi
Xiajin
Hekou
LANZHOU
Heichengzhen
Huan Xian
Huan Jiang
Liupan Shan
Quzi
Yanchang
Fenxi
Xi Xian
Huozhou
Zhaocheng
Huo Shan
Daning
Pu Xian
Xiangquan
Qinyuan
Licheng
She Xian
Wu'an
Shahe
Yongnian
Handan
Feixiang
Guantao
Liaocheng
JINAN
Guyuan
Qingyang
Luo He
Linzhenzhen
Ganquan
Anze
Tunliu
Fengfeng
Ci Xian
Daming
Shen Xian
Yanggu
Dingxi
Huining
Lintao
Fu Xian
Yichuan
Luochuan
Linfen
Hongtong
Changzhi
Lucheng
Linzhou
Anyang
Shuiye
Tangyin
Hebi
Chaocheng
Wating
Jingning
Migang Shan
Longde
Pingliang
Zhenyuan
Jing He
Xifeng
Heshui
Ning Xian
Huangling
Huanglong
Ji Xian
Jishan
Xiangning
Fushan
Hejin
Xinjiang
Yicheng
Gaoping
Lingchuan
Linqi
Qingfeng
Fan Xian
Wenshang
Weiyuan
Tongwei
Jingchuan
Lingtai
Changwu
Xunyi
Yijun
Hancheng
Chengcheng
Wanrong
Houma
Qinshui
Jincheng
Huixian
Xun Xian
Hua Xian
Puyang
Yuncheng
Jiaxiang
Zoucheng
Jining
Longxi
Wushan
Wei He
Qin'an
Qingshui
Long Xian
Bin Xian
Tongchuan
Yao Xian
Fuping
Dali
Wenxi
Xia Xian
Yuanqu
Yangcheng
Jiaozuo
Ji Xian
Xinxiang
Heze
Juye
Dingtao
Jinxiang
Min Xian
Gangu
Tianshui
Qianyang
Qian Xian
Fengxiang
Qishan
Jingyang
Sanyuan
Huayin
Yongji
Zhongtiao Shan
Anyi
Jiyuan
Mengjin
Qinyang
Wen Xian
Yuanyang
Fengqiu
Lankao
Chengwu
Li Xian
Xihe
Baoji
Fufeng
Xingping
Xianyang
Lintong
Weinan
Hua Xian
Tongguan
Mianchi
Yima
Sanmenxia
Luoning
Luoyang
Sishui
ZHENGZHOU
Kaifeng
Cao Xian
Shan Xian
Xingyang
Dengfeng
Qi Xian
Ningling
Shangqiu
Dangshan
Feng Xian
Mei Xian
Taibai Shan
Zhouzhi
XI'AN
Hu Xian
Lantian
Hua Shan
Luonan
Lingbao
Chuankou
Lushi
Luo He
Song Xian
Ruyang
Linru
Yuzhou
Baisha
Xinzheng
Weichuan
Sui Xian
Liangdang
Hui Xian
Cheng Xian
Feng Xian
Qinling Shandi
Zhuggu
Wudu
Liuba
Foping
Shangzhou
HENAN
Changge
Taikang
Huiting
Zhecheng
Yongcheng
Xiao Xian
Jia Xian
Xuchang
Fugou
Xihua
Huaiyang
Bozhou
Huaibei
Lueyang
Mian Xian
Ningshan
Zhashui
Zhen'an
Shanyang
Danfeng
Taipingzhen
Funiu Shan
Lushan
Xiangcheng
Pingdingshan
Zhoukou
Shangshui
Suzhou
Guoyang
Wen Xian
Yangpingguan
Baocheng
Yang Xian
Chenggu
Hanzhong
Ningqiang
Xixiang
Shiquan
Shangnan
Xiping
Xixia
Ye Xian
Yancheng
Luohe
Wuyang
Jingziguan
Hanyin
Xunyang
Baihe
Yunxi
Yun Xian
Neixiang
Xichuan
Zhenping
Fangcheng
Sheqi
Nanyang
Zhumadian
Suiping
Xiping
Shenqiu
Jieshou
Taihe
Fuyang
Mengcheng
Pingwu
Qingchuan
Guangyuan
Ankang
Ziyang
Bainiu
Wodian
Tangbe
Biyang
Queshan
Runan
Hong He
Ying He
Xifei He
ANHUI
3582 2825 2187 2174 2870 2149 3556 3058 2831 2347 2322 2942 3670 4843 3100 3767 2160 2192 3002 5588
102 104 106 108 110 112 114 116 44 42 40 38 36 34
ft m
12 000 4000
9000 3000
6000 2000
4500 1500
3000 1000
1200 400
600 200
0 0
200 600
2000 6000
m ft
Projection: Conical with two standard parallels

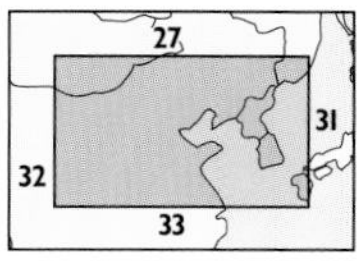
27
31
32
33

9
10
11
12
13
14
15
16
B
C
D
E
F
G
H
HARBIN
CHANGCHUN
JILIN
SHENYANG
FUSHUN
ANSHAN
DALIAN
P'YŎNGYANG
SOUL
INCH'ŎN
TAEJŎN
TAEGU
PUSAN
KWANGJU
QINGDAO
ZIBO
TIANJIN
NORTH KOREA
SOUTH KOREA
JAPAN
RUSSIA
HEILONGJIANG
JILIN
LIAONING
SHANDONG
JIANGSU
Dongbei (Manchuria)
SEA OF JAPAN
HUANG HAI
(Yellow Sea)
Bo Hai
Korea Bay
Korea Strait
Liaodong Wan
Laizhou Wan
Liaodong Bandao
Shandong Bandao
Changbai Shan
Zhangguangcai Ling
Tongjosŏn Man
Horqin Youyi Qianqi (Ulanhot)
Baicheng
Taonan
Da'an
Zhenlai
Hulingol
Tongliao
Chifeng
Fuxin
Jinzhou
Huludao
Qinhuangdao
Siping
Liaoyuan
Tonghua
Dandong
Sinŭiju
Yingkou
Benxi
Liaoyang
Mudanjiang
Jixi
Vladivostok
Ussuriysk
Yanji
Tumen
Hamhŭng
Chŏngjin
Kimch'aek
Wŏnsan
Kaesŏng
Haeju
Namp'o
Chunch'ŏn
Kangnŭng
Suwŏn
Ch'ŏngju
Chŏnju
Kunsan
Mokp'o
Yŏsu
Masan
Ulsan
P'ohang
Andong
Cheju
Cheju-do
Hallasan 1950
Tsushima
Iki
Sasebo
Nagasaki
Yantai
Weihai
Weifang
Linyi
Lianyungang
Xuzhou
Huai'an
Yancheng
Paektu-san 2744
Panmunjŏm
COPYRIGHT GEORGE PHILIP LTD.
East from Greenwich

INDONESIA AND THE PHILIPPINES 1:12 500 000

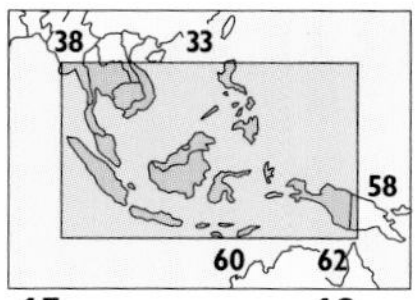
38
33
58
60
62

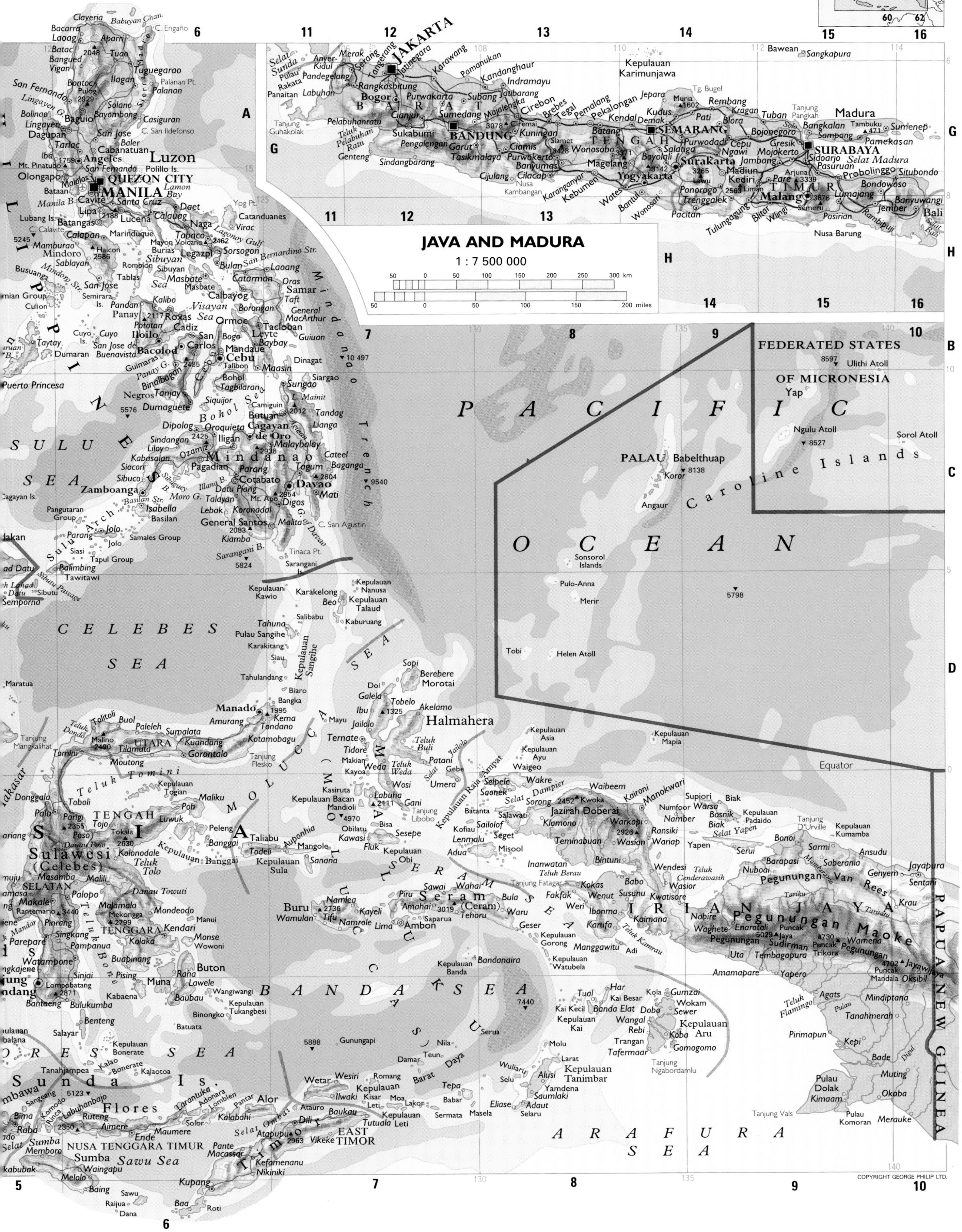
JAVA AND MADURA
1 : 7 500 000
JAKARTA
BANDUNG
SEMARANG
SURABAYA
Yogyakarta
Surakarta
Malang
Madura
Bali
Kepulauan Karimunjawa
Nusa Barung
PACIFIC OCEAN
FEDERATED STATES OF MICRONESIA
PALAU
Babelthuap
Koror
Caroline Islands
Yap
Ulithi Atoll
Ngulu Atoll
Sorol Atoll
Sonsorol Islands
Pulo-Anna
Merir
Tobi
Helen Atoll
Equator
Luzon
QUEZON CITY
MANILA
Mindoro
Samar
Panay
Negros
Cebu
Leyte
Bohol
Mindanao
Davao
Zamboanga
Sulu Arch.
Mindanao Trench
SULU SEA
CELEBES SEA
Kepulauan Talaud
Kepulauan Sangihe
Manado
Halmahera
Morotai
MOLUCCA SEA
Sulawesi (Celebes)
Teluk Tomini
Kepulauan Sula
Buru
Seram (Ceram)
Ambon
BANDA SEA
Kepulauan Aru
Kepulauan Tanimbar
Kepulauan Kai
IRIAN JAYA
Jazirah Doberai
Pegunungan Maoke
Puncak Jaya
PAPUA NEW GUINEA
ARAFURA SEA
Flores
Sumba
Sawu Sea
Timor
EAST TIMOR
Dili
Kupang
NUSA TENGGARA TIMUR
FLORES SEA
Sunda Is.
COPYRIGHT GEORGE PHILIP LTD.

MAINLAND SOUTH-EAST ASIA 1:6 000 000

50 0 50 100 150 200 km

50 0 50 100 150 miles

Gulf of Thailand
SOUTH CHINA SEA
MALAYSIA
PENINSULAR MALAYSIA
INDONESIA
Strait of Malacca
Myeik Kyunzu (Mergui Archipelago)
Malay Peninsula
Sumatera
Nam (Cochin China) Phan
Phnom Penh
THANH PHO HO CHI MINH (SAIGON)
Kuala Lumpur
SINGAPORE
Johor Baharu
George Town
Medan
Ipoh
Kota Baharu
Kuala Terengganu
Kuantan
Melaka
Seremban
Songkhla
Hat Yai
Nakhon Si Thammarat
Surat Thani
Phuket
Can Tho
Bac Lieu
Long Xuyen
My Tho
Bien Hoa
Vung Tau
Phan Thiet
Nha Trang
Da Lat
Kepulauan Anambas (Indonesia)
Kepulauan Natuna Besar (Indonesia)
Kepulauan Natuna Selatan (Indonesia)
Borneo
SARAWAK (Malaysia)
Kucing
Cameron Highlands
Mekong
Projection: Conical with two standard parallels
East from Greenwich
COPYRIGHT GEORGE PHILIP LTD.

TURKMENISTAN
AFGHANISTAN
PAKISTAN
IRAN
ARABIAN SEA
Tropic of Cancer
KARACHI
Hyderabad
Quetta
Kabul
Herat
Qandahar
Peshawar
RAWALPINDI
Islamabad
LAHORE
FAISALABAD
Multan
Gujranwala
Amritsar
DELHI
Jaipur
Agra
Gwalior
Kanpur
Ahmadabad
Vadodara (Baroda)
Surat
MUMBAI (BOMBAY)
Pune (Poona)
Nagpur
HYDERABAD
Bangalore
Chennai (Madras)
Mysore
Madurai
Cochin (Kochi)
Calicut (Kozhikode)
Mangalore
Colombo
SRI LANKA
Jaffna
Kandy
Trincomalee
Srinagar
Gilgit
KASHMIR
JAMMU
Northern Areas
NORTH WEST FRONTIER
PUNJAB
HARYANA
HIMACHAL PRADESH
UTTARANCHAL
RAJASTHAN
GUJARAT
MADHYA PRADESH
MAHARASHTRA
KARNATAKA
TAMIL NADU
KERALA
ANDHRA PRADESH
GOA
SIND
BALUCHISTAN
Thar or Great Indian Desert
Hindu Kush
Karakoram
Aksai Chin
Rann of Kachchh
Gulf of Kachchh
Gulf of Khambhat
Gulf of Mannar
Palk Strait
Adam's Bridge
Malabar Coast
Coromandel Coast
Western Ghats
Eastern Ghats
Makran Coast Range
Central Makran Range
Siahan Range
Kirthar Range
Sulaiman Range
Vindhya Range
Satpura Range
Ajanta Range
Satmala Hills
Indus
Mouths of the Indus
C. Comorin
Dondra Head
Continuation Southwards on same scale
Projection: Conical with two standard parallels

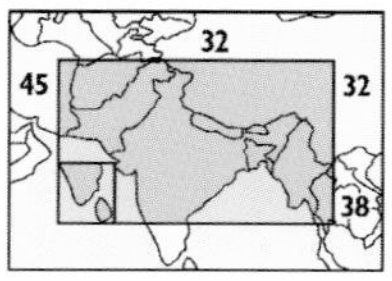
32
45
32
38

C H I N A
X I Z A N G Z I Z H I Q U (T I B E T)
Q I N G H A I
Tanggula (Dangla) Shan
Huh Xil Shan
Bayan Har Shan
Nyainqentanglha Shan
Gangdisê Shan
Dogai Coring
Siling Co
Nam Co
Gyaring Co
Tangra Yumco
Gyaring Hu
Ngoring Hu
Yushu
Dainkog
Nangqen
Gamtog
Garzê
Baiyü
Qamdo
Dêngqên
Baqên
Nagqu
Xainza
Ombu
Coqên
Lhari
Lhinzub
Gongbo'gyamda
Lhasa
Xigazê
Gyangzê
Lhazê
Saga
Zhongba
Nang Xian
Lhunzê
Comai
Gamba
Dinggyê
Riga
Jido
Zhaxizê
Lhorong
Coqên
Ningjing
Yidun
Litang
Yajiang
Xinlong
S I C H U A N
Y U N N A N
Muli Zangzu Zizhixian
Zhongdian
Zhizhixian
Weixi
Lijiang
Jianchuan
Yunlong
Baoshan
Tengchong
Longling
Changning
Nu Jiang
Lancang Jiang (Mekong)
Yarlung Zangbo Jiang (Brahmaputra)
Mainkung
Dzhiuk
N E P A L
Mt. Everest 8850
Kanchenjunga 8598
Katmandu
Bhaktapur
Nepalganj
Nuwakot
Gurkha
Nawakot
Dhaulagiri 8172
Muktinath
Mustang
Jumla
Mugu
Simikot
Karnali
Siwalik Range
Biratnagar
Dhankuta
Birganj
Raxaul
S I K K I M
Gangtok
Darjiling
Thimphu
Punakha
Tongsa Dzong
B H U T A N
Taga Dzong
A R U N A C H A L P R A D E S H
Towang
Rupa
Kangto
Itanagar
Dibrugarh
Tinsukia
North Lakhimpur
Sibsagar
Jorhat
Dergaon
Tezpur
Balipara
A S S A M
Gauhati
Nowgong
Rangia
Barpeta
Mairabari
Dhubri
Goalpara
Brahmaputra
M E G H A L A Y A
Shillong
Cherrapunji
Tura
N A G A L A N D
Kohima
Mokokchung
M A N I P U R
Imphal
Ukhrul
Tamenglong
Churachandpur
Silchar
Haflong
Barail Range
M I Z O R A M
Aizawl
Lunglei
T R I P U R A
Agartala
B A N G L A D E S H
DHAKA
Mymensingh
Sylhet
Rajshahi
Bogra
Rangpur
Dinajpur
Pabna
Kushtia
Jessore
Khulna
Barisal
Chandpur
Comilla
Noakhali
Chittagong
Cox's Bazar
Bhola
Hatia
Patuakhali
Narayanganj
Brahmanbaria
Sundarbans
Mouths of the Ganges
East Bengal
W E S T B E N G A L
KOLKATA (CALCUTTA)
Haora
Barddhaman
Durgapur
Asansol
Bankura
Krishnanagar
Barakpur
Shrirampur
Haldia
Contai
Diamond Harbour
Bhatpara
Siliguri
Jalpaiguri
Koch Bihar
Alipur Duar
Balurghat
Kishanganj
Purnia
Katihar
Saidpur
Ingraj Bazar
Baharampur
B I H A R
Patna
Gaya
Muzaffarpur
Darbhanga
Chhapra
Arrah
Bhagalpur
Munger
Begusarai
Jamalpur
Bihar
Sasaram
Aurangabad
Siwan
Gorakhpur
Deoria
Motihari
Bettiah
J H A R K H A N D
Ranchi
Jamshedpur
Dhanbad
Bokaro
Hazaribag
Giridih
Deoghar
Lohardaga
Ramgarh
Purulia
Chaibasa
Gumla
Chakradharpur
U T T A R P R A D E S H
Lucknow
Varanasi
Allahabad
Faizabad
Gonda
Basti
Bahraich
Sultanpur
Azamgarh
Jaunpur
Mirzapur
Rae Bareli
Fatehpur
Rewa
Satna
Dudhi
C H H A T T I S G A R H
Raipur
Bilaspur
Durg
Dhamtari
Kanker
Raigarh
Korba
Ambikapur
Chirmiri
Kawardha
Jagdalpur
O R I S S A
Cuttack
Bhubaneshwar
Puri
Chilka L.
Paradip
Kendrapara
Balasore
Baleshwar
Bhadrakh
Sambalpur
Jharsuguda
Rourkela
Keonjhargarh
Dhenkanal
Talcher
Angul
Mahanadi
Brahmani
Brahmapur
Rayagada
Jeypore
Bhawanipatna
Titlagarh
Balangir
Sonepur
Russellkonda
Ichchapuram
Tekkali
Srikakulam
Vizianagaram
Vishakhapatnam
Anakapalle
Kakinada
Godavari Point
Pithapuram
Narasapur
Machilipatnam
Eastern Ghats
Northern Circars
B A Y O F B E N G A L
I N D I A N O C E A N
Preparis North Channel
Preparis South Channel
Preparis Kyun (Burma)
Koko Kyunzu (Burma)
Moscos Is.
Maungmagan
Kyunzu
Launglon Bok
B U R M A (M Y A N M A R)
K A C H I N
Myitkyina
Putao
Sumprabum
Bhamo
Katha
Mogaung
Hkakabo Razi
Kawngtim
Hukawng Valley
Hkamti
Maingkwan
S A G A I N G
Shwebo
Monywa
Sagaing
Mandalay
Kalewa
Mawlaik
Tamu
Homalin
Chindwin
Mogok
Mong Mit
Lashio
Hsenwi
Kunlong
Namtu
S H A N
Taunggyi
Kengtung
Mong Hsu
Mong Kung
Mong Hpayak
Mong Pan
Mong Ton
Mong Nai
Loi-kaw
K A Y A H
Bawlake
Toungoo
K A Y I N
Pyinmana
Meiktila
Thazi
Yamethin
M A G W E
Magwe
Minbu
Yenangyaung
Kyaukpadaung
Pakokku
Pauk
Myingyan
Taungdwingyi
Thayetmyo
Prome
Pyu
Pegu
Madauk
Thaton
Martaban
Moulmein
Pa-an
MON
RANGOON (YANGON)
Letpadan
Tharrawaddy
Henzada
Kyongpyaw
Yandoon
Bassein
Ma-ubin
Pyapon
Myaungmya
I R R A W A D D Y
Mouths of the Irrawaddy
G. of Martaban
Maudin Sun
Gwa
Sandoway
Taungup
Cheduba I.
Ramree I.
Kyaukpyu
Sittwe (Akyab)
Paletwa
A R A K A N
Arakan Coast
Arakan Yoma
Pegu Yoma
Irrawaddy
Sittang Myit
Salween
Dawna Range
C H I N
Falam
Hakha
Tiddim
Gangaw
Mindat
Kanpetlet
Mt. Victoria 3053
Ponnyadaung
Kalegauk Kyun
Lamaing
Ye
Natkyizin
Sangkhla Buri
Nam Tok
Yebyu
Tavoy
T H A I L A N D
Chiang Rai
Chiang Mai
Mae Hong Son
Lampang
Muang Lamphun
Tak
Mae Klong
Tropic of Cancer
East from Greenwich
12 13 14 15 16 17 18 19 20 21 22
B C D E F G H J K L M

THE INDO-GANGETIC PLAIN 1:6 000 000

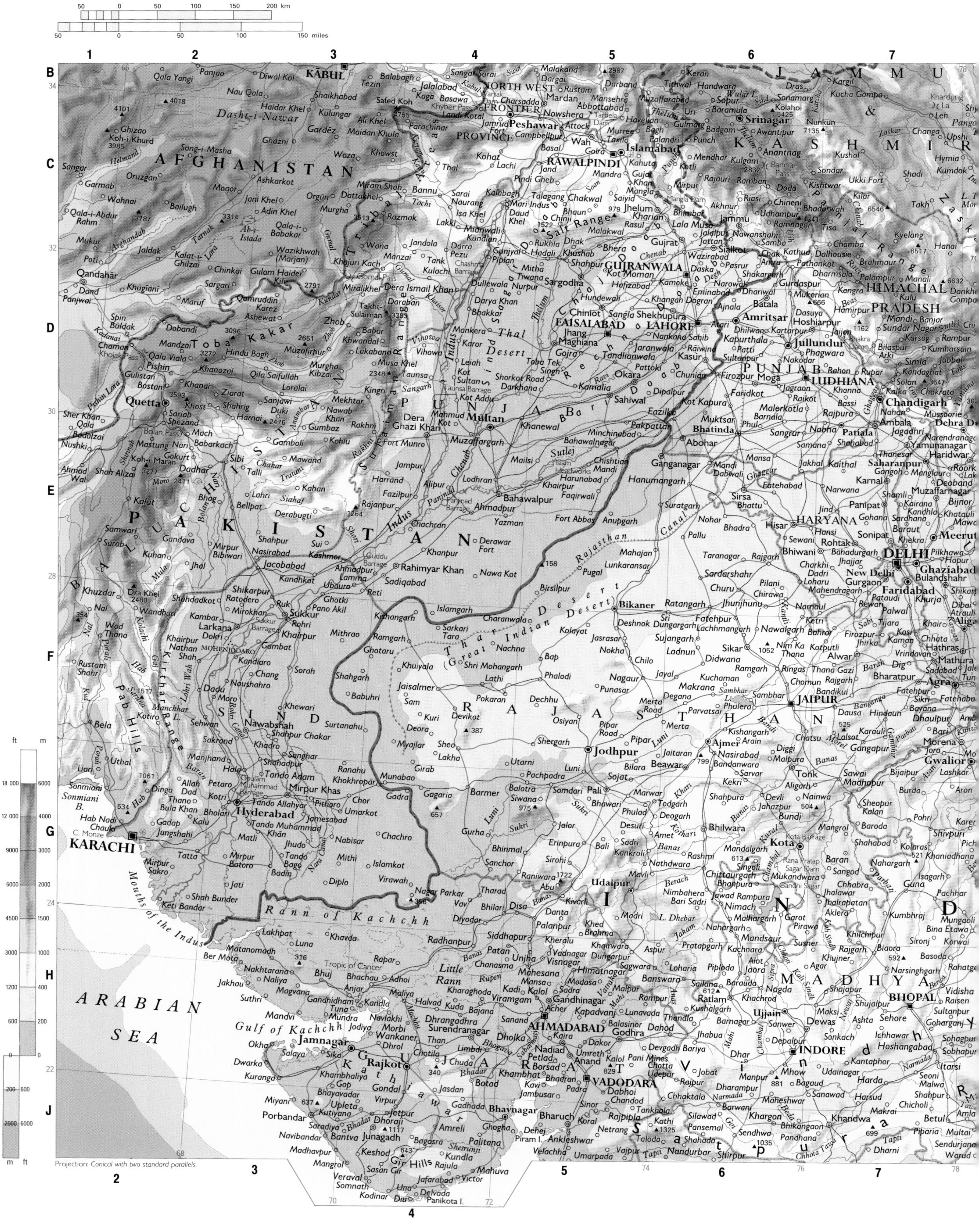

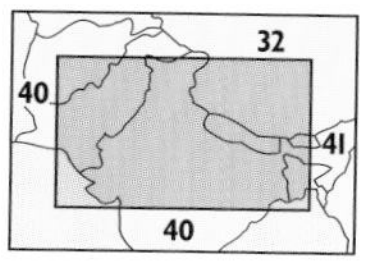
32
40
41
40

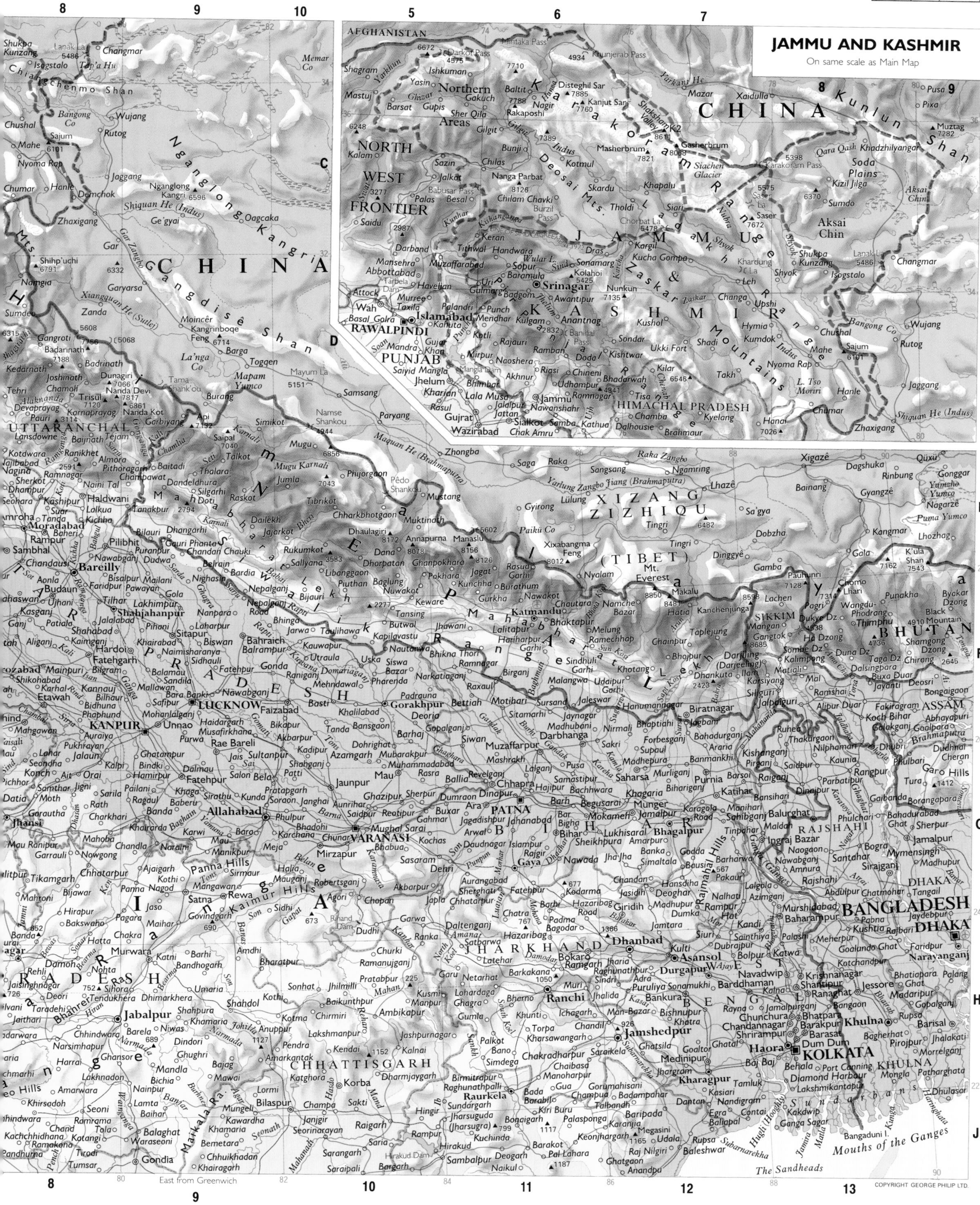
JAMMU AND KASHMIR
On same scale as Main Map
AFGHANISTAN
CHINA
NORTH WEST FRONTIER
Northern Areas
PUNJAB
JAMMU & KASHMIR
HIMACHAL PRADESH
Karakoram Range
Ladakh Range
Zaskar Mountains
Kunlun Shan
Aksai Chin
Soda Plains
Islamabad
RAWALPINDI
Srinagar
Jammu
Gilgit
Leh
K2 8611
Gasherbrum 8068
Nanga Parbat 8126
Siachen Glacier
Deosai Mts.
CHINA
Ngangong Kangri
Gangdisê Shan
XIZANG ZIZHIQU
(TIBET)
Yarlung Zangbo Jiang (Brahmaputra)
NEPAL
Mahabharat Lekh
Siwalik Range
Katmandu
Mt. Everest 8850
Makalu 8481
Kanchenjunga 8598
Annapurna 8078
Dhaulagiri 8172
Manaslu 8156
SIKKIM
Gangtok
BHUTAN
Thimphu
UTTARANCHAL
Nanda Devi 7817
UTTAR PRADESH
LUCKNOW
KANPUR
Allahabad
VARANASI
Bareilly
Moradabad
BIHAR
PATNA
Gaya
Bhagalpur
JHARKHAND
Ranchi
Jamshedpur
Dhanbad
WEST BENGAL
KOLKATA
Haora
Kharagpur
Durgapur
Asansol
CHHATTISGARH
Bilaspur
Korba
MADHYA PRADESH
Jabalpur
Kaimur Hills
Panna Hills
Rajmahal Hills
BANGLADESH
DHAKA
RAJSHAHI
KHULNA
Khulna
Narayanganj
ASSAM
Garo Hills
Sundarbans
Mouths of the Ganges
The Sandheads
East from Greenwich
8
9
10
11
12
13
A
B
C
D
E
F
G
H
J

THE MIDDLE EAST 1:7 000 000

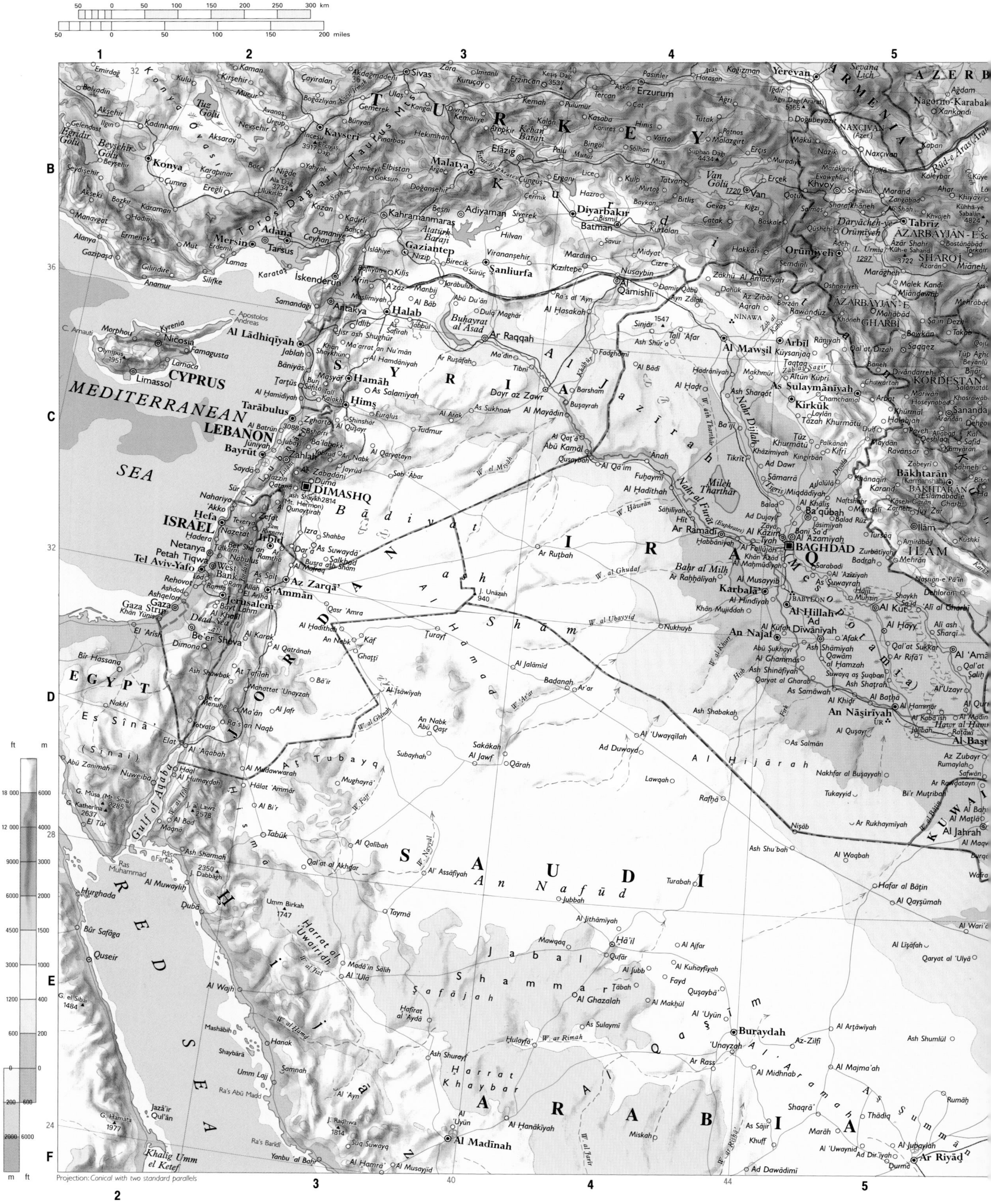

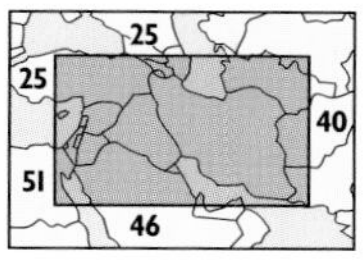
25
25
40
51
46

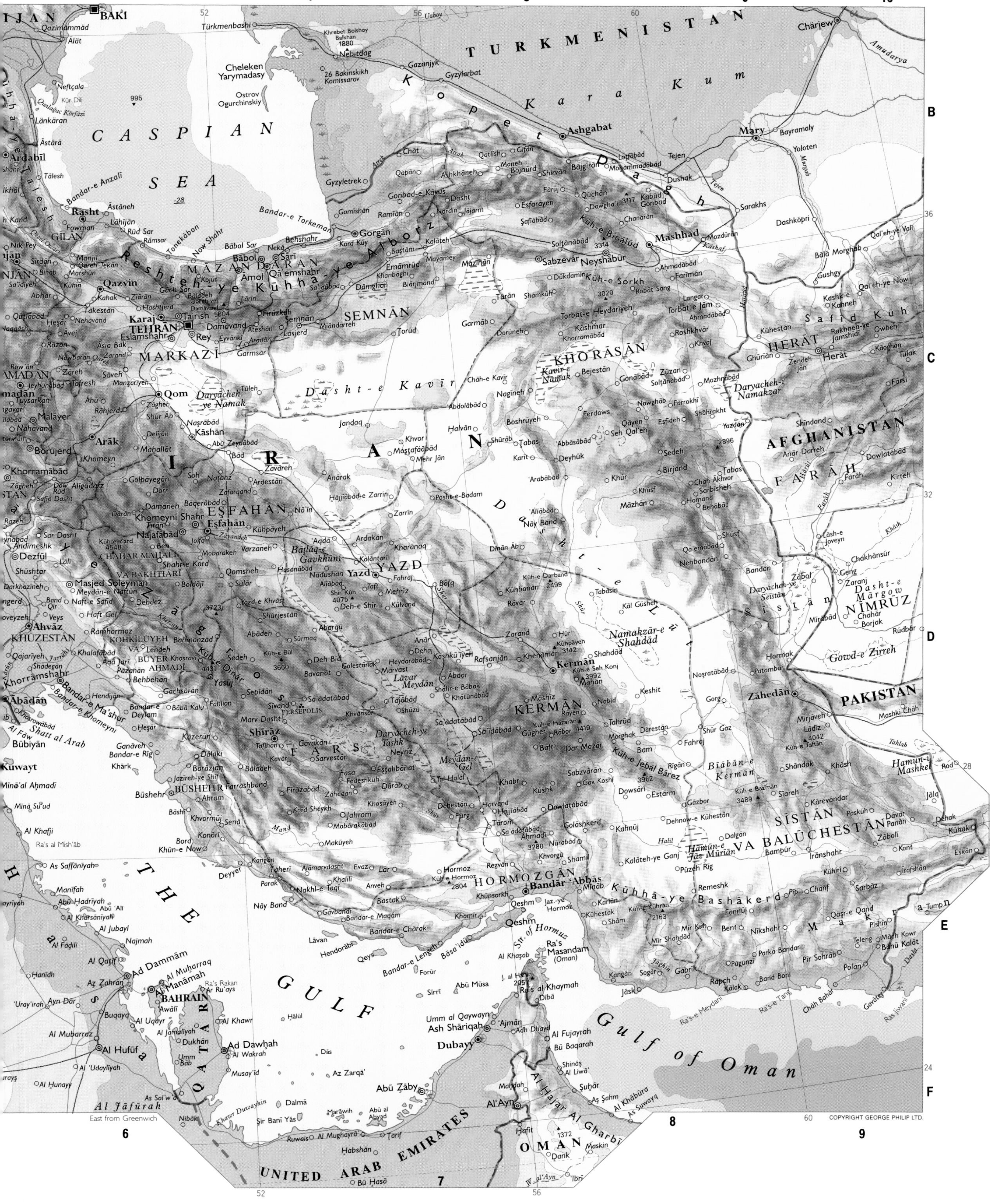
TURKMENISTAN
Kara Kum
Kopet Dagh
CASPIAN SEA
Ashgabat
Mary
Chärjew
Amudarya
Türkmenbashi
BAKI
Reshteh-ye Kūhha-ye Alborz
MAZANDARAN
TEHRĀN
Tehrān
Qom
MARKAZĪ
SEMNĀN
KHORĀSĀN
Mashhad
Dasht-e Kavīr
Dasht-e Lūt
IRAN
EŞFAHĀN
Eşfahān
YAZD
Yazd
KERMĀN
Kermān
FĀRS
Shīrāz
KHŪZESTĀN
Ahvāz
Ābādān
Zāgros
HERĀT
Herāt
AFGHANISTAN
FARĀH
NĪMRŪZ
Dasht-e Mārgow
Zāhedān
SĪSTĀN VA BALŪCHESTĀN
PAKISTAN
HORMOZGĀN
Bandar-e 'Abbās
Kūhhā-ye Bashākerd
Str. of Hormuz
THE GULF
Gulf of Oman
Kuwayt
Ad Dammām
BAHRAIN
Al Manāmah
QATAR
Ad Dawhah
Al Hufūf
Al Jāfūrah
Dubayy
Abū Zaby
Ash Shāriqah
UNITED ARAB EMIRATES
Al Hajar Al Gharbī
OMAN
Shatt al Arab
Bushehr
East from Greenwich
6
7
8
9
10
B
C
D
E
F
COPYRIGHT GEORGE PHILIP LTD.

ARABIA AND THE HORN OF AFRICA 1:15 000 000

100 0 100 200 300 400 500 600 km

100 0 100 200 300 400 miles

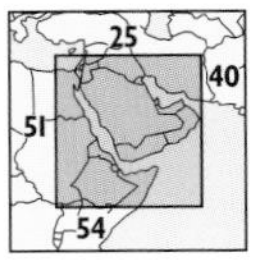
25
40
51
54

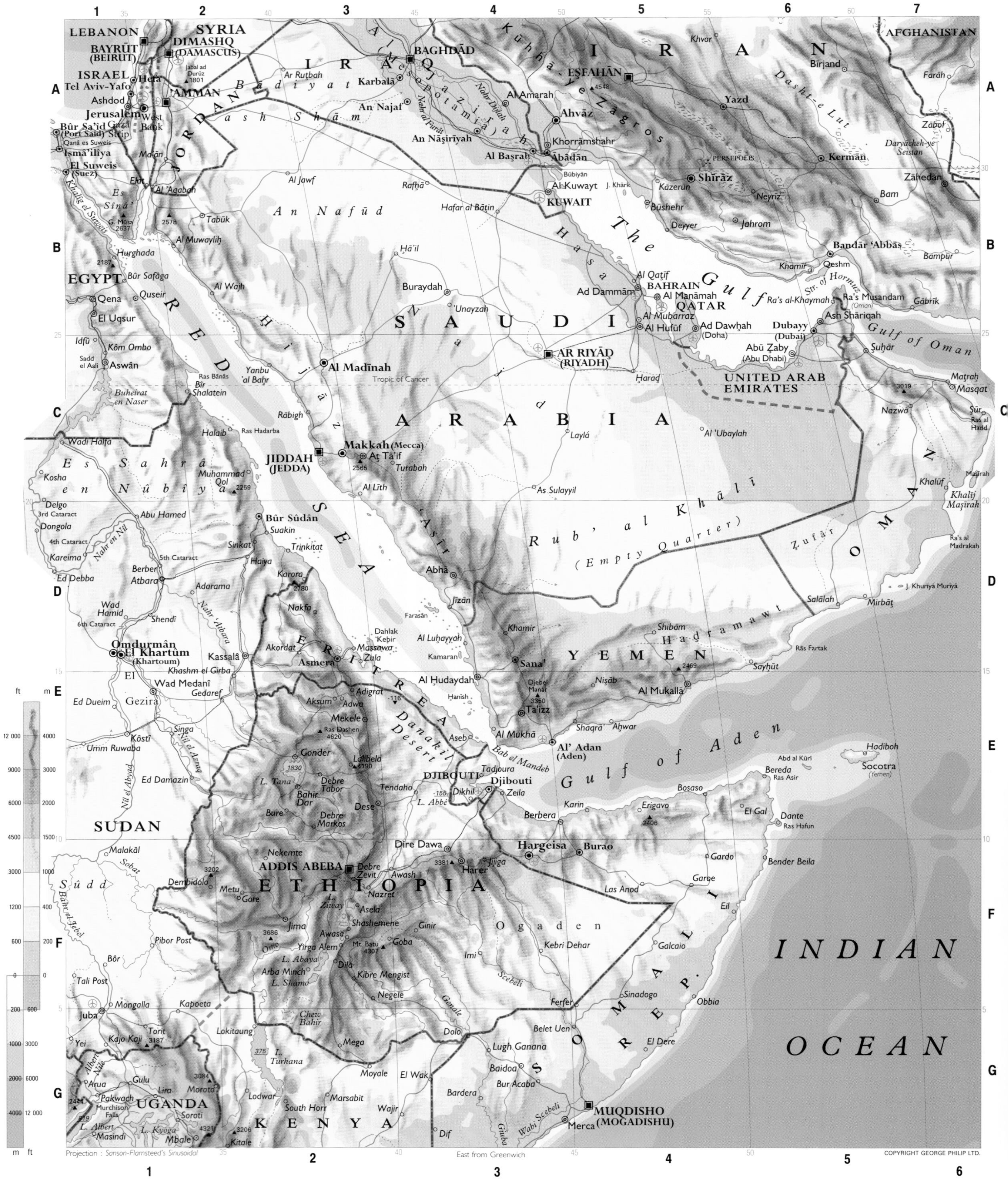
1 2 3 4 5 6 7
A B C D E F G
LEBANON
BAYRŪT (BEIRUT)
SYRIA
DIMASHQ (DAMASCUS)
ISRAEL
Hefa
Tel Aviv-Yafo
Ashdod
Jerusalem
West Bank
Gaza Strip
'AMMĀN
JORDAN
Jabal ad Durūz 1801
Bûr Sa'îd (Port Said)
Qanâ es Suweis
Isma'ilîya
El Suweis (Suez)
Ma'ān
Elat
Al 'Aqabah
Es Sînâ'
G. Mûsa 2637
2578
Tabūk
Khalîg el Suweis
Al Muwaylih
Hurghada
2187
EGYPT
Bûr Safâga
Quseir
Qena
El Uqsur
Idfû
Kôm Ombo
Sadd el Aali
Aswân
Ras Bânâs
Bîr Shalatein
Buheirat en Naser
RED SEA
Halaib
Ras Hadarba
Wadi Halfa
Es Sahrâ en Nûbîya
Kosha
Muhammad Qol
2259
Delgo
3rd Cataract
Dongola
4th Cataract
Nahr en Nil
Kareima
Abu Hamed
Bûr Sûdân
Suakin
Sinkat
Trinkitat
5th Cataract
Berber
Atbara
Ed Debba
Haiya
Adarama
Nahr 'Atbara
Wad Hamid
6th Cataract
Shendî
Omdurmân
El Khartûm (Khartoum)
Kassalâ
Khashm el Girba
El Gezira
Wad Medanî
Gedaref
Ed Dueim
Kôstî
Umm Ruwaba
Singa
Nîl el Azraq
Nîl el Abyad
Ed Damazin
SUDAN
Malakâl
Sobat
Sûdd
Bahr el Jebel
Pibor Post
Bôr
Tali Post
Mongalla
Kapoeta
Juba
Torit
Kajo Kaji
3187
Yei
Albert Nile
Arua
Pakwach
Murchison Falls
2444
L. Albert
Masindi
Gulu
Lira
Moroto
3084
UGANDA
Soroti
L. Kyoga
Mbale
4321
Lokitaung
L. Turkana
375
Lodwar
South Horr
Marsabit
KENYA
3206
Kitale
Moyale
El Wak
Wajir
Bardera
Dif
Giuba
Wabi Scebeli
Merca
MUQDISHO (MOGADISHU)
Baidoa
Bur Acaba
Lugh Ganana
Dolo
Belet Uen
Ferfer
SOMALI REP.
El Dere
Obbia
Sinadogo
Galcaio
Eil
Garoe
Las Anod
Gardo
Bender Beila
El Gal
Dante
Ras Hafun
Bereda
Ras Asir
Bosaso
Erigavo
2406
Karin
Berbera
Burao
Hargeisa
Jijiga
Harer
3381
Dire Dawa
Ogaden
Kebri Dehar
Imi
Scebeli
Genale
Negele
Kibre Mengist
Goba
Mt. Batu 4307
Dila
Yirga Alem
Awasa
Shashemene
Ginir
Asela
Nazret
L. Ziway
Awash
Debre Zevit
ADDIS ABEBA
Nekemte
ETHIOPIA
Dembidolo
3202
Metu
Gore
Jima
3686
Omo
L. Abaya
Arba Minch
L. Shamo
Chew Bahir
Mega
Bure
Debre Markos
Bahir Dar
L. Tana
1830
Debre Tabor
Gonder
Lalibela
4190
Ras Dashen 4620
Mekele
Aksum
Adwa
Adigrat
Asmera
Akordat
Nakfa
2780
Karora
ERITREA
Massawa
Zula
Dahlak Kebir
Danakil Desert
-116
Aseb
Dese
Tendaho
L. Abbé
-155
Dikhil
Tadjoura
DJIBOUTI
Djibouti
Zeila
Bab el Mandeb
Gulf of Aden
Socotra (Yemen)
Hadiboh
Abd al Kūri
Al' Adan (Aden)
Al Mukhā
Ta'izz
Djebel Manar 3350
Shaqrā'
Ahwar
Nisāb
Al Mukallā
2469
Sayhūt
Rās Fartak
YEMEN
Hadramawt
Shibām
Sana'
Khamir
Al Hudaydah
Kamaran
Al Luhayyah
Hanish
Farasān
Jīzān
Abhā
'Asīr
Salālah
Mirbāt
J. Khuriyā Muriyā
Zufār
OMAN
Ra's al Madrakah
Khalīj Masīrah
Masīrah
Khalūf
Şūr
Ra's al Hadd
Nazwá
Matrah
Masqat
3019
Gulf of Oman
Şuhār
Ash Shāriqah
Ra's Musandam (Oman)
Dubayy (Dubai)
Abū Zaby (Abu Dhabi)
UNITED ARAB EMIRATES
Ad Dawhah (Doha)
QATAR
BAHRAIN
Al Manāmah
Al Qatīf
Ad Dammām
Al Mubarraz
Al Hufūf
Harad
Al 'Ubaylah
Rub' al Khālī (Empty Quarter)
As Sulayyil
Laylá
AR RIYĀD (RIYADH)
SAUDI ARABIA
Najd
Hasa
'Unayzah
Buraydah
Hā'il
An Nafūd
Al Jawf
Rafhā
Hafar al Bātin
Al Wajh
Hijāz
Al Madīnah
Yanbu 'al Bahr
Tropic of Cancer
Rābigh
JIDDAH (JEDDA)
Makkah (Mecca)
At Tā'if
2565
Turabah
Al Līth
Badiyat ash Shām
Ar Rutbah
IRAQ
BAGHDĀD
Karbalā'
An Najaf
Al Mesopotamia
Nahr al Furāt
Nahr Dijlah
An Nāşirīyah
Al 'Amarah
Al Başrah
KUWAIT
Al Kuwayt
Būbiyān
Khorramshahr
Ābādān
Ahvāz
J. Khārk
The Gulf
Kāzerūn
Būshehr
Deyyer
Jahrom
Shīrāz
PERSEPOLIS
Neyrīz
IRAN
Kūhhā-ye Zāgros
Eşfahān
4548
Yazd
Khvor
Bīrjand
Dasht-e Lut
Kermān
Bam
Bandār 'Abbās
Qeshm
Khamir
Str. of Hormuz
Ra's al-Khaymah
Bampūr
Gābrīk
Zāhedān
Zābol
Daryācheh-ye Sīstan
Farāh
AFGHANISTAN
INDIAN OCEAN
ft m
12 000 4000
9000 3000
6000 2000
4500 1500
3000 1000
1200 400
600 200
0 0
200 600
1000 3000
2000 6000
4000 12 000
m ft
Projection : Sanson-Flamsteed's Sinusoidal
East from Greenwich
35 40 45 50 55 60
30 25 20 15 10 5

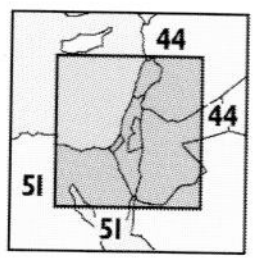

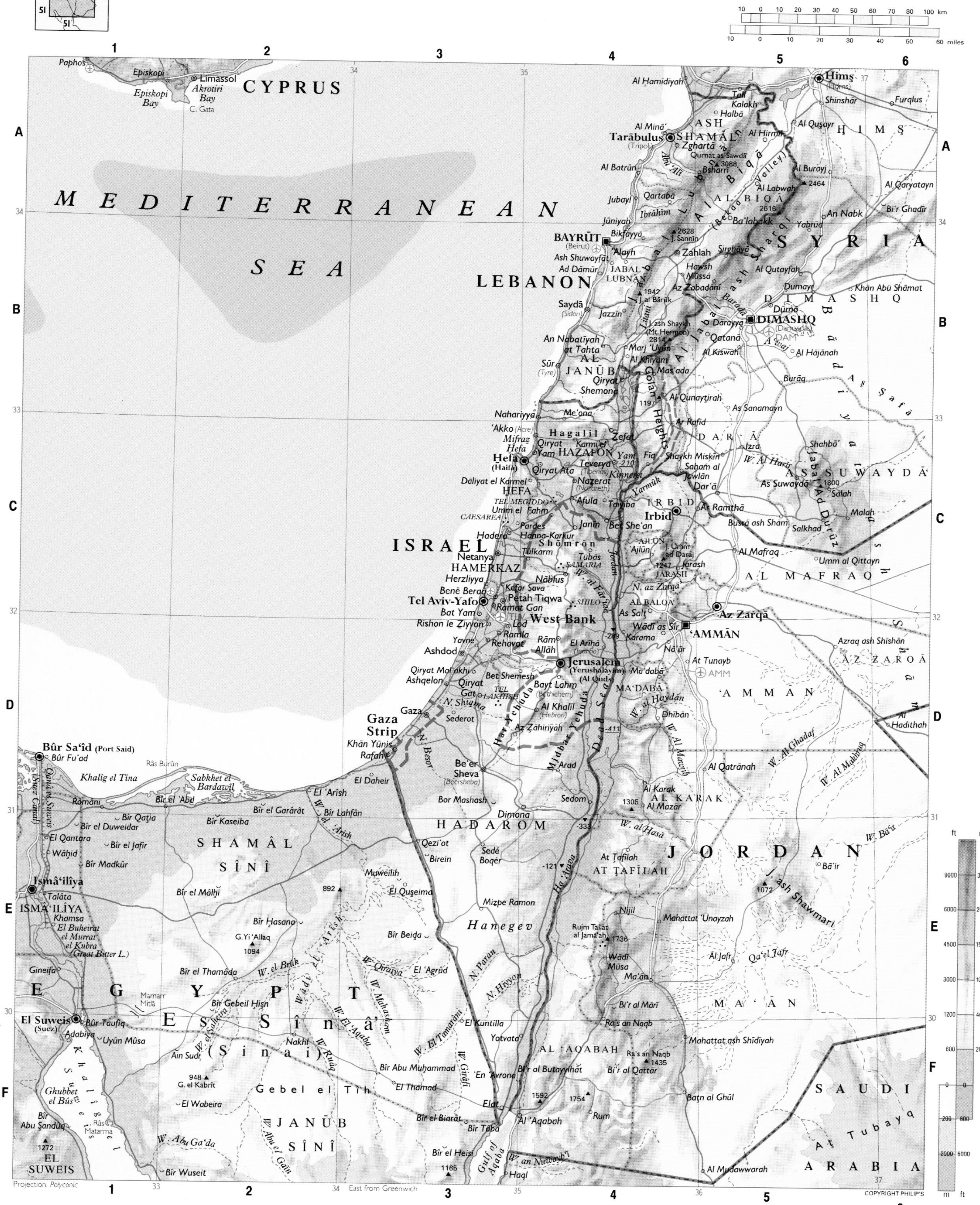

1974 Cease Fire Lines

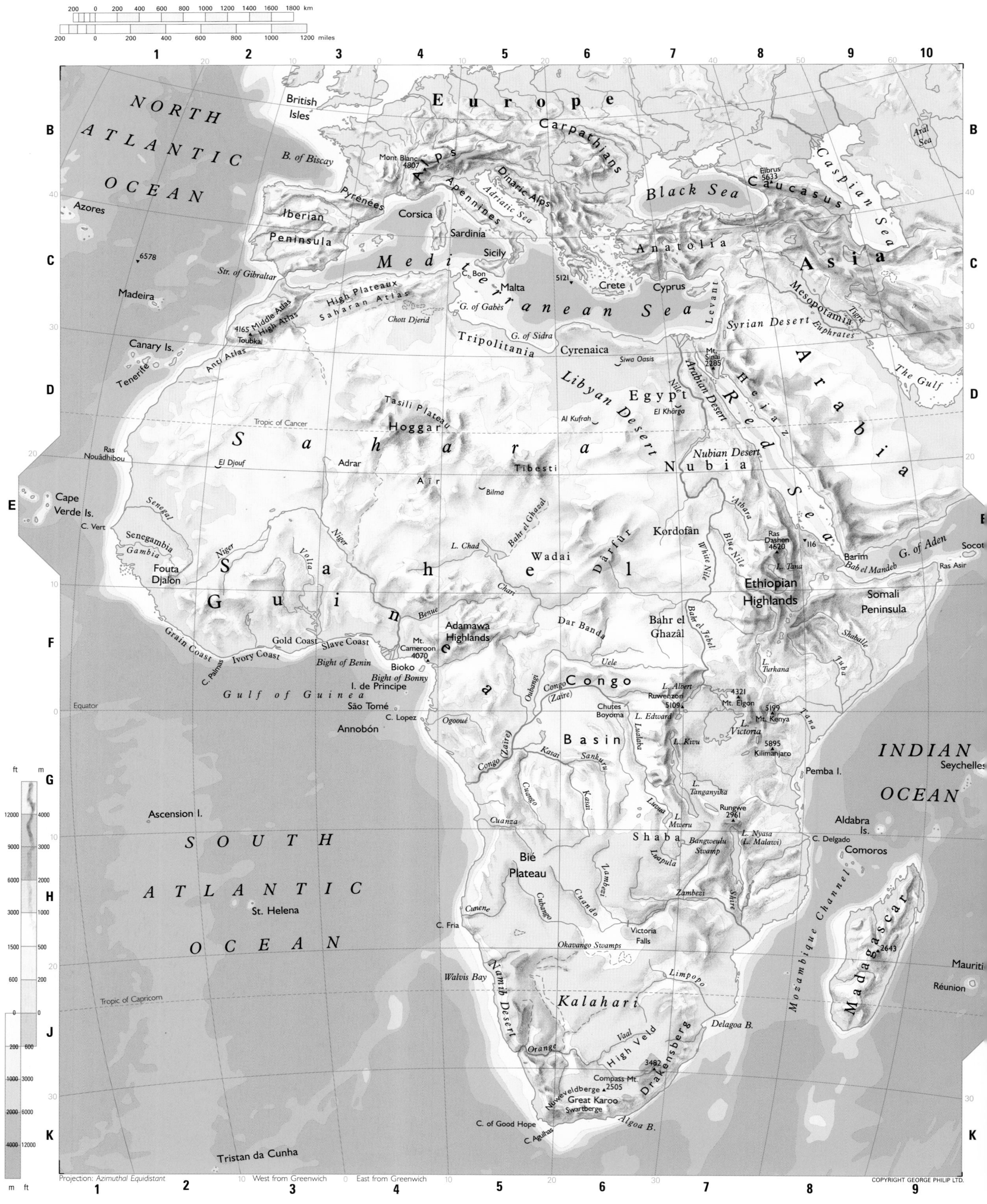

200 0 200 400 600 800 1000 1200 1400 1600 1800 km
200 0 200 400 600 800 1000 1200 miles
Europe
British Isles
NORTH ATLANTIC OCEAN
B. of Biscay
Mont Blanc 4807
Alps
Carpathians
Dinaric Alps
Adriatic Sea
Apennines
Black Sea
Elbrus 5633
Caucasus
Caspian Sea
Aral Sea
Azores
Pyrénées
Iberian Peninsula
Corsica
Sardinia
Sicily
Anatolia
Asia
6578
Str. of Gibraltar
Mediterranean Sea
C. Bon
Malta
5121
Crete
Cyprus
Levant
Mesopotamia
Tigris
Madeira
High Plateaux
Saharan Atlas
Middle Atlas
High Atlas
4165
Toubkal
Chott Djerid
G. of Gabès
Syrian Desert
Euphrates
Canary Is.
Anti Atlas
Tripolitania
G. of Sidra
Cyrenaica
Siwa Oasis
Mt. Sinai 2285
Arabia
The Gulf
Tenerife
Libyan Desert
Egypt
Nile
Arabian Desert
Hejaz
Red Sea
Tasili Plateau
Hoggar
Tropic of Cancer
Al Kufrah
El Khârga
Sahara
Ras Nouâdhibou
El Djouf
Adrar
Tibesti
Nubian Desert
Nubia
Aïr
Bilma
Cape Verde Is.
C. Vert
Senegal
Bahr el Ghazal
Atbara
Kordofân
Senegambia
Gambia
Niger
Volta
L. Chad
Wadai
Dârfûr
White Nile
Blue Nile
Ras Dashen 4620
116
Barim
Bab el Mandeb
G. of Aden
Ras Asir
Fouta Djalon
Sahel
Guinea
Chari
L. Tana
Ethiopian Highlands
Somali Peninsula
Benue
Dar Banda
Bahr el Ghazâl
Bahr el Jebel
Grain Coast
Gold Coast
Slave Coast
Ivory Coast
Adamawa Highlands
Mt. Cameroon 4070
Bight of Benin
Bioko
Bight of Bonny
C. Palmas
Shabeelle
Juba
L. Turkana
Uele
Oubangui
Congo (Zaïre)
Congo Basin
L. Albert
4321
Ruwenzori 5109
Mt. Elgon
Gulf of Guinea
I. de Principe
São Tomé
Equator
Chutes Boyoma
L. Edward
5199
Mt. Kenya
Tana
C. Lopez
Ogooué
L. Victoria
Annobón
Lualaba
L. Kivu
5895
Kilimanjaro
INDIAN OCEAN
Seychelles
Kasai
Sankuru
Pemba I.
Cuango
L. Tanganyika
Ascension I.
Luvua
Rungwe 2961
Cuanza
L. Mweru
Aldabra Is.
SOUTH ATLANTIC OCEAN
Shaba
L. Nyasa (L. Malawi)
C. Delgado
Bangweulu Swamp
Luapula
Comoros
Bié Plateau
Zambezi
Mozambique Channel
Cunene
Cubango
Cuando
Shire
St. Helena
C. Fria
Victoria Falls
Okavango Swamps
Madagascar
2643
Walvis Bay
Namib Desert
Limpopo
Mauriti
Réunion
Tropic of Capricorn
Kalahari
Delagoa B.
Vaal
High Veld
Drakensberg
Orange
3482
Compass Mt. 2505
Nuweveldberge
Great Karoo
Swartberge
C. of Good Hope
C. Agulhas
Algoa B.
Tristan da Cunha
ft m
12000 4000
9000 3000
6000 2000
3000 1000
1500 500
600 200
0 0
200 600
1000 3000
2000 6000
4000 12000
m ft
Projection: Azimuthal Equidistant
West from Greenwich
East from Greenwich
COPYRIGHT GEORGE PHILIP LTD.

NORTH ATLANTIC OCEAN
SOUTH ATLANTIC OCEAN
INDIAN OCEAN
Mediterranean Sea
Black Sea
Caspian Sea
Red Sea
Sahara
ALGERIA
LIBYA
EGYPT
MOROCCO
TUNISIA
WESTERN SAHARA
MAURITANIA
MALI
NIGER
CHAD
SUDAN
ERITREA
DJIBOUTI
ETHIOPIA
SOMALI REP.
SENEGAL
GAMBIA
GUINEA-BISSAU
GUINEA
SIERRA LEONE
LIBERIA
IVORY COAST
BURKINA FASO
GHANA
TOGO
BENIN
NIGERIA
CAMEROON
CENTRAL AFRICAN REP.
EQUATORIAL GUINEA
SÃO TOMÉ & PRINCIPE
GABON
CONGO
CONGO (DEM. REP. OF THE)
UGANDA
KENYA
RWANDA
BURUNDI
TANZANIA
ANGOLA
ZAMBIA
MALAWI
MOZAMBIQUE
ZIMBABWE
NAMIBIA
BOTSWANA
SOUTH AFRICA
LESOTHO
SWAZ.
MADAGASCAR
COMOROS
SEYCHELLES
MAURITIUS
Cairo
Algiers
Tunis
Tripoli
Rabat
Nouakchott
Dakar
Banjul
Bamako
Niamey
Ndjamena
Khartoum
Asmera
Addis Ababa
Mogadishu
Nairobi
Kampala
Kinshasa
Brazzaville
Luanda
Lusaka
Harare
Pretoria
Maputo
Cape Town
Antananarivo
Canary Is.
Madeira
Azores
Ascension I.
St. Helena
Tristan da Cunha
Tropic of Cancer
Equator
Tropic of Capricorn
Gulf of Guinea
Bight of Benin
Mozambique Channel
Dakar Capital Cities
Projection: Azimuthal Equidistant
West from Greenwich
East from Greenwich
COPYRIGHT GEORGE PHILIP LTD.

 1:15 000 000

100 0 100 200 300 400 500 600 km

100 0 100 200 300 400 miles

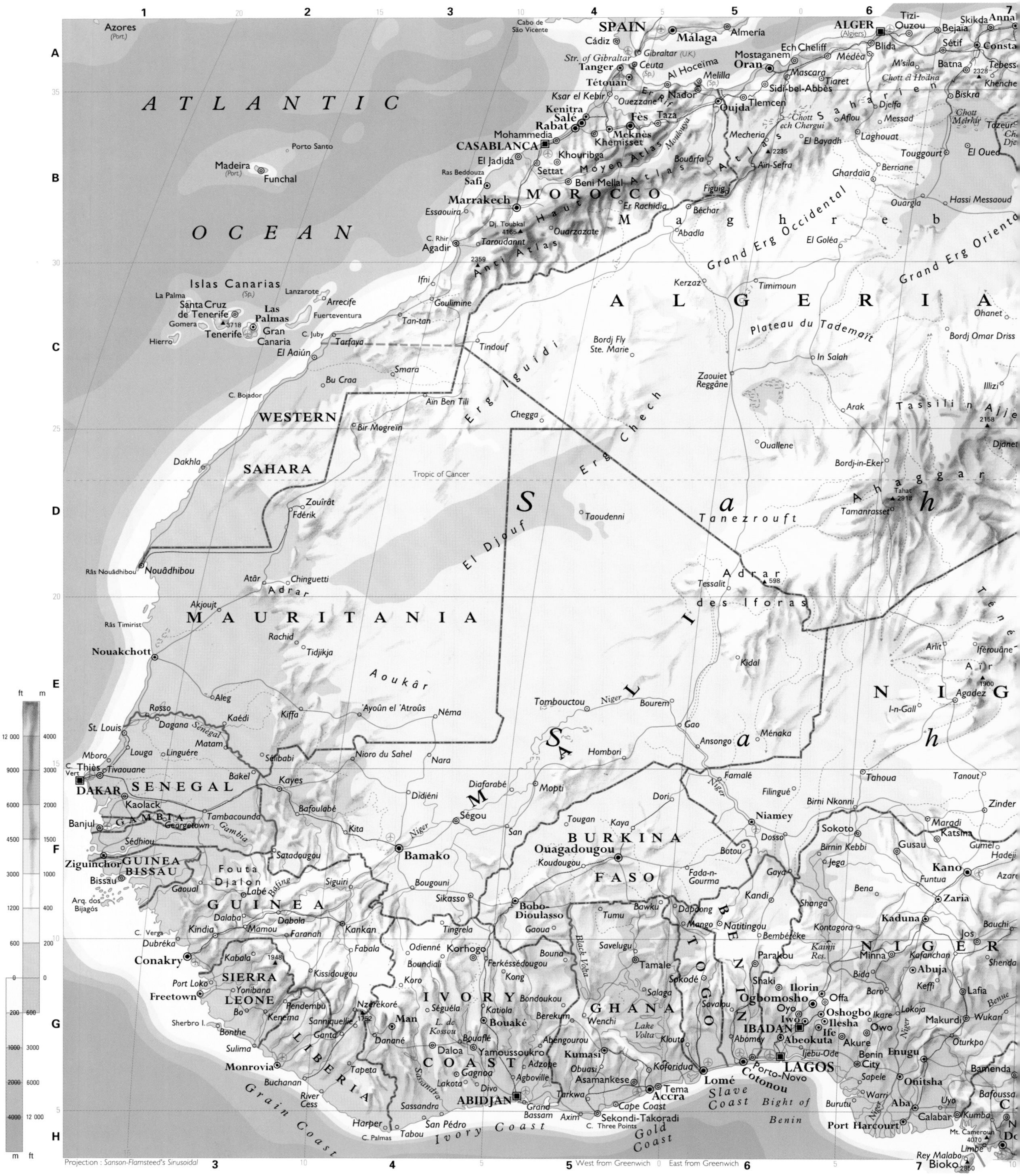

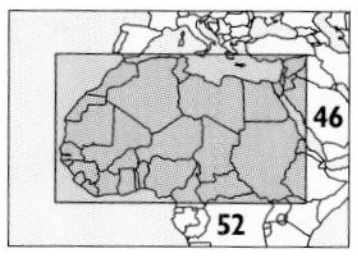
46
52

MEDITERRANEAN SEA
RED SEA
GREECE
TURKEY
CYPRUS
SYRIA
LEBANON
ISRAEL
JORDAN
IRAQ
SAUDI ARABIA
MALTA
LIBYA
EGYPT
SUDAN
CHAD
CENTRAL AFRICAN REPUBLIC
ETHIOPIA
ERITREA
CAMEROON
Sahara
Sicilia
Bizerte
Ariana
CARTHAGE
TUNIS
Béja
Nabeul
Sousse
Kairouan
Mahdia
Sfax
Golfe de Gabès
Gabès
Île de Djerba
Médenine
Zarzis
Tataouine
Dehibat
Zuwārah
Az Zāwiyah
Tarābulus (Tripoli)
Al Khums
Gharyān
968
Misrātah
Mizdah
Tripolitania
Daraj
Ghudāmis
Surt
Khalīj Surt
Valletta
Banghāzī
Zāwiyat al Baydā
Al Marj
Darnah
Sulūq
Tubruq
Bardīyah
Ajdābiyā
Cyrenaica
Al Jaghbūb
Awjilah
Hūn
Zillah
Idehan-awbārī
Brach
Sabhah
Awbārī
1200
Marzūq
Fezzan
Wāw al Kabīr
Ghat
Al Qaţrūn
Sahrâ' Rebiana
Al Jawf
Al Kufrah
Sahrâ' Lîbîya
Iráklion
Kríti
Ródhos
Antalya
ADANA
Antakya
HALAB
Nahr al Furāt
Al Lādhiqīyah
Nicosia
Tarābulus
Hims
BAYRŪT (Beirut)
DIMASHQ (Damascus)
Jabal ad Durūz
1801
Ar Rutbah
Bādiyat ash Shām
Haifa
Tel Aviv-Yafo
Ashdod
Jerusalem
West Bank
'AMMĀN
Ma'ān
Al Jawf
Salûm
EL ISKANDARÎYA (Alexandria)
El Mahalla el Kubra
Damanhûr
Dumyât
Bûr Sa'îd
El Mansûra
Qanâ es Suweis
Ismâ'ilîya
Tanta
Zagazig
Marsâ Matrûh
El Alamein
EL GÎZA
EL QAHIRA (Cairo)
El Suweis
Helwân
El Faiyûm
Beni Suef
Maghâgha
El Minyâ
Mallawi
Manfalût
Asyût
Tahta
Sohâg
Girga
Qena
THEBES
KARNAK
El Uqsur
Idfû
Kom Ombo
Sadd el Aali
Aswân
Buheirat en Naser
ABU SIMBEL
Wâdi Halfa
-133
Munkhafed el Qattâra
Sîwa
Qasr Farâfra
Mût
El Wâhât el-Dakhla
El Khârga
El Wâhât el-Khârga
Es Sahrâ' Esh Sharqîya
Nahr en Nîl
Khalîg el Suweis
Es Sinâ'
G. Mûsa 2637
Elat
Al 'Aqabah
2578
Tabūk
Al Muwaylih
2187
Hurghada
Bûr Safâga
Quseir
Al Wajh
Hijaz
Yanbu 'al Bahr
Râbigh
Ras Bânâs
Bîr Shalatein
Halaib
Ras Hadarba
1082
J. Uweinat 1893
Ma'tan as Sarra
El Wâhât el Selîma
Es Sahrâ en Nûbîya
Kosha
Muhammad Qol
2259
Bûr Sûdân
Suakin
Trinkitat
Sinkat
Haiya
Karora
2780
Nakfa
Delgo
3rd Cataract
Dongola
Abu Hamed
4th Cataract
Kareima
5th Cataract
Berber
Atbara
Ed Debba
Bir 'Atrun
Adarama
Nahr 'Atbara
Wad Hamid
Shendi
6th Cataract
Omdurmân
El Khartûm (Khartoum)
Kassalâ
Akordat
Khashm el Girba
El Wuz
Sodiri
El Gezira
Wâd Medanî
Gedaref
Ed Dueim
Umm Keddada
El Obeid
Kôstî
Singa
Nil el Azraq
Umm Ruwaba
En Nahud
Er Rahad
El Odaiya
Abû Zabad
Kordofân
Ed Damazin
Nil el Abyad
1325
Kâdugli
Gonder
1830
L. Tana
Bahir Dar
Bure
Debre Markos
Nekemte
Toummo
Madama
Aozou Strip
Aozou
Bardai
Pic Toussidé 3265
3150
Tarso Emissi
Tibesti
Zouar
Emi Koussi 3415
Chirfa
Bilma
Grand Erg du Bilma
Fachi
Borkou
Ounianga Sérir
Dépression du Mourdi
Faya-Largeau
Fada
Ennedi
1310
Erg du Djourab
Zagaoua
Oum Chalouba
Biltine
Zigey
Bahr el Ghazal
Nguigmi
Mao
Lac Tchad
Bosso
Moussoro
Ati
Abéché
Oum Hadjer
Massakory
Gashua
Geidam
Maiduguri
Ndjamena
Bokoro
Mongo
Kousseri
Massenya
Potiskum
Bama
Bajoga
Abou-Deïa
Am Timan
Goz Beïda
Chari
Bongor
Maroua
Biu
Kumo
Mubi
Guider
Numan
Garoua
Yola
Pala
Laï
Logone
Sarh
Moundou
Koumra
Doba
Birao
Ndélé
Malha
1954
Kutum
Al Junaynah
Dârfûr
Jebel Mara 3088
El Fâsher
Zalingei
Nyâlâ
Bahr el Arab
Songo
1226
Sa'id Bundas
Raga
Bahr el Ghazâl
Jur
Gogriâl
Wâw
Tonj
Sûdd
Bahr el Jebel
Rumbêk
Malakâl
Sobat
Dembidolo
3202
Metu
Gore
Jima
3686
Omo
L. Abaya
Arba Minch
L. Shamo
Chew Bahir
Pibor Post
Bôr
Toinya
Amadi
Tali Post
El Istiwa'iya
Mongalla
Kapoeta
Juba
Yambiô
Yei
Kajo Kaji
Torit
3187
Lokitaung
L. Turkana
Baïbokoum
Gashaka
Ngaoundéré
Banyo
Massif de Adamaoua
Paoua
Kaga Bandoro
Bossangoa
Bozoum
Bouar
Bétaré Oya
Foumban
Yoko
Sibut
Bambari
Ippy
Yalinga
Bakouma
Carnot
Bossembélé
Bangassou
Oubangi
Bomu
Mobaye
Mobayi
Obo
Bertoua
Batouri
Nanga-Eboko
Abong-Mbang
Berbérati
Bangui
Zongo
Bosobolo
Bondo
Angoumbé
Uele
Dungu
Faradje
Mbaïki
Libenge
Yaoundé
Sanaga
A
B
C
D
E
F
G
H
8
9
10
11
12
13
14
15
20
25
30
35
40
5
10
15
20
25
30
35

CENTRAL AND SOUTHERN AFRICA 1:15 000 000

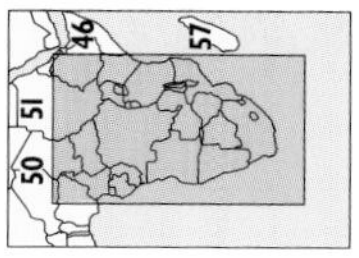
46
50
51
57

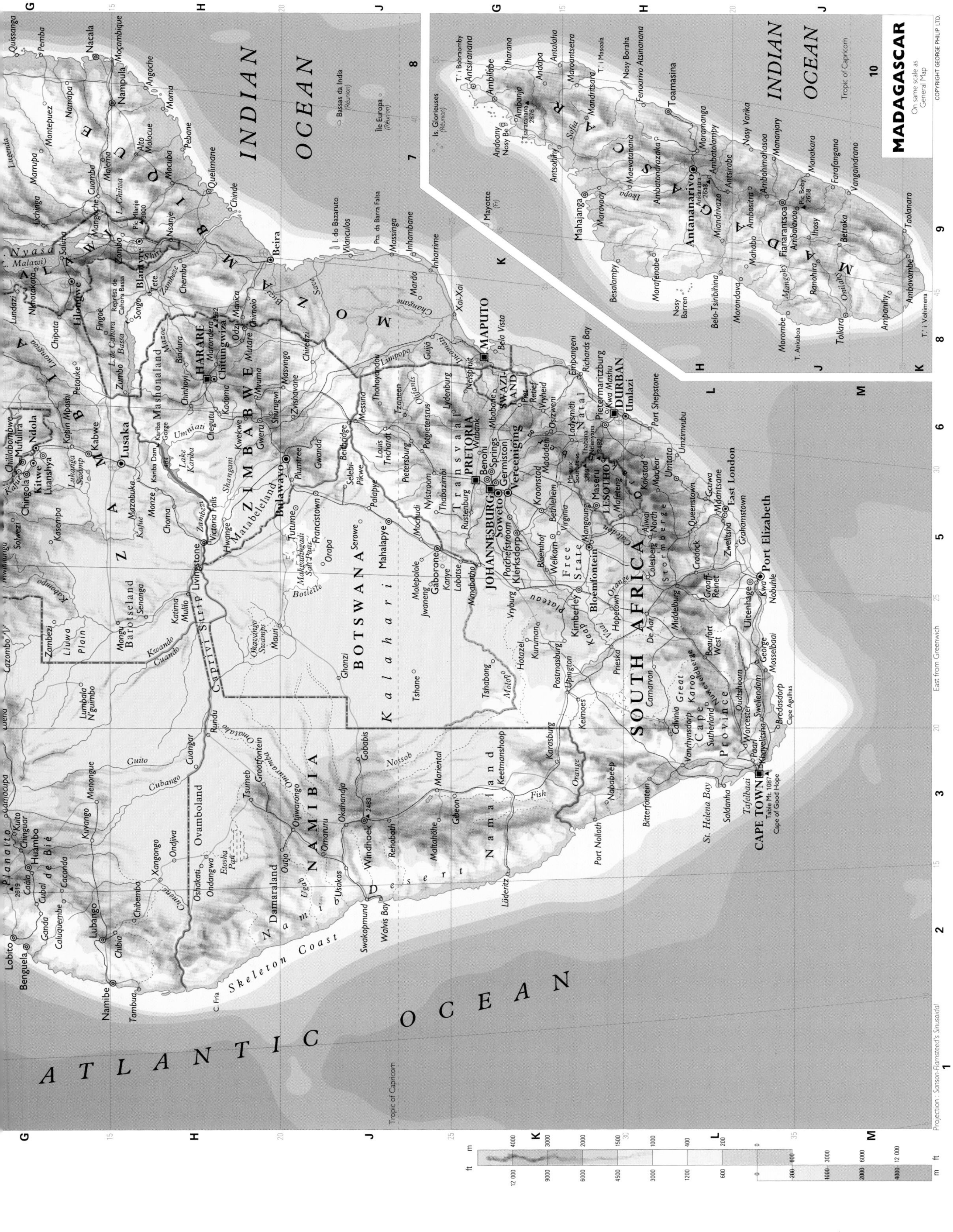
ATLANTIC OCEAN
INDIAN OCEAN
SOUTH AFRICA
NAMIBIA
BOTSWANA
ZIMBABWE
ZAMBIA
MOZAMBIQUE
MALAWI
LESOTHO
SWAZILAND
MADAGASCAR
On same scale as General Map
Kalahari
Namib Desert
Skeleton Coast
Transvaal
Free State
Natal
Cape Province
Great Karoo
Namaland
Damaraland
Ovamboland
Matabeleland
Mashonaland
Barotseland
Caprivi Strip
Planalto de Bié
CAPE TOWN
Table Mt. 1087
Cape of Good Hope
Cape Agulhas
Port Elizabeth
East London
DURBAN
Pietermaritzburg
Bloemfontein
Kimberley
JOHANNESBURG
Soweto
PRETORIA
Vereeniging
Germiston
Benoni
Springs
Maseru
MAPUTO
Beira
HARARE
Bulawayo
Lusaka
Livingstone
Victoria Falls
Lake Kariba
Gaborone
Windhoek
Walvis Bay
Swakopmund
Lüderitz
Keetmanshoop
Lubango
Namibe
Benguela
Lobito
Huambo
Blantyre
Zomba
Lilongwe
Nampula
Moçambique
Nacala
Quelimane
Inhambane
Antananarivo
Toamasina
Mahajanga
Fianarantsoa
Toliara
Taolanaro
Antsiranana
Bassas da India (Réunion)
Île Europa (Réunion)
Mayotte (Fr.)
Is. Glorieuses (Réunion)
Orange
Limpopo
Zambezi
Okavango Swamps
Etosha Pan
Tropic of Capricorn
East from Greenwich
Projection: Sanson-Flamsteed's Sinusoidal
m
ft
4000
3000
2000
1500
1000
400
200
0
12 000
9000
6000
4500
3000
1200
600
COPYRIGHT GEORGE PHILIP LTD.

EAST AFRICA 1:8 000 000

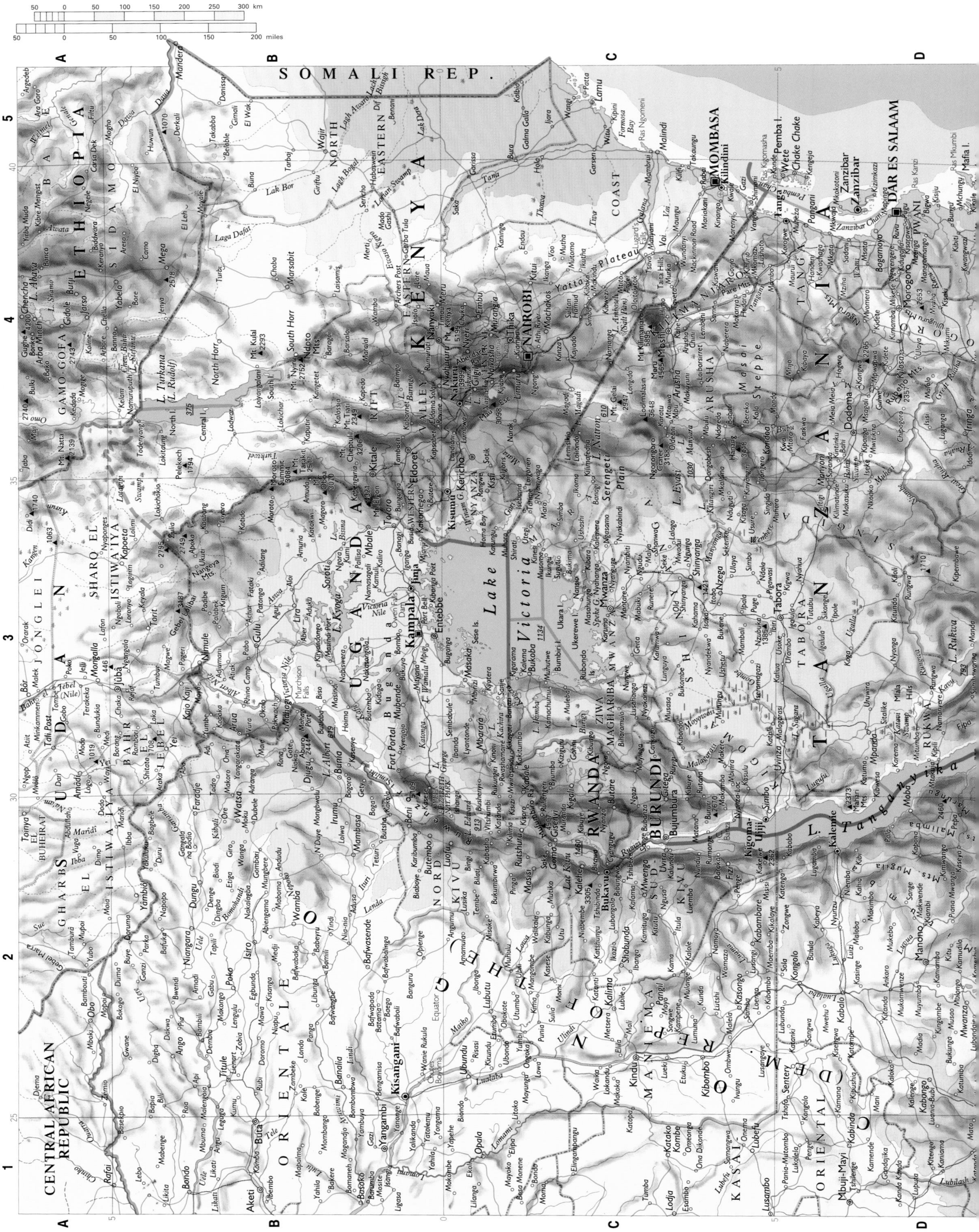

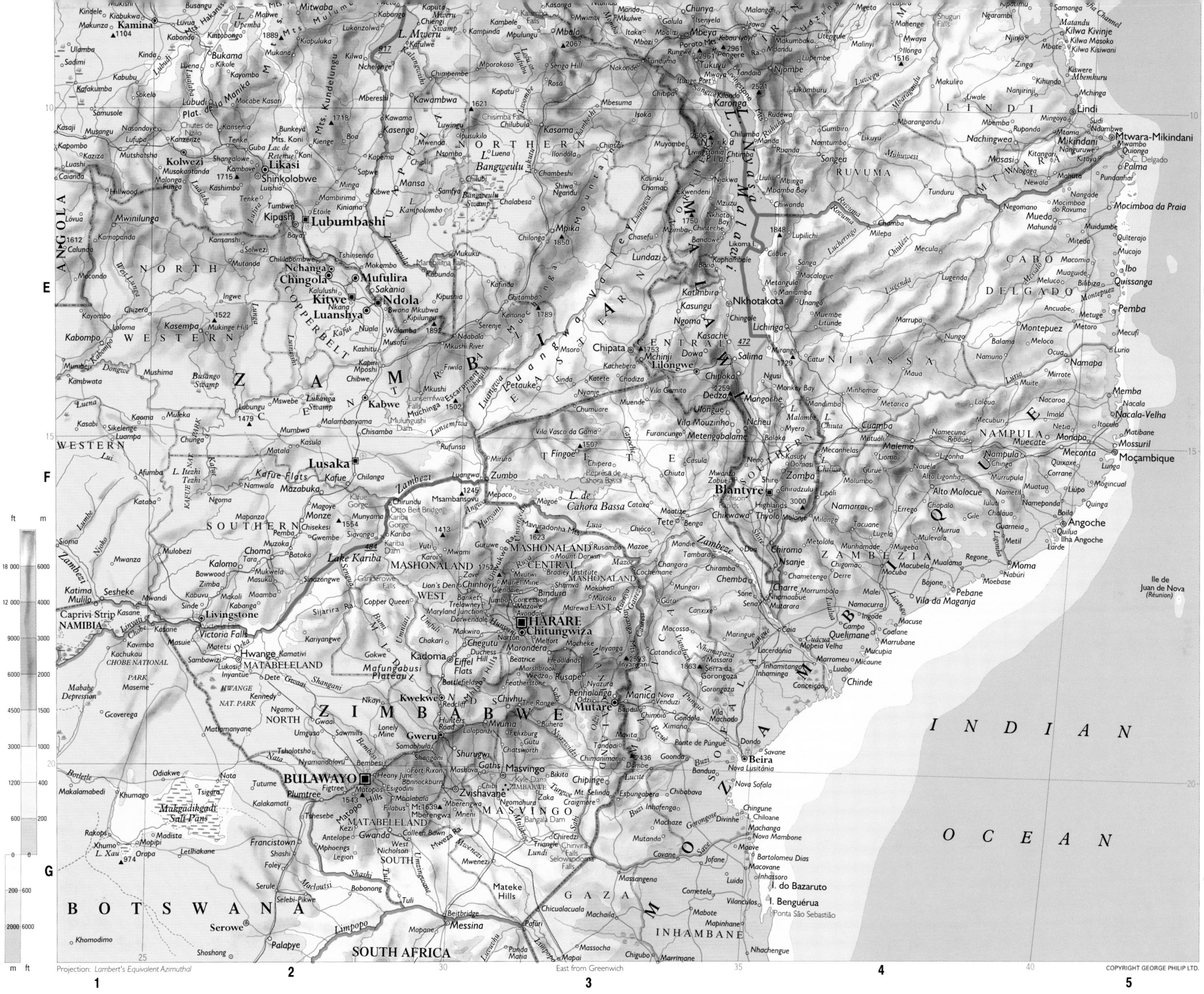
ANGOLA
ZAMBIA
MALAWI
MOZAMBIQUE
ZIMBABWE
BOTSWANA
SOUTH AFRICA
NAMIBIA
INDIAN OCEAN
L. Nyasa
Malawi
L. Mweru
Lake Kariba
L. de Cahora Bassa
Zambezi
Limpopo
Lusaka
Harare
Chitungwiza
Bulawayo
Lubumbashi
Likasi
Kolwezi
Ndola
Kitwe
Mufulira
Chingola
Luanshya
Kabwe
Livingstone
Victoria Falls
Hwange
Kadoma
Kwekwe
Gweru
Mutare
Masvingo
Blantyre
Zomba
Lilongwe
Nkhotakota
Beira
Quelimane
Nampula
Moçambique
Pemba
Lindi
Mtwara-Mikindani
Tete
Chipata
Mbeya
Messina
Serowe
Palapye
Francistown
Makgadikgadi Salt Pans
Caprivi Strip
Ile de Juan de Nova (Réunion)
I. do Bazaruto
I. Benguérua
CABO DELGADO
NIASSA
NAMPULA
ZAMBEZIA
MANICA
SOFALA
TETE
GAZA
INHAMBANE
LINDI
MTWARA
RUVUMA
NORTHERN
COPPERBELT
CENTRAL
EASTERN
SOUTHERN
WESTERN
NORTH WESTERN
MASHONALAND CENTRAL
MASHONALAND EAST
MASHONALAND WEST
MATABELELAND NORTH
MATABELELAND SOUTH
MASVINGO
ft
m
18 000
12 000
9000
6000
4500
3000
1200
600
0
200
2000
6000
4000
3000
2000
1500
1000
400
200
Projection: Lambert's Equivalent Azimuthal
East from Greenwich
COPYRIGHT GEORGE PHILIP LTD.

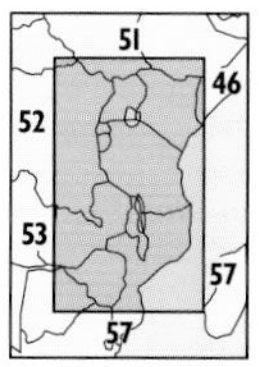
51
46
52
53
57
57

SOUTHERN AFRICA 1:8 000 000

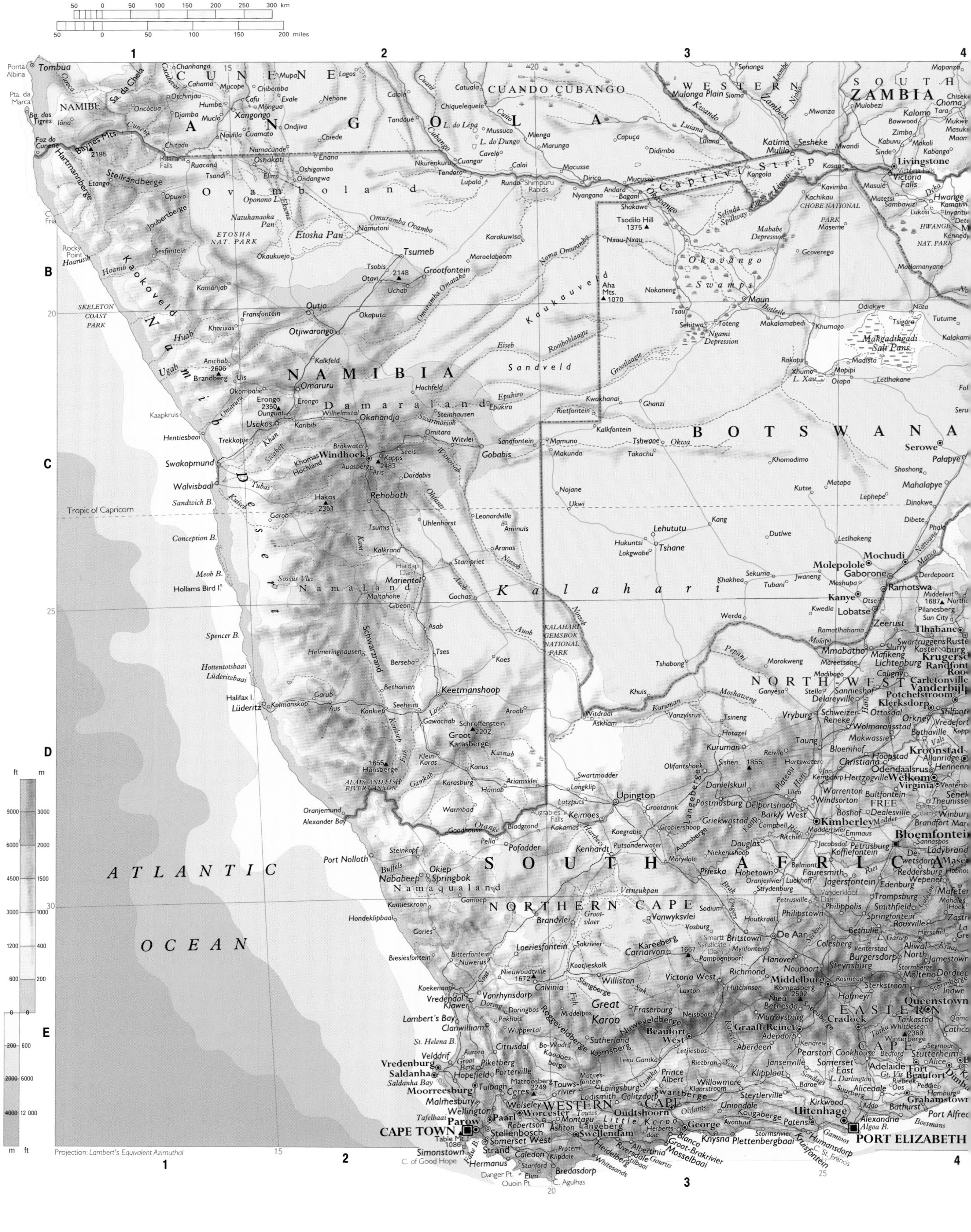

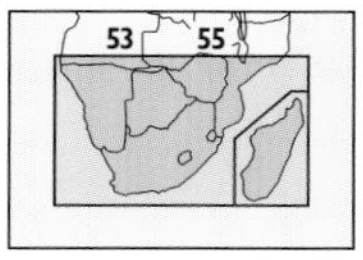
53
55

MADAGASCAR
On same scale as General Map
MOZAMBIQUE CHANNEL
INDIAN OCEAN
MOZAMBIQUE
ZIMBABWE
MALAWI
SWAZILAND
MADAGASCAR
TETE
ZAMBEZIA
MANICA
SOFALA
INHAMBANE
GAZA
MAPUTO
MASHONALAND CENTRAL
MASHONALAND WEST
MASHONALAND EAST
MASVINGO
MATABELELAND
NORTHERN
MPUMALANGA
GAUTENG
KWAZULU NATAL
LESOTHO
EASTERN CAPE
HARARE
Chitungwiza
Mutare
Masvingo
Beira
Maputo
Inhambane
Xai-Xai
Quelimane
Pebane
Angoche
Chinde
PRETORIA
JOHANNESBURG
Benoni
Springs
Vereeniging
Pietermaritzburg
DURBAN
KwaMashu
Umlazi
Empangeni
East London
Pietersburg
Nelspruit
Messina
Mbabane
Manzini
ANTANANARIVO
Antsiranana
Mahajanga
Toamasina
Fianarantsoa
Antsirabe
Toliara
Taolanaro
Morondava
Maintirano
Manakara
Mananjary
Farafangana
Maroantsetra
Sambava
Antalaha
Iharana
Is. Glorieuses (Fr.)
Ile de Júan de Nova (Fr.)
I. do Bazaruto
I. Benguérua
Tropic of Capricorn
East from Greenwich
5
6
7
8
9
A
B
C
D
E

COPYRIGHT GEORGE PHILIP LTD.

AUSTRALIA AND OCEANIA : Physical and Political 1:50 000 000

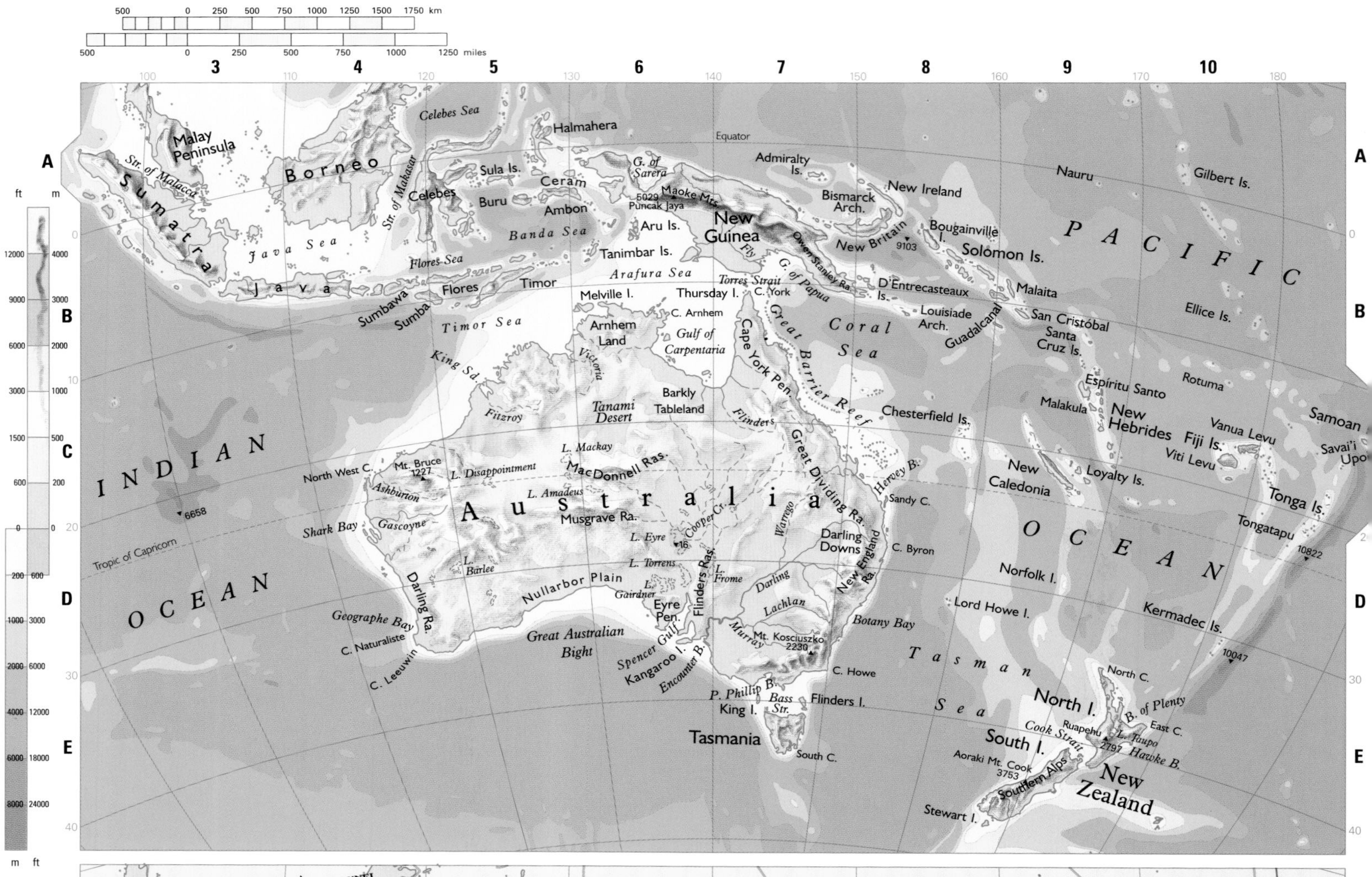
500 0 250 500 750 1000 1250 1500 1750 km
500 0 250 500 750 1000 1250 miles
ft m
12000 4000
9000 3000
6000 2000
3000 1000
1500 500
600 200
0 0
200 600
1000 3000
2000 6000
4000 12000
6000 18000
8000 24000
m ft
Malay Peninsula
Str. of Malacca
Sumatra
Borneo
Celebes Sea
Str. of Makasar
Celebes
Halmahera
Sula Is.
Buru
Ceram
Ambon
Banda Sea
Java Sea
Java
Flores Sea
Sumbawa
Sumba
Flores
Timor
Timor Sea
G. of Sarera
Maoke Mts.
5029 Puncak Jaya
Aru Is.
Tanimbar Is.
Arafura Sea
New Guinea
Fly
Torres Strait
Thursday I.
C. York
G. of Papua
Owen Stanley Ra.
Admiralty Is.
Bismarck Arch.
New Ireland
New Britain
9103
Bougainville I.
Solomon Is.
D'Entrecasteaux Is.
Louisiade Arch.
Malaita
Guadalcanal
San Cristóbal
Santa Cruz Is.
Equator
Nauru
Gilbert Is.
Ellice Is.
PACIFIC
OCEAN
Melville I.
C. Arnhem
Arnhem Land
Gulf of Carpentaria
Victoria
King Sd.
Fitzroy
Tanami Desert
Barkly Tableland
Cape York Pen.
Great Barrier Reef
Coral Sea
Flinders
Chesterfield Is.
Espíritu Santo
Malakula
New Hebrides
Rotuma
Fiji Is.
Vanua Levu
Viti Levu
Samoan
Savai'i
Upo
Tonga Is.
Tongatapu
10822
INDIAN
OCEAN
6658
Tropic of Capricorn
North West C.
Mt. Bruce 1227
Ashburton
L. Disappointment
L. Mackay
MacDonnell Ras.
L. Amadeus
Australia
Musgrave Ra.
Gascoyne
Shark Bay
L. Eyre
-16
Cooper Cr.
L. Torrens
L. Barlee
L. Frome
Great Dividing Ra.
Warrego
Darling Downs
Hervey B.
Sandy C.
C. Byron
New England Ra.
Darling
Lachlan
Murray
Nullarbor Plain
L. Gairdner
Eyre Pen.
Flinders Ras.
Darling Ra.
Geographe Bay
C. Naturaliste
C. Leeuwin
Great Australian Bight
Spencer Gulf
Kangaroo I.
Encounter B.
Mt. Kosciuszko 2230
Botany Bay
C. Howe
P. Phillip B.
King I.
Bass Str.
Flinders I.
Tasmania
South C.
New Caledonia
Loyalty Is.
Norfolk I.
Lord Howe I.
Kermadec Is.
10047
Tasman Sea
North C.
North I.
B. of Plenty
East C.
Ruapehu 2797
L. Taupo
Hawke B.
Cook Strait
South I.
Aoraki Mt. Cook 3753
Southern Alps
New Zealand
Stewart I.

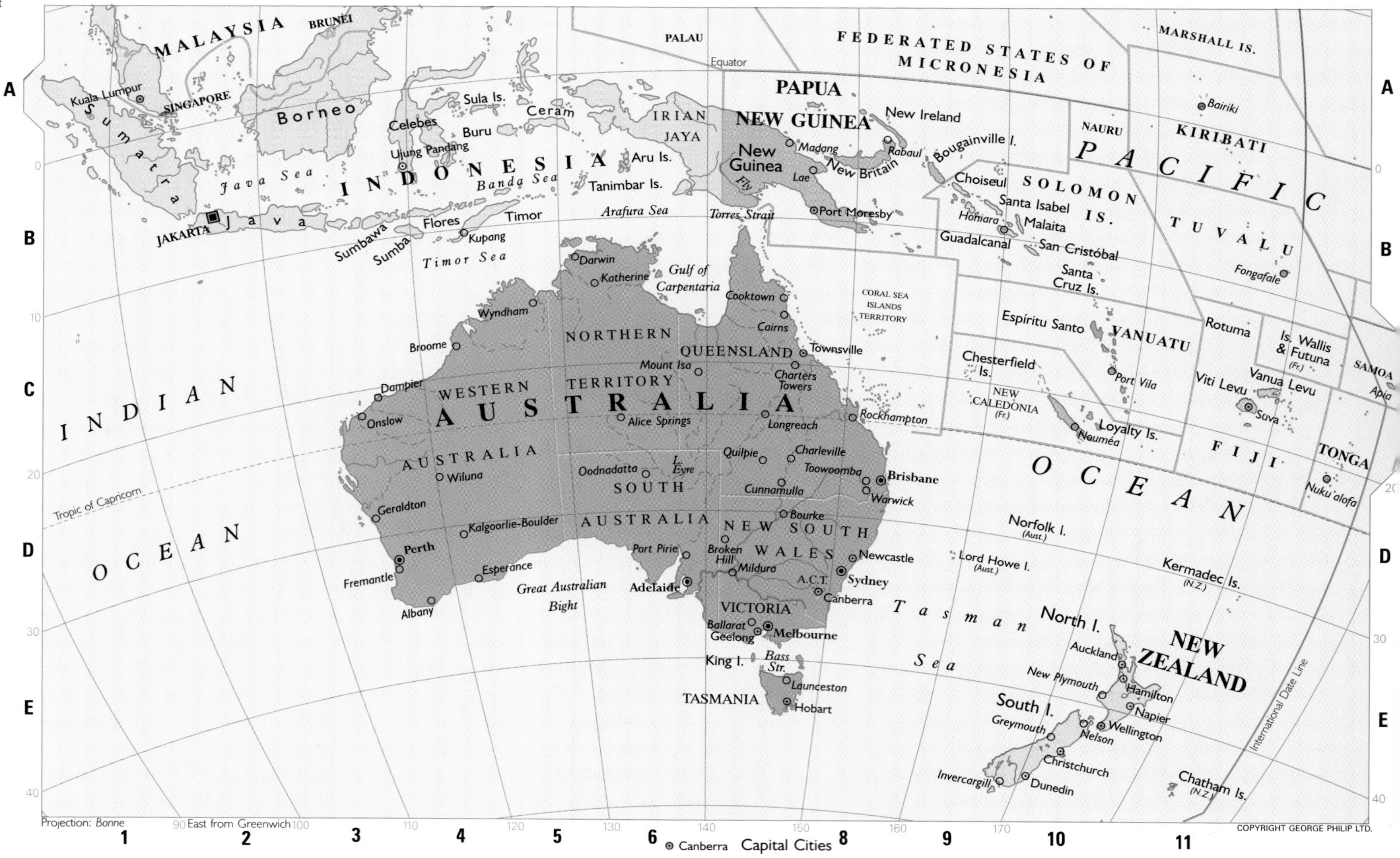
MALAYSIA
BRUNEI
Kuala Lumpur
SINGAPORE
Sumatra
Borneo
Celebes
Sula Is.
Buru
Ceram
Ujung Pandang
INDONESIA
IRIAN JAYA
Aru Is.
Banda Sea
Tanimbar Is.
Java Sea
JAKARTA
Java
Sumbawa
Sumba
Flores
Timor
Kupang
Timor Sea
Arafura Sea
Torres Strait
PALAU
FEDERATED STATES OF MICRONESIA
MARSHALL IS.
Equator
PAPUA NEW GUINEA
New Guinea
Madang
Lae
Fly
Port Moresby
New Ireland
Rabaul
New Britain
Bougainville I.
Choiseul
SOLOMON IS.
Santa Isabel
Honiara
Malaita
Guadalcanal
San Cristóbal
Santa Cruz Is.
NAURU
Bairiki
KIRIBATI
PACIFIC
TUVALU
Fongafale
CORAL SEA ISLANDS TERRITORY
Darwin
Katherine
Gulf of Carpentaria
Cooktown
Cairns
Wyndham
NORTHERN TERRITORY
QUEENSLAND
Townsville
Mount Isa
Charters Towers
Broome
Dampier
WESTERN AUSTRALIA
AUSTRALIA
Onslow
Alice Springs
Longreach
Rockhampton
Espíritu Santo
VANUATU
Port Vila
Chesterfield Is.
NEW CALEDONIA (Fr.)
Nouméa
Loyalty Is.
Rotuma
Is. Wallis & Futuna (Fr.)
SAMOA
Apia
Viti Levu
Vanua Levu
Suva
FIJI
TONGA
Nuku'alofa
Wiluna
Quilpie
Charleville
Toowoomba
Brisbane
Warwick
Oodnadatta
L. Eyre
SOUTH AUSTRALIA
Cunnamulla
Bourke
Geraldton
Kalgoorlie-Boulder
NEW SOUTH WALES
Perth
Port Pirie
Broken Hill
Mildura
Newcastle
Sydney
A.C.T.
Canberra
Fremantle
Esperance
Adelaide
Albany
Great Australian Bight
VICTORIA
Ballarat
Geelong
Melbourne
King I.
Bass Str.
Launceston
TASMANIA
Hobart
INDIAN
OCEAN
Tropic of Capricorn
Norfolk I. (Aust.)
Lord Howe I. (Aust.)
Kermadec Is. (N.Z.)
Tasman Sea
North I.
Auckland
NEW ZEALAND
New Plymouth
Hamilton
Napier
Wellington
Nelson
South I.
Greymouth
Christchurch
Invercargill
Dunedin
Chatham Is. (N.Z.)
International Date Line

Projection: Bonne

East from Greenwich

⊛ Canberra Capital Cities

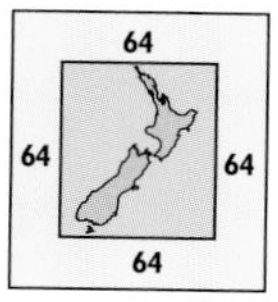
64
64
64
64

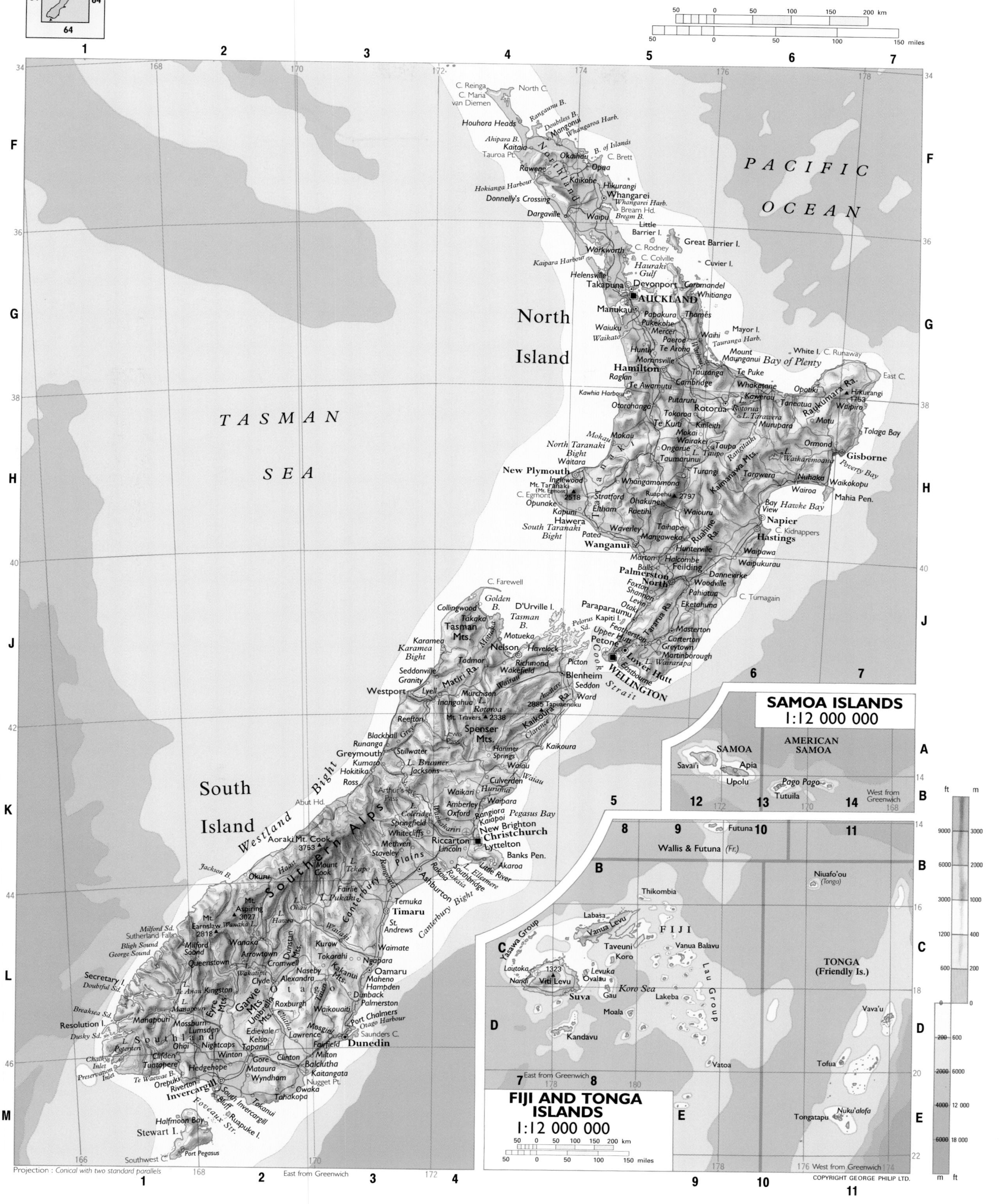
PACIFIC OCEAN
TASMAN SEA
North Island
South Island
C. Reinga
C. Maria van Diemen
North C.
Houhora Heads
Rangaunu B.
Doubtless B.
Mangonui
Whangaroa Harb.
Ahipara B.
Kaitaia
Tauroa Pt.
Northland
Okaihau
B. of Islands
C. Brett
Rawene
Opua
Hokianga Harbour
Kaikohe
Hikurangi
Whangarei
Whangarei Harb.
Donnelly's Crossing
Bream Hd.
Dargaville
Waipu
Bream B.
Little Barrier I.
Great Barrier I.
Warkworth
C. Rodney
C. Colville
Kaipara Harbour
Hauraki Gulf
Cuvier I.
Helensville
Takapuna
Devonport
Coromandel
AUCKLAND
Whitianga
Manukau
Papakura
Thames
Pukekohe
Waiuku
Mercer
Mayor I.
Waikato
Waihi
Paeroa
Tauranga Harb.
Huntly
Te Aroha
Mount Maunganui
Bay of Plenty
White I.
C. Runaway
Morrinsville
Hamilton
Tauranga
Te Puke
East C.
Raglan
Cambridge
Whakatane
Opotiki
Hikurangi 1753
Kawhia Harbour
Te Awamutu
Kawerau
Raukumara Ra.
Otorohanga
Putaruru
Rotorua
L. Rotorua
L. Tarawera
Tarleatua
Waipiro
Tokoroa
Murupara
Motu
Te Kuiti
Kinleith
Tolaga Bay
Mokau
Mokai
Wairakei
Ormond
North Taranaki Bight
Ongarue
Taupo
L. Taupo
L. Waikaremoana
Gisborne
Waitara
Taumarunui
Poverty Bay
New Plymouth
Turangi
Tarawera
Nuhaka
Inglewood
Whangamomona
Waikokopu
Mt. Taranaki (Mt. Egmont) 2518
Ruapehu 2797
Kaimanawa Mts.
Wairoa
C. Egmont
Stratford
Ohakune
Mahia Pen.
Opunake
Eltham
Raetihi
Waiouru
Bay View
Hawke Bay
Kaponi
Hawera
Napier
South Taranaki Bight
Patea
Waverley
Taihape
Ruahine Ra.
C. Kidnappers
Hastings
Wanganui
Mangaweka
Hunterville
Waipawa
Marton
Halcombe
Bulls
Feilding
Waipukurau
Palmerston North
Dannevirke
Foxton
Woodville
C. Farewell
Shannon
Pahiatua
C. Turnagain
Golden B.
D'Urville I.
Levin
Collingwood
Otaki
Eketahuna
Tasman B.
Paraparaumu
Takaka
Kapiti I.
Tararua Ra.
Tasman Mts.
Pelorus Sd.
Featherston
Masterton
Karamea
Motueka
Upper Hutt
Carterton
Karamea Bight
Greytown
Nelson
Havelock
Petone
Martinborough
Tadmor
Richmond
Lower Hutt
Seddonville
Wakefield
Picton
L. Wairarapa
Granity
Matiri Ra.
Blenheim
Eastbourne
Westport
Lyell
Seddon
WELLINGTON
Murchison
Cook Strait
Inangahua
L. Rotoroa
Ward
2885 Tapuaenuku
Reefton
Mt. Travers 2338
Kaikoura Ra.
Blackball
Spenser Mts.
Runanga
Clarence
Greymouth
Stillwater
Hanmer Springs
Kaikoura
Kumara
L. Brunner
Hokitika
Jacksons
Waiau
Ross
Culverden
Westland Bight
Arthur's Pass
Hurunui
Abut Hd.
Waikari
Coleridge
Amberley
Pegasus Bay
Springfield
Oxford
Rangiora
Kaiapoi
New Brighton
Whitecliffs
Christchurch
Aoraki Mt. Cook 3753
Methven
Riccarton
Lyttelton
Staveley
Lincoln
Banks Pen.
Southern Alps
Plains
Akaroa
Jackson B.
Mount Cook
L. Ellesmere
Little River
Okuru
L. Tekapo
Rakaia
Southbridge
Ashburton
Fairlie
Canterbury
Temuka
Mt. Aspiring 3027
L. Pukaki
Timaru
L. Ohau
Canterbury Bight
Mt. Earnslaw 2818
Wanaka L.
L. Hawea
St. Andrews
Milford Sd.
Sutherland Falls
Bligh Sound
George Sound
Milford Sound
Wanaka
Waitaki
Waimate
Queenstown
Arrowtown
Dunstan Mts.
Kurow
Cromwell
Tokarahi
Ngapara
Secretary I.
Doubtful Sd.
Naseby
Kakanui Mts.
Oamaru
Te Anau
Kingston
Clyde
Alexandra
Maheno
L. Manapouri
Eyre Mts.
Garvie Mts.
Otago
Hampden
Breaksea Sd.
Roxburgh
Dunback
Manapouri
Umbrella Mts.
Waikouaiti
Resolution I.
Mossburn
Palmerston
Dusky Sd.
Lumsden
Edievale
Lawrence
Mosgiel
Port Chalmers
Otago Harbour
Southland
Saunders C.
L. Poteriteri
Nightcaps
Kelso
Tapanui
Fairfield
Dunedin
Ohai
Clifden
Winton
Clinton
Chalky Inlet
Tuatapere
Hedgehope
Gore
Balclutha
Milton
Preservation Inlet
Mataura
Kaitangata
Te Waewae B.
Orepuki
Wyndham
Nugget Pt.
Riverton
Invercargill
South Invercargill
Owaka
Bluff
Tahakopa
Foveaux Str.
Tokanui
Ruapuke I.
Halfmoon Bay
Stewart I.
Port Pegasus
Southwest C.
Projection : Conical with two standard parallels
East from Greenwich
SAMOA ISLANDS
1:12 000 000
SAMOA
AMERICAN SAMOA
Savai'i
Apia
Upolu
Pago Pago
Tutuila
West from Greenwich
Futuna
Wallis & Futuna (Fr.)
Niuafo'ou (Tonga)
Thikombia
Labasa
Vanua Levu
FIJI
Yasawa Group
Taveuni
Vanua Balavu
Koro
TONGA (Friendly Is.)
Lautoka
1323
Levuka
Nandi
Viti Levu
Ovalau
Lau Group
Koro Sea
Suva
Gau
Lakeba
Moala
Vava'u
Kandavu
Vatoa
Tofua
East from Greenwich
FIJI AND TONGA ISLANDS
1:12 000 000
Nuku'alofa
Tongatapu
176 West from Greenwich 174
COPYRIGHT GEORGE PHILIP LTD.
ft
m
9000
3000
6000
2000
3000
1000
1200
400
600
200
0
0
200
600
2000
6000
4000
12 000
6000
18 000
m
ft

WESTERN AUSTRALIA 1:8 000 000

WESTERN AUSTRALIA
SOUTH AUSTRALIA
INDIAN OCEAN
SOUTHERN OCEAN
Great Australian Bight
Great Victoria Desert
Nullarbor Plain
Hampton Tableland
PERTH
Fremantle
Kwinana
Rockingham
Mandurah
Geraldton
Carnarvon
Kalgoorlie-Boulder
Bunbury
Busselton
Albany
Esperance
Norseman
Northam
Merredin
Katanning
Collie
Eucla
Nullarbor
Penong
Ayers Rock 868
Mt. Olga 1069
ULURU NAT. PARK
Yulara
Petermann Ranges
Musgrave Ranges
Mt. Woodroffe 1440
Everard Ranges
Mt. Augustus 1105
Mt. Essendon 906
Mt. Fraser 799
Mt. Eureka 499
Mt. Redcliffe 576
Mt. Burges 554
Mt. Ragged 585
Pt. Lillian 466
Mt. Aloysius 1058
L. Carnegie
L. Wells
L. Austin
L. Moore
L. Barlee
L. Ballard
L. Carey
L. Cowan
L. Dundas
L. Minigwal
Shark Bay
Dirk Hartog I.
Archipelago of the Recherche
Houtman Abrolhos
Leeuwin
C. Leeuwin
Pt. D'Entrecasteaux
West Cape Howe
Wilson Bluff
Head of Bight
▼ 5632
25
30
35
115
120
125
130
E
F
G
1
2
3
4
5
East from Greenwich
Projection: Bonne
COPYRIGHT GEORGE PHILIP LTD.
ft
m
3000
1200
600
0
1000
400
200
200
600
2000
6000
4000
12 000
37
62
63

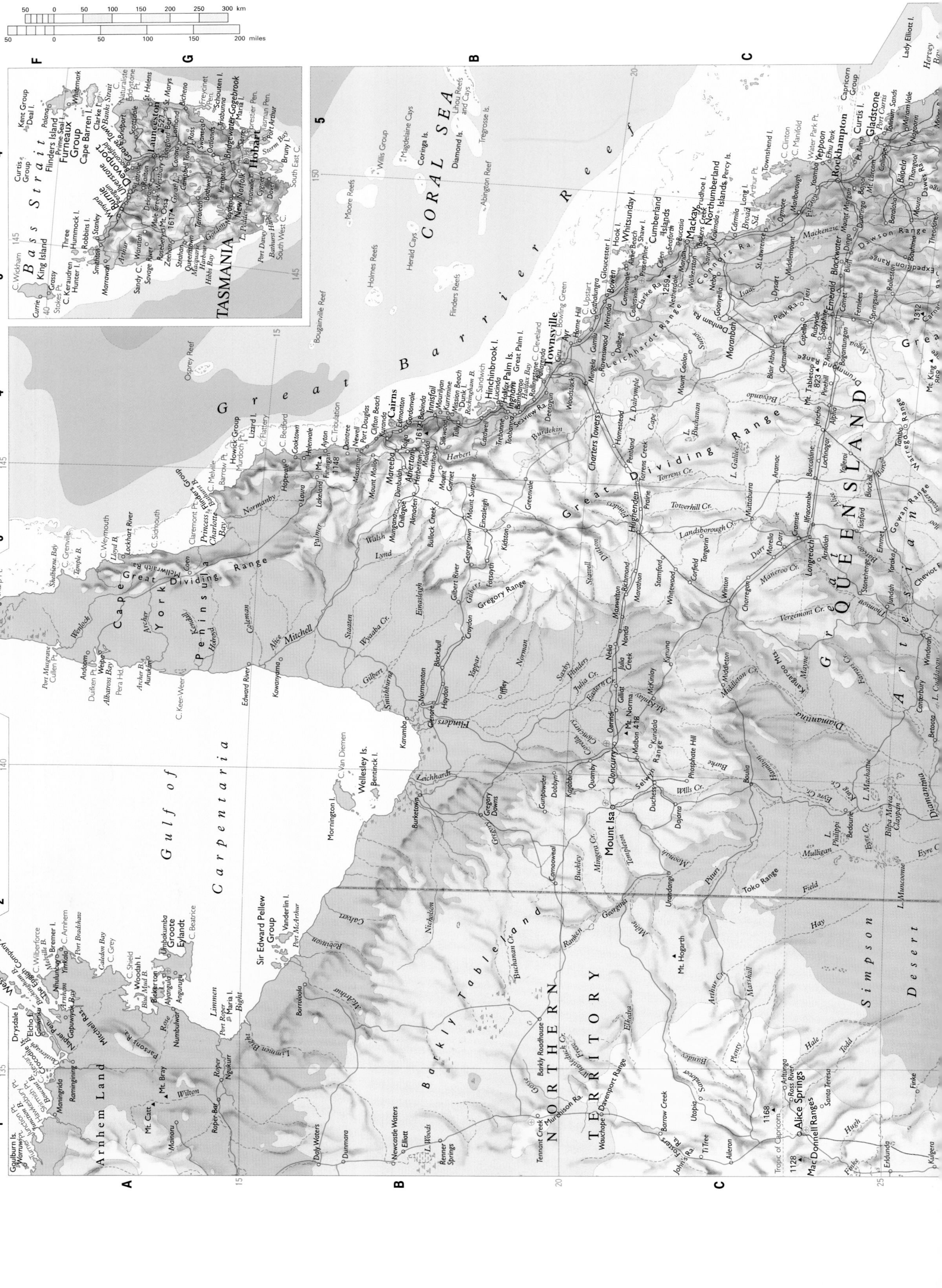
50 0 50 100 150 200 250 300 km
50 0 50 100 150 200 miles
TASMANIA
Bass Strait
Flinders Island
Furneaux Group
King Island
Launceston
Hobart
Devonport
Burnie
CORAL SEA
Great Barrier Reef
Gulf of Carpentaria
Cape York Peninsula
Great Dividing Range
QUEENSLAND
NORTHERN TERRITORY
Barkly Tableland
Simpson Desert
Arnhem Land
Groote Eylandt
Wellesley Is.
Mornington I.
Cairns
Townsville
Mackay
Rockhampton
Gladstone
Mount Isa
Cloncurry
Longreach
Hughenden
Charters Towers
Alice Springs
Tennant Creek
Karumba
Normanton
Weipa
Cooktown
Bowen
Emerald
Winton
Thursday I.
Horn I.
Turtle Head I.
Sir Edward Pellew Group
Wessel Is.
MacDonnell Ranges
Great Artesian Basin

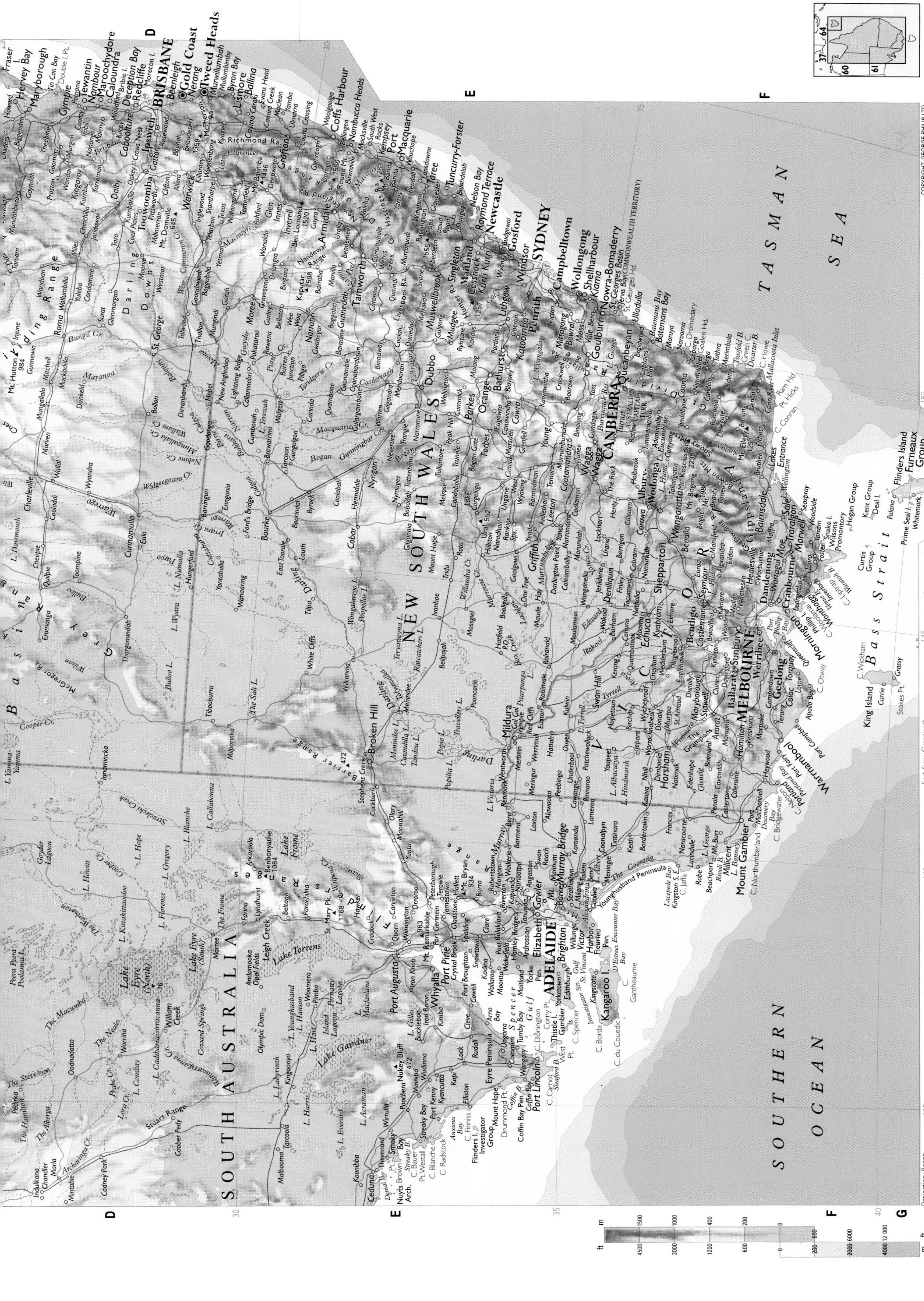

SOUTH AUSTRALIA
NEW SOUTH WALES
VICTORIA
TASMAN SEA
SOUTHERN OCEAN
Bass Strait
SYDNEY
MELBOURNE
CANBERRA
ADELAIDE
BRISBANE
Newcastle
Wollongong
Geelong
Gold Coast
Tweed Heads
Toowoomba
Ipswich
Warwick
Lismore
Grafton
Coffs Harbour
Armidale
Tamworth
Dubbo
Orange
Bathurst
Wagga Wagga
Albury
Wodonga
Shepparton
Bendigo
Ballarat
Mildura
Broken Hill
Port Augusta
Port Pirie
Whyalla
Port Lincoln
Mount Gambier
Warrnambool
Kangaroo I.
King Island
Flinders Island
Furneaux Group
Cape Barren I.
Spencer Gulf
Great Dividing Range
Lake Eyre (North)
Lake Eyre (South)
Lake Torrens
Lake Frome
Lake Gairdner
Darling
Murray
Grey Range
Darling Downs
Gippsland
Mt. Kosciuszko 2230
Projection: Bonne
East from Greenwich
COPYRIGHT, GEORGE PHILIP LTD.

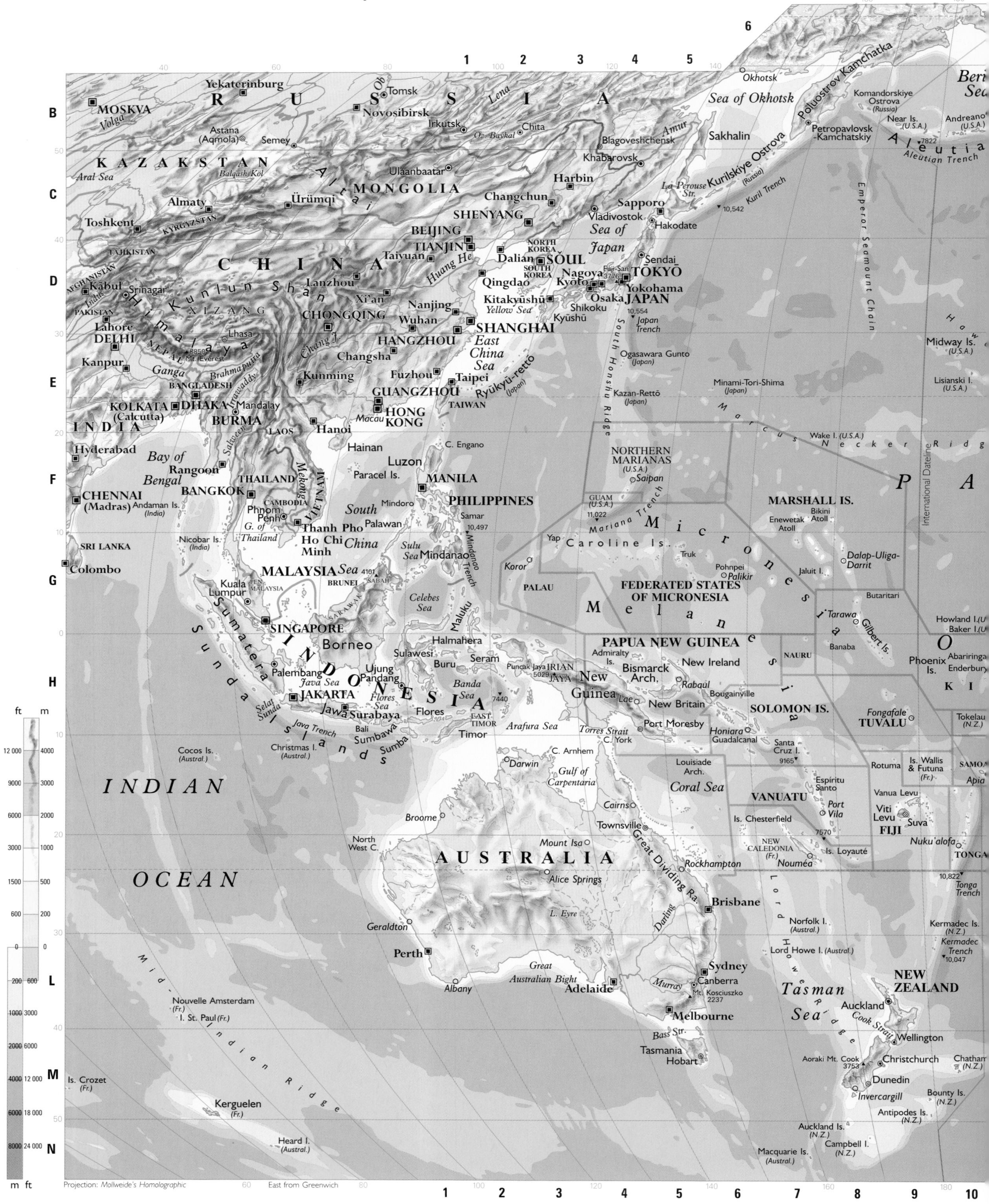

ft m
12 000 4000
9000 3000
6000 2000
3000 1000
1500 500
600 200
0 0
200 600
1000 3000
2000 6000
4000 12 000
6000 18 000
8000 24 000
m ft
Projection: Mollweide's Homolographic
East from Greenwich
Yekaterinburg
MOSKVA
Volga
R U S S I A
Tomsk
Ob
Novosibirsk
Lena
Irkutsk
O. Baykal
Chita
Astana (Aqmola)
Semey
KAZAKSTAN
Aral Sea
Balqash Köl
Altai
Ulaanbaatar
MONGOLIA
Amur
Blagoveshchensk
Khabarovsk
Harbin
Changchun
Almaty
Ürümqi
KYRGYZSTAN
Toshkent
TAJIKISTAN
SHENYANG
BEIJING
TIANJIN
Taiyuan
Huang He
Vladivostok
Sapporo
Hakodate
Sea of Japan
NORTH KOREA
SOUTH KOREA
SÖUL
Dalian
Qingdao
Sendai
Nagoya
Fuji-San 3776
TOKYO
Kyoto
Yokohama
Osaka
JAPAN
Kitakyushu
Shikoku
Kyushu
Yellow Sea
AFGHANISTAN
Kabul
Indus
Srinagar
PAKISTAN
Lahore
DELHI
CHINA
Kunlun Shan
XIZANG
Lanzhou
Xi'an
Himalaya
NEPAL
Lhasa
8850 Mt. Everest
Kanpur
Ganga
Brahmaputra
BANGLADESH
CHONGQING
Nanjing
Wuhan
SHANGHAI
HANGZHOU
Chang J.
Changsha
East China Sea
Kunming
Fuzhou
Taipei
TAIWAN
Ryukyu-retto (Japan)
GUANGZHOU
HONG KONG
Macau
KOLKATA (Calcutta)
DHAKA
Mandalay
Irrawaddy
BURMA
INDIA
Hanoi
LAOS
Hainan
Hyderabad
Bay of Bengal
Rangoon
Salween
THAILAND
Mekong
VIETNAM
BANGKOK
CAMBODIA
Phnom Penh
CHENNAI (Madras)
Andaman Is. (India)
G. of Thailand
Thanh Pho Ho Chi Minh
Nicobar Is. (India)
SRI LANKA
Colombo
Paracel Is.
Luzon
C. Engano
MANILA
PHILIPPINES
Mindoro
South China Sea
Palawan
Samar
10,497
Sulu Sea
Mindanao
Mindanao Trench
MALAYSIA
BRUNEI
SABAH
Kuala Lumpur
PEN. MALAYSIA
SARAWAK
Celebes Sea
4101
Sumatera
SINGAPORE
Borneo
INDONESIA
Maluku
Halmahera
Sulawesi
Seram
Buru
Palembang
Ujung Pandang
Java Sea
JAKARTA
Flores Sea
Banda Sea
7440
Jawa
Surabaya
Flores
EAST TIMOR
Timor
Selat Sunda
Sunda Islands
Java Trench
Bali
Sumbawa
Sumba
Christmas I. (Austral.)
Cocos Is. (Austral.)
Okhotsk
Sea of Okhotsk
Poluostrov Kamchatka
Komandorskiye Ostrova (Russia)
Bering Sea
Petropavlovsk-Kamchatskiy
Near Is. (U.S.A.)
Andreanof Is. (U.S.A.)
7822
Aleutian Is.
Aleutian Trench
Sakhalin
La Perouse Str.
Kurilskiye Ostrova (Russia)
Kuril Trench
10,542
Emperor Seamount Chain
Hawaiian Ridge
Midway Is. (U.S.A.)
Japan Trench
10,554
South Honshu Ridge
Ogasawara Gunto (Japan)
Minami-Tori-Shima (Japan)
Lisianski I. (U.S.A.)
Kazan-Retto (Japan)
Marcus Necker Ridge
Wake I. (U.S.A.)
International Dateline
NORTHERN MARIANAS (U.S.A.)
Saipan
GUAM (U.S.A.)
11,022
Mariana Trench
MARSHALL IS.
Bikini Atoll
Enewetak Atoll
PACIFIC
Micronesia
Yap
Caroline Is.
Truk
Koror
PALAU
Pohnpei
Palikir
Dalap-Uliga-Darrit
Jaluit I.
FEDERATED STATES OF MICRONESIA
Melanesia
Butaritari
Tarawa
Gilbert Is.
Howland I. (U.S.A.)
Baker I. (U.S.A.)
Banaba
NAURU
PAPUA NEW GUINEA
Admiralty Is.
Bismarck Arch.
New Ireland
Rabaul
Puncak Jaya 5029
IRIAN JAYA
New Guinea
Lae
New Britain
Bougainville
SOLOMON IS.
Phoenix Is.
Abariringa
Enderbury
KIRIBATI
Arafura Sea
Torres Strait
C. York
Port Moresby
Honiara
Guadalcanal
Fongafale
TUVALU
Tokelau (N.Z.)
Santa Cruz I.
9165
Rotuma
Is. Wallis & Futuna (Fr.)
SAMOA
Apia
C. Arnhem
Darwin
Gulf of Carpentaria
Louisiade Arch.
Coral Sea
Espiritu Santo
VANUATU
Port Vila
Vanua Levu
Viti Levu
Suva
FIJI
Cairns
Is. Chesterfield
Townsville
7570
Broome
Nuku'alofa
TONGA
NEW CALEDONIA (Fr.)
Nouméa
Is. Loyauté
North West C.
Mount Isa
AUSTRALIA
Great Dividing Ra.
Rockhampton
Alice Springs
10,822
Tonga Trench
Brisbane
Lord Howe Rise
Darling
L. Eyre
Norfolk I. (Austral.)
Kermadec Is. (N.Z.)
Kermadec Trench
10,047
Geraldton
Perth
Lord Howe I. (Austral.)
Great Australian Bight
Sydney
Canberra
Mt. Kosciuszko 2237
Murray
Adelaide
Albany
NEW ZEALAND
Tasman Sea
Auckland
Cook Strait
Wellington
Melbourne
Bass Str.
Tasmania
Hobart
Aoraki Mt. Cook 3753
Christchurch
Chatham Is. (N.Z.)
Dunedin
Invercargill
Bounty Is. (N.Z.)
Antipodes Is. (N.Z.)
Auckland Is. (N.Z.)
Campbell I. (N.Z.)
Macquarie Is. (Austral.)
INDIAN OCEAN
Mid-Indian Ridge
Nouvelle Amsterdam (Fr.)
I. St. Paul (Fr.)
Is. Crozet (Fr.)
Kerguelen (Fr.)
Heard I. (Austral.)

Arctic Circle
ALASKA
(U.S.A.)
Anchorage
5959
Bristol Bay
Gulf of Alaska
Juneau
Prince of Wales I.
(U.S.A.)
Prince Rupert
Queen Charlotte Is.
(Canada)
Is. (U.S.A.)
Vancouver
Vancouver I.
Victoria
Seattle
Portland
Rocky Mts
C A N A D A
Edmonton
Calgary
Regina
L. Winnipeg
Winnipeg
Newfoundland
St. Lawrence
St. John's
NORTH
L. Superior
Québec
Montréal
Ottawa
L. Huron
L. Michigan
Toronto
L. Ontario
Boston
Minneapolis
Missouri
Snake
Boise
Detroit
Buffalo
Salt Lake City
CHICAGO
L. Erie
C. Mendocino
Denver
Pittsburgh
NEW YORK CITY
PHILADELPHIA
Baltimore
Washington D.C.
Sacramento
Colorado
Kansas City
St. Louis
Cincinnati
Appalachian Mts.
SAN FRANCISCO
4418
UNITED STATES
ATLANTIC
6741
Oklahoma City
Memphis
Atlanta
C. Hatteras
LOS ANGELES
Phoenix
Dallas
Mississippi
San Diego
Bermuda
(U.K.)
Ciudad Juárez
Houston
Jacksonville
Guadalupe
(Mex.)
San Antonio
New Orleans
Sargasso Sea
Baja California
MEXICO
Gulf of Mexico
Miami
Florida Str.
BAHAMAS
OCEAN
Golfo de California
Monterrey
Tropic of Cancer
La Habana
West Indies
CUBA
C. San Lucas
Canal de Yucatan
Ridge
Honolulu
Oahu
HAWAIIAN IS.
(U.S.A.)
4205
Hawaii
Guadalajara
MEXICO
5700
Puebla
Mérida
7680
9200
HAITI
DOMINICAN REP.
JAMAICA
Kingston
Leeward Is.
Is. Revilla Gigedo
(Mex.)
Johnston I.
(U.S.A.)
Acapulco
BELIZE
PUERTO RICO
(U.S.A.)
CIFIC
HONDURAS
Caribbean Sea
GUATEMALA
Guatemala
San Salvador
EL SALVADOR
NICARAGUA
BARBADOS
Windward Is.
North West Christmas I. Ridge
I. Clipperton
(Fr.)
Managua
Barranquilla
Maracaibo
San José
Caracas
COSTA RICA
Colón
Panamá
Orinoco
PANAMA
Palmyra Is.
(U.S.A.)
VENEZUELA
I. del Coco
(Costa Rica)
Medellín
Bogotá
Teraina
Tabuaeran
Kiritimati
Cali
I. de Malpelo
(Colombia)
COLOMBIA
Equator
Galápagos
(Ecuador)
Quito
Jarvis I.
(U.S.A.)
EAN
ECUADOR
Amazonas
Guayaquil
Iquitos
Malden I.
Starbuck I.
C. Paliñas
BRAZIL
KIRIBATI
East Pacific Ridge
Tongareva
Caroline I.
Is. Marquises
Trujillo
Pukapuka
Manihiki
Vostok I.
6369
PERU
Flint I.
LIMA
AMER. SAMOA
(U.S.A.)
Cuzco
L. Titicaca
Nevada Ancohuma
6550
Suwarrow Is.
Is. de la Société
Tuamotu Ridge
Is. Tuamotu
Arequipa
La Paz
Tahiti
6866
Papeete
Peru-
Arica
BOLIVIA
Niue
(N.Z.)
Cook Is.
(N.Z.)
FRENCH POLYNESIA
Iquique
Chile
Mururoa
Austral Seamount Chain
Tropic of Capricorn
Antofagasta
PARAGUAY
Rarotonga
Is. Tubuai
Ducie I.
8050
Trench
Asunción
Pitcairn I.
(U.K.)
San Felix
(Chile)
San Ambrosio
(Chile)
San Miguel de Tucumán
Sala-y-Gómez
(Chile)
Rapa
I. de Pascua
(Chile)
Pôrto Alegre
Córdoba
Arch. de Juan Fernández
(Chile)
Aconcagua
6960
Valparaíso
Rosario
URUGUAY
SANTIAGO
BUENOS AIRES
Montevideo
Río de la Plata
Concepción
ARGENTINA
Chile Rise
Andes
SOUTH ATLANTIC OCEAN
Patagonia
6212
Pacific-Antarctic Ridge
Falkland Is.
(U.K.)
Punta Arenas
Est. de Magallanes
South Georgia
(U.K.)
Tierra del Fuego
C. de Hornos
West from Greenwich

COPYRIGHT GEORGE PHILIP LTD.

NORTH AMERICA : Physical 1:35 000 000

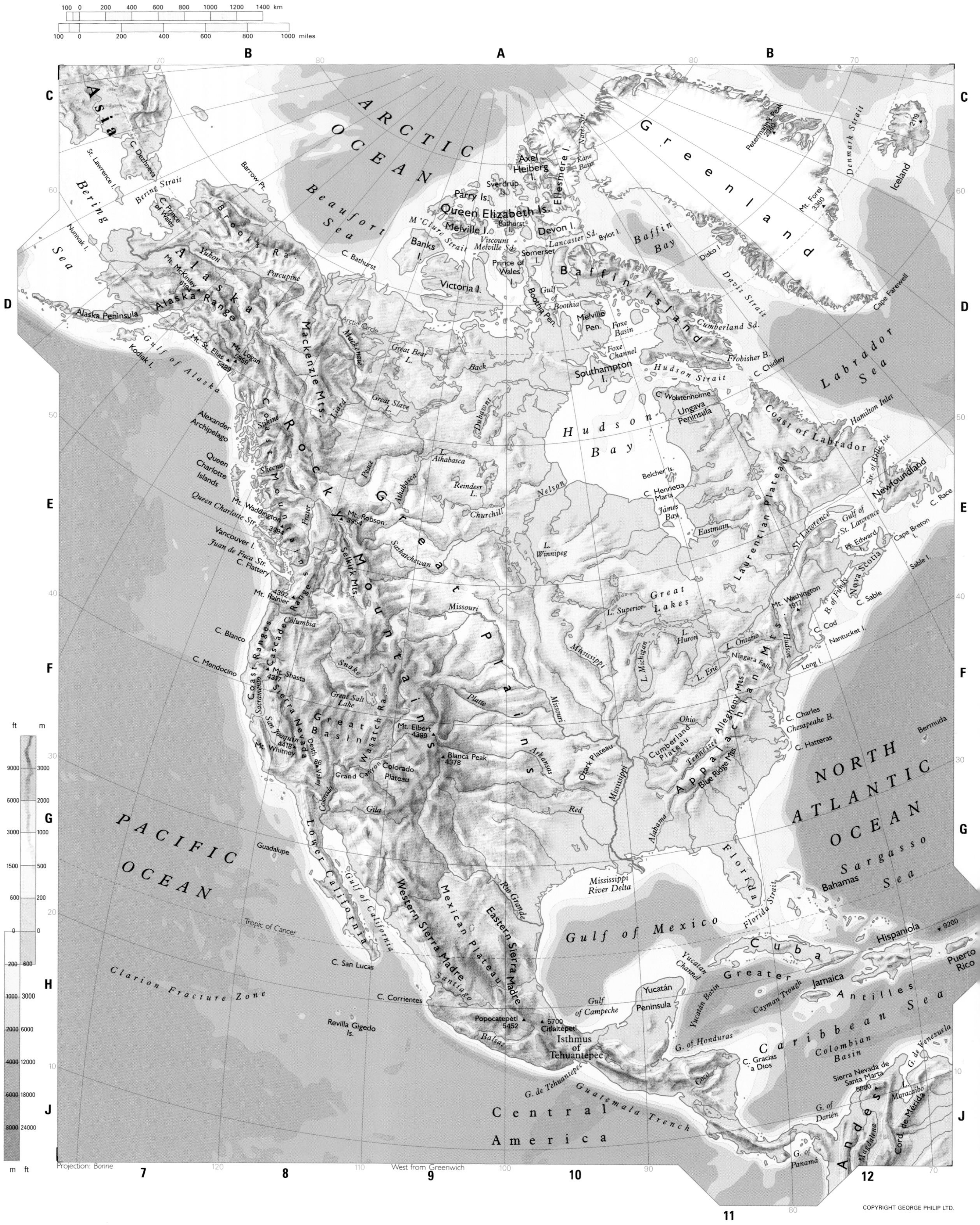

COPYRIGHT GEORGE PHILIP LTD.

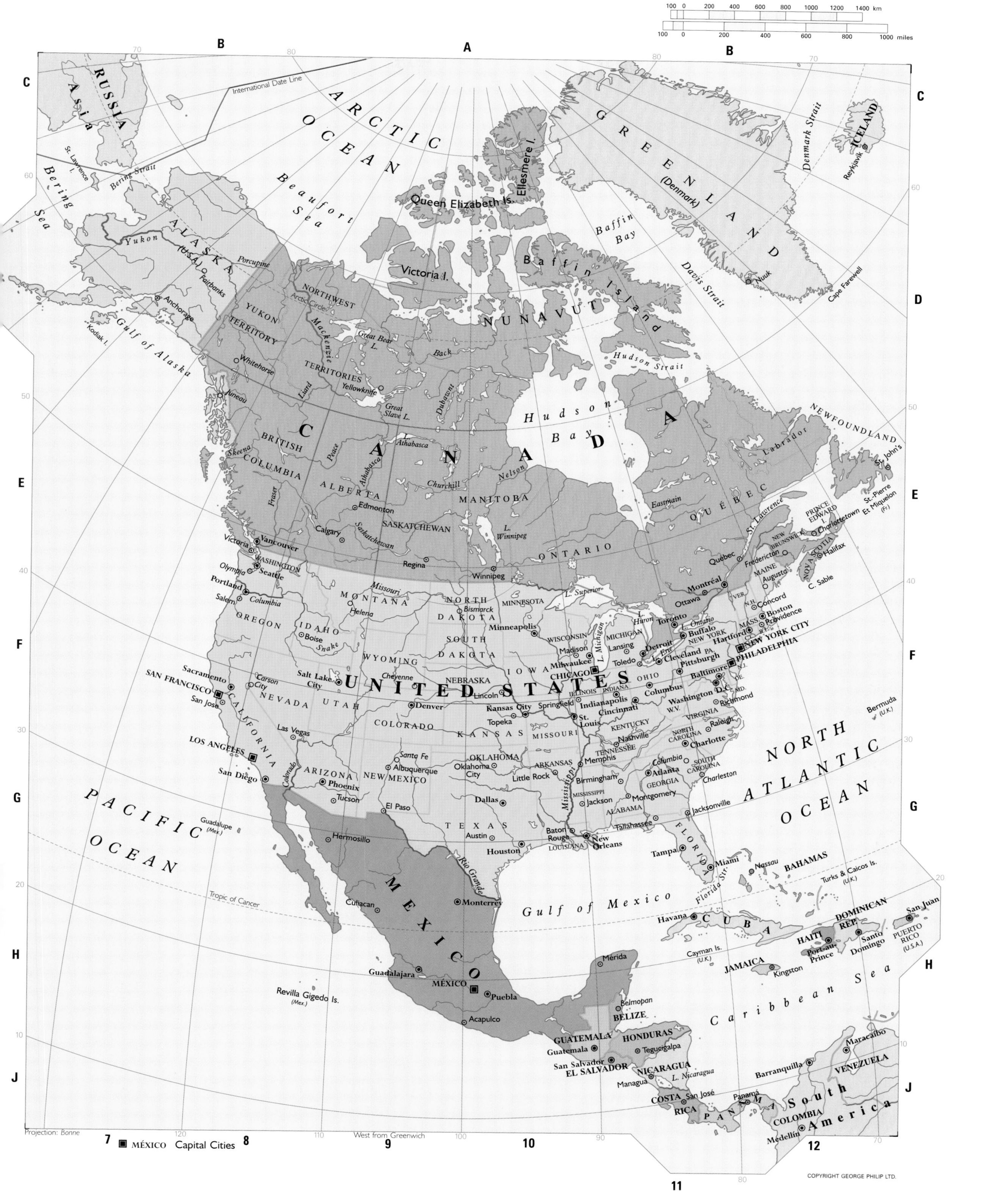

100 0 200 400 600 800 1000 1200 1400 km
100 0 200 400 600 800 1000 miles
ARCTIC OCEAN
Beaufort Sea
RUSSIA
Asia
International Date Line
St. Lawrence I.
Bering Strait
Bering Sea
ALASKA (U.S.A.)
Yukon
Porcupine
Fairbanks
Anchorage
Kodiak I.
Gulf of Alaska
Queen Elizabeth Is.
Ellesmere I.
Victoria I.
Baffin Island
Baffin Bay
GREENLAND (Denmark)
Nuuk
Davis Strait
Cape Farewell
Denmark Strait
ICELAND
Reykjavik
NUNAVUT
NORTHWEST TERRITORIES
Arctic Circle
Mackenzie
YUKON TERRITORY
Whitehorse
Juneau
Great Bear L.
Back
Yellowknife
Great Slave L.
Liard
Dubawnt
Hudson Strait
Hudson Bay
NEWFOUNDLAND
Labrador
St. John's
CANADA
BRITISH COLUMBIA
Skeena
Peace
Athabasca
L. Athabasca
Churchill
Nelson
ALBERTA
Edmonton
Calgary
Saskatchewan
SASKATCHEWAN
MANITOBA
L. Winnipeg
Fraser
Vancouver
Victoria
Regina
Winnipeg
ONTARIO
QUÉBEC
Eastmain
St. Lawrence
PRINCE EDWARD I.
Charlottetown
St.-Pierre Et Miquelon (Fr.)
NEW BRUNSWICK
Fredericton
NOVA SCOTIA
Halifax
C. Sable
Québec
Montréal
Ottawa
MAINE
Augusta
VER.
N.H.
Concord
MASS.
Boston
Providence
CONN.
R.I.
Hartford
NEW YORK CITY
PHILADELPHIA
WASHINGTON
Olympia
Seattle
Portland
Salem
Columbia
OREGON
MONTANA
Missouri
Helena
IDAHO
Boise
Snake
NORTH DAKOTA
Bismarck
MINNESOTA
Minneapolis
SOUTH DAKOTA
WYOMING
Cheyenne
NEBRASKA
Lincoln
IOWA
WISCONSIN
Madison
Milwaukee
L. Superior
L. Michigan
L. Huron
MICHIGAN
Lansing
Detroit
L. Erie
L. Ontario
Toronto
Buffalo
NEW YORK
Cleveland
PA.
Pittsburgh
Toledo
OHIO
Columbus
CHICAGO
ILLINOIS
INDIANA
Indianapolis
Cincinnati
Springfield
St. Louis
Baltimore
N.J.
DE.
MD.
Washington D.C.
Richmond
W.V.
VIRGINIA
Raleigh
KENTUCKY
Nashville
TENNESSEE
Memphis
NORTH CAROLINA
Charlotte
SOUTH CAROLINA
Columbia
Charleston
Atlanta
GEORGIA
Birmingham
ALABAMA
Montgomery
MISSISSIPPI
Jackson
Mississippi
Jacksonville
Tallahassee
FLORIDA
Tampa
Miami
Florida Str.
UNITED STATES
Sacramento
SAN FRANCISCO
San Jose
Carson City
NEVADA
CALIFORNIA
Salt Lake City
UTAH
Denver
COLORADO
Kansas City
Topeka
KANSAS
MISSOURI
Las Vegas
LOS ANGELES
San Diego
Colorado
ARIZONA
Phoenix
Tucson
NEW MEXICO
Santa Fe
Albuquerque
OKLAHOMA
Oklahoma City
ARKANSAS
Little Rock
Dallas
El Paso
TEXAS
Austin
Houston
Baton Rouge
LOUISIANA
New Orleans
Bermuda (U.K.)
NORTH ATLANTIC OCEAN
PACIFIC OCEAN
Guadalupe (Mex.)
Tropic of Cancer
Hermosillo
Rio Grande
Monterrey
Culiacan
MEXICO
Guadalajara
MÉXICO
Puebla
Acapulco
Revilla Gigedo Is. (Mex.)
Gulf of Mexico
Mérida
Belmopan
BELIZE
GUATEMALA
Guatemala
HONDURAS
Tegucigalpa
San Salvador
EL SALVADOR
NICARAGUA
Managua
L. Nicaragua
COSTA RICA
San José
PANAMA
Panamá
BAHAMAS
Nassau
Turks & Caicos Is. (U.K.)
Havana
CUBA
Cayman Is. (U.K.)
JAMAICA
Kingston
HAITI
Port-au-Prince
DOMINICAN REP.
Santo Domingo
San Juan
PUERTO RICO (U.S.A.)
Caribbean Sea
Maracaibo
Barranquilla
VENEZUELA
COLOMBIA
Medellín
South America
Projection: Bonne
West from Greenwich
MÉXICO Capital Cities

100 0 100 200 300 400 500 600 km
100 0 100 200 300 400 miles
PACIFIC OCEAN
ALASKA
YUKON TERRITORY
NORTHWEST TERRITORIES
BRITISH COLUMBIA
ALBERTA
SASKATCHEWAN
MANITOBA
CANADA
UNITED STATES
WASHINGTON
MONTANA
NORTH DAKOTA
SOUTH DAKOTA
MINNESOTA
NEBRASKA
IOWA
Anchorage
Kenai
Homer
Seward
Valdez
Cordova
Fairbanks
Delta Junction
Tok
Dawson
Whitehorse
Juneau
Sitka
Ketchikan
Prince Rupert
Inuvik
Tuktoyaktuk
Aklavik
Old Crow
Fort McPherson
Norman Wells
Fort Good Hope
Yellowknife
Hay River
Fort Smith
Fort Simpson
Fort Nelson
Fort St. John
Dawson Creek
Prince George
Kamloops
Kelowna
Penticton
VANCOUVER
Victoria
Nanaimo
SEATTLE
Tacoma
Olympia
Spokane
Edmonton
Calgary
Red Deer
Lethbridge
Medicine Hat
Grande Prairie
Fort McMurray
Saskatoon
Regina
Moose Jaw
Swift Current
Prince Albert
North Battleford
Lloydminster
Flin Flon
The Pas
Thompson
Churchill
Winnipeg
Brandon
Portage la Prairie
Selkirk
Kenora
Dryden
Minot
Bismarck
Fargo
Grand Forks
Williston
Pierre
Rapid City
Sioux Falls
Sioux City
MINNEAPOLIS
ST. PAUL
Omaha
Des Moines
Great Bear L.
Great Slave L.
Lake Athabasca
Lake Winnipeg
L. Winnipegosis
L. Manitoba
Reindeer Lake
Victoria Island
Banks Island
Prince of Wales I.
Boothia Peninsula
King William I.
Coronation Gulf
Amundsen Gulf
Queen Maud Gulf
Rankin Inlet
Baker Lake
Arviat
Kugluktuk
Cambridge Bay
Gjoa Haven
Mackenzie Mountains
Selwyn Mts.
Rocky Mountains
Coast Mountains
Cassiar Mountains
St. Elias Mts.
Wrangell Mts.
Mt. Logan 5959
Mt. Robson 3954
Vancouver I.
Queen Charlotte Is.
Alexander Archipelago
Projection : Bonne
ALASKA
1:30 000 000
100 0 100 200 300 400 500 600 km
100 0 100 200 300 400 miles
CHUKCHI SEA
BERING SEA
GULF OF ALASKA
PACIFIC OCEAN
RUSSIA
Brooks Range
Alaska Range
Mt. McKinley 6194
Barrow
Prudhoe Bay
Point Hope
Kotzebue
Nome
Bethel
Dillingham
Kodiak
Dutch Harbor
Aleutian Is.
Alaska Peninsula
West from Greenwich

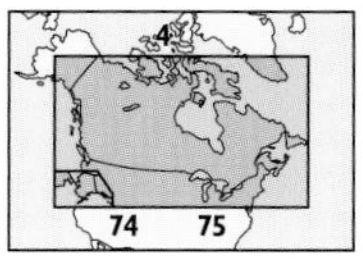
74
75

11
12
13
14
15
16
B
C
D
E
Devon I.
Lancaster Sound
Baffin Bay
Nunavik
Uummannaq
Bylot I.
Arctic Bay
Nanisivik
Borden Pen.
Brodeur Peninsula
Pond Inlet
C. Adair
Clyde River
Qeqertarsuaq
Ilulissat
Qasigiannguit
GREENLAND
(KALAALLIT NUNAAT)
(Denmark)
Kangerlussuaq
Tasiilaq
Kong Frederik VI's Kyst
C. Raper
Davis Strait
Sisimiut
Maniitsoq
Nuuk
Qeqertarsuatsiaat
Paamiut
Arsuk
Qaqortoq
Nanortalik
Alluitsup Paa
Uummannarsuaq
Baffin Island
Home B.
Fury and Hecla Str.
Igloolik
Qikiqtarjuaq
C. Dyer
Cumberland Peninsula
Pangnirtung
Hoare B.
Mercy C.
Cumberland Sd.
Simpson Pen.
Pelly Bay
Committee B.
Melville Peninsula
Sanirajak
Foxe Basin
Prince Charles I.
Air Force I.
Nettilling L.
Rae Isthmus
Repulse Bay
NUNAVUT
C. Dorchester
Amadjuak L.
Foxe Pen.
Iqaluit
Hall Peninsula
Wager B.
Roes Welcome Sd.
Foxe Channel
Cape Dorset
Meta Incognita Peninsula
Kimmirut
Frobisher Bay
Resolution I.
Southampton I.
Salliq
Bell Pen.
Salisbury I.
Hudson Strait
Nottingham I.
Coats I.
Ivujivik
Salluit
Quaqtaq
C. Chidley
Akpatok I.
Labrador Sea
ATLANTIC OCEAN
Mansel I.
Kangiqsujuaq
Péninsule d'Ungava
Kangirsuk
Ungava Bay
Kangiqsualujjuaq
Hebron
Puvirnituq
Arnaud
L. Payne
Hudson Bay
Ottawa Is.
Feuilles
Koksoak
Kuujjuaq
Baleine
George
Nain
NEWFOUNDLAND
Hopedale
C. Harrison
Rigolet
Cartwright
Inukjuak
Mélèzes
Caniapiscau
L. Minto
Smallwood Res.
Labrador
North West River
Happy Valley-Goose Bay
Port Hope Simpson
Belle Isle
C. Bauld
St. Anthony
Sleeper Is.
King George Is.
Baker's Dozen Is.
Sanikiluaq
Belcher Is.
Tatnam
L. à l'Eau Claire
L. Bienville
Schefferville
Petitsikapau L.
Churchill Falls
Churchill
Esker
Kuujjuarapik
Grande Baleine
C. Henrietta Maria
Kanaaupscow
Rés. de Caniapiscau
Labrador City
Fermont
Ashuanipi L.
Natashquan
St-Augustin
Str. of Belle Isle
Notre Dame B.
Lewisporte
Gander
Bonavista
Trinity B.
Carbonear
St. John's
Baie Verte
Deer Lake
Grand Falls
Corner Brook
Newfoundland
Stephenville
Placentia
Marystown
Placentia B.
C. Race
Channel-Port aux Basques
Peawanuck
Winisk
Severn
Pte. Louis XIV
La Grande
Chisasibi
James Bay
Akimiski I.
Wemindji
1135
Gagnon
QUÉBEC
Moisie
Romaine
Havre-St-Pierre
Rés. Manicouagan
Î. d'Anticosti
Natashquan
Big Trout L.
Attawapiskat
Eastmain
Fort Albany
Charlton I.
Waskaganish
Rupert
L. Mistassini
L. Albanel
Manicouagan
Sept-Îles
Port-Cartier
Gulf of St. Lawrence
Cabot Str.
ST.-PIERRE et MIQUELON (Fr.)
ONTARIO
Albany
Moosonee
Nottaway
Harricana
Chibougamau
Péribonca
Baie Comeau
St. Lawrence
Matane
Gaspé
Pén. de Gaspé
Îs. de la Madeleine
North C.
Cape Breton I.
Glace Bay
St. Joseph
Missinaibi
Matagami
Dolbeau
L. St-Jean
Rimouski
Campbellton
Bathurst
PR. EDWARD I.
Sydney
Port Hawkesbury
Antigonish
Nakina
Kenogami
Hearst
L. Matagami
Chicoutimi
Rivière-du-Loup
Edmundston
Miramichi
Summerside
Charlottetown
Northumberland Str.
NOVA SCOTIA
L. Nipigon
Geraldton
Kapuskasing
Cochrane
Abitibi L.
Rés. Gouin
Roberval
Jonquière
NEW BRUNSWICK
Moncton
New Glasgow
Nipigon
Marathon
Oba
Timmins
Amos
1190
Grand Falls
Truro
Sable I. (Nova Scotia)
Kirkland Lake
Rouyn-Noranda
Val-d'Or
La Tuque
Québec
Lévis
Woodstock
Fredericton
Amherst
Kentville
Dartmouth
Thunder Bay
Chapleau
New Liskeard
Rés. Cabonga
Mont-Laurier
Shawinigan
Trois-Rivières
Thetford Mines
Saint John
Digby
Halifax
Wawa
Lake Superior
Joliette
St-Hyacinthe
MAINE
Bay of Fundy
Bridgewater
Liverpool
Houghton
Sault Ste. Marie
Elliot Lake
Sudbury
Outaouais
MONTRÉAL
Sherbrooke
Bangor
Yarmouth
Ironwood
Marquette
MICHIGAN
Manitoulin I.
L. Nipissing
North Bay
Hull
Granby
L. Champlain
Augusta
C. Sable
Parry Sound
Georgian Bay
Pembroke
Ottawa
Cornwall
Montpelier
Lewiston
Portland
Manistique
Huntsville
Burlington
VERMONT
NEW HAMPSHIRE
Escanaba
Menominee
Petoskey
Lake Huron
Barrie
Peterborough
Kingston
Concord
Wausau
Traverse City
Owen Sound
Belleville
Manchester
WISCONSIN
Green Bay
Cadillac
Oshawa
L. Ontario
Syracuse
MASS.
BOSTON
C. Cod
Appleton
TORONTO
Kitchener
Hamilton
Rochester
Albany
Springfield
Providence
Sheboygan
Saginaw
Lake Michigan
London
Niagara Falls
NEW YORK
HARTFORD
R.I.
MILWAUKEE
Grand Rapids
Flint
BUFFALO
CONN.
Madison
Racine
Lansing
Sarnia
Elmira
Binghamton
New Haven
Kenosha
DETROIT
Windsor
L. Erie
Jamestown
Bridgeport
Rockford
CHICAGO
Erie
Scranton
NEW YORK
Gary
South Bend
Toledo
CLEVELAND
PENNSYLVANIA
Newark
N.J.
Allentown
Trenton
ILLINOIS
INDIANA
OHIO
2136
1890
2850
2591
3809
1852
257
814
6309
60
50
40
30
80
70
90
West from Greenwich
11
12
13
14

EASTERN CANADA 1:7 000 000

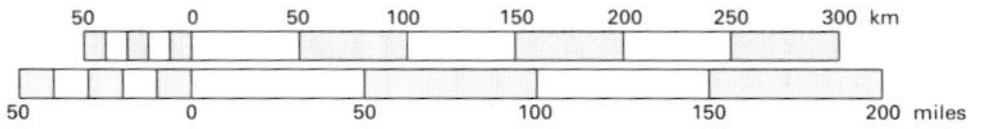

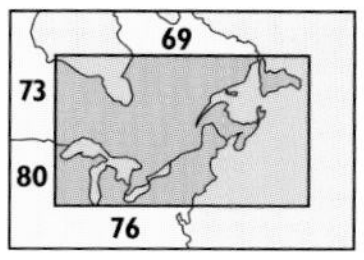
69
73
80
76

6
7
8
9
A
B
C
D
L A B R A D O R
S E A
N E W F O U N D L A N D
Labrador
Q U É B E C
Newfoundland
Smallwood Reservoir
Nain
South Aulatsivik I.
Paul I.
Voisey B.
Tunungayualok I.
Nunaksaluk I.
Davis Inlet
Big Bay
Hopedale
Kaipokok B.
Aillik
Makkovik
Adlavik Is.
C. Harrison
Postville
Holton
Indian Harbour
Groswater B.
Rigolet
Hamilton Inlet
Cartwright
Table B.
Black Tickle
Island of Ponds
Mealy Mts.
1128
Paradise River
Square Islands
Charlottetown
Williams harbour
Port Hope Simpson
Battle Harbour
Mary's Harbour
Lodge Bay
Belle Isle
Red Bay
L'Anse aux Meadows
St. Anthony
L'Anse au Loup
Forteau
Blanc-Sablon
Str. of Belle Isle
North West River
Goose
Happy Valley-Goose Bay
Churchill Falls
Twin Falls
Esker
Menihek
Schefferville
Attikamagen L.
Labrador City
Wabush
Fermont
Ashuanipi L.
Minipi L.
Natashquan
Little Mecatina
St-Augustin
Petit Mécatina
Rivière St-Paul
St. Barbe
Roddickton
Englee
Groais I.
Bell I.
Horse Is.
Port au Choix
Hawke's Bay
Harbour Deep
Daniel's Harbour
Long Range Mts.
GROS MORNE NAT. PARK
Rocky Harbour
Norris Point
Trout River
Deer Lake
Corner Brook
Pasadena
Stephenville
St. George's B.
C. St. George
Port au Port B.
Petit Jardin
South Branch
Great Codroy
C. Ray
Channel-Port aux Basques
Rose Blanche
Isle aux Morts
Burgeo
François
Harbour Breton
Belleoram
Grand Bank
Fortune
Marystown
Burin
St. Lawrence
C. St. Mary's
Placentia
St. Bride's
Argentia
Ferryland
Trepassey
Avalon Peninsula
C. Race
C. Pine
St. John's
Mt. Pearl
Torbay
Holyrood
Whitless Bay
Conception B.
Carbonear
Heart's Content
Bay Roberts
Trinity B.
Old Perlican
Clarenville
Port Blandford
TERRA NOVA NAT. PARK
Glovertown
Trinity
Bonavista
C. Bonavista
Catalina
Bonavista B.
Gander
Gambo
Glenwood
Wesleyville
Musgrave Harbour
C. Freels
Fogo I.
Fogo
Twillingate
Lewisporte
Botwood
Bishop's Falls
Grand Falls-Windsor
Badger
Buchans
Red Indian L.
Meelpaeg Res.
Jeddore L.
Victoria L.
Grey
Granite L.
St. Alban's
Terrenceville
Springdale
Baie Verte
Jackson's Arm
Notre Dame B.
La Scie
C. St. John
White B.
Hare B.
Miquelon
Langlade
St-Pierre
ST-PIERRE ET MIQUELON (France)
Cabot Strait
St. Paul I.
Cape North
Cape Breton Island
CAPE BRETON HIGHLANDS NAT. PARK
Pleasant Bay
Ingonish
St. Ann's B.
Chéticamp
Sydney Mines
New Waterford
Glace Bay
Sydney
North Sydney
Louisbourg
Bras d'Or L.
Inverness
Port Hood
Port Hawkesbury
St. Peters
I. Madame
Chedabucto B.
Canso
Mulgrave
Antigonish
Sherbrooke
Guysborough
NOVA SCOTIA
Halifax
Dartmouth
Sheet Harbour
Musquodoboit Harbour
Upper Musquodoboit
Enfield
Truro
Stewiacke
Stellarton
New Glasgow
Pictou
Amherst
Springhill
Parrsboro
Minas Basin
Kentville
Windsor
Middleton
Annapolis Royal
Digby
Bridgetown
Middle Sackville
Mahone Bay
Lunenburg
Bridgewater
Liverpool
Milton
KEJIMKUJIK NAT. PARK
Rossignol L.
Weymouth
St. Mary's Bay
Shelburne
Lockeport
Yarmouth
Wedgeport
Clark's Harbour
C. Sable
Sable I. (Nova Scotia)
Bay of Fundy
PRINCE EDWARD ISLAND
North Cape
Tignish
Alberton
Summerside
Kensington
Borden
Charlottetown
Souris
St. Peters
East Pt.
Georgetown
Montague
Murray Hr.
Cape Tormentine
Northumberland Str.
Îs. de la Madeleine (Québec)
Fatima
Cap-aux-Meules
Havre-Aubert
Grande-Entrée
Î. Brion
GULF OF ST. LAWRENCE
Î. d'Anticosti
Port-Menier
Pte. de l'Ouest
Pte. du Sud-Ouest
Pte. Heath
Pte. du Sud
Dét. de Jacques-Cartier
Dét. d'Honguedo
572
C. de Gaspé
Gaspé
Percé
Grande-Rivière
Chandler
Pén. de Gaspé
Mts. Chic-Chocs
Mt. Jacques Cartier
1268
PARC DE CONSERVATION DE LA GASPÉSIE
Rivière-au-Renard
Grande-Vallée
Mont-Louis
Ste-Anne-des-Monts
Cap-Chat
Matane
Mont-Joli
Sayabec
Amqui
Causapscal
Rimouski
Bic
Trois-Pistoles
Rivière-du-Loup
Cabano
Dégelis
Matapédia
Atholville
Campbellton
Dalhousie
Chaleur Bay
New Richmond
Bonaventure
Paspébiac
Miscou I.
Lamèque
Shippegan
Caraquet
Tracadie-Sheila
Bathurst
Neguac
Miramichi B.
Miramichi
Newcastle
Rogersville
Richibucto
Bouctouche
Shediac
Moncton
St. Antoine
Doaktown
Chipman
Grand L.
Petitcodiac
Sackville
Chignecto B.
Sussex
Hampton
Rothesay
Saint John
St. George
St. Stephen
Blacks Hr.
Eastport
Grand Manan I.
Fredericton
Fredericton Junc.
Oromocto
Minto
Woodstock
Hartland
Perth-Andover
Plaster Rock
Grand Falls
St. Leonard
Edmundston
Mt. Carleton
820
St. Quentin
Kedgwick
NEW BRUNSWICK
Saint John
St. Lawrence
Sept-Îles
Port-Cartier
Moisie
Clarke City
Rivière-Pentecôte
Sainte-Anne
Baie Trinité
Pte. des Monts
Godbout
Baie Comeau
Chute-aux-Outardes
Betsiamites
Forestville
Les Escoumins
Tadoussac
Chicoutimi
Alma
Jonquière
La Baie
Saguenay
Petite Saguenay
St-Siméon
La Malbaie
Baie-St-Paul
La Pocatière
St. Pascal
St-Jean-Port-Joli
Montmagny
Québec
I. d'Orléans
Levis
Charny
Beauceville
St-Georges
Thetford Mines
Lac-Mégantic
Sherbrooke
Magog
Coaticook
East Angus
Asbestos
Plessisville
Victoriaville
Deschaillons
Ste-Marie
Beaupré
PARC PROV. DES GRANDS JARDINS
1190
Lac Bouchette
Sheldrake
Mingan
Havre-St-Pierre
Natashquan
Kegaska
Romaine
Harrington Harbour
I. du Petit Mécatina
St-Augustin
Musquaro
Olomane
Aguanus
Nabisipi
Magpie
St-Jean
Romaine
Manitou
1048
Walker
Mistassini
Rés. Manicouagan
Petit Lac Manicouagan
Gagnon
Rés. de Caniapiscau
Rés. Pipmuacan
Manicouagan
Outardes
Betsiamites
Péribonca
Manouane
Plétipi
1135
Caniapiscau
Petitsikapau L.
Menihek Lakes
Wakuach
Champdoré
610
Tudor
Whitegull
Mistinibi
Mistastin L.
Kogaluk
Fraser
L. de la Hutte Sauvage
L. Nachicapau
Chakonipau
Otelnuk
Le Moyne
Baleine
George
Châteauguay
Sérigny
Sable
Néret
Bermen
Dalmas
Nitchequon
Nichicun
Naocoçane
Opiscotéo
Joseph
Winokapau
Ossokmanuan L.
Atikonak L.
Burnt L.
Churchill
Naskaupi
Kanairiktok
Seal L.
Nipishish L.
Grand L.
Melville
Harp L.
Eagle
Paradise
Sandwich B.
North River
MAINE
Van Buren
Fort Kent
Caribou
Presque Isle
Ashland
Eagle Lake
Houlton
Patten
Chamberlain L.
Chesuncook L.
1606
Millinocket
Moosehead L.
Jackman
Greenville
Lincoln
Dover-Foxcroft
Calais
Machias
Old Town
Bangor
Brewer
Bingham
Mooselookmeguntic L.
Skowhegan
Waterville
Ellsworth
Bar Harbor
Mount Desert I.
Belfast
Camden
Rockland
Augusta
Rumford
Berlin
Norway
Auburn
Lewiston
Brunswick
Bath
Portland
Sebago L.
Conway
Saco
Biddeford
Sanford
Rochester
Concord
Dover
Portsmouth
Manchester
Nashua
Haverhill
Lawrence
Gloucester
Lynn
Lowell
Newton
BOSTON
Quincy
Brockton
Worcester
Woonsocket
C. Cod
NEW HAMPSHIRE
MASS.
UNITED STATES
Laconia
Hanover
St. Johnsbury
Island Pond
Newport
ATLANTIC OCEAN
55
50
45
70
65
60
West from Greenwich
6
7
8

WESTERN CANADA 1:7 000 000

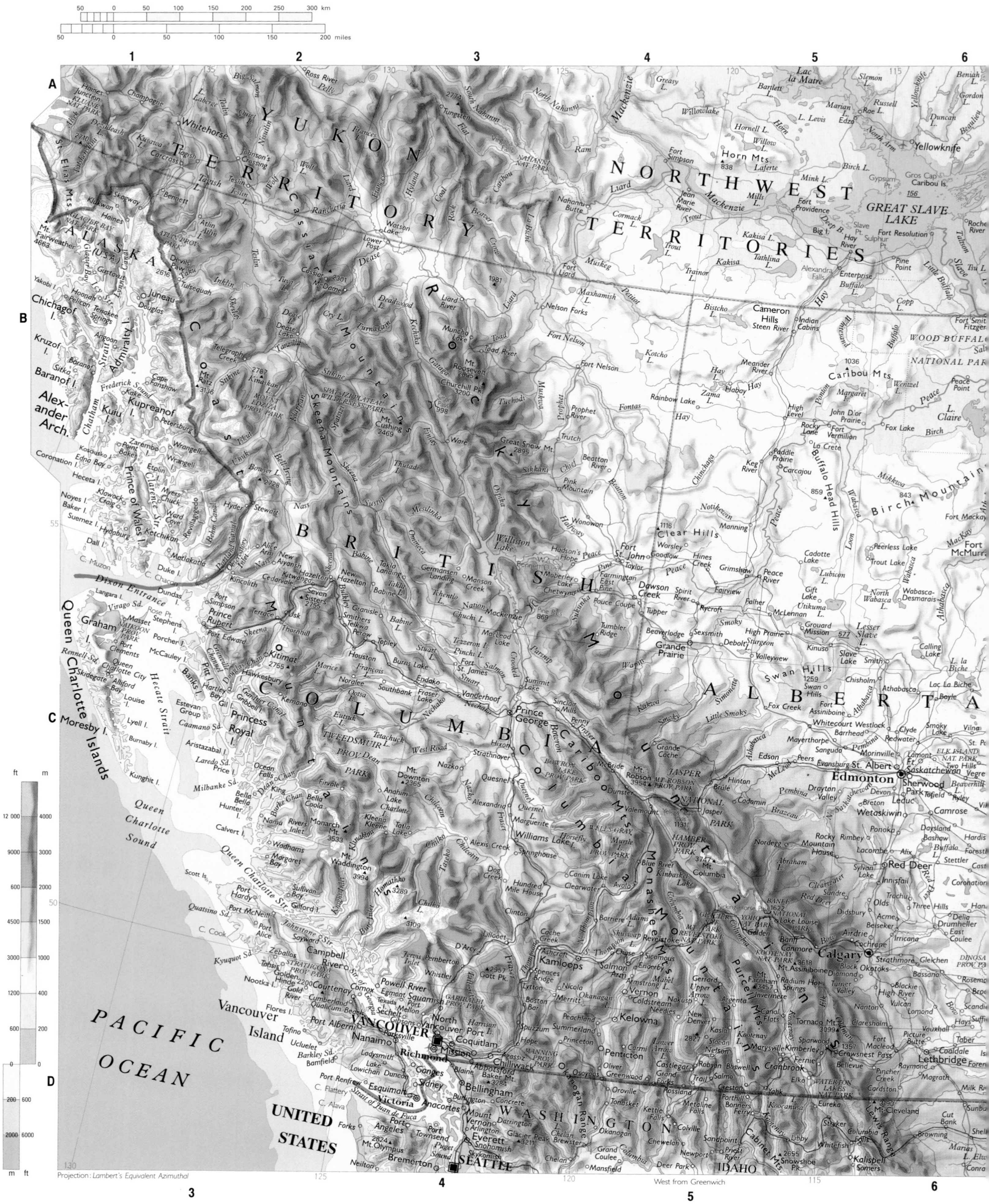

Projection: *Lambert's Equivalent Azimuthal*

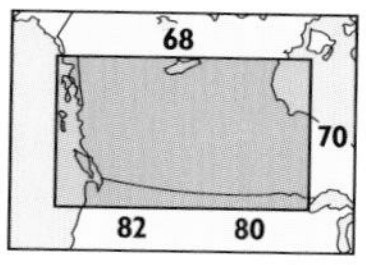
68
70
82
80

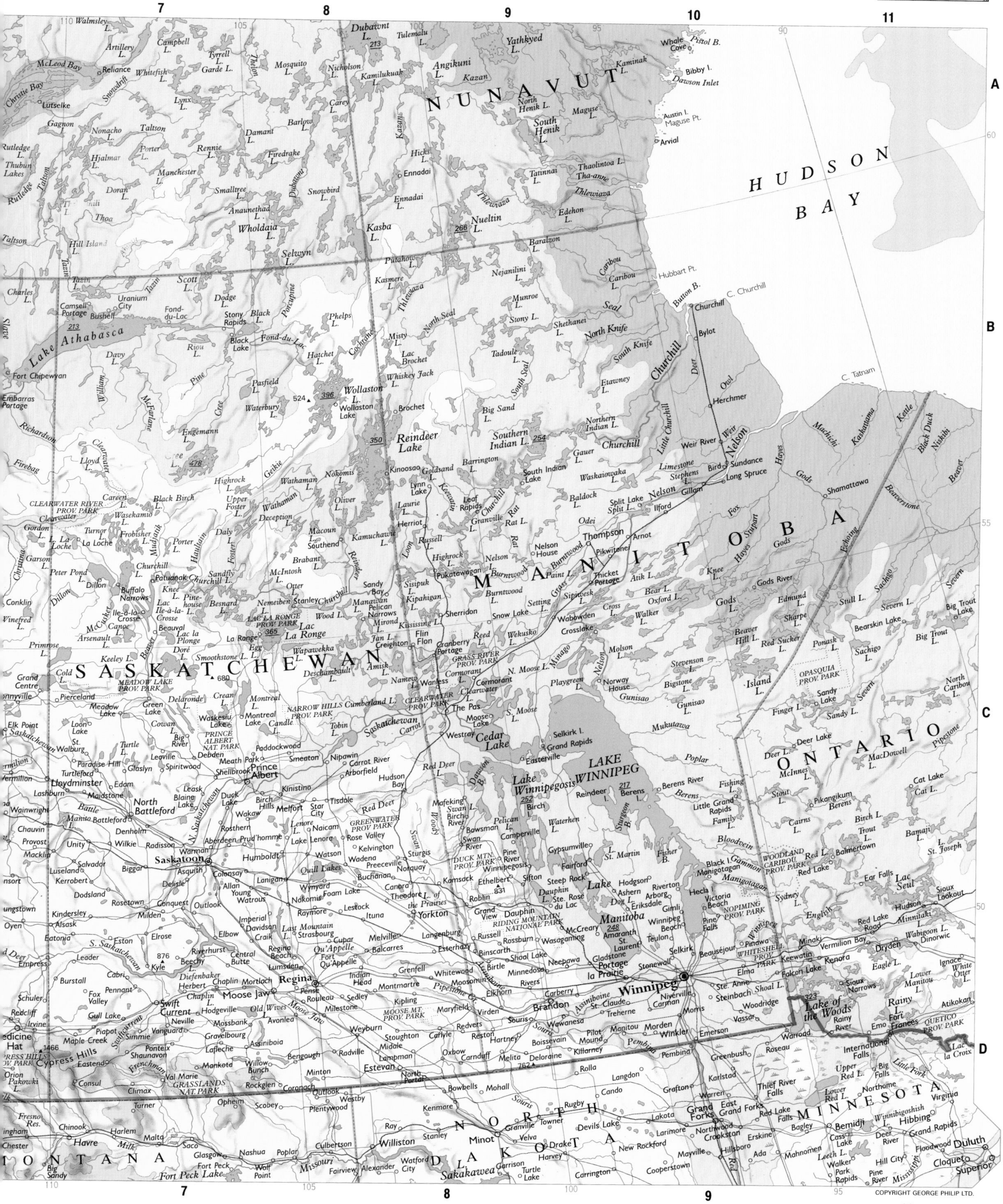
7
8
9
10
11
A
B
C
D
NUNAVUT
HUDSON BAY
MANITOBA
SASKATCHEWAN
ONTARIO
MINNESOTA
NORTH DAKOTA
MONTANA
Walmsley L.
Artillery L.
Campbell L.
Tyrrell L.
Garde L.
Thelon
Mosquito L.
Nicholson L.
Dubawnt L.
Tulemalu L.
Yathkyed L.
Whale Cove
Pistol B.
Kaminak L.
Bibby I.
Dawson Inlet
McLeod Bay
Reliance
Whitefish L.
Snowdrift
Christie Bay
Lutselke
Lynx L.
Kamilukuak L.
Angikuni L.
Kazan
North Henik L.
South Henik L.
Maguse L.
Austin I.
Maguse Pt.
Arviat
Gagnon
Nonacho L.
Taltson
Damant L.
Barlow L.
Carey L.
Rutledge L.
Thubun Lakes
Hjalmar L.
Porter L.
Rennie L.
Firedrake L.
Hicks L.
Ennadai
Thaolintoa L.
Tha-anne
Tatinnai L.
Manchester L.
Doran L.
Smalltree L.
Dubawnt
Snowbird L.
Ennadai L.
Thlewiaza
Edehon L.
Thoa
Anaunethad L.
Wholdaia L.
Kasba L.
Nueltin L.
266
213
Hill Island L.
Selwyn L.
Baralzon L.
Putahow L.
Tazin L.
Scott L.
Kasmere L.
Nejanilini L.
Caribou L.
Hubbart Pt.
Charles L.
Uranium City
Dodge L.
Fond-du-Lac
Camsell Portage
Bushell
Stony Rapids
Black L.
Porcupine
Phelps L.
Munroe L.
Stony L.
Seal
Button B.
C. Churchill
Churchill
Bylot
Lake Athabasca
Black Lake
Fond-du-Lac
Riou L.
Hatchet L.
Cochrane
Misty L.
North Seal
Lac Brochet
Tadoule L.
Shethanei L.
North Knife
South Knife
Davy L.
Fort Chipewyan
Pine
Pasfield L.
Waterbury L.
524
396
Wollaston L.
Wollaston Lake
Whiskey Jack
South Seal
Etawney L.
Deer
Owl
C. Tatnam
Herchmer
Embarras Portage
William
McFarlane
Cree
Brochet
Big Sand L.
Northern Indian L.
Little Churchill
Richardson
Clearwater
Engemann L.
350
Reindeer Lake
Southern Indian L.
254
Churchill
Weir River
Weir
Nelson
Machichi
Kaskattama
Kettle
Black Duck
Niskibi
Firebag
Lloyd L.
478
Highrock L.
Geikie
Nokomis L.
Kinoosao
Goldsand L.
Barrington L.
South Indian Lake
Gauer L.
Waskaiowaka L.
Limestone
Stephens L.
Bird
Sundance
Long Spruce
Hayes
Gods
Beaver
Careen L.
Black Birch
Wathaman L.
Upper Foster L.
Lynn Lake
Leaf Rapids
Baldock L.
Split Lake
Nelson
Gillam
Shamattawa
Beaverstone
CLEARWATER RIVER PROV. PARK
Wasekamio L.
Wathaman
Deception L.
Oliver L.
Laurie L.
Keewatin
Churchill
Rat
Split L.
Ilford
Fox
Stupart
Gordon L.
Turnor L.
Frobisher L.
Mudjatik
Macoun L.
Herriot
Granville L.
Rat L.
Odei
Arnot
Thompson
La Loche
Daly L.
Southend
Kamuchawie L.
Russell L.
Nelson House
Pikwitonei
Gods
Echoing
Garson L.
Porter L.
Haultain
Foster
Brabant L.
Reindeer
Loon
Highrock L.
Nelson L.
Burntwood
Christina
Peter Pond L.
Churchill L.
Patuanak
Churchill
Sandfly L.
McIntosh L.
Otter L.
Sandy Bay
Sisipuk L.
Pukatawagan L.
Paint L.
Thicket Portage
Atik L.
Knee L.
Gods River
Severn
Dillon
Buffalo Narrows
Knee L.
Pinehouse L.
Bear L.
Oxford L.
Edmund L.
Sachigo
Conklin
Dillon
Ile-à-la-Crosse
Lac Ile-à-la-Crosse
Besnard L.
Nemeiben L.
Stanley
Churchill
Kipahigan L.
Burntwood L.
Setting L.
Grass
Sipiwesk L.
Gods L.
Still L.
Severn L.
Big Trout Lake
Winefred L.
McCusker
Canoe L.
LAC LA RONGE PROV. PARK
Manawan L.
Pelican Narrows
Mirond L.
Wood L.
Kississing L.
Sherridon
Snow Lake
Wabowden
Cross L.
Walker L.
Sharpe L.
Bearskin Lake
Arsenault L.
Beauval
Lac la Plonge
La Ronge
365
Lac La Ronge
Jan L.
Flin Flon
Reed L.
Wekusko L.
Crosslake
Beaver Hill L.
Big Trout L.
Primrose L.
Doré L.
Egg L.
Smoothstone L.
Wapawekka L.
Creighton
Cranberry Portage
GRASS RIVER PROV. PARK
Minago
Nelson
Molson L.
Red Sucker L.
Ponask L.
Sachigo L.
Keeley L.
Beaver
Deschambault L.
Amisk L.
Cormorant L.
N. Moose L.
Stevenson L.
Island L.
Cold L.
680
Namew L.
Wanless
Cormorant
Playgreen L.
Norway House
Bigstone L.
OPASQUIA PROV. PARK
North Caribou L.
Grand Centre
Pierceland
MEADOW LAKE PROV. PARK
Crean L.
Delaronde L.
Montreal L.
NARROW HILLS PROV. PARK
Cumberland L.
Clearwater
CLEARWATER PROV. PARK
The Pas
Gunisao
Gunisao L.
Sandy Lake
Finger L.
Sandy L.
Meadow Lake
Green Lake
Waskesiu Lake
Montreal Lake
Candle L.
Tobin L.
Saskatchewan
Carrot
Moose Lake
S. Moose L.
Mukutawa
Elk Point
Loon Lake
Cowan L.
PRINCE ALBERT NAT. PARK
Big River
Westray
Cedar Lake
Selkirk I.
Grand Rapids
Deer L.
Deer Lake
Pipestone
St. Walburg
Turtle L.
Paddockwood
Easterville
Poplar
MacDowell L.
Paradise Hill
Glaslyn
Leoville
Spiritwood
Debden
Smeaton
Nipawin
Carrot River
LAKE WINNIPEG
McInnes L.
Turtleford
Meath Park
Shellbrook
Prince Albert
Arborfield
Red Deer L.
Dawson B.
Lloydminster
Edam
Hudson Bay
Lake Winnipegosis
217
Berens River
Fishing L.
Cat Lake
Cat L.
Lashburn
Maidstone
Leask
Blaine Lake
Duck Lake
Kinistino
Birch Hills
Star City
Tisdale
Red Deer
Mafeking
Swan L.
Birch River
252
Birch
Reindeer L.
Berens I.
Berens
Little Grand Rapids
Stout L.
Pikangikum
Berens
Wainwright
Battle
North Battleford
Wakaw
Melfort
Woody
Family L.
Chauvin
Manito
Battleford
Denholm
Rosthern
Lenore L.
Naicam
GREENWATER PROV. PARK
Bowsman
Pelican L.
Waterhen L.
Sturgeon B.
Cairns L.
Birch L.
Trout L.
Bamaji L.
Provost
Unity
Wilkie
Radisson
Aberdeen
Prud'homme
Lake Lenore
Rose Valley
Swan River
Camperville
Bloodvein
Macklin
Salvador
Saskatoon
Humboldt
Watson
Kelvington
Gypsumville
St. Martin L.
Fisher B.
Gammon
WOODLAND CARIBOU PROV. PARK
Red L.
Balmertown
St. Joseph L.
Luseland
Biggar
Asquith
Colonsay
Quill Lakes
Wadena
Preeceville
Sturgis
DUCK MTN. PROV. PARK
Pine River
Winnipegosis
Fairford
Black L.
Manigotagan
Red Lake
Kerrobert
Delisle
Lanigan
Buchanan
Norquay
Kamsack
Ethelbert
Sifton
Steep Rock
Hodgson
Riverton
Manigotagan
Ear Falls
Lac Seul
Sioux Lookout
Dodsland
Allan
Young
Watrous
Wynyard
Foam Lake
Canora
Theodore
L. of the Prairies
831
Lake
Ashern
Arborg
Hecla I.
Victoria Beach
Sydney L.
Rosetown
Conquest
Outlook
Nokomis
Roblin
Dauphin L.
Ste. Rose du Lac
Dog L.
Eriksdale
NOPIMING PROV. PARK
English
Hudson
Minnitaki L.
Kindersley
Alsask
Milden
Raymore
Lestock
Ituna
Yorkton
Grand View
Dauphin
RIDING MOUNTAIN NATIONAL PARK
Manitoba
248
Gimli
Winnipeg Beach
Pine Falls
Winnipeg
Red Lake Road
Wabigoon L.
Dinorwic
Oyen
Imperial
Davidson
Last Mountain L.
Strasbourg
Langenburg
Russell
McCreary
Amaranth
Teulon
Minaki
Vermilion Bay
Dryden
Eatonia
Eston
Elrose
Elbow
Craik
Cupar
Melville
Esterhazy
Rossburn
Wasagaming
St. Laurent
Beausejour
WHITESHELL PROV. PARK
Keewatin
Kenora
Eagle L.
Ignace
White Otter L.
Empress
S. Saskatchewan
Leader
876
Kyle
Riverhurst
Beechy
Central Butte
Regina Beach
Qu'Appelle
Fort Qu'Appelle
Balcarres
Binscarth
Shoal Lake
Neepawa
Gladstone
Portage la Prairie
Stonewall
Selkirk
Elma
Falcon Lake
Lower Manitou L.
Burstall
Cabri
Diefenbaker
Herbert
Chaplin
Mortlach
Lumsden
Regina
Indian Head
Grenfell
Whitewood
Moosomin
Birtle
Minnedosa
Rivers
Ste. Anne
Steinbach
Shoal L.
Sioux Narrows
Schuler
Fox Valley
Pennant
Swift Current
Chaplin L.
Moose Jaw
Pense
Rouleau
Montmartre
Sedley
Pipestone Cr.
Elkhorn
Brandon
Carberry
Assiniboine
St. Claude
Niverville
Carman
323
Lake of the Woods
Rainy L.
Atikokan
Redcliff
Irvine
Gull Lake
Hodgeville
Old Wives L.
Moose Jaw
Milestone
Kipling
MOOSE MT. PROV. PARK
Maryfield
Virden
Souris
Wawanesa
Treherne
Morris
Woodridge
Vassar
Rainy River
Emo
Fort Frances
QUETICO PROV. PARK
Medicine Hat
Piapot
Neville
Mossbank
Avonlea
Weyburn
Redvers
Reston
Hartney
Pilot Mound
Manitou
Morden
Winkler
Emerson
Warroad
Maple Creek
Simmie
Vanguard
Gravelbourg
Assiniboia
Stoughton
Carlyle
Boissevain
Pembina
1466
Cypress Hills
Eastend
Pontelx
Shaunavon
Bengough
Radville
Midale
Lampman
Oxbow
Carnduff
Melita
Deloraine
Killarney
Roseau
International Falls
Lac la Croix
Frenchman
Mankota
Willow Bunch
Minton
Estevan
762
Pembina
Greenbush
Orion
Pakowki L.
Consul
Val Marie
GRASSLANDS NAT. PARK
Rockglen
Coronach
North Portal
Rolla
Langdon
Karlstad
Upper Red L.
Big Falls
Little Fork
Climax
Outlook
Westby
Bowbells
Mohall
Cando
Grafton
Thief River Falls
Lower Red L.
Northome
Virginia
Turner
Opheim
Scobey
Plentywood
Souris
Rugby
Warren
East Grand Forks
Grand Forks
Red Lake Falls
Fresno Res.
Kenmare
Towner
Devils Lake
Lakota
Winnibigoshish L.
Bemidji
Hibbing
Chinook
Harlem
Malta
Ray
Granville
Minot
Velva
Larimore
Northwood
Crookston
Erskine
Bagley
Cass Lake
Grand Rapids
Havre
Milk
Saco
Glasgow
Nashua
Poplar
Culbertson
Williston
Stanley
Drake
Harvey
New Rockford
Mayville
Hillsboro
Ada
Mahnomen
Leech L.
Deer River
Floodwood
Duluth
Big Sandy
Fort Peck
Fort Peck Lake
Wolf Point
Missouri
Fairview
Alexander
Watford City
Sakakawea
Garrison
Turtle Lake
Carrington
Cooperstown
Walker
Park Rapids
Pine River
Mississippi
Hill City
Cloquet
Superior
Red
60
55
50
110
105
100
95
90

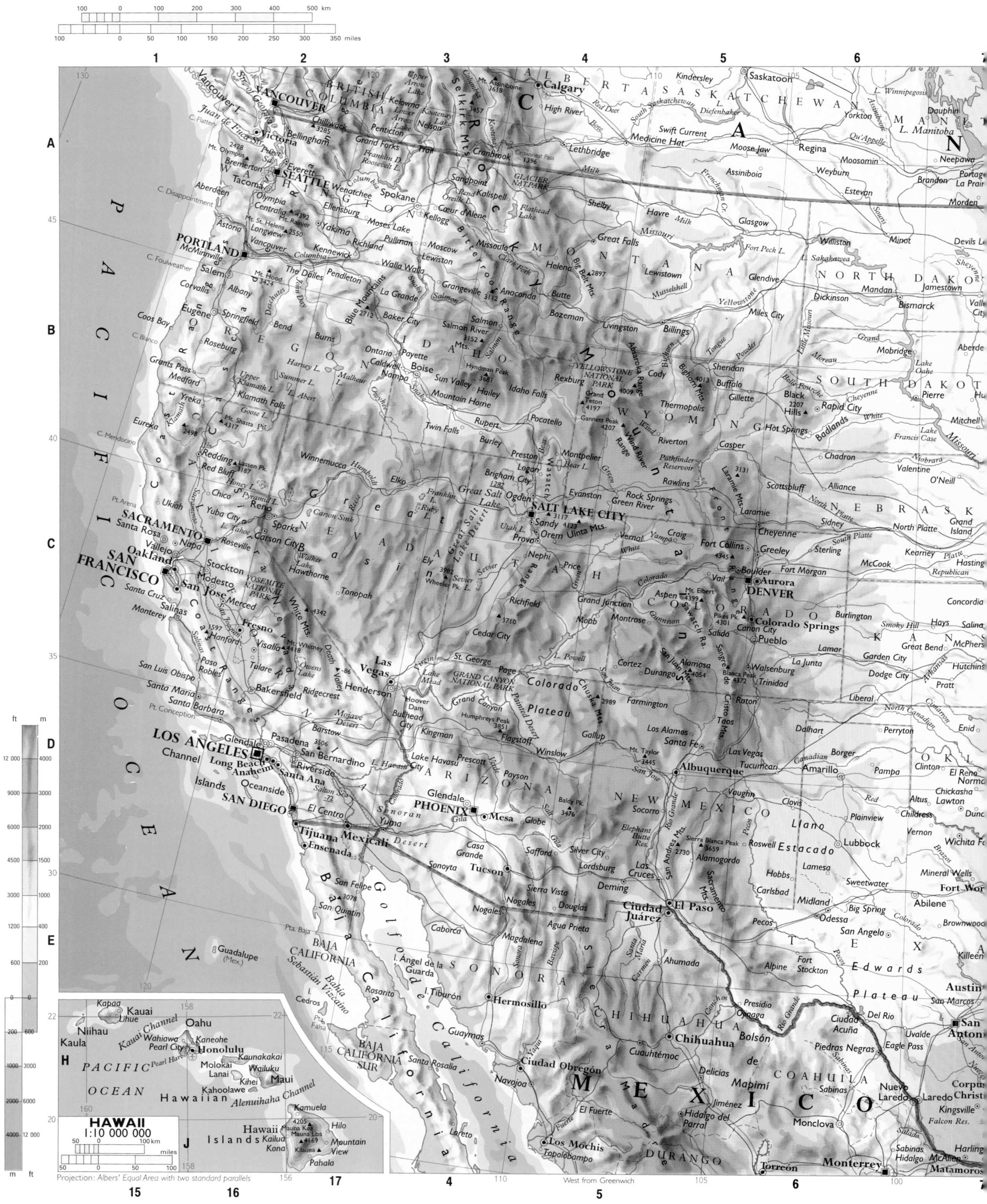
100 0 100 200 300 400 500 km
100 0 50 100 150 200 250 300 350 miles
1 2 3 4 5 6 7
A B C D E H J
ft m
12 000 4000
9000 3000
6000 2000
4500 1500
3000 1000
1200 400
600 200
0 0
200 600
1000 3000
2000 6000
4000 12 000
PACIFIC OCEAN
BRITISH COLUMBIA
ALBERTA
SASKATCHEWAN
CANADA
MANITOBA
WASHINGTON
OREGON
IDAHO
MONTANA
WYOMING
NORTH DAKOTA
SOUTH DAKOTA
NEBRASKA
KANSAS
COLORADO
UTAH
NEVADA
CALIFORNIA
ARIZONA
NEW MEXICO
TEXAS
OKLAHOMA
MEXICO
BAJA CALIFORNIA
BAJA CALIFORNIA SUR
SONORA
CHIHUAHUA
COAHUILA
DURANGO
ROCKY MOUNTAINS
Great Basin
Colorado Plateau
Llano Estacado
Edwards Plateau
Sonoran Desert
Mojave Desert
Golfo de California
Great Salt Lake
Great Salt Lake Desert
Coast Ranges
Sierra Nevada
Cascade Range
Bitterroot Range
Wind River Range
Bighorn Mts.
Uinta Mts.
Sangre de Cristo Mts.
San Juan Mts.
Sierra Madre
YELLOWSTONE NATIONAL PARK
GRAND CANYON NATIONAL PARK
YOSEMITE NATIONAL PARK
GLACIER NAT. PARK
Black Hills
Badlands
VANCOUVER
Victoria
SEATTLE
Tacoma
Spokane
PORTLAND
Salem
Eugene
Boise
Calgary
Saskatoon
Regina
Medicine Hat
Lethbridge
Great Falls
Helena
Missoula
Billings
Bismarck
Pierre
Rapid City
Casper
Cheyenne
SALT LAKE CITY
Ogden
Provo
Reno
Carson City
SACRAMENTO
SAN FRANCISCO
Oakland
San Jose
Fresno
Bakersfield
Las Vegas
LOS ANGELES
Long Beach
Anaheim
Santa Ana
San Bernardino
SAN DIEGO
Tijuana
Mexicali
Ensenada
PHOENIX
Mesa
Tucson
Flagstaff
Albuquerque
Santa Fe
DENVER
Boulder
Colorado Springs
Pueblo
El Paso
Ciudad Juárez
Chihuahua
Hermosillo
Ciudad Obregón
Los Mochis
Torreón
Monterrey
Amarillo
Lubbock
Odessa
Midland
San Angelo
Abilene
Austin
San Antonio
Nuevo Laredo
Laredo
Corpus Christi
Matamoros
HAWAII
1:10 000 000
Kauai
Oahu
Honolulu
Niihau
Molokai
Lanai
Maui
Kahoolawe
Hawaii
Hilo
Hawaiian Islands
PACIFIC OCEAN
Projection: Albers' Equal Area with two standard parallels
West from Greenwich
15 16 17 4 5 6

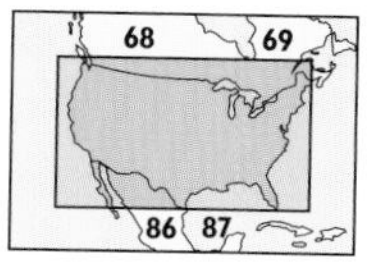
68
69
86
87

8
9
10
11
12
13
A
B
C
D
E
F
95
90
85
80
75
65
45
40
35
30
25
C A N A D A
O N T A R I O
Q U E B E C
Lake Winnipeg
Winnipeg
Lake of the Woods
Kenora
Dryden
Sioux Lookout
Lake Nipigon
Nipigon
Thunder Bay
Nakina
Hearst
Geraldton
Marathon
Wawa
Moosonee
Cochrane
Timmins
Kirkland Lake
Rouyn-Noranda
Amos
L. Abitibi
L. Matagami
Chibougamau
L. Chibougamau
Baie-Comeau
Matane
Rimouski
Rivière-du-Loup
Edmundston
Chicoutimi
Alma
Jonquière
Roberval
La Tuque
Québec
Shawinigan
Trois-Rivières
Joliette
Drummondville
Sherbrooke
Mont-Laurier
MONTREAL
Ottawa
Hull
Pembroke
North Bay
Sudbury
Sault Ste. Marie
L. Nipissing
Huntsville
Manitoulin I.
Parry Sound
Georgian Bay
Orillia
Peterborough
Kingston
Barrie
Owen Sound
Oshawa
TORONTO
Kitchener
Hamilton
London
Windsor
Lake Superior
Lake Michigan
Lake Huron
Lake Erie
Lake Ontario
I. Royale
NEW BRUNSWICK
Saint John
Fort Kent
Caribou
Presque Isle
Houlton
Millinocket
Moosehead L.
Calais
MAINE
Bangor
Waterville
Belfast
Penobscot Bay
Augusta
Lewiston
Portland
Farmington
Berlin
White Mts.
NEW HAMPSHIRE
VERMONT
Montpelier
Burlington
Plattsburgh
L. Champlain
Adirondack Mts.
Rutland
Concord
Manchester
Nashua
Lawrence
Lowell
BOSTON
C. Cod
Worcester
Providence
Fall River
New Bedford
Nantucket I.
Martha's Vineyard
HARTFORD
Springfield
New Haven
Bridgeport
Yonkers
Long I.
NEW YORK
Newark
Paterson
Jersey City
Trenton
PHILADELPHIA
Atlantic City
Albany
Troy
Schenectady
Utica
Syracuse
Rochester
Niagara Falls
BUFFALO
Oswego
Watertown
Glens Falls
Catskill Mts.
Poughkeepsie
Binghamton
Ithaca
Elmira
Jamestown
Erie
Bradford
Scranton
Wilkes-Barre
Allentown
Reading
Lancaster
Harrisburg
Williamsport
Altoona
Johnstown
PITTSBURGH
PENNSYLVANIA
Wilmington
Dover
BALTIMORE
Annapolis
WASHINGTON D.C.
C. May
Delaware B.
Salisbury
Chesapeake Bay
Frederick
Cumberland
Morgantown
Clarksburg
Elkins
WEST VIRGINIA
Parkersburg
Charleston
Huntington
Beckley
Bluefield
Harrisonburg
Charlottesville
Richmond
Lynchburg
Petersburg
Roanoke
Newport News
Virginia Beach
Norfolk
Elizabeth City
Albemarle Sd.
Pamlico Sd.
C. Hatteras
Rocky Mount
Greenville
Goldsboro
Raleigh
Durham
Greensboro
Winston-Salem
Danville
Hickory
NORTH CAROLINA
CHARLOTTE
Fayetteville
New Bern
Jacksonville
Onslow Bay
Wilmington
C. Fear
Rock Hill
Florence
Myrtle Beach
Long Bay
Sumter
Columbia
SOUTH CAROLINA
Georgetown
C. Romain
Orangeburg
Charleston
Spartanburg
Greenville
Anderson
Asheville
Knoxville
Johnson City
Kingsport
CLEVELAND
Akron
Youngstown
Canton
Mansfield
Sandusky
Toledo
Findlay
Lima
Marion
COLUMBUS
Zanesville
Wheeling
Dayton
Springfield
CINCINNATI
Portsmouth
Maysville
Ashtabula
Warren
Oil City
DETROIT
Ann Arbor
Flint
Port Huron
Lansing
Jackson
Battle Creek
Kalamazoo
Grand Rapids
Muskegon
Midland
Saginaw
Bay City
Saginaw Bay
Alpena
Petoskey
Traverse City
Manistee
Cadillac
Ludington
Escanaba
Manistique
Marquette
Ishpeming
Iron Mountain
Houghton
Keweenaw Bay
Whitefish Bay
Michipicoten I.
North Channel
Apostle Is.
Ironwood
Ashland
Superior
Duluth
Two Harbors
Hibbing
Virginia
Ely
International Falls
Fort Frances
Rainy L.
Thief River Falls
Grand Forks
Red Lake
Bemidji
Leech L.
Moorhead
Fargo
MINNESOTA
Fergus Falls
Brainerd
Mille Lacs
St. Cloud
Big Stone Lake
Watertown
Willmar
MINNEAPOLIS
ST. PAUL
Red Wing
Coon Rapids
Brookings
Mankato
Owatonna
Rochester
Austin
Winona
La Crosse
Madison
Sioux Falls
Worthington
Albert Lea
Mason City
Charles City
Spencer
Cherokee
Fort Dodge
Sioux City
Waterloo
Cedar Rapids
Dubuque
IOWA
Des Moines
Ames
Iowa City
Davenport
Rock Island
Clinton
Council Bluffs
Omaha
Lincoln
Norfolk
Columbus
Red Oak
Creston
Ottumwa
Burlington
Galesburg
Maryville
Kirksville
Beatrice
St. Joseph
Chillicothe
Hannibal
Quincy
Manhattan
Topeka
Leavenworth
KANSAS CITY
Lawrence
Sedalia
Jefferson City
Columbia
MISSOURI
ST. LOUIS
East St. Louis
Alton
L. of the Ozarks
Emporia
Rolla
Wichita
Newton
Fort Scott
Nevada
Pittsburg
Joplin
Springfield
Parsons
Arkansas City
Bartlesville
Ponca City
Tulsa
Muskogee
Lebanon
Ozark Plateau
West Plains
Poplar Bluff
Cape Girardeau
Carbondale
Paragould
Fayetteville
Boston Mts.
Jonesboro
Blytheville
Newport
Russellville
Conway
Fort Smith
McAlester
Ouachita Mts.
Little Rock
Stuttgart
Hot Springs
ARKANSAS
Pine Bluff
Oklahoma City
Shawnee
Ardmore
Durant
Paris
Sherman
Texarkana
Hope
Camden
El Dorado
Denton
DALLAS
Arlington
Marshall
Longview
Tyler
Shreveport
Monroe
Vicksburg
Corsicana
Palestine
Waco
Nacogdoches
Lufkin
Natchitoches
Alexandria
Natchez
De Ridder
Huntsville
Temple
Bryan
LOUISIANA
Lake Charles
Baton Rouge
Lafayette
Beaumont
Port Arthur
HOUSTON
Pasadena
Galveston
New Iberia
Houma
Marsh I.
Atchafalaya B.
Morgan City
NEW ORLEANS
L. Pontchartrain
Breton Sd.
Mississippi River Delta
Freeport
Port Lavaca
Matagorda I.
Aransas Pass
Laguna Madre
Brownsville
Rio Grande
GULF OF MEXICO
WISCONSIN
Eau Claire
Wausau
Stevens Point
Rhinelander
Merrill
Menominee
Green Bay
Appleton
Manitowoc
Oshkosh
Sheboygan
Portage
MILWAUKEE
Janesville
Racine
Kenosha
Rockford
Elgin
CHICAGO
Aurora
Joliet
Gary
South Bend
Elkhart
Fort Wayne
Kankakee
Midwest
Peoria
Bloomington
Champaign
Springfield
Decatur
Danville
Kokomo
Muncie
Lafayette
INDIANAPOLIS
Richmond
ILLINOIS
INDIANA
Terre Haute
Mattoon
Effingham
Bloomington
Columbus
Vincennes
Louisville
Frankfort
Lexington
Richmond
Evansville
Owensboro
Mount Vernon
Henderson
Danville
KENTUCKY
Hazard
Somerset
Bowling Green
Hopkinsville
Paducah
Mayfield
Clarksville
Nashville
Murfreesboro
Oak Ridge
Middlesboro
Dyersburg
TENNESSEE
Jackson
Memphis
Columbia
Chattanooga
Athens
Corinth
Florence
Huntsville
Clarksdale
Oxford
Tupelo
Decatur
Greenwood
Cleveland
Greenville
MISSISSIPPI
Yazoo City
Columbus
Birmingham
Tuscaloosa
ALABAMA
Anniston
Gadsden
Meridian
Demopolis
Selma
Montgomery
Jackson
McComb
Laurel
Hattiesburg
Bogalusa
Gulfport
Biloxi
Mobile
Greenville
Troy
Andalusia
Dothan
Pensacola
Panama City
Apalachicola
C. San Blas
Tallahassee
Thomasville
Valdosta
Tifton
Albany
Cordele
Columbus
Auburn
La Grange
Macon
Dublin
GEORGIA
ATLANTA
Rome
Gainesville
Roswell
Athens
Augusta
Statesboro
Savannah
Douglas
Waycross
Brunswick
Lake City
Jacksonville
St. Augustine
Gainesville
Ocala
Daytona Beach
Deltona
C. Canaveral
Orlando
Melbourne
Lakeland
TAMPA
Clearwater
St. Petersburg
Tampa B.
Sarasota
Palm Bay
Fort Pierce
West Palm Beach
Fort Lauderdale
MIAMI
Fort Myers
Cape Coral
Charlotte Harbor
Naples
L. Okeechobee
The Everglades
C. Sable
Florida Bay
Florida Keys
Key West
Straits of Florida
FLORIDA
Apalachee B.
Grand Bahama I.
Freeport
Little Abaco I.
Great Abaco I.
N.E. Providence Channel
N.W. Providence Channel
BAHAMAS
Eleuthera I.
Nassau
New Providence I.
Cat I.
Exuma Sound
Andros I.
Great Exuma I.
Long I.
ATLANTIC OCEAN
Appalachian Mts.
Allegheny Mts.
Blue Ridge
Cumberland Plateau

8
9
10
11
12

50 0 50 100 150 200 km
50 0 50 100 150 miles
LAKE SUPERIOR
LAKE MICHIGAN
LAKE HURON
Georgian Bay
LAKE ERIE
LAKE ONTARIO
ONTARIO
QUEBEC
CANADA
MICHIGAN
WISCONSIN
ILLINOIS
INDIANA
OHIO
KENTUCKY
WEST VIRGINIA
VIRGINIA
PENNSYLVANIA
NEW YORK
VERMONT
NEW HAMPSHIRE
MASS.
CONN.
R.I.
NEW JERSEY
DELAWARE
MARYLAND
Chesapeake Bay
Delaware Bay
Long Island
Cape Cod
MONTREAL
OTTAWA
TORONTO
Québec
CHICAGO
MILWAUKEE
DETROIT
CLEVELAND
PITTSBURGH
BUFFALO
COLUMBUS
INDIANAPOLIS
CINCINNATI
NEW YORK CITY
PHILADELPHIA
BALTIMORE
WASHINGTON D.C.
BOSTON
HARTFORD
Norfolk
Richmond
Sudbury
Sault Ste. Marie
Hamilton
London
Toledo
Dayton
Louisville
Lexington
Erie
Rochester
Syracuse
Albany
Scranton
Harrisburg
Allentown
Trenton
Newark
Providence
Worcester
Springfield
Lansing
Grand Rapids
Flint
Saginaw
Green Bay
Akron
Youngstown
Fort Wayne
Charleston
Roanoke
Virginia Beach

TENNESSEE
NORTH CAROLINA
SOUTH CAROLINA
GEORGIA
ALABAMA
MISSISSIPPI
FLORIDA
MAINE
NEW HAMPSHIRE
CANADA
ATLANTIC OCEAN
GULF OF MEXICO
BAHAMAS
Nashville
ATLANTA
CHARLOTTE
Jacksonville
TAMPA
MIAMI
Birmingham
Montgomery
Columbus
Macon
Savannah
Charleston
Columbia
Raleigh
Durham
Greensboro
Winston-Salem
Knoxville
Chattanooga
Huntsville
Mobile
Pensacola
Tallahassee
Orlando
St. Petersburg
Clearwater
Fort Lauderdale
Hialeah
Wilmington
Myrtle Beach
Greenville
Spartanburg
Augusta
Portland
Bangor
Lewiston
Okefenokee Swamp
BIG CYPRESS NAT. PRESERVE
EVERGLADES NAT. PARK
GREAT SMOKY MTS. NAT. PARK
ACADIA NAT. PARK
Continuation Eastwards On same scale.
West from Greenwich
Projection: Albers' Equal Area with two standard parallels
COPYRIGHT GEORGE PHILIP LTD.

NORTH-EASTERN UNITED STATES 1:2 500 000

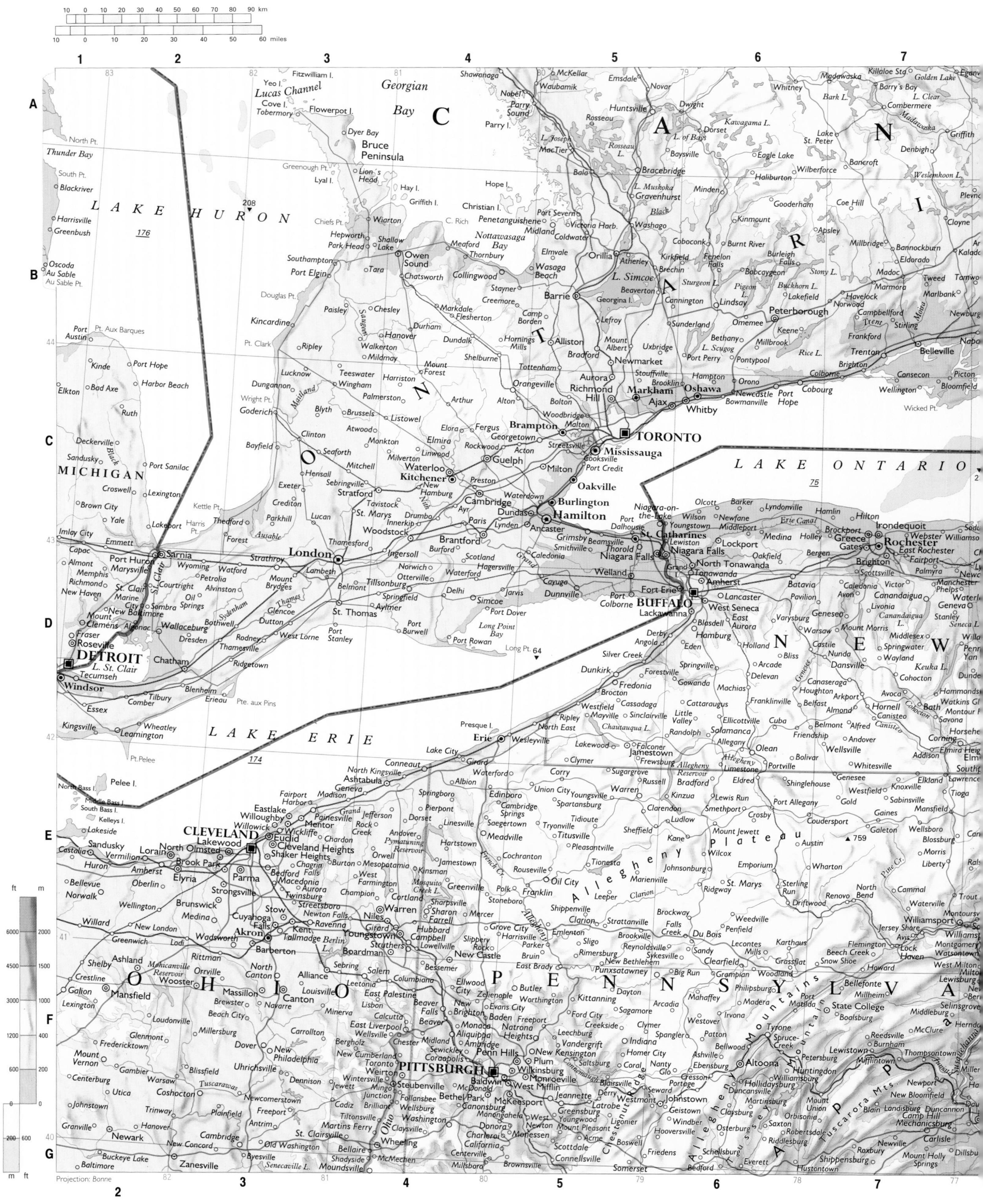

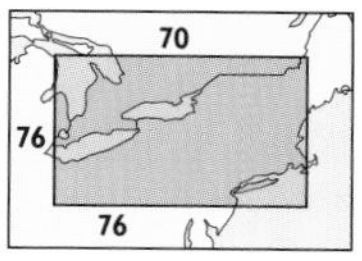
70
76
76

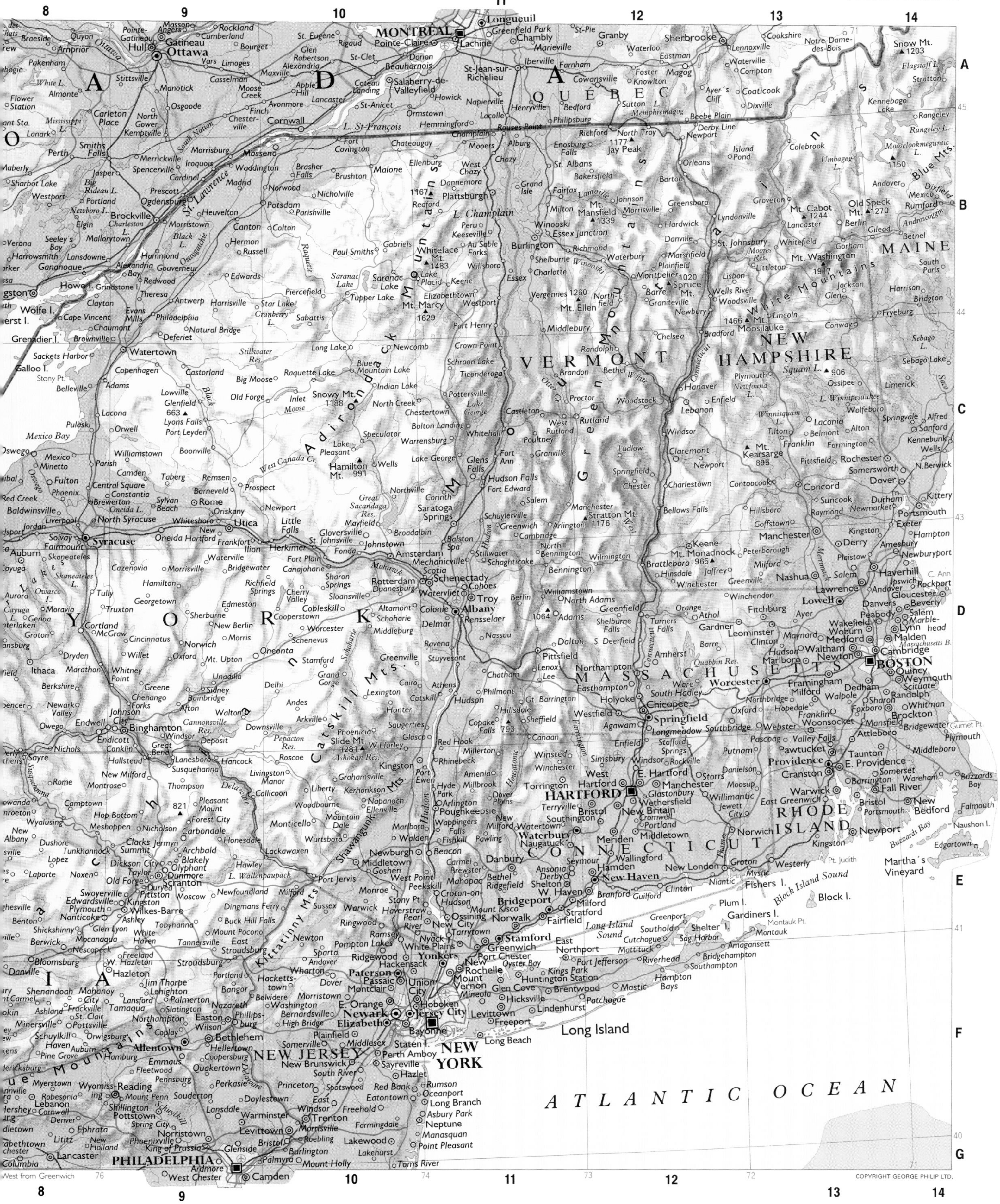
8
9
10
11
12
13
14
A
B
C
D
E
F
G
MONTREAL
Ottawa
Gatineau
Hull
Longueuil
Lachine
Pointe-Claire
Sherbrooke
Granby
Magog
Coaticook
QUÉBEC
CANADA
Cornwall
Massena
Malone
Plattsburgh
Ogdensburg
Brockville
Kingston
Watertown
Syracuse
Utica
Rome
Oswego
Auburn
Ithaca
Binghamton
Elmira
Scranton
Wilkes-Barre
Allentown
Bethlehem
Reading
PHILADELPHIA
Camden
Trenton
NEW JERSEY
Newark
Jersey City
Paterson
Elizabeth
NEW YORK
Yonkers
Long Island
Long Beach
Albany
Schenectady
Troy
Saratoga Springs
Glens Falls
Poughkeepsie
Newburgh
Kingston
Middletown
Catskill Mts.
Adirondack Mountains
Mt. Marcy 1629
L. Champlain
Burlington
Montpelier
Barre
Rutland
VERMONT
Green Mountains
Mt. Mansfield 1339
Bennington
Brattleboro
NEW HAMPSHIRE
White Mountains
Mt. Washington 1917
Concord
Manchester
Nashua
Portsmouth
MAINE
Berlin
MASSACHUSETTS
BOSTON
Cambridge
Lowell
Lawrence
Worcester
Springfield
Pittsfield
Fall River
New Bedford
RHODE ISLAND
Providence
Newport
CONNECTICUT
HARTFORD
New Haven
Bridgeport
Stamford
Waterbury
New London
Long Island Sound
Block Island Sound
Martha´s Vineyard
ATLANTIC OCEAN
West from Greenwich
76
75
74
73
72
71
45
44
43
42
41
40

COPYRIGHT GEORGE PHILIP LTD.

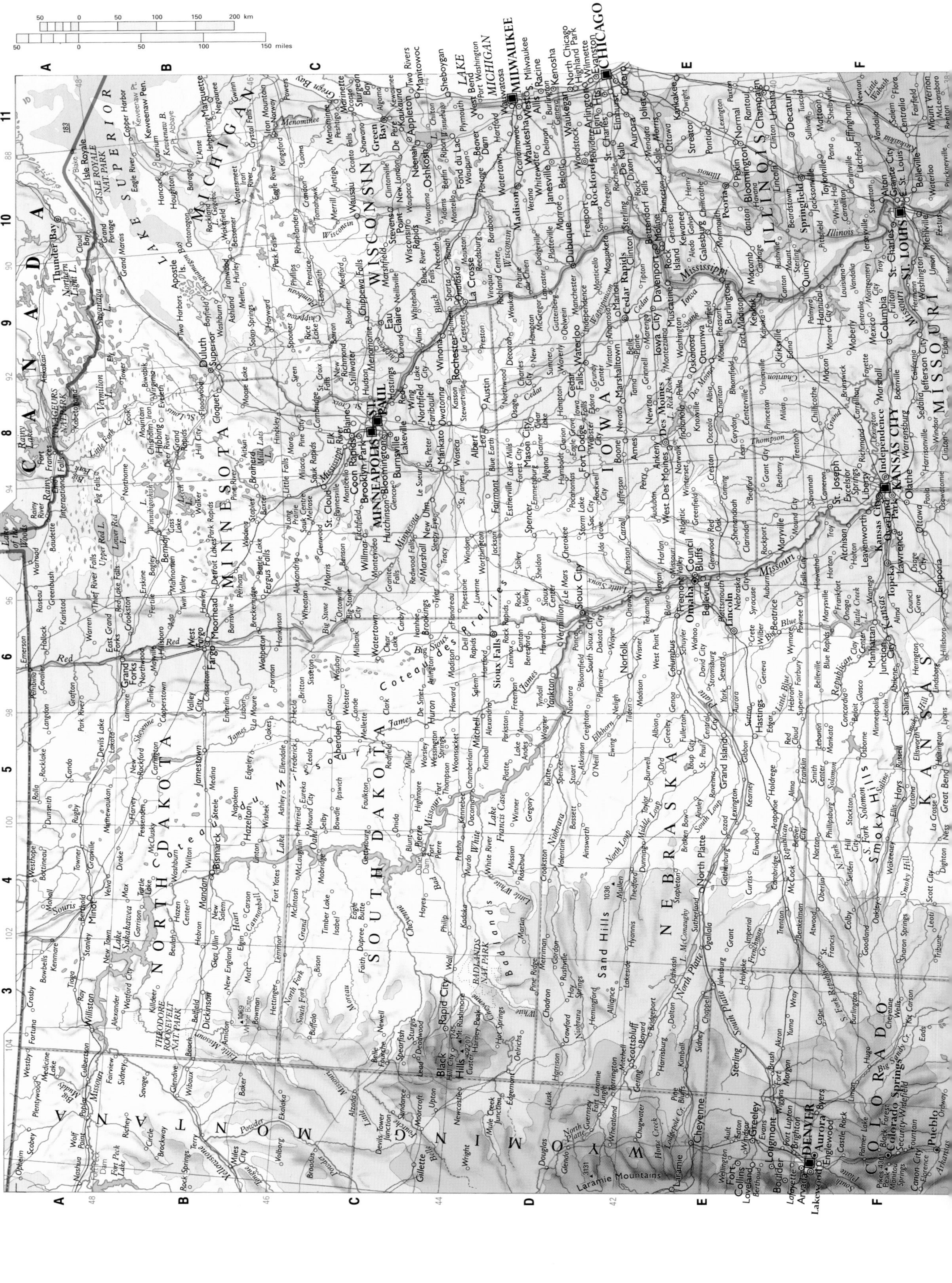
50 0 50 100 150 200 km
50 0 50 100 150 miles
CANADA
LAKE SUPERIOR
MICHIGAN
LAKE MICHIGAN
MINNESOTA
WISCONSIN
IOWA
ILLINOIS
MISSOURI
NORTH DAKOTA
SOUTH DAKOTA
NEBRASKA
KANSAS
MONTANA
WYOMING
COLORADO
MILWAUKEE
CHICAGO
MINNEAPOLIS
ST. PAUL
KANSAS CITY
ST. LOUIS
DENVER
Sand Hills
Badlands
Laramie Mountains
Smoky Hills
Coteau des Prairies
Missouri
Mississippi
Lake of the Woods

OKLAHOMA
ARKANSAS
MISSISSIPPI
LOUISIANA
TENNESSEE
TEXAS
NEW MEXICO
MEXICO
COAHUILA
CHIHUAHUA
GULF OF MEXICO
Oklahoma City
Tulsa
Wichita
Dallas
Fort Worth
Houston
San Antonio
Austin
Memphis
Little Rock
New Orleans
Shreveport
Jackson
Baton Rouge
Corpus Christi
Amarillo
Lubbock
Abilene
Waco
Laredo
Galveston
Sangre de Cristo Mts.
Llano Estacado
Edwards Plateau
Stockton Plateau
Balcones Escarpment
Boston Mts.
Ouachita Mts.
Ozark Plateau
Bolsón de Mapimí
Rio Grande
Red
Arkansas
Mississippi
Canadian
Brazos
Colorado
Pecos
Carlsbad Caverns Nat. Park
Guadalupe Mts. Nat. Park
Big Bend National Park
Continuation Southwards on same scale
ft
m
12 000
9000
6000
4500
3000
1200
600
200
0
4000
3000
2000
1500
1000
400
Projection: Albers' Equal Area with two standard parallels
West from Greenwich
COPYRIGHT GEORGE PHILIP LTD.

WESTERN UNITED STATES 1:6 000 000

50 0 50 100 150 200 km

50 0 50 100 150 miles

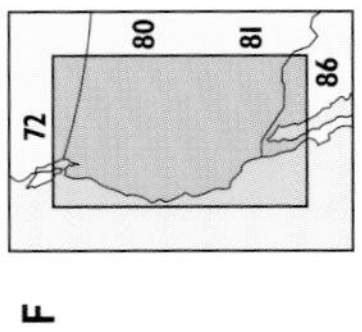

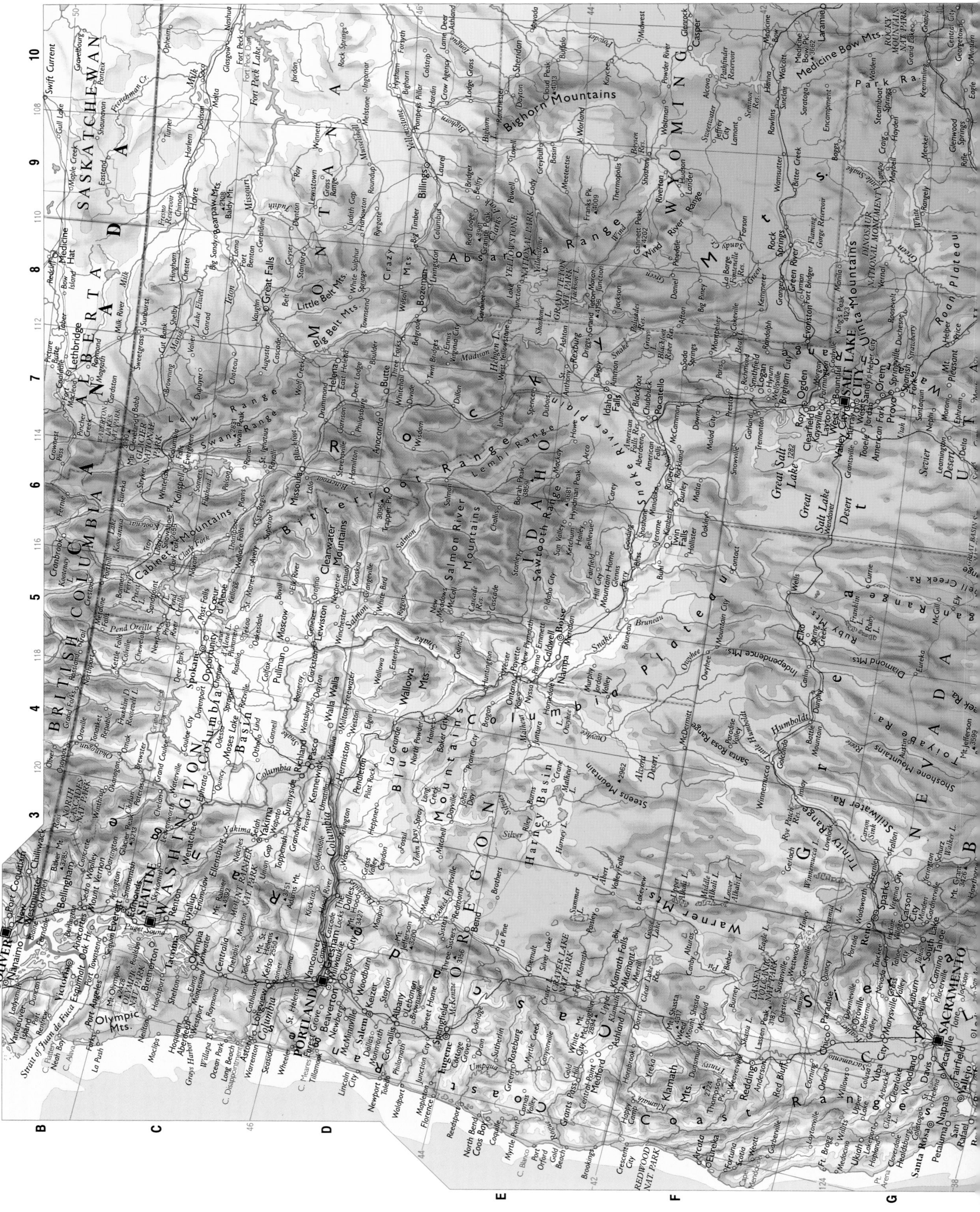

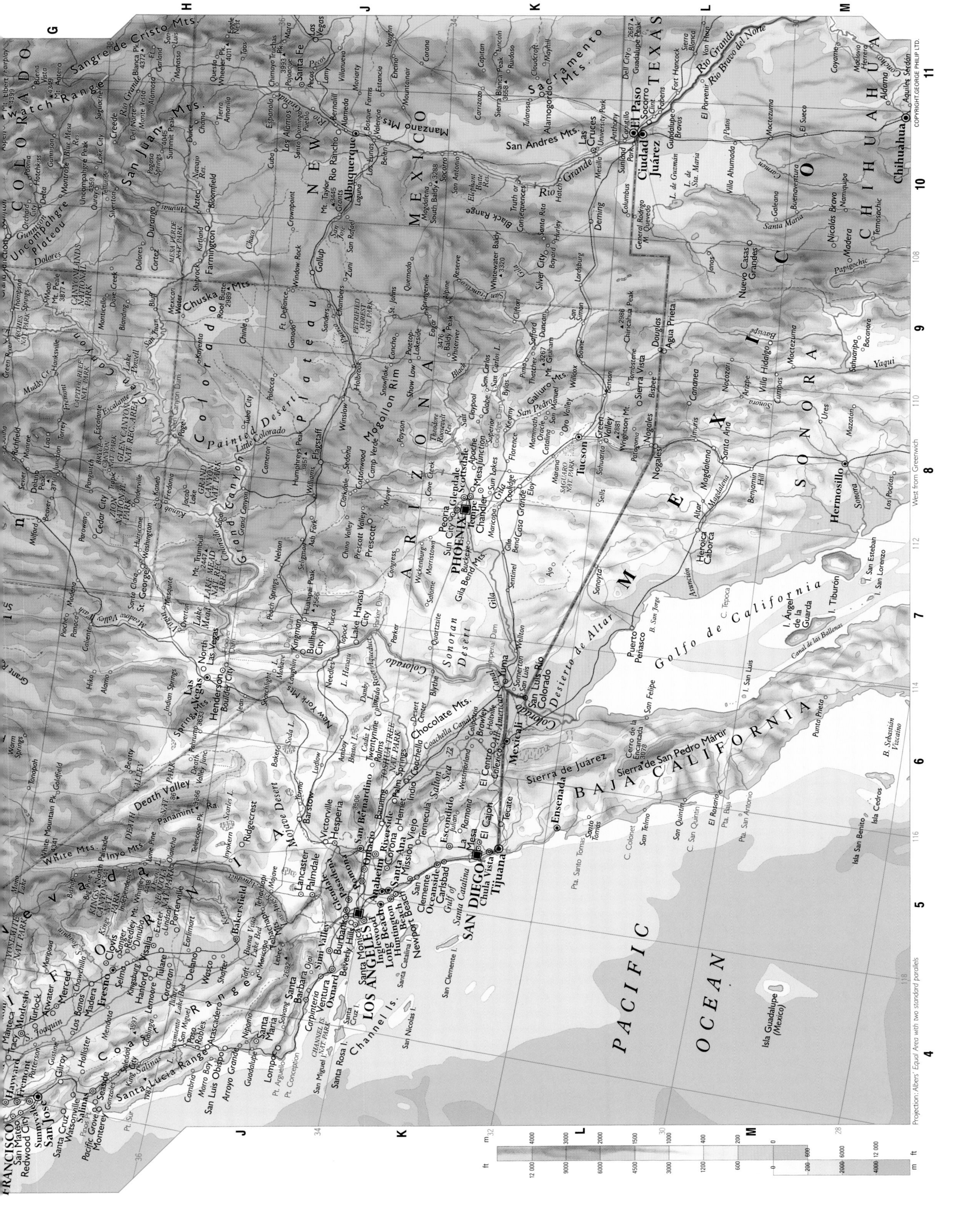
PACIFIC OCEAN
ARIZONA
NEW MEXICO
COLORADO
TEXAS
CHIHUAHUA
SONORA
BAJA CALIFORNIA
MEXICO
Golfo de California
Colorado Plateau
Painted Desert
Mojave Desert
Sonoran Desert
Desierto de Altar
Death Valley
Sangre de Cristo Mts.
San Juan Mts.
Sacramento Mts.
Chocolate Mts.
Sierra de Juárez
Sierra de San Pedro Martir
Mogollon Rim
Grand Canyon
Rio Grande
Colorado
LOS ANGELES
SAN DIEGO
PHOENIX
Albuquerque
Tucson
El Paso
Ciudad Juárez
Las Vegas
Hermosillo
Chihuahua
Tijuana
Mexicali
Santa Fe
Fresno
Bakersfield
San Bernardino
Ensenada
Channel Is.
Isla Guadalupe (Mexico)
Projection: Albers' Equal Area with two standard parallels
West from Greenwich
COPYRIGHT GEORGE PHILIP LTD.

CENTRAL AND SOUTHERN CALIFORNIA AND WESTERN WASHINGTON 1:2 500 000

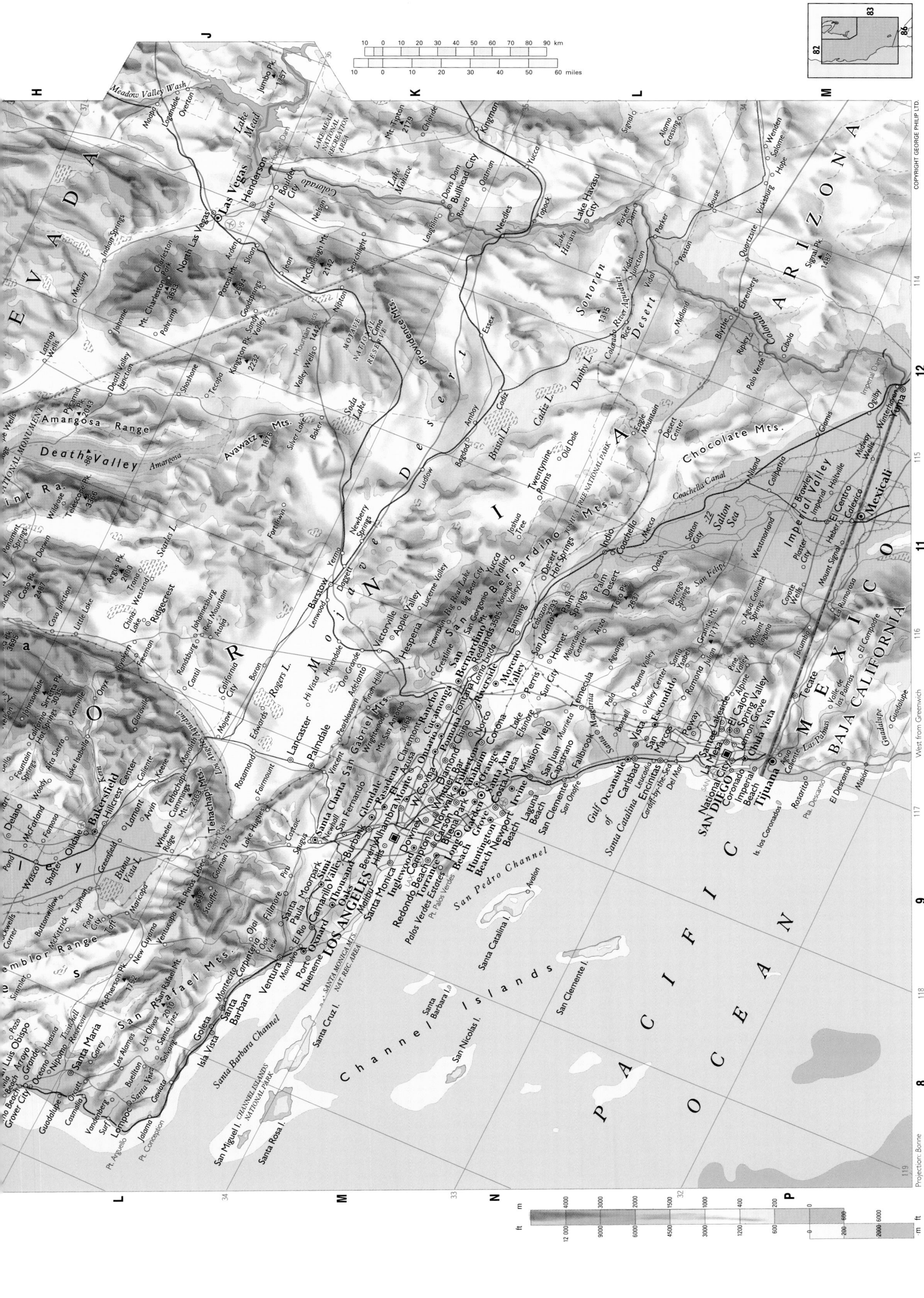
NEVADA
CALIFORNIA
ARIZONA
MEXICO
BAJA CALIFORNIA
PACIFIC OCEAN
Mojave Desert
Sonoran Desert
Death Valley
Amargosa Range
Chocolate Mts.
San Bernardino Mts.
San Gabriel Mts.
San Rafael Mts.
Temblor Range
Tehachapi Mts.
Channel Islands
Santa Barbara Channel
San Pedro Channel
Gulf of Santa Catalina
Salton Sea
Imperial Valley
Lake Mead
Lake Mohave
Las Vegas
Henderson
Kingman
Needles
Lake Havasu City
Bullhead City
Barstow
Victorville
Palmdale
Lancaster
Bakersfield
Ridgecrest
San Bernardino
Riverside
Palm Springs
Indio
LOS ANGELES
Long Beach
Santa Ana
Anaheim
Oxnard
Ventura
Santa Barbara
Santa Maria
San Luis Obispo
Oceanside
Escondido
SAN DIEGO
Chula Vista
Tijuana
Mexicali
El Centro
Yuma
Blythe
Ensenada
Santa Catalina I.
San Clemente I.
San Nicolas I.
Santa Cruz I.
Santa Rosa I.
San Miguel I.
Projection: Bonne
West from Greenwich
COPYRIGHT GEORGE PHILIP LTD.
km
miles

MEXICO 1:8 000 000

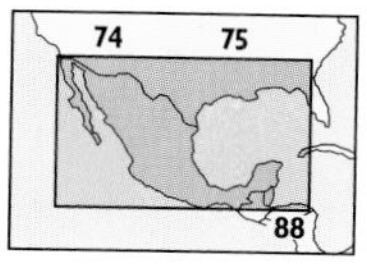
74
75
88

5
6
7
8
A
B
C
D
E
GULF OF MEXICO
Golfo de Campeche
Golfo de Tehuantepec
Golfo de Honduras
UNITED STATES
TEXAS
ARKANSAS
LOUISIANA
MISSISSIPPI
ALABAMA
GEORGIA
FLORIDA
TAMAULIPAS
VERACRUZ
PUEBLA
OAXACA
CHIAPAS
TABASCO
CAMPECHE
YUCATÁN
QUINTANA ROO
GUATEMALA
BELIZE
HONDURAS
CUBA
Wichita Falls
Denison
Sherman
Paris
Hope
Camden
Texarkana
El Dorado
Greenville
Tuscaloosa
Opelika
Columbus
McRae
Denton
Greenville
FORT WORTH
DALLAS
Possum Kingdom Res.
Ranger
Abilene
Cleburne
Marshall
Longview
Tyler
Shreveport
Monroe
Tallulah
Vicksburg
Jackson
Meridian
Selma
Montgomery
Phenix City
Troy
Americus
Cordele
Albany
Tifton
Waycross
Hillsboro
Corsicana
Palestine
Toledo Bend Res.
Natchez
Laurel
Hattiesburg
Dothan
Jim Woodruff Res.
Valdosta
Chattahoochee
Tallahassee
Brownwood
Waco
Nacogdoches
Sam Rayburn Reservoir
Lufkin
Jewett
Alexandria
McComb
Flomaton
Bogalusa
MOBILE
Pensacola
Panama City
Lake City
Temple
Huntsville
Bryan
Baton Rouge
Hammond
Biloxi
Gulfport
Austin
Navasota
Lake Charles
Lafayette
Beaumont
L. Pontchartrain
NEW ORLEANS
Mobile Bay
C. San Blas
Apalachee Bay
Suwannee
HOUSTON
Port Arthur
Breton Sd.
Atchafalaya Bay
Terrebonne Bay
Mississippi River Delta
Rosenberg
Galveston
SAN ANTONIO
Victoria
Clearwater
Dilley
Nueces
Alice
Corpus Christi
Laredo
Kingsville
Nuevo Laredo
Zapata
Laguna Madre
Camargo
McAllen
Harlingen
Brownsville
Reynosa
Matamoros
Valle Hermoso
Santa Teresa
Laguna Madre
Montemorelos
Mendez
San Fernando
Linares
Villagrán
Hidalgo
Santander Jiménez
Zaragoza
La Pesca
Soto la Marina
Ciudad Victoria
Sierra de Tamaulipas
Llera
Calles
Aldama
Pta. Jerez
Ocampo
Ciudad Mante
Altamira
Ciudad Madero
Tampico
Ciudad de Valles
Cárdenas
Pánuco
L. de Tamiahua
Ozuluama
Tempoal
Magozal
Tantoyuca
C. Rojo
Tamazunchale
Chicontepec
Tuxpan
Zimapán
Zacualtipán
Poza Rica
Papantla
San Juan del Río
Huichapán
Pachuca
Huauchinango
Nautla
Misantla
Tula
Tulancingo
Teziutlán
Zumpango
Jalapa Enríquez
MÉXICO
Tlaxcala
Apizaco
Coatepec
Veracruz
Amecameca
PUEBLA
Citlaltépetl 5700
Popocatépetl 5452
Córdoba
Orizaba
Alvarado
Tlacotalpan
San Andrés Tuxtla
1879
Cuernavaca
Jojutla
Izúcar de Matamoros
Tehuacán
Cosamaloapan
Tres Valles
Coatzacoalcos
Comalcalco
Paraíso
Frontera
Ciudad del Carmen
L. de Términos
Chilac
Ajalpan
Acatlán
Iguala
Chiautla
Huautla de Jiménez
Presa Miguel Alemán
Acayucan
Minatitlán
Cárdenas
Villahermosa
Macuspana
Palizada
Balancán
Tenosique
Huajuapan de León
Asunción Nochixtlán
San Juan Bautista Valle Nacional
Istmo de Tehuantepec
Jesús Carranza
Presa Netzahualcóyotl
Raudales de Malpaso
Teapa
Simojovel
Ocosingo
Chilapa
Chilpancingo
Silacayoapan
Tlaxiaco
Oaxaca
Tlacolula
Tehuantepec
Tuxtla Gutiérrez
Chiapa de Corzo
San Cristóbal de las Casas
La Independencia
Tierra Colorada
Ayutla
Acapulco
Ometepec
Ocotlán
Ejutla
San Jerónimo Taviche
Ixtepec
Matías Romero
Comitán
Juchitán
Arriaga
Tonalá
Miahuatlán
Pinotepa Nacional
Jamiltepec
Tututepec
San Pedro Mixtepec
Puerto Escondido
Pochutla
Puerto Ángel
Salina Cruz
Puerto Arista
Pijijiapan
Mapastepec
La Concordia
Motozintla
Huixtla
Tapachula
Coatepeque
Retalhuleu
Punta Maldonado
Papagayo
Verde
3139
3993
4220
Tropic of Cancer
La Esperanza
Guane
La Fe
C. San Antonio
C. Corrientes
Canal de Yucatán
I. Desterrada
I. Pérez (Mexico)
Pta. Yalkubul
Rio Lagartos
C. Catoche
Cancún
Puerto Juárez
Dzilam de Bravo
El Cuyo
Tizimín
Progreso
Motul
Temax
Izamal
Espita
Puerto Morelos
Mérida
Valladolid
Isla Cozumel
Cozumel
Maxcanú
Sotuta
Ticul
Peto
Tenabo
Tekax
Vigía Chico
B. de la Ascensión
Bolonchenticul
Campeche
Hopelchén
Felipe Carrillo Puerto
B. del Espíritu Santo
Champotón
Chenkán
Bacalar
Chetumal
B. de Chetumal
Banco Chinchorro
Matamoros
Corozal
Ambergris Cay
Orange Walk
Hondo
Concepción
Turneffe Is.
Belize City
Uaxactún
San Ignacio
Belmopan
Benque Viejo
Dangriga
L. Petén Itzá
La Libertad
Flores
Maya Mts.
Is. de la Bahía
Monkey River
Roatán
Puerto Castilla
Iriona
San Antonio
Trujillo
San Luis
Punta Gorda
Puerto Barrios
Tela
Balfate
Livingston
Sebol
Olanchito
San Pedro Sula
El Progreso
Arenal
Cuchumatanes
Cobán
L. de Izabal
Santa Bárbara
Yoro
Cuilco
Huehuetenango
Sierra de las Minas
Gualán
Zacapa
Juticalpa
Catacamas
San Marcos
Totonicapán
Santa Rosa de Copán
Comayagua
Sololá
Jalapa
Chiquimula
Antigua
Mazatenango
GUATEMALA
Amatitlán
La Esperanza
La Paz
Tegucigalpa
Yuscarán
Danlí
Patuca
Brazos
Colorado
Trinity
Sabine
Guadalupe
Red
Mississippi
Pearl
Tombigbee
Alabama
Coosa
Chattahoochee
Ocmulgee
Usumacinta
Lacantún
Salinas
Grijalva
Motagua
Ulúa
Sulaco
Conchos
Presa Falcón
Presa M. R. Gómez
Nuevo Guerrero
General Treviño
Cadereyta
Mezcala
Balsas
Papaloapan
30
25
20
15
95
90
85
100

COPYRIGHT GEORGE PHILIP LTD.

CENTRAL AMERICA AND THE WEST INDIES

1:8 000 000

Projection: Conical with two standard parallels

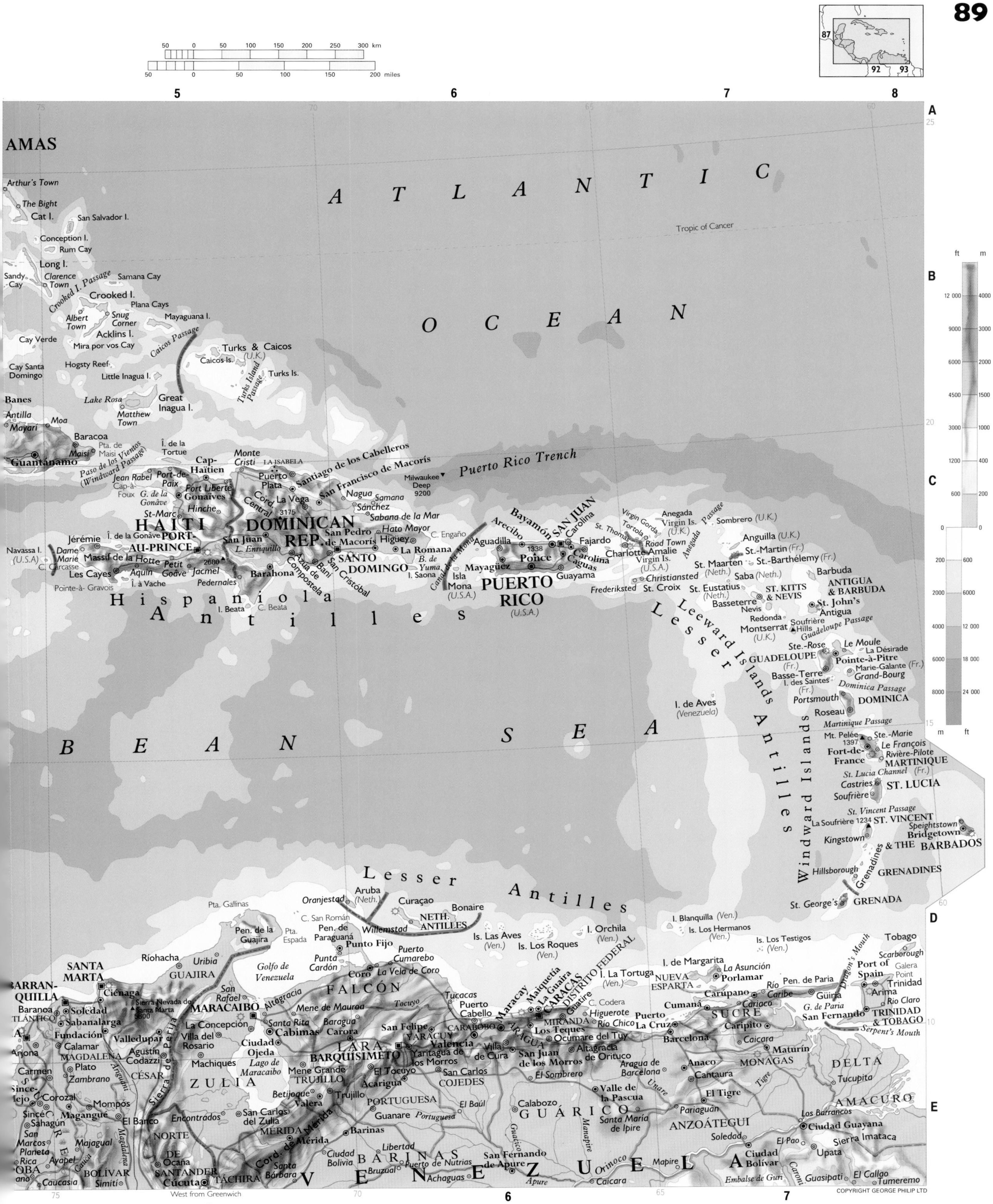
87
92
93
50 0 50 100 150 200 250 300 km
50 0 50 100 150 200 miles
5
6
7
8
A
B
C
D
E
AMAS
Arthur's Town
The Bight
Cat I.
San Salvador I.
Conception I.
Rum Cay
Long I.
Sandy Cay
Clarence Town
Crooked I. Passage
Samana Cay
Crooked I.
Plana Cays
Albert Town
Snug Corner
Mayaguana I.
Acklins I.
Cay Verde
Mira por vos Cay
Caicos Passage
Turks & Caicos (U.K.)
Caicos Is.
Turks Island Passage
Turks Is.
Cay Santa Domingo
Hogsty Reef
Little Inagua I.
Banes
Lake Rosa
Great Inagua I.
Antilla
Moa
Matthew Town
Mayarí
Baracoa
Pta. de Maisí
Maisí
Guantánamo
Paso de los Vientos (Windward Passage)
Î. de la Tortue
Cap-Haïtien
Monte Cristi
LA ISABELA
Jean Rabel
Port-de-Paix
Cap-à-Foux
G. de la Gonâve
Fort Liberté
Gonaïves
Hinche
St-Marc
Puerto Plata
Santiago de los Caballeros
San Francisco de Macorís
Cord. Central
La Vega
Nagua
Samana
Sánchez
Milwaukee Deep 9200
Puerto Rico Trench
ATLANTIC
OCEAN
Tropic of Cancer
HAITI
DOMINICAN REP.
Jérémie
Î. de la Gonâve
PORT-AU-PRINCE
San Juan
L. Enriquillo
Sabana de la Mar
Hato Mayor
Higüey
San Pedro de Macorís
C. Engaño
La Romana
SANTO DOMINGO
B. de Yuma
I. Saona
Navassa I. (U.S.A)
Dame Marie
C. Carcasse
Massif de la Hotte
Petit Goâve
Jacmel
2680
Les Cayes
Aquin
Î. à Vache
Pointe-à-Gravois
Pernedales
Barahona
Azua de Compostela
Baní
San Cristóbal
Hispaniola
I. Beata
C. Beata
Antilles
Canal de la Mona
Isla Mona (U.S.A.)
Aguadilla
Arecibo
Bayamón
SAN JUAN
Carolina
1338
Ponce
Mayagüez
Caguas
Fajardo
Guayama
PUERTO RICO (U.S.A.)
St. Thomas
Tortola
Virgin Gorda
Anegada
Virgin Is. (U.K.)
Anegada Passage
Sombrero (U.K.)
Road Town
Charlotte Amalie
Virgin Is. (U.S.A.)
Christiansted
Frederiksted
St. Croix
Anguilla (U.K.)
St.-Martin (Fr.)
St. Maarten (Neth.)
St.-Barthélemy (Fr.)
Saba (Neth.)
Barbuda
St. Eustatius (Neth.)
ST. KITTS & NEVIS
ANTIGUA & BARBUDA
Basseterre
Nevis
St. John's
Antigua
Redonda
Montserrat (U.K.)
Soufrière Hills
Guadeloupe Passage
Ste.-Rose
Le Moule
La Désirade
GUADELOUPE (Fr.)
Pointe-à-Pitre
Basse-Terre
Marie-Galante (Fr.)
Grand-Bourg
I. des Saintes (Fr.)
Dominica Passage
Portsmouth
DOMINICA
Roseau
Leeward Islands
Lesser Antilles
I. de Aves (Venezuela)
Martinique Passage
Mt. Pelée 1397
Ste.-Marie
Le François
Fort-de-France
Rivière-Pilote
MARTINIQUE (Fr.)
St. Lucia Channel
Castries
ST. LUCIA
Soufrière
Windward Islands
St. Vincent Passage
La Soufrière 1234
ST. VINCENT
Speightstown
Bridgetown
Kingstown
& THE
BARBADOS
Grenadines
Hillsborough
GRENADINES
St. George's
GRENADA
CARIBBEAN SEA
Lesser Antilles
Aruba (Neth.)
Oranjestad
Curaçao
Bonaire
NETH. ANTILLES
Willemstad
Pta. Gallinas
C. San Román
Pen. de la Guajira
Pta. Espada
Pen. de Paraguaná
Punto Fijo
Is. Las Aves (Ven.)
Is. Los Roques (Ven.)
I. Orchila (Ven.)
I. Blanquilla (Ven.)
Is. Los Hermanos (Ven.)
Is. Los Testigos (Ven.)
Tobago
Scarborough
Dragon's Mouth
Ríohacha
Uribia
Golfo de Venezuela
Punta Cardón
Puerto Cumarebo
GUAJIRA
Coro
La Vela de Coro
I. de Margarita
La Asunción
Porlamar
I. La Tortuga (Ven.)
NUEVA ESPARTA
SANTA MARTA
BARRANQUILLA
Ciénaga
Sierra Nevada de Santa Marta 5800
San Rafael
Altagracia
FALCÓN
Mene de Mauroa
Tocuyo
Tucacas
Maracay
Maiquetía
La Guaira
CARACAS
DISTRITO FEDERAL
Guatire
C. Codera
Carúpano
Río Caribe
Pen. de Paria
Güiria
Port of Spain
Galera Point
Trinidad
Arima
Río Claro
Baranoa
Soledad
MARACAIBO
Puerto Cabello
Cumaná
Cariaco
G. de Paria
TRINIDAD & TOBAGO
Sabanalarga
La Concepción
Santa Rita
Baragua
Carora
San Felipe
YARACUY
CARABOBO
Higuerote
Puerto La Cruz
SUCRE
San Fernando
Serpent's Mouth
Fundación
Valledupar
Cabimas
MIRANDA
Los Teques
Río Chico
Caripito
Calamar
Agustín Codazzi
Villa del Rosario
Ciudad Ojeda
LARA
Valencia
ARAGUA
Ocumare del Tuy
Barcelona
Caicara
MAGDALENA
BARQUISIMETO
Yaritagua
Villa de Cura
Altagracia de Orituco
Maturín
Arjona
Plato
Lago de Maracaibo
Mene Grande
El Tocuyo
San Juan de los Morros
Aragua de Barcelona
Anaco
MONAGAS
DELTA
Carmen
Machiques
TRUJILLO
San Carlos
COJEDES
El Sombrero
Cantaura
Zambrano
CÉSAR
Acarigua
ZULIA
Valle de la Pascua
Unare
Tucupita
Corozal
Mompós
Betijoque
Valera
Trujillo
PORTUGUESA
El Baúl
Tigre
El Tigre
AMACURO
Sincé
Magangué
Sahagún
El Banco
Encontrados
San Carlos del Zulia
Guanare
Calabozo
GUÁRICO
Pariaguán
Los Barrancos
Santa María de Ipire
ANZOÁTEGUI
Ciudad Guayana
NORTE DE SANTANDER
MÉRIDA
Barinas
Cord. de Mérida
Sierra Imataca
San Marcos
Planeta Rica
Majagual
Ocaña
Mérida
Ciudad Bolivia
Libertad
Puerto de Nutrias
San Fernando de Apure
Manapire
Soledad
El Pao
Upata
Ayapel
Santa Bárbara
BARINAS
Orinoco
Mapire
Ciudad Bolívar
Cúcuta
TÁCHIRA
BOLÍVAR
Simití
Caucasia
Bruzual
Achaguas
Apure
Caicara
Embalse de Guri
Caroní
Guasipati
El Callao
Tumeremo
VENEZUELA
West from Greenwich
75
70
65
60
25
20
15
10
ft
m
12 000
9000
6000
4500
3000
1200
600
4000
3000
2000
1500
1000
400
200
0
200
2000
4000
6000
8000
600
6000
12 000
18 000
24 000
COPYRIGHT GEORGE PHILIP LTD

100 0 200 400 600 800 1000 1200 1400 km
100 0 200 400 600 800 1000 miles
NORTH ATLANTIC OCEAN
Caribbean Sea
Cuba
Greater Antilles
Lesser Antilles
Turks & Caicos Is.
Hispaniola
Puerto Rico
Jamaica
Guadeloupe
Dominica
Martinique
St. Lucia
Barbados
St. Vincent
Grenada
Tobago
Trinidad
I. Margarita
Yucatan Channel
Gulf of Campeche
Yucatán Peninsula
Isthmus of Tehuantepec
G. de Honduras
C. Gracias a Dios
Guatemala Trench
L. Nicaragua
Panama Canal
G. of Darién
Gulf of Panamá
C. de la Aguja
Sierra Nevada de Santa Marta
L. Maracaibo
Cord. de Mérida
Cordillera Occidental
Cordillera Central
Cordillera Oriental
Magdalena
Llanos
Orinoco
Meta
Guiana Highlands
Mt. Roraima
Sierra Pacaraima
Serra Tumucumaque
Essequibo
Courantyne
Branco
C. Orange
Guaviare
C. de San Francisco
Caquetá
Negro
Marajó I.
Equator
Cotopaxi
Chimborazo
Japurá
Putumayo
Amazon
Galapagos Is.
G. of Guayaquil
Napo
Pta. Pariñas
Pta. Negra
Marañón
Juruá
Ucayali
Selvas
Purus
Madeira
Tapajós
Xingu
Tocantins
Parnaíba
C. de São Roque
Aripuanã
Roosevelt
Teles Pires
Araguaia
Huascarán
Plat. of Borborema
São Francisco
Madre de Dios
Arinos
Guaporé
Mamoré
Plateau of Mato Grosso
Brazilian Highlands
Chile Peru Trench
Chincha Alta
L. Titicaca
Nevada Ancohuma
Bolivian Plateau
L. de Poopó
PACIFIC OCEAN
Abrolhos Bank
Gran Chaco
Paraguay
Paraná
Serra da Mantiqueira
Pico da Bandeira
C. Frio
Tropic of Capricorn
Tropic of Cancer
Atacama Desert
Pilcomayo
Cerro Ojos del Salado
Iguaçu Falls
San Félix
San Ambrosio
Salado
Uruguay
Serra do Mar
Salinas Grandes
Entre Ríos
Andes
L. Mar Chiquita
Sierra de Córdoba
Mt. Aconcagua
L. dos Patos
Pampas
Arch. de Juan Fernández
Río de la Plata
Colorado
Bahía Blanca
Negro
SOUTH ATLANTIC OCEAN
G. San Matías
Valdés Peninsula
Chile Rise
Chiloé I.
Chubut
Patagonia
Chonos Archipelago
Mte. San Valentín
Argentine Basin
Taitao Peninsula
Gulf of San Jorge
Gulf of Penas
Wellington I.
Madre de Dios I.
Falkland Is.
West Falkland
East Falkland
Magellan's Str.
Santa Inés I.
Tierra del Fuego
Staten I.
Canal Cockburn
Canal Beagle
C. Horn
South Georgia
West from Greenwich
ft m
CARTOGRAPHY BY PHILIP'S.

Projection: *Lambert's Azimuthal Equal Area*

100 0 200 400 600 800 1000 1200 1400 km
100 0 200 400 600 800 1000 miles
Tropic of Cancer
NORTH ATLANTIC OCEAN
Havana
CUBA
BAHAMAS
Turks & Caicos Is. (U.K.)
MEXICO
BELIZE
GUATEMALA
Guatemala
HONDURAS
Tegucigalpa
San Salvador
EL SALVADOR
NICARAGUA
Managua
COSTA RICA
San José
Panamá
PANAMA
JAMAICA
Kingston
HAITI
Port-au-Prince
DOMINICAN REP.
San Juan
PUERTO RICO (U.S.A.)
Virgin Is. (U.K.)
ST. KITTS & NEVIS
Basse-Terre
ANTIGUA & BARBUDA
GUADELOUPE (Fr.)
DOMINICA
Fort-de-France
MARTINIQUE (Fr.)
Castries
ST. LUCIA
ST. VINCENT
Kingstown
BARBADOS
Bridgetown
GRENADA
St. George's
Port of Spain
TRINIDAD & TOBAGO
Caribbean Sea
Aruba
Curaçao
Barranquilla
C. de la Aguja
Cartagena
G. of Darién
Maracaibo
Barquisimeto
Valencia
Caracas
Orinoco
Ciudad Guayana
Cúcuta
San Cristóbal
Bucaramanga
Medellín
VENEZUELA
Georgetown
GUYANA
Paramaribo
SURINAM
Cayenne
C. Orange
FRENCH GUIANA
Gulf of Panamá
Bogotá
Cali
Magdalena
COLOMBIA
RORAIMA
Branco
Essequibo
AMAPÁ
Galapagos Is. (Ecuador)
Quito
ECUADOR
Guayaquil
G. of Guayaquil
Equator
Marajó I.
Belém
Putumayo
Japurá
Napo
Amazon
Manaus
Santarém
São Luís
Iquitos
Marañón
AMAZONAS
PARÁ
Tapajós
Xingu
Tocantins
Fortaleza
MARANHÃO
Teresina
C. de São Roque
CEARÁ
RIO G. DO NORTE
Natal
PARAÍBA
Juruá
Purus
Madeira
Parnaíba
PIAUÍ
Campina Grande
Recife
PERNAMBUCO
ALAGOAS
Maceió
SERGIPE
Aracaju
Chiclayo
Trujillo
Chimbote
Ucayali
ACRE
Pôrto Velho
PERU
Callao
LIMA
Madre de Dios
RONDÔNIA
BRAZIL
TOCANTINS
Araguaia
Cuzco
L. Titicaca
MATO GROSSO
BAHÍA
Salvador
São Francisco
Mamoré
BOLIVIA
Cuiabá
GOIÁS
DIS. FED.
Brasília
Goiânia
Arequipa
La Paz
Cochabamba
Santa Cruz
Sucre
Paraguay
MINAS GERAIS
MATO GROSSO DO SUL
Belo Horizonte
ESPIRITO SANTO
Vitória
Iquique
Ribeirão Prêto
Juiz de Fora
PACIFIC OCEAN
Paraná
SÃO PAULO
Campinas
Campos
R. DE J.
Niterói
SÃO PAULO
RIO DE JANEIRO
Antofagasta
PARAGUAY
Pilcomayo
Salta
Asunción
PARANÁ
Curitiba
Tropic of Capricorn
San Félix (Chile)
San Ambrosio (Chile)
San Miguel de Tucumán
Resistencia
Corrientes
SANTA CATARINA
Uruguay
RIO GRANDE DO SUL
Salado
Pôrto Alegre
Córdoba
Santa Fe
San Juan
Paraná
Pelotas
Viña del Mar
Valparaíso
SANTIAGO
Mendoza
Rosario
URUGUAY
Arch. de Juan Fernández (Chile)
BUENOS AIRES
Montevideo
La Plata
Río de la Plata
Talca
Concepción
Bahía Blanca
Mar del Plata
Colorado
CHILE
ARGENTINA
SOUTH ATLANTIC OCEAN
Valdivia
Negro
Viedma
Puerto Montt
Chubut
Comodoro Rivadavia
Gulf of San Jorge
Gulf of Penas
West Falkland
FALKLAND IS. (U.K.)
Stanley
East Falkland
Magellan's Str.
Punta Arenas
Tierra del Fuego
C. Horn
South Georgia (U.K.)
Projection: Lambert's Azimuthal Equal Area
LIMA Capital Cities
West from Greenwich
CARTOGRAPHY BY PHILIP'S.

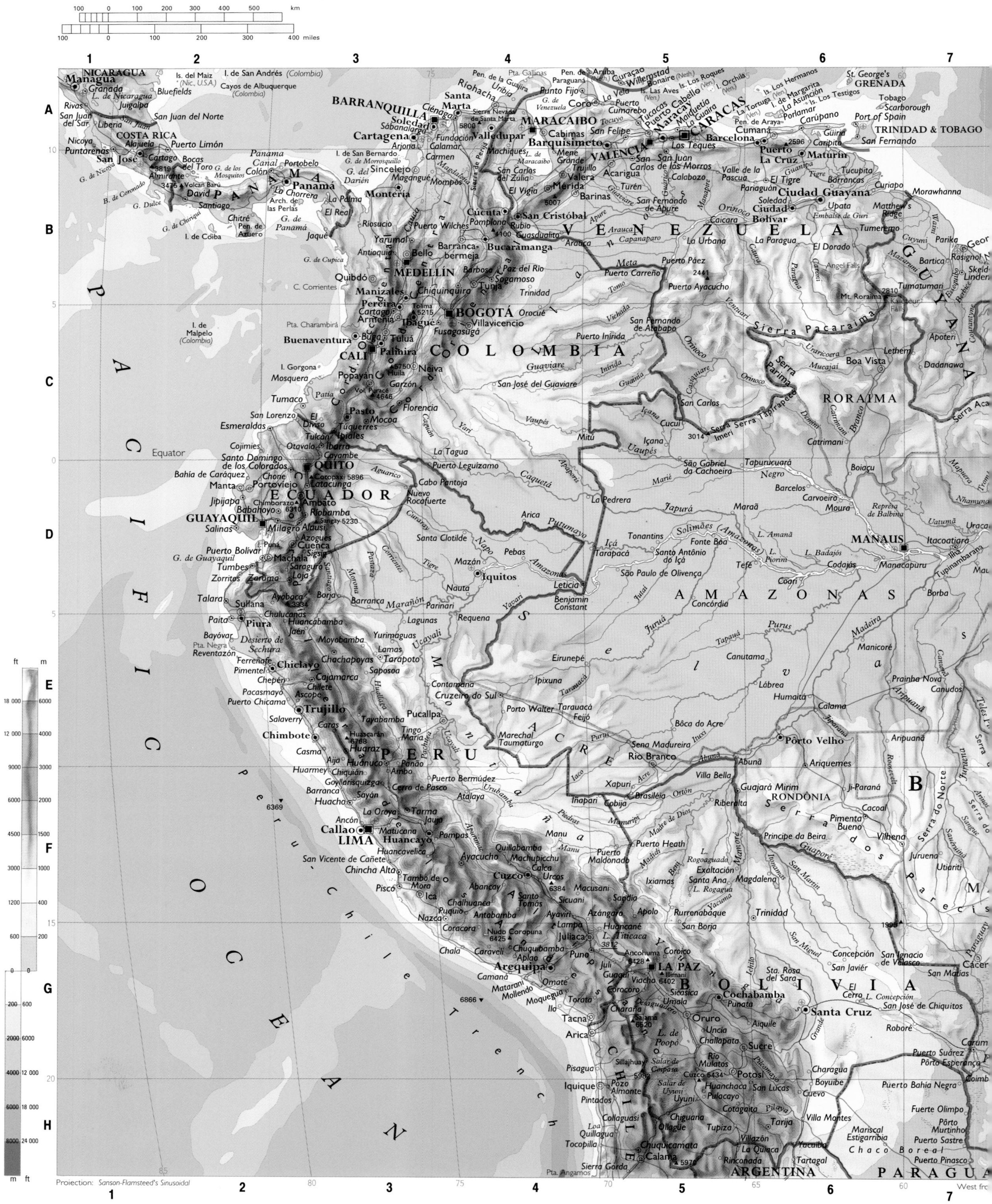
km 100 0 100 200 300 400 500
100 0 100 200 300 400 miles
NICARAGUA
Managua
Granada
L. de Nicaragua
COSTA RICA
San José
PANAMA
Panamá
BARRANQUILLA
Cartagena
MARACAIBO
CARACAS
Barquisimeto
VALENCIA
Barcelona
Ciudad Guayana
TRINIDAD & TOBAGO
GRENADA
VENEZUELA
GUYANA
MEDELLÍN
BOGOTÁ
CALI
COLOMBIA
QUITO
ECUADOR
GUAYAQUIL
Equator
PACIFIC OCEAN
Peru-Chile Trench
PERU
Trujillo
Chimbote
Callao
LIMA
Cuzco
Arequipa
L. Titicaca
LA PAZ
BOLIVIA
Cochabamba
Santa Cruz
Oruro
Sucre
Potosí
CHILE
ARGENTINA
PARAGUAY
AMAZONAS
MANAUS
Iquitos
RORAIMA
RONDÔNIA
Pôrto Velho
Rio Branco
ACRE
Leticia
Amazonas
Orinoco
Sierra Pacaraima
Serra Parima
Mt. Roraima
Angel Falls
Projection: Sanson-Flamsteed's Sinusoidal
ft m
18 000 6000
12 000 4000
9000 3000
6000 2000
4500 1500
3000 1000
1200 400
600 200
0 0
200 600
2000 6000
4000 12 000
6000 18 000
8000 24 000
m ft

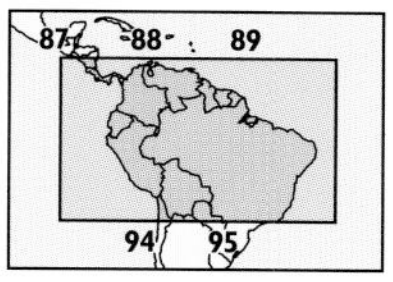
87
88
89
94
95

8
9
10
11
12
13
A
B
C
D
E
F
G
H
A T L A N T I C
O C E A N
Equator
São Paulo (Braz.)
Rocas
Fernando de Noronha (Braz.)
Trindade (Braz.)
6059
SURINAM
FRENCH GUIANA
Paramaribo
Nieuw Amsterdam
Nieuw Nickerie
Totness
Moengo
Kwakoegron
Albina
St-Laurent
Iracoubo
Sinnamary
Kourou
Cayenne
Approuague
Kaw
C. Orange
St-Georges
Oiapoque
Camopi
Prof. Van Blommestein-meer
Serra Tumucumaque
AMAPÁ
Amapá
I. de Maracá
Araguari
Meriruma
Serra do Navio
Macapá
I. Caviana
I. Mexiana
Mazagão
Chaves
C. Maguarinho
Afuá
I. de Marajó
Soure
Curuçá
Salinópolis
Vigia
Bragança
I. Grande de Gurupá
Almeirim
Gurupá
Breves
BELÉM
Castanhal
Viseu
Turiaçu
Cururupu
Óbidos
Monte Alegre
Prainha
Pôrto de Móz
Curralinho
Abaetetuba
Alenquer
Amazonas (Amazon)
Xingu
Cametá
Juruti
Parintins
Santarém
Belterra
Aveiro
Brasília Legal
Altamira
Baião
P A R Á
Tucuruí
Represa de Tucuruí
Itaituba
Iriri
Tapajós
B. de São Marcos
Alcântara
São Luís
Barreirinhas
Tutóia
Luís Correia
Camocim
Pinheiro
Rosário
Itapecuru-Mirim
Viana
Parnaíba
Granja
Itapipoca
Caucaia
FORTALEZA
Santa Inês
Brejo
Piracuruca
Sobral
Maranguape
Cascavel
Bacabal
Coroatá
Codó
Piripiri
Baturité
Russas
Aracati
Pedreiras
Caxias
Campo Maior
Oiticica
Ipu
Quixadá
Açailândia
Areia Branca
Marabá
Tocantins
MARANHÃO
Teresina
Crateús
Mossoró
Macau
Ceará Mirim
C. de São Roque
São João do Araguaia
Imperatriz
Barra do Corda
Senador Pompeu
CEARÁ
RIO GRANDE DO NORTE
Natal
Carajás
Tocantinópolis
Grajaú
Pôrto Franco
Colinas
Amarante
Valença do Piauí
Iguatu
Caraúbas
Caicó
Currais Novos
Canguaretama
Mamanguape
Estreito
Carolina
Floriano
Oeiras
Picos
Crato
Cajàzeiras
Sousa
Patos
Alagoa Grande
Cabedelo
João Pessoa
Loreto
Nova Iorque
PARAÍBA
Campina Grande
Araguaína
Riachão
Uruçuí
PIAUÍ
Ouricuri
Chapada do Araripe
Juàzeiro do Norte
Olinda
RECIFE
Jaboatão
Conceição do Araguaia
Paulistana
Salgueiro
Caruaru
Pesqueira
PERNAMBUCO
Vitória de Santo Antão
Serra do Penitente
São João do Piauí
Santa Filomena
Araguacema
Pedro Afonso
Caracol
Petrolina
Juàzeiro
Garanhuns
Palmares
Petrolândia
Palmeira dos Índios
Rio Largo
Maceió
Serra do Cachimbo
Serra do Estrondo
Novo Remanso
Nova Casa Nova
Represa de Sobradinho
Paulo Afonso
Arapiraca
ALAGOAS
Penedo
Chapada das Mangabeiras
Parnaguá
Senhor-do-Bonfim
Propriá
SERGIPE
Capela
Aracaju
Palmas
BRAZIL
Pôrto Nacional
TOCANTINS
Serra da Tabatinga
Barra
Xique-Xique
Jacobina
Queimadas
São Cristóvão
Estância
Serrinha
Mundo Novo
Alagoinhas
Feira de Santana
Santa Isabel do Morro
I. do Bananal
Gurupi
Peixe
Manuel Alves
Taguatinga
Barreiras
Ibotirama
BAHIA
Itaberaba
Cachoeira
Santo Amaro
SALVADOR
B. de Todos os Santos
Serra Formosa
Serra do Roncador
Paranã
Campos Belos
São Domingos
Serra Geral de Goiás
Santa Maria da Vitória
Bom Jesus da Lapa
Serra do Sincorá
Castro Alves
Valença
Nazaré
Serra Dourada
Jequié
Posse
Carinhanha
Caetité
Brumado
Ubaitaba
MATO GROSSO
Planalto do Mato Grosso
Niquelândia
1678
Uruaçu
Aruanã
Condeúba
Vitória da Conquista
Itabuna
Ilhéus
Canavieiras
Belmonte
Pôrto Seguro
DIST. FED.
Formosa
BRASÍLIA
Januária
Monte Azul
São Francisco
Pedra Azul
Jequitinhonha
Santo Antonio
Barra do Garças
Goiás
Taguatinga
Anápolis
Luziânia
Janaúba
Montes Claros
Salinas
Rondonópolis
Goiânia
Vianópolis
GOIÁS
Itamaraju
Prado
Caravelas
Araçuaí
Teófilo Otoni
Nanuque
Mucuri
Alto Araguaia
Morrinhos
Paracatu
Pirapora
Serra do Espinhaço
MATO GROSSO DO SUL
Ipameri
Patos de Minas
Corinto
1340
Diamantina
Governador Valadares
Conceição da Barra
São Mateus
Coxim
Jataí
Rio Verde
Catalão
Quirinópolis
Itumbiara
Araguari
MINAS GERAIS
Nova Venécia
Linhares
ESPÍRITO SANTO
Uberlândia
Patrocínio
Curvelo
Ipatinga
Colatina
Campo Grande
Paranaíba
Ituiutaba
Prata
Uberaba
Araxá
Ibiá
Sete Lagoas
Itabira
Caratinga
Santa Fé do Sul
Água Clara
BELO HORIZONTE
Sabará
Miranda
São José do Barretos
Igarapava
Divinópolis
Nova Lima
Ponte Nova
Cariacica
Vitória
Vila Velha
Aquidauana
Ribas do Rio Pardo
Três Lagoas
Rio Prêto
Andradina
Passos
Conselheiro Lafaiete
Ouro Prêto
2890
Ubá
Cachoeiro de Itapemirim
Araçatuba
Ribeirão Prêto
Panorama
Presidente Epitácio
Penápolis
Catanduva
Lins
Araraquara
Poços de Caldas
Guaxupé
São João del Rei
Barbacena
Itaperuna
Juiz de Fora
Campos
Dourados
Presidente Prudente
Marília
SÃO PAULO
São Carlos
Três Rios
Nova Friburgo
Ponta Porã
Assis
Bauru
Jaú
Moji-Mirim
São Lourenço
2787
Petrópolis
Pedro Juan Caballero
Paranapanema
Botucatu
Piracicaba
Limeira
Campinas
Volta Redonda
RIO DE JANEIRO
Niterói
Cabo Frio
Greenwich
55
50
45
40
35
30
10
5
0
15
20

CENTRAL SOUTH AMERICA 1:8 000 000

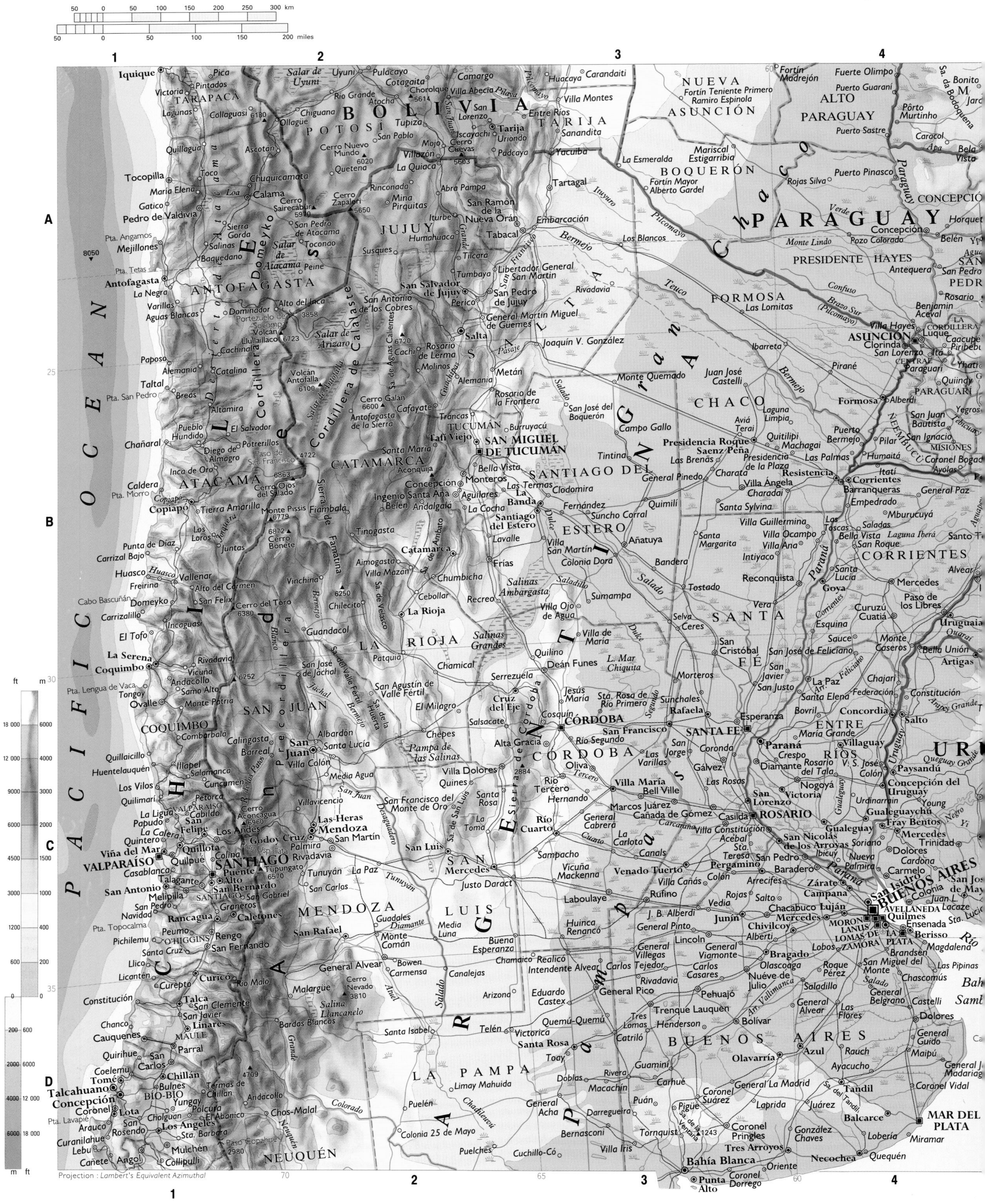

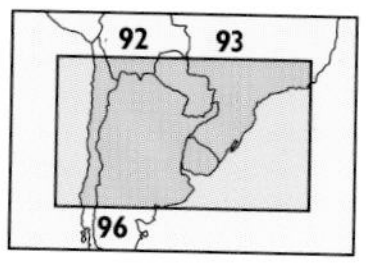
92
93
96

5
6
7
A
B
C
D
BELO HORIZONTE
Nova Lima
Itabirito
Congonhas
Conselheiro Lafaiete
Ouro Prêto
Vitória
Itaquari
Vila Velha
Guarapari
Pico da Bandeira 2890
Ponte Nova
Castelo
Carangola
Muriaé
Alegre
Cachoeiro de Itapemirim
Itaperuna
Cambuci
Guarus
CAMPOS
Cabo de São Tomé
Macaé
Nova Friburgo
Petrópolis
Além Paraíba
Três Rios
Leopoldina
Cataguases
Ubá
Juiz de Fora
São João del Rei
Barbacena
Santos Dumont
Lavras
Três Corações
São Lourenço
Mantiqueira
Oliveira
Campo Belo
Represa de Furnas
Três Pontas
Varginha
Alfenas
Guaxupé
Passos
São Sebastião do Paraíso
Batatais
Franca
Andradina
Três Lagoas
Mirassol
Olímpia
São José do Rio Prêto
Bebedouro
Ribeirão Prêto
Araçatuba
Birigui
Catanduva
Taquaritinga
Novo Horizonte
Jaboticabal
Mococa
Casa Branca
São João da Boa Vista
Poços de Caldas
Pouso Alegre
Itajubá
Ouro Fino
Mogi-Mirim
Araras
Pinhal
Limeira
Americana
Rio Claro
Piracicaba
CAMPINAS
Bragança Paulista
Guaratinguetá
Cruzeiro
Volta Redonda
Barra Mansa
Barra do Piraí
RIO DE JANEIRO
DUQUE DE CAXIAS
NOVA IGUAÇU
SÃO GONÇALO
NITERÓI
Cabo Frio
La. de Araruama
Angra dos Reis
Ilha Grande
Bahia da Ilha Grande
Pta. de Juatinga
Tropic of Capricorn
Taubaté
São José dos Campos
Jacareí
Moji das Cruzes
SÃO PAULO
SANTO ANDRÉ
São Bernardo do Campo
SANTOS
São Vicente
Guarujá
Ilha de São Sebastião
Pta. de Boi
Itanhaém
Jundiaí
Itu
Sorocaba
Tatuí
Botucatu
Tietê
Avaré
Ourinhos
Jacarèzinho
Santa Cruz do Rio Pardo
Assis
Marília
Paraguaçu Paulista
Bauru
Jaú
Lins
Araraquara
São Carlos
Garça
Bariri
Pirajuí
Penápolis
Tupã
Martinópolis
Presidente Prudente
Presidente Epitácio
Adamantina
Santo Anastácio
Rancharia
Porecatu
Cambará
Cornélio Procópio
Londrina
Rolândia
Arapongas
Apucarana
Maringá
Nova Esperança
Paranavaí
Sertanópolis
Centenário do Sul
Umuarama
Cianorte
Cruzeiro do Oeste
Mandaguari
Joaquim Távora
Itaporanga
Itapetininga
Itapeva
Itararé
Paranapiacaba
Juquiá
Registro
Iguape
Ilha Comprida
Ilha do Cardoso
Apiaí
Jaguariaíva
Tibagi
Ibaiti
Castro
Ponta Grossa
Prudentópolis
Guarapuava
CURITIBA
Palmeira
Antonina
Paranaguá
Matinhos
Guaratuba
Joinville
São Francisco do Sul
Rio Negro
Mafra
São Mateus do Sul
Lapa
Irati
União da Vitória
Pôrto União
Palmas
Pato Branco
Clevelândia
Caçador
Blumenau
Itajaí
Brusque
Santa Cecília
Curitibanos
Rio do Sul
SANTA CATARINA
Campos Novos
Lajes
São José
Ilha de Santa Catarina
Florianópolis
Laguna
Cabo Santa Marta Grande
Tubarão
Criciúma
Araranguá
Torres
São Joaquim
Vacaria
Bento Gonçalves
Caxias do Sul
Nôvo Hamburgo
Taquara
São Leopoldo
Canoas
Osorio
PÔRTO ALEGRE
Viamão
Montenegro
Santa Cruz do Sul
Cachoeira do Sul
Rio Pardo
Santa Maria
Alegrete
Santiago
São Borja
São Luís Gonzaga
Santo Ângelo
Cruz Alta
Passo Fundo
Carazinho
Erechim
Palmeira das Missões
Santa Rosa
Frederico Westphalen
Chapecó
Joaçaba
Xanxerê
São Miguel do Oeste
RIO GRANDE DO SUL
São Gabriel
Santana do Livramento
Rivera
Dom Pedrito
Bagé
Caçapava do Sul
Camaquã
Encantadas
Tapes
Mostardas
São Lourenço do Sul
Canguçu
Pelotas
Pinheiro Machado
Lagoa dos Patos
São José do Norte
Rio Grande
Jaguarão
Lagoa Mirim
Lagoa Mangueira
Santa Vitória do Palmar
Chuy
Tres
Treinta y Tres
Melo
Fraile Muerto
Rio Branco
Vergara
Cerro Chato
San Gregorio
Blanquillo
Tacuarembó
Sarandí del Yi
José Batlle y Ordóñez
Lascano
Aigua
Castillos
Rocha
Minas
San Carlos
Maldonado
Pando
MONTEVIDEO
Plata
Antonio
TO GROSSO DO SUL
Sidrolândia
Nioaque
Guia Lopes da Laguna
Maracaju
Nova Alvorada do Sul
Rio Brilhante
Dourados
Ponta Porã
Pedro Juan Caballero
Amambai
Capitán Bado
Naviraí
Ivinhema
Nova Andradina
Euclides da Cunha Paulista
Rosana
Pôrto São José
Mundo Novo
Salto del Guairá
Guaíra
Goio-Erê
Campo Mourão
Cândido de Abreu
Ubiratã
Pitanga
Cascavel
Toledo
Porto Mendes
Represa de Itaipu
CANINDEYU
Curuguaty
Igatimi
ALTO PARANÁ
Hernandarias
Ciudad del Este
Foz do Iguaçu
Cat. del Iguaçu
Medianeira
Laranjeiras do Sul
Francisco Beltrão
Bernardo de Irigoyen
Irala
Abai
Eldorado
ITAPUÁ
San Pedro
MISIONES
Encarnación
Oberá
Candelaria
Leandro N. Alem
Apóstoles
San Javier
Corpus
Monteagudo
BRAZIL
PARANÁ
SÃO PAULO
Serra do Mar
Serra Geral
ATLANTIC
OCEAN
1889
1808
1340
2787
5304
55
50
45
40
25
30
35
West from Greenwich
COPYRIGHT GEORGE PHILIP LTD

SOUTH AMERICA-SOUTH 1:16 000 000

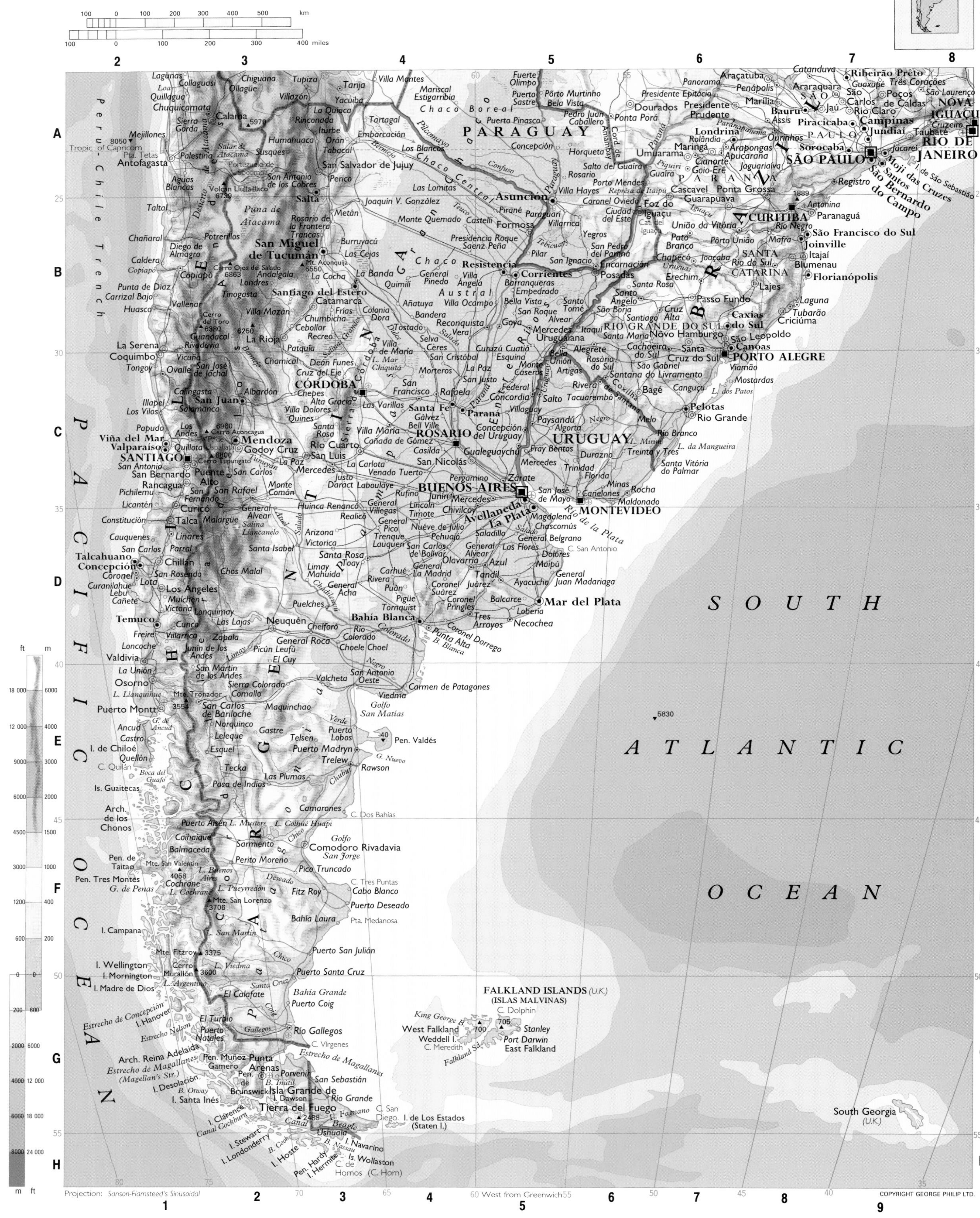

INDEX

The index contains the names of all the principal places and features shown on the World Maps. Each name is followed by an additional entry in italics giving the country or region within which it is located. The alphabetical order of names composed of two or more words is governed primarily by the first word and then by the second. This is an example of the rule:

Mīr Kūh, *Iran*	**45 E8**	26 22N	58 55 E
Mīr Shahdād, *Iran*	**45 E8**	26 15N	58 29 E
Mira, *Italy*	**20 B5**	45 26N	12 8 E
Mira por vos Cay, *Bahamas*	**89 B5**	22 9N	74 30W
Miraj, *India*	**40 L9**	16 50N	74 45 E

Physical features composed of a proper name (Erie) and a description (Lake) are positioned alphabetically by the proper name. The description is positioned after the proper name and is usually abbreviated:

Erie, L., *N. Amer.*	**78 D4**	42 15N	81 0W

Where a description forms part of a settlement or administrative name however, it is always written in full and put in its true alphabetic position:

Mount Morris, *U.S.A.*	**78 D7**	42 44N	77 52W

Names beginning with M' and Mc are indexed as if they were spelled Mac. Names beginning St. are alphabetised under Saint, but Sankt, Sint, Sant', Santa and San are all spelt in full and are alphabetised accordingly. If the same place name occurs two or more times in the index and all are in the same country, each is followed by the name of the administrative subdivision in which it is located. The names are placed in the alphabetical order of the subdivisions. For example:

Jackson, *Ky., U.S.A.*	**76 G4**	37 33N	83 23W
Jackson, *Mich., U.S.A.*	**76 D3**	42 15N	84 24W
Jackson, *Minn., U.S.A.*	**80 D7**	43 37N	95 1W

The number in bold type which follows each name in the index refers to the number of the map page where that feature or place will be found. This is usually the largest scale at which the place or feature appears.

The letter and figure which are in bold type immediately after the page number give the grid square on the map page, within which the feature is situated. The letter represents the latitude and the figure the longitude.

In some cases the feature itself may fall within the specified square, while the name is outside. This is usually the case only with features which are larger than a grid square.

For a more precise location the geographical coordinates which follow the letter/figure references give the latitude and the longitude of each place. The first set of figures represent the latitude which is the distance north or south of the Equator measured as an angle at the centre of the earth. The Equator is latitude 0°, the North Pole is 90°N, and the South Pole 90°S.

The second set of figures represent the longitude, which is the distance East or West of the prime meridian, which runs through Greenwich, England. Longitude is also measured as an angle at the centre of the earth and is given East or West of the prime meridian, from 0° to 180° in either direction.

The unit of measurement for latitude and longitude is the degree, which is subdivided into 60 minutes. Each index entry states the position of a place in degrees and minutes, a space being left between the degrees and the minutes.

The latitude is followed by N(orth) or S(outh) and the longitude by E(ast) or W(est).

Rivers are indexed to their mouths or confluences, and carry the symbol → after their names. A solid square ■ follows the name of a country, while an open square □ refers to a first order administrative area.

Abbreviations used in the index

A.C.T. – Australian Capital Territory
Afghan. – Afghanistan
Ala. – Alabama
Alta. – Alberta
Amer. – America(n)
Arch. – Archipelago
Ariz. – Arizona
Ark. – Arkansas
Atl. Oc. – Atlantic Ocean
B. – Baie, Bahía, Bay, Bucht, Bugt
B.C. – British Columbia
Bangla. – Bangladesh
Barr. – Barrage
Bos.-H. – Bosnia-Herzegovina
C. – Cabo, Cap, Cape, Coast
C.A.R. – Central African Republic
C. Prov. – Cape Province
Calif. – California
Cent. – Central
Chan. – Channel
Colo. – Colorado
Conn. – Connecticut
Cord. – Cordillera
Cr. – Creek
Czech. – Czech Republic
D.C. – District of Columbia
Del. – Delaware
Dep. – Dependency
Des. – Desert
Dist. – District
Dj. – Djebel
Domin. – Dominica
Dom. Rep. – Dominican Republic
E. – East
E. Salv. – El Salvador
Eq. Guin. – Equatorial Guinea
Fla. – Florida
Falk. Is. – Falkland Is.
G. – Golfe, Golfo, Gulf, Guba, Gebel
Ga. – Georgia
Gt. – Great, Greater
Guinea-Biss. – Guinea-Bissau
H.K. – Hong Kong
H.P. – Himachal Pradesh
Hants. – Hampshire
Harb. – Harbor, Harbour
Hd. – Head
Hts. – Heights
I.(s). – Île, Ilha, Insel, Isla, Island, Isle
Ill. – Illinois
Ind. – Indiana
Ind. Oc. – Indian Ocean
Ivory C. – Ivory Coast
J. – Jabal, Jebel, Jazira
Junc. – Junction
K. – Kap, Kapp
Kans. – Kansas
Kep. – Kepulauan
Ky. – Kentucky
L. – Lac, Lacul, Lago, Lagoa, Lake, Limni, Loch, Lough
La. – Louisiana
Liech. – Liechtenstein
Lux. – Luxembourg
Mad. P. – Madhya Pradesh
Madag. – Madagascar
Man. – Manitoba
Mass. – Massachusetts
Md. – Maryland
Me. – Maine
Medit. S. – Mediterranean Sea
Mich. – Michigan
Minn. – Minnesota
Miss. – Mississippi
Mo. – Missouri
Mont. – Montana
Mozam. – Mozambique
Mt.(e) – Mont, Monte, Monti, Montaña, Mountain
N. – Nord, Norte, North, Northern, Nouveau
N.B. – New Brunswick
N.C. – North Carolina
N. Cal. – New Caledonia
N. Dak. – North Dakota
N.H. – New Hampshire
N.I. – North Island
N.J. – New Jersey
N. Mex. – New Mexico
N.S. – Nova Scotia
N.S.W. – New South Wales
N.W.T. – North West Territory
N.Y. – New York
N.Z. – New Zealand
Nebr. – Nebraska
Neths. – Netherlands
Nev. – Nevada
Nfld. – Newfoundland
Nic. – Nicaragua
O. – Oued, Ouadi
Occ. – Occidentale
Okla. – Oklahoma
Ont. – Ontario
Or. – Orientale
Oreg. – Oregon
Os. – Ostrov
Oz. – Ozero
P. – Pass, Passo, Pasul, Pulau
P.E.I. – Prince Edward Island
Pa. – Pennsylvania
Pac. Oc. – Pacific Ocean
Papua N.G. – Papua New Guinea
Pass. – Passage
Pen. – Peninsula, Péninsule
Phil. – Philippines
Pk. – Park, Peak
Plat. – Plateau
Prov. – Province, Provincial
Pt. – Point
Pta. – Ponta, Punta
Pte. – Pointe
Qué. – Québec
Queens. – Queensland
R. – Rio, River
R.I. – Rhode Island
Ra.(s). – Range(s)
Raj. – Rajasthan
Reg. – Region
Rep. – Republic
Res. – Reserve, Reservoir
S. – San, South, Sea
Si. Arabia – Saudi Arabia
S.C. – South Carolina
S. Dak. – South Dakota
S.I. – South Island
S. Leone – Sierra Leone
Sa. – Serra, Sierra
Sask. – Saskatchewan
Scot. – Scotland
Sd. – Sound
Sev. – Severnaya
Sib. – Siberia
Sprs. – Springs
St. – Saint
Sta. – Santa, Station
Ste. – Sainte
Sto. – Santo
Str. – Strait, Stretto
Switz. – Switzerland
Tas. – Tasmania
Tenn. – Tennessee
Tex. – Texas
Tg. – Tanjung
Trin. & Tob. – Trinidad & Tobago
U.A.E. – United Arab Emirates
U.K. – United Kingdom
U.S.A. – United States of America
Ut. P. – Uttar Pradesh
Va. – Virginia
Vdkhr. – Vodokhranilishche
Vf. – Vírful
Vic. – Victoria
Vol. – Volcano
Vt. – Vermont
W. – Wadi, West
W. Va. – West Virginia
Wash. – Washington
Wis. – Wisconsin
Wlkp. – Wielkopolski
Wyo. – Wyoming
Yorks. – Yorkshire
Yug. – Yugoslavia

A

A Coruña, Spain 19 A1 43 20N 8 25W
A Estrada, Spain 19 A1 42 43N 8 27W
A Fonsagrada, Spain 19 A2 43 8N 7 4W
Aachen, Germany 16 C4 50 45N 6 6 E
Aalborg = Ålborg, Denmark 9 H13 57 2N 9 54 E
Aalen, Germany 16 D6 48 51N 10 6 E
Aalst, Belgium 15 D4 50 56N 4 2 E
Aalten, Neths. 15 C6 51 56N 6 35 E
Aalter, Belgium 15 C3 51 5N 3 28 E
Äänekoski, Finland 9 E21 62 36N 25 44 E
Aarau, Switz. 18 C8 47 23N 8 4 E
Aare →, Switz. 18 C8 47 33N 8 14 E
Aarhus = Århus, Denmark 9 H14 56 8N 10 11 E
Aarschot, Belgium 15 D4 50 59N 4 49 E
Aba, Dem. Rep. of the Congo 54 B3 3 58N 30 17 E
Aba, Nigeria 50 G7 5 10N 7 19 E
Ābādān, Iran 45 D6 30 22N 48 20 E
Ābādeh, Iran 45 D7 31 8N 52 40 E
Abadla, Algeria 50 B5 31 2N 2 45W
Abaetetuba, Brazil 93 D9 1 40S 48 50W
Abagnar Qi, China 34 C9 43 52N 116 2 E
Abai, Paraguay 95 B4 25 58S 55 54W
Abakan, Russia 27 D10 53 40N 91 10 E
Abancay, Peru 92 F4 13 35S 72 55W
Abariringa, Kiribati 64 H10 2 50S 171 40W
Abarqū, Iran 45 D7 31 10N 53 20 E
Abashiri, Japan 30 B12 44 0N 144 15 E
Abashiri-Wan, Japan 30 C12 44 0N 144 30 E
Ābay = Nîl el Azraq →, Sudan 51 E12 15 38N 32 31 E
Abay, Kazakstan 26 E8 49 38N 72 53 E
Abaya, L., Ethiopia 46 F2 6 30N 37 50 E
Abaza, Russia 26 D9 52 39N 90 6 E
'Abbāsābād, Iran 45 C8 33 34N 58 23 E
Abbay = Nîl el Azraq →, Sudan 51 E12 15 38N 32 31 E
Abbaye, Pt., U.S.A. 76 B1 46 58N 88 8W
Abbé, L., Ethiopia 46 E3 11 8N 41 47 E
Abbeville, France 18 A4 50 6N 1 49 E
Abbeville, Ala., U.S.A. 77 K3 31 34N 85 15W
Abbeville, La., U.S.A. 81 L8 29 58N 92 8W
Abbeville, S.C., U.S.A. 77 H4 34 11N 82 23W
Abbot Ice Shelf, Antarctica 5 D16 73 0S 92 0W
Abbottabad, Pakistan 42 B5 34 10N 73 15 E
Abd al Kūrī, Yemen 46 E5 12 5N 52 20 E
Ābdar, Iran 45 D7 30 16N 55 19 E
'Abdolābād, Iran 45 C8 34 12N 56 30 E
Abdulpur, Bangla. 43 G13 24 15N 88 59 E
Abéché, Chad 51 F10 13 50N 20 35 E
Abengourou, Ivory C. 50 G5 6 42N 3 27W
Åbenrå, Denmark 9 J13 55 3N 9 25 E
Abeokuta, Nigeria 50 G6 7 3N 3 19 E
Aber, Uganda 54 B3 2 12N 32 25 E
Aberaeron, U.K. 11 E3 52 15N 4 15W
Aberayron = Aberaeron, U.K. 11 E3 52 15N 4 15W
Aberchirder, U.K. 12 D6 57 34N 2 37W
Abercorn = Mbala, Zambia 55 D3 8 46S 31 24 E
Abercorn, Australia 63 D5 25 12S 151 5 E
Aberdare, U.K. 11 F4 51 43N 3 27W
Aberdare Ra., Kenya 54 C4 0 15S 36 50 E
Aberdeen, Australia 63 E5 32 9S 150 56 E
Aberdeen, Canada 73 C7 52 20N 106 8W
Aberdeen, S. Africa 56 E3 32 28S 24 2 E
Aberdeen, U.K. 12 D6 57 9N 2 5W
Aberdeen, Ala., U.S.A. 77 J1 33 49N 88 33W
Aberdeen, Idaho, U.S.A. 82 E7 42 57N 112 50W
Aberdeen, Md., U.S.A. 76 F7 39 31N 76 10W
Aberdeen, S. Dak., U.S.A. 80 C5 45 28N 98 29W
Aberdeen, Wash., U.S.A. 84 D3 46 59N 123 50W
Aberdeen, City of □, U.K. 12 D6 57 10N 2 10W
Aberdeenshire □, U.K. 12 D6 57 17N 2 36W
Aberdovey = Aberdyfi, U.K. 11 E3 52 33N 4 3W
Aberdyfi, U.K. 11 E3 52 33N 4 3W
Aberfeldy, U.K. 12 E5 56 37N 3 51W
Abergavenny, U.K. 11 F4 51 49N 3 1W
Abergele, U.K. 10 D4 53 17N 3 35W
Abernathy, U.S.A. 81 J4 33 50N 101 51W
Abert, L., U.S.A. 82 E3 42 38N 120 14W
Aberystwyth, U.K. 11 E3 52 25N 4 5W
Abhā, Si. Arabia 46 D3 18 0N 42 34 E
Abhar, Iran 45 B6 36 9N 49 13 E
Abhayapuri, India 43 F14 26 24N 90 38 E
Abidjan, Ivory C. 50 G5 5 26N 3 58W
Abilene, Kans., U.S.A. 80 F6 38 55N 97 13W
Abilene, Tex., U.S.A. 81 J5 32 28N 99 43W
Abingdon, U.K. 11 F6 51 40N 1 17W
Abingdon, U.S.A. 77 G5 36 43N 81 59W
Abington Reef, Australia 62 B4 18 0S 149 35 E
Abitau →, Canada 73 B7 59 53N 109 3W
Abitibi →, Canada 70 B3 51 3N 80 55W
Abitibi, L., Canada 70 C4 48 40N 79 40W
Abkhaz Republic = Abkhazia □, Georgia 25 F7 43 12N 41 5 E
Abkhazia □, Georgia 25 F7 43 12N 41 5 E
Abminga, Australia 63 D1 26 8S 134 51 E
Åbo = Turku, Finland 9 F20 60 30N 22 19 E
Abohar, India 42 D6 30 10N 74 10 E
Abomey, Benin 50 G6 7 10N 2 5 E
Abong-Mbang, Cameroon 52 D2 4 0N 13 8 E
Abou-Deïa, Chad 51 F9 11 20N 19 20 E
Aboyne, U.K. 12 D6 57 4N 2 47W
Abra Pampa, Argentina 94 A2 22 43S 65 42W
Abraham L., Canada 72 C5 52 15N 116 35W
Abreojos, Pta., Mexico 86 B2 26 50N 113 40W
Abrud, Romania 17 E12 46 19N 23 5 E
Absaroka Range, U.S.A. 82 D9 44 45N 109 50W
Abu, India 42 G5 24 41N 72 50 E
Abū al Abyad, U.A.E. 45 E7 24 11N 53 50 E
Abū al Khaşīb, Iraq 45 D6 30 25N 48 0 E
Abū 'Alī, Si. Arabia 45 E6 27 20N 49 27 E
Abū 'Alī →, Lebanon 47 A4 34 25N 35 50 E
Abu Dhabi = Abū Ẓāby, U.A.E. 46 C5 24 28N 54 22 E
Abū Du'ān, Syria 44 B3 36 25N 38 15 E
Abu el Gairi, W. →, Egypt 47 F2 29 35N 33 30 E
Abu Ga'da, W. →, Egypt 47 F1 29 15N 32 53 E
Abū Ḩadrīyah, Si. Arabia 45 E6 27 20N 48 58 E
Abu Hamed, Sudan 51 E12 19 32N 33 13 E
Abū Kamāl, Syria 44 C4 34 30N 41 0 E
Abū Madd, Ra's, Si. Arabia 44 E3 24 50N 37 7 E
Abū Mūsā, U.A.E. 45 E7 25 52N 55 3 E
Abū Qaşr, Si. Arabia 44 D3 30 21N 38 34 E
Abu Şafāt, W. →, Jordan 47 E5 30 24N 36 7 E
Abu Simbel, Egypt 51 D12 22 18N 31 40 E
Abū Şukhayr, Iraq 44 D5 31 54N 44 30 E
Abu Zabad, Sudan 51 F11 12 25N 29 10 E
Abū Ẓāby, U.A.E. 46 C5 24 28N 54 22 E
Abū Zeydābād, Iran 45 C6 33 54N 51 45 E
Abuja, Nigeria 50 G7 9 5N 7 32 E
Abukuma-Gawa →, Japan 30 E10 38 6N 140 52 E
Abukuma-Sammyaku, Japan 30 F10 37 30N 140 45 E
Abunã, Brazil 92 E5 9 40S 65 20W
Abunã →, Brazil 92 E5 9 41S 65 20W
Aburo, Dem. Rep. of the Congo 54 B3 2 4N 30 53 E
Abut Hd., N.Z. 59 K3 43 7S 170 15 E
Acadia Nat. Park, U.S.A. 77 C11 44 20N 68 13W
Açailândia, Brazil 93 D9 4 57S 47 0W
Acajutla, El Salv. 88 D2 13 36N 89 50W
Acámbaro, Mexico 86 D4 20 0N 100 40W
Acaponeta, Mexico 86 C3 22 30N 105 20W
Acapulco, Mexico 87 D5 16 51N 99 56W
Acarai, Serra, Brazil 92 C7 1 50N 57 50W
Acarigua, Venezuela 92 B5 9 33N 69 12W
Acatlán, Mexico 87 D5 18 10N 98 3W
Acayucan, Mexico 87 D6 17 59N 94 58W
Accomac, U.S.A. 76 G8 37 43N 75 40W
Accra, Ghana 50 G5 5 35N 0 6W
Accrington, U.K. 10 D5 53 45N 2 22W
Acebal, Argentina 94 C3 33 20S 60 50W
Aceh □, Indonesia 36 D1 4 15N 97 30 E
Achalpur, India 40 J10 21 22N 77 32 E
Acheng, China 35 B14 45 30N 126 58 E
Acher, India 42 H5 23 10N 72 32 E
Achill Hd., Ireland 13 C1 53 58N 10 15W
Achill I., Ireland 13 C1 53 58N 10 1W
Achinsk, Russia 27 D10 56 20N 90 20 E
Acireale, Italy 20 F6 37 37N 15 10 E
Ackerman, U.S.A. 81 J10 33 19N 89 11W
Acklins I., Bahamas 89 B5 22 30N 74 0W
Acme, Canada 72 C6 51 33N 113 30W
Acme, U.S.A. 78 F5 40 8N 79 26W
Aconcagua, Cerro, Argentina 94 C2 32 39S 70 0W
Aconquija, Mt., Argentina 94 B2 27 0S 66 0W
Açores, Is. dos, Atl. Oc. 50 A1 38 0N 27 0W
Acornhoek, S. Africa 57 C5 24 37S 31 2 E
Acraman, L., Australia 63 E2 32 2S 135 23 E
Acre = 'Akko, Israel 47 C4 32 55N 35 4 E
Acre □, Brazil 92 E4 9 1S 71 0W
Acre →, Brazil 92 E5 8 45S 67 22W
Acton, Canada 78 C4 43 38N 80 3W
Acuña, Mexico 86 B4 29 18N 100 55W
Ad Dammām, Si. Arabia 45 E6 26 20N 50 5 E
Ad Dāmūr, Lebanon 47 B4 33 44N 35 27 E
Ad Dawādimi, Si. Arabia 44 E5 24 35N 44 15 E
Ad Dawḩah, Qatar 46 B5 25 15N 51 35 E
Ad Dawr, Iraq 44 C4 34 27N 43 47 E
Ad Dir'īyah, Si. Arabia 44 E5 24 44N 46 35 E
Ad Dīwānīyah, Iraq 44 D5 32 0N 45 0 E
Ad Dujayl, Iraq 44 C5 33 51N 44 14 E
Ad Duwayd, Si. Arabia 44 D4 30 15N 42 17 E
Ada, Minn., U.S.A. 80 B6 47 18N 96 31W
Ada, Okla., U.S.A. 81 H6 34 46N 96 41W
Adabiya, Egypt 47 F1 29 53N 32 28 E
Adair, C., Canada 69 A12 71 31N 71 24W
Adaja →, Spain 19 B3 41 32N 4 52W
Adak I., U.S.A. 68 C2 51 45N 176 45W
Adamaoua, Massif de l', Cameroon 51 G7 7 20N 12 20 E
Adamawa Highlands = Adamaoua, Massif de l', Cameroon 51 G7 7 20N 12 20 E
Adamello, Mte., Italy 18 C9 46 9N 10 30 E
Adaminaby, Australia 63 F4 36 0S 148 45 E
Adams, Mass., U.S.A. 79 D11 42 38N 73 7W
Adams, N.Y., U.S.A. 79 C8 43 49N 76 1W
Adams, Wis., U.S.A. 80 D10 43 57N 89 49W
Adam's Bridge, Sri Lanka 40 Q11 9 15N 79 40 E
Adams L., Canada 72 C5 51 10N 119 40W
Adams Mt., U.S.A. 84 D5 46 12N 121 30W
Adam's Peak, Sri Lanka 40 R12 6 48N 80 30 E
Adana, Turkey 25 G6 37 0N 35 16 E
Adapazarı = Sakarya, Turkey 25 F5 40 48N 30 25 E
Adarama, Sudan 51 E12 17 10N 34 52 E
Adare, C., Antarctica 5 D11 71 0S 171 0 E
Adaut, Indonesia 37 F8 8 8S 131 7 E
Adavale, Australia 63 D3 25 52S 144 32 E
Adda →, Italy 18 D8 45 8N 9 53 E
Addis Ababa = Addis Abeba, Ethiopia 46 F2 9 2N 38 42 E
Addis Abeba, Ethiopia 46 F2 9 2N 38 42 E
Addison, U.S.A. 78 D7 42 1N 77 14W
Addo, S. Africa 56 E4 33 32S 25 45 E
Ādeh, Iran 44 B5 37 42N 45 11 E
Adel, U.S.A. 77 K4 31 8N 83 25W
Adelaide, Australia 63 E2 34 52S 138 30 E
Adelaide, Bahamas 88 A4 25 4N 77 31W
Adelaide, S. Africa 56 E4 32 42S 26 20 E
Adelaide I., Antarctica 5 C17 67 15S 68 30W
Adelaide Pen., Canada 68 B10 68 15N 97 30W
Adelaide River, Australia 60 B5 13 15S 131 7 E
Adelanto, U.S.A. 85 L9 34 35N 117 22W
Adele I., Australia 60 C3 15 32S 123 9 E
Adélie, Terre, Antarctica 5 C10 68 0S 140 0 E
Adélie Land = Adélie, Terre, Antarctica 5 C10 68 0S 140 0 E
Aden = Al 'Adan, Yemen 46 E4 12 45N 45 0 E
Aden, G. of, Asia 46 E4 12 30N 47 30 E
Adendorp, S. Africa 56 E3 32 15S 24 30 E
Adh Dhayd, U.A.E. 45 E7 25 17N 55 53 E
Adhoi, India 42 H4 23 26N 70 32 E
Adi, Indonesia 37 E8 4 15S 133 30 E
Adieu, C., Australia 61 F5 32 0S 132 10 E
Adieu Pt., Australia 60 C3 15 14S 124 35 E
Adige →, Italy 20 B5 45 9N 12 20 E
Adigrat, Ethiopia 46 E2 14 20N 39 26 E
Adilabad, India 40 K11 19 33N 78 20 E
Adirondack Mts., U.S.A. 79 C10 44 0N 74 0W
Adjumani, Uganda 54 B3 3 20N 31 50 E
Adlavik Is., Canada 71 B8 55 0N 58 40W
Admiralty G., Australia 60 B4 14 20S 125 55 E
Admiralty I., U.S.A. 72 B2 57 30N 134 30W
Admiralty Is., Papua N. G. 64 H6 2 0S 147 0 E
Adonara, Indonesia 37 F6 8 15S 123 5 E
Adoni, India 40 M10 15 33N 77 18 E
Adour →, France 18 E3 43 32N 1 32W
Adra, India 43 H12 23 30N 86 42 E
Adra, Spain 19 D4 36 43N 3 3W
Adrano, Italy 20 F6 37 40N 14 50 E
Adrar, Mauritania 50 D3 20 30N 7 30 E
Adrar des Iforas, Algeria 50 C5 27 51N 0 11 E
Adrian, Mich., U.S.A. 76 E3 41 54N 84 2W
Adrian, Tex., U.S.A. 81 H3 35 16N 102 40W
Adriatic Sea, Medit. S. 20 C6 43 0N 16 0 E
Adua, Indonesia 37 E7 1 45S 129 50 E
Adwa, Ethiopia 46 E2 14 15N 38 52 E
Adygea □, Russia 25 F7 45 0N 40 0 E
Adzhar Republic = Ajaria □, Georgia 25 F7 41 30N 42 0 E
Adzopé, Ivory C. 50 G5 6 7N 3 49W
Ægean Sea, Medit. S. 21 E11 38 30N 25 0 E
Aerhtai Shan, Mongolia 32 B4 46 40N 92 45 E
'Afak, Iraq 44 C5 32 4N 45 15 E
Afándou, Greece 23 C10 36 18N 28 12 E
Afghanistan ■, Asia 40 C4 33 0N 65 0 E
Aflou, Algeria 50 B6 34 7N 2 3 E
Africa 48 E6 10 0N 20 0 E
'Afrīn, Syria 44 B3 36 32N 36 50 E
Afton, N.Y., U.S.A. 79 D9 42 14N 75 32W
Afton, Wyo., U.S.A. 82 E8 42 44N 110 56W
Afuá, Brazil 93 D8 0 15S 50 20W
'Afula, Israel 47 C4 32 37N 35 17 E
Afyon, Turkey 25 G5 38 45N 30 33 E
Afyonkarahisar = Afyon, Turkey 25 G5 38 45N 30 33 E
Agadès = Agadez, Niger 50 E7 16 58N 7 59 E
Agadez, Niger 50 E7 16 58N 7 59 E
Agadir, Morocco 50 B4 30 28N 9 55W
Agaete, Canary Is. 22 F4 28 6N 15 43W
Agar, India 42 H7 23 40N 76 2 E
Agartala, India 41 H17 23 50N 91 23 E
Agassiz, Canada 72 D4 49 14N 121 46W
Agats, Indonesia 37 F9 5 33S 138 0 E
Agawam, U.S.A. 79 D12 42 5N 72 37W
Agboville, Ivory C. 50 G5 5 55N 4 15W
Ağdam, Azerbaijan 44 B5 40 0N 46 58 E
Agde, France 18 E5 43 19N 3 28 E
Agen, France 18 D4 44 12N 0 38 E
Āgh Kand, Iran 45 B6 37 15N 48 4 E
Aginskoye, Russia 27 D12 51 6N 114 32 E
Agnew, Australia 61 E3 28 1S 120 31 E
Agori, India 43 G10 24 33N 82 57 E
Agra, India 42 F7 27 17N 77 58 E
Ağri, Turkey 25 G7 39 44N 43 3 E
Agri →, Italy 20 D7 40 13N 16 44 E
Ağrı Dağı, Turkey 25 G7 39 50N 44 15 E
Ağri Karakose = Ağri, Turkey 25 G7 39 44N 43 3 E
Agrigento, Italy 20 F5 37 19N 13 34 E
Agrinion, Greece 21 E9 38 37N 21 27 E
Agua Caliente, Baja Calif., Mexico 85 N10 32 29N 116 59W
Agua Caliente, Sinaloa, Mexico 86 B3 26 30N 108 20W
Agua Caliente Springs, U.S.A. 85 N10 32 56N 116 19W
Água Clara, Brazil 93 H8 20 25S 52 45W
Agua Hechicero, Mexico 85 N10 32 26N 116 14W
Agua Prieta, Mexico 86 A3 31 20N 109 32W
Aguadilla, Puerto Rico 89 C6 18 26N 67 10W
Aguadulce, Panama 88 E3 8 15N 80 32W
Aguanga, U.S.A. 85 M10 33 27N 116 51W
Aguanish, Canada 71 B7 50 14N 62 2W
Aguanus →, Canada 71 B7 50 13N 62 5W
Aguapey →, Argentina 94 B4 29 7S 56 36W
Aguaray Guazú →, Paraguay 94 A4 24 47S 57 19W
Aguarico →, Ecuador 92 D3 0 59S 75 11W
Aguas Blancas, Chile 94 A2 24 15S 69 55W
Aguas Calientes, Sierra de, Argentina 94 B2 25 26S 66 40W
Aguascalientes, Mexico 86 C4 21 53N 102 12W
Aguascalientes □, Mexico 86 C4 22 0N 102 20W
Aguilares, Argentina 94 B2 27 26S 65 35W
Aguilas, Spain 19 D5 37 23N 1 35W
Agüimes, Canary Is. 22 G4 27 58N 15 27W
Aguja, C. de la, Colombia 90 B3 11 18N 74 12W
Agulhas, C., S. Africa 56 E3 34 52S 20 0 E
Agulo, Canary Is. 22 F2 28 11N 17 12W
Agung, Gunung, Indonesia 36 F5 8 20S 115 28 E
Agur, Uganda 54 B3 2 28N 32 55 E
Agusan →, Phil. 37 C7 9 0N 125 30 E
Aha Mts., Botswana 56 B3 19 45S 21 0 E
Ahaggar, Algeria 50 D7 23 0N 6 30 E
Ahar, Iran 44 B5 38 35N 47 0 E
Ahipara B., N.Z. 59 F4 35 5S 173 5 E
Ahiri, India 40 K12 19 30N 80 0 E
Ahmad Wal, Pakistan 42 E1 29 18N 65 58 E
Ahmadabad, India 42 H5 23 0N 72 40 E
Aḩmadābād, Khorāsān, Iran 45 C9 35 3N 60 50 E
Aḩmadābād, Khorāsān, Iran 45 C8 35 49N 59 42 E
Aḩmadī, Iran 45 E8 27 56N 56 42 E
Ahmadnagar, India 40 K9 19 7N 74 46 E
Ahmadpur, Pakistan 42 E4 29 12N 71 10 E
Ahmadpur Lamma, Pakistan 42 E4 28 19N 70 3 E
Ahmedabad = Ahmadabad, India 42 H5 23 0N 72 40 E
Ahmednagar = Ahmadnagar, India 40 K9 19 7N 74 46 E
Ahome, Mexico 86 B3 25 55N 109 11W
Ahoskie, U.S.A. 77 G7 36 17N 76 59W
Ahram, Iran 45 D6 28 52N 51 16 E
Ahrax Pt., Malta 23 D1 36 0N 14 22 E
Āhū, Iran 45 C6 34 33N 50 2 E
Ahuachapán, El Salv. 88 D2 13 54N 89 52W
Ahvāz, Iran 45 D6 31 20N 48 40 E
Ahvenanmaa = Åland, Finland 9 F19 60 15N 20 0 E
Aḩwar, Yemen 46 E4 13 30N 46 40 E
Ai →, India 43 F14 26 26N 90 44 E
Ai-Ais, Namibia 56 D2 27 54S 17 59 E
Aichi □, Japan 31 G8 35 0N 137 15 E
Aigua, Uruguay 95 C5 34 13S 54 46W
Aigues-Mortes, France 18 E6 43 35N 4 12 E
Aihui, China 33 A7 50 10N 127 30 E
Aija, Peru 92 E3 9 50S 77 45W
Aikawa, Japan 30 E9 38 2N 138 15 E
Aiken, U.S.A. 77 J5 33 34N 81 43W
Aileron, Australia 62 C1 22 39S 133 20 E
Aillik, Canada 71 A8 55 11N 59 18W
Ailsa Craig, U.K. 12 F3 55 15N 5 6W
'Ailūn, Jordan 47 C4 32 18N 35 47 E
Aim, Russia 27 D14 59 0N 133 55 E
Aimere, Indonesia 37 F6 8 45S 121 3 E
Aimogasta, Argentina 94 B2 28 33S 66 50W
Aïn Ben Tili, Mauritania 50 C4 25 59N 9 27W
Aïn Sefra, Algeria 50 B5 32 47N 0 37W
Ain Sudr, Egypt 47 F2 29 50N 33 6 E
Ainaži, Latvia 9 H21 57 50N 24 24 E
Ainsworth, U.S.A. 80 D5 42 33N 99 52W
Aiquile, Bolivia 92 G5 18 10S 65 10W
Aïr, Niger 50 E7 18 30N 8 0 E
Air Force I., Canada 69 B12 67 58N 74 5W
Air Hitam, Malaysia 39 M4 1 55N 103 11 E
Airdrie, Canada 72 C6 51 18N 114 2W
Airdrie, U.K. 12 F5 55 52N 3 57W
Aire →, U.K. 10 D7 53 43N 0 55W
Aire, I. de l', Spain 22 B11 39 48N 4 16 E
Airlie Beach, Australia 62 C4 20 16S 148 43 E
Aisne →, France 18 B5 49 26N 2 50 E
Ait, India 43 G8 25 54N 79 14 E
Aitkin, U.S.A. 80 B8 46 32N 93 42W
Aiud, Romania 17 E12 46 19N 23 44 E
Aix-en-Provence, France 18 E6 43 32N 5 27 E
Aix-la-Chapelle = Aachen, Germany 16 C4 50 45N 6 6 E
Aix-les-Bains, France 18 D6 45 41N 5 53 E
Aíyion, Greece 21 E10 38 15N 22 5 E
Aizawl, India 41 H18 23 40N 92 44 E
Aizkraukle, Latvia 9 H21 56 36N 25 11 E
Aizpute, Latvia 9 H19 56 43N 21 40 E
Aizuwakamatsu, Japan 30 F9 37 30N 139 56 E
Ajaccio, France 18 F8 41 55N 8 40 E
Ajaigarh, India 43 G9 24 52N 80 16 E
Ajalpan, Mexico 87 D5 18 22N 97 15W
Ajanta Ra., India 40 J9 20 28N 75 50 E
Ajari Rep. = Ajaria □, Georgia 25 F7 41 30N 42 0 E
Ajaria □, Georgia 25 F7 41 30N 42 0 E
Ajax, Canada 78 C5 43 50N 79 1W
Ajdābiyā, Libya 51 B10 30 54N 20 4 E
Ajka, Hungary 17 E9 47 4N 17 31 E
'Ajmān, U.A.E. 45 E7 25 25N 55 30 E
Ajmer, India 42 F6 26 28N 74 37 E
Ajnala, India 42 D6 31 50N 74 48 E
Ajo, U.S.A. 83 K7 32 22N 112 52W
Ajo, C. de, Spain 19 A4 43 31N 3 35W
Akabira, Japan 30 C11 43 33N 142 5 E
Akamas, Cyprus 23 D11 35 3N 32 18 E
Akanthou, Cyprus 23 D12 35 22N 33 45 E
Akaroa, N.Z. 59 K4 43 49S 172 59 E
Akashi, Japan 31 G7 34 45N 134 58 E
Akbarpur, Bihar, India 43 G10 24 39N 83 58 E
Akbarpur, Ut. P., India 43 F10 26 25N 82 32 E
Akelamo, Indonesia 37 D7 1 35N 129 40 E
Aketi, Dem. Rep. of the Congo 52 D4 2 38N 23 47 E
Akharnai, Greece 21 E10 38 5N 23 44 E
Akhelóös →, Greece 21 E9 38 19N 21 7 E
Akhisar, Turkey 21 E12 38 56N 27 48 E
Akhnur, India 43 C6 32 52N 74 45 E
Akhtyrka = Okhtyrka, Ukraine 25 D5 50 25N 35 0 E
Aki, Japan 31 H6 33 30N 133 54 E
Akimiski I., Canada 70 B3 52 50N 81 30W
Akita, Japan 30 E10 39 45N 140 7 E
Akita □, Japan 30 E10 39 40N 140 30 E
Akjoujt, Mauritania 50 E3 19 45N 14 15W
Akkeshi, Japan 30 C12 43 2N 144 51 E
'Akko, Israel 47 C4 32 55N 35 4 E
Aklavik, Canada 68 B6 68 12N 135 0W
Aklera, India 42 G7 24 26N 76 32 E
Akmolinsk = Astana, Kazakstan 26 D8 51 10N 71 30 E
Akō, Japan 31 G7 34 45N 134 24 E
Akola, India 40 J10 20 42N 77 2 E
Akordat, Eritrea 46 D2 15 30N 37 40 E
Akpatok I., Canada 69 B13 60 25N 68 8W
Åkrahamn, Norway 9 G11 59 15N 5 10 E
Akranes, Iceland 8 D2 64 19N 22 5W
Akron, Colo., U.S.A. 80 E3 40 10N 103 13W
Akron, Ohio, U.S.A. 78 E3 41 5N 81 31W
Akrotiri, Cyprus 23 E11 34 36N 32 57 E
Akrotiri Bay, Cyprus 23 E12 34 35N 33 10 E
Aksai Chin, China 43 B8 35 15N 79 55 E
Aksaray, Turkey 25 G5 38 25N 34 2 E
Aksay, Kazakstan 25 D9 51 11N 53 0 E
Akşehir, Turkey 44 B1 38 18N 31 30 E
Akşehir Gölü, Turkey 25 G5 38 30N 31 25 E
Aksu, China 32 B3 41 5N 80 10 E
Aksum, Ethiopia 46 E2 14 5N 38 40 E
Aktogay, Kazakstan 26 E8 46 57N 79 40 E
Aktsyabrski, Belarus 17 B15 52 38N 28 53 E
Aktyubinsk = Aqtöbe, Kazakstan 25 D10 50 17N 57 10 E
Akure, Nigeria 50 G7 7 15N 5 5 E
Akureyri, Iceland 8 D4 65 40N 18 6W
Akuseki-Shima, Japan 31 K4 29 27N 129 37 E
Akyab = Sittwe, Burma 41 J18 20 18N 92 45 E
Al 'Adan, Yemen 46 E4 12 45N 45 0 E
Al Aḩsā = Hasa □, Si. Arabia 45 E6 25 50N 49 0 E
Al Ajfar, Si. Arabia 44 E4 27 26N 43 0 E
Al Amādīyah, Iraq 44 B4 37 5N 43 30 E
Al 'Amārah, Iraq 44 D5 31 55N 47 15 E
Al 'Aqabah, Jordan 47 F4 29 31N 35 0 E
Al Arak, Syria 44 C3 34 38N 38 35 E
Al 'Aramah, Si. Arabia 44 E5 25 30N 46 0 E
Al Arţāwīyah, Si. Arabia 44 E5 26 31N 45 20 E
Al 'Āşimah = 'Ammān □, Jordan 47 D5 31 40N 36 30 E
Al 'Assāfīyah, Si. Arabia 44 D3 28 17N 38 59 E
Al 'Ayn, Oman 45 E7 24 15N 55 45 E
Al 'Ayn, Si. Arabia 44 E3 25 4N 38 6 E
Al 'Aẓamīyah, Iraq 44 C5 33 22N 44 22 E
Al 'Azīzīyah, Iraq 44 C5 32 54N 45 4 E
Al Bāb, Syria 44 B3 36 23N 37 29 E
Al Bad', Si. Arabia 44 D2 28 28N 35 1 E
Al Bādī, Iraq 44 C4 35 56N 41 32 E
Al Baḩrah, Kuwait 44 D5 29 40N 47 52 E
Al Baḩral Mayyit = Dead Sea, Asia 47 D4 31 30N 35 30 E
Al Balqā' □, Jordan 47 C4 32 5N 35 45 E
Al Bārūk, J., Lebanon 47 B4 33 39N 35 40 E
Al Başrah, Iraq 44 D5 30 30N 47 50 E
Al Baţḩā, Iraq 44 D5 31 6N 45 53 E
Al Batrūn, Lebanon 47 A4 34 15N 35 40 E
Al Bayḑā, Libya 51 B10 32 50N 21 44 E
Al Biqā, Lebanon 47 A5 34 10N 36 10 E
Al Bi'r, Si. Arabia 44 D3 28 51N 36 16 E
Al Burayj, Syria 47 A5 34 15N 36 46 E
Al Faḑilī, Si. Arabia 45 E6 26 58N 49 10 E
Al Fallūjah, Iraq 44 C4 33 20N 43 55 E
Al Fāw, Iraq 45 D6 30 0N 48 30 E
Al Fujayrah, U.A.E. 45 E8 25 7N 56 18 E
Al Ghadaf, W. →, Jordan 47 D5 31 26N 36 43 E
Al Ghammās, Iraq 44 D5 31 45N 44 37 E

Al Ghazālah, *Si. Arabia* **44 E4** 26 48N 41 19 E
Al Ḩadīthah, *Iraq* **44 C4** 34 0N 41 13 E
Al Ḩadīthah, *Si. Arabia* **47 D6** 31 28N 37 8 E
Al Ḩaḑr, *Iraq* **44 C4** 35 35N 42 44 E
Al Ḩājānah, *Syria* **47 B5** 33 20N 36 33 E
Al Ḩajar al Gharbī, *Oman* **45 E8** 24 10N 56 15 E
Al Hāmad, *Si. Arabia* **44 D3** 31 30N 39 30 E
Al Hamdāniyah, *Syria* **44 C3** 35 25N 36 50 E
Al Ḩamīdīyah, *Syria* **47 A4** 34 42N 35 57 E
Al Ḩammār, *Iraq* **44 D5** 30 57N 46 51 E
Al Ḩamrā', *Si. Arabia* **44 E3** 24 2N 38 55 E
Al Ḩanākīyah, *Si. Arabia* **44 E4** 24 51N 40 31 E
Al Harīr, W. →, *Syria* **47 C4** 32 44N 35 59 E
Al Ḩasā, W. →, *Jordan* **47 D4** 31 4N 35 29 E
Al Ḩasakah, *Syria* **44 B4** 36 35N 40 45 E
Al Haydān, W. →, *Jordan* **47 D4** 31 29N 35 34 E
Al Ḩayy, *Iraq* **44 C5** 32 5N 46 5 E
Al Ḩijarah, *Asia* **44 D4** 30 0N 44 0 E
Al Ḩillah, *Iraq* **44 C5** 32 30N 44 25 E
Al Ḩillah, *Si. Arabia* **46 B4** 23 35N 46 50 E
Al Hindīyah, *Iraq* **44 C5** 32 30N 44 10 E
Al Hirmil, *Lebanon* **47 A5** 34 26N 36 24 E
Al Hoceïma, *Morocco* **50 A5** 35 8N 3 58W
Al Ḩudaydah, *Yemen* **46 E3** 14 50N 43 0 E
Al Hufūf, *Si. Arabia* **46 B4** 25 25N 49 45 E
Al Ḩumayḑah, *Si. Arabia* **44 D2** 29 14N 34 56 E
Al Ḩunayy, *Si. Arabia* **45 E6** 25 58N 48 45 E
Al Īsāwīyah, *Si. Arabia* **44 D3** 30 43N 37 59 E
Al Jafr, *Jordan* **47 E5** 30 18N 36 14 E
Al Jāfūrah, *Si. Arabia* **45 E7** 25 0N 50 15 E
Al Jaghbūb, *Libya* **51 C10** 29 42N 24 38 E
Al Jahrah, *Kuwait* **44 D5** 29 25N 47 40 E
Al Jalāmīd, *Si. Arabia* **44 D3** 31 20N 40 6 E
Al Jamalīyah, *Qatar* **45 E6** 25 37N 51 5 E
Al Janūb □, *Lebanon* **47 B4** 33 20N 35 20 E
Al Jawf, *Libya* **51 D10** 24 10N 23 24 E
Al Jawf, *Si. Arabia* **44 D3** 29 55N 39 40 E
Al Jazirah, *Iraq* **44 C5** 33 30N 44 0 E
Al Jithāmīyah, *Si. Arabia* **44 E4** 27 41N 41 43 E
Al Jubayl, *Si. Arabia* **45 E6** 27 0N 49 50 E
Al Jubaylah, *Si. Arabia* **44 E5** 24 55N 46 25 E
Al Jubb, *Si. Arabia* **44 E4** 27 11N 42 17 E
Al Junaynah, *Sudan* **51 F10** 13 27N 22 45 E
Al Kabā'ish, *Iraq* **44 D5** 30 58N 47 0 E
Al Karak, *Jordan* **47 D4** 31 11N 35 42 E
Al Karak □, *Jordan* **47 E5** 31 0N 36 0 E
Al Kāzim Tyah, *Iraq* **44 C5** 33 22N 44 12 E
Al Khābūra, *Oman* **45 F8** 23 57N 57 5 E
Al Khafji, *Si. Arabia* **45 E6** 28 24N 48 29 E
Al Khalīl, *West Bank* **47 D4** 31 32N 35 6 E
Al Khāliş, *Iraq* **44 C5** 33 49N 44 32 E
Al Kharsānīyah, *Si. Arabia* **45 E6** 27 13N 49 18 E
Al Khaşab, *Oman* **45 E8** 26 14N 56 15 E
Al Khawr, *Qatar* **45 E6** 25 41N 51 30 E
Al Khiḑr, *Iraq* **44 D5** 31 12N 45 33 E
Al Khiyām, *Lebanon* **47 B4** 33 20N 35 36 E
Al Kiswah, *Syria* **47 B5** 33 23N 36 14 E
Al Kūfah, *Iraq* **44 C5** 32 2N 44 24 E
Al Kufrah, *Libya* **51 D10** 24 17N 23 15 E
Al Kuhayfīyah, *Si. Arabia* **44 E4** 27 12N 43 3 E
Al Kūt, *Iraq* **44 C5** 32 30N 46 0 E
Al Kuwayt, *Kuwait* **46 B4** 29 30N 48 0 E
Al Labwah, *Lebanon* **47 A5** 34 11N 36 20 E
Al Lādhiqīyah, *Syria* **44 C2** 35 30N 35 45 E
Al Līth, *Si. Arabia* **46 C3** 20 9N 40 15 E
Al Liwā', *Oman* **45 E8** 24 31N 56 36 E
Al Luḩayyah, *Yemen* **46 D3** 15 45N 42 40 E
Al Madīnah, *Iraq* **44 D5** 30 57N 47 16 E
Al Madīnah, *Si. Arabia* **46 C2** 24 35N 39 52 E
Al Mafraq, *Jordan* **47 C5** 32 17N 36 14 E
Al Maḩmūdīyah, *Iraq* **44 C5** 33 3N 44 21 E
Al Majma'ah, *Si. Arabia* **44 E5** 25 57N 45 22 E
Al Makhruq, W. →, *Jordan* **47 D6** 31 28N 37 0 E
Al Makḩūl, *Si. Arabia* **44 E4** 26 37N 42 39 E
Al Manāmah, *Bahrain* **46 B5** 26 10N 50 30 E
Al Maqwa', *Kuwait* **44 D5** 29 10N 47 59 E
Al Marj, *Libya* **51 B10** 32 25N 20 30 E
Al Maţlā, *Kuwait* **44 D5** 29 24N 47 40 E
Al Mawjib, W. →, *Jordan* **47 D4** 31 28N 35 36 E
Al Mawşil, *Iraq* **44 B4** 36 15N 43 5 E
Al Mayādin, *Syria* **44 C4** 35 1N 40 27 E
Al Mazār, *Jordan* **47 D4** 31 4N 35 41 E
Al Midhnab, *Si. Arabia* **44 E5** 25 50N 44 18 E
Al Minā', *Lebanon* **47 A4** 34 24N 35 49 E
Al Miqdādīyah, *Iraq* **44 C5** 34 0N 45 0 E
Al Mubarraz, *Si. Arabia* **45 E6** 25 30N 49 40 E
Al Mudawwarah, *Jordan* **47 F5** 29 19N 36 0 E
Al Mughayrā', *U.A.E.* **45 E7** 24 5N 53 32 E
Al Muḩarraq, *Bahrain* **45 E6** 26 15N 50 40 E
Al Mukallā, *Yemen* **46 E4** 14 33N 49 2 E
Al Mukhā, *Yemen* **46 E3** 13 18N 43 15 E
Al Musayjīd, *Si. Arabia* **44 E3** 24 5N 39 5 E
Al Musayyib, *Iraq* **44 C5** 32 49N 44 20 E
Al Muwayliḩ, *Si. Arabia* **44 E2** 27 40N 35 30 E
Al Qā'im, *Iraq* **44 C4** 34 21N 41 7 E
Al Qalībah, *Si. Arabia* **44 D3** 28 24N 37 42 E
Al Qāmishlī, *Syria* **44 B4** 37 2N 41 14 E
Al Qaryatayn, *Syria* **47 A6** 34 12N 37 13 E
Al Qaşīm, *Si. Arabia* **44 E4** 26 0N 43 0 E
Al Qaţ'ā, *Syria* **44 C4** 34 40N 40 48 E
Al Qaţīf, *Si. Arabia* **45 E6** 26 35N 50 0 E
Al Qatrānah, *Jordan* **47 D5** 31 12N 36 6 E
Al Qaţrūn, *Libya* **51 D9** 24 56N 15 3 E
Al Qayşūmah, *Si. Arabia* **44 D5** 28 20N 46 7 E
Al Quds = Jerusalem, *Israel* **47 D4** 31 47N 35 10 E
Al Qunayţirah, *Syria* **47 C4** 32 55N 35 45 E
Al Qurnah, *Iraq* **44 D5** 31 1N 47 25 E
Al Quşayr, *Iraq* **44 D5** 30 39N 45 50 E
Al Quşayr, *Syria* **47 A5** 34 31N 36 34 E
Al Quţayfah, *Syria* **47 B5** 33 44N 36 36 E
Al 'Ubaylah, *Si. Arabia* **46 C5** 21 59N 50 57 E
Al 'Uḑaylīyah, *Si. Arabia* **45 E6** 25 8N 49 18 E
Al 'Ulā, *Si. Arabia* **44 E3** 26 35N 38 0 E
Al 'Uqayr, *Si. Arabia* **45 E6** 25 40N 50 15 E
Al 'Uwaynid, *Si. Arabia* **44 E5** 24 50N 46 0 E
Al 'Uwayqīlah, *Si. Arabia* **44 D4** 30 30N 42 10 E
Al 'Uyūn, *Ḩijāz, Si. Arabia* **44 E3** 24 33N 39 35 E
Al 'Uyūn, *Najd, Si. Arabia* **44 E4** 26 30N 43 50 E
Al 'Uzayr, *Iraq* **44 D5** 31 19N 47 25 E
Al Wajh, *Si. Arabia* **44 E3** 26 10N 36 30 E
Al Wakrah, *Qatar* **45 E6** 25 10N 51 40 E
Al Waqbah, *Si. Arabia* **44 D5** 28 48N 45 33 E
Al Wari'āh, *Si. Arabia* **44 E5** 27 51N 47 25 E
Ala Dağ, *Turkey* **44 B2** 37 44N 35 9 E
Ala Tau Shankou = Dzungarian Gates, *Asia* **32 B3** 45 0N 82 0 E
Alabama □, *U.S.A.* **77 J2** 33 0N 87 0W
Alabama →, *U.S.A.* **77 K2** 31 8N 87 57W
Alabaster, *U.S.A.* **77 J2** 33 15N 86 49W
Alaçam Dağları, *Turkey* **21 E13** 39 18N 28 49 E
Alachua, *U.S.A.* **77 L4** 29 47N 82 30W
Alaérma, *Greece* **23 C9** 36 9N 27 57 E
Alagoa Grande, *Brazil* **93 E11** 7 3S 35 35W
Alagoas □, *Brazil* **93 E11** 9 0S 36 0W
Alagoinhas, *Brazil* **93 F11** 12 7S 38 20W
Alaior, *Spain* **22 B11** 39 57N 4 8 E
Alajero, *Canary Is.* **22 F2** 28 3N 17 13W
Alajuela, *Costa Rica* **88 D3** 10 2N 84 8W
Alakamisy, *Madag.* **57 C8** 21 19S 47 14 E
Alaknanda →, *India* **43 D8** 30 8N 78 36 E
Alakurtti, *Russia* **24 A5** 67 0N 30 30 E
Alamarvdasht, *Iran* **45 E7** 27 37N 52 59 E
Alameda, *Calif., U.S.A.* **84 H4** 37 46N 122 15W
Alameda, *N. Mex., U.S.A.* **83 J10** 35 11N 106 37W
Alamo, *U.S.A.* **85 J11** 37 22N 115 10W
Alamo Crossing, *U.S.A.* **85 L13** 34 16N 113 33W
Alamogordo, *U.S.A.* **83 K11** 32 54N 105 57W
Alamos, *Mexico* **86 B3** 27 0N 109 0W
Alamosa, *U.S.A.* **83 H11** 37 28N 105 52W
Åland, *Finland* **9 F19** 60 15N 20 0 E
Ålands hav, *Sweden* **9 F18** 60 0N 19 30 E
Alania = North Ossetia □, *Russia* **25 F7** 43 30N 44 30 E
Alanya, *Turkey* **25 G5** 36 38N 32 0 E
Alaotra, Farihin', *Madag.* **57 B8** 17 30S 48 30 E
Alapayevsk, *Russia* **26 D7** 57 52N 61 42 E
Alappuzha = Alleppey, *India* **40 Q10** 9 30N 76 28 E
Alarobia-Vohiposa, *Madag.* **57 C8** 20 59S 47 9 E
Alaşehir, *Turkey* **21 E13** 38 23N 28 30 E
Alaska □, *U.S.A.* **68 B5** 64 0N 154 0W
Alaska, G. of, *Pac. Oc.* **68 C5** 58 0N 145 0W
Alaska Peninsula, *U.S.A.* **68 C4** 56 0N 159 0W
Alaska Range, *U.S.A.* **68 B4** 62 50N 151 0W
Ālāt, *Azerbaijan* **25 G8** 39 58N 49 25 E
Alatyr, *Russia* **24 D8** 54 55N 46 35 E
Alausi, *Ecuador* **92 D3** 2 0S 78 50W
Alava, C., *U.S.A.* **82 B1** 48 10N 124 44W
Alavus, *Finland* **9 E20** 62 35N 23 36 E
Alawoona, *Australia* **63 E3** 34 45S 140 30 E
'Alayh, *Lebanon* **47 B4** 33 46N 35 33 E
Alba, *Italy* **18 D8** 44 42N 8 2 E
Alba-Iulia, *Romania* **17 E12** 46 8N 23 39 E
Albacete, *Spain* **19 C5** 39 0N 1 50W
Albacutya, L., *Australia* **63 F3** 35 45S 141 58 E
Albanel, L., *Canada* **70 B5** 50 55N 73 12W
Albania ■, *Europe* **21 D9** 41 0N 20 0 E
Albany, *Australia* **61 G2** 35 1S 117 58 E
Albany, *Ga., U.S.A.* **77 K3** 31 35N 84 10W
Albany, *N.Y., U.S.A.* **79 D11** 42 39N 73 45W
Albany, *Oreg., U.S.A.* **82 D2** 44 38N 123 6W
Albany, *Tex., U.S.A.* **81 J5** 32 44N 99 18W
Albany →, *Canada* **70 B3** 52 17N 81 31W
Albardón, *Argentina* **94 C2** 31 20S 68 30W
Albatross B., *Australia* **62 A3** 12 45S 141 30 E
Albemarle, *U.S.A.* **77 H5** 35 21N 80 11W
Albemarle Sd., *U.S.A.* **77 H7** 36 5N 76 0W
Alberche →, *Spain* **19 C3** 39 58N 4 46W
Alberdi, *Paraguay* **94 B4** 26 14S 58 20W
Albert, L., *Africa* **54 B3** 1 30N 31 0 E
Albert, L., *Australia* **63 F2** 35 30S 139 10 E
Albert Edward Ra., *Australia* **60 C4** 18 17S 127 57 E
Albert Lea, *U.S.A.* **80 D8** 43 39N 93 22W
Albert Nile →, *Uganda* **54 B3** 3 36N 32 2 E
Albert Town, *Bahamas* **89 B5** 22 37N 74 33W
Alberta □, *Canada* **72 C6** 54 40N 115 0W
Alberti, *Argentina* **94 D3** 35 1S 60 16W
Albertinia, *S. Africa* **56 E3** 34 11S 21 34 E
Alberton, *Canada* **71 C7** 46 50N 64 0W
Albertville = Kalemie, *Dem. Rep. of the Congo* **54 D2** 5 55S 29 9 E
Albertville, *France* **18 D7** 45 40N 6 22 E
Albertville, *U.S.A.* **77 H2** 34 16N 86 13W
Albi, *France* **18 E5** 43 56N 2 9 E
Albia, *U.S.A.* **80 E8** 41 2N 92 48W
Albina, *Surinam* **93 B8** 5 37N 54 15W
Albina, Ponta, *Angola* **56 B1** 15 52S 11 44 E
Albion, *Mich., U.S.A.* **76 D3** 42 15N 84 45W
Albion, *Nebr., U.S.A.* **80 E6** 41 42N 98 0W
Albion, *Pa., U.S.A.* **78 E4** 41 53N 80 22W
Alborán, *Medit. S.* **19 E4** 35 57N 3 0W
Ålborg, *Denmark* **9 H13** 57 2N 9 54 E
Alborz, Reshteh-ye Kūhhā-ye, *Iran* **45 C7** 36 0N 52 0 E
Albuquerque, *U.S.A.* **83 J10** 35 5N 106 39W
Albuquerque, Cayos de, *Caribbean* **88 D3** 12 10N 81 50W
Alburg, *U.S.A.* **79 B11** 44 59N 73 18W
Albury = Albury-Wodonga, *Australia* **63 F4** 36 3S 146 56 E
Albury-Wodonga, *Australia* **63 F4** 36 3S 146 56 E
Alcalá de Henares, *Spain* **19 B4** 40 28N 3 22W
Alcalá la Real, *Spain* **19 D4** 37 27N 3 57W
Álcamo, *Italy* **20 F5** 37 59N 12 55 E
Alcañiz, *Spain* **19 B5** 41 2N 0 8W
Alcântara, *Brazil* **93 D10** 2 20S 44 30W
Alcántara, Embalse de, *Spain* **19 C2** 39 44N 6 50W
Alcantarilla, *Spain* **19 D5** 37 59N 1 12W
Alcaraz, Sierra de, *Spain* **19 C4** 38 40N 2 20W
Alcaudete, *Spain* **19 D3** 37 35N 4 5W
Alcázar de San Juan, *Spain* **19 C4** 39 24N 3 12W
Alchevsk, *Ukraine* **25 E6** 48 30N 38 45 E
Alcira = Alzira, *Spain* **19 C5** 39 9N 0 30W
Alcova, *U.S.A.* **82 E10** 42 34N 106 43W
Alcoy, *Spain* **19 C5** 38 43N 0 30W
Alcúdia, *Spain* **22 B10** 39 51N 3 7 E
Alcúdia, B. d', *Spain* **22 B10** 39 47N 3 15 E
Aldabra Is., *Seychelles* **49 G8** 9 22S 46 28 E
Aldama, *Mexico* **87 C5** 23 0N 98 4W
Aldan, *Russia* **27 D13** 58 40N 125 30 E
Aldan →, *Russia* **27 C13** 63 28N 129 35 E
Aldea, Pta. de la, *Canary Is.* **22 G4** 28 0N 15 50W
Aldeburgh, *U.K.* **11 E9** 52 10N 1 37 E
Alder Pk., *U.S.A.* **84 K5** 35 53N 121 22W
Alderney, *U.K.* **11 H5** 49 42N 2 11W
Aldershot, *U.K.* **11 F7** 51 15N 0 44W
Aledo, *U.S.A.* **80 E9** 41 12N 90 45W
Aleg, *Mauritania* **50 E3** 17 3N 13 55W
Alegranza, *Canary Is.* **22 E6** 29 23N 13 32W
Alegranza, I., *Canary Is.* **22 E6** 29 23N 13 32W
Alegre, *Brazil* **95 A7** 20 50S 41 30W
Alegrete, *Brazil* **95 B4** 29 40S 56 0W
Aleisk, *Russia* **26 D9** 52 40N 83 0 E
Aleksandriya = Oleksandriya, *Ukraine* **17 C14** 50 37N 26 19 E
Aleksandrov Gay, *Russia* **25 D8** 50 9N 48 34 E
Aleksandrovsk-Sakhalinskiy, *Russia* **27 D15** 50 50N 142 20 E
Além Paraíba, *Brazil* **95 A7** 21 52S 42 41W
Alemania, *Argentina* **94 B2** 25 40S 65 30W
Alemania, *Chile* **94 B2** 25 10S 69 55W
Alençon, *France* **18 B4** 48 27N 0 4 E
Alenquer, *Brazil* **93 D8** 1 56S 54 46W
Alenuihaha Channel, *U.S.A.* **74 H17** 20 30N 156 0W
Aleppo = Ḩalab, *Syria* **44 B3** 36 10N 37 15 E
Alès, *France* **18 D6** 44 9N 4 5 E
Alessándria, *Italy* **18 D8** 44 54N 8 37 E
Ålesund, *Norway* **9 E12** 62 28N 6 12 E
Aleutian Is., *Pac. Oc.* **68 C2** 52 0N 175 0W
Aleutian Trench, *Pac. Oc.* **64 C10** 48 0N 180 0 E
Alexander, *U.S.A.* **80 B3** 47 51N 103 39W
Alexander, Mt., *Australia* **61 E3** 28 58S 120 16 E
Alexander Arch., *U.S.A.* **68 C6** 56 0N 136 0W
Alexander Bay, *S. Africa* **56 D2** 28 40S 16 30 E
Alexander City, *U.S.A.* **77 J3** 32 56N 85 58W
Alexander I., *Antarctica* **5 C17** 69 0S 70 0W
Alexandra, *Australia* **63 F4** 37 8S 145 40 E
Alexandra, *N.Z.* **59 L2** 45 14S 169 25 E
Alexandra Falls, *Canada* **72 A5** 60 29N 116 18W
Alexandria = El Iskandarîya, *Egypt* **51 B11** 31 13N 29 58 E
Alexandria, *B.C., Canada* **72 C4** 52 35N 122 27W
Alexandria, *Ont., Canada* **79 A10** 45 19N 74 38W
Alexandria, *Romania* **17 G13** 43 57N 25 24 E
Alexandria, *S. Africa* **56 E4** 33 38S 26 28 E
Alexandria, *U.K.* **12 F4** 55 59N 4 35W
Alexandria, *La., U.S.A.* **81 K8** 31 18N 92 27W
Alexandria, *Minn., U.S.A.* **80 C7** 45 53N 95 22W
Alexandria, *S. Dak., U.S.A.* **80 D6** 43 39N 97 47W
Alexandria, *Va., U.S.A.* **76 F7** 38 48N 77 3W
Alexandria Bay, *U.S.A.* **79 B9** 44 20N 75 55W
Alexandrina, L., *Australia* **63 F2** 35 25S 139 10 E
Alexandroúpolis, *Greece* **21 D11** 40 50N 25 54 E
Alexis →, *Canada* **71 B8** 52 33N 56 8W
Alexis Creek, *Canada* **72 C4** 52 10N 123 20W
Alfabia, *Spain* **22 B9** 39 44N 2 44 E
Alfenas, *Brazil* **95 A6** 21 20S 46 10W
Alford, *Aberds., U.K.* **12 D6** 57 14N 2 41W
Alford, *Lincs., U.K.* **10 D8** 53 15N 0 10 E
Alfred, *Maine, U.S.A.* **79 C14** 43 29N 70 43W
Alfred, *N.Y., U.S.A.* **78 D7** 42 16N 77 48W
Alfreton, *U.K.* **10 D6** 53 6N 1 24W
Alga, *Kazakstan* **25 E10** 49 53N 57 20 E
Algaida, *Spain* **22 B9** 39 33N 2 53 E
Ålgård, *Norway* **9 G11** 58 46N 5 53 E
Algarve, *Portugal* **19 D1** 36 58N 8 20W
Algeciras, *Spain* **19 D3** 36 9N 5 28W
Algemesí, *Spain* **19 C5** 39 11N 0 27W
Alger, *Algeria* **50 A6** 36 42N 3 8 E
Algeria ■, *Africa* **50 C6** 28 30N 2 0 E
Alghero, *Italy* **20 D3** 40 33N 8 19 E
Algiers = Alger, *Algeria* **50 A6** 36 42N 3 8 E
Algoa B., *S. Africa* **56 E4** 33 50S 25 45 E
Algoma, *U.S.A.* **76 C2** 44 36N 87 26W
Algona, *U.S.A.* **80 D7** 43 4N 94 14W
Algonac, *U.S.A.* **78 D2** 42 37N 82 32W
Algonquin Prov. Park, *Canada* **70 C4** 45 50N 78 30W
Algorta, *Uruguay* **96 C5** 32 25S 57 23W
Alhambra, *U.S.A.* **85 L8** 34 8N 118 6W
Alhucemas = Al Hoceïma, *Morocco* **50 A5** 35 8N 3 58W
'Alī al Gharbī, *Iraq* **44 C5** 32 30N 46 45 E
'Alī ash Sharqī, *Iraq* **44 C5** 32 7N 46 44 E
'Alī Khēl, *Afghan.* **42 C3** 33 57N 69 43 E
Alī Shāh, *Iran* **44 B5** 38 9N 45 50 E
'Alīābād, *Khorāsān, Iran* **45 C8** 32 30N 57 30 E
'Alīābād, *Kordestān, Iran* **44 C5** 35 4N 46 58 E
'Alīābād, *Yazd, Iran* **45 D7** 31 41N 53 49 E
Aliağa, *Turkey* **21 E12** 38 47N 26 59 E
Aliákmon →, *Greece* **21 D10** 40 30N 22 36 E
Alicante, *Spain* **19 C5** 38 23N 0 30W
Alice, *S. Africa* **56 E4** 32 48S 26 55 E
Alice, *U.S.A.* **81 M5** 27 45N 98 5W
Alice →, *Queens., Australia* **62 C3** 24 2S 144 50 E
Alice →, *Queens., Australia* **62 B3** 15 35S 142 20 E
Alice Arm, *Canada* **72 B3** 55 29N 129 31W
Alice Springs, *Australia* **62 C1** 23 40S 133 50 E
Alicedale, *S. Africa* **56 E4** 33 15S 26 4 E
Aliceville, *U.S.A.* **77 J1** 33 8N 88 9W
Aliganj, *India* **43 F8** 27 30N 79 10 E
Aligarh, *Raj., India* **42 G7** 25 55N 76 15 E
Aligarh, *Ut. P., India* **42 F8** 27 55N 78 10 E
Alīgūdarz, *Iran* **45 C6** 33 25N 49 45 E
Alimnia, *Greece* **23 C9** 36 16N 27 43 E
Alingsås, *Sweden* **9 H15** 57 56N 12 31 E
Alipur, *Pakistan* **42 E4** 29 25N 70 55 E
Alipur Duar, *India* **41 F16** 26 30N 89 35 E
Aliquippa, *U.S.A.* **78 F4** 40 37N 80 15W
Alitus = Alytus, *Lithuania* **9 J21** 54 24N 24 3 E
Aliwal North, *S. Africa* **56 E4** 30 45S 26 45 E
Alix, *Canada* **72 C6** 52 24N 113 11W
Aljustrel, *Portugal* **19 D1** 37 55N 8 10W
Alkmaar, *Neths.* **15 B4** 52 37N 4 45 E
All American Canal, *U.S.A.* **83 K6** 32 45N 115 15W
Allagash →, *U.S.A.* **77 B11** 47 5N 69 3W
Allah Dad, *Pakistan* **42 G2** 25 38N 67 34 E
Allahabad, *India* **43 G9** 25 25N 81 58 E
Allan, *Canada* **73 C7** 51 53N 106 4W
Allanridge, *S. Africa* **56 D4** 27 45S 26 40 E
Allegany, *U.S.A.* **78 D6** 42 6N 78 30W
Allegheny →, *U.S.A.* **78 F5** 40 27N 80 1W
Allegheny Mts., *U.S.A.* **76 G6** 38 15N 80 10W
Allegheny Reservoir, *U.S.A.* **78 E6** 41 50N 79 0W
Allen, Bog of, *Ireland* **13 C5** 53 15N 7 0W
Allen, L., *Ireland* **13 B3** 54 8N 8 4W
Allendale, *U.S.A.* **77 J5** 33 1N 81 18W
Allende, *Mexico* **86 B4** 28 20N 100 50W
Allentown, *U.S.A.* **79 F9** 40 37N 75 29W
Alleppey, *India* **40 Q10** 9 30N 76 28 E
Aller →, *Germany* **16 B5** 52 56N 9 12 E
Alliance, *Nebr., U.S.A.* **80 D3** 42 6N 102 52W
Alliance, *Ohio, U.S.A.* **78 F3** 40 55N 81 6W
Allier →, *France* **18 C5** 46 57N 3 4 E
Alliford Bay, *Canada* **72 C2** 53 12N 131 58W
Alliston, *Canada* **78 B5** 44 9N 79 52W
Alloa, *U.K.* **12 E5** 56 7N 3 47W
Allora, *Australia* **63 D5** 28 2S 152 0 E
Alluitsup Paa, *Greenland* **4 C5** 60 30N 45 35W
Alma, *Canada* **71 C5** 48 35N 71 40W
Alma, *Ga., U.S.A.* **77 K4** 31 33N 82 28W
Alma, *Kans., U.S.A.* **80 F6** 39 1N 96 17W
Alma, *Mich., U.S.A.* **76 D3** 43 23N 84 39W
Alma, *Nebr., U.S.A.* **80 E5** 40 6N 99 22W
Alma Ata = Almaty, *Kazakstan* **26 E8** 43 15N 76 57 E
Almada, *Portugal* **19 C1** 38 40N 9 9W
Almaden, *Australia* **62 B3** 17 22S 144 40 E
Almadén, *Spain* **19 C3** 38 49N 4 52W
Almanor, L., *U.S.A.* **82 F3** 40 14N 121 9W
Almansa, *Spain* **19 C5** 38 51N 1 5W
Almanzor, Pico, *Spain* **19 B3** 40 15N 5 18W
Almanzora →, *Spain* **19 D5** 37 14N 1 46W
Almaty, *Kazakstan* **26 E8** 43 15N 76 57 E
Almazán, *Spain* **19 B4** 41 30N 2 30W
Almeirim, *Brazil* **93 D8** 1 30S 52 34W
Almelo, *Neths.* **15 B6** 52 22N 6 42 E
Almendralejo, *Spain* **19 C2** 38 41N 6 26W
Almere-Stad, *Neths.* **15 B5** 52 20N 5 15 E
Almería, *Spain* **19 D4** 36 52N 2 27W
Almirante, *Panama* **88 E3** 9 10N 82 30W
Almiroú, Kólpos, *Greece* **23 D6** 35 23N 24 20 E
Almond, *U.S.A.* **78 D7** 42 19N 77 44W
Almont, *U.S.A.* **78 D1** 42 55N 83 3W
Almonte, *Canada* **79 A8** 45 14N 76 12W
Almora, *India* **43 E8** 29 38N 79 40 E
Alness, *U.K.* **12 D4** 57 41N 4 16W
Alnmouth, *U.K.* **10 B6** 55 24N 1 37W
Alnwick, *U.K.* **10 B6** 55 24N 1 42W
Aloi, *Uganda* **54 B3** 2 16N 33 10 E
Alon, *Burma* **41 H19** 22 12N 95 5 E
Alor, *Indonesia* **37 F6** 8 15S 124 30 E
Alor Setar, *Malaysia* **39 J3** 6 7N 100 22 E
Alot, *India* **42 H6** 23 56N 75 40 E
Aloysius, Mt., *Australia* **61 E4** 26 0S 128 38 E
Alpaugh, *U.S.A.* **84 K7** 35 53N 119 29W
Alpena, *U.S.A.* **76 C4** 45 4N 83 27W
Alpha, *Australia* **62 C4** 23 39S 146 37 E
Alphen aan den Rijn, *Neths.* **15 B4** 52 7N 4 40 E
Alpine, *Ariz., U.S.A.* **83 K9** 33 51N 109 9W
Alpine, *Calif., U.S.A.* **85 N10** 32 50N 116 46W
Alpine, *Tex., U.S.A.* **81 K3** 30 22N 103 40W
Alps, *Europe* **18 C8** 46 30N 9 30 E
Alsace, *France* **18 B7** 48 15N 7 25 E
Alsask, *Canada* **73 C7** 51 21N 109 59W
Alsasua, *Spain* **19 A4** 42 54N 2 10W
Alsek →, *U.S.A.* **72 B1** 59 10N 138 12W
Alsten, *Norway* **8 D15** 65 58N 12 40 E
Alston, *U.K.* **10 C5** 54 49N 2 25W
Alta, *Norway* **8 B20** 69 57N 23 10 E
Alta Gracia, *Argentina* **94 C3** 31 40S 64 30W
Alta Sierra, *U.S.A.* **85 K8** 35 42N 118 33W
Altaelva →, *Norway* **8 B20** 69 54N 23 17 E
Altafjorden, *Norway* **8 A20** 70 5N 23 5 E
Altai = Aerhtai Shan, *Mongolia* **32 B4** 46 40N 92 45 E
Altamaha →, *U.S.A.* **77 K5** 31 20N 81 20W
Altamira, *Brazil* **93 D8** 3 12S 52 10W
Altamira, *Chile* **94 B2** 25 47S 69 51W
Altamira, *Mexico* **87 C5** 22 24N 97 55W
Altamont, *U.S.A.* **79 D10** 42 43N 74 3W
Altamura, *Italy* **20 D7** 40 49N 16 33 E
Altanbulag, *Mongolia* **32 A5** 50 16N 106 30 E
Altar, *Mexico* **86 A2** 30 40N 111 50W
Altar, Desierto de, *Mexico* **86 B2** 30 10N 112 0W
Altata, *Mexico* **86 C3** 24 30N 108 0W
Altavista, *U.S.A.* **76 G6** 37 6N 79 17W
Altay, *China* **32 B3** 47 48N 88 10 E
Altea, *Spain* **19 C5** 38 38N 0 2W
Altiplano = Bolivian Plateau, *S. Amer.* **90 E4** 20 0S 67 30W
Alto Araguaia, *Brazil* **93 G8** 17 15S 53 20W
Alto Cuchumatanes = Cuchumatanes, Sierra de los, *Guatemala* **88 C1** 15 35N 91 25W
Alto del Carmen, *Chile* **94 B1** 28 46S 70 30W
Alto del Inca, *Chile* **94 A2** 24 10S 68 10W
Alto Ligonha, *Mozam.* **55 F4** 15 30S 38 11 E
Alto Molocue, *Mozam.* **55 F4** 15 50S 37 35 E
Alto Paraguay □, *Paraguay* **94 A4** 21 0S 58 30W
Alto Paraná □, *Paraguay* **95 B5** 25 30S 54 50W
Alton, *Canada* **78 C4** 43 54N 80 5W
Alton, *U.K.* **11 F7** 51 9N 0 59W
Alton, *Ill., U.S.A.* **80 F9** 38 53N 90 11W
Alton, *N.H., U.S.A.* **79 C13** 43 27N 71 13W
Altoona, *U.S.A.* **78 F6** 40 31N 78 24W
Altūn Kūprī, *Iraq* **44 C5** 35 45N 44 9 E
Altun Shan, *China* **32 C3** 38 30N 88 0 E
Alturas, *U.S.A.* **82 F3** 41 29N 120 32W
Altus, *U.S.A.* **81 H5** 34 38N 99 20W
Alucra, *Turkey* **25 F6** 40 22N 38 47 E
Alūksne, *Latvia* **9 H22** 57 24N 27 3 E
Alunite, *U.S.A.* **85 K12** 35 59N 114 55W
Alusi, *Indonesia* **37 F8** 7 35S 131 40 E
Alva, *U.S.A.* **81 G5** 36 48N 98 40W
Alvarado, *Mexico* **87 D5** 18 40N 95 50W
Alvarado, *U.S.A.* **81 J6** 32 24N 97 13W
Alvaro Obregón, Presa, *Mexico* **86 B3** 27 55N 109 52W
Alvear, *Argentina* **94 B4** 29 5S 56 30W
Alvesta, *Sweden* **9 H16** 56 54N 14 35 E
Alvin, *U.S.A.* **81 L7** 29 26N 95 15W
Alvinston, *Canada* **78 D3** 42 49N 81 52W
Älvkarleby, *Sweden* **9 F17** 60 34N 17 26 E
Alvord Desert, *U.S.A.* **82 E4** 42 30N 118 25W
Älvsbyn, *Sweden* **8 D19** 65 40N 21 0 E
Alwar, *India* **42 F7** 27 38N 76 34 E
Alxa Zuoqi, *China* **34 E3** 38 50N 105 40 E
Alyangula, *Australia* **62 A2** 13 55S 136 30 E
Alyata = Ālāt, *Azerbaijan* **25 G8** 39 58N 49 25 E
Alyth, *U.K.* **12 E5** 56 38N 3 13W
Alytus, *Lithuania* **9 J21** 54 24N 24 3 E
Alzada, *U.S.A.* **80 C2** 45 2N 104 25W
Alzira, *Spain* **19 C5** 39 9N 0 30W
Am Timan, *Chad* **51 F10** 11 0N 20 10 E
Amadeus, L., *Australia* **61 D5** 24 54S 131 0 E
Amadi, *Dem. Rep. of the Congo* **54 B2** 3 40N 26 40 E
Amâdi, *Sudan* **51 G12** 5 29N 30 25 E
Amadjuak L., *Canada* **69 B12** 65 0N 71 8W
Amagansett, *U.S.A.* **79 F12** 40 59N 72 9W
Amagasaki, *Japan* **31 G7** 34 42N 135 20 E
Amahai, *Indonesia* **37 E7** 3 20S 128 55 E
Amakusa-Shotō, *Japan* **31 H5** 32 15N 130 10 E

Åmål, *Sweden* **9 G15** 59 3N 12 42 E
Amaliás, *Greece* **21 F9** 37 47N 21 22 E
Amalner, *India* **40 J9** 21 5N 75 5 E
Amamapare, *Indonesia* **37 E9** 4 53S 136 38 E
Amambaí, *Brazil* **95 A5** 23 5S 55 13W
Amambaí →, *Brazil* **95 A5** 23 22S 53 56W
Amambay □, *Paraguay* **95 A4** 23 0S 56 0W
Amambay, Cordillera de, *S. Amer.* **95 A4** 23 0S 55 45W
Amami-Guntō, *Japan* **31 L4** 27 16N 129 21 E
Amami-Ō-Shima, *Japan* **31 L4** 28 0N 129 0 E
Amaná, L., *Brazil* **92 D6** 2 35S 64 40W
Amanat →, *India* **43 G11** 24 7N 84 4 E
Amanda Park, *U.S.A.* **84 C3** 47 28N 123 55W
Amangeldy, *Kazakstan* **26 D7** 50 10N 65 10 E
Amapá, *Brazil* **93 C8** 2 5N 50 50W
Amapá □, *Brazil* **93 C8** 1 40N 52 0W
Amarante, *Brazil* **93 E10** 6 14S 42 50W
Amaranth, *Canada* **73 C9** 50 36N 98 43W
Amargosa →, *U.S.A.* **85 J10** 36 14N 116 51W
Amargosa Range, *U.S.A.* **85 J10** 36 20N 116 45W
Amári, *Greece* **23 D6** 35 13N 24 40 E
Amarillo, *U.S.A.* **81 H4** 35 13N 101 50W
Amarkantak, *India* **43 H9** 22 40N 81 45 E
Amaro, Mte., *Italy* **20 C6** 42 5N 14 5 E
Amarpur, *India* **43 G12** 25 5N 87 0 E
Amarwara, *India* **43 H8** 22 18N 79 10 E
Amasya □, *Turkey* **25 F6** 40 40N 35 50 E
Amata, *Australia* **61 E5** 26 9S 131 9 E
Amatikulu, *S. Africa* **57 D5** 29 3S 31 33 E
Amatitlán, *Guatemala* **88 D1** 14 29N 90 38W
Amay, *Belgium* **15 D5** 50 33N 5 19 E
Amazon = Amazonas →, *S. Amer.* **93 D9** 0 5S 50 0W
Amazonas □, *Brazil* **92 E6** 5 0S 65 0W
Amazonas →, *S. Amer.* **93 D9** 0 5S 50 0W
Ambah, *India* **42 F8** 26 43N 78 13 E
Ambahakily, *Madag.* **57 C7** 21 36S 43 41 E
Ambahita, *Madag.* **57 C8** 24 1S 45 16 E
Ambala, *India* **42 D7** 30 23N 76 56 E
Ambalavao, *Madag.* **57 C8** 21 50S 46 56 E
Ambanja, *Madag.* **57 A8** 13 40S 48 27 E
Ambararata, *Madag.* **57 B8** 15 3S 48 33 E
Ambarchik, *Russia* **27 C17** 69 40N 162 20 E
Ambarijeby, *Madag.* **57 A8** 14 56S 47 41 E
Ambaro, Helodranon', *Madag.* **57 A8** 13 23S 48 38 E
Ambato, *Ecuador* **92 D3** 1 5S 78 42W
Ambato, *Madag.* **57 A8** 13 24S 48 29 E
Ambato, Sierra de, *Argentina* **94 B2** 28 25S 66 10W
Ambato Boeny, *Madag.* **57 B8** 16 28S 46 43 E
Ambatofinandrahana, *Madag.* **57 C8** 20 33S 46 48 E
Ambatolampy, *Madag.* **57 B8** 19 20S 47 35 E
Ambatomainty, *Madag.* **57 B8** 17 41S 45 40 E
Ambatomanoina, *Madag.* **57 B8** 18 18S 47 37 E
Ambatondrazaka, *Madag.* **57 B8** 17 55S 48 28 E
Ambatosoratra, *Madag.* **57 B8** 17 37S 48 31 E
Ambenja, *Madag.* **57 B8** 15 17S 46 58 E
Amberg, *Germany* **16 D6** 49 26N 11 52 E
Ambergris Cay, *Belize* **87 D7** 18 0N 88 0W
Amberley, *N.Z.* **59 K4** 43 9S 172 44 E
Ambikapur, *India* **43 H10** 23 15N 83 15 E
Ambilobé, *Madag.* **57 A8** 13 10S 49 3 E
Ambinanindrano, *Madag.* **57 C8** 20 5S 48 23 E
Ambinanitelo, *Madag.* **57 B8** 15 21S 49 35 E
Ambinda, *Madag.* **57 B8** 16 25S 45 52 E
Amble, *U.K.* **10 B6** 55 20N 1 36W
Ambleside, *U.K.* **10 C5** 54 26N 2 58W
Ambo, *Peru* **92 F3** 10 5S 76 10W
Amboahangy, *Madag.* **57 C8** 24 15S 46 22 E
Ambodifototra, *Madag.* **57 B8** 16 59S 49 52 E
Ambodilazana, *Madag.* **57 B8** 18 6S 49 10 E
Ambodiriana, *Madag.* **57 B8** 17 55S 49 18 E
Ambohidratrimo, *Madag.* **57 B8** 18 50S 47 26 E
Ambohidray, *Madag.* **57 B8** 18 36S 48 18 E
Ambohimahamasina, *Madag.* **57 C8** 21 56S 47 11 E
Ambohimahasoa, *Madag.* **57 C8** 21 7S 47 13 E
Ambohimanga, *Madag.* **57 C8** 20 52S 47 36 E
Ambohimitombo, *Madag.* **57 C8** 20 43S 47 26 E
Ambohitra, *Madag.* **57 A8** 12 30S 49 10 E
Amboise, *France* **18 C4** 47 24N 1 2 E
Ambon, *Indonesia* **37 E7** 3 43S 128 12 E
Ambondro, *Madag.* **57 D8** 25 13S 45 44 E
Amboseli, L., *Kenya* **54 C4** 2 40S 37 10 E
Ambositra, *Madag.* **57 C8** 20 31S 47 25 E
Ambovombe, *Madag.* **57 D8** 25 11S 46 5 E
Amboy, *U.S.A.* **85 L11** 34 33N 115 45W
Amboyna Cay, *S. China Sea* **36 C4** 7 50N 112 50 E
Ambridge, *U.S.A.* **78 F4** 40 36N 80 14W
Ambriz, *Angola* **52 F2** 7 48S 13 8 E
Amchitka I., *U.S.A.* **68 C1** 51 32N 179 0 E
Amderma, *Russia* **26 C7** 69 45N 61 30 E
Amdhi, *India* **43 H9** 23 51N 81 27 E
Ameca, *Mexico* **86 C4** 20 30N 104 0W
Ameca →, *Mexico* **86 C3** 20 40N 105 15W
Amecameca, *Mexico* **87 D5** 19 7N 98 46W
Ameland, *Neths.* **15 A5** 53 27N 5 45 E
Amenia, *U.S.A.* **79 E11** 41 51N 73 33W
American Falls, *U.S.A.* **82 E7** 42 47N 112 51W
American Falls Reservoir, *U.S.A.* **82 E7** 42 47N 112 52W
American Fork, *U.S.A.* **82 F8** 40 23N 111 48W
American Highland, *Antarctica* **5 D6** 73 0S 75 0 E
American Samoa ■, *Pac. Oc.* **59 B13** 14 20S 170 40W
Americana, *Brazil* **95 A6** 22 45S 47 20W
Americus, *U.S.A.* **77 K3** 32 4N 84 14W
Amersfoort, *Neths.* **15 B5** 52 9N 5 23 E
Amersfoort, *S. Africa* **57 D4** 26 59S 29 53 E
Amery Ice Shelf, *Antarctica* **5 C6** 69 30S 72 0 E
Ames, *U.S.A.* **80 E8** 42 2N 93 37W
Amesbury, *U.S.A.* **79 D14** 42 51N 70 56W
Amet, *India* **42 G5** 25 18N 73 56 E
Amga, *Russia* **27 C14** 60 50N 132 0 E
Amga →, *Russia* **27 C14** 62 38N 134 32 E
Amgu, *Russia* **27 E14** 45 45N 137 15 E
Amgun →, *Russia* **27 D14** 52 56N 139 38 E
Amherst, *Canada* **71 C7** 45 48N 64 8W
Amherst, *Mass., U.S.A.* **79 D12** 42 23N 72 31W
Amherst, *N.Y., U.S.A.* **78 D6** 42 59N 78 48W
Amherst, *Ohio, U.S.A.* **78 E2** 41 24N 82 14W
Amherst I., *Canada* **79 B8** 44 8N 76 43W
Amherstburg, *Canada* **70 D3** 42 6N 83 6W
Amiata, Mte., *Italy* **20 C4** 42 53N 11 37 E
Amidon, *U.S.A.* **80 B3** 46 29N 103 19W
Amiens, *France* **18 B5** 49 54N 2 16 E
Aminuis, *Namibia* **56 C2** 23 43S 19 21 E
Amīrābād, *Iran* **44 C5** 33 20N 46 16 E
Amirante Is., *Seychelles* **28 K9** 6 0S 53 0 E
Amisk L., *Canada* **73 C8** 54 35N 102 15W
Amistad, Presa de la, *Mexico* **86 B4** 29 24N 101 0W
Amite, *U.S.A.* **81 K9** 30 44N 90 30W
Amla, *India* **42 J8** 21 56N 78 7 E
Amlia I., *U.S.A.* **68 C2** 52 4N 173 30W
Amlwch, *U.K.* **10 D3** 53 24N 4 20W
'Ammān, *Jordan* **47 D4** 31 57N 35 52 E
'Ammān □, *Jordan* **47 D5** 31 40N 36 30 E
Ammanford, *U.K.* **11 F4** 51 48N 3 59W
Ammassalik = Tasiilaq, *Greenland* **4 C6** 65 40N 37 20W
Ammochostos = Famagusta, *Cyprus* **23 D12** 35 8N 33 55 E
Ammon, *U.S.A.* **82 E8** 43 28N 111 58W
Amnat Charoen, *Thailand* **38 E5** 15 51N 104 38 E
Amnura, *Bangla.* **43 G13** 24 37N 88 25 E
Āmol, *Iran* **45 B7** 36 23N 52 20 E
Amorgós, *Greece* **21 F11** 36 50N 25 57 E
Amory, *U.S.A.* **77 J1** 33 59N 88 29W
Amos, *Canada* **70 C4** 48 35N 78 5W
Åmot, *Norway* **9 G13** 59 57N 9 54 E
Amoy = Xiamen, *China* **33 D6** 24 25N 118 4 E
Ampanavoana, *Madag.* **57 B9** 15 41S 50 22 E
Ampang, *Malaysia* **39 L3** 3 8N 101 45 E
Ampangalana, Lakandranon', *Madag.* **57 C8** 22 48S 47 50 E
Ampanihy, *Madag.* **57 C7** 24 40S 44 45 E
Amparafaravola, *Madag.* **57 B8** 17 35S 48 13 E
Ampasinambo, *Madag.* **57 C8** 20 31S 48 0 E
Ampasindava, Helodranon', *Madag.* **57 A8** 13 40S 48 15 E
Ampasindava, Saikanosy, *Madag.* **57 A8** 13 42S 47 55 E
Ampenan, *Indonesia* **36 F5** 8 34S 116 4 E
Amper →, *Germany* **16 D6** 48 29N 11 55 E
Ampitsikinana, *Réunion* **57 A8** 12 57S 49 49 E
Ampombiantambo, *Madag.* **57 A8** 12 42S 48 57 E
Ampotaka, *Madag.* **57 D7** 25 3S 44 41 E
Ampoza, *Madag.* **57 C7** 22 20S 44 44 E
Amqui, *Canada* **71 C6** 48 28N 67 27W
Amravati, *India* **40 J10** 20 55N 77 45 E
Amreli, *India* **42 J4** 21 35N 71 17 E
Amritsar, *India* **42 D6** 31 35N 74 57 E
Amroha, *India* **43 E8** 28 53N 78 30 E
Amsterdam, *Neths.* **15 B4** 52 23N 4 54 E
Amsterdam, *U.S.A.* **79 D10** 42 56N 74 11W
Amsterdam, I. = Nouvelle-Amsterdam, I., *Ind. Oc.* **3 F13** 38 30S 77 30 E
Amstetten, *Austria* **16 D8** 48 7N 14 51 E
Amudarya →, *Uzbekistan* **26 E6** 43 58N 59 34 E
Amundsen Gulf, *Canada* **68 A7** 71 0N 124 0W
Amundsen Sea, *Antarctica* **5 D15** 72 0S 115 0W
Amuntai, *Indonesia* **36 E5** 2 28S 115 25 E
Amur →, *Russia* **27 D15** 52 56N 141 10 E
Amurang, *Indonesia* **37 D6** 1 5N 124 40 E
Amursk, *Russia* **27 D14** 50 14N 136 54 E
Amyderya = Amudarya →, *Uzbekistan* **26 E6** 43 58N 59 34 E
An Bien, *Vietnam* **39 H5** 9 45N 105 0 E
An Hoa, *Vietnam* **38 E7** 15 40N 108 5 E
An Nabatīyah at Tahta, *Lebanon* **47 B4** 33 23N 35 27 E
An Nabk, *Si. Arabia* **44 D3** 31 20N 37 20 E
An Nabk, *Syria* **47 A5** 34 2N 36 44 E
An Nafūd, *Si. Arabia* **44 D4** 28 15N 41 0 E
An Najaf, *Iraq* **44 C5** 32 3N 44 15 E
An Nāṣirīyah, *Iraq* **44 D5** 31 0N 46 15 E
An Nhon, *Vietnam* **38 F7** 13 55N 109 7 E
An Nu'ayrīyah, *Si. Arabia* **45 E6** 27 30N 48 30 E
An Nuwayb'ī, W. →, *Si. Arabia* **47 F3** 29 18N 34 57 E
An Thoi, Dao, *Vietnam* **39 H4** 9 58N 104 0 E
An Uaimh, *Ireland* **13 C5** 53 39N 6 41W
Anabar →, *Russia* **27 B12** 73 8N 113 36 E
'Anabtā, *West Bank* **47 C4** 32 19N 35 7 E
Anaconda, *U.S.A.* **82 C7** 46 8N 112 57W
Anacortes, *U.S.A.* **84 B4** 48 30N 122 37W
Anadarko, *U.S.A.* **81 H5** 35 4N 98 15W
Anadolu, *Turkey* **25 G5** 39 0N 30 0 E
Anadyr, *Russia* **27 C18** 64 35N 177 20 E
Anadyr →, *Russia* **27 C18** 64 55N 176 5 E
Anadyrskiy Zaliv, *Russia* **27 C19** 64 0N 180 0 E
Anaga, Pta. de, *Canary Is.* **22 F3** 28 34N 16 9W
'Ānah, *Iraq* **44 C4** 34 25N 42 0 E
Anaheim, *U.S.A.* **85 M9** 33 50N 117 55W
Anahim Lake, *Canada* **72 C3** 52 28N 125 18W
Anáhuac, *Mexico* **86 B4** 27 14N 100 9W
Anakapalle, *India* **41 L13** 17 42N 83 6 E
Anakie, *Australia* **62 C4** 23 32S 147 45 E
Analalava, *Madag.* **57 A8** 14 35S 48 0 E
Analavoka, *Madag.* **57 C8** 22 23S 46 30 E
Análipsis, *Greece* **23 A3** 39 36N 19 55 E
Anambar →, *Pakistan* **42 D3** 30 15N 68 50 E
Anambas, Kepulauan, *Indonesia* **39 L6** 3 20N 106 30 E
Anambas Is. = Anambas, Kepulauan, *Indonesia* **39 L6** 3 20N 106 30 E
Anamosa, *U.S.A.* **80 D9** 42 7N 91 17W
Anamur, *Turkey* **25 G5** 36 8N 32 58 E
Anan, *Japan* **31 H7** 33 54N 134 40 E
Anand, *India* **42 H5** 22 32N 72 59 E
Anantnag, *India* **43 C6** 33 45N 75 10 E
Ananyiv, *Ukraine* **17 E15** 47 44N 29 58 E
Anapodháris →, *Greece* **23 E7** 34 59N 25 20 E
Anápolis, *Brazil* **93 G9** 16 15S 48 50W
Anapu →, *Brazil* **93 D8** 1 53S 50 53W
Anār, *Iran* **45 D7** 30 55N 55 13 E
Anārak, *Iran* **45 C7** 33 25N 53 40 E
Anas →, *India* **42 H5** 23 26N 74 0 E
Anatolia = Anadolu, *Turkey* **25 G5** 39 0N 30 0 E
Anatsogno, *Madag.* **57 C7** 23 33S 43 46 E
Añatuya, *Argentina* **94 B3** 28 20S 62 50W
Anaunethad L., *Canada* **73 A8** 60 55N 104 25W
Anbyŏn, *N. Korea* **35 E14** 39 1N 127 35 E
Ancaster, *Canada* **78 C5** 43 13N 79 59W
Anchor Bay, *U.S.A.* **84 G3** 38 48N 123 34W
Anchorage, *U.S.A.* **68 B5** 61 13N 149 54W
Anci, *China* **34 E9** 39 20N 116 40 E
Ancohuma, Nevada, *Bolivia* **92 G5** 16 0S 68 50W
Ancón, *Peru* **92 F3** 11 50S 77 10W
Ancona, *Italy* **20 C5** 43 38N 13 30 E
Ancud, *Chile* **96 E2** 42 0S 73 50W
Ancud, G. de, *Chile* **96 E2** 42 0S 73 0W
Anda, *China* **33 B7** 46 24N 125 19 E
Andacollo, *Argentina* **94 D1** 37 10S 70 42W
Andacollo, *Chile* **94 C1** 30 14S 71 6W
Andaingo, *Madag.* **57 B8** 18 12S 48 17 E
Andalgalá, *Argentina* **94 B2** 27 40S 66 30W
Åndalsnes, *Norway* **9 E12** 62 35N 7 43 E
Andalucía □, *Spain* **19 D3** 37 35N 5 0W
Andalusia = Andalucía □, *Spain* **19 D3** 37 35N 5 0W
Andalusia, *U.S.A.* **77 K2** 31 18N 86 29W
Andaman Is., *Ind. Oc.* **29 H13** 12 30N 92 45 E
Andaman Sea, *Ind. Oc.* **36 B1** 13 0N 96 0 E
Andamooka Opal Fields, *Australia* **63 E2** 30 27S 137 9 E
Andapa, *Madag.* **57 A8** 14 39S 49 39 E
Andara, *Namibia* **56 B3** 18 2S 21 9 E
Andenes, *Norway* **8 B17** 69 19N 16 18 E
Andenne, *Belgium* **15 D5** 50 28N 5 5 E
Anderson, *Alaska, U.S.A.* **68 B5** 64 25N 149 15W
Anderson, *Calif., U.S.A.* **82 F2** 40 27N 122 18W
Anderson, *Ind., U.S.A.* **76 E3** 40 10N 85 41W
Anderson, *Mo., U.S.A.* **81 G7** 36 39N 94 27W
Anderson, *S.C., U.S.A.* **77 H4** 34 31N 82 39W
Anderson →, *Canada* **68 B7** 69 42N 129 0W
Andes, *U.S.A.* **79 D10** 42 12N 74 47W
Andes, Cord. de los, *S. Amer.* **92 H5** 20 0S 68 0W
Andfjorden, *Norway* **8 B17** 69 10N 16 20 E
Andhra Pradesh □, *India* **40 L11** 18 0N 79 0 E
Andijon, *Uzbekistan* **26 E8** 41 10N 72 15 E
Andikíthira, *Greece* **21 G10** 35 52N 23 15 E
Andilamena, *Madag.* **57 B8** 17 1S 48 35 E
Andīmeshk, *Iran* **45 C6** 32 27N 48 21 E
Andizhan = Andijon, *Uzbekistan* **26 E8** 41 10N 72 15 E
Andoany, *Madag.* **57 A8** 13 25S 48 16 E
Andong, *S. Korea* **35 F15** 36 40N 128 43 E
Andongwei, *China* **35 G10** 35 6N 119 20 E
Andoom, *Australia* **62 A3** 12 25S 141 53 E
Andorra ■, *Europe* **18 E4** 42 30N 1 30 E
Andorra La Vella, *Andorra* **18 E4** 42 31N 1 32 E
Andover, *U.K.* **11 F6** 51 12N 1 29W
Andover, *Maine, U.S.A.* **79 B14** 44 38N 70 45W
Andover, *Mass., U.S.A.* **79 D13** 42 40N 71 8W
Andover, *N.J., U.S.A.* **79 F10** 40 59N 74 45W
Andover, *N.Y., U.S.A.* **78 D7** 42 10N 77 48W
Andover, *Ohio, U.S.A.* **78 E4** 41 36N 80 34W
Andøya, *Norway* **8 B16** 69 10N 15 50 E
Andradina, *Brazil* **93 H8** 20 54S 51 23W
Andrahary, Mt., *Madag.* **57 A8** 13 37S 49 17 E
Andramasina, *Madag.* **57 B8** 19 11S 47 35 E
Andranopasy, *Madag.* **57 C7** 21 17S 43 44 E
Andranovory, *Madag.* **57 C7** 23 8S 44 10 E
Andratx, *Spain* **22 B9** 39 39N 2 25 E
Andreanof Is., *U.S.A.* **68 C2** 51 30N 176 0W
Andrews, *S.C., U.S.A.* **77 J6** 33 27N 79 34W
Andrews, *Tex., U.S.A.* **81 J3** 32 19N 102 33W
Ándria, *Italy* **20 D7** 41 13N 16 17 E
Andriamena, *Madag.* **57 B8** 17 26S 47 30 E
Andriandampy, *Madag.* **57 C8** 22 45S 45 41 E
Andriba, *Madag.* **57 B8** 17 30S 46 58 E
Androka, *Madag.* **57 C7** 24 58S 44 2 E
Andropov = Rybinsk, *Russia* **24 C6** 58 5N 38 50 E
Ándros, *Greece* **21 F11** 37 50N 24 57 E
Andros I., *Bahamas* **88 B4** 24 30N 78 0W
Andros Town, *Bahamas* **88 B4** 24 43N 77 47W
Androscoggin →, *U.S.A.* **79 C14** 43 58N 70 0W
Andselv, *Norway* **8 B18** 69 4N 18 34 E
Andújar, *Spain* **19 C3** 38 3N 4 5W
Andulo, *Angola* **52 G3** 11 25S 16 45 E
Anegada I., *Br. Virgin Is.* **89 C7** 18 45N 64 20W
Anegada Passage, *W. Indies* **89 C7** 18 15N 63 45W
Aneto, Pico de, *Spain* **19 A6** 42 37N 0 40 E
Ang Thong, *Thailand* **38 E3** 14 35N 100 31 E
Angamos, Punta, *Chile* **94 A1** 23 1S 70 32W
Angara →, *Russia* **27 D10** 58 5N 94 20 E
Angarsk, *Russia* **27 D11** 52 30N 104 0 E
Angas Hills, *Australia* **60 D4** 23 0S 127 50 E
Angaston, *Australia* **63 E2** 34 30S 139 8 E
Ånge, *Sweden* **9 E16** 62 31N 15 35 E
Ángel, Salto = Angel Falls, *Venezuela* **92 B6** 5 57N 62 30W
Ángel de la Guarda, I., *Mexico* **86 B2** 29 30N 113 30W
Angel Falls, *Venezuela* **92 B6** 5 57N 62 30W
Angeles, *Phil.* **37 A6** 15 9N 120 33 E
Ängelholm, *Sweden* **9 H15** 56 15N 12 58 E
Angels Camp, *U.S.A.* **84 G6** 38 4N 120 32W
Ångermanälven →, *Sweden* **8 E17** 62 40N 18 0 E
Ångermanland, *Sweden* **8 E18** 63 36N 17 45 E
Angers, *Canada* **79 A9** 45 31N 75 29W
Angers, *France* **18 C3** 47 30N 0 35W
Ångesån →, *Sweden* **8 C20** 66 16N 22 47 E
Angikuni L., *Canada* **73 A9** 62 0N 100 0W
Angkor, *Cambodia* **38 F4** 13 22N 103 50 E
Anglesey, Isle of □, *U.K.* **10 D3** 53 16N 4 18W
Angleton, *U.S.A.* **81 L7** 29 10N 95 26W
Anglisidhes, *Cyprus* **23 E12** 34 51N 33 27 E
Angmagssalik = Tasiilaq, *Greenland* **4 C6** 65 40N 37 20W
Ango, *Dem. Rep. of the Congo* **54 B2** 4 10N 26 5 E
Angoche, *Mozam.* **55 F4** 16 8S 39 55 E
Angoche, I., *Mozam.* **55 F4** 16 20S 39 50 E
Angol, *Chile* **94 D1** 37 56S 72 45W
Angola, *Ind., U.S.A.* **76 E3** 41 38N 85 0W
Angola, *N.Y., U.S.A.* **78 D5** 42 38N 79 2W
Angola ■, *Africa* **53 G3** 12 0S 18 0 E
Angoulême, *France* **18 D4** 45 39N 0 10 E
Angoumois, *France* **18 D3** 45 50N 0 25 E
Angra dos Reis, *Brazil* **95 A7** 23 0S 44 10W
Angren, *Uzbekistan* **26 E8** 41 1N 70 12 E
Angtassom, *Cambodia* **39 G5** 11 1N 104 41 E
Angu, *Dem. Rep. of the Congo* **54 B1** 3 23N 24 30 E
Anguang, *China* **35 B12** 45 15N 123 45 E
Anguilla ■, *W. Indies* **89 C7** 18 14N 63 5W
Anguo, *China* **34 E8** 38 28N 115 15 E
Angurugu, *Australia* **62 A2** 14 0S 136 25 E
Angus □, *U.K.* **12 E6** 56 46N 2 56W
Angwa →, *Zimbabwe* **57 B5** 16 0S 30 23 E
Anhanduí →, *Brazil* **95 A5** 21 46S 52 9W
Anholt, *Denmark* **9 H14** 56 42N 11 33 E
Anhui □, *China* **33 C6** 32 0N 117 0 E
Anhwei = Anhui □, *China* **33 C6** 32 0N 117 0 E
Anichab, *Namibia* **56 C1** 21 0S 14 46 E
Animas →, *U.S.A.* **83 H9** 36 43N 108 13W
Anivorano, *Madag.* **57 B8** 18 44S 48 58 E
Anjalankoski, *Finland* **9 F22** 60 45N 26 51 E
Anjar, *India* **42 H4** 23 6N 70 10 E
Anjou, *France* **18 C3** 47 20N 0 15W
Anjozorobe, *Madag.* **57 B8** 18 22S 47 52 E
Anju, *N. Korea* **35 E13** 39 36N 125 40 E
Ankaboa, Tanjona, *Madag.* **57 C7** 21 58S 43 20 E
Ankang, *China* **34 H5** 32 40N 109 1 E
Ankara, *Turkey* **25 G5** 39 57N 32 54 E
Ankaramena, *Madag.* **57 C8** 21 57S 46 39 E
Ankaratra, *Madag.* **53 H9** 19 25S 47 12 E
Ankasakasa, *Madag.* **57 B7** 16 21S 44 52 E
Ankavandra, *Madag.* **57 B8** 18 46S 45 18 E
Ankazoabo, *Madag.* **57 C7** 22 18S 44 31 E
Ankazobe, *Madag.* **57 B8** 18 20S 47 10 E
Ankeny, *U.S.A.* **80 E8** 41 44N 93 36W
Ankilimalinika, *Madag.* **57 C7** 22 58S 43 45 E
Ankilizato, *Madag.* **57 C8** 20 25S 45 1 E
Ankisabe, *Madag.* **57 B8** 19 17S 46 29 E
Ankoro, *Dem. Rep. of the Congo* **54 D2** 6 45S 26 55 E
Ankororoka, *Madag.* **57 D8** 25 30S 45 11 E
Anmyŏn-do, *S. Korea* **35 F14** 36 25N 126 25 E
Ann, C., *U.S.A.* **79 D14** 42 38N 70 35W
Ann Arbor, *U.S.A.* **76 D4** 42 17N 83 45W
Anna, *U.S.A.* **81 G10** 37 28N 89 15W
Annaba, *Algeria* **50 A7** 36 50N 7 46 E
Annalee →, *Ireland* **13 B4** 54 2N 7 24W
Annam, *Vietnam* **38 E7** 16 0N 108 0 E
Annamitique, Chaîne, *Asia* **38 D6** 17 0N 106 0 E
Annan, *U.K.* **12 G5** 54 59N 3 16W
Annan →, *U.K.* **12 G5** 54 58N 3 16W
Annapolis, *U.S.A.* **76 F7** 38 59N 76 30W
Annapolis Royal, *Canada* **71 D6** 44 44N 65 32W
Annapurna, *Nepal* **43 E10** 28 34N 83 50 E
Annean, L., *Australia* **61 E2** 26 54S 118 14 E
Annecy, *France* **18 D7** 45 55N 6 8 E
Anning, *China* **32 D5** 24 55N 102 26 E
Anniston, *U.S.A.* **77 J3** 33 39N 85 50W
Annobón, *Atl. Oc.* **49 G4** 1 25S 5 36 E
Annotto Bay, *Jamaica* **88 C4** 18 17N 76 45W
Annville, *U.S.A.* **79 F8** 40 20N 76 31W
Áno Viánnos, *Greece* **23 D7** 35 2N 25 21 E
Anorotsangana, *Madag.* **57 A8** 13 56S 47 55 E
Anosibe, *Madag.* **57 B8** 19 26S 48 13 E
Anóyia, *Greece* **23 D6** 35 16N 24 52 E
Anping, *Hebei, China* **34 E8** 38 15N 115 30 E
Anping, *Liaoning, China* **35 D12** 41 5N 123 30 E
Anqing, *China* **33 C6** 30 30N 117 3 E
Anqiu, *China* **35 F10** 36 25N 119 10 E
Ansai, *China* **34 F5** 36 50N 109 20 E
Ansbach, *Germany* **16 D6** 49 28N 10 34 E
Anshan, *China* **35 D12** 41 5N 122 58 E
Anshun, *China* **32 D5** 26 18N 105 57 E
Ansley, *U.S.A.* **80 E5** 41 18N 99 23W
Anson, *U.S.A.* **81 J5** 32 45N 99 54W
Anson B., *Australia* **60 B5** 13 20S 130 6 E
Ansongo, *Mali* **50 E6** 15 25N 0 35 E
Ansonia, *U.S.A.* **79 E11** 41 21N 73 5W
Anstruther, *U.K.* **12 E6** 56 14N 2 41W
Ansudu, *Indonesia* **37 E9** 2 11S 139 22 E
Antabamba, *Peru* **92 F4** 14 40S 73 0W
Antakya, *Turkey* **25 G6** 36 14N 36 10 E
Antalaha, *Madag.* **57 A9** 14 57S 50 20 E
Antalya, *Turkey* **25 G5** 36 52N 30 45 E
Antalya Körfezi, *Turkey* **25 G5** 36 15N 31 30 E
Antambohobe, *Madag.* **57 C8** 22 20S 46 47 E
Antanambao-Manampotsy, *Madag.* **57 B8** 19 29S 48 34 E
Antanambe, *Madag.* **57 B8** 16 26S 49 52 E
Antananarivo, *Madag.* **57 B8** 18 55S 47 31 E
Antananarivo □, *Madag.* **57 B8** 19 0S 47 0 E
Antanifotsy, *Madag.* **57 B8** 19 39S 47 19 E
Antanimbaribe, *Madag.* **57 C7** 21 30S 44 48 E
Antanimora, *Madag.* **57 C8** 24 49S 45 40 E
Antarctic Pen., *Antarctica* **5 C18** 67 0S 60 0W
Antarctica **5 E3** 90 0S 0 0W
Antelope, *Zimbabwe* **55 G2** 21 2S 28 31 E
Antequera, *Paraguay* **94 A4** 24 8S 57 7W
Antequera, *Spain* **19 D3** 37 5N 4 33W
Antero, Mt., *U.S.A.* **83 G10** 38 41N 106 15W
Antevamena, *Madag.* **57 C7** 21 2S 44 8 E
Anthony, *Kans., U.S.A.* **81 G5** 37 9N 98 2W
Anthony, *N. Mex., U.S.A.* **83 K10** 32 0N 106 36W
Anti Atlas, *Morocco* **50 C4** 30 0N 8 30W
Anti-Lebanon = Ash Sharqi, Al Jabal, *Lebanon* **47 B5** 33 40N 36 10 E
Antibes, *France* **18 E7** 43 34N 7 6 E
Anticosti, Î. d', *Canada* **71 C7** 49 30N 63 0W
Antigo, *U.S.A.* **80 C10** 45 9N 89 9W
Antigonish, *Canada* **71 C7** 45 38N 61 58W
Antigua, *Canary Is.* **22 F5** 28 24N 14 1W
Antigua, *Guatemala* **88 D1** 14 34N 90 41W
Antigua, *W. Indies* **89 C7** 17 0N 61 50W
Antigua & Barbuda ■, *W. Indies* **89 C7** 17 20N 61 48W
Antilla, *Cuba* **88 B4** 20 40N 75 50W
Antilles = West Indies, *Cent. Amer.* **89 D7** 15 0N 65 0W
Antioch, *U.S.A.* **84 G5** 38 1N 121 48W
Antioquia, *Colombia* **92 B3** 6 40N 75 55W
Antipodes Is., *Pac. Oc.* **64 M9** 49 45S 178 40 E
Antlers, *U.S.A.* **81 H7** 34 14N 95 37W
Antoetra, *Madag.* **57 C8** 20 46S 47 20 E
Antofagasta, *Chile* **94 A1** 23 50S 70 30W
Antofagasta □, *Chile* **94 A2** 24 0S 69 0W
Antofagasta de la Sierra, *Argentina* **94 B2** 26 5S 67 20W
Antofalla, *Argentina* **94 B2** 25 30S 68 5W
Antofalla, Salar de, *Argentina* **94 B2** 25 40S 67 45W
Anton, *U.S.A.* **81 J3** 33 49N 102 10W
Antongila, Helodrano, *Madag.* **57 B8** 15 30S 49 50 E
Antonibé, *Madag.* **57 B8** 15 7S 47 24 E
Antonibé, Presqu'île d', *Madag.* **57 A8** 14 55S 47 20 E
Antonina, *Brazil* **95 B6** 25 26S 48 42W
Antrim, *U.K.* **13 B5** 54 43N 6 14W
Antrim, *U.S.A.* **78 F3** 40 7N 81 21W
Antrim □, *U.K.* **13 B5** 54 56N 6 25W
Antrim, Mts. of, *U.K.* **13 A5** 55 3N 6 14W
Antrim Plateau, *Australia* **60 C4** 18 8S 128 20 E
Antsakabary, *Madag.* **57 B8** 15 3S 48 56 E
Antsalova, *Madag.* **57 B7** 18 40S 44 37 E

B

Bagamoyo, *Tanzania* 54 D4 6 28S 38 55 E
Bagan Datoh, *Malaysia* 39 L3 3 59N 100 47 E
Bagan Serai, *Malaysia* 39 K3 5 1N 100 32 E
Baganga, *Phil.* 37 C7 7 34N 126 33 E
Bagani, *Namibia* 56 B3 18 7S 21 41 E
Bagansiapiapi, *Indonesia* 36 D2 2 12N 100 50 E
Bagasra, *India* 42 J4 21 30N 71 0 E
Bagaud, *India* 42 H6 22 19N 75 53 E
Bagdad, *U.S.A.* 85 L11 34 35N 115 53W
Bagdarin, *Russia* 27 D12 54 26N 113 36 E
Bagé, *Brazil* 95 C5 31 20S 54 15W
Bagenalstown = Muine Bheag, *Ireland* 13 D5 52 42N 6 58W
Baggs, *U.S.A.* 82 F10 41 2N 107 39W
Bagh, *Pakistan* 43 C5 33 59N 73 45 E
Baghain →, *India* 43 G9 25 32N 81 1 E
Baghdād, *Iraq* 44 C5 33 20N 44 30 E
Bagheria, *Italy* 20 E5 38 5N 13 30 E
Baghlān, *Afghan.* 40 A6 32 12N 68 46 E
Baghlān □, *Afghan.* 40 B6 36 0N 68 30 E
Bagley, *U.S.A.* 80 B7 47 32N 95 24W
Bago = Pegu, *Burma* 41 L20 17 20N 96 29 E
Bagodar, *India* 43 G11 24 5N 85 52 E
Bagrationovsk, *Russia* 9 J19 54 23N 20 39 E
Baguio, *Phil.* 37 A6 16 26N 120 34 E
Bah, *India* 43 F8 26 53N 78 36 E
Bahadurganj, *India* 43 F12 26 16N 87 49 E
Bahadurgarh, *India* 42 E7 28 40N 76 57 E
Bahama, Canal Viejo de, *W. Indies* 88 B4 22 10N 77 30W
Bahamas ■, *N. Amer.* 89 B5 24 0N 75 0W
Baharampur, *India* 43 G13 24 2N 88 27 E
Bahawalnagar, *Pakistan* 42 E5 30 0N 73 15 E
Bahawalpur, *Pakistan* 42 E4 29 24N 71 40 E
Baheri, *India* 43 E8 28 45N 79 34 E
Bahgul →, *India* 43 F8 27 45N 79 36 E
Bahi, *Tanzania* 54 D4 5 58S 35 21 E
Bahi Swamp, *Tanzania* 54 D4 6 10S 35 0 E
Bahía = Salvador, *Brazil* 93 F11 13 0S 38 30W
Bahía □, *Brazil* 93 F10 12 0S 42 0W
Bahía, Is. de la, *Honduras* 88 C2 16 45N 86 15W
Bahía Blanca, *Argentina* 94 D3 38 35S 62 13W
Bahía de Caráquez, *Ecuador* 92 D2 0 40S 80 27W
Bahía Honda, *Cuba* 88 B3 22 54N 83 10W
Bahía Laura, *Argentina* 96 F3 48 10S 66 30W
Bahía Negra, *Paraguay* 92 H7 20 5S 58 5W
Bahir Dar, *Ethiopia* 46 E2 11 37N 37 10 E
Bahmanzād, *Iran* 45 D6 31 15N 51 47 E
Bahr el Ghazâl □, *Sudan* 51 G11 7 0N 28 0 E
Bahraich, *India* 43 F9 27 38N 81 37 E
Bahrain ■, *Asia* 46 B5 26 0N 50 35 E
Bahror, *India* 42 F7 27 51N 76 20 E
Bāhū Kalāt, *Iran* 45 E9 25 43N 61 25 E
Bai Bung, Mui = Ca Mau, Mui, *Vietnam* 39 H5 8 38N 104 44 E
Bai Duc, *Vietnam* 38 C5 18 3N 105 49 E
Bai Thuong, *Vietnam* 38 C5 19 54N 105 23 E
Baia Mare, *Romania* 17 E12 47 40N 23 35 E
Baião, *Brazil* 93 D9 2 40S 49 40W
Baïbokoum, *Chad* 51 G9 7 46N 15 43 E
Baicheng, *China* 35 B12 45 38N 122 42 E
Baidoa, *Somali Rep.* 46 G3 3 8N 43 30 E
Baie Comeau, *Canada* 71 C6 49 12N 68 10W
Baie-St-Paul, *Canada* 71 C5 47 28N 70 32W
Baie Trinité, *Canada* 71 C6 49 25N 67 20W
Baie Verte, *Canada* 71 C8 49 55N 56 12W
Baihar, *India* 43 H9 22 6N 80 33 E
Baihe, *China* 34 H6 32 50N 110 5 E
Ba'iji, *Iraq* 44 C4 35 0N 43 30 E
Baijnath, *India* 43 E8 29 55N 79 37 E
Baikal, L. = Baykal, Oz., *Russia* 27 D11 53 0N 108 0 E
Baikunthpur, *India* 43 H10 23 15N 82 33 E
Baile Atha Cliath = Dublin, *Ireland* 13 C5 53 21N 6 15W
Băileşti, *Romania* 17 F12 44 1N 23 20 E
Bainbridge, *Ga., U.S.A.* 77 K3 30 55N 84 35W
Bainbridge, *N.Y., U.S.A.* 79 D9 42 18N 75 29W
Baing, *Indonesia* 37 F6 10 14S 120 34 E
Bainiu, *China* 34 H7 32 50N 112 15 E
Bā'ir, *Jordan* 47 E5 30 45N 36 55 E
Bairin Youqi, *China* 35 C10 43 30N 118 35 E
Bairin Zuoqi, *China* 35 C10 43 58N 119 15 E
Bairnsdale, *Australia* 63 F4 37 48S 147 36 E
Baisha, *China* 34 G7 34 20N 112 32 E
Baitadi, *Nepal* 43 E9 29 35N 80 25 E
Baiyin, *China* 34 F3 36 45N 104 14 E
Baiyu Shan, *China* 34 F4 37 15N 107 30 E
Baj Baj, *India* 43 H13 22 30N 88 5 E
Baja, *Hungary* 17 E10 46 12N 18 59 E
Baja, Pta., *Mexico* 86 B1 29 50N 116 0W
Baja California, *Mexico* 86 A1 31 10N 115 12W
Baja California □, *Mexico* 86 B2 30 0N 115 0W
Baja California Sur □, *Mexico* 86 B2 25 50N 111 50W
Bajag, *India* 43 H9 22 40N 81 21 E
Bajamar, *Canary Is.* 22 F3 28 33N 16 20W
Bajana, *India* 42 H4 23 7N 71 49 E
Bājgīrān, *Iran* 45 B8 37 36N 58 24 E
Bajimba, Mt., *Australia* 63 D5 29 17S 152 6 E
Bajo Nuevo, *Caribbean* 88 C4 15 40N 78 50W
Bajoga, *Nigeria* 51 F8 10 57N 11 20 E
Bajool, *Australia* 62 C5 23 40S 150 35 E
Bakel, *Senegal* 50 F3 14 56N 12 20W
Baker, *Calif., U.S.A.* 85 K10 35 16N 116 4W
Baker, *Mont., U.S.A.* 80 B2 46 22N 104 17W
Baker, L., *Canada* 68 B10 64 0N 96 0W
Baker City, *U.S.A.* 82 D5 44 47N 117 50W
Baker I., *Pac. Oc.* 64 G10 0 10N 176 35W
Baker I., *U.S.A.* 72 B2 55 20N 133 40W
Baker L., *Australia* 61 E4 26 54S 126 5 E
Baker Lake, *Canada* 68 B10 64 20N 96 3W
Baker Mt., *U.S.A.* 82 B3 48 50N 121 49W
Bakers Creek, *Australia* 62 C4 21 13S 149 7 E
Baker's Dozen Is., *Canada* 70 A4 56 45N 78 45W
Bakersfield, *Calif., U.S.A.* 85 K8 35 23N 119 1W
Bakersfield, *Vt., U.S.A.* 79 B12 44 45N 72 48W
Bākhtarān, *Iran* 44 C5 34 23N 47 0 E
Bākhtarān □, *Iran* 44 C5 34 0N 46 30 E
Bakı, *Azerbaijan* 25 F8 40 29N 49 56 E
Bakkafjörður, *Iceland* 8 C6 66 2N 14 48W
Bakony, *Hungary* 17 E9 47 10N 17 30 E
Bakony Forest = Bakony, *Hungary* 17 E9 47 10N 17 30 E
Bakouma, *C.A.R.* 52 C4 5 40N 22 56 E
Bakswaho, *India* 43 G8 24 15N 79 18 E
Baku = Bakı, *Azerbaijan* 25 F8 40 29N 49 56 E
Bakutis Coast, *Antarctica* 5 D15 74 0S 120 0W
Baky = Bakı, *Azerbaijan* 25 F8 40 29N 49 56 E
Bala, *Canada* 78 A5 45 1N 79 37W
Bala, *U.K.* 10 E4 52 54N 3 36W
Bala, L., *U.K.* 10 E4 52 53N 3 37W
Balabac I., *Phil.* 36 C5 8 0N 117 0 E
Balabac Str., *E. Indies* 36 C5 7 53N 117 5 E
Balabagh, *Afghan.* 42 B4 34 25N 70 12 E
Ba'labakk, *Lebanon* 47 B5 34 0N 36 10 E
Balabalangan, Kepulauan, *Indonesia* 36 E5 2 20S 117 30 E
Balad, *Iraq* 44 C5 34 1N 44 9 E
Balad Rūz, *Iraq* 44 C5 33 42N 45 5 E
Bālādeh, *Fārs, Iran* 45 D6 29 17N 51 56 E
Bālādeh, *Māzandaran, Iran* 45 B6 36 12N 51 48 E
Balaghat, *India* 40 J12 21 49N 80 12 E
Balaghat Ra., *India* 40 K10 18 50N 76 30 E
Balaguer, *Spain* 19 B6 41 50N 0 50 E
Balaklava, *Ukraine* 25 F5 44 30N 33 30 E
Balakovo, *Russia* 24 D8 52 4N 47 55 E
Balamau, *India* 43 F9 27 10N 80 21 E
Balancán, *Mexico* 87 D6 17 48N 91 32W
Balashov, *Russia* 25 D7 51 30N 43 10 E
Balasinor, *India* 42 H5 22 57N 73 23 E
Balasore = Baleshwar, *India* 41 J15 21 35N 87 3 E
Balaton, *Hungary* 17 E9 46 50N 17 40 E
Balbina, Reprêsa de, *Brazil* 92 D7 2 0S 59 30W
Balboa, *Panama* 88 E4 8 57N 79 34W
Balbriggan, *Ireland* 13 C5 53 37N 6 11W
Balcarce, *Argentina* 94 D4 38 0S 58 10W
Balcarres, *Canada* 73 C8 50 50N 103 35W
Balchik, *Bulgaria* 21 C13 43 28N 28 11 E
Balclutha, *N.Z.* 59 M2 46 15S 169 45 E
Balcones Escarpment, *U.S.A.* 81 L5 29 30N 99 15W
Bald Hd., *Australia* 61 G2 35 6S 118 1 E
Bald I., *Australia* 61 F2 34 57S 118 27 E
Bald Knob, *U.S.A.* 81 H9 35 19N 91 34W
Baldock L., *Canada* 73 B9 56 33N 97 57W
Baldwin, *Mich., U.S.A.* 76 D3 43 54N 85 51W
Baldwin, *Pa., U.S.A.* 78 F5 40 23N 79 59W
Baldwinsville, *U.S.A.* 79 C8 43 10N 76 20W
Baldy Mt., *U.S.A.* 82 B9 48 9N 109 39W
Baldy Peak, *U.S.A.* 83 K9 33 54N 109 34W
Baleares, Is., *Spain* 22 B10 39 30N 3 0 E
Balearic Is. = Baleares, Is., *Spain* 22 B10 39 30N 3 0 E
Baleine = Whale →, *Canada* 71 A6 58 15N 67 40W
Baler, *Phil.* 37 A6 15 46N 121 34 E
Baleshare, *U.K.* 12 D1 57 31N 7 22W
Baleshwar, *India* 41 J15 21 35N 87 3 E
Balfate, *Honduras* 88 C2 15 48N 86 25W
Bali, *Greece* 23 D6 35 25N 24 47 E
Bali, *India* 42 G5 25 11N 73 17 E
Bali, *Indonesia* 36 F4 8 20S 115 0 E
Bali □, *Indonesia* 36 F5 8 20S 115 0 E
Bali, Selat, *Indonesia* 37 H16 8 18S 114 25 E
Baliapal, *India* 43 J12 21 40N 87 17 E
Balikeşir, *Turkey* 21 E12 39 39N 27 53 E
Balikpapan, *Indonesia* 36 E5 1 10S 116 55 E
Balimbing, *Phil.* 37 C5 5 5N 119 58 E
Baling, *Malaysia* 39 K3 5 41N 100 55 E
Balipara, *India* 41 F18 26 50N 92 45 E
Balkan Mts. = Stara Planina, *Bulgaria* 21 C10 43 15N 23 0 E
Balkhash = Balqash, *Kazakstan* 26 E8 46 50N 74 50 E
Balkhash, Ozero = Balqash Köl, *Kazakstan* 26 E8 46 0N 74 50 E
Balla, *Bangla.* 41 G17 24 10N 91 35 E
Ballachulish, *U.K.* 12 E3 56 41N 5 8W
Balladonia, *Australia* 61 F3 32 27S 123 51 E
Ballaghaderreen, *Ireland* 13 C3 53 55N 8 34W
Ballarat, *Australia* 63 F3 37 33S 143 50 E
Ballard, L., *Australia* 61 E3 29 20S 120 40 E
Ballater, *U.K.* 12 D5 57 3N 3 3W
Ballenas, Canal de, *Mexico* 86 B2 29 10N 113 45W
Balleny Is., *Antarctica* 5 C11 66 30S 163 0 E
Ballia, *India* 43 G11 25 46N 84 12 E
Ballina, *Australia* 63 D5 28 50S 153 31 E
Ballina, *Ireland* 13 B2 54 7N 9 9W
Ballinasloe, *Ireland* 13 C3 53 20N 8 13W
Ballinger, *U.S.A.* 81 K5 31 45N 99 57W
Ballinrobe, *Ireland* 13 C2 53 38N 9 13W
Ballinskelligs B., *Ireland* 13 E1 51 48N 10 13W
Ballston Spa, *U.S.A.* 79 D11 43 0N 73 51W
Ballycastle, *U.K.* 13 A5 55 12N 6 15W
Ballyclare, *U.K.* 13 B5 54 46N 6 0W
Ballyhaunis, *Ireland* 13 C3 53 46N 8 46W
Ballymena, *U.K.* 13 B5 54 52N 6 17W
Ballymoney, *U.K.* 13 A5 55 5N 6 31W
Ballymote, *Ireland* 13 B3 54 5N 8 31W
Ballynahinch, *U.K.* 13 B6 54 24N 5 54W
Ballyquintin Pt., *U.K.* 13 B6 54 20N 5 30W
Ballyshannon, *Ireland* 13 B3 54 30N 8 11W
Balmaceda, *Chile* 96 F2 46 0S 71 50W
Balmertown, *Canada* 73 C10 51 4N 93 41W
Balmoral, *Australia* 63 F3 37 15S 141 48 E
Balmorhea, *U.S.A.* 81 K3 30 59N 103 45W
Balochistan = Baluchistan □, *Pakistan* 40 F4 27 30N 65 0 E
Balonne →, *Australia* 63 D4 28 47S 147 56 E
Balotra, *India* 42 G5 25 50N 72 14 E
Balqash, *Kazakstan* 26 E8 46 50N 74 50 E
Balqash Köl, *Kazakstan* 26 E8 46 0N 74 50 E
Balrampur, *India* 43 F10 27 30N 82 20 E
Balranald, *Australia* 63 E3 34 38S 143 33 E
Balsas, *Mexico* 87 D5 18 0N 99 40W
Balsas →, *Brazil* 93 E9 7 15S 44 35W
Balsas →, *Mexico* 86 D4 17 55N 102 10W
Balston Spa, *U.S.A.* 79 D11 43 0N 73 52W
Balta, *Ukraine* 17 D15 48 2N 29 45 E
Bălţi, *Moldova* 17 E14 47 48N 27 58 E
Baltic Sea, *Europe* 9 H18 57 0N 19 0 E
Baltimore, *Ireland* 13 E2 51 29N 9 22W
Baltimore, *Md., U.S.A.* 76 F7 39 17N 76 37W
Baltimore, *Ohio, U.S.A.* 78 G2 39 51N 82 36W
Baltit, *Pakistan* 43 A6 36 15N 74 40 E
Baltiysk, *Russia* 9 J18 54 41N 19 58 E
Baluchistan □, *Pakistan* 40 F4 27 30N 65 0 E
Balurghat, *India* 43 G13 25 15N 88 44 E
Balvi, *Latvia* 9 H22 57 8N 27 15 E
Balya, *Turkey* 21 E12 39 44N 27 35 E
Bam, *Iran* 45 D8 29 7N 58 14 E
Bama, *Nigeria* 51 F8 11 33N 13 41 E
Bamaga, *Australia* 62 A3 10 50S 142 25 E
Bamaji L., *Canada* 70 B1 51 9N 91 25W
Bamako, *Mali* 50 F4 12 34N 7 55W
Bambari, *C.A.R.* 52 C4 5 40N 20 35 E
Bambaroo, *Australia* 62 B4 18 50S 146 10 E
Bamberg, *Germany* 16 D6 49 54N 10 54 E
Bamberg, *U.S.A.* 77 J5 33 18N 81 2W
Bambili, *Dem. Rep. of the Congo* 54 B2 3 40N 26 0 E
Bamfield, *Canada* 72 D3 48 45N 125 10W
Bāmīān □, *Afghan.* 40 B5 35 0N 67 0 E
Bamiancheng, *China* 35 C13 43 15N 124 2 E
Bampūr, *Iran* 45 E9 27 15N 60 21 E
Ban Ban, *Laos* 38 C4 19 31N 103 30 E
Ban Bang Hin, *Thailand* 39 H2 9 32N 98 35 E
Ban Chiang Klang, *Thailand* 38 C3 19 25N 100 55 E
Ban Chik, *Laos* 38 D4 17 15N 102 22 E
Ban Choho, *Thailand* 38 E4 15 2N 102 9 E
Ban Dan Lan Hoi, *Thailand* 38 D2 17 0N 99 35 E
Ban Don = Surat Thani, *Thailand* 39 H2 9 6N 99 20 E
Ban Don, *Vietnam* 38 F6 12 53N 107 48 E
Ban Don, Ao →, *Thailand* 39 H2 9 20N 99 25 E
Ban Dong, *Thailand* 38 C3 19 30N 100 59 E
Ban Hong, *Thailand* 38 C2 18 18N 98 50 E
Ban Kaeng, *Thailand* 38 D3 17 29N 100 7 E
Ban Kantang, *Thailand* 39 J2 7 25N 99 31 E
Ban Keun, *Laos* 38 C4 18 22N 102 35 E
Ban Khai, *Thailand* 38 F3 12 46N 101 18 E
Ban Kheun, *Laos* 38 B3 20 13N 101 7 E
Ban Khlong Kua, *Thailand* 39 J3 6 57N 100 8 E
Ban Khuan Mao, *Thailand* 39 J2 7 50N 99 37 E
Ban Ko Yai Chim, *Thailand* 39 G2 11 17N 99 26 E
Ban Kok, *Thailand* 38 D4 16 40N 103 40 E
Ban Laem, *Thailand* 38 F2 13 13N 99 59 E
Ban Lao Ngam, *Laos* 38 E6 15 28N 106 10 E
Ban Le Kathe, *Thailand* 38 E2 15 49N 98 53 E
Ban Mae Chedi, *Thailand* 38 C2 19 11N 99 31 E
Ban Mae Laeng, *Thailand* 38 B2 20 1N 99 17 E
Ban Mae Sariang, *Thailand* 38 C1 18 10N 97 56 E
Ban Mê Thuôt = Buon Ma Thuot, *Vietnam* 38 F7 12 40N 108 3 E
Ban Mi, *Thailand* 38 E3 15 3N 100 32 E
Ban Muong Mo, *Laos* 38 C4 19 4N 103 58 E
Ban Na Mo, *Laos* 38 D5 17 7N 105 40 E
Ban Na San, *Thailand* 39 H2 8 53N 99 52 E
Ban Na Tong, *Laos* 38 B3 20 56N 101 47 E
Ban Nam Bac, *Laos* 38 B4 20 38N 102 20 E
Ban Nam Ma, *Laos* 38 A3 22 2N 101 37 E
Ban Ngang, *Laos* 38 E6 15 59N 106 11 E
Ban Nong Bok, *Laos* 38 D5 17 5N 104 48 E
Ban Nong Boua, *Laos* 38 E6 15 40N 106 33 E
Ban Nong Pling, *Thailand* 38 E3 15 40N 100 10 E
Ban Pak Chan, *Thailand* 39 G2 10 32N 98 51 E
Ban Phai, *Thailand* 38 D4 16 4N 102 44 E
Ban Pong, *Thailand* 38 F2 13 50N 99 55 E
Ban Ron Phibun, *Thailand* 39 H2 8 9N 99 51 E
Ban Sanam Chai, *Thailand* 39 J3 7 33N 100 25 E
Ban Sangkha, *Thailand* 38 E4 14 37N 103 52 E
Ban Tak, *Thailand* 38 D2 17 2N 99 4 E
Ban Tako, *Thailand* 38 E4 14 5N 102 40 E
Ban Tha Dua, *Thailand* 38 D2 17 59N 98 39 E
Ban Tha Li, *Thailand* 38 D3 17 37N 101 25 E
Ban Tha Nun, *Thailand* 39 H2 8 12N 98 18 E
Ban Thahine, *Laos* 38 E5 14 12N 105 33 E
Ban Xien Kok, *Laos* 38 B3 20 54N 100 39 E
Ban Yen Nhan, *Vietnam* 38 B6 20 57N 106 2 E
Banaba, *Kiribati* 64 H8 0 45S 169 50 E
Banalia, *Dem. Rep. of the Congo* 54 B2 1 32N 25 5 E
Banam, *Cambodia* 39 G5 11 20N 105 17 E
Bananal, I. do, *Brazil* 93 F8 11 30S 50 30W
Banaras = Varanasi, *India* 43 G10 25 22N 83 0 E
Banas →, *Gujarat, India* 42 H4 23 45N 71 25 E
Banas →, *Mad. P., India* 43 G9 24 15N 81 30 E
Bânâs, Ras, *Egypt* 51 D13 23 57N 35 59 E
Banbridge, *U.K.* 13 B5 54 22N 6 16W
Banbury, *U.K.* 11 E6 52 4N 1 20W
Banchory, *U.K.* 12 D6 57 3N 2 29W
Bancroft, *Canada* 78 A7 45 3N 77 51W
Band Bonī, *Iran* 45 E8 25 30N 59 33 E
Band Qīr, *Iran* 45 D6 31 39N 48 53 E
Banda, *Mad. P., India* 43 G8 24 3N 78 57 E
Banda, *Ut. P., India* 43 G9 25 30N 80 26 E
Banda, Kepulauan, *Indonesia* 37 E7 4 37S 129 50 E
Banda Aceh, *Indonesia* 36 C1 5 35N 95 20 E
Banda Banda, Mt., *Australia* 63 E5 31 10S 152 28 E
Banda Elat, *Indonesia* 37 F8 5 40S 133 5 E
Banda Is. = Banda, Kepulauan, *Indonesia* 37 E7 4 37S 129 50 E
Banda Sea, *Indonesia* 37 F7 6 0S 130 0 E
Bandai-San, *Japan* 30 F10 37 36N 140 4 E
Bandān, *Iran* 45 D9 31 23N 60 44 E
Bandanaira, *Indonesia* 37 E7 4 32S 129 54 E
Bandanwara, *India* 42 F6 26 9N 74 38 E
Bandar = Machilipatnam, *India* 41 L12 16 12N 81 8 E
Bandār 'Abbās, *Iran* 45 E8 27 15N 56 15 E
Bandar-e Anzalī, *Iran* 45 B6 37 30N 49 30 E
Bandar-e Bushehr = Būshehr, *Iran* 45 D6 28 55N 50 55 E
Bandar-e Chārak, *Iran* 45 E7 26 45N 54 20 E
Bandar-e Deylam, *Iran* 45 D6 30 5N 50 10 E
Bandar-e Khomeynı, *Iran* 45 D6 30 30N 49 5 E
Bandar-e Lengeh, *Iran* 45 E7 26 35N 54 58 E
Bandar-e Maqām, *Iran* 45 E7 26 56N 53 29 E
Bandar-e Ma'shur, *Iran* 45 D6 30 35N 49 10 E
Bandar-e Rīg, *Iran* 45 D6 29 29N 50 38 E
Bandar-e Torkeman, *Iran* 45 B7 37 0N 54 10 E
Bandar Maharani = Muar, *Malaysia* 39 L4 2 3N 102 34 E
Bandar Penggaram = Batu Pahat, *Malaysia* 39 M4 1 50N 102 56 E
Bandar Seri Begawan, *Brunei* 36 C4 4 52N 115 0 E
Bandar Sri Aman, *Malaysia* 36 D4 1 15N 111 32 E
Bandawe, *Malawi* 55 E3 11 58S 34 5 E
Bandeira, Pico da, *Brazil* 95 A7 20 26S 41 47W
Bandera, *Argentina* 94 B3 28 55S 62 20W
Banderas, B. de, *Mexico* 86 C3 20 40N 105 30W
Bandhogarh, *India* 43 H9 23 40N 81 2 E
Bandi →, *India* 42 F6 26 12N 75 47 E
Bandikui, *India* 42 F7 27 3N 76 34 E
Bandırma, *Turkey* 21 D13 40 20N 28 0 E
Bandon, *Ireland* 13 E3 51 44N 8 44W
Bandon →, *Ireland* 13 E3 51 43N 8 37W
Bandula, *Mozam.* 55 F3 19 0S 33 7 E
Bandundu, *Dem. Rep. of the Congo* 52 E3 3 15S 17 22 E
Bandung, *Indonesia* 36 F3 6 54S 107 36 E
Bāneh, *Iran* 44 C5 35 59N 45 53 E
Banes, *Cuba* 89 B4 21 0N 75 42W
Banff, *Canada* 72 C5 51 10N 115 34W
Banff, *U.K.* 12 D6 57 40N 2 33W
Banff Nat. Park, *Canada* 72 C5 51 30N 116 15W
Bang Fai →, *Laos* 38 D5 16 57N 104 45 E
Bang Hieng →, *Laos* 38 D5 16 10N 105 10 E
Bang Krathum, *Thailand* 38 D3 16 34N 100 18 E
Bang Lamung, *Thailand* 38 F3 13 3N 100 56 E
Bang Mun Nak, *Thailand* 38 D3 16 2N 100 23 E
Bang Pa In, *Thailand* 38 E3 14 14N 100 35 E
Bang Rakam, *Thailand* 38 D3 16 45N 100 7 E
Bang Saphan, *Thailand* 39 G2 11 14N 99 28 E
Bangaduni I., *India* 43 J13 21 34N 88 52 E
Bangala Dam, *Zimbabwe* 55 G3 21 7S 31 25 E
Bangalore, *India* 40 N10 12 59N 77 40 E
Banganga →, *India* 42 F6 27 6N 77 25 E
Bangaon, *India* 43 H13 23 0N 88 47 E
Bangassou, *C.A.R.* 52 D4 4 55N 23 7 E
Banggai, *Indonesia* 37 E6 1 34S 123 30 E
Banggai, Kepulauan, *Indonesia* 37 E6 1 40S 123 30 E
Banggai Arch. = Banggai, Kepulauan, *Indonesia* 37 E6 1 40S 123 30 E
Banggi, *Malaysia* 36 C5 7 17N 117 12 E
Banghāzī, *Libya* 51 B10 32 11N 20 3 E
Bangka, *Sulawesi, Indonesia* 37 D7 1 50N 125 5 E
Bangka, *Sumatera, Indonesia* 36 E3 2 0S 105 50 E
Bangka, Selat, *Indonesia* 36 E3 2 30S 105 30 E
Bangkalan, *Indonesia* 37 G15 7 2S 112 46 E
Bangkinang, *Indonesia* 36 D2 0 18N 101 5 E
Bangko, *Indonesia* 36 E2 2 5S 102 9 E
Bangkok, *Thailand* 38 F3 13 45N 100 35 E
Bangladesh ■, *Asia* 41 H17 24 0N 90 0 E
Bangong Co, *India* 43 B8 35 50N 79 20 E
Bangor, *Down, U.K.* 13 B6 54 40N 5 40W
Bangor, *Gwynedd, U.K.* 10 D3 53 14N 4 8W
Bangor, *Maine, U.S.A.* 69 D13 44 48N 68 46W
Bangor, *Pa., U.S.A.* 79 F9 40 52N 75 13W
Bangued, *Phil.* 37 A6 17 40N 120 37 E
Bangui, *C.A.R.* 52 D3 4 23N 18 35 E
Banguru, *Dem. Rep. of the Congo* 54 B2 0 30N 27 10 E
Bangweulu, L., *Zambia* 55 E3 11 0S 30 0 E
Bangweulu Swamp, *Zambia* 55 E3 11 20S 30 15 E
Bani, *Dom. Rep.* 89 C5 18 16N 70 22W
Banī Sa'd, *Iraq* 44 C5 33 34N 44 32 E
Banihal Pass, *India* 43 C6 33 30N 75 12 E
Bāniyās, *Syria* 44 C3 35 10N 36 0 E
Banja Luka, *Bos.-H.* 20 B7 44 49N 17 11 E
Banjar, *India* 42 D7 31 38N 77 21 E
Banjar →, *India* 43 H9 22 36N 80 22 E
Banjarmasin, *Indonesia* 36 E4 3 20S 114 35 E
Banjul, *Gambia* 50 F2 13 28N 16 40W
Banka, *India* 43 G12 24 53N 86 55 E
Banket, *Zimbabwe* 55 F3 17 27S 30 19 E
Bankipore, *India* 41 G14 25 35N 85 10 E
Banks I., *B.C., Canada* 72 C3 53 20N 130 0W
Banks I., *N.W.T., Canada* 68 A7 73 15N 121 30W
Banks Pen., *N.Z.* 59 K4 43 45S 173 15 E
Banks Str., *Australia* 62 G4 40 40S 148 10 E
Bankura, *India* 43 H12 23 11N 87 18 E
Banmankhi, *India* 43 G12 25 53N 87 11 E
Bann →, *Arm., U.K.* 13 B5 54 30N 6 31W
Bann →, *L'derry., U.K.* 13 A5 55 8N 6 41W
Bannang Sata, *Thailand* 39 J3 6 16N 101 16 E
Banning, *U.S.A.* 85 M10 33 56N 116 53W
Banningville = Bandundu, *Dem. Rep. of the Congo* 52 E3 3 15S 17 22 E
Bannockburn, *Canada* 78 B7 44 39N 77 33W
Bannockburn, *U.K.* 12 E5 56 5N 3 55W
Bannockburn, *Zimbabwe* 55 G2 20 17S 29 48 E
Bannu, *Pakistan* 40 C7 33 0N 70 18 E
Bano, *India* 43 H11 22 40N 84 55 E
Bansgaon, *India* 43 F10 26 33N 83 21 E
Banská Bystrica, *Slovak Rep.* 17 D10 48 46N 19 14 E
Banswara, *India* 42 H6 23 32N 74 24 E
Bantaeng, *Indonesia* 37 F5 5 32S 119 56 E
Bantry, *Ireland* 13 E2 51 41N 9 27W
Bantry B., *Ireland* 13 E2 51 37N 9 44W
Bantul, *Indonesia* 37 G14 7 55S 110 19 E
Bantva, *India* 42 J4 21 29N 70 12 E
Banyak, Kepulauan, *Indonesia* 36 D1 2 10N 97 10 E
Banyalbufar, *Spain* 22 B9 39 42N 2 31 E
Banyo, *Cameroon* 52 C2 6 52N 11 45 E
Banyumas, *Indonesia* 37 G13 7 32S 109 18 E
Banyuwangi, *Indonesia* 37 H16 8 13S 114 21 E
Banzare Coast, *Antarctica* 5 C9 68 0S 125 0 E
Bao Ha, *Vietnam* 38 A5 22 11N 104 21 E
Bao Lac, *Vietnam* 38 A5 22 57N 105 40 E
Bao Loc, *Vietnam* 39 G6 11 32N 107 48 E
Baocheng, *China* 34 H4 33 12N 106 56 E
Baode, *China* 34 E6 39 1N 111 5 E
Baodi, *China* 35 E9 39 38N 117 20 E
Baoding, *China* 34 E8 38 50N 115 28 E
Baoji, *China* 34 G4 34 20N 107 5 E
Baoshan, *China* 32 D4 25 10N 99 5 E
Baotou, *China* 34 D6 40 32N 110 2 E
Baoying, *China* 35 H10 33 17N 119 20 E
Bap, *India* 42 F5 27 23N 72 18 E
Bapatla, *India* 41 M12 15 55N 80 30 E
Bāqerābād, *Iran* 45 C6 33 2N 51 58 E
Ba'qūbah, *Iraq* 44 C5 33 45N 44 50 E
Baquedano, *Chile* 94 A2 23 20S 69 52W
Bar, *Montenegro, Yug.* 21 C8 42 8N 19 6 E
Bar, *Ukraine* 17 D14 49 4N 27 40 E
Bar Bigha, *India* 43 G11 25 21N 85 47 E
Bar Harbor, *U.S.A.* 77 C11 44 23N 68 13W
Bar-le-Duc, *France* 18 B6 48 47N 5 10 E
Bara, *India* 43 G9 25 16N 81 43 E
Bara Banki, *India* 43 F9 26 55N 81 12 E
Barabai, *Indonesia* 36 E5 2 32S 115 34 E
Baraboo, *U.S.A.* 80 D10 43 28N 89 45W
Baracoa, *Cuba* 89 B5 20 20N 74 30W
Baradā →, *Syria* 47 B5 33 33N 36 34 E
Baradero, *Argentina* 94 C4 33 52S 59 29W
Baraga, *U.S.A.* 80 B10 46 47N 88 30W
Barah →, *India* 42 F6 27 42N 77 5 E
Barahona, *Dom. Rep.* 89 C5 18 13N 71 7W
Barail Range, *India* 41 G18 25 15N 93 20 E
Barakaldo, *Spain* 19 A4 43 18N 2 59W
Barakar →, *India* 43 G12 24 7N 86 14 E
Barakhola, *India* 41 G18 25 0N 92 45 E
Barakot, *India* 43 J11 21 33N 84 59 E

Barakpur, India 43 H13 22 44N 88 30 E
Baralaba, Australia 62 C4 24 13S 149 50 E
Baralzon L., Canada 73 B9 60 0N 98 3W
Baramula, India 43 B6 34 15N 74 20 E
Baran, India 42 G7 25 9N 76 40 E
Baran →, Pakistan 42 G3 25 13N 68 17 E
Baranavichy, Belarus 17 B14 53 10N 26 0 E
Baranof, U.S.A. 72 B2 57 5N 134 50W
Baranof I., U.S.A. 68 C6 57 0N 135 0W
Barapasi, Indonesia 37 E9 2 15S 137 5 E
Barasat, India 43 H13 22 46N 88 31 E
Barat Daya, Kepulauan, Indonesia 37 F7 7 30S 128 0 E
Barataria B., U.S.A. 81 L10 29 20N 89 55W
Barauda, India 42 H6 23 33N 75 15 E
Baraut, India 42 E7 29 13N 77 7 E
Barbacena, Brazil 95 A7 21 15S 43 56W
Barbados ■, W. Indies 89 D8 13 10N 59 30W
Barbària, C. de, Spain 22 C7 38 39N 1 24 E
Barbastro, Spain 19 A6 42 2N 0 5 E
Barberton, S. Africa 57 D5 25 42S 31 2 E
Barberton, U.S.A. 78 E3 41 0N 81 39W
Barbosa, Colombia 92 B4 5 57N 73 37W
Barbourville, U.S.A. 77 G4 36 52N 83 53W
Barbuda, W. Indies 89 C7 17 30N 61 40W
Barcaldine, Australia 62 C4 23 43S 145 6 E
Barcellona Pozzo di Gotto, Italy 20 E6 38 9N 15 13 E
Barcelona, Spain 19 B7 41 21N 2 10 E
Barcelona, Venezuela 92 A6 10 10N 64 40W
Barcelos, Brazil 92 D6 1 0S 63 0W
Barcoo →, Australia 62 D3 25 30S 142 50 E
Bardaï, Chad 51 D9 21 25N 17 0 E
Bardas Blancas, Argentina 94 D2 35 49S 69 45W
Bardawîl, Sabkhet el, Egypt 47 D2 31 10N 33 15 E
Barddhaman, India 43 H12 23 14N 87 39 E
Bardejov, Slovak Rep. 17 D11 49 18N 21 15 E
Bardera, Somali Rep. 46 G3 2 20N 42 27 E
Bardīyah, Libya 51 B10 31 45N 25 5 E
Bardsey I., U.K. 10 E3 52 45N 4 47W
Bardstown, U.S.A. 76 G3 37 49N 85 28W
Bareilly, India 43 E8 28 22N 79 27 E
Barela, India 43 H9 23 6N 80 3 E
Barents Sea, Arctic 4 B9 73 0N 39 0 E
Barfleur, Pte. de, France 18 B3 49 42N 1 16W
Bargara, Australia 62 C5 24 50S 152 25 E
Barguzin, Russia 27 D11 53 37N 109 37 E
Barh, India 43 G11 25 29N 85 46 E
Barhaj, India 43 F10 26 18N 83 44 E
Barharwa, India 43 G12 24 52N 87 47 E
Barhi, India 43 G11 24 15N 85 25 E
Bari, India 42 F7 26 39N 77 39 E
Bari, Italy 20 D7 41 8N 16 51 E
Bari Doab, Pakistan 42 D5 30 20N 73 0 E
Bari Sadri, India 42 G6 24 28N 74 30 E
Barīdī, Ra's, Si. Arabia 44 E3 24 17N 37 31 E
Barīm, Yemen 48 E8 12 39N 43 25 E
Barinas, Venezuela 92 B4 8 36N 70 15W
Baring, C., Canada 68 B8 70 0N 117 30W
Baringo, Kenya 54 B4 0 47N 36 16 E
Baringo, L., Kenya 54 B4 0 47N 36 16 E
Barisal, Bangla. 41 H17 22 45N 90 20 E
Barisan, Bukit, Indonesia 36 E2 3 30S 102 15 E
Barito →, Indonesia 36 E4 4 0S 114 50 E
Bark L., Canada 78 A7 45 27N 77 51W
Barkakana, India 43 H11 23 37N 85 29 E
Barker, U.S.A. 78 C6 43 20N 78 33W
Barkley, L., U.S.A. 77 G2 37 1N 88 14W
Barkley Sound, Canada 72 D3 48 50N 125 10W
Barkly East, S. Africa 56 E4 30 58S 27 33 E
Barkly Roadhouse, Australia 62 B2 19 52S 135 50 E
Barkly Tableland, Australia 62 B2 17 50S 136 40 E
Barkly West, S. Africa 56 D3 28 5S 24 31 E
Barkol Kazak Zizhixian, China 32 B4 43 37N 93 2 E
Bârlad, Romania 17 E14 46 15N 27 38 E
Bârlad →, Romania 17 F14 45 38N 27 32 E
Barlee, L., Australia 61 E2 29 15S 119 30 E
Barlee, Mt., Australia 61 D4 24 38S 128 13 E
Barletta, Italy 20 D7 41 19N 16 17 E
Barlovento, Canary Is. 22 F2 28 48N 17 48W
Barlow L., Canada 73 A8 62 0N 103 0W
Barmedman, Australia 63 E4 34 9S 147 21 E
Barmer, India 42 G4 25 45N 71 20 E
Barmera, Australia 63 E3 34 15S 140 28 E
Barmouth, U.K. 10 E3 52 44N 4 4W
Barna →, India 43 G10 25 21N 83 3 E
Barnagar, India 42 H6 23 7N 75 19 E
Barnala, India 42 D6 30 23N 75 33 E
Barnard Castle, U.K. 10 C6 54 33N 1 55W
Barnaul, Russia 26 D9 53 20N 83 40 E
Barnesville, U.S.A. 77 J3 33 3N 84 9W
Barnet □, U.K. 11 F7 51 38N 0 9W
Barneveld, Neths. 15 B5 52 7N 5 36 E
Barneveld, U.S.A. 79 C9 43 16N 75 14W
Barnhart, U.S.A. 81 K4 31 8N 101 10W
Barnsley, U.K. 10 D6 53 34N 1 27W
Barnstaple, U.K. 11 F3 51 5N 4 4W
Barnstaple Bay = Bideford Bay, U.K. 11 F3 51 5N 4 20W
Barnsville, U.S.A. 80 B6 46 43N 96 28W
Barnwell, U.S.A. 77 J5 33 15N 81 23W
Baro, Nigeria 50 G7 8 35N 6 18 E
Baroda = Vadodara, India 42 H5 22 20N 73 10 E
Baroda, India 42 G7 25 29N 76 35 E
Baroe, S. Africa 56 E3 33 13S 24 33 E
Baron Ra., Australia 60 D4 23 30S 127 45 E
Barotseland, Zambia 53 H4 15 0S 24 0 E
Barpeta, India 41 F17 26 20N 91 10 E
Barques, Pt. Aux, U.S.A. 78 B2 44 4N 82 58W
Barquísimeto, Venezuela 92 A5 10 4N 69 19W
Barr Smith Range, Australia 61 E3 27 4S 120 20 E
Barra, Brazil 93 F10 11 5S 43 10W
Barra, U.K. 12 E1 57 0N 7 29W
Barra, Sd. of, U.K. 12 D1 57 4N 7 25W
Barra de Navidad, Mexico 86 D4 19 12N 104 41W
Barra do Corda, Brazil 93 E9 5 30S 45 10W
Barra do Piraí, Brazil 95 A7 22 30S 43 50W
Barra Falsa, Pta. da, Mozam. 57 C6 22 58S 35 37 E
Barra Hd., U.K. 12 E1 56 47N 7 40W
Barra Mansa, Brazil 95 A7 22 35S 44 12W
Barraba, Australia 63 E5 30 21S 150 35 E
Barrackpur = Barakpur, India 43 H13 22 44N 88 30 E
Barradale Roadhouse, Australia 60 D1 22 42S 114 58 E
Barraigh = Barra, U.K. 12 E1 57 0N 7 29W
Barranca, Lima, Peru 92 F3 10 45S 77 50W
Barranca, Loreto, Peru 92 D3 4 50S 76 50W
Barrancabermeja, Colombia 92 B4 7 0N 73 50W
Barrancas, Venezuela 92 B6 8 55N 62 5W
Barrancos, Portugal 19 C2 38 10N 6 58W
Barranqueras, Argentina 94 B4 27 30S 59 0W
Barranquilla, Colombia 92 A4 11 0N 74 50W
Barraute, Canada 70 C4 48 26N 77 38W
Barre, Mass., U.S.A. 79 D12 42 25N 72 6W
Barre, Vt., U.S.A. 79 B12 44 12N 72 30W
Barreal, Argentina 94 C2 31 33S 69 28W
Barreiras, Brazil 93 F10 12 8S 45 0W
Barreirinhas, Brazil 93 D10 2 30S 42 50W
Barreiro, Portugal 19 C1 38 40N 9 6W
Barren, Nosy, Madag. 57 B7 18 25S 43 40 E
Barretos, Brazil 93 H9 20 30S 48 35W
Barrhead, Canada 72 C6 54 10N 114 24W
Barrie, Canada 78 B5 44 24N 79 40W
Barrier Ra., Australia 63 E3 31 0S 141 30 E
Barrière, Canada 72 C4 51 12N 120 7W
Barrington, U.S.A. 79 E13 41 44N 71 18W
Barrington L., Canada 73 B8 56 55N 100 15W
Barrington Tops, Australia 63 E5 32 6S 151 28 E
Barringun, Australia 63 D4 29 1S 145 41 E
Barro do Garças, Brazil 93 G8 15 54S 52 16W
Barron, U.S.A. 80 C9 45 24N 91 51W
Barrow, U.S.A. 68 A4 71 18N 156 47W
Barrow →, Ireland 13 D5 52 25N 6 58W
Barrow Creek, Australia 62 C1 21 30S 133 55 E
Barrow I., Australia 60 D2 20 45S 115 20 E
Barrow-in-Furness, U.K. 10 C4 54 7N 3 14W
Barrow Pt., Australia 62 A3 14 20S 144 40 E
Barrow Pt., U.S.A. 66 B4 71 10N 156 20W
Barrow Ra., Australia 61 E4 26 0S 127 40 E
Barrow Str., Canada 4 B3 74 20N 95 0W
Barry, U.K. 11 F4 51 24N 3 16W
Barry's Bay, Canada 78 A7 45 29N 77 41W
Barsat, Pakistan 43 A5 36 10N 72 45 E
Barsham, Syria 44 C4 35 21N 40 33 E
Barsi, India 40 K9 18 10N 75 50 E
Barsoi, India 41 G15 25 48N 87 57 E
Barstow, U.S.A. 85 L9 34 54N 117 1W
Barthélemy, Col, Vietnam 38 C5 19 26N 104 6 E
Bartica, Guyana 92 B7 6 25N 58 40W
Bartlesville, U.S.A. 81 G7 36 45N 95 59W
Bartlett, U.S.A. 84 J8 36 29N 118 2W
Bartlett, L., Canada 72 A5 63 5N 118 20W
Bartolomeu Dias, Mozam. 55 G4 21 10S 35 8 E
Barton, U.S.A. 79 B12 44 45N 72 11W
Barton upon Humber, U.K. 10 D7 53 41N 0 25W
Bartow, U.S.A. 77 M5 27 54N 81 50W
Barú, Volcan, Panama 88 E3 8 55N 82 35W
Barumba, Dem. Rep. of the Congo 54 B1 1 3N 23 37 E
Baruunsuu, Mongolia 34 C3 43 43N 105 35 E
Barwani, India 42 H6 22 2N 74 57 E
Barysaw, Belarus 17 A15 54 17N 28 28 E
Barzān, Iraq 44 B5 36 55N 44 3 E
Bâsa'idū, Iran 45 E7 26 35N 55 20 E
Basal, Pakistan 42 C5 33 33N 72 13 E
Basankusa, Dem. Rep. of the Congo 52 D3 1 5N 19 50 E
Basarabeasca, Moldova 17 E15 46 21N 28 58 E
Basarabia = Bessarabiya, Moldova 17 E15 47 0N 28 10 E
Basawa, Afghan. 42 B4 34 15N 70 50 E
Bascuñán, C., Chile 94 B1 28 52S 71 35W
Basel, Switz. 18 C7 47 35N 7 35 E
Bashākerd, Kūhhā-ye, Iran 45 E8 26 42N 58 35 E
Bashaw, Canada 72 C6 52 35N 112 58W
Bāshī, Iran 45 D6 28 41N 51 4 E
Bashkir Republic = Bashkortostan □, Russia 24 D10 54 0N 57 0 E
Bashkortostan □, Russia 24 D10 54 0N 57 0 E
Basibasy, Madag. 57 C7 22 10S 43 40 E
Basilan I., Phil. 37 C6 6 35N 122 0 E
Basilan Str., Phil. 37 C6 6 50N 122 0 E
Basildon, U.K. 11 F8 51 34N 0 28 E
Basim = Washim, India 40 J10 20 3N 77 0 E
Basin, U.S.A. 82 D9 44 23N 108 2W
Basingstoke, U.K. 11 F6 51 15N 1 5W
Baskatong, Rés., Canada 70 C4 46 46N 75 50W
Basle = Basel, Switz. 18 C7 47 35N 7 35 E
Basoda, India 42 H7 23 52N 77 54 E
Basoko, Dem. Rep. of the Congo 54 B1 1 16N 23 40 E
Basque Provinces = País Vasco □, Spain 19 A4 42 50N 2 45W
Basra = Al Başrah, Iraq 44 D5 30 30N 47 50 E
Bass Str., Australia 62 F4 39 15S 146 30 E
Bassano, Canada 72 C6 50 48N 112 20W
Bassano del Grappa, Italy 20 B4 45 46N 11 44 E
Bassas da India, Ind. Oc. 53 J7 22 0S 39 0 E
Basse-Terre, Guadeloupe 89 C7 16 0N 61 44W
Bassein, Burma 41 L19 16 45N 94 30 E
Basseterre, St. Kitts & Nevis 89 C7 17 17N 62 43W
Bassett, U.S.A. 80 D5 42 35N 99 32W
Bassi, India 42 D7 30 44N 76 21 E
Bastak, Iran 45 E7 27 15N 54 25 E
Baştām, Iran 45 B7 36 29N 55 4 E
Bastar, India 41 K12 19 15N 81 40 E
Basti, India 43 F10 26 52N 82 55 E
Bastia, France 18 E8 42 40N 9 30 E
Bastogne, Belgium 15 D5 50 1N 5 43 E
Bastrop, La., U.S.A. 81 J9 32 47N 91 55W
Bastrop, Tex., U.S.A. 81 K6 30 7N 97 19W
Bat Yam, Israel 47 C3 32 2N 34 44 E
Bata, Eq. Guin. 52 D1 1 57N 9 50 E
Bataan □, Phil. 37 B6 14 40N 120 25 E
Batabanó, Cuba 88 B3 22 40N 82 20W
Batabanó, G. de, Cuba 88 B3 22 30N 82 30W
Batac, Phil. 37 A6 18 3N 120 34 E
Batagai, Russia 27 C14 67 38N 134 38 E
Batala, India 42 D6 31 48N 75 12 E
Batama, Dem. Rep. of the Congo 54 B2 0 58N 26 33 E
Batamay, Russia 27 C13 63 30N 129 15 E
Batang, Indonesia 37 G13 6 55S 109 45 E
Batangas, Phil. 37 B6 13 35N 121 10 E
Batanta, Indonesia 37 E8 0 55S 130 40 E
Batatais, Brazil 95 A6 20 54S 47 37W
Batavia, U.S.A. 78 D6 43 0N 78 11W
Batchelor, Australia 60 B5 13 4S 131 1 E
Battdambang, Cambodia 38 F4 13 7N 103 12 E
Batemans B., Australia 63 F5 35 40S 150 12 E
Batemans Bay, Australia 63 F5 35 44S 150 11 E
Bates Ra., Australia 61 E3 27 27S 121 5 E
Batesburg-Leesville, U.S.A. 77 J5 33 54N 81 33W
Batesville, Ark., U.S.A. 81 H9 35 46N 91 39W
Batesville, Miss., U.S.A. 81 H10 34 19N 89 57W
Batesville, Tex., U.S.A. 81 L5 28 58N 99 37W
Bath, Canada 79 B8 44 11N 76 47W
Bath, U.K. 11 F5 51 23N 2 22W
Bath, Maine, U.S.A. 77 D11 43 55N 69 49W
Bath, N.Y., U.S.A. 78 D7 42 20N 77 19W
Bath & North East Somerset □, U.K. 11 F5 51 21N 2 27W
Batheay, Cambodia 39 G5 11 59N 104 57 E
Bathurst = Banjul, Gambia 50 F2 13 28N 16 40W
Bathurst, Australia 63 E4 33 25S 149 31 E
Bathurst, Canada 71 C6 47 37N 65 43W
Bathurst, S. Africa 56 E4 33 30S 26 50 E
Bathurst, C., Canada 68 A7 70 34N 128 0W
Bathurst B., Australia 62 A3 14 16S 144 25 E
Bathurst Harb., Australia 62 G4 43 15S 146 10 E
Bathurst I., Australia 60 B5 11 30S 130 10 E
Bathurst I., Canada 4 B2 76 0N 100 30W
Bathurst Inlet, Canada 68 B9 66 50N 108 1W
Batlow, Australia 63 F4 35 31S 148 9 E
Batman, Turkey 25 G7 37 55N 41 5 E
Baţn al Ghūl, Jordan 47 F4 29 36N 35 56 E
Batna, Algeria 50 A7 35 34N 6 15 E
Batoka, Zambia 55 F2 16 45S 27 15 E
Baton Rouge, U.S.A. 81 K9 30 27N 91 11W
Batong, Ko, Thailand 39 J2 6 32N 99 12 E
Batopilas, Mexico 86 B3 27 0N 107 45W
Batouri, Cameroon 52 D2 4 30N 14 25 E
Båtsfjord, Norway 8 A23 70 38N 29 39 E
Battambang = Batdambang, Cambodia 38 F4 13 7N 103 12 E
Batticaloa, Sri Lanka 40 R12 7 43N 81 45 E
Battipáglia, Italy 20 D6 40 37N 14 58 E
Battle, U.K. 11 G8 50 55N 0 30 E
Battle →, Canada 73 C7 52 43N 108 15W
Battle Creek, U.S.A. 76 D3 42 19N 85 11W
Battle Ground, U.S.A. 84 E4 45 47N 122 32W
Battle Harbour, Canada 71 B8 52 16N 55 35W
Battle Lake, U.S.A. 80 B7 46 17N 95 43W
Battle Mountain, U.S.A. 82 F5 40 38N 116 56W
Battlefields, Zimbabwe 55 F2 18 37S 29 47 E
Battleford, Canada 73 C7 52 45N 108 15W
Batu, Ethiopia 46 F2 6 55N 39 45 E
Batu, Kepulauan, Indonesia 36 E1 0 30S 98 25 E
Batu Caves, Malaysia 39 L3 3 15N 101 40 E
Batu Gajah, Malaysia 39 K3 4 28N 101 3 E
Batu Is. = Batu, Kepulauan, Indonesia 36 E1 0 30S 98 25 E
Batu Pahat, Malaysia 39 M4 1 50N 102 56 E
Batuata, Indonesia 37 F6 6 12S 122 42 E
Batumi, Georgia 25 F7 41 39N 41 44 E
Baturaja, Indonesia 36 E2 4 11S 104 15 E
Baturité, Brazil 93 D11 4 28S 38 45W
Bau, Malaysia 36 D4 1 25N 110 9 E
Baubau, Indonesia 37 F6 5 25S 122 38 E
Baucau, E. Timor 37 F7 8 27S 126 27 E
Bauchi, Nigeria 50 F7 10 22N 9 48 E
Baudette, U.S.A. 80 A7 48 43N 94 36W
Bauer, C., Australia 63 E1 32 44S 134 4 E
Bauhinia, Australia 62 C4 24 35S 149 18 E
Baukau = Baucau, E. Timor 37 F7 8 27S 126 27 E
Bauld, C., Canada 69 C14 51 38N 55 26W
Bauru, Brazil 95 A6 22 10S 49 0W
Bausi, India 43 G12 24 48N 87 1 E
Bauska, Latvia 9 H21 56 24N 24 15 E
Bautzen, Germany 16 C8 51 10N 14 26 E
Bavānāt, Iran 45 D7 30 28N 53 27 E
Bavaria = Bayern □, Germany 16 D6 48 50N 12 0 E
Bavispe →, Mexico 86 B3 29 30N 109 11W
Bawdwin, Burma 41 H20 23 5N 97 20 E
Bawean, Indonesia 36 F4 5 46S 112 35 E
Bawku, Ghana 50 F5 11 3N 0 19W
Bawlake, Burma 41 K20 19 11N 97 21 E
Baxley, U.S.A. 77 K4 31 47N 82 21W
Baxter, U.S.A. 80 B7 46 21N 94 17W
Baxter Springs, U.S.A. 81 G7 37 2N 94 44W
Bay City, Mich., U.S.A. 76 D4 43 36N 83 54W
Bay City, Tex., U.S.A. 81 L7 28 59N 95 58W
Bay Minette, U.S.A. 77 K2 30 53N 87 46W
Bay Roberts, Canada 71 C9 47 36N 53 16W
Bay St. Louis, U.S.A. 81 K10 30 19N 89 20W
Bay Springs, U.S.A. 81 K10 31 59N 89 17W
Bay View, N.Z. 59 H6 39 25S 176 50 E
Baya, Dem. Rep. of the Congo 55 E2 11 53S 27 25 E
Bayamo, Cuba 88 B4 20 20N 76 40W
Bayamón, Puerto Rico 89 C6 18 24N 66 10W
Bayan Har Shan, China 32 C4 34 0N 98 0 E
Bayan Hot = Alxa Zuoqi, China 34 E3 38 50N 105 40 E
Bayan Obo, China 34 D5 41 52N 109 59 E
Bayan-Ovoo = Erdenetsogt, Mongolia 34 C4 42 55N 106 5 E
Bayana, India 42 F7 26 55N 77 18 E
Bayanaūyl, Kazakstan 26 D8 50 45N 75 45 E
Bayandalay, Mongolia 34 C2 43 30N 103 29 E
Bayanhongor, Mongolia 32 B5 46 8N 102 43 E
Bayard, N. Mex., U.S.A. 83 K9 32 46N 108 8W
Bayard, Nebr., U.S.A. 80 E3 41 45N 103 20W
Baybay, Phil. 37 B6 10 40N 124 55 E
Baydhabo = Baidoa, Somali Rep. 46 G3 3 8N 43 30 E
Bayern □, Germany 16 D6 48 50N 12 0 E
Bayeux, France 18 B3 49 17N 0 42W
Bayfield, Canada 78 C3 43 34N 81 42W
Bayfield, U.S.A. 80 B9 46 49N 90 49W
Bayındır, Turkey 21 E12 38 13N 27 39 E
Baykal, Oz., Russia 27 D11 53 0N 108 0 E
Baykan, Turkey 44 B4 38 7N 41 44 E
Baykonur = Bayqongyr, Kazakstan 26 E7 47 48N 65 50 E
Baymak, Russia 24 D10 52 36N 58 19 E
Baynes Mts., Namibia 56 B1 17 15S 13 0 E
Bayombong, Phil. 37 A6 16 30N 121 10 E
Bayonne, France 18 E3 43 30N 1 28W
Bayonne, U.S.A. 79 F10 40 40N 74 7W
Bayovar, Peru 92 E2 5 50S 81 0W
Bayqongyr, Kazakstan 26 E7 47 48N 65 50 E
Bayram-Ali = Bayramaly, Turkmenistan 26 F7 37 37N 62 10 E
Bayramaly, Turkmenistan 26 F7 37 37N 62 10 E
Bayramiç, Turkey 21 E12 39 48N 26 36 E
Bayreuth, Germany 16 D6 49 56N 11 35 E
Bayrūt, Lebanon 47 B4 33 53N 35 31 E
Bays, L. of, Canada 78 A5 45 15N 79 4W
Baysville, Canada 78 A5 45 9N 79 7W
Bayt Lahm, West Bank 47 D4 31 43N 35 12 E
Baytown, U.S.A. 81 L7 29 43N 94 59W
Baza, Spain 19 D4 37 30N 2 47W
Bazaruto, I. do, Mozam. 57 C6 21 40S 35 28 E
Bazhou, China 34 E9 39 8N 116 22 E
Bazmān, Kūh-e, Iran 45 D9 28 4N 60 1 E
Beach, U.S.A. 80 B3 46 58N 104 0W
Beach City, U.S.A. 78 F3 40 39N 81 35W
Beachport, Australia 63 F3 37 29S 140 0 E
Beachy Hd., U.K. 11 G8 50 44N 0 15 E
Beacon, Australia 61 F2 30 26S 117 52 E
Beacon, U.S.A. 79 E11 41 30N 73 58W
Beaconsfield, Australia 62 G4 41 11S 146 48 E
Beagle, Canal, S. Amer. 96 H3 55 0S 68 30W
Beagle Bay, Australia 60 C3 16 58S 122 40 E
Bealanana, Madag. 57 A8 14 33S 48 44 E
Beals Cr. →, U.S.A. 81 J4 32 10N 100 51W
Beamsville, Canada 78 C5 43 12N 79 28W
Bear →, Calif., U.S.A. 84 G5 38 56N 121 36W
Bear →, Utah, U.S.A. 74 B4 41 30N 112 8W
Bear I., Ireland 13 E2 51 38N 9 50W
Bear L., Canada 73 B9 55 8N 96 0W
Bear L., U.S.A. 82 F8 41 59N 111 21W
Beardmore, Canada 70 C2 49 36N 87 57W
Beardmore Glacier, Antarctica 5 E11 84 30S 170 0 E
Beardstown, U.S.A. 80 F9 40 1N 90 26W
Bearma →, India 43 G8 24 20N 79 51 E
Béarn, France 18 E3 43 20N 0 30W
Bearpaw Mts., U.S.A. 82 B9 48 12N 109 30W
Bearskin Lake, Canada 70 B1 53 58N 91 2W
Beas →, India 42 D6 31 10N 74 59 E
Beata, C., Dom. Rep. 89 C5 17 40N 71 30W
Beata, I., Dom. Rep. 89 C5 17 34N 71 31W
Beatrice, U.S.A. 80 E6 40 16N 96 45W
Beatrice, Zimbabwe 55 F3 18 15S 30 55 E
Beatrice, C., Australia 62 A2 14 20S 136 55 E
Beatton →, Canada 72 B4 56 15N 120 45W
Beatton River, Canada 72 B4 57 26N 121 20W
Beatty, U.S.A. 84 J10 36 54N 116 46W
Beauce, Plaine de la, France 18 B4 48 10N 1 45 E
Beauceville, Canada 71 C5 46 13N 70 46W
Beaudesert, Australia 63 D5 27 59S 153 0 E
Beaufort, Malaysia 36 C5 5 30N 115 40 E
Beaufort, N.C., U.S.A. 77 H7 34 43N 76 40W
Beaufort, S.C., U.S.A. 77 J5 32 26N 80 40W
Beaufort Sea, Arctic 4 B1 72 0N 140 0W
Beaufort West, S. Africa 56 E3 32 18S 22 36 E
Beauharnois, Canada 79 A11 45 20N 73 52W
Beaulieu →, Canada 72 A6 62 3N 113 11W
Beauly, U.K. 12 D4 57 30N 4 28W
Beauly →, U.K. 12 D4 57 29N 4 27W
Beaumaris, U.K. 10 D3 53 16N 4 6W
Beaumont, Belgium 15 D4 50 15N 4 14 E
Beaumont, U.S.A. 81 K7 30 5N 94 6W
Beaune, France 18 C6 47 2N 4 50 E
Beaupré, Canada 71 C5 47 3N 70 54W
Beauraing, Belgium 15 D4 50 7N 4 57 E
Beauséjour, Canada 73 C9 50 5N 96 35W
Beauvais, France 18 B5 49 25N 2 8 E
Beauval, Canada 73 B7 55 9N 107 37W
Beaver, Okla., U.S.A. 81 G4 36 49N 100 31W
Beaver, Pa., U.S.A. 78 F4 40 42N 80 19W
Beaver, Utah, U.S.A. 83 G7 38 17N 112 38W
Beaver →, B.C., Canada 72 B4 59 52N 124 20W
Beaver →, Ont., Canada 70 A2 55 55N 87 48W
Beaver →, Sask., Canada 73 B7 55 26N 107 45W
Beaver →, U.S.A. 81 G5 36 35N 99 30W
Beaver City, U.S.A. 80 E5 40 8N 99 50W
Beaver Creek, Canada 68 B5 63 0N 141 0W
Beaver Dam, U.S.A. 80 D10 43 28N 88 50W
Beaver Falls, U.S.A. 78 F4 40 46N 80 20W
Beaver Hill L., Canada 73 C10 54 5N 94 50W
Beaver I., U.S.A. 76 C3 45 40N 85 33W
Beaverhill L., Canada 72 C6 53 27N 112 32W
Beaverlodge, Canada 72 B5 55 11N 119 29W
Beaverstone →, Canada 70 B2 54 59N 89 25W
Beaverton, Canada 78 B5 44 26N 79 9W
Beaverton, U.S.A. 84 E4 45 29N 122 48W
Beawar, India 42 F6 26 3N 74 18 E
Bebedouro, Brazil 95 A6 21 0S 48 25W
Beboa, Madag. 57 B7 17 22S 44 33 E
Beccles, U.K. 11 E9 52 27N 1 35 E
Bečej, Serbia, Yug. 21 B9 45 36N 20 3 E
Béchar, Algeria 50 B5 31 38N 2 18W
Beckley, U.S.A. 76 G5 37 47N 81 11W
Beddouza, Ras, Morocco 50 B4 32 33N 9 9W
Bedford, Canada 79 A12 45 7N 72 59W
Bedford, S. Africa 56 E4 32 40S 26 10 E
Bedford, U.K. 11 E7 52 8N 0 28W
Bedford, Ind., U.S.A. 76 F2 38 52N 86 29W
Bedford, Iowa, U.S.A. 80 E7 40 40N 94 44W
Bedford, Ohio, U.S.A. 78 E3 41 23N 81 32W
Bedford, Pa., U.S.A. 78 F6 40 1N 78 30W
Bedford, Va., U.S.A. 76 G6 37 20N 79 31W
Bedford, C., Australia 62 B4 15 14S 145 21 E
Bedfordshire □, U.K. 11 E7 52 4N 0 28W
Bedourie, Australia 62 C2 24 30S 139 30 E
Bedum, Neths. 15 A6 53 18N 6 36 E
Beebe Plain, Canada 79 A12 45 1N 72 9W
Beech Creek, U.S.A. 78 E7 41 5N 77 36W
Beenleigh, Australia 63 D5 27 43S 153 10 E
Be'er Menuha, Israel 44 D2 30 19N 35 8 E
Be'er Sheva, Israel 47 D3 31 15N 34 48 E
Beersheba = Be'er Sheva, Israel 47 D3 31 15N 34 48 E
Beestekraal, S. Africa 57 D4 25 23S 27 38 E
Beeston, U.K. 10 E6 52 56N 1 14W
Beeville, U.S.A. 81 L6 28 24N 97 45W
Befale, Dem. Rep. of the Congo 52 D4 0 25N 20 45 E
Befandriana, Mahajanga, Madag. 57 B8 15 16S 48 32 E
Befandriana, Toliara, Madag. 57 C7 21 55S 44 0 E
Befasy, Madag. 57 C7 20 33S 44 23 E
Befotaka, Antsiranana, Madag. 57 A8 13 15S 48 16 E
Befotaka, Fianarantsoa, Madag. 57 C8 23 49S 47 0 E
Bega, Australia 63 F4 36 41S 149 51 E
Begusarai, India 43 G12 25 24N 86 9 E
Behābād, Iran 45 C8 32 24N 59 47 E

Bīārjmand, *Iran* 45 B7 36 6N 55 53 E
Biaro, *Indonesia* 37 D7 2 5N 125 26 E
Biarritz, *France* 18 E3 43 29N 1 33W
Bibai, *Japan* 30 C10 43 19N 141 52 E
Bibby I., *Canada* 73 A10 61 55N 93 0W
Biberach, *Germany* 16 D5 48 5N 9 47 E
Bibungwa, *Dem. Rep. of the Congo* 54 C2 2 40S 28 15 E
Bic, *Canada* 71 C6 48 20N 68 41W
Bicester, *U.K.* 11 F6 51 54N 1 9W
Bicheno, *Australia* 62 G4 41 52S 148 18 E
Bichia, *India* 43 H9 22 27N 80 42 E
Bickerton I., *Australia* 62 A2 13 45S 136 10 E
Bida, *Nigeria* 50 G7 9 3N 5 58 E
Bidar, *India* 40 L10 17 55N 77 35 E
Biddeford, *U.S.A.* 77 D10 43 30N 70 28W
Bideford, *U.K.* 11 F3 51 1N 4 13W
Bideford Bay, *U.K.* 11 F3 51 5N 4 20W
Bidhuna, *India* 43 F8 26 49N 79 31 E
Bidor, *Malaysia* 39 K3 4 6N 101 15 E
Bié, Planalto de, *Angola* 53 G3 12 0S 16 0 E
Bieber, *U.S.A.* 82 F3 41 7N 121 8W
Biel, *Switz.* 18 C7 47 8N 7 14 E
Bielefeld, *Germany* 16 B5 52 1N 8 33 E
Biella, *Italy* 18 D8 45 34N 8 3 E
Bielsk Podlaski, *Poland* 17 B12 52 47N 23 12 E
Bielsko-Biała, *Poland* 17 D10 49 50N 19 2 E
Bien Hoa, *Vietnam* 39 G6 10 57N 106 49 E
Bienne = Biel, *Switz.* 18 C7 47 8N 7 14 E
Bienville, L., *Canada* 70 A5 55 5N 72 40W
Biesiesfontein, *S. Africa* 56 E2 30 57S 17 58 E
Big →, *Canada* 71 B8 54 50N 58 55W
Big B., *Canada* 71 A7 55 43N 60 35W
Big Bear City, *U.S.A.* 85 L10 34 16N 116 51W
Big Bear Lake, *U.S.A.* 85 L10 34 15N 116 56W
Big Belt Mts., *U.S.A.* 82 C8 46 30N 111 25W
Big Bend, *Swaziland* 57 D5 26 50S 31 58 E
Big Bend Nat. Park, *U.S.A.* 81 L3 29 20N 103 5W
Big Black →, *U.S.A.* 81 K9 32 3N 91 4W
Big Blue →, *U.S.A.* 80 F6 39 35N 96 34W
Big Creek, *U.S.A.* 84 H7 37 11N 119 14W
Big Cypress Nat. Preserve, *U.S.A.* 77 M5 26 0N 81 10W
Big Cypress Swamp, *U.S.A.* 77 M5 26 15N 81 30W
Big Falls, *U.S.A.* 80 A8 48 12N 93 48W
Big Fork →, *U.S.A.* 80 A8 48 31N 93 43W
Big Horn Mts. = Bighorn Mts., *U.S.A.* 82 D10 44 30N 107 30W
Big I., *Canada* 72 A5 61 7N 116 45W
Big Lake, *U.S.A.* 81 K4 31 12N 101 28W
Big Moose, *U.S.A.* 79 C10 43 49N 74 58W
Big Muddy Cr. →, *U.S.A.* 80 A2 48 8N 104 36W
Big Pine, *U.S.A.* 84 H8 37 10N 118 17W
Big Piney, *U.S.A.* 82 E8 42 32N 110 7W
Big Rapids, *U.S.A.* 76 D3 43 42N 85 29W
Big Rideau L., *Canada* 79 B8 44 40N 76 15W
Big River, *Canada* 73 C7 53 50N 107 0W
Big Run, *U.S.A.* 78 F6 40 57N 78 55W
Big Sable Pt., *U.S.A.* 76 C2 44 3N 86 1W
Big Salmon →, *Canada* 72 A2 61 52N 134 55W
Big Sand L., *Canada* 73 B9 57 45N 99 45W
Big Sandy, *U.S.A.* 82 B8 48 11N 110 7W
Big Sandy →, *U.S.A.* 76 F4 38 25N 82 36W
Big Sandy Cr. →, *U.S.A.* 80 F3 38 7N 102 29W
Big Sioux →, *U.S.A.* 80 D6 42 29N 96 27W
Big Spring, *U.S.A.* 81 J4 32 15N 101 28W
Big Stone City, *U.S.A.* 80 C6 45 18N 96 28W
Big Stone Gap, *U.S.A.* 77 G4 36 52N 82 47W
Big Stone L., *U.S.A.* 80 C6 45 30N 96 35W
Big Sur, *U.S.A.* 84 J5 36 15N 121 48W
Big Timber, *U.S.A.* 82 D9 45 50N 109 57W
Big Trout L., *Canada* 70 B2 53 40N 90 0W
Big Trout Lake, *Canada* 70 B2 53 45N 90 0W
Biğa, *Turkey* 21 D12 40 13N 27 14 E
Bigadiç, *Turkey* 21 E13 39 22N 28 7 E
Biggar, *Canada* 73 C7 52 4N 108 0W
Biggar, *U.K.* 12 F5 55 38N 3 32W
Bigge I., *Australia* 60 B4 14 35S 125 10 E
Biggenden, *Australia* 63 D5 25 31S 152 4 E
Biggleswade, *U.K.* 11 E7 52 5N 0 14W
Biggs, *U.S.A.* 84 F5 39 25N 121 43W
Bighorn, *U.S.A.* 82 C10 46 10N 107 27W
Bighorn →, *U.S.A.* 82 C10 46 10N 107 28W
Bighorn L., *U.S.A.* 82 D9 44 55N 108 15W
Bighorn Mts., *U.S.A.* 82 D10 44 30N 107 30W
Bigstone L., *Canada* 73 C9 53 42N 95 44W
Bigwa, *Tanzania* 54 D4 7 10S 39 10 E
Bihać, *Bos.-H.* 16 F8 44 49N 15 57 E
Bihar, *India* 43 G11 25 5N 85 40 E
Bihar □, *India* 43 G12 25 0N 86 0 E
Biharamulo, *Tanzania* 54 C3 2 25S 31 25 E
Bihariganj, *India* 43 G12 25 44N 86 59 E
Bihor, Munţii, *Romania* 17 E12 46 29N 22 47 E
Bijagós, Arquipélago dos, *Guinea-Biss.* 50 F2 11 15N 16 10W
Bijaipur, *India* 42 F7 26 2N 77 20 E
Bijapur, *Chhattisgarh, India* 41 K12 18 50N 80 50 E
Bijapur, *Karnataka, India* 40 L9 16 50N 75 55 E
Bījār, *Iran* 44 C5 35 52N 47 35 E
Bijawar, *India* 43 G8 24 38N 79 30 E
Bijeljina, *Bos.-H.* 21 B8 44 46N 19 14 E
Bijnor, *India* 42 E8 29 27N 78 11 E
Bikaner, *India* 42 E5 28 2N 73 18 E
Bikapur, *India* 43 F10 26 30N 82 7 E
Bikeqi, *China* 34 D6 40 43N 111 20 E
Bikfayyā, *Lebanon* 47 B4 33 55N 35 41 E
Bikin, *Russia* 27 E14 46 50N 134 20 E
Bikin →, *Russia* 30 A7 46 51N 134 2 E
Bikini Atoll, *Marshall Is.* 64 F8 12 0N 167 30 E
Bikita, *Zimbabwe* 57 C5 20 6S 31 41 E
Bila Tserkva, *Ukraine* 17 D16 49 45N 30 10 E
Bilara, *India* 42 F5 26 14N 73 53 E
Bilaspur, *Chhattisgarh, India* 43 H10 22 2N 82 15 E
Bilaspur, *Punjab, India* 42 D7 31 19N 76 50 E
Bilauk Taungdan, *Thailand* 38 F2 13 0N 99 0 E
Bilbao, *Spain* 19 A4 43 16N 2 56W
Bilbo = Bilbao, *Spain* 19 A4 43 16N 2 56W
Bíldudalur, *Iceland* 8 D2 65 41N 23 36W
Bílé Karpaty, *Europe* 17 D9 49 5N 18 0 E
Bilecik, *Turkey* 25 F5 40 5N 30 5 E
Bilgram, *India* 43 F9 27 11N 80 2 E
Bilhaur, *India* 43 F9 26 51N 80 5 E
Bilhorod-Dnistrovskyy, *Ukraine* 25 E5 46 11N 30 23 E
Bilibino, *Russia* 27 C17 68 3N 166 20 E
Bilibiza, *Mozam.* 55 E5 12 30S 40 20 E
Billabalong Roadhouse, *Australia* 61 E2 27 25S 115 49 E
Billiluna, *Australia* 60 C4 19 37S 127 41 E
Billings, *U.S.A.* 82 D9 45 47N 108 30W
Billiton Is. = Belitung, *Indonesia* 36 E3 3 10S 107 50 E
Bilma, *Niger* 51 E8 18 50N 13 30 E
Biloela, *Australia* 62 C5 24 24S 150 31 E
Biloxi, *U.S.A.* 81 K10 30 24N 88 53W
Bilpa Morea Claypan, *Australia* 62 D3 25 0S 140 0 E
Biltine, *Chad* 51 F10 14 40N 20 50 E
Bima, *Indonesia* 37 F5 8 22S 118 49 E
Bimini Is., *Bahamas* 88 A4 25 42N 79 25W
Bin Xian, *Heilongjiang, China* 35 B14 45 42N 127 32 E
Bin Xian, *Shaanxi, China* 34 G5 35 2N 108 4 E
Bina-Etawah, *India* 42 G8 24 13N 78 14 E
Bināb, *Iran* 45 B6 36 35N 48 41 E
Binalbagan, *Phil.* 37 B6 10 12N 122 50 E
Binalong, *Australia* 63 E4 34 40S 148 39 E
Bīnālūd, Kūh-e, *Iran* 45 B8 36 30N 58 30 E
Binatang = Bintangor, *Malaysia* 36 D4 2 10N 111 40 E
Binche, *Belgium* 15 D4 50 26N 4 10 E
Bindki, *India* 43 F9 26 2N 80 36 E
Bindura, *Zimbabwe* 55 F3 17 18S 31 18 E
Bingara, *Australia* 63 D5 29 52S 150 36 E
Bingham, *U.S.A.* 77 C11 45 3N 69 53W
Binghamton, *U.S.A.* 79 D9 42 6N 75 55W
Bingöl, *Turkey* 44 B4 38 53N 40 29 E
Binh Dinh = An Nhon, *Vietnam* 38 F7 13 55N 109 7 E
Binh Khe, *Vietnam* 38 F7 13 57N 108 51 E
Binh Son, *Vietnam* 38 E7 15 20N 108 40 E
Binhai, *China* 35 G10 34 2N 119 49 E
Binisatua, *Spain* 22 B11 39 50N 4 11 E
Binjai, *Indonesia* 36 D3 3 20N 98 30 E
Binnaway, *Australia* 63 E4 31 28S 149 24 E
Binongko, *Indonesia* 37 F6 5 57S 124 2 E
Binscarth, *Canada* 73 C8 50 37N 101 17W
Bintan, *Indonesia* 36 D2 1 0N 104 0 E
Bintangor, *Malaysia* 36 D4 2 10N 111 40 E
Bintulu, *Malaysia* 36 D4 3 10N 113 0 E
Bintuni, *Indonesia* 37 E8 2 7S 133 32 E
Binzert = Bizerte, *Tunisia* 51 A7 37 15N 9 50 E
Binzhou, *China* 35 F10 37 20N 118 2 E
Bío Bío □, *Chile* 94 D1 37 35S 72 0W
Bioko, *Eq. Guin.* 52 D1 3 30N 8 40 E
Bir, *India* 40 K9 19 4N 75 46 E
Bîr Abu Muḩammad, *Egypt* 47 F3 29 44N 34 14 E
Bi'r ad Dabbāghāt, *Jordan* 47 E4 30 26N 35 32 E
Bi'r al Butayyihāt, *Jordan* 47 F4 29 47N 35 20 E
Bi'r al Mārī, *Jordan* 47 E4 30 4N 35 33 E
Bi'r al Qattār, *Jordan* 47 F4 29 47N 35 32 E
Bir Atrun, *Sudan* 51 E11 18 15N 26 40 E
Bîr Beiḍa, *Egypt* 47 E3 30 25N 34 29 E
Bîr el 'Abd, *Egypt* 47 D2 31 2N 33 0 E
Bîr el Biarât, *Egypt* 47 F3 29 30N 34 43 E
Bîr el Duweidar, *Egypt* 47 E1 30 56N 32 32 E
Bîr el Garârât, *Egypt* 47 D2 31 3N 33 34 E
Bîr el Heisi, *Egypt* 47 F3 29 22N 34 36 E
Bîr el Jafir, *Egypt* 47 E1 30 50N 32 41 E
Bîr el Mâlḩi, *Egypt* 47 E2 30 38N 33 19 E
Bîr el Thamâda, *Egypt* 47 E2 30 12N 33 27 E
Bîr Gebeil Ḩişn, *Egypt* 47 E2 30 2N 33 18 E
Bi'r Ghadīr, *Syria* 47 A6 34 6N 37 3 E
Bîr Ḩasana, *Egypt* 47 E2 30 29N 33 46 E
Bîr Kaseiba, *Egypt* 47 E2 31 0N 33 17 E
Bîr Lahfân, *Egypt* 47 E2 31 0N 33 51 E
Bîr Madkûr, *Egypt* 47 E1 30 44N 32 33 E
Bîr Mogreïn, *Mauritania* 50 C3 25 10N 11 25W
Bi'r Muţribah, *Kuwait* 44 D5 29 54N 47 17 E
Bîr Qaţia, *Egypt* 47 E1 30 58N 32 45 E
Bîr Shalatein, *Egypt* 51 D13 23 5N 35 25 E
Biratnagar, *Nepal* 43 F12 26 27N 87 17 E
Birawa, *Dem. Rep. of the Congo* 54 C2 2 20S 28 48 E
Birch →, *Canada* 72 B6 58 28N 112 17W
Birch Hills, *Canada* 73 C7 52 59N 105 25W
Birch I., *Canada* 73 C9 52 26N 99 54W
Birch L., *N.W.T., Canada* 72 A5 62 4N 116 33W
Birch L., *Ont., Canada* 70 B1 51 23N 92 18W
Birch Mts., *Canada* 72 B6 57 30N 113 10W
Birch River, *Canada* 73 C8 52 24N 101 6W
Birchip, *Australia* 63 F3 35 56S 142 55 E
Bird, *Canada* 73 B10 56 30N 94 13W
Bird I. = Las Aves, Is., *W. Indies* 89 C7 15 45N 63 55W
Birdsville, *Australia* 62 D2 25 51S 139 20 E
Birdum Cr. →, *Australia* 60 C5 15 14S 133 0 E
Birecik, *Turkey* 44 B3 37 2N 38 0 E
Birein, *Israel* 47 E3 30 50N 34 28 E
Bireuen, *Indonesia* 36 C1 5 14N 96 39 E
Birigui, *Brazil* 95 A5 21 18S 50 16W
Birjand, *Iran* 45 C8 32 53N 59 13 E
Birkenhead, *U.K.* 10 D4 53 23N 3 2W
Bîrlad = Bârlad, *Romania* 17 E14 46 15N 27 38 E
Birmingham, *U.K.* 11 E6 52 29N 1 52W
Birmingham, *U.S.A.* 77 J2 33 31N 86 48W
Birmitrapur, *India* 41 H14 22 24N 84 46 E
Birni Nkonni, *Niger* 50 F7 13 55N 5 15 E
Birnin Kebbi, *Nigeria* 50 F6 12 32N 4 12 E
Birobidzhan, *Russia* 27 E14 48 50N 132 50 E
Birr, *Ireland* 13 C4 53 6N 7 54W
Birrie →, *Australia* 63 D4 29 43S 146 37 E
Birsilpur, *India* 42 E5 28 11N 72 15 E
Birsk, *Russia* 24 C10 55 25N 55 30 E
Birtle, *Canada* 73 C8 50 30N 101 5W
Birur, *India* 40 N9 13 30N 75 55 E
Biržai, *Lithuania* 9 H21 56 11N 24 45 E
Birzebbugga, *Malta* 23 D2 35 50N 14 32 E
Bisa, *Indonesia* 37 E7 1 15S 127 28 E
Bisalpur, *India* 43 E8 28 14N 79 48 E
Bisbee, *U.S.A.* 83 L9 31 27N 109 55W
Biscay, B. of, *Atl. Oc.* 18 D1 45 0N 2 0W
Biscayne B., *U.S.A.* 77 N5 25 40N 80 12W
Biscoe Bay, *Antarctica* 5 D13 77 0S 152 0W
Biscoe Is., *Antarctica* 5 C17 66 0S 67 0W
Biscostasing, *Canada* 70 C3 47 18N 82 9W
Bishkek, *Kyrgyzstan* 26 E8 42 54N 74 46 E
Bishnupur, *India* 43 H12 23 8N 87 20 E
Bisho, *S. Africa* 57 E4 32 50S 27 23 E
Bishop, *Calif., U.S.A.* 84 H8 37 22N 118 24W
Bishop, *Tex., U.S.A.* 81 M6 27 35N 97 48W
Bishop Auckland, *U.K.* 10 C6 54 39N 1 40W
Bishop's Falls, *Canada* 71 C8 49 2N 55 30W
Bishop's Stortford, *U.K.* 11 F8 51 52N 0 10 E
Bisina, L., *Uganda* 54 B3 1 38N 33 56 E
Biskra, *Algeria* 50 B7 34 50N 5 44 E
Bismarck, *U.S.A.* 80 B4 46 48N 100 47W
Bismarck Arch., *Papua N. G.* 64 H7 2 30S 150 0 E
Biso, *Uganda* 54 B3 1 44N 31 26 E
Bison, *U.S.A.* 80 C3 45 31N 102 28W
Bīsotūn, *Iran* 44 C5 34 23N 47 26 E
Bissagos = Bijagós, Arquipélago dos, *Guinea-Biss.* 50 F2 11 15N 16 10W
Bissau, *Guinea-Biss.* 50 F2 11 45N 15 45W
Bistcho L., *Canada* 72 B5 59 45N 118 50W
Bistriţa, *Romania* 17 E13 47 9N 24 35 E
Bistriţa →, *Romania* 17 E14 46 30N 26 57 E
Biswan, *India* 43 F9 27 29N 81 2 E
Bitlis, *Turkey* 44 B4 38 20N 42 3 E
Bitola, *Macedonia* 21 D9 41 1N 21 20 E
Bitolj = Bitola, *Macedonia* 21 D9 41 1N 21 20 E
Bitter Creek, *U.S.A.* 82 F9 41 33N 108 33W
Bitterfontein, *S. Africa* 56 E2 31 1S 18 32 E
Bitterroot →, *U.S.A.* 82 C6 46 52N 114 7W
Bitterroot Range, *U.S.A.* 82 D6 46 0N 114 20W
Bitterwater, *U.S.A.* 84 J6 36 23N 121 0W
Biu, *Nigeria* 51 F8 10 40N 12 3 E
Biwa-Ko, *Japan* 31 G8 35 15N 136 10 E
Biwabik, *U.S.A.* 80 B8 47 32N 92 21W
Bixby, *U.S.A.* 81 H7 35 57N 95 53W
Biyang, *China* 34 H7 32 38N 113 21 E
Biysk, *Russia* 26 D9 52 40N 85 0 E
Bizana, *S. Africa* 57 E4 30 50S 29 52 E
Bizen, *Japan* 31 G7 34 43N 134 8 E
Bizerte, *Tunisia* 51 A7 37 15N 9 50 E
Bjargtangar, *Iceland* 8 D1 65 30N 24 30W
Bjelovar, *Croatia* 20 B7 45 56N 16 49 E
Bjørnevatn, *Norway* 8 B23 69 40N 30 0 E
Bjørnøya, *Arctic* 4 B8 74 30N 19 0 E
Black = Da →, *Vietnam* 38 B5 21 15N 105 20 E
Black →, *Canada* 78 B5 44 42N 79 19W
Black →, *Ariz., U.S.A.* 83 K8 33 44N 110 13W
Black →, *Ark., U.S.A.* 81 H9 35 38N 91 20W
Black →, *Mich., U.S.A.* 78 D2 42 59N 82 27W
Black →, *N.Y., U.S.A.* 79 C8 43 59N 76 4W
Black →, *Wis., U.S.A.* 80 D9 43 57N 91 22W
Black Bay Pen., *Canada* 70 C2 48 38N 88 21W
Black Birch L., *Canada* 73 B7 56 53N 107 45W
Black Diamond, *Canada* 72 C6 50 45N 114 14W
Black Duck →, *Canada* 70 A2 56 51N 89 2W
Black Forest = Schwarzwald, *Germany* 16 D5 48 30N 8 20 E
Black Forest, *U.S.A.* 80 F2 39 0N 104 43W
Black Hd., *Ireland* 13 C2 53 9N 9 16W
Black Hills, *U.S.A.* 80 D3 44 0N 103 45W
Black I., *Canada* 73 C9 51 12N 96 30W
Black L., *Canada* 73 B7 59 12N 105 15W
Black L., *Mich., U.S.A.* 76 C3 45 28N 84 16W
Black L., *N.Y., U.S.A.* 79 B9 44 31N 75 36W
Black Lake, *Canada* 73 B7 59 11N 105 20W
Black Mesa, *U.S.A.* 81 G3 36 58N 102 58W
Black Mt. = Mynydd Du, *U.K.* 11 F4 51 52N 3 50W
Black Mts., *U.K.* 11 F4 51 55N 3 7W
Black Range, *U.S.A.* 83 K10 33 15N 107 50W
Black River, *Jamaica* 88 C4 18 0N 77 50W
Black River Falls, *U.S.A.* 80 C9 44 18N 90 51W
Black Sea, *Eurasia* 25 F6 43 30N 35 0 E
Black Tickle, *Canada* 71 B8 53 28N 55 45W
Black Volta →, *Africa* 50 G5 8 41N 1 33W
Black Warrior →, *U.S.A.* 77 J2 32 32N 87 51W
Blackall, *Australia* 62 C4 24 25S 145 45 E
Blackball, *N.Z.* 59 K3 42 22S 171 26 E
Blackbull, *Australia* 62 B3 17 55S 141 45 E
Blackburn, *U.K.* 10 D5 53 45N 2 29W
Blackburn with Darwen □, *U.K.* 10 D5 53 45N 2 29W
Blackfoot, *U.S.A.* 82 E7 43 11N 112 21W
Blackfoot →, *U.S.A.* 82 C7 46 52N 113 53W
Blackfoot River Reservoir, *U.S.A.* 82 E8 43 0N 111 43W
Blackpool, *U.K.* 10 D4 53 49N 3 3W
Blackpool □, *U.K.* 10 D4 53 49N 3 3W
Blackriver, *U.S.A.* 78 B1 44 46N 83 17W
Blacks Harbour, *Canada* 71 C6 45 3N 66 49W
Blacksburg, *U.S.A.* 76 G5 37 14N 80 25W
Blacksod B., *Ireland* 13 B1 54 6N 10 0W
Blackstone, *U.S.A.* 76 G7 37 4N 78 0W
Blackstone Ra., *Australia* 61 E4 26 0S 128 30 E
Blackwater, *Australia* 62 C4 23 35S 148 53 E
Blackwater →, *Meath, Ireland* 13 C4 53 39N 6 41W
Blackwater →, *Waterford, Ireland* 13 D4 52 4N 7 52W
Blackwater →, *U.K.* 13 B5 54 31N 6 35W
Blackwell, *U.S.A.* 81 G6 36 48N 97 17W
Blackwells Corner, *U.S.A.* 85 K7 35 37N 119 47W
Blaenau Ffestiniog, *U.K.* 10 E4 53 0N 3 56W
Blaenau Gwent □, *U.K.* 11 F4 51 48N 3 12W
Blagodarnoye = Blagodarnyy, *Russia* 25 E7 45 7N 43 37 E
Blagodarnyy, *Russia* 25 E7 45 7N 43 37 E
Blagoevgrad, *Bulgaria* 21 C10 42 2N 23 5 E
Blagoveshchensk, *Russia* 27 D13 50 20N 127 30 E
Blain, *U.S.A.* 78 F7 40 20N 77 31W
Blaine, *Minn., U.S.A.* 80 C8 45 10N 93 13W
Blaine, *Wash., U.S.A.* 84 B4 48 59N 122 45W
Blaine Lake, *Canada* 73 C7 52 51N 106 52W
Blair, *U.S.A.* 80 E6 41 33N 96 8W
Blair Athol, *Australia* 62 C4 22 42S 147 31 E
Blair Atholl, *U.K.* 12 E5 56 46N 3 50W
Blairgowrie, *U.K.* 12 E5 56 35N 3 21W
Blairsden, *U.S.A.* 84 F6 39 47N 120 37W
Blairsville, *U.S.A.* 78 F5 40 26N 79 16W
Blake Pt., *U.S.A.* 80 A10 48 11N 88 25W
Blakely, *Ga., U.S.A.* 77 K3 31 23N 84 56W
Blakely, *Pa., U.S.A.* 79 E9 41 28N 75 37W
Blanc, C., *Spain* 22 B9 39 21N 2 51 E
Blanc, Mont, *Alps* 18 D7 45 48N 6 50 E
Blanc-Sablon, *Canada* 71 B8 51 24N 57 12W
Blanca, B., *Argentina* 96 D4 39 10S 61 30W
Blanca Peak, *U.S.A.* 83 H11 37 35N 105 29W
Blanche, C., *Australia* 63 E1 33 1S 134 9 E
Blanche, L., *S. Austral., Australia* 63 D2 29 15S 139 40 E
Blanche, L., *W. Austral., Australia* 60 D3 22 25S 123 17 E
Blanco, *S. Africa* 56 E3 33 55S 22 23 E
Blanco, *U.S.A.* 81 K5 30 6N 98 25W
Blanco →, *Argentina* 94 C2 30 20S 68 42W
Blanco, C., *Costa Rica* 88 E2 9 34N 85 8W
Blanco, C., *U.S.A.* 82 E1 42 51N 124 34W
Blanda →, *Iceland* 8 D3 65 37N 20 9W
Blandford Forum, *U.K.* 11 G5 50 51N 2 9W
Blanding, *U.S.A.* 83 H9 37 37N 109 29W
Blanes, *Spain* 19 B7 41 40N 2 48 E
Blankenberge, *Belgium* 15 C3 51 20N 3 9 E
Blanquilla, I., *Venezuela* 89 D7 11 51N 64 37W
Blanquillo, *Uruguay* 95 C4 32 53S 55 37W
Blantyre, *Malawi* 55 F4 15 45S 35 0 E
Blarney, *Ireland* 13 E3 51 56N 8 33W
Blasdell, *U.S.A.* 78 D6 42 48N 78 50W
Blåvands Huk, *Denmark* 9 J13 55 33N 8 4 E
Blaydon, *U.K.* 10 C6 54 58N 1 42W
Blayney, *Australia* 63 E4 33 32S 149 14 E
Blaze, Pt., *Australia* 60 B5 12 56S 130 11 E
Blekinge, *Sweden* 9 H16 56 25N 15 20 E
Blenheim, *Canada* 78 D3 42 20N 82 0W
Blenheim, *N.Z.* 59 J4 41 38S 173 57 E
Bletchley, *U.K.* 11 F7 51 59N 0 44W
Blida, *Algeria* 50 A6 36 30N 2 49 E
Bligh Sound, *N.Z.* 59 L1 44 47S 167 32 E
Blind River, *Canada* 70 C3 46 10N 82 58W
Bliss, *Idaho, U.S.A.* 82 E6 42 56N 114 57W
Bliss, *N.Y., U.S.A.* 78 D6 42 34N 78 15W
Blissfield, *U.S.A.* 78 F3 40 24N 81 58W
Blitar, *Indonesia* 37 H15 8 5S 112 11 E
Block I., *U.S.A.* 79 E13 41 11N 71 35W
Block Island Sd., *U.S.A.* 79 E13 41 15N 71 40W
Bloemfontein, *S. Africa* 56 D4 29 6S 26 7 E
Bloemhof, *S. Africa* 56 D4 27 38S 25 32 E
Blois, *France* 18 C4 47 35N 1 20 E
Blönduós, *Iceland* 8 D3 65 40N 20 12W
Bloodvein →, *Canada* 73 C9 51 47N 96 43W
Bloody Foreland, *Ireland* 13 A3 55 10N 8 17W
Bloomer, *U.S.A.* 80 C9 45 6N 91 29W
Bloomfield, *Canada* 78 C7 43 59N 77 14W
Bloomfield, *Iowa, U.S.A.* 80 E8 40 45N 92 25W
Bloomfield, *N. Mex., U.S.A.* 83 H10 36 43N 107 59W
Bloomfield, *Nebr., U.S.A.* 80 D6 42 36N 97 39W
Bloomington, *Ill., U.S.A.* 80 E10 40 28N 89 0W
Bloomington, *Ind., U.S.A.* 76 F2 39 10N 86 32W
Bloomington, *Minn., U.S.A.* 80 C8 44 50N 93 17W
Bloomsburg, *U.S.A.* 79 F8 41 0N 76 27W
Blora, *Indonesia* 37 G14 6 57S 111 25 E
Blossburg, *U.S.A.* 78 E7 41 41N 77 4W
Blouberg, *S. Africa* 57 C4 23 8S 28 59 E
Blountstown, *U.S.A.* 77 K3 30 27N 85 3W
Blue Earth, *U.S.A.* 80 D8 43 38N 94 6W
Blue Mesa Reservoir, *U.S.A.* 83 G10 38 28N 107 20W
Blue Mountain Lake, *U.S.A.* 79 C10 43 52N 74 30W
Blue Mts., *Maine, U.S.A.* 79 B14 44 50N 70 35W
Blue Mts., *Oreg., U.S.A.* 82 D4 45 15N 119 0W
Blue Mts., *Pa., U.S.A.* 79 F8 40 30N 76 30W
Blue Mud B., *Australia* 62 A2 13 30S 136 0 E
Blue Nile = Nîl el Azraq →, *Sudan* 51 E12 15 38N 32 31 E
Blue Rapids, *U.S.A.* 80 F6 39 41N 96 39W
Blue Ridge Mts., *U.S.A.* 77 G5 36 30N 80 15W
Blue River, *Canada* 72 C5 52 6N 119 18W
Bluefield, *U.S.A.* 76 G5 37 15N 81 17W
Bluefields, *Nic.* 88 D3 12 20N 83 50W
Bluff, *Australia* 62 C4 23 35S 149 4 E
Bluff, *N.Z.* 59 M2 46 37S 168 20 E
Bluff, *U.S.A.* 83 H9 37 17N 109 33W
Bluff Knoll, *Australia* 61 F2 34 24S 118 15 E
Bluff Pt., *Australia* 61 E1 27 50S 114 5 E
Bluffton, *U.S.A.* 76 E3 40 44N 85 11W
Blumenau, *Brazil* 95 B6 27 0S 49 0W
Blunt, *U.S.A.* 80 C5 44 31N 99 59W
Bly, *U.S.A.* 82 E3 42 24N 121 3W
Blyth, *Canada* 78 C3 43 44N 81 26W
Blyth, *U.K.* 10 B6 55 8N 1 31W
Blythe, *U.S.A.* 85 M12 33 37N 114 36W
Blytheville, *U.S.A.* 81 H10 35 56N 89 55W
Bo, *S. Leone* 50 G3 7 55N 11 50W
Bo Duc, *Vietnam* 39 G6 11 58N 106 50 E
Bo Hai, *China* 35 E10 39 0N 119 0 E
Bo Xian = Bozhou, *China* 34 H8 33 55N 115 41 E
Boa Vista, *Brazil* 92 C6 2 48N 60 30W
Boaco, *Nic.* 88 D2 12 29N 85 35W
Bo'ai, *China* 34 G7 35 10N 113 3 E
Boalsburg, *U.S.A.* 78 F7 40 46N 77 47W
Boane, *Mozam.* 57 D5 26 6S 32 19 E
Boardman, *U.S.A.* 78 E4 41 2N 80 40W
Bobadah, *Australia* 63 E4 32 19S 146 41 E
Bobbili, *India* 41 K13 18 35N 83 30 E
Bobcaygeon, *Canada* 78 B6 44 33N 78 33W
Bobo-Dioulasso, *Burkina Faso* 50 F5 11 8N 4 13W
Bóbr →, *Poland* 16 B8 52 4N 15 4 E
Bobraomby, Tanjon' i, *Madag.* 57 A8 12 40S 49 10 E
Bobruysk = Babruysk, *Belarus* 17 B15 53 10N 29 15 E
Boby, Pic, *Madag.* 53 J9 22 12S 46 55 E
Bôca do Acre, *Brazil* 92 E5 8 50S 67 27W
Boca Raton, *U.S.A.* 77 M5 26 21N 80 5W
Bocas del Toro, *Panama* 88 E3 9 15N 82 20W
Bochnia, *Poland* 17 D11 49 58N 20 27 E
Bochum, *Germany* 16 C4 51 28N 7 13 E
Bocoyna, *Mexico* 86 B3 27 52N 107 35W
Bodaybo, *Russia* 27 D12 57 50N 114 0 E
Boddam, *U.K.* 12 B7 59 56N 1 17W
Boddington, *Australia* 61 F2 32 50S 116 30 E
Bodega Bay, *U.S.A.* 84 G3 38 20N 123 3W
Boden, *Sweden* 8 D19 65 50N 21 42 E
Bodensee, *Europe* 18 C8 47 35N 9 25 E
Bodhan, *India* 40 K10 18 40N 77 44 E
Bodmin, *U.K.* 11 G3 50 28N 4 43W
Bodmin Moor, *U.K.* 11 G3 50 33N 4 36W
Bodø, *Norway* 8 C16 67 17N 14 24 E
Bodrog →, *Hungary* 17 D11 48 11N 21 22 E
Bodrum, *Turkey* 21 F12 37 3N 27 30 E
Boende, *Dem. Rep. of the Congo* 52 E4 0 24S 21 12 E
Boerne, *U.S.A.* 81 L5 29 47N 98 44W
Boesmans →, *S. Africa* 56 E4 33 42S 26 39 E
Bogalusa, *U.S.A.* 81 K10 30 47N 89 52W
Bogan →, *Australia* 63 D4 29 59S 146 17 E
Bogan Gate, *Australia* 63 E4 33 7S 147 49 E
Bogantungan, *Australia* 62 C4 23 41S 147 17 E
Bogata, *U.S.A.* 81 J7 33 28N 95 13W
Boggabilla, *Australia* 63 D5 28 36S 150 24 E

Boggabri, *Australia* **63 E5** 30 45S 150 5 E
Boggeragh Mts., *Ireland* **13 D3** 52 2N 8 55W
Boglan = Solhan, *Turkey* **44 B4** 38 57N 41 3 E
Bognor Regis, *U.K.* **11 G7** 50 47N 0 40W
Bogo, *Phil.* **37 B6** 11 3N 124 0 E
Bogong, Mt., *Australia* **63 F4** 36 47S 147 17 E
Bogor, *Indonesia* **36 F3** 6 36S 106 48 E
Bogotá, *Colombia* **92 C4** 4 34N 74 0W
Bogotol, *Russia* **26 D9** 56 15N 89 50 E
Bogra, *Bangla.* **41 G16** 24 51N 89 22 E
Boguchany, *Russia* **27 D10** 58 40N 97 30 E
Bohemian Forest = Böhmerwald, *Germany* **16 D7** 49 8N 13 14 E
Böhmerwald, *Germany* **16 D7** 49 8N 13 14 E
Bohol □, *Phil.* **37 C6** 9 50N 124 10 E
Bohol Sea, *Phil.* **37 C6** 9 0N 124 0 E
Bohuslän, *Sweden* **9 G14** 58 25N 12 0 E
Boi, Pta. de, *Brazil* **95 A6** 23 55S 45 15W
Boiaçu, *Brazil* **92 D6** 0 27S 61 46W
Boileau, C., *Australia* **60 C3** 17 40S 122 7 E
Boise, *U.S.A.* **82 E5** 43 37N 116 13W
Boise City, *U.S.A.* **81 G3** 36 44N 102 31W
Boissevain, *Canada* **73 D8** 49 15N 100 5W
Bojador, C., *W. Sahara* **50 C3** 26 0N 14 30W
Bojana →, *Albania* **21 D8** 41 52N 19 22 E
Bojnūrd, *Iran* **45 B8** 37 30N 57 20 E
Bojonegoro, *Indonesia* **37 G14** 7 11S 111 54 E
Bokaro, *India* **43 H11** 23 46N 85 55 E
Bokhara →, *Australia* **63 D4** 29 55S 146 42 E
Boknafjorden, *Norway* **9 G11** 59 14N 5 40 E
Bokoro, *Chad* **51 F9** 12 25N 17 14 E
Bokpyin, *Burma* **39 G2** 11 18N 98 42 E
Bolan →, *Pakistan* **42 E2** 28 38N 67 42 E
Bolan Pass, *Pakistan* **40 E5** 29 50N 67 20 E
Bolaños →, *Mexico* **86 C4** 21 14N 104 8W
Bolbec, *France* **18 B4** 49 30N 0 30 E
Boldājī, *Iran* **45 D6** 31 56N 51 3 E
Bole, *China* **32 B3** 45 11N 81 37 E
Bolekhiv, *Ukraine* **17 D12** 49 0N 23 57 E
Bolesławiec, *Poland* **16 C8** 51 17N 15 37 E
Bolgrad = Bolhrad, *Ukraine* **17 F15** 45 40N 28 32 E
Bolhrad, *Ukraine* **17 F15** 45 40N 28 32 E
Bolívar, *Argentina* **94 D3** 36 15S 60 53W
Bolivar, *Mo., U.S.A.* **81 G8** 37 37N 93 25W
Bolivar, *N.Y., U.S.A.* **78 D6** 42 4N 78 10W
Bolivar, *Tenn., U.S.A.* **81 H10** 35 12N 89 0W
Bolivia ■, *S. Amer.* **92 G6** 17 6S 64 0W
Bolivian Plateau, *S. Amer.* **90 E4** 20 0S 67 30W
Bollnäs, *Sweden* **9 F17** 61 21N 16 24 E
Bollon, *Australia* **63 D4** 28 2S 147 29 E
Bolmen, *Sweden* **9 H15** 56 55N 13 40 E
Bolobo, *Dem. Rep. of the Congo* **52 E3** 2 6S 16 20 E
Bologna, *Italy* **20 B4** 44 29N 11 20 E
Bologoye, *Russia* **24 C5** 57 55N 34 5 E
Bolonchenticul, *Mexico* **87 D7** 20 0N 89 49W
Boloven, Cao Nguyen, *Laos* **38 E6** 15 10N 106 30 E
Bolpur, *India* **43 H12** 23 40N 87 45 E
Bolsena, L. di, *Italy* **20 C4** 42 36N 11 56 E
Bolshevik, Ostrov, *Russia* **27 B11** 78 30N 102 0 E
Bolshoi Kavkas = Caucasus Mountains, *Eurasia* **25 F7** 42 50N 44 0 E
Bolshoy Anyuy →, *Russia* **27 C17** 68 30N 160 49 E
Bolshoy Begichev, Ostrov, *Russia* **27 B12** 74 20N 112 30 E
Bolshoy Lyakhovskiy, Ostrov, *Russia* **27 B15** 73 35N 142 0 E
Bolshoy Tyuters, Ostrov, *Russia* **9 G22** 59 51N 27 13 E
Bolsward, *Neths.* **15 A5** 53 3N 5 32 E
Bolt Head, *U.K.* **11 G4** 50 12N 3 48W
Bolton, *Canada* **78 C5** 43 54N 79 45W
Bolton, *U.K.* **10 D5** 53 35N 2 26W
Bolton Landing, *U.S.A.* **79 C11** 43 32N 73 35W
Bolu, *Turkey* **25 F5** 40 45N 31 35 E
Bolungavík, *Iceland* **8 C2** 66 9N 23 15W
Bolvadin, *Turkey* **25 G5** 38 45N 31 4 E
Bolzano, *Italy* **20 A4** 46 31N 11 22 E
Bom Jesus da Lapa, *Brazil* **93 F10** 13 15S 43 25W
Boma, *Dem. Rep. of the Congo* **52 F2** 5 50S 13 4 E
Bombala, *Australia* **63 F4** 36 56S 149 15 E
Bombay = Mumbai, *India* **40 K8** 18 55N 72 50 E
Bomboma, *Dem. Rep. of the Congo* **52 D3** 2 25N 18 55 E
Bombombwa, *Dem. Rep. of the Congo* **54 B2** 1 40N 25 40 E
Bomili, *Dem. Rep. of the Congo* **54 B2** 1 45N 27 5 E
Bømlo, *Norway* **9 G11** 59 37N 5 13 E
Bomokandi →, *Dem. Rep. of the Congo* **54 B2** 3 39N 26 8 E
Bomu →, *C.A.R.* **52 D4** 4 40N 22 30 E
Bon, C., *Tunisia* **48 C5** 37 1N 11 2 E
Bon Sar Pa, *Vietnam* **38 F6** 12 24N 107 35 E
Bonaigarh, *India* **43 J11** 21 50N 84 57 E
Bonaire, *Neth. Ant.* **89 D6** 12 10N 68 15W
Bonang, *Australia* **63 F4** 37 11S 148 41 E
Bonanza, *Nic.* **88 D3** 13 54N 84 35W
Bonaparte Arch., *Australia* **60 B3** 14 0S 124 30 E
Bonaventure, *Canada* **71 C6** 48 5N 65 32W
Bonavista, *Canada* **71 C9** 48 40N 53 5W
Bonavista, C., *Canada* **71 C9** 48 42N 53 5W
Bonavista B., *Canada* **71 C9** 48 45N 53 25W
Bondo, *Dem. Rep. of the Congo* **54 B1** 3 55N 23 53 E
Bondoukou, *Ivory C.* **50 G5** 8 2N 2 47W
Bondowoso, *Indonesia* **37 G15** 7 55S 113 49 E
Bone, Teluk, *Indonesia* **37 E6** 4 10S 120 50 E
Bonerate, *Indonesia* **37 F6** 7 25S 121 5 E
Bonerate, Kepulauan, *Indonesia* **37 F6** 6 30S 121 10 E
Bo'ness, *U.K.* **12 E5** 56 1N 3 37W
Bonete, Cerro, *Argentina* **94 B2** 27 55S 68 40W
Bong Son = Hoai Nhon, *Vietnam* **38 E7** 14 28N 109 1 E
Bongor, *Chad* **51 F9** 10 35N 15 20 E
Bonham, *U.S.A.* **81 J6** 33 35N 96 11W
Bonifacio, *France* **18 F8** 41 24N 9 10 E
Bonifacio, Bouches de, *Medit. S.* **20 D3** 41 12N 9 15 E
Bonin Is. = Ogasawara Gunto, *Pac. Oc.* **28 G18** 27 0N 142 0 E
Bonn, *Germany* **16 C4** 50 46N 7 6 E
Bonne Terre, *U.S.A.* **81 G9** 37 55N 90 33W
Bonners Ferry, *U.S.A.* **82 B5** 48 42N 116 19W
Bonney, L., *Australia* **63 F3** 37 50S 140 20 E
Bonnie Rock, *Australia* **61 F2** 30 29S 118 22 E
Bonny, Bight of, *Africa* **52 D1** 3 30N 9 20 E
Bonnyrigg, *U.K.* **12 F5** 55 53N 3 6W
Bonnyville, *Canada* **73 C6** 54 20N 110 45W
Bonoi, *Indonesia* **37 E9** 1 45S 137 41 E
Bonsall, *U.S.A.* **85 M9** 33 16N 117 14W
Bontang, *Indonesia* **36 D5** 0 10N 117 30 E
Bonthe, *S. Leone* **50 G3** 7 30N 12 33W
Bontoc, *Phil.* **37 A6** 17 7N 120 58 E
Bonython Ra., *Australia* **60 D4** 23 40S 128 45 E
Bookabie, *Australia* **61 F5** 31 50S 132 41 E
Booker, *U.S.A.* **81 G4** 36 27N 100 32W
Boolaboolka L., *Australia* **63 E3** 32 38S 143 10 E
Booligal, *Australia* **63 E3** 33 58S 144 53 E
Boonah, *Australia* **63 D5** 27 58S 152 41 E
Boone, *Iowa, U.S.A.* **80 D8** 42 4N 93 53W
Boone, *N.C., U.S.A.* **77 G5** 36 13N 81 41W
Booneville, *Ark., U.S.A.* **81 H8** 35 8N 93 55W
Booneville, *Miss., U.S.A.* **77 H1** 34 39N 88 34W
Boonville, *Calif., U.S.A.* **84 F3** 39 1N 123 22W
Boonville, *Ind., U.S.A.* **76 F2** 38 3N 87 16W
Boonville, *Mo., U.S.A.* **80 F8** 38 58N 92 44W
Boonville, *N.Y., U.S.A.* **79 C9** 43 29N 75 20W
Boorindal, *Australia* **63 E4** 30 22S 146 11 E
Boorowa, *Australia* **63 E4** 34 28S 148 44 E
Boosaaso = Bosaso, *Somali Rep.* **46 E4** 11 12N 49 18 E
Boothia, Gulf of, *Canada* **69 A11** 71 0N 90 0W
Boothia Pen., *Canada* **68 A10** 71 0N 94 0W
Bootle, *U.K.* **10 D4** 53 28N 3 1W
Booué, *Gabon* **52 E2** 0 5S 11 55 E
Boquete, *Panama* **88 E3** 8 46N 82 27W
Boquilla, Presa de la, *Mexico* **86 B3** 27 40N 105 30W
Boquillas del Carmen, *Mexico* **86 B4** 29 17N 102 53W
Bor, *Serbia, Yug.* **21 B10** 44 5N 22 7 E
Bôr, *Sudan* **51 G12** 6 10N 31 40 E
Bor Mashash, *Israel* **47 D3** 31 7N 34 50 E
Borah Peak, *U.S.A.* **82 D7** 44 8N 113 47W
Borås, *Sweden* **9 H15** 57 43N 12 56 E
Borāzjān, *Iran* **45 D6** 29 22N 51 10 E
Borba, *Brazil* **92 D7** 4 12S 59 34W
Borborema, Planalto da, *Brazil* **90 D7** 7 0S 37 0W
Bord Khūn-e Now, *Iran* **45 D6** 28 3N 51 28 E
Borda, C., *Australia* **63 F2** 35 45S 136 34 E
Bordeaux, *France* **18 D3** 44 50N 0 36W
Borden, *Australia* **61 F2** 34 3S 118 12 E
Borden, *Canada* **71 C7** 46 18N 63 47W
Borden I., *Canada* **4 B2** 78 30N 111 30W
Borden Pen., *Canada* **69 A11** 73 0N 83 0W
Borders = Scottish Borders □, *U.K.* **12 F6** 55 35N 2 50W
Bordertown, *Australia* **63 F3** 36 19S 140 45 E
Borðeyri, *Iceland* **8 D3** 65 12N 21 6W
Bordj Fly Ste. Marie, *Algeria* **50 C5** 27 19N 2 32W
Bordj-in-Eker, *Algeria* **50 D7** 24 9N 5 3 E
Bordj Omar Driss, *Algeria* **50 C7** 28 10N 6 40 E
Borehamwood, *U.K.* **11 F7** 51 40N 0 15W
Borgå = Porvoo, *Finland* **9 F21** 60 24N 25 40 E
Borgarfjörður, *Iceland* **8 D7** 65 31N 13 49W
Borgarnes, *Iceland* **8 D3** 64 32N 21 55W
Børgefjellet, *Norway* **8 D15** 65 20N 13 45 E
Borger, *Neths.* **15 B6** 52 54N 6 44 E
Borger, *U.S.A.* **81 H4** 35 39N 101 24W
Borgholm, *Sweden* **9 H17** 56 52N 16 39 E
Borhoyn Tal, *Mongolia* **34 C6** 43 50N 111 58 E
Borikhane, *Laos* **38 C4** 18 33N 103 43 E
Borisoglebsk, *Russia* **25 D7** 51 27N 42 5 E
Borisov = Barysaw, *Belarus* **17 A15** 54 17N 28 28 E
Borja, *Peru* **92 D3** 4 20S 77 40W
Borkou, *Chad* **51 E9** 18 15N 18 50 E
Borkum, *Germany* **16 B4** 53 34N 6 40 E
Borlänge, *Sweden* **9 F16** 60 29N 15 26 E
Borley, C., *Antarctica* **5 C5** 66 15S 52 30 E
Borneo, *E. Indies* **36 D5** 1 0N 115 0 E
Bornholm, *Denmark* **9 J16** 55 10N 15 0 E
Borogontsy, *Russia* **27 C14** 62 42N 131 8 E
Boron, *U.S.A.* **85 L9** 35 0N 117 39W
Borongan, *Phil.* **37 B7** 11 37N 125 26 E
Borovichi, *Russia* **24 C5** 58 25N 33 55 E
Borrego Springs, *U.S.A.* **85 M10** 33 15N 116 23W
Borroloola, *Australia* **62 B2** 16 4S 136 17 E
Borşa, *Romania* **17 E13** 47 41N 24 50 E
Borsad, *India* **42 H5** 22 25N 72 54 E
Borth, *U.K.* **11 E3** 52 29N 4 2W
Borūjerd, *Iran* **45 C6** 33 55N 48 50 E
Boryslav, *Ukraine* **17 D12** 49 18N 23 28 E
Borzya, *Russia* **27 D12** 50 24N 116 31 E
Bosa, *Italy* **20 D3** 40 18N 8 30 E
Bosanska Gradiška, *Bos.-H.* **20 B7** 45 10N 17 15 E
Bosaso, *Somali Rep.* **46 E4** 11 12N 49 18 E
Boscastle, *U.K.* **11 G3** 50 41N 4 42W
Boshan, *China* **35 F9** 36 28N 117 49 E
Boshof, *S. Africa* **56 D4** 28 31S 25 13 E
Boshrūyeh, *Iran* **45 C8** 33 50N 57 30 E
Bosna →, *Bos.-H.* **21 B8** 45 4N 18 29 E
Bosna i Hercegovina = Bosnia-Herzegovina ■, *Europe* **20 B7** 44 0N 18 0 E
Bosnia-Herzegovina ■, *Europe* **20 B7** 44 0N 18 0 E
Bosnik, *Indonesia* **37 E9** 1 5S 136 10 E
Bosobolo, *Dem. Rep. of the Congo* **52 D3** 4 15N 19 50 E
Bosporus = İstanbul Boğazı, *Turkey* **21 D13** 41 10N 29 10 E
Bosque Farms, *U.S.A.* **83 J10** 34 53N 106 40W
Bossangoa, *C.A.R.* **52 C3** 6 35N 17 30 E
Bossier City, *U.S.A.* **81 J8** 32 31N 93 44W
Bosso, *Niger* **51 F8** 13 43N 13 19 E
Bostan, *Pakistan* **42 D2** 30 26N 67 2 E
Bostānābād, *Iran* **44 B5** 37 50N 46 50 E
Bosten Hu, *China* **32 B3** 41 55N 87 40 E
Boston, *U.K.* **10 E7** 52 59N 0 2W
Boston, *U.S.A.* **79 D13** 42 22N 71 4W
Boston Bar, *Canada* **72 D4** 49 52N 121 30W
Boston Mts., *U.S.A.* **81 H8** 35 42N 93 15W
Boswell, *Canada* **72 D5** 49 28N 116 45W
Boswell, *U.S.A.* **78 F5** 40 10N 79 2W
Botad, *India* **42 H4** 22 15N 71 40 E
Botene, *Laos* **38 D3** 17 35N 101 12 E
Bothaville, *S. Africa* **56 D4** 27 23S 26 34 E
Bothnia, G. of, *Europe* **8 E19** 63 0N 20 15 E
Bothwell, *Australia* **62 G4** 42 20S 147 1 E
Bothwell, *Canada* **78 D3** 42 38N 81 52W
Botletle →, *Botswana* **56 C3** 20 10S 23 15 E
Botoşani, *Romania* **17 E14** 47 42N 26 41 E
Botou, *Burkina Faso* **50 F6** 12 42N 1 59 E
Botswana ■, *Africa* **56 C3** 22 0S 24 0 E
Bottineau, *U.S.A.* **80 A4** 48 50N 100 27W
Bottrop, *Germany* **15 C6** 51 31N 6 58 E
Botucatu, *Brazil* **95 A6** 22 55S 48 30W
Botwood, *Canada* **71 C8** 49 6N 55 23W
Bouaflé, *Ivory C.* **50 G4** 7 1N 5 47W
Bouaké, *Ivory C.* **50 G4** 7 40N 5 2W
Bouar, *C.A.R.* **52 C3** 6 0N 15 40 E
Bouârfa, *Morocco* **50 B5** 32 32N 1 58W
Boucaut B., *Australia* **62 A1** 12 0S 134 25 E
Bougainville, C., *Australia* **60 B4** 13 57S 126 4 E
Bougainville I., *Papua N. G.* **64 H7** 6 0S 155 0 E
Bougainville Reef, *Australia* **62 B4** 15 30S 147 5 E
Bougie = Bejaïa, *Algeria* **50 A7** 36 42N 5 2 E
Bougouni, *Mali* **50 F4** 11 30N 7 20W
Bouillon, *Belgium* **15 E5** 49 44N 5 3 E
Boulder, *Colo., U.S.A.* **80 E2** 40 1N 105 17W
Boulder, *Mont., U.S.A.* **82 C7** 46 14N 112 7W
Boulder City, *U.S.A.* **85 K12** 35 59N 114 50W
Boulder Creek, *U.S.A.* **84 H4** 37 7N 122 7W
Boulder Dam = Hoover Dam, *U.S.A.* **85 K12** 36 1N 114 44W
Boulia, *Australia* **62 C2** 22 52S 139 51 E
Boulogne-sur-Mer, *France* **18 A4** 50 42N 1 36 E
Boultoum, *Niger* **51 F8** 14 45N 10 25 E
Boun Neua, *Laos* **38 B3** 21 38N 101 54 E
Boun Tai, *Laos* **38 B3** 21 23N 101 58 E
Bouna, *Ivory C.* **50 G5** 9 10N 3 0W
Boundary Peak, *U.S.A.* **84 H8** 37 51N 118 21W
Boundiali, *Ivory C.* **50 G4** 9 30N 6 20W
Bountiful, *U.S.A.* **82 F8** 40 53N 111 53W
Bounty Is., *Pac. Oc.* **64 M9** 48 0S 178 30 E
Bourbonnais, *France* **18 C5** 46 28N 3 0 E
Bourdel L., *Canada* **70 A5** 56 43N 74 10W
Bourem, *Mali* **50 E5** 17 0N 0 24W
Bourg-en-Bresse, *France* **18 C6** 46 13N 5 12 E
Bourg-St.-Maurice, *France* **18 D7** 45 35N 6 46 E
Bourges, *France* **18 C5** 47 9N 2 25 E
Bourget, *Canada* **79 A9** 45 26N 75 9W
Bourgogne, *France* **18 C6** 47 0N 4 50 E
Bourke, *Australia* **63 E4** 30 8S 145 55 E
Bourne, *U.K.* **10 E7** 52 47N 0 22W
Bournemouth, *U.K.* **11 G6** 50 43N 1 52W
Bournemouth □, *U.K.* **11 G6** 50 43N 1 52W
Bouse, *U.S.A.* **85 M13** 33 56N 114 0W
Bouvet I. = Bouvetøya, *Antarctica* **3 G10** 54 26S 3 24 E
Bouvetøya, *Antarctica* **3 G10** 54 26S 3 24 E
Bovill, *U.S.A.* **82 C5** 46 51N 116 24W
Bovril, *Argentina* **94 C4** 31 21S 59 26W
Bow →, *Canada* **72 C6** 49 57N 111 41W
Bow Island, *Canada* **72 D6** 49 50N 111 23W
Bowbells, *U.S.A.* **80 A3** 48 48N 102 15W
Bowdle, *U.S.A.* **80 C5** 45 27N 99 39W
Bowelling, *Australia* **61 F2** 33 25S 116 30 E
Bowen, *Argentina* **94 D2** 35 0S 67 31W
Bowen, *Australia* **62 C4** 20 0S 148 16 E
Bowen Mts., *Australia* **63 F4** 37 0S 147 50 E
Bowie, *Ariz., U.S.A.* **83 K9** 32 19N 109 29W
Bowie, *Tex., U.S.A.* **81 J6** 33 34N 97 51W
Bowkān, *Iran* **44 B5** 36 31N 46 12 E
Bowland, Forest of, *U.K.* **10 D5** 54 0N 2 30W
Bowling Green, *Ky., U.S.A.* **76 G2** 36 59N 86 27W
Bowling Green, *Ohio, U.S.A.* **76 E4** 41 23N 83 39W
Bowling Green, C., *Australia* **62 B4** 19 19S 147 25 E
Bowman, *U.S.A.* **80 B3** 46 11N 103 24W
Bowman I., *Antarctica* **5 C8** 65 0S 104 0 E
Bowmanville, *Canada* **78 C6** 43 55N 78 41W
Bowmore, *U.K.* **12 F2** 55 45N 6 17W
Bowral, *Australia* **63 E5** 34 26S 150 27 E
Bowraville, *Australia* **63 E5** 30 37S 152 52 E
Bowron →, *Canada* **72 C4** 54 3N 121 50W
Bowron Lake Prov. Park, *Canada* **72 C4** 53 10N 121 5W
Bowser L., *Canada* **72 B3** 56 30N 129 30W
Bowsman, *Canada* **73 C8** 52 14N 101 12W
Bowwood, *Zambia* **55 F2** 17 5S 26 20 E
Box Cr. →, *Australia* **63 E3** 34 10S 143 50 E
Boxmeer, *Neths.* **15 C5** 51 38N 5 56 E
Boxtel, *Neths.* **15 C5** 51 36N 5 20 E
Boyce, *U.S.A.* **81 K8** 31 23N 92 40W
Boyd L., *Canada* **70 B4** 52 46N 76 42W
Boyle, *Canada* **72 C6** 54 35N 112 49W
Boyle, *Ireland* **13 C3** 53 59N 8 18W
Boyne →, *Ireland* **13 C5** 53 43N 6 15W
Boyne City, *U.S.A.* **76 C3** 45 13N 85 1W
Boynton Beach, *U.S.A.* **77 M5** 26 32N 80 4W
Boyolali, *Indonesia* **37 G14** 7 32S 110 35 E
Boyoma, Chutes, *Dem. Rep. of the Congo* **54 B2** 0 35N 25 23 E
Boysen Reservoir, *U.S.A.* **82 E9** 43 25N 108 11W
Boyuibe, *Bolivia* **92 G6** 20 25S 63 17W
Boyup Brook, *Australia* **61 F2** 33 50S 116 23 E
Boz Dağları, *Turkey* **21 E13** 38 20N 28 0 E
Bozburun, *Turkey* **21 F13** 36 43N 28 4 E
Bozcaada, *Turkey* **21 E12** 39 49N 26 3 E
Bozdoğan, *Turkey* **21 F13** 37 40N 28 17 E
Bozeman, *U.S.A.* **82 D8** 45 41N 111 2W
Bozen = Bolzano, *Italy* **20 A4** 46 31N 11 22 E
Bozhou, *China* **34 H8** 33 55N 115 41 E
Bozoum, *C.A.R.* **52 C3** 6 25N 16 35 E
Bra, *Italy* **18 D7** 44 42N 7 51 E
Brabant □, *Belgium* **15 D4** 50 46N 4 30 E
Brabant L., *Canada* **73 B8** 55 58N 103 43W
Brač, *Croatia* **20 C7** 43 20N 16 40 E
Bracadale, L., *U.K.* **12 D2** 57 20N 6 30W
Bracciano, L. di, *Italy* **20 C5** 42 7N 12 14 E
Bracebridge, *Canada* **78 A5** 45 2N 79 19W
Brach, *Libya* **51 C8** 27 31N 14 20 E
Bräcke, *Sweden* **9 E16** 62 45N 15 26 E
Brackettville, *U.S.A.* **81 L4** 29 19N 100 25W
Bracknell, *U.K.* **11 F7** 51 25N 0 43W
Bracknell Forest □, *U.K.* **11 F7** 51 25N 0 44W
Brad, *Romania* **17 E12** 46 10N 22 50 E
Bradenton, *U.S.A.* **77 M4** 27 30N 82 34W
Bradford, *Canada* **78 B5** 44 7N 79 34W
Bradford, *U.K.* **10 D6** 53 47N 1 45W
Bradford, *Pa., U.S.A.* **78 E6** 41 58N 78 38W
Bradford, *Vt., U.S.A.* **79 C12** 43 59N 72 9W
Bradley, *Ark., U.S.A.* **81 J8** 33 6N 93 39W
Bradley, *Calif., U.S.A.* **84 K6** 35 52N 120 48W
Bradley Institute, *Zimbabwe* **55 F3** 17 7S 31 25 E
Brady, *U.S.A.* **81 K5** 31 9N 99 20W
Braeside, *Canada* **79 A8** 45 28N 76 24W
Braga, *Portugal* **19 B1** 41 35N 8 25W
Bragado, *Argentina* **94 D3** 35 2S 60 27W
Bragança, *Brazil* **93 D9** 1 0S 47 2W
Bragança, *Portugal* **19 B2** 41 48N 6 50W
Bragança Paulista, *Brazil* **95 A6** 22 55S 46 32W
Brahmanbaria, *Bangla.* **41 H17** 23 58N 91 15 E
Brahmani →, *India* **41 J15** 20 39N 86 46 E
Brahmapur, *India* **41 K14** 19 15N 84 54 E
Brahmaputra →, *India* **41 F19** 27 48N 95 30 E
Braich-y-pwll, *U.K.* **10 E3** 52 47N 4 46W
Braidwood, *Australia* **63 F4** 35 27S 149 49 E
Brăila, *Romania* **17 F14** 45 19N 27 59 E
Brainerd, *U.S.A.* **80 B7** 46 22N 94 12W
Braintree, *U.K.* **11 F8** 51 53N 0 34 E
Braintree, *U.S.A.* **79 D14** 42 13N 71 0W
Brak →, *S. Africa* **56 D3** 29 35S 22 55 E
Brakwater, *Namibia* **56 C2** 22 28S 17 3 E
Brampton, *Canada* **78 C5** 43 45N 79 45W
Brampton, *U.K.* **10 C5** 54 57N 2 44W
Branco →, *Brazil* **92 D6** 1 20S 61 50W
Brandberg, *Namibia* **56 B2** 21 10S 14 33 E
Brandenburg = Neubrandenburg, *Germany* **16 B7** 53 33N 13 15 E
Brandenburg, *Germany* **16 B7** 52 25N 12 33 E
Brandenburg □, *Germany* **16 B6** 52 50N 13 0 E
Brandfort, *S. Africa* **56 D4** 28 40S 26 30 E
Brandon, *Canada* **73 D9** 49 50N 99 57W
Brandon, *U.S.A.* **79 C11** 43 48N 73 4W
Brandon B., *Ireland* **13 D1** 52 17N 10 8W
Brandon Mt., *Ireland* **13 D1** 52 15N 10 15W
Brandsen, *Argentina* **94 D4** 35 10S 58 15W
Brandvlei, *S. Africa* **56 E3** 30 25S 20 30 E
Branford, *U.S.A.* **79 E12** 41 17N 72 49W
Braniewo, *Poland* **17 A10** 54 25N 19 50 E
Bransfield Str., *Antarctica* **5 C18** 63 0S 59 0W
Branson, *U.S.A.* **81 G8** 36 39N 93 13W
Brantford, *Canada* **78 C4** 43 10N 80 15W
Bras d'Or L., *Canada* **71 C7** 45 50N 60 50W
Brasher Falls, *U.S.A.* **79 B10** 44 49N 74 47W
Brasil, Planalto, *Brazil* **90 E6** 18 0S 46 30W
Brasiléia, *Brazil* **92 F5** 11 0S 68 45W
Brasília, *Brazil* **93 G9** 15 47S 47 55W
Brasília Legal, *Brazil* **93 D7** 3 49S 55 36W
Braslaw, *Belarus* **9 J22** 55 38N 27 0 E
Braşov, *Romania* **17 F13** 45 38N 25 35 E
Brasschaat, *Belgium* **15 C4** 51 19N 4 27 E
Brassey, Banjaran, *Malaysia* **36 D5** 5 0N 117 15 E
Brassey Ra., *Australia* **61 E3** 25 8S 122 15 E
Brasstown Bald, *U.S.A.* **77 H4** 34 53N 83 49W
Brastad, *Sweden* **9 G14** 58 23N 11 30 E
Bratislava, *Slovak Rep.* **17 D9** 48 10N 17 7 E
Bratsk, *Russia* **27 D11** 56 10N 101 30 E
Brattleboro, *U.S.A.* **79 D12** 42 51N 72 34W
Braunau, *Austria* **16 D7** 48 15N 13 3 E
Braunschweig, *Germany* **16 B6** 52 15N 10 31 E
Braunton, *U.K.* **11 F3** 51 7N 4 10W
Bravo del Norte, Rio = Grande, Rio →, *U.S.A.* **81 N6** 25 58N 97 9W
Brawley, *U.S.A.* **85 N11** 32 59N 115 31W
Bray, *Ireland* **13 C5** 53 13N 6 7W
Bray, Mt., *Australia* **62 A1** 14 0S 134 30 E
Bray, Pays de, *France* **18 B4** 49 46N 1 26 E
Brazeau →, *Canada* **72 C5** 52 55N 115 14W
Brazil, *U.S.A.* **76 F2** 39 32N 87 8W
Brazil ■, *S. Amer.* **93 F9** 12 0S 50 0W
Brazilian Highlands = Brasil, Planalto, *Brazil* **90 E6** 18 0S 46 30W
Brazo Sur →, *S. Amer.* **94 B4** 25 21S 57 42W
Brazos →, *U.S.A.* **81 L7** 28 53N 95 23W
Brazzaville, *Congo* **52 E3** 4 9S 15 12 E
Brčko, *Bos.-H.* **21 B8** 44 54N 18 46 E
Breaden, L., *Australia* **61 E4** 25 51S 125 28 E
Breaksea Sd., *N.Z.* **59 L1** 45 35S 166 35 E
Bream B., *N.Z.* **59 F5** 35 56S 174 28 E
Bream Hd., *N.Z.* **59 F5** 35 51S 174 36 E
Breas, *Chile* **94 B1** 25 29S 70 24W
Brebes, *Indonesia* **37 G13** 6 52S 109 3 E
Brechin, *Canada* **78 B5** 44 32N 79 10W
Brechin, *U.K.* **12 E6** 56 44N 2 39W
Brecht, *Belgium* **15 C4** 51 21N 4 38 E
Breckenridge, *Colo., U.S.A.* **82 G10** 39 29N 106 3W
Breckenridge, *Minn., U.S.A.* **80 B6** 46 16N 96 35W
Breckenridge, *Tex., U.S.A.* **81 J5** 32 45N 98 54W
Breckland, *U.K.* **11 E8** 52 30N 0 40 E
Brecon, *U.K.* **11 F4** 51 57N 3 23W
Brecon Beacons, *U.K.* **11 F4** 51 53N 3 26W
Breda, *Neths.* **15 C4** 51 35N 4 45 E
Bredasdorp, *S. Africa* **56 E3** 34 33S 20 2 E
Bree, *Belgium* **15 C5** 51 8N 5 35 E
Bregenz, *Austria* **16 E5** 47 30N 9 45 E
Breiðafjörður, *Iceland* **8 D2** 65 15N 23 15W
Brejo, *Brazil* **93 D10** 3 41S 42 47W
Bremen, *Germany* **16 B5** 53 4N 8 47 E
Bremer Bay, *Australia* **61 F2** 34 21S 119 20 E
Bremer I., *Australia* **62 A2** 12 5S 136 45 E
Bremerhaven, *Germany* **16 B5** 53 33N 8 36 E
Bremerton, *U.S.A.* **84 C4** 47 34N 122 38W
Brenham, *U.S.A.* **81 K6** 30 10N 96 24W
Brennerpass, *Austria* **16 E6** 47 2N 11 30 E
Brent, *U.S.A.* **77 J2** 32 56N 87 10W
Brentwood, *U.K.* **11 F8** 51 37N 0 19 E
Brentwood, *Calif., U.S.A.* **84 H5** 37 56N 121 42W
Brentwood, *N.Y., U.S.A.* **79 F11** 40 47N 73 15W
Bréscia, *Italy* **18 D9** 45 33N 10 15 E
Breskens, *Neths.* **15 C3** 51 23N 3 33 E
Breslau = Wrocław, *Poland* **17 C9** 51 5N 17 5 E
Bressanone, *Italy* **20 A4** 46 43N 11 39 E
Bressay, *U.K.* **12 A7** 60 9N 1 6W
Brest, *Belarus* **17 B12** 52 10N 23 40 E
Brest, *France* **18 B1** 48 24N 4 31W
Brest-Litovsk = Brest, *Belarus* **17 B12** 52 10N 23 40 E
Bretagne, *France* **18 B2** 48 10N 3 0W
Breton, *Canada* **72 C6** 53 7N 114 28W
Breton Sd., *U.S.A.* **81 L10** 29 35N 89 15W
Brett, C., *N.Z.* **59 F5** 35 10S 174 20 E
Brevard, *U.S.A.* **77 H4** 35 14N 82 44W
Breves, *Brazil* **93 D8** 1 40S 50 29W
Brewarrina, *Australia* **63 E4** 30 0S 146 51 E
Brewer, *U.S.A.* **77 C11** 44 48N 68 46W
Brewer, Mt., *U.S.A.* **84 J8** 36 44N 118 22W
Brewster, *N.Y., U.S.A.* **79 E11** 41 23N 73 37W

Brewster, Ohio, U.S.A. 78 F3 40 43N 81 36W
Brewster, Wash., U.S.A. 82 B4 48 6N 119 47W
Brewster, Kap = Kangikajik, Greenland 4 B6 70 7N 22 0W
Brewton, U.S.A. 77 K2 31 7N 87 4W
Breyten, S. Africa 57 D5 26 16S 30 0 E
Brezhnev = Naberezhnyye Chelny, Russia 24 C9 55 42N 52 19 E
Briançon, France 18 D7 44 54N 6 39 E
Bribie I., Australia 63 D5 27 0S 153 10 E
Bribri, Costa Rica 88 E3 9 38N 82 50W
Bridgehampton, U.S.A. 79 F12 40 56N 72 19W
Bridgend, U.K. 11 F4 51 30N 3 34W
Bridgend □, U.K. 11 F4 51 36N 3 36W
Bridgeport, Calif., U.S.A. 84 G7 38 15N 119 14W
Bridgeport, Conn., U.S.A. 79 E11 41 11N 73 12W
Bridgeport, Nebr., U.S.A. 80 E3 41 40N 103 6W
Bridgeport, Tex., U.S.A. 81 J6 33 13N 97 45W
Bridger, U.S.A. 82 D9 45 18N 108 55W
Bridgeton, U.S.A. 76 F8 39 26N 75 14W
Bridgetown, Australia 61 F2 33 58S 116 7 E
Bridgetown, Barbados 89 D8 13 5N 59 30W
Bridgetown, Canada 71 D6 44 55N 65 18W
Bridgewater, Canada 71 D7 44 25N 64 31W
Bridgewater, Mass., U.S.A. 79 E14 41 59N 70 58W
Bridgewater, N.Y., U.S.A. 79 D9 42 53N 75 15W
Bridgewater, C., Australia 63 F3 38 23S 141 23 E
Bridgewater-Gagebrook, Australia 62 G4 42 44S 147 14 E
Bridgnorth, U.K. 11 E5 52 32N 2 25W
Bridgton, U.S.A. 79 B14 44 3N 70 42W
Bridgwater, U.K. 11 F5 51 8N 2 59W
Bridgwater B., U.K. 11 F4 51 15N 3 15W
Bridlington, U.K. 10 C7 54 5N 0 12W
Bridlington B., U.K. 10 C7 54 4N 0 10W
Bridport, Australia 62 G4 40 59S 147 23 E
Bridport, U.K. 11 G5 50 44N 2 45W
Brig, Switz. 18 C7 46 18N 7 59 E
Brigg, U.K. 10 D7 53 34N 0 28W
Brigham City, U.S.A. 82 F7 41 31N 112 1W
Bright, Australia 63 F4 36 42S 146 56 E
Brighton, Australia 63 F2 35 5S 138 30 E
Brighton, Canada 78 B7 44 2N 77 44W
Brighton, U.K. 11 G7 50 49N 0 7W
Brighton, Colo., U.S.A. 80 F2 39 59N 104 49W
Brighton, N.Y., U.S.A. 78 C7 43 8N 77 34W
Brilliant, U.S.A. 78 F4 40 15N 80 39W
Bríndisi, Italy 21 D7 40 39N 17 55 E
Brinkley, U.S.A. 81 H9 34 53N 91 12W
Brinnon, U.S.A. 84 C4 47 41N 122 54W
Brion, I., Canada 71 C7 47 46N 61 26W
Brisbane, Australia 63 D5 27 25S 153 2 E
Brisbane →, Australia 63 D5 27 24S 153 9 E
Bristol, U.K. 11 F5 51 26N 2 35W
Bristol, Conn., U.S.A. 79 E12 41 40N 72 57W
Bristol, Pa., U.S.A. 79 F10 40 6N 74 51W
Bristol, R.I., U.S.A. 79 E13 41 40N 71 16W
Bristol, Tenn., U.S.A. 77 G4 36 36N 82 11W
Bristol, City of □, U.K. 11 F5 51 27N 2 36W
Bristol B., U.S.A. 68 C4 58 0N 160 0W
Bristol Channel, U.K. 11 F3 51 18N 4 30W
Bristol I., Antarctica 5 B1 58 45S 28 0W
Bristol L., U.S.A. 83 J5 34 23N 116 50W
Bristow, U.S.A. 81 H6 35 50N 96 23W
Britain = Great Britain, Europe 6 E5 54 0N 2 15W
British Columbia □, Canada 72 C3 55 0N 125 15W
British Indian Ocean Terr. = Chagos Arch., Ind. Oc. 29 K11 6 0S 72 0 E
British Isles, Europe 6 E5 54 0N 4 0W
Brits, S. Africa 57 D4 25 37S 27 48 E
Britstown, S. Africa 56 E3 30 37S 23 30 E
Britt, Canada 70 C3 45 46N 80 34W
Brittany = Bretagne, France 18 B2 48 10N 3 0W
Britton, U.S.A. 80 C6 45 48N 97 45W
Brive-la-Gaillarde, France 18 D4 45 10N 1 32 E
Brixen = Bressanone, Italy 20 A4 46 43N 11 39 E
Brixham, U.K. 11 G4 50 23N 3 31W
Brno, Czech Rep. 17 D9 49 10N 16 35 E
Broad →, U.S.A. 77 J5 34 1N 81 4W
Broad Arrow, Australia 61 F3 30 23S 121 15 E
Broad B., U.K. 12 C2 58 14N 6 18W
Broad Haven, Ireland 13 B2 54 20N 9 55W
Broad Law, U.K. 12 F5 55 30N 3 21W
Broad Sd., Australia 62 C4 22 0S 149 45 E
Broadalbin, U.S.A. 79 C10 43 4N 74 12W
Broadback →, Canada 70 B4 51 21N 78 52W
Broadhurst Ra., Australia 60 D3 22 30S 122 30 E
Broads, The, U.K. 10 E9 52 45N 1 30 E
Broadus, U.S.A. 80 C2 45 27N 105 25W
Brochet, Canada 73 B8 57 53N 101 40W
Brochet, L., Canada 73 B8 58 36N 101 35W
Brocken, Germany 16 C6 51 47N 10 37 E
Brockport, U.S.A. 78 C7 43 13N 77 56W
Brockton, U.S.A. 79 D13 42 5N 71 1W
Brockville, Canada 79 B9 44 35N 75 41W
Brockway, Mont., U.S.A. 80 B2 47 18N 105 45W
Brockway, Pa., U.S.A. 78 E6 41 15N 78 47W
Brocton, U.S.A. 78 D5 42 23N 79 26W
Brodeur Pen., Canada 69 A11 72 30N 88 10W
Brodhead, Mt., U.S.A. 78 E7 41 39N 77 47W
Brodick, U.K. 12 F3 55 35N 5 9W
Brodnica, Poland 17 B10 53 15N 19 25 E
Brody, Ukraine 17 C13 50 5N 25 10 E
Brogan, U.S.A. 82 D5 44 15N 117 31W
Broken Arrow, U.S.A. 81 G7 36 3N 95 48W
Broken Bow, Nebr., U.S.A. 80 E5 41 24N 99 38W
Broken Bow, Okla., U.S.A. 81 H7 34 2N 94 44W
Broken Bow Lake, U.S.A. 81 H7 34 9N 94 40W
Broken Hill = Kabwe, Zambia 55 E2 14 30S 28 29 E
Broken Hill, Australia 63 E3 31 58S 141 29 E
Bromley □, U.K. 11 F8 51 24N 0 2 E
Bromsgrove, U.K. 11 E5 52 21N 2 2W
Brønderslev, Denmark 9 H13 57 16N 9 57 E
Bronkhorstspruit, S. Africa 57 D4 25 46S 28 45 E
Brønnøysund, Norway 8 D15 65 28N 12 14 E
Brook Park, U.S.A. 78 E4 41 24N 81 51W
Brookhaven, U.S.A. 81 K9 31 35N 90 26W
Brookings, Oreg., U.S.A. 82 E1 42 3N 124 17W
Brookings, S. Dak., U.S.A. 80 C6 44 19N 96 48W
Brooklin, Canada 78 C6 43 55N 78 55W
Brooklyn Park, U.S.A. 80 C8 45 6N 93 23W
Brooks, Canada 72 C6 50 35N 111 55W
Brooks Range, U.S.A. 68 B5 68 0N 152 0W
Brooksville, U.S.A. 77 L4 28 33N 82 23W
Brookton, Australia 61 F2 32 22S 117 0 E
Brookville, U.S.A. 78 E5 41 10N 79 5W
Broom, L., U.K. 12 D3 57 55N 5 15W
Broome, Australia 60 C3 18 0S 122 15 E
Brora, U.K. 12 C5 58 0N 3 52W
Brora →, U.K. 12 C5 58 0N 3 51W
Brosna →, Ireland 13 C4 53 14N 7 58W
Brothers, U.S.A. 82 E3 43 49N 120 36W
Brough, U.K. 10 C5 54 32N 2 18W
Brough Hd., U.K. 12 B5 59 8N 3 20W
Broughton Island = Qikiqtarjuaq, Canada 69 B13 67 33N 63 0W
Brown, L., Australia 61 F2 31 5S 118 15 E
Brown, Pt., Australia 63 E1 32 32S 133 50 E
Brown City, U.S.A. 78 C2 43 13N 82 59W
Brown Willy, U.K. 11 G3 50 35N 4 37W
Brownfield, U.S.A. 81 J3 33 11N 102 17W
Browning, U.S.A. 82 B7 48 34N 113 1W
Brownsville, Oreg., U.S.A. 82 D2 44 24N 122 59W
Brownsville, Pa., U.S.A. 78 F5 40 1N 79 53W
Brownsville, Tenn., U.S.A. 81 H10 35 36N 89 16W
Brownsville, Tex., U.S.A. 81 N6 25 54N 97 30W
Brownville, U.S.A. 79 C9 44 0N 75 59W
Brownwood, U.S.A. 81 K5 31 43N 98 59W
Browse I., Australia 60 B3 14 7S 123 33 E
Bruas, Malaysia 39 K3 4 30N 100 47 E
Bruay-la-Buissière, France 18 A5 50 29N 2 33 E
Bruce, Mt., Australia 60 D2 22 37S 118 8 E
Bruce Pen., Canada 78 B3 45 0N 81 30W
Bruce Rock, Australia 61 F2 31 52S 118 8 E
Bruck an der Leitha, Austria 17 D9 48 1N 16 47 E
Bruck an der Mur, Austria 16 E8 47 24N 15 16 E
Brue →, U.K. 11 F5 51 13N 2 59W
Bruges = Brugge, Belgium 15 C3 51 13N 3 13 E
Brugge, Belgium 15 C3 51 13N 3 13 E
Bruin, U.S.A. 78 E5 41 3N 79 43W
Brûlé, Canada 72 C5 53 15N 117 58W
Brumado, Brazil 93 F10 14 14S 41 40W
Brumunddal, Norway 9 F14 60 53N 10 56 E
Bruneau, U.S.A. 82 E6 42 53N 115 48W
Bruneau →, U.S.A. 82 E6 42 56N 115 57W
Brunei = Bandar Seri Begawan, Brunei 36 C4 4 52N 115 0 E
Brunei ■, Asia 36 D4 4 50N 115 0 E
Brunner, L., N.Z. 59 K3 42 37S 171 27 E
Brunssum, Neths. 15 D5 50 57N 5 59 E
Brunswick = Braunschweig, Germany 16 B6 52 15N 10 31 E
Brunswick, Ga., U.S.A. 77 K5 31 10N 81 30W
Brunswick, Maine, U.S.A. 77 D11 43 55N 69 58W
Brunswick, Md., U.S.A. 76 F7 39 19N 77 38W
Brunswick, Mo., U.S.A. 80 F8 39 26N 93 8W
Brunswick, Ohio, U.S.A. 78 E3 41 14N 81 51W
Brunswick, Pen. de, Chile 96 G2 53 30S 71 30W
Brunswick B., Australia 60 C3 15 15S 124 50 E
Brunswick Junction, Australia 61 F2 33 15S 115 50 E
Bruny I., Australia 62 G4 43 20S 147 15 E
Brus Laguna, Honduras 88 C3 15 47N 84 35W
Brush, U.S.A. 80 E3 40 15N 103 37W
Brushton, U.S.A. 79 B10 44 50N 74 31W
Brusque, Brazil 95 B6 27 5S 49 0W
Brussel, Belgium 15 D4 50 51N 4 21 E
Brussels = Brussel, Belgium 15 D4 50 51N 4 21 E
Brussels, Canada 78 C3 43 44N 81 15W
Bruthen, Australia 63 F4 37 42S 147 50 E
Bruxelles = Brussel, Belgium 15 D4 50 51N 4 21 E
Bryan, Ohio, U.S.A. 76 E3 41 28N 84 33W
Bryan, Tex., U.S.A. 81 K6 30 40N 96 22W
Bryan, Mt., Australia 63 E2 33 30S 139 0 E
Bryansk, Russia 24 D4 53 13N 34 25 E
Bryce Canyon Nat. Park, U.S.A. 83 H7 37 30N 112 10W
Bryne, Norway 9 G11 58 44N 5 38 E
Bryson City, U.S.A. 77 H4 35 26N 83 27W
Bsharri, Lebanon 47 A5 34 15N 36 0 E
Bū Baqarah, U.A.E. 45 E8 25 35N 56 25 E
Bu Craa, W. Sahara 50 C3 26 45N 12 50W
Bū Ḩasā, U.A.E. 45 F7 23 30N 53 20 E
Bua Yai, Thailand 38 E4 15 33N 102 26 E
Buapinang, Indonesia 37 E6 4 40S 121 30 E
Bubanza, Burundi 54 C2 3 6S 29 23 E
Būbiyān, Kuwait 46 B4 29 45N 48 15 E
Bucaramanga, Colombia 92 B4 7 0N 73 0W
Bucasia, Australia 62 C4 21 2S 149 10 E
Buccaneer Arch., Australia 60 C3 16 7S 123 20 E
Buchach, Ukraine 17 D13 49 5N 25 25 E
Buchan, U.K. 12 D6 57 32N 2 21W
Buchan Ness, U.K. 12 D7 57 29N 1 46W
Buchanan, Canada 73 C8 51 40N 102 45W
Buchanan, Liberia 50 G3 5 57N 10 2W
Buchanan, L., Queens., Australia 62 C4 21 35S 145 52 E
Buchanan, L., W. Austral., Australia 61 E3 25 33S 123 2 E
Buchanan, L., U.S.A. 81 K5 30 45N 98 25W
Buchanan Cr. →, Australia 62 B2 19 13S 136 33 E
Buchans, Canada 71 C8 48 50N 56 52W
Bucharest = Bucureşti, Romania 17 F14 44 27N 26 10 E
Buchon, Pt., U.S.A. 84 K6 35 15N 120 54W
Buck Hill Falls, U.S.A. 79 E9 41 11N 75 16W
Buckeye, U.S.A. 83 K7 33 22N 112 35W
Buckeye Lake, U.S.A. 78 G2 39 55N 82 29W
Buckhannon, U.S.A. 76 F5 39 0N 80 8W
Buckhaven, U.K. 12 E5 56 11N 3 3W
Buckhorn L., Canada 78 B6 44 29N 78 23W
Buckie, U.K. 12 D6 57 41N 2 58W
Buckingham, Canada 70 C4 45 37N 75 24W
Buckingham, U.K. 11 F7 51 59N 0 57W
Buckingham B., Australia 62 A2 12 10S 135 40 E
Buckinghamshire □, U.K. 11 F7 51 53N 0 55W
Buckle Hd., Australia 60 B4 14 26S 127 52 E
Buckleboo, Australia 63 E2 32 54S 136 12 E
Buckley, U.K. 10 D4 53 10N 3 5W
Buckley →, Australia 62 C2 20 10S 138 49 E
Bucklin, U.S.A. 81 G5 37 33N 99 38W
Bucks L., U.S.A. 84 F5 39 54N 121 12W
Buctouche, Canada 71 C7 46 30N 64 45W
Bucureşti, Romania 17 F14 44 27N 26 10 E
Bucyrus, U.S.A. 76 E4 40 48N 82 59W
Budalin, Burma 41 H19 22 20N 95 10 E
Budapest, Hungary 17 E10 47 29N 19 5 E
Budaun, India 43 E8 28 5N 79 10 E
Budd Coast, Antarctica 5 C8 68 0S 112 0 E
Bude, U.K. 11 G3 50 49N 4 34W
Budennovsk, Russia 25 F7 44 50N 44 10 E
Budge Budge = Baj Baj, India 43 H13 22 30N 88 5 E
Budgewoi, Australia 63 E5 33 13S 151 34 E
Budjala, Dem. Rep. of the Congo 52 D3 2 50N 19 40 E
Buellton, U.S.A. 85 L6 34 37N 120 12W
Buena Esperanza, Argentina 94 C2 34 45S 65 15W
Buena Park, U.S.A. 85 M9 33 52N 117 59W
Buena Vista, Colo., U.S.A. 83 G10 38 51N 106 8W
Buena Vista, Va., U.S.A. 76 G6 37 44N 79 21W
Buena Vista Lake Bed, U.S.A. 85 K7 35 12N 119 18W
Buenaventura, Colombia 92 C3 3 53N 77 4W
Buenaventura, Mexico 86 B3 29 50N 107 30W
Buenos Aires, Argentina 94 C4 34 30S 58 20W
Buenos Aires, Costa Rica 88 E3 9 10N 83 20W
Buenos Aires □, Argentina 94 D4 36 30S 60 0W
Buenos Aires, L., Chile 96 F2 46 35S 72 30W
Buffalo, Mo., U.S.A. 81 G8 37 39N 93 6W
Buffalo, N.Y., U.S.A. 78 D6 42 53N 78 53W
Buffalo, Okla., U.S.A. 81 G5 36 50N 99 38W
Buffalo, S. Dak., U.S.A. 80 C3 45 35N 103 33W
Buffalo, Wyo., U.S.A. 82 D10 44 21N 106 42W
Buffalo →, Canada 72 A5 60 5N 115 5W
Buffalo →, S. Africa 57 D5 28 43S 30 37 E
Buffalo Head Hills, Canada 72 B5 57 25N 115 55W
Buffalo L., Alta., Canada 72 C6 52 27N 112 54W
Buffalo L., N.W.T., Canada 72 A5 60 12N 115 25W
Buffalo Narrows, Canada 73 B7 55 51N 108 29W
Buffels →, S. Africa 56 D2 29 36S 17 3 E
Buford, U.S.A. 77 H4 34 10N 84 0W
Bug = Buh →, Ukraine 25 E5 46 59N 31 58 E
Bug →, Poland 17 B11 52 31N 21 5 E
Buga, Colombia 92 C3 4 0N 76 15W
Bugala I., Uganda 54 C3 0 40S 32 20 E
Buganda, Uganda 54 C3 0 0 31 30 E
Buganga, Uganda 54 C3 0 3S 32 0 E
Bugel, Tanjung, Indonesia 37 G14 6 26S 111 3 E
Bugibba, Malta 23 D1 35 57N 14 25 E
Bugsuk, Phil. 36 C5 8 15N 117 15 E
Bugulma, Russia 24 D9 54 33N 52 48 E
Bugun Shara, Mongolia 32 B5 49 0N 104 0 E
Buguruslan, Russia 24 D9 53 39N 52 26 E
Buh →, Ukraine 25 E5 46 59N 31 58 E
Buhera, Zimbabwe 57 B5 19 18S 31 29 E
Buhl, U.S.A. 82 E6 42 36N 114 46W
Builth Wells, U.K. 11 E4 52 9N 3 25W
Buir Nur, Mongolia 33 B6 47 50N 117 42 E
Bujumbura, Burundi 54 C2 3 16S 29 18 E
Bukachacha, Russia 27 D12 52 55N 116 50 E
Bukama, Dem. Rep. of the Congo 55 D2 9 10S 25 50 E
Bukavu, Dem. Rep. of the Congo 54 C2 2 20S 28 52 E
Bukene, Tanzania 54 C3 4 15S 32 48 E
Bukhara = Bukhoro, Uzbekistan 26 F7 39 48N 64 25 E
Bukhoro, Uzbekistan 26 F7 39 48N 64 25 E
Bukima, Tanzania 54 C3 1 50S 33 25 E
Bukit Mertajam, Malaysia 39 K3 5 22N 100 28 E
Bukittinggi, Indonesia 36 E2 0 20S 100 20 E
Bukoba, Tanzania 54 C3 1 20S 31 49 E
Bukuya, Uganda 54 B3 0 40N 31 52 E
Būl, Kuh-e, Iran 45 D7 30 48N 52 45 E
Bula, Indonesia 37 E8 3 6S 130 30 E
Bulahdelah, Australia 63 E5 32 23S 152 13 E
Bulan, Phil. 37 B6 12 40N 123 52 E
Bulandshahr, India 42 E7 28 28N 77 51 E
Bulawayo, Zimbabwe 55 G2 20 7S 28 32 E
Buldan, Turkey 21 E13 38 2N 28 50 E
Bulgar, Russia 24 D8 54 57N 49 4 E
Bulgaria ■, Europe 21 C11 42 35N 25 30 E
Buli, Teluk, Indonesia 37 D7 0 48N 128 25 E
Buliluyan, C., Phil. 36 C5 8 20N 117 15 E
Bulkley →, Canada 72 B3 55 15N 127 40W
Bull Shoals L., U.S.A. 81 G8 36 22N 92 35W
Bullhead City, U.S.A. 85 K12 35 8N 114 32W
Büllingen, Belgium 15 D6 50 25N 6 16 E
Bullock Creek, Australia 62 B3 17 43S 144 31 E
Bulloo →, Australia 63 D3 28 43S 142 30 E
Bulloo L., Australia 63 D3 28 43S 142 25 E
Bulls, N.Z. 59 J5 40 10S 175 24 E
Bulnes, Chile 94 D1 36 42S 72 19W
Bulsar = Valsad, India 40 J8 20 40N 72 58 E
Bultfontein, S. Africa 56 D4 28 18S 26 10 E
Bulukumba, Indonesia 37 F6 5 33S 120 11 E
Bulun, Russia 27 B13 70 37N 127 30 E
Bumba, Dem. Rep. of the Congo 52 D4 2 13N 22 30 E
Bumbiri I., Tanzania 54 C3 1 40S 31 55 E
Bumhpa Bum, Burma 41 F20 26 51N 97 14 E
Bumi →, Zimbabwe 55 F2 17 0S 28 20 E
Buna, Kenya 54 B4 2 58N 39 30 E
Bunazi, Tanzania 54 C3 1 3S 31 23 E
Bunbury, Australia 61 F2 33 20S 115 35 E
Bunclody, Ireland 13 D5 52 39N 6 40W
Buncrana, Ireland 13 A4 55 8N 7 27W
Bundaberg, Australia 63 C5 24 54S 152 22 E
Bundey →, Australia 62 C2 21 46S 135 37 E
Bundi, India 42 G6 25 30N 75 35 E
Bundoran, Ireland 13 B3 54 28N 8 16W
Bung Kan, Thailand 38 C4 18 23N 103 37 E
Bungay, U.K. 11 E9 52 27N 1 28 E
Bungil Cr. →, Australia 63 D4 27 5S 149 5 E
Bungo-Suidō, Japan 31 H6 33 0N 132 15 E
Bungoma, Kenya 54 B3 0 34N 34 34 E
Bungotakada, Japan 31 H5 33 35N 131 25 E
Bungu, Tanzania 54 D4 7 35S 39 0 E
Bunia, Dem. Rep. of the Congo 54 B3 1 35N 30 20 E
Bunji, Pakistan 43 B6 35 45N 74 40 E
Bunkie, U.S.A. 81 K8 30 57N 92 11W
Bunnell, U.S.A. 77 L5 29 28N 81 16W
Buntok, Indonesia 36 E4 1 40S 114 58 E
Bunyu, Indonesia 36 D5 3 35N 117 50 E
Buol, Indonesia 37 D6 1 15N 121 32 E
Buon Brieng, Vietnam 38 F7 13 9N 108 12 E
Buon Ma Thuot, Vietnam 38 F7 12 40N 108 3 E
Buong Long, Cambodia 38 F6 13 44N 106 59 E
Buorkhaya, Mys, Russia 27 B14 71 50N 132 40 E
Buqayq, Si. Arabia 45 E6 26 0N 49 45 E
Bur Acaba, Somali Rep. 46 G3 3 12N 44 20 E
Bûr Safâga, Egypt 44 E2 26 43N 33 57 E
Bûr Sa'îd, Egypt 51 B12 31 16N 32 18 E
Bûr Sûdân, Sudan 51 E13 19 32N 37 9 E
Bura, Kenya 54 C4 1 4S 39 58 E
Burakin, Australia 61 F2 30 31S 117 10 E
Burao, Somali Rep. 46 F4 9 32N 45 32 E
Burāq, Syria 47 B5 33 11N 36 29 E
Buraydah, Si. Arabia 44 E4 26 20N 43 59 E
Burbank, U.S.A. 85 L8 34 11N 118 19W
Burda, India 42 G6 25 50N 77 35 E
Burdekin →, Australia 62 B4 19 38S 147 25 E
Burdur, Turkey 25 G5 37 45N 30 17 E
Burdwan = Barddhaman, India 43 H12 23 14N 87 39 E
Bure, Ethiopia 46 E2 10 40N 37 4 E
Bure →, U.K. 10 E9 52 38N 1 43 E
Bureya →, Russia 27 E13 49 27N 129 30 E
Burford, Canada 78 C4 43 7N 80 27W
Burgas, Bulgaria 21 C12 42 33N 27 29 E
Burgeo, Canada 71 C8 47 37N 57 38W
Burgersdorp, S. Africa 56 E4 31 0S 26 20 E
Burges, Mt., Australia 61 F3 30 50S 121 5 E
Burgos, Spain 19 A4 42 21N 3 41W
Burgsvik, Sweden 9 H18 57 3N 18 19 E
Burgundy = Bourgogne, France 18 C6 47 0N 4 50 E
Burhaniye, Turkey 21 E12 39 30N 26 58 E
Burhanpur, India 40 J10 21 18N 76 14 E
Burhi Gandak →, India 43 G12 25 20N 86 37 E
Burhner →, India 43 H9 22 43N 80 31 E
Burias I., Phil. 37 B6 12 55N 123 5 E
Burica, Pta., Costa Rica 88 E3 8 3N 82 51W
Burien, U.S.A. 84 C4 47 28N 122 21W
Burigi, L., Tanzania 54 C3 2 2S 31 22 E
Burin, Canada 71 C8 47 1N 55 14W
Buriram, Thailand 38 E4 15 0N 103 0 E
Burj Sāfitā, Syria 44 C3 34 48N 36 7 E
Burkburnett, U.S.A. 81 H5 34 6N 98 34W
Burke →, Australia 62 C2 23 12S 139 33 E
Burke Chan., Canada 72 C3 52 10N 127 30W
Burketown, Australia 62 B2 17 45S 139 33 E
Burkina Faso ■, Africa 50 F5 12 0N 1 0W
Burk's Falls, Canada 70 C4 45 37N 79 24W
Burleigh Falls, Canada 78 B6 44 33N 78 12W
Burley, U.S.A. 82 E7 42 32N 113 48W
Burlingame, U.S.A. 84 H4 37 35N 122 21W
Burlington, Canada 78 C5 43 18N 79 45W
Burlington, Colo., U.S.A. 80 F3 39 18N 102 16W
Burlington, Iowa, U.S.A. 80 E9 40 49N 91 14W
Burlington, Kans., U.S.A. 80 F7 38 12N 95 45W
Burlington, N.C., U.S.A. 77 G6 36 6N 79 26W
Burlington, N.J., U.S.A. 79 F10 40 4N 74 51W
Burlington, Vt., U.S.A. 79 B11 44 29N 73 12W
Burlington, Wash., U.S.A. 84 B4 48 28N 122 20W
Burlington, Wis., U.S.A. 76 D1 42 41N 88 17W
Burlyu-Tyube, Kazakstan 26 E8 46 30N 79 10 E
Burma ■, Asia 41 J20 21 0N 96 30 E
Burnaby I., Canada 72 C2 52 25N 131 19W
Burnet, U.S.A. 81 K5 30 45N 98 14W
Burney, U.S.A. 82 F3 40 53N 121 40W
Burnham, U.S.A. 78 F7 40 38N 77 34W
Burnham-on-Sea, U.K. 11 F5 51 14N 3 0W
Burnie, Australia 62 G4 41 4S 145 56 E
Burnley, U.K. 10 D5 53 47N 2 14W
Burns, U.S.A. 82 E4 43 35N 119 3W
Burns Lake, Canada 72 C3 54 20N 125 45W
Burnside →, Canada 68 B9 66 51N 108 4W
Burnside, L., Australia 61 E3 25 22S 123 0 E
Burnsville, U.S.A. 80 C8 44 47N 93 17W
Burnt L., Canada 71 B7 53 35N 64 4W
Burnt River, Canada 78 B6 44 41N 78 42W
Burntwood →, Canada 73 B9 56 8N 96 34W
Burntwood L., Canada 73 B8 55 22N 100 26W
Burqān, Kuwait 44 D5 29 0N 47 57 E
Burra, Australia 63 E2 33 40S 138 55 E
Burray, U.K. 12 C6 58 51N 2 54W
Burren Junction, Australia 63 E4 30 7S 148 59 E
Burrinjuck Res., Australia 63 F4 35 0S 148 36 E
Burro, Serranías del, Mexico 86 B4 29 0N 102 0W
Burrow Hd., U.K. 12 G4 54 41N 4 24W
Burruyacú, Argentina 94 B3 26 30S 64 40W
Burry Port, U.K. 11 F3 51 41N 4 15W
Bursa, Turkey 21 D13 40 15N 29 5 E
Burstall, Canada 73 C7 50 39N 109 54W
Burton, Ohio, U.S.A. 78 E3 41 28N 81 8W
Burton, S.C., U.S.A. 77 J5 32 25N 80 45W
Burton, L., Canada 70 B4 54 45N 78 20W
Burton upon Trent, U.K. 10 E6 52 48N 1 38W
Buru, Indonesia 37 E7 3 30S 126 30 E
Burûn, Râs, Egypt 47 D2 31 14N 33 7 E
Burundi ■, Africa 54 C3 3 15S 30 0 E
Bururi, Burundi 54 C2 3 57S 29 37 E
Burutu, Nigeria 50 G7 5 20N 5 29 E
Burwell, U.S.A. 80 E5 41 47N 99 8W
Burwick, U.K. 12 C5 58 45N 2 58W
Bury, U.K. 10 D5 53 35N 2 17W
Bury St. Edmunds, U.K. 11 E8 52 15N 0 43 E
Buryatia □, Russia 27 D11 53 0N 110 0 E
Busan = Pusan, S. Korea 35 G15 35 5N 129 0 E
Busango Swamp, Zambia 55 E2 14 15S 25 45 E
Buşayrah, Syria 44 C4 35 9N 40 26 E
Būshehr, Iran 45 D6 28 55N 50 55 E
Būshehr □, Iran 45 D6 28 20N 51 45 E
Bushell, Canada 73 B7 59 31N 108 45W
Bushenyi, Uganda 54 C3 0 35S 30 10 E
Bushire = Būshehr, Iran 45 D6 28 55N 50 55 E
Businga, Dem. Rep. of the Congo 52 D4 3 16N 20 59 E
Buşra ash Shām, Syria 47 C5 32 30N 36 25 E
Busselton, Australia 61 F2 33 42S 115 15 E
Bussum, Neths. 15 B5 52 16N 5 10 E
Busto Arsizio, Italy 18 D8 45 37N 8 51 E
Busu Djanoa, Dem. Rep. of the Congo 52 D4 1 43N 21 23 E
Busuanga I., Phil. 37 B5 12 10N 120 0 E
Buta, Dem. Rep. of the Congo 54 B1 2 50N 24 53 E
Butare, Rwanda 54 C2 2 31S 29 52 E
Butaritari, Kiribati 64 G9 3 30N 174 0 E
Bute, U.K. 12 F3 55 48N 5 2W
Bute Inlet, Canada 72 C4 50 40N 124 53W
Butemba, Uganda 54 B3 1 9N 31 37 E
Butembo, Dem. Rep. of the Congo 54 B2 0 9N 29 18 E
Butha Qi, China 33 B7 48 0N 122 32 E
Butiaba, Uganda 54 B3 1 50N 31 20 E
Butler, Mo., U.S.A. 80 F7 38 16N 94 20W
Butler, Pa., U.S.A. 78 F5 40 52N 79 52W
Buton, Indonesia 37 E6 5 0S 122 45 E
Butte, Mont., U.S.A. 82 C7 46 0N 112 32W
Butte, Nebr., U.S.A. 80 D5 42 58N 98 51W

Butte Creek →, U.S.A. 84 F5 39 12N 121 56W
Butterworth = Gcuwa, S. Africa 57 E4 32 20S 28 11 E
Butterworth, Malaysia 39 K3 5 24N 100 23 E
Buttevant, Ireland 13 D3 52 14N 8 40W
Buttfield, Mt., Australia 61 D4 24 45S 128 9 E
Button B., Canada 73 B10 58 45N 94 23W
Buttonwillow, U.S.A. 85 K7 35 24N 119 28W
Butty Hd., Australia 61 F3 33 54S 121 39 E
Butuan, Phil. 37 C7 8 57N 125 33 E
Butung = Buton, Indonesia 37 E6 5 0S 122 45 E
Buturlinovka, Russia 25 D7 50 50N 40 35 E
Buur Hakaba = Bur Acaba, Somali Rep. 46 G3 3 12N 44 20 E
Buxa Duar, India 43 F13 27 45N 89 35 E
Buxar, India 43 G10 25 34N 83 58 E
Buxtehude, Germany 16 B5 53 28N 9 39 E
Buxton, U.K. 10 D6 53 16N 1 54W
Buy, Russia 24 C7 58 28N 41 28 E
Büyük Menderes →, Turkey 21 F12 37 28N 27 11 E
Büyükçekmece, Turkey 21 D13 41 2N 28 35 E
Buzău, Romania 17 F14 45 10N 26 50 E
Buzău →, Romania 17 F14 45 26N 27 44 E
Buzen, Japan 31 H5 33 35N 131 5 E
Buzi →, Mozam. 55 F3 19 50S 34 43 E
Buzuluk, Russia 24 D9 52 48N 52 12 E
Buzzards B., U.S.A. 79 E14 41 45N 70 37W
Buzzards Bay, U.S.A. 79 E14 41 44N 70 37W
Bwana Mkubwe, Dem. Rep. of the Congo 55 E2 13 8S 28 38 E
Byarezina →, Belarus 17 B16 52 33N 30 14 E
Byaroza, Belarus 17 B13 52 31N 24 51 E
Bydgoszcz, Poland 17 B9 53 10N 18 0 E
Byelarus = Belarus ■, Europe 17 B14 53 30N 27 0 E
Byelorussia = Belarus ■, Europe 17 B14 53 30N 27 0 E
Byers, U.S.A. 80 F2 39 43N 104 14W
Byesville, U.S.A. 78 G3 39 58N 81 32W
Byford, Australia 61 F2 32 15S 116 0 E
Bykhaw, Belarus 17 B16 53 31N 30 14 E
Bykhov = Bykhaw, Belarus 17 B16 53 31N 30 14 E
Bylas, U.S.A. 83 K8 33 8N 110 7W
Bylot, Canada 73 B10 58 25N 94 8W
Bylot I., Canada 69 A12 73 13N 78 34W
Byrd, C., Antarctica 5 C17 69 38S 76 7W
Byrock, Australia 63 E4 30 40S 146 27 E
Byron Bay, Australia 63 D5 28 43S 153 37 E
Byrranga, Gory, Russia 27 B11 75 0N 100 0 E
Byrranga Mts. = Byrranga, Gory, Russia 27 B11 75 0N 100 0 E
Byske, Sweden 8 D19 64 57N 21 11 E
Byske älv →, Sweden 8 D19 64 57N 21 13 E
Bytom, Poland 17 C10 50 25N 18 54 E
Bytów, Poland 17 A9 54 10N 17 30 E
Byumba, Rwanda 54 C3 1 35S 30 4 E

C

Ca →, Vietnam 38 C5 18 45N 105 45 E
Ca Mau, Vietnam 39 H5 9 7N 105 8 E
Ca Mau, Mui, Vietnam 39 H5 8 38N 104 44 E
Ca Na, Vietnam 39 G7 11 20N 108 54 E
Caacupé, Paraguay 94 B4 25 23S 57 5W
Caála, Angola 53 G3 12 46S 15 30 E
Caamano Sd., Canada 72 C3 52 55N 129 25W
Caazapá, Paraguay 94 B4 26 8S 56 19W
Caazapá □, Paraguay 95 B4 26 10S 56 0W
Caballeria, C. de, Spain 22 A11 40 5N 4 5 E
Cabanatuan, Phil. 37 A6 15 30N 120 58 E
Cabano, Canada 71 C6 47 40N 68 56W
Cabazon, U.S.A. 85 M10 33 55N 116 47W
Cabedelo, Brazil 93 E12 7 0S 34 50W
Cabildo, Chile 94 C1 32 30S 71 5W
Cabimas, Venezuela 92 A4 10 23N 71 25W
Cabinda, Angola 52 F2 5 33S 12 11 E
Cabinda □, Angola 52 F2 5 0S 12 30 E
Cabinet Mts., U.S.A. 82 C6 48 0N 115 30W
Cabo Blanco, Argentina 96 F3 47 15S 65 47W
Cabo Frio, Brazil 95 A7 22 51S 42 3W
Cabo Pantoja, Peru 92 D3 1 0S 75 10W
Cabonga, Réservoir, Canada 70 C4 47 20N 76 40W
Cabool, U.S.A. 81 G8 37 7N 92 6W
Caboolture, Australia 63 D5 27 5S 152 58 E
Cabora Bassa Dam = Cahora Bassa, Représa de, Mozam. 55 F3 15 20S 32 50 E
Caborca, Mexico 86 A2 30 40N 112 10W
Cabot, Mt., U.S.A. 79 B13 44 30N 71 25W
Cabot Hd., Canada 78 A3 45 14N 81 17W
Cabot Str., Canada 71 C8 47 15N 59 40W
Cabra, Spain 19 D3 37 30N 4 28W
Cabrera, Spain 22 B9 39 8N 2 57 E
Cabri, Canada 73 C7 50 35N 108 25W
Cabriel →, Spain 19 C5 39 14N 1 3W
Caçador, Brazil 95 B5 26 47S 51 0W
Čačak, Serbia, Yug. 21 C9 43 54N 20 20 E
Caçapava do Sul, Brazil 95 C5 30 30S 53 30W
Cáceres, Brazil 92 G7 16 5S 57 40W
Cáceres, Spain 19 C2 39 26N 6 23W
Cache Bay, Canada 70 C4 46 22N 80 0W
Cache Cr. →, U.S.A. 84 G5 38 42N 121 42W
Cache Creek, Canada 72 C4 50 48N 121 19W
Cachi, Argentina 94 B2 25 5S 66 10W
Cachimbo, Serra do, Brazil 93 E7 9 30S 55 30W
Cachinal de la Sierra, Chile 94 A2 24 58S 69 32W
Cachoeira, Brazil 93 F11 12 30S 39 0W
Cachoeira do Sul, Brazil 95 C5 30 3S 52 53W
Cachoeiro de Itapemirim, Brazil 95 A7 20 51S 41 7W
Cacoal, Brazil 92 F6 11 32S 61 18W
Cacólo, Angola 52 G3 10 9S 19 21 E
Caconda, Angola 53 G3 13 48S 15 8 E
Caddo, U.S.A. 81 H6 34 7N 96 16W
Cader Idris, U.K. 11 E4 52 42N 3 53W
Cadereyta, Mexico 86 B5 25 36N 100 0W
Cadibarrawirracanna, L., Australia 63 D2 28 52S 135 27 E
Cadillac, U.S.A. 76 C3 44 15N 85 24W
Cadiz, Phil. 37 B6 10 57N 123 15 E
Cádiz, Spain 19 D2 36 30N 6 20W
Cadiz, Calif., U.S.A. 85 L11 34 30N 115 28W
Cadiz, Ohio, U.S.A. 78 F4 40 22N 81 0W
Cádiz, G. de, Spain 19 D2 36 40N 7 0W
Cadiz L., U.S.A. 83 J6 34 18N 115 24W
Cadney Park, Australia 63 D1 27 55S 134 3 E
Cadomin, Canada 72 C5 53 2N 117 20W
Cadotte Lake, Canada 72 B5 56 26N 116 23W
Cadoux, Australia 61 F2 30 46S 117 7 E
Caen, France 18 B3 49 10N 0 22W
Caernarfon, U.K. 10 D3 53 8N 4 16W
Caernarfon B., U.K. 10 D3 53 4N 4 40W
Caernarvon = Caernarfon, U.K. 10 D3 53 8N 4 16W
Caerphilly, U.K. 11 F4 51 35N 3 13W
Caerphilly □, U.K. 11 F4 51 37N 3 12W
Caesarea, Israel 47 C3 32 30N 34 53 E
Caetité, Brazil 93 F10 13 50S 42 32W
Cafayate, Argentina 94 B2 26 2S 66 0W
Cafu, Angola 56 B2 16 30S 15 8 E
Cagayan de Oro, Phil. 37 C6 8 30N 124 40 E
Cagayan Is., Phil. 37 C5 9 40N 121 16 E
Cágliari, Italy 20 E3 39 13N 9 7 E
Cágliari, G. di, Italy 20 E3 39 8N 9 11 E
Caguán →, Colombia 92 D4 0 8S 74 18W
Caguas, Puerto Rico 89 C6 18 14N 66 2W
Caha Mts., Ireland 13 E2 51 45N 9 40W
Cahama, Angola 56 B1 16 17S 14 19 E
Caher, Ireland 13 D4 52 22N 7 56W
Caherciveen, Ireland 13 E1 51 56N 10 14W
Cahora Bassa, L. de, Mozam. 55 F3 15 35S 32 0 E
Cahora Bassa, Représa de, Mozam. 55 F3 15 20S 32 50 E
Cahore Pt., Ireland 13 D5 52 33N 6 12W
Cahors, France 18 D4 44 27N 1 27 E
Cahul, Moldova 17 F15 45 50N 28 15 E
Cai Bau, Dao, Vietnam 38 B6 21 10N 107 27 E
Cai Nuoc, Vietnam 39 H5 8 56N 105 1 E
Caia, Mozam. 55 F4 17 51S 35 24 E
Caianda, Angola 55 E1 11 2S 23 31 E
Caibarién, Cuba 88 B4 22 30N 79 30W
Caicara, Venezuela 92 B5 7 38N 66 10W
Caicó, Brazil 93 E11 6 20S 37 0W
Caicos Is., Turks & Caicos 89 B5 21 40N 71 40W
Caicos Passage, W. Indies 89 B5 22 45N 72 45W
Caird Coast, Antarctica 5 D1 75 0S 25 0W
Cairn Gorm, U.K. 12 D5 57 7N 3 39W
Cairngorm Mts., U.K. 12 D5 57 6N 3 42W
Cairnryan, U.K. 12 G3 54 59N 5 1W
Cairns, Australia 62 B4 16 57S 145 45 E
Cairns L., Canada 73 C10 51 42N 94 30W
Cairo = El Qâhira, Egypt 51 B12 30 1N 31 14 E
Cairo, Ga., U.S.A. 77 K3 30 52N 84 13W
Cairo, Ill., U.S.A. 81 G10 37 0N 89 11W
Cairo, N.Y., U.S.A. 79 D11 42 18N 74 0W
Caithness, Ord of, U.K. 12 C5 58 8N 3 36W
Cajamarca, Peru 92 E3 7 5S 78 28W
Cajàzeiras, Brazil 93 E11 6 52S 38 30W
Cala d'Or, Spain 22 B10 39 23N 3 14 E
Cala en Porter, Spain 22 B11 39 52N 4 8 E
Cala Figuera, C. de, Spain 22 B9 39 27N 2 31 E
Cala Forcat, Spain 22 B10 40 0N 3 47 E
Cala Major, Spain 22 B9 39 33N 2 37 E
Cala Mezquida = Sa Mesquida, Spain 22 B11 39 55N 4 16 E
Cala Millor, Spain 22 B10 39 35N 3 22 E
Cala Ratjada, Spain 22 B10 39 43N 3 27 E
Cala Santa Galdana, Spain 22 B10 39 56N 3 58 E
Calabar, Nigeria 50 H7 4 57N 8 20 E
Calabogie, Canada 79 A8 45 18N 76 43W
Calabozo, Venezuela 92 B5 9 0N 67 28W
Calábria □, Italy 20 E7 39 0N 16 30 E
Calafate, Argentina 96 G2 50 19S 72 15W
Calahorra, Spain 19 A5 42 18N 1 59W
Calais, France 18 A4 50 57N 1 56 E
Calais, U.S.A. 77 C12 45 11N 67 17W
Calalaste, Cord. de, Argentina 94 B2 25 0S 67 0W
Calama, Brazil 92 E6 8 0S 62 50W
Calama, Chile 94 A2 22 30S 68 55W
Calamar, Colombia 92 A4 10 15N 74 55W
Calamian Group, Phil. 37 B5 11 50N 119 55 E
Calamocha, Spain 19 B5 40 50N 1 17W
Calang, Indonesia 36 D1 4 37N 95 37 E
Calapan, Phil. 37 B6 13 25N 121 7 E
Călăraşi, Romania 17 F14 44 12N 27 20 E
Calatayud, Spain 19 B5 41 20N 1 40W
Calauag, Phil. 37 B6 13 55N 122 15 E
Calavite, C., Phil. 37 B6 13 26N 120 20 E
Calbayog, Phil. 37 B6 12 4N 124 38 E
Calca, Peru 92 F4 13 22S 72 0W
Calcasieu L., U.S.A. 81 L8 29 55N 93 18W
Calcutta = Kolkata, India 43 H13 22 36N 88 24 E
Calcutta, U.S.A. 78 F4 40 40N 80 34W
Caldas da Rainha, Portugal 19 C1 39 24N 9 8W
Calder →, U.K. 10 D6 53 44N 1 22W
Caldera, Chile 94 B1 27 5S 70 55W
Caldwell, Idaho, U.S.A. 82 E5 43 40N 116 41W
Caldwell, Kans., U.S.A. 81 G6 37 2N 97 37W
Caldwell, Tex., U.S.A. 81 K6 30 32N 96 42W
Caledon, S. Africa 56 E2 34 14S 19 26 E
Caledon →, S. Africa 56 E4 30 31S 26 5 E
Caledon B., Australia 62 A2 12 45S 137 0 E
Caledonia, Canada 78 C5 43 7N 79 58W
Caledonia, U.S.A. 78 D7 42 58N 77 51W
Calemba, Angola 56 B2 16 0S 15 44 E
Calen, Australia 62 C4 20 56S 148 48 E
Caletones, Chile 94 C1 34 6S 70 27W
Calexico, U.S.A. 85 N11 32 40N 115 30W
Calf of Man, U.K. 10 C3 54 3N 4 48W
Calgary, Canada 72 C6 51 0N 114 10W
Calheta, Madeira 22 D2 32 44N 17 11W
Calhoun, U.S.A. 77 H3 34 30N 84 57W
Cali, Colombia 92 C3 3 25N 76 35W
Calicut, India 40 P9 11 15N 75 43 E
Caliente, U.S.A. 83 H6 37 37N 114 31W
California, Mo., U.S.A. 80 F8 38 38N 92 34W
California, Pa., U.S.A. 78 F5 40 4N 79 54W
California □, U.S.A. 84 H7 37 30N 119 30W
California, Baja, Mexico 86 A1 32 10N 115 12W
California, Baja, T.N. = Baja California □, Mexico 86 B2 30 0N 115 0W
California, Baja, T.S. = Baja California Sur □, Mexico 86 B2 25 50N 111 50W
California, G. de, Mexico 86 B2 27 0N 111 0W
California City, U.S.A. 85 K9 35 10N 117 55W
California Hot Springs, U.S.A. 85 K8 35 51N 118 41W
Calingasta, Argentina 94 C2 31 15S 69 30W
Calipatria, U.S.A. 85 M11 33 8N 115 31W
Calistoga, U.S.A. 84 G4 38 35N 122 35W
Calitzdorp, S. Africa 56 E3 33 33S 21 42 E
Callabonna, L., Australia 63 D3 29 40S 140 5 E
Callan, Ireland 13 D4 52 32N 7 24W
Callander, U.K. 12 E4 56 15N 4 13W
Callao, Peru 92 F3 12 0S 77 0W
Calles, Mexico 87 C5 23 2N 98 42W
Callicoon, U.S.A. 79 E9 41 46N 75 3W
Calling Lake, Canada 72 B6 55 15N 113 12W
Calliope, Australia 62 C5 24 0S 151 16 E
Calne, U.K. 11 F6 51 26N 2 0W
Calola, Angola 56 B2 16 25S 17 48 E
Caloundra, Australia 63 D5 26 45S 153 10 E
Calpella, U.S.A. 84 F3 39 14N 123 12W
Calpine, U.S.A. 84 F6 39 40N 120 27W
Calstock, Canada 70 C3 49 47N 84 9W
Caltagirone, Italy 20 F6 37 14N 14 31 E
Caltanissetta, Italy 20 F6 37 29N 14 4 E
Calulo, Angola 52 G2 10 1S 14 56 E
Calvert →, Australia 62 B2 16 17S 137 44 E
Calvert I., Canada 72 C3 51 30N 128 0W
Calvert Ra., Australia 60 D3 24 0S 122 30 E
Calvi, France 18 E8 42 34N 8 45 E
Calviá, Spain 19 C7 39 34N 2 31 E
Calvillo, Mexico 86 C4 21 51N 102 43W
Calvinia, S. Africa 56 E2 31 28S 19 45 E
Calwa, U.S.A. 84 J7 36 42N 119 46W
Cam →, U.K. 11 E8 52 21N 0 16 E
Cam Lam, Vietnam 39 G7 11 54N 109 10 E
Cam Pha, Vietnam 38 B6 21 7N 107 18 E
Cam Ranh, Vietnam 39 G7 11 54N 109 12 E
Cam Xuyen, Vietnam 38 C6 18 15N 106 0 E
Camabatela, Angola 52 F3 8 20S 15 26 E
Camacha, Madeira 22 D3 32 41N 16 49W
Camacho, Mexico 86 C4 24 25N 102 18W
Camacupa, Angola 53 G3 11 58S 17 22 E
Camagüey, Cuba 88 B4 21 20N 78 0W
Camaná, Peru 92 G4 16 30S 72 50W
Camanche Reservoir, U.S.A. 84 G6 38 14N 121 1W
Camaquã, Brazil 95 C5 30 51S 51 49W
Camaquã →, Brazil 95 C5 31 17S 51 47W
Câmara de Lobos, Madeira 22 D3 32 39N 16 59W
Camargo, Mexico 87 B5 26 19N 98 50W
Camargue, France 18 E6 43 34N 4 34 E
Camarillo, U.S.A. 85 L7 34 13N 119 2W
Camarón, C., Honduras 88 C2 16 0N 85 5W
Camarones, Argentina 96 E3 44 50S 65 40W
Camas, U.S.A. 84 E4 45 35N 122 24W
Camas Valley, U.S.A. 82 E2 43 2N 123 40W
Camballin, Australia 60 C3 17 59S 124 12 E
Cambará, Brazil 95 A5 23 2S 50 5W
Cambay = Khambhat, India 42 H5 22 23N 72 33 E
Cambay, G. of = Khambhat, G. of, India 40 J8 20 45N 72 30 E
Cambodia ■, Asia 38 F5 12 15N 105 0 E
Camborne, U.K. 11 G2 50 12N 5 19W
Cambrai, France 18 A5 50 11N 3 14 E
Cambria, U.S.A. 84 K5 35 34N 121 5W
Cambrian Mts., U.K. 11 E4 52 3N 3 57W
Cambridge, Canada 78 C4 43 23N 80 15W
Cambridge, Jamaica 88 C4 18 18N 77 54W
Cambridge, N.Z. 59 G5 37 54S 175 29 E
Cambridge, U.K. 11 E8 52 12N 0 8 E
Cambridge, Mass., U.S.A. 79 D13 42 22N 71 6W
Cambridge, Minn., U.S.A. 80 C8 45 34N 93 13W
Cambridge, N.Y., U.S.A. 79 C11 43 2N 73 22W
Cambridge, Nebr., U.S.A. 80 E4 40 17N 100 10W
Cambridge, Ohio, U.S.A. 78 F3 40 2N 81 35W
Cambridge Bay = Ikaluktutiak, Canada 68 B9 69 10N 105 0W
Cambridge G., Australia 60 B4 14 55S 128 15 E
Cambridge Springs, U.S.A. 78 E4 41 48N 80 4W
Cambridgeshire □, U.K. 11 E7 52 25N 0 7W
Cambuci, Brazil 95 A7 21 35S 41 55W
Cambundi-Catembo, Angola 52 G3 10 10S 17 35 E
Camden, Ala., U.S.A. 77 K2 31 59N 87 17W
Camden, Ark., U.S.A. 81 J8 33 35N 92 50W
Camden, Maine, U.S.A. 77 C11 44 13N 69 4W
Camden, N.J., U.S.A. 79 G9 39 56N 75 7W
Camden, N.Y., U.S.A. 79 C9 43 20N 75 45W
Camden, S.C., U.S.A. 77 H5 34 16N 80 36W
Camden Sd., Australia 60 C3 15 27S 124 25 E
Camdenton, U.S.A. 81 F8 38 1N 92 45W
Cameron, Ariz., U.S.A. 83 J8 35 53N 111 25W
Cameron, La., U.S.A. 81 L8 29 48N 93 20W
Cameron, Mo., U.S.A. 80 F7 39 44N 94 14W
Cameron, Tex., U.S.A. 81 K6 30 51N 96 59W
Cameron Highlands, Malaysia 39 K3 4 27N 101 22 E
Cameron Hills, Canada 72 B5 59 48N 118 0W
Cameroon ■, Africa 52 C2 6 0N 12 30 E
Cameroun, Mt., Cameroon 52 D1 4 13N 9 10 E
Cametá, Brazil 93 D9 2 12S 49 30W
Camiguin I., Phil. 37 C6 18 56N 121 55 E
Camilla, U.S.A. 77 K3 31 14N 84 12W
Caminha, Portugal 19 B1 41 50N 8 50W
Camino, U.S.A. 84 G6 38 44N 120 41W
Camira Creek, Australia 63 D5 29 15S 152 58 E
Cammal, U.S.A. 78 E7 41 24N 77 28W
Camocim, Brazil 93 D10 2 55S 40 50W
Camooweal, Australia 62 B2 19 56S 138 7 E
Camopi, Fr. Guiana 93 C8 3 12N 52 17W
Camp Borden, Canada 78 B5 44 18N 79 56W
Camp Hill, U.S.A. 78 F8 40 14N 76 55W
Camp Nelson, U.S.A. 85 J8 36 8N 118 39W
Camp Pendleton, U.S.A. 85 M9 33 16N 117 23W
Camp Verde, U.S.A. 83 J8 34 34N 111 51W
Camp Wood, U.S.A. 81 L5 29 40N 100 1W
Campana, Argentina 94 C4 34 10S 58 55W
Campana, I., Chile 96 F1 48 20S 75 20W
Campanário, Madeira 22 D2 32 39N 17 2W
Campánia □, Italy 20 D6 41 0N 14 30 E
Campbell, S. Africa 56 D3 28 48S 23 44 E
Campbell, Calif., U.S.A. 84 H5 37 17N 121 57W
Campbell, Ohio, U.S.A. 78 E4 41 5N 80 37W
Campbell I., Pac. Oc. 64 N8 52 30S 169 0 E
Campbell L., Canada 73 A7 63 14N 106 55W
Campbell River, Canada 72 C3 50 5N 125 20W
Campbell Town, Australia 62 G4 41 52S 147 30 E
Campbellford, Canada 78 B7 44 18N 77 48W
Campbellpur, Pakistan 42 C5 33 46N 72 26 E
Campbellsville, U.S.A. 76 G3 37 21N 85 20W
Campbellton, Canada 71 C6 47 57N 66 43W
Campbelltown, Australia 63 E5 34 4S 150 49 E
Campbeltown, U.K. 12 F3 55 26N 5 36W
Campeche, Mexico 87 D6 19 50N 90 32W
Campeche □, Mexico 87 D6 19 50N 90 32W
Campeche, Golfo de, Mexico 87 D6 19 30N 93 0W
Camperdown, Australia 63 F3 38 14S 143 9 E
Camperville, Canada 73 C8 51 59N 100 9W
Câmpina, Romania 17 F13 45 10N 25 45 E
Campina Grande, Brazil 93 E11 7 20S 35 47W
Campinas, Brazil 95 A6 22 50S 47 0W
Campo Grande, Brazil 93 H8 20 25S 54 40W
Campo Maíor, Brazil 93 D10 4 50S 42 12W
Campo Mourão, Brazil 95 A5 24 3S 52 22W
Campobasso, Italy 20 D6 41 34N 14 39 E
Campos, Brazil 95 A7 21 50S 41 20W
Campos Belos, Brazil 93 F9 13 10S 47 3W
Campos del Port, Spain 22 B10 39 26N 3 1 E
Campos Novos, Brazil 95 B5 27 21S 51 50W
Camptonville, U.S.A. 84 F5 39 27N 121 3W
Camptown, U.S.A. 79 E8 41 44N 76 14W
Câmpulung, Romania 17 F13 45 17N 25 3 E
Camrose, Canada 72 C6 53 0N 112 50W
Camsell Portage, Canada 73 B7 59 37N 109 15W
Çan, Turkey 21 D12 40 2N 27 3 E
Can Clavo, Spain 22 C7 38 57N 1 27 E
Can Creu, Spain 22 C7 38 58N 1 28 E
Can Gio, Vietnam 39 G6 10 25N 106 58 E
Can Tho, Vietnam 39 G5 10 2N 105 46 E
Canaan, U.S.A. 79 D11 42 2N 73 20W
Canada ■, N. Amer. 68 C10 60 0N 100 0W
Cañada de Gómez, Argentina 94 C3 32 40S 61 30W
Canadian, U.S.A. 81 H4 35 55N 100 23W
Canadian →, U.S.A. 81 H7 35 28N 95 3W
Canajoharie, U.S.A. 79 D10 42 54N 74 35W
Çanakkale, Turkey 21 D12 40 8N 26 24 E
Çanakkale Boğazı, Turkey 21 D12 40 17N 26 32 E
Canal Flats, Canada 72 C5 50 10N 115 48W
Canalejas, Argentina 94 D2 35 15S 66 34W
Canals, Argentina 94 C3 33 35S 62 53W
Canandaigua, U.S.A. 78 D7 42 54N 77 17W
Canandaigua L., U.S.A. 78 D7 42 47N 77 19W
Cananea, Mexico 86 A2 31 0N 110 20W
Canarias, Is., Atl. Oc. 22 F4 28 30N 16 0W
Canarreos, Arch. de los, Cuba 88 B3 21 35N 81 40W
Canary Is. = Canarias, Is., Atl. Oc. 22 F4 28 30N 16 0W
Canaseraga, U.S.A. 78 D7 42 27N 77 45W
Canatlán, Mexico 86 C4 24 31N 104 47W
Canaveral, C., U.S.A. 77 L5 28 27N 80 32W
Canavieiras, Brazil 93 G11 15 39S 39 0W
Canberra, Australia 63 F4 35 15S 149 8 E
Canby, Calif., U.S.A. 82 F3 41 27N 120 52W
Canby, Minn., U.S.A. 80 C6 44 43N 96 16W
Canby, Oreg., U.S.A. 84 E4 45 16N 122 42W
Cancún, Mexico 87 C7 21 8N 86 44W
Candelaria, Argentina 95 B4 27 29S 55 44W
Candelaria, Canary Is. 22 F3 28 22N 16 22W
Candelo, Australia 63 F4 36 47S 149 43 E
Candia = Iráklion, Greece 23 D7 35 20N 25 12 E
Candle L., Canada 73 C7 53 50N 105 18W
Candlemas I., Antarctica 5 B1 57 3S 26 40W
Cando, U.S.A. 80 A5 48 32N 99 12W
Canea = Khaniá, Greece 23 D6 35 30N 24 4 E
Canelones, Uruguay 95 C4 34 32S 56 17W
Cañete, Chile 94 D1 37 50S 73 30W
Cañete, Peru 92 F3 13 8S 76 30W
Cangas de Narcea, Spain 19 A2 43 10N 6 32W
Canguaretama, Brazil 93 E11 6 20S 35 5W
Canguçu, Brazil 95 C5 31 22S 52 43W
Canguçu, Serra do, Brazil 95 C5 31 20S 52 40W
Cangzhou, China 34 E9 38 19N 116 52 E
Caniapiscau →, Canada 71 A6 56 40N 69 30W
Caniapiscau, Rés. de, Canada 71 B6 54 10N 69 55W
Canicattì, Italy 20 F5 37 21N 13 51 E
Canim Lake, Canada 72 C4 51 47N 120 54W
Canindeyu □, Paraguay 95 A5 24 10S 55 0W
Canisteo, U.S.A. 78 D7 42 16N 77 36W
Canisteo →, U.S.A. 78 D7 42 7N 77 8W
Cañitas, Mexico 86 C4 23 36N 102 43W
Çankırı, Turkey 25 F5 40 40N 33 37 E
Cankuzo, Burundi 54 C3 3 10S 30 31 E
Canmore, Canada 72 C5 51 7N 115 18W
Cann River, Australia 63 F4 37 35S 149 7 E
Canna, U.K. 12 D2 57 3N 6 33W
Cannanore, India 40 P9 11 53N 75 27 E
Cannes, France 18 E7 43 32N 7 1 E
Canning Town = Port Canning, India 43 H13 22 23N 88 40 E
Cannington, Canada 78 B5 44 20N 79 2W
Cannock, U.K. 11 E5 52 41N 2 1W
Cannon Ball →, U.S.A. 80 B4 46 20N 100 38W
Cannondale Mt., Australia 62 D4 25 13S 148 57 E
Cannonsville Reservoir, U.S.A. 79 D9 42 4N 75 22W
Cannonvale, Australia 62 C4 20 17S 148 43 E
Canoas, Brazil 95 B5 29 56S 51 11W
Canoe L., Canada 73 B7 55 10N 108 15W
Canon City, U.S.A. 80 F2 38 27N 105 14W
Canora, Canada 73 C8 51 40N 102 30W
Canowindra, Australia 63 E4 33 35S 148 38 E
Canso, Canada 71 C7 45 20N 61 0W
Cantabria □, Spain 19 A4 43 10N 4 0W
Cantabrian Mts. = Cantábrica, Cordillera, Spain 19 A3 43 0N 5 10W
Cantábrica, Cordillera, Spain 19 A3 43 0N 5 10W
Cantal, Plomb du, France 18 D5 45 3N 2 45 E
Canterbury, Australia 62 D3 25 23S 141 53 E
Canterbury, U.K. 11 F9 51 16N 1 6 E
Canterbury Bight, N.Z. 59 L3 44 16S 171 55 E
Canterbury Plains, N.Z. 59 K3 43 55S 171 22 E
Cantil, U.S.A. 85 K9 35 18N 117 58W
Canton = Guangzhou, China 33 D6 23 5N 113 10 E
Canton, Ga., U.S.A. 77 H3 34 14N 84 29W
Canton, Ill., U.S.A. 80 E9 40 33N 90 2W
Canton, Miss., U.S.A. 81 J9 32 37N 90 2W
Canton, Mo., U.S.A. 80 E9 40 8N 91 32W
Canton, N.Y., U.S.A. 79 B9 44 36N 75 10W
Canton, Ohio, U.S.A. 78 F3 40 48N 81 23W
Canton, Pa., U.S.A. 78 E8 41 39N 76 51W
Canton, S. Dak., U.S.A. 80 D6 43 18N 96 35W
Canton L., U.S.A. 81 G5 36 6N 98 35W
Canudos, Brazil 92 E7 7 13S 58 5W
Canumã →, Brazil 92 D7 3 55S 59 10W
Canutama, Brazil 92 E6 6 30S 64 20W
Canutillo, U.S.A. 83 L10 31 55N 106 36W
Canvey, U.K. 11 F8 51 31N 0 37 E
Canyon, U.S.A. 81 H4 34 59N 101 55W
Canyonlands Nat. Park, U.S.A. 83 G9 38 15N 110 0W
Canyonville, U.S.A. 82 E2 42 56N 123 17W

Cha-am, *Thailand* **38 F2** 12 48N 99 58 E
Cha Pa, *Vietnam* **38 A4** 22 20N 103 47 E
Chacabuco, *Argentina* **94 C3** 34 40S 60 27W
Chachapoyas, *Peru* **92 E3** 6 15S 77 50W
Chachoengsao, *Thailand* **38 F3** 13 42N 101 5 E
Chachran, *Pakistan* **40 E7** 28 55N 70 30 E
Chachro, *Pakistan* **42 G4** 25 5N 70 15 E
Chaco □, *Argentina* **94 B3** 26 30S 61 0W
Chaco □, *Paraguay* **94 B4** 26 0S 60 0W
Chaco →, *U.S.A.* **83 H9** 36 46N 108 39W
Chaco Austral, *S. Amer.* **96 B4** 27 0S 61 30W
Chaco Boreal, *S. Amer.* **92 H6** 22 0S 60 0W
Chaco Central, *S. Amer.* **96 A4** 24 0S 61 0W
Chacon, C., *U.S.A.* **72 C2** 54 42N 132 0W
Chad ■, *Africa* **51 F8** 15 0N 17 15 E
Chad, L. = Tchad, L., *Chad* **51 F8** 13 30N 14 30 E
Chadan, *Russia* **27 D10** 51 17N 91 35 E
Chadileuvú →, *Argentina* **94 D2** 37 46S 66 0W
Chadiza, *Zambia* **55 E3** 14 45S 32 27 E
Chadron, *U.S.A.* **80 D3** 42 50N 103 0W
Chadyr-Lunga = Ciadâr-Lunga, *Moldova* **17 E15** 46 3N 28 51 E
Chae Hom, *Thailand* **38 C2** 18 43N 99 35 E
Chaem →, *Thailand* **38 C2** 18 11N 98 38 E
Chaeryŏng, *N. Korea* **35 E13** 38 24N 125 36 E
Chagai Hills = Chāh Gay Hills, *Afghan.* **40 E3** 29 30N 64 0 E
Chagda, *Russia* **27 D14** 58 45N 130 38 E
Chaghcharān, *Afghan.* **40 B4** 34 31N 65 15 E
Chagos Arch., *Ind. Oc.* **29 K11** 6 0S 72 0 E
Chagrin Falls, *U.S.A.* **78 E3** 41 26N 81 24W
Chāh Ākhvor, *Iran* **45 C8** 32 41N 59 40 E
Chāh Bahar, *Iran* **45 E9** 25 20N 60 40 E
Chāh-e Kavīr, *Iran* **45 C8** 34 29N 56 52 E
Chāh Gay Hills, *Afghan.* **40 E3** 29 30N 64 0 E
Chahar Burjak, *Afghan.* **40 D3** 30 15N 62 0 E
Chahār Mahāll va Bakhtīarī □, *Iran* **45 C6** 32 0N 49 0 E
Chaibasa, *India* **41 H14** 22 42N 85 49 E
Chainat, *Thailand* **38 E3** 15 11N 100 8 E
Chaiya, *Thailand* **39 H2** 9 23N 99 14 E
Chaj Doab, *Pakistan* **42 C5** 32 15N 73 0 E
Chajari, *Argentina* **94 C4** 30 42S 58 0W
Chak Amru, *Pakistan* **42 C6** 32 22N 75 11 E
Chakar →, *Pakistan* **42 E3** 29 29N 68 2 E
Chakari, *Zimbabwe* **57 B4** 18 5S 29 51 E
Chake Chake, *Tanzania* **54 D4** 5 15S 39 45 E
Chakhānsūr, *Afghan.* **40 D3** 31 10N 62 0 E
Chakonipau, L., *Canada* **71 A6** 56 18N 68 30W
Chakradharpur, *India* **43 H11** 22 45N 85 40 E
Chakrata, *India* **42 D7** 30 42N 77 51 E
Chakwal, *Pakistan* **42 C5** 32 56N 72 53 E
Chala, *Peru* **92 G4** 15 48S 74 20W
Chalchihuites, *Mexico* **86 C4** 23 29N 103 53W
Chalcis = Khalkis, *Greece* **21 E10** 38 27N 23 42 E
Chaleur B., *Canada* **71 C6** 47 55N 65 30W
Chalfant, *U.S.A.* **84 H8** 37 32N 118 21W
Chalhuanca, *Peru* **92 F4** 14 15S 73 15W
Chalisgaon, *India* **40 J9** 20 30N 75 10 E
Chalk River, *Canada* **70 C4** 46 1N 77 27W
Chalky Inlet, *N.Z.* **59 M1** 46 3S 166 31 E
Challapata, *Bolivia* **92 G5** 18 53S 66 50W
Challis, *U.S.A.* **82 D6** 44 30N 114 14W
Chalmette, *U.S.A.* **81 L10** 29 56N 89 58W
Chalon-sur-Saône, *France* **18 C6** 46 48N 4 50 E
Châlons-en-Champagne, *France* **18 B6** 48 58N 4 20 E
Chalyaphum, *Thailand* **38 E4** 15 48N 102 2 E
Cham, Cu Lao, *Vietnam* **38 E7** 15 57N 108 30 E
Chama, *U.S.A.* **83 H10** 36 54N 106 35W
Chamaicó, *Argentina* **94 D3** 35 3S 64 58W
Chaman, *Pakistan* **40 D5** 30 58N 66 25 E
Chamba, *India* **42 C7** 32 35N 76 10 E
Chamba, *Tanzania* **55 E4** 11 37S 37 0 E
Chambal →, *India* **43 F8** 26 29N 79 15 E
Chamberlain, *U.S.A.* **80 D5** 43 49N 99 20W
Chamberlain →, *Australia* **60 C4** 15 30S 127 54 E
Chamberlain L., *U.S.A.* **77 B11** 46 14N 69 19W
Chambers, *U.S.A.* **83 J9** 35 11N 109 26W
Chambersburg, *U.S.A.* **76 F7** 39 56N 77 40W
Chambéry, *France* **18 D6** 45 34N 5 55 E
Chambeshi →, *Zambia* **52 G6** 11 53S 29 48 E
Chambly, *Canada* **79 A11** 45 27N 73 17W
Chambord, *Canada* **71 C5** 48 25N 72 6W
Chamchamal, *Iraq* **44 C5** 35 32N 44 50 E
Chamela, *Mexico* **86 D3** 19 32N 105 5W
Chamical, *Argentina* **94 C2** 30 22S 66 27W
Chamkar Luong, *Cambodia* **39 G4** 11 0N 103 45 E
Chamoli, *India* **43 D8** 30 24N 79 21 E
Chamonix-Mont Blanc, *France* **18 D7** 45 55N 6 51 E
Chamouchouane →, *Canada* **70 C5** 48 37N 72 20W
Champa, *India* **43 H10** 22 2N 82 43 E
Champagne, *Canada* **72 A1** 60 49N 136 30W
Champagne, *France* **18 B6** 48 40N 4 20 E
Champaign, *U.S.A.* **76 E1** 40 7N 88 15W
Champassak, *Laos* **38 E5** 14 53N 105 52 E
Champawat, *India* **43 E9** 29 20N 80 6 E
Champdoré, L., *Canada* **71 A6** 55 55N 65 49W
Champion, *U.S.A.* **78 E4** 41 19N 80 51W
Champlain, *U.S.A.* **79 B11** 44 59N 73 27W
Champlain, L., *U.S.A.* **79 B11** 44 40N 73 20W
Champotón, *Mexico* **87 D6** 19 20N 90 50W
Champua, *India* **43 H11** 22 5N 85 40 E
Chana, *Thailand* **39 J3** 6 55N 100 44 E
Chañaral, *Chile* **94 B1** 26 23S 70 40W
Chanārān, *Iran* **45 B8** 36 39N 59 6 E
Chanasma, *India* **42 H5** 23 44N 72 5 E
Chanco, *Chile* **94 D1** 35 44S 72 32W
Chand, *India* **43 J8** 21 57N 79 7 E
Chandan, *India* **43 G12** 24 38N 86 40 E
Chandan Chauki, *India* **43 E9** 28 33N 80 47 E
Chandannagar, *India* **43 H13** 22 52N 88 24 E
Chandausi, *India* **43 E8** 28 27N 78 49 E
Chandeleur Is., *U.S.A.* **81 L10** 29 55N 88 57W
Chandeleur Sd., *U.S.A.* **81 L10** 29 55N 89 0W
Chandigarh, *India* **42 D7** 30 43N 76 47 E
Chandil, *India* **43 H12** 22 58N 86 3 E
Chandler, *Australia* **63 D1** 27 0S 133 19 E
Chandler, *Canada* **71 C7** 48 18N 64 46W
Chandler, *Ariz., U.S.A.* **83 K8** 33 18N 111 50W
Chandler, *Okla., U.S.A.* **81 H6** 35 42N 96 53W
Chandod, *India* **42 J5** 21 59N 73 28 E
Chandpur, *Bangla.* **41 H17** 23 8N 90 45 E
Chandrapur, *India* **40 K11** 19 57N 79 25 E
Chānf, *Iran* **45 E9** 26 38N 60 29 E
Chang, *Pakistan* **42 F3** 26 59N 68 30 E
Chang, Ko, *Thailand* **39 F4** 12 0N 102 23 E
Ch'ang Chiang = Chang Jiang →, *China* **33 C7** 31 48N 121 10 E
Chang Jiang →, *China* **33 C7** 31 48N 121 10 E
Changa, *India* **43 C7** 33 53N 77 35 E
Changanacheri, *India* **40 Q10** 9 25N 76 31 E
Changane →, *Mozam.* **57 C5** 24 30S 33 30 E
Changbai, *China* **35 D15** 41 25N 128 5 E
Changbai Shan, *China* **35 C15** 42 20N 129 0 E
Changchiak'ou = Zhangjiakou, *China* **34 D8** 40 48N 114 55 E
Ch'angchou = Changzhou, *China* **33 C6** 31 47N 119 58 E
Changchun, *China* **35 C13** 43 57N 125 17 E
Changchunling, *China* **35 B13** 45 18N 125 27 E
Changde, *China* **33 D6** 29 4N 111 35 E
Changdo-ri, *N. Korea* **35 E14** 38 30N 127 40 E
Changhai = Shanghai, *China* **33 C7** 31 15N 121 26 E
Changhua, *Taiwan* **33 D7** 24 2N 120 30 E
Changhŭng, *S. Korea* **35 G14** 34 41N 126 52 E
Changhŭngni, *N. Korea* **35 D15** 40 24N 128 19 E
Changjiang, *China* **38 C7** 19 20N 108 55 E
Changjin, *N. Korea* **35 D14** 40 23N 127 15 E
Changjin-chŏsuji, *N. Korea* **35 D14** 40 30N 127 15 E
Changli, *China* **35 E10** 39 40N 119 13 E
Changling, *China* **35 B12** 44 20N 123 58 E
Changlun, *Malaysia* **39 J3** 6 25N 100 26 E
Changping, *China* **34 D9** 40 14N 116 12 E
Changsha, *China* **33 D6** 28 12N 113 0 E
Changwu, *China* **34 G4** 35 10N 107 45 E
Changyi, *China* **35 F10** 36 40N 119 30 E
Changyŏn, *N. Korea* **35 E13** 38 15N 125 6 E
Changyuan, *China* **34 G8** 35 15N 114 42 E
Changzhi, *China* **34 F7** 36 10N 113 6 E
Changzhou, *China* **33 C6** 31 47N 119 58 E
Chanhanga, *Angola* **56 B1** 16 0S 14 8 E
Channapatna, *India* **40 N10** 12 40N 77 15 E
Channel Is., *U.K.* **11 H5** 49 19N 2 24W
Channel Is., *U.S.A.* **85 M7** 33 40N 119 15W
Channel Islands Nat. Park, *U.S.A.* **85 M8** 33 30N 119 0W
Channel-Port aux Basques, *Canada* **71 C8** 47 30N 59 9W
Channel Tunnel, *Europe* **11 F9** 51 0N 1 30 E
Channing, *U.S.A.* **81 H3** 35 41N 102 20W
Chantada, *Spain* **19 A2** 42 36N 7 46W
Chanthaburi, *Thailand* **38 F4** 12 38N 102 12 E
Chantrey Inlet, *Canada* **68 B10** 67 48N 96 20W
Chanute, *U.S.A.* **81 G7** 37 41N 95 27W
Chao Phraya →, *Thailand* **38 F3** 13 32N 100 36 E
Chao Phraya Lowlands, *Thailand* **38 E3** 15 30N 100 0 E
Chaocheng, *China* **34 F8** 36 4N 115 37 E
Chaoyang, *China* **35 D11** 41 35N 120 22 E
Chaozhou, *China* **33 D6** 23 42N 116 32 E
Chapais, *Canada* **70 C5** 49 47N 74 51W
Chapala, *Mozam.* **55 F4** 15 50S 37 35 E
Chapala, L. de, *Mexico* **86 C4** 20 10N 103 20W
Chapayev, *Kazakstan* **25 D9** 50 25N 51 10 E
Chapayevsk, *Russia* **24 D8** 53 0N 49 40 E
Chapecó, *Brazil* **95 B5** 27 14S 52 41W
Chapel Hill, *U.S.A.* **77 H6** 35 55N 79 4W
Chapleau, *Canada* **70 C3** 47 50N 83 24W
Chaplin, *Canada* **73 C7** 50 28N 106 40W
Chaplin L., *Canada* **73 C7** 50 22N 106 36W
Chappell, *U.S.A.* **80 E3** 41 6N 102 28W
Chapra = Chhapra, *India* **43 G11** 25 48N 84 44 E
Chara, *Russia* **27 D12** 56 54N 118 20 E
Charadai, *Argentina* **94 B4** 27 35S 59 55W
Charagua, *Bolivia* **92 G6** 19 45S 63 10W
Charambirá, Punta, *Colombia* **92 C3** 4 16N 77 32W
Charaña, *Bolivia* **92 G5** 17 30S 69 25W
Charanwala, *India* **42 F5** 27 51N 72 10 E
Charata, *Argentina* **94 B3** 27 13S 61 14W
Charcas, *Mexico* **86 C4** 23 10N 101 20W
Chard, *U.K.* **11 G5** 50 52N 2 58W
Chardon, *U.S.A.* **78 E3** 41 35N 81 12W
Chardzhou = Chärjew, *Turkmenistan* **26 F7** 39 6N 63 34 E
Charente →, *France* **18 D3** 45 57N 1 5W
Chari →, *Chad* **51 F8** 12 58N 14 31 E
Chārīkār, *Afghan.* **40 B6** 35 0N 69 10 E
Chariton →, *U.S.A.* **80 F8** 39 19N 92 58W
Chärjew, *Turkmenistan* **26 F7** 39 6N 63 34 E
Charkhari, *India* **43 G8** 25 24N 79 45 E
Charkhi Dadri, *India* **42 E7** 28 37N 76 17 E
Charleroi, *Belgium* **15 D4** 50 24N 4 27 E
Charleroi, *U.S.A.* **78 F5** 40 9N 79 57W
Charles, C., *U.S.A.* **76 G8** 37 7N 75 58W
Charles City, *U.S.A.* **80 D8** 43 4N 92 41W
Charles L., *Canada* **73 B6** 59 50N 110 33W
Charles Town, *U.S.A.* **76 F7** 39 17N 77 52W
Charleston, *Ill., U.S.A.* **76 F1** 39 30N 88 10W
Charleston, *Miss., U.S.A.* **81 H9** 34 1N 90 4W
Charleston, *Mo., U.S.A.* **81 G10** 36 55N 89 21W
Charleston, *S.C., U.S.A.* **77 J6** 32 46N 79 56W
Charleston, *W. Va., U.S.A.* **76 F5** 38 21N 81 38W
Charleston L., *Canada* **79 B9** 44 32N 76 0W
Charleston Peak, *U.S.A.* **85 J11** 36 16N 115 42W
Charlestown, *Ireland* **13 C3** 53 58N 8 48W
Charlestown, *S. Africa* **57 D4** 27 26S 29 53 E
Charlestown, *Ind., U.S.A.* **76 F3** 38 27N 85 40W
Charlestown, *N.H., U.S.A.* **79 C12** 43 14N 72 25W
Charleville = Rath Luirc, *Ireland* **13 D3** 52 21N 8 40W
Charleville, *Australia* **63 D4** 26 24S 146 15 E
Charleville-Mézières, *France* **18 B6** 49 44N 4 40 E
Charlevoix, *U.S.A.* **76 C3** 45 19N 85 16W
Charlotte, *Mich., U.S.A.* **76 D3** 42 34N 84 50W
Charlotte, *N.C., U.S.A.* **77 H5** 35 13N 80 51W
Charlotte, *Vt., U.S.A.* **79 B11** 44 19N 73 14W
Charlotte Amalie, *U.S. Virgin Is.* **89 C7** 18 21N 64 56W
Charlotte Harbor, *U.S.A.* **77 M4** 26 50N 82 10W
Charlotte L., *Canada* **72 C3** 52 12N 125 19W
Charlottesville, *U.S.A.* **76 F6** 38 2N 78 30W
Charlottetown, *Nfld., Canada* **71 B8** 52 46N 56 7W
Charlottetown, *P.E.I., Canada* **71 C7** 46 14N 63 8W
Charlton, *Australia* **63 F3** 36 16S 143 24 E
Charlton, *U.S.A.* **80 E8** 40 59N 93 20W
Charlton I., *Canada* **70 B4** 52 0N 79 20W
Charny, *Canada* **71 C5** 46 43N 71 15W
Charolles, *France* **18 C6** 46 27N 4 16 E
Charre, *Mozam.* **55 F4** 17 13S 35 10 E
Charsadda, *Pakistan* **42 B4** 34 7N 71 45 E
Charters Towers, *Australia* **62 C4** 20 5S 146 13 E
Chartres, *France* **18 B4** 48 29N 1 30 E
Chascomús, *Argentina* **94 D4** 35 30S 58 0W
Chasefu, *Zambia* **55 E3** 11 55S 33 8 E
Chashma Barrage, *Pakistan* **42 C4** 32 27N 71 20 E
Chāt, *Iran* **45 B7** 37 59N 55 16 E
Châteaubriant, *France* **18 C3** 47 43N 1 23W
Chateaugay, *U.S.A.* **79 B10** 44 56N 74 5W
Châteauguay, L., *Canada* **71 A5** 56 26N 70 3W
Châteaulin, *France* **18 B1** 48 11N 4 8W
Châteauroux, *France* **18 C4** 46 50N 1 40 E
Châtellerault, *France* **18 C4** 46 50N 0 30 E
Chatham = Miramichi, *Canada* **71 C6** 47 2N 65 28W
Chatham, *Canada* **78 D2** 42 24N 82 11W
Chatham, *U.K.* **11 F8** 51 22N 0 32 E
Chatham, *U.S.A.* **79 D11** 42 21N 73 36W
Chatham Is., *Pac. Oc.* **64 M10** 44 0S 176 40W
Chatmohar, *Bangla.* **43 G13** 24 15N 89 15 E
Chatra, *India* **43 G11** 24 12N 84 56 E
Chatrapur, *India* **41 K14** 19 22N 85 2 E
Chats, L. des, *Canada* **79 A8** 45 30N 76 20W
Chatsu, *India* **42 F6** 26 36N 75 57 E
Chatsworth, *Canada* **78 B4** 44 27N 80 54W
Chatsworth, *Zimbabwe* **55 F3** 19 38S 31 13 E
Chattahoochee, *U.S.A.* **77 K3** 30 42N 84 51W
Chattahoochee →, *U.S.A.* **77 K3** 30 54N 84 57W
Chattanooga, *U.S.A.* **77 H3** 35 3N 85 19W
Chatteris, *U.K.* **11 E8** 52 28N 0 2 E
Chaturat, *Thailand* **38 E3** 15 40N 101 51 E
Chau Doc, *Vietnam* **39 G5** 10 42N 105 7 E
Chaukan Pass, *Burma* **41 F20** 27 0N 97 15 E
Chaumont, *France* **18 B6** 48 7N 5 8 E
Chaumont, *U.S.A.* **79 B8** 44 4N 76 8W
Chautauqua L., *U.S.A.* **78 D5** 42 10N 79 24W
Chauvin, *Canada* **73 C6** 52 45N 110 10W
Chaves, *Brazil* **93 D9** 0 15S 49 55W
Chaves, *Portugal* **19 B2** 41 45N 7 32W
Chawang, *Thailand* **39 H2** 8 25N 99 30 E
Chaykovskiy, *Russia* **24 C9** 56 47N 54 9 E
Chazy, *U.S.A.* **79 B11** 44 53N 73 26W
Cheb, *Czech Rep.* **16 C7** 50 9N 12 28 E
Cheboksary, *Russia* **24 C8** 56 8N 47 12 E
Cheboygan, *U.S.A.* **76 C3** 45 39N 84 29W
Chech, Erg, *Africa* **50 D5** 25 0N 2 15W
Chechenia □, *Russia* **25 F8** 43 30N 45 29 E
Checheno-Ingush Republic = Chechenia □, *Russia* **25 F8** 43 30N 45 29 E
Chechnya = Chechenia □, *Russia* **25 F8** 43 30N 45 29 E
Chech'ŏn, *S. Korea* **35 F15** 37 8N 128 12 E
Checotah, *U.S.A.* **81 H7** 35 28N 95 31W
Chedabucto B., *Canada* **71 C7** 45 25N 61 8W
Cheduba I., *Burma* **41 K18** 18 45N 93 40 E
Cheepie, *Australia* **63 D4** 26 33S 145 1 E
Chegdomyn, *Russia* **27 D14** 51 7N 133 1 E
Chegga, *Mauritania* **50 C4** 25 27N 5 40W
Chegutu, *Zimbabwe* **55 F3** 18 10S 30 14 E
Chehalis, *U.S.A.* **84 D4** 46 40N 122 58W
Chehalis →, *U.S.A.* **84 D3** 46 57N 123 50W
Cheju do, *S. Korea* **35 H14** 33 29N 126 34 E
Chekiang = Zhejiang □, *China* **33 D7** 29 0N 120 0 E
Chela, Sa. da, *Angola* **56 B1** 16 20S 13 20 E
Chelan, *U.S.A.* **82 C4** 47 51N 120 1W
Chelan, L., *U.S.A.* **82 B3** 48 11N 120 30W
Cheleken, *Turkmenistan* **25 G9** 39 34N 53 16 E
Cheleken Yarymadasy, *Turkmenistan* **45 B7** 39 30N 53 15 E
Chelforó, *Argentina* **96 D3** 39 0S 66 33W
Chelkar = Shalqar, *Kazakstan* **26 E6** 47 48N 59 39 E
Chelkar Tengiz, Solonchak, *Kazakstan* **26 E7** 48 5N 63 7 E
Chełm, *Poland* **17 C12** 51 8N 23 30 E
Chełmno, *Poland* **17 B10** 53 20N 18 30 E
Chelmsford, *U.K.* **11 F8** 51 44N 0 29 E
Chelsea, *U.S.A.* **79 C12** 43 59N 72 27W
Cheltenham, *U.K.* **11 F5** 51 54N 2 4W
Chelyabinsk, *Russia* **26 D7** 55 10N 61 24 E
Chelyuskin, C., *Russia* **28 B14** 77 30N 103 0 E
Chemainus, *Canada* **84 B3** 48 55N 123 42W
Chemba, *Mozam.* **53 H6** 17 9S 34 53 E
Chemnitz, *Germany* **16 C7** 50 51N 12 54 E
Chemult, *U.S.A.* **82 E3** 43 14N 121 47W
Chen, Gora, *Russia* **27 C15** 65 16N 141 50 E
Chenab →, *Pakistan* **42 D4** 30 23N 71 2 E
Chenango Forks, *U.S.A.* **79 D9** 42 15N 75 51W
Cheney, *U.S.A.* **82 C5** 47 30N 117 35W
Cheng Xian, *China* **34 H3** 33 43N 105 42 E
Chengcheng, *China* **34 G5** 35 8N 109 56 E
Chengchou = Zhengzhou, *China* **34 G7** 34 45N 113 34 E
Chengde, *China* **35 D9** 40 59N 117 58 E
Chengdu, *China* **32 C5** 30 38N 104 2 E
Chenggu, *China* **34 H4** 33 10N 107 21 E
Chengjiang, *China* **32 D5** 24 39N 103 0 E
Ch'engmai, *China* **38 C7** 19 50N 109 58 E
Ch'engtu = Chengdu, *China* **32 C5** 30 38N 104 2 E
Chengwu, *China* **34 G8** 34 58N 115 50 E
Chengyang, *China* **35 F11** 36 18N 120 21 E
Chenjiagang, *China* **35 G10** 34 23N 119 47 E
Chenkán, *Mexico* **87 D6** 19 8N 90 58W
Chennai, *India* **40 N12** 13 8N 80 19 E
Cheo Reo, *Vietnam* **36 B3** 13 25N 108 28 E
Cheom Ksan, *Cambodia* **38 E5** 14 13N 104 56 E
Chepén, *Peru* **92 E3** 7 15S 79 23W
Chepes, *Argentina* **94 C2** 31 20S 66 35W
Chepo, *Panama* **88 E4** 9 10N 79 6W
Chepstow, *U.K.* **11 F5** 51 38N 2 41W
Cheptulil, Mt., *Kenya* **54 B4** 1 25N 35 35 E
Chequamegon B., *U.S.A.* **80 B9** 46 40N 90 30W
Cher →, *France* **18 C4** 47 21N 0 29 E
Cheraw, *U.S.A.* **77 H6** 34 42N 79 53W
Cherbourg, *France* **18 B3** 49 39N 1 40W
Cherdyn, *Russia* **24 B10** 60 24N 56 29 E
Cheremkhovo, *Russia* **27 D11** 53 8N 103 1 E
Cherepanovo, *Russia* **26 D9** 54 15N 83 30 E
Cherepovets, *Russia* **24 C6** 59 5N 37 55 E
Chergui, Chott ech, *Algeria* **50 B6** 34 21N 0 25 E
Cherikov = Cherykaw, *Belarus* **17 B16** 53 32N 31 20 E
Cherkasy, *Ukraine* **25 E5** 49 27N 32 4 E
Cherkessk, *Russia* **25 F7** 44 15N 42 5 E
Cherlak, *Russia* **26 D8** 54 15N 74 55 E
Chernaya, *Russia* **27 B9** 70 30N 89 10 E
Chernigov = Chernihiv, *Ukraine* **24 D5** 51 28N 31 20 E
Chernihiv, *Ukraine* **24 D5** 51 28N 31 20 E
Chernivtsi, *Ukraine* **17 D13** 48 15N 25 52 E
Chernobyl = Chornobyl, *Ukraine* **17 C16** 51 20N 30 15 E
Chernogorsk, *Russia* **27 D10** 53 49N 91 18 E
Chernovtsy = Chernivtsi, *Ukraine* **17 D13** 48 15N 25 52 E
Chernyakhovsk, *Russia* **9 J19** 54 36N 21 48 E
Chernysheyskiy, *Russia* **27 C12** 63 0N 112 30 E
Cherokee, *Iowa, U.S.A.* **80 D7** 42 45N 95 33W
Cherokee, *Okla., U.S.A.* **81 G5** 36 45N 98 21W
Cherokee Village, *U.S.A.* **81 G9** 36 17N 91 30W
Cherokees, Grand Lake O' The, *U.S.A.* **81 G7** 36 28N 95 2W
Cherrapunji, *India* **41 G17** 25 17N 91 47 E
Cherry Valley, *Calif., U.S.A.* **85 M10** 33 59N 116 57W
Cherry Valley, *N.Y., U.S.A.* **79 D10** 42 48N 74 45W
Cherskiy, *Russia* **27 C17** 68 45N 161 18 E
Cherskogo Khrebet, *Russia* **27 C15** 65 0N 143 0 E
Cherven, *Belarus* **17 B15** 53 45N 28 28 E
Chervonohrad, *Ukraine* **17 C13** 50 25N 24 10 E
Cherwell →, *U.K.* **11 F6** 51 44N 1 14W
Cherykaw, *Belarus* **17 B16** 53 32N 31 20 E
Chesapeake, *U.S.A.* **76 G7** 36 50N 76 17W
Chesapeake B., *U.S.A.* **76 G7** 38 0N 76 10W
Cheshire □, *U.K.* **10 D5** 53 14N 2 30W
Cheshskaya Guba, *Russia* **24 A8** 67 20N 47 0 E
Cheshunt, *U.K.* **11 F7** 51 43N 0 1W
Chesil Beach, *U.K.* **11 G5** 50 37N 2 33W
Chesley, *Canada* **78 B3** 44 17N 81 5W
Chester, *U.K.* **10 D5** 53 12N 2 53W
Chester, *Calif., U.S.A.* **82 F3** 40 19N 121 14W
Chester, *Ill., U.S.A.* **81 G10** 37 55N 89 49W
Chester, *Mont., U.S.A.* **82 B8** 48 31N 110 58W
Chester, *Pa., U.S.A.* **76 F8** 39 51N 75 22W
Chester, *S.C., U.S.A.* **77 H5** 34 43N 81 12W
Chester, *Vt., U.S.A.* **79 C12** 43 16N 72 36W
Chester, *W. Va., U.S.A.* **78 F4** 40 37N 80 34W
Chester-le-Street, *U.K.* **10 C6** 54 51N 1 34W
Chesterfield, *U.K.* **10 D6** 53 15N 1 25W
Chesterfield, Is., *N. Cal.* **64 J7** 19 52S 158 15 E
Chesterfield Inlet, *Canada* **68 B10** 63 30N 90 45W
Chesterton Ra., *Australia* **63 D4** 25 30S 147 27 E
Chestertown, *U.S.A.* **79 C11** 43 40N 73 48W
Chesterville, *Canada* **79 A9** 45 6N 75 14W
Chestnut Ridge, *U.S.A.* **78 F5** 40 20N 79 10W
Chesuncook L., *U.S.A.* **77 C11** 46 0N 69 21W
Chéticamp, *Canada* **71 C7** 46 37N 60 59W
Chetumal, *Mexico* **87 D7** 18 30N 88 20W
Chetumal, B. de, *Mexico* **87 D7** 18 40N 88 10W
Chetwynd, *Canada* **72 B4** 55 45N 121 36W
Cheviot, The, *U.K.* **10 B5** 55 29N 2 9W
Cheviot Hills, *U.K.* **10 B5** 55 20N 2 30W
Cheviot Ra., *Australia* **62 D3** 25 20S 143 45 E
Chew Bahir, *Ethiopia* **46 G2** 4 40N 36 50 E
Chewelah, *U.S.A.* **82 B5** 48 17N 117 43W
Cheyenne, *Okla., U.S.A.* **81 H5** 35 37N 99 40W
Cheyenne, *Wyo., U.S.A.* **80 E2** 41 8N 104 49W
Cheyenne →, *U.S.A.* **80 C4** 44 41N 101 18W
Cheyenne Wells, *U.S.A.* **80 F3** 38 49N 102 21W
Cheyne B., *Australia* **61 F2** 34 35S 118 50 E
Chhabra, *India* **42 G7** 24 40N 76 54 E
Chhaktala, *India* **42 H6** 22 6N 74 11 E
Chhapra, *India* **43 G11** 25 48N 84 44 E
Chhata, *India* **42 F7** 27 42N 77 30 E
Chhatarpur, *Jharkhand, India* **43 G11** 24 23N 84 11 E
Chhatarpur, *Mad. P., India* **43 G8** 24 55N 79 35 E
Chhattisgarh □, *India* **43 J10** 22 0N 82 0 E
Chhep, *Cambodia* **38 F5** 13 45N 105 24 E
Chhindwara, *Mad. P., India* **43 H8** 23 3N 79 29 E
Chhindwara, *Mad. P., India* **43 H8** 22 2N 78 59 E
Chhlong, *Cambodia* **39 F5** 12 15N 105 58 E
Chhota Tawa →, *India* **42 H7** 22 14N 76 36 E
Chhoti Kali Sindh →, *India* **42 G6** 24 2N 75 31 E
Chhuikhadan, *India* **43 J9** 21 32N 80 59 E
Chhuk, *Cambodia* **39 G5** 10 46N 104 28 E
Chi →, *Thailand* **38 E5** 15 11N 104 43 E
Chiai, *Taiwan* **33 D7** 23 29N 120 25 E
Chiamboni, *Somali Rep.* **52 E8** 1 39S 41 35 E
Chiamussu = Jiamusi, *China* **33 B8** 46 40N 130 26 E
Chiang Dao, *Thailand* **38 C2** 19 22N 98 58 E
Chiang Kham, *Thailand* **38 C3** 19 32N 100 18 E
Chiang Khan, *Thailand* **38 D3** 17 52N 101 36 E
Chiang Khong, *Thailand* **38 B3** 20 17N 100 24 E
Chiang Mai, *Thailand* **38 C2** 18 47N 98 59 E
Chiang Rai, *Thailand* **38 C2** 19 52N 99 50 E
Chiang Saen, *Thailand* **38 B3** 20 16N 100 5 E
Chiapa →, *Mexico* **87 D6** 16 42N 93 0W
Chiapa de Corzo, *Mexico* **87 D6** 16 42N 93 0W
Chiapas □, *Mexico* **87 D6** 17 0N 92 45W
Chiautla, *Mexico* **87 D5** 18 18N 98 34W
Chiávari, *Italy* **18 D8** 44 19N 9 19 E
Chiavenna, *Italy* **18 C8** 46 19N 9 24 E
Chiba, *Japan* **31 G10** 35 30N 140 7 E
Chiba □, *Japan* **31 G10** 35 30N 140 20 E
Chibabava, *Mozam.* **57 C5** 20 17S 33 35 E
Chibemba, *Cunene, Angola* **53 H2** 15 48S 14 8 E
Chibemba, *Huila, Angola* **56 B2** 16 20S 15 20 E
Chibi, *Zimbabwe* **57 C5** 20 18S 30 25 E
Chibia, *Angola* **53 H2** 15 10S 13 42 E
Chibougamau, *Canada* **70 C5** 49 56N 74 24W
Chibougamau, L., *Canada* **70 C5** 49 50N 74 20W
Chibuto, *Mozam.* **57 C5** 24 40S 33 33 E
Chic-Chocs, Mts., *Canada* **71 C6** 48 55N 66 0W
Chicacole = Srikakulam, *India* **41 K13** 18 14N 83 58 E
Chicago, *U.S.A.* **76 E2** 41 53N 87 38W
Chicago Heights, *U.S.A.* **76 E2** 41 30N 87 38W
Chichagof I., *U.S.A.* **68 C6** 57 30N 135 30W
Chichén-Itzá, *Mexico* **87 C7** 20 40N 88 36W
Chicheng, *China* **34 D8** 40 55N 115 55 E
Chichester, *U.K.* **11 G7** 50 50N 0 47W
Chichester Ra., *Australia* **60 D2** 22 12S 119 15 E
Chichibu, *Japan* **31 F9** 35 59N 139 10 E
Ch'ich'ihaerh = Qiqihar, *China* **27 E13** 47 26N 124 0 E
Chicholi, *India* **42 H8** 22 1N 77 40 E
Chickasha, *U.S.A.* **81 H6** 35 3N 97 58W
Chiclana de la Frontera, *Spain* **19 D2** 36 26N 6 9W
Chiclayo, *Peru* **92 E3** 6 42S 79 50W
Chico, *U.S.A.* **84 F5** 39 44N 121 50W
Chico →, *Chubut, Argentina* **96 E3** 44 0S 67 0W
Chico →, *Santa Cruz, Argentina* **96 G3** 50 0S 68 30W
Chicomo, *Mozam.* **57 C5** 24 31S 34 6 E
Chicontepec, *Mexico* **87 C5** 20 58N 98 10W
Chicopee, *U.S.A.* **79 D12** 42 9N 72 37W

Chicoutimi, *Canada* **71 C5** 48 28N 71 5W
Chicualacuala, *Mozam.* **57 C5** 22 6S 31 42 E
Chidambaram, *India* **40 P11** 11 20N 79 45 E
Chidenguele, *Mozam.* **57 C5** 24 55S 34 11 E
Chidley, C., *Canada* **69 B13** 60 23N 64 26W
Chiducuane, *Mozam.* **57 C5** 24 35S 34 25 E
Chiede, *Angola* **56 B2** 17 15S 16 22 E
Chiefs Pt., *Canada* **78 B3** 44 41N 81 18W
Chiem Hoa, *Vietnam* **38 A5** 22 12N 105 17 E
Chiemsee, *Germany* **16 E7** 47 53N 12 28 E
Chiengi, *Zambia* **55 D2** 8 45S 29 10 E
Chiengmai = Chiang Mai, *Thailand* **38 C2** 18 47N 98 59 E
Chiese →, *Italy* **18 D9** 45 8N 10 25 E
Chieti, *Italy* **20 C6** 42 21N 14 10 E
Chifeng, *China* **35 C10** 42 18N 118 58 E
Chignecto B., *Canada* **71 C7** 45 30N 64 40W
Chiguana, *Bolivia* **94 A2** 21 0S 67 58W
Chigwell, *U.K.* **11 F8** 51 37N 0 5 E
Chiha-ri, *N. Korea* **35 E14** 38 40N 126 30 E
Chihli, G. of = Bo Hai, *China* **35 E10** 39 0N 119 0 E
Chihuahua, *Mexico* **86 B3** 28 40N 106 3W
Chihuahua □, *Mexico* **86 B3** 28 40N 106 3W
Chiili = Shīeli, *Kazakstan* **26 E7** 44 20N 66 15 E
Chik Bollapur, *India* **40 N10** 13 25N 77 45 E
Chikmagalur, *India* **40 N9** 13 15N 75 45 E
Chikwawa, *Malawi* **55 F3** 16 2S 34 50 E
Chilac, *Mexico* **87 D5** 18 20N 97 24W
Chilam Chavki, *Pakistan* **43 B6** 35 5N 75 5 E
Chilanga, *Zambia* **55 F2** 15 33S 28 16 E
Chilapa, *Mexico* **87 D5** 17 40N 99 11W
Chilas, *Pakistan* **43 B6** 35 25N 74 5 E
Chilaw, *Sri Lanka* **40 R11** 7 30N 79 50 E
Chilcotin →, *Canada* **72 C4** 51 44N 122 23W
Childers, *Australia* **63 D5** 25 15S 152 17 E
Childress, *U.S.A.* **81 H4** 34 25N 100 13W
Chile ■, *S. Amer.* **96 D2** 35 0S 72 0W
Chile Rise, *Pac. Oc.* **65 L18** 38 0S 92 0W
Chilecito, *Argentina* **94 B2** 29 10S 67 30W
Chilete, *Peru* **92 E3** 7 10S 78 50W
Chililabombwe, *Zambia* **55 E2** 12 18S 27 43 E
Chilin = Jilin, *China* **35 C14** 43 44N 126 30 E
Chilka L., *India* **41 K14** 19 40N 85 25 E
Chilko →, *Canada* **72 C4** 52 0N 123 40W
Chilko L., *Canada* **72 C4** 51 20N 124 10W
Chillagoe, *Australia* **62 B3** 17 7S 144 33 E
Chillán, *Chile* **94 D1** 36 40S 72 10W
Chillicothe, *Ill., U.S.A.* **80 E10** 40 55N 89 29W
Chillicothe, *Mo., U.S.A.* **80 F8** 39 48N 93 33W
Chillicothe, *Ohio, U.S.A.* **76 F4** 39 20N 82 59W
Chilliwack, *Canada* **72 D4** 49 10N 121 54W
Chilo, *India* **42 F5** 27 25N 73 32 E
Chiloane, I., *Mozam.* **57 C5** 20 40S 34 55 E
Chiloé, I. de, *Chile* **96 E2** 42 30S 73 50W
Chilpancingo, *Mexico* **87 D5** 17 30N 99 30W
Chiltern Hills, *U.K.* **11 F7** 51 40N 0 53W
Chilton, *U.S.A.* **76 C1** 44 2N 88 10W
Chilubi, *Zambia* **55 E2** 11 5S 29 58 E
Chilubula, *Zambia* **55 E3** 10 14S 30 51 E
Chilumba, *Malawi* **55 E3** 10 28S 34 12 E
Chilung, *Taiwan* **33 D7** 25 3N 121 45 E
Chilwa, L., *Malawi* **55 F4** 15 15S 35 40 E
Chimaltitán, *Mexico* **86 C4** 21 46N 103 50W
Chimán, *Panama* **88 E4** 8 45N 78 40W
Chimanimani, *Zimbabwe* **57 B5** 19 48S 32 52 E
Chimay, *Belgium* **15 D4** 50 3N 4 20 E
Chimayo, *U.S.A.* **83 H11** 36 0N 105 56W
Chimbay, *Uzbekistan* **26 E6** 42 57N 59 47 E
Chimborazo, *Ecuador* **92 D3** 1 29S 78 55W
Chimbote, *Peru* **92 E3** 9 0S 78 35W
Chimkent = Shymkent, *Kazakstan* **26 E7** 42 18N 69 36 E
Chimoio, *Mozam.* **55 F3** 19 4S 33 30 E
Chimpembe, *Zambia* **55 D2** 9 31S 29 33 E
Chin □, *Burma* **41 J18** 22 0N 93 0 E
Chin Ling Shan = Qinling Shandi, *China* **34 H5** 33 50N 108 10 E
China, *Mexico* **87 B5** 25 40N 99 20W
China ■, *Asia* **33 C6** 30 0N 110 0 E
China Lake, *U.S.A.* **85 K9** 35 44N 117 37W
Chinan = Jinan, *China* **34 F9** 36 38N 117 1 E
Chinandega, *Nic.* **88 D2** 12 35N 87 12W
Chinati Peak, *U.S.A.* **81 L2** 29 57N 104 29W
Chincha Alta, *Peru* **92 F3** 13 25S 76 7W
Chinchaga →, *Canada* **72 B5** 58 53N 118 20W
Chinchilla, *Australia* **63 D5** 26 45S 150 38 E
Chinchorro, Banco, *Mexico* **87 D7** 18 35N 87 20W
Chinchou = Jinzhou, *China* **35 D11** 41 5N 121 3 E
Chincoteague, *U.S.A.* **76 G8** 37 56N 75 23W
Chinde, *Mozam.* **55 F4** 18 35S 36 30 E
Chindo, *S. Korea* **35 G14** 34 28N 126 15 E
Chindwin →, *Burma* **41 J19** 21 26N 95 15 E
Chineni, *India* **43 C6** 33 2N 75 15 E
Chinga, *Mozam.* **55 F4** 15 13S 38 35 E
Chingola, *Zambia* **55 E2** 12 31S 27 53 E
Chingole, *Malawi* **55 E3** 13 4S 34 17 E
Ch'ingtao = Qingdao, *China* **35 F11** 36 5N 120 20 E
Chinguetti, *Mauritania* **50 D3** 20 25N 12 24W
Chingune, *Mozam.* **57 C5** 20 33S 34 58 E
Chinhae, *S. Korea* **35 G15** 35 9N 128 47 E
Chinhanguanine, *Mozam.* **57 D5** 25 21S 32 30 E
Chinhoyi, *Zimbabwe* **55 F3** 17 20S 30 8 E
Chini, *India* **42 D8** 31 32N 78 15 E
Chiniot, *Pakistan* **42 D5** 31 45N 73 0 E
Chínipas, *Mexico* **86 B3** 27 22N 108 32W
Chinji, *Pakistan* **42 C5** 32 42N 72 22 E
Chinju, *S. Korea* **35 G15** 35 12N 128 2 E
Chinle, *U.S.A.* **83 H9** 36 9N 109 33W
Chinnampo = Namp'o, *N. Korea* **35 E13** 38 52N 125 10 E
Chino, *Japan* **31 G9** 35 59N 138 9 E
Chino, *U.S.A.* **85 L9** 34 1N 117 41W
Chino Valley, *U.S.A.* **83 J7** 34 45N 112 27W
Chinon, *France* **18 C4** 47 10N 0 15 E
Chinook, *U.S.A.* **82 B9** 48 35N 109 14W
Chinsali, *Zambia* **55 E3** 10 30S 32 2 E
Chióggia, *Italy* **20 B5** 45 13N 12 17 E
Chíos = Khíos, *Greece* **21 E12** 38 27N 26 9 E
Chipata, *Zambia* **55 E3** 13 38S 32 28 E
Chipinge, *Zimbabwe* **55 G3** 20 13S 32 28 E
Chipley, *U.S.A.* **77 K3** 30 47N 85 32W
Chipman, *Canada* **71 C6** 46 6N 65 53W
Chipoka, *Malawi* **55 E3** 13 57S 34 28 E
Chippenham, *U.K.* **11 F5** 51 27N 2 6W
Chippewa →, *U.S.A.* **80 C8** 44 25N 92 5W
Chippewa Falls, *U.S.A.* **80 C9** 44 56N 91 24W
Chipping Norton, *U.K.* **11 F6** 51 56N 1 32W
Chiputneticook Lakes, *U.S.A.* **77 C11** 45 35N 67 35W
Chiquián, *Peru* **92 F3** 10 10S 77 0W
Chiquimula, *Guatemala* **88 D2** 14 51N 89 37W
Chiquinquira, *Colombia* **92 B4** 5 37N 73 50W
Chirala, *India* **40 M12** 15 50N 80 26 E
Chiramba, *Mozam.* **55 F3** 16 55S 34 39 E
Chirawa, *India* **42 E6** 28 14N 75 42 E
Chirchiq, *Uzbekistan* **26 E7** 41 29N 69 35 E
Chiredzi, *Zimbabwe* **57 C5** 21 0S 31 38 E
Chiricahua Peak, *U.S.A.* **83 L9** 31 51N 109 18W
Chiriquí, G. de, *Panama* **88 E3** 8 0N 82 10W
Chiriquí, L. de, *Panama* **88 E3** 9 10N 82 0W
Chirivira Falls, *Zimbabwe* **55 G3** 21 10S 32 12 E
Chirmiri, *India* **41 H13** 23 15N 82 20 E
Chirripó Grande, Cerro, *Costa Rica* **88 E3** 9 29N 83 29W
Chirundu, *Zimbabwe* **57 B4** 16 3S 28 50 E
Chisamba, *Zambia* **55 E2** 14 55S 28 20 E
Chisapani Garhi, *Nepal* **41 F14** 27 30N 84 2 E
Chisasibi, *Canada* **70 B4** 53 50N 79 0W
Chisholm, *Canada* **72 C6** 54 55N 114 10W
Chisholm, *U.S.A.* **80 B8** 47 29N 92 53W
Chishtian Mandi, *Pakistan* **42 E5** 29 50N 72 55 E
Chisimaio, *Somali Rep.* **49 G8** 0 22S 42 32 E
Chisimba Falls, *Zambia* **55 E3** 10 12S 30 56 E
Chişinău, *Moldova* **17 E15** 47 2N 28 50 E
Chisos Mts., *U.S.A.* **81 L3** 29 5N 103 15W
Chistopol, *Russia* **24 C9** 55 25N 50 38 E
Chita, *Russia* **27 D12** 52 0N 113 35 E
Chitipa, *Malawi* **55 D3** 9 41S 33 19 E
Chitose, *Japan* **30 C10** 42 49N 141 39 E
Chitral, *Pakistan* **40 B7** 35 50N 71 56 E
Chitré, *Panama* **88 E3** 7 59N 80 27W
Chittagong, *Bangla.* **41 H17** 22 19N 91 48 E
Chittagong □, *Bangla.* **41 G17** 24 5N 91 0 E
Chittaurgarh, *India* **42 G6** 24 52N 74 38 E
Chittoor, *India* **40 N11** 13 15N 79 5 E
Chitungwiza, *Zimbabwe* **55 F3** 18 0S 31 6 E
Chiusi, *Italy* **20 C4** 43 1N 11 57 E
Chivasso, *Italy* **18 D7** 45 11N 7 53 E
Chivhu, *Zimbabwe* **55 F3** 19 2S 30 52 E
Chivilcoy, *Argentina* **94 C4** 34 55S 60 0W
Chiwanda, *Tanzania* **55 E3** 11 23S 34 55 E
Chizarira, *Zimbabwe* **55 F2** 17 36S 27 45 E
Chizera, *Zambia* **55 E2** 13 10S 25 0 E
Chkalov = Orenburg, *Russia* **24 D10** 51 45N 55 6 E
Chloride, *U.S.A.* **85 K12** 35 25N 114 12W
Cho Bo, *Vietnam* **38 B5** 20 46N 105 10 E
Cho-do, *N. Korea* **35 E13** 38 30N 124 40 E
Cho Phuoc Hai, *Vietnam* **39 G6** 10 26N 107 18 E
Choba, *Kenya* **54 B4** 2 30N 38 5 E
Choch'iwŏn, *S. Korea* **35 F14** 36 37N 127 18 E
Chocolate Mts., *U.S.A.* **85 M11** 33 15N 115 15W
Choctawhatchee →, *U.S.A.* **77 K3** 30 25N 86 8W
Choele Choel, *Argentina* **96 D3** 39 11S 65 40W
Choix, *Mexico* **86 B3** 26 40N 108 23W
Chojnice, *Poland* **17 B9** 53 42N 17 32 E
Chōkai-San, *Japan* **30 E10** 39 6N 140 3 E
Choke Canyon L., *U.S.A.* **81 L5** 28 30N 98 20W
Chokurdakh, *Russia* **27 B15** 70 38N 147 55 E
Cholame, *U.S.A.* **84 K6** 35 44N 120 18W
Cholet, *France* **18 C3** 47 4N 0 52W
Cholguan, *Chile* **94 D1** 37 10S 72 3W
Choluteca, *Honduras* **88 D2** 13 20N 87 14W
Choluteca →, *Honduras* **88 D2** 13 0N 87 20W
Chom Bung, *Thailand* **38 F2** 13 37N 99 36 E
Chom Thong, *Thailand* **38 C2** 18 25N 98 41 E
Choma, *Zambia* **55 F2** 16 48S 26 59 E
Chomun, *India* **42 F6** 27 15N 75 40 E
Chomutov, *Czech Rep.* **16 C7** 50 28N 13 23 E
Chon Buri, *Thailand* **38 F3** 13 21N 101 1 E
Chon Thanh, *Vietnam* **39 G6** 11 24N 106 36 E
Ch'onan, *S. Korea* **35 F14** 36 48N 127 9 E
Chone, *Ecuador* **92 D3** 0 40S 80 0W
Chong Kai, *Cambodia* **38 F4** 13 57N 103 35 E
Chong Mek, *Thailand* **38 E5** 15 10N 105 27 E
Chŏngdo, *S. Korea* **35 G15** 35 38N 128 42 E
Chŏngha, *S. Korea* **35 F15** 36 12N 129 21 E
Chŏngjin, *N. Korea* **35 D15** 41 47N 129 50 E
Chŏngju, *S. Korea* **35 F14** 36 39N 127 27 E
Chŏngju, *N. Korea* **35 E13** 39 40N 125 5 E
Chongli, *China* **34 D8** 40 58N 115 15 E
Chongqing, *China* **32 D5** 29 35N 106 25 E
Chongqing Shi □, *China* **32 C5** 30 0N 108 0 E
Chonguene, *Mozam.* **57 C5** 25 3S 33 49 E
Chŏngŭp, *S. Korea* **35 G14** 35 35N 126 50 E
Chŏnju, *S. Korea* **35 G14** 35 50N 127 4 E
Chonos, Arch. de los, *Chile* **96 F2** 45 0S 75 0W
Chop, *Ukraine* **17 D12** 48 26N 22 12 E
Chopim →, *Brazil* **95 B5** 25 35S 53 5W
Chor, *Pakistan* **42 G3** 25 31N 69 46 E
Chorbat La, *India* **43 B7** 34 42N 76 37 E
Chorley, *U.K.* **10 D5** 53 39N 2 38W
Chornobyl, *Ukraine* **17 C16** 51 20N 30 15 E
Chorolque, Cerro, *Bolivia* **94 A2** 20 59S 66 5W
Chorregon, *Australia* **62 C3** 22 40S 143 32 E
Chortkiv, *Ukraine* **17 D13** 49 2N 25 46 E
Ch'ŏrwŏn, *S. Korea* **35 E14** 38 15N 127 10 E
Chorzów, *Poland* **17 C10** 50 18N 18 57 E
Chos-Malal, *Argentina* **94 D1** 37 20S 70 15W
Ch'osan, *N. Korea* **35 D13** 40 50N 125 47 E
Choszczno, *Poland* **16 B8** 53 7N 15 25 E
Choteau, *U.S.A.* **82 C7** 47 49N 112 11W
Chotila, *India* **42 H4** 22 23N 71 15 E
Chotta Udepur, *India* **42 H6** 22 19N 74 1 E
Chowchilla, *U.S.A.* **84 H6** 37 7N 120 16W
Choybalsan, *Mongolia* **33 B6** 48 4N 114 30 E
Christchurch, *N.Z.* **59 K4** 43 33S 172 47 E
Christchurch, *U.K.* **11 G6** 50 44N 1 47W
Christian I., *Canada* **78 B4** 44 50N 80 12W
Christiana, *S. Africa* **56 D4** 27 52S 25 8 E
Christiansted, *U.S. Virgin Is.* **89 C7** 17 45N 64 42W
Christie B., *Canada* **73 A6** 62 32N 111 10W
Christina →, *Canada* **73 B6** 56 40N 111 3W
Christmas Cr. →, *Australia* **60 C4** 18 29S 125 23 E
Christmas I. = Kiritimati, *Kiribati* **65 G12** 1 58N 157 27W
Christmas I., *Ind. Oc.* **64 J2** 10 30S 105 40 E
Christopher L., *Australia* **61 D4** 24 49S 127 42 E
Chtimba, *Malawi* **55 E3** 10 35S 34 13 E
Chu = Shū, *Kazakstan* **26 E8** 43 36N 73 42 E
Chu →, *Vietnam* **38 C5** 19 53N 105 45 E
Chu Lai, *Vietnam* **38 E7** 15 28N 108 45 E
Ch'uanchou = Quanzhou, *China* **33 D6** 24 55N 118 34 E
Chuankou, *China* **34 G6** 34 20N 110 59 E
Chubbuck, *U.S.A.* **82 E7** 42 55N 112 28W
Chūbu □, *Japan* **31 F8** 36 45N 137 30 E
Chubut →, *Argentina* **96 E3** 43 20S 65 5W
Chuchi L., *Canada* **72 B4** 55 12N 124 30W
Chuda, *India* **42 H4** 22 29N 71 41 E
Chudskoye, Ozero, *Russia* **9 G22** 58 13N 27 30 E
Chūgoku □, *Japan* **31 G6** 35 0N 133 0 E
Chūgoku-Sanchi, *Japan* **31 G6** 35 0N 133 0 E
Chugwater, *U.S.A.* **80 E2** 41 46N 104 50W
Chukchi Sea, *Russia* **27 C19** 68 0N 175 0W
Chukotskoye Nagorye, *Russia* **27 C18** 68 0N 175 0 E
Chula Vista, *U.S.A.* **85 N9** 32 39N 117 5W
Chulucanas, *Peru* **92 E2** 5 8S 80 10W
Chulym →, *Russia* **26 D9** 57 43N 83 51 E
Chum Phae, *Thailand* **38 D4** 16 40N 102 6 E
Chum Saeng, *Thailand* **38 E3** 15 55N 100 15 E
Chumar, *India* **43 C8** 32 40N 78 35 E
Chumbicha, *Argentina* **94 B2** 29 0S 66 10W
Chumikan, *Russia* **27 D14** 54 40N 135 10 E
Chumphon, *Thailand* **39 G2** 10 35N 99 14 E
Chumuare, *Mozam.* **55 E3** 14 31S 31 50 E
Chumunjin, *S. Korea* **35 F15** 37 55N 128 54 E
Chuna →, *Russia* **27 D10** 57 47N 94 37 E
Ch'unch'ŏn, *S. Korea* **35 F14** 37 58N 127 44 E
Chunchura, *India* **43 H13** 22 53N 88 27 E
Chunga, *Zambia* **55 F2** 15 0S 26 2 E
Chunggang-ŭp, *N. Korea* **35 D14** 41 48N 126 48 E
Chunghwa, *N. Korea* **35 E13** 38 52N 125 47 E
Ch'ungju, *S. Korea* **35 F14** 36 58N 127 58 E
Chungking = Chongqing, *China* **32 D5** 29 35N 106 25 E
Ch'ungmu, *S. Korea* **35 G15** 34 50N 128 20 E
Chungt'iaoshan = Zhongtiao Shan, *China* **34 G6** 35 0N 111 10 E
Chunian, *Pakistan* **42 D6** 30 57N 74 0 E
Chunya, *Tanzania* **55 D3** 8 30S 33 27 E
Chunyang, *China* **35 C15** 43 38N 129 23 E
Chuquibamba, *Peru* **92 G4** 15 47S 72 44W
Chuquicamata, *Chile* **94 A2** 22 15S 69 0W
Chur, *Switz.* **18 C8** 46 52N 9 32 E
Churachandpur, *India* **41 G18** 24 20N 93 40 E
Churchill, *Canada* **73 B10** 58 47N 94 11W
Churchill →, *Man., Canada* **73 B10** 58 47N 94 12W
Churchill →, *Nfld., Canada* **71 B7** 53 19N 60 10W
Churchill, C., *Canada* **73 B10** 58 46N 93 12W
Churchill Falls, *Canada* **71 B7** 53 36N 64 19W
Churchill L., *Canada* **73 B7** 55 55N 108 20W
Churchill Pk., *Canada* **72 B3** 58 10N 125 10W
Churki, *India* **43 H10** 23 50N 83 12 E
Churu, *India* **42 E6** 28 20N 74 50 E
Churún Merú = Angel Falls, *Venezuela* **92 B6** 5 57N 62 30W
Chushal, *India* **43 C8** 33 40N 78 40 E
Chuska Mts., *U.S.A.* **83 H9** 36 15N 108 50W
Chusovoy, *Russia* **24 C10** 58 22N 57 50 E
Chute-aux-Outardes, *Canada* **71 C6** 49 7N 68 24W
Chuuronjang, *N. Korea* **35 D15** 41 35N 129 40 E
Chuvash Republic = Chuvashia □, *Russia* **24 C8** 55 30N 47 0 E
Chuvashia □, *Russia* **24 C8** 55 30N 47 0 E
Chuwārtah, *Iraq* **44 C5** 35 43N 45 34 E
Chūy = Shū →, *Kazakstan* **28 E10** 45 0N 67 44 E
Chuy, *Uruguay* **95 C5** 33 41S 53 27W
Ci Xian, *China* **34 F8** 36 20N 114 25 E
Ciadâr-Lunga, *Moldova* **17 E15** 46 3N 28 51 E
Ciamis, *Indonesia* **37 G13** 7 20S 108 21 E
Cianjur, *Indonesia* **37 G12** 6 49S 107 8 E
Cianorte, *Brazil* **95 A5** 23 37S 52 37W
Cibola, *U.S.A.* **85 M12** 33 17N 114 42W
Cicero, *U.S.A.* **76 E2** 41 51N 87 45W
Ciechanów, *Poland* **17 B11** 52 52N 20 38 E
Ciego de Avila, *Cuba* **88 B4** 21 50N 78 50W
Ciénaga, *Colombia* **92 A4** 11 1N 74 15W
Cienfuegos, *Cuba* **88 B3** 22 10N 80 30W
Cieszyn, *Poland* **17 D10** 49 45N 18 35 E
Cieza, *Spain* **19 C5** 38 17N 1 23W
Cihuatlán, *Mexico* **86 D4** 19 14N 104 35W
Cijara, Embalse de, *Spain* **19 C3** 39 18N 4 52W
Cijulang, *Indonesia* **37 G13** 7 42S 108 27 E
Cilacap, *Indonesia* **37 G13** 7 43S 109 0 E
Cill Chainnigh = Kilkenny, *Ireland* **13 D4** 52 39N 7 15W
Cilo Dağı, *Turkey* **25 G7** 37 28N 43 55 E
Cima, *U.S.A.* **85 K11** 35 14N 115 30W
Cimarron, *Kans., U.S.A.* **81 G4** 37 48N 100 21W
Cimarron, *N. Mex., U.S.A.* **81 G2** 36 31N 104 55W
Cimarron →, *U.S.A.* **81 G6** 36 10N 96 17W
Cimişlia, *Moldova* **17 E15** 46 34N 28 44 E
Cimone, Mte., *Italy* **20 B4** 44 12N 10 42 E
Cinca →, *Spain* **19 B6** 41 26N 0 21 E
Cincar, *Bos.-H.* **20 C7** 43 55N 17 5 E
Cincinnati, *U.S.A.* **76 F3** 39 6N 84 31W
Cincinnatus, *U.S.A.* **79 D9** 42 33N 75 54W
Çine, *Turkey* **21 F13** 37 37N 28 2 E
Ciney, *Belgium* **15 D5** 50 18N 5 5 E
Cinto, Mte., *France* **18 E8** 42 24N 8 54 E
Circle, *Alaska, U.S.A.* **68 B5** 65 50N 144 4W
Circle, *Mont., U.S.A.* **80 B2** 47 25N 105 35W
Circleville, *U.S.A.* **76 F4** 39 36N 82 57W
Cirebon, *Indonesia* **36 F3** 6 45S 108 32 E
Ciremai, *Indonesia* **37 G13** 6 55S 108 27 E
Cirencester, *U.K.* **11 F6** 51 43N 1 57W
Cirium, *Cyprus* **23 E11** 34 40N 32 53 E
Cisco, *U.S.A.* **81 J5** 32 23N 98 59W
Citlaltépetl, *Mexico* **87 D5** 19 0N 97 20W
Citrus Heights, *U.S.A.* **84 G5** 38 42N 121 17W
Citrusdal, *S. Africa* **56 E2** 32 35S 19 0 E
Città di Castello, *Italy* **20 C5** 43 27N 12 14 E
Ciudad Altamirano, *Mexico* **86 D4** 18 20N 100 40W
Ciudad Bolívar, *Venezuela* **92 B6** 8 5N 63 36W
Ciudad Camargo, *Mexico* **86 B3** 27 41N 105 10W
Ciudad de Valles, *Mexico* **87 C5** 22 0N 99 0W
Ciudad del Carmen, *Mexico* **87 D6** 18 38N 91 50W
Ciudad del Este, *Paraguay* **95 B5** 25 30S 54 50W
Ciudad Delicias = Delicias, *Mexico* **86 B3** 28 10N 105 30W
Ciudad Guayana, *Venezuela* **92 B6** 8 0N 62 30W
Ciudad Guerrero, *Mexico* **86 B3** 28 33N 107 28W
Ciudad Guzmán, *Mexico* **86 D4** 19 40N 103 30W
Ciudad Juárez, *Mexico* **86 A3** 31 40N 106 28W
Ciudad Madero, *Mexico* **87 C5** 22 19N 97 50W
Ciudad Mante, *Mexico* **87 C5** 22 50N 99 0W
Ciudad Obregón, *Mexico* **86 B3** 27 28N 109 59W
Ciudad Real, *Spain* **19 C4** 38 59N 3 55W
Ciudad Rodrigo, *Spain* **19 B2** 40 35N 6 32W
Ciudad Trujillo = Santo Domingo, *Dom. Rep.* **89 C6** 18 30N 69 59W
Ciudad Victoria, *Mexico* **87 C5** 23 41N 99 9W
Ciudadela, *Spain* **22 B10** 40 0N 3 50 E
Civitanova Marche, *Italy* **20 C5** 43 18N 13 44 E
Civitavécchia, *Italy* **20 C4** 42 6N 11 48 E
Cizre, *Turkey* **25 G7** 37 19N 42 10 E
Clackmannanshire □, *U.K.* **12 E5** 56 10N 3 43W
Clacton-on-Sea, *U.K.* **11 F9** 51 47N 1 11 E
Claire, L., *Canada* **72 B6** 58 35N 112 5W
Clairton, *U.S.A.* **78 F5** 40 18N 79 53W
Clallam Bay, *U.S.A.* **84 B2** 48 15N 124 16W
Clanton, *U.S.A.* **77 J2** 32 51N 86 38W
Clanwilliam, *S. Africa* **56 E2** 32 11S 18 52 E
Clara, *Ireland* **13 C4** 53 21N 7 37W
Claraville, *U.S.A.* **85 K8** 35 24N 118 20W
Clare, *Australia* **63 E2** 33 50S 138 37 E
Clare, *U.S.A.* **76 D3** 43 49N 84 46W
Clare □, *Ireland* **13 D3** 52 45N 9 0W
Clare →, *Ireland* **13 C2** 53 20N 9 2W
Clare I., *Ireland* **13 C1** 53 49N 10 0W
Claremont, *Calif., U.S.A.* **85 L9** 34 6N 117 43W
Claremont, *N.H., U.S.A.* **79 C12** 43 23N 72 20W
Claremont Pt., *Australia* **62 A3** 14 1S 143 41 E
Claremore, *U.S.A.* **81 G7** 36 19N 95 36W
Claremorris, *Ireland* **13 C3** 53 45N 9 0W
Clarence →, *Australia* **63 D5** 29 25S 153 22 E
Clarence →, *N.Z.* **59 K4** 42 10S 173 56 E
Clarence, I., *Chile* **96 G2** 54 0S 72 0W
Clarence I., *Antarctica* **5 C18** 61 10S 54 0W
Clarence Str., *Australia* **60 B5** 12 0S 131 0 E
Clarence Town, *Bahamas* **89 B5** 23 6N 74 59W
Clarendon, *Pa., U.S.A.* **78 E5** 41 47N 79 6W
Clarendon, *Tex., U.S.A.* **81 H4** 34 56N 100 53W
Clarenville, *Canada* **71 C9** 48 10N 54 1W
Claresholm, *Canada* **72 D6** 50 0N 113 33W
Clarie Coast, *Antarctica* **5 C9** 68 0S 135 0 E
Clarinda, *U.S.A.* **80 E7** 40 44N 95 2W
Clarion, *Iowa, U.S.A.* **80 D8** 42 44N 93 44W
Clarion, *Pa., U.S.A.* **78 E5** 41 13N 79 23W
Clarion →, *U.S.A.* **78 E5** 41 7N 79 41W
Clark, *U.S.A.* **80 C6** 44 53N 97 44W
Clark, Pt., *Canada* **78 B3** 44 4N 81 45W
Clark Fork, *U.S.A.* **82 B5** 48 9N 116 11W
Clark Fork →, *U.S.A.* **82 B5** 48 9N 116 15W
Clarkdale, *U.S.A.* **83 J7** 34 46N 112 3W
Clarke City, *Canada* **71 B6** 50 12N 66 38W
Clarke I., *Australia* **62 G4** 40 32S 148 10 E
Clarke Ra., *Australia* **62 C4** 20 40S 148 30 E
Clark's Fork →, *U.S.A.* **82 D9** 45 39N 108 43W
Clark's Harbour, *Canada* **71 D6** 43 25N 65 38W
Clarks Hill L., *U.S.A.* **77 J4** 33 40N 82 12W
Clarks Summit, *U.S.A.* **79 E9** 41 30N 75 42W
Clarksburg, *U.S.A.* **76 F5** 39 17N 80 30W
Clarksdale, *U.S.A.* **81 H9** 34 12N 90 35W
Clarksville, *Ark., U.S.A.* **81 H8** 35 28N 93 28W
Clarksville, *Tenn., U.S.A.* **77 G2** 36 32N 87 21W
Clarksville, *Tex., U.S.A.* **81 J7** 33 37N 95 3W
Clatskanie, *U.S.A.* **84 D3** 46 6N 123 12W
Claude, *U.S.A.* **81 H4** 35 7N 101 22W
Claveria, *Phil.* **37 A6** 18 37N 121 4 E
Clay, *U.S.A.* **84 G5** 38 17N 121 10W
Clay Center, *U.S.A.* **80 F6** 39 23N 97 8W
Claypool, *U.S.A.* **83 K8** 33 25N 110 51W
Claysburg, *U.S.A.* **78 F6** 40 17N 78 27W
Claysville, *U.S.A.* **78 F4** 40 7N 80 25W
Clayton, *N. Mex., U.S.A.* **81 G3** 36 27N 103 11W
Clayton, *N.Y., U.S.A.* **79 B8** 44 14N 76 5W
Clear, C., *Ireland* **13 E2** 51 25N 9 32W
Clear, L., *Canada* **78 A7** 45 26N 77 12W
Clear Hills, *Canada* **72 B5** 56 40N 119 30W
Clear I., *Ireland* **13 E2** 51 26N 9 30W
Clear L., *U.S.A.* **84 F4** 39 2N 122 47W
Clear Lake, *Iowa, U.S.A.* **80 D8** 43 8N 93 23W
Clear Lake, *S. Dak., U.S.A.* **80 C6** 44 45N 96 41W
Clear Lake Reservoir, *U.S.A.* **82 F3** 41 56N 121 5W
Clearfield, *Pa., U.S.A.* **78 E6** 41 2N 78 27W
Clearfield, *Utah, U.S.A.* **82 F8** 41 7N 112 2W
Clearlake, *U.S.A.* **82 G2** 38 57N 122 38W
Clearlake Highlands, *U.S.A.* **84 G4** 38 57N 122 38W
Clearwater, *Canada* **72 C4** 51 38N 120 2W
Clearwater, *U.S.A.* **77 M4** 27 58N 82 48W
Clearwater →, *Alta., Canada* **72 C6** 52 22N 114 57W
Clearwater →, *Alta., Canada* **73 B6** 56 44N 111 23W
Clearwater L., *Canada* **73 C9** 53 34N 99 49W
Clearwater Mts., *U.S.A.* **82 C6** 46 5N 115 20W
Clearwater Prov. Park, *Canada* **73 C8** 54 0N 101 0W
Clearwater River Prov. Park, *Canada* **73 B7** 56 55N 109 10W
Cleburne, *U.S.A.* **81 J6** 32 21N 97 23W
Clee Hills, *U.K.* **11 E5** 52 26N 2 35W
Cleethorpes, *U.K.* **10 D7** 53 33N 0 3W
Cleeve Cloud, *U.K.* **11 F6** 51 56N 2 0W
Clemson, *U.S.A.* **77 H4** 34 41N 82 50W
Clerke Reef, *Australia* **60 C2** 17 22S 119 20 E
Clermont, *Australia* **62 C4** 22 49S 147 39 E
Clermont, *U.S.A.* **77 L5** 28 33N 81 46W
Clermont-Ferrand, *France* **18 D5** 45 46N 3 4 E
Clervaux, *Lux.* **15 D6** 50 4N 6 2 E
Clevedon, *U.K.* **11 F5** 51 26N 2 52W
Cleveland, *Miss., U.S.A.* **81 J9** 33 45N 90 43W
Cleveland, *Ohio, U.S.A.* **78 E3** 41 30N 81 42W
Cleveland, *Okla., U.S.A.* **81 G6** 36 19N 96 28W
Cleveland, *Tenn., U.S.A.* **77 H3** 35 10N 84 53W
Cleveland, *Tex., U.S.A.* **81 K7** 30 21N 95 5W
Cleveland, C., *Australia* **62 B4** 19 11S 147 1 E
Cleveland, Mt., *U.S.A.* **82 B7** 48 56N 113 51W
Cleveland Heights, *U.S.A.* **78 E3** 41 30N 81 34W
Clevelândia, *Brazil* **95 B5** 26 24S 52 23W
Clew B., *Ireland* **13 C2** 53 50N 9 49W
Clewiston, *U.S.A.* **77 M5** 26 45N 80 56W
Clifden, *Ireland* **13 C1** 53 29N 10 1W
Clifden, *N.Z.* **59 M1** 46 1S 167 42 E
Cliffdell, *U.S.A.* **84 D5** 46 56N 121 5W
Cliffy Hd., *Australia* **61 G2** 35 1S 116 29 E
Clifton, *Australia* **63 D5** 27 59S 151 53 E
Clifton, *Ariz., U.S.A.* **83 K9** 33 3N 109 18W
Clifton, *Colo., U.S.A.* **83 G9** 39 7N 108 25W
Clifton, *Tex., U.S.A.* **81 K6** 31 47N 97 35W
Clifton Beach, *Australia* **62 B4** 16 46S 145 39 E
Climax, *Canada* **73 D7** 49 10N 108 20W

Clinch →, U.S.A. 77 H3 35 53N 84 29W
Clingmans Dome, U.S.A. 77 H4 35 34N 83 30W
Clint, U.S.A. 83 L10 31 35N 106 14W
Clinton, B.C., Canada 72 C4 51 6N 121 35W
Clinton, Ont., Canada 78 C3 43 37N 81 32W
Clinton, N.Z. 59 M2 46 12S 169 23 E
Clinton, Ark., U.S.A. 81 H8 35 36N 92 28W
Clinton, Conn., U.S.A. 79 E12 41 17N 72 32W
Clinton, Ill., U.S.A. 80 E10 40 9N 88 57W
Clinton, Ind., U.S.A. 76 F2 39 40N 87 24W
Clinton, Iowa, U.S.A. 80 E9 41 51N 90 12W
Clinton, Mass., U.S.A. 79 D13 42 25N 71 41W
Clinton, Miss., U.S.A. 81 J9 32 20N 90 20W
Clinton, Mo., U.S.A. 80 F8 38 22N 93 46W
Clinton, N.C., U.S.A. 77 H6 35 0N 78 22W
Clinton, Okla., U.S.A. 81 H5 35 31N 98 58W
Clinton, S.C., U.S.A. 77 H5 34 29N 81 53W
Clinton, Tenn., U.S.A. 77 G3 36 6N 84 8W
Clinton, Wash., U.S.A. 84 C4 47 59N 122 21W
Clinton C., Australia 62 C5 22 30S 150 45 E
Clinton Colden L., Canada 68 B9 63 58N 107 27W
Clintonville, U.S.A. 80 C10 44 37N 88 46W
Clipperton, I., Pac. Oc. 65 F17 10 18N 109 13W
Clisham, U.K. 12 D2 57 57N 6 49W
Clitheroe, U.K. 10 D5 53 53N 2 22W
Clo-oose, Canada 84 B2 48 39N 124 49W
Cloates, Pt., Australia 60 D1 22 43S 113 40 E
Clocolan, S. Africa 57 D4 28 55S 27 34 E
Clodomira, Argentina 94 B3 27 35S 64 14W
Clogher Hd., Ireland 13 C5 53 48N 6 14W
Clonakilty, Ireland 13 E3 51 37N 8 53W
Clonakilty B., Ireland 13 E3 51 35N 8 51W
Cloncurry, Australia 62 C3 20 40S 140 28 E
Cloncurry →, Australia 62 B3 18 37S 140 40 E
Clondalkin, Ireland 13 C5 53 19N 6 25W
Clones, Ireland 13 B4 54 11N 7 15W
Clonmel, Ireland 13 D4 52 21N 7 42W
Cloquet, U.S.A. 80 B8 46 43N 92 28W
Clorinda, Argentina 94 B4 25 16S 57 45W
Cloud Bay, Canada 70 C2 48 5N 89 26W
Cloud Peak, U.S.A. 82 D10 44 23N 107 11W
Cloudcroft, U.S.A. 83 K11 32 58N 105 45W
Cloverdale, U.S.A. 84 G4 38 48N 123 1W
Clovis, Calif., U.S.A. 84 J7 36 49N 119 42W
Clovis, N. Mex., U.S.A. 81 H3 34 24N 103 12W
Cloyne, Canada 78 B7 44 49N 77 11W
Cluj-Napoca, Romania 17 E12 46 47N 23 38 E
Clunes, Australia 63 F3 37 20S 143 45 E
Clutha →, N.Z. 59 M2 46 20S 169 49 E
Clwyd →, U.K. 10 D4 53 19N 3 31W
Clyde, Canada 72 C6 54 9N 113 39W
Clyde, N.Z. 59 L2 45 12S 169 20 E
Clyde, U.S.A. 78 C8 43 5N 76 52W
Clyde →, U.K. 12 F4 55 55N 4 30W
Clyde, Firth of, U.K. 12 F3 55 22N 5 1W
Clyde River, Canada 69 A13 70 30N 68 30W
Clydebank, U.K. 12 F4 55 54N 4 23W
Clymer, N.Y., U.S.A. 78 D5 42 1N 79 37W
Clymer, Pa., U.S.A. 78 D5 40 40N 79 1W
Coachella, U.S.A. 85 M10 33 41N 116 10W
Coachella Canal, U.S.A. 85 N12 32 43N 114 57W
Coahoma, U.S.A. 81 J4 32 18N 101 18W
Coahuayana →, Mexico 86 D4 18 41N 103 45W
Coahuila □, Mexico 86 B4 27 0N 103 0W
Coal →, Canada 72 B3 59 39N 126 57W
Coalane, Mozam. 55 F4 17 48S 37 2 E
Coalcomán, Mexico 86 D4 18 40N 103 10W
Coaldale, Canada 72 D6 49 45N 112 35W
Coalgate, U.S.A. 81 H6 34 32N 96 13W
Coalinga, U.S.A. 84 J6 36 9N 120 21W
Coalisland, U.K. 13 B5 54 33N 6 42W
Coalville, U.K. 10 E6 52 44N 1 23W
Coalville, U.S.A. 82 F8 40 55N 111 24W
Coari, Brazil 92 D6 4 8S 63 7W
Coast □, Kenya 54 C4 2 40S 39 45 E
Coast Mts., Canada 72 C3 55 0N 129 20W
Coast Ranges, U.S.A. 84 G4 39 0N 123 0W
Coatbridge, U.K. 12 F4 55 52N 4 6W
Coatepec, Mexico 87 D5 19 27N 96 58W
Coatepeque, Guatemala 88 D1 14 46N 91 55W
Coatesville, U.S.A. 76 F8 39 59N 75 50W
Coaticook, Canada 79 A13 45 10N 71 46W
Coats I., Canada 69 B11 62 30N 83 0W
Coats Land, Antarctica 5 D1 77 0S 25 0W
Coatzacoalcos, Mexico 87 D6 18 7N 94 25W
Cobalt, Canada 70 C4 47 25N 79 42W
Cobán, Guatemala 88 C1 15 30N 90 21W
Cobar, Australia 63 E4 31 27S 145 48 E
Cóbh, Ireland 13 E3 51 51N 8 17W
Cobija, Bolivia 92 F5 11 0S 68 50W
Cobleskill, U.S.A. 79 D10 42 41N 74 29W
Coboconk, Canada 78 B6 44 39N 78 48W
Cobourg, Canada 78 C6 43 58N 78 10W
Cobourg Pen., Australia 60 B5 11 20S 132 15 E
Cobram, Australia 63 F4 35 54S 145 40 E
Cóbué, Mozam. 55 E3 12 0S 34 58 E
Coburg, Germany 16 C6 50 15N 10 58 E
Cocanada = Kakinada, India 41 L13 16 57N 82 11 E
Cochabamba, Bolivia 92 G5 17 26S 66 10W
Cochemane, Mozam. 55 F3 17 0S 32 54 E
Cochin, India 40 Q10 9 58N 76 20 E
Cochin China = Nam-Phan, Vietnam 39 G6 10 30N 106 0 E
Cochran, U.S.A. 77 J4 32 23N 83 21W
Cochrane, Alta., Canada 72 C6 51 11N 114 30W
Cochrane, Ont., Canada 70 C3 49 0N 81 0W
Cochrane, Chile 96 F2 47 15S 72 33W
Cochrane →, Canada 73 B8 59 0N 103 40W
Cochrane, L., Chile 96 F2 47 10S 72 0W
Cochranton, U.S.A. 78 E4 41 31N 80 3W
Cockburn, Australia 63 E3 32 5S 141 0 E
Cockburn, Canal, Chile 96 G2 54 30S 72 0W
Cockburn I., Canada 70 C3 45 55N 83 22W
Cockburn Ra., Australia 60 C4 15 46S 128 0 E
Cockermouth, U.K. 10 C4 54 40N 3 22W
Cocklebiddy, Australia 61 F4 32 0S 126 3 E
Coco →, Cent. Amer. 88 D3 15 0N 83 8W
Coco, I. del, Pac. Oc. 65 G19 5 25N 87 55W
Cocoa, U.S.A. 77 L5 28 21N 80 44W
Cocobeach, Gabon 52 D1 0 59N 9 34 E
Cocos Is., Ind. Oc. 64 J1 12 10S 96 55 E
Cod, C., U.S.A. 76 D10 42 5N 70 10W
Codajás, Brazil 92 D6 3 55S 62 0W
Codó, Brazil 93 D10 4 30S 43 55W
Cody, U.S.A. 82 D9 44 32N 109 3W
Coe Hill, Canada 78 B7 44 52N 77 50W
Coelemu, Chile 94 D1 36 30S 72 48W
Coen, Australia 62 A3 13 52S 143 12 E
Cœur d'Alene, U.S.A. 82 C5 47 45N 116 51W
Cœur d'Alene L., U.S.A. 82 C5 47 32N 116 48W
Coevorden, Neths. 15 B6 52 40N 6 44 E
Cofete, Canary Is. 22 F5 28 6N 14 23W
Coffeyville, U.S.A. 81 G7 37 2N 95 37W
Coffin B., Australia 63 E2 34 38S 135 28 E
Coffin Bay, Australia 63 E2 34 37S 135 29 E
Coffin Bay Peninsula, Australia 63 E2 34 32S 135 15 E
Coffs Harbour, Australia 63 E5 30 16S 153 5 E
Cognac, France 18 D3 45 41N 0 20W
Cohocton, U.S.A. 78 D7 42 30N 77 30W
Cohocton →, U.S.A. 78 D7 42 9N 77 6W
Cohoes, U.S.A. 79 D11 42 46N 73 42W
Cohuna, Australia 63 F3 35 45S 144 15 E
Coiba, I., Panama 88 E3 7 30N 81 40W
Coig →, Argentina 96 G3 51 0S 69 10W
Coigeach, Rubha, U.K. 12 C3 58 6N 5 26W
Coihaique, Chile 96 F2 45 30S 71 45W
Coimbatore, India 40 P10 11 2N 76 59 E
Coimbra, Brazil 92 G7 19 55S 57 48W
Coimbra, Portugal 19 B1 40 15N 8 27W
Coín, Spain 19 D3 36 40N 4 48W
Coipasa, Salar de, Bolivia 92 G5 19 26S 68 9W
Cojimies, Ecuador 92 C3 0 20N 80 0W
Cojutepequé, El Salv. 88 D2 13 41N 88 54W
Cokeville, U.S.A. 82 E8 42 5N 110 57W
Colac, Australia 63 F3 38 21S 143 35 E
Colatina, Brazil 93 G10 19 32S 40 37W
Colbeck, C., Antarctica 5 D13 77 6S 157 48W
Colborne, Canada 78 C7 44 0N 77 53W
Colby, U.S.A. 80 F4 39 24N 101 3W
Colchester, U.K. 11 F8 51 54N 0 55 E
Cold L., Canada 73 C7 54 33N 110 5W
Coldstream, Canada 72 C5 50 13N 119 11W
Coldstream, U.K. 12 F6 55 39N 2 15W
Coldwater, Canada 78 B5 44 42N 79 40W
Coldwater, Kans., U.S.A. 81 G5 37 16N 99 20W
Coldwater, Mich., U.S.A. 76 E3 41 57N 85 0W
Colebrook, U.S.A. 79 B13 44 54N 71 30W
Coleman, U.S.A. 81 K5 31 50N 99 26W
Coleman →, Australia 62 B3 15 6S 141 38 E
Colenso, S. Africa 57 D4 28 44S 29 50 E
Coleraine, Australia 63 F3 37 36S 141 40 E
Coleraine, U.K. 13 A5 55 8N 6 41W
Coleridge, L., N.Z. 59 K3 43 17S 171 30 E
Colesberg, S. Africa 56 E4 30 45S 25 5 E
Coleville, U.S.A. 84 G7 38 34N 119 30W
Colfax, Calif., U.S.A. 84 F6 39 6N 120 57W
Colfax, La., U.S.A. 81 K8 31 31N 92 42W
Colfax, Wash., U.S.A. 82 C5 46 53N 117 22W
Colhué Huapi, L., Argentina 96 F3 45 30S 69 0W
Coligny, S. Africa 57 D4 26 17S 26 15 E
Colima, Mexico 86 D4 19 14N 103 43W
Colima □, Mexico 86 D4 19 10N 103 40W
Colima, Nevado de, Mexico 86 D4 19 35N 103 45W
Colina, Chile 94 C1 33 13S 70 45W
Colinas, Brazil 93 E10 6 0S 44 10W
Coll, U.K. 12 E2 56 39N 6 34W
Collaguasi, Chile 94 A2 21 5S 68 45W
Collarenebri, Australia 63 D4 29 33S 148 34 E
Colleen Bawn, Zimbabwe 55 G2 21 0S 29 12 E
College Park, U.S.A. 77 J3 33 40N 84 27W
College Station, U.S.A. 81 K6 30 37N 96 21W
Collie, Australia 61 F2 33 22S 116 8 E
Collier B., Australia 60 C3 16 10S 124 15 E
Collier Ra., Australia 61 D2 24 45S 119 10 E
Collina, Passo di, Italy 20 B4 44 2N 10 56 E
Collingwood, Canada 78 B4 44 29N 80 13W
Collingwood, N.Z. 59 J4 40 41S 172 40 E
Collins, Canada 70 B2 50 17N 89 27W
Collinsville, Australia 62 C4 20 30S 147 56 E
Collipulli, Chile 94 D1 37 55S 72 30W
Collooney, Ireland 13 B3 54 11N 8 29W
Colmar, France 18 B7 48 5N 7 20 E
Colo →, Australia 63 E5 33 25S 150 52 E
Cologne = Köln, Germany 16 C4 50 56N 6 57 E
Colom, I. d'en, Spain 22 B11 39 58N 4 16 E
Coloma, U.S.A. 84 G6 38 48N 120 53W
Colomb-Béchar = Béchar, Algeria 50 B5 31 38N 2 18W
Colombia ■, S. Amer. 92 C4 3 45N 73 0W
Colombian Basin, S. Amer. 66 H12 14 0N 76 0W
Colombo, Sri Lanka 40 R11 6 56N 79 58 E
Colón, Buenos Aires, Argentina 94 C3 33 53S 61 7W
Colón, Entre Ríos, Argentina 94 C4 32 12S 58 10W
Colón, Cuba 88 B3 22 42N 80 54W
Colón, Panama 88 E4 9 20N 79 54W
Colònia de Sant Jordi, Spain 22 B9 39 19N 2 59 E
Colonia del Sacramento, Uruguay 94 C4 34 25S 57 50W
Colonia Dora, Argentina 94 B3 28 34S 62 59W
Colonial Beach, U.S.A. 76 F7 38 15N 76 58W
Colonie, U.S.A. 79 D11 42 43N 73 50W
Colonsay, Canada 73 C7 51 59N 105 52W
Colonsay, U.K. 12 E2 56 5N 6 12W
Colorado □, U.S.A. 83 G10 39 30N 105 30W
Colorado →, Argentina 96 D4 39 50S 62 8W
Colorado →, N. Amer. 83 L6 31 45N 114 40W
Colorado →, U.S.A. 81 L7 28 36N 95 59W
Colorado City, U.S.A. 81 J4 32 24N 100 52W
Colorado Plateau, U.S.A. 83 H8 37 0N 111 0W
Colorado River Aqueduct, U.S.A. 85 L12 34 17N 114 10W
Colorado Springs, U.S.A. 80 F2 38 50N 104 49W
Colotlán, Mexico 86 C4 22 6N 103 16W
Colstrip, U.S.A. 82 D10 45 53N 106 38W
Colton, U.S.A. 79 B10 44 33N 74 56W
Columbia, Ky., U.S.A. 76 G3 37 6N 85 18W
Columbia, La., U.S.A. 81 J8 32 6N 92 5W
Columbia, Miss., U.S.A. 81 K10 31 15N 89 50W
Columbia, Mo., U.S.A. 80 F8 38 57N 92 20W
Columbia, Pa., U.S.A. 79 F8 40 2N 76 30W
Columbia, S.C., U.S.A. 77 J5 34 0N 81 2W
Columbia, Tenn., U.S.A. 77 H2 35 37N 87 2W
Columbia →, N. Amer. 84 D2 46 15N 124 5W
Columbia, C., Canada 4 A4 83 0N 70 0W
Columbia, District of □, U.S.A. 76 F7 38 55N 77 0W
Columbia, Mt., Canada 72 C5 52 8N 117 20W
Columbia Basin, U.S.A. 82 C4 46 45N 119 5W
Columbia Falls, U.S.A. 82 B6 48 23N 114 11W
Columbia Mts., Canada 72 C5 52 0N 119 0W
Columbia Plateau, U.S.A. 82 D5 44 0N 117 30W
Columbiana, U.S.A. 78 F4 40 53N 80 42W
Columbretes, Is., Spain 19 C6 39 50N 0 50 E
Columbus, Ga., U.S.A. 77 J3 32 28N 84 59W
Columbus, Ind., U.S.A. 76 F3 39 13N 85 55W
Columbus, Kans., U.S.A. 81 G7 37 10N 94 50W
Columbus, Miss., U.S.A. 77 J1 33 30N 88 25W
Columbus, Mont., U.S.A. 82 D9 45 38N 109 15W
Columbus, N. Mex., U.S.A. 83 L10 31 50N 107 38W
Columbus, Nebr., U.S.A. 80 E6 41 26N 97 22W
Columbus, Ohio, U.S.A. 76 F4 39 58N 83 0W
Columbus, Tex., U.S.A. 81 L6 29 42N 96 33W
Colusa, U.S.A. 84 F4 39 13N 122 1W
Colville, U.S.A. 82 B5 48 33N 117 54W
Colville →, U.S.A. 68 A4 70 25N 150 30W
Colville, C., N.Z. 59 G5 36 29S 175 21 E
Colwood, Canada 84 B3 48 26N 123 29W
Colwyn Bay, U.K. 10 D4 53 18N 3 44W
Comácchio, Italy 20 B5 44 42N 12 11 E
Comalcalco, Mexico 87 D6 18 16N 93 13W
Comallo, Argentina 96 E2 41 0S 70 5W
Comanche, U.S.A. 81 K5 31 54N 98 36W
Comayagua, Honduras 88 D2 14 25N 87 37W
Combahee →, U.S.A. 77 J5 32 30N 80 31W
Combarbalá, Chile 94 C1 31 11S 71 2W
Comber, Canada 78 D2 42 14N 82 33W
Comber, U.K. 13 B6 54 33N 5 45W
Combermere, Canada 78 A7 45 22N 77 37W
Comblain-au-Pont, Belgium 15 D5 50 29N 5 35 E
Comeragh Mts., Ireland 13 D4 52 18N 7 34W
Comet, Australia 62 C4 23 36S 148 38 E
Comilla, Bangla. 41 H17 23 28N 91 10 E
Comino, Malta 23 C1 36 1N 14 20 E
Comino, C., Italy 20 D3 40 32N 9 49 E
Comitán, Mexico 87 D6 16 18N 92 9W
Commerce, Ga., U.S.A. 77 H4 34 12N 83 28W
Commerce, Tex., U.S.A. 81 J7 33 15N 95 54W
Committee B., Canada 69 B11 68 30N 86 30W
Commonwealth B., Antarctica 5 C10 67 0S 144 0 E
Commoron Cr. →, Australia 63 D5 28 22S 150 8 E
Communism Pk. = Kommunizma, Pik, Tajikistan 26 F8 39 0N 72 2 E
Como, Italy 18 D8 45 47N 9 5 E
Como, Lago di, Italy 18 D8 46 0N 9 11 E
Comodoro Rivadavia, Argentina 96 F3 45 50S 67 40W
Comorin, C., India 40 Q10 8 3N 77 40 E
Comoro Is. = Comoros ■, Ind. Oc. 49 H8 12 10S 44 15 E
Comoros ■, Ind. Oc. 49 H8 12 10S 44 15 E
Comox, Canada 72 D4 49 42N 124 55W
Compiègne, France 18 B5 49 24N 2 50 E
Compostela, Mexico 86 C4 21 15N 104 53W
Comprida, I., Brazil 95 A6 24 50S 47 42W
Compton, Canada 79 A13 45 14N 71 49W
Compton, U.S.A. 85 M8 33 54N 118 13W
Comrat, Moldova 17 E15 46 18N 28 40 E
Con Cuong, Vietnam 38 C5 19 2N 104 54 E
Con Son, Vietnam 39 H6 8 41N 106 37 E
Conakry, Guinea 50 G3 9 29N 13 49W
Conara, Australia 62 G4 41 50S 147 26 E
Concarneau, France 18 C2 47 52N 3 56W
Conceição, Mozam. 55 F4 18 47S 36 7 E
Conceição da Barra, Brazil 93 G11 18 35S 39 45W
Conceição do Araguaia, Brazil 93 E9 8 0S 49 2W
Concepción, Argentina 94 B2 27 20S 65 35W
Concepción, Bolivia 92 G6 16 15S 62 8W
Concepción, Chile 94 D1 36 50S 73 0W
Concepción, Mexico 87 D6 18 15N 90 5W
Concepción, Paraguay 94 A4 23 22S 57 26W
Concepción □, Chile 94 D1 37 0S 72 30W
Concepción →, Mexico 86 A2 30 32N 113 2W
Concepción, Est. de, Chile 96 G2 50 30S 74 55W
Concepción, L., Bolivia 92 G6 17 20S 61 20W
Concepción, Punta, Mexico 86 B2 26 55N 111 59W
Concepción del Oro, Mexico 86 C4 24 40N 101 30W
Concepción del Uruguay, Argentina 94 C4 32 35S 58 20W
Conception, Pt., U.S.A. 85 L6 34 27N 120 28W
Conception B., Canada 71 C9 47 45N 53 0W
Conception B., Namibia 56 C1 23 55S 14 22 E
Conception I., Bahamas 89 B4 23 52N 75 9W
Concession, Zimbabwe 55 F3 17 27S 30 56 E
Conchas Dam, U.S.A. 81 H2 35 22N 104 11W
Concho, U.S.A. 83 J9 34 28N 109 36W
Concho →, U.S.A. 81 K5 31 34N 99 43W
Conchos →, Chihuahua, Mexico 86 B4 29 32N 105 0W
Conchos →, Tamaulipas, Mexico 87 B5 25 9N 98 35W
Concord, Calif., U.S.A. 84 H4 37 59N 122 2W
Concord, N.C., U.S.A. 77 H5 35 25N 80 35W
Concord, N.H., U.S.A. 79 C13 43 12N 71 32W
Concordia, Argentina 94 C4 31 20S 58 2W
Concórdia, Brazil 92 D5 4 36S 66 36W
Concordia, Mexico 86 C3 23 18N 106 2W
Concordia, U.S.A. 80 F6 39 34N 97 40W
Concrete, U.S.A. 82 B3 48 32N 121 45W
Condamine, Australia 63 D5 26 56S 150 9 E
Conde, U.S.A. 80 C5 45 9N 98 6W
Condeúba, Brazil 93 F10 14 52S 42 0W
Condobolin, Australia 63 E4 33 4S 147 6 E
Condon, U.S.A. 82 D3 45 14N 120 11W
Conegliano, Italy 20 B5 45 53N 12 18 E
Conejera, I. = Conills, I. des, Spain 22 B9 39 11N 2 58 E
Conejos, Mexico 86 B4 26 14N 103 53W
Confuso →, Paraguay 94 B4 25 9S 57 34W
Congleton, U.K. 10 D5 53 10N 2 13W
Congo (Kinshasa) = Congo, Dem. Rep. of the ■, Africa 52 E4 3 0S 23 0 E
Congo ■, Africa 52 E3 1 0S 16 0 E
Congo →, Africa 52 F2 6 4S 12 24 E
Congo, Dem. Rep. of the ■, Africa 52 E4 3 0S 23 0 E
Congo Basin, Africa 52 E4 0 10S 24 30 E
Congonhas, Brazil 95 A7 20 30S 43 52W
Congress, U.S.A. 83 J7 34 9N 112 51W
Conills, I. des, Spain 22 B9 39 11N 2 58 E
Coniston, Canada 70 C3 46 29N 80 51W
Conjeeveram = Kanchipuram, India 40 N11 12 52N 79 45 E
Conklin, Canada 73 B6 55 38N 111 5W
Conklin, U.S.A. 79 D9 42 2N 75 49W
Conn, L., Ireland 13 B2 54 3N 9 15W
Connacht □, Ireland 13 C2 53 43N 9 12W
Conneaut, U.S.A. 78 E4 41 57N 80 34W
Connecticut □, U.S.A. 79 E12 41 30N 72 45W
Connecticut →, U.S.A. 79 E12 41 16N 72 20W
Connell, U.S.A. 82 C4 46 40N 118 52W
Connellsville, U.S.A. 78 F5 40 1N 79 35W
Connemara, Ireland 13 C2 53 29N 9 45W
Connemaugh →, U.S.A. 78 F5 40 28N 79 19W
Connersville, U.S.A. 76 F3 39 39N 85 8W
Connors Ra., Australia 62 C4 21 40S 149 10 E
Conquest, Canada 73 C7 51 32N 107 14W
Conrad, U.S.A. 82 B8 48 10N 111 57W
Conran, C., Australia 63 F4 37 49S 148 44 E
Conroe, U.S.A. 81 K7 30 19N 95 27W
Consecon, Canada 78 C7 44 0N 77 31W
Conselheiro Lafaiete, Brazil 95 A7 20 40S 43 48W
Consett, U.K. 10 C6 54 51N 1 50W
Consort, Canada 73 C6 52 1N 110 46W
Constance = Konstanz, Germany 16 E5 47 40N 9 10 E
Constance, L. = Bodensee, Europe 18 C8 47 35N 9 25 E
Constanța, Romania 17 F15 44 14N 28 38 E
Constantia, U.S.A. 79 C8 43 15N 76 1W
Constantine, Algeria 50 A7 36 25N 6 42 E
Constitución, Chile 94 D1 35 20S 72 30W
Constitución, Uruguay 94 C4 31 0S 57 50W
Consul, Canada 73 D7 49 20N 109 30W
Contact, U.S.A. 82 F6 41 46N 114 45W
Contai, India 43 J12 21 54N 87 46 E
Contamana, Peru 92 E4 7 19S 74 55W
Contas →, Brazil 93 F11 14 17S 39 1W
Contoocook, U.S.A. 79 C13 43 13N 71 45W
Contra Costa, Mozam. 57 D5 25 9S 33 30 E
Contwoyto L., Canada 68 B8 65 42N 110 50W
Conway = Conwy, U.K. 10 D4 53 17N 3 50W
Conway = Conwy →, U.K. 10 D4 53 17N 3 50W
Conway, Ark., U.S.A. 81 H8 35 5N 92 26W
Conway, N.H., U.S.A. 79 C13 43 59N 71 7W
Conway, S.C., U.S.A. 77 J6 33 51N 79 3W
Conway, L., Australia 63 D2 28 17S 135 35 E
Conwy, U.K. 10 D4 53 17N 3 50W
Conwy □, U.K. 10 D4 53 10N 3 44W
Conwy →, U.K. 10 D4 53 17N 3 50W
Coober Pedy, Australia 63 D1 29 1S 134 43 E
Cooch Behar = Koch Bihar, India 41 F16 26 22N 89 29 E
Cooinda, Australia 60 B5 13 15S 130 5 E
Cook, Australia 61 F5 30 37S 130 25 E
Cook, U.S.A. 80 B8 47 49N 92 39W
Cook, B., Chile 96 H3 55 10S 70 0W
Cook, C., Canada 72 C3 50 8N 127 55W
Cook, Mt. = Aoraki Mount Cook, N.Z. 59 K3 43 36S 170 9 E
Cook Inlet, U.S.A. 68 C4 60 0N 152 0W
Cook Is., Pac. Oc. 65 J12 17 0S 160 0W
Cook Strait, N.Z. 59 J5 41 15S 174 29 E
Cookeville, U.S.A. 77 G3 36 10N 85 30W
Cookhouse, S. Africa 56 E4 32 44S 25 47 E
Cookshire, Canada 79 A13 45 25N 71 38W
Cookstown, U.K. 13 B5 54 39N 6 45W
Cooksville, Canada 78 C5 43 36N 79 35W
Cooktown, Australia 62 B4 15 30S 145 16 E
Coolabah, Australia 63 E4 31 1S 146 43 E
Cooladdi, Australia 63 D4 26 37S 145 23 E
Coolah, Australia 63 E4 31 48S 149 41 E
Coolamon, Australia 63 E4 34 46S 147 8 E
Coolgardie, Australia 61 F3 30 55S 121 8 E
Coolidge, U.S.A. 83 K8 32 59N 111 31W
Coolidge Dam, U.S.A. 83 K8 33 0N 110 20W
Cooma, Australia 63 F4 36 12S 149 8 E
Coon Rapids, U.S.A. 80 C8 45 9N 93 19W
Coonabarabran, Australia 63 E4 31 14S 149 18 E
Coonamble, Australia 63 E4 30 56S 148 27 E
Coonana, Australia 61 F3 31 0S 123 0 E
Coondapoor, India 40 N9 13 42N 74 40 E
Cooninie, L., Australia 63 D2 26 4S 139 59 E
Cooper, U.S.A. 81 J7 33 23N 95 42W
Cooper Cr. →, Australia 63 D2 28 29S 137 46 E
Cooperstown, N. Dak., U.S.A. 80 B5 47 27N 98 8W
Cooperstown, N.Y., U.S.A. 79 D10 42 42N 74 56W
Coorabie, Australia 61 F5 31 54S 132 18 E
Coorong, The, Australia 63 F2 35 50S 139 20 E
Coorow, Australia 61 E2 29 53S 116 2 E
Cooroy, Australia 63 D5 26 22S 152 54 E
Coos Bay, U.S.A. 82 E1 43 22N 124 13W
Coosa →, U.S.A. 77 J2 32 30N 86 16W
Cootamundra, Australia 63 E4 34 36S 148 1 E
Cootehill, Ireland 13 B4 54 4N 7 5W
Copahue Paso, Argentina 94 D1 37 49S 71 8W
Copainalá, Mexico 87 D6 17 8N 93 11W
Copake Falls, U.S.A. 79 D11 42 7N 73 31W
Copán, Honduras 88 D2 14 50N 89 9W
Cope, U.S.A. 80 F3 39 40N 102 51W
Copenhagen = København, Denmark 9 J15 55 41N 12 34 E
Copenhagen, U.S.A. 79 C9 43 54N 75 41W
Copiapó, Chile 94 B1 27 30S 70 20W
Copiapó →, Chile 94 B1 27 19S 70 56W
Coplay, U.S.A. 79 F9 40 44N 75 29W
Copp L., Canada 72 A6 60 14N 114 40W
Coppename →, Surinam 93 B7 5 48N 55 55W
Copper Harbor, U.S.A. 76 B2 47 28N 87 53W
Copper Queen, Zimbabwe 55 F2 17 29S 29 18 E
Copperas Cove, U.S.A. 81 K6 31 8N 97 54W
Copperbelt □, Zambia 55 E2 13 15S 27 30 E
Coppermine = Kugluktuk, Canada 68 B8 67 50N 115 5W
Coppermine →, Canada 68 B8 67 49N 116 4W
Copperopolis, U.S.A. 84 H6 37 58N 120 38W
Coquet →, U.K. 10 B6 55 20N 1 32W
Coquille, U.S.A. 82 E1 43 11N 124 11W
Coquimbo, Chile 94 C1 30 0S 71 20W
Coquimbo □, Chile 94 C1 31 0S 71 0W
Corabia, Romania 17 G13 43 48N 24 30 E
Coracora, Peru 92 G4 15 5S 73 45W
Coraki, Australia 63 D5 28 59S 153 17 E
Coral, U.S.A. 78 F5 40 29N 79 10W
Coral Gables, U.S.A. 77 N5 25 45N 80 16W
Coral Harbour = Salliq, Canada 69 B11 64 8N 83 10W
Coral Sea, Pac. Oc. 64 J7 15 0S 150 0 E

Coral Springs, *U.S.A.* 77 M5 26 16N 80 13W
Coraopolis, *U.S.A.* 78 F4 40 31N 80 10W
Corato, *Italy* 20 D7 41 9N 16 25 E
Corbin, *U.S.A.* 76 G3 36 57N 84 6W
Corby, *U.K.* 11 E7 52 30N 0 41W
Corcaigh = Cork, *Ireland* 13 E3 51 54N 8 29W
Corcoran, *U.S.A.* 84 J7 36 6N 119 33W
Corcubión, *Spain* 19 A1 42 56N 9 12W
Cordele, *U.S.A.* 77 K4 31 58N 83 47W
Cordell, *U.S.A.* 81 H5 35 17N 98 59W
Córdoba, *Argentina* 94 C3 31 20S 64 10W
Córdoba, *Mexico* 87 D5 18 50N 97 0W
Córdoba, *Spain* 19 D3 37 50N 4 50W
Córdoba □, *Argentina* 94 C3 31 22S 64 15W
Córdoba, Sierra de, *Argentina* 94 C3 31 10S 64 25W
Cordova, *U.S.A.* 68 B5 60 33N 145 45W
Corella →, *Australia* 62 B3 19 34S 140 47 E
Corfield, *Australia* 62 C3 21 40S 143 21 E
Corfu = Kérkira, *Greece* 23 A3 39 38N 19 50 E
Corfu, Str. of, *Greece* 23 A4 39 34N 20 0 E
Coria, *Spain* 19 C2 39 58N 6 33W
Corigliano Cálabro, *Italy* 20 E7 39 36N 16 31 E
Coringa Is., *Australia* 62 B4 16 58S 149 58 E
Corinth = Kórinthos, *Greece* 21 F10 37 56N 22 55 E
Corinth, *Miss., U.S.A.* 77 H1 34 56N 88 31W
Corinth, *N.Y., U.S.A.* 79 C11 43 15N 73 49W
Corinth, G. of = Korinthiakós Kólpos, *Greece* 21 E10 38 16N 22 30 E
Corinto, *Brazil* 93 G10 18 20S 44 30W
Corinto, *Nic.* 88 D2 12 30N 87 10W
Cork, *Ireland* 13 E3 51 54N 8 29W
Cork □, *Ireland* 13 E3 51 57N 8 40W
Cork Harbour, *Ireland* 13 E3 51 47N 8 16W
Çorlu, *Turkey* 21 D12 41 11N 27 49 E
Cormack L., *Canada* 72 A4 60 56N 121 37W
Cormorant, *Canada* 73 C8 54 14N 100 35W
Cormorant L., *Canada* 73 C8 54 15N 100 50W
Corn Is. = Maiz, Is. del, *Nic.* 88 D3 12 15N 83 4W
Cornélio Procópio, *Brazil* 95 A5 23 7S 50 40W
Corner Brook, *Canada* 71 C8 48 57N 57 58W
Corneşti, *Moldova* 17 E15 47 21N 28 1 E
Corning, *Ark., U.S.A.* 81 G9 36 25N 90 35W
Corning, *Calif., U.S.A.* 82 G2 39 56N 122 11W
Corning, *Iowa, U.S.A.* 80 E7 40 59N 94 44W
Corning, *N.Y., U.S.A.* 78 D7 42 9N 77 3W
Cornwall, *Canada* 79 A10 45 2N 74 44W
Cornwall, *U.S.A.* 79 F8 40 17N 76 25W
Cornwall □, *U.K.* 11 G3 50 26N 4 40W
Corny Pt., *Australia* 63 E2 34 55S 137 0 E
Coro, *Venezuela* 92 A5 11 25N 69 41W
Coroatá, *Brazil* 93 D10 4 8S 44 0W
Corocoro, *Bolivia* 92 G5 17 15S 68 28W
Coroico, *Bolivia* 92 G5 16 0S 67 50W
Coromandel, *N.Z.* 59 G5 36 45S 175 31 E
Coromandel Coast, *India* 40 N12 12 30N 81 0 E
Corona, *Calif., U.S.A.* 85 M9 33 53N 117 34W
Corona, *N. Mex., U.S.A.* 83 J11 34 15N 105 36W
Coronach, *Canada* 73 D7 49 7N 105 31W
Coronado, *U.S.A.* 85 N9 32 41N 117 11W
Coronado, B. de, *Costa Rica* 88 E3 9 0N 83 40W
Coronados, Is. los, *U.S.A.* 85 N9 32 25N 117 15W
Coronation, *Canada* 72 C6 52 5N 111 27W
Coronation Gulf, *Canada* 68 B8 68 25N 110 0W
Coronation I., *Antarctica* 5 C18 60 45S 46 0W
Coronation Is., *Australia* 60 B3 14 57S 124 55 E
Coronda, *Argentina* 94 C3 31 58S 60 56W
Coronel, *Chile* 94 D1 37 0S 73 10W
Coronel Bogado, *Paraguay* 94 B4 27 11S 56 18W
Coronel Dorrego, *Argentina* 94 D3 38 40S 61 10W
Coronel Oviedo, *Paraguay* 94 B4 25 24S 56 30W
Coronel Pringles, *Argentina* 94 D3 38 0S 61 30W
Coronel Suárez, *Argentina* 94 D3 37 30S 61 52W
Coronel Vidal, *Argentina* 94 D4 37 28S 57 45W
Coropuna, Nevado, *Peru* 92 G4 15 30S 72 41W
Corowa, *Australia* 63 F4 35 58S 146 21 E
Corozal, *Belize* 87 D7 18 23N 88 23W
Corpus, *Argentina* 95 B4 27 10S 55 30W
Corpus Christi, *U.S.A.* 81 M6 27 47N 97 24W
Corpus Christi, L., *U.S.A.* 81 L6 28 2N 97 52W
Corralejo, *Canary Is.* 22 F6 28 43N 13 53W
Corraun Pen., *Ireland* 13 C2 53 54N 9 54W
Correntes, C. das, *Mozam.* 57 C6 24 6S 35 34 E
Corrib, L., *Ireland* 13 C2 53 27N 9 16W
Corrientes, *Argentina* 94 B4 27 30S 58 45W
Corrientes □, *Argentina* 94 B4 28 0S 57 0W
Corrientes →, *Argentina* 94 C4 30 42S 59 38W
Corrientes →, *Peru* 92 D4 3 43S 74 35W
Corrientes, C., *Colombia* 92 B3 5 30N 77 34W
Corrientes, C., *Cuba* 88 B3 21 43N 84 30W
Corrientes, C., *Mexico* 86 C3 20 25N 105 42W
Corrigan, *U.S.A.* 81 K7 31 0N 94 52W
Corrigin, *Australia* 61 F2 32 20S 117 53 E
Corry, *U.S.A.* 78 E5 41 55N 79 39W
Corse, *France* 18 F8 42 0N 9 0 E
Corse, C., *France* 18 E8 43 1N 9 25 E
Corsica = Corse, *France* 18 F8 42 0N 9 0 E
Corsicana, *U.S.A.* 81 J6 32 6N 96 28W
Corte, *France* 18 E8 42 19N 9 11 E
Cortez, *U.S.A.* 83 H9 37 21N 108 35W
Cortland, *N.Y., U.S.A.* 79 D8 42 36N 76 11W
Cortland, *Ohio, U.S.A.* 78 E4 41 20N 80 44W
Çorum, *Turkey* 25 F5 40 30N 34 57 E
Corumbá, *Brazil* 92 G7 19 0S 57 30W
Corunna = A Coruña, *Spain* 19 A1 43 20N 8 25W
Corvallis, *U.S.A.* 82 D2 44 34N 123 16W
Corvette, L. de la, *Canada* 70 B5 53 25N 74 3W
Corydon, *U.S.A.* 80 E8 40 46N 93 19W
Cosalá, *Mexico* 86 C3 24 28N 106 40W
Cosamaloapan, *Mexico* 87 D5 18 23N 95 50W
Cosenza, *Italy* 20 E7 39 18N 16 15 E
Coshocton, *U.S.A.* 78 F3 40 16N 81 51W
Cosmo Newberry, *Australia* 61 E3 28 0S 122 54 E
Coso Junction, *U.S.A.* 85 J9 36 3N 117 57W
Coso Pk., *U.S.A.* 85 J9 36 13N 117 44W
Cosquín, *Argentina* 94 C3 31 15S 64 30W
Costa Blanca, *Spain* 19 C5 38 25N 0 10W
Costa Brava, *Spain* 19 B7 41 30N 3 0 E
Costa del Sol, *Spain* 19 D3 36 30N 4 30W
Costa Dorada, *Spain* 19 B6 41 12N 1 15 E
Costa Mesa, *U.S.A.* 85 M9 33 38N 117 55W
Costa Rica ■, *Cent. Amer.* 88 E3 10 0N 84 0W
Cosumnes →, *U.S.A.* 84 G5 38 16N 121 26W
Cotabato, *Phil.* 37 C6 7 14N 124 15 E
Cotagaita, *Bolivia* 94 A2 20 45S 65 40W
Côte d'Azur, *France* 18 E7 43 25N 7 10 E
Côte-d'Ivoire = Ivory Coast ■, *Africa* 50 G4 7 30N 5 0W
Coteau des Prairies, *U.S.A.* 80 C6 45 20N 97 50W
Coteau du Missouri, *U.S.A.* 80 B4 47 0N 100 0W
Coteau Landing, *Canada* 79 A10 45 15N 74 13W
Cotentin, *France* 18 B3 49 15N 1 30W
Cotillo, *Canary Is.* 22 F5 28 41N 14 1W
Cotonou, *Benin* 50 G6 6 20N 2 25 E
Cotopaxi, *Ecuador* 92 D3 0 40S 78 30W
Cotswold Hills, *U.K.* 11 F5 51 42N 2 10W
Cottage Grove, *U.S.A.* 82 E2 43 48N 123 3W
Cottbus, *Germany* 16 C8 51 45N 14 20 E
Cottonwood, *U.S.A.* 83 J7 34 45N 112 1W
Cotulla, *U.S.A.* 81 L5 28 26N 99 14W
Coudersport, *U.S.A.* 78 E6 41 46N 78 1W
Couedic, C. du, *Australia* 63 F2 36 5S 136 40 E
Coulee City, *U.S.A.* 82 C4 47 37N 119 17W
Coulman I., *Antarctica* 5 D11 73 35S 170 0 E
Coulonge →, *Canada* 70 C4 45 52N 76 46W
Coulterville, *U.S.A.* 84 H6 37 43N 120 12W
Council, *U.S.A.* 82 D5 44 44N 116 26W
Council Bluffs, *U.S.A.* 80 E7 41 16N 95 52W
Council Grove, *U.S.A.* 80 F6 38 40N 96 29W
Coupeville, *U.S.A.* 84 B4 48 13N 122 41W
Courantyne →, *S. Amer.* 92 B7 5 55N 57 5W
Courcelles, *Belgium* 15 D4 50 28N 4 22 E
Courtenay, *Canada* 72 D4 49 45N 125 0W
Courtland, *U.S.A.* 84 G5 38 20N 121 34W
Courtrai = Kortrijk, *Belgium* 15 D3 50 50N 3 17 E
Courtright, *Canada* 78 D2 42 49N 82 28W
Coushatta, *U.S.A.* 81 J8 32 1N 93 21W
Coutts Crossing, *Australia* 63 D5 29 49S 152 55 E
Couvin, *Belgium* 15 D4 50 3N 4 29 E
Cove I., *Canada* 78 A3 45 17N 81 44W
Coventry, *U.K.* 11 E6 52 25N 1 28W
Covilhã, *Portugal* 19 B2 40 17N 7 31W
Covington, *Ga., U.S.A.* 77 J4 33 36N 83 51W
Covington, *Ky., U.S.A.* 76 F3 39 5N 84 31W
Covington, *Okla., U.S.A.* 81 G6 36 18N 97 35W
Covington, *Tenn., U.S.A.* 81 H10 35 34N 89 39W
Covington, *Va., U.S.A.* 76 G5 37 47N 79 59W
Cowal, L., *Australia* 63 E4 33 40S 147 25 E
Cowan, L., *Australia* 61 F3 31 45S 121 45 E
Cowan L., *Canada* 73 C7 54 0N 107 15W
Cowangie, *Australia* 63 F3 35 12S 141 26 E
Cowansville, *Canada* 79 A12 45 14N 72 46W
Coward Springs, *Australia* 63 D2 29 24S 136 49 E
Cowcowing Lakes, *Australia* 61 F2 30 55S 117 20 E
Cowdenbeath, *U.K.* 12 E5 56 7N 3 21W
Cowell, *Australia* 63 E2 33 39S 136 56 E
Cowes, *U.K.* 11 G6 50 45N 1 18W
Cowichan L., *Canada* 84 B2 48 53N 124 17W
Cowlitz →, *U.S.A.* 84 D4 46 6N 122 55W
Cowra, *Australia* 63 E4 33 49S 148 42 E
Coxilha Grande, *Brazil* 95 B5 28 18S 51 30W
Coxim, *Brazil* 93 G8 18 30S 54 55W
Cox's Bazar, *Bangla.* 41 J17 21 26N 91 59 E
Coyote Wells, *U.S.A.* 85 N11 32 44N 115 58W
Coyuca de Benítez, *Mexico* 87 D4 17 1N 100 8W
Coyuca de Catalan, *Mexico* 86 D4 18 18N 100 41W
Cozad, *U.S.A.* 80 E5 40 52N 99 59W
Cozumel, *Mexico* 87 C7 20 31N 86 55W
Cozumel, Isla, *Mexico* 87 C7 20 30N 86 40W
Cracow = Kraków, *Poland* 17 C10 50 4N 19 57 E
Cracow, *Australia* 63 D5 25 17S 150 17 E
Cradock, *Australia* 63 E2 32 6S 138 31 E
Cradock, *S. Africa* 56 E4 32 8S 25 36 E
Craig, *U.S.A.* 82 F10 40 31N 107 33W
Craigavon, *U.K.* 13 B5 54 27N 6 23W
Craigmore, *Zimbabwe* 55 G3 20 28S 32 50 E
Craik, *Canada* 73 C7 51 3N 105 49W
Crailsheim, *Germany* 16 D6 49 8N 10 5 E
Craiova, *Romania* 17 F12 44 21N 23 48 E
Cramsie, *Australia* 62 C3 23 20S 144 15 E
Cranberry L., *U.S.A.* 79 B10 44 11N 74 50W
Cranberry Portage, *Canada* 73 C8 54 35N 101 23W
Cranbrook, *Australia* 61 F2 34 18S 117 33 E
Cranbrook, *Canada* 72 D5 49 30N 115 46W
Crandon, *U.S.A.* 80 C10 45 34N 88 54W
Crane, *Oreg., U.S.A.* 82 E4 43 25N 118 35W
Crane, *Tex., U.S.A.* 81 K3 31 24N 102 21W
Cranston, *U.S.A.* 79 E13 41 47N 71 26W
Crater L., *U.S.A.* 82 E2 42 56N 122 6W
Crater Lake Nat. Park, *U.S.A.* 82 E2 42 55N 122 10W
Crateús, *Brazil* 93 E10 5 10S 40 39W
Crato, *Brazil* 93 E11 7 10S 39 25W
Craven, L., *Canada* 70 B4 54 20N 76 56W
Crawford, *U.S.A.* 80 D3 42 41N 103 25W
Crawfordsville, *U.S.A.* 76 E2 40 2N 86 54W
Crawley, *U.K.* 11 F7 51 7N 0 11W
Crazy Mts., *U.S.A.* 82 C8 46 12N 110 20W
Crean L., *Canada* 73 C7 54 5N 106 9W
Crediton, *Canada* 78 C3 43 17N 81 33W
Cree →, *Canada* 73 B7 58 57N 105 47W
Cree →, *U.K.* 12 G4 54 55N 4 25W
Cree L., *Canada* 73 B7 57 30N 106 30W
Creede, *U.S.A.* 83 H10 37 51N 106 56W
Creekside, *U.S.A.* 78 F5 40 40N 79 11W
Creel, *Mexico* 86 B3 27 45N 107 38W
Creemore, *Canada* 78 B4 44 19N 80 6W
Creighton, *Canada* 73 C8 54 45N 101 54W
Creighton, *U.S.A.* 80 D6 42 28N 97 54W
Crema, *Italy* 18 D8 45 22N 9 41 E
Cremona, *Italy* 18 D9 45 7N 10 2 E
Cres, *Croatia* 16 F8 44 58N 14 25 E
Crescent City, *U.S.A.* 82 F1 41 45N 124 12W
Crespo, *Argentina* 94 C3 32 2S 60 19W
Cresson, *U.S.A.* 78 F6 40 28N 78 36W
Crestline, *Calif., U.S.A.* 85 L9 34 14N 117 18W
Crestline, *Ohio, U.S.A.* 78 F2 40 47N 82 44W
Creston, *Canada* 72 D5 49 10N 116 31W
Creston, *Calif., U.S.A.* 84 K6 35 32N 120 33W
Creston, *Iowa, U.S.A.* 80 E7 41 4N 94 22W
Crestview, *Calif., U.S.A.* 84 H8 37 46N 118 58W
Crestview, *Fla., U.S.A.* 77 K2 30 46N 86 34W
Crete = Kríti, *Greece* 23 D7 35 15N 25 0 E
Crete, *U.S.A.* 80 E6 40 38N 96 58W
Créteil, *France* 18 B5 48 47N 2 28 E
Creus, C. de, *Spain* 19 A7 42 20N 3 19 E
Creuse →, *France* 18 C4 47 0N 0 34 E
Crewe, *U.K.* 10 D5 53 6N 2 26W
Crewkerne, *U.K.* 11 G5 50 53N 2 48W
Criciúma, *Brazil* 95 B6 28 40S 49 23W
Crieff, *U.K.* 12 E5 56 22N 3 50W
Crimea □, *Ukraine* 25 E5 45 30N 33 10 E
Crimean Pen. = Krymskyy Pivostriv, *Ukraine* 25 F5 45 0N 34 0 E
Crişul Alb →, *Romania* 17 E11 46 42N 21 17 E
Crişul Negru →, *Romania* 17 E11 46 42N 21 16 E
Crna →, *Macedonia* 21 D9 41 33N 21 59 E
Crna Gora = Montenegro □, *Yugoslavia* 21 C8 42 40N 19 20 E
Crna Gora, *Macedonia* 21 C9 42 10N 21 30 E
Crna Reka = Crna →, *Macedonia* 21 D9 41 33N 21 59 E
Croagh Patrick, *Ireland* 13 C2 53 46N 9 40W
Croatia ■, *Europe* 16 F9 45 20N 16 0 E
Crocker, Banjaran, *Malaysia* 36 C5 5 40N 116 30 E
Crockett, *U.S.A.* 81 K7 31 19N 95 27W
Crocodile = Krokodil →, *Mozam.* 57 D5 25 14S 32 18 E
Crocodile Is., *Australia* 62 A1 12 3S 134 58 E
Crohy Hd., *Ireland* 13 B3 54 55N 8 26W
Croix, L. La, *Canada* 70 C1 48 20N 92 15W
Croker, C., *Australia* 60 B5 10 58S 132 35 E
Croker, C., *Canada* 78 B4 44 58N 80 59W
Croker I., *Australia* 60 B5 11 12S 132 32 E
Cromarty, *U.K.* 12 D4 57 40N 4 2W
Cromer, *U.K.* 10 E9 52 56N 1 17 E
Cromwell, *N.Z.* 59 L2 45 3S 169 14 E
Cromwell, *U.S.A.* 79 E12 41 36N 72 39W
Crook, *U.K.* 10 C6 54 43N 1 45W
Crooked →, *Canada* 72 C4 54 50N 122 54W
Crooked →, *U.S.A.* 82 D3 44 32N 121 16W
Crooked I., *Bahamas* 89 B5 22 50N 74 10W
Crooked Island Passage, *Bahamas* 89 B5 23 0N 74 30W
Crookston, *Minn., U.S.A.* 80 B6 47 47N 96 37W
Crookston, *Nebr., U.S.A.* 80 D4 42 56N 100 45W
Crookwell, *Australia* 63 E4 34 28S 149 24 E
Crosby, *U.K.* 10 D4 53 30N 3 3W
Crosby, *N. Dak., U.S.A.* 80 A3 48 55N 103 18W
Crosby, *Pa., U.S.A.* 78 E6 41 45N 78 23W
Crosbyton, *U.S.A.* 81 J4 33 40N 101 14W
Cross City, *U.S.A.* 77 L4 29 38N 83 7W
Cross Fell, *U.K.* 10 C5 54 43N 2 28W
Cross L., *Canada* 73 C9 54 45N 97 30W
Cross Lake, *Canada* 73 C9 54 37N 97 47W
Cross Sound, *U.S.A.* 68 C6 58 0N 135 0W
Crossett, *U.S.A.* 81 J9 33 8N 91 58W
Crosshaven, *Ireland* 13 E3 51 47N 8 17W
Crossville, *U.S.A.* 77 G3 35 57N 85 2W
Croswell, *U.S.A.* 78 C2 43 16N 82 37W
Croton-on-Hudson, *U.S.A.* 79 E11 41 12N 73 55W
Crotone, *Italy* 20 E7 39 5N 17 8 E
Crow →, *Canada* 72 B4 59 41N 124 20W
Crow Agency, *U.S.A.* 82 D10 45 36N 107 28W
Crow Hd., *Ireland* 13 E1 51 35N 10 9W
Crowell, *U.S.A.* 81 J5 33 59N 99 43W
Crowley, *U.S.A.* 81 K8 30 13N 92 22W
Crowley, L., *U.S.A.* 84 H8 37 35N 118 42W
Crown Point, *Ind., U.S.A.* 76 E2 41 25N 87 22W
Crown Point, *N.Y., U.S.A.* 79 C11 43 57N 73 26W
Crownpoint, *U.S.A.* 83 J9 35 41N 108 9W
Crows Landing, *U.S.A.* 84 H5 37 23N 121 6W
Crows Nest, *Australia* 63 D5 27 16S 152 4 E
Crowsnest Pass, *Canada* 72 D6 49 40N 114 40W
Croydon, *Australia* 62 B3 18 13S 142 14 E
Croydon □, *U.K.* 11 F7 51 22N 0 5W
Crozet, Is., *Ind. Oc.* 3 G12 46 27S 52 0 E
Cruz, C., *Cuba* 88 C4 19 50N 77 50W
Cruz Alta, *Brazil* 95 B5 28 45S 53 40W
Cruz del Eje, *Argentina* 94 C3 30 45S 64 50W
Cruzeiro, *Brazil* 95 A7 22 33S 45 0W
Cruzeiro do Oeste, *Brazil* 95 A5 23 46S 53 4W
Cruzeiro do Sul, *Brazil* 92 E4 7 35S 72 35W
Cry L., *Canada* 72 B3 58 45N 129 0W
Crystal Bay, *U.S.A.* 84 F7 39 15N 120 0W
Crystal Brook, *Australia* 63 E2 33 21S 138 12 E
Crystal City, *U.S.A.* 81 L5 28 41N 99 50W
Crystal Falls, *U.S.A.* 76 B1 46 5N 88 20W
Crystal River, *U.S.A.* 77 L4 28 54N 82 35W
Crystal Springs, *U.S.A.* 81 K9 31 59N 90 21W
Csongrád, *Hungary* 17 E11 46 43N 20 12 E
Cu Lao Hon, *Vietnam* 39 G7 10 54N 108 18 E
Cua Rao, *Vietnam* 38 C5 19 16N 104 27 E
Cuácua →, *Mozam.* 55 F4 17 54S 37 0 E
Cuamato, *Angola* 56 B2 17 2S 15 7 E
Cuamba, *Mozam.* 55 E4 14 45S 36 22 E
Cuando →, *Angola* 53 H4 17 30S 23 15 E
Cuando Cubango □, *Angola* 56 B3 16 25S 20 0 E
Cuangar, *Angola* 56 B2 17 36S 18 39 E
Cuango = Kwango →, *Dem. Rep. of the Congo* 52 E3 3 14S 17 22 E
Cuanza →, *Angola* 52 F2 9 21S 13 9 E
Cuarto →, *Argentina* 94 C3 33 25S 63 2W
Cuatrociénegas, *Mexico* 86 B4 26 59N 102 5W
Cuauhtémoc, *Mexico* 86 B3 28 25N 106 52W
Cuba, *N. Mex., U.S.A.* 83 J10 36 1N 107 4W
Cuba, *N.Y., U.S.A.* 78 D6 42 13N 78 17W
Cuba ■, *W. Indies* 88 B4 22 0N 79 0W
Cubango →, *Africa* 56 B3 18 50S 22 25 E
Cuchumatanes, Sierra de los, *Guatemala* 88 C1 15 35N 91 25W
Cuckfield, *U.K.* 11 F7 51 1N 0 8W
Cucuí, *Brazil* 92 C5 1 12N 66 50W
Cucurpe, *Mexico* 86 A2 30 20N 110 43W
Cúcuta, *Colombia* 92 B4 7 54N 72 31W
Cuddalore, *India* 40 P11 11 46N 79 45 E
Cuddapah, *India* 40 M11 14 30N 78 47 E
Cuddapan, L., *Australia* 62 D3 25 45S 141 26 E
Cue, *Australia* 61 E2 27 25S 117 54 E
Cuenca, *Ecuador* 92 D3 2 50S 79 9W
Cuenca, *Spain* 19 B4 40 5N 2 10W
Cuenca, Serranía de, *Spain* 19 C5 39 55N 1 50W
Cuernavaca, *Mexico* 87 D5 18 55N 99 15W
Cuero, *U.S.A.* 81 L6 29 6N 97 17W
Cuevas del Almanzora, *Spain* 19 D5 37 18N 1 58W
Cuevo, *Bolivia* 92 H6 20 15S 63 30W
Cuiabá, *Brazil* 93 G7 15 30S 56 0W
Cuiabá →, *Brazil* 93 G7 17 5S 56 36W
Cuijk, *Neths.* 15 C5 51 44N 5 50 E
Cuilco, *Guatemala* 88 C1 15 24N 91 58W
Cuillin Hills, *U.K.* 12 D2 57 13N 6 15W
Cuillin Sd., *U.K.* 12 D2 57 4N 6 20W
Cuito →, *Angola* 56 B3 18 1S 20 48 E
Cuitzeo, L. de, *Mexico* 86 D4 19 55N 101 5W
Cukai, *Malaysia* 39 K4 4 13N 103 25 E
Culbertson, *U.S.A.* 80 A2 48 9N 104 31W
Culcairn, *Australia* 63 F4 35 41S 147 3 E
Culgoa →, *Australia* 63 D4 29 56S 146 20 E
Culiacán, *Mexico* 86 C3 24 50N 107 23W
Culiacán →, *Mexico* 86 C3 24 30N 107 42W
Culion, *Phil.* 37 B6 11 54N 119 58 E
Cullarin Ra., *Australia* 63 E4 34 30S 149 30 E
Cullen, *U.K.* 12 D6 57 42N 2 49W
Cullen Pt., *Australia* 62 A3 11 57S 141 54 E
Cullera, *Spain* 19 C5 39 9N 0 17W
Cullman, *U.S.A.* 77 H2 34 11N 86 51W
Culpeper, *U.S.A.* 76 F7 38 30N 78 0W
Culuene →, *Brazil* 93 F8 12 56S 52 51W
Culver, Pt., *Australia* 61 F3 32 54S 124 43 E
Culverden, *N.Z.* 59 K4 42 47S 172 49 E
Cumaná, *Venezuela* 92 A6 10 30N 64 5W
Cumberland, *B.C., Canada* 72 D4 49 40N 125 0W
Cumberland, *Ont., Canada* 79 A9 45 29N 75 24W
Cumberland, *U.S.A.* 76 F6 39 39N 78 46W
Cumberland →, *U.S.A.* 77 G2 36 15N 87 0W
Cumberland, L., *U.S.A.* 77 G3 36 57N 84 55W
Cumberland I., *U.S.A.* 77 K5 30 50N 81 25W
Cumberland Is., *Australia* 62 C4 20 35S 149 10 E
Cumberland L., *Canada* 73 C8 54 3N 102 18W
Cumberland Pen., *Canada* 69 B13 67 0N 64 0W
Cumberland Plateau, *U.S.A.* 77 H3 36 0N 85 0W
Cumberland Sd., *Canada* 69 B13 65 30N 66 0W
Cumbernauld, *U.K.* 12 F5 55 57N 3 58W
Cumborah, *Australia* 63 D4 29 40S 147 45 E
Cumbria □, *U.K.* 10 C5 54 42N 2 52W
Cumbrian Mts., *U.K.* 10 C5 54 30N 3 0W
Cumbum, *India* 40 M11 15 40N 79 10 E
Cuminá →, *Brazil* 93 D7 1 30S 56 0W
Cummings Mt., *U.S.A.* 85 K8 35 2N 118 34W
Cummins, *Australia* 63 E2 34 16S 135 43 E
Cumnock, *Australia* 63 E4 32 59S 148 46 E
Cumnock, *U.K.* 12 F4 55 28N 4 17W
Cumpas, *Mexico* 86 B3 30 0N 109 48W
Cumplida, Pta., *Canary Is.* 22 F2 28 50N 17 48W
Cunco, *Chile* 96 D2 38 55S 72 2W
Cuncumén, *Chile* 94 C1 31 53S 70 38W
Cunderdin, *Australia* 61 F2 31 37S 117 12 E
Cunene →, *Angola* 56 B1 17 20S 11 50 E
Cúneo, *Italy* 18 D7 44 23N 7 32 E
Çüngüş, *Turkey* 44 B3 38 13N 39 17 E
Cunillera, I. = Sa Conillera, *Spain* 22 C7 38 59N 1 13 E
Cunnamulla, *Australia* 63 D4 28 2S 145 38 E
Cupar, *Canada* 73 C8 50 57N 104 10W
Cupar, *U.K.* 12 E5 56 19N 3 1W
Cupica, G. de, *Colombia* 92 B3 6 25N 77 30W
Curaçao, *Neth. Ant.* 89 D6 12 10N 69 0W
Curanilahue, *Chile* 94 D1 37 29S 73 28W
Curaray →, *Peru* 92 D4 2 20S 74 5W
Curepto, *Chile* 94 D1 35 8S 72 1W
Curiapo, *Venezuela* 92 B6 8 33N 61 5W
Curicó, *Chile* 94 C1 34 55S 71 20W
Curitiba, *Brazil* 95 B6 25 20S 49 10W
Curitibanos, *Brazil* 95 B5 27 18S 50 36W
Currabubula, *Australia* 63 E5 31 16S 150 44 E
Currais Novos, *Brazil* 93 E11 6 13S 36 30W
Curralinho, *Brazil* 93 D9 1 45S 49 46W
Currant, *U.S.A.* 82 G6 38 51N 115 32W
Current →, *U.S.A.* 81 G9 36 15N 90 55W
Currie, *Australia* 62 F3 39 56S 143 53 E
Currie, *U.S.A.* 82 F6 40 16N 114 45W
Curtea de Argeş, *Romania* 17 F13 45 12N 24 42 E
Curtis, *U.S.A.* 80 E4 40 38N 100 31W
Curtis Group, *Australia* 62 F4 39 30S 146 37 E
Curtis I., *Australia* 62 C5 23 35S 151 10 E
Curuápanema →, *Brazil* 93 D7 2 25S 55 2W
Curuçá, *Brazil* 93 D9 0 43S 47 50W
Curuguaty, *Paraguay* 95 A4 24 31S 55 42W
Curup, *Indonesia* 36 E2 4 26S 102 13 E
Cururupu, *Brazil* 93 D10 1 50S 44 50W
Curuzú Cuatiá, *Argentina* 94 B4 29 50S 58 5W
Curvelo, *Brazil* 93 G10 18 45S 44 27W
Cushing, *U.S.A.* 81 H6 35 59N 96 46W
Cushing, Mt., *Canada* 72 B3 57 35N 126 57W
Cusihuiriáchic, *Mexico* 86 B3 28 10N 106 50W
Custer, *U.S.A.* 80 D3 43 46N 103 36W
Cut Bank, *U.S.A.* 82 B7 48 38N 112 20W
Cutchogue, *U.S.A.* 79 E12 41 1N 72 30W
Cuthbert, *U.S.A.* 77 K3 31 46N 84 48W
Cutler, *U.S.A.* 84 J7 36 31N 119 17W
Cuttaburra →, *Australia* 63 D3 29 43S 144 22 E
Cuttack, *India* 41 J14 20 25N 85 57 E
Cuvier, C., *Australia* 61 D1 23 14S 113 22 E
Cuvier I., *N.Z.* 59 G5 36 27S 175 50 E
Cuxhaven, *Germany* 16 B5 53 51N 8 41 E
Cuyahoga Falls, *U.S.A.* 78 E3 41 8N 81 29W
Cuyo, *Phil.* 37 B6 10 50N 121 5 E
Cuyuni →, *Guyana* 92 B7 6 23N 58 41W
Cuzco, *Bolivia* 92 H5 20 0S 66 50W
Cuzco, *Peru* 92 F4 13 32S 72 0W
Cwmbran, *U.K.* 11 F4 51 39N 3 2W
Cyangugu, *Rwanda* 54 C2 2 29S 28 54 E
Cyclades = Kikládhes, *Greece* 21 F11 37 0N 24 30 E
Cygnet, *Australia* 62 G4 43 8S 147 1 E
Cynthiana, *U.S.A.* 76 F3 38 23N 84 18W
Cypress Hills, *Canada* 73 D7 49 40N 109 30W
Cypress Hills Prov. Park, *Canada* 73 D7 49 40N 109 30W
Cyprus ■, *Asia* 23 E12 35 0N 33 0 E
Cyrenaica, *Libya* 51 C10 27 0N 23 0 E
Czar, *Canada* 73 C6 52 27N 110 50W
Czech Rep. ■, *Europe* 16 D8 50 0N 15 0 E
Częstochowa, *Poland* 17 C10 50 49N 19 7 E

D

Da →, *Vietnam* 38 B5 21 15N 105 20 E
Da Hinggan Ling, *China* 33 B7 48 0N 121 0 E
Da Lat, *Vietnam* 39 G7 11 56N 108 25 E
Da Nang, *Vietnam* 38 D7 16 4N 108 13 E
Da Qaidam, *China* 32 C4 37 50N 95 15 E
Da Yunhe →, *China* 35 G11 34 25N 120 5 E
Da'an, *China* 35 B13 45 30N 124 7 E
Daba Shan, *China* 33 C5 32 0N 109 0 E
Dabbagh, Jabal, *Si. Arabia* 44 E2 27 52N 35 45 E
Dabhoi, *India* 42 H5 22 10N 73 20 E
Dabo = Pasirkuning, *Indonesia* 36 E2 0 30S 104 33 E
Dabola, *Guinea* 50 F3 10 50N 11 5W
Dabung, *Malaysia* 39 K4 5 23N 102 1 E

E

Enfield, Canada 71 D7 44 56N 63 32W
Enfield, Conn., U.S.A. 79 E12 41 58N 72 36W
Enfield, N.H., U.S.A. 79 C12 43 39N 72 9W
Engadin, Switz. 18 C9 46 45N 10 10 E
Engaño, C., Dom. Rep. 89 C6 18 30N 68 20W
Engaño, C., Phil. 37 A6 18 35N 122 23 E
Engaru, Japan 30 B11 44 3N 143 31 E
Engcobo, S. Africa 57 E4 31 37S 28 0 E
Engels, Russia 25 D8 51 28N 46 6 E
Engemann L., Canada 73 B7 58 0N 106 55W
Enggano, Indonesia 36 F2 5 20S 102 40 E
England, U.S.A. 81 H9 34 33N 91 58W
England □, U.K. 10 D7 53 0N 2 0W
Englee, Canada 71 B8 50 45N 56 5W
Englehart, Canada 70 C4 47 49N 79 52W
Englewood, U.S.A. 80 F2 39 39N 104 59W
English →, Canada 73 C10 50 35N 93 30W
English Bazar = Ingraj Bazar, India 43 G13 24 58N 88 10 E
English Channel, Europe 11 G6 50 0N 2 0W
English River, Canada 70 C1 49 14N 91 0W
Enid, U.S.A. 81 G6 36 24N 97 53W
Enkhuizen, Neths. 15 B5 52 42N 5 17 E
Enna, Italy 20 F6 37 34N 14 16 E
Ennadai, Canada 73 A8 61 8N 100 53W
Ennadai L., Canada 73 A8 61 0N 101 0W
Ennedi, Chad 51 E10 17 15N 22 0 E
Enngonia, Australia 63 D4 29 21S 145 50 E
Ennis, Ireland 13 D3 52 51N 8 59W
Ennis, Mont., U.S.A. 82 D8 45 21N 111 44W
Ennis, Tex., U.S.A. 81 J6 32 20N 96 38W
Enniscorthy, Ireland 13 D5 52 30N 6 34W
Enniskillen, U.K. 13 B4 54 21N 7 39W
Ennistimon, Ireland 13 D2 52 57N 9 17W
Enns →, Austria 16 D8 48 14N 14 32 E
Enontekiö, Finland 8 B20 68 23N 23 37 E
Enosburg Falls, U.S.A. 79 B12 44 55N 72 48W
Enriquillo, L., Dom. Rep. 89 C5 18 20N 72 5W
Enschede, Neths. 15 B6 52 13N 6 53 E
Ensenada, Argentina 94 C4 34 55S 57 55W
Ensenada, Mexico 86 A1 31 50N 116 50W
Ensenada de los Muertos, Mexico 86 C2 23 59N 109 50W
Ensiola, Pta. de n', Spain 22 B9 39 7N 2 55 E
Entebbe, Uganda 54 B3 0 4N 32 28 E
Enterprise, Canada 72 A5 60 47N 115 45W
Enterprise, Ala., U.S.A. 77 K3 31 19N 85 51W
Enterprise, Oreg., U.S.A. 82 D5 45 25N 117 17W
Entre Ríos, Bolivia 94 A3 21 30S 64 25W
Entre Ríos □, Argentina 94 C4 30 30S 58 30W
Entroncamento, Portugal 19 C1 39 28N 8 28W
Enugu, Nigeria 50 G7 6 30N 7 30 E
Enumclaw, U.S.A. 84 C5 47 12N 121 59W
Eólie, Ís., Italy 20 E6 38 30N 14 57 E
Epe, Neths. 15 B5 52 21N 5 59 E
Épernay, France 18 B5 49 3N 3 56 E
Ephesus, Turkey 21 F12 37 55N 27 22 E
Ephraim, U.S.A. 82 G8 39 22N 111 35W
Ephrata, Pa., U.S.A. 79 F8 40 11N 76 11W
Ephrata, Wash., U.S.A. 82 C4 47 19N 119 33W
Épinal, France 18 B7 48 10N 6 27 E
Episkopi, Cyprus 23 E11 34 40N 32 54 E
Episkopi, Greece 23 D6 35 20N 24 20 E
Episkopi Bay, Cyprus 23 E11 34 35N 32 50 E
Epsom, U.K. 11 F7 51 19N 0 16W
Epukiro, Namibia 56 C2 21 40S 19 9 E
Equatorial Guinea ■, Africa 52 D1 2 0N 8 0 E
Er Rachidia, Morocco 50 B5 31 58N 4 20W
Er Rahad, Sudan 51 F12 12 45N 30 32 E
Er Rif, Morocco 50 A5 35 1N 4 1W
Erāwadī Myit = Irrawaddy →, Burma 41 M19 15 50N 95 6 E
Erāwadī Myitwanya = Irrawaddy, Mouths of the, Burma 41 M19 15 30N 95 0 E
Erbil = Arbīl, Iraq 44 B5 36 15N 44 5 E
Erçek, Turkey 44 B4 38 39N 43 36 E
Erciyaş Dağı, Turkey 25 G6 38 30N 35 30 E
Érd, Hungary 17 E10 47 22N 18 56 E
Erdao Jiang →, China 35 C14 43 0N 127 0 E
Erdek, Turkey 21 D12 40 23N 27 47 E
Erdene = Ulaan-Uul, Mongolia 34 B6 44 13N 111 10 E
Erdenetsogt, Mongolia 34 C4 42 55N 106 5 E
Erebus, Mt., Antarctica 5 D11 77 35S 167 0 E
Erechim, Brazil 95 B5 27 35S 52 15W
Ereğli, Konya, Turkey 25 G5 37 31N 34 4 E
Ereğli, Zonguldak, Turkey 25 F5 41 15N 31 24 E
Erenhot, China 34 C7 43 48N 112 2 E
Eresma →, Spain 19 B3 41 26N 4 45W
Erfenisdam, S. Africa 56 D4 28 30S 26 50 E
Erfurt, Germany 16 C6 50 58N 11 2 E
Erg Iguidi, Africa 50 C4 27 0N 7 0 E
Ergani, Turkey 44 B3 38 17N 39 49 E
Ergel, Mongolia 34 C5 43 8N 109 5 E
Ergeni Vozvyshennost, Russia 25 E7 47 0N 44 0 E
Ērgli, Latvia 9 H21 56 54N 25 38 E
Eriboll, L., U.K. 12 C4 58 30N 4 42W
Érice, Italy 20 E5 38 2N 12 35 E
Erie, U.S.A. 78 D4 42 8N 80 5W
Erie, L., N. Amer. 78 D4 42 15N 81 0W
Erie Canal, U.S.A. 78 C7 43 5N 78 43W
Erieau, Canada 78 D3 42 16N 81 57W
Erigavo, Somali Rep. 46 E4 10 35N 47 20 E
Erikoúsa, Greece 23 A3 39 53N 19 34 E
Eriksdale, Canada 73 C9 50 52N 98 7W
Erímanthos, Greece 21 F9 37 57N 21 50 E
Erimo-misaki, Japan 30 D11 41 50N 143 15 E
Erinpura, India 42 G5 25 9N 73 3 E
Eriskay, U.K. 12 D1 57 4N 7 18W
Eritrea ■, Africa 46 D2 14 0N 38 30 E
Erlangen, Germany 16 D6 49 36N 11 0 E
Erldunda, Australia 62 D1 25 14S 133 12 E
Ermelo, Neths. 15 B5 52 18N 5 35 E
Ermelo, S. Africa 57 D4 26 31S 29 59 E
Ermenek, Turkey 44 B2 36 38N 33 0 E
Ermones, Greece 23 A3 39 37N 19 46 E
Ermoúpolis = Síros, Greece 21 F11 37 28N 24 57 E
Erne →, Ireland 13 B3 54 30N 8 16W
Erne, Lower L., U.K. 13 B4 54 28N 7 47W
Erne, Upper L., U.K. 13 B4 54 14N 7 32W
Ernest Giles Ra., Australia 61 E3 27 0S 123 45 E
Erode, India 40 P10 11 24N 77 45 E
Eromanga, Australia 63 D3 26 40S 143 11 E
Erongo, Namibia 56 C2 21 39S 15 58 E
Erramala Hills, India 40 M11 15 30N 78 15 E
Errigal, Ireland 13 A3 55 2N 8 6W
Erris Hd., Ireland 13 B1 54 19N 10 0W
Erskine, U.S.A. 80 B7 47 40N 96 0W
Ertis = Irtysh →, Russia 26 C7 61 4N 68 52 E
Erwin, U.S.A. 77 G4 36 9N 82 25W
Erzgebirge, Germany 16 C7 50 27N 12 55 E
Erzin, Russia 27 D10 50 15N 95 10 E
Erzincan, Turkey 25 G6 39 46N 39 30 E
Erzurum, Turkey 25 G7 39 57N 41 15 E
Es Caló, Spain 22 C8 38 40N 1 30 E
Es Canar, Spain 22 B8 39 2N 1 36 E
Es Mercadal, Spain 22 B11 39 59N 4 5 E
Es Migjorn Gran, Spain 22 B11 39 57N 4 3 E
Es Sahrâ' Esh Sharqîya, Egypt 51 C12 27 30N 32 30 E
Es Sînâ', Egypt 47 F3 29 0N 34 0 E
Es Vedrà, Spain 22 C7 38 52N 1 12 E
Esambo, Dem. Rep. of the Congo 54 C1 3 48S 23 30 E
Esan-Misaki, Japan 30 D10 41 40N 141 10 E
Esashi, Hokkaidō, Japan 30 B11 44 56N 142 35 E
Esashi, Hokkaidō, Japan 30 D10 41 52N 140 7 E
Esbjerg, Denmark 9 J13 55 29N 8 29 E
Escalante, U.S.A. 83 H8 37 47N 111 36W
Escalante →, U.S.A. 83 H8 37 24N 110 57W
Escalón, Mexico 86 B4 26 46N 104 20W
Escambia →, U.S.A. 77 K2 30 32N 87 11W
Escanaba, U.S.A. 76 C2 45 45N 87 4W
Esch-sur-Alzette, Lux. 18 B6 49 32N 6 0 E
Escondido, U.S.A. 85 M9 33 7N 117 5W
Escuinapa, Mexico 86 C3 22 50N 105 50W
Escuintla, Guatemala 88 D1 14 20N 90 48W
Esenguly, Turkmenistan 26 F6 37 37N 53 59 E
Eşfahān, Iran 45 C6 32 39N 51 43 E
Eşfahān □, Iran 45 C6 32 50N 51 50 E
Esfarāyen, Iran 45 B8 37 4N 57 30 E
Esfideh, Iran 45 C8 33 39N 59 46 E
Esh Sham = Dimashq, Syria 47 B5 33 30N 36 18 E
Esha Ness, U.K. 12 A7 60 29N 1 38W
Esher, U.K. 11 F7 51 21N 0 20W
Eshowe, S. Africa 57 D5 28 50S 31 30 E
Esigodini, Zimbabwe 57 C4 20 18S 28 56 E
Esil = Ishim →, Russia 26 D8 57 45N 71 10 E
Esira, Madag. 57 C8 24 20S 46 42 E
Esk →, Cumb., U.K. 12 G5 54 58N 3 2W
Esk →, N. Yorks., U.K. 10 C7 54 30N 0 37W
Eskān, Iran 45 E9 26 48N 63 9 E
Esker, Canada 71 B6 53 53N 66 25W
Eskifjörður, Iceland 8 D7 65 3N 13 55W
Eskilstuna, Sweden 9 G17 59 22N 16 32 E
Eskimo Pt., Canada 68 B10 61 10N 94 15W
Eskişehir, Turkey 25 G5 39 50N 30 30 E
Esla →, Spain 19 B2 41 29N 6 3W
Eslāmābād-e Gharb, Iran 44 C5 34 10N 46 30 E
Eslāmshahr, Iran 45 C6 35 40N 51 10 E
Eşme, Turkey 21 E13 38 23N 28 58 E
Esmeraldas, Ecuador 92 C3 1 0N 79 40W
Esnagi L., Canada 70 C3 48 36N 84 33W
Espanola, Canada 70 C3 46 15N 81 46W
Espanola, U.S.A. 83 H10 35 59N 106 5W
Esparta, Costa Rica 88 E3 9 59N 84 40W
Esperance, Australia 61 F3 33 45S 121 55 E
Esperance B., Australia 61 F3 33 48S 121 55 E
Esperanza, Argentina 94 C3 31 29S 61 3W
Espichel, C., Portugal 19 C1 38 22N 9 16W
Espigão, Serra do, Brazil 95 B5 26 35S 50 30W
Espinazo, Sierra del = Espinhaço, Serra do, Brazil 93 G10 17 30S 43 30W
Espinhaço, Serra do, Brazil 93 G10 17 30S 43 30W
Espinilho, Serra do, Brazil 95 B5 28 30S 55 0W
Espírito Santo □, Brazil 93 H10 20 0S 40 45W
Espíritu Santo, Vanuatu 64 J8 15 15S 166 50 E
Espíritu Santo, B. del, Mexico 87 D7 19 15N 87 0W
Espíritu Santo, I., Mexico 86 C2 24 30N 110 23W
Espita, Mexico 87 C7 21 1N 88 19W
Espoo, Finland 9 F21 60 12N 24 40 E
Espungabera, Mozam. 57 C5 20 29S 32 45 E
Esquel, Argentina 96 E2 42 55S 71 20W
Esquimalt, Canada 72 D4 48 26N 123 25W
Esquina, Argentina 94 C4 30 0S 59 30W
Essaouira, Morocco 50 B4 31 32N 9 42W
Essebie, Dem. Rep. of the Congo 54 B3 2 58N 30 40 E
Essen, Belgium 15 C4 51 28N 4 28 E
Essen, Germany 16 C4 51 28N 7 2 E
Essendon, Mt., Australia 61 E3 25 0S 120 29 E
Essequibo →, Guyana 92 B7 6 50N 58 30W
Essex, Canada 78 D2 42 10N 82 49W
Essex, Calif., U.S.A. 85 L11 34 44N 115 15W
Essex, N.Y., U.S.A. 79 B11 44 19N 73 21W
Essex □, U.K. 11 F8 51 54N 0 27 E
Essex Junction, U.S.A. 79 B11 44 29N 73 7W
Esslingen, Germany 16 D5 48 44N 9 18 E
Estados, I. de Los, Argentina 96 G4 54 40S 64 30W
Eşţahbānāt, Iran 45 D7 29 8N 54 4 E
Estância, Brazil 93 F11 11 16S 37 26W
Estancia, U.S.A. 83 J10 34 46N 106 4W
Estārm, Iran 45 D8 28 21N 58 21 E
Estcourt, S. Africa 57 D4 29 0S 29 53 E
Estelí, Nic. 88 D2 13 9N 86 22W
Estellencs, Spain 22 B9 39 39N 2 29 E
Esterhazy, Canada 73 C8 50 37N 102 5W
Estevan, Canada 73 D8 49 10N 102 59W
Estevan Group, Canada 72 C3 53 3N 129 38W
Estherville, U.S.A. 80 D7 43 24N 94 50W
Eston, Canada 73 C7 51 8N 108 40W
Estonia ■, Europe 9 G21 58 30N 25 30 E
Estreito, Brazil 93 E9 6 32S 47 25W
Estrela, Serra da, Portugal 19 B2 40 10N 7 45W
Estremoz, Portugal 19 C2 38 51N 7 39W
Estrondo, Serra do, Brazil 93 E9 7 20S 48 0W
Esztergom, Hungary 17 E10 47 47N 18 44 E
Etah, India 43 F8 27 35N 78 40 E
Étampes, France 18 B5 48 26N 2 10 E
Etanga, Namibia 56 B1 17 55S 13 0 E
Etawah, India 43 F8 26 48N 79 6 E
Etawney L., Canada 73 B9 57 50N 96 50W
Ethel, U.S.A. 84 D4 46 32N 122 46W
Ethelbert, Canada 73 C8 51 32N 100 25W
Ethiopia ■, Africa 46 F3 8 0N 40 0 E
Ethiopian Highlands, Ethiopia 28 J7 10 0N 37 0 E
Etive, L., U.K. 12 E3 56 29N 5 10W
Etna, Italy 20 F6 37 50N 14 55 E
Etoile, Dem. Rep. of the Congo 55 E2 11 33S 27 30 E
Etosha Pan, Namibia 56 B2 18 40S 16 30 E
Etowah, U.S.A. 77 H3 35 20N 84 32W
Ettelbruck, Lux. 15 E6 49 51N 6 5 E
Ettrick Water →, U.K. 12 F6 55 31N 2 55W
Etuku, Dem. Rep. of the Congo 54 C2 3 42S 25 45 E
Etzatlán, Mexico 86 C4 20 48N 104 5W
Etzná, Mexico 87 D6 19 35N 90 15W
Euboea = Évvoia, Greece 21 E11 38 30N 24 0 E
Eucla, Australia 61 F4 31 41S 128 52 E
Euclid, U.S.A. 78 E3 41 34N 81 32W
Eucumbene, L., Australia 63 F4 36 2S 148 40 E
Eudora, U.S.A. 81 J9 33 7N 91 16W
Eufaula, Ala., U.S.A. 77 K3 31 54N 85 9W
Eufaula, Okla., U.S.A. 81 H7 35 17N 95 35W
Eufaula L., U.S.A. 81 H7 35 18N 95 21W
Eugene, U.S.A. 82 E2 44 5N 123 4W
Eugowra, Australia 63 E4 33 22S 148 24 E
Eulo, Australia 63 D4 28 10S 145 3 E
Eunice, La., U.S.A. 81 K8 30 30N 92 25W
Eunice, N. Mex., U.S.A. 81 J3 32 26N 103 10W
Eupen, Belgium 15 D6 50 37N 6 3 E
Euphrates = Furāt, Nahr al →, Asia 44 D5 31 0N 47 25 E
Eureka, Canada 4 B3 80 0N 85 56W
Eureka, Calif., U.S.A. 82 F1 40 47N 124 9W
Eureka, Kans., U.S.A. 81 G6 37 49N 96 17W
Eureka, Mont., U.S.A. 82 B6 48 53N 115 3W
Eureka, Nev., U.S.A. 82 G5 39 31N 115 58W
Eureka, S. Dak., U.S.A. 80 C5 45 46N 99 38W
Eureka, Mt., Australia 61 E3 26 35S 121 35 E
Euroa, Australia 63 F4 36 44S 145 35 E
Europa, Île, Ind. Oc. 53 J8 22 20S 40 22 E
Europa, Picos de, Spain 19 A3 43 10N 4 49W
Europa, Pta. de, Gib. 19 D3 36 3N 5 21W
Europe 6 E10 50 0N 20 0 E
Europoort, Neths. 15 C4 51 57N 4 10 E
Eustis, U.S.A. 77 L5 28 51N 81 41W
Eutsuk L., Canada 72 C3 53 20N 126 45W
Evale, Angola 56 B2 16 33S 15 44 E
Evans, U.S.A. 80 E2 40 23N 104 41W
Evans, L., Canada 70 B4 50 50N 77 0W
Evans City, U.S.A. 78 F4 40 46N 80 4W
Evans Head, Australia 63 D5 29 7S 153 27 E
Evans Mills, U.S.A. 79 B9 44 6N 75 48W
Evansburg, Canada 72 C5 53 36N 114 59W
Evanston, Ill., U.S.A. 76 E2 42 3N 87 41W
Evanston, Wyo., U.S.A. 82 F8 41 16N 110 58W
Evansville, U.S.A. 76 G2 37 58N 87 35W
Evaz, Iran 45 E7 27 46N 53 59 E
Eveleth, U.S.A. 80 B8 47 28N 92 32W
Evensk, Russia 27 C16 62 12N 159 30 E
Everard, L., Australia 63 E2 31 30S 135 0 E
Everard Ranges, Australia 61 E5 27 5S 132 28 E
Everest, Mt., Nepal 43 E12 28 5N 86 58 E
Everett, Pa., U.S.A. 78 F6 40 1N 78 23W
Everett, Wash., U.S.A. 84 C4 47 59N 122 12W
Everglades, The, U.S.A. 77 N5 25 50N 81 0W
Everglades City, U.S.A. 77 N5 25 52N 81 23W
Everglades Nat. Park, U.S.A. 77 N5 25 30N 81 0W
Evergreen, Ala., U.S.A. 77 K2 31 26N 86 57W
Evergreen, Mont., U.S.A. 82 B6 48 9N 114 13W
Evesham, U.K. 11 E6 52 6N 1 56W
Evje, Norway 9 G12 58 36N 7 51 E
Évora, Portugal 19 C2 38 33N 7 57W
Evowghlī, Iran 44 B5 38 43N 45 13 E
Évreux, France 18 B4 49 3N 1 8 E
Évros →, Greece 21 D12 41 40N 26 34 E
Évry, France 18 B5 48 38N 2 27 E
Évvoia, Greece 21 E11 38 30N 24 0 E
Ewe, L., U.K. 12 D3 57 49N 5 38W
Ewing, U.S.A. 80 D5 42 16N 98 21W
Ewo, Congo 52 E2 0 48S 14 45 E
Exaltación, Bolivia 92 F5 13 10S 65 20W
Excelsior Springs, U.S.A. 80 F7 39 20N 94 13W
Exe →, U.K. 11 G4 50 41N 3 29W
Exeter, Canada 78 C3 43 21N 81 29W
Exeter, U.K. 11 G4 50 43N 3 31W
Exeter, Calif., U.S.A. 84 J7 36 18N 119 9W
Exeter, N.H., U.S.A. 79 D14 42 59N 70 57W
Exmoor, U.K. 11 F4 51 12N 3 45W
Exmouth, Australia 60 D1 21 54S 114 10 E
Exmouth, U.K. 11 G4 50 37N 3 25W
Exmouth G., Australia 60 D1 22 15S 114 15 E
Expedition Ra., Australia 62 C4 24 30S 149 12 E
Extremadura □, Spain 19 C2 39 30N 6 5W
Exuma Sound, Bahamas 88 B4 24 30N 76 20W
Eyasi, L., Tanzania 54 C4 3 30S 35 0 E
Eye Pen., U.K. 12 C2 58 13N 6 10W
Eyemouth, U.K. 12 F6 55 52N 2 5W
Eyjafjörður, Iceland 8 C4 66 15N 18 30W
Eyre (North), L., Australia 63 D2 28 30S 137 20 E
Eyre (South), L., Australia 63 D2 29 18S 137 25 E
Eyre Mts., N.Z. 59 L2 45 25S 168 25 E
Eyre Pen., Australia 63 E2 33 30S 136 17 E
Eysturoy, Færoe Is. 8 E9 62 13N 6 54W
Eyvānkī, Iran 45 C6 35 24N 51 56 E
Ezine, Turkey 21 E12 39 48N 26 20 E
Ezouza →, Cyprus 23 E11 34 44N 32 27 E

F

F.Y.R.O.M. = Macedonia ■, Europe 21 D9 41 53N 21 40 E
Fabala, Guinea 50 G4 9 44N 9 5W
Fabens, U.S.A. 83 L10 31 30N 106 10W
Fabriano, Italy 20 C5 43 20N 12 54 E
Fachi, Niger 51 E8 18 6N 11 34 E
Fada, Chad 51 E10 17 13N 21 34 E
Fada-n-Gourma, Burkina Faso 50 F6 12 10N 0 30 E
Faddeyevskiy, Ostrov, Russia 27 B15 76 0N 144 0 E
Fadghāmī, Syria 44 C4 35 53N 40 52 E
Faenza, Italy 20 B4 44 17N 11 53 E
Færoe Is. = Føroyar, Atl. Oc. 8 F9 62 0N 7 0W
Făgăras, Romania 17 F13 45 48N 24 58 E
Fagersta, Sweden 9 F16 60 1N 15 46 E
Fagnano, L., Argentina 96 G3 54 30S 68 0W
Fahliān, Iran 45 D6 30 11N 51 28 E
Fahraj, Kermān, Iran 45 D8 29 0N 59 0 E
Fahraj, Yazd, Iran 45 D7 31 46N 54 36 E
Faial, Madeira 22 D3 32 47N 16 53W
Fair Haven, U.S.A. 76 D9 43 36N 73 16W
Fair Hd., U.K. 13 A5 55 14N 6 9W
Fair Oaks, U.S.A. 84 G5 38 39N 121 16W
Fairbanks, U.S.A. 68 B5 64 51N 147 43W
Fairbury, U.S.A. 80 E6 40 8N 97 11W
Fairfax, U.S.A. 79 B11 44 40N 73 1W
Fairfield, Ala., U.S.A. 77 J2 33 29N 86 55W
Fairfield, Calif., U.S.A. 84 G4 38 15N 122 3W
Fairfield, Conn., U.S.A. 79 E11 41 9N 73 16W
Fairfield, Idaho, U.S.A. 82 E6 43 21N 114 44W
Fairfield, Ill., U.S.A. 76 F1 38 23N 88 22W
Fairfield, Iowa, U.S.A. 80 E9 40 56N 91 57W
Fairfield, Tex., U.S.A. 81 K7 31 44N 96 10W
Fairford, Canada 73 C9 51 37N 98 38W
Fairhope, U.S.A. 77 K2 30 31N 87 54W
Fairlie, N.Z. 59 L3 44 5S 170 49 E
Fairmead, U.S.A. 84 H6 37 5N 120 10W
Fairmont, Minn., U.S.A. 80 D7 43 39N 94 28W
Fairmont, W. Va., U.S.A. 76 F5 39 29N 80 9W
Fairmount, Calif., U.S.A. 85 L8 34 45N 118 26W
Fairmount, N.Y., U.S.A. 79 C8 43 5N 76 12W
Fairplay, U.S.A. 83 G11 39 15N 106 2W
Fairport, U.S.A. 78 C7 43 6N 77 27W
Fairport Harbor, U.S.A. 78 E3 41 45N 81 17W
Fairview, Canada 72 B5 56 5N 118 25W
Fairview, Mont., U.S.A. 80 B2 47 51N 104 3W
Fairview, Okla., U.S.A. 81 G5 36 16N 98 29W
Fairweather, Mt., U.S.A. 72 B1 58 55N 137 32W
Faisalabad, Pakistan 42 D5 31 30N 73 5 E
Faith, U.S.A. 80 C3 45 2N 102 2W
Faizabad, India 43 F10 26 45N 82 10 E
Fajardo, Puerto Rico 89 C6 18 20N 65 39W
Fajr, W. →, Si. Arabia 44 D3 29 10N 38 10 E
Fakenham, U.K. 10 E8 52 51N 0 51 E
Fakfak, Indonesia 37 E8 2 55S 132 18 E
Faku, China 35 C12 42 32N 123 21 E
Falaise, France 18 B3 48 54N 0 12W
Falaise, Mui, Vietnam 38 C5 19 6N 105 45 E
Falam, Burma 41 H18 23 0N 93 45 E
Falcó, C. des, Spain 22 C7 38 50N 1 23 E
Falcón, Presa, Mexico 87 B5 26 35N 99 10W
Falcon Lake, Canada 73 D9 49 42N 95 15W
Falcon Reservoir, U.S.A. 81 M5 26 34N 99 10W
Falconara Marittima, Italy 20 C5 43 37N 13 24 E
Falcone, C. del, Italy 20 D3 40 58N 8 12 E
Falconer, U.S.A. 78 D5 42 7N 79 13W
Faleshty = Făleşti, Moldova 17 E14 47 32N 27 44 E
Făleşti, Moldova 17 E14 47 32N 27 44 E
Falfurrias, U.S.A. 81 M5 27 14N 98 9W
Falher, Canada 72 B5 55 44N 117 15W
Falirakí, Greece 23 C10 36 22N 28 12 E
Falkenberg, Sweden 9 H15 56 54N 12 30 E
Falkirk, U.K. 12 F5 56 0N 3 47W
Falkirk □, U.K. 12 F5 55 58N 3 49W
Falkland, U.K. 12 E5 56 16N 3 12W
Falkland Is. □, Atl. Oc. 96 G5 51 30S 59 0W
Falkland Sd., Falk. Is. 96 G5 52 0S 60 0W
Falköping, Sweden 9 G15 58 12N 13 33 E
Fall River, U.S.A. 79 E13 41 43N 71 10W
Fallbrook, U.S.A. 85 M9 33 23N 117 15W
Fallon, U.S.A. 82 G4 39 28N 118 47W
Falls City, U.S.A. 80 E7 40 3N 95 36W
Falls Creek, U.S.A. 78 E6 41 9N 78 48W
Falmouth, Jamaica 88 C4 18 30N 77 40W
Falmouth, U.K. 11 G2 50 9N 5 5W
Falmouth, U.S.A. 79 E14 41 33N 70 37W
Falsa, Pta., Mexico 86 B1 27 51N 115 3W
False B., S. Africa 56 E2 34 15S 18 40 E
Falso, C., Honduras 88 C3 15 12N 83 21W
Falster, Denmark 9 J14 54 45N 11 55 E
Falsterbo, Sweden 9 J15 55 23N 12 50 E
Fălticeni, Romania 17 E14 47 21N 26 20 E
Falun, Sweden 9 F16 60 37N 15 37 E
Famagusta, Cyprus 23 D12 35 8N 33 55 E
Famagusta Bay, Cyprus 23 D13 35 15N 34 0 E
Famalé, Niger 50 F6 14 33N 1 5 E
Famatina, Sierra de, Argentina 94 B2 27 30S 68 0W
Family L., Canada 73 C9 51 54N 95 27W
Famoso, U.S.A. 85 K7 35 37N 119 12W
Fan Xian, China 34 G8 35 55N 115 38 E
Fanad Hd., Ireland 13 A4 55 17N 7 38W
Fandriana, Madag. 57 C8 20 14S 47 21 E
Fang, Thailand 38 C2 19 55N 99 13 E
Fangcheng, China 34 H7 33 18N 112 59 E
Fangshan, China 34 E6 38 3N 111 25 E
Fangzi, China 35 F10 36 33N 119 10 E
Fanjakana, Madag. 57 C8 21 10S 46 53 E
Fanjiatun, China 35 C13 43 40N 125 15 E
Fannich, L., U.K. 12 D4 57 38N 4 59W
Fannūj, Iran 45 E8 26 35N 59 38 E
Fanø, Denmark 9 J13 55 25N 8 25 E
Fano, Italy 20 C5 43 50N 13 1 E
Fanshi, China 34 E7 39 12N 113 20 E
Fao = Al Fāw, Iraq 45 D6 30 0N 48 30 E
Faqirwali, Pakistan 42 E5 29 27N 73 0 E
Faradje, Dem. Rep. of the Congo 54 B2 3 50N 29 45 E
Farafangana, Madag. 57 C8 22 49S 47 50 E
Farāh, Afghan. 40 C3 32 20N 62 7 E
Farāh □, Afghan. 40 C3 32 25N 62 10 E
Farahalana, Madag. 57 A9 14 26S 50 10 E
Faranah, Guinea 50 F3 10 3N 10 45W
Farasān, Jazā'ir, Si. Arabia 46 D3 16 45N 41 55 E
Farasan Is. = Farasān, Jazā'ir, Si. Arabia 46 D3 16 45N 41 55 E
Faratsiho, Madag. 57 B8 19 24S 46 57 E
Fareham, U.K. 11 G6 50 51N 1 11W
Farewell, C., N.Z. 59 J4 40 29S 172 43 E
Farewell C. = Nunap Isua, Greenland 69 C15 59 48N 43 55W
Farghona, Uzbekistan 26 E8 40 23N 71 19 E
Fargo, U.S.A. 80 B6 46 53N 96 48W
Fār'iah, W. al →, West Bank 47 C4 32 12N 35 27 E
Faribault, U.S.A. 80 C8 44 18N 93 16W
Faridabad, India 42 E6 28 26N 77 19 E
Faridkot, India 42 D6 30 44N 74 45 E
Faridpur, Bangla. 43 H13 23 15N 89 55 E
Faridpur, India 43 E8 28 13N 79 33 E
Farimān, Iran 45 C8 35 40N 59 49 E
Farina, Australia 63 E2 30 3S 138 15 E
Fariones, Pta., Canary Is. 22 E6 29 13N 13 28W
Farmerville, U.S.A. 81 J8 32 47N 92 24W
Farmingdale, U.S.A. 79 F10 40 12N 74 10W
Farmington, Canada 72 B4 55 54N 120 30W
Farmington, Calif., U.S.A. 84 H6 37 55N 120 59W
Farmington, Maine, U.S.A. 77 C10 44 40N 70 9W

Farmington, Mo., U.S.A. 81 G9 37 47N 90 25W
Farmington, N.H., U.S.A. 79 C13 43 24N 71 4W
Farmington, N. Mex., U.S.A. 83 H9 36 44N 108 12W
Farmington, Utah, U.S.A. 82 F8 41 0N 111 12W
Farmington →, U.S.A. 79 E12 41 51N 72 38W
Farmville, U.S.A. 76 G6 37 18N 78 24W
Farne Is., U.K. 10 B6 55 38N 1 37W
Farnham, Canada 79 A12 45 17N 72 59W
Farnham, Mt., Canada 72 C5 50 29N 116 30W
Faro, Brazil 93 D7 2 10S 56 39W
Faro, Canada 68 B6 62 11N 133 22W
Faro, Portugal 19 D2 37 2N 7 55W
Fårö, Sweden 9 H18 57 55N 19 5 E
Farquhar, C., Australia 61 D1 23 50S 113 36 E
Farrars Cr. →, Australia 62 D3 25 35S 140 43 E
Farrāshband, Iran 45 D7 28 57N 52 5 E
Farrell, U.S.A. 78 E4 41 13N 80 30W
Farrokhī, Iran 45 C8 33 50N 59 31 E
Farruch, C. = Ferrutx, C., Spain 22 B10 39 47N 3 21 E
Fārs □, Iran 45 D7 29 30N 55 0 E
Fársala, Greece 21 E10 39 17N 22 23 E
Farson, U.S.A. 82 E9 42 6N 109 27W
Farsund, Norway 9 G12 58 5N 6 55 E
Fartak, Rās, Si. Arabia 44 D2 28 5N 34 34 E
Fartak, Ra's, Yemen 46 D5 15 38N 52 15 E
Fartura, Serra da, Brazil 95 B5 26 21S 52 52W
Fārūj, Iran 45 B8 37 14N 58 14 E
Farvel, Kap = Nunap Isua, Greenland 69 C15 59 48N 43 55W
Farwell, U.S.A. 81 H3 34 23N 103 2W
Fāryāb □, Afghan. 40 B4 36 0N 65 0 E
Fasā, Iran 45 D7 29 0N 53 39 E
Fasano, Italy 20 D7 40 50N 17 22 E
Fastiv, Ukraine 17 C15 50 7N 29 57 E
Fastov = Fastiv, Ukraine 17 C15 50 7N 29 57 E
Fatagar, Tanjung, Indonesia 37 E8 2 46S 131 57 E
Fatehabad, Haryana, India 42 E6 29 31N 75 27 E
Fatehabad, Ut. P., India 42 F8 27 1N 78 19 E
Fatehgarh, India 43 F8 27 25N 79 35 E
Fatehpur, Bihar, India 43 G11 24 38N 85 14 E
Fatehpur, Raj., India 42 F6 28 0N 74 40 E
Fatehpur, Ut. P., India 43 G9 25 56N 81 13 E
Fatehpur, Ut. P., India 43 F9 27 10N 81 13 E
Fatehpur Sikri, India 42 F6 27 6N 77 40 E
Fatima, Canada 71 C7 47 24N 61 53W
Faulkton, U.S.A. 80 C5 45 2N 99 8W
Faure I., Australia 61 E1 25 52S 113 50 E
Fauresmith, S. Africa 56 D4 29 44S 25 17 E
Fauske, Norway 8 C16 67 17N 15 25 E
Favara, Italy 20 F5 37 19N 13 39 E
Favàritx, C. de, Spain 22 B11 40 0N 4 15 E
Favignana, Italy 20 F5 37 56N 12 20 E
Fawcett, Pt., Australia 60 B5 11 46S 130 2 E
Fawn →, Canada 70 A2 55 20N 87 35W
Fawnskin, U.S.A. 85 L10 34 16N 116 56W
Faxaflói, Iceland 8 D2 64 29N 23 0W
Faya-Largeau, Chad 51 E9 17 58N 19 6 E
Fayd, Si. Arabia 44 E4 27 1N 42 52 E
Fayette, Ala., U.S.A. 77 J2 33 41N 87 50W
Fayette, Mo., U.S.A. 80 F8 39 9N 92 41W
Fayetteville, Ark., U.S.A. 81 G7 36 4N 94 10W
Fayetteville, N.C., U.S.A. 77 H6 35 3N 78 53W
Fayetteville, Tenn., U.S.A. 77 H2 35 9N 86 34W
Fazilka, India 42 D6 30 27N 74 2 E
Fazilpur, Pakistan 42 E4 29 18N 70 29 E
Fdérik, Mauritania 50 D3 22 40N 12 45W
Feale →, Ireland 13 D2 52 27N 9 37W
Fear, C., U.S.A. 77 J7 33 50N 77 58W
Feather →, U.S.A. 82 G3 38 47N 121 36W
Feather Falls, U.S.A. 84 F5 39 36N 121 16W
Featherston, N.Z. 59 J5 41 6S 175 20 E
Featherstone, Zimbabwe 55 F3 18 42S 30 55 E
Fécamp, France 18 B4 49 45N 0 22 E
Fedala = Mohammedia, Morocco 50 B4 33 44N 7 21W
Federación, Argentina 94 C4 31 0S 57 55W
Féderal, Argentina 96 C5 30 57S 58 48W
Federal Way, U.S.A. 84 C4 47 18N 122 19W
Fedeshkūh, Iran 45 D7 28 49N 53 50 E
Fehmarn, Germany 16 A6 54 27N 11 7 E
Fehmarn Bælt, Europe 9 J14 54 35N 11 20 E
Fehmarn Belt = Fehmarn Bælt, Europe 9 J14 54 35N 11 20 E
Fei Xian, China 35 G9 35 18N 117 59 E
Feijó, Brazil 92 E4 8 9S 70 21W
Feilding, N.Z. 59 J5 40 13S 175 35 E
Feira de Santana, Brazil 93 F11 12 15S 38 57W
Feixiang, China 34 F8 36 30N 114 45 E
Felanitx, Spain 22 B10 39 28N 3 9 E
Feldkirch, Austria 16 E5 47 15N 9 37 E
Felipe Carrillo Puerto, Mexico 87 D7 19 38N 88 3W
Felixburg, Zimbabwe 57 B5 19 29S 30 51 E
Felixstowe, U.K. 11 F9 51 58N 1 23 E
Felton, U.S.A. 84 H4 37 3N 122 4W
Femer Bælt = Fehmarn Bælt, Europe 9 J14 54 35N 11 20 E
Femunden, Norway 9 E14 62 10N 11 53 E
Fen He →, China 34 G6 35 36N 110 42 E
Fenelon Falls, Canada 78 B6 44 32N 78 45W
Feng Xian, Jiangsu, China 34 G9 34 43N 116 35 E
Feng Xian, Shaanxi, China 34 H4 33 54N 106 40 E
Fengcheng, China 35 D13 40 28N 124 5 E
Fengfeng, China 34 F8 36 28N 114 8 E
Fengning, China 34 D9 41 10N 116 33 E
Fengqiu, China 34 G8 35 2N 114 25 E
Fengrun, China 35 E10 39 48N 118 8 E
Fengtai, China 34 E9 39 50N 116 18 E
Fengxiang, China 34 G4 34 29N 107 25 E
Fengyang, China 35 H9 32 51N 117 29 E
Fengzhen, China 34 D7 40 25N 113 2 E
Fenoarivo, Fianarantsoa, Madag. 57 C8 21 43S 46 24 E
Fenoarivo, Fianarantsoa, Madag. 57 C8 20 52S 46 53 E
Fenoarivo Afovoany, Madag. 57 B8 18 26S 46 34 E
Fenoarivo Atsinanana, Madag. 57 B8 17 22S 49 25 E
Fens, The, U.K. 10 E7 52 38N 0 2W
Fenton, U.S.A. 76 D4 42 48N 83 42W
Fenxi, China 34 F6 36 40N 111 31 E
Fenyang, China 34 F6 37 18N 111 48 E
Feodosiya, Ukraine 25 E6 45 2N 35 16 E
Ferdows, Iran 45 C8 33 58N 58 2 E
Ferfer, Somali Rep. 46 F4 5 4N 45 9 E
Fergana = Farghona, Uzbekistan 26 E8 40 23N 71 19 E
Fergus, Canada 78 C4 43 43N 80 24W
Fergus Falls, U.S.A. 80 B6 46 17N 96 4W
Ferkéssédougou, Ivory C. 50 G4 9 35N 5 6W
Ferland, Canada 70 B2 50 19N 88 27W
Fermanagh □, U.K. 13 B4 54 21N 7 40W
Fermo, Italy 20 C5 43 9N 13 43 E
Fermont, Canada 71 B6 52 47N 67 5W
Fermoy, Ireland 13 D3 52 9N 8 16W
Fernández, Argentina 94 B3 27 55S 63 50W
Fernandina Beach, U.S.A. 77 K5 30 40N 81 27W
Fernando de Noronha, Brazil 93 D12 4 0S 33 10W
Fernando Póo = Bioko, Eq. Guin. 52 D1 3 30N 8 40 E
Ferndale, U.S.A. 84 B4 48 51N 122 36W
Fernie, Canada 72 D5 49 30N 115 5W
Fernlees, Australia 62 C4 23 51S 148 7 E
Fernley, U.S.A. 82 G4 39 36N 119 15W
Ferozepore = Firozpur, India 42 D6 30 55N 74 40 E
Ferrara, Italy 20 B4 44 50N 11 35 E
Ferreñafe, Peru 92 E3 6 42S 79 50W
Ferrerías, Spain 22 B11 39 59N 4 1 E
Ferret, C., France 18 D3 44 38N 1 15W
Ferriday, U.S.A. 81 K9 31 38N 91 33W
Ferrol, Spain 19 A1 43 29N 8 15W
Ferron, U.S.A. 83 G8 39 5N 111 8W
Ferrutx, C., Spain 22 B10 39 47N 3 21 E
Ferryland, Canada 71 C9 47 2N 52 53W
Fertile, U.S.A. 80 B6 47 32N 96 17W
Fès, Morocco 50 B5 34 0N 5 0W
Fessenden, U.S.A. 80 B5 47 39N 99 38W
Festus, U.S.A. 80 F9 38 13N 90 24W
Feteşti, Romania 17 F14 44 22N 27 51 E
Fethiye, Turkey 25 G4 36 36N 29 6 E
Fetlar, U.K. 12 A8 60 36N 0 52W
Feuilles →, Canada 69 C12 58 47N 70 4W
Fez = Fès, Morocco 50 B5 34 0N 5 0W
Fezzan, Libya 51 C8 27 0N 13 0 E
Fiambalá, Argentina 94 B2 27 45S 67 37W
Fianarantsoa, Madag. 57 C8 21 26S 47 5 E
Fianarantsoa □, Madag. 57 B8 19 30S 47 0 E
Ficksburg, S. Africa 57 D4 28 51S 27 53 E
Field →, Australia 62 C2 23 48S 138 0 E
Field I., Australia 60 B5 12 5S 132 23 E
Fier, Albania 21 D8 40 43N 19 33 E
Fife □, U.K. 12 E5 56 16N 3 1W
Fife Ness, U.K. 12 E6 56 17N 2 35W
Fifth Cataract, Sudan 51 E12 18 22N 33 50 E
Figeac, France 18 D5 44 37N 2 2 E
Figtree, Zimbabwe 55 G2 20 22S 28 20 E
Figueira da Foz, Portugal 19 B1 40 7N 8 54W
Figueres, Spain 19 A7 42 18N 2 58 E
Figuig, Morocco 50 B5 32 5N 1 11W
Fihaonana, Madag. 57 B8 18 36S 47 12 E
Fiherenana, Madag. 57 B8 18 29S 48 24 E
Fiherenana →, Madag. 57 C7 23 19S 43 37 E
Fiji ■, Pac. Oc. 59 C8 17 20S 179 0 E
Filabusi, Zimbabwe 57 C4 20 34S 29 20 E
Filey, U.K. 10 C7 54 12N 0 18W
Filey B., U.K. 10 C7 54 12N 0 15W
Filfla, Malta 23 D1 35 47N 14 24 E
Filiatrá, Greece 21 F9 37 9N 21 35 E
Filingué, Niger 50 F6 14 21N 3 22 E
Filipstad, Sweden 9 G16 59 43N 14 9 E
Fillmore, Calif., U.S.A. 85 L8 34 24N 118 55W
Fillmore, Utah, U.S.A. 83 G7 38 58N 112 20W
Finch, Canada 79 A9 45 11N 75 7W
Findhorn →, U.K. 12 D5 57 38N 3 38W
Findlay, U.S.A. 76 E4 41 2N 83 39W
Finger L., Canada 70 B1 53 33N 93 30W
Finger Lakes, U.S.A. 79 D8 42 40N 76 30W
Fingoè, Mozam. 55 E3 14 55S 31 50 E
Finisterre, C. = Fisterra, C., Spain 19 A1 42 50N 9 19W
Finke, Australia 62 D1 25 34S 134 35 E
Finland ■, Europe 8 E22 63 0N 27 0 E
Finland, G. of, Europe 9 G21 60 0N 26 0 E
Finlay →, Canada 72 B3 57 0N 125 10W
Finley, Australia 63 F4 35 38S 145 35 E
Finley, U.S.A. 80 B6 47 31N 97 50W
Finn →, Ireland 13 B4 54 51N 7 28W
Finnigan, Mt., Australia 62 B4 15 49S 145 17 E
Finniss, C., Australia 63 E1 33 8S 134 51 E
Finnmark, Norway 8 B20 69 37N 23 57 E
Finnsnes, Norway 8 B18 69 14N 18 0 E
Finspång, Sweden 9 G16 58 43N 15 47 E
Fiora →, Italy 20 C4 42 20N 11 34 E
Fiq, Syria 47 C4 32 46N 35 41 E
Firat = Furāt, Nahr al →, Asia 44 D5 31 0N 47 25 E
Firebag →, Canada 73 B6 57 45N 111 21W
Firebaugh, U.S.A. 84 J6 36 52N 120 27W
Firedrake L., Canada 73 A8 61 25N 104 30W
Firenze, Italy 20 C4 43 46N 11 15 E
Firk →, Iraq 44 D5 30 59N 44 34 E
Firozabad, India 43 F8 27 10N 78 25 E
Firozpur, India 42 D6 30 55N 74 40 E
Firozpur-Jhirka, India 42 F7 27 48N 76 57 E
Fīrūzābād, Iran 45 D7 28 52N 52 35 E
Fīrūzkūh, Iran 45 C7 35 50N 52 50 E
Firvale, Canada 72 C3 52 27N 126 13W
Fish →, Namibia 56 D2 28 7S 17 10 E
Fish →, S. Africa 56 E3 31 30S 20 16 E
Fish River Canyon, Namibia 56 D2 27 40S 17 35 E
Fisher, Australia 61 F5 30 30S 131 0 E
Fisher B., Canada 73 C9 51 35N 97 13W
Fishers I., U.S.A. 79 E13 41 15N 72 0W
Fishguard, U.K. 11 E3 52 0N 4 58W
Fishing L., Canada 73 C9 52 10N 95 24W
Fishkill, U.S.A. 79 E11 41 32N 73 53W
Fisterra, C., Spain 19 A1 42 50N 9 19W
Fitchburg, U.S.A. 79 D13 42 35N 71 48W
Fitz Roy, Argentina 96 F3 47 0S 67 0W
Fitzgerald, Canada 72 B6 59 51N 111 36W
Fitzgerald, U.S.A. 77 K4 31 43N 83 15W
Fitzmaurice →, Australia 60 B5 14 45S 130 5 E
Fitzroy →, Queens., Australia 62 C5 23 32S 150 52 E
Fitzroy →, W. Austral., Australia 60 C3 17 31S 123 35 E
Fitzroy, Mte., Argentina 96 F2 49 17S 73 5W
Fitzroy Crossing, Australia 60 C4 18 9S 125 38 E
Fitzwilliam I., Canada 78 A3 45 30N 81 45W
Fiume = Rijeka, Croatia 16 F8 45 20N 14 21 E
Five Points, U.S.A. 84 J6 36 26N 120 6W
Fizi, Dem. Rep. of the Congo 54 C2 4 17S 28 55 E
Flagstaff, U.S.A. 83 J8 35 12N 111 39W
Flagstaff L., U.S.A. 77 C10 45 12N 70 18W
Flaherty I., Canada 70 A4 56 15N 79 15W
Flåm, Norway 9 F12 60 50N 7 7 E
Flambeau →, U.S.A. 80 C9 45 18N 91 14W
Flamborough Hd., U.K. 10 C7 54 7N 0 5W
Flaming Gorge Reservoir, U.S.A. 82 F9 41 10N 109 25W
Flamingo, Teluk, Indonesia 37 F9 5 30S 138 0 E
Flanders = Flandre, Europe 18 A5 50 50N 2 30 E
Flandre, Europe 18 A5 50 50N 2 30 E
Flandre Occidentale = West-Vlaanderen □, Belgium 15 D2 51 0N 3 0 E
Flandre Orientale = Oost-Vlaanderen □, Belgium 15 C3 51 5N 3 50 E
Flandreau, U.S.A. 80 C6 44 3N 96 36W
Flanigan, U.S.A. 84 E7 40 10N 119 53W
Flannan Is., U.K. 12 C1 58 9N 7 52W
Flåsjön, Sweden 8 D16 64 5N 15 40 E
Flat →, Canada 72 A3 61 33N 125 18W
Flathead L., U.S.A. 82 C7 47 51N 114 8W
Flattery, C., Australia 62 A4 14 58S 145 21 E
Flattery, C., U.S.A. 84 B2 48 23N 124 29W
Flatwoods, U.S.A. 76 F4 38 31N 82 43W
Fleetwood, U.K. 10 D4 53 55N 3 1W
Fleetwood, U.S.A. 79 F9 40 27N 75 49W
Flekkefjord, Norway 9 G12 58 18N 6 39 E
Flemington, U.S.A. 78 E7 41 7N 77 28W
Flensburg, Germany 16 A5 54 47N 9 27 E
Flers, France 18 B3 48 47N 0 33W
Flesherton, Canada 78 B4 44 16N 80 33W
Flesko, Tanjung, Indonesia 37 D6 0 29N 124 30 E
Fleurieu Pen., Australia 63 F2 35 40S 138 5 E
Flevoland □, Neths. 15 B5 52 30N 5 30 E
Flin Flon, Canada 73 C8 54 46N 101 53W
Flinders →, Australia 62 B3 17 36S 140 36 E
Flinders B., Australia 61 F2 34 19S 115 19 E
Flinders Group, Australia 62 A3 14 11S 144 15 E
Flinders I., S. Austral., Australia 63 E1 33 44S 134 41 E
Flinders I., Tas., Australia 62 G4 40 0S 148 0 E
Flinders Ranges, Australia 63 E2 31 30S 138 30 E
Flinders Reefs, Australia 62 B4 17 37S 148 31 E
Flint, U.K. 10 D4 53 15N 3 8W
Flint, U.S.A. 76 D4 43 1N 83 41W
Flint →, U.S.A. 77 K3 30 57N 84 34W
Flint I., Kiribati 65 J12 11 26S 151 48W
Flintshire □, U.K. 10 D4 53 17N 3 17W
Flodden, U.K. 10 B5 55 37N 2 8W
Floodwood, U.S.A. 80 B8 46 55N 92 55W
Flora, U.S.A. 76 F1 38 40N 88 29W
Florala, U.S.A. 77 K2 31 0N 86 20W
Florence = Firenze, Italy 20 C4 43 46N 11 15 E
Florence, Ala., U.S.A. 77 H2 34 48N 87 41W
Florence, Ariz., U.S.A. 83 K8 33 2N 111 23W
Florence, Colo., U.S.A. 80 F2 38 23N 105 8W
Florence, Oreg., U.S.A. 82 E1 43 58N 124 7W
Florence, S.C., U.S.A. 77 H6 34 12N 79 46W
Florence, L., Australia 63 D2 28 53S 138 9 E
Florencia, Colombia 92 C3 1 36N 75 36W
Florennes, Belgium 15 D4 50 15N 4 35 E
Florenville, Belgium 15 E5 49 40N 5 19 E
Flores, Guatemala 88 C2 16 59N 89 50W
Flores, Indonesia 37 F6 8 35S 121 0 E
Flores I., Canada 72 D3 49 20N 126 10W
Flores Sea, Indonesia 37 F6 6 30S 120 0 E
Floreşti, Moldova 17 E15 47 53N 28 17 E
Floresville, U.S.A. 81 L5 29 8N 98 10W
Floriano, Brazil 93 E10 6 50S 43 0W
Florianópolis, Brazil 95 B6 27 30S 48 30W
Florida, Cuba 88 B4 21 32N 78 14W
Florida, Uruguay 95 C4 34 7S 56 10W
Florida □, U.S.A. 77 L5 28 0N 82 0W
Florida, Straits of, U.S.A. 88 B4 25 0N 80 0W
Florida B., U.S.A. 88 B3 25 0N 80 45W
Florida Keys, U.S.A. 77 N5 24 40N 81 0W
Flórina, Greece 21 D9 40 48N 21 26 E
Florø, Norway 9 F11 61 35N 5 1 E
Flower Station, Canada 79 A8 45 10N 76 41W
Flowerpot I., Canada 78 A3 45 18N 81 38W
Floydada, U.S.A. 81 J4 33 59N 101 20W
Fluk, Indonesia 37 E7 1 42S 127 44 E
Flushing = Vlissingen, Neths. 15 C3 51 26N 3 34 E
Flying Fish, C., Antarctica 5 D15 72 6S 102 29W
Foam Lake, Canada 73 C8 51 40N 103 32W
Foça, Turkey 21 E12 38 39N 26 46 E
Focşani, Romania 17 F14 45 41N 27 15 E
Fóggia, Italy 20 D6 41 27N 15 34 E
Fogo, Canada 71 C9 49 43N 54 17W
Fogo I., Canada 71 C9 49 40N 54 5W
Föhr, Germany 16 A5 54 43N 8 30 E
Foix, France 18 E4 42 58N 1 38 E
Folda, Nord-Trøndelag, Norway 8 D14 64 32N 10 30 E
Folda, Nordland, Norway 8 C16 67 38N 14 50 E
Foley, Botswana 56 C4 21 34S 27 21 E
Foley, U.S.A. 77 K2 30 24N 87 41W
Foleyet, Canada 70 C3 48 15N 82 25W
Folgefonni, Norway 9 F12 60 3N 6 23 E
Foligno, Italy 20 C5 42 57N 12 42 E
Folkestone, U.K. 11 F9 51 5N 1 12 E
Folkston, U.S.A. 77 K5 30 50N 82 0W
Follansbee, U.S.A. 78 F4 40 19N 80 35W
Folsom L., U.S.A. 84 G5 38 42N 121 9W
Fond-du-Lac, Canada 73 B7 59 19N 107 12W
Fond du Lac, U.S.A. 80 D10 43 47N 88 27W
Fond-du-Lac →, Canada 73 B7 59 17N 106 0W
Fonda, U.S.A. 79 D10 42 57N 74 22W
Fondi, Italy 20 D5 41 21N 13 25 E
Fongafale, Tuvalu 64 H9 8 31S 179 13 E
Fonsagrada = A Fonsagrada, Spain 19 A2 43 8N 7 4W
Fonseca, G. de, Cent. Amer. 88 D2 13 10N 87 40W
Fontainebleau, France 18 B5 48 24N 2 40 E
Fontana, U.S.A. 85 L9 34 6N 117 26W
Fontas →, Canada 72 B4 58 14N 121 48W
Fonte Boa, Brazil 92 D5 2 33S 66 0W
Fontenay-le-Comte, France 18 C3 46 28N 0 48W
Fontenelle Reservoir, U.S.A. 82 E8 42 1N 110 3W
Fontur, Iceland 8 C6 66 23N 14 32W
Foochow = Fuzhou, China 33 D6 26 5N 119 16 E
Foping, China 34 H5 33 41N 108 0 E
Forbes, Australia 63 E4 33 22S 148 5 E
Forbesganj, India 43 F12 26 17N 87 18 E
Ford City, Calif., U.S.A. 85 K7 35 9N 119 27W
Ford City, Pa., U.S.A. 78 F5 40 46N 79 32W
Førde, Norway 9 F11 61 27N 5 53 E
Ford's Bridge, Australia 63 D4 29 41S 145 29 E
Fordyce, U.S.A. 81 J8 33 49N 92 25W
Forel, Mt., Greenland 4 C6 66 52N 36 55W
Foremost, Canada 72 D6 49 26N 111 34W
Forest, Canada 78 C3 43 6N 82 0W
Forest, U.S.A. 81 J10 32 22N 89 29W
Forest City, Iowa, U.S.A. 80 D8 43 16N 93 39W
Forest City, N.C., U.S.A. 77 H5 35 20N 81 52W
Forest City, Pa., U.S.A. 79 E9 41 39N 75 28W
Forest Grove, U.S.A. 84 E3 45 31N 123 7W
Forestburg, Canada 72 C6 52 35N 112 1W
Foresthill, U.S.A. 84 F6 39 1N 120 49W
Forestier Pen., Australia 62 G4 43 0S 148 0 E
Forestville, Canada 71 C6 48 48N 69 2W
Forestville, Calif., U.S.A. 84 G4 38 28N 122 54W
Forestville, N.Y., U.S.A. 78 D5 42 28N 79 10W
Forfar, U.K. 12 E6 56 39N 2 53W
Forks, U.S.A. 84 C2 47 57N 124 23W
Forksville, U.S.A. 79 E8 41 29N 76 35W
Forlì, Italy 20 B5 44 13N 12 3 E
Forman, U.S.A. 80 B6 46 7N 97 38W
Formby Pt., U.K. 10 D4 53 33N 3 6W
Formentera, Spain 22 C7 38 43N 1 27 E
Formentor, C. de, Spain 22 B10 39 58N 3 13 E
Former Yugoslav Republic of Macedonia = Macedonia ■, Europe 21 D9 41 53N 21 40 E
Fórmia, Italy 20 D5 41 15N 13 37 E
Formosa = Taiwan ■, Asia 33 D7 23 30N 121 0 E
Formosa, Argentina 94 B4 26 15S 58 10W
Formosa, Brazil 93 G9 15 32S 47 20W
Formosa □, Argentina 94 B4 25 0S 60 0W
Formosa, Serra, Brazil 93 F8 12 0S 55 0W
Formosa Bay, Kenya 54 C5 2 40S 40 20 E
Fornells, Spain 22 A11 40 3N 4 7 E
Føroyar, Atl. Oc. 8 F9 62 0N 7 0W
Forres, U.K. 12 D5 57 37N 3 37W
Forrest, Australia 61 F4 30 51S 128 6 E
Forrest, Mt., Australia 61 D4 24 48S 127 45 E
Forrest City, U.S.A. 81 H9 35 1N 90 47W
Forsayth, Australia 62 B3 18 33S 143 34 E
Forssa, Finland 9 F20 60 49N 23 38 E
Forst, Germany 16 C8 51 45N 14 37 E
Forsyth, U.S.A. 82 C10 46 16N 106 41W
Fort Abbas, Pakistan 42 E5 29 12N 72 52 E
Fort Albany, Canada 70 B3 52 15N 81 35W
Fort Ann, U.S.A. 79 C11 43 25N 73 30W
Fort Assiniboine, Canada 72 C6 54 20N 114 45W
Fort Augustus, U.K. 12 D4 57 9N 4 42W
Fort Beaufort, S. Africa 56 E4 32 46S 26 40 E
Fort Benton, U.S.A. 82 C8 47 49N 110 40W
Fort Bragg, U.S.A. 82 G2 39 26N 123 48W
Fort Bridger, U.S.A. 82 F8 41 19N 110 23W
Fort Chipewyan, Canada 73 B6 58 42N 111 8W
Fort Collins, U.S.A. 80 E2 40 35N 105 5W
Fort-Coulonge, Canada 70 C4 45 50N 76 45W
Fort Covington, U.S.A. 79 B10 44 59N 74 29W
Fort Davis, U.S.A. 81 K3 30 35N 103 54W
Fort-de-France, Martinique 89 D7 14 36N 61 2W
Fort Defiance, U.S.A. 83 J9 35 45N 109 5W
Fort Dodge, U.S.A. 80 D7 42 30N 94 11W
Fort Edward, U.S.A. 79 C11 43 16N 73 35W
Fort Erie, Canada 78 D6 42 54N 78 56W
Fort Fairfield, U.S.A. 77 B12 46 46N 67 50W
Fort Frances, Canada 73 D10 48 36N 93 24W
Fort Garland, U.S.A. 83 H11 37 26N 105 26W
Fort George = Chisasibi, Canada 70 B4 53 50N 79 0W
Fort Good-Hope, Canada 68 B7 66 14N 128 40W
Fort Hancock, U.S.A. 83 L11 31 18N 105 51W
Fort Hertz = Putao, Burma 41 F20 27 28N 97 30 E
Fort Hope, Canada 70 B2 51 30N 88 0W
Fort Irwin, U.S.A. 85 K10 35 16N 116 34W
Fort Kent, U.S.A. 77 B11 47 15N 68 36W
Fort Klamath, U.S.A. 82 E3 42 42N 122 0W
Fort Laramie, U.S.A. 80 D2 42 13N 104 31W
Fort Lauderdale, U.S.A. 77 M5 26 7N 80 8W
Fort Liard, Canada 72 A4 60 14N 123 30W
Fort Liberté, Haiti 89 C5 19 42N 71 51W
Fort Lupton, U.S.A. 80 E2 40 5N 104 49W
Fort Mackay, Canada 72 B6 57 12N 111 41W
Fort Macleod, Canada 72 D6 49 45N 113 30W
Fort McMurray, Canada 72 B6 56 44N 111 7W
Fort McPherson, Canada 68 B6 67 30N 134 55W
Fort Madison, U.S.A. 80 E9 40 38N 91 27W
Fort Meade, U.S.A. 77 M5 27 45N 81 48W
Fort Morgan, U.S.A. 80 E3 40 15N 103 48W
Fort Myers, U.S.A. 77 M5 26 39N 81 52W
Fort Nelson, Canada 72 B4 58 50N 122 44W
Fort Nelson →, Canada 72 B4 59 32N 124 0W
Fort Norman = Tulita, Canada 68 B7 64 57N 125 30W
Fort Payne, U.S.A. 77 H3 34 26N 85 43W
Fort Peck, U.S.A. 82 B10 48 1N 106 27W
Fort Peck Dam, U.S.A. 82 C10 48 0N 106 26W
Fort Peck L., U.S.A. 82 C10 48 0N 106 26W
Fort Pierce, U.S.A. 77 M5 27 27N 80 20W
Fort Pierre, U.S.A. 80 C4 44 21N 100 22W
Fort Plain, U.S.A. 79 D10 42 56N 74 37W
Fort Portal, Uganda 54 B3 0 40N 30 20 E
Fort Providence, Canada 72 A5 61 3N 117 40W
Fort Qu'Appelle, Canada 73 C8 50 45N 103 50W
Fort Resolution, Canada 72 A6 61 10N 113 40W
Fort Rixon, Zimbabwe 55 G2 20 2S 29 17 E
Fort Ross, U.S.A. 84 G3 38 32N 123 13W
Fort Rupert = Waskaganish, Canada 70 B4 51 30N 78 40W
Fort St. James, Canada 72 C4 54 30N 124 10W
Fort St. John, Canada 72 B4 56 15N 120 50W
Fort Saskatchewan, Canada 72 C6 53 40N 113 15W
Fort Scott, U.S.A. 81 G7 37 50N 94 42W
Fort Severn, Canada 70 A2 56 0N 87 40W
Fort Shevchenko, Kazakstan 25 F9 44 35N 50 23 E
Fort Simpson, Canada 72 A4 61 45N 121 15W
Fort Smith, Canada 72 B6 60 0N 111 51W
Fort Smith, U.S.A. 81 H7 35 23N 94 25W
Fort Stockton, U.S.A. 81 K3 30 53N 102 53W
Fort Sumner, U.S.A. 81 H2 34 28N 104 15W
Fort Thompson, U.S.A. 80 C5 44 3N 99 26W
Fort Valley, U.S.A. 77 J4 32 33N 83 53W
Fort Vermilion, Canada 72 B5 58 24N 116 0W
Fort Walton Beach, U.S.A. 77 K2 30 25N 86 36W
Fort Wayne, U.S.A. 76 E3 41 4N 85 9W
Fort William, U.K. 12 E3 56 49N 5 7W
Fort Worth, U.S.A. 81 J6 32 45N 97 18W
Fort Yates, U.S.A. 80 B4 46 5N 100 38W

Fort Yukon, U.S.A. 68 B5 66 34N 145 16W
Fortaleza, Brazil 93 D11 3 45S 38 35W
Forteau, Canada 71 B8 51 28N 56 58W
Fortescue →, Australia 60 D2 21 0S 116 4 E
Forth →, U.K. 12 E5 56 9N 3 50W
Forth, Firth of, U.K. 12 E6 56 5N 2 55W
Fortrose, U.K. 12 D4 57 35N 4 9W
Fortuna, Calif., U.S.A. 82 F1 40 36N 124 9W
Fortuna, N. Dak., U.S.A. 80 A3 48 55N 103 47W
Fortune, Canada 71 C8 47 4N 55 50W
Fortune B., Canada 71 C8 47 30N 55 22W
Forūr, Iran 45 E7 26 17N 54 32 E
Foshan, China 33 D6 23 4N 113 5 E
Fosna, Norway 8 E14 63 50N 10 20 E
Fosnavåg, Norway 9 E11 62 22N 5 38 E
Fossano, Italy 18 D7 44 33N 7 43 E
Fossil, U.S.A. 82 D3 45 0N 120 9W
Foster, Canada 79 A12 45 17N 72 30W
Foster →, Canada 73 B7 55 47N 105 49W
Fosters Ra., Australia 62 C1 21 35S 133 48 E
Fostoria, U.S.A. 76 E4 41 10N 83 25W
Fotadrevo, Madag. 57 C8 24 3S 45 1 E
Fougères, France 18 B3 48 21N 1 14W
Foul Pt., Sri Lanka 40 Q12 8 35N 81 18 E
Foula, U.K. 12 A6 60 10N 2 5W
Foulness I., U.K. 11 F8 51 36N 0 55 E
Foulpointe, Madag. 57 B8 17 41S 49 31 E
Foulweather, C., U.S.A. 74 B2 44 50N 124 5W
Foumban, Cameroon 52 C2 5 45N 10 50 E
Fountain, U.S.A. 80 F2 38 41N 104 42W
Fountain Springs, U.S.A. 85 K8 35 54N 118 51W
Fouriesburg, S. Africa 56 D4 28 38S 28 14 E
Foúrnoi, Greece 21 F12 37 36N 26 32 E
Fourth Cataract, Sudan 51 E12 18 47N 32 3 E
Fouta Djalon, Guinea 50 F3 11 20N 12 10W
Foux, Cap-à-, Haiti 89 C5 19 43N 73 27W
Foveaux Str., N.Z. 59 M2 46 42S 168 10 E
Fowey, U.K. 11 G3 50 20N 4 39W
Fowler, Calif., U.S.A. 84 J7 36 38N 119 41W
Fowler, Colo., U.S.A. 80 F3 38 8N 104 2W
Fowlers B., Australia 61 F5 31 59S 132 34 E
Fowman, Iran 45 B6 37 13N 49 19 E
Fox →, Canada 73 B10 56 3N 93 18W
Fox Creek, Canada 72 C5 54 24N 116 48W
Fox Lake, Canada 72 B6 58 28N 114 31W
Fox Valley, Canada 73 C7 50 30N 109 25W
Foxboro, U.S.A. 79 D13 42 4N 71 16W
Foxe Basin, Canada 69 B12 66 0N 77 0W
Foxe Chan., Canada 69 B11 65 0N 80 0W
Foxe Pen., Canada 69 B12 65 0N 76 0W
Foxton, N.Z. 59 J5 40 29S 175 18 E
Foyle, Lough, U.K. 13 A4 55 7N 7 4W
Foynes, Ireland 13 D2 52 37N 9 7W
Foz do Cunene, Angola 56 B1 17 15S 11 48 E
Foz do Iguaçu, Brazil 95 B5 25 30S 54 30W
Frackville, U.S.A. 79 F8 40 47N 76 14W
Fraile Muerto, Uruguay 95 C5 32 31S 54 32W
Framingham, U.S.A. 79 D13 42 17N 71 25W
Franca, Brazil 93 H9 20 33S 47 30W
Francavilla Fontana, Italy 21 D7 40 32N 17 35 E
France ■, Europe 18 C5 47 0N 3 0 E
Frances, Australia 63 F3 36 41S 140 55 E
Frances →, Canada 72 A3 60 16N 129 10W
Frances L., Canada 72 A3 61 23N 129 30W
Franceville, Gabon 52 E2 1 40S 13 32 E
Franche-Comté, France 18 C6 46 50N 5 55 E
Francis Case, L., U.S.A. 80 D5 43 4N 98 34W
Francisco Beltrão, Brazil 95 B5 26 5S 53 4W
Francisco I. Madero, Coahuila, Mexico 86 B4 25 48N 103 18W
Francisco I. Madero, Durango, Mexico 86 C4 24 32N 104 22W
Francistown, Botswana 57 C4 21 7S 27 33 E
François, Canada 71 C8 47 35N 56 45W
François L., Canada 72 C3 54 0N 125 30W
Franeker, Neths. 15 A5 53 12N 5 33 E
Frankford, Canada 78 B7 44 12N 77 36W
Frankfort, S. Africa 57 D4 27 17S 28 30 E
Frankfort, Ind., U.S.A. 76 E2 40 17N 86 31W
Frankfort, Kans., U.S.A. 80 F6 39 42N 96 25W
Frankfort, Ky., U.S.A. 76 F3 38 12N 84 52W
Frankfort, N.Y., U.S.A. 79 C9 43 2N 75 4W
Frankfurt, Brandenburg, Germany 16 B8 52 20N 14 32 E
Frankfurt, Hessen, Germany 16 C5 50 7N 8 41 E
Fränkische Alb, Germany 16 D6 49 10N 11 23 E
Frankland →, Australia 61 G2 35 0S 116 48 E
Franklin, Ky., U.S.A. 77 G2 36 43N 86 35W
Franklin, La., U.S.A. 81 L9 29 48N 91 30W
Franklin, Mass., U.S.A. 79 D13 42 5N 71 24W
Franklin, N.H., U.S.A. 79 C13 43 27N 71 39W
Franklin, Nebr., U.S.A. 80 E5 40 6N 98 57W
Franklin, Pa., U.S.A. 78 E5 41 24N 79 50W
Franklin, Va., U.S.A. 77 G7 36 41N 76 56W
Franklin, W. Va., U.S.A. 76 F6 38 39N 79 20W
Franklin B., Canada 68 B7 69 45N 126 0W
Franklin D. Roosevelt L., U.S.A. 82 B4 48 18N 118 9W
Franklin I., Antarctica 5 D11 76 10S 168 30 E
Franklin L., U.S.A. 82 F6 40 25N 115 22W
Franklin Mts., Canada 68 B7 65 0N 125 0W
Franklin Str., Canada 68 A10 72 0N 96 0W
Franklinton, U.S.A. 81 K9 30 51N 90 9W
Franklinville, U.S.A. 78 D6 42 20N 78 27W
Franks Pk., U.S.A. 82 E9 43 58N 109 18W
Frankston, Australia 63 F4 38 8S 145 8 E
Fransfontein, Namibia 56 C2 20 12S 15 1 E
Frantsa Iosifa, Zemlya, Russia 26 A6 82 0N 55 0 E
Franz, Canada 70 C3 48 25N 84 30W
Franz Josef Land = Frantsa Iosifa, Zemlya, Russia 26 A6 82 0N 55 0 E
Fraser, U.S.A. 78 D2 42 32N 82 57W
Fraser →, B.C., Canada 72 D4 49 7N 123 11W
Fraser →, Nfld., Canada 71 A7 56 39N 62 10W
Fraser, Mt., Australia 61 E2 25 35S 118 20 E
Fraser I., Australia 63 D5 25 15S 153 10 E
Fraser Lake, Canada 72 C4 54 0N 124 50W
Fraserburg, S. Africa 56 E3 31 55S 21 30 E
Fraserburgh, U.K. 12 D6 57 42N 2 1W
Fraserdale, Canada 70 C3 49 55N 81 37W
Fray Bentos, Uruguay 94 C4 33 10S 58 15W
Fredericia, Denmark 9 J13 55 34N 9 45 E
Frederick, Md., U.S.A. 76 F7 39 25N 77 25W
Frederick, Okla., U.S.A. 81 H5 34 23N 99 1W
Frederick, S. Dak., U.S.A. 80 C5 45 50N 98 31W
Fredericksburg, Pa., U.S.A. 79 F8 40 27N 76 26W
Fredericksburg, Tex., U.S.A. 81 K5 30 16N 98 52W
Fredericksburg, Va., U.S.A. 76 F7 38 18N 77 28W
Fredericktown, Mo., U.S.A. 81 G9 37 34N 90 18W
Fredericktown, Ohio, U.S.A. 78 F2 40 29N 82 33W
Frederico I. Madero, Presa, Mexico 86 B3 28 7N 105 40W
Frederico Westphalen, Brazil 95 B5 27 22S 53 24W
Fredericton, Canada 71 C6 45 57N 66 40W
Fredericton Junction, Canada 71 C6 45 41N 66 40W
Frederikshåb = Paamiut, Greenland 4 C5 62 0N 49 43W
Frederikshavn, Denmark 9 H14 57 28N 10 31 E
Frederiksted, U.S. Virgin Is. 89 C7 17 43N 64 53W
Fredonia, Ariz., U.S.A. 83 H7 36 57N 112 32W
Fredonia, Kans., U.S.A. 81 G7 37 32N 95 49W
Fredonia, N.Y., U.S.A. 78 D5 42 26N 79 20W
Fredrikstad, Norway 9 G14 59 13N 10 57 E
Free State □, S. Africa 56 D4 28 30S 27 0 E
Freehold, U.S.A. 79 F10 40 16N 74 17W
Freel Peak, U.S.A. 84 G7 38 52N 119 54W
Freeland, U.S.A. 79 E9 41 1N 75 54W
Freels, C., Canada 71 C9 49 15N 53 30W
Freeman, Calif., U.S.A. 85 K9 35 35N 117 53W
Freeman, S. Dak., U.S.A. 80 D6 43 21N 97 26W
Freeport, Bahamas 88 A4 26 30N 78 47W
Freeport, Ill., U.S.A. 80 D10 42 17N 89 36W
Freeport, N.Y., U.S.A. 79 F11 40 39N 73 35W
Freeport, Ohio, U.S.A. 78 F3 40 12N 81 15W
Freeport, Pa., U.S.A. 78 F5 40 41N 79 41W
Freeport, Tex., U.S.A. 81 L7 28 57N 95 21W
Freetown, S. Leone 50 G3 8 30N 13 17W
Frégate, L., Canada 70 B5 53 15N 74 45W
Fregenal de la Sierra, Spain 19 C2 38 10N 6 39W
Freibourg = Fribourg, Switz. 18 C7 46 49N 7 9 E
Freiburg, Germany 16 E4 47 59N 7 51 E
Freire, Chile 96 D2 38 54S 72 38W
Freirina, Chile 94 B1 28 30S 71 10W
Freising, Germany 16 D6 48 24N 11 45 E
Freistadt, Austria 16 D8 48 30N 14 30 E
Fréjus, France 18 E7 43 25N 6 44 E
Fremantle, Australia 61 F2 32 7S 115 47 E
Fremont, Calif., U.S.A. 84 H4 37 32N 121 57W
Fremont, Mich., U.S.A. 76 D3 43 28N 85 57W
Fremont, Nebr., U.S.A. 80 E6 41 26N 96 30W
Fremont, Ohio, U.S.A. 76 E4 41 21N 83 7W
Fremont →, U.S.A. 83 G8 38 24N 110 42W
French Camp, U.S.A. 84 H5 37 53N 121 16W
French Creek →, U.S.A. 78 E5 41 24N 79 50W
French Guiana ■, S. Amer. 93 C8 4 0N 53 0W
French Polynesia ■, Pac. Oc. 65 K13 20 0S 145 0W
Frenchman Cr. →, N. Amer. 82 B10 48 31N 107 10W
Frenchman Cr. →, U.S.A. 80 E4 40 14N 100 50W
Fresco →, Brazil 93 E8 7 15S 51 30W
Freshfield, C., Antarctica 5 C10 68 25S 151 10 E
Fresnillo, Mexico 86 C4 23 10N 103 0W
Fresno, U.S.A. 84 J7 36 44N 119 47W
Fresno Reservoir, U.S.A. 82 B9 48 36N 109 57W
Frew →, Australia 62 C2 20 0S 135 38 E
Frewsburg, U.S.A. 78 D5 42 3N 79 10W
Freycinet Pen., Australia 62 G4 42 10S 148 25 E
Fria, C., Namibia 56 B1 18 0S 12 0 E
Friant, U.S.A. 84 J7 36 59N 119 43W
Frías, Argentina 94 B2 28 40S 65 5W
Fribourg, Switz. 18 C7 46 49N 7 9 E
Friday Harbor, U.S.A. 84 B3 48 32N 123 1W
Friedens, U.S.A. 78 F6 40 3N 78 59W
Friedrichshafen, Germany 16 E5 47 39N 9 30 E
Friendly Is. = Tonga ■, Pac. Oc. 59 D11 19 50S 174 30W
Friendship, U.S.A. 78 D6 42 12N 78 8W
Friesland □, Neths. 15 A5 53 5N 5 50 E
Frio →, U.S.A. 81 L5 28 26N 98 11W
Frio, C., Brazil 90 F6 22 50S 41 50W
Friona, U.S.A. 81 H3 34 38N 102 43W
Fritch, U.S.A. 81 H4 35 38N 101 36W
Frobisher B., Canada 69 B13 62 30N 66 0W
Frobisher Bay = Iqaluit, Canada 69 B13 63 44N 68 31W
Frobisher L., Canada 73 B7 56 20N 108 15W
Frohavet, Norway 8 E13 64 0N 9 30 E
Frome, U.K. 11 F5 51 14N 2 19W
Frome →, U.K. 11 G5 50 41N 2 6W
Frome, L., Australia 63 E2 30 45S 139 45 E
Front Range, U.S.A. 74 C5 40 25N 105 45W
Front Royal, U.S.A. 76 F6 38 55N 78 12W
Frontera, Canary Is. 22 G2 27 47N 17 59W
Frontera, Mexico 87 D6 18 30N 92 40W
Fronteras, Mexico 86 A3 30 56N 109 31W
Frosinone, Italy 20 D5 41 38N 13 19 E
Frostburg, U.S.A. 76 F6 39 39N 78 56W
Frostisen, Norway 8 B17 68 14N 17 10 E
Frøya, Norway 8 E13 63 43N 8 40 E
Frunze = Bishkek, Kyrgyzstan 26 E8 42 54N 74 46 E
Frutal, Brazil 93 H9 20 0S 49 0W
Frýdek-Místek, Czech Rep. 17 D10 49 40N 18 20 E
Fryeburg, U.S.A. 79 B14 44 1N 70 59W
Fu Xian = Wafangdian, China 35 E11 39 38N 121 58 E
Fu Xian, China 34 G5 36 0N 109 20 E
Fucheng, China 34 F9 37 50N 116 10 E
Fuchou = Fuzhou, China 33 D6 26 5N 119 16 E
Fuchū, Japan 31 G6 34 34N 133 14 E
Fuencaliente, Canary Is. 22 F2 28 28N 17 50W
Fuencaliente, Pta., Canary Is. 22 F2 28 27N 17 51W
Fuengirola, Spain 19 D3 36 32N 4 41W
Fuentes de Oñoro, Spain 19 B2 40 33N 6 52W
Fuerte →, Mexico 86 B3 25 50N 109 25W
Fuerte Olimpo, Paraguay 94 A4 21 0S 57 51W
Fuerteventura, Canary Is. 22 F6 28 30N 14 0W
Fufeng, China 34 G5 34 22N 108 0 E
Fugou, China 34 G8 34 3N 114 25 E
Fugu, China 34 E6 39 2N 111 3 E
Fuhai, China 32 B3 47 2N 87 25 E
Fuḩaymī, Iraq 44 C4 34 16N 42 10 E
Fuji, Japan 31 G9 35 9N 138 39 E
Fuji-San, Japan 31 G9 35 22N 138 44 E
Fuji-Yoshida, Japan 31 G9 35 30N 138 46 E
Fujian □, China 33 D6 26 0N 118 0 E
Fujinomiya, Japan 31 G9 35 10N 138 40 E
Fujisawa, Japan 31 G9 35 22N 139 29 E
Fujiyama, Mt. = Fuji-San, Japan 31 G9 35 22N 138 44 E
Fukien = Fujian □, China 33 D6 26 0N 118 0 E
Fukuchiyama, Japan 31 G7 35 19N 135 9 E
Fukue-Shima, Japan 31 H4 32 40N 128 45 E
Fukui, Japan 31 F8 36 5N 136 10 E
Fukui □, Japan 31 G8 36 0N 136 12 E
Fukuoka, Japan 31 H5 33 39N 130 21 E
Fukuoka □, Japan 31 H5 33 30N 131 0 E
Fukushima, Japan 30 F10 37 44N 140 28 E
Fukushima □, Japan 30 F10 37 30N 140 15 E
Fukuyama, Japan 31 G6 34 35N 133 20 E
Fulda, Germany 16 C5 50 32N 9 40 E
Fulda →, Germany 16 C5 51 25N 9 39 E
Fulford Harbour, Canada 84 B3 48 47N 123 27W
Fullerton, Calif., U.S.A. 85 M9 33 53N 117 56W
Fullerton, Nebr., U.S.A. 80 E6 41 22N 97 58W
Fulongquan, China 35 B13 44 20N 124 42 E
Fulton, Mo., U.S.A. 80 F9 38 52N 91 57W
Fulton, N.Y., U.S.A. 79 C8 43 19N 76 25W
Funabashi, Japan 31 G10 35 45N 140 0 E
Funafuti = Fongafale, Tuvalu 64 H9 8 31S 179 13 E
Funchal, Madeira 22 D3 32 38N 16 54W
Fundación, Colombia 92 A4 10 31N 74 11W
Fundão, Portugal 19 B2 40 8N 7 30W
Fundy, B. of, Canada 71 D6 45 0N 66 0W
Funhalouro, Mozam. 57 C5 23 3S 34 25 E
Funing, Hebei, China 35 E10 39 53N 119 12 E
Funing, Jiangsu, China 35 H10 33 45N 119 50 E
Funiu Shan, China 34 H7 33 30N 112 20 E
Funtua, Nigeria 50 F7 11 30N 7 18 E
Fuping, Hebei, China 34 E8 38 48N 114 12 E
Fuping, Shaanxi, China 34 G5 34 42N 109 10 E
Furano, Japan 30 C11 43 21N 142 23 E
Furāt, Nahr al →, Asia 44 D5 31 0N 47 25 E
Fūrg, Iran 45 D7 28 18N 55 13 E
Furnás, Spain 22 B8 39 3N 1 32 E
Furnas, Represa de, Brazil 95 A6 20 50S 45 30W
Furneaux Group, Australia 62 G4 40 10S 147 50 E
Furqlus, Syria 47 A6 34 36N 37 8 E
Fürstenwalde, Germany 16 B8 52 22N 14 3 E
Fürth, Germany 16 D6 49 28N 10 59 E
Furukawa, Japan 30 E10 38 34N 140 58 E
Fury and Hecla Str., Canada 69 B11 69 56N 84 0W
Fusagasuga, Colombia 92 C4 4 21N 74 22W
Fushan, Shandong, China 35 F11 37 30N 121 15 E
Fushan, Shanxi, China 34 G6 35 58N 111 51 E
Fushun, China 35 D12 41 50N 123 56 E
Fusong, China 35 C14 42 20N 127 15 E
Futuna, Wall. & F. Is. 59 B8 14 25S 178 20W
Fuxin, China 35 C11 42 5N 121 48 E
Fuyang, China 34 H8 33 0N 115 48 E
Fuyang He →, China 34 E9 38 12N 117 0 E
Fuyu, China 35 B13 45 12N 124 43 E
Fuzhou, China 33 D6 26 5N 119 16 E
Fylde, U.K. 10 D5 53 50N 2 58W
Fyn, Denmark 9 J14 55 20N 10 30 E
Fyne, L., U.K. 12 F3 55 59N 5 23W

G

Gabela, Angola 52 G2 11 0S 14 24 E
Gabès, Tunisia 51 B8 33 53N 10 2 E
Gabès, G. de, Tunisia 51 B8 34 0N 10 30 E
Gabon ■, Africa 52 E2 0 10S 10 0 E
Gaborone, Botswana 56 C4 24 45S 25 57 E
Gabriels, U.S.A. 79 B10 44 26N 74 12W
Gābrīk, Iran 45 E8 25 44N 58 28 E
Gabrovo, Bulgaria 21 C11 42 52N 25 19 E
Gāch Sār, Iran 45 B6 36 7N 51 19 E
Gachsārān, Iran 45 D6 30 15N 50 45 E
Gadag, India 40 M9 15 30N 75 45 E
Gadap, Pakistan 42 G2 25 5N 67 28 E
Gadarwara, India 43 H8 22 50N 78 50 E
Gadhada, India 42 J4 22 0N 71 35 E
Gadra, Pakistan 42 G4 25 40N 70 38 E
Gadsden, U.S.A. 77 H3 34 1N 86 1W
Gadwal, India 40 L10 16 10N 77 50 E
Gaffney, U.S.A. 77 H5 35 5N 81 39W
Gafsa, Tunisia 50 B7 34 24N 8 43 E
Gagaria, India 42 G4 25 43N 70 46 E
Gagnoa, Ivory C. 50 G4 6 56N 5 16W
Gagnon, Canada 71 B6 51 50N 68 5W
Gagnon, L., Canada 73 A6 62 3N 110 27W
Gahini, Rwanda 54 C3 1 50S 30 30 E
Gahmar, India 43 G10 25 27N 83 49 E
Gai Xian = Gaizhou, China 35 D12 40 22N 122 20 E
Gaïdhouronísi, Greece 23 E7 34 53N 25 41 E
Gail, U.S.A. 81 J4 32 46N 101 27W
Gaillimh = Galway, Ireland 13 C2 53 17N 9 3W
Gaines, U.S.A. 78 E7 41 46N 77 35W
Gainesville, Fla., U.S.A. 77 L4 29 40N 82 20W
Gainesville, Ga., U.S.A. 77 H4 34 18N 83 50W
Gainesville, Mo., U.S.A. 81 G8 36 36N 92 26W
Gainesville, Tex., U.S.A. 81 J6 33 38N 97 8W
Gainsborough, U.K. 10 D7 53 24N 0 46W
Gairdner, L., Australia 63 E2 31 30S 136 0 E
Gairloch, L., U.K. 12 D3 57 43N 5 45W
Gaizhou, China 35 D12 40 22N 122 20 E
Gaj →, Pakistan 42 F2 26 26N 67 21 E
Gakuch, Pakistan 43 A5 36 7N 73 45 E
Galán, Cerro, Argentina 94 B2 25 55S 66 52W
Galana →, Kenya 54 C5 3 9S 40 8 E
Galápagos, Pac. Oc. 90 D1 0 0 91 0W
Galashiels, U.K. 12 F6 55 37N 2 49W
Galaţi, Romania 17 F15 45 27N 28 2 E
Galatina, Italy 21 D8 40 10N 18 10 E
Galax, U.S.A. 77 G5 36 40N 80 56W
Galcaio, Somali Rep. 46 F4 6 30N 47 30 E
Galdhøpiggen, Norway 9 F12 61 38N 8 18 E
Galeana, Chihuahua, Mexico 86 A3 30 7N 107 38W
Galeana, Nuevo León, Mexico 86 A3 24 50N 100 4W
Galela, Indonesia 37 D7 1 50N 127 49 E
Galena, U.S.A. 68 B4 64 44N 156 56W
Galera Pt., Trin. & Tob. 89 D7 10 49N 60 54W
Galesburg, U.S.A. 80 E9 40 57N 90 22W
Galeton, U.S.A. 78 E7 41 44N 77 39W
Galich, Russia 24 C7 58 22N 42 24 E
Galicia □, Spain 19 A2 42 43N 7 45W
Galilee = Hagalil, Israel 47 C4 32 53N 35 18 E
Galilee, L., Australia 62 C4 22 20S 145 50 E
Galilee, Sea of = Yam Kinneret, Israel 47 C4 32 45N 35 35 E
Galinoporni, Cyprus 23 D13 35 31N 34 18 E
Galion, U.S.A. 78 F2 40 44N 82 47W
Galiuro Mts., U.S.A. 83 K8 32 30N 110 20W
Galiwinku, Australia 62 A2 12 2S 135 34 E
Gallan Hd., U.K. 12 C1 58 15N 7 2W
Gallatin, U.S.A. 77 G2 36 24N 86 27W
Galle, Sri Lanka 40 R12 6 5N 80 10 E
Gállego →, Spain 19 B5 41 39N 0 51W
Gallegos →, Argentina 96 G3 51 35S 69 0W
Galley Hd., Ireland 13 E3 51 32N 8 55W
Gallinas, Pta., Colombia 92 A4 12 28N 71 40W
Gallipoli = Gelibolu, Turkey 21 D12 40 28N 26 43 E
Gallipoli, Italy 21 D8 40 3N 17 58 E
Gallipolis, U.S.A. 76 F4 38 49N 82 12W
Gällivare, Sweden 8 C19 67 9N 20 40 E
Galloo I., U.S.A. 79 C8 43 55N 76 25W
Galloway, U.K. 12 F4 55 1N 4 29W
Galloway, Mull of, U.K. 12 G4 54 39N 4 52W
Gallup, U.S.A. 83 J9 35 32N 108 45W
Galoya, Sri Lanka 40 Q12 8 10N 80 55 E
Galt, U.S.A. 84 G5 38 15N 121 18W
Galty Mts., Ireland 13 D3 52 22N 8 10W
Galtymore, Ireland 13 D3 52 21N 8 11W
Galva, U.S.A. 80 E9 41 10N 90 3W
Galveston, U.S.A. 81 L7 29 18N 94 48W
Galveston B., U.S.A. 81 L7 29 36N 94 50W
Gálvez, Argentina 94 C3 32 0S 61 14W
Galway, Ireland 13 C2 53 17N 9 3W
Galway □, Ireland 13 C2 53 22N 9 1W
Galway B., Ireland 13 C2 53 13N 9 10W
Gam →, Vietnam 38 B5 21 55N 105 12 E
Gamagōri, Japan 31 G8 34 50N 137 14 E
Gambat, Pakistan 42 F3 27 17N 68 26 E
Gambhir →, India 42 F6 26 58N 77 27 E
Gambia ■, W. Afr. 50 F2 13 25N 16 0W
Gambia →, W. Afr. 50 F2 13 28N 16 34W
Gambier, U.S.A. 78 F2 40 22N 82 23W
Gambier, C., Australia 60 B5 11 56S 130 57 E
Gambier Is., Australia 63 F2 35 3S 136 30 E
Gambo, Canada 71 C9 48 47N 54 13W
Gamboli, Pakistan 42 E3 29 53N 68 24 E
Gamboma, Congo 52 E3 1 55S 15 52 E
Gamka →, S. Africa 56 E3 33 18S 21 39 E
Gamkab →, Namibia 56 D2 28 4S 17 54 E
Gamlakarleby = Kokkola, Finland 8 E20 63 50N 23 8 E
Gammon →, Canada 73 C9 51 24N 95 44W
Gamtoos →, S. Africa 56 E4 33 58S 25 1 E
Gan Jiang →, China 33 D6 29 15N 116 0 E
Ganado, U.S.A. 83 J9 35 43N 109 33W
Gananoque, Canada 79 B8 44 20N 76 10W
Ganāveh, Iran 45 D6 29 35N 50 35 E
Gäncä, Azerbaijan 25 F8 40 45N 46 20 E
Gancheng, China 38 C7 18 51N 108 37 E
Gand = Gent, Belgium 15 C3 51 2N 3 42 E
Ganda, Angola 53 G2 13 3S 14 35 E
Gandajika, Dem. Rep. of the Congo 52 F4 6 45S 23 57 E
Gandak →, India 43 G11 25 39N 85 13 E
Gandava, Pakistan 42 E2 28 32N 67 32 E
Gander, Canada 71 C9 48 58N 54 35W
Gander L., Canada 71 C9 48 58N 54 35W
Ganderowe Falls, Zimbabwe 55 F2 17 20S 29 10 E
Gandhi Sagar, India 42 G6 24 40N 75 40 E
Gandhinagar, India 42 H5 23 15N 72 45 E
Gandía, Spain 19 C5 38 58N 0 9W
Gando, Pta., Canary Is. 22 G4 27 55N 15 22W
Ganedidalem = Gani, Indonesia 37 E7 0 48S 128 14 E
Ganga →, India 43 H14 23 20N 90 30 E
Ganga Sagar, India 43 J13 21 38N 88 5 E
Gangan →, India 43 E8 28 38N 78 58 E
Ganganagar, India 42 E5 29 56N 73 56 E
Gangapur, India 42 F7 26 32N 76 49 E
Gangaw, Burma 41 H19 22 5N 94 5 E
Gangdisê Shan, China 41 D12 31 20N 81 0 E
Ganges = Ganga →, India 43 H14 23 20N 90 30 E
Ganges, Canada 72 D4 48 51N 123 31W
Ganges, Mouths of the, India 43 J14 21 30N 90 0 E
Gangoh, India 42 E7 29 46N 77 18 E
Gangroti, India 43 D8 30 50N 79 10 E
Gangtok, India 41 F16 27 20N 88 37 E
Gangu, China 34 G3 34 40N 105 15 E
Gangyao, China 35 B14 44 12N 126 37 E
Gani, Indonesia 37 E7 0 48S 128 14 E
Ganj, India 43 F8 27 45N 78 57 E
Gannett Peak, U.S.A. 82 E9 43 11N 109 39W
Ganquan, China 34 F5 36 20N 109 20 E
Gansu □, China 34 G3 36 0N 104 0 E
Ganta, Liberia 50 G4 7 15N 8 59W
Gantheaume, C., Australia 63 F2 36 4S 137 32 E
Gantheaume B., Australia 61 E1 27 40S 114 10 E
Gantsevichi = Hantsavichy, Belarus 17 B14 52 49N 26 30 E
Ganyem = Genyem, Indonesia 37 E10 2 46S 140 12 E
Ganyu, China 35 G10 34 50N 119 8 E
Ganzhou, China 33 D6 25 51N 114 56 E
Gao, Mali 50 E5 16 15N 0 5W
Gaomi, China 35 F10 36 20N 119 42 E
Gaoping, China 34 G7 35 45N 112 55 E
Gaotang, China 34 F9 36 50N 116 15 E
Gaoua, Burkina Faso 50 F5 10 20N 3 8W
Gaoual, Guinea 50 F3 11 45N 13 25W
Gaoxiong = Kaohsiung, Taiwan 33 D7 22 35N 120 16 E
Gaoyang, China 34 E8 38 40N 115 45 E
Gaoyou Hu, China 35 H10 32 45N 119 20 E
Gaoyuan, China 35 F9 37 8N 117 58 E
Gap, France 18 D7 44 33N 6 5 E
Gapat →, India 43 G10 24 30N 82 28 E
Gapuwiyak, Australia 62 A2 12 25S 135 43 E
Gar, China 32 C2 32 10N 79 58 E
Garabogazköl Aylagy, Turkmenistan 25 F9 41 0N 53 30 E
Garachico, Canary Is. 22 F3 28 22N 16 46W
Garachiné, Panama 88 E4 8 0N 78 12W
Garafia, Canary Is. 22 F2 28 48N 17 57W
Garah, Australia 63 D4 29 5S 149 38 E
Garajonay, Canary Is. 22 F2 28 7N 17 14W
Garanhuns, Brazil 93 E11 8 50S 36 30W
Garautha, India 43 G8 25 34N 79 18 E
Garba Tula, Kenya 54 B4 0 30N 38 32 E
Garberville, U.S.A. 82 F2 40 6N 123 48W
Garbiyang, India 43 D9 30 8N 80 54 E
Garda, L. di, Italy 20 B4 45 40N 10 41 E
Garde L., Canada 73 A7 62 50N 106 13W
Garden City, Ga., U.S.A. 77 J5 32 6N 81 9W
Garden City, Kans., U.S.A. 81 G4 37 58N 100 53W
Garden City, Tex., U.S.A. 81 K4 31 52N 101 29W

H

Hailuoto, Finland 8 D21 65 3N 24 45 E
Hainan □, China 33 E5 19 0N 109 30 E
Hainaut □, Belgium 15 D4 50 30N 4 0 E
Haines, Alaska, U.S.A. 72 B1 59 14N 135 26W
Haines, Oreg., U.S.A. 82 D5 44 55N 117 56W
Haines City, U.S.A. 77 L5 28 7N 81 38W
Haines Junction, Canada 72 A1 60 45N 137 30W
Haiphong, Vietnam 32 D5 20 47N 106 41 E
Haiti ■, W. Indies 89 C5 19 0N 72 30W
Haiya, Sudan 51 E13 18 20N 36 21 E
Haiyang, China 35 F11 36 47N 121 9 E
Haiyuan, China 34 F3 36 35N 105 52 E
Haizhou, China 35 G10 34 37N 119 7 E
Haizhou Wan, China 35 G10 34 50N 119 20 E
Hajdúböszörmény, Hungary 17 E11 47 40N 21 30 E
Hajipur, India 43 G11 25 45N 85 13 E
Hājjī Muḩsin, Iraq 44 C5 32 35N 45 29 E
Ḩājjīābād, Iran 45 D7 28 19N 55 55 E
Ḩājjīābād-e Zarrīn, Iran 45 C7 33 9N 54 51 E
Hajnówka, Poland 17 B12 52 47N 23 35 E
Hakansson, Mts., Dem. Rep. of the Congo 55 D2 8 40S 25 45 E
Hakkâri, Turkey 44 B4 37 34N 43 44 E
Hakken-Zan, Japan 31 G7 34 10N 135 54 E
Hakodate, Japan 30 D10 41 45N 140 44 E
Hakos, Namibia 56 C2 23 13S 16 21 E
Haku-San, Japan 31 F8 36 9N 136 46 E
Hakui, Japan 31 F8 36 53N 136 47 E
Hala, Pakistan 40 G6 25 43N 68 20 E
Ḩalab, Syria 44 B3 36 10N 37 15 E
Ḩalabjah, Iraq 44 C5 35 10N 45 58 E
Halaib, Sudan 51 D13 22 12N 36 30 E
Hālat 'Ammār, Si. Arabia 44 D3 29 10N 36 4 E
Halbā, Lebanon 47 A5 34 34N 36 6 E
Halberstadt, Germany 16 C6 51 54N 11 3 E
Halcombe, N.Z. 59 J5 40 8S 175 30 E
Halcon, Phil. 37 B6 13 0N 121 30 E
Halden, Norway 9 G14 59 9N 11 23 E
Haldia, India 41 H16 22 5N 88 3 E
Haldwani, India 43 E8 29 31N 79 30 E
Hale ✈, Australia 62 C2 24 56S 135 53 E
Halesowen, U.K. 11 E5 52 27N 2 3W
Haleyville, U.S.A. 77 H2 34 14N 87 37W
Halfmoon Bay, N.Z. 59 M2 46 50S 168 5 E
Halfway ✈, Canada 72 B4 56 12N 121 32W
Halia, India 43 G10 24 50N 82 19 E
Haliburton, Canada 78 A6 45 3N 78 30W
Halifax, Australia 62 B4 18 32S 146 22 E
Halifax, Canada 71 D7 44 38N 63 35W
Halifax, U.K. 10 D6 53 43N 1 52W
Halifax, U.S.A. 78 F8 40 25N 76 55W
Halifax B., Australia 62 B4 18 50S 147 0 E
Halifax I., Namibia 56 D2 26 38S 15 4 E
Halīl ✈, Iran 45 E8 27 40N 58 30 E
Halkirk, U.K. 12 C5 58 30N 3 29W
Hall Beach = Sanirajak, Canada 69 B11 68 46N 81 12W
Hall Pen., Canada 69 B13 63 30N 66 0W
Hall Pt., Australia 60 C3 15 40S 124 23 E
Halland, Sweden 9 H15 57 8N 12 47 E
Halle, Belgium 15 D4 50 44N 4 13 E
Halle, Germany 16 C6 51 30N 11 56 E
Hällefors, Sweden 9 G16 59 47N 14 31 E
Hallett, Australia 63 E2 33 25S 138 55 E
Hallettsville, U.S.A. 81 L6 29 27N 96 57W
Hallim, S. Korea 35 H14 33 24N 126 15 E
Hallingdalselvi ✈, Norway 9 F13 60 23N 9 35 E
Hallock, U.S.A. 80 A6 48 47N 96 57W
Halls Creek, Australia 60 C4 18 16S 127 38 E
Hallsberg, Sweden 9 G16 59 5N 15 7 E
Hallstead, U.S.A. 79 E9 41 58N 75 45W
Halmahera, Indonesia 37 D7 0 40N 128 0 E
Halmstad, Sweden 9 H15 56 41N 12 52 E
Hälsingborg = Helsingborg, Sweden 9 H15 56 3N 12 42 E
Hälsingland, Sweden 9 F16 61 40N 16 5 E
Halstead, U.K. 11 F8 51 57N 0 40 E
Halti, Finland 8 B19 69 17N 21 18 E
Halton □, U.K. 10 D5 53 22N 2 45W
Haltwhistle, U.K. 10 C5 54 58N 2 26W
Ḩālūl, Qatar 45 E7 25 40N 52 40 E
Halvad, India 42 H4 23 1N 71 11 E
Ḩalvān, Iran 45 C8 33 57N 56 15 E
Ham Tan, Vietnam 39 G6 10 40N 107 45 E
Ham Yen, Vietnam 38 A5 22 4N 105 3 E
Hamab, Namibia 56 D2 28 7S 19 16 E
Hamada, Japan 31 G6 34 56N 132 4 E
Hamadān, Iran 45 C6 34 52N 48 32 E
Hamadān □, Iran 45 C6 35 0N 49 0 E
Ḩamāh, Syria 44 C3 35 5N 36 40 E
Hamamatsu, Japan 31 G8 34 45N 137 45 E
Hamar, Norway 9 F14 60 48N 11 7 E
Hamâta, Gebel, Egypt 44 E2 24 17N 35 0 E
Hambantota, Sri Lanka 40 R12 6 10N 81 10 E
Hamber Prov. Park, Canada 72 C5 52 20N 118 0W
Hamburg, Germany 16 B5 53 33N 9 59 E
Hamburg, Ark., U.S.A. 81 J9 33 14N 91 48W
Hamburg, N.Y., U.S.A. 78 D6 42 43N 78 50W
Hamburg, Pa., U.S.A. 79 F9 40 33N 75 59W
Ḩamḑ, W. al ✈, Si. Arabia 44 E3 24 55N 36 20 E
Hamden, U.S.A. 79 E12 41 23N 72 54W
Häme, Finland 9 F20 61 38N 25 10 E
Hämeenlinna, Finland 9 F21 61 0N 24 28 E
Hamelin Pool, Australia 61 E1 26 22S 114 20 E
Hameln, Germany 16 B5 52 6N 9 21 E
Hamerkaz □, Israel 47 C3 32 15N 34 55 E
Hamersley Ra., Australia 60 D2 22 0S 117 45 E
Hamhung, N. Korea 35 E14 39 54N 127 30 E
Hami, China 32 B4 42 55N 93 25 E
Hamilton, Australia 63 F3 37 45S 142 2 E
Hamilton, Canada 78 C5 43 15N 79 50W
Hamilton, N.Z. 59 G5 37 47S 175 19 E
Hamilton, U.K. 12 F4 55 46N 4 2W
Hamilton, Ala., U.S.A. 77 H1 34 9N 87 59W
Hamilton, Mont., U.S.A. 82 C6 46 15N 114 10W
Hamilton, N.Y., U.S.A. 79 D9 42 50N 75 33W
Hamilton, Ohio, U.S.A. 76 F3 39 24N 84 34W
Hamilton, Tex., U.S.A. 81 K5 31 42N 98 7W
Hamilton ✈, Australia 62 C2 23 30S 139 47 E
Hamilton City, U.S.A. 84 F4 39 45N 122 1W
Hamilton Inlet, Canada 71 B8 54 0N 57 30W
Hamilton Mt., U.S.A. 79 C10 43 25N 74 22W
Hamina, Finland 9 F22 60 34N 27 12 E
Hamirpur, H.P., India 42 D7 31 41N 76 31 E
Hamirpur, Ut. P., India 43 G9 25 57N 80 9 E
Hamlet, U.S.A. 77 H6 34 53N 79 42W
Hamley Bridge, Australia 63 E2 34 17S 138 35 E
Hamlin = Hameln, Germany 16 B5 52 6N 9 21 E
Hamlin, N.Y., U.S.A. 78 C7 43 17N 77 55W
Hamlin, Tex., U.S.A. 81 J4 32 53N 100 8W
Hamm, Germany 16 C4 51 40N 7 50 E
Ḩammār, Hawr al, Iraq 44 D5 30 50N 47 10 E
Hammerfest, Norway 8 A20 70 39N 23 41 E
Hammond, Ind., U.S.A. 76 E2 41 38N 87 30W
Hammond, La., U.S.A. 81 K9 30 30N 90 28W
Hammond, N.Y., U.S.A. 79 B9 44 27N 75 42W
Hammondsport, U.S.A. 78 D7 42 25N 77 13W
Hammonton, U.S.A. 76 F8 39 39N 74 48W
Hampden, N.Z. 59 L3 45 18S 170 50 E
Hampshire □, U.K. 11 F6 51 7N 1 23W
Hampshire Downs, U.K. 11 F6 51 15N 1 10W
Hampton, N.B., Canada 71 C6 45 32N 65 51W
Hampton, Ont., Canada 78 C6 43 58N 78 45W
Hampton, Ark., U.S.A. 81 J8 33 32N 92 28W
Hampton, Iowa, U.S.A. 80 D8 42 45N 93 13W
Hampton, N.H., U.S.A. 79 D14 42 57N 70 50W
Hampton, S.C., U.S.A. 77 J5 32 52N 81 7W
Hampton, Va., U.S.A. 76 G7 37 2N 76 21W
Hampton Bays, U.S.A. 79 F12 40 53N 72 30W
Hampton Tableland, Australia 61 F4 32 0S 127 0 E
Hamyang, S. Korea 35 G14 35 32N 127 42 E
Han Pijesak, Bos.-H. 21 B8 44 5N 18 57 E
Hanak, Si. Arabia 44 E3 25 32N 37 0 E
Hanamaki, Japan 30 E10 39 23N 141 7 E
Hanang, Tanzania 54 C4 4 30S 35 25 E
Hanau, Germany 16 C5 50 7N 8 56 E
Hanbogd = Ihbulag, Mongolia 34 C4 43 11N 107 10 E
Hancheng, China 34 G6 35 31N 110 25 E
Hancock, Mich., U.S.A. 80 B10 47 8N 88 35W
Hancock, N.Y., U.S.A. 79 E9 41 57N 75 17W
Handa, Japan 31 G8 34 53N 136 55 E
Handan, China 34 F8 36 35N 114 28 E
Handeni, Tanzania 54 D4 5 25S 38 2 E
Handwara, India 43 B6 34 21N 74 20 E
Hanegev, Israel 47 E4 30 50N 35 0 E
Hanford, U.S.A. 84 J7 36 20N 119 39W
Hang Chat, Thailand 38 C2 18 20N 99 21 E
Hang Dong, Thailand 38 C2 18 41N 98 55 E
Hangang ✈, S. Korea 35 F14 37 50N 126 30 E
Hangayn Nuruu, Mongolia 32 B4 47 30N 99 0 E
Hangchou = Hangzhou, China 33 C7 30 18N 120 11 E
Hanggin Houqi, China 34 D4 40 58N 107 4 E
Hanggin Qi, China 34 E5 39 52N 108 50 E
Hangu, China 35 E9 39 18N 117 53 E
Hangzhou, China 33 C7 30 18N 120 11 E
Hangzhou Wan, China 33 C7 30 15N 120 45 E
Hanhongor, Mongolia 34 C3 43 55N 104 28 E
Ḩanīdh, Si. Arabia 45 E6 26 35N 48 38 E
Ḩanīsh, Yemen 46 E3 13 45N 42 46 E
Hankinson, U.S.A. 80 B6 46 4N 96 54W
Hanko, Finland 9 G20 59 50N 22 57 E
Hanksville, U.S.A. 83 G8 38 22N 110 43W
Hanle, India 43 C8 32 42N 79 4 E
Hanmer Springs, N.Z. 59 K4 42 32S 172 50 E
Hann ✈, Australia 60 C4 17 26S 126 17 E
Hann, Mt., Australia 60 C4 15 45S 126 0 E
Hanna, Canada 72 C6 51 40N 111 54W
Hanna, U.S.A. 82 F10 41 52N 106 34W
Hannah B., Canada 70 B4 51 40N 80 0W
Hannibal, Mo., U.S.A. 80 F9 39 42N 91 22W
Hannibal, N.Y., U.S.A. 79 C8 43 19N 76 35W
Hannover, Germany 16 B5 52 22N 9 46 E
Hanoi, Vietnam 32 D5 21 5N 105 55 E
Hanover = Hannover, Germany 16 B5 52 22N 9 46 E
Hanover, Canada 78 B3 44 9N 81 2W
Hanover, S. Africa 56 E3 31 4S 24 29 E
Hanover, N.H., U.S.A. 79 C12 43 42N 72 17W
Hanover, Ohio, U.S.A. 78 F2 40 4N 82 16W
Hanover, Pa., U.S.A. 76 F7 39 48N 76 59W
Hanover, I., Chile 96 G2 51 0S 74 50W
Hansdiha, India 43 G12 24 36N 87 5 E
Hansi, India 42 E6 29 10N 75 57 E
Hanson, L., Australia 63 E2 31 0S 136 15 E
Hantsavichy, Belarus 17 B14 52 49N 26 30 E
Hanumangarh, India 42 E6 29 35N 74 19 E
Hanzhong, China 34 H4 33 10N 107 1 E
Hanzhuang, China 35 G9 34 33N 117 23 E
Haora, India 43 H13 22 37N 88 20 E
Haparanda, Sweden 8 D21 65 52N 24 8 E
Happy, U.S.A. 81 H4 34 45N 101 52W
Happy Camp, U.S.A. 82 F2 41 48N 123 23W
Happy Valley-Goose Bay, Canada 71 B7 53 15N 60 20W
Hapsu, N. Korea 35 D15 41 13N 128 51 E
Hapur, India 42 E7 28 45N 77 45 E
Ḩaql, Si. Arabia 47 F3 29 10N 34 58 E
Har, Indonesia 37 F8 5 16S 133 14 E
Har-Ayrag, Mongolia 34 B5 45 47N 109 16 E
Har Hu, China 32 C4 38 20N 97 38 E
Har Us Nuur, Mongolia 32 B4 48 0N 92 0 E
Har Yehuda, Israel 47 D3 31 35N 34 57 E
Ḩaraḑ, Si. Arabia 46 C4 24 22N 49 0 E
Haranomachi, Japan 30 F10 37 38N 140 58 E
Harare, Zimbabwe 55 F3 17 43S 31 2 E
Harbin, China 35 B14 45 48N 126 40 E
Harbor Beach, U.S.A. 78 C2 43 51N 82 39W
Harbour Breton, Canada 71 C8 47 29N 55 50W
Harbour Deep, Canada 71 B8 50 25N 56 32W
Harda, India 42 H7 22 27N 77 5 E
Hardangerfjorden, Norway 9 F12 60 5N 6 0 E
Hardangervidda, Norway 9 F12 60 7N 7 20 E
Hardap Dam, Namibia 56 C2 24 32S 17 50 E
Hardenberg, Neths. 15 B6 52 34N 6 37 E
Harderwijk, Neths. 15 B5 52 21N 5 38 E
Hardey ✈, Australia 60 D2 22 45S 116 8 E
Hardin, U.S.A. 82 D10 45 44N 107 37W
Harding, S. Africa 57 E4 30 35S 29 55 E
Harding Ra., Australia 60 C3 16 17S 124 55 E
Hardisty, Canada 72 C6 52 40N 111 18W
Hardoi, India 43 F9 27 26N 80 6 E
Hardwar = Haridwar, India 42 E8 29 58N 78 9 E
Hardwick, U.S.A. 79 B12 44 30N 72 22W
Hardy, Pen., Chile 96 H3 55 30S 68 20W
Hare B., Canada 71 B8 51 15N 55 45W
Hareid, Norway 9 E12 62 22N 6 1 E
Harer, Ethiopia 46 F3 9 20N 42 8 E
Hargeisa, Somali Rep. 46 F3 9 30N 44 2 E
Hari ✈, Indonesia 36 E2 1 16S 104 5 E
Haria, Canary Is. 22 E6 29 8N 13 32W
Haridwar, India 42 E8 29 58N 78 9 E
Harim, Jabal al, Oman 45 E8 25 58N 56 14 E
Haringhata ✈, Bangla. 41 J16 22 0N 89 58 E
Harīrūd ✈, Asia 40 A2 37 24N 60 38 E
Härjedalen, Sweden 9 E15 62 22N 13 5 E
Harlan, Iowa, U.S.A. 80 E7 41 39N 95 19W
Harlan, Ky., U.S.A. 77 G4 36 51N 83 19W
Harlech, U.K. 10 E3 52 52N 4 6W
Harlem, U.S.A. 82 B9 48 32N 108 47W
Harlingen, Neths. 15 A5 53 11N 5 25 E
Harlingen, U.S.A. 81 M6 26 12N 97 42W
Harlow, U.K. 11 F8 51 46N 0 8 E
Harlowton, U.S.A. 82 C9 46 26N 109 50W
Harnai, Pakistan 42 D2 30 6N 67 56 E
Harney Basin, U.S.A. 82 E4 43 30N 119 0W
Harney L., U.S.A. 82 E4 43 14N 119 8W
Harney Peak, U.S.A. 80 D3 43 52N 103 32W
Härnösand, Sweden 9 E17 62 38N 17 55 E
Haroldswick, U.K. 12 A8 60 48N 0 50W
Harp L., Canada 71 A7 55 5N 61 50W
Harper, Liberia 50 H4 4 25N 7 43W
Harrai, India 43 H8 22 37N 79 13 E
Harrand, Pakistan 42 E4 29 28N 70 3 E
Harricana ✈, Canada 70 B4 50 56N 79 32W
Harriman, U.S.A. 77 H3 35 56N 84 33W
Harrington Harbour, Canada 71 B8 50 31N 59 30W
Harris, U.K. 12 D2 57 50N 6 55W
Harris, Sd. of, U.K. 12 D1 57 44N 7 6W
Harris L., Australia 63 E2 31 10S 135 10 E
Harris Pt., Canada 78 C2 43 6N 82 9W
Harrisburg, Ill., U.S.A. 81 G10 37 44N 88 32W
Harrisburg, Nebr., U.S.A. 80 E3 41 33N 103 44W
Harrisburg, Pa., U.S.A. 78 F8 40 16N 76 53W
Harrismith, S. Africa 57 D4 28 15S 29 8 E
Harrison, Ark., U.S.A. 81 G8 36 14N 93 7W
Harrison, Maine, U.S.A. 79 B14 44 7N 70 39W
Harrison, Nebr., U.S.A. 80 D3 42 41N 103 53W
Harrison, C., Canada 71 B8 54 55N 57 55W
Harrison L., Canada 72 D4 49 33N 121 50W
Harrisonburg, U.S.A. 76 F6 38 27N 78 52W
Harrisonville, U.S.A. 80 F7 38 39N 94 21W
Harriston, Canada 78 C4 43 57N 80 53W
Harrisville, Mich., U.S.A. 78 B1 44 39N 83 17W
Harrisville, N.Y., U.S.A. 79 B9 44 9N 75 19W
Harrisville, Pa., U.S.A. 78 E5 41 8N 80 0W
Harrodsburg, U.S.A. 76 G3 37 46N 84 51W
Harrogate, U.K. 10 C6 54 0N 1 33W
Harrow □, U.K. 11 F7 51 35N 0 21W
Harrowsmith, Canada 79 B8 44 24N 76 40W
Harry S. Truman Reservoir, U.S.A. 80 F7 38 16N 93 24W
Harsīn, Iran 44 C5 34 18N 47 33 E
Harstad, Norway 8 B17 68 48N 16 30 E
Harsud, India 42 H7 22 6N 76 44 E
Hart, U.S.A. 76 D2 43 42N 86 22W
Hart, L., Australia 63 E2 31 10S 136 25 E
Hartbees ✈, S. Africa 56 D3 28 45S 20 32 E
Hartford, Conn., U.S.A. 79 E12 41 46N 72 41W
Hartford, Ky., U.S.A. 76 G2 37 27N 86 55W
Hartford, S. Dak., U.S.A. 80 D6 43 38N 96 57W
Hartford, Wis., U.S.A. 80 D10 43 19N 88 22W
Hartford City, U.S.A. 76 E3 40 27N 85 22W
Hartland, Canada 71 C6 46 20N 67 32W
Hartland Pt., U.K. 11 F3 51 1N 4 32W
Hartlepool, U.K. 10 C6 54 42N 1 13W
Hartlepool □, U.K. 10 C6 54 42N 1 17W
Hartley Bay, Canada 72 C3 53 25N 129 15W
Hartmannberge, Namibia 56 B1 17 0S 13 0 E
Hartney, Canada 73 D8 49 30N 100 35W
Harts ✈, S. Africa 56 D3 28 24S 24 17 E
Hartselle, U.S.A. 77 H2 34 27N 86 56W
Hartshorne, U.S.A. 81 H7 34 51N 95 34W
Hartstown, U.S.A. 78 E4 41 33N 80 23W
Hartsville, U.S.A. 77 H5 34 23N 80 4W
Hartswater, S. Africa 56 D3 27 34S 24 43 E
Hartwell, U.S.A. 77 H4 34 21N 82 56W
Harunabad, Pakistan 42 E5 29 35N 73 8 E
Harvand, Iran 45 D7 28 25N 55 43 E
Harvey, Australia 61 F2 33 5S 115 54 E
Harvey, Ill., U.S.A. 76 E2 41 36N 87 50W
Harvey, N. Dak., U.S.A. 80 B5 47 47N 99 56W
Harwich, U.K. 11 F9 51 56N 1 17 E
Haryana □, India 42 E7 29 0N 76 10 E
Haryn ✈, Belarus 17 B14 52 7N 27 17 E
Harz, Germany 16 C6 51 38N 10 44 E
Hasa □, Si. Arabia 45 E6 25 50N 49 0 E
Ḩasanābād, Iran 45 C7 32 8N 52 44 E
Hasdo ✈, India 43 J10 21 44N 82 44 E
Hashimoto, Japan 31 G7 34 19N 135 37 E
Hashtjerd, Iran 45 C6 35 52N 50 40 E
Haskell, U.S.A. 81 J5 33 10N 99 44W
Haslemere, U.K. 11 F7 51 5N 0 43W
Hasselt, Belgium 15 D5 50 56N 5 21 E
Hassi Messaoud, Algeria 50 B7 31 51N 6 1 E
Hässleholm, Sweden 9 H15 56 10N 13 46 E
Hastings, N.Z. 59 H6 39 39S 176 52 E
Hastings, U.K. 11 G8 50 51N 0 35 E
Hastings, Mich., U.S.A. 76 D3 42 39N 85 17W
Hastings, Minn., U.S.A. 80 C8 44 44N 92 51W
Hastings, Nebr., U.S.A. 80 E5 40 35N 98 23W
Hastings Ra., Australia 63 E5 31 15S 152 14 E
Hat Yai, Thailand 39 J3 7 1N 100 27 E
Hatanbulag = Ergel, Mongolia 34 C5 43 8N 109 5 E
Hatay = Antalya, Turkey 25 G5 36 52N 30 45 E
Hatch, U.S.A. 83 K10 32 40N 107 9W
Hatchet L., Canada 73 B8 58 36N 103 40W
Hateruma-Shima, Japan 31 M1 24 3N 123 47 E
Hatfield P.O., Australia 63 E3 33 54S 143 49 E
Hatgal, Mongolia 32 A5 50 26N 100 9 E
Hathras, India 42 F8 27 36N 78 6 E
Hatia, Bangla. 41 H17 22 30N 91 5 E
Hato Mayor, Dom. Rep. 89 C6 18 46N 69 15W
Hatta, India 43 G8 24 7N 79 36 E
Hattah, Australia 63 E3 34 48S 142 17 E
Hatteras, C., U.S.A. 77 H8 35 14N 75 32W
Hattiesburg, U.S.A. 81 K10 31 20N 89 17W
Hatvan, Hungary 17 E10 47 40N 19 45 E
Hau Bon = Cheo Reo, Vietnam 36 B3 13 25N 108 28 E
Hau Duc, Vietnam 38 E7 15 20N 108 13 E
Haugesund, Norway 9 G11 59 23N 5 13 E
Haukipudas, Finland 8 D21 65 12N 25 20 E
Haultain ✈, Canada 73 B7 55 51N 106 46W
Hauraki G., N.Z. 59 G5 36 35S 175 5 E
Haut Atlas, Morocco 50 B4 32 30N 5 0W
Haut-Zaïre = Orientale □, Dem. Rep. of the Congo 54 B2 2 20N 26 0 E
Hautes Fagnes = Hohe Venn, Belgium 15 D6 50 30N 6 5 E
Hauts Plateaux, Algeria 48 C4 35 0N 1 0 E
Havana = La Habana, Cuba 88 B3 23 8N 82 22W
Havana, U.S.A. 80 E9 40 18N 90 4W
Havant, U.K. 11 G7 50 51N 0 58W
Havasu, L., U.S.A. 85 L12 34 18N 114 28W
Havel ✈, Germany 16 B7 52 50N 12 3 E
Havelian, Pakistan 42 B5 34 2N 73 10 E
Havelock, Canada 78 B7 44 26N 77 53W
Havelock, N.Z. 59 J4 41 17S 173 48 E
Havelock, U.S.A. 77 H7 34 53N 76 54W
Haverfordwest, U.K. 11 F3 51 48N 4 58W
Haverhill, U.S.A. 79 D13 42 47N 71 5W
Haverstraw, U.S.A. 79 E11 41 12N 73 58W
Havirga, Mongolia 34 B7 45 41N 113 5 E
Havířov, Czech Rep. 17 D10 49 46N 18 20 E
Havlíčkův Brod, Czech Rep. 16 D8 49 36N 15 33 E
Havre, U.S.A. 82 B9 48 33N 109 41W
Havre-Aubert, Canada 71 C7 47 12N 61 56W
Havre-St.-Pierre, Canada 71 B7 50 18N 63 33W
Haw ✈, U.S.A. 77 H6 35 36N 79 3W
Hawaii □, U.S.A. 74 H16 19 30N 156 30W
Hawaii I., Pac. Oc. 74 J17 20 0N 155 0W
Hawaiian Is., Pac. Oc. 74 H17 20 30N 156 0W
Hawaiian Ridge, Pac. Oc. 65 E11 24 0N 165 0W
Hawarden, U.S.A. 80 D6 43 0N 96 29W
Hawea, L., N.Z. 59 L2 44 28S 169 19 E
Hawera, N.Z. 59 H5 39 35S 174 19 E
Hawick, U.K. 12 F6 55 26N 2 47W
Hawk Junction, Canada 70 C3 48 5N 84 38W
Hawke B., N.Z. 59 H6 39 25S 177 20 E
Hawker, Australia 63 E2 31 59S 138 22 E
Hawkesbury, Canada 70 C5 45 37N 74 37W
Hawkesbury I., Canada 72 C3 53 37N 129 3W
Hawkesbury Pt., Australia 62 A1 11 55S 134 5 E
Hawkinsville, U.S.A. 77 J4 32 17N 83 28W
Hawley, Minn., U.S.A. 80 B6 46 53N 96 19W
Hawley, Pa., U.S.A. 79 E9 41 28N 75 11W
Ḩawrān, W. ✈, Iraq 44 C4 33 58N 42 34 E
Hawsh Mūssá, Lebanon 47 B4 33 45N 35 55 E
Hawthorne, U.S.A. 82 G4 38 32N 118 38W
Hay, Australia 63 E3 34 30S 144 51 E
Hay ✈, Australia 62 C2 24 50S 138 0 E
Hay ✈, Canada 72 A5 60 50N 116 26W
Hay, C., Australia 60 B4 14 5S 129 29 E
Hay I., Canada 78 B4 44 53N 80 58W
Hay L., Canada 72 B5 58 50N 118 50W
Hay-on-Wye, U.K. 11 E4 52 5N 3 8W
Hay River, Canada 72 A5 60 51N 115 44W
Hay Springs, U.S.A. 80 D3 42 41N 102 41W
Haya = Tehoru, Indonesia 37 E7 3 23S 129 30 E
Hayachine-San, Japan 30 E10 39 34N 141 29 E
Hayden, U.S.A. 82 F10 40 30N 107 16W
Haydon, Australia 62 B3 18 0S 141 30 E
Hayes, U.S.A. 80 C4 44 23N 101 1W
Hayes ✈, Canada 70 A1 57 3N 92 12W
Hayes Creek, Australia 60 B5 13 43S 131 22 E
Hayle, U.K. 11 G2 50 11N 5 26W
Hayling I., U.K. 11 G7 50 48N 0 59W
Hayrabolu, Turkey 21 D12 41 12N 27 5 E
Hays, Canada 72 C6 50 6N 111 48W
Hays, U.S.A. 80 F5 38 53N 99 20W
Haysyn, Ukraine 17 D15 48 57N 29 25 E
Hayvoron, Ukraine 17 D15 48 22N 29 52 E
Hayward, Calif., U.S.A. 84 H4 37 40N 122 5W
Hayward, Wis., U.S.A. 80 B9 46 1N 91 29W
Haywards Heath, U.K. 11 G7 51 0N 0 5W
Hazafon □, Israel 47 C4 32 40N 35 20 E
Hazārān, Kūh-e, Iran 45 D8 29 35N 57 20 E
Hazard, U.S.A. 76 G4 37 15N 83 12W
Hazaribag, India 43 H11 23 58N 85 26 E
Hazaribag Road, India 43 G11 24 12N 85 57 E
Hazelton, Canada 72 B3 55 20N 127 42W
Hazelton, U.S.A. 80 B4 46 29N 100 17W
Hazen, U.S.A. 80 B4 47 18N 101 38W
Hazlehurst, Ga., U.S.A. 77 K4 31 52N 82 36W
Hazlehurst, Miss., U.S.A. 81 K9 31 52N 90 24W
Hazlet, U.S.A. 79 F10 40 25N 74 12W
Hazleton, U.S.A. 79 F9 40 57N 75 59W
Hazlett, L., Australia 60 D4 21 30S 128 48 E
Hazro, Turkey 44 B4 38 15N 40 47 E
Head of Bight, Australia 61 F5 31 30S 131 25 E
Headlands, Zimbabwe 55 F3 18 15S 32 2 E
Healdsburg, U.S.A. 84 G4 38 37N 122 52W
Healdton, U.S.A. 81 H6 34 14N 97 29W
Healesville, Australia 63 F4 37 35S 145 30 E
Heany Junction, Zimbabwe 57 C4 20 6S 28 54 E
Heard I., Ind. Oc. 3 G13 53 0S 74 0 E
Hearne, U.S.A. 81 K6 30 53N 96 36W
Hearst, Canada 70 C3 49 40N 83 41W
Heart ✈, U.S.A. 80 B4 46 46N 100 50W
Heart's Content, Canada 71 C9 47 54N 53 27W
Heath Pt., Canada 71 C7 49 8N 61 40W
Heavener, U.S.A. 81 H7 34 53N 94 36W
Hebbronville, U.S.A. 81 M5 27 18N 98 41W
Hebei □, China 34 E9 39 0N 116 0 E
Hebel, Australia 63 D4 28 58S 147 47 E
Heber, U.S.A. 85 N11 32 44N 115 32W
Heber City, U.S.A. 82 F8 40 31N 111 25W
Heber Springs, U.S.A. 81 H9 35 30N 92 2W
Hebert, Canada 73 C7 50 30N 107 10W
Hebgen L., U.S.A. 82 D8 44 52N 111 20W
Hebi, China 34 G8 35 57N 114 7 E
Hebrides, U.K. 6 D4 57 30N 7 0W
Hebrides, Sea of the, U.K. 12 D2 57 5N 7 0W
Hebron = Al Khalīl, West Bank 47 D4 31 32N 35 6 E
Hebron, Canada 69 C13 58 5N 62 30W
Hebron, N. Dak., U.S.A. 80 B3 46 54N 102 3W
Hebron, Nebr., U.S.A. 80 E6 40 10N 97 35W
Hecate Str., Canada 72 C2 53 10N 130 30W
Heceta I., U.S.A. 72 B2 55 46N 133 40W
Hechi, China 32 D5 24 40N 108 2 E
Hechuan, China 32 C5 30 2N 106 12 E
Hecla, U.S.A. 80 C5 45 53N 98 9W
Hecla I., Canada 73 C9 51 10N 96 43W
Hede, Sweden 9 E15 62 23N 13 30 E
Hedemora, Sweden 9 F16 60 18N 15 58 E
Heerde, Neths. 15 B6 52 24N 6 2 E
Heerenveen, Neths. 15 B5 52 57N 5 55 E
Heerhugowaard, Neths. 15 B4 52 40N 4 51 E
Heerlen, Neths. 18 A6 50 55N 5 58 E
Ḩefa, Israel 47 C4 32 46N 35 0 E
Ḩefa □, Israel 47 C4 32 40N 35 0 E
Hefei, China 33 C6 31 52N 117 18 E

Hegang, *China* 33 B8 47 20N 130 19 E
Heichengzhen, *China* 34 F4 36 24N 106 3 E
Heidelberg, *Germany* 16 D5 49 24N 8 42 E
Heidelberg, *S. Africa* 56 E3 34 6S 20 59 E
Heilbron, *S. Africa* 57 D4 27 16S 27 59 E
Heilbronn, *Germany* 16 D5 49 9N 9 13 E
Heilongjiang □, *China* 33 B7 48 0N 126 0 E
Heilunkiang = Heilongjiang □, *China* 33 B7 48 0N 126 0 E
Heimaey, *Iceland* 8 E3 63 26N 20 17W
Heinola, *Finland* 9 F22 61 13N 26 2 E
Heinze Kyun, *Burma* 38 E1 14 25N 97 45 E
Heishan, *China* 35 D12 41 40N 122 5 E
Heishui, *China* 35 C10 42 8N 119 30 E
Hejaz = Ḩijāz □, *Si. Arabia* 46 C2 24 0N 40 0 E
Hejian, *China* 34 E9 38 25N 116 5 E
Hejin, *China* 34 G6 35 35N 110 42 E
Hekimhan, *Turkey* 44 B3 38 50N 37 55 E
Hekla, *Iceland* 8 E4 63 56N 19 35W
Hekou, *China* 32 D5 22 30N 103 59 E
Helan Shan, *China* 34 E3 38 30N 105 55 E
Helen Atoll, *Pac. Oc.* 37 D8 2 40N 132 0 E
Helena, *Ark., U.S.A.* 81 H9 34 32N 90 36W
Helena, *Mont., U.S.A.* 82 C7 46 36N 112 2W
Helendale, *U.S.A.* 85 L9 34 44N 117 19W
Helensburgh, *U.K.* 12 E4 56 1N 4 43W
Helensville, *N.Z.* 59 G5 36 41S 174 29 E
Helenvale, *Australia* 62 B4 15 43S 145 14 E
Helgeland, *Norway* 8 C15 66 7N 13 29 E
Helgoland, *Germany* 16 A4 54 10N 7 53 E
Heligoland = Helgoland, *Germany* 16 A4 54 10N 7 53 E
Heligoland B. = Deutsche Bucht, *Germany* 16 A5 54 15N 8 0 E
Hella, *Iceland* 8 E3 63 50N 20 24W
Hellertown, *U.S.A.* 79 F9 40 35N 75 21W
Hellespont = Çanakkale Boğazı, *Turkey* 21 D12 40 17N 26 32 E
Hellevoetsluis, *Neths.* 15 C4 51 50N 4 8 E
Hellín, *Spain* 19 C5 38 31N 1 40W
Helmand □, *Afghan.* 40 D4 31 20N 64 0 E
Helmand →, *Afghan.* 40 D2 31 12N 61 34 E
Helmeringhausen, *Namibia* 56 D2 25 54S 16 57 E
Helmond, *Neths.* 15 C5 51 29N 5 41 E
Helmsdale, *U.K.* 12 C5 58 7N 3 39W
Helmsdale →, *U.K.* 12 C5 58 7N 3 40W
Helong, *China* 35 C15 42 40N 129 0 E
Helper, *U.S.A.* 82 G8 39 41N 110 51W
Helsingborg, *Sweden* 9 H15 56 3N 12 42 E
Helsingfors = Helsinki, *Finland* 9 F21 60 15N 25 3 E
Helsingør, *Denmark* 9 H15 56 2N 12 35 E
Helsinki, *Finland* 9 F21 60 15N 25 3 E
Helston, *U.K.* 11 G2 50 6N 5 17W
Helvellyn, *U.K.* 10 C4 54 32N 3 1W
Helwân, *Egypt* 51 C12 29 50N 31 20 E
Hemel Hempstead, *U.K.* 11 F7 51 44N 0 28W
Hemet, *U.S.A.* 85 M10 33 45N 116 58W
Hemingford, *U.S.A.* 80 D3 42 19N 103 4W
Hemmingford, *Canada* 79 A11 45 3N 73 35W
Hempstead, *U.S.A.* 81 K6 30 6N 96 5W
Hemse, *Sweden* 9 H18 57 15N 18 22 E
Henan □, *China* 34 H8 34 0N 114 0 E
Henares →, *Spain* 19 B4 40 24N 3 30W
Henashi-Misaki, *Japan* 30 D9 40 37N 139 51 E
Henderson, *Argentina* 94 D3 36 18S 61 43W
Henderson, *Ky., U.S.A.* 76 G2 37 50N 87 35W
Henderson, *N.C., U.S.A.* 77 G6 36 20N 78 25W
Henderson, *Nev., U.S.A.* 85 J12 36 2N 114 59W
Henderson, *Tenn., U.S.A.* 77 H1 35 26N 88 38W
Henderson, *Tex., U.S.A.* 81 J7 32 9N 94 48W
Hendersonville, *N.C., U.S.A.* 77 H4 35 19N 82 28W
Hendersonville, *Tenn., U.S.A.* 77 G2 36 18N 86 37W
Hendījān, *Iran* 45 D6 30 14N 49 43 E
Hendorābī, *Iran* 45 E7 26 40N 53 37 E
Hengcheng, *China* 34 E4 38 18N 106 28 E
Hengdaohezi, *China* 35 B15 44 52N 129 0 E
Hengelo, *Neths.* 15 B6 52 16N 6 48 E
Hengshan, *China* 34 F5 37 58N 109 5 E
Hengshui, *China* 34 F8 37 41N 115 40 E
Hengyang, *China* 33 D6 26 59N 112 22 E
Henlopen, C., *U.S.A.* 76 F8 38 48N 75 6W
Hennenman, *S. Africa* 56 D4 27 59S 27 1 E
Hennessey, *U.S.A.* 81 G6 36 6N 97 54W
Henrietta, *U.S.A.* 81 J5 33 49N 98 12W
Henrietta, Ostrov = Genriyetty, Ostrov, *Russia* 27 B16 77 6N 156 30 E
Henrietta Maria, C., *Canada* 70 A3 55 9N 82 20W
Henry, *U.S.A.* 80 E10 41 7N 89 22W
Henryetta, *U.S.A.* 81 H7 35 27N 95 59W
Henryville, *Canada* 79 A11 45 8N 73 11W
Hensall, *Canada* 78 C3 43 26N 81 30W
Hentiesbaai, *Namibia* 56 C1 22 8S 14 18 E
Hentiyn Nuruu, *Mongolia* 33 B5 48 30N 108 30 E
Henty, *Australia* 63 F4 35 30S 147 0 E
Henzada, *Burma* 41 L19 17 38N 95 26 E
Heppner, *U.S.A.* 82 D4 45 21N 119 33W
Hepworth, *Canada* 78 B3 44 37N 81 9W
Hequ, *China* 34 E6 39 20N 111 15 E
Héraðsflói, *Iceland* 8 D6 65 42N 14 12W
Héraðsvötn →, *Iceland* 8 D4 65 45N 19 25W
Herald Cays, *Australia* 62 B4 16 58S 149 9 E
Herāt, *Afghan.* 40 B3 34 20N 62 7 E
Herāt □, *Afghan.* 40 B3 35 0N 62 0 E
Herbert →, *Australia* 62 B4 18 31S 146 17 E
Herberton, *Australia* 62 B4 17 20S 145 25 E
Herbertsdale, *S. Africa* 56 E3 34 1S 21 46 E
Herceg-Novi, *Montenegro, Yug.* 21 C8 42 30N 18 33 E
Herchmer, *Canada* 73 B10 57 22N 94 10W
Herðubreið, *Iceland* 8 D5 65 11N 16 21W
Hereford, *U.K.* 11 E5 52 4N 2 43W
Hereford, *U.S.A.* 81 H3 34 49N 102 24W
Herefordshire □, *U.K.* 11 E5 52 8N 2 40W
Herentals, *Belgium* 15 C4 51 12N 4 51 E
Herford, *Germany* 16 B5 52 7N 8 39 E
Herington, *U.S.A.* 80 F6 38 40N 96 57W
Herkimer, *U.S.A.* 79 D10 43 0N 74 59W
Herlong, *U.S.A.* 84 E6 40 8N 120 8W
Herm, *U.K.* 11 H5 49 30N 2 28W
Hermann, *U.S.A.* 80 F9 38 42N 91 27W
Hermannsburg, *Australia* 60 D5 23 57S 132 45 E
Hermanus, *S. Africa* 56 E2 34 27S 19 12 E
Hermidale, *Australia* 63 E4 31 30S 146 42 E
Hermiston, *U.S.A.* 82 D4 45 51N 119 17W
Hermite, I., *Chile* 96 H3 55 50S 68 0W
Hermon, *U.S.A.* 79 B9 44 28N 75 14W
Hermon, Mt. = Shaykh, J. ash, *Lebanon* 47 B4 33 25N 35 50 E
Hermosillo, *Mexico* 86 B2 29 10N 111 0W
Hernád →, *Hungary* 17 D11 47 56N 21 8 E
Hernandarias, *Paraguay* 95 B5 25 20S 54 40W
Hernandez, *U.S.A.* 84 J6 36 24N 120 46W
Hernando, *Argentina* 94 C3 32 28S 63 40W
Hernando, *U.S.A.* 81 H10 34 50N 90 0W
Herndon, *U.S.A.* 78 F8 40 43N 76 51W
Herne, *Germany* 15 C7 51 32N 7 14 E
Herne Bay, *U.K.* 11 F9 51 21N 1 8 E
Herning, *Denmark* 9 H13 56 8N 8 58 E
Heroica = Caborca, *Mexico* 86 A2 30 40N 112 10W
Heroica Nogales = Nogales, *Mexico* 86 A2 31 20N 110 56W
Heron Bay, *Canada* 70 C2 48 40N 86 25W
Herradura, Pta. de la, *Canary Is.* 22 F5 28 26N 14 8W
Herreid, *U.S.A.* 80 C4 45 50N 100 4W
Herrin, *U.S.A.* 81 G10 37 48N 89 2W
Herriot, *Canada* 73 B8 56 22N 101 16W
Hershey, *U.S.A.* 79 F8 40 17N 76 39W
Hersonissos, *Greece* 23 D7 35 18N 25 22 E
Herstal, *Belgium* 15 D5 50 40N 5 38 E
Hertford, *U.K.* 11 F7 51 48N 0 4W
Hertfordshire □, *U.K.* 11 F7 51 51N 0 5W
's-Hertogenbosch, *Neths.* 15 C5 51 42N 5 17 E
Hertzogville, *S. Africa* 56 D4 28 9S 25 30 E
Hervey B., *Australia* 62 C5 25 0S 152 52 E
Herzliyya, *Israel* 47 C3 32 10N 34 50 E
Ḩeṣār, *Fārs, Iran* 45 D6 29 52N 50 16 E
Ḩeṣār, *Markazī, Iran* 45 C6 35 50N 49 12 E
Heshui, *China* 34 G5 35 48N 108 0 E
Heshun, *China* 34 F7 37 22N 113 32 E
Hesperia, *U.S.A.* 85 L9 34 25N 117 18W
Hesse = Hessen □, *Germany* 16 C5 50 30N 9 0 E
Hessen □, *Germany* 16 C5 50 30N 9 0 E
Hetch Hetchy Aqueduct, *U.S.A.* 84 H5 37 29N 122 19W
Hettinger, *U.S.A.* 80 C3 46 0N 102 42W
Heuvelton, *U.S.A.* 79 B9 44 37N 75 25W
Hewitt, *U.S.A.* 81 K6 31 27N 97 11W
Hexham, *U.K.* 10 C5 54 58N 2 4W
Hexigten Qi, *China* 35 C9 43 18N 117 30 E
Ḩeydarābād, *Iran* 45 D7 30 33N 55 38 E
Heysham, *U.K.* 10 C5 54 3N 2 53W
Heywood, *Australia* 63 F3 38 8S 141 37 E
Heze, *China* 34 G8 35 14N 115 20 E
Hi Vista, *U.S.A.* 85 L9 34 45N 117 46W
Hialeah, *U.S.A.* 77 N5 25 50N 80 17W
Hiawatha, *U.S.A.* 80 F7 39 51N 95 32W
Hibbing, *U.S.A.* 80 B8 47 25N 92 56W
Hibbs B., *Australia* 62 G4 42 35S 145 15 E
Hibernia Reef, *Australia* 60 B3 12 0S 123 23 E
Hickman, *U.S.A.* 81 G10 36 34N 89 11W
Hickory, *U.S.A.* 77 H5 35 44N 81 21W
Hicks, Pt., *Australia* 63 F4 37 49S 149 17 E
Hicks L., *Canada* 73 A9 61 25N 100 0W
Hicksville, *U.S.A.* 79 F11 40 46N 73 32W
Hida-Gawa →, *Japan* 31 G8 35 26N 137 3 E
Hida-Sammyaku, *Japan* 31 F8 36 30N 137 40 E
Hidaka-Sammyaku, *Japan* 30 C11 42 35N 142 45 E
Hidalgo, *Mexico* 87 C5 24 15N 99 26W
Hidalgo □, *Mexico* 87 C5 20 30N 99 10W
Hidalgo, Presa M., *Mexico* 86 B3 26 30N 108 35W
Hidalgo del Parral, *Mexico* 86 B3 26 58N 105 40W
Hierro, *Canary Is.* 22 G1 27 44N 18 0W
Higashiajima-San, *Japan* 30 F10 37 40N 140 10 E
Higashiōsaka, *Japan* 31 G7 34 40N 135 37 E
Higgins, *U.S.A.* 81 G4 36 7N 100 2W
Higgins Corner, *U.S.A.* 84 F5 39 2N 121 5W
High Atlas = Haut Atlas, *Morocco* 50 B4 32 30N 5 0W
High Bridge, *U.S.A.* 79 F10 40 40N 74 54W
High Level, *Canada* 72 B5 58 31N 117 8W
High Point, *U.S.A.* 77 H6 35 57N 80 0W
High Prairie, *Canada* 72 B5 55 30N 116 30W
High River, *Canada* 72 C6 50 30N 113 50W
High Tatra = Tatry, *Slovak Rep.* 17 D11 49 20N 20 0 E
High Veld, *Africa* 48 J6 27 0S 27 0 E
High Wycombe, *U.K.* 11 F7 51 37N 0 45W
Highland □, *U.K.* 12 D4 57 17N 4 21W
Highland Park, *U.S.A.* 76 D2 42 11N 87 48W
Highmore, *U.S.A.* 80 C5 44 31N 99 27W
Highrock L., *Man., Canada* 73 B8 55 45N 100 30W
Highrock L., *Sask., Canada* 73 B7 57 5N 105 32W
Higüey, *Dom. Rep.* 89 C6 18 37N 68 42W
Hiiumaa, *Estonia* 9 G20 58 50N 22 45 E
Ḩijāz □, *Si. Arabia* 46 C2 24 0N 40 0 E
Hijo = Tagum, *Phil.* 37 C7 7 33N 125 53 E
Hikari, *Japan* 31 H5 33 58N 131 58 E
Hiko, *U.S.A.* 84 H11 37 32N 115 14W
Hikone, *Japan* 31 G8 35 15N 136 10 E
Hikurangi, *Gisborne, N.Z.* 59 H6 37 55S 178 4 E
Hikurangi, *Northland, N.Z.* 59 F5 35 36S 174 17 E
Hildesheim, *Germany* 16 B5 52 9N 9 56 E
Hill →, *Australia* 61 F2 30 23S 115 3 E
Hill City, *Idaho, U.S.A.* 82 E6 43 18N 115 3W
Hill City, *Kans., U.S.A.* 80 F5 39 22N 99 51W
Hill City, *S. Dak., U.S.A.* 80 D3 43 56N 103 35W
Hill Island L., *Canada* 73 A7 60 30N 109 50W
Hillcrest Center, *U.S.A.* 85 K8 35 23N 118 57W
Hillegom, *Neths.* 15 B4 52 18N 4 35 E
Hillerød, *Denmark* 9 J15 55 56N 12 19 E
Hillsboro, *Kans., U.S.A.* 80 F6 38 21N 97 12W
Hillsboro, *N. Dak., U.S.A.* 80 B6 47 26N 97 3W
Hillsboro, *N.H., U.S.A.* 79 C13 43 7N 71 54W
Hillsboro, *Ohio, U.S.A.* 76 F4 39 12N 83 37W
Hillsboro, *Oreg., U.S.A.* 84 E4 45 31N 122 59W
Hillsboro, *Tex., U.S.A.* 81 J6 32 1N 97 8W
Hillsborough, *Grenada* 89 D7 12 28N 61 28W
Hillsdale, *Mich., U.S.A.* 76 E3 41 56N 84 38W
Hillsdale, *N.Y., U.S.A.* 79 D11 42 11N 73 30W
Hillsport, *Canada* 70 C2 49 27N 85 34W
Hillston, *Australia* 63 E4 33 30S 145 31 E
Hilo, *U.S.A.* 74 J17 19 44N 155 5W
Hilton, *U.S.A.* 78 C7 43 17N 77 48W
Hilton Head Island, *U.S.A.* 77 J5 32 13N 80 45W
Hilversum, *Neths.* 15 B5 52 14N 5 10 E
Himachal Pradesh □, *India* 42 D7 31 30N 77 0 E
Himalaya, *Asia* 43 E11 29 0N 84 0 E
Himatnagar, *India* 40 H8 23 37N 72 57 E
Himeji, *Japan* 31 G7 34 50N 134 40 E
Himi, *Japan* 31 F8 36 50N 136 55 E
Ḩimş, *Syria* 47 A5 34 40N 36 45 E
Ḩimş □, *Syria* 47 A6 34 30N 37 0 E
Hinche, *Haiti* 89 C5 19 9N 72 1W
Hinchinbrook I., *Australia* 62 B4 18 20S 146 15 E
Hinckley, *U.K.* 11 E6 52 33N 1 22W
Hinckley, *U.S.A.* 80 B8 46 1N 92 56W
Hindaun, *India* 42 F7 26 44N 77 5 E
Hindmarsh, L., *Australia* 63 F3 36 5S 141 55 E
Hindu Bagh, *Pakistan* 42 D2 30 56N 67 50 E
Hindu Kush, *Asia* 40 B7 36 0N 71 0 E
Hindubagh, *Pakistan* 40 D5 30 56N 67 57 E
Hindupur, *India* 40 N10 13 49N 77 32 E
Hines Creek, *Canada* 72 B5 56 20N 118 40W
Hinesville, *U.S.A.* 77 K5 31 51N 81 36W
Hinganghat, *India* 40 J11 20 30N 78 52 E
Hingham, *U.S.A.* 82 B8 48 33N 110 25W
Hingir, *India* 43 J10 21 57N 83 41 E
Hingoli, *India* 40 K10 19 41N 77 15 E
Hinna = Imi, *Ethiopia* 46 F3 6 28N 42 10 E
Hinnøya, *Norway* 8 B16 68 35N 15 50 E
Hinojosa del Duque, *Spain* 19 C3 38 30N 5 9W
Hinsdale, *U.S.A.* 79 D12 42 47N 72 29W
Hinton, *Canada* 72 C5 53 26N 117 34W
Hinton, *U.S.A.* 76 G5 37 40N 80 54W
Hirado, *Japan* 31 H4 33 22N 129 33 E
Hirakud Dam, *India* 41 J13 21 32N 83 45 E
Hiran →, *India* 43 H8 23 6N 79 21 E
Hirapur, *India* 43 G8 24 22N 79 13 E
Hiratsuka, *Japan* 31 G9 35 19N 139 21 E
Hiroo, *Japan* 30 C11 42 17N 143 19 E
Hirosaki, *Japan* 30 D10 40 34N 140 28 E
Hiroshima, *Japan* 31 G6 34 24N 132 30 E
Hiroshima □, *Japan* 31 G6 34 50N 133 0 E
Hisar, *India* 42 E6 29 12N 75 45 E
Hisb →, *Iraq* 44 D5 31 45N 44 17 E
Ḩismá, *Si. Arabia* 44 D3 28 30N 36 0 E
Hispaniola, *W. Indies* 89 C5 19 0N 71 0W
Hīt, *Iraq* 44 C4 33 38N 42 49 E
Hita, *Japan* 31 H5 33 20N 130 58 E
Hitachi, *Japan* 31 F10 36 36N 140 39 E
Hitchin, *U.K.* 11 F7 51 58N 0 16W
Hitoyoshi, *Japan* 31 H5 32 13N 130 45 E
Hitra, *Norway* 8 E13 63 30N 8 45 E
Hixon, *Canada* 72 C4 53 25N 122 35W
Ḩiyyon, N. →, *Israel* 47 E4 30 25N 35 10 E
Hjalmar L., *Canada* 73 A7 61 33N 109 25W
Hjälmaren, *Sweden* 9 G16 59 18N 15 40 E
Hjørring, *Denmark* 9 H13 57 29N 9 59 E
Hkakabo Razi, *Burma* 41 E20 28 25N 97 23 E
Hlobane, *S. Africa* 57 D5 27 42S 31 0 E
Hluhluwe, *S. Africa* 57 D5 28 1S 32 15 E
Hlyboka, *Ukraine* 17 D13 48 5N 25 56 E
Ho Chi Minh City = Thanh Pho Ho Chi Minh, *Vietnam* 39 G6 10 58N 106 40 E
Ho Thuong, *Vietnam* 38 C5 19 32N 105 48 E
Hoa Binh, *Vietnam* 38 B5 20 50N 105 20 E
Hoa Da, *Vietnam* 39 G7 11 16N 108 40 E
Hoa Hiep, *Vietnam* 39 G5 11 34N 105 51 E
Hoai Nhon, *Vietnam* 38 E7 14 28N 109 1 E
Hoang Lien Son, *Vietnam* 38 A4 22 0N 104 0 E
Hoanib →, *Namibia* 56 B2 19 27S 12 46 E
Hoare B., *Canada* 69 B13 65 17N 62 30W
Hoarusib →, *Namibia* 56 B2 19 3S 12 36 E
Hobart, *Australia* 62 G4 42 50S 147 21 E
Hobart, *U.S.A.* 81 H5 35 1N 99 6W
Hobbs, *U.S.A.* 81 J3 32 42N 103 8W
Hobbs Coast, *Antarctica* 5 D14 74 50S 131 0W
Hobe Sound, *U.S.A.* 77 M5 27 4N 80 8W
Hoboken, *U.S.A.* 79 F10 40 45N 74 4W
Hobro, *Denmark* 9 H13 56 39N 9 46 E
Hoburgen, *Sweden* 9 H18 56 55N 18 7 E
Hochfeld, *Namibia* 56 C2 21 28S 17 58 E
Hodaka-Dake, *Japan* 31 F8 36 17N 137 39 E
Hodeida = Al Ḩudaydah, *Yemen* 46 E3 14 50N 43 0 E
Hodgeville, *Canada* 73 C7 50 7N 106 58W
Hodgson, *Canada* 73 C9 51 13N 97 36W
Hódmezővásárhely, *Hungary* 17 E11 46 28N 20 22 E
Hodna, Chott el, *Algeria* 50 A6 35 26N 4 43 E
Hodonín, *Czech Rep.* 17 D9 48 50N 17 10 E
Hoeamdong, *N. Korea* 35 C16 42 30N 130 16 E
Hoek van Holland, *Neths.* 15 C4 52 0N 4 7 E
Hoengsŏng, *S. Korea* 35 F14 37 29N 127 59 E
Hoeryong, *N. Korea* 35 C15 42 30N 129 45 E
Hoeyang, *N. Korea* 35 E14 38 43N 127 36 E
Hof, *Germany* 16 C6 50 19N 11 55 E
Hofmeyr, *S. Africa* 56 E4 31 39S 25 50 E
Höfn, *Iceland* 8 D6 64 15N 15 13W
Hofors, *Sweden* 9 F17 60 31N 16 15 E
Hofsjökull, *Iceland* 8 D4 64 49N 18 48W
Hōfu, *Japan* 31 G5 34 3N 131 34 E
Hogan Group, *Australia* 63 F4 39 13S 147 1 E
Hogarth, Mt., *Australia* 62 C2 21 48S 136 58 E
Hoggar = Ahaggar, *Algeria* 50 D7 23 0N 6 30 E
Hogsty Reef, *Bahamas* 89 B5 21 41N 73 48W
Hoh →, *U.S.A.* 84 C2 47 45N 124 29W
Hohe Venn, *Belgium* 15 D6 50 30N 6 5 E
Hohenwald, *U.S.A.* 77 H2 35 33N 87 33W
Hoher Rhön = Rhön, *Germany* 16 C5 50 24N 9 58 E
Hohhot, *China* 34 D6 40 52N 111 40 E
Hóhlakas, *Greece* 23 D9 35 57N 27 53 E
Hoi An, *Vietnam* 38 E7 15 30N 108 19 E
Hoi Xuan, *Vietnam* 38 B5 20 25N 105 9 E
Hoisington, *U.S.A.* 80 F5 38 31N 98 47W
Hōjō, *Japan* 31 H6 33 58N 132 46 E
Hokianga Harbour, *N.Z.* 59 F4 35 31S 173 22 E
Hokitika, *N.Z.* 59 K3 42 42S 171 0 E
Hokkaidō □, *Japan* 30 C11 43 30N 143 0 E
Holbrook, *Australia* 63 F4 35 42S 147 18 E
Holbrook, *U.S.A.* 83 J8 34 54N 110 10W
Holden, *U.S.A.* 82 G7 39 6N 112 16W
Holdenville, *U.S.A.* 81 H6 35 5N 96 24W
Holdrege, *U.S.A.* 80 E5 40 26N 99 23W
Holguín, *Cuba* 88 B4 20 50N 76 20W
Hollams Bird I., *Namibia* 56 C1 24 40S 14 30 E
Holland, *Mich., U.S.A.* 76 D2 42 47N 86 7W
Holland, *N.Y., U.S.A.* 78 D6 42 38N 78 32W
Hollandale, *U.S.A.* 81 J9 33 10N 90 51W
Hollandia = Jayapura, *Indonesia* 37 E10 2 28S 140 38 E
Holley, *U.S.A.* 78 C6 43 14N 78 2W
Hollidaysburg, *U.S.A.* 78 F6 40 26N 78 24W
Hollis, *U.S.A.* 81 H5 34 41N 99 55W
Hollister, *Calif., U.S.A.* 84 J5 36 51N 121 24W
Hollister, *Idaho, U.S.A.* 82 E6 42 21N 114 35W
Holly Hill, *U.S.A.* 77 L5 29 16N 81 3W
Holly Springs, *U.S.A.* 81 H10 34 46N 89 27W
Hollywood, *U.S.A.* 77 N5 26 1N 80 9W
Holman, *Canada* 68 A8 70 44N 117 44W
Hólmavík, *Iceland* 8 D3 65 42N 21 40W
Holmen, *U.S.A.* 80 D9 43 58N 91 15W
Holmes Reefs, *Australia* 62 B4 16 27S 148 0 E
Holmsund, *Sweden* 8 E19 63 41N 20 20 E
Holroyd →, *Australia* 62 A3 14 10S 141 36 E
Holstebro, *Denmark* 9 H13 56 22N 8 37 E
Holsworthy, *U.K.* 11 G3 50 48N 4 22W
Holton, *Canada* 71 B8 54 31N 57 12W
Holton, *U.S.A.* 80 F7 39 28N 95 44W
Holtville, *U.S.A.* 85 N11 32 49N 115 23W
Holwerd, *Neths.* 15 A5 53 22N 5 54 E
Holy I., *Angl., U.K.* 10 D3 53 17N 4 37W
Holy I., *Northumb., U.K.* 10 B6 55 40N 1 47W
Holyhead, *U.K.* 10 D3 53 18N 4 38W
Holyoke, *Colo., U.S.A.* 80 E3 40 35N 102 18W
Holyoke, *Mass., U.S.A.* 79 D12 42 12N 72 37W
Holyrood, *Canada* 71 C9 47 27N 53 8W
Homa Bay, *Kenya* 54 C3 0 36S 34 30 E
Homalin, *Burma* 41 G19 24 55N 95 0 E
Homand, *Iran* 45 C8 32 28N 59 37 E
Homathko →, *Canada* 72 C4 51 0N 124 56W
Hombori, *Mali* 50 E5 15 20N 1 38W
Home B., *Canada* 69 B13 68 40N 67 10W
Home Hill, *Australia* 62 B4 19 43S 147 25 E
Homedale, *U.S.A.* 82 E5 43 37N 116 56W
Homer, *Alaska, U.S.A.* 68 C4 59 39N 151 33W
Homer, *La., U.S.A.* 81 J8 32 48N 93 4W
Homer City, *U.S.A.* 78 F5 40 32N 79 10W
Homestead, *Australia* 62 C4 20 20S 145 40 E
Homestead, *U.S.A.* 77 N5 25 28N 80 29W
Homewood, *U.S.A.* 84 F6 39 4N 120 8W
Homoine, *Mozam.* 57 C6 23 55S 35 8 E
Homs = Ḩimş, *Syria* 47 A5 34 40N 36 45 E
Homyel, *Belarus* 17 B16 52 28N 31 0 E
Hon Chong, *Vietnam* 39 G5 10 25N 104 30 E
Hon Me, *Vietnam* 38 C5 19 23N 105 56 E
Honan = Henan □, *China* 34 H8 34 0N 114 0 E
Honbetsu, *Japan* 30 C11 43 7N 143 37 E
Honcut, *U.S.A.* 84 F5 39 20N 121 32W
Hondeklipbaai, *S. Africa* 56 E2 30 19S 17 17 E
Hondo, *Japan* 31 H5 32 27N 130 12 E
Hondo, *U.S.A.* 81 L5 29 21N 99 9W
Hondo →, *Belize* 87 D7 18 25N 88 21W
Honduras ■, *Cent. Amer.* 88 D2 14 40N 86 30W
Honduras, G. de, *Caribbean* 88 C2 16 50N 87 0W
Hønefoss, *Norway* 9 F14 60 10N 10 18 E
Honesdale, *U.S.A.* 79 E9 41 34N 75 16W
Honey L., *U.S.A.* 84 E6 40 15N 120 19W
Honfleur, *France* 18 B4 49 25N 0 13 E
Hong →, *Vietnam* 32 D5 22 0N 104 0 E
Hong Gai, *Vietnam* 38 B6 20 57N 107 5 E
Hong He →, *China* 34 H8 32 25N 115 35 E
Hong Kong □, *China* 33 D6 22 11N 114 14 E
Hongch'ŏn, *S. Korea* 35 F14 37 44N 127 53 E
Hongjiang, *China* 33 D5 27 7N 109 59 E
Hongliu He →, *China* 34 F5 38 0N 109 50 E
Hongor, *Mongolia* 34 B7 45 45N 112 50 E
Hongsa, *Laos* 38 C3 19 43N 101 20 E
Hongshui He →, *China* 33 D5 23 48N 109 30 E
Hongsŏng, *S. Korea* 35 F14 36 37N 126 38 E
Hongtong, *China* 34 F6 36 16N 111 40 E
Honguedo, Détroit d', *Canada* 71 C7 49 15N 64 0W
Hongwon, *N. Korea* 35 E14 40 0N 127 56 E
Hongze Hu, *China* 35 H10 33 15N 118 35 E
Honiara, *Solomon Is.* 64 H7 9 27S 159 57 E
Honiton, *U.K.* 11 G4 50 47N 3 11W
Honjō, *Japan* 30 E10 39 23N 140 3 E
Honningsvåg, *Norway* 8 A21 70 59N 25 59 E
Honolulu, *U.S.A.* 74 H16 21 19N 157 52W
Honshū, *Japan* 33 C8 36 0N 138 0 E
Hood, Mt., *U.S.A.* 82 D3 45 23N 121 42W
Hood, Pt., *Australia* 61 F2 34 23S 119 34 E
Hood River, *U.S.A.* 82 D3 45 43N 121 31W
Hoodsport, *U.S.A.* 84 C3 47 24N 123 9W
Hoogeveen, *Neths.* 15 B6 52 44N 6 28 E
Hoogezand-Sappemeer, *Neths.* 15 A6 53 9N 6 45 E
Hooghly = Hugli →, *India* 43 J13 21 56N 88 4 E
Hooghly-Chinsura = Chunchura, *India* 43 H13 22 53N 88 27 E
Hook Hd., *Ireland* 13 D5 52 7N 6 56W
Hook I., *Australia* 62 C4 20 4S 149 0 E
Hook of Holland = Hoek van Holland, *Neths.* 15 C4 52 0N 4 7 E
Hooker, *U.S.A.* 81 G4 36 52N 101 13W
Hooker Creek, *Australia* 60 C5 18 23S 130 38 E
Hoonah, *U.S.A.* 72 B1 58 7N 135 27W
Hooper Bay, *U.S.A.* 68 B3 61 32N 166 6W
Hoopeston, *U.S.A.* 76 E2 40 28N 87 40W
Hoopstad, *S. Africa* 56 D4 27 50S 25 55 E
Hoorn, *Neths.* 15 B5 52 38N 5 4 E
Hoover, *U.S.A.* 77 J2 33 20N 86 11W
Hoover Dam, *U.S.A.* 85 K12 36 1N 114 44W
Hooversville, *U.S.A.* 78 F6 40 9N 78 55W
Hop Bottom, *U.S.A.* 79 E9 41 42N 75 46W
Hope, *Canada* 72 D4 49 25N 121 25W
Hope, *Ariz., U.S.A.* 85 M13 33 43N 113 42W
Hope, *Ark., U.S.A.* 81 J8 33 40N 93 36W
Hope, L., *S. Austral., Australia* 63 D2 28 24S 139 18 E
Hope, L., *W. Austral., Australia* 61 F3 32 35S 120 15 E
Hope I., *Canada* 78 B4 44 55N 80 11W
Hope Town, *Bahamas* 88 A4 26 35N 76 57W
Hopedale, *Canada* 71 A7 55 28N 60 13W
Hopedale, *U.S.A.* 79 D13 42 8N 71 33W
Hopefield, *S. Africa* 56 E2 33 3S 18 22 E
Hopei = Hebei □, *China* 34 E9 39 0N 116 0 E
Hopelchén, *Mexico* 87 D7 19 46N 89 50W
Hopetoun, *Vic., Australia* 63 F3 35 42S 142 22 E
Hopetoun, *W. Austral., Australia* 61 F3 33 57S 120 7 E
Hopetown, *S. Africa* 56 D3 29 34S 24 3 E
Hopevale, *Australia* 62 B4 15 16S 145 20 E
Hopewell, *U.S.A.* 76 G7 37 18N 77 17W
Hopkins, L., *Australia* 60 D4 24 15S 128 35 E
Hopkinsville, *U.S.A.* 77 G2 36 52N 87 29W
Hopland, *U.S.A.* 84 G3 38 58N 123 7W
Hoquiam, *U.S.A.* 84 D3 46 59N 123 53W
Horden Hills, *Australia* 60 D5 20 15S 130 0 E

I

Ilfracombe, U.K. 11 F3 51 12N 4 8W
Ilhéus, Brazil 93 F11 14 49S 39 2W
Ili = Ile →, Kazakstan 26 E8 45 53N 77 10 E
Iliamna L., U.S.A. 68 C4 59 30N 155 0W
Iligan, Phil. 37 C6 8 12N 124 13 E
Ilion, U.S.A. 79 D9 43 1N 75 2W
Ilkeston, U.K. 10 E6 52 58N 1 19W
Ilkley, U.K. 10 D6 53 56N 1 48W
Illampu = Ancohuma, Nevada, Bolivia 92 G5 16 0S 68 50W
Illana B., Phil. 37 C6 7 35N 123 45 E
Illapel, Chile 94 C1 32 0S 71 10W
Iller →, Germany 16 D6 48 23N 9 58 E
Illetas, Spain 22 B9 39 32N 2 35 E
Illimani, Nevado, Bolivia 92 G5 16 30S 67 50W
Illinois □, U.S.A. 80 E10 40 15N 89 30W
Illinois →, U.S.A. 80 F9 38 58N 90 28W
Illium = Troy, Turkey 21 E12 39 57N 26 12 E
Illizi, Algeria 50 C7 26 31N 8 32 E
Ilmajoki, Finland 9 E20 62 44N 22 34 E
Ilmen, Ozero, Russia 24 C5 58 15N 31 10 E
Ilo, Peru 92 G4 17 40S 71 20W
Iloilo, Phil. 37 B6 10 45N 122 33 E
Ilorin, Nigeria 50 G6 8 30N 4 35 E
Ilwaco, U.S.A. 84 D2 46 19N 124 3W
Ilwaki, Indonesia 37 F7 7 55S 126 30 E
Imabari, Japan 31 G6 34 4N 133 0 E
Imaloto →, Madag. 57 C8 23 27S 45 13 E
Imandra, Ozero, Russia 24 A5 67 30N 33 0 E
Imanombo, Madag. 57 C8 24 26S 45 49 E
Imari, Japan 31 H4 33 15N 129 52 E
Imatra, Finland 24 B4 61 12N 28 48 E
Imbil, Australia 63 D5 26 22S 152 32 E
imeni 26 Bakinskikh Komissarov = Neftçala, Azerbaijan 25 G8 39 19N 49 12 E
imeni 26 Bakinskikh Komissarov, Turkmenistan 45 B7 39 22N 54 10 E
Imeri, Serra, Brazil 92 C5 0 50N 65 25W
Imerimandroso, Madag. 57 B8 17 26S 48 35 E
Imi, Ethiopia 46 F3 6 28N 42 10 E
Imlay, U.S.A. 82 F4 40 40N 118 9W
Imlay City, U.S.A. 78 D1 43 2N 83 5W
Immingham, U.K. 10 D7 53 37N 0 13W
Immokalee, U.S.A. 77 M5 26 25N 81 25W
Ímola, Italy 20 B4 44 20N 11 42 E
Imperatriz, Brazil 93 E9 5 30S 47 29W
Impéria, Italy 18 E8 43 53N 8 3 E
Imperial, Canada 73 C7 51 21N 105 28W
Imperial, Calif., U.S.A. 85 N11 32 51N 115 34W
Imperial, Nebr., U.S.A. 80 E4 40 31N 101 39W
Imperial Beach, U.S.A. 85 N9 32 35N 117 8W
Imperial Dam, U.S.A. 85 N12 32 55N 114 25W
Imperial Reservoir, U.S.A. 85 N12 32 53N 114 28W
Imperial Valley, U.S.A. 85 N11 33 0N 115 30W
Imperieuse Reef, Australia 60 C2 17 36S 118 50 E
Impfondo, Congo 52 D3 1 40N 18 0 E
Imphal, India 41 G18 24 48N 93 56 E
İmroz = Gökçeada, Turkey 21 D11 40 10N 25 50 E
Imuris, Mexico 86 A2 30 47N 110 52W
Imuruan B., Phil. 37 B5 10 40N 119 10 E
In Salah, Algeria 50 C6 27 10N 2 32 E
Ina, Japan 31 G8 35 50N 137 55 E
Inangahua, N.Z. 59 J3 41 52S 171 59 E
Inanwatan, Indonesia 37 E8 2 8S 132 10 E
Iñapari, Peru 92 F5 11 0S 69 40W
Inari, Finland 8 B22 68 54N 27 5 E
Inarijärvi, Finland 8 B22 69 0N 28 0 E
Inawashiro-Ko, Japan 30 F10 37 29N 140 6 E
Inca, Spain 22 B9 39 43N 2 54 E
Inca de Oro, Chile 94 B2 26 45S 69 54W
Incaguasi, Chile 94 B1 29 12S 71 5W
İnce Burun, Turkey 25 F5 42 7N 34 56 E
İncesu, Turkey 44 B2 38 38N 35 11 E
Inch'ŏn, S. Korea 35 F14 37 27N 126 40 E
İncirliova, Turkey 21 F12 37 50N 27 41 E
Incline Village, U.S.A. 82 G4 39 10N 119 58W
Incomáti →, Mozam. 57 D5 25 46S 32 43 E
Indalsälven →, Sweden 9 E17 62 36N 17 30 E
Indaw, Burma 41 G20 24 15N 96 5 E
Independence, Calif., U.S.A. 84 J8 36 48N 118 12W
Independence, Iowa, U.S.A. 80 D9 42 28N 91 54W
Independence, Kans., U.S.A. 81 G7 37 14N 95 42W
Independence, Ky., U.S.A. 76 F3 38 57N 84 33W
Independence, Mo., U.S.A. 80 F7 39 6N 94 25W
Independence Fjord, Greenland 4 A6 82 10N 29 0W
Independence Mts., U.S.A. 82 F5 41 20N 116 0W
Index, U.S.A. 84 C5 47 50N 121 33W
India ■, Asia 40 K11 20 0N 78 0 E
Indian →, U.S.A. 77 M5 27 59N 80 34W
Indian Cabins, Canada 72 B5 59 52N 117 40W
Indian Harbour, Canada 71 B8 54 27N 57 13W
Indian Head, Canada 73 C8 50 30N 103 41W
Indian Lake, U.S.A. 79 C10 43 47N 74 16W
Indian Ocean 28 K11 5 0S 75 0 E
Indian Springs, U.S.A. 85 J11 36 35N 115 40W
Indiana, U.S.A. 78 F5 40 37N 79 9W
Indiana □, U.S.A. 76 F3 40 0N 86 0W
Indianapolis, U.S.A. 76 F2 39 46N 86 9W
Indianola, Iowa, U.S.A. 80 E8 41 22N 93 34W
Indianola, Miss., U.S.A. 81 J9 33 27N 90 39W
Indiga, Russia 24 A8 67 38N 49 9 E
Indigirka →, Russia 27 B15 70 48N 148 54 E
Indio, U.S.A. 85 M10 33 43N 116 13W
Indo-China, Asia 28 H14 15 0N 102 0 E
Indonesia ■, Asia 36 F5 5 0S 115 0 E
Indore, India 42 H6 22 42N 75 53 E
Indramayu, Indonesia 37 G13 6 20S 108 19 E
Indravati →, India 41 K12 19 20N 80 20 E
Indre →, France 18 C4 47 16N 0 11 E
Indulkana, Australia 63 D1 26 58S 133 5 E
Indus →, Pakistan 42 G2 24 20N 67 47 E
Indus, Mouths of the, Pakistan 42 H3 24 0N 68 0 E
İnebolu, Turkey 25 F5 41 55N 33 40 E
Infiernillo, Presa del, Mexico 86 D4 18 9N 102 0W
Ingenio, Canary Is. 22 G4 27 55N 15 26W
Ingenio Santa Ana, Argentina 94 B2 27 25S 65 40W
Ingersoll, Canada 78 C4 43 4N 80 55W
Ingham, Australia 62 B4 18 43S 146 10 E
Ingleborough, U.K. 10 C5 54 10N 2 22W
Inglewood, Queens., Australia 63 D5 28 25S 151 2 E
Inglewood, Vic., Australia 63 F3 36 29S 143 53 E
Inglewood, N.Z. 59 H5 39 9S 174 14 E
Inglewood, U.S.A. 85 M8 33 58N 118 21W
Ingólfshöfði, Iceland 8 E5 63 48N 16 39W
Ingolstadt, Germany 16 D6 48 46N 11 26 E
Ingomar, U.S.A. 82 C10 46 35N 107 23W
Ingonish, Canada 71 C7 46 42N 60 18W
Ingraj Bazar, India 43 G13 24 58N 88 10 E
Ingrid Christensen Coast, Antarctica 5 C6 69 30S 76 0 E
Ingulec = Inhulec, Ukraine 25 E5 47 42N 33 14 E
Ingushetia □, Russia 25 F8 43 20N 44 50 E
Ingwavuma, S. Africa 57 D5 27 9S 31 59 E
Inhaca, Mozam. 57 D5 26 1S 32 57 E
Inhafenga, Mozam. 57 C5 20 36S 33 53 E
Inhambane, Mozam. 57 C6 23 54S 35 30 E
Inhambane □, Mozam. 57 C5 22 30S 34 20 E
Inhaminga, Mozam. 55 F4 18 26S 35 0 E
Inharrime, Mozam. 57 C6 24 30S 35 0 E
Inharrime →, Mozam. 57 C6 24 30S 35 0 E
Inhulec, Ukraine 25 E5 47 42N 33 14 E
Ining = Yining, China 26 E9 43 58N 81 10 E
Inírida →, Colombia 92 C5 3 55N 67 52W
Inishbofin, Ireland 13 C1 53 37N 10 13W
Inisheer, Ireland 13 C2 53 3N 9 32W
Inishfree B., Ireland 13 A3 55 4N 8 23W
Inishkea North, Ireland 13 B1 54 9N 10 11W
Inishkea South, Ireland 13 B1 54 7N 10 12W
Inishmaan, Ireland 13 C2 53 5N 9 35W
Inishmore, Ireland 13 C2 53 8N 9 45W
Inishowen Pen., Ireland 13 A4 55 14N 7 15W
Inishshark, Ireland 13 C1 53 37N 10 16W
Inishturk, Ireland 13 C1 53 42N 10 7W
Inishvickillane, Ireland 13 D1 52 3N 10 37W
Injune, Australia 63 D4 25 53S 148 32 E
Inklin →, Canada 72 B2 58 50N 133 10W
Inland Sea = Setonaikai, Japan 31 G6 34 20N 133 30 E
Inle L., Burma 41 J20 20 30N 96 58 E
Inlet, U.S.A. 79 C10 43 45N 74 48W
Inn →, Austria 16 D7 48 35N 13 28 E
Innamincka, Australia 63 D3 27 44S 140 46 E
Inner Hebrides, U.K. 12 E2 57 0N 6 30W
Inner Mongolia = Nei Monggol Zizhiqu □, China 34 D7 42 0N 112 0 E
Inner Sound, U.K. 12 D3 57 30N 5 55W
Innerkip, Canada 78 C4 43 13N 80 42W
Innetalling I., Canada 70 A4 56 0N 79 0W
Innisfail, Australia 62 B4 17 33S 146 5 E
Innisfail, Canada 72 C6 52 0N 113 57W
In'noshima, Japan 31 G6 34 19N 133 10 E
Innsbruck, Austria 16 E6 47 16N 11 23 E
Inny →, Ireland 13 C4 53 30N 7 50W
Inongo, Dem. Rep. of the Congo 52 E3 1 55S 18 30 E
Inoucdjouac = Inukjuak, Canada 69 C12 58 25N 78 15W
Inowrocław, Poland 17 B10 52 50N 18 12 E
Inpundong, N. Korea 35 D14 41 25N 126 34 E
Inscription, C., Australia 61 E1 25 29S 112 59 E
Insein, Burma 41 L20 16 50N 96 5 E
Inta, Russia 24 A11 66 5N 60 8 E
Intendente Alvear, Argentina 94 D3 35 12S 63 32W
Interlaken, Switz. 18 C7 46 41N 7 50 E
Interlaken, U.S.A. 79 D8 42 37N 76 44W
International Falls, U.S.A. 80 A8 48 36N 93 25W
Intiyaco, Argentina 94 B3 28 43S 60 5W
Inukjuak, Canada 69 C12 58 25N 78 15W
Inútil, B., Chile 96 G2 53 30S 70 15W
Inuvik, Canada 68 B6 68 16N 133 40W
Inveraray, U.K. 12 E3 56 14N 5 5W
Inverbervie, U.K. 12 E6 56 51N 2 17W
Invercargill, N.Z. 59 M2 46 24S 168 24 E
Inverclyde □, U.K. 12 F4 55 55N 4 49W
Inverell, Australia 63 D5 29 45S 151 8 E
Invergordon, U.K. 12 D4 57 41N 4 10W
Inverloch, Australia 63 F4 38 38S 145 45 E
Invermere, Canada 72 C5 50 30N 116 2W
Inverness, Canada 71 C7 46 15N 61 19W
Inverness, U.K. 12 D4 57 29N 4 13W
Inverness, U.S.A. 77 L4 28 50N 82 20W
Inverurie, U.K. 12 D6 57 17N 2 23W
Investigator Group, Australia 63 E1 34 45S 134 20 E
Investigator Str., Australia 63 F2 35 30S 137 0 E
Inya, Russia 26 D9 50 28N 86 37 E
Inyanga, Zimbabwe 55 F3 18 12S 32 40 E
Inyangani, Zimbabwe 55 F3 18 5S 32 50 E
Inyantue, Zimbabwe 56 B4 18 33S 26 39 E
Inyo Mts., U.S.A. 84 J9 36 40N 118 0W
Inyokern, U.S.A. 85 K9 35 39N 117 49W
Inza, Russia 24 D8 53 55N 46 25 E
Iō-Jima, Japan 31 J5 30 48N 130 18 E
Ioánnina, Greece 21 E9 39 42N 20 47 E
Iola, U.S.A. 81 G7 37 55N 95 24W
Iona, U.K. 12 E2 56 20N 6 25W
Ione, U.S.A. 84 G6 38 21N 120 56W
Ionia, U.S.A. 76 D3 42 59N 85 4W
Ionian Is. = Iónioi Nísoi, Greece 21 E9 38 40N 20 0 E
Ionian Sea, Medit. S. 21 E7 37 30N 17 30 E
Iónioi Nísoi, Greece 21 E9 38 40N 20 0 E
Íos, Greece 21 F11 36 41N 25 20 E
Iowa □, U.S.A. 80 D8 42 18N 93 30W
Iowa →, U.S.A. 80 E9 41 10N 91 1W
Iowa City, U.S.A. 80 E9 41 40N 91 32W
Iowa Falls, U.S.A. 80 D8 42 31N 93 16W
Iowa Park, U.S.A. 81 J5 33 57N 98 40W
Ipala, Tanzania 54 C3 4 30S 32 52 E
Ipameri, Brazil 93 G9 17 44S 48 9W
Ipatinga, Brazil 93 G10 19 32S 42 30W
Ipiales, Colombia 92 C3 0 50N 77 37W
Ipin = Yibin, China 32 D5 28 45N 104 32 E
Ipixuna, Brazil 92 E4 7 0S 71 40W
Ipoh, Malaysia 39 K3 4 35N 101 5 E
Ippy, C.A.R. 52 C4 6 5N 21 7 E
İpsala, Turkey 21 D12 40 55N 26 23 E
Ipswich, Australia 63 D5 27 35S 152 40 E
Ipswich, U.K. 11 E9 52 4N 1 10 E
Ipswich, Mass., U.S.A. 79 D14 42 41N 70 50W
Ipswich, S. Dak., U.S.A. 80 C5 45 27N 99 2W
Ipu, Brazil 93 D10 4 23S 40 44W
Iqaluit, Canada 69 B13 63 44N 68 31W
Iquique, Chile 92 H4 20 19S 70 5W
Iquitos, Peru 92 D4 3 45S 73 10W
Irabu-Jima, Japan 31 M2 24 50N 125 10 E
Iracoubo, Fr. Guiana 93 B8 5 30N 53 10W
Īrafshān, Iran 45 E9 26 42N 61 56 E
Iráklion, Greece 23 D7 35 20N 25 12 E
Iráklion □, Greece 23 D7 35 10N 25 10 E
Irala, Paraguay 95 B5 25 55S 54 35W
Iran ■, Asia 45 C7 33 0N 53 0 E
Iran, Gunung-Gunung, Malaysia 36 D4 2 20N 114 50 E
Iran, Plateau of, Asia 28 F9 32 0N 55 0 E
Iran Ra. = Iran, Gunung-Gunung, Malaysia 36 D4 2 20N 114 50 E
Īrānshahr, Iran 45 E9 27 15N 60 40 E
Irapuato, Mexico 86 C4 20 40N 101 30W
Iraq ■, Asia 44 C5 33 0N 44 0 E
Irati, Brazil 95 B5 25 25S 50 38W
Irbid, Jordan 47 C4 32 35N 35 48 E
Irbid □, Jordan 47 C5 32 15N 36 35 E
Ireland ■, Europe 13 C4 53 50N 7 52W
Irhyangdong, N. Korea 35 D15 41 15N 129 30 E
Iri, S. Korea 35 G14 35 59N 127 0 E
Irian Jaya □, Indonesia 37 E9 4 0S 137 0 E
Iringa, Tanzania 54 D4 7 48S 35 43 E
Iringa □, Tanzania 54 D4 7 48S 35 43 E
Iriomote-Jima, Japan 31 M1 24 19N 123 48 E
Iriona, Honduras 88 C2 15 57N 85 11W
Iriri →, Brazil 93 D8 3 52S 52 37W
Irish Republic ■, Europe 13 C3 53 0N 8 0W
Irish Sea, U.K. 10 D3 53 38N 4 48W
Irkutsk, Russia 27 D11 52 18N 104 20 E
Irma, Canada 73 C6 52 55N 111 14W
Irō-Zaki, Japan 31 G9 34 36N 138 51 E
Iron Baron, Australia 63 E2 32 58S 137 11 E
Iron Gate = Portile de Fier, Europe 17 F12 44 44N 22 30 E
Iron Knob, Australia 63 E2 32 46S 137 8 E
Iron Mountain, U.S.A. 76 C1 45 49N 88 4W
Iron River, U.S.A. 80 B10 46 6N 88 39W
Irondequoit, U.S.A. 78 C7 43 13N 77 35W
Ironton, Mo., U.S.A. 81 G9 37 36N 90 38W
Ironton, Ohio, U.S.A. 76 F4 38 32N 82 41W
Ironwood, U.S.A. 80 B9 46 27N 90 9W
Iroquois, Canada 79 B9 44 51N 75 19W
Iroquois Falls, Canada 70 C3 48 46N 80 41W
Irpin, Ukraine 17 C16 50 30N 30 15 E
Irrara Cr. →, Australia 63 D4 29 35S 145 31 E
Irrawaddy □, Burma 41 L19 17 0N 95 0 E
Irrawaddy →, Burma 41 M19 15 50N 95 6 E
Irrawaddy, Mouths of the, Burma 41 M19 15 30N 95 0 E
Irricana, Canada 72 C6 51 19N 113 37W
Irtysh →, Russia 26 C7 61 4N 68 52 E
Irumu, Dem. Rep. of the Congo 54 B2 1 32N 29 53 E
Irún, Spain 19 A5 43 20N 1 52W
Irunea = Pamplona, Spain 19 A5 42 48N 1 38W
Irvine, U.K. 12 F4 55 37N 4 41W
Irvine, Calif., U.S.A. 85 M9 33 41N 117 46W
Irvine, Ky., U.S.A. 76 G4 37 42N 83 58W
Irvinestown, U.K. 13 B4 54 28N 7 39W
Irving, U.S.A. 81 J6 32 49N 96 56W
Irvona, U.S.A. 78 F6 40 46N 78 33W
Irwin →, Australia 61 E1 29 15S 114 54 E
Irymple, Australia 63 E3 34 14S 142 8 E
Isa Khel, Pakistan 42 C4 32 41N 71 17 E
Isaac →, Australia 62 C4 22 55S 149 20 E
Isabel, U.S.A. 80 C4 45 24N 101 26W
Isabela, Phil. 37 C6 6 40N 121 59 E
Isabela, I., Mexico 86 C3 21 51N 105 55W
Isabelia, Cord., Nic. 88 D2 13 30N 85 25W
Isabella Ra., Australia 60 D3 21 0S 121 4 E
Ísafjarðardjúp, Iceland 8 C2 66 10N 23 0W
Ísafjörður, Iceland 8 C2 66 5N 23 9W
Isagarh, India 42 G7 24 48N 77 51 E
Isahaya, Japan 31 H5 32 52N 130 2 E
Isaka, Tanzania 54 C3 3 56S 32 59 E
Isan →, India 43 F9 26 51N 80 7 E
Isana = Içana →, Brazil 92 C5 0 26N 67 19W
Isar →, Germany 16 D7 48 48N 12 57 E
Íschia, Italy 20 D5 40 44N 13 57 E
Isdell →, Australia 60 C3 16 27S 124 51 E
Ise, Japan 31 G8 34 25N 136 45 E
Ise-Wan, Japan 31 G8 34 43N 136 43 E
Iseramagazi, Tanzania 54 C3 4 37S 32 10 E
Isère →, France 18 D6 44 59N 4 51 E
Isérnia, Italy 20 D6 41 36N 14 14 E
Isfahan = Eşfahān, Iran 45 C6 32 39N 51 43 E
Ishigaki-Shima, Japan 31 M2 24 20N 124 10 E
Ishikari-Gawa →, Japan 30 C10 43 15N 141 23 E
Ishikari-Sammyaku, Japan 30 C11 43 30N 143 0 E
Ishikari-Wan, Japan 30 C10 43 25N 141 1 E
Ishikawa □, Japan 31 F8 36 30N 136 30 E
Ishim, Russia 26 D7 56 10N 69 30 E
Ishim →, Russia 26 D8 57 45N 71 10 E
Ishinomaki, Japan 30 E10 38 32N 141 20 E
Ishioka, Japan 31 F10 36 11N 140 16 E
Ishkuman, Pakistan 43 A5 36 30N 73 50 E
Ishpeming, U.S.A. 76 B2 46 29N 87 40W
Isil Kul, Russia 26 D8 54 55N 71 16 E
Isiolo, Kenya 54 B4 0 24N 37 33 E
Isiro, Dem. Rep. of the Congo 54 B2 2 53N 27 40 E
Isisford, Australia 62 C3 24 15S 144 21 E
İskenderun, Turkey 25 G6 36 32N 36 10 E
İskenderun Körfezi, Turkey 25 G6 36 40N 35 50 E
Iskŭr →, Bulgaria 21 C11 43 45N 24 25 E
Iskut →, Canada 72 B2 56 45N 131 49W
Isla →, U.K. 12 E5 56 32N 3 20W
Isla Vista, U.S.A. 85 L7 34 25N 119 53W
Islam Headworks, Pakistan 42 E5 29 49N 72 33 E
Islamabad, Pakistan 42 C5 33 40N 73 10 E
Islamgarh, Pakistan 42 F4 27 51N 70 48 E
Islamkot, Pakistan 42 G4 24 42N 70 13 E
Islampur, India 43 G11 25 9N 85 12 E
Island L., Canada 73 C10 53 47N 94 25W
Island Lagoon, Australia 63 E2 31 30S 136 40 E
Island Pond, U.S.A. 79 B13 44 49N 71 53W
Islands, B. of, Canada 71 C8 49 11N 58 15W
Islands, B. of, N.Z. 59 F5 35 15S 174 6 E
Islay, U.K. 12 F2 55 46N 6 10W
Isle →, France 18 D3 44 55N 0 15W
Isle aux Morts, Canada 71 C8 47 35N 59 0W
Isle of Wight □, U.K. 11 G6 50 41N 1 17W
Isle Royale Nat. Park, U.S.A. 80 B10 48 0N 88 55W
Isleton, U.S.A. 84 G5 38 10N 121 37W
Ismail = Izmayil, Ukraine 17 F15 45 22N 28 46 E
Ismâ'ilîya, Egypt 51 B12 30 37N 32 18 E
Isoanala, Madag. 57 C8 23 50S 45 44 E
Isogstalo, India 43 B8 34 15N 78 46 E
Isparta, Turkey 25 G5 37 47N 30 30 E
Íspica, Italy 20 F6 36 47N 14 55 E
Israel ■, Asia 47 D3 32 0N 34 50 E
Issoire, France 18 D5 45 32N 3 15 E
Issyk-Kul, Ozero = Ysyk-Köl, Kyrgyzstan 26 E8 42 25N 77 15 E
İstanbul, Turkey 21 D13 41 0N 29 0 E
İstanbul Boğazı, Turkey 21 D13 41 10N 29 10 E
Istiaía, Greece 21 E10 38 57N 23 9 E
Istokpoga, L., U.S.A. 77 M5 27 23N 81 17W
Istra, Croatia 16 F7 45 10N 14 0 E
Istres, France 18 E6 43 31N 4 59 E
Istria = Istra, Croatia 16 F7 45 10N 14 0 E
Itá, Paraguay 94 B4 25 29S 57 21W
Itaberaba, Brazil 93 F10 12 32S 40 18W
Itabira, Brazil 93 G10 19 37S 43 13W
Itabirito, Brazil 95 A7 20 15S 43 48W
Itabuna, Brazil 93 F11 14 48S 39 16W
Itacaunas →, Brazil 93 E9 5 21S 49 8W
Itacoatiara, Brazil 92 D7 3 8S 58 25W
Itaipú, Représa de, Brazil 95 B5 25 30S 54 30W
Itaituba, Brazil 93 D7 4 10S 55 50W
Itajaí, Brazil 95 B6 27 50S 48 39W
Itajubá, Brazil 95 A6 22 24S 45 30W
Itaka, Tanzania 55 D3 8 50S 32 49 E
Italy ■, Europe 20 C5 42 0N 13 0 E
Itamaraju, Brazil 93 G11 17 5S 39 31W
Itampolo, Madag. 57 C7 24 41S 43 57 E
Itandrano, Madag. 57 C8 21 47S 45 17 E
Itapecuru-Mirim, Brazil 93 D10 3 24S 44 20W
Itaperuna, Brazil 95 A7 21 10S 41 54W
Itapetininga, Brazil 95 A6 23 36S 48 7W
Itapeva, Brazil 95 A6 23 59S 48 59W
Itapicuru →, Bahia, Brazil 93 F11 11 47S 37 32W
Itapicuru →, Maranhão, Brazil 93 D10 2 52S 44 12W
Itapipoca, Brazil 93 D11 3 30S 39 35W
Itapuá □, Paraguay 95 B4 26 40S 55 40W
Itaquari, Brazil 95 A7 20 20S 40 25W
Itaquí, Brazil 94 B4 29 8S 56 30W
Itararé, Brazil 95 A6 24 6S 49 23W
Itarsi, India 42 H7 22 36N 77 51 E
Itatí, Argentina 94 B4 27 16S 58 15W
Itchen →, U.K. 11 G6 50 55N 1 22W
Itezhi Tezhi, L., Zambia 55 F2 15 30S 25 30 E
Ithaca = Itháki, Greece 21 E9 38 25N 20 40 E
Ithaca, U.S.A. 79 D8 42 27N 76 30W
Itháki, Greece 21 E9 38 25N 20 40 E
Itiquira →, Brazil 93 G7 17 18S 56 44W
Itō, Japan 31 G9 34 58N 139 5 E
Itoigawa, Japan 31 F8 37 2N 137 51 E
Itonamas →, Bolivia 92 F6 12 28S 64 24W
Ittoqqortoormiit, Greenland 4 B6 70 20N 23 0W
Itu, Brazil 95 A6 23 17S 47 15W
Itu Aba I., S. China Sea 36 B4 10 23N 114 21 E
Ituiutaba, Brazil 93 G9 19 0S 49 25W
Itumbiara, Brazil 93 G9 18 20S 49 10W
Ituna, Canada 73 C8 51 10N 103 24W
Itunge Port, Tanzania 55 D3 9 40S 33 55 E
Iturbe, Argentina 94 A2 23 0S 65 25W
Ituri →, Dem. Rep. of the Congo 54 B2 1 40N 27 1 E
Iturup, Ostrov, Russia 27 E15 45 0N 148 0 E
Ituxi →, Brazil 92 E6 7 18S 64 51W
Ituyuro →, Argentina 94 A3 22 40S 63 50W
Itzehoe, Germany 16 B5 53 55N 9 31 E
Ivahona, Madag. 57 C8 23 27S 46 10 E
Ivaí →, Brazil 95 A5 23 18S 53 42W
Ivalo, Finland 8 B22 68 38N 27 35 E
Ivalojoki →, Finland 8 B22 68 40N 27 40 E
Ivanava, Belarus 17 B13 52 7N 25 29 E
Ivanhoe, Australia 63 E3 32 56S 144 20 E
Ivanhoe, Calif., U.S.A. 84 J7 36 23N 119 13W
Ivanhoe, Minn., U.S.A. 80 C6 44 28N 96 15W
Ivano-Frankivsk, Ukraine 17 D13 48 40N 24 40 E
Ivano-Frankovsk = Ivano-Frankivsk, Ukraine 17 D13 48 40N 24 40 E
Ivanovo = Ivanava, Belarus 17 B13 52 7N 25 29 E
Ivanovo, Russia 24 C7 57 5N 41 0 E
Ivato, Madag. 57 C8 20 37S 47 10 E
Ivatsevichy, Belarus 17 B13 52 43N 25 21 E
Ivdel, Russia 24 B11 60 42N 60 24 E
Ivinheima →, Brazil 95 A5 23 14S 53 42W
Ivinhema, Brazil 95 A5 22 10S 53 37W
Ivohibe, Madag. 57 C8 22 31S 46 57 E
Ivory Coast, W. Afr. 50 H4 4 20N 5 0W
Ivory Coast ■, Africa 50 G4 7 30N 5 0W
Ivrea, Italy 18 D7 45 28N 7 52 E
Ivujivik, Canada 69 B12 62 24N 77 55W
Ivybridge, U.K. 11 G4 50 23N 3 56W
Iwaizumi, Japan 30 E10 39 50N 141 45 E
Iwaki, Japan 31 F10 37 3N 140 55 E
Iwakuni, Japan 31 G6 34 15N 132 8 E
Iwamizawa, Japan 30 C10 43 12N 141 46 E
Iwanai, Japan 30 C10 42 58N 140 30 E
Iwata, Japan 31 G8 34 42N 137 51 E
Iwate □, Japan 30 E10 39 30N 141 30 E
Iwate-San, Japan 30 E10 39 51N 141 0 E
Iwo, Nigeria 50 G6 7 39N 4 9 E
Ixiamas, Bolivia 92 F5 13 50S 68 5W
Ixopo, S. Africa 57 E5 30 11S 30 5 E
Ixtepec, Mexico 87 D5 16 32N 95 10W
Ixtlán del Río, Mexico 86 C4 21 5N 104 21W
Iyo, Japan 31 H6 33 45N 132 45 E
Izabal, L. de, Guatemala 88 C2 15 30N 89 10W
Izamal, Mexico 87 C7 20 56N 89 1W
Izena-Shima, Japan 31 L3 26 56N 127 56 E
Izhevsk, Russia 24 C9 56 51N 53 14 E
Izhma →, Russia 24 A9 65 19N 52 54 E
Izmayil, Ukraine 17 F15 45 22N 28 46 E
İzmir, Turkey 21 E12 38 25N 27 8 E
İzmit = Kocaeli, Turkey 25 F4 40 45N 29 50 E
İznik Gölü, Turkey 21 D13 40 27N 29 30 E
Izra, Syria 47 C5 32 51N 36 15 E
Izu-Shotō, Japan 31 G10 34 30N 140 0 E
Izúcar de Matamoros, Mexico 87 D5 18 36N 98 28W
Izumi-Sano, Japan 31 G7 34 23N 135 18 E
Izumo, Japan 31 G6 35 20N 132 46 E
Izyaslav, Ukraine 17 C14 50 5N 26 50 E

J

Jabalpur, India 43 H8 23 9N 79 58 E
Jabbūl, Syria 44 B3 36 4N 37 30 E
Jabiru, Australia 60 B5 12 40S 132 53 E
Jablah, Syria 44 C3 35 20N 36 0 E
Jablonec nad Nisou, Czech Rep. 16 C8 50 43N 15 10 E

K

Keene, N.Y., U.S.A. 79 B11 44 16N 73 46W
Keeper Hill, Ireland 13 D3 52 45N 8 16W
Keer-Weer, C., Australia 62 A3 14 0S 141 32 E
Keeseville, U.S.A. 79 B11 44 29N 73 30W
Keetmanshoop, Namibia 56 D2 26 35S 18 8 E
Keewatin, Canada 73 D10 49 46N 94 34W
Keewatin →, Canada 73 B8 56 29N 100 46W
Kefallinia, Greece 21 E9 38 15N 20 30 E
Kefamenanu, Indonesia 37 F6 9 28S 124 29 E
Kefar Sava, Israel 47 C3 32 11N 34 54 E
Keffi, Nigeria 50 G7 8 55N 7 43 E
Keflavík, Iceland 8 D2 64 2N 22 35W
Keg River, Canada 72 B5 57 54N 117 55W
Kegaska, Canada 71 B7 50 9N 61 18W
Keighley, U.K. 10 D6 53 52N 1 54W
Keila, Estonia 9 G21 59 18N 24 25 E
Keimoes, S. Africa 56 D3 28 41S 20 59 E
Keitele, Finland 8 E22 63 10N 26 20 E
Keith, Australia 63 F3 36 6S 140 20 E
Keith, U.K. 12 D6 57 32N 2 57W
Keizer, U.S.A. 82 D2 44 57N 123 1W
Kejimkujik Nat. Park, Canada 71 D6 44 25N 65 25W
Kejserr Franz Joseph Fd., Greenland 4 B6 73 30N 24 30W
Kekri, India 42 G6 26 0N 75 10 E
Kelan, China 34 E6 38 43N 111 31 E
Kelang, Malaysia 39 L3 3 2N 101 26 E
Kelantan →, Malaysia 39 J4 6 13N 102 14 E
Kelkit →, Turkey 25 F6 40 45N 36 32 E
Kellerberrin, Australia 61 F2 31 36S 117 38 E
Kellett, C., Canada 4 B1 72 0N 126 0W
Kelleys I., U.S.A. 78 E2 41 36N 82 42W
Kellogg, U.S.A. 82 C5 47 32N 116 7W
Kells = Ceanannus Mor, Ireland 13 C5 53 44N 6 53W
Kelokedhara, Cyprus 23 E11 34 48N 32 39 E
Kelowna, Canada 72 D5 49 50N 119 25W
Kelseyville, U.S.A. 84 G4 38 59N 122 50W
Kelso, N.Z. 59 L2 45 54S 169 15 E
Kelso, U.K. 12 F6 55 36N 2 26W
Kelso, U.S.A. 84 D4 46 9N 122 54W
Keluang, Malaysia 39 L4 2 3N 103 18 E
Kelvington, Canada 73 C8 52 10N 103 30W
Kem, Russia 24 B5 65 0N 34 38 E
Kem →, Russia 24 B5 64 57N 34 41 E
Kema, Indonesia 37 D7 1 22N 125 8 E
Kemah, Turkey 44 B3 39 32N 39 5 E
Kemaman, Malaysia 36 D2 4 12N 103 18 E
Kemano, Canada 72 C3 53 35N 128 0W
Kemasik, Malaysia 39 K4 4 25N 103 27 E
Kemerovo, Russia 26 D9 55 20N 86 5 E
Kemi, Finland 8 D21 65 44N 24 34 E
Kemi älv = Kemijoki →, Finland 8 D21 65 47N 24 32 E
Kemijärvi, Finland 8 C22 66 43N 27 22 E
Kemijoki →, Finland 8 D21 65 47N 24 32 E
Kemmerer, U.S.A. 82 F8 41 48N 110 32W
Kemmuna = Comino, Malta 23 C1 36 1N 14 20 E
Kemp, L., U.S.A. 81 J5 33 46N 99 9W
Kemp Land, Antarctica 5 C5 69 0S 55 0 E
Kempsey, Australia 63 E5 31 1S 152 50 E
Kempt, L., Canada 70 C5 47 25N 74 22W
Kempten, Germany 16 E6 47 45N 10 17 E
Kempton, Australia 62 G4 42 31S 147 12 E
Kemptville, Canada 79 B9 45 0N 75 38W
Ken →, India 43 G9 25 13N 80 27 E
Kenai, U.S.A. 68 B4 60 33N 151 16W
Kendai, India 43 H10 22 45N 82 37 E
Kendal, Indonesia 37 G14 6 56S 110 14 E
Kendal, U.K. 10 C5 54 20N 2 44W
Kendall, Australia 63 E5 31 35S 152 44 E
Kendall, U.S.A. 77 N5 25 41N 80 19W
Kendall →, Australia 62 A3 14 4S 141 35 E
Kendallville, U.S.A. 76 E3 41 27N 85 16W
Kendari, Indonesia 37 E6 3 50S 122 30 E
Kendawangan, Indonesia 36 E4 2 32S 110 17 E
Kendrapara, India 41 J15 20 35N 86 30 E
Kendrew, S. Africa 56 E3 32 32S 24 30 E
Kene Thao, Laos 38 D3 17 44N 101 10 E
Kenedy, U.S.A. 81 L6 28 49N 97 51W
Kenema, S. Leone 50 G3 7 50N 11 14W
Keng Kok, Laos 38 D5 16 26N 105 12 E
Keng Tawng, Burma 41 J21 20 45N 98 18 E
Keng Tung, Burma 41 J21 21 0N 99 30 E
Kengeja, Tanzania 54 D4 5 26S 39 45 E
Kenhardt, S. Africa 56 D3 29 19S 21 12 E
Kenitra, Morocco 50 B4 34 15N 6 40W
Kenli, China 35 F10 37 30N 118 20 E
Kenmare, Ireland 13 E2 51 53N 9 36W
Kenmare, U.S.A. 80 A3 48 41N 102 5W
Kenmare River, Ireland 13 E2 51 48N 9 51W
Kennebago Lake, U.S.A. 79 A14 45 4N 70 40W
Kennebec, U.S.A. 80 D5 43 54N 99 52W
Kennebec →, U.S.A. 77 D11 43 45N 69 46W
Kennebunk, U.S.A. 79 C14 43 23N 70 33W
Kennedy, Zimbabwe 56 B4 18 52S 27 10 E
Kennedy Ra., Australia 61 D2 24 45S 115 10 E
Kennedy Taungdeik, Burma 41 H18 23 15N 93 45 E
Kenner, U.S.A. 81 L9 29 59N 90 15W
Kennet →, U.K. 11 F7 51 27N 0 57W
Kenneth Ra., Australia 61 D2 23 50S 117 8 E
Kennett, U.S.A. 81 G9 36 14N 90 3W
Kennewick, U.S.A. 82 C4 46 12N 119 7W
Kenogami →, Canada 70 B3 51 6N 84 28W
Kenora, Canada 73 D10 49 47N 94 29W
Kenosha, U.S.A. 76 D2 42 35N 87 49W
Kensington, Canada 71 C7 46 28N 63 34W
Kent, Ohio, U.S.A. 78 E3 41 9N 81 22W
Kent, Tex., U.S.A. 81 K2 31 4N 104 13W
Kent, Wash., U.S.A. 84 C4 47 23N 122 14W
Kent □, U.K. 11 F8 51 12N 0 40 E
Kent Group, Australia 62 F4 39 30S 147 20 E
Kent Pen., Canada 68 B9 68 30N 107 0W
Kentaū, Kazakstan 26 E7 43 32N 68 36 E
Kentland, U.S.A. 76 E2 40 46N 87 27W
Kenton, U.S.A. 76 E4 40 39N 83 37W
Kentucky □, U.S.A. 76 G3 37 0N 84 0W
Kentucky →, U.S.A. 76 F3 38 41N 85 11W
Kentucky L., U.S.A. 77 G2 37 1N 88 16W
Kentville, Canada 71 C7 45 6N 64 29W
Kentwood, U.S.A. 81 K9 30 56N 90 31W
Kenya ■, Africa 54 B4 1 0N 38 0 E
Kenya, Mt., Kenya 54 C4 0 10S 37 18 E
Keo Neua, Deo, Vietnam 38 C5 18 23N 105 10 E
Keokuk, U.S.A. 80 E9 40 24N 91 24W
Keonjhargarh, India 43 J11 21 28N 85 35 E
Kep, Cambodia 39 G5 10 29N 104 19 E
Kep, Vietnam 38 B6 21 24N 106 16 E
Kepi, Indonesia 37 F9 6 32S 139 19 E
Kerala □, India 40 P10 11 0N 76 15 E
Kerama-Rettō, Japan 31 L3 26 5N 127 15 E
Keran, Pakistan 43 B5 34 35N 73 59 E
Kerang, Australia 63 F3 35 40S 143 55 E
Keraudren, C., Australia 60 C2 19 58S 119 45 E
Kerava, Finland 9 F21 60 25N 25 5 E
Kerch, Ukraine 25 E6 45 20N 36 20 E
Kerguelen, Ind. Oc. 3 G13 49 15S 69 10 E
Kericho, Kenya 54 C4 0 22S 35 15 E
Kerinci, Indonesia 36 E2 1 40S 101 15 E
Kerki, Turkmenistan 26 F7 37 50N 65 12 E
Kérkira, Greece 23 A3 39 38N 19 50 E
Kerkrade, Neths. 15 D6 50 53N 6 4 E
Kermadec Is., Pac. Oc. 64 L10 30 0S 178 15W
Kermadec Trench, Pac. Oc. 64 L10 30 30S 176 0W
Kermān, Iran 45 D8 30 15N 57 1 E
Kerman, U.S.A. 84 J6 36 43N 120 4W
Kermān □, Iran 45 D8 30 0N 57 0 E
Kermān, Bīābān-e, Iran 45 D8 28 45N 59 45 E
Kermānshāh = Bākhtarān, Iran 44 C5 34 23N 47 0 E
Kermit, U.S.A. 81 K3 31 52N 103 6W
Kern →, U.S.A. 85 K7 35 16N 119 18W
Kernow = Cornwall □, U.K. 11 G3 50 26N 4 40W
Kernville, U.S.A. 85 K8 35 45N 118 26W
Keroh, Malaysia 39 K3 5 43N 101 1 E
Kerrera, U.K. 12 E3 56 24N 5 33W
Kerrobert, Canada 73 C7 51 56N 109 8W
Kerrville, U.S.A. 81 K5 30 3N 99 8W
Kerry □, Ireland 13 D2 52 7N 9 35W
Kerry Hd., Ireland 13 D2 52 25N 9 56W
Kerulen →, Asia 33 B6 48 48N 117 0 E
Kerzaz, Algeria 50 C5 29 29N 1 37W
Kesagami →, Canada 70 B4 51 40N 79 45W
Kesagami L., Canada 70 B3 50 23N 80 15W
Keşan, Turkey 21 D12 40 49N 26 38 E
Kesennuma, Japan 30 E10 38 54N 141 35 E
Keshit, Iran 45 D8 29 43N 58 17 E
Kestell, S. Africa 57 D4 28 17S 28 42 E
Kestenga, Russia 24 A5 65 50N 31 45 E
Keswick, U.K. 10 C4 54 36N 3 8W
Ket →, Russia 26 D9 58 55N 81 32 E
Ketapang, Indonesia 36 E4 1 55S 110 0 E
Ketchikan, U.S.A. 72 B2 55 21N 131 39W
Ketchum, U.S.A. 82 E6 43 41N 114 22W
Ketef, Khalîg Umm el, Egypt 44 F2 23 40N 35 35 E
Keti Bandar, Pakistan 42 G2 24 8N 67 27 E
Ketri, India 42 E6 28 1N 75 50 E
Kętrzyn, Poland 17 A11 54 7N 21 22 E
Kettering, U.K. 11 E7 52 24N 0 43W
Kettering, U.S.A. 76 F3 39 41N 84 10W
Kettle →, Canada 73 B11 56 40N 89 34W
Kettle Falls, U.S.A. 82 B4 48 37N 118 3W
Kettle Pt., Canada 78 C2 43 13N 82 1W
Kettleman City, U.S.A. 84 J7 36 1N 119 58W
Keuka L., U.S.A. 78 D7 42 30N 77 9W
Keuruu, Finland 9 E21 62 16N 24 41 E
Kewanee, U.S.A. 80 E10 41 14N 89 56W
Kewaunee, U.S.A. 76 C2 44 27N 87 31W
Keweenaw B., U.S.A. 76 B1 47 0N 88 15W
Keweenaw Pen., U.S.A. 76 B2 47 30N 88 0W
Keweenaw Pt., U.S.A. 76 B2 47 25N 87 43W
Key Largo, U.S.A. 77 N5 25 5N 80 27W
Key West, U.S.A. 75 F10 24 33N 81 48W
Keynsham, U.K. 11 F5 51 24N 2 29W
Keyser, U.S.A. 76 F6 39 26N 78 59W
Kezhma, Russia 27 D11 58 59N 101 9 E
Kezi, Zimbabwe 57 C4 20 58S 28 32 E
Khabarovsk, Russia 27 E14 48 30N 135 5 E
Khabr, Iran 45 D8 28 51N 56 22 E
Khābūr →, Syria 44 C4 35 17N 40 35 E
Khachmas = Xaçmaz, Azerbaijan 25 F8 41 31N 48 42 E
Khachrod, India 42 H6 23 25N 75 20 E
Khadro, Pakistan 42 F3 26 11N 68 50 E
Khadzhilyangar, China 43 B8 35 45N 79 20 E
Khaga, India 43 G9 25 47N 81 7 E
Khagaria, India 43 G12 25 30N 86 32 E
Khaipur, Pakistan 42 E5 29 34N 72 17 E
Khair, India 42 F7 27 57N 77 46 E
Khairabad, India 43 F9 27 33N 80 47 E
Khairagarh, India 43 J9 21 27N 81 2 E
Khairpur, Pakistan 42 F3 27 32N 68 49 E
Khairpur Nathan Shah, Pakistan 42 F2 27 6N 67 44 E
Khairwara, India 42 H5 23 58N 73 38 E
Khaisor →, Pakistan 42 D3 31 17N 68 59 E
Khajuri Kach, Pakistan 42 C3 32 4N 69 51 E
Khakassia □, Russia 26 D9 53 0N 90 0 E
Khakhea, Botswana 56 C3 24 48S 23 22 E
Khalafābād, Iran 45 D6 30 54N 49 24 E
Khalilabad, India 43 F10 26 48N 83 5 E
Khalīlī, Iran 45 E7 27 38N 53 17 E
Khalkhāl, Iran 45 B6 37 37N 48 32 E
Khalkís, Greece 21 E10 38 27N 23 42 E
Khalmer-Sede = Tazovskiy, Russia 26 C8 67 30N 78 44 E
Khalmer Yu, Russia 26 C7 67 58N 65 1 E
Khalturin, Russia 24 C8 58 40N 48 50 E
Khalūf, Oman 46 C6 20 30N 58 13 E
Kham Keut, Laos 38 C5 18 15N 104 43 E
Khamaria, India 43 H9 23 5N 80 48 E
Khambhaliya, India 42 H3 22 14N 69 41 E
Khambhat, India 42 H5 22 23N 72 33 E
Khambhat, G. of, India 40 J8 20 45N 72 30 E
Khamīr, Iran 45 E7 26 57N 55 36 E
Khamir, Yemen 46 D3 16 2N 44 0 E
Khamsa, Egypt 47 E1 30 27N 32 23 E
Khan →, Namibia 56 C2 22 37S 14 56 E
Khān Abū Shāmat, Syria 47 B5 33 39N 36 53 E
Khān Azād, Iraq 44 C5 33 7N 44 22 E
Khān Mujiddah, Iraq 44 C4 32 21N 43 48 E
Khān Shaykhūn, Syria 44 C3 35 26N 36 38 E
Khān Yūnis, Gaza Strip 47 D3 31 21N 34 18 E
Khanai, Pakistan 42 D2 30 30N 67 8 E
Khānaqīn, Iraq 44 C5 34 23N 45 25 E
Khānbāghī, Iran 45 B7 36 10N 55 25 E
Khandwa, India 40 J10 21 49N 76 22 E
Khandyga, Russia 27 C14 62 42N 135 35 E
Khāneh, Iran 44 B5 36 41N 45 8 E
Khanewal, Pakistan 42 D4 30 20N 71 55 E
Khangah Dogran, Pakistan 42 D5 31 50N 73 37 E
Khanh Duong, Vietnam 38 F7 12 44N 108 44 E
Khaniá, Greece 23 D6 35 30N 24 4 E
Khaniá □, Greece 23 D6 35 30N 24 0 E
Khaniadhana, India 42 G8 25 1N 78 8 E
Khaníon, Kólpos, Greece 23 D5 35 33N 23 55 E
Khanka, L., Asia 27 E14 45 0N 132 24 E
Khankendy = Xankändi, Azerbaijan 25 G8 39 52N 46 49 E
Khanna, India 42 D7 30 42N 76 16 E
Khanozai, Pakistan 42 D2 30 37N 67 19 E
Khanpur, Pakistan 42 E4 28 42N 70 35 E
Khanty-Mansiysk, Russia 26 C7 61 0N 69 0 E
Khapalu, Pakistan 43 B7 35 10N 76 20 E
Khapcheranga, Russia 27 E12 49 42N 112 24 E
Kharaghoda, India 42 H4 23 11N 71 46 E
Kharagpur, India 43 H12 22 20N 87 25 E
Khárakas, Greece 23 D7 35 1N 25 7 E
Kharan Kalat, Pakistan 40 E4 28 34N 65 21 E
Kharānaq, Iran 45 C7 32 20N 54 45 E
Kharda, India 40 K9 18 40N 75 34 E
Khardung La, India 43 B7 34 20N 77 43 E
Khârga, El Wâhât-el, Egypt 51 C12 25 10N 30 35 E
Khargon, India 40 J9 21 45N 75 40 E
Khari →, India 42 G6 25 54N 74 31 E
Kharian, Pakistan 42 C5 32 49N 73 52 E
Khārk, Jazīreh-ye, Iran 45 D6 29 15N 50 28 E
Kharkiv, Ukraine 25 E6 49 58N 36 20 E
Kharkov = Kharkiv, Ukraine 25 E6 49 58N 36 20 E
Kharovsk, Russia 24 C7 59 56N 40 13 E
Kharsawangarh, India 43 H11 22 48N 85 50 E
Kharta, Turkey 21 D13 40 55N 29 7 E
Khartoum = El Khartûm, Sudan 51 E12 15 31N 32 35 E
Khasan, Russia 30 C5 42 25N 130 40 E
Khāsh, Iran 40 E2 28 15N 61 15 E
Khashm el Girba, Sudan 51 F13 14 59N 35 58 E
Khaskovo, Bulgaria 21 D11 41 56N 25 30 E
Khatanga, Russia 27 B11 72 0N 102 20 E
Khatanga →, Russia 27 B11 72 55N 106 0 E
Khatauli, India 42 E7 29 17N 77 43 E
Khatra, India 43 H12 22 59N 86 51 E
Khātūnābād, Iran 45 D7 30 1N 55 25 E
Khatyrka, Russia 27 C18 62 3N 175 15 E
Khavda, India 42 H3 23 51N 69 43 E
Khaybar, Ḥarrat, Si. Arabia 44 E4 25 45N 40 0 E
Khayelitsha, S. Africa 53 L3 34 5S 18 42 E
Khāzimiyah, Iraq 44 C4 34 46N 43 37 E
Khe Bo, Vietnam 38 C5 19 8N 104 41 E
Khe Long, Vietnam 38 B5 21 29N 104 46 E
Khed Brahma, India 40 G8 24 7N 73 5 E
Khekra, India 42 E7 28 52N 77 20 E
Khemarak Phouminville, Cambodia 39 G4 11 37N 102 59 E
Khemisset, Morocco 50 B4 33 50N 6 1W
Khemmarat, Thailand 38 D5 16 10N 105 15 E
Khenāmān, Iran 45 D8 30 27N 56 29 E
Khenchela, Algeria 50 A7 35 28N 7 11 E
Khersān →, Iran 45 D6 31 33N 50 22 E
Kherson, Ukraine 25 E5 46 35N 32 35 E
Khersónisos Akrotíri, Greece 23 D6 35 30N 24 10 E
Kheta →, Russia 27 B11 71 54N 102 6 E
Khewari, Pakistan 42 F3 26 36N 68 52 E
Khilchipur, India 42 G7 24 2N 76 34 E
Khilok, Russia 27 D12 51 30N 110 45 E
Khíos, Greece 21 E12 38 27N 26 9 E
Khirsadoh, India 43 H8 22 11N 78 47 E
Khiuma = Hiiumaa, Estonia 9 G20 58 50N 22 45 E
Khiva, Uzbekistan 26 E7 41 30N 60 18 E
Khīyāv, Iran 44 B5 38 30N 47 45 E
Khlong Khlung, Thailand 38 D2 16 12N 99 43 E
Khmelnik, Ukraine 17 D14 49 33N 27 58 E
Khmelnitskiy = Khmelnytskyy, Ukraine 17 D14 49 23N 27 0 E
Khmelnytskyy, Ukraine 17 D14 49 23N 27 0 E
Khmer Rep. = Cambodia ■, Asia 38 F5 12 15N 105 0 E
Khoai, Hon, Vietnam 39 H5 8 26N 104 50 E
Khodoriv, Ukraine 17 D13 49 24N 24 19 E
Khodzent = Khŭjand, Tajikistan 26 E7 40 17N 69 37 E
Khojak Pass, Afghan. 42 D2 30 51N 66 34 E
Khok Kloi, Thailand 39 H2 8 17N 98 19 E
Khok Pho, Thailand 39 J3 6 43N 101 6 E
Kholm, Russia 24 C5 57 10N 31 15 E
Kholmsk, Russia 27 E15 47 40N 142 5 E
Khomas Hochland, Namibia 56 C2 22 40S 16 0 E
Khomeyn, Iran 45 C6 33 40N 50 7 E
Khomeyni Shahr, Iran 45 C6 32 41N 51 31 E
Khomodino, Botswana 56 C3 22 46S 23 52 E
Khon Kaen, Thailand 38 D4 16 30N 102 47 E
Khong →, Cambodia 38 F5 13 32N 105 58 E
Khong Sedone, Laos 38 E5 15 34N 105 49 E
Khonuu, Russia 27 C15 66 30N 143 12 E
Khoper →, Russia 25 D6 49 30N 42 20 E
Khóra Sfakíon, Greece 23 D6 35 15N 24 9 E
Khorāsān □, Iran 45 C8 34 0N 58 0 E
Khorat = Nakhon Ratchasima, Thailand 38 E4 14 59N 102 12 E
Khorat, Cao Nguyen, Thailand 38 E4 15 30N 102 50 E
Khorixas, Namibia 56 C1 20 16S 14 59 E
Khorramābād, Khorāsān, Iran 45 C8 35 6N 57 57 E
Khorramābād, Lorestān, Iran 45 C6 33 30N 48 25 E
Khorrāmshahr, Iran 45 D6 30 29N 48 15 E
Khorugh, Tajikistan 26 F8 37 30N 71 36 E
Khosravī, Iran 45 D6 30 48N 51 28 E
Khosrowābād, Khuzestān, Iran 45 D6 30 10N 48 25 E
Khosrowābād, Kordestān, Iran 44 C5 35 31N 47 38 E
Khost, Pakistan 42 D2 30 13N 67 35 E
Khosūyeh, Iran 45 D7 28 32N 54 26 E
Khotyn, Ukraine 17 D14 48 31N 26 27 E
Khouribga, Morocco 50 B4 32 58N 6 57W
Khowst, Afghan. 42 C3 33 22N 69 58 E
Khowst □, Afghan. 40 C6 33 20N 70 0 E
Khoyniki, Belarus 17 C15 51 54N 29 55 E
Khrysokhou B., Cyprus 23 D11 35 6N 32 25 E
Khu Khan, Thailand 38 E5 14 42N 104 12 E
Khudzhand = Khŭjand, Tajikistan 26 E7 40 17N 69 37 E
Khuff, Si. Arabia 44 E5 24 55N 44 53 E
Khūgīānī, Afghan. 42 D2 31 37N 65 4 E
Khuis, Botswana 56 D3 26 40S 21 49 E
Khuiyala, India 42 F4 27 9N 70 25 E
Khŭjand, Tajikistan 26 E7 40 17N 69 37 E
Khujner, India 42 H7 23 47N 76 36 E
Khulna, Bangla. 41 H16 22 45N 89 34 E
Khulna □, Bangla. 41 H16 22 25N 89 35 E
Khumago, Botswana 56 C3 20 26S 24 32 E
Khūnsorkh, Iran 45 E8 27 9N 56 7 E
Khunti, India 43 H11 23 5N 85 17 E
Khūr, Iran 45 C8 32 55N 58 18 E
Khurai, India 42 G8 24 3N 78 23 E
Khurayş, Si. Arabia 45 E6 25 6N 48 2 E
Khurīyā Murīyā, Jazā'ir, Oman 46 D6 17 30N 55 58 E
Khurja, India 42 E7 28 15N 77 58 E
Khūrmāl, Iraq 44 C5 35 18N 46 2 E
Khurr, Wādī al, Iraq 44 C4 32 3N 43 52 E
Khūsf, Iran 45 C8 32 46N 58 53 E
Khush, Afghan. 40 C3 32 55N 62 10 E
Khushab, Pakistan 42 C5 32 20N 72 20 E
Khust, Ukraine 17 D12 48 10N 23 18 E
Khuzdar, Pakistan 42 F2 27 52N 66 30 E
Khūzestān □, Iran 45 D6 31 0N 49 0 E
Khvāf, Iran 45 C9 34 33N 60 8 E
Khvājeh, Iran 44 B5 38 9N 46 35 E
Khvānsār, Iran 45 D7 29 56N 54 8 E
Khvor, Iran 45 C7 33 45N 55 0 E
Khvorgū, Iran 45 E8 27 34N 56 27 E
Khvormūj, Iran 45 D6 28 40N 51 30 E
Khvoy, Iran 44 B5 38 35N 45 0 E
Khyber Pass, Afghan. 42 B4 34 10N 71 8 E
Kiabukwa, Dem. Rep. of the Congo 55 D1 8 40S 24 48 E
Kiama, Australia 63 E5 34 40S 150 50 E
Kiamba, Phil. 37 C6 6 2N 124 46 E
Kiambi, Dem. Rep. of the Congo 54 D2 7 15S 28 0 E
Kiambu, Kenya 54 C4 1 8S 36 50 E
Kiangara, Madag. 57 B8 17 58S 47 2 E
Kiangsi = Jiangxi □, China 33 D6 27 30N 116 0 E
Kiangsu = Jiangsu □, China 35 H11 33 0N 120 0 E
Kibanga Port, Uganda 54 B3 0 10N 32 58 E
Kibara, Tanzania 54 C3 2 8S 33 30 E
Kibare, Mts., Dem. Rep. of the Congo 54 D2 8 25S 27 10 E
Kibombo, Dem. Rep. of the Congo 54 C2 3 57S 25 53 E
Kibondo, Tanzania 54 C3 3 35S 30 45 E
Kibre Mengist, Ethiopia 46 F2 5 54N 38 59 E
Kibumbu, Burundi 54 C2 3 32S 29 45 E
Kibungo, Rwanda 54 C3 2 10S 30 32 E
Kibuye, Burundi 54 C2 3 39S 29 59 E
Kibuye, Rwanda 54 C2 2 3S 29 21 E
Kibwesa, Tanzania 54 D2 6 30S 29 58 E
Kibwezi, Kenya 54 C4 2 27S 37 57 E
Kichha, India 43 E8 28 53N 79 30 E
Kichha →, India 43 E8 28 41N 79 18 E
Kichmengskiy Gorodok, Russia 24 B8 59 59N 45 48 E
Kicking Horse Pass, Canada 72 C5 51 28N 116 16W
Kidal, Mali 50 E6 18 26N 1 22 E
Kidderminster, U.K. 11 E5 52 24N 2 15W
Kidete, Tanzania 54 D4 6 25S 37 17 E
Kidnappers, C., N.Z. 59 H6 39 38S 177 5 E
Kidsgrove, U.K. 10 D5 53 5N 2 14W
Kidston, Australia 62 B3 18 52S 144 8 E
Kidugallo, Tanzania 54 D4 6 49S 38 15 E
Kiel, Germany 16 A6 54 19N 10 8 E
Kiel Canal = Nord-Ostsee-Kanal, Germany 16 A5 54 12N 9 32 E
Kielce, Poland 17 C11 50 52N 20 42 E
Kielder Water, U.K. 10 B5 55 11N 2 31W
Kieler Bucht, Germany 16 A6 54 35N 10 25 E
Kien Binh, Vietnam 39 H5 9 55N 105 19 E
Kien Tan, Vietnam 39 G5 10 7N 105 17 E
Kienge, Dem. Rep. of the Congo 55 E2 10 30S 27 30 E
Kiev = Kyyiv, Ukraine 17 C16 50 30N 30 28 E
Kiffa, Mauritania 50 E3 16 37N 11 24W
Kifrī, Iraq 44 C5 34 45N 45 0 E
Kigali, Rwanda 54 C3 1 59S 30 4 E
Kigarama, Tanzania 54 C3 1 1S 31 50 E
Kigoma □, Tanzania 54 D3 5 0S 30 0 E
Kigoma-Ujiji, Tanzania 54 C2 4 55S 29 36 E
Kigomasha, Ras, Tanzania 54 C4 4 58S 38 58 E
Kığı, Turkey 44 B4 39 18N 40 21 E
Kihei, U.S.A. 74 H16 20 47N 156 28W
Kihnu, Estonia 9 G21 58 9N 24 1 E
Kii-Sanchi, Japan 31 G8 34 20N 136 0 E
Kii-Suidō, Japan 31 H7 33 40N 134 45 E
Kikaiga-Shima, Japan 31 K4 28 19N 129 59 E
Kikinda, Serbia, Yug. 21 B9 45 50N 20 30 E
Kikládhes, Greece 21 F11 37 0N 24 30 E
Kikwit, Dem. Rep. of the Congo 52 E3 5 0S 18 45 E
Kilar, India 42 C7 33 6N 76 25 E
Kilauea Crater, U.S.A. 74 J17 19 25N 155 17W
Kilbrannan Sd., U.K. 12 F3 55 37N 5 26W
Kilchu, N. Korea 35 D15 40 57N 129 25 E
Kilcoy, Australia 63 D5 26 59S 152 30 E
Kildare, Ireland 13 C5 53 9N 6 55W
Kildare □, Ireland 13 C5 53 10N 6 50W
Kilfinnane, Ireland 13 D3 52 21N 8 28W
Kilgore, U.S.A. 81 J7 32 23N 94 53W
Kilifi, Kenya 54 C4 3 40S 39 48 E
Kilimanjaro, Tanzania 54 C4 3 7S 37 20 E
Kilimanjaro □, Tanzania 54 C4 4 0S 38 0 E
Kilindini, Kenya 54 C4 4 4S 39 40 E
Kilis, Turkey 44 B3 36 42N 37 6 E
Kiliya, Ukraine 17 F15 45 28N 29 16 E
Kilkee, Ireland 13 D2 52 41N 9 39W
Kilkeel, U.K. 13 B5 54 4N 6 0W
Kilkenny, Ireland 13 D4 52 39N 7 15W
Kilkenny □, Ireland 13 D4 52 35N 7 15W
Kilkieran B., Ireland 13 C2 53 20N 9 41W
Kilkís, Greece 21 D10 40 58N 22 57 E
Killala, Ireland 13 B2 54 13N 9 12W
Killala B., Ireland 13 B2 54 16N 9 8W
Killaloe, Ireland 13 D3 52 48N 8 28W
Killaloe Station, Canada 78 A7 45 33N 77 25W
Killarney, Australia 63 D5 28 20S 152 18 E
Killarney, Canada 73 D9 49 10N 99 40W
Killarney, Ireland 13 D2 52 4N 9 30W
Killary Harbour, Ireland 13 C2 53 38N 9 52W
Killdeer, U.S.A. 80 B3 47 26N 102 48W
Killeen, U.S.A. 81 K6 31 7N 97 44W
Killin, U.K. 12 E4 56 28N 4 19W
Killíni, Greece 21 F10 37 54N 22 25 E
Killorglin, Ireland 13 D2 52 6N 9 47W
Killybegs, Ireland 13 B3 54 38N 8 26W
Kilmarnock, U.K. 12 F4 55 37N 4 29W
Kilmore, Australia 63 F3 37 25S 144 53 E

L

Lewiston, Maine, U.S.A. 77 C11 44 6N 70 13W
Lewiston, N.Y., U.S.A. 78 C5 43 11N 79 3W
Lewistown, Mont., U.S.A. 82 C9 47 4N 109 26W
Lewistown, Pa., U.S.A. 78 F7 40 36N 77 34W
Lexington, Ill., U.S.A. 80 E10 40 39N 88 47W
Lexington, Ky., U.S.A. 76 F3 38 3N 84 30W
Lexington, Mich., U.S.A. 78 C2 43 16N 82 32W
Lexington, Mo., U.S.A. 80 F8 39 11N 93 52W
Lexington, N.C., U.S.A. 77 H5 35 49N 80 15W
Lexington, N.Y., U.S.A. 79 D10 42 15N 74 22W
Lexington, Nebr., U.S.A. 80 E5 40 47N 99 45W
Lexington, Ohio, U.S.A. 78 F2 40 41N 82 35W
Lexington, Tenn., U.S.A. 77 H1 35 39N 88 24W
Lexington, Va., U.S.A. 76 G6 37 47N 79 27W
Lexington Park, U.S.A. 76 F7 38 16N 76 27W
Leyburn, U.K. 10 C6 54 19N 1 48W
Leyland, U.K. 10 D5 53 42N 2 43W
Leyte □, Phil. 37 B6 11 0N 125 0 E
Lezhë, Albania 21 D8 41 47N 19 39 E
Lhasa, China 32 D4 29 25N 90 58 E
Lhazê, China 32 D3 29 5N 87 38 E
Lhokkruet, Indonesia 36 D1 4 55N 95 24 E
Lhokseumawe, Indonesia 36 C1 5 10N 97 10 E
L'Hospitalet de Llobregat, Spain 19 B7 41 21N 2 6 E
Li, Thailand 38 D2 17 48N 98 57 E
Li Xian, Gansu, China 34 G3 34 10N 105 5 E
Li Xian, Hebei, China 34 E8 38 30N 115 35 E
Lianga, Phil. 37 C7 8 38N 126 6 E
Liangcheng, Nei Monggol Zizhiqu, China 34 D7 40 28N 112 25 E
Liangcheng, Shandong, China 35 G10 35 32N 119 37 E
Liangdang, China 34 H4 33 56N 106 18 E
Liangpran, Indonesia 36 D4 1 4N 114 23 E
Lianshanguan, China 35 D12 40 53N 123 43 E
Lianshui, China 35 H10 33 42N 119 20 E
Lianyungang, China 35 G10 34 40N 119 11 E
Liao He →, China 35 D11 41 0N 121 50 E
Liaocheng, China 34 F8 36 28N 115 58 E
Liaodong Bandao, China 35 E12 40 0N 122 30 E
Liaodong Wan, China 35 D11 40 20N 121 10 E
Liaoning □, China 35 D12 41 40N 122 30 E
Liaoyang, China 35 D12 41 15N 122 58 E
Liaoyuan, China 35 C13 42 58N 125 2 E
Liaozhong, China 35 D12 41 23N 122 50 E
Liard →, Canada 72 A4 61 51N 121 18W
Liard River, Canada 72 B3 59 25N 126 5W
Liari, Pakistan 42 G2 25 37N 66 30 E
Libau = Liepāja, Latvia 9 H19 56 30N 21 0 E
Libby, U.S.A. 82 B6 48 23N 115 33W
Libenge, Dem. Rep. of the Congo 52 D3 3 40N 18 55 E
Liberal, U.S.A. 81 G4 37 3N 100 55W
Liberec, Czech Rep. 16 C8 50 47N 15 7 E
Liberia, Costa Rica 88 D2 10 40N 85 30W
Liberia ■, W. Afr. 50 G4 6 30N 9 30W
Liberty, Mo., U.S.A. 80 F7 39 15N 94 25W
Liberty, N.Y., U.S.A. 79 E10 41 48N 74 45W
Liberty, Pa., U.S.A. 78 E7 41 34N 77 6W
Liberty, Tex., U.S.A. 81 K7 30 3N 94 48W
Lībīya, Sahrâ', Africa 51 C10 25 0N 25 0 E
Libobo, Tanjung, Indonesia 37 E7 0 54S 128 28 E
Libode, S. Africa 57 E4 31 33S 29 2 E
Libourne, France 18 D3 44 55N 0 14W
Libramont, Belgium 15 E5 49 55N 5 23 E
Libreville, Gabon 52 D1 0 25N 9 26 E
Libya ■, N. Afr. 51 C9 27 0N 17 0 E
Libyan Desert = Lībīya, Sahrâ', Africa 51 C10 25 0N 25 0 E
Licantén, Chile 94 D1 35 55S 72 0W
Licata, Italy 20 F5 37 6N 13 56 E
Licheng, China 34 F7 36 28N 113 20 E
Lichfield, U.K. 11 E6 52 41N 1 49W
Lichinga, Mozam. 55 E4 13 13S 35 11 E
Lichtenburg, S. Africa 56 D4 26 8S 26 8 E
Licking →, U.S.A. 76 F3 39 6N 84 30W
Licungo →, Mozam. 55 F4 17 40S 37 15 E
Lida, Belarus 9 K21 53 53N 25 15 E
Lidköping, Sweden 9 G15 58 31N 13 7 E
Liebig, Mt., Australia 60 D5 23 18S 131 22 E
Liechtenstein ■, Europe 18 C8 47 8N 9 35 E
Liège, Belgium 15 D5 50 38N 5 35 E
Liège □, Belgium 15 D5 50 32N 5 35 E
Liegnitz = Legnica, Poland 16 C9 51 12N 16 10 E
Lienart, Dem. Rep. of the Congo 54 B2 3 3N 25 31 E
Lienyünchiangshih = Lianyungang, China 35 G10 34 40N 119 11 E
Lienz, Austria 16 E7 46 50N 12 46 E
Liepāja, Latvia 9 H19 56 30N 21 0 E
Lier, Belgium 15 C4 51 7N 4 34 E
Lièvre →, Canada 70 C4 45 31N 75 26W
Liffey →, Ireland 13 C5 53 21N 6 13W
Lifford, Ireland 13 B4 54 51N 7 29W
Lifudzin, Russia 30 B7 44 21N 134 58 E
Lightning Ridge, Australia 63 D4 29 22S 148 0 E
Ligonha →, Mozam. 55 F4 16 54S 39 9 E
Ligonier, U.S.A. 78 F5 40 15N 79 14W
Liguria □, Italy 18 D8 44 30N 8 50 E
Ligurian Sea, Medit. S. 20 C3 43 20N 9 0 E
Lihou Reefs and Cays, Australia 62 B5 17 25S 151 40 E
Lihue, U.S.A. 74 H15 21 59N 159 23W
Lijiang, China 32 D5 26 55N 100 20 E
Likasi, Dem. Rep. of the Congo 55 E2 10 55S 26 48 E
Likoma I., Malawi 55 E3 12 3S 34 45 E
Likumburu, Tanzania 55 D4 9 43S 35 8 E
Lille, France 18 A5 50 38N 3 3 E
Lille Bælt, Denmark 9 J13 55 20N 9 45 E
Lillehammer, Norway 9 F14 61 8N 10 30 E
Lillesand, Norway 9 G13 58 15N 8 23 E
Lillian Pt., Australia 61 E4 27 40S 126 6 E
Lillooet, Canada 72 C4 50 44N 121 57W
Lillooet →, Canada 72 D4 49 15N 121 57W
Lilongwe, Malawi 55 E3 14 0S 33 48 E
Liloy, Phil. 37 C6 8 4N 122 39 E
Lim →, Bos.-H. 21 C8 43 45N 19 15 E
Lima, Indonesia 37 E7 3 39S 127 58 E
Lima, Peru 92 F3 12 0S 77 0W
Lima, Mont., U.S.A. 82 D7 44 38N 112 36W
Lima, Ohio, U.S.A. 76 E3 40 44N 84 6W
Lima →, Portugal 19 B1 41 41N 8 50W
Liman, Indonesia 37 G14 7 48S 111 45 E
Limassol, Cyprus 23 E12 34 42N 33 1 E
Limavady, U.K. 13 A5 55 3N 6 56W
Limay →, Argentina 96 D3 39 0S 68 0W
Limay Mahuida, Argentina 94 D2 37 10S 66 45W
Limbang, Brunei 36 D5 4 42N 115 6 E
Limbaži, Latvia 9 H21 57 31N 24 42 E
Limbdi, India 42 H4 22 34N 71 51 E
Limbe, Cameroon 52 D1 4 1N 9 10 E
Limburg, Germany 16 C5 50 22N 8 4 E
Limburg □, Belgium 15 C5 51 2N 5 25 E
Limburg □, Neths. 15 C5 51 20N 5 55 E
Limeira, Brazil 95 A6 22 35S 47 28W
Limerick, Ireland 13 D3 52 40N 8 37W
Limerick, U.S.A. 79 C14 43 41N 70 48W
Limerick □, Ireland 13 D3 52 30N 8 50W
Limestone, U.S.A. 78 D6 42 2N 78 38W
Limestone →, Canada 73 B10 56 31N 94 7W
Limfjorden, Denmark 9 H13 56 55N 9 0 E
Limia = Lima →, Portugal 19 B1 41 41N 8 50W
Limingen, Norway 8 D15 64 48N 13 35 E
Limmen Bight, Australia 62 A2 14 40S 135 35 E
Limmen Bight →, Australia 62 B2 15 7S 135 44 E
Límnos, Greece 21 E11 39 50N 25 5 E
Limoges, Canada 79 A9 45 20N 75 16W
Limoges, France 18 D4 45 50N 1 15 E
Limón, Costa Rica 88 E3 10 0N 83 2W
Limon, U.S.A. 80 F3 39 16N 103 41W
Limousin, France 18 D4 45 30N 1 30 E
Limoux, France 18 E5 43 4N 2 12 E
Limpopo →, Africa 57 D5 25 5S 33 30 E
Limuru, Kenya 54 C4 1 2S 36 35 E
Lin Xian, China 34 F6 37 57N 110 58 E
Linares, Chile 94 D1 35 50S 71 40W
Linares, Mexico 87 C5 24 50N 99 40W
Linares, Spain 19 C4 38 10N 3 40W
Lincheng, China 34 F8 37 25N 114 30 E
Lincoln, Argentina 94 C3 34 55S 61 30W
Lincoln, N.Z. 59 K4 43 38S 172 30 E
Lincoln, U.K. 10 D7 53 14N 0 32W
Lincoln, Calif., U.S.A. 84 G5 38 54N 121 17W
Lincoln, Ill., U.S.A. 80 E10 40 9N 89 22W
Lincoln, Kans., U.S.A. 80 F5 39 3N 98 9W
Lincoln, Maine, U.S.A. 77 C11 45 22N 68 30W
Lincoln, N.H., U.S.A. 79 B13 44 3N 71 40W
Lincoln, N. Mex., U.S.A. 83 K11 33 30N 105 23W
Lincoln, Nebr., U.S.A. 80 E6 40 49N 96 41W
Lincoln City, U.S.A. 82 D1 44 57N 124 1W
Lincoln Hav = Lincoln Sea, Arctic 4 A5 84 0N 55 0W
Lincoln Sea, Arctic 4 A5 84 0N 55 0W
Lincolnshire □, U.K. 10 D7 53 14N 0 32W
Lincolnshire Wolds, U.K. 10 D7 53 26N 0 13W
Lincolnton, U.S.A. 77 H5 35 29N 81 16W
Lind, U.S.A. 82 C4 46 58N 118 37W
Linda, U.S.A. 84 F5 39 8N 121 34W
Linden, Guyana 92 B7 6 0N 58 10W
Linden, Ala., U.S.A. 77 J2 32 18N 87 48W
Linden, Calif., U.S.A. 84 G5 38 1N 121 5W
Linden, Tex., U.S.A. 81 J7 33 1N 94 22W
Lindenhurst, U.S.A. 79 F11 40 41N 73 23W
Lindesnes, Norway 9 H12 57 58N 7 3 E
Líndhos, Greece 23 C10 36 6N 28 4 E
Líndhos, Ákra, Greece 23 C10 36 4N 28 10 E
Lindi, Tanzania 55 D4 9 58S 39 38 E
Lindi □, Tanzania 55 D4 9 40S 38 30 E
Lindi →, Dem. Rep. of the Congo 54 B2 0 33N 25 5 E
Lindsay, Canada 78 B6 44 22N 78 43W
Lindsay, Calif., U.S.A. 84 J7 36 12N 119 5W
Lindsay, Okla., U.S.A. 81 H6 34 50N 97 38W
Lindsborg, U.S.A. 80 F6 38 35N 97 40W
Linesville, U.S.A. 78 E4 41 39N 80 26W
Linfen, China 34 F6 36 3N 111 30 E
Ling Xian, China 34 F9 37 22N 116 30 E
Lingao, China 38 C7 19 56N 109 42 E
Lingayen, Phil. 37 A6 16 1N 120 14 E
Lingayen G., Phil. 37 A6 16 10N 120 15 E
Lingbi, China 35 H9 33 33N 117 33 E
Lingchuan, China 34 G7 35 45N 113 12 E
Lingen, Germany 16 B4 52 31N 7 19 E
Lingga, Indonesia 36 E2 0 12S 104 37 E
Lingga, Kepulauan, Indonesia 36 E2 0 10S 104 30 E
Lingga Arch. = Lingga, Kepulauan, Indonesia 36 E2 0 10S 104 30 E
Lingle, U.S.A. 80 D2 42 8N 104 21W
Lingqiu, China 34 E8 39 28N 114 22 E
Lingshi, China 34 F6 36 48N 111 48 E
Lingshou, China 34 E8 38 20N 114 20 E
Lingshui, China 38 C8 18 27N 110 0 E
Lingtai, China 34 G4 35 0N 107 40 E
Linguère, Senegal 50 E2 15 25N 15 5W
Lingwu, China 34 E4 38 6N 106 20 E
Lingyuan, China 35 D10 41 10N 119 15 E
Linhai, China 33 D7 28 50N 121 8 E
Linhares, Brazil 93 G10 19 25S 40 4W
Linhe, China 34 D4 40 48N 107 20 E
Linjiang, China 35 D14 41 50N 127 0 E
Linköping, Sweden 9 G16 58 28N 15 36 E
Linkou, China 35 B16 45 15N 130 18 E
Linnhe, L., U.K. 12 E3 56 36N 5 25W
Linosa, Medit. S. 20 G5 35 51N 12 50 E
Linqi, China 34 G7 35 45N 113 52 E
Linqing, China 34 F8 36 50N 115 42 E
Linqu, China 35 F10 36 25N 118 30 E
Linru, China 34 G7 34 11N 112 52 E
Lins, Brazil 95 A6 21 40S 49 44W
Linta →, Madag. 57 D7 25 2S 44 5 E
Linton, Ind., U.S.A. 76 F2 39 2N 87 10W
Linton, N. Dak., U.S.A. 80 B4 46 16N 100 14W
Lintong, China 34 G5 34 20N 109 10 E
Linwood, Canada 78 C4 43 35N 80 43W
Linxi, China 35 C10 43 36N 118 2 E
Linxia, China 32 C5 35 36N 103 10 E
Linyanti →, Africa 56 B4 17 50S 25 5 E
Linyi, China 35 G10 35 5N 118 21 E
Linz, Austria 16 D8 48 18N 14 18 E
Linzhenzhen, China 34 F5 36 30N 109 59 E
Linzi, China 35 F10 36 50N 118 20 E
Lion, G. du, France 18 E6 43 10N 4 0 E
Lionárisso, Cyprus 23 D13 35 28N 34 8 E
Lions, G. of = Lion, G. du, France 18 E6 43 10N 4 0 E
Lion's Den, Zimbabwe 55 F3 17 15S 30 5 E
Lion's Head, Canada 78 B3 44 58N 81 15W
Lipa, Phil. 37 B6 13 57N 121 10 E
Lipali, Mozam. 55 F4 15 50S 35 50 E
Lípari, Italy 20 E6 38 26N 14 58 E
Lípari, Is. = Eólie, Ís., Italy 20 E6 38 30N 14 57 E
Lipcani, Moldova 17 D14 48 14N 26 48 E
Lipetsk, Russia 24 D6 52 37N 39 35 E
Lipkany = Lipcani, Moldova 17 D14 48 14N 26 48 E
Lipovcy Manzovka, Russia 30 B6 44 12N 132 26 E
Lipovets, Ukraine 17 D15 49 12N 29 1 E
Lippe →, Germany 16 C4 51 39N 6 36 E
Lipscomb, U.S.A. 81 G4 36 14N 100 16W
Liptrap C., Australia 63 F4 38 50S 145 55 E
Lira, Uganda 54 B3 2 17N 32 57 E
Liria = Lliria, Spain 19 C5 39 37N 0 35W
Lisala, Dem. Rep. of the Congo 52 D4 2 12N 21 38 E
Lisboa, Portugal 19 C1 38 42N 9 10W
Lisbon = Lisboa, Portugal 19 C1 38 42N 9 10W
Lisbon, N. Dak., U.S.A. 80 B6 46 27N 97 41W
Lisbon, N.H., U.S.A. 79 B13 44 13N 71 55W
Lisbon, Ohio, U.S.A. 78 F4 40 46N 80 46W
Lisbon Falls, U.S.A. 77 D10 44 0N 70 4W
Lisburn, U.K. 13 B5 54 31N 6 3W
Liscannor B., Ireland 13 D2 52 55N 9 24W
Lishi, China 34 F6 37 31N 111 8 E
Lishu, China 35 C13 43 20N 124 18 E
Lisianski I., Pac. Oc. 64 E10 26 2N 174 0W
Lisichansk = Lysychansk, Ukraine 25 E6 48 55N 38 30 E
Lisieux, France 18 B4 49 10N 0 12 E
Liski, Russia 25 D6 51 3N 39 30 E
Lismore, Australia 63 D5 28 44S 153 21 E
Lismore, Ireland 13 D4 52 8N 7 55W
Lista, Norway 9 G12 58 7N 6 39 E
Lister, Mt., Antarctica 5 D11 78 0S 162 0 E
Liston, Australia 63 D5 28 39S 152 6 E
Listowel, Canada 78 C4 43 44N 80 58W
Listowel, Ireland 13 D2 52 27N 9 29W
Litani →, Lebanon 47 B4 33 20N 35 15 E
Litchfield, Calif., U.S.A. 84 E6 40 24N 120 23W
Litchfield, Conn., U.S.A. 79 E11 41 45N 73 11W
Litchfield, Ill., U.S.A. 80 F10 39 11N 89 39W
Litchfield, Minn., U.S.A. 80 C7 45 8N 94 32W
Lithgow, Australia 63 E5 33 25S 150 8 E
Líthinon, Ákra, Greece 23 E6 34 55N 24 44 E
Lithuania ■, Europe 9 J20 55 30N 24 0 E
Lititz, U.S.A. 79 F8 40 9N 76 18W
Litoměřice, Czech Rep. 16 C8 50 33N 14 10 E
Little Abaco I., Bahamas 88 A4 26 50N 77 30W
Little Barrier I., N.Z. 59 G5 36 12S 175 8 E
Little Belt Mts., U.S.A. 82 C8 46 40N 110 45W
Little Blue →, U.S.A. 80 F6 39 42N 96 41W
Little Buffalo →, Canada 72 A6 61 0N 113 46W
Little Cayman, Cayman Is. 88 C3 19 41N 80 3W
Little Churchill →, Canada 73 B9 57 30N 95 22W
Little Colorado →, U.S.A. 83 H8 36 12N 111 48W
Little Current, Canada 70 C3 45 55N 82 0W
Little Current →, Canada 70 B3 50 57N 84 36W
Little Falls, Minn., U.S.A. 80 C7 45 59N 94 22W
Little Falls, N.Y., U.S.A. 79 C10 43 3N 74 51W
Little Fork →, U.S.A. 80 A8 48 31N 93 35W
Little Grand Rapids, Canada 73 C9 52 0N 95 29W
Little Humboldt →, U.S.A. 82 F5 41 1N 117 43W
Little Inagua I., Bahamas 89 B5 21 40N 73 50W
Little Karoo, S. Africa 56 E3 33 45S 21 0 E
Little Lake, U.S.A. 85 K9 35 56N 117 55W
Little Laut Is. = Laut Kecil, Kepulauan, Indonesia 36 E5 4 45S 115 40 E
Little Mecatina = Petit-Mécatina →, Canada 71 B8 50 40N 59 30W
Little Minch, U.K. 12 D2 57 35N 6 45W
Little Missouri →, U.S.A. 80 B3 47 36N 102 25W
Little Ouse →, U.K. 11 E9 52 22N 1 12 E
Little Rann, India 42 H4 23 25N 71 25 E
Little Red →, U.S.A. 81 H9 35 11N 91 27W
Little River, N.Z. 59 K4 43 45S 172 49 E
Little Rock, U.S.A. 81 H8 34 45N 92 17W
Little Ruaha →, Tanzania 54 D4 7 57S 37 53 E
Little Sable Pt., U.S.A. 76 D2 43 38N 86 33W
Little Sioux →, U.S.A. 80 E6 41 48N 96 4W
Little Smoky →, Canada 72 C5 54 44N 117 11W
Little Snake →, U.S.A. 82 F9 40 27N 108 26W
Little Valley, U.S.A. 78 D6 42 15N 78 48W
Little Wabash →, U.S.A. 76 G1 37 55N 88 5W
Little White →, U.S.A. 80 D4 43 40N 100 40W
Littlefield, U.S.A. 81 J3 33 55N 102 20W
Littlehampton, U.K. 11 G7 50 49N 0 32W
Littleton, U.S.A. 79 B13 44 18N 71 46W
Liu He →, China 35 D11 40 55N 121 35 E
Liuba, China 34 H4 33 38N 106 55 E
Liugou, China 35 D10 40 57N 118 15 E
Liuhe, China 35 C13 42 17N 125 43 E
Liukang Tenggaja = Sabalana, Kepulauan, Indonesia 37 F5 6 45S 118 50 E
Liuli, Tanzania 55 E3 11 3S 34 38 E
Liuwa Plain, Zambia 53 G4 14 20S 22 30 E
Liuzhou, China 33 D5 24 22N 109 22 E
Liuzhuang, China 35 H11 33 12N 120 18 E
Livadhia, Cyprus 23 E12 34 57N 33 38 E
Live Oak, Calif., U.S.A. 84 F5 39 17N 121 40W
Live Oak, Fla., U.S.A. 77 K4 30 18N 82 59W
Liveras, Cyprus 23 D11 35 23N 32 57 E
Livermore, U.S.A. 84 H5 37 41N 121 47W
Livermore, Mt., U.S.A. 81 K2 30 38N 104 11W
Livermore Falls, U.S.A. 77 C11 44 29N 70 11W
Liverpool, Canada 71 D7 44 5N 64 41W
Liverpool, U.K. 10 D4 53 25N 3 0W
Liverpool, U.S.A. 79 C8 43 6N 76 13W
Liverpool Bay, U.K. 10 D4 53 30N 3 20W
Liverpool Plains, Australia 63 E5 31 15S 150 15 E
Liverpool Ra., Australia 63 E5 31 50S 150 30 E
Livingston, Guatemala 88 C2 15 50N 88 50W
Livingston, U.K. 12 F5 55 54N 3 30W
Livingston, Ala., U.S.A. 77 J1 32 35N 88 11W
Livingston, Calif., U.S.A. 84 H6 37 23N 120 43W
Livingston, Mont., U.S.A. 82 D8 45 40N 110 34W
Livingston, S.C., U.S.A. 77 J5 33 32N 80 53W
Livingston, Tenn., U.S.A. 77 G3 36 23N 85 19W
Livingston, Tex., U.S.A. 81 K7 30 43N 94 56W
Livingston, L., U.S.A. 81 K7 30 50N 95 10W
Livingston Manor, U.S.A. 79 E10 41 54N 74 50W
Livingstone, Zambia 55 F2 17 46S 25 52 E
Livingstone Mts., Tanzania 55 D3 9 40S 34 20 E
Livingstonia, Malawi 55 E3 10 38S 34 5 E
Livny, Russia 24 D6 52 30N 37 30 E
Livonia, Mich., U.S.A. 76 D4 42 23N 83 23W
Livonia, N.Y., U.S.A. 78 D7 42 49N 77 40W
Livorno, Italy 20 C4 43 33N 10 19 E
Livramento, Brazil 95 C4 30 55S 55 30W
Liwale, Tanzania 55 D4 9 48S 37 58 E
Lizard I., Australia 62 A4 14 42S 145 30 E
Lizard Pt., U.K. 11 H2 49 57N 5 13W
Ljubljana, Slovenia 16 E8 46 4N 14 33 E
Ljungan →, Sweden 9 E17 62 18N 17 23 E
Ljungby, Sweden 9 H15 56 49N 13 55 E
Ljusdal, Sweden 9 F17 61 46N 16 3 E
Ljusnan →, Sweden 9 F17 61 12N 17 8 E
Ljusne, Sweden 9 F17 61 13N 17 7 E
Llancanelo, Salina, Argentina 94 D2 35 40S 69 8W
Llandeilo, U.K. 11 F4 51 53N 3 59W
Llandovery, U.K. 11 F4 51 59N 3 48W
Llandrindod Wells, U.K. 11 E4 52 14N 3 22W
Llandudno, U.K. 10 D4 53 19N 3 50W
Llanelli, U.K. 11 F3 51 41N 4 10W
Llanes, Spain 19 A3 43 25N 4 50W
Llangollen, U.K. 10 E4 52 58N 3 11W
Llanidloes, U.K. 11 E4 52 27N 3 31W
Llano, U.S.A. 81 K5 30 45N 98 41W
Llano →, U.S.A. 81 K5 30 39N 98 26W
Llano Estacado, U.S.A. 81 J3 33 30N 103 0W
Llanos, S. Amer. 92 C4 5 0N 71 35W
Llanquihue, L., Chile 96 E1 41 10S 72 50W
Llanwrtyd Wells, U.K. 11 E4 52 7N 3 38W
Llebeig, C. des, Spain 22 B9 39 33N 2 18 E
Lleida, Spain 19 B6 41 37N 0 39 E
Llentrisca, C., Spain 22 C7 38 52N 1 15 E
Llera, Mexico 87 C5 23 19N 99 1W
Lleyn Peninsula, U.K. 10 E3 52 51N 4 36W
Llico, Chile 94 C1 34 46S 72 5W
Lliria, Spain 19 C5 39 37N 0 35W
Llobregat →, Spain 19 B7 41 19N 2 9 E
Lloret de Mar, Spain 19 B7 41 41N 2 53 E
Lloyd B., Australia 62 A3 12 45S 143 27 E
Lloyd L., Canada 73 B7 57 22N 108 57W
Lloydminster, Canada 73 C7 53 17N 110 0W
Llucmajor, Spain 22 B9 39 29N 2 53 E
Llullaillaco, Volcán, S. Amer. 94 A2 24 43S 68 30W
Lo →, Vietnam 38 B5 21 18N 105 25 E
Loa, U.S.A. 83 G8 38 24N 111 39W
Loa →, Chile 94 A1 21 26S 70 41W
Loaita I., S. China Sea 36 B4 10 41N 114 25 E
Loange →, Dem. Rep. of the Congo 52 E4 4 17S 20 2 E
Lobatse, Botswana 56 D4 25 12S 25 40 E
Lobería, Argentina 94 D4 38 10S 58 40W
Lobito, Angola 53 G2 12 18S 13 35 E
Lobos, Argentina 94 D4 35 10S 59 0W
Lobos, I., Mexico 86 B2 27 15N 110 30W
Lobos, I. de, Canary Is. 22 F6 28 45N 13 50W
Loc Binh, Vietnam 38 B6 21 46N 106 54 E
Loc Ninh, Vietnam 39 G6 11 50N 106 34 E
Locarno, Switz. 18 C8 46 10N 8 47 E
Loch Baghasdail = Lochboisdale, U.K. 12 D1 57 9N 7 20W
Loch Garman = Wexford, Ireland 13 D5 52 20N 6 28W
Loch Nam Madadh = Lochmaddy, U.K. 12 D1 57 36N 7 10W
Lochaber, U.K. 12 E3 56 59N 5 1W
Locharbriggs, U.K. 12 F5 55 7N 3 35W
Lochboisdale, U.K. 12 D1 57 9N 7 20W
Loche, L. La, Canada 73 B7 56 30N 109 30W
Lochem, Neths. 15 B6 52 9N 6 26 E
Loches, France 18 C4 47 7N 1 0 E
Lochgilphead, U.K. 12 E3 56 2N 5 26W
Lochinver, U.K. 12 C3 58 9N 5 14W
Lochmaddy, U.K. 12 D1 57 36N 7 10W
Lochnagar, Australia 62 C4 23 33S 145 38 E
Lochnagar, U.K. 12 E5 56 57N 3 15W
Lochy, L., U.K. 12 E4 57 0N 4 53W
Lock, Australia 63 E2 33 34S 135 46 E
Lock Haven, U.S.A. 78 E7 41 8N 77 28W
Lockeford, U.S.A. 84 G5 38 10N 121 9W
Lockeport, Canada 71 D6 43 47N 65 4W
Lockerbie, U.K. 12 F5 55 7N 3 21W
Lockhart, U.S.A. 81 L6 29 53N 97 40W
Lockhart, L., Australia 61 F2 33 15S 119 3 E
Lockhart River, Australia 62 A3 12 58S 143 30 E
Lockney, U.S.A. 81 H4 34 7N 101 27W
Lockport, U.S.A. 78 C6 43 10N 78 42W
Lod, Israel 47 D3 31 57N 34 54 E
Lodeinoye Pole, Russia 24 B5 60 44N 33 33 E
Lodge Bay, Canada 71 B8 52 14N 55 51W
Lodge Grass, U.S.A. 82 D10 45 19N 107 22W
Lodgepole Cr. →, U.S.A. 80 E2 41 20N 104 30W
Lodhran, Pakistan 42 E4 29 32N 71 30 E
Lodi, Italy 18 D8 45 19N 9 30 E
Lodi, Calif., U.S.A. 84 G5 38 8N 121 16W
Lodi, Ohio, U.S.A. 78 E3 41 2N 82 0W
Lodja, Dem. Rep. of the Congo 54 C1 3 30S 23 23 E
Lodwar, Kenya 54 B4 3 10N 35 40 E
Łódź, Poland 17 C10 51 45N 19 27 E
Loei, Thailand 38 D3 17 29N 101 35 E
Loengo, Dem. Rep. of the Congo 54 C2 4 48S 26 30 E
Loeriesfontein, S. Africa 56 E2 31 0S 19 26 E
Lofoten, Norway 8 B15 68 30N 14 0 E
Logan, Iowa, U.S.A. 80 E7 41 39N 95 47W
Logan, Ohio, U.S.A. 76 F4 39 32N 82 25W
Logan, Utah, U.S.A. 82 F8 41 44N 111 50W
Logan, W. Va., U.S.A. 76 G5 37 51N 81 59W
Logan, Mt., Canada 68 B5 60 31N 140 22W
Logandale, U.S.A. 85 J12 36 36N 114 29W
Logansport, Ind., U.S.A. 76 E2 40 45N 86 22W
Logansport, La., U.S.A. 81 K8 31 58N 94 0W
Logone →, Chad 51 F9 12 6N 15 2 E
Logroño, Spain 19 A4 42 28N 2 27W
Lohardaga, India 43 H11 23 27N 84 45 E
Loharia, India 42 H6 23 45N 74 14 E
Loharu, India 42 E6 28 27N 75 49 E
Lohja, Finland 9 F21 60 12N 24 5 E
Lohri Wah →, Pakistan 42 F2 27 27N 67 37 E
Loi-kaw, Burma 41 K20 19 40N 97 17 E
Loimaa, Finland 9 F20 60 50N 23 5 E
Loir →, France 18 C3 47 33N 0 32W
Loire →, France 18 C2 47 16N 2 10W
Loja, Ecuador 92 D3 3 59S 79 16W
Loja, Spain 19 D3 37 10N 4 10W
Loji = Kawasi, Indonesia 37 E7 1 38S 127 28 E
Lokandu, Dem. Rep. of the Congo 54 C2 2 30S 25 45 E
Lokeren, Belgium 15 C3 51 6N 3 59 E
Lokgwabe, Botswana 56 C3 24 10S 21 50 E
Lokichokio, Kenya 54 B3 4 19N 34 13 E
Lokitaung, Kenya 54 B4 4 12N 35 48 E

Lokkan tekojärvi, Finland 8 C22 67 55N 27 35 E
Lokoja, Nigeria 50 G7 7 47N 6 45 E
Lola, Mt., U.S.A. 84 F6 39 26N 120 22W
Loliondo, Tanzania 54 C4 2 2S 35 39 E
Lolland, Denmark 9 J14 54 45N 11 30 E
Lolo, U.S.A. 82 C6 46 45N 114 5W
Lom, Bulgaria 21 C10 43 48N 23 12 E
Lom Kao, Thailand 38 D3 16 53N 101 14 E
Lom Sak, Thailand 38 D3 16 47N 101 15 E
Loma, U.S.A. 82 C8 47 56N 110 30W
Loma Linda, U.S.A. 85 L9 34 3N 117 16W
Lomami →, Dem. Rep. of the Congo 54 B1 0 46N 24 16 E
Lomas de Zamóra, Argentina 94 C4 34 45S 58 25W
Lombadina, Australia 60 C3 16 31S 122 54 E
Lombárdia □, Italy 18 D8 45 40N 9 30 E
Lombardy = Lombárdia □, Italy 18 D8 45 40N 9 30 E
Lomblen, Indonesia 37 F6 8 30S 123 32 E
Lombok, Indonesia 36 F5 8 45S 116 30 E
Lomé, Togo 50 G6 6 9N 1 20 E
Lomela, Dem. Rep. of the Congo 52 E4 2 19S 23 15 E
Lomela →, Dem. Rep. of the Congo 52 E4 0 15S 20 40 E
Lommel, Belgium 15 C5 51 14N 5 19 E
Lomond, Canada 72 C6 50 24N 112 36W
Lomond, L., U.K. 12 E4 56 8N 4 38W
Lomphat, Cambodia 38 F6 13 30N 106 59 E
Lompobatang, Indonesia 37 F5 5 24S 119 56 E
Lompoc, U.S.A. 85 L6 34 38N 120 28W
Łomża, Poland 17 B12 53 10N 22 2 E
Loncoche, Chile 96 D2 39 20S 72 50W
Londa, India 40 M9 15 30N 74 30 E
Londiani, Kenya 54 C4 0 10S 35 33 E
London, Canada 78 D3 42 59N 81 15W
London, U.K. 11 F7 51 30N 0 3W
London, Ky., U.S.A. 76 G3 37 8N 84 5W
London, Ohio, U.S.A. 76 F4 39 53N 83 27W
London, Greater □, U.K. 11 F7 51 36N 0 5W
Londonderry, U.K. 13 B4 55 0N 7 20W
Londonderry □, U.K. 13 B4 55 0N 7 20W
Londonderry, C., Australia 60 B4 13 45S 126 55 E
Londonderry, I., Chile 96 H2 55 0S 71 0W
Londres, Argentina 96 B3 27 43S 67 7W
Londrina, Brazil 95 A5 23 18S 51 10W
Lone Pine, U.S.A. 84 J8 36 36N 118 4W
Lonely Mine, Zimbabwe 57 B4 19 30S 28 49 E
Long B., U.S.A. 77 J6 33 35N 78 45W
Long Beach, Calif., U.S.A. 85 M8 33 47N 118 11W
Long Beach, N.Y., U.S.A. 79 F11 40 35N 73 39W
Long Beach, Wash., U.S.A. 84 D2 46 21N 124 3W
Long Branch, U.S.A. 79 F11 40 18N 74 0W
Long Creek, U.S.A. 82 D4 44 43N 119 6W
Long Eaton, U.K. 10 E6 52 53N 1 15W
Long I., Australia 62 C4 20 22S 148 51 E
Long I., Bahamas 89 B4 23 20N 75 10W
Long I., Canada 70 B4 54 50N 79 20W
Long I., Ireland 13 E2 51 30N 9 34W
Long I., U.S.A. 79 F11 40 45N 73 30W
Long Island Sd., U.S.A. 79 E12 41 10N 73 0W
Long L., Canada 70 C2 49 30N 86 50W
Long Lake, U.S.A. 79 C10 43 58N 74 25W
Long Point B., Canada 78 D4 42 40N 80 10W
Long Prairie →, U.S.A. 80 C7 46 20N 94 36W
Long Pt., Canada 78 D4 42 35N 80 2W
Long Range Mts., Canada 71 C8 49 30N 57 30W
Long Reef, Australia 60 B4 14 1S 125 48 E
Long Spruce, Canada 73 B10 56 24N 94 21W
Long Str. = Longa, Proliv, Russia 4 C16 70 0N 175 0 E
Long Thanh, Vietnam 39 G6 10 47N 106 57 E
Long Xian, China 34 G4 34 55N 106 55 E
Long Xuyen, Vietnam 39 G5 10 19N 105 28 E
Longa, Proliv, Russia 4 C16 70 0N 175 0 E
Longbenton, U.K. 10 B6 55 1N 1 31W
Longboat Key, U.S.A. 77 M4 27 23N 82 39W
Longde, China 34 G4 35 30N 106 20 E
Longford, Australia 62 G4 41 32S 147 3 E
Longford, Ireland 13 C4 53 43N 7 49W
Longford □, Ireland 13 C4 53 42N 7 45W
Longhua, China 35 D9 41 18N 117 45 E
Longido, Tanzania 54 C4 2 43S 36 42 E
Longiram, Indonesia 36 E5 0 5S 115 45 E
Longkou, China 35 F11 37 40N 120 18 E
Longlac, Canada 70 C2 49 45N 86 25W
Longmeadow, U.S.A. 79 D12 42 3N 72 34W
Longmont, U.S.A. 80 E2 40 10N 105 6W
Longnawan, Indonesia 36 D4 1 51N 114 55 E
Longreach, Australia 62 C3 23 28S 144 14 E
Longueuil, Canada 79 A11 45 32N 73 28W
Longview, Tex., U.S.A. 81 J7 32 30N 94 44W
Longview, Wash., U.S.A. 84 D4 46 8N 122 57W
Longxi, China 34 G3 34 53N 104 40 E
Lonoke, U.S.A. 81 H9 34 47N 91 54W
Lonquimay, Chile 96 D2 38 26S 71 14W
Lons-le-Saunier, France 18 C6 46 40N 5 31 E
Looe, U.K. 11 G3 50 22N 4 28W
Lookout, C., Canada 70 A3 55 18N 83 56W
Lookout, C., U.S.A. 77 H7 34 35N 76 32W
Loolmalasin, Tanzania 54 C4 3 0S 35 53 E
Loon →, Alta., Canada 72 B5 57 8N 115 3W
Loon →, Man., Canada 73 B8 55 53N 101 59W
Loon Lake, Canada 73 C7 54 2N 109 10W
Loongana, Australia 61 F4 30 52S 127 5 E
Loop Hd., Ireland 13 D2 52 34N 9 56W
Lop Buri, Thailand 38 E3 14 48N 100 37 E
Lop Nor = Lop Nur, China 32 B4 40 20N 90 10 E
Lop Nur, China 32 B4 40 20N 90 10 E
Lopatina, Gora, Russia 27 D15 50 47N 143 10 E
Lopez, U.S.A. 79 E8 41 27N 76 20W
Lopez, C., Gabon 52 E1 0 47S 8 40 E
Lopphavet, Norway 8 A19 70 27N 21 15 E
Lora →, Afghan. 40 D4 31 35N 66 32 E
Lora, Hāmūn-i-, Pakistan 40 E4 29 38N 64 58 E
Lora Cr. →, Australia 63 D2 28 10S 135 22 E
Lora del Río, Spain 19 D3 37 39N 5 33W
Lorain, U.S.A. 78 E2 41 28N 82 11W
Loralai, Pakistan 42 D3 30 20N 68 41 E
Lorca, Spain 19 D5 37 41N 1 42W
Lord Howe I., Pac. Oc. 64 L7 31 33S 159 6 E
Lord Howe Ridge, Pac. Oc. 64 L8 30 0S 162 30 E
Lordsburg, U.S.A. 83 K9 32 21N 108 43W
Lorestan □, Iran 45 C6 33 30N 48 40 E
Loreto, Brazil 93 E9 7 5S 45 10W
Loreto, Mexico 86 B2 26 1N 111 21W
Lorient, France 18 C2 47 45N 3 23W
Lormi, India 43 H9 22 17N 81 41 E
Lorn, U.K. 12 E3 56 26N 5 10W
Lorn, Firth of, U.K. 12 E3 56 20N 5 40W
Lorne, Australia 63 F3 38 33S 143 59 E
Lorovouno, Cyprus 23 D11 35 8N 32 36 E
Lorraine □, France 18 B7 48 53N 6 0 E
Los Alamos, Calif., U.S.A. 85 L6 34 44N 120 17W
Los Alamos, N. Mex., U.S.A. 83 J10 35 53N 106 19W
Los Altos, U.S.A. 84 H4 37 23N 122 7W
Los Andes, Chile 94 C1 32 50S 70 40W
Los Angeles, Chile 94 D1 37 28S 72 23W
Los Angeles, U.S.A. 85 M8 34 4N 118 15W
Los Angeles, Bahia de, Mexico 86 B2 28 56N 113 34W
Los Angeles Aqueduct, U.S.A. 85 K9 35 22N 118 5W
Los Banos, U.S.A. 84 H6 37 4N 120 51W
Los Blancos, Argentina 94 A3 23 40S 62 30W
Los Chiles, Costa Rica 88 D3 11 2N 84 43W
Los Cristianos, Canary Is. 22 F3 28 3N 16 42W
Los Gatos, U.S.A. 84 H5 37 14N 121 59W
Los Hermanos Is., Venezuela 89 D7 11 45N 64 25W
Los Islotes, Canary Is. 22 E6 29 4N 13 44W
Los Llanos de Aridane, Canary Is. 22 F2 28 38N 17 54W
Los Loros, Chile 94 B1 27 50S 70 6W
Los Lunas, U.S.A. 83 J10 34 48N 106 44W
Los Mochis, Mexico 86 B3 25 45N 108 57W
Los Olivos, U.S.A. 85 L6 34 40N 120 7W
Los Palacios, Cuba 88 B3 22 35N 83 15W
Los Reyes, Mexico 86 D4 19 34N 102 30W
Los Roques Is., Venezuela 89 D6 11 50N 66 45W
Los Teques, Venezuela 92 A5 10 21N 67 2W
Los Testigos, Is., Venezuela 92 A6 11 23N 63 6W
Los Vilos, Chile 94 C1 32 10S 71 30W
Lošinj, Croatia 16 F8 44 30N 14 30 E
Loskop Dam, S. Africa 57 D4 25 23S 29 20 E
Lossiemouth, U.K. 12 D5 57 42N 3 17W
Lostwithiel, U.K. 11 G3 50 24N 4 41W
Lot →, France 18 D4 44 18N 0 20 E
Lota, Chile 94 D1 37 5S 73 10W
Lotfābād, Iran 45 B8 37 32N 59 20 E
Lothair, S. Africa 57 D5 26 22S 30 27 E
Loubomo, Congo 52 E2 4 9S 12 47 E
Loudonville, U.S.A. 78 F2 40 38N 82 14W
Louga, Senegal 50 E2 15 45N 16 5W
Loughborough, U.K. 10 E6 52 47N 1 11W
Loughrea, Ireland 13 C3 53 12N 8 33W
Loughros More B., Ireland 13 B3 54 48N 8 32W
Louis Trichardt, S. Africa 57 C4 23 1S 29 43 E
Louis XIV, Pte., Canada 70 B4 54 37N 79 45W
Louisa, U.S.A. 76 F4 38 7N 82 36W
Louisbourg, Canada 71 C8 45 55N 60 0W
Louise I., Canada 72 C2 52 55N 131 50W
Louiseville, Canada 70 C5 46 20N 72 56W
Louisiade Arch., Papua N. G. 64 J7 11 10S 153 0 E
Louisiana, U.S.A. 80 F9 39 27N 91 3W
Louisiana □, U.S.A. 81 K9 30 50N 92 0W
Louisville, Ky., U.S.A. 76 F3 38 15N 85 46W
Louisville, Miss., U.S.A. 81 J10 33 7N 89 3W
Louisville, Ohio, U.S.A. 78 F3 40 50N 81 16W
Loulé, Portugal 19 D1 37 9N 8 0W
Loup City, U.S.A. 80 E5 41 17N 98 58W
Loups Marins, Lacs des, Canada 70 A5 56 30N 73 45W
Lourdes, France 18 E3 43 6N 0 3W
Louth, Australia 63 E4 30 30S 145 8 E
Louth, Ireland 13 C5 53 58N 6 32W
Louth, U.K. 10 D7 53 22N 0 1W
Louth □, Ireland 13 C5 53 56N 6 34W
Louvain = Leuven, Belgium 15 D4 50 52N 4 42 E
Louwsburg, S. Africa 57 D5 27 37S 31 7 E
Lovech, Bulgaria 21 C11 43 8N 24 42 E
Loveland, U.S.A. 80 E2 40 24N 105 5W
Lovell, U.S.A. 82 D9 44 50N 108 24W
Lovelock, U.S.A. 82 F4 40 11N 118 28W
Loviisa, Finland 9 F22 60 28N 26 12 E
Loving, U.S.A. 81 J2 32 17N 104 6W
Lovington, U.S.A. 81 J3 32 57N 103 21W
Lovisa = Loviisa, Finland 9 F22 60 28N 26 12 E
Low, L., Canada 70 B4 52 29N 76 17W
Low Pt., Australia 61 F4 32 25S 127 25 E
Low Tatra = Nízké Tatry, Slovak Rep. 17 D10 48 55N 19 30 E
Lowa, Dem. Rep. of the Congo 54 C2 1 25S 25 47 E
Lowa →, Dem. Rep. of the Congo 54 C2 1 24S 25 51 E
Lowell, U.S.A. 79 D13 42 38N 71 19W
Lowellville, U.S.A. 78 E4 41 2N 80 32W
Löwen →, Namibia 56 D2 26 51S 18 17 E
Lower Alkali L., U.S.A. 82 F3 41 16N 120 2W
Lower Arrow L., Canada 72 D5 49 40N 118 5W
Lower California = Baja California, Mexico 86 A1 31 10N 115 12W
Lower Hutt, N.Z. 59 J5 41 10S 174 55 E
Lower Lake, U.S.A. 84 G4 38 55N 122 37W
Lower Manitou L., Canada 73 D10 49 15N 93 0W
Lower Post, Canada 72 B3 59 58N 128 30W
Lower Red L., U.S.A. 80 B7 47 58N 95 0W
Lower Saxony = Niedersachsen □, Germany 16 B5 52 50N 9 0 E
Lower Tunguska = Tunguska, Nizhnyaya →, Russia 27 C9 65 48N 88 4 E
Lowestoft, U.K. 11 E9 52 29N 1 45 E
Lowgar □, Afghan. 40 B6 34 0N 69 0 E
Łowicz, Poland 17 B10 52 6N 19 55 E
Lowville, U.S.A. 79 C9 43 47N 75 29W
Loxton, Australia 63 E3 34 28S 140 31 E
Loxton, S. Africa 56 E3 31 30S 22 22 E
Loyalton, U.S.A. 84 F6 39 41N 120 14W
Loyalty Is. = Loyauté, Îs., N. Cal. 64 K8 20 50S 166 30 E
Loyang = Luoyang, China 34 G7 34 40N 112 26 E
Loyauté, Îs., N. Cal. 64 K8 20 50S 166 30 E
Loyev = Loyew, Belarus 17 C16 51 56N 30 46 E
Loyew, Belarus 17 C16 51 56N 30 46 E
Loyoro, Uganda 54 B3 3 22N 34 14 E
Luachimo, Angola 52 F4 7 23S 20 48 E
Luajan →, India 43 G11 24 44N 85 1 E
Lualaba →, Dem. Rep. of the Congo 54 B2 0 26N 25 20 E
Luampa, Zambia 55 F1 15 4S 24 20 E
Luan Chau, Vietnam 38 B4 21 38N 103 24 E
Luan He →, China 35 E10 39 20N 119 5 E
Luan Xian, China 35 E10 39 40N 118 40 E
Luancheng, China 34 F8 37 53N 114 40 E
Luanda, Angola 52 F2 8 50S 13 15 E
Luang, Thale, Thailand 39 J3 7 30N 100 15 E
Luang Prabang, Laos 38 C4 19 52N 102 10 E
Luangwa, Zambia 55 F3 15 35S 30 16 E
Luangwa →, Zambia 55 E3 14 25S 30 25 E
Luangwa Valley, Zambia 55 E3 13 30S 31 30 E
Luanne, China 35 D9 40 55N 117 40 E
Luanping, China 35 D9 40 53N 117 23 E
Luanshya, Zambia 55 E2 13 3S 28 28 E
Luapula □, Zambia 55 E2 11 0S 29 0 E
Luapula →, Africa 55 D2 9 26S 28 33 E
Luarca, Spain 19 A2 43 32N 6 32W
Luashi, Dem. Rep. of the Congo 55 E1 10 50S 23 36 E
Luau, Angola 52 G4 10 40S 22 10 E
Lubana, Ozero = Lubānas Ezers, Latvia 9 H22 56 45N 27 0 E
Lubānas Ezers, Latvia 9 H22 56 45N 27 0 E
Lubang Is., Phil. 37 B6 13 50N 120 12 E
Lubao, Dem. Rep. of the Congo 54 D2 5 17S 25 42 E
Lubbock, U.S.A. 81 J4 33 35N 101 51W
Lübeck, Germany 16 B6 53 52N 10 40 E
Lubefu, Dem. Rep. of the Congo 54 C1 4 47S 24 27 E
Lubefu →, Dem. Rep. of the Congo 54 C1 4 10S 23 0 E
Lubero = Luofu, Dem. Rep. of the Congo 54 C2 0 10S 29 15 E
Lubicon L., Canada 72 B5 56 23N 115 56W
Lubilash →, Dem. Rep. of the Congo 52 F4 6 2S 23 45 E
Lubin, Poland 16 C9 51 24N 16 11 E
Lublin, Poland 17 C12 51 12N 22 38 E
Lubnān, Jabal, Lebanon 47 B4 33 45N 35 40 E
Lubny, Ukraine 26 D4 50 3N 32 58 E
Lubongola, Dem. Rep. of the Congo 54 C2 2 35S 27 50 E
Lubudi, Dem. Rep. of the Congo 52 F5 9 57S 25 58 E
Lubudi →, Dem. Rep. of the Congo 55 D2 9 0S 25 35 E
Lubuklinggau, Indonesia 36 E2 3 15S 102 55 E
Lubuksikaping, Indonesia 36 D2 0 10N 100 15 E
Lubumbashi, Dem. Rep. of the Congo 55 E2 11 40S 27 28 E
Lubunda, Dem. Rep. of the Congo 54 D2 5 12S 26 41 E
Lubungu, Zambia 55 E2 14 35S 26 24 E
Lubutu, Dem. Rep. of the Congo 54 C2 0 45S 26 30 E
Luc An Chau, Vietnam 38 A5 22 6N 104 43 E
Lucan, Canada 78 C3 43 11N 81 24W
Lucania, Mt., Canada 68 B5 61 1N 140 29W
Lucas Channel, Canada 78 A3 45 21N 81 45W
Lucca, Italy 20 C4 43 50N 10 29 E
Luce Bay, U.K. 12 G4 54 45N 4 48W
Lucea, Jamaica 88 C4 18 25N 78 10W
Lucedale, U.S.A. 77 K1 30 56N 88 35W
Lucena, Phil. 37 B6 13 56N 121 37 E
Lucena, Spain 19 D3 37 27N 4 31W
Lučenec, Slovak Rep. 17 D10 48 18N 19 42 E
Lucerne = Luzern, Switz. 18 C8 47 3N 8 18 E
Lucerne, U.S.A. 84 F4 39 6N 122 48W
Lucerne Valley, U.S.A. 85 L10 34 27N 116 57W
Lucero, Mexico 86 A3 30 49N 106 30W
Lucheng, China 34 F7 36 20N 113 11 E
Lucheringo →, Mozam. 55 E4 11 43S 36 17 E
Lucia, U.S.A. 84 J5 36 2N 121 33W
Lucinda, Australia 62 B4 18 32S 146 20 E
Luckenwalde, Germany 16 B7 52 5N 13 10 E
Luckhoff, S. Africa 56 D3 29 44S 24 43 E
Lucknow, Canada 78 C3 43 57N 81 31W
Lucknow, India 43 F9 26 50N 81 0 E
Lüda = Dalian, China 35 E11 38 50N 121 40 E
Lüderitz, Namibia 56 D2 26 41S 15 8 E
Lüderitzbaai, Namibia 56 D2 26 36S 15 8 E
Ludhiana, India 42 D6 30 57N 75 56 E
Ludington, U.S.A. 76 D2 43 57N 86 27W
Ludlow, U.K. 11 E5 52 22N 2 42W
Ludlow, Calif., U.S.A. 85 L10 34 43N 116 10W
Ludlow, Pa., U.S.A. 78 E6 41 43N 78 56W
Ludlow, Vt., U.S.A. 79 C12 43 24N 72 42W
Ludvika, Sweden 9 F16 60 8N 15 14 E
Ludwigsburg, Germany 16 D5 48 53N 9 11 E
Ludwigshafen, Germany 16 D5 49 29N 8 26 E
Lueki, Dem. Rep. of the Congo 54 C2 3 20S 25 48 E
Luena, Dem. Rep. of the Congo 55 D2 9 28S 25 43 E
Luena, Zambia 55 E3 10 40S 30 25 E
Lüeyang, China 34 H4 33 22N 106 10 E
Lufira →, Dem. Rep. of the Congo 55 D2 9 30S 27 0 E
Lufkin, U.S.A. 81 K7 31 21N 94 44W
Lufupa, Dem. Rep. of the Congo 55 E1 10 37S 24 56 E
Luga, Russia 24 C4 58 40N 29 55 E
Lugano, Switz. 18 C8 46 1N 8 57 E
Lugansk = Luhansk, Ukraine 25 E6 48 38N 39 15 E
Lugard's Falls, Kenya 54 C4 3 6S 38 41 E
Lugela, Mozam. 55 F4 16 25S 36 43 E
Lugenda →, Mozam. 55 E4 11 25S 38 33 E
Lugh Ganana, Somali Rep. 46 G3 3 48N 42 34 E
Lugnaquilla, Ireland 13 D5 52 58N 6 28W
Lugo, Italy 20 B4 44 25N 11 54 E
Lugo, Spain 19 A2 43 2N 7 35W
Lugoj, Romania 17 F11 45 42N 21 57 E
Lugovoy = Qulan, Kazakstan 26 E8 42 55N 72 43 E
Luhansk, Ukraine 25 E6 48 38N 39 15 E
Luiana, Angola 56 B3 17 25S 22 59 E
Luimneach = Limerick, Ireland 13 D3 52 40N 8 37W
Luing, U.K. 12 E3 56 14N 5 39W
Luis Correia, Brazil 93 D10 3 0S 41 35W
Luitpold Coast, Antarctica 5 D1 78 30S 32 0W
Luiza, Dem. Rep. of the Congo 52 F4 7 40S 22 30 E
Luizi, Dem. Rep. of the Congo 54 D2 6 0S 27 25 E
Luján, Argentina 94 C4 34 45S 59 5W
Lukanga Swamp, Zambia 55 E2 14 30S 27 40 E
Lukenie →, Dem. Rep. of the Congo 52 E3 3 0S 18 50 E
Lukhisaral, India 43 G12 25 11N 86 5 E
Lukolela, Dem. Rep. of the Congo 54 D1 5 23S 24 32 E
Lukosi, Zimbabwe 55 F2 18 30S 26 30 E
Łuków, Poland 17 C12 51 55N 22 23 E
Lule älv →, Sweden 8 D19 65 35N 22 10 E
Luleå, Sweden 8 D20 65 35N 22 10 E
Lüleburgaz, Turkey 21 D12 41 23N 27 22 E
Luling, U.S.A. 81 L6 29 41N 97 39W
Lulong, China 35 E10 39 53N 118 51 E
Lulonga →, Dem. Rep. of the Congo 52 D3 1 0N 18 10 E
Lulua →, Dem. Rep. of the Congo 52 E4 4 30S 20 30 E
Lumajang, Indonesia 37 H15 8 8S 113 13 E
Lumbala N'guimbo, Angola 53 G4 14 18S 21 18 E
Lumberton, U.S.A. 77 H6 34 37N 79 0W
Lumbwa, Kenya 54 C4 0 12S 35 28 E
Lumsden, Canada 73 C8 50 39N 104 52W
Lumsden, N.Z. 59 L2 45 44S 168 27 E
Lumut, Malaysia 39 K3 4 13N 100 37 E
Lumut, Tanjung, Indonesia 36 E3 3 50S 105 58 E
Luna, India 42 H3 23 43N 69 16 E
Lunavada, India 42 H5 23 8N 73 37 E
Lund, Sweden 9 J15 55 44N 13 12 E
Lundazi, Zambia 55 E3 12 20S 33 7 E
Lundi →, Zimbabwe 55 G3 21 43S 32 34 E
Lundu, Malaysia 36 D3 1 40N 109 50 E
Lundy, U.K. 11 F3 51 10N 4 41W
Lune →, U.K. 10 C5 54 0N 2 51W
Lüneburg, Germany 16 B6 53 15N 10 24 E
Lüneburg Heath = Lüneburger Heide, Germany 16 B6 53 10N 10 12 E
Lüneburger Heide, Germany 16 B6 53 10N 10 12 E
Lunenburg, Canada 71 D7 44 22N 64 18W
Lunéville, France 18 B7 48 36N 6 30 E
Lunga →, Zambia 55 E2 14 34S 26 25 E
Lunglei, India 41 H18 22 55N 92 45 E
Luni, India 42 G5 26 0N 73 6 E
Luni →, India 42 G4 24 41N 71 14 E
Luninets = Luninyets, Belarus 17 B14 52 15N 26 50 E
Luning, U.S.A. 82 G4 38 30N 118 11W
Luninyets, Belarus 17 B14 52 15N 26 50 E
Lunkaransar, India 42 E5 28 29N 73 44 E
Lunsemfwa →, Zambia 55 E3 14 54S 30 12 E
Lunsemfwa Falls, Zambia 55 E2 14 30S 29 6 E
Luo He →, China 34 G6 34 35N 110 20 E
Luochuan, China 34 G5 35 45N 109 26 E
Luofu, Dem. Rep. of the Congo 54 C2 0 10S 29 15 E
Luohe, China 34 H8 33 32N 114 2 E
Luonan, China 34 G6 34 5N 110 10 E
Luoning, China 34 G6 34 35N 111 40 E
Luoyang, China 34 G7 34 40N 112 26 E
Luozigou, China 35 C16 43 42N 130 18 E
Lupanshui, China 32 D5 26 38N 104 48 E
Lupilichi, Mozam. 55 E4 11 47S 35 13 E
Luque, Paraguay 94 B4 25 19S 57 25W
Luray, U.S.A. 76 F6 38 40N 78 28W
Lurgan, U.K. 13 B5 54 28N 6 19W
Lusaka, Zambia 55 F2 15 28S 28 16 E
Lusambo, Dem. Rep. of the Congo 54 C1 4 58S 23 28 E
Lusangaye, Dem. Rep. of the Congo 54 C2 4 54S 26 0 E
Luseland, Canada 73 C7 52 5N 109 24W
Lushan, China 34 H7 33 45N 112 55 E
Lushi, China 34 G6 34 3N 111 3 E
Lushnjë, Albania 21 D8 40 55N 19 41 E
Lushoto, Tanzania 54 C4 4 47S 38 20 E
Lüshun, China 35 E11 38 45N 121 15 E
Lusk, U.S.A. 80 D2 42 46N 104 27W
Lūt, Dasht-e, Iran 45 D8 31 30N 58 0 E
Luta = Dalian, China 35 E11 38 50N 121 40 E
Lutherstadt Wittenberg, Germany 16 C7 51 53N 12 39 E
Luton, U.K. 11 F7 51 53N 0 24W
Luton □, U.K. 11 F7 51 53N 0 24W
Lutselke, Canada 73 A6 62 24N 110 44W
Lutsk, Ukraine 17 C13 50 50N 25 15 E
Lützow Holmbukta, Antarctica 5 C4 69 10S 37 30 E
Lutzputs, S. Africa 56 D3 28 3S 20 40 E
Luuq = Lugh Ganana, Somali Rep. 46 G3 3 48N 42 34 E
Luverne, Ala., U.S.A. 77 K2 31 43N 86 16W
Luverne, Minn., U.S.A. 80 D6 43 39N 96 13W
Luvua, Dem. Rep. of the Congo 55 D2 8 48S 25 17 E
Luvua →, Dem. Rep. of the Congo 54 D2 6 50S 27 30 E
Luvuvhu →, S. Africa 57 C5 22 25S 31 18 E
Luwegu →, Tanzania 55 D4 8 31S 37 23 E
Luwuk, Indonesia 37 E6 0 56S 122 47 E
Luxembourg, Lux. 18 B7 49 37N 6 9 E
Luxembourg □, Belgium 15 E5 49 58N 5 30 E
Luxembourg ■, Europe 18 B7 49 45N 6 0 E
Luxi, China 32 D4 24 27N 98 36 E
Luxor = El Uqsur, Egypt 51 C12 25 41N 32 38 E
Luyi, China 34 H8 33 50N 115 35 E
Luza, Russia 24 B8 60 39N 47 10 E
Luzern, Switz. 18 C8 47 3N 8 18 E
Luzhou, China 32 D5 28 52N 105 20 E
Luziânia, Brazil 93 G9 16 20S 48 0W
Luzon, Phil. 37 A6 16 0N 121 0 E
Lviv, Ukraine 17 D13 49 50N 24 0 E
Lvov = Lviv, Ukraine 17 D13 49 50N 24 0 E
Lyakhavichy, Belarus 17 B14 53 2N 26 32 E
Lyakhovskiye, Ostrova, Russia 27 B15 73 40N 141 0 E
Lyal I., Canada 78 B3 44 57N 81 24W
Lyallpur = Faisalabad, Pakistan 42 D5 31 30N 73 5 E
Lybster, U.K. 12 C5 58 18N 3 15W
Lycksele, Sweden 8 D18 64 38N 18 40 E
Lydda = Lod, Israel 47 D3 31 57N 34 54 E
Lydenburg, S. Africa 57 D5 25 10S 30 29 E
Lydia, Turkey 21 E13 38 48N 28 19 E
Lyell, N.Z. 59 J4 41 48S 172 4 E
Lyell I., Canada 72 C2 52 40N 131 35W
Lyepyel, Belarus 24 D4 54 50N 28 40 E
Lykens, U.S.A. 79 F8 40 34N 76 42W
Lyman, U.S.A. 82 F8 41 20N 110 18W
Lyme B., U.K. 11 G4 50 42N 2 53W
Lyme Regis, U.K. 11 G5 50 43N 2 57W
Lymington, U.K. 11 G6 50 45N 1 32W
Łyna →, Poland 9 J19 54 37N 21 14 E
Lynchburg, U.S.A. 76 G6 37 25N 79 9W
Lynd →, Australia 62 B3 16 28S 143 18 E
Lynd Ra., Australia 63 D4 25 30S 149 20 E
Lynden, Canada 78 C4 43 14N 80 9W

Milford Haven, *U.K.* **11 F2** 51 42N 5 7W
Milford Sd., *N.Z.* **59 L1** 44 41S 167 47 E
Milḩ, Baḩr al, *Iraq* **44 C4** 32 40N 43 35 E
Milikapiti, *Australia* **60 B5** 11 26S 130 40 E
Miling, *Australia* **61 F2** 30 30S 116 17 E
Milk →, *U.S.A.* **82 B10** 48 4N 106 19W
Milk River, *Canada* **72 D6** 49 10N 112 5W
Mill I., *Antarctica* **5 C8** 66 0S 101 30 E
Mill Valley, *U.S.A.* **84 H4** 37 54N 122 32W
Millau, *France* **18 D5** 44 8N 3 4 E
Millbridge, *Canada* **78 B7** 44 41N 77 36W
Millbrook, *Canada* **78 B6** 44 10N 78 29W
Millbrook, *U.S.A.* **79 E11** 41 47N 73 42W
Mille Lacs, L. des, *Canada* **70 C1** 48 45N 90 35W
Mille Lacs L., *U.S.A.* **80 B8** 46 15N 93 39W
Milledgeville, *U.S.A.* **77 J4** 33 5N 83 14W
Millen, *U.S.A.* **77 J5** 32 48N 81 57W
Millennium I. = Caroline I., *Kiribati* **65 H12** 9 58S 150 13W
Miller, *U.S.A.* **80 C5** 44 31N 98 59W
Millersburg, *Ohio, U.S.A.* **78 F3** 40 33N 81 55W
Millersburg, *Pa., U.S.A.* **78 F8** 40 32N 76 58W
Millerton, *U.S.A.* **79 E11** 41 57N 73 31W
Millerton L., *U.S.A.* **84 J7** 37 1N 119 41W
Millheim, *U.S.A.* **78 F7** 40 54N 77 29W
Millicent, *Australia* **63 F3** 37 34S 140 21 E
Millington, *U.S.A.* **81 H10** 35 20N 89 53W
Millinocket, *U.S.A.* **77 C11** 45 39N 68 43W
Millmerran, *Australia* **63 D5** 27 53S 151 16 E
Millom, *U.K.* **10 C4** 54 13N 3 16W
Mills L., *Canada* **72 A5** 61 30N 118 20W
Millsboro, *U.S.A.* **78 G5** 40 0N 80 0W
Milltown Malbay, *Ireland* **13 D2** 52 52N 9 24W
Millville, *N.J., U.S.A.* **76 F8** 39 24N 75 2W
Millville, *Pa., U.S.A.* **79 E8** 41 7N 76 32W
Millwood L., *U.S.A.* **81 J8** 33 42N 93 58W
Milne →, *Australia* **62 C2** 21 10S 137 33 E
Milo, *U.S.A.* **77 C11** 45 15N 68 59W
Milos, *Greece* **21 F11** 36 44N 24 25 E
Milparinka, *Australia* **63 D3** 29 46S 141 57 E
Milton, *N.S., Canada* **71 D7** 44 4N 64 45W
Milton, *Ont., Canada* **78 C5** 43 31N 79 53W
Milton, *N.Z.* **59 M2** 46 7S 169 59 E
Milton, *Calif., U.S.A.* **84 G6** 38 3N 120 51W
Milton, *Fla., U.S.A.* **77 K2** 30 38N 87 3W
Milton, *Pa., U.S.A.* **78 F8** 41 1N 76 51W
Milton, *Vt., U.S.A.* **79 B11** 44 38N 73 7W
Milton-Freewater, *U.S.A.* **82 D4** 45 56N 118 23W
Milton Keynes, *U.K.* **11 E7** 52 1N 0 44W
Milton Keynes □, *U.K.* **11 E7** 52 1N 0 44W
Milverton, *Canada* **78 C4** 43 34N 80 55W
Milwaukee, *U.S.A.* **76 D2** 43 2N 87 55W
Milwaukee Deep, *Atl. Oc.* **89 C6** 19 50N 68 0W
Milwaukie, *U.S.A.* **84 E4** 45 27N 122 38W
Min Jiang →, *Fujian, China* **33 D6** 26 0N 119 35 E
Min Jiang →, *Sichuan, China* **32 D5** 28 45N 104 40 E
Min Xian, *China* **34 G3** 34 25N 104 5 E
Mina Pirquitas, *Argentina* **94 A2** 22 40S 66 30W
Mīnā Su'ud, *Si. Arabia* **45 D6** 28 45N 48 28 E
Mīnā'al Aḩmadī, *Kuwait* **45 D6** 29 5N 48 10 E
Minago →, *Canada* **73 C9** 54 33N 98 59W
Minaki, *Canada* **73 D10** 49 59N 94 40W
Minamata, *Japan* **31 H5** 32 10N 130 30 E
Minami-Tori-Shima, *Pac. Oc.* **64 E7** 24 20N 153 58 E
Minas, *Uruguay* **95 C4** 34 20S 55 10W
Minas, Sierra de las, *Guatemala* **88 C2** 15 9N 89 31W
Minas Basin, *Canada* **71 C7** 45 20N 64 12W
Minas Gerais □, *Brazil* **93 G9** 18 50S 46 0W
Minatitlán, *Mexico* **87 D6** 17 59N 94 31W
Minbu, *Burma* **41 J19** 20 10N 94 52 E
Minchinabad, *Pakistan* **42 D5** 30 10N 73 34 E
Mindanao, *Phil.* **37 C6** 8 0N 125 0 E
Mindanao Sea = Bohol Sea, *Phil.* **37 C6** 9 0N 124 0 E
Mindanao Trench, *Pac. Oc.* **37 B7** 12 0N 126 6 E
Minden, *Canada* **78 B6** 44 55N 78 43W
Minden, *Germany* **16 B5** 52 17N 8 55 E
Minden, *La., U.S.A.* **81 J8** 32 37N 93 17W
Minden, *Nev., U.S.A.* **84 G7** 38 57N 119 46W
Mindiptana, *Indonesia* **37 F10** 5 55S 140 22 E
Mindoro, *Phil.* **37 B6** 13 0N 121 0 E
Mindoro Str., *Phil.* **37 B6** 12 30N 120 30 E
Mine, *Japan* **31 G5** 34 12N 131 7 E
Minehead, *U.K.* **11 F4** 51 12N 3 29W
Mineola, *N.Y., U.S.A.* **79 F11** 40 45N 73 39W
Mineola, *Tex., U.S.A.* **81 J7** 32 40N 95 29W
Mineral King, *U.S.A.* **84 J8** 36 27N 118 36W
Mineral Wells, *U.S.A.* **81 J5** 32 48N 98 7W
Minersville, *U.S.A.* **79 F8** 40 41N 76 16W
Minerva, *U.S.A.* **78 F3** 40 44N 81 6W
Minetto, *U.S.A.* **79 C8** 43 24N 76 28W
Mingäçevir Su Anbarı, *Azerbaijan* **25 F8** 40 57N 46 50 E
Mingan, *Canada* **71 B7** 50 20N 64 0W
Mingechaurskoye Vdkhr. = Mingäçevir Su Anbarı, *Azerbaijan* **25 F8** 40 57N 46 50 E
Mingela, *Australia* **62 B4** 19 52S 146 38 E
Mingenew, *Australia* **61 E2** 29 12S 115 21 E
Mingera Cr. →, *Australia* **62 C2** 20 38S 137 45 E
Mingin, *Burma* **41 H19** 22 50N 94 30 E
Mingo Junction, *U.S.A.* **78 F4** 40 19N 80 37W
Mingteke Daban = Mintaka Pass, *Pakistan* **43 A6** 37 0N 74 58 E
Mingyuegue, *China* **35 C15** 43 2N 128 50 E
Minho = Miño →, *Spain* **19 A2** 41 52N 8 40W
Minho, *Portugal* **19 B1** 41 25N 8 20W
Minidoka, *U.S.A.* **82 E7** 42 45N 113 29W
Minigwal, L., *Australia* **61 E3** 29 31S 123 14 E
Minilya →, *Australia* **61 D1** 23 45S 114 0 E
Minilya Roadhouse, *Australia* **61 D1** 23 55S 114 0 E
Minipi L., *Canada* **71 B7** 52 25N 60 45W
Mink L., *Canada* **72 A5** 61 54N 117 40W
Minna, *Nigeria* **50 G7** 9 37N 6 30 E
Minneapolis, *Kans., U.S.A.* **80 F6** 39 8N 97 42W
Minneapolis, *Minn., U.S.A.* **80 C8** 44 59N 93 16W
Minnedosa, *Canada* **73 C9** 50 14N 99 50W
Minnesota □, *U.S.A.* **80 B8** 46 0N 94 15W
Minnesota →, *U.S.A.* **80 C8** 44 54N 93 9W
Minnewaukan, *U.S.A.* **80 A5** 48 4N 99 15W
Minnipa, *Australia* **63 E2** 32 51S 135 9 E
Minnitaki L., *Canada* **70 C1** 49 57N 92 10W
Mino, *Japan* **31 G8** 35 32N 136 55 E
Miño →, *Spain* **19 A2** 41 52N 8 40W
Minorca = Menorca, *Spain* **22 B11** 40 0N 4 0 E
Minot, *U.S.A.* **80 A4** 48 14N 101 18W
Minqin, *China* **34 E2** 38 38N 103 20 E
Minsk, *Belarus* **17 B14** 53 52N 27 30 E
Mińsk Mazowiecki, *Poland* **17 B11** 52 10N 21 33 E
Mintabie, *Australia* **63 D1** 27 15S 133 7 E
Mintaka Pass, *Pakistan* **43 A6** 37 0N 74 58 E
Minto, *Canada* **71 C6** 46 5N 66 5W
Minto, L., *Canada* **70 A5** 57 13N 75 0W
Minton, *Canada* **73 D8** 49 10N 104 35W
Minturn, *U.S.A.* **82 G10** 39 35N 106 26W
Minusinsk, *Russia* **27 D10** 53 43N 91 20 E
Minutang, *India* **41 E20** 28 15N 96 30 E
Miquelon, *Canada* **70 C4** 49 25N 76 27W
Miquelon, *St- P. & M.* **71 C8** 47 8N 56 22W
Mīr Kūh, *Iran* **45 E8** 26 22N 58 55 E
Mīr Shahdād, *Iran* **45 E8** 26 15N 58 29 E
Mira, *Italy* **20 B5** 45 26N 12 8 E
Mira por vos Cay, *Bahamas* **89 B5** 22 9N 74 30W
Miraj, *India* **40 L9** 16 50N 74 45 E
Miram Shah, *Pakistan* **42 C4** 33 0N 70 2 E
Miramar, *Argentina* **94 D4** 38 15S 57 50W
Miramar, *Mozam.* **57 C6** 23 50S 35 35 E
Miramichi, *Canada* **71 C6** 47 2N 65 28W
Miramichi B., *Canada* **71 C7** 47 15N 65 0W
Miranda, *Brazil* **93 H7** 20 10S 56 15W
Miranda →, *Brazil* **92 G7** 19 25S 57 20W
Miranda de Ebro, *Spain* **19 A4** 42 41N 2 57W
Miranda do Douro, *Portugal* **19 B2** 41 30N 6 16W
Mirandópolis, *Brazil* **95 A5** 21 9S 51 6W
Mirango, *Malawi* **55 E3** 13 32S 34 58 E
Mirassol, *Brazil* **95 A6** 20 46S 49 28W
Mirbāţ, *Oman* **46 D5** 17 0N 54 45 E
Miri, *Malaysia* **36 D4** 4 23N 113 59 E
Miriam Vale, *Australia* **62 C5** 24 20S 151 33 E
Mirim, L., *S. Amer.* **95 C5** 32 45S 52 50W
Mirnyy, *Russia* **27 C12** 62 33N 113 53 E
Mirokhan, *Pakistan* **42 F3** 27 46N 68 6 E
Mirond L., *Canada* **73 B8** 55 6N 102 47W
Mirpur, *Pakistan* **43 C5** 33 32N 73 56 E
Mirpur Batoro, *Pakistan* **42 G3** 24 44N 68 16 E
Mirpur Bibiwari, *Pakistan* **42 E2** 28 33N 67 44 E
Mirpur Khas, *Pakistan* **42 G3** 25 30N 69 0 E
Mirpur Sakro, *Pakistan* **42 G2** 24 33N 67 41 E
Mirtağ, *Turkey* **44 B4** 38 23N 41 56 E
Miryang, *S. Korea* **35 G15** 35 31N 128 44 E
Mirzapur, *India* **43 G10** 25 10N 82 34 E
Mirzapur-cum-Vindhyachal = Mirzapur, *India* **43 G10** 25 10N 82 34 E
Misantla, *Mexico* **87 D5** 19 56N 96 50W
Misawa, *Japan* **30 D10** 40 41N 141 24 E
Miscou I., *Canada* **71 C7** 47 57N 64 31W
Mish'āb, Ra's al, *Si. Arabia* **45 D6** 28 15N 48 43 E
Mishan, *China* **33 B8** 45 37N 131 48 E
Mishawaka, *U.S.A.* **76 E2** 41 40N 86 11W
Mishima, *Japan* **31 G9** 35 10N 138 52 E
Misión, *Mexico* **85 N10** 32 6N 116 53W
Misiones □, *Argentina* **95 B5** 27 0S 55 0W
Misiones □, *Paraguay* **94 B4** 27 0S 56 0W
Miskah, *Si. Arabia* **44 E4** 24 49N 42 56 E
Miskitos, Cayos, *Nic.* **88 D3** 14 26N 82 50W
Miskolc, *Hungary* **17 D11** 48 7N 20 50 E
Misoke, *Dem. Rep. of the Congo* **54 C2** 0 42S 28 2 E
Misool, *Indonesia* **37 E8** 1 52S 130 10 E
Mişrātah, *Libya* **51 B9** 32 24N 15 3 E
Missanabie, *Canada* **70 C3** 48 20N 84 6W
Missinaibi →, *Canada* **70 B3** 50 43N 81 29W
Missinaibi L., *Canada* **70 C3** 48 23N 83 40W
Mission, *Canada* **72 D4** 49 10N 122 15W
Mission, *S. Dak., U.S.A.* **80 D4** 43 18N 100 39W
Mission, *Tex., U.S.A.* **81 M5** 26 13N 98 20W
Mission Beach, *Australia* **62 B4** 17 53S 146 6 E
Mission Viejo, *U.S.A.* **85 M9** 33 36N 117 40W
Missisa L., *Canada* **70 B2** 52 20N 85 7W
Missisicabi →, *Canada* **70 B4** 51 14N 79 31W
Mississagi →, *Canada* **70 C3** 46 15N 83 9W
Mississauga, *Canada* **78 C5** 43 32N 79 35W
Mississippi □, *U.S.A.* **81 J10** 33 0N 90 0W
Mississippi →, *U.S.A.* **81 L10** 29 9N 89 15W
Mississippi L., *Canada* **79 A8** 45 5N 76 10W
Mississippi River Delta, *U.S.A.* **81 L9** 29 10N 89 15W
Mississippi Sd., *U.S.A.* **81 K10** 30 20N 89 0W
Missoula, *U.S.A.* **82 C7** 46 52N 114 1W
Missouri □, *U.S.A.* **80 F8** 38 25N 92 30W
Missouri →, *U.S.A.* **80 F9** 38 49N 90 7W
Missouri City, *U.S.A.* **81 L7** 29 37N 95 32W
Missouri Valley, *U.S.A.* **80 E7** 41 34N 95 53W
Mist, *U.S.A.* **84 E3** 45 59N 123 15W
Mistassibi →, *Canada* **71 B5** 48 53N 72 13W
Mistassini, *Canada* **71 C5** 48 53N 72 12W
Mistassini →, *Canada* **71 C5** 48 42N 72 20W
Mistassini, L., *Canada* **70 B5** 51 0N 73 30W
Mistastin L., *Canada* **71 A7** 55 57N 63 20W
Mistinibi, L., *Canada* **71 A7** 55 56N 64 17W
Misty L., *Canada* **73 B8** 58 53N 101 40W
Misurata = Mişrātah, *Libya* **51 B9** 32 24N 15 3 E
Mitchell, *Australia* **63 D4** 26 29S 147 58 E
Mitchell, *Canada* **78 C3** 43 28N 81 12W
Mitchell, *Nebr., U.S.A.* **80 E3** 41 57N 103 49W
Mitchell, *Oreg., U.S.A.* **82 D3** 44 34N 120 9W
Mitchell, *S. Dak., U.S.A.* **80 D6** 43 43N 98 2W
Mitchell →, *Australia* **62 B3** 15 12S 141 35 E
Mitchell, Mt., *U.S.A.* **77 H4** 35 46N 82 16W
Mitchell Ranges, *Australia* **62 A2** 12 49S 135 36 E
Mitchelstown, *Ireland* **13 D3** 52 15N 8 16W
Mitha Tiwana, *Pakistan* **42 C5** 32 13N 72 6 E
Mithi, *Pakistan* **42 G3** 24 44N 69 48 E
Mithrao, *Pakistan* **42 F3** 27 28N 69 40 E
Mitilíni, *Greece* **21 E12** 39 6N 26 35 E
Mito, *Japan* **31 F10** 36 20N 140 30 E
Mitrovica = Kosovska Mitrovica, *Kosovo, Yug.* **21 C9** 42 54N 20 52 E
Mitsinjo, *Madag.* **57 B8** 16 1S 45 52 E
Mitsiwa, *Eritrea* **46 D2** 15 35N 39 25 E
Mitsukaidō, *Japan* **31 F9** 36 1N 139 59 E
Mittagong, *Australia* **63 E5** 34 28S 150 29 E
Mittimatalik = Pond Inlet, *Canada* **69 A12** 72 40N 77 0W
Mitú, *Colombia* **92 C4** 1 15N 70 13W
Mitumba, *Tanzania* **54 D3** 7 8S 31 2 E
Mitumba, Mts., *Dem. Rep. of the Congo* **54 D2** 7 0S 27 30 E
Mitwaba, *Dem. Rep. of the Congo* **55 D2** 8 2S 27 17 E
Mityana, *Uganda* **54 B3** 0 23N 32 2 E
Mixteco →, *Mexico* **87 D5** 18 11N 98 30W
Miyagi □, *Japan* **30 E10** 38 15N 140 45 E
Miyāh, W. el →, *Syria* **44 C3** 34 44N 39 57 E
Miyake-Jima, *Japan* **31 G9** 34 5N 139 30 E
Miyako, *Japan* **30 E10** 39 40N 141 59 E
Miyako-Jima, *Japan* **31 M2** 24 45N 125 20 E
Miyako-Rettō, *Japan* **31 M2** 24 24N 125 0 E
Miyakonojō, *Japan* **31 J5** 31 40N 131 5 E
Miyani, *India* **42 J3** 21 50N 69 26 E
Miyanoura-Dake, *Japan* **31 J5** 30 20N 130 31 E
Miyazaki, *Japan* **31 J5** 31 56N 131 30 E
Miyazaki □, *Japan* **31 H5** 32 30N 131 30 E
Miyazu, *Japan* **31 G7** 35 35N 135 10 E
Miyet, Bahr el = Dead Sea, *Asia* **47 D4** 31 30N 35 30 E
Miyoshi, *Japan* **31 G6** 34 48N 132 51 E
Miyun, *China* **34 D9** 40 28N 116 50 E
Miyun Shuiku, *China* **35 D9** 40 30N 117 0 E
Mizdah, *Libya* **51 B8** 31 30N 13 0 E
Mizen Hd., *Cork, Ireland* **13 E2** 51 27N 9 50W
Mizen Hd., *Wick., Ireland* **13 D5** 52 51N 6 4W
Mizhi, *China* **34 F6** 37 47N 110 12 E
Mizoram □, *India* **41 H18** 23 30N 92 40 E
Mizpe Ramon, *Israel* **47 E3** 30 34N 34 49 E
Mizusawa, *Japan* **30 E10** 39 8N 141 8 E
Mjölby, *Sweden* **9 G16** 58 20N 15 10 E
Mjøsa, *Norway* **9 F14** 60 40N 11 0 E
Mkata, *Tanzania* **54 D4** 5 45S 38 20 E
Mkokotoni, *Tanzania* **54 D4** 5 55S 39 15 E
Mkomazi, *Tanzania* **54 C4** 4 40S 38 7 E
Mkomazi →, *S. Africa* **57 E5** 30 12S 30 50 E
Mkulwe, *Tanzania* **55 D3** 8 37S 32 20 E
Mkumbi, Ras, *Tanzania* **54 D4** 7 38S 39 55 E
Mkushi, *Zambia* **55 E2** 14 25S 29 15 E
Mkushi River, *Zambia* **55 E2** 13 32S 29 45 E
Mkuze, *S. Africa* **57 D5** 27 10S 32 0 E
Mladá Boleslav, *Czech Rep.* **16 C8** 50 27N 14 53 E
Mlala Hills, *Tanzania* **54 D3** 6 50S 31 40 E
Mlange = Mulanje, *Malawi* **55 F4** 16 2S 35 33 E
Mlanje, Pic, *Malawi* **53 H7** 15 57S 35 38 E
Mława, *Poland* **17 B11** 53 9N 20 25 E
Mljet, *Croatia* **20 C7** 42 43N 17 30 E
Mmabatho, *S. Africa* **56 D4** 25 49S 25 30 E
Mo i Rana, *Norway* **8 C16** 66 20N 14 7 E
Moa, *Cuba* **89 B4** 20 40N 74 56W
Moa, *Indonesia* **37 F7** 8 0S 128 0 E
Moab, *U.S.A.* **83 G9** 38 35N 109 33W
Moala, *Fiji* **59 D8** 18 36S 179 53 E
Moama, *Australia* **63 F3** 36 7S 144 46 E
Moamba, *Mozam.* **57 D5** 25 36S 32 15 E
Moapa, *U.S.A.* **85 J12** 36 40N 114 37W
Moate, *Ireland* **13 C4** 53 24N 7 44W
Moba, *Dem. Rep. of the Congo* **54 D2** 7 0S 29 48 E
Mobārakābād, *Iran* **45 D7** 28 24N 53 20 E
Mobaye, *C.A.R.* **52 D4** 4 25N 21 5 E
Mobayi, *Dem. Rep. of the Congo* **52 D4** 4 15N 21 8 E
Moberley Lake, *Canada* **72 B4** 55 50N 121 44W
Moberly, *U.S.A.* **80 F8** 39 25N 92 26W
Mobile, *U.S.A.* **77 K1** 30 41N 88 3W
Mobile B., *U.S.A.* **77 K2** 30 30N 88 0W
Mobridge, *U.S.A.* **80 C4** 45 32N 100 26W
Mobutu Sese Seko, L. = Albert, L., *Africa* **54 B3** 1 30N 31 0 E
Moc Chau, *Vietnam* **38 B5** 20 50N 104 38 E
Moc Hoa, *Vietnam* **39 G5** 10 46N 105 56 E
Mocabe Kasari, *Dem. Rep. of the Congo* **55 D2** 9 58S 26 12 E
Moçambique, *Mozam.* **55 F5** 15 3S 40 42 E
Moçâmedes = Namibe, *Angola* **53 H2** 15 7S 12 11 E
Mocanaqua, *U.S.A.* **79 E8** 41 9N 76 8W
Mochudi, *Botswana* **56 C4** 24 27S 26 7 E
Mocimboa da Praia, *Mozam.* **55 E5** 11 25S 40 20 E
Moclips, *U.S.A.* **84 C2** 47 14N 124 13W
Mocoa, *Colombia* **92 C3** 1 7N 76 35W
Mococa, *Brazil* **95 A6** 21 28S 47 0W
Mocorito, *Mexico* **86 B3** 25 30N 107 53W
Moctezuma, *Mexico* **86 B3** 29 50N 109 0W
Moctezuma →, *Mexico* **87 C5** 21 59N 98 34W
Mocuba, *Mozam.* **55 F4** 16 54S 36 57 E
Mocúzari, Presa, *Mexico* **86 B3** 27 10N 109 10W
Modane, *France* **18 D7** 45 12N 6 40 E
Modasa, *India* **42 H5** 23 30N 73 21 E
Modder →, *S. Africa* **56 D3** 29 2S 24 37 E
Modderrivier, *S. Africa* **56 D3** 29 2S 24 38 E
Módena, *Italy* **20 B4** 44 40N 10 55 E
Modena, *U.S.A.* **83 H7** 37 48N 113 56W
Modesto, *U.S.A.* **84 H6** 37 39N 121 0W
Módica, *Italy* **20 F6** 36 52N 14 46 E
Moe, *Australia* **63 F4** 38 12S 146 19 E
Moebase, *Mozam.* **55 F4** 17 3S 38 41 E
Moengo, *Surinam* **93 B8** 5 45N 54 20W
Moffat, *U.K.* **12 F5** 55 21N 3 27W
Moga, *India* **42 D6** 30 48N 75 8 E
Mogadishu = Muqdisho, *Somali Rep.* **46 G4** 2 2N 45 25 E
Mogador = Essaouira, *Morocco* **50 B4** 31 32N 9 42W
Mogalakwena →, *S. Africa* **57 C4** 22 38S 28 40 E
Mogami-Gawa →, *Japan* **30 E10** 38 45N 140 0 E
Mogán, *Canary Is.* **22 G4** 27 53N 15 43W
Mogaung, *Burma* **41 G20** 25 20N 97 0 E
Mogi das Cruzes, *Brazil* **95 A6** 23 31S 46 11W
Mogi-Guaçu →, *Brazil* **95 A6** 20 53S 48 10W
Mogi-Mirim, *Brazil* **95 A6** 22 29S 47 0W
Mogilev = Mahilyow, *Belarus* **17 B16** 53 55N 30 18 E
Mogilev-Podolskiy = Mohyliv-Podilskyy, *Ukraine* **17 D14** 48 26N 27 48 E
Mogincual, *Mozam.* **55 F5** 15 35S 40 25 E
Mogocha, *Russia* **27 D12** 53 40N 119 50 E
Mogok, *Burma* **41 H20** 23 0N 96 40 E
Mogollon Rim, *U.S.A.* **83 J8** 34 10N 110 50W
Mogumber, *Australia* **61 F2** 31 2S 116 3 E
Mohács, *Hungary* **17 F10** 45 58N 18 41 E
Mohales Hoek, *Lesotho* **56 E4** 30 7S 27 26 E
Mohall, *U.S.A.* **80 A4** 48 46N 101 31W
Moḩammadābād, *Iran* **45 B8** 37 52N 59 5 E
Mohammedia, *Morocco* **50 B4** 33 44N 7 21W
Mohana →, *India* **43 G11** 24 43N 85 0 E
Mohanlalganj, *India* **43 F9** 26 41N 80 58 E
Mohave, L., *U.S.A.* **85 K12** 35 12N 114 34W
Mohawk →, *U.S.A.* **79 D11** 42 47N 73 41W
Mohenjodaro, *Pakistan* **42 F3** 27 19N 68 7 E
Mohicanville Reservoir, *U.S.A.* **78 F3** 40 45N 82 0W
Mohoro, *Tanzania* **54 D4** 8 6S 39 8 E
Mohyliv-Podilskyy, *Ukraine* **17 D14** 48 26N 27 48 E
Moidart, L., *U.K.* **12 E3** 56 47N 5 52W
Moira →, *Canada* **78 B7** 44 21N 77 24W
Moires, *Greece* **23 D6** 35 4N 24 56 E
Moisaküla, *Estonia* **9 G21** 58 3N 25 12 E
Moisie, *Canada* **71 B6** 50 12N 66 1W
Moisie →, *Canada* **71 B6** 50 14N 66 5W
Mojave, *U.S.A.* **85 K8** 35 3N 118 10W
Mojave Desert, *U.S.A.* **85 L10** 35 0N 116 30W
Mojo, *Bolivia* **94 A2** 21 48S 65 33W
Mojokerto, *Indonesia* **37 G15** 7 28S 112 26 E
Mokai, *N.Z.* **59 H5** 38 32S 175 56 E
Mokambo, *Dem. Rep. of the Congo* **55 E2** 12 25S 28 20 E
Mokameh, *India* **43 G11** 25 24N 85 55 E
Mokau, *N.Z.* **59 H5** 38 42S 174 39 E
Mokelumne →, *U.S.A.* **84 G5** 38 13N 121 28W
Mokelumne Hill, *U.S.A.* **84 G6** 38 18N 120 43W
Mokhós, *Greece* **23 D7** 35 16N 25 27 E
Mokhotlong, *Lesotho* **57 D4** 29 22S 29 2 E
Mokokchung, *India* **41 F19** 26 15N 94 30 E
Mokolo →, *S. Africa* **57 C4** 23 14S 27 43 E
Mokp'o, *S. Korea* **35 G14** 34 50N 126 25 E
Mokra Gora, *Yugoslavia* **21 C9** 42 50N 20 30 E
Mol, *Belgium* **15 C5** 51 11N 5 5 E
Molchanovo, *Russia* **26 D9** 57 40N 83 50 E
Mold, *U.K.* **10 D4** 53 9N 3 8W
Moldavia = Moldova ■, *Europe* **17 E15** 47 0N 28 0 E
Molde, *Norway* **8 E12** 62 45N 7 9 E
Moldova ■, *Europe* **17 E15** 47 0N 28 0 E
Moldoveanu, Vf., *Romania* **17 F13** 45 36N 24 45 E
Mole →, *U.K.* **11 F7** 51 24N 0 21W
Mole Creek, *Australia* **62 G4** 41 34S 146 24 E
Molepolole, *Botswana* **56 C4** 24 28S 25 28 E
Molfetta, *Italy* **20 D7** 41 12N 16 36 E
Moline, *U.S.A.* **80 E9** 41 30N 90 31W
Molinos, *Argentina* **94 B2** 25 28S 66 15W
Moliro, *Dem. Rep. of the Congo* **54 D3** 8 12S 30 30 E
Mollendo, *Peru* **92 G4** 17 0S 72 0W
Mollerin, L., *Australia* **61 F2** 30 30S 117 35 E
Molodechno = Maladzyechna, *Belarus* **17 A14** 54 20N 26 50 E
Molokai, *U.S.A.* **74 H16** 21 8N 157 0W
Molong, *Australia* **63 E4** 33 5S 148 54 E
Molopo →, *Africa* **56 D3** 27 30S 20 13 E
Molotov = Perm, *Russia* **24 C10** 58 0N 56 10 E
Molson L., *Canada* **73 C9** 54 22N 96 40W
Molteno, *S. Africa* **56 E4** 31 22S 26 22 E
Molu, *Indonesia* **37 F8** 6 45S 131 40 E
Molucca Sea, *Indonesia* **37 E6** 0 0 125 0 E
Moluccas = Maluku, *Indonesia* **37 E7** 1 0S 127 0 E
Moma, *Dem. Rep. of the Congo* **54 C1** 1 35S 23 52 E
Moma, *Mozam.* **55 F4** 16 47S 39 4 E
Mombasa, *Kenya* **54 C4** 4 2S 39 43 E
Mombetsu, *Japan* **30 B11** 44 21N 143 22 E
Momchilgrad, *Bulgaria* **21 D11** 41 33N 25 23 E
Momi, *Dem. Rep. of the Congo* **54 C2** 1 42S 27 0 E
Mompós, *Colombia* **92 B4** 9 14N 74 26W
Møn, *Denmark* **9 J15** 54 57N 12 20 E
Mon □, *Burma* **41 L20** 16 0N 97 30 E
Mona, Canal de la, *W. Indies* **89 C6** 18 30N 67 45W
Mona, Isla, *Puerto Rico* **89 C6** 18 5N 67 54W
Mona, Pta., *Costa Rica* **88 E3** 9 37N 82 36W
Monaca, *U.S.A.* **78 F4** 40 41N 80 17W
Monaco ■, *Europe* **18 E7** 43 46N 7 23 E
Monadhliath Mts., *U.K.* **12 D4** 57 10N 4 4W
Monadnock, Mt., *U.S.A.* **79 D12** 42 52N 72 7W
Monaghan, *Ireland* **13 B5** 54 15N 6 57W
Monaghan □, *Ireland* **13 B5** 54 11N 6 56W
Monahans, *U.S.A.* **81 K3** 31 36N 102 54W
Monapo, *Mozam.* **55 E5** 14 56S 40 19 E
Monar, L., *U.K.* **12 D3** 57 26N 5 8W
Monarch Mt., *Canada* **72 C3** 51 55N 125 57W
Monashee Mts., *Canada* **72 C5** 51 0N 118 43W
Monasterevin, *Ireland* **13 C4** 53 8N 7 4W
Monastir = Bitola, *Macedonia* **21 D9** 41 1N 21 20 E
Moncayo, Sierra del, *Spain* **19 B5** 41 48N 1 50W
Monchegorsk, *Russia* **24 A5** 67 54N 32 58 E
Mönchengladbach, *Germany* **16 C4** 51 11N 6 27 E
Monchique, *Portugal* **19 D1** 37 19N 8 38W
Moncks Corner, *U.S.A.* **77 J5** 33 12N 80 1W
Monclova, *Mexico* **86 B4** 26 50N 101 30W
Moncton, *Canada* **71 C7** 46 7N 64 51W
Mondego →, *Portugal* **19 B1** 40 9N 8 52W
Mondeodo, *Indonesia* **37 E6** 3 34S 122 9 E
Mondovì, *Italy* **18 D7** 44 23N 7 49 E
Mondrain I., *Australia* **61 F3** 34 9S 122 14 E
Monessen, *U.S.A.* **78 F5** 40 9N 79 54W
Monett, *U.S.A.* **81 G8** 36 55N 93 55W
Moneymore, *U.K.* **13 B5** 54 41N 6 40W
Monforte de Lemos, *Spain* **19 A2** 42 31N 7 33W
Möng Hsu, *Burma* **41 J21** 21 54N 98 30 E
Mong Kung, *Burma* **41 J20** 21 35N 97 35 E
Mong Nai, *Burma* **41 J20** 20 32N 97 46 E
Mong Pawk, *Burma* **41 H21** 22 4N 99 16 E
Mong Ton, *Burma* **41 J21** 20 17N 98 45 E
Mong Wa, *Burma* **41 J22** 21 26N 100 27 E
Mong Yai, *Burma* **41 H21** 22 21N 98 3 E
Mongalla, *Sudan* **51 G12** 5 8N 31 42 E
Mongers, L., *Australia* **61 E2** 29 25S 117 5 E
Monghyr = Munger, *India* **43 G12** 25 23N 86 30 E
Mongibello = Etna, *Italy* **20 F6** 37 50N 14 55 E
Mongo, *Chad* **51 F9** 12 14N 18 43 E
Mongolia ■, *Asia* **27 E10** 47 0N 103 0 E
Mongu, *Zambia* **53 H4** 15 16S 23 12 E
Môngua, *Angola* **56 B2** 16 43S 15 20 E
Monifieth, *U.K.* **12 E6** 56 30N 2 48W
Monkey Bay, *Malawi* **55 E4** 14 7S 35 1 E
Monkey Mia, *Australia* **61 E1** 25 48S 113 43 E
Monkey River, *Belize* **87 D7** 16 22N 88 29W
Monkoto, *Dem. Rep. of the Congo* **52 E4** 1 38S 20 35 E
Monkton, *Canada* **78 C3** 43 35N 81 5W
Monmouth, *U.K.* **11 F5** 51 48N 2 42W
Monmouth, *Ill., U.S.A.* **80 E9** 40 55N 90 39W
Monmouth, *Oreg., U.S.A.* **82 D2** 44 51N 123 14W
Monmouthshire □, *U.K.* **11 F5** 51 48N 2 54W
Mono L., *U.S.A.* **84 H7** 38 1N 119 1W

Mtama, *Tanzania* 55 E4 10 17S 39 21 E
Mtamvuna →, *S. Africa* 57 E5 31 6S 30 12 E
Mtilikwe →, *Zimbabwe* 55 G3 21 9S 31 30 E
Mtubatuba, *S. Africa* 57 D5 28 30S 32 8 E
Mtwalume, *S. Africa* 57 E5 30 30S 30 38 E
Mtwara-Mikindani, *Tanzania* 55 E5 10 20S 40 20 E
Mu Gia, Deo, *Vietnam* 38 D5 17 40N 105 47 E
Mu Us Shamo, *China* 34 E5 39 0N 109 0 E
Muang Chiang Rai = Chiang Rai, *Thailand* 38 C2 19 52N 99 50 E
Muang Khong, *Laos* 38 E5 14 7N 105 51 E
Muang Lamphun, *Thailand* 38 C2 18 40N 99 2 E
Muang Pak Beng, *Laos* 38 C3 19 54N 101 8 E
Muar, *Malaysia* 39 L4 2 3N 102 34 E
Muarabungo, *Indonesia* 36 E2 1 28S 102 52 E
Muaraenim, *Indonesia* 36 E2 3 40S 103 50 E
Muarajuloi, *Indonesia* 36 E4 0 12S 114 3 E
Muarakaman, *Indonesia* 36 E5 0 2S 116 45 E
Muaratebo, *Indonesia* 36 E2 1 30S 102 26 E
Muaratembesi, *Indonesia* 36 E2 1 42S 103 8 E
Muaratewe, *Indonesia* 36 E4 0 58S 114 52 E
Mubarakpur, *India* 43 F10 26 6N 83 18 E
Mubarraz = Al Mubarraz, *Si. Arabia* 45 E6 25 30N 49 40 E
Mubende, *Uganda* 54 B3 0 33N 31 22 E
Mubi, *Nigeria* 51 F8 10 18N 13 16 E
Mubur, Pulau, *Indonesia* 39 L6 3 20N 106 12 E
Mucajaí →, *Brazil* 92 C6 2 25N 60 52W
Muchachos, Roque de los, *Canary Is.* 22 F2 28 44N 17 52W
Muchinga Mts., *Zambia* 55 E3 11 30S 31 30 E
Muck, *U.K.* 12 E2 56 50N 6 15W
Muckadilla, *Australia* 63 D4 26 35S 148 23 E
Mucuri, *Brazil* 93 G11 18 0S 39 36W
Mucusso, *Angola* 56 B3 18 1S 21 25 E
Muda, *Canary Is.* 22 F6 28 34N 13 57W
Mudanjiang, *China* 35 B15 44 38N 129 30 E
Mudanya, *Turkey* 21 D13 40 25N 28 50 E
Muddy Cr. →, *U.S.A.* 83 H8 38 24N 110 42W
Mudgee, *Australia* 63 E4 32 32S 149 31 E
Mudjatik →, *Canada* 73 B7 56 1N 107 36W
Muecate, *Mozam.* 55 E4 14 55S 39 40 E
Mueda, *Mozam.* 55 E4 11 36S 39 28 E
Mueller Ra., *Australia* 60 C4 18 18S 126 46 E
Muende, *Mozam.* 55 E3 14 28S 33 0 E
Muerto, Mar, *Mexico* 87 D6 16 10N 94 10W
Mufulira, *Zambia* 55 E2 12 32S 28 15 E
Mufumbiro Range, *Africa* 54 C2 1 25S 29 30 E
Mughal Sarai, *India* 43 G10 25 18N 83 7 E
Mughayrā', *Si. Arabia* 44 D3 29 17N 37 41 E
Mugi, *Japan* 31 H7 33 40N 134 25 E
Mugila, Mts., *Dem. Rep. of the Congo* 54 D2 7 0S 28 50 E
Muğla, *Turkey* 21 F13 37 15N 28 22 E
Mugu, *Nepal* 43 E10 29 45N 82 30 E
Muhammad, Râs, *Egypt* 44 E2 27 44N 34 16 E
Muhammad Qol, *Sudan* 51 D13 20 53N 37 9 E
Muhammadabad, *India* 43 F10 26 4N 83 25 E
Muhesi →, *Tanzania* 54 D4 7 0S 35 20 E
Mühlhausen, *Germany* 16 C6 51 12N 10 27 E
Mühlig Hofmann fjell, *Antarctica* 5 D3 72 30S 5 0 E
Muhos, *Finland* 8 D22 64 47N 25 59 E
Muhu, *Estonia* 9 G20 58 36N 23 11 E
Muhutwe, *Tanzania* 54 C3 1 35S 31 45 E
Muine Bheag, *Ireland* 13 D5 52 42N 6 58W
Muir, L., *Australia* 61 F2 34 30S 116 40 E
Mujnak = Muynak, *Uzbekistan* 26 E6 43 44N 59 10 E
Mukacheve, *Ukraine* 17 D12 48 27N 22 45 E
Mukachevo = Mukacheve, *Ukraine* 17 D12 48 27N 22 45 E
Mukah, *Malaysia* 36 D4 2 55N 112 5 E
Mukandwara, *India* 42 G6 24 49N 75 59 E
Mukdahan, *Thailand* 38 D5 16 32N 104 43 E
Mukden = Shenyang, *China* 35 D12 41 48N 123 27 E
Mukerian, *India* 42 D6 31 57N 75 37 E
Mukhtuya = Lensk, *Russia* 27 C12 60 48N 114 55 E
Mukinbudin, *Australia* 61 F2 30 55S 118 5 E
Mukishi, *Dem. Rep. of the Congo* 55 D1 8 30S 24 44 E
Mukomuko, *Indonesia* 36 E2 2 30S 101 10 E
Mukomwenze, *Dem. Rep. of the Congo* 54 D2 6 49S 27 15 E
Muktsar, *India* 42 D6 30 30N 74 30 E
Mukur = Moqor, *Afghan.* 42 C2 32 50N 67 42 E
Mukutawa →, *Canada* 73 C9 53 10N 97 24W
Mukwela, *Zambia* 55 F2 17 0S 26 40 E
Mula, *Spain* 19 C5 38 3N 1 33W
Mula →, *Pakistan* 42 F2 27 57N 67 36 E
Mulange, *Dem. Rep. of the Congo* 54 C2 3 40S 27 10 E
Mulanje, *Malawi* 55 F4 16 2S 35 33 E
Mulchén, *Chile* 94 D1 37 45S 72 20W
Mulde →, *Germany* 16 C7 51 53N 12 15 E
Mule Creek Junction, *U.S.A.* 80 D2 43 19N 104 8W
Muleba, *Tanzania* 54 C3 1 50S 31 37 E
Mulejé, *Mexico* 86 B2 26 53N 112 1W
Muleshoe, *U.S.A.* 81 H3 34 13N 102 43W
Mulgrave, *Canada* 71 C7 45 38N 61 31W
Mulhacén, *Spain* 19 D4 37 4N 3 20W
Mülheim, *Germany* 33 C6 51 25N 6 54 E
Mulhouse, *France* 18 C7 47 40N 7 20 E
Muling, *China* 35 B16 44 35N 130 10 E
Mull, *U.K.* 12 E3 56 25N 5 56W
Mull, Sound of, *U.K.* 12 E3 56 30N 5 50W
Mullaittivu, *Sri Lanka* 40 Q12 9 15N 80 49 E
Mullen, *U.S.A.* 80 D4 42 3N 101 1W
Mullens, *U.S.A.* 76 G5 37 35N 81 23W
Muller, Pegunungan, *Indonesia* 36 D4 0 30N 113 30 E
Mullet Pen., *Ireland* 13 B1 54 13N 10 2W
Mullewa, *Australia* 61 E2 28 29S 115 30 E
Mulligan →, *Australia* 62 D2 25 0S 139 0 E
Mullingar, *Ireland* 13 C4 53 31N 7 21W
Mullins, *U.S.A.* 77 H6 34 12N 79 15W
Mullumbimby, *Australia* 63 D5 28 30S 153 30 E
Mulobezi, *Zambia* 55 F2 16 45S 25 7 E
Mulroy B., *Ireland* 13 A4 55 15N 7 46W
Multan, *Pakistan* 42 D4 30 15N 71 36 E
Mulumbe, Mts., *Dem. Rep. of the Congo* 55 D2 8 40S 27 30 E
Mulungushi Dam, *Zambia* 55 E2 14 48S 28 48 E
Mulvane, *U.S.A.* 81 G6 37 29N 97 15W
Mumbai, *India* 40 K8 18 55N 72 50 E
Mumbwa, *Zambia* 55 F2 15 0S 27 0 E
Mun →, *Thailand* 38 E5 15 19N 105 30 E
Muna, *Indonesia* 37 F6 5 0S 122 30 E
Munabao, *India* 42 G4 25 45N 70 17 E
Munamagi, *Estonia* 9 H22 57 43N 27 4 E
München, *Germany* 16 D6 48 8N 11 34 E
Munchen-Gladbach = Mönchengladbach, *Germany* 16 C4 51 11N 6 27 E
Muncho Lake, *Canada* 72 B3 59 0N 125 50W
Munch'ŏn, *N. Korea* 35 E14 39 14N 127 19 E
Muncie, *U.S.A.* 76 E3 40 12N 85 23W
Muncoonie, L., *Australia* 62 D2 25 12S 138 40 E
Mundabbera, *Australia* 63 D5 25 36S 151 18 E
Munday, *U.S.A.* 81 J5 33 27N 99 38W
Münden, *Germany* 16 C5 51 25N 9 38 E
Mundiwindi, *Australia* 60 D3 23 47S 120 9 E
Mundo Novo, *Brazil* 93 F10 11 50S 40 29W
Mundra, *India* 42 H3 22 54N 69 48 E
Mundrabilla, *Australia* 61 F4 31 52S 127 51 E
Mungallala, *Australia* 63 D4 26 28S 147 34 E
Mungallala Cr. →, *Australia* 63 D4 28 53S 147 5 E
Mungana, *Australia* 62 B3 17 8S 144 27 E
Mungaoli, *India* 42 G8 24 24N 78 7 E
Mungari, *Mozam.* 55 F3 17 12S 33 30 E
Mungbere, *Dem. Rep. of the Congo* 54 B2 2 36N 28 28 E
Mungeli, *India* 43 H9 22 4N 81 41 E
Munger, *India* 43 G12 25 23N 86 30 E
Munich = München, *Germany* 16 D6 48 8N 11 34 E
Munising, *U.S.A.* 76 B2 46 25N 86 40W
Munku-Sardyk, *Russia* 27 D11 51 45N 100 20 E
Muñoz Gamero, Pen., *Chile* 96 G2 52 30S 73 5W
Munroe L., *Canada* 73 B9 59 13N 98 35W
Munsan, *S. Korea* 35 F14 37 51N 126 48 E
Münster, *Germany* 16 C4 51 58N 7 37 E
Munster □, *Ireland* 13 D3 52 18N 8 44W
Muntadgin, *Australia* 61 F2 31 45S 118 33 E
Muntok, *Indonesia* 36 E3 2 5S 105 10 E
Munyama, *Zambia* 55 F2 16 5S 28 31 E
Muong Beng, *Laos* 38 B3 20 23N 101 46 E
Muong Boum, *Vietnam* 38 A4 22 24N 102 49 E
Muong Et, *Laos* 38 B5 20 49N 104 1 E
Muong Hai, *Laos* 38 B3 21 3N 101 49 E
Muong Hiem, *Laos* 38 B4 20 5N 103 22 E
Muong Houn, *Laos* 38 B3 20 8N 101 23 E
Muong Hung, *Vietnam* 38 B4 20 56N 103 53 E
Muong Kau, *Laos* 38 E5 15 6N 105 47 E
Muong Khao, *Laos* 38 C4 19 38N 103 32 E
Muong Khoua, *Laos* 38 B4 21 5N 102 31 E
Muong Liep, *Laos* 38 C3 18 29N 101 40 E
Muong May, *Laos* 38 E6 14 49N 106 56 E
Muong Ngeun, *Laos* 38 B3 20 36N 101 3 E
Muong Ngoi, *Laos* 38 B4 20 43N 102 41 E
Muong Nhie, *Vietnam* 38 A4 22 12N 102 28 E
Muong Nong, *Laos* 38 D6 16 22N 106 30 E
Muong Ou Tay, *Laos* 38 A3 22 7N 101 48 E
Muong Oua, *Laos* 38 C3 18 18N 101 20 E
Muong Peun, *Laos* 38 B4 20 13N 103 52 E
Muong Phalane, *Laos* 38 D5 16 39N 105 34 E
Muong Phieng, *Laos* 38 C3 19 6N 101 32 E
Muong Phine, *Laos* 38 D6 16 32N 106 2 E
Muong Sai, *Laos* 38 B3 20 42N 101 59 E
Muong Saiapoun, *Laos* 38 C3 18 24N 101 31 E
Muong Sen, *Vietnam* 38 C5 19 24N 104 8 E
Muong Sing, *Laos* 38 B3 21 11N 101 9 E
Muong Son, *Laos* 38 B4 20 27N 103 19 E
Muong Soui, *Laos* 38 C4 19 33N 102 52 E
Muong Va, *Laos* 38 B4 21 53N 102 19 E
Muong Xia, *Vietnam* 38 B5 20 19N 104 50 E
Muonio, *Finland* 8 C20 67 57N 23 40 E
Muonionjoki →, *Finland* 8 C20 67 11N 23 34 E
Muping, *China* 35 F11 37 22N 121 36 E
Muqdisho, *Somali Rep.* 46 G4 2 2N 45 25 E
Mur →, *Austria* 17 E9 46 18N 16 52 E
Murakami, *Japan* 30 E9 38 14N 139 29 E
Murallón, Cerro, *Chile* 96 F2 49 48S 73 30W
Muranda, *Rwanda* 54 C2 1 52S 29 20 E
Murang'a, *Kenya* 54 C4 0 45S 37 9 E
Murashi, *Russia* 24 C8 59 30N 49 0 E
Murat →, *Turkey* 25 G7 38 46N 40 0 E
Muratlı, *Turkey* 21 D12 41 10N 27 29 E
Murayama, *Japan* 30 E10 38 30N 140 25 E
Murchison →, *Australia* 61 E1 27 45S 114 0 E
Murchison, Mt., *Antarctica* 5 D11 73 0S 168 0 E
Murchison Falls, *Uganda* 54 B3 2 15N 31 30 E
Murchison Ra., *Australia* 62 C1 20 0S 134 10 E
Murchison Rapids, *Malawi* 55 F3 15 55S 34 35 E
Murcia, *Spain* 19 D5 38 5N 1 10W
Murcia □, *Spain* 19 D5 37 50N 1 30W
Murdo, *U.S.A.* 80 D4 43 53N 100 43W
Murdoch Pt., *Australia* 62 A3 14 37S 144 55 E
Mureş →, *Romania* 17 E11 46 15N 20 13 E
Mureşul = Mureş →, *Romania* 17 E11 46 15N 20 13 E
Murewa, *Zimbabwe* 57 B5 17 39S 31 47 E
Murfreesboro, *N.C., U.S.A.* 77 G7 36 27N 77 6W
Murfreesboro, *Tenn., U.S.A.* 77 H2 35 51N 86 24W
Murgab = Murghob, *Tajikistan* 26 F8 38 10N 74 2 E
Murgab →, *Turkmenistan* 45 B9 38 18N 61 12 E
Murgenella, *Australia* 60 B5 11 34S 132 56 E
Murgha Kibzai, *Pakistan* 42 D3 30 44N 69 25 E
Murghob, *Tajikistan* 26 F8 38 10N 74 2 E
Murgon, *Australia* 63 D5 26 15S 151 54 E
Muri, *India* 43 H11 23 22N 85 52 E
Muria, *Indonesia* 37 G14 6 36S 110 53 E
Muriaé, *Brazil* 95 A7 21 8S 42 23W
Muriel Mine, *Zimbabwe* 55 F3 17 14S 30 40 E
Müritz, *Germany* 16 B7 53 25N 12 42 E
Murka, *Kenya* 54 C4 3 27S 38 0 E
Murliganj, *India* 43 G12 25 54N 86 59 E
Murmansk, *Russia* 24 A5 68 57N 33 10 E
Muro, *Spain* 22 B10 39 44N 3 3 E
Murom, *Russia* 24 C7 55 35N 42 3 E
Muroran, *Japan* 30 C10 42 25N 141 0 E
Muroto, *Japan* 31 H7 33 18N 134 9 E
Muroto-Misaki, *Japan* 31 H7 33 15N 134 10 E
Murphy, *U.S.A.* 82 E5 43 13N 116 33W
Murphys, *U.S.A.* 84 G6 38 8N 120 28W
Murray, *Ky., U.S.A.* 77 G1 36 37N 88 19W
Murray, *Utah, U.S.A.* 82 F8 40 40N 111 53W
Murray →, *Australia* 63 F2 35 20S 139 22 E
Murray, L., *U.S.A.* 77 H5 34 3N 81 13W
Murray Bridge, *Australia* 63 F2 35 6S 139 14 E
Murray Harbour, *Canada* 71 C7 46 0N 62 28W
Murraysburg, *S. Africa* 56 E3 31 58S 23 47 E
Murree, *Pakistan* 42 C5 33 56N 73 28 E
Murrieta, *U.S.A.* 85 M9 33 33N 117 13W
Murrumbidgee →, *Australia* 63 E3 34 43S 143 12 E
Murrumburrah, *Australia* 63 E4 34 32S 148 22 E
Murrurundi, *Australia* 63 E5 31 42S 150 51 E
Murshidabad, *India* 43 G13 24 11N 88 19 E
Murtle L., *Canada* 72 C5 52 8N 119 38W
Murtoa, *Australia* 63 F3 36 35S 142 28 E
Murungu, *Tanzania* 54 C3 4 12S 31 10 E
Mururoa, *Pac. Oc.* 65 K14 21 52S 138 55W
Murwara, *India* 43 H9 23 46N 80 28 E
Murwillumbah, *Australia* 63 D5 28 18S 153 27 E
Mürzzuschlag, *Austria* 16 E8 47 36N 15 41 E
Muş, *Turkey* 25 G7 38 45N 41 30 E
Mûsa, Gebel, *Egypt* 44 D2 28 33N 33 59 E
Musa Khel, *Pakistan* 42 D3 30 59N 69 52 E
Mūsa Qal'eh, *Afghan.* 40 C4 32 20N 64 50 E
Musafirkhana, *India* 43 F9 26 22N 81 48 E
Musala, *Bulgaria* 21 C10 42 13N 23 37 E
Musala, *Indonesia* 36 D1 1 41N 98 28 E
Musan, *N. Korea* 35 C15 42 12N 129 12 E
Musangu, *Dem. Rep. of the Congo* 55 E1 10 28S 23 55 E
Musasa, *Tanzania* 54 C3 3 25S 31 30 E
Musay'īd, *Qatar* 45 E6 25 0N 51 33 E
Muscat = Masqat, *Oman* 46 C6 23 37N 58 36 E
Muscat & Oman = Oman ■, *Asia* 46 C6 23 0N 58 0 E
Muscatine, *U.S.A.* 80 E9 41 25N 91 3W
Musgrave Harbour, *Canada* 71 C9 49 27N 53 58W
Musgrave Ranges, *Australia* 61 E5 26 0S 132 0 E
Mushie, *Dem. Rep. of the Congo* 52 E3 2 56S 16 55 E
Musi →, *Indonesia* 36 E2 2 20S 104 56 E
Muskeg →, *Canada* 72 A4 60 20N 123 20W
Muskegon, *U.S.A.* 76 D2 43 14N 86 16W
Muskegon →, *U.S.A.* 76 D2 43 14N 86 21W
Muskegon Heights, *U.S.A.* 76 D2 43 12N 86 16W
Muskogee, *U.S.A.* 81 H7 35 45N 95 22W
Muskoka, L., *Canada* 78 B5 45 0N 79 25W
Muskwa →, *Canada* 72 B4 58 47N 122 48W
Muslīmiyah, *Syria* 44 B3 36 19N 37 12 E
Musofu, *Zambia* 55 E2 13 30S 29 0 E
Musoma, *Tanzania* 54 C3 1 30S 33 48 E
Musquaro, L., *Canada* 71 B7 50 38N 61 5W
Musquodoboit Harbour, *Canada* 71 D7 44 50N 63 9W
Musselburgh, *U.K.* 12 F5 55 57N 3 2W
Musselshell →, *U.S.A.* 82 C10 47 21N 107 57W
Mussoorie, *India* 42 D8 30 27N 78 6 E
Mussuco, *Angola* 56 B2 17 2S 19 3 E
Mustafakemalpaşa, *Turkey* 21 D13 40 2N 28 24 E
Mustang, *Nepal* 43 E10 29 10N 83 55 E
Musters, L., *Argentina* 96 F3 45 20S 69 25W
Musudan, *N. Korea* 35 D15 40 50N 129 43 E
Muswellbrook, *Australia* 63 E5 32 16S 150 56 E
Mût, *Egypt* 51 C11 25 28N 28 58 E
Mut, *Turkey* 44 B2 36 40N 33 28 E
Mutanda, *Mozam.* 57 C5 21 0S 33 34 E
Mutanda, *Zambia* 55 E2 12 24S 26 13 E
Mutare, *Zimbabwe* 55 F3 18 58S 32 38 E
Muting, *Indonesia* 37 F10 7 23S 140 20 E
Mutoko, *Zimbabwe* 57 B5 17 24S 32 13 E
Mutoray, *Russia* 27 C11 60 56N 101 0 E
Mutshatsha, *Dem. Rep. of the Congo* 55 E1 10 35S 24 20 E
Mutsu, *Japan* 30 D10 41 5N 140 55 E
Mutsu-Wan, *Japan* 30 D10 41 5N 140 55 E
Muttaburra, *Australia* 62 C3 22 38S 144 29 E
Mutton I., *Ireland* 13 D2 52 49N 9 32W
Mutuáli, *Mozam.* 55 E4 14 55S 37 0 E
Muweilih, *Egypt* 47 E3 30 42N 34 19 E
Muy Muy, *Nic.* 88 D2 12 39N 85 36W
Muyinga, *Burundi* 54 C3 3 14S 30 33 E
Muynak, *Uzbekistan* 26 E6 43 44N 59 10 E
Muzaffarabad, *Pakistan* 43 B5 34 25N 73 30 E
Muzaffargarh, *Pakistan* 42 D4 30 5N 71 14 E
Muzaffarnagar, *India* 42 E7 29 26N 77 40 E
Muzaffarpur, *India* 43 F11 26 7N 85 23 E
Muzafirpur, *Pakistan* 42 D3 30 58N 69 9 E
Muzhi, *Russia* 24 A11 65 25N 64 40 E
Mvuma, *Zimbabwe* 55 F3 19 16S 30 30 E
Mvurwi, *Zimbabwe* 55 F3 17 0S 30 57 E
Mwadui, *Tanzania* 54 C3 3 26S 33 32 E
Mwambo, *Tanzania* 55 E5 10 30S 40 22 E
Mwandi, *Zambia* 55 F1 17 30S 24 51 E
Mwanza, *Dem. Rep. of the Congo* 54 D2 7 55S 26 43 E
Mwanza, *Tanzania* 54 C3 2 30S 32 58 E
Mwanza, *Zambia* 55 F1 16 58S 24 28 E
Mwanza □, *Tanzania* 54 C3 2 0S 33 0 E
Mwaya, *Tanzania* 55 D3 9 32S 33 55 E
Mweelrea, *Ireland* 13 C2 53 39N 9 49W
Mweka, *Dem. Rep. of the Congo* 52 E4 4 50S 21 34 E
Mwenezi, *Zimbabwe* 55 G3 21 15S 30 48 E
Mwenezi →, *Mozam.* 55 G3 22 40S 31 50 E
Mwenga, *Dem. Rep. of the Congo* 54 C2 3 1S 28 28 E
Mweru, L., *Zambia* 55 D2 9 0S 28 40 E
Mweza Range, *Zimbabwe* 55 G3 21 0S 30 0 E
Mwilambwe, *Dem. Rep. of the Congo* 54 D2 8 7S 25 5 E
Mwimbi, *Tanzania* 55 D3 8 38S 31 39 E
Mwinilunga, *Zambia* 55 E1 11 43S 24 25 E
My Tho, *Vietnam* 39 G6 10 29N 106 23 E
Myajlar, *India* 42 F4 26 15N 70 20 E
Myanaung, *Burma* 41 K19 18 18N 95 22 E
Myanmar = Burma ■, *Asia* 41 J20 21 0N 96 30 E
Myaungmya, *Burma* 41 L19 16 30N 94 40 E
Mycenæ, *Greece* 21 F10 37 39N 22 52 E
Myeik Kyunzu, *Burma* 39 G1 11 30N 97 30 E
Myers Chuck, *U.S.A.* 72 B2 55 44N 132 11W
Myerstown, *U.S.A.* 79 F8 40 22N 76 19W
Myingyan, *Burma* 41 J19 21 30N 95 20 E
Myitkyina, *Burma* 41 G20 25 24N 97 26 E
Mykines, *Færoe Is.* 8 E9 62 7N 7 35W
Mykolayiv, *Ukraine* 25 E5 46 58N 32 0 E
Mymensingh, *Bangla.* 41 G17 24 45N 90 24 E
Mynydd Du, *U.K.* 11 F4 51 52N 3 50W
Mýrdalsjökull, *Iceland* 8 E4 63 40N 19 6W
Myrtle Beach, *U.S.A.* 77 J6 33 42N 78 53W
Myrtle Creek, *U.S.A.* 82 E2 43 1N 123 17W
Myrtle Point, *U.S.A.* 82 E1 43 4N 124 8W
Myrtou, *Cyprus* 23 D12 35 18N 33 4 E
Mysia, *Turkey* 21 E12 39 50N 27 0 E
Mysore = Karnataka □, *India* 40 N10 13 15N 77 0 E
Mysore, *India* 40 N10 12 17N 76 41 E
Mystic, *U.S.A.* 79 E13 41 21N 71 58W
Myszków, *Poland* 17 C10 50 45N 19 22 E
Mytishchi, *Russia* 24 C6 55 50N 37 50 E
Mývatn, *Iceland* 8 D5 65 36N 17 0W
Mzimba, *Malawi* 55 E3 11 55S 33 39 E
Mzimkulu →, *S. Africa* 57 E5 30 44S 30 28 E
Mzimvubu →, *S. Africa* 57 E4 31 38S 29 33 E
Mzuzu, *Malawi* 55 E3 11 30S 33 55 E

N

Na Hearadh = Harris, *U.K.* 12 D2 57 50N 6 55W
Na Noi, *Thailand* 38 C3 18 19N 100 43 E
Na Phao, *Laos* 38 D5 17 35N 105 44 E
Na Sam, *Vietnam* 38 A6 22 3N 106 37 E
Na San, *Vietnam* 38 B5 21 12N 104 2 E
Naab →, *Germany* 16 D6 49 1N 12 2 E
Naantali, *Finland* 9 F19 60 29N 22 2 E
Naas, *Ireland* 13 C5 53 12N 6 40W
Nababeep, *S. Africa* 56 D2 29 36S 17 46 E
Nabadwip = Navadwip, *India* 43 H13 23 34N 88 20 E
Nabari, *Japan* 31 G8 34 37N 136 5 E
Nabawa, *Australia* 61 E1 28 30S 114 48 E
Nabberu, L., *Australia* 61 E3 25 50S 120 30 E
Naberezhnyye Chelny, *Russia* 24 C9 55 42N 52 19 E
Nabeul, *Tunisia* 51 A8 36 30N 10 44 E
Nabha, *India* 42 D7 30 26N 76 14 E
Nabīd, *Iran* 45 D8 29 40N 57 38 E
Nabire, *Indonesia* 37 E9 3 15S 135 26 E
Nabisar, *Pakistan* 42 G3 25 8N 69 40 E
Nabisipi →, *Canada* 71 B7 50 14N 62 13W
Nabiswera, *Uganda* 54 B3 1 27N 32 15 E
Nablus = Nābulus, *West Bank* 47 C4 32 14N 35 15 E
Naboomspruit, *S. Africa* 57 C4 24 32S 28 40 E
Nābulus, *West Bank* 47 C4 32 14N 35 15 E
Nacala, *Mozam.* 55 E5 14 31S 40 34 E
Nacala-Velha, *Mozam.* 55 E5 14 32S 40 34 E
Nacaome, *Honduras* 88 D2 13 31N 87 30W
Nacaroa, *Mozam.* 55 E4 14 22S 39 56 E
Naches, *U.S.A.* 82 C3 46 44N 120 42W
Naches →, *U.S.A.* 84 D6 46 38N 120 31W
Nachicapau, L., *Canada* 71 A6 56 40N 68 5W
Nachingwea, *Tanzania* 55 E4 10 23S 38 49 E
Nachna, *India* 42 F4 27 34N 71 41 E
Nacimiento L., *U.S.A.* 84 K6 35 46N 120 53W
Naco, *Mexico* 86 A3 31 20N 109 56W
Nacogdoches, *U.S.A.* 81 K7 31 36N 94 39W
Nácori Chico, *Mexico* 86 B3 29 39N 109 1W
Nacozari, *Mexico* 86 A3 30 24N 109 39W
Nadi, *Fiji* 59 C7 17 42S 177 20 E
Nadiad, *India* 42 H5 22 41N 72 56 E
Nador, *Morocco* 50 B5 35 14N 2 58W
Nadur, *Malta* 23 C1 36 2N 14 18 E
Nadūshan, *Iran* 45 C7 32 2N 53 35 E
Nadvirna, *Ukraine* 17 D13 48 37N 24 30 E
Nadvoitsy, *Russia* 24 B5 63 52N 34 14 E
Nadvornaya = Nadvirna, *Ukraine* 17 D13 48 37N 24 30 E
Nadym, *Russia* 26 C8 65 35N 72 42 E
Nadym →, *Russia* 26 C8 66 12N 72 0 E
Nærbø, *Norway* 9 G11 58 40N 5 39 E
Næstved, *Denmark* 9 J14 55 13N 11 44 E
Naft-e Safīd, *Iran* 45 D6 31 40N 49 17 E
Naftshahr, *Iran* 44 C5 34 0N 45 30 E
Nafud Desert = An Nafūd, *Si. Arabia* 44 D4 28 15N 41 0 E
Naga, *Phil.* 37 B6 13 38N 123 15 E
Nagahama, *Japan* 31 G8 35 23N 136 16 E
Nagai, *Japan* 30 E10 38 6N 140 2 E
Nagaland □, *India* 41 G19 26 0N 94 30 E
Nagano, *Japan* 31 F9 36 40N 138 10 E
Nagano □, *Japan* 31 F9 36 15N 138 0 E
Nagaoka, *Japan* 31 F9 37 27N 138 51 E
Nagappattinam, *India* 40 P11 10 46N 79 51 E
Nagar →, *Bangla.* 43 G13 24 27N 89 12 E
Nagar Parkar, *Pakistan* 42 G4 24 28N 70 46 E
Nagasaki, *Japan* 31 H4 32 47N 129 50 E
Nagasaki □, *Japan* 31 H4 32 50N 129 40 E
Nagato, *Japan* 31 G5 34 19N 131 5 E
Nagaur, *India* 42 F5 27 15N 73 45 E
Nagda, *India* 42 H6 23 27N 75 25 E
Nagercoil, *India* 40 Q10 8 12N 77 26 E
Nagina, *India* 43 E8 29 30N 78 30 E
Nagineh, *Iran* 45 C8 34 20N 57 15 E
Nagir, *Pakistan* 43 A6 36 12N 74 42 E
Nagod, *India* 43 G9 24 34N 80 36 E
Nagoorin, *Australia* 62 C5 24 17S 151 15 E
Nagorno-Karabakh, *Azerbaijan* 25 F8 39 55N 46 45 E
Nagornyy, *Russia* 27 D13 55 58N 124 57 E
Nagoya, *Japan* 31 G8 35 10N 136 50 E
Nagpur, *India* 40 J11 21 8N 79 10 E
Nagua, *Dom. Rep.* 89 C6 19 23N 69 50W
Nagykanizsa, *Hungary* 17 E9 46 28N 17 0 E
Nagykőrös, *Hungary* 17 E10 47 5N 19 48 E
Naha, *Japan* 31 L3 26 13N 127 42 E
Nahan, *India* 42 D7 30 33N 77 18 E
Nahanni Butte, *Canada* 72 A4 61 2N 123 31W
Nahanni Nat. Park, *Canada* 72 A4 61 15N 125 0W
Nahargarh, *Mad. P., India* 42 G6 24 10N 75 14 E
Nahargarh, *Raj., India* 42 G7 24 55N 76 50 E
Nahariyya, *Israel* 44 C2 33 1N 35 5 E
Nahāvand, *Iran* 45 C6 34 10N 48 22 E
Naicá, *Mexico* 86 B3 27 53N 105 31W
Naicam, *Canada* 73 C8 52 30N 104 30W
Naikoon Prov. Park, *Canada* 72 C2 53 55N 131 55W
Naimisharanya, *India* 43 F9 27 21N 80 30 E
Nain, *Canada* 71 A7 56 34N 61 40W
Nā'īn, *Iran* 45 C7 32 54N 53 0 E
Naini Tal, *India* 43 E8 29 30N 79 30 E
Nainpur, *India* 40 H12 22 30N 80 10 E
Nainwa, *India* 42 G6 25 46N 75 51 E
Nairn, *U.K.* 12 D5 57 35N 3 53W
Nairobi, *Kenya* 54 C4 1 17S 36 48 E
Naissaar, *Estonia* 9 G21 59 34N 24 29 E
Naivasha, *Kenya* 54 C4 0 40S 36 30 E
Naivasha, L., *Kenya* 54 C4 0 48S 36 20 E
Najafābād, *Iran* 45 C6 32 40N 51 15 E
Najd, *Si. Arabia* 46 B3 26 30N 42 0 E
Najibabad, *India* 42 E8 29 40N 78 20 E
Najin, *N. Korea* 35 C16 42 12N 130 15 E
Najmah, *Si. Arabia* 45 E6 26 42N 50 6 E

Neuquén □, Argentina 94 D2 38 0S 69 50W
Neuruppin, Germany 16 B7 52 55N 12 48 E
Neuse →, U.S.A. 77 H7 35 6N 76 29W
Neusiedler See, Austria 17 E9 47 50N 16 47 E
Neustrelitz, Germany 16 B7 53 21N 13 4 E
Neva →, Russia 24 C5 59 50N 30 30 E
Nevada, Iowa, U.S.A. 80 D8 42 1N 93 27W
Nevada, Mo., U.S.A. 81 G7 37 51N 94 22W
Nevada □, U.S.A. 82 G5 39 0N 117 0W
Nevada City, U.S.A. 84 F6 39 16N 121 1W
Nevado, Cerro, Argentina 94 D2 35 30S 68 32W
Nevel, Russia 24 C4 56 0N 29 55 E
Nevers, France 18 C5 47 0N 3 9 E
Nevertire, Australia 63 E4 31 50S 147 44 E
Neville, Canada 73 D7 49 58N 107 39W
Nevinnomyssk, Russia 25 F7 44 40N 42 0 E
Nevis, St. Kitts & Nevis 89 C7 17 0N 62 30W
Nevşehir, Turkey 44 B2 38 33N 34 40 E
Nevyansk, Russia 24 C11 57 30N 60 13 E
New →, U.S.A. 76 F5 38 10N 81 12W
New Aiyansh, Canada 72 B3 55 12N 129 4W
New Albany, Ind., U.S.A. 76 F3 38 18N 85 49W
New Albany, Miss., U.S.A. 81 H10 34 29N 89 0W
New Albany, Pa., U.S.A. 79 E8 41 36N 76 27W
New Amsterdam, Guyana 92 B7 6 15N 57 36W
New Angledool, Australia 63 D4 29 5S 147 55 E
New Baltimore, U.S.A. 78 D2 42 41N 82 44W
New Bedford, U.S.A. 79 E14 41 38N 70 56W
New Berlin, N.Y., U.S.A. 79 D9 42 37N 75 20W
New Berlin, Pa., U.S.A. 78 F8 40 50N 76 57W
New Bern, U.S.A. 77 H7 35 7N 77 3W
New Bethlehem, U.S.A. 78 F5 41 0N 79 20W
New Bloomfield, U.S.A. 78 F7 40 25N 77 11W
New Boston, U.S.A. 81 J7 33 28N 94 25W
New Braunfels, U.S.A. 81 L5 29 42N 98 8W
New Brighton, N.Z. 59 K4 43 29S 172 43 E
New Brighton, U.S.A. 78 F4 40 42N 80 19W
New Britain, Papua N. G. 64 H7 5 50S 150 20 E
New Britain, U.S.A. 79 E12 41 40N 72 47W
New Brunswick, U.S.A. 79 F10 40 30N 74 27W
New Brunswick □, Canada 71 C6 46 50N 66 30W
New Caledonia ■, Pac. Oc. 64 K8 21 0S 165 0 E
New Castile = Castilla-La Mancha □, Spain 19 C4 39 30N 3 30W
New Castle, Ind., U.S.A. 76 F3 39 55N 85 22W
New Castle, Pa., U.S.A. 78 F4 41 0N 80 21W
New City, U.S.A. 79 E11 41 9N 73 59W
New Concord, U.S.A. 78 G3 39 59N 81 54W
New Cumberland, U.S.A. 78 F4 40 30N 80 36W
New Cuyama, U.S.A. 85 L7 34 57N 119 38W
New Delhi, India 42 E7 28 37N 77 13 E
New Denver, Canada 72 D5 50 0N 117 25W
New Don Pedro Reservoir, U.S.A. 84 H6 37 43N 120 24W
New England, U.S.A. 80 B3 46 32N 102 52W
New England Ra., Australia 63 E5 30 20S 151 45 E
New Forest, U.K. 11 G6 50 53N 1 34W
New Galloway, U.K. 12 F4 55 5N 4 9W
New Glasgow, Canada 71 C7 45 35N 62 36W
New Guinea, Oceania 28 K17 4 0S 136 0 E
New Hamburg, Canada 78 C4 43 23N 80 42W
New Hampshire □, U.S.A. 79 C13 44 0N 71 30W
New Hampton, U.S.A. 80 D8 43 3N 92 19W
New Hanover, S. Africa 57 D5 29 22S 30 31 E
New Hartford, U.S.A. 79 C9 43 4N 75 18W
New Haven, Conn., U.S.A. 79 E12 41 18N 72 55W
New Haven, Mich., U.S.A. 78 D2 42 44N 82 48W
New Hazelton, Canada 72 B3 55 20N 127 30W
New Hebrides = Vanuatu ■, Pac. Oc. 64 J8 15 0S 168 0 E
New Holland, U.S.A. 79 F8 40 6N 76 5W
New Iberia, U.S.A. 81 K9 30 1N 91 49W
New Ireland, Papua N. G. 64 H7 3 20S 151 50 E
New Jersey □, U.S.A. 76 E8 40 0N 74 30W
New Kensington, U.S.A. 78 F5 40 34N 79 46W
New Lexington, U.S.A. 76 F4 39 43N 82 13W
New Liskeard, Canada 70 C4 47 31N 79 41W
New London, Conn., U.S.A. 79 E12 41 22N 72 6W
New London, Ohio, U.S.A. 78 E2 41 5N 82 24W
New London, Wis., U.S.A. 80 C10 44 23N 88 45W
New Madrid, U.S.A. 81 G10 36 36N 89 32W
New Martinsville, U.S.A. 76 F5 39 39N 80 52W
New Meadows, U.S.A. 82 D5 44 58N 116 18W
New Melones L., U.S.A. 84 H6 37 57N 120 31W
New Mexico □, U.S.A. 83 J10 34 30N 106 0W
New Milford, Conn., U.S.A. 79 E11 41 35N 73 25W
New Milford, Pa., U.S.A. 79 E9 41 52N 75 44W
New Norcia, Australia 61 F2 30 57S 116 13 E
New Norfolk, Australia 62 G4 42 46S 147 2 E
New Orleans, U.S.A. 81 L9 29 58N 90 4W
New Philadelphia, U.S.A. 78 F3 40 30N 81 27W
New Plymouth, N.Z. 59 H5 39 4S 174 5 E
New Plymouth, U.S.A. 82 E5 43 58N 116 49W
New Port Richey, U.S.A. 77 L4 28 16N 82 43W
New Providence, Bahamas 88 A4 25 25N 78 35W
New Quay, U.K. 11 E3 52 13N 4 21W
New Radnor, U.K. 11 E4 52 15N 3 9W
New Richmond, Canada 71 C6 48 15N 65 45W
New Richmond, U.S.A. 80 C8 45 7N 92 32W
New Roads, U.S.A. 81 K9 30 42N 91 26W
New Rochelle, U.S.A. 79 F11 40 55N 73 47W
New Rockford, U.S.A. 80 B5 47 41N 99 8W
New Romney, U.K. 11 G8 50 59N 0 57 E
New Ross, Ireland 13 D5 52 23N 6 57W
New Salem, U.S.A. 80 B4 46 51N 101 25W
New Scone, U.K. 12 E5 56 25N 3 24W
New Siberian I. = Novaya Sibir, Ostrov, Russia 27 B16 75 10N 150 0 E
New Siberian Is. = Novosibirskiye Ostrova, Russia 27 B15 75 0N 142 0 E
New Smyrna Beach, U.S.A. 77 L5 29 1N 80 56W
New South Wales □, Australia 63 E4 33 0S 146 0 E
New Town, U.S.A. 80 B3 47 59N 102 30W
New Tredegar, U.K. 11 F4 51 44N 3 16W
New Ulm, U.S.A. 80 C7 44 19N 94 28W
New Waterford, Canada 71 C7 46 13N 60 4W
New Westminster, Canada 84 A4 49 13N 122 55W
New York, U.S.A. 79 F11 40 45N 74 0W
New York □, U.S.A. 79 D9 43 0N 75 0W
New York Mts., U.S.A. 83 J6 35 0N 115 20W
New Zealand ■, Oceania 59 J6 40 0S 176 0 E
Newaj →, India 42 G7 24 24N 76 49 E
Newala, Tanzania 55 E4 10 58S 39 18 E
Newark, Del., U.S.A. 76 F8 39 41N 75 46W
Newark, N.J., U.S.A. 79 F10 40 44N 74 10W
Newark, N.Y., U.S.A. 78 C7 43 3N 77 6W
Newark, Ohio, U.S.A. 78 F2 40 3N 82 24W
Newark-on-Trent, U.K. 10 D7 53 5N 0 48W
Newark Valley, U.S.A. 79 D8 42 14N 76 11W
Newberg, U.S.A. 82 D2 45 18N 122 58W
Newberry, Mich., U.S.A. 76 B3 46 21N 85 30W
Newberry, S.C., U.S.A. 77 H5 34 17N 81 37W
Newberry Springs, U.S.A. 85 L10 34 50N 116 41W
Newboro L., Canada 79 B8 44 38N 76 20W
Newbridge = Droichead Nua, Ireland 13 C5 53 11N 6 48W
Newburgh, Canada 78 B8 44 19N 76 52W
Newburgh, U.S.A. 79 E10 41 30N 74 1W
Newbury, U.K. 11 F6 51 24N 1 20W
Newbury, N.H., U.S.A. 79 B12 43 19N 72 3W
Newbury, Vt., U.S.A. 79 B12 44 5N 72 4W
Newburyport, U.S.A. 77 D10 42 49N 70 53W
Newcastle, Australia 63 E5 33 0S 151 46 E
Newcastle, N.B., Canada 71 C6 47 1N 65 38W
Newcastle, Ont., Canada 70 D4 43 55N 78 35W
Newcastle, S. Africa 57 D4 27 45S 29 58 E
Newcastle, U.K. 13 B6 54 13N 5 54W
Newcastle, Calif., U.S.A. 84 G5 38 53N 121 8W
Newcastle, Wyo., U.S.A. 80 D2 43 50N 104 11W
Newcastle Emlyn, U.K. 11 E3 52 2N 4 28W
Newcastle Ra., Australia 60 C5 15 45S 130 15 E
Newcastle-under-Lyme, U.K. 10 D5 53 1N 2 14W
Newcastle-upon-Tyne, U.K. 10 C6 54 58N 1 36W
Newcastle Waters, Australia 62 B1 17 30S 133 28 E
Newcastle West, Ireland 13 D2 52 27N 9 3W
Newcomb, U.S.A. 79 C10 43 58N 74 10W
Newcomerstown, U.S.A. 78 F3 40 16N 81 36W
Newdegate, Australia 61 F2 33 6S 119 0 E
Newell, Australia 62 B4 16 20S 145 16 E
Newell, U.S.A. 80 C3 44 43N 103 25W
Newfane, U.S.A. 78 C6 43 17N 78 43W
Newfield, U.S.A. 79 D8 42 18N 76 33W
Newfound L., U.S.A. 79 C13 43 40N 71 47W
Newfoundland, Canada 66 E14 49 0N 55 0W
Newfoundland, U.S.A. 79 E9 41 18N 75 19W
Newfoundland □, Canada 71 B8 53 0N 58 0W
Newhall, U.S.A. 85 L8 34 23N 118 32W
Newhaven, U.K. 11 G8 50 47N 0 3 E
Newkirk, U.S.A. 81 G6 36 53N 97 3W
Newlyn, U.K. 11 G2 50 6N 5 34W
Newman, Australia 60 D2 23 18S 119 45 E
Newman, U.S.A. 84 H5 37 19N 121 1W
Newmarket, Canada 78 B5 44 3N 79 28W
Newmarket, Ireland 13 D2 52 13N 9 0W
Newmarket, U.K. 11 E8 52 15N 0 25 E
Newmarket, U.S.A. 79 C14 43 4N 70 56W
Newnan, U.S.A. 77 J3 33 23N 84 48W
Newport, Ireland 13 C2 53 53N 9 33W
Newport, I. of W., U.K. 11 G6 50 42N 1 17W
Newport, Newp., U.K. 11 F5 51 35N 3 0W
Newport, Ark., U.S.A. 81 H9 35 37N 91 16W
Newport, Ky., U.S.A. 76 F3 39 5N 84 30W
Newport, N.H., U.S.A. 79 C12 43 22N 72 10W
Newport, N.Y., U.S.A. 79 C9 43 11N 75 1W
Newport, Oreg., U.S.A. 82 D1 44 39N 124 3W
Newport, Pa., U.S.A. 78 F7 40 29N 77 8W
Newport, R.I., U.S.A. 79 E13 41 29N 71 19W
Newport, Tenn., U.S.A. 77 H4 35 58N 83 11W
Newport, Vt., U.S.A. 79 B12 44 56N 72 13W
Newport, Wash., U.S.A. 82 B5 48 11N 117 3W
Newport □, U.K. 11 F4 51 33N 3 1W
Newport Beach, U.S.A. 85 M9 33 37N 117 56W
Newport News, U.S.A. 76 G7 36 59N 76 25W
Newport Pagnell, U.K. 11 E7 52 5N 0 43W
Newquay, U.K. 11 G2 50 25N 5 6W
Newry, U.K. 13 B5 54 11N 6 21W
Newton, Ill., U.S.A. 80 F10 38 59N 88 10W
Newton, Iowa, U.S.A. 80 E8 41 42N 93 3W
Newton, Kans., U.S.A. 81 F6 38 3N 97 21W
Newton, Mass., U.S.A. 79 D13 42 21N 71 12W
Newton, Miss., U.S.A. 81 J10 32 19N 89 10W
Newton, N.C., U.S.A. 77 H5 35 40N 81 13W
Newton, N.J., U.S.A. 79 E10 41 3N 74 45W
Newton, Tex., U.S.A. 81 K8 30 51N 93 46W
Newton Abbot, U.K. 11 G4 50 32N 3 37W
Newton Aycliffe, U.K. 10 C6 54 37N 1 34W
Newton Falls, U.S.A. 78 E4 41 11N 80 59W
Newton Stewart, U.K. 12 G4 54 57N 4 30W
Newtonmore, U.K. 12 D4 57 4N 4 8W
Newtown, U.K. 11 E4 52 31N 3 19W
Newtownabbey, U.K. 13 B6 54 40N 5 56W
Newtownards, U.K. 13 B6 54 36N 5 42W
Newtownbarry = Bunclody, Ireland 13 D5 52 39N 6 40W
Newtownstewart, U.K. 13 B4 54 43N 7 23W
Newville, U.S.A. 78 F7 40 10N 77 24W
Neya, Russia 24 C7 58 21N 43 49 E
Neyrīz, Iran 45 D7 29 15N 54 19 E
Neyshābūr, Iran 45 B8 36 10N 58 50 E
Nezhin = Nizhyn, Ukraine 25 D5 51 5N 31 55 E
Nezperce, U.S.A. 82 C5 46 14N 116 14W
Ngabang, Indonesia 36 D3 0 23N 109 55 E
Ngabordamlu, Tanjung, Indonesia 37 F8 6 56S 134 11 E
N'Gage, Angola 52 F3 7 46S 15 16 E
Ngami Depression, Botswana 56 C3 20 30S 22 46 E
Ngamo, Zimbabwe 55 F2 19 3S 27 32 E
Nganglong Kangri, China 41 C12 33 0N 81 0 E
Ngao, Thailand 38 C2 18 46N 99 59 E
Ngaoundéré, Cameroon 52 C2 7 15N 13 35 E
Ngapara, N.Z. 59 L3 44 57S 170 46 E
Ngara, Tanzania 54 C3 2 29S 30 40 E
Ngawi, Indonesia 37 G14 7 24S 111 26 E
Nghia Lo, Vietnam 38 B5 21 33N 104 28 E
Ngoma, Malawi 55 E3 13 8S 33 45 E
Ngomahura, Zimbabwe 55 G3 20 26S 30 43 E
Ngomba, Tanzania 55 D3 8 20S 32 53 E
Ngoring Hu, China 32 C4 34 55N 97 5 E
Ngorongoro, Tanzania 54 C4 3 11S 35 32 E
Ngozi, Burundi 54 C2 2 54S 29 50 E
Ngudu, Tanzania 54 C3 2 58S 33 25 E
Nguigmi, Niger 51 F8 14 20N 13 20 E
Nguiu, Australia 60 B5 11 46S 130 38 E
Ngukurr, Australia 62 A1 14 44S 134 44 E
Ngunga, Tanzania 54 C3 3 37S 33 37 E
Nguru, Nigeria 51 F8 12 56N 10 29 E
Nguru Mts., Tanzania 54 D4 6 0S 37 30 E
Ngusi, Malawi 55 E3 14 0S 34 50 E
Nguyen Binh, Vietnam 38 A5 22 39N 105 56 E
Nha Trang, Vietnam 39 F7 12 16N 109 10 E
Nhacoongo, Mozam. 57 C6 24 18S 35 14 E
Nhamaabué, Mozam. 55 F4 17 25S 35 5 E
Nhamundá →, Brazil 93 D7 2 12S 56 41W
Nhangulaze, L., Mozam. 57 C5 24 0S 34 30 E
Nhill, Australia 63 F3 36 18S 141 40 E
Nho Quan, Vietnam 38 B5 20 18N 105 45 E
Nhulunbuy, Australia 62 A2 12 10S 137 20 E
Nia-nia, Dem. Rep. of the Congo 54 B2 1 30N 27 40 E
Niagara Falls, Canada 78 C5 43 7N 79 5W
Niagara Falls, U.S.A. 78 C6 43 5N 79 4W
Niagara-on-the-Lake, Canada 78 C5 43 15N 79 4W
Niah, Malaysia 36 D4 3 58N 113 46 E
Niamey, Niger 50 F6 13 27N 2 6 E
Niangara, Dem. Rep. of the Congo 54 B2 3 42N 27 50 E
Niantic, U.S.A. 79 E12 41 20N 72 11W
Nias, Indonesia 36 D1 1 0N 97 30 E
Niassa □, Mozam. 55 E4 13 30S 36 0 E
Nibāk, Si. Arabia 45 E7 24 25N 50 50 E
Nicaragua ■, Cent. Amer. 88 D2 11 40N 85 30W
Nicaragua, L. de, Nic. 88 D2 12 0N 85 30W
Nicastro, Italy 20 E7 38 59N 16 19 E
Nice, France 18 E7 43 42N 7 14 E
Niceville, U.S.A. 77 K2 30 31N 86 30W
Nichicun, L., Canada 71 B5 53 5N 71 0W
Nichinan, Japan 31 J5 31 38N 131 23 E
Nicholás, Canal, W. Indies 88 B3 23 30N 80 5W
Nicholasville, U.S.A. 76 G3 37 53N 84 34W
Nichols, U.S.A. 79 D8 42 1N 76 22W
Nicholson, Australia 60 C4 18 2S 128 54 E
Nicholson, U.S.A. 79 E9 41 37N 75 47W
Nicholson →, Australia 62 B2 17 31S 139 36 E
Nicholson L., Canada 73 A8 62 40N 102 40W
Nicholson Ra., Australia 61 E2 27 15S 116 45 E
Nicholville, U.S.A. 79 B10 44 41N 74 39W
Nicobar Is., Ind. Oc. 29 J13 8 0N 93 30 E
Nicola, Canada 72 C4 50 12N 120 40W
Nicolls Town, Bahamas 88 A4 25 8N 78 0W
Nicosia, Cyprus 23 D12 35 10N 33 25 E
Nicoya, Costa Rica 88 D2 10 9N 85 27W
Nicoya, G. de, Costa Rica 88 E3 10 0N 85 0W
Nicoya, Pen. de, Costa Rica 88 E2 9 45N 85 40W
Nidd →, U.K. 10 D6 53 59N 1 23W
Niedersachsen □, Germany 16 B5 52 50N 9 0 E
Niekerkshoop, S. Africa 56 D3 29 19S 22 51 E
Niemba, Dem. Rep. of the Congo 54 D2 5 58S 28 24 E
Niemen = Neman →, Lithuania 9 J19 55 25N 21 10 E
Nienburg, Germany 16 B5 52 39N 9 13 E
Nieu Bethesda, S. Africa 56 E3 31 51S 24 34 E
Nieuw Amsterdam, Surinam 93 B7 5 53N 55 5W
Nieuw Nickerie, Surinam 93 B7 6 0N 56 59W
Nieuwoudtville, S. Africa 56 E2 31 23S 19 7 E
Nieuwpoort, Belgium 15 C2 51 8N 2 45 E
Nieves, Pico de las, Canary Is. 22 G4 27 57N 15 35W
Niğde, Turkey 25 G5 37 58N 34 40 E
Nigel, S. Africa 57 D4 26 27S 28 25 E
Niger ■, W. Afr. 50 E7 17 30N 10 0 E
Niger →, W. Afr. 50 G7 5 33N 6 33 E
Nigeria ■, W. Afr. 50 G7 8 30N 8 0 E
Nighasin, India 43 E9 28 14N 80 52 E
Nightcaps, N.Z. 59 L2 45 57S 168 2 E
Nii-Jima, Japan 31 G9 34 20N 139 15 E
Niigata, Japan 30 F9 37 58N 139 0 E
Niigata □, Japan 31 F9 37 15N 138 45 E
Niihama, Japan 31 H6 33 55N 133 16 E
Niihau, U.S.A. 74 H14 21 54N 160 9W
Niimi, Japan 31 G6 34 59N 133 28 E
Niitsu, Japan 30 F9 37 48N 139 7 E
Nijil, Jordan 47 E4 30 32N 35 33 E
Nijkerk, Neths. 15 B5 52 13N 5 30 E
Nijmegen, Neths. 15 C5 51 50N 5 52 E
Nijverdal, Neths. 15 B6 52 22N 6 28 E
Nīk Pey, Iran 45 B6 36 50N 48 10 E
Nikiniki, Indonesia 37 F6 9 49S 124 30 E
Nikkō, Japan 31 F9 36 45N 139 35 E
Nikolayev = Mykolayiv, Ukraine 25 E5 46 58N 32 0 E
Nikolayevsk, Russia 25 E8 50 0N 45 35 E
Nikolayevsk-na-Amur, Russia 27 D15 53 8N 140 44 E
Nikolskoye, Russia 27 D17 55 12N 166 0 E
Nikopol, Ukraine 25 E5 47 35N 34 25 E
Nīkshahr, Iran 45 E9 26 15N 60 10 E
Nikšić, Montenegro, Yug. 21 C8 42 50N 18 57 E
Nîl, Nahr en →, Africa 51 B12 30 10N 31 6 E
Nîl el Abyad →, Sudan 51 E12 15 38N 32 31 E
Nîl el Azraq →, Sudan 51 E12 15 38N 32 31 E
Nila, Indonesia 37 F7 6 44S 129 31 E
Niland, U.S.A. 85 M11 33 14N 115 31W
Nile = Nîl, Nahr en →, Africa 51 B12 30 10N 31 6 E
Niles, Mich., U.S.A. 76 E2 41 50N 86 15W
Niles, Ohio, U.S.A. 78 E4 41 11N 80 46W
Nim Ka Thana, India 42 F6 27 44N 75 48 E
Nimach, India 42 G6 24 30N 74 56 E
Nimbahera, India 42 G6 24 37N 74 45 E
Nîmes, France 18 E6 43 50N 4 23 E
Nimfaíon, Ákra = Pínnes, Ákra, Greece 21 D11 40 5N 24 20 E
Nimmitabel, Australia 63 F4 36 29S 149 15 E
Nīnawá, Iraq 44 B4 36 25N 43 10 E
Nindigully, Australia 63 D4 28 21S 148 50 E
Nineveh = Nīnawá, Iraq 44 B4 36 25N 43 10 E
Ning Xian, China 34 G4 35 30N 107 58 E
Ning'an, China 35 B15 44 22N 129 20 E
Ningbo, China 33 D7 29 51N 121 28 E
Ningcheng, China 35 D10 41 32N 119 53 E
Ningjin, China 34 F8 37 35N 114 57 E
Ningjing Shan, China 32 D4 30 0N 98 20 E
Ningling, China 34 G8 34 25N 115 22 E
Ningpo = Ningbo, China 33 D7 29 51N 121 28 E
Ningqiang, China 34 H4 32 47N 106 15 E
Ningshan, China 34 H5 33 21N 108 21 E
Ningsia Hui A.R. = Ningxia Huizu Zizhiqu □, China 34 F4 38 0N 106 0 E
Ningwu, China 34 E7 39 0N 112 18 E
Ningxia Huizu Zizhiqu □, China 34 F4 38 0N 106 0 E
Ningyang, China 34 G9 35 47N 116 45 E
Ninh Binh, Vietnam 38 B5 20 15N 105 55 E
Ninh Giang, Vietnam 38 B6 20 44N 106 24 E
Ninh Hoa, Vietnam 38 F7 12 30N 109 7 E
Ninh Ma, Vietnam 38 F7 12 48N 109 21 E
Ninove, Belgium 15 D4 50 51N 4 2 E
Nioaque, Brazil 95 A4 21 5S 55 50W
Niobrara, U.S.A. 80 D6 42 45N 98 2W
Niobrara →, U.S.A. 80 D6 42 46N 98 3W
Nioro du Sahel, Mali 50 E4 15 15N 9 30W
Niort, France 18 C3 46 19N 0 29W
Nipawin, Canada 73 C8 53 20N 104 0W
Nipigon, Canada 70 C2 49 0N 88 17W
Nipigon, L., Canada 70 C2 49 50N 88 30W
Nipishish L., Canada 71 B7 54 12N 60 45W
Nipissing, L., Canada 70 C4 46 20N 80 0W
Nipomo, U.S.A. 85 K6 35 3N 120 29W
Nipton, U.S.A. 85 K11 35 28N 115 16W
Niquelândia, Brazil 93 F9 14 33S 48 23W
Nīr, Iran 44 B5 38 2N 47 59 E
Nirasaki, Japan 31 G9 35 42N 138 27 E
Nirmal, India 40 K11 19 3N 78 20 E
Nirmali, India 43 F12 26 20N 86 35 E
Niš, Serbia, Yug. 21 C9 43 19N 21 58 E
Nişāb, Si. Arabia 44 D5 29 11N 44 43 E
Nişāb, Yemen 46 E4 14 25N 46 29 E
Nishinomiya, Japan 31 G7 34 45N 135 20 E
Nishino'omote, Japan 31 J5 30 43N 130 59 E
Nishiwaki, Japan 31 G7 34 59N 134 58 E
Niskibi →, Canada 70 A2 56 29N 88 9W
Nisqually →, U.S.A. 84 C4 47 6N 122 42W
Nissáki, Greece 23 A3 39 43N 19 52 E
Nissum Bredning, Denmark 9 H13 56 40N 8 20 E
Nistru = Dnister →, Europe 17 E16 46 18N 30 17 E
Nisutlin →, Canada 72 A2 60 14N 132 34W
Nitchequon, Canada 71 B5 53 10N 70 58W
Niterói, Brazil 95 A7 22 52S 43 0W
Nith →, Canada 78 C4 43 12N 80 23W
Nith →, U.K. 12 F5 55 14N 3 33W
Nitra, Slovak Rep. 17 D10 48 19N 18 4 E
Nitra →, Slovak Rep. 17 E10 47 46N 18 10 E
Niuafo'ou, Tonga 59 B11 15 30S 175 58W
Niue, Cook Is. 65 J11 19 2S 169 54W
Niut, Indonesia 36 D4 0 55N 110 6 E
Niuzhuang, China 35 D12 40 58N 122 28 E
Nivala, Finland 8 E21 63 56N 24 57 E
Nivelles, Belgium 15 D4 50 35N 4 20 E
Nivernais, France 18 C5 47 15N 3 30 E
Niwas, India 43 H9 23 3N 80 26 E
Nixon, U.S.A. 81 L6 29 16N 97 46W
Nizamabad, India 40 K11 18 45N 78 7 E
Nizamghat, India 41 E19 28 20N 95 45 E
Nizhne Kolymsk, Russia 27 C17 68 34N 160 55 E
Nizhnekamsk, Russia 24 C9 55 38N 51 49 E
Nizhneudinsk, Russia 27 D10 54 54N 99 3 E
Nizhnevartovsk, Russia 26 C8 60 56N 76 38 E
Nizhniy Novgorod, Russia 24 C7 56 20N 44 0 E
Nizhniy Tagil, Russia 24 C10 57 55N 59 57 E
Nizhyn, Ukraine 25 D5 51 5N 31 55 E
Nizip, Turkey 44 B3 37 5N 37 50 E
Nízké Tatry, Slovak Rep. 17 D10 48 55N 19 30 E
Njakwa, Malawi 55 E3 11 1S 33 56 E
Njanji, Zambia 55 E3 14 25S 31 46 E
Njinjo, Tanzania 55 D4 8 48S 38 54 E
Njombe, Tanzania 55 D3 9 20S 34 50 E
Njombe →, Tanzania 54 D4 6 56S 35 6 E
Nkana, Zambia 55 E2 12 50S 28 8 E
Nkandla, S. Africa 57 D5 28 37S 31 5 E
Nkayi, Zimbabwe 55 F2 19 41S 29 20 E
Nkhotakota, Malawi 55 E3 12 56S 34 15 E
Nkongsamba, Cameroon 52 D1 4 55N 9 55 E
Nkurenkuru, Namibia 56 B2 17 42S 18 32 E
Nmai →, Burma 41 G20 25 30N 97 25 E
Noakhali = Maijdi, Bangla. 41 H17 22 48N 91 10 E
Nobel, Canada 78 A4 45 25N 80 6W
Nobeoka, Japan 31 H5 32 36N 131 41 E
Noblesville, U.S.A. 76 E3 40 3N 86 1W
Nocera Inferiore, Italy 20 D6 40 44N 14 38 E
Nocona, U.S.A. 81 J6 33 47N 97 44W
Noda, Japan 31 G9 35 56N 139 52 E
Nogales, Mexico 86 A2 31 20N 110 56W
Nogales, U.S.A. 83 L8 31 20N 110 56W
Nōgata, Japan 31 H5 33 48N 130 44 E
Noggerup, Australia 61 F2 33 32S 116 5 E
Noginsk, Russia 27 C10 64 30N 90 50 E
Nogoa →, Australia 62 C4 23 40S 147 55 E
Nogoyá, Argentina 94 C4 32 24S 59 48W
Nohar, India 42 E6 29 11N 74 49 E
Nohta, India 43 H8 23 40N 79 34 E
Noires, Mts., France 18 B2 48 11N 3 40W
Noirmoutier, Î. de, France 18 C2 46 58N 2 10W
Nojane, Botswana 56 C3 23 15S 20 14 E
Nojima-Zaki, Japan 31 G9 34 54N 139 53 E
Nok Kundi, Pakistan 40 E3 28 50N 62 45 E
Nokaneng, Botswana 56 B3 19 40S 22 17 E
Nokia, Finland 9 F20 61 30N 23 30 E
Nokomis, Canada 73 C8 51 35N 105 0W
Nokomis L., Canada 73 B8 57 0N 103 0W
Nola, C.A.R. 52 D3 3 35N 16 4 E
Noma Omuramba →, Namibia 56 B3 18 52S 20 53 E
Nombre de Dios, Panama 88 E4 9 34N 79 28W
Nome, U.S.A. 68 B3 64 30N 165 25W
Nomo-Zaki, Japan 31 H4 32 35N 129 44 E
Nonacho L., Canada 73 A7 61 42N 109 40W
Nonda, Australia 62 C3 20 40S 142 28 E
Nong Chang, Thailand 38 E2 15 23N 99 51 E
Nong Het, Laos 38 C4 19 29N 103 59 E
Nong Khai, Thailand 38 D4 17 50N 102 46 E
Nong'an, China 35 B13 44 25N 125 5 E
Nongoma, S. Africa 57 D5 27 58S 31 35 E
Nonoava, Mexico 86 B3 27 28N 106 44W
Nonoava →, Mexico 86 B3 27 29N 106 45W
Nonthaburi, Thailand 38 F3 13 51N 100 34 E
Noonamah, Australia 60 B5 12 40S 131 4 E
Noord Brabant □, Neths. 15 C5 51 40N 5 0 E
Noord Holland □, Neths. 15 B4 52 30N 4 45 E
Noordbeveland, Neths. 15 C3 51 35N 3 50 E
Noordoostpolder, Neths. 15 B5 52 45N 5 45 E
Noordwijk, Neths. 15 B4 52 14N 4 26 E
Nootka I., Canada 72 D3 49 32N 126 42W
Nopiming Prov. Park, Canada 73 C9 50 30N 95 37W
Noralee, Canada 72 C3 53 59N 126 26W
Noranda = Rouyn-Noranda, Canada 70 C4 48 20N 79 0W
Norco, U.S.A. 85 M9 33 56N 117 33W
Nord-Kivu □, Dem. Rep. of the Congo 54 C2 1 0S 29 0 E
Nord-Ostsee-Kanal, Germany 16 A5 54 12N 9 32 E
Nordaustlandet, Svalbard 4 B9 79 14N 23 0 E
Nordegg, Canada 72 C5 52 29N 116 5W
Norderney, Germany 16 B4 53 42N 7 9 E
Norderstedt, Germany 16 B5 53 42N 10 1 E

O

Oakhurst, U.S.A. **84 H7** 37 19N 119 40W
Oakland, U.S.A. **84 H4** 37 49N 122 16W
Oakley, Idaho, U.S.A. **82 E7** 42 15N 113 53W
Oakley, Kans., U.S.A. **80 F4** 39 8N 100 51W
Oakover →, Australia **60 D3** 21 0S 120 40 E
Oakridge, U.S.A. **82 E2** 43 45N 122 28W
Oakville, Canada **78 C5** 43 27N 79 41W
Oakville, U.S.A. **84 D3** 46 51N 123 14W
Oamaru, N.Z. **59 L3** 45 5S 170 59 E
Oasis, Calif., U.S.A. **85 M10** 33 28N 116 6W
Oasis, Nev., U.S.A. **84 H9** 37 29N 117 55W
Oates Land, Antarctica **5 C11** 69 0S 160 0 E
Oatlands, Australia **62 G4** 42 17S 147 21 E
Oatman, U.S.A. **85 K12** 35 1N 114 19W
Oaxaca, Mexico **87 D5** 17 2N 96 40W
Oaxaca □, Mexico **87 D5** 17 0N 97 0W
Ob →, Russia **26 C7** 66 45N 69 30 E
Oba, Canada **70 C3** 49 4N 84 7W
Obama, Japan **31 G7** 35 30N 135 45 E
Oban, U.K. **12 E3** 56 25N 5 29W
Obbia, Somali Rep. **46 F4** 5 25N 48 30 E
Obera, Argentina **95 B4** 27 21S 55 2W
Oberhausen, Germany **16 C4** 51 28N 6 51 E
Oberlin, Kans., U.S.A. **80 F4** 39 49N 100 32W
Oberlin, La., U.S.A. **81 K8** 30 37N 92 46W
Oberlin, Ohio, U.S.A. **78 E2** 41 18N 82 13W
Oberon, Australia **63 E4** 33 45S 149 52 E
Obi, Indonesia **37 E7** 1 23S 127 45 E
Óbidos, Brazil **93 D7** 1 50S 55 30W
Obihiro, Japan **30 C11** 42 56N 143 12 E
Obilatu, Indonesia **37 E7** 1 25S 127 20 E
Obluchye, Russia **27 E14** 49 1N 131 4 E
Obo, C.A.R. **54 A2** 5 20N 26 32 E
Oboa, Mt., Uganda **54 B3** 1 45N 34 45 E
Oboyan, Russia **26 D4** 51 15N 36 21 E
Obozerskaya = Obozerskiy, Russia **24 B7** 63 34N 40 21 E
Obozerskiy, Russia **24 B7** 63 34N 40 21 E
Observatory Inlet, Canada **72 B3** 55 10N 129 54W
Obshchi Syrt, Russia **6 E16** 52 0N 53 0 E
Obskaya Guba, Russia **26 C8** 69 0N 73 0 E
Obuasi, Ghana **50 G5** 6 17N 1 40W
Ocala, U.S.A. **77 L4** 29 11N 82 8W
Ocampo, Chihuahua, Mexico **86 B3** 28 9N 108 24W
Ocampo, Tamaulipas, Mexico **87 C5** 22 50N 99 20W
Ocaña, Spain **19 C4** 39 55N 3 30W
Ocanomowoc, U.S.A. **80 D10** 43 7N 88 30W
Occidental, Cordillera, Colombia **92 C3** 5 0N 76 0W
Occidental, Grand Erg, Algeria **50 B6** 30 20N 1 0 E
Ocean City, Md., U.S.A. **76 F8** 38 20N 75 5W
Ocean City, N.J., U.S.A. **76 F8** 39 17N 74 35W
Ocean City, Wash., U.S.A. **84 C2** 47 4N 124 10W
Ocean Falls, Canada **72 C3** 52 18N 127 48W
Ocean I. = Banaba, Kiribati **64 H8** 0 45S 169 50 E
Ocean Park, U.S.A. **84 D2** 46 30N 124 3W
Oceano, U.S.A. **85 K6** 35 6N 120 37W
Oceanport, U.S.A. **79 F10** 40 19N 74 3W
Oceanside, U.S.A. **85 M9** 33 12N 117 23W
Ochil Hills, U.K. **12 E5** 56 14N 3 40W
Ocilla, U.S.A. **77 K4** 31 36N 83 15W
Ocmulgee →, U.S.A. **77 K4** 31 58N 82 33W
Ocniţa, Moldova **17 D14** 48 25N 27 30 E
Oconee →, U.S.A. **77 K4** 31 58N 82 33W
Oconto, U.S.A. **76 C2** 44 53N 87 52W
Oconto Falls, U.S.A. **76 C1** 44 52N 88 9W
Ocosingo, Mexico **87 D6** 17 10N 92 15W
Ocotal, Nic. **88 D2** 13 41N 86 31W
Ocotlán, Mexico **86 C4** 20 21N 102 42W
Ocotlán de Morelos, Mexico **87 D5** 16 48N 96 40W
Ōda, Japan **31 G6** 35 11N 132 30 E
Ódáðahraun, Iceland **8 D5** 65 5N 17 0W
Odate, Japan **30 D10** 40 16N 140 34 E
Odawara, Japan **31 G9** 35 20N 139 6 E
Odda, Norway **9 F12** 60 3N 6 35 E
Odei →, Canada **73 B9** 56 6N 96 54W
Ödemiş, Turkey **21 E13** 38 15N 28 0 E
Odendaalsrus, S. Africa **56 D4** 27 48S 26 45 E
Odense, Denmark **9 J14** 55 22N 10 23 E
Oder →, Europe **16 B8** 53 33N 14 38 E
Odesa, Ukraine **25 E5** 46 30N 30 45 E
Odessa = Odesa, Ukraine **25 E5** 46 30N 30 45 E
Odessa, Canada **79 B8** 44 17N 76 43W
Odessa, Tex., U.S.A. **81 K3** 31 52N 102 23W
Odessa, Wash., U.S.A. **82 C4** 47 20N 118 41W
Odiakwe, Botswana **56 C4** 20 12S 25 17 E
Odienné, Ivory C. **50 G4** 9 30N 7 34W
Odintsovo, Russia **24 C6** 55 39N 37 15 E
O'Donnell, U.S.A. **81 J4** 32 58N 101 50W
Odorheiu Secuiesc, Romania **17 E13** 46 21N 25 21 E
Odra = Oder →, Europe **16 B8** 53 33N 14 38 E
Odzi, Zimbabwe **57 B5** 19 0S 32 20 E
Odzi →, Zimbabwe **57 B5** 19 45S 32 23 E
Oeiras, Brazil **93 E10** 7 0S 42 8W
Oelrichs, U.S.A. **80 D3** 43 11N 103 14W
Oelwein, U.S.A. **80 D9** 42 41N 91 55W
Oenpelli, Australia **60 B5** 12 20S 133 4 E
Ofanto →, Italy **20 D7** 41 22N 16 13 E
Offa, Nigeria **50 G6** 8 13N 4 42 E
Offaly □, Ireland **13 C4** 53 15N 7 30W
Offenbach, Germany **16 C5** 50 6N 8 44 E
Offenburg, Germany **16 D4** 48 28N 7 56 E
Ofotfjorden, Norway **8 B17** 68 27N 17 0 E
Ōfunato, Japan **30 E10** 39 4N 141 43 E
Oga, Japan **30 E9** 39 55N 139 50 E
Oga-Hantō, Japan **30 E9** 39 58N 139 47 E
Ogaden, Ethiopia **46 F3** 7 30N 45 30 E
Ōgaki, Japan **31 G8** 35 21N 136 37 E
Ogallala, U.S.A. **80 E4** 41 8N 101 43W
Ogasawara Gunto, Pac. Oc. **28 G18** 27 0N 142 0 E
Ogbomosho, Nigeria **50 G6** 8 1N 4 11 E
Ogden, U.S.A. **82 F7** 41 13N 111 58W
Ogdensburg, U.S.A. **79 B9** 44 42N 75 30W
Ogeechee →, U.S.A. **77 K5** 31 50N 81 3W
Ogilby, U.S.A. **85 N12** 32 49N 114 50W
Oglio →, Italy **20 B4** 45 2N 10 39 E
Ogmore, Australia **62 C4** 22 37S 149 35 E
Ogoki, Canada **70 B2** 51 38N 85 58W
Ogoki →, Canada **70 B2** 51 38N 85 57W
Ogoki L., Canada **70 B2** 50 50N 87 10W
Ogoki Res., Canada **70 B2** 50 45N 88 15W
Ogooué →, Gabon **52 E1** 1 0S 9 0 E
Ogowe = Ogooué →, Gabon **52 E1** 1 0S 9 0 E
Ogre, Latvia **9 H21** 56 49N 24 36 E
Ogurchinskiy, Ostrov, Turkmenistan **45 B7** 38 55N 53 2 E
Ohai, N.Z. **59 L2** 45 55S 168 0 E
Ohakune, N.Z. **59 H5** 39 24S 175 24 E
Ohata, Japan **30 D10** 41 24N 141 10 E
Ohau, L., N.Z. **59 L2** 44 15S 169 53 E
Ohio □, U.S.A. **78 F2** 40 15N 82 45W
Ohio →, U.S.A. **76 G1** 36 59N 89 8W
Ohře →, Czech Rep. **16 C8** 50 30N 14 10 E
Ohrid, Macedonia **21 D9** 41 8N 20 52 E
Ohridsko Jezero, Macedonia **21 D9** 41 8N 20 52 E
Ohrigstad, S. Africa **57 C5** 24 39S 30 36 E
Oiapoque, Brazil **93** 3 50N 51 50W
Oikou, China **35 E9** 38 35N 117 42 E
Oil City, U.S.A. **78 E5** 41 26N 79 42W
Oil Springs, Canada **78 D2** 42 47N 82 7W
Oildale, U.S.A. **85 K7** 35 25N 119 1W
Oise →, France **18 B5** 49 0N 2 4 E
Ōita, Japan **31 H5** 33 14N 131 36 E
Ōita □, Japan **31 H5** 33 15N 131 30 E
Oiticica, Brazil **93 E10** 5 3S 41 5W
Ojacaliente, Mexico **86 C4** 22 34N 102 15W
Ojai, U.S.A. **85 L7** 34 27N 119 15W
Ojinaga, Mexico **86 B4** 29 34N 104 25W
Ojiya, Japan **31 F9** 37 18N 138 48 E
Ojos del Salado, Cerro, Argentina **94 B2** 27 0S 68 40W
Oka →, Russia **24 C7** 56 20N 43 59 E
Okaba, Indonesia **37 F9** 8 6S 139 42 E
Okahandja, Namibia **56 C2** 22 0S 16 59 E
Okanagan L., Canada **72 D5** 50 0N 119 30W
Okanogan, U.S.A. **82 B4** 48 22N 119 35W
Okanogan →, U.S.A. **82 B4** 48 6N 119 44W
Okaputa, Namibia **56 C2** 20 5S 17 0 E
Okara, Pakistan **42 D5** 30 50N 73 31 E
Okaukuejo, Namibia **56 B2** 19 10S 16 0 E
Okavango Delta, Botswana **56 B3** 18 45S 22 45 E
Okavango Swamp = Okavango Delta, Botswana **56 B3** 18 45S 22 45 E
Okaya, Japan **31 F9** 36 5N 138 10 E
Okayama, Japan **31 G6** 34 40N 133 54 E
Okayama □, Japan **31 G6** 35 0N 133 50 E
Okazaki, Japan **31 G8** 34 57N 137 10 E
Okeechobee, U.S.A. **77 M5** 27 15N 80 50W
Okeechobee, L., U.S.A. **77 M5** 27 0N 80 50W
Okefenokee Swamp, U.S.A. **77 K4** 30 40N 82 20W
Okehampton, U.K. **11 G4** 50 44N 4 0W
Okha, India **42 H3** 22 27N 69 4 E
Okha, Russia **27 D15** 53 40N 143 0 E
Okhotsk, Russia **27 D15** 59 20N 143 10 E
Okhotsk, Sea of, Asia **27 D15** 55 0N 145 0 E
Okhotskiy Perevoz, Russia **27 C14** 61 52N 135 35 E
Okhtyrka, Ukraine **25 D5** 50 25N 35 0 E
Oki-Shotō, Japan **31 F6** 36 5N 133 15 E
Okiep, S. Africa **56 D2** 29 39S 17 53 E
Okinawa □, Japan **31 L4** 26 40N 128 0 E
Okinawa-Guntō, Japan **31 L4** 26 40N 128 0 E
Okinawa-Jima, Japan **31 L4** 26 32N 128 0 E
Okino-erabu-Shima, Japan **31 L4** 27 21N 128 33 E
Oklahoma □, U.S.A. **81 H6** 35 20N 97 30W
Oklahoma City, U.S.A. **81 H6** 35 30N 97 30W
Okmulgee, U.S.A. **81 H7** 35 37N 95 58W
Oknitsa = Ocniţa, Moldova **17 D14** 48 25N 27 30 E
Okolo, Uganda **54 B3** 2 37N 31 8 E
Okolona, U.S.A. **81 J10** 34 0N 88 45W
Okombahe, Namibia **56 C2** 21 23S 15 22 E
Okotoks, Canada **72 C6** 50 43N 113 58W
Oksibil, Indonesia **37 E10** 4 59S 140 35 E
Oksovskiy, Russia **24 B6** 62 33N 39 57 E
Oktabrsk = Oktyabrsk, Kazakstan **25 E10** 49 28N 57 25 E
Oktyabrsk, Kazakstan **25 E10** 49 28N 57 25 E
Oktyabrskiy = Aktsyabrski, Belarus **17 B15** 52 38N 28 53 E
Oktyabrskiy, Russia **24 D9** 54 28N 53 28 E
Oktyabrskoy Revolyutsii, Ostrov, Russia **27 B10** 79 30N 97 0 E
Okuru, N.Z. **59 K2** 43 55S 168 55 E
Okushiri-Tō, Japan **30 C9** 42 15N 139 30 E
Okwa →, Botswana **56 C3** 22 30S 23 0 E
Ola, U.S.A. **81 H8** 35 2N 93 13W
Ólafsfjörður, Iceland **8 C4** 66 4N 18 39W
Ólafsvík, Iceland **8 D2** 64 53N 23 43W
Olancha, U.S.A. **85 J8** 36 17N 118 1W
Olancha Pk., U.S.A. **85 J8** 36 15N 118 7W
Olanchito, Honduras **88 C2** 15 30N 86 30W
Öland, Sweden **9 H17** 56 45N 16 38 E
Olary, Australia **63 E3** 32 18S 140 19 E
Olascoaga, Argentina **94 D3** 35 15S 60 39W
Olathe, U.S.A. **80 F7** 38 53N 94 49W
Olavarría, Argentina **94 D3** 36 55S 60 20W
Oława, Poland **17 C9** 50 57N 17 20 E
Ólbia, Italy **20 D3** 40 55N 9 31 E
Olcott, U.S.A. **78 C6** 43 20N 78 42W
Old Bahama Chan. = Bahama, Canal Viejo de, W. Indies **88 B4** 22 10N 77 30W
Old Baldy Pk. = San Antonio, Mt., U.S.A. **85 L9** 34 17N 117 38W
Old Castile = Castilla y Leon □, Spain **19 B3** 42 0N 5 0W
Old Crow, Canada **68 B6** 67 30N 139 55W
Old Dale, U.S.A. **85 L11** 34 8N 115 47W
Old Forge, N.Y., U.S.A. **79 C10** 43 43N 74 58W
Old Forge, Pa., U.S.A. **79 E9** 41 22N 75 45W
Old Perlican, Canada **71 C9** 48 5N 53 1W
Old Shinyanga, Tanzania **54 C3** 3 33S 33 27 E
Old Speck Mt., U.S.A. **79 B14** 44 34N 70 57W
Old Town, U.S.A. **77 C11** 44 56N 68 39W
Old Washington, U.S.A. **78 F3** 40 2N 81 27W
Old Wives L., Canada **73 C7** 50 5N 106 0W
Oldbury, U.K. **11 F5** 51 38N 2 33W
Oldcastle, Ireland **13 C4** 53 46N 7 10W
Oldeani, Tanzania **54 C4** 3 22S 35 35 E
Oldenburg, Germany **16 B5** 53 9N 8 13 E
Oldenzaal, Neths. **15 B6** 52 19N 6 53 E
Oldham, U.K. **10 D5** 53 33N 2 7W
Oldman →, Canada **72 D6** 49 57N 111 42W
Oldmeldrum, U.K. **12 D6** 57 20N 2 19W
Olds, Canada **72 C6** 51 50N 114 10W
Oldziyt, Mongolia **34 B5** 44 40N 109 1 E
Olean, U.S.A. **78 D6** 42 5N 78 26W
Olekma →, Russia **27 C13** 60 22N 120 42 E
Olekminsk, Russia **27 C13** 60 25N 120 30 E
Oleksandriya, Ukraine **17 C14** 50 37N 26 19 E
Olema, U.S.A. **84 G4** 38 3N 122 47W
Olenegorsk, Russia **24 A5** 68 9N 33 18 E
Olenek, Russia **27 C12** 68 28N 112 18 E
Olenek →, Russia **27 B13** 73 0N 120 10 E
Oléron, Î. d', France **18 D3** 45 55N 1 15W
Oleśnica, Poland **17 C9** 51 13N 17 22 E
Olevsk, Ukraine **17 C14** 51 12N 27 39 E
Olga, Russia **27 E14** 43 50N 135 14 E
Olga, L., Canada **70 C4** 49 47N 77 15W
Olga, Mt., Australia **61 E5** 25 20S 130 50 E
Olhão, Portugal **19 D2** 37 3N 7 48W
Olifants →, Africa **57 C5** 23 57S 31 58 E
Olifants →, Namibia **56 C2** 25 30S 19 30 E
Olifantshoek, S. Africa **56 D3** 27 57S 22 42 E
Ólimbos, Óros, Greece **21 D10** 40 6N 22 23 E
Olímpia, Brazil **95 A6** 20 44S 48 54W
Olinda, Brazil **93 E12** 8 1S 34 51W
Oliva, Argentina **94 C3** 32 0S 63 38W
Olivehurst, U.S.A. **84 F5** 39 6N 121 34W
Olivenza, Spain **19 C2** 38 41N 7 9W
Oliver, Canada **72 D5** 49 13N 119 37W
Oliver L., Canada **73 B8** 56 56N 103 22W
Ollagüe, Chile **94 A2** 21 15S 68 10W
Olney, Ill., U.S.A. **76 F1** 38 44N 88 5W
Olney, Tex., U.S.A. **81 J5** 33 22N 98 45W
Olomane →, Canada **71 B7** 50 14N 60 37W
Olomouc, Czech Rep. **17 D9** 49 38N 17 12 E
Olonets, Russia **24 B5** 61 0N 32 54 E
Olongapo, Phil. **37 B6** 14 50N 120 18 E
Olot, Spain **19 A7** 42 11N 2 30 E
Olovyannaya, Russia **27 D12** 50 58N 115 35 E
Oloy →, Russia **27 C16** 66 29N 159 29 E
Olsztyn, Poland **17 B11** 53 48N 20 29 E
Olt →, Romania **17 G13** 43 43N 24 51 E
Olteniţa, Romania **17 F14** 44 7N 26 42 E
Olton, U.S.A. **81 H3** 34 11N 102 8W
Olymbos, Cyprus **23 D12** 35 21N 33 45 E
Olympia, Greece **21 F9** 37 39N 21 39 E
Olympia, U.S.A. **84 D4** 47 3N 122 53W
Olympic Dam, Australia **63 E2** 30 30S 136 55 E
Olympic Mts., U.S.A. **84 C3** 47 55N 123 45W
Olympic Nat. Park, U.S.A. **84 C3** 47 48N 123 30W
Olympus, Cyprus **23 E11** 34 56N 32 52 E
Olympus, Mt. = Ólimbos, Óros, Greece **21 D10** 40 6N 22 23 E
Olympus, Mt. = Uludağ, Turkey **21 D13** 40 4N 29 13 E
Olympus, Mt., U.S.A. **84 C3** 47 48N 123 43W
Olyphant, U.S.A. **79 E9** 41 27N 75 36W
Om →, Russia **26 D8** 54 59N 73 22 E
Om Koi, Thailand **38 D2** 17 48N 98 22 E
Ōma, Japan **30 D10** 41 45N 141 5 E
Ōmachi, Japan **31 F8** 36 30N 137 50 E
Omae-Zaki, Japan **31 G9** 34 36N 138 14 E
Ōmagari, Japan **30 E10** 39 27N 140 29 E
Omagh, U.K. **13 B4** 54 36N 7 19W
Omagh □, U.K. **13 B4** 54 35N 7 15W
Omaha, U.S.A. **80 E7** 41 17N 95 58W
Omak, U.S.A. **82 B4** 48 25N 119 31W
Omalos, Greece **23 D5** 35 19N 23 55 E
Oman ■, Asia **46 C6** 23 0N 58 0 E
Oman, G. of, Asia **45 E8** 24 30N 58 30 E
Omaruru, Namibia **56 C2** 21 26S 16 0 E
Omaruru →, Namibia **56 C1** 22 7S 14 15 E
Omate, Peru **92 G4** 16 45S 71 0W
Ombai, Selat, Indonesia **37 F6** 8 30S 124 50 E
Omboué, Gabon **52 E1** 1 35S 9 15 E
Ombrone →, Italy **20 C4** 42 42N 11 5 E
Omdurmân, Sudan **51 E12** 15 40N 32 28 E
Omemee, Canada **78 B6** 44 18N 78 33W
Omeonga, Dem. Rep. of the Congo **54 C1** 3 40S 24 22 E
Ometepe, I. de, Nic. **88 D2** 11 32N 85 35W
Ometepec, Mexico **87 D5** 16 39N 98 23W
Ominato, Japan **30 D10** 41 17N 141 10 E
Omineca →, Canada **72 B4** 56 3N 124 16W
Omitara, Namibia **56 C2** 22 16S 18 2 E
Ōmiya, Japan **31 G9** 35 54N 139 38 E
Ommen, Neths. **15 B6** 52 31N 6 26 E
Ömnögovĭ □, Mongolia **34 C3** 43 15N 104 0 E
Omo →, Ethiopia **46 F2** 6 25N 36 10 E
Omodhos, Cyprus **23 E11** 34 51N 32 48 E
Omolon →, Russia **27 C16** 68 42N 158 36 E
Omono-Gawa →, Japan **30 E10** 39 46N 140 3 E
Omsk, Russia **26 D8** 55 0N 73 12 E
Omsukchan, Russia **27 C16** 62 32N 155 48 E
Ōmu, Japan **30 B11** 44 34N 142 58 E
Omul, Vf., Romania **17 F13** 45 27N 25 29 E
Ōmura, Japan **31 H4** 32 56N 129 57 E
Omuramba Omatako →, Namibia **56 B2** 17 45S 20 25 E
Omuramba Ovambo →, Namibia **56 B2** 18 45S 16 59 E
Ōmuta, Japan **31 H5** 33 5N 130 26 E
Onaga, U.S.A. **80 F6** 39 29N 96 10W
Onalaska, U.S.A. **80 D9** 43 53N 91 14W
Onancock, U.S.A. **76 G8** 37 43N 75 45W
Onang, Indonesia **37 E5** 3 2S 118 49 E
Onaping L., Canada **70 C3** 47 3N 81 30W
Onavas, Mexico **86 B3** 28 28N 109 30W
Onawa, U.S.A. **80 D6** 42 2N 96 6W
Oncócua, Angola **56 B1** 16 30S 13 25 E
Onda, Spain **19 C5** 39 55N 0 17W
Ondaejin, N. Korea **35 D15** 41 34N 129 40 E
Ondangwa, Namibia **56 B2** 17 57S 16 4 E
Ondjiva, Angola **56 B2** 16 48S 15 50 E
Öndörshil, Mongolia **34 B5** 45 13N 108 5 E
Öndverðarnes, Iceland **8 D1** 64 52N 24 0W
One Tree, Australia **63 E3** 34 11S 144 43 E
Onega, Russia **24 B6** 64 0N 38 10 E
Onega →, Russia **24 B6** 63 58N 38 2 E
Onega, G. of = Onezhskaya Guba, Russia **24 B6** 64 24N 36 38 E
Onega, L. = Onezhskoye Ozero, Russia **24 B6** 61 44N 35 22 E
Oneida, U.S.A. **79 C9** 43 6N 75 39W
Oneida L., U.S.A. **79 C9** 43 12N 75 54W
O'Neill, U.S.A. **80 D5** 42 27N 98 39W
Onekotan, Ostrov, Russia **27 E16** 49 25N 154 45 E
Onema, Dem. Rep. of the Congo **54 C1** 4 35S 24 30 E
Oneonta, U.S.A. **79 D9** 42 27N 75 4W
Oneşti, Romania **17 E14** 46 17N 26 47 E
Onezhskaya Guba, Russia **24 B6** 64 24N 36 38 E
Onezhskoye Ozero, Russia **24 B6** 61 44N 35 22 E
Ongarue, N.Z. **59 H5** 38 42S 175 19 E
Ongers →, S. Africa **56 E3** 31 4S 23 13 E
Ongerup, Australia **61 F2** 33 58S 118 28 E
Ongjin, N. Korea **35 F13** 37 56N 125 21 E
Ongkharak, Thailand **38 E3** 14 8N 101 1 E
Ongniud Qi, China **35 C10** 43 0N 118 38 E
Ongoka, Dem. Rep. of the Congo **54 C2** 1 20S 26 0 E
Ongole, India **40 M12** 15 33N 80 2 E
Ongon = Havirga, Mongolia **34 B7** 45 41N 113 5 E
Onida, U.S.A. **80 C4** 44 42N 100 4W
Onilahy →, Madag. **57 C7** 23 34S 43 45 E
Onitsha, Nigeria **50 G7** 6 6N 6 42 E
Onoda, Japan **31 G5** 33 59N 131 11 E
Onpyŏng-ni, S. Korea **35 H14** 33 25N 126 55 E
Onslow, Australia **60 D2** 21 40S 115 12 E
Onslow B., U.S.A. **77 H7** 34 20N 77 15W
Ontake-San, Japan **31 G8** 35 53N 137 29 E
Ontario, Calif., U.S.A. **85 L9** 34 4N 117 39W
Ontario, Oreg., U.S.A. **82 D5** 44 2N 116 58W
Ontario □, Canada **70 B2** 48 0N 83 0W
Ontario, L., N. Amer. **78 C7** 43 20N 78 0W
Ontonagon, U.S.A. **80 B10** 46 52N 89 19W
Onyx, U.S.A. **85 K8** 35 41N 118 14W
Oodnadatta, Australia **63 D2** 27 33S 135 30 E
Ooldea, Australia **61 F5** 30 27S 131 50 E
Oombulgurri, Australia **60 C4** 15 15S 127 45 E
Oorindi, Australia **62 C3** 20 40S 141 1 E
Oost-Vlaanderen □, Belgium **15 C3** 51 5N 3 50 E
Oostende, Belgium **15 C2** 51 15N 2 54 E
Oosterhout, Neths. **15 C4** 51 39N 4 47 E
Oosterschelde →, Neths. **15 C4** 51 33N 4 0 E
Oosterwolde, Neths. **15 B6** 53 0N 6 17 E
Ootacamund = Udagamandalam, India **40 P10** 11 30N 76 44 E
Ootsa L., Canada **72 C3** 53 50N 126 2W
Opala, Dem. Rep. of the Congo **54 C1** 0 40S 24 20 E
Opanake, Sri Lanka **40 R12** 6 35N 80 40 E
Opasatika, Canada **70 C3** 49 30N 82 50W
Opasquia Prov. Park, Canada **70 B1** 53 33N 93 5W
Opava, Czech Rep. **17 D9** 49 57N 17 58 E
Opelika, U.S.A. **77 J3** 32 39N 85 23W
Opelousas, U.S.A. **81 K8** 30 32N 92 5W
Opémisca, L., Canada **70 C5** 49 56N 74 52W
Opheim, U.S.A. **82 B10** 48 51N 106 24W
Ophthalmia Ra., Australia **60 D2** 23 15S 119 30 E
Opinaca →, Canada **70 B4** 52 15N 78 2W
Opinaca, Rés., Canada **70 B4** 52 39N 76 20W
Opinnagau →, Canada **70 B3** 54 12N 82 25W
Opiscoteo, L., Canada **71 B6** 53 10N 68 10W
Opole, Poland **17 C9** 50 42N 17 58 E
Oponono L., Namibia **56 B2** 18 8S 15 45 E
Oporto = Porto, Portugal **19 B1** 41 8N 8 40W
Opotiki, N.Z. **59 H6** 38 1S 177 19 E
Opp, U.S.A. **77 K2** 31 17N 86 16W
Oppdal, Norway **9 E13** 62 35N 9 41 E
Opportunity, U.S.A. **82 C5** 47 39N 117 15W
Opua, N.Z. **59 F5** 35 19S 174 9 E
Opunake, N.Z. **59 H4** 39 26S 173 52 E
Opuwo, Namibia **56 B1** 18 3S 13 45 E
Ora, Cyprus **23 E12** 34 51N 33 12 E
Oracle, U.S.A. **83 K8** 32 37N 110 46W
Oradea, Romania **17 E11** 47 2N 21 58 E
Öræfajökull, Iceland **8 D5** 64 2N 16 39W
Orai, India **43 G8** 25 58N 79 30 E
Oral = Zhayyq →, Kazakstan **25 E9** 47 0N 51 48 E
Oral, Kazakstan **25 D9** 51 20N 51 20 E
Oran, Algeria **50 A5** 35 45N 0 39W
Orange, Australia **63 E4** 33 15S 149 7 E
Orange, France **18 D6** 44 8N 4 47 E
Orange, Calif., U.S.A. **85 M9** 33 47N 117 51W
Orange, Mass., U.S.A. **79 D12** 42 35N 72 19W
Orange, Tex., U.S.A. **81 K8** 30 6N 93 44W
Orange, Va., U.S.A. **76 F6** 38 15N 78 7W
Orange →, S. Africa **56 D2** 28 41S 16 28 E
Orange, C., Brazil **93 C8** 4 20N 51 30W
Orange Cove, U.S.A. **84 J7** 36 38N 119 19W
Orange Free State = Free State □, S. Africa **56 D4** 28 30S 27 0 E
Orange Grove, U.S.A. **81 M6** 27 58N 97 56W
Orange Walk, Belize **87 D7** 18 6N 88 33W
Orangeburg, U.S.A. **77 J5** 33 30N 80 52W
Orangeville, Canada **78 C4** 43 55N 80 5W
Oranienburg, Germany **16 B7** 52 45N 13 14 E
Oranje = Orange →, S. Africa **56 D2** 28 41S 16 28 E
Oranje Vrystaat = Free State □, S. Africa **56 D4** 28 30S 27 0 E
Oranjemund, Namibia **56 D2** 28 38S 16 29 E
Oranjerivier, S. Africa **56 D3** 29 40S 24 12 E
Oranjestad, Aruba **89 D5** 12 32N 70 2W
Orapa, Botswana **53 J5** 21 15S 25 30 E
Oras, Phil. **37 B7** 12 9N 125 28 E
Oraşul Stalin = Braşov, Romania **17 F13** 45 38N 25 35 E
Orbetello, Italy **20 C4** 42 27N 11 13 E
Orbisonia, U.S.A. **78 F7** 40 15N 77 54W
Orbost, Australia **63 F4** 37 40S 148 29 E
Orcas I., U.S.A. **84 B4** 48 42N 122 56W
Orchard City, U.S.A. **83 G10** 38 50N 107 58W
Orchila, I., Venezuela **89 D6** 11 48N 66 10W
Orcutt, U.S.A. **85 L6** 34 52N 120 27W
Ord, U.S.A. **80 E5** 41 36N 98 56W
Ord →, Australia **60 C4** 15 33S 128 15 E
Ord, Mt., Australia **60 C4** 17 20S 125 34 E
Orderville, U.S.A. **83 H7** 37 17N 112 38W
Ordos = Mu Us Shamo, China **34 E5** 39 0N 109 0 E
Ordu, Turkey **25 F6** 40 55N 37 53 E
Ordway, U.S.A. **80 F3** 38 13N 103 46W
Ordzhonikidze = Vladikavkaz, Russia **25 F7** 43 0N 44 35 E
Ore, Dem. Rep. of the Congo **54 B2** 3 17N 29 30 E
Ore Mts. = Erzgebirge, Germany **16 C7** 50 27N 12 55 E
Örebro, Sweden **9 G16** 59 20N 15 18 E
Oregon, U.S.A. **80 D10** 42 1N 89 20W
Oregon □, U.S.A. **82 E3** 44 0N 121 0W
Oregon City, U.S.A. **84 E4** 45 21N 122 36W
Orekhovo-Zuyevo, Russia **24 C6** 55 50N 38 55 E
Orel, Russia **24 D6** 52 57N 36 3 E
Orem, U.S.A. **82 F8** 40 19N 111 42W
Ören, Turkey **21 F12** 37 3N 27 57 E
Orenburg, Russia **24 D10** 51 45N 55 6 E
Orense = Ourense, Spain **19 A2** 42 19N 7 55W
Orepuki, N.Z. **59 M1** 46 19S 167 46 E
Orestiás, Greece **21 D12** 41 30N 26 33 E
Orestos Pereyra, Mexico **86 B3** 26 31N 105 40W
Orford Ness, U.K. **11 E9** 52 5N 1 35 E

Organos, Pta. de los, Canary Is. 22 F2 28 12N 17 17W
Orgaz, Spain 19 C4 39 39N 3 53W
Orgeyev = Orhei, Moldova 17 E15 47 24N 28 50 E
Orhaneli, Turkey 21 E13 39 54N 28 59 E
Orhangazi, Turkey 21 D13 40 29N 29 18 E
Orhei, Moldova 17 E15 47 24N 28 50 E
Orhon Gol →, Mongolia 32 A5 50 21N 106 0 E
Oriental, Cordillera, Colombia 92 B4 6 0N 73 0W
Oriental, Grand Erg, Algeria 50 B7 30 0N 6 30 E
Orientale □, Dem. Rep. of the Congo 54 B2 2 20N 26 0 E
Oriente, Argentina 94 D3 38 44S 60 37W
Orihuela, Spain 19 C5 38 7N 0 55W
Orillia, Canada 78 B5 44 40N 79 24W
Orinoco →, Venezuela 92 B6 9 15N 61 30W
Orion, Canada 73 D6 49 27N 110 49W
Oriskany, U.S.A. 79 C9 43 10N 75 20W
Orissa □, India 41 K14 20 0N 84 0 E
Orissaare, Estonia 9 G20 58 34N 23 5 E
Oristano, Italy 20 E3 39 54N 8 36 E
Oristano, G. di, Italy 20 E3 39 50N 8 29 E
Orizaba, Mexico 87 D5 18 51N 97 6W
Orkanger, Norway 8 E13 63 18N 9 52 E
Orkla →, Norway 8 E13 63 18N 9 51 E
Orkney, S. Africa 56 D4 26 58S 26 40 E
Orkney □, U.K. 12 B5 59 2N 3 13W
Orkney Is., U.K. 12 B6 59 0N 3 0W
Orland, U.S.A. 84 F4 39 45N 122 12W
Orlando, U.S.A. 77 L5 28 33N 81 23W
Orléanais, France 18 C5 48 0N 2 0 E
Orléans, France 18 C4 47 54N 1 52 E
Orleans, U.S.A. 79 B12 44 49N 72 12W
Orléans, I. d', Canada 71 C5 46 54N 70 58W
Ormara, Pakistan 40 G4 25 16N 64 33 E
Ormoc, Phil. 37 B6 11 0N 124 37 E
Ormond, N.Z. 59 H6 38 33S 177 56 E
Ormond Beach, U.S.A. 77 L5 29 17N 81 3W
Ormskirk, U.K. 10 D5 53 35N 2 54W
Ormstown, Canada 79 A11 45 8N 74 0W
Örnsköldsvik, Sweden 8 E18 63 17N 18 40 E
Oro, N. Korea 35 D14 40 1N 127 27 E
Oro →, Mexico 86 B3 25 35N 105 2W
Oro Grande, U.S.A. 85 L9 34 36N 117 20W
Oro Valley, U.S.A. 83 K8 32 26N 110 58W
Orocué, Colombia 92 C4 4 48N 71 20W
Orofino, U.S.A. 82 C5 46 29N 116 15W
Orol Dengizi = Aral Sea, Asia 26 E7 44 30N 60 0 E
Oromocto, Canada 71 C6 45 54N 66 29W
Orono, Canada 78 C6 43 59N 78 37W
Orono, U.S.A. 77 C11 44 53N 68 40W
Oronsay, U.K. 12 E2 56 1N 6 15W
Oroqen Zizhiqi, China 33 A7 50 34N 123 43 E
Oroquieta, Phil. 37 C6 8 32N 123 44 E
Orosháza, Hungary 17 E11 46 32N 20 42 E
Orotukan, Russia 27 C16 62 16N 151 42 E
Oroville, Calif., U.S.A. 84 F5 39 31N 121 33W
Oroville, Wash., U.S.A. 82 B4 48 56N 119 26W
Oroville, L., U.S.A. 84 F5 39 33N 121 29W
Orroroo, Australia 63 E2 32 43S 138 38 E
Orrville, U.S.A. 78 F3 40 50N 81 46W
Orsha, Belarus 24 D5 54 30N 30 25 E
Orsk, Russia 26 D6 51 12N 58 34 E
Orşova, Romania 17 F12 44 41N 22 25 E
Ortaca, Turkey 21 F13 36 49N 28 45 E
Ortegal, C., Spain 19 A2 43 43N 7 52W
Orthez, France 18 E3 43 29N 0 48W
Ortigueira, Spain 19 A2 43 40N 7 50W
Orting, U.S.A. 84 C4 47 6N 122 12W
Ortles, Italy 18 C9 46 31N 10 33 E
Ortón →, Bolivia 92 F5 10 50S 67 0W
Ortonville, U.S.A. 80 C6 45 19N 96 27W
Orūmīyeh, Iran 44 B5 37 40N 45 0 E
Orūmīyeh, Daryācheh-ye, Iran 44 B5 37 50N 45 30 E
Oruro, Bolivia 92 G5 18 0S 67 9W
Orust, Sweden 9 G14 58 10N 11 40 E
Oruzgān □, Afghan. 40 C5 33 30N 66 0 E
Orvieto, Italy 20 C5 42 43N 12 7 E
Orwell, N.Y., U.S.A. 79 C9 43 35N 75 50W
Orwell, Ohio, U.S.A. 78 E4 41 32N 80 52W
Orwell →, U.K. 11 F9 51 59N 1 18 E
Orwigsburg, U.S.A. 79 F8 40 38N 76 6W
Oryakhovo, Bulgaria 21 C10 43 40N 23 57 E
Osa, Russia 24 C10 57 17N 55 26 E
Osa, Pen. de, Costa Rica 88 E3 8 0N 84 0W
Osage, U.S.A. 80 D8 43 17N 92 49W
Osage →, U.S.A. 80 F9 38 35N 91 57W
Osage City, U.S.A. 80 F7 38 38N 95 50W
Ōsaka, Japan 31 G7 34 40N 135 30 E
Osan, S. Korea 35 F14 37 11N 127 4 E
Osawatomie, U.S.A. 80 F7 38 31N 94 57W
Osborne, U.S.A. 80 F5 39 26N 98 42W
Osceola, Ark., U.S.A. 81 H10 35 42N 89 58W
Osceola, Iowa, U.S.A. 80 E8 41 2N 93 46W
Oscoda, U.S.A. 78 B1 44 26N 83 20W
Ösel = Saaremaa, Estonia 9 G20 58 30N 22 30 E
Osgoode, Canada 79 A9 45 8N 75 36W
Osh, Kyrgyzstan 26 E8 40 37N 72 49 E
Oshakati, Namibia 53 H3 17 45S 15 40 E
Oshawa, Canada 78 C6 43 50N 78 50W
Oshigambo, Namibia 56 B2 17 45S 16 5 E
Oshkosh, Nebr., U.S.A. 80 E3 41 24N 102 21W
Oshkosh, Wis., U.S.A. 80 C10 44 1N 88 33W
Oshmyany = Ashmyany, Belarus 9 J21 54 26N 25 52 E
Oshnovīyeh, Iran 44 B5 37 2N 45 6 E
Oshogbo, Nigeria 50 G6 7 48N 4 37 E
Oshtorīnān, Iran 45 C6 34 1N 48 38 E
Oshwe, Dem. Rep. of the Congo 52 E3 3 25S 19 28 E
Osijek, Croatia 21 B8 45 34N 18 41 E
Osipenko = Berdyansk, Ukraine 25 E6 46 45N 36 50 E
Osipovichi = Asipovichy, Belarus 17 B15 53 19N 28 33 E
Osiyan, India 42 F5 26 43N 72 55 E
Osizweni, S. Africa 57 D5 27 49S 30 7 E
Oskaloosa, U.S.A. 80 E8 41 18N 92 39W
Oskarshamn, Sweden 9 H17 57 15N 16 27 E
Oskélanéo, Canada 70 C4 48 5N 75 15W
Öskemen, Kazakstan 26 E9 50 0N 82 36 E
Oslo, Norway 9 G14 59 55N 10 45 E
Oslofjorden, Norway 9 G14 59 20N 10 35 E
Osmanabad, India 40 K10 18 5N 76 10 E
Osmaniye, Turkey 25 G6 37 5N 36 10 E
Osnabrück, Germany 16 B5 52 17N 8 3 E
Osorio, Brazil 95 B5 29 53S 50 17W
Osorno, Chile 96 E2 40 25S 73 0W
Osoyoos, Canada 72 D5 49 0N 119 30W
Osøyro, Norway 9 F11 60 9N 5 30 E
Ospika →, Canada 72 B4 56 20N 124 0W
Osprey Reef, Australia 62 A4 13 52S 146 36 E
Oss, Neths. 15 C5 51 46N 5 32 E
Ossa, Mt., Australia 62 G4 41 52S 146 3 E
Óssa, Óros, Greece 21 E10 39 47N 22 42 E
Ossabaw I., U.S.A. 77 K5 31 50N 81 5W
Ossining, U.S.A. 79 E11 41 10N 73 55W
Ossipee, U.S.A. 79 C13 43 41N 71 7W
Ossokmanuan L., Canada 71 B7 53 25N 65 0W
Ossora, Russia 27 D17 59 20N 163 13 E
Ostend = Oostende, Belgium 15 C2 51 15N 2 54 E
Oster, Ukraine 17 C16 50 57N 30 53 E
Osterburg, U.S.A. 78 F6 40 16N 78 31W
Österdalälven, Sweden 9 F16 61 30N 13 45 E
Østerdalen, Norway 9 F14 61 40N 10 50 E
Östersund, Sweden 8 E16 63 10N 14 38 E
Ostfriesische Inseln, Germany 16 B4 53 42N 7 0 E
Ostrava, Czech Rep. 17 D10 49 51N 18 18 E
Ostróda, Poland 17 B10 53 42N 19 58 E
Ostroh, Ukraine 17 C14 50 20N 26 30 E
Ostrołęka, Poland 17 B11 53 4N 21 32 E
Ostrów Mazowiecka, Poland 17 B11 52 50N 21 51 E
Ostrów Wielkopolski, Poland 17 C9 51 36N 17 44 E
Ostrowiec-Świętokrzyski, Poland 17 C11 50 55N 21 22 E
Ostuni, Italy 21 D7 40 44N 17 35 E
Ōsumi-Kaikyō, Japan 31 J5 30 55N 131 0 E
Ōsumi-Shotō, Japan 31 J5 30 30N 130 0 E
Osuna, Spain 19 D3 37 14N 5 8W
Oswegatchie →, U.S.A. 79 B9 44 42N 75 30W
Oswego, U.S.A. 79 C8 43 27N 76 31W
Oswego →, U.S.A. 79 C8 43 27N 76 30W
Oswestry, U.K. 10 E4 52 52N 3 3W
Oświęcim, Poland 17 C10 50 2N 19 11 E
Otago □, N.Z. 59 L2 45 15S 170 0 E
Otago Harbour, N.Z. 59 L3 45 47S 170 42 E
Ōtake, Japan 31 G6 34 12N 132 13 E
Otaki, N.Z. 59 J5 40 45S 175 10 E
Otaru, Japan 30 C10 43 10N 141 0 E
Otaru-Wan = Ishikari-Wan, Japan 30 C10 43 25N 141 1 E
Otavalo, Ecuador 92 C3 0 13N 78 20W
Otavi, Namibia 56 B2 19 40S 17 24 E
Otchinjau, Angola 56 B1 16 30S 13 56 E
Otelnuk L., Canada 71 A6 56 9N 68 12W
Othello, U.S.A. 82 C4 46 50N 119 10W
Otjiwarongo, Namibia 56 C2 20 30S 16 33 E
Otoineppu, Japan 30 B11 44 44N 142 16 E
Otorohanga, N.Z. 59 H5 38 12S 175 14 E
Otoskwin →, Canada 70 B2 52 13N 88 6W
Otra →, Norway 9 G13 58 9N 8 1 E
Otranto, Italy 21 D8 40 9N 18 28 E
Otranto, C. d', Italy 21 D8 40 7N 18 30 E
Otranto, Str. of, Italy 21 D8 40 15N 18 40 E
Otse, S. Africa 56 D4 25 2S 25 45 E
Ōtsu, Japan 31 G7 35 0N 135 50 E
Ōtsuki, Japan 31 G9 35 36N 138 57 E
Ottawa = Outaouais →, Canada 70 C5 45 27N 74 8W
Ottawa, Canada 79 A9 45 27N 75 42W
Ottawa, Ill., U.S.A. 80 E10 41 21N 88 51W
Ottawa, Kans., U.S.A. 80 F7 38 37N 95 16W
Ottawa Is., Canada 69 C11 59 35N 80 10W
Otter Cr. →, U.S.A. 79 B11 44 13N 73 17W
Otter L., Canada 73 B8 55 35N 104 39W
Otterville, Canada 78 D4 42 55N 80 36W
Ottery St. Mary, U.K. 11 G4 50 44N 3 17W
Otto Beit Bridge, Zimbabwe 55 F2 15 59S 28 56 E
Ottosdal, S. Africa 56 D4 26 46S 25 59 E
Ottumwa, U.S.A. 80 E8 41 1N 92 25W
Oturkpo, Nigeria 50 G7 7 16N 8 8 E
Otway, B., Chile 96 G2 53 30S 74 0W
Otway, C., Australia 63 F3 38 52S 143 30 E
Otwock, Poland 17 B11 52 5N 21 20 E
Ou →, Laos 38 B4 20 4N 102 13 E
Ou Neua, Laos 38 A3 22 18N 101 48 E
Ou-Sammyaku, Japan 30 E10 39 20N 140 35 E
Ouachita →, U.S.A. 81 K9 31 38N 91 49W
Ouachita, L., U.S.A. 81 H8 34 34N 93 12W
Ouachita Mts., U.S.A. 81 H7 34 40N 94 25W
Ouagadougou, Burkina Faso 50 F5 12 25N 1 30W
Ouahran = Oran, Algeria 50 A5 35 45N 0 39W
Ouallene, Algeria 50 D6 24 41N 1 11 E
Ouargla, Algeria 50 B7 31 59N 5 16 E
Ouarzazate, Morocco 50 B4 30 55N 6 50W
Oubangi →, Dem. Rep. of the Congo 52 E3 0 30S 17 50 E
Ouddorp, Neths. 15 C3 51 50N 3 57 E
Oude Rijn →, Neths. 15 B4 52 12N 4 24 E
Oudenaarde, Belgium 15 D3 50 50N 3 37 E
Oudtshoorn, S. Africa 56 E3 33 35S 22 14 E
Ouessant, Î. d', France 18 B1 48 28N 5 6W
Ouesso, Congo 52 D3 1 37N 16 5 E
Ouest, Pte. de l', Canada 71 C7 49 52N 64 40W
Ouezzane, Morocco 50 B4 34 51N 5 35W
Oughterard, Ireland 13 C2 53 26N 9 18W
Oujda, Morocco 50 B5 34 41N 1 55W
Oulainen, Finland 8 D21 64 17N 24 47 E
Oulu, Finland 8 D21 65 1N 25 29 E
Oulujärvi, Finland 8 D22 64 25N 27 15 E
Oulujoki →, Finland 8 D21 65 1N 25 30 E
Oum Chalouba, Chad 51 E10 15 48N 20 46 E
Oum Hadjer, Chad 51 F9 13 18N 19 41 E
Ounasjoki →, Finland 8 C21 66 31N 25 40 E
Ounguati, Namibia 56 C2 22 0S 15 46 E
Ounianga Sérir, Chad 51 E10 18 54N 20 51 E
Our →, Lux. 15 E6 49 55N 6 5 E
Ouray, U.S.A. 83 G10 38 1N 107 40W
Ourense, Spain 19 A2 42 19N 7 55W
Ouricuri, Brazil 93 E10 7 53S 40 5W
Ourinhos, Brazil 95 A6 23 0S 49 54W
Ouro Fino, Brazil 95 A6 22 16S 46 25W
Ouro Prêto, Brazil 95 A7 20 20S 43 30W
Ourthe →, Belgium 15 D5 50 29N 5 35 E
Ouse →, E. Susx., U.K. 11 G8 50 47N 0 4 E
Ouse →, N. Yorks., U.K. 10 D7 53 44N 0 55W
Outaouais →, Canada 70 C5 45 27N 74 8W
Outardes →, Canada 71 C6 49 24N 69 30W
Outer Hebrides, U.K. 12 D1 57 30N 7 40W
Outjo, Namibia 56 C2 20 5S 16 7 E
Outlook, Canada 73 C7 51 30N 107 0W
Outokumpu, Finland 8 E23 62 43N 29 1 E
Ouyen, Australia 63 F3 35 1S 142 22 E
Ovalau, Fiji 59 C8 17 40S 178 48 E
Ovalle, Chile 94 C1 30 33S 71 18W
Ovamboland, Namibia 56 B2 18 30S 16 0 E
Overflakkee, Neths. 15 C4 51 44N 4 10 E
Overijssel □, Neths. 15 B6 52 25N 6 35 E
Overland Park, U.S.A. 80 F7 38 55N 94 50W
Overton, U.S.A. 85 J12 36 33N 114 27W
Övertorneå, Sweden 8 C20 66 23N 23 38 E
Ovid, U.S.A. 79 D8 42 41N 76 49W
Oviedo, Spain 19 A3 43 25N 5 50W
Oviši, Latvia 9 H19 57 33N 21 44 E
Ovoot, Mongolia 34 B7 45 21N 113 45 E
Övör Hangay □, Mongolia 34 B2 45 0N 102 30 E
Øvre Årdal, Norway 9 F12 61 19N 7 48 E
Ovruch, Ukraine 17 C15 51 25N 28 45 E
Owaka, N.Z. 59 M2 46 27S 169 40 E
Owambo = Ovamboland, Namibia 56 B2 18 30S 16 0 E
Owasco L., U.S.A. 79 D8 42 50N 76 31W
Owase, Japan 31 G8 34 7N 136 12 E
Owatonna, U.S.A. 80 C8 44 5N 93 14W
Owbeh, Afghan. 40 B3 34 28N 63 10 E
Owego, U.S.A. 79 D8 42 6N 76 16W
Owen Falls Dam, Uganda 54 B3 0 30N 33 5 E
Owen Sound, Canada 78 B4 44 35N 80 55W
Owens →, U.S.A. 84 J9 36 32N 117 59W
Owens L., U.S.A. 85 J9 36 26N 117 57W
Owensboro, U.S.A. 76 G2 37 46N 87 7W
Owl →, Canada 73 B10 57 51N 92 44W
Owo, Nigeria 50 G7 7 10N 5 39 E
Owosso, U.S.A. 76 D3 43 0N 84 10W
Owyhee, U.S.A. 82 F5 41 57N 116 6W
Owyhee →, U.S.A. 82 E5 43 49N 117 2W
Owyhee, L., U.S.A. 82 E5 43 38N 117 14W
Ox Mts. = Slieve Gamph, Ireland 13 B3 54 6N 9 0W
Öxarfjörður, Iceland 8 C5 66 15N 16 45W
Oxbow, Canada 73 D8 49 14N 102 10W
Oxelösund, Sweden 9 G17 58 43N 17 5 E
Oxford, N.Z. 59 K4 43 18S 172 11 E
Oxford, U.K. 11 F6 51 46N 1 15W
Oxford, Mass., U.S.A. 79 D13 42 7N 71 52W
Oxford, Miss., U.S.A. 81 H10 34 22N 89 31W
Oxford, N.C., U.S.A. 77 G6 36 19N 78 35W
Oxford, N.Y., U.S.A. 79 D9 42 27N 75 36W
Oxford, Ohio, U.S.A. 76 F3 39 31N 84 45W
Oxford L., Canada 73 C9 54 51N 95 37W
Oxfordshire □, U.K. 11 F6 51 48N 1 16W
Oxnard, U.S.A. 85 L7 34 12N 119 11W
Oxus = Amudarya →, Uzbekistan 26 E6 43 58N 59 34 E
Oya, Malaysia 36 D4 2 55N 111 55 E
Oyama, Japan 31 F9 36 18N 139 48 E
Oyem, Gabon 52 D2 1 34N 11 31 E
Oyen, Canada 73 C6 51 22N 110 28W
Oykel →, U.K. 12 D4 57 56N 4 26W
Oymyakon, Russia 27 C15 63 25N 142 44 E
Oyo, Nigeria 50 G6 7 46N 3 56 E
Oyster Bay, U.S.A. 79 F11 40 52N 73 32W
Ōyübari, Japan 30 C11 43 1N 142 5 E
Ozamiz, Phil. 37 C6 8 15N 123 50 E
Ozark, Ala., U.S.A. 77 K3 31 28N 85 39W
Ozark, Ark., U.S.A. 81 H8 35 29N 93 50W
Ozark, Mo., U.S.A. 81 G8 37 1N 93 12W
Ozark Plateau, U.S.A. 81 G9 37 20N 91 40W
Ozarks, L. of the, U.S.A. 80 F8 38 12N 92 38W
Ózd, Hungary 17 D11 48 14N 20 15 E
Ozette L., U.S.A. 84 B2 48 6N 124 38W
Ozona, U.S.A. 81 K4 30 43N 101 12W
Ozuluama, Mexico 87 C5 21 40N 97 50W

P

Pa-an, Burma 41 L20 16 51N 97 40 E
Pa Mong Dam, Thailand 38 D4 18 0N 102 22 E
Pa Sak →, Thailand 36 B2 15 30N 101 0 E
Paamiut, Greenland 4 C5 62 0N 49 43W
Paarl, S. Africa 56 E2 33 45S 18 56 E
Pab Hills, Pakistan 42 F2 26 30N 66 45 E
Pabbay, U.K. 12 D1 57 46N 7 14W
Pabianice, Poland 17 C10 51 40N 19 20 E
Pabna, Bangla. 41 G16 24 1N 89 18 E
Pabo, Uganda 54 B3 3 1N 32 10 E
Pacaja →, Brazil 93 D8 1 56S 50 50W
Pacaraima, Sa., S. Amer. 92 C6 4 0N 62 30W
Pacasmayo, Peru 92 E3 7 20S 79 35W
Pachhar, India 42 G7 24 40N 77 42 E
Pachitea →, Peru 92 E4 8 46S 74 33W
Pachmarhi, India 43 H8 22 28N 78 26 E
Pachpadra, India 40 G8 25 58N 72 10 E
Pachuca, Mexico 87 C5 20 10N 98 40W
Pacific, Canada 72 C3 54 48N 128 28W
Pacific-Antarctic Ridge, Pac. Oc. 65 M16 43 0S 115 0W
Pacific Grove, U.S.A. 84 J5 36 38N 121 56W
Pacific Ocean, Pac. Oc. 65 G14 10 0N 140 0W
Pacific Rim Nat. Park, Canada 84 B2 48 40N 124 45W
Pacifica, U.S.A. 84 H4 37 36N 122 30W
Pacitan, Indonesia 37 H14 8 12S 111 7 E
Packwood, U.S.A. 84 D5 46 36N 121 40W
Padaido, Kepulauan, Indonesia 37 E9 1 15S 136 30 E
Padang, Indonesia 36 E2 1 0S 100 20 E
Padang Endau, Malaysia 39 L4 2 40N 103 38 E
Padangpanjang, Indonesia 36 E2 0 40S 100 20 E
Padangsidempuan, Indonesia 36 D1 1 30N 99 15 E
Paddle Prairie, Canada 72 B5 57 57N 117 29W
Paddockwood, Canada 73 C7 53 30N 105 30W
Paderborn, Germany 16 C5 51 42N 8 45 E
Padma, India 43 G11 24 12N 85 22 E
Pádova, Italy 20 B4 45 25N 11 53 E
Padra, India 42 H5 22 15N 73 7 E
Padrauna, India 43 F10 26 54N 83 59 E
Padre I., U.S.A. 81 M6 27 10N 97 25W
Padstow, U.K. 11 G3 50 33N 4 58W
Padua = Pádova, Italy 20 B4 45 25N 11 53 E
Paducah, Ky., U.S.A. 76 G1 37 5N 88 37W
Paducah, Tex., U.S.A. 81 H4 34 1N 100 18W
Paengnyŏng-do, S. Korea 35 F13 37 57N 124 40 E
Paeroa, N.Z. 59 G5 37 23S 175 41 E
Pafúri, Mozam. 57 C5 22 28S 31 17 E
Pag, Croatia 16 F8 44 25N 15 3 E
Pagadian, Phil. 37 C6 7 55N 123 30 E
Pagai Selatan, Pulau, Indonesia 36 E2 3 0S 100 15 E
Pagai Utara, Pulau, Indonesia 36 E2 2 35S 100 0 E
Pagalu = Annobón, Atl. Oc. 49 G4 1 25S 5 36 E
Pagara, India 43 G9 24 22N 80 1 E
Pagastikós Kólpos, Greece 21 E10 39 15N 23 0 E
Pagatan, Indonesia 36 E5 3 33S 115 59 E
Page, U.S.A. 83 H8 36 57N 111 27W
Pago Pago, Amer. Samoa 59 B13 14 16S 170 43W
Pagosa Springs, U.S.A. 83 H10 37 16N 107 1W
Pagwa River, Canada 70 B2 50 2N 85 14W
Pahala, U.S.A. 74 J17 19 12N 155 29W
Pahang →, Malaysia 39 L4 3 30N 103 9 E
Pahiatua, N.Z. 59 J5 40 27S 175 50 E
Pahokee, U.S.A. 77 M5 26 50N 80 40W
Pahrump, U.S.A. 85 J11 36 12N 115 59W
Pahute Mesa, U.S.A. 84 H10 37 20N 116 45W
Pai, Thailand 38 C2 19 19N 98 27 E
Paicines, U.S.A. 84 J5 36 44N 121 17W
Paide, Estonia 9 G21 58 57N 25 31 E
Paignton, U.K. 11 G4 50 26N 3 35W
Päijänne, Finland 9 F21 61 30N 25 30 E
Pailani, India 43 G9 25 45N 80 26 E
Pailin, Cambodia 38 F4 12 46N 102 36 E
Painan, Indonesia 36 E2 1 21S 100 34 E
Painesville, U.S.A. 78 E3 41 43N 81 15W
Paint Hills = Wemindji, Canada 70 B4 53 0N 78 49W
Paint L., Canada 73 B9 55 28N 97 57W
Painted Desert, U.S.A. 83 J8 36 0N 111 0W
Paintsville, U.S.A. 76 G4 37 49N 82 48W
País Vasco □, Spain 19 A4 42 50N 2 45W
Paisley, Canada 78 B3 44 18N 81 16W
Paisley, U.K. 12 F4 55 50N 4 25W
Paisley, U.S.A. 82 E3 42 42N 120 32W
Paita, Peru 92 E2 5 11S 81 9W
Pajares, Puerto de, Spain 19 A3 42 58N 5 46W
Pak Lay, Laos 38 C3 18 15N 101 27 E
Pak Phanang, Thailand 39 H3 8 21N 100 12 E
Pak Sane, Laos 38 C4 18 22N 103 39 E
Pak Song, Laos 38 E6 15 11N 106 14 E
Pak Suong, Laos 38 C3 19 58N 102 15 E
Pakaur, India 43 G12 24 38N 87 51 E
Pakenham, Canada 79 A8 45 18N 76 18W
Pákhnes, Greece 23 D6 35 16N 24 4 E
Pakhuis, S. Africa 56 E2 32 9S 19 5 E
Pakistan ■, Asia 42 E4 30 0N 70 0 E
Pakkading, Laos 38 C4 18 19N 103 59 E
Pakokku, Burma 41 J19 21 20N 95 0 E
Pakowki L., Canada 73 D6 49 20N 111 0W
Pakpattan, Pakistan 42 D5 30 25N 73 27 E
Paktīā □, Afghan. 40 C6 33 30N 69 15 E
Paktīkā □, Afghan. 40 C6 32 30N 69 0 E
Pakwach, Uganda 54 B3 2 28N 31 27 E
Pakxe, Laos 38 E5 15 5N 105 52 E
Pal Lahara, India 43 J11 21 27N 85 11 E
Pala, Chad 51 G9 9 25N 15 5 E
Pala, Dem. Rep. of the Congo 54 D2 6 45S 29 30 E
Pala, U.S.A. 85 M9 33 22N 117 5W
Palabek, Uganda 54 B3 3 22N 32 33 E
Palacios, U.S.A. 81 L6 28 42N 96 13W
Palagruža, Croatia 20 C7 42 24N 16 15 E
Palaiókastron, Greece 23 D8 35 12N 26 15 E
Palaiokhóra, Greece 23 D5 35 16N 23 39 E
Palam, India 40 K10 19 0N 77 0 E
Palampur, India 42 C7 32 10N 76 30 E
Palana, Australia 62 F4 39 45S 147 55 E
Palana, Russia 27 D16 59 10N 159 59 E
Palanan, Phil. 37 A6 17 8N 122 29 E
Palanan Pt., Phil. 37 A6 17 17N 122 30 E
Palandri, Pakistan 43 C5 33 42N 73 40 E
Palanga, Lithuania 9 J19 55 58N 21 3 E
Palangkaraya, Indonesia 36 E4 2 16S 113 56 E
Palani Hills, India 40 P10 10 14N 77 33 E
Palanpur, India 42 G5 24 10N 72 25 E
Palapye, Botswana 56 C4 22 30S 27 7 E
Palas, Pakistan 43 B5 35 4N 73 14 E
Palashi, India 43 H13 23 47N 88 15 E
Palasponga, India 43 J11 21 47N 85 34 E
Palatka, Russia 27 C16 60 6N 150 54 E
Palatka, U.S.A. 77 L5 29 39N 81 38W
Palau ■, Pac. Oc. 28 J17 7 30N 134 30 E
Palauk, Burma 38 F2 13 10N 98 40 E
Palawan, Phil. 36 C5 9 30N 118 30 E
Palayankottai, India 40 Q10 8 45N 77 45 E
Paldiski, Estonia 9 G21 59 23N 24 9 E
Paleleh, Indonesia 37 D6 1 10N 121 50 E
Palembang, Indonesia 36 E2 3 0S 104 50 E
Palencia, Spain 19 A3 42 1N 4 34W
Palenque, Mexico 87 D6 17 31N 91 58W
Paleokastrítsa, Greece 23 A3 39 40N 19 41 E
Paleometokho, Cyprus 23 D12 35 7N 33 11 E
Palermo, Italy 20 E5 38 7N 13 22 E
Palermo, U.S.A. 82 G3 39 26N 121 33W
Palestina, Chile 96 A3 23 50S 69 47W
Palestine, Asia 47 D4 32 0N 35 0 E
Palestine, U.S.A. 81 K7 31 46N 95 38W
Paletwa, Burma 41 J18 21 10N 92 50 E
Palghat, India 40 P10 10 46N 76 42 E
Palgrave, Mt., Australia 60 D2 23 22S 115 58 E
Pali, India 42 G5 25 50N 73 20 E
Palikir, Micronesia 64 G7 6 55N 158 9 E
Palioúrion, Ákra, Greece 21 E10 39 57N 23 45 E
Palisades Reservoir, U.S.A. 82 E8 43 20N 111 12W
Paliseul, Belgium 15 E5 49 54N 5 8 E
Palitana, India 42 J4 21 32N 71 49 E
Palizada, Mexico 87 D6 18 18N 92 8W
Palk Bay, Asia 40 Q11 9 30N 79 15 E
Palk Strait, Asia 40 Q11 10 0N 79 45 E
Palkānah, Iraq 44 C5 35 49N 44 26 E
Palkot, India 43 H11 22 53N 84 39 E
Palla Road = Dinokwe, Botswana 56 C4 23 29S 26 37 E
Pallanza = Verbánia, Italy 18 D8 45 56N 8 33 E
Pallarenda, Australia 62 B4 19 12S 146 46 E
Pallinup →, Australia 61 F2 34 27S 118 50 E
Pallisa, Uganda 54 B3 1 12N 33 43 E
Pallu, India 42 E6 28 59N 74 14 E
Palm Bay, U.S.A. 77 L5 28 2N 80 35W
Palm Beach, U.S.A. 77 M6 26 43N 80 2W
Palm Coast, U.S.A. 77 L5 29 32N 81 10W
Palm Desert, U.S.A. 85 M10 33 43N 116 22W
Palm Is., Australia 62 B4 18 40S 146 35 E
Palm Springs, U.S.A. 85 M10 33 50N 116 33W
Palma, Mozam. 55 E5 10 46S 40 29 E
Palma, B. de, Spain 22 B9 39 30N 2 39 E

Port Weld = Kuala Sepetang, *Malaysia* **39 K3** 4 49N 100 28 E
Porta Orientalis, *Romania* **17 F12** 45 6N 22 18 E
Portadown, *U.K.* **13 B5** 54 25N 6 27W
Portaferry, *U.K.* **13 B6** 54 23N 5 33W
Portage, *Pa., U.S.A.* **78 F6** 40 23N 78 41W
Portage, *Wis., U.S.A.* **80 D10** 43 33N 89 28W
Portage La Prairie, *Canada* **73 D9** 49 58N 98 18W
Portageville, *U.S.A.* **81 G10** 36 26N 89 42W
Portalegre, *Portugal* **19 C2** 39 19N 7 25W
Portales, *U.S.A.* **81 H3** 34 11N 103 20W
Portarlington, *Ireland* **13 C4** 53 9N 7 14W
Portbou, *Spain* **19 A7** 42 25N 3 9 E
Porter L., *N.W.T., Canada* **73 A7** 61 41N 108 5W
Porter L., *Sask., Canada* **73 B7** 56 20N 107 20W
Porterville, *S. Africa* **56 E2** 33 0S 19 0 E
Porterville, *U.S.A.* **84 J8** 36 4N 119 1W
Porthcawl, *U.K.* **11 F4** 51 29N 3 42W
Porthill, *U.S.A.* **82 B5** 48 59N 116 30W
Porthmadog, *U.K.* **10 E3** 52 55N 4 8W
Portile de Fier, *Europe* **17 F12** 44 44N 22 30 E
Portimão, *Portugal* **19 D1** 37 8N 8 32W
Portishead, *U.K.* **11 F5** 51 29N 2 46W
Portknockie, *U.K.* **12 D6** 57 42N 2 51W
Portland, *N.S.W., Australia* **63 E5** 33 20S 150 0 E
Portland, *Vic., Australia* **63 F3** 38 20S 141 35 E
Portland, *Canada* **79 B8** 44 42N 76 12W
Portland, *Conn., U.S.A.* **79 E12** 41 34N 72 38W
Portland, *Maine, U.S.A.* **69 D12** 43 39N 70 16W
Portland, *Mich., U.S.A.* **76 D3** 42 52N 84 54W
Portland, *Oreg., U.S.A.* **84 E4** 45 32N 122 37W
Portland, *Pa., U.S.A.* **79 F9** 40 55N 75 6W
Portland, *Tex., U.S.A.* **81 M6** 27 53N 97 20W
Portland, I. of, *U.K.* **11 G5** 50 33N 2 26W
Portland B., *Australia* **63 F3** 38 15S 141 45 E
Portland Bill, *U.K.* **11 G5** 50 31N 2 28W
Portland Canal, *U.S.A.* **72 B2** 55 56N 130 0W
Portmadoc = Porthmadog, *U.K.* **10 E3** 52 55N 4 8W
Porto, *Portugal* **19 B1** 41 8N 8 40W
Pôrto Alegre, *Brazil* **95 C5** 30 5S 51 10W
Porto Amboim = Gunza, *Angola* **52 G2** 10 50S 13 50 E
Porto Cristo, *Spain* **22 B10** 39 33N 3 20 E
Pôrto de Móz, *Brazil* **93 D8** 1 41S 52 13W
Porto Empédocle, *Italy* **20 F5** 37 17N 13 32 E
Pôrto Esperança, *Brazil* **92 G7** 19 37S 57 29W
Pôrto Franco, *Brazil* **93 E9** 6 20S 47 24W
Pôrto Mendes, *Brazil* **95 A5** 24 30S 54 15W
Porto Moniz, *Madeira* **22 D2** 32 52N 17 11W
Pôrto Murtinho, *Brazil* **92 H7** 21 45S 57 55W
Pôrto Nacional, *Brazil* **93 F9** 10 40S 48 30W
Porto-Novo, *Benin* **50 G6** 6 23N 2 42 E
Porto Petro, *Spain* **22 B10** 39 22N 3 13 E
Porto Santo, I. de, *Madeira* **50 B2** 33 45N 16 25W
Pôrto São José, *Brazil* **95 A5** 22 43S 53 10W
Pôrto Seguro, *Brazil* **93 G11** 16 26S 39 5W
Porto Tórres, *Italy* **20 D3** 40 50N 8 24 E
Pôrto União, *Brazil* **95 B5** 26 10S 51 10W
Pôrto Válter, *Brazil* **92 E4** 8 15S 72 40W
Porto-Vecchio, *France* **18 F8** 41 35N 9 16 E
Pôrto Velho, *Brazil* **92 E6** 8 46S 63 54W
Portobelo, *Panama* **88 E4** 9 35N 79 42W
Portoferráio, *Italy* **20 C4** 42 48N 10 20 E
Portola, *U.S.A.* **84 F6** 39 49N 120 28W
Portoscuso, *Italy* **20 E3** 39 12N 8 24 E
Portoviejo, *Ecuador* **92 D2** 1 7S 80 28W
Portpatrick, *U.K.* **12 G3** 54 51N 5 7W
Portree, *U.K.* **12 D2** 57 25N 6 12W
Portrush, *U.K.* **13 A5** 55 12N 6 40W
Portsmouth, *Domin.* **89 C7** 15 34N 61 27W
Portsmouth, *U.K.* **11 G6** 50 48N 1 6W
Portsmouth, *N.H., U.S.A.* **77 D10** 43 5N 70 45W
Portsmouth, *Ohio, U.S.A.* **76 F4** 38 44N 82 57W
Portsmouth, *R.I., U.S.A.* **79 E13** 41 36N 71 15W
Portsmouth, *Va., U.S.A.* **76 G7** 36 50N 76 18W
Portsmouth ☐, *U.K.* **11 G6** 50 48N 1 6W
Portsoy, *U.K.* **12 D6** 57 41N 2 41W
Portstewart, *U.K.* **13 A5** 55 11N 6 43W
Porttipahtan tekojärvi, *Finland* **8 B22** 68 5N 26 40 E
Portugal ■, *Europe* **19 C1** 40 0N 8 0W
Portumna, *Ireland* **13 C3** 53 6N 8 14W
Portville, *U.S.A.* **78 D6** 42 3N 78 20W
Porvenir, *Chile* **96 G2** 53 10S 70 16W
Porvoo, *Finland* **9 F21** 60 24N 25 40 E
Posadas, *Argentina* **95 B4** 27 30S 55 50W
Poshan = Boshan, *China* **35 F9** 36 28N 117 49 E
Posht-e-Badam, *Iran* **45 C7** 33 2N 55 23 E
Poso, *Indonesia* **37 E6** 1 20S 120 55 E
Posong, *S. Korea* **35 G14** 34 46N 127 5 E
Posse, *Brazil* **93 F9** 14 4S 46 18W
Possession I., *Antarctica* **5 D11** 72 4S 172 0 E
Possum Kingdom L., *U.S.A.* **81 J5** 32 52N 98 26W
Post, *U.S.A.* **81 J4** 33 12N 101 23W
Post Falls, *U.S.A.* **82 C5** 47 43N 116 57W
Postavy = Pastavy, *Belarus* **9 J22** 55 4N 26 50 E
Poste-de-la-Baleine = Kuujjuarapik, *Canada* **70 A4** 55 20N 77 35W
Postmasburg, *S. Africa* **56 D3** 28 18S 23 5 E
Postojna, *Slovenia* **16 F8** 45 46N 14 12 E
Poston, *U.S.A.* **85 M12** 34 0N 114 24W
Postville, *Canada* **71 B8** 54 54N 59 47W
Potchefstroom, *S. Africa* **56 D4** 26 41S 27 7 E
Poteau, *U.S.A.* **81 H7** 35 3N 94 37W
Poteet, *U.S.A.* **81 L5** 29 2N 98 35W
Potenza, *Italy* **20 D6** 40 38N 15 48 E
Poteriteri, L., *N.Z.* **59 M1** 46 5S 167 10 E
Potgietersrus, *S. Africa* **57 C4** 24 10S 28 55 E
Poti, *Georgia* **25 F7** 42 10N 41 38 E
Potiskum, *Nigeria* **51 F8** 11 39N 11 2 E
Potomac →, *U.S.A.* **76 G7** 38 0N 76 23W
Potosí, *Bolivia* **92 G5** 19 38S 65 50W
Potosi Mt., *U.S.A.* **85 K11** 35 57N 115 29W
Pototan, *Phil.* **37 B6** 10 54N 122 38 E
Potrerillos, *Chile* **94 B2** 26 30S 69 30W
Potsdam, *Germany* **16 B7** 52 25N 13 4 E
Potsdam, *U.S.A.* **79 B10** 44 40N 74 59W
Pottersville, *U.S.A.* **79 C11** 43 43N 73 50W
Pottstown, *U.S.A.* **79 F9** 40 15N 75 39W
Pottsville, *U.S.A.* **79 F8** 40 41N 76 12W
Pottuvil, *Sri Lanka* **40 R12** 6 55N 81 50 E
Pouce Coupé, *Canada* **72 B4** 55 40N 120 10W
Poughkeepsie, *U.S.A.* **79 E11** 41 42N 73 56W
Poulaphouca Res., *Ireland* **13 C5** 53 8N 6 30W
Poulsbo, *U.S.A.* **84 C4** 47 44N 122 39W
Poultney, *U.S.A.* **79 C11** 43 31N 73 14W
Poulton-le-Fylde, *U.K.* **10 D5** 53 51N 2 58W
Pouso Alegre, *Brazil* **95 A6** 22 14S 45 57W
Pouthisat, *Cambodia* **38 F4** 12 34N 103 50 E
Považská Bystrica, *Slovak Rep.* **17 D10** 49 8N 18 27 E
Povenets, *Russia* **24 B5** 62 50N 34 50 E
Poverty B., *N.Z.* **59 H7** 38 43S 178 2 E
Póvoa de Varzim, *Portugal* **19 B1** 41 25N 8 46W
Povungnituk = Puvirnituq, *Canada* **69 B12** 60 2N 77 10W
Powassan, *Canada* **70 C4** 46 5N 79 25W
Poway, *U.S.A.* **85 N9** 32 58N 117 2W
Powder →, *U.S.A.* **80 B2** 46 45N 105 26W
Powder River, *U.S.A.* **82 E10** 43 2N 106 59W
Powell, *U.S.A.* **82 D9** 44 45N 108 46W
Powell, L., *U.S.A.* **83 H8** 36 57N 111 29W
Powell River, *Canada* **72 D4** 49 50N 124 35W
Powers, *U.S.A.* **76 C2** 45 41N 87 32W
Powys ☐, *U.K.* **11 E4** 52 20N 3 20W
Poyang Hu, *China* **33 D6** 29 5N 116 20 E
Poyarkovo, *Russia* **27 E13** 49 36N 128 41 E
Poza Rica, *Mexico* **87 C5** 20 33N 97 27W
Požarevac, *Serbia, Yug.* **21 B9** 44 35N 21 18 E
Poznań, *Poland* **17 B9** 52 25N 16 55 E
Pozo, *U.S.A.* **85 K6** 35 20N 120 24W
Pozo Almonte, *Chile* **92 H5** 20 10S 69 50W
Pozo Colorado, *Paraguay* **94 A4** 23 30S 58 45W
Pozoblanco, *Spain* **19 C3** 38 23N 4 51W
Pozzuoli, *Italy* **20 D6** 40 49N 14 7 E
Prachin Buri, *Thailand* **38 E3** 14 0N 101 25 E
Prachuap Khiri Khan, *Thailand* **39 G2** 11 49N 99 48 E
Prado, *Brazil* **93 G11** 17 20S 39 13W
Prague = Praha, *Czech Rep.* **16 C8** 50 5N 14 22 E
Praha, *Czech Rep.* **16 C8** 50 5N 14 22 E
Praia, *C. Verde Is.* **49 E1** 15 2N 23 34W
Prainha, *Amazonas, Brazil* **92 E6** 7 10S 60 30W
Prainha, *Pará, Brazil* **93 D8** 1 45S 53 30W
Prairie, *Australia* **62 C3** 20 50S 144 35 E
Prairie City, *U.S.A.* **82 D4** 44 28N 118 43W
Prairie Dog Town Fork →, *U.S.A.* **81 H5** 34 30N 99 23W
Prairie du Chien, *U.S.A.* **80 D9** 43 3N 91 9W
Prairies, L. of the, *Canada* **73 C8** 51 16N 101 32W
Pran Buri, *Thailand* **38 F2** 12 23N 99 55 E
Prapat, *Indonesia* **36 D1** 2 41N 98 58 E
Prasonísi, Ákra, *Greece* **23 D9** 35 42N 27 46 E
Prata, *Brazil* **93 G9** 19 25S 48 54W
Pratabpur, *India* **43 H10** 23 28N 83 15 E
Pratapgarh, *Raj., India* **42 G6** 24 2N 74 40 E
Pratapgarh, *Ut. P., India* **43 G9** 25 56N 81 59 E
Prato, *Italy* **20 C4** 43 53N 11 6 E
Pratt, *U.S.A.* **81 G5** 37 39N 98 44W
Prattville, *U.S.A.* **77 J2** 32 28N 86 29W
Pravia, *Spain* **19 A2** 43 30N 6 12W
Praya, *Indonesia* **36 F5** 8 39S 116 17 E
Precordillera, *Argentina* **94 C2** 30 0S 69 1W
Preeceville, *Canada* **73 C8** 51 57N 102 40W
Preiļi, *Latvia* **9 H22** 56 18N 26 43 E
Premont, *U.S.A.* **81 M5** 27 22N 98 7W
Prentice, *U.S.A.* **80 C9** 45 33N 90 17W
Preobrazheniye, *Russia* **30 C6** 42 54N 133 54 E
Preparis North Channel, *Ind. Oc.* **41 M18** 15 12N 93 40 E
Preparis South Channel, *Ind. Oc.* **41 M18** 14 36N 93 40 E
Přerov, *Czech Rep.* **17 D9** 49 28N 17 27 E
Prescott, *Canada* **79 B9** 44 45N 75 30W
Prescott, *Ariz., U.S.A.* **83 J7** 34 33N 112 28W
Prescott, *Ark., U.S.A.* **81 J8** 33 48N 93 23W
Prescott Valley, *U.S.A.* **83 J7** 34 40N 112 18W
Preservation Inlet, *N.Z.* **59 M1** 46 8S 166 35 E
Presho, *U.S.A.* **80 D4** 43 54N 100 3W
Presidencia de la Plaza, *Argentina* **94 B4** 27 0S 59 50W
Presidencia Roque Saenz Peña, *Argentina* **94 B3** 26 45S 60 30W
Presidente Epitácio, *Brazil* **93 H8** 21 56S 52 6W
Presidente Hayes ☐, *Paraguay* **94 A4** 24 0S 59 0W
Presidente Prudente, *Brazil* **95 A5** 22 5S 51 25W
Presidio, *Mexico* **86 B4** 29 29N 104 23W
Presidio, *U.S.A.* **81 L2** 29 34N 104 22W
Prešov, *Slovak Rep.* **17 D11** 49 0N 21 15 E
Prespa, L. = Prespansko Jezero, *Macedonia* **21 D9** 40 55N 21 0 E
Prespansko Jezero, *Macedonia* **21 D9** 40 55N 21 0 E
Presque I., *U.S.A.* **78 D4** 42 9N 80 6W
Presque Isle, *U.S.A.* **77 B12** 46 41N 68 1W
Prestatyn, *U.K.* **10 D4** 53 20N 3 24W
Presteigne, *U.K.* **11 E5** 52 17N 3 0W
Preston, *Canada* **78 C4** 43 23N 80 21W
Preston, *U.K.* **10 D5** 53 46N 2 42W
Preston, *Idaho, U.S.A.* **82 E8** 42 6N 111 53W
Preston, *Minn., U.S.A.* **80 D8** 43 40N 92 5W
Preston, C., *Australia* **60 D2** 20 51S 116 12 E
Prestonburg, *U.S.A.* **76 G4** 37 39N 82 46W
Prestwick, *U.K.* **12 F4** 55 29N 4 37W
Pretoria, *S. Africa* **57 D4** 25 44S 28 12 E
Préveza, *Greece* **21 E9** 38 57N 20 45 E
Prey Veng, *Cambodia* **39 G5** 11 35N 105 29 E
Pribilof Is., *U.S.A.* **68 C2** 57 0N 170 0W
Příbram, *Czech Rep.* **16 D8** 49 41N 14 2 E
Price, *U.S.A.* **82 G8** 39 36N 110 49W
Price I., *Canada* **72 C3** 52 23N 128 41W
Prichard, *U.S.A.* **77 K1** 30 44N 88 5W
Priekule, *Latvia* **9 H19** 56 26N 21 35 E
Prienai, *Lithuania* **9 J20** 54 38N 23 57 E
Prieska, *S. Africa* **56 D3** 29 40S 22 42 E
Priest L., *U.S.A.* **82 B5** 48 35N 116 52W
Priest River, *U.S.A.* **82 B5** 48 10N 116 54W
Priest Valley, *U.S.A.* **84 J6** 36 10N 120 39W
Prievidza, *Slovak Rep.* **17 D10** 48 46N 18 36 E
Prikaspiyskaya Nizmennost = Caspian Depression, *Eurasia* **25 E8** 47 0N 48 0 E
Prilep, *Macedonia* **21 D9** 41 21N 21 32 E
Priluki = Pryluky, *Ukraine* **25 D5** 50 30N 32 24 E
Prime Seal I., *Australia* **62 G4** 40 3S 147 43 E
Primrose L., *Canada* **73 C7** 54 55N 109 45W
Prince Albert, *Canada* **73 C7** 53 15N 105 50W
Prince Albert, *S. Africa* **56 E3** 33 12S 22 2 E
Prince Albert Mts., *Antarctica* **5 D11** 76 0S 161 30 E
Prince Albert Nat. Park, *Canada* **73 C7** 54 0N 106 25W
Prince Albert Pen., *Canada* **68 A8** 72 30N 116 0W
Prince Albert Sd., *Canada* **68 A8** 70 25N 115 0W
Prince Alfred, C., *Canada* **4 B1** 74 20N 124 40W
Prince Charles I., *Canada* **69 B12** 67 47N 76 12W
Prince Charles Mts., *Antarctica* **5 D6** 72 0S 67 0 E
Prince Edward I. ☐, *Canada* **71 C7** 46 20N 63 20W
Prince Edward Is., *Ind. Oc.* **3 G11** 46 35S 38 0 E
Prince Edward Pt., *Canada* **78 C8** 43 56N 76 52W
Prince George, *Canada* **72 C4** 53 55N 122 50W
Prince of Wales, C., *U.S.A.* **66 C3** 65 36N 168 5W
Prince of Wales I., *Australia* **62 A3** 10 40S 142 10 E
Prince of Wales I., *Canada* **68 A10** 73 0N 99 0W
Prince of Wales I., *U.S.A.* **68 C6** 55 47N 132 50W
Prince Patrick I., *Canada* **4 B2** 77 0N 120 0W
Prince Regent Inlet, *Canada* **4 B3** 73 0N 90 0W
Prince Rupert, *Canada* **72 C2** 54 20N 130 20W
Princess Charlotte B., *Australia* **62 A3** 14 25S 144 0 E
Princess May Ranges, *Australia* **60 C4** 15 30S 125 30 E
Princess Royal I., *Canada* **72 C3** 53 0N 128 40W
Princeton, *Canada* **72 D4** 49 27N 120 30W
Princeton, *Calif., U.S.A.* **84 F4** 39 24N 122 1W
Princeton, *Ill., U.S.A.* **80 E10** 41 23N 89 28W
Princeton, *Ind., U.S.A.* **76 F2** 38 21N 87 34W
Princeton, *Ky., U.S.A.* **76 G2** 37 7N 87 53W
Princeton, *Mo., U.S.A.* **80 E8** 40 24N 93 35W
Princeton, *N.J., U.S.A.* **79 F10** 40 21N 74 39W
Princeton, *W. Va., U.S.A.* **76 G5** 37 22N 81 6W
Príncipe, I. de, *Atl. Oc.* **48 F4** 1 37N 7 27 E
Principe da Beira, *Brazil* **92 F6** 12 20S 64 30W
Prineville, *U.S.A.* **82 D3** 44 18N 120 51W
Prins Harald Kyst, *Antarctica* **5 D4** 70 0S 35 1 E
Prinsesse Astrid Kyst, *Antarctica* **5 D3** 70 45S 12 30 E
Prinsesse Ragnhild Kyst, *Antarctica* **5 D4** 70 15S 27 30 E
Prinzapolca, *Nic.* **88 D3** 13 20N 83 35W
Priozersk, *Russia* **24 B5** 61 2N 30 7 E
Pripet = Prypyat →, *Europe* **17 C16** 51 20N 30 15 E
Pripet Marshes, *Europe* **17 B15** 52 10N 28 10 E
Pripyat Marshes = Pripet Marshes, *Europe* **17 B15** 52 10N 28 10 E
Pripyats = Prypyat →, *Europe* **17 C16** 51 20N 30 15 E
Priština, *Kosovo, Yug.* **21 C9** 42 40N 21 13 E
Privas, *France* **18 D6** 44 45N 4 37 E
Privolzhskaya Vozvyshennost, *Russia* **25 D8** 51 0N 46 0 E
Prizren, *Kosovo, Yug.* **21 C9** 42 13N 20 45 E
Probolinggo, *Indonesia* **37 G15** 7 46S 113 13 E
Proctor, *U.S.A.* **79 C11** 43 40N 73 2W
Proddatur, *India* **40 M11** 14 45N 78 30 E
Prodhromos, *Cyprus* **23 E11** 34 57N 32 50 E
Profitis Ilías, *Greece* **23 C9** 36 17N 27 56 E
Profondeville, *Belgium* **15 D4** 50 23N 4 52 E
Progreso, *Coahuila, Mexico* **86 B4** 27 28N 101 4W
Progreso, *Yucatán, Mexico* **87 C7** 21 20N 89 40W
Prokopyevsk, *Russia* **26 D9** 54 0N 86 45 E
Prokuplje, *Serbia, Yug.* **21 C9** 43 16N 21 36 E
Prome, *Burma* **41 K19** 18 49N 95 13 E
Prophet →, *Canada* **72 B4** 58 48N 122 40W
Prophet River, *Canada* **72 B4** 58 6N 122 43W
Propriá, *Brazil* **93 F11** 10 13S 36 51W
Proserpine, *Australia* **62 C4** 20 21S 148 36 E
Prosna →, *Poland* **17 B9** 52 6N 17 44 E
Prospect, *U.S.A.* **79 C9** 43 18N 75 9W
Prosser, *U.S.A.* **82 C4** 46 12N 119 46W
Prostějov, *Czech Rep.* **17 D9** 49 30N 17 9 E
Proston, *Australia* **63 D5** 26 8S 151 32 E
Provence, *France* **18 E6** 43 40N 5 46 E
Providence, *Ky., U.S.A.* **76 G2** 37 24N 87 46W
Providence, *R.I., U.S.A.* **79 E13** 41 49N 71 24W
Providence Bay, *Canada* **70 C3** 45 41N 82 15W
Providence Mts., *U.S.A.* **85 K11** 35 10N 115 15W
Providencia, I. de, *Colombia* **88 D3** 13 25N 81 26W
Provideniya, *Russia* **27 C19** 64 23N 173 18W
Provins, *France* **18 B5** 48 33N 3 15 E
Provo, *U.S.A.* **82 F8** 40 14N 111 39W
Provost, *Canada* **73 C6** 52 25N 110 20W
Prudhoe Bay, *U.S.A.* **68 A5** 70 18N 148 22W
Prudhoe I., *Australia* **62 C4** 21 19S 149 41 E
Prud'homme, *Canada* **73 C7** 52 20N 105 54W
Pruszków, *Poland* **17 B11** 52 9N 20 49 E
Prut →, *Romania* **17 F15** 45 28N 28 10 E
Pruzhany, *Belarus* **17 B13** 52 33N 24 28 E
Prydz B., *Antarctica* **5 C6** 69 0S 74 0 E
Pryluky, *Ukraine* **25 D5** 50 30N 32 24 E
Pryor, *U.S.A.* **81 G7** 36 19N 95 19W
Prypyat →, *Europe* **17 C16** 51 20N 30 15 E
Przemyśl, *Poland* **17 D12** 49 50N 22 45 E
Przhevalsk = Karakol, *Kyrgyzstan* **26 E8** 42 30N 78 20 E
Psará, *Greece* **21 E11** 38 37N 25 38 E
Psíra, *Greece* **23 D7** 35 12N 25 52 E
Pskov, *Russia* **24 C4** 57 50N 28 25 E
Ptich = Ptsich →, *Belarus* **17 B15** 52 9N 28 52 E
Ptolemaís, *Greece* **21 D9** 40 30N 21 43 E
Ptsich →, *Belarus* **17 B15** 52 9N 28 52 E
Pu Xian, *China* **34 F6** 36 24N 111 6 E
Pua, *Thailand* **38 C3** 19 11N 100 55 E
Puán, *Argentina* **94 D3** 37 30S 62 45W
Puan, *S. Korea* **35 G14** 35 44N 126 44 E
Pucallpa, *Peru* **92 E4** 8 25S 74 30W
Pudasjärvi, *Finland* **8 D22** 65 23N 26 53 E
Pudozh, *Russia* **24 B6** 61 48N 36 32 E
Puduchcheri = Pondicherry, *India* **40 P11** 11 59N 79 50 E
Pudukkottai, *India* **40 P11** 10 28N 78 47 E
Puebla, *Mexico* **87 D5** 19 3N 98 12W
Puebla ☐, *Mexico* **87 D5** 18 30N 98 0W
Pueblo, *U.S.A.* **80 F2** 38 16N 104 37W
Pueblo Hundido, *Chile* **94 B1** 26 20S 70 5W
Puelches, *Argentina* **94 D2** 38 5S 65 51W
Puelén, *Argentina* **94 D2** 37 32S 67 38W
Puente Alto, *Chile* **94 C1** 33 32S 70 35W
Puente-Genil, *Spain* **19 D3** 37 22N 4 47W
Puerco →, *U.S.A.* **83 J10** 34 22N 107 50W
Puerto, *Canary Is.* **22 F2** 28 5N 17 20W
Puerto Aisén, *Chile* **96 F2** 45 27S 73 0W
Puerto Ángel, *Mexico* **87 D5** 15 40N 96 29W
Puerto Arista, *Mexico* **87 D6** 15 56N 93 48W
Puerto Armuelles, *Panama* **88 E3** 8 20N 82 51W
Puerto Ayacucho, *Venezuela* **92 B5** 5 40N 67 35W
Puerto Barrios, *Guatemala* **88 C2** 15 40N 88 32W
Puerto Bermejo, *Argentina* **94 B4** 26 55S 58 34W
Puerto Bermúdez, *Peru* **92 F4** 10 20S 74 58W
Puerto Bolívar, *Ecuador* **92 D3** 3 19S 79 55W
Puerto Cabello, *Venezuela* **92 A5** 10 28N 68 1W
Puerto Cabezas, *Nic.* **88 D3** 14 0N 83 30W
Puerto Cabo Gracias á Dios, *Nic.* **88 D3** 15 0N 83 10W
Puerto Carreño, *Colombia* **92 B5** 6 12N 67 22W
Puerto Castilla, *Honduras* **88 C2** 16 0N 86 0W
Puerto Chicama, *Peru* **92 E3** 7 45S 79 20W
Puerto Coig, *Argentina* **96 G3** 50 54S 69 15W
Puerto Cortés, *Costa Rica* **88 E3** 8 55N 84 0W
Puerto Cortés, *Honduras* **88 C2** 15 51N 88 0W
Puerto Cumarebo, *Venezuela* **92 A5** 11 29N 69 30W
Puerto de Alcudia = Port d'Alcúdia, *Spain* **22 B10** 39 50N 3 7 E
Puerto de Cabrera, *Spain* **22 B9** 39 8N 2 56 E
Puerto de Gran Tarajal, *Canary Is.* **22 F5** 28 13N 14 1W
Puerto de la Cruz, *Canary Is.* **22 F3** 28 24N 16 32W
Puerto de Pozo Negro, *Canary Is.* **22 F6** 28 19N 13 55W
Puerto de Sóller = Port de Sóller, *Spain* **22 B9** 39 48N 2 42 E
Puerto del Carmen, *Canary Is.* **22 F6** 28 55N 13 38W
Puerto del Rosario, *Canary Is.* **22 F6** 28 30N 13 52W
Puerto Deseado, *Argentina* **96 F3** 47 55S 66 0W
Puerto Escondido, *Mexico* **87 D5** 15 50N 97 3W
Puerto Heath, *Bolivia* **92 F5** 12 34S 68 39W
Puerto Inírida, *Colombia* **92 C5** 3 53N 67 52W
Puerto Juárez, *Mexico* **87 C7** 21 11N 86 49W
Puerto La Cruz, *Venezuela* **92 A6** 10 13N 64 38W
Puerto Leguízamo, *Colombia* **92 D4** 0 12S 74 46W
Puerto Limón, *Colombia* **92 C4** 3 23N 73 30W
Puerto Lobos, *Argentina* **96 E3** 42 0S 65 3W
Puerto Madryn, *Argentina* **96 E3** 42 48S 65 4W
Puerto Maldonado, *Peru* **92 F5** 12 30S 69 10W
Puerto Manotí, *Cuba* **88 B4** 21 22N 76 50W
Puerto Montt, *Chile* **96 E2** 41 28S 73 0W
Puerto Morazán, *Nic.* **88 D2** 12 51N 87 11W
Puerto Morelos, *Mexico* **87 C7** 20 49N 86 52W
Puerto Natales, *Chile* **96 G2** 51 45S 72 15W
Puerto Padre, *Cuba* **88 B4** 21 13N 76 35W
Puerto Páez, *Venezuela* **92 B5** 6 13N 67 28W
Puerto Peñasco, *Mexico* **86 A2** 31 20N 113 33W
Puerto Pinasco, *Paraguay* **94 A4** 22 36S 57 50W
Puerto Plata, *Dom. Rep.* **89 C5** 19 48N 70 45W
Puerto Pollensa = Port de Pollença, *Spain* **22 B10** 39 54N 3 4 E
Puerto Princesa, *Phil.* **37 C5** 9 46N 118 45 E
Puerto Quepos, *Costa Rica* **88 E3** 9 29N 84 6W
Puerto Rico, *Canary Is.* **22 G4** 27 47N 15 42W
Puerto Rico ■, *W. Indies* **89 C6** 18 15N 66 45W
Puerto Rico Trench, *Atl. Oc.* **89 C6** 19 50N 66 0W
Puerto San Julián, *Argentina* **96 F3** 49 18S 67 43W
Puerto Sastre, *Paraguay* **94 A4** 22 2S 57 55W
Puerto Suárez, *Bolivia* **92 G7** 18 58S 57 52W
Puerto Vallarta, *Mexico* **86 C3** 20 36N 105 15W
Puerto Wilches, *Colombia* **92 B4** 7 21N 73 54W
Puertollano, *Spain* **19 C3** 38 43N 4 7W
Pueyrredón, L., *Argentina* **96 F2** 47 20S 72 0W
Puffin I., *Ireland* **13 E1** 51 50N 10 24W
Pugachev, *Russia* **24 D8** 52 0N 48 49 E
Pugal, *India* **42 E5** 28 30N 72 48 E
Puge, *Tanzania* **54 C3** 4 45S 33 11 E
Puget Sound, *U.S.A.* **82 C2** 47 50N 122 30W
Pugŏdong, *N. Korea* **35 C16** 42 5N 130 0 E
Pugu, *Tanzania* **54 D4** 6 55S 39 4 E
Pūgūnzī, *Iran* **45 E8** 25 49N 59 10 E
Puig Major, *Spain* **22 B9** 39 48N 2 47 E
Puigcerdà, *Spain* **19 A6** 42 24N 1 50 E
Puigpunyent, *Spain* **22 B9** 39 38N 2 32 E
Pujon-chŏsuji, *N. Korea* **35 D14** 40 35N 127 35 E
Pukaki, L., *N.Z.* **59 L3** 44 4S 170 1 E
Pukapuka, *Cook Is.* **65 J11** 10 53S 165 49W
Pukaskwa Nat. Park, *Canada* **70 C2** 48 20N 86 0W
Pukatawagan, *Canada* **73 B8** 55 45N 101 20W
Pukchin, *N. Korea* **35 D13** 40 12N 125 45 E
Pukch'ŏng, *N. Korea* **35 D15** 40 14N 128 10 E
Pukekohe, *N.Z.* **59 G5** 37 12S 174 55 E
Pukhrayan, *India* **43 F8** 26 14N 79 51 E
Pula, *Croatia* **16 F7** 44 54N 13 57 E
Pulacayo, *Bolivia* **92 H5** 20 25S 66 41W
Pulandian, *China* **35 E11** 39 25N 121 58 E
Pularumpi, *Australia* **60 B5** 11 24S 130 26 E
Pulaski, *N.Y., U.S.A.* **79 C8** 43 34N 76 8W
Pulaski, *Tenn., U.S.A.* **77 H2** 35 12N 87 2W
Pulaski, *Va., U.S.A.* **76 G5** 37 3N 80 47W
Pulau →, *Indonesia* **37 F9** 5 50S 138 15 E
Puławy, *Poland* **17 C11** 51 23N 21 59 E
Pulga, *U.S.A.* **84 F5** 39 48N 121 29W
Pulicat L., *India* **40 N12** 13 40N 80 15 E
Pullman, *U.S.A.* **82 C5** 46 44N 117 10W
Pulog, Mt., *Phil.* **37 A6** 16 40N 120 50 E
Pułtusk, *Poland* **17 B11** 52 43N 21 6 E
Pumlumon Fawr, *U.K.* **11 E4** 52 28N 3 46W
Puná, I., *Ecuador* **92 D2** 2 55S 80 5W
Punakha, *Bhutan* **41 F16** 27 42N 89 52 E
Punasar, *India* **42 F5** 27 6N 73 6 E
Punata, *Bolivia* **92 G5** 17 32S 65 50W
Punch, *India* **43 C6** 33 48N 74 4 E
Punch →, *Pakistan* **42 C5** 33 12N 73 40 E
Punda Maria, *S. Africa* **57 C5** 22 40S 31 5 E
Pune, *India* **40 K8** 18 29N 73 57 E
P'ungsan, *N. Korea* **35 D15** 40 50N 128 9 E
Pungue, Ponte de, *Mozam.* **55 F3** 19 0S 34 0 E
Punjab ☐, *India* **42 D7** 31 0N 76 0 E
Punjab ☐, *Pakistan* **42 E6** 32 0N 72 30 E
Puno, *Peru* **92 G4** 15 55S 70 3W
Punpun →, *India* **43 G11** 25 31N 85 18 E
Punta Alta, *Argentina* **96 D4** 38 53S 62 4W
Punta Arenas, *Chile* **96 G2** 53 10S 71 0W
Punta de Díaz, *Chile* **94 B1** 28 0S 70 45W
Punta del Hidalgo, *Canary Is.* **22 F3** 28 33N 16 19W
Punta Gorda, *Belize* **87 D7** 16 10N 88 45W
Punta Gorda, *U.S.A.* **77 M5** 26 56N 82 3W
Punta Prieta, *Mexico* **86 B2** 28 58N 114 17W
Punta Prima, *Spain* **22 B11** 39 48N 4 16 E
Puntarenas, *Costa Rica* **88 E3** 10 0N 84 50W
Punto Fijo, *Venezuela* **92 A4** 11 50N 70 13W
Punxsatawney, *U.S.A.* **78 F6** 40 57N 78 59W
Puquio, *Peru* **92 F4** 14 45S 74 10W
Pur →, *Russia* **26 C8** 67 31N 77 55 E
Purace, Vol., *Colombia* **92 C3** 2 21N 76 23W
Puralia = Puruliya, *India* **43 H12** 23 17N 86 24 E
Puranpur, *India* **43 E9** 28 31N 80 9 E
Purbeck, Isle of, *U.K.* **11 G6** 50 39N 1 59W

Q

R

Randers, *Denmark* **9 H14** 56 29N 10 1 E
Randfontein, *S. Africa* **57 D4** 26 8S 27 45 E
Randle, *U.S.A.* **84 D5** 46 32N 121 57W
Randolph, *Mass., U.S.A.* **79 D13** 42 10N 71 2W
Randolph, *N.Y., U.S.A.* **78 D6** 42 10N 78 59W
Randolph, *Utah, U.S.A.* **82 F8** 41 40N 111 11W
Randolph, *Vt., U.S.A.* **79 C12** 43 55N 72 40W
Randsburg, *U.S.A.* **85 K9** 35 22N 117 39W
Råne älv →, *Sweden* **8 D20** 65 50N 22 20 E
Rangae, *Thailand* **39 J3** 6 19N 101 44 E
Rangaunu B., *N.Z.* **59 F4** 34 51S 173 15 E
Rangeley, *U.S.A.* **79 B14** 44 58N 70 39W
Rangeley L., *U.S.A.* **79 B14** 44 55N 70 43W
Rangely, *U.S.A.* **82 F9** 40 5N 108 48W
Ranger, *U.S.A.* **81 J5** 32 28N 98 41W
Rangia, *India* **41 F17** 26 28N 91 38 E
Rangiora, *N.Z.* **59 K4** 43 19S 172 36 E
Rangitaiki →, *N.Z.* **59 G6** 37 54S 176 49 E
Rangitata →, *N.Z.* **59 K3** 43 45S 171 15 E
Rangkasbitung, *Indonesia* **37 G12** 6 21S 106 15 E
Rangon →, *Burma* **41 L20** 16 28N 96 40 E
Rangoon, *Burma* **41 L20** 16 45N 96 20 E
Rangpur, *Bangla.* **41 G16** 25 42N 89 22 E
Rangsit, *Thailand* **38 F3** 13 59N 100 37 E
Ranibennur, *India* **40 M9** 14 35N 75 30 E
Raniganj, *Ut. P., India* **43 F9** 27 3N 82 13 E
Raniganj, *W. Bengal, India* **41 H15** 23 40N 87 5 E
Ranikhet, *India* **43 E8** 29 39N 79 25 E
Raniwara, *India* **40 G8** 24 50N 72 10 E
Rāniyah, *Iraq* **44 B5** 36 15N 44 53 E
Ranka, *India* **43 H10** 23 59N 83 47 E
Ranken →, *Australia* **62 C2** 20 31S 137 36 E
Rankin, *U.S.A.* **81 K4** 31 13N 101 56W
Rankin Inlet, *Canada* **68 B10** 62 30N 93 0W
Rankins Springs, *Australia* **63 E4** 33 49S 146 14 E
Rannoch, L., *U.K.* **12 E4** 56 41N 4 20W
Rannoch Moor, *U.K.* **12 E4** 56 38N 4 48W
Ranobe, Helodranon' i, *Madag.* **57 C7** 23 3S 43 33 E
Ranohira, *Madag.* **57 C8** 22 29S 45 24 E
Ranomafana, *Toamasina, Madag.* **57 B8** 18 57S 48 50 E
Ranomafana, *Toliara, Madag.* **57 C8** 24 34S 47 0 E
Ranomena, *Madag.* **57 C8** 23 25S 47 17 E
Ranong, *Thailand* **39 H2** 9 56N 98 40 E
Ranotsara Nord, *Madag.* **57 C8** 22 48S 46 36 E
Rānsa, *Iran* **45 C6** 33 39N 48 18 E
Ransiki, *Indonesia* **37 E8** 1 30S 134 10 E
Rantabe, *Madag.* **57 B8** 15 42S 49 39 E
Rantauprapat, *Indonesia* **36 D1** 2 15N 99 50 E
Rantemario, *Indonesia* **37 E5** 3 15S 119 57 E
Rantoul, *U.S.A.* **76 E1** 40 19N 88 9W
Raoyang, *China* **34 E8** 38 15N 115 45 E
Rapa, *Pac. Oc.* **65 K13** 27 35S 144 20W
Rapa Nui = Pascua, I. de, *Chile* **65 K17** 27 7S 109 23W
Rapallo, *Italy* **18 D8** 44 21N 9 14 E
Rapar, *India* **42 H4** 23 34N 70 38 E
Rāpch, *Iran* **45 E8** 25 40N 59 15 E
Raper, C., *Canada* **69 B13** 69 44N 67 6W
Rapid City, *U.S.A.* **80 D3** 44 5N 103 14W
Rapid River, *U.S.A.* **76 C2** 45 55N 86 58W
Rapla, *Estonia* **9 G21** 59 1N 24 52 E
Rapti →, *India* **43 F10** 26 18N 83 41 E
Raquette →, *U.S.A.* **79 B10** 45 0N 74 42W
Raquette Lake, *U.S.A.* **79 C10** 43 49N 74 40W
Rarotonga, *Cook Is.* **65 K12** 21 30S 160 0W
Ra's al 'Ayn, *Syria* **44 B4** 36 45N 40 12 E
Ra's al Khaymah, *U.A.E.* **46 B6** 25 50N 55 59 E
Rasca, Pta. de la, *Canary Is.* **22 G3** 27 59N 16 41W
Raseiniai, *Lithuania* **9 J20** 55 25N 23 5 E
Rashmi, *India* **42 G6** 25 4N 74 22 E
Rasht, *Iran* **45 B6** 37 20N 49 40 E
Rasi Salai, *Thailand* **38 E5** 15 20N 104 9 E
Rason L., *Australia* **61 E3** 28 45S 124 25 E
Rasra, *India* **43 G10** 25 50N 83 50 E
Rasul, *Pakistan* **42 C5** 32 42N 73 34 E
Rat Buri, *Thailand* **38 F2** 13 30N 99 54 E
Rat Islands, *U.S.A.* **68 C1** 52 0N 178 0 E
Rat L., *Canada* **73 B9** 56 10N 99 40W
Ratangarh, *India* **42 E6** 28 5N 74 35 E
Raṭāwī, *Iraq* **44 D5** 30 38N 47 13 E
Rath, *India* **43 G8** 25 36N 79 37 E
Rath Luirc, *Ireland* **13 D3** 52 21N 8 40W
Rathdrum, *Ireland* **13 D5** 52 56N 6 14W
Rathenow, *Germany* **16 B7** 52 37N 12 19 E
Rathkeale, *Ireland* **13 D3** 52 32N 8 56W
Rathlin I., *U.K.* **13 A5** 55 18N 6 14W
Rathmelton, *Ireland* **13 A4** 55 2N 7 38W
Ratibor = Racibórz, *Poland* **17 C10** 50 7N 18 18 E
Ratlam, *India* **42 H6** 23 20N 75 0 E
Ratnagiri, *India* **40 L8** 16 57N 73 18 E
Ratodero, *Pakistan* **42 F3** 27 48N 68 18 E
Raton, *U.S.A.* **81 G2** 36 54N 104 24W
Rattaphum, *Thailand* **39 J3** 7 8N 100 16 E
Rattray Hd., *U.K.* **12 D7** 57 38N 1 50W
Ratz, Mt., *Canada* **72 B2** 57 23N 132 12W
Raub, *Malaysia* **39 L3** 3 47N 101 52 E
Rauch, *Argentina* **94 D4** 36 45S 59 5W
Raudales de Malpaso, *Mexico* **87 D6** 17 30N 23 30W
Raufarhöfn, *Iceland* **8 C6** 66 27N 15 57W
Raufoss, *Norway* **9 F14** 60 44N 10 37 E
Raukumara Ra., *N.Z.* **59 H6** 38 5S 177 55 E
Rauma, *Finland* **9 F19** 61 10N 21 30 E
Raurkela, *India* **43 H11** 22 14N 84 50 E
Rausu-Dake, *Japan* **30 B12** 44 4N 145 7 E
Rava-Ruska, *Poland* **17 C12** 50 15N 23 42 E
Rava Russkaya = Rava-Ruska, *Poland* **17 C12** 50 15N 23 42 E
Ravalli, *U.S.A.* **82 C6** 47 17N 114 11W
Ravānsar, *Iran* **44 C5** 34 43N 46 40 E
Rāvar, *Iran* **45 D8** 31 20N 56 51 E
Ravena, *U.S.A.* **79 D11** 42 28N 73 49W
Ravenna, *Italy* **20 B5** 44 25N 12 12 E
Ravenna, *Nebr., U.S.A.* **80 E5** 41 1N 98 55W
Ravenna, *Ohio, U.S.A.* **78 E3** 41 9N 81 15W
Ravensburg, *Germany* **16 E5** 47 46N 9 36 E
Ravenshoe, *Australia* **62 B4** 17 37S 145 29 E
Ravensthorpe, *Australia* **61 F3** 33 35S 120 2 E
Ravenswood, *Australia* **62 C4** 20 6S 146 54 E
Ravenswood, *U.S.A.* **76 F5** 38 57N 81 46W
Ravi →, *Pakistan* **42 D4** 30 35N 71 49 E
Rawalpindi, *Pakistan* **42 C5** 33 38N 73 8 E
Rawāndūz, *Iraq* **44 B5** 36 40N 44 30 E
Rawang, *Malaysia* **39 L3** 3 20N 101 35 E
Rawene, *N.Z.* **59 F4** 35 25S 173 32 E
Rawlinna, *Australia* **61 F4** 30 58S 125 28 E
Rawlins, *U.S.A.* **82 F10** 41 47N 107 14W
Rawlinson Ra., *Australia* **61 D4** 24 40S 128 30 E
Rawson, *Argentina* **96 E3** 43 15S 65 5W
Raxaul, *India* **43 F11** 26 59N 84 51 E
Ray, *U.S.A.* **80 A3** 48 21N 103 10W
Ray, C., *Canada* **71 C8** 47 33N 59 15W
Rayadurg, *India* **40 M10** 14 40N 76 50 E
Rayagada, *India* **41 K13** 19 15N 83 20 E
Raychikhinsk, *Russia* **27 E13** 49 46N 129 25 E
Rāyen, *Iran* **45 D8** 29 34N 57 26 E
Rayleigh, *U.K.* **11 F8** 51 36N 0 37 E
Raymond, *Canada* **72 D6** 49 30N 112 35W
Raymond, *Calif., U.S.A.* **84 H7** 37 13N 119 54W
Raymond, *N.H., U.S.A.* **79 C13** 43 2N 71 11W
Raymond, *Wash., U.S.A.* **84 D3** 46 41N 123 44W
Raymondville, *U.S.A.* **81 M6** 26 29N 97 47W
Raymore, *Canada* **73 C8** 51 25N 104 31W
Rayón, *Mexico* **86 B2** 29 43N 110 35W
Rayong, *Thailand* **38 F3** 12 40N 101 20 E
Rayville, *U.S.A.* **81 J9** 32 29N 91 46W
Raz, Pte. du, *France* **18 C1** 48 2N 4 47W
Razan, *Iran* **45 C6** 35 23N 49 2 E
Razdel'naya = Rozdilna, *Ukraine* **17 E16** 46 50N 30 2 E
Razdolnoye, *Russia* **30 C5** 43 30N 131 52 E
Razeh, *Iran* **45 C6** 32 47N 48 9 E
Razgrad, *Bulgaria* **21 C12** 43 33N 26 34 E
Razim, Lacul, *Romania* **17 F15** 44 50N 29 0 E
Razmak, *Pakistan* **42 C3** 32 45N 69 50 E
Ré, Î. de, *France* **18 C3** 46 12N 1 30W
Reading, *U.K.* **11 F7** 51 27N 0 58W
Reading, *U.S.A.* **79 F9** 40 20N 75 56W
Reading □, *U.K.* **11 F7** 51 27N 0 58W
Realicó, *Argentina* **94 D3** 35 0S 64 15W
Ream, *Cambodia* **39 G4** 10 34N 103 39 E
Reata, *Mexico* **86 B4** 26 8N 101 5W
Reay Forest, *U.K.* **12 C4** 58 22N 4 55W
Rebi, *Indonesia* **37 F8** 6 23S 134 7 E
Rebiana, *Libya* **51 D10** 24 12N 22 10 E
Rebun-Tō, *Japan* **30 B10** 45 23N 141 2 E
Recherche, Arch. of the, *Australia* **61 F3** 34 15S 122 50 E
Rechna Doab, *Pakistan* **42 D5** 31 35N 73 30 E
Rechytsa, *Belarus* **17 B16** 52 21N 30 24 E
Recife, *Brazil* **93 E12** 8 0S 35 0W
Recklinghausen, *Germany* **15 C7** 51 37N 7 12 E
Reconquista, *Argentina* **94 B4** 29 10S 59 45W
Recreo, *Argentina* **94 B2** 29 25S 65 10W
Red →, *La., U.S.A.* **81 K9** 31 1N 91 45W
Red →, *N. Dak., U.S.A.* **68 C10** 49 0N 97 15W
Red Bank, *U.S.A.* **79 F10** 40 21N 74 5W
Red Bay, *Canada* **71 B8** 51 44N 56 25W
Red Bluff, *U.S.A.* **82 F2** 40 11N 122 15W
Red Bluff L., *U.S.A.* **81 K3** 31 54N 103 55W
Red Cliffs, *Australia* **63 E3** 34 19S 142 11 E
Red Cloud, *U.S.A.* **80 E5** 40 5N 98 32W
Red Creek, *U.S.A.* **79 C8** 43 14N 76 45W
Red Deer, *Canada* **72 C6** 52 20N 113 50W
Red Deer →, *Alta., Canada* **73 C7** 50 58N 110 0W
Red Deer →, *Man., Canada* **73 C8** 52 53N 101 1W
Red Deer L., *Canada* **73 C8** 52 55N 101 20W
Red Hook, *U.S.A.* **79 E11** 41 55N 73 53W
Red Indian L., *Canada* **71 C8** 48 35N 57 0W
Red L., *Canada* **73 C10** 51 3N 93 49W
Red Lake, *Canada* **73 C10** 51 3N 93 49W
Red Lake Falls, *U.S.A.* **80 B6** 47 53N 96 16W
Red Lake Road, *Canada* **73 C10** 49 59N 93 25W
Red Lodge, *U.S.A.* **82 D9** 45 11N 109 15W
Red Mountain, *U.S.A.* **85 K9** 35 37N 117 38W
Red Oak, *U.S.A.* **80 E7** 41 1N 95 14W
Red Rock, *Canada* **70 C2** 48 55N 88 15W
Red Rock, L., *U.S.A.* **80 E8** 41 22N 92 59W
Red Rocks Pt., *Australia* **61 F4** 32 13S 127 32 E
Red Sea, *Asia* **46 C2** 25 0N 36 0 E
Red Slate Mt., *U.S.A.* **84 H8** 37 31N 118 52W
Red Sucker L., *Canada* **70 B1** 54 9N 93 40W
Red Tower Pass = Turnu Roşu, P., *Romania* **17 F13** 45 33N 24 17 E
Red Wing, *U.S.A.* **80 C8** 44 34N 92 31W
Redang, *Malaysia* **36 C2** 5 49N 103 2 E
Redange, *Lux.* **15 E5** 49 46N 5 52 E
Redcar, *U.K.* **10 C6** 54 37N 1 4W
Redcar & Cleveland □, *U.K.* **10 C7** 54 29N 1 0W
Redcliff, *Canada* **73 C6** 50 10N 110 50W
Redcliffe, *Australia* **63 D5** 27 12S 153 0 E
Redcliffe, Mt., *Australia* **61 E3** 28 30S 121 30 E
Reddersburg, *S. Africa* **56 D4** 29 41S 26 10 E
Redding, *U.S.A.* **82 F2** 40 35N 122 24W
Redditch, *U.K.* **11 E6** 52 18N 1 55W
Redfield, *U.S.A.* **80 C5** 44 53N 98 31W
Redford, *U.S.A.* **79 B11** 44 38N 73 48W
Redlands, *U.S.A.* **85 M9** 34 4N 117 11W
Redmond, *Oreg., U.S.A.* **82 D3** 44 17N 121 11W
Redmond, *Wash., U.S.A.* **84 C4** 47 41N 122 7W
Redon, *France* **18 C2** 47 40N 2 6W
Redonda, *Antigua* **89 C7** 16 58N 62 19W
Redondela, *Spain* **19 A1** 42 15N 8 38W
Redondo Beach, *U.S.A.* **85 M8** 33 50N 118 23W
Redruth, *U.K.* **11 G2** 50 14N 5 14W
Redvers, *Canada* **73 D8** 49 35N 101 40W
Redwater, *Canada* **72 C6** 53 55N 113 6W
Redwood, *U.S.A.* **79 B9** 44 18N 75 48W
Redwood City, *U.S.A.* **84 H4** 37 30N 122 15W
Redwood Falls, *U.S.A.* **80 C7** 44 32N 95 7W
Redwood Nat. Park, *U.S.A.* **82 F1** 41 40N 124 5W
Ree, L., *Ireland* **13 C3** 53 35N 8 0W
Reed, L., *Canada* **73 C8** 54 38N 100 30W
Reed City, *U.S.A.* **76 D3** 43 53N 85 31W
Reedley, *U.S.A.* **84 J7** 36 36N 119 27W
Reedsburg, *U.S.A.* **80 D9** 43 32N 90 0W
Reedsport, *U.S.A.* **82 E1** 43 42N 124 6W
Reedsville, *U.S.A.* **78 F7** 40 39N 77 35W
Reefton, *N.Z.* **59 K3** 42 6S 171 51 E
Reese →, *U.S.A.* **82 F5** 40 48N 117 4W
Refugio, *U.S.A.* **81 L6** 28 18N 97 17W
Regensburg, *Germany* **16 D7** 49 1N 12 6 E
Reggâne = Zaouiet Reggâne, *Algeria* **50 C6** 26 32N 0 3 E
Réggio di Calábria, *Italy* **20 E6** 38 6N 15 39 E
Réggio nell'Emilia, *Italy* **20 B4** 44 43N 10 36 E
Reghin, *Romania* **17 E13** 46 46N 24 42 E
Regina, *Canada* **73 C8** 50 27N 104 35W
Regina Beach, *Canada* **73 C8** 50 47N 105 0W
Registro, *Brazil* **95 A6** 24 29S 47 49W
Rehar →, *India* **43 H10** 23 55N 82 40 E
Rehli, *India* **43 H8** 23 38N 79 5 E
Rehoboth, *Namibia* **56 C2** 23 15S 17 4 E
Rehovot, *Israel* **47 D3** 31 54N 34 48 E
Reichenbach, *Germany* **16 C7** 50 37N 12 17 E
Reid, *Australia* **61 F4** 30 49S 128 26 E
Reidsville, *U.S.A.* **77 G6** 36 21N 79 40W
Reigate, *U.K.* **11 F7** 51 14N 0 12W
Reims, *France* **18 B6** 49 15N 4 1 E
Reina Adelaida, Arch., *Chile* **96 G2** 52 20S 74 0W
Reindeer →, *Canada* **73 B8** 55 36N 103 11W
Reindeer I., *Canada* **73 C9** 52 30N 98 0W
Reindeer L., *Canada* **73 B8** 57 15N 102 15W
Reinga, C., *N.Z.* **59 F4** 34 25S 172 43 E
Reinosa, *Spain* **19 A3** 43 2N 4 15W
Reitz, *S. Africa* **57 D4** 27 48S 28 29 E
Reivilo, *S. Africa* **56 D3** 27 36S 24 8 E
Reliance, *Canada* **73 A7** 63 0N 109 20W
Remarkable, Mt., *Australia* **63 E2** 32 48S 138 10 E
Rembang, *Indonesia* **37 G14** 6 42S 111 21 E
Remedios, *Panama* **88 E3** 8 15N 81 50W
Remeshk, *Iran* **45 E8** 26 55N 58 50 E
Remich, *Lux.* **15 E6** 49 32N 6 22 E
Remscheid, *Germany* **15 C7** 51 11N 7 12 E
Ren Xian, *China* **34 F8** 37 8N 114 40 E
Rendsburg, *Germany* **16 A5** 54 17N 9 39 E
Renfrew, *Canada* **79 A8** 45 30N 76 40W
Renfrewshire □, *U.K.* **12 F4** 55 49N 4 38W
Rengat, *Indonesia* **36 E2** 0 30S 102 45 E
Rengo, *Chile* **94 C1** 34 24S 70 50W
Reni, *Ukraine* **17 F15** 45 28N 28 15 E
Renmark, *Australia* **63 E3** 34 11S 140 43 E
Rennell Sd., *Canada* **72 C2** 53 23N 132 35W
Renner Springs, *Australia* **62 B1** 18 20S 133 47 E
Rennes, *France* **18 B3** 48 7N 1 41W
Rennie L., *Canada* **73 A7** 61 32N 105 35W
Reno, *U.S.A.* **84 F7** 39 31N 119 48W
Reno →, *Italy* **20 B5** 44 38N 12 16 E
Renovo, *U.S.A.* **78 E7** 41 20N 77 45W
Renqiu, *China* **34 E9** 38 43N 116 5 E
Rensselaer, *Ind., U.S.A.* **76 E2** 40 57N 87 9W
Rensselaer, *N.Y., U.S.A.* **79 D11** 42 38N 73 45W
Rentería, *Spain* **19 A5** 43 19N 1 54W
Renton, *U.S.A.* **84 C4** 47 29N 122 12W
Reotipur, *India* **43 G10** 25 33N 83 45 E
Republic, *Mo., U.S.A.* **81 G8** 37 7N 93 29W
Republic, *Wash., U.S.A.* **82 B4** 48 39N 118 44W
Republican →, *U.S.A.* **80 F6** 39 4N 96 48W
Repulse Bay, *Canada* **69 B11** 66 30N 86 30W
Requena, *Peru* **92 E4** 5 5S 73 52W
Requena, *Spain* **19 C5** 39 30N 1 4W
Reşadiye = Datça, *Turkey* **21 F12** 36 46N 27 40 E
Reserve, *U.S.A.* **83 K9** 33 43N 108 45W
Resht = Rasht, *Iran* **45 B6** 37 20N 49 40 E
Resistencia, *Argentina* **94 B4** 27 30S 59 0W
Reşiţa, *Romania* **17 F11** 45 18N 21 53 E
Resolution I., *Canada* **69 B13** 61 30N 65 0W
Resolution I., *N.Z.* **59 L1** 45 40S 166 40 E
Ressano Garcia, *Mozam.* **57 D5** 25 25S 32 0 E
Reston, *Canada* **73 D8** 49 33N 101 6W
Retalhuleu, *Guatemala* **88 D1** 14 33N 91 46W
Retenue, L. de, *Dem. Rep. of the Congo* **55 E2** 11 0S 27 0 E
Retford, *U.K.* **10 D7** 53 19N 0 56W
Réthímnon, *Greece* **23 D6** 35 18N 24 30 E
Réthímnon □, *Greece* **23 D6** 35 23N 24 28 E
Reti, *Pakistan* **42 E3** 28 5N 69 48 E
Réunion ■, *Ind. Oc.* **49 J9** 21 0S 56 0 E
Reus, *Spain* **19 B6** 41 10N 1 5 E
Reutlingen, *Germany* **16 D5** 48 29N 9 12 E
Reval = Tallinn, *Estonia* **9 G21** 59 22N 24 48 E
Revda, *Russia* **24 C10** 56 48N 59 57 E
Revelganj, *India* **43 G11** 25 50N 84 40 E
Revelstoke, *Canada* **72 C5** 51 0N 118 10W
Reventazón, *Peru* **92 E2** 6 10S 80 58W
Revillagigedo, Is. de, *Pac. Oc.* **86 D2** 18 40N 112 0W
Revuè →, *Mozam.* **55 F3** 19 50S 34 0 E
Rewa, *India* **43 G9** 24 33N 81 25 E
Rewari, *India* **42 E7** 28 15N 76 40 E
Rexburg, *U.S.A.* **82 E8** 43 49N 111 47W
Rey, *Iran* **45 C6** 35 35N 51 25 E
Rey, I. del, *Panama* **88 E4** 8 20N 78 30W
Rey Malabo, *Eq. Guin.* **52 D1** 3 45N 8 50 E
Reyðarfjörður, *Iceland* **8 D6** 65 2N 14 13W
Reyes, Pt., *U.S.A.* **84 H3** 38 0N 123 0W
Reykjahlið, *Iceland* **8 D5** 65 40N 16 55W
Reykjanes, *Iceland* **8 E2** 63 48N 22 40W
Reykjavík, *Iceland* **8 D3** 64 10N 21 57W
Reynolds Ra., *Australia* **60 D5** 22 30S 133 0 E
Reynoldsville, *U.S.A.* **78 E6** 41 5N 78 58W
Reynosa, *Mexico* **87 B5** 26 5N 98 18W
Rēzekne, *Latvia* **9 H22** 56 30N 27 17 E
Rezvān, *Iran* **45 E8** 27 34N 56 6 E
Rhayader, *U.K.* **11 E4** 52 18N 3 29W
Rhein →, *Europe* **15 C6** 51 52N 6 2 E
Rhein-Main-Donau-Kanal, *Germany* **16 D6** 49 1N 11 27 E
Rheine, *Germany* **16 B4** 52 17N 7 26 E
Rheinland-Pfalz □, *Germany* **16 C4** 50 0N 7 0 E
Rhin = Rhein →, *Europe* **15 C6** 51 52N 6 2 E
Rhine = Rhein →, *Europe* **15 C6** 51 52N 6 2 E
Rhinebeck, *U.S.A.* **79 E11** 41 56N 73 55W
Rhineland-Palatinate = Rheinland-Pfalz □, *Germany* **16 C4** 50 0N 7 0 E
Rhinelander, *U.S.A.* **80 C10** 45 38N 89 25W
Rhinns Pt., *U.K.* **12 F2** 55 40N 6 29W
Rhino Camp, *Uganda* **54 B3** 3 0N 31 22 E
Rhir, Cap, *Morocco* **50 B4** 30 38N 9 54W
Rhode Island □, *U.S.A.* **79 E13** 41 40N 71 30W
Rhodes = Ródhos, *Greece* **23 C10** 36 15N 28 10 E
Rhodesia = Zimbabwe ■, *Africa* **55 F3** 19 0S 30 0 E
Rhodope Mts. = Rhodopi Planina, *Bulgaria* **21 D11** 41 40N 24 20 E
Rhodopi Planina, *Bulgaria* **21 D11** 41 40N 24 20 E
Rhön, *Germany* **16 C5** 50 24N 9 58 E
Rhondda, *U.K.* **11 F4** 51 39N 3 31W
Rhondda Cynon Taff □, *U.K.* **11 F4** 51 42N 3 27W
Rhône →, *France* **18 E6** 43 28N 4 42 E
Rhum, *U.K.* **12 E2** 57 0N 6 20W
Rhyl, *U.K.* **10 D4** 53 20N 3 29W
Riachão, *Brazil* **93 E9** 7 20S 46 37W
Riasi, *India* **43 C6** 33 10N 74 50 E
Riau □, *Indonesia* **36 D2** 0 0 102 35 E
Riau, Kepulauan, *Indonesia* **36 D2** 0 30N 104 20 E
Riau Arch. = Riau, Kepulauan, *Indonesia* **36 D2** 0 30N 104 20 E
Ribadeo, *Spain* **19 A2** 43 35N 7 5W
Ribas do Rio Pardo, *Brazil* **93 H8** 20 27S 53 46W
Ribauè, *Mozam.* **55 E4** 14 57S 38 17 E
Ribble →, *U.K.* **10 D5** 53 52N 2 25W
Ribe, *Denmark* **9 J13** 55 19N 8 44 E
Ribeira Brava, *Madeira* **22 D2** 32 41N 17 4W
Ribeirão Prêto, *Brazil* **95 A6** 21 10S 47 50W
Riberalta, *Bolivia* **92 F5** 11 0S 66 0W
Riccarton, *N.Z.* **59 K4** 43 32S 172 37 E
Rice, *U.S.A.* **85 L12** 34 5N 114 51W
Rice L., *Canada* **78 B6** 44 12N 78 10W
Rice Lake, *U.S.A.* **80 C9** 45 30N 91 44W
Rich, C., *Canada* **78 B4** 44 43N 80 38W
Richards Bay, *S. Africa* **57 D5** 28 48S 32 6 E
Richardson →, *Canada* **73 B6** 58 25N 111 14W
Richardson Lakes, *U.S.A.* **76 C10** 44 46N 70 58W
Richardson Springs, *U.S.A.* **84 F5** 39 51N 121 46W
Riche, C., *Australia* **61 F2** 34 36S 118 47 E
Richey, *U.S.A.* **80 B2** 47 39N 105 4W
Richfield, *U.S.A.* **83 G8** 38 46N 112 5W
Richfield Springs, *U.S.A.* **79 D10** 42 51N 74 59W
Richford, *U.S.A.* **79 B12** 45 0N 72 40W
Richibucto, *Canada* **71 C7** 46 42N 64 54W
Richland, *Ga., U.S.A.* **77 J3** 32 5N 84 40W
Richland, *Wash., U.S.A.* **82 C4** 46 17N 119 18W
Richland Center, *U.S.A.* **80 D9** 43 21N 90 23W
Richlands, *U.S.A.* **76 G5** 37 6N 81 48W
Richmond, *Australia* **62 C3** 20 43S 143 8 E
Richmond, *N.Z.* **59 J4** 41 20S 173 12 E
Richmond, *U.K.* **10 C6** 54 25N 1 43W
Richmond, *Calif., U.S.A.* **84 H4** 37 56N 122 21W
Richmond, *Ind., U.S.A.* **76 F3** 39 50N 84 53W
Richmond, *Ky., U.S.A.* **76 G3** 37 45N 84 18W
Richmond, *Mich., U.S.A.* **78 D2** 42 49N 82 45W
Richmond, *Mo., U.S.A.* **80 F8** 39 17N 93 58W
Richmond, *Tex., U.S.A.* **81 L7** 29 35N 95 46W
Richmond, *Utah, U.S.A.* **82 F8** 41 56N 111 48W
Richmond, *Va., U.S.A.* **76 G7** 37 33N 77 27W
Richmond, *Vt., U.S.A.* **79 B12** 44 24N 72 59W
Richmond Hill, *Canada* **78 C5** 43 52N 79 27W
Richmond Ra., *Australia* **63 D5** 29 0S 152 45 E
Richwood, *U.S.A.* **76 F5** 38 14N 80 32W
Ridder = Leninogorsk, *Kazakstan* **26 D9** 50 20N 83 30 E
Riddlesburg, *U.S.A.* **78 F6** 40 9N 78 15W
Ridgecrest, *U.S.A.* **85 K9** 35 38N 117 40W
Ridgefield, *Conn., U.S.A.* **79 E11** 41 17N 73 30W
Ridgefield, *Wash., U.S.A.* **84 E4** 45 49N 122 45W
Ridgeland, *U.S.A.* **77 J5** 32 29N 80 59W
Ridgetown, *Canada* **78 D3** 42 26N 81 52W
Ridgewood, *U.S.A.* **79 F10** 40 59N 74 7W
Ridgway, *U.S.A.* **78 E6** 41 25N 78 44W
Riding Mountain Nat. Park, *Canada* **73 C9** 50 50N 100 0W
Ridley, Mt., *Australia* **61 F3** 33 12S 122 7 E
Riebeek-Oos, *S. Africa* **56 E4** 33 10S 26 10 E
Ried, *Austria* **16 D7** 48 14N 13 30 E
Riesa, *Germany* **16 C7** 51 17N 13 17 E
Riet →, *S. Africa* **56 D3** 29 0S 23 54 E
Rietbron, *S. Africa* **56 E3** 32 54S 23 10 E
Rietfontein, *Namibia* **56 C3** 21 58S 20 58 E
Rieti, *Italy* **20 C5** 42 24N 12 51 E
Rif, Er = Er Rif, *Morocco* **50 A5** 35 1N 4 1W
Riffe L., *U.S.A.* **84 D4** 46 32N 122 26W
Rifle, *U.S.A.* **82 G10** 39 32N 107 47W
Rift Valley □, *Kenya* **54 B4** 0 20N 36 0 E
Rīga, *Latvia* **9 H21** 56 53N 24 8 E
Riga, G. of, *Latvia* **9 H20** 57 40N 23 45 E
Rīgān, *Iran* **45 D8** 28 37N 58 58 E
Rīgas Jūras Līcis = Riga, G. of, *Latvia* **9 H20** 57 40N 23 45 E
Rigaud, *Canada* **79 A10** 45 29N 74 18W
Rigby, *U.S.A.* **82 E8** 43 40N 111 55W
Rīgestān, *Afghan.* **40 D4** 30 15N 65 0 E
Riggins, *U.S.A.* **82 D5** 45 25N 116 19W
Rigolet, *Canada* **71 B8** 54 10N 58 23W
Rihand Dam, *India* **43 G10** 24 9N 83 2 E
Riihimäki, *Finland* **9 F21** 60 45N 24 48 E
Riiser-Larsen-halvøya, *Antarctica* **5 C4** 68 0S 35 0 E
Rijeka, *Croatia* **16 F8** 45 20N 14 21 E
Rijssen, *Neths.* **15 B6** 52 19N 6 31 E
Rikuzentakada, *Japan* **30 E10** 39 0N 141 40 E
Riley, *U.S.A.* **82 E4** 43 32N 119 28W
Rimah, Wadi ar →, *Si. Arabia* **44 E4** 26 5N 41 30 E
Rimbey, *Canada* **72 C6** 52 35N 114 15W
Rimersburg, *U.S.A.* **78 E5** 41 3N 79 30W
Rímini, *Italy* **20 B5** 44 3N 12 33 E
Rimouski, *Canada* **71 C6** 48 27N 68 30W
Rimrock, *U.S.A.* **84 D5** 46 38N 121 10W
Rinca, *Indonesia* **37 F5** 8 45S 119 35 E
Rincón de Romos, *Mexico* **86 C4** 22 14N 102 18W
Rinconada, *Argentina* **94 A2** 22 26S 66 10W
Rind →, *India* **43 G9** 25 53N 80 33 E
Ringas, *India* **42 F6** 27 21N 75 34 E
Ringkøbing, *Denmark* **9 H13** 56 5N 8 15 E
Ringvassøy, *Norway* **8 B18** 69 56N 19 15 E
Ringwood, *U.S.A.* **79 E10** 41 7N 74 15W
Rinjani, *Indonesia* **36 F5** 8 24S 116 28 E
Rio Branco, *Brazil* **92 E5** 9 58S 67 49W
Río Branco, *Uruguay* **95 C5** 32 40S 53 40W
Río Bravo del Norte →, *Mexico* **87 B5** 25 57N 97 9W
Rio Brilhante, *Brazil* **95 A5** 21 48S 54 33W
Rio Claro, *Brazil* **95 A6** 22 19S 47 35W
Rio Claro, *Trin. & Tob.* **89 D7** 10 20N 61 25W
Río Colorado, *Argentina* **96 D4** 39 0S 64 0W
Río Cuarto, *Argentina* **94 C3** 33 10S 64 25W
Rio das Pedras, *Mozam.* **57 C6** 23 8S 35 28 E
Rio de Janeiro, *Brazil* **95 A7** 23 0S 43 12W
Rio de Janeiro □, *Brazil* **95 A7** 22 50S 43 0W
Rio do Sul, *Brazil* **95 B6** 27 13S 49 37W
Río Gallegos, *Argentina* **96 G3** 51 35S 69 15W
Rio Grande = Grande, Rio →, *U.S.A.* **81 N6** 25 58N 97 9W
Río Grande, *Argentina* **96 G3** 53 50S 67 45W
Rio Grande, *Brazil* **95 C5** 32 0S 52 20W
Río Grande, *Mexico* **86 C4** 23 50N 103 2W
Río Grande, *Nic.* **88 D3** 12 54N 83 33W
Rio Grande City, *U.S.A.* **81 M5** 26 23N 98 49W
Río Grande de Santiago →, *Mexico* **86 C3** 21 36N 105 26W
Rio Grande do Norte □, *Brazil* **93 E11** 5 40S 36 0W
Rio Grande do Sul □, *Brazil* **95 C5** 30 0S 53 0W

S

Sálakhos, *Greece* **23 C9** 36 17N 27 57 E
Salālah, *Oman* **46 D5** 16 56N 53 59 E
Salamanca, *Chile* **94 C1** 31 46S 70 59W
Salamanca, *Spain* **19 B3** 40 58N 5 39W
Salamanca, *U.S.A.* **78 D6** 42 10N 78 43W
Salāmatābād, *Iran* **44 C5** 35 39N 47 50 E
Salamis, *Cyprus* **23 D12** 35 11N 33 54 E
Salamís, *Greece* **21 F10** 37 56N 23 30 E
Salar de Atacama, *Chile* **94 A2** 23 30S 68 25W
Salar de Uyuni, *Bolivia* **92 H5** 20 30S 67 45W
Salatiga, *Indonesia* **37 G14** 7 19S 110 30 E
Salavat, *Russia* **24 D10** 53 21N 55 55 E
Salaverry, *Peru* **92 E3** 8 15S 79 0W
Salawati, *Indonesia* **37 E8** 1 7S 130 52 E
Salaya, *India* **42 H3** 22 19N 69 35 E
Salayar, *Indonesia* **37 F6** 6 7S 120 30 E
Salcombe, *U.K.* **11 G4** 50 14N 3 47W
Saldanha, *S. Africa* **56 E2** 33 0S 17 58 E
Saldanha B., *S. Africa* **56 E2** 33 6S 18 0 E
Saldus, *Latvia* **9 H20** 56 38N 22 30 E
Sale, *Australia* **63 F4** 38 6S 147 6 E
Salé, *Morocco* **50 B4** 34 3N 6 48W
Sale, *U.K.* **10 D5** 53 26N 2 19W
Salekhard, *Russia* **26 C7** 66 30N 66 35 E
Salem, *India* **40 P11** 11 40N 78 11 E
Salem, *Ill., U.S.A.* **76 F1** 38 38N 88 57W
Salem, *Ind., U.S.A.* **76 F2** 38 36N 86 6W
Salem, *Mass., U.S.A.* **79 D14** 42 31N 70 53W
Salem, *Mo., U.S.A.* **81 G9** 37 39N 91 32W
Salem, *N.H., U.S.A.* **79 D13** 42 45N 71 12W
Salem, *N.J., U.S.A.* **76 F8** 39 34N 75 28W
Salem, *N.Y., U.S.A.* **79 C11** 43 10N 73 20W
Salem, *Ohio, U.S.A.* **78 F4** 40 54N 80 52W
Salem, *Oreg., U.S.A.* **82 D2** 44 56N 123 2W
Salem, *S. Dak., U.S.A.* **80 D6** 43 44N 97 23W
Salem, *Va., U.S.A.* **76 G5** 37 18N 80 3W
Salerno, *Italy* **20 D6** 40 41N 14 47 E
Salford, *U.K.* **10 D5** 53 30N 2 18W
Salgótarján, *Hungary* **17 D10** 48 5N 19 47 E
Salgueiro, *Brazil* **93 E11** 8 4S 39 6W
Salibabu, *Indonesia* **37 D7** 3 51N 126 40 E
Salida, *U.S.A.* **74 C5** 38 32N 106 0W
Salihli, *Turkey* **21 E13** 38 28N 28 8 E
Salihorsk, *Belarus* **17 B14** 52 51N 27 27 E
Salima, *Malawi* **53 G6** 13 47S 34 28 E
Salina, *Italy* **20 E6** 38 34N 14 50 E
Salina, *Kans., U.S.A.* **80 F6** 38 50N 97 37W
Salina, *Utah, U.S.A.* **83 G8** 38 58N 111 51W
Salina Cruz, *Mexico* **87 D5** 16 10N 95 10W
Salinas, *Brazil* **93 G10** 16 10S 42 10W
Salinas, *Chile* **94 A2** 23 31S 69 29W
Salinas, *Ecuador* **92 D2** 2 10S 80 58W
Salinas, *U.S.A.* **84 J5** 36 40N 121 39W
Salinas →, *Guatemala* **87 D6** 16 28N 90 31W
Salinas →, *U.S.A.* **84 J5** 36 45N 121 48W
Salinas, B. de, *Nic.* **88 D2** 11 4N 85 45W
Salinas, Pampa de las, *Argentina* **94 C2** 31 58S 66 42W
Salinas Ambargasta, *Argentina* **94 B3** 29 0S 65 0W
Salinas de Hidalgo, *Mexico* **86 C4** 22 30N 101 40W
Salinas Grandes, *Argentina* **94 C3** 30 0S 65 0W
Saline →, *Ark., U.S.A.* **81 J8** 33 10N 92 8W
Saline →, *Kans., U.S.A.* **80 F6** 38 52N 97 30W
Salines, C. de ses, *Spain* **22 B10** 39 16N 3 4 E
Salinópolis, *Brazil* **93 D9** 0 40S 47 20W
Salisbury = Harare, *Zimbabwe* **55 F3** 17 43S 31 2 E
Salisbury, *U.K.* **11 F6** 51 4N 1 47W
Salisbury, *Md., U.S.A.* **76 F8** 38 22N 75 36W
Salisbury, *N.C., U.S.A.* **77 H5** 35 40N 80 29W
Salisbury I., *Canada* **69 B12** 63 30N 77 0W
Salisbury Plain, *U.K.* **11 F6** 51 14N 1 55W
Şalkhad, *Syria* **47 C5** 32 29N 36 43 E
Salla, *Finland* **8 C23** 66 50N 28 49 E
Salliq, *Canada* **69 B11** 64 8N 83 10W
Sallisaw, *U.S.A.* **81 H7** 35 28N 94 47W
Salluit, *Canada* **69 B12** 62 14N 75 38W
Salmās, *Iran* **44 B5** 38 11N 44 47 E
Salmo, *Canada* **72 D5** 49 10N 117 20W
Salmon, *U.S.A.* **82 D7** 45 11N 113 54W
Salmon →, *Canada* **72 C4** 54 3N 122 40W
Salmon →, *U.S.A.* **82 D5** 45 51N 116 47W
Salmon Arm, *Canada* **72 C5** 50 40N 119 15W
Salmon Gums, *Australia* **61 F3** 32 59S 121 38 E
Salmon River Mts., *U.S.A.* **82 D6** 45 0N 114 30W
Salo, *Finland* **9 F20** 60 22N 23 10 E
Salome, *U.S.A.* **85 M13** 33 47N 113 37W
Salon, *India* **43 F9** 26 2N 81 27 E
Salon-de-Provence, *France* **18 E6** 43 39N 5 6 E
Salonica = Thessaloníki, *Greece* **21 D10** 40 38N 22 58 E
Salonta, *Romania* **17 E11** 46 49N 21 42 E
Salpausselkä, *Finland* **9 F22** 61 0N 27 0 E
Salsacate, *Argentina* **94 C2** 31 20S 65 5W
Salsk, *Russia* **25 E7** 46 28N 41 30 E
Salso →, *Italy* **20 F5** 37 6N 13 57 E
Salt →, *Canada* **72 B6** 60 0N 112 25W
Salt →, *U.S.A.* **83 K7** 33 23N 112 19W
Salt Lake City, *U.S.A.* **82 F8** 40 45N 111 53W
Salt Range, *Pakistan* **42 C5** 32 30N 72 25 E
Salta, *Argentina* **94 A2** 24 57S 65 25W
Salta □, *Argentina* **94 A2** 24 48S 65 30W
Saltash, *U.K.* **11 G3** 50 24N 4 14W
Saltburn by the Sea, *U.K.* **10 C7** 54 35N 0 58W
Saltcoats, *U.K.* **12 F4** 55 38N 4 47W
Saltee Is., *Ireland* **13 D5** 52 7N 6 37W
Saltfjellet, *Norway* **8 C16** 66 40N 15 15 E
Saltfjorden, *Norway* **8 C16** 67 15N 14 10 E
Saltillo, *Mexico* **86 B4** 25 25N 101 0W
Salto, *Argentina* **94 C3** 34 20S 60 15W
Salto, *Uruguay* **94 C4** 31 27S 57 50W
Salto →, *Italy* **20 C5** 42 26N 12 25 E
Salto del Guaíra, *Paraguay* **95 A5** 24 3S 54 17W
Salton City, *U.S.A.* **85 M11** 33 29N 115 51W
Salton Sea, *U.S.A.* **85 M11** 33 15N 115 45W
Saltsburg, *U.S.A.* **78 F5** 40 29N 79 27W
Saluda →, *U.S.A.* **77 J5** 34 1N 81 4W
Salûm, *Egypt* **51 B11** 31 31N 25 7 E
Salur, *India* **41 K13** 18 27N 83 18 E
Salvador, *Brazil* **93 F11** 13 0S 38 30W
Salvador, *Canada* **73 C7** 52 10N 109 32W
Salvador, L., *U.S.A.* **81 L9** 29 43N 90 15W
Salween →, *Burma* **41 L20** 16 31N 97 37 E
Salyan, *Azerbaijan* **25 G8** 39 33N 48 59 E
Salzach →, *Austria* **16 D7** 48 12N 12 56 E
Salzburg, *Austria* **16 E7** 47 48N 13 2 E
Salzgitter, *Germany* **16 B6** 52 9N 10 19 E
Salzwedel, *Germany* **16 B6** 52 52N 11 10 E
Sam, *India* **42 F4** 26 50N 70 31 E
Sam Neua, *Laos* **38 B5** 20 29N 104 5 E
Sam Ngao, *Thailand* **38 D2** 17 18N 99 0 E
Sam Rayburn Reservoir, *U.S.A.* **81 K7** 31 4N 94 5W
Sam Son, *Vietnam* **38 C5** 19 44N 105 54 E
Sam Teu, *Laos* **38 C5** 19 59N 104 38 E
Sama de Langreo = Langreo, *Spain* **19 A3** 43 18N 5 40W
Samagaltay, *Russia* **27 D10** 50 36N 95 3 E
Samales Group, *Phil.* **37 C6** 6 0N 122 0 E
Samana, *India* **42 D7** 30 10N 76 13 E
Samana Cay, *Bahamas* **89 B5** 23 3N 73 45W
Samanga, *Tanzania* **55 D4** 8 20S 39 13 E
Samangān □, *Afghan.* **40 B5** 36 15N 68 3 E
Samangwa, *Dem. Rep. of the Congo* **54 C1** 4 23S 24 10 E
Samani, *Japan* **30 C11** 42 7N 142 56 E
Samar, *Phil.* **37 B7** 12 0N 125 0 E
Samara, *Russia* **24 D9** 53 8N 50 6 E
Samaria = Shōmrōn, *West Bank* **47 C4** 32 15N 35 13 E
Samariá, *Greece* **23 D5** 35 17N 23 58 E
Samarinda, *Indonesia* **36 E5** 0 30S 117 9 E
Samarkand = Samarqand, *Uzbekistan* **26 F7** 39 40N 66 55 E
Samarqand, *Uzbekistan* **26 F7** 39 40N 66 55 E
Sāmarrā, *Iraq* **44 C4** 34 12N 43 52 E
Samastipur, *India* **43 G11** 25 50N 85 50 E
Samba, *Dem. Rep. of the Congo* **54 C2** 4 38S 26 22 E
Samba, *India* **43 C6** 32 32N 75 10 E
Sambalpur, *India* **41 J14** 21 28N 84 4 E
Sambar, Tanjung, *Indonesia* **36 E4** 2 59S 110 19 E
Sambas, *Indonesia* **36 D3** 1 20N 109 20 E
Sambava, *Madag.* **57 A9** 14 16S 50 10 E
Sambawizi, *Zimbabwe* **55 F2** 18 24S 26 13 E
Sambhal, *India* **43 E8** 28 35N 78 37 E
Sambhar, *India* **42 F6** 26 52N 75 6 E
Sambhar L., *India* **42 F6** 26 55N 75 12 E
Sambiase, *Italy* **20 E7** 38 58N 16 17 E
Sambir, *Ukraine* **17 D12** 49 30N 23 10 E
Sambor, *Cambodia* **38 F6** 12 46N 106 0 E
Samborombón, B., *Argentina* **94 D4** 36 5S 57 20W
Samch'ŏk, *S. Korea* **35 F15** 37 30N 129 10 E
Samch'onp'o, *S. Korea* **35 G15** 35 0N 128 6 E
Same, *Tanzania* **54 C4** 4 2S 37 38 E
Samfya, *Zambia* **55 E2** 11 22S 29 31 E
Samnah, *Si. Arabia* **44 E3** 25 10N 37 15 E
Samo Alto, *Chile* **94 C1** 30 22S 71 0W
Samoa ■, *Pac. Oc.* **59 B13** 14 0S 172 0W
Samokov, *Bulgaria* **21 C10** 42 18N 23 35 E
Sámos, *Greece* **21 F12** 37 45N 26 50 E
Samothráki = Mathráki, *Greece* **23 A3** 39 48N 19 31 E
Samothráki, *Greece* **21 D11** 40 28N 25 28 E
Sampacho, *Argentina* **94 C3** 33 20S 64 50W
Sampang, *Indonesia* **37 G15** 7 11S 113 13 E
Sampit, *Indonesia* **36 E4** 2 34S 113 0 E
Sampit, Teluk, *Indonesia* **36 E4** 3 5S 113 3 E
Samrong, *Cambodia* **38 E4** 14 15N 103 30 E
Samrong, *Thailand* **38 E3** 15 10N 100 40 E
Samsø, *Denmark* **9 J14** 55 50N 10 35 E
Samsun, *Turkey* **25 F6** 41 15N 36 22 E
Samui, Ko, *Thailand* **39 H3** 9 30N 100 0 E
Samusole, *Dem. Rep. of the Congo* **55 E1** 10 2S 24 0 E
Samut Prakan, *Thailand* **38 F3** 13 32N 100 40 E
Samut Songkhram →, *Thailand* **36 B1** 13 24N 100 1 E
Samwari, *Pakistan* **42 E2** 28 30N 66 46 E
San, *Mali* **50 F5** 13 15N 4 57W
San →, *Cambodia* **38 F5** 13 32N 105 57 E
San →, *Poland* **17 C11** 50 45N 21 51 E
San Agustin, C., *Phil.* **37 C7** 6 20N 126 13 E
San Agustín de Valle Fértil, *Argentina* **94 C2** 30 35S 67 30W
San Ambrosio, *Pac. Oc.* **90 F3** 26 28S 79 53W
San Andreas, *U.S.A.* **84 G6** 38 12N 120 41W
San Andrés, I. de, *Caribbean* **88 D3** 12 42N 81 46W
San Andres Mts., *U.S.A.* **83 K10** 33 0N 106 30W
San Andrés Tuxtla, *Mexico* **87 D5** 18 30N 95 20W
San Angelo, *U.S.A.* **81 K4** 31 28N 100 26W
San Anselmo, *U.S.A.* **84 H4** 37 59N 122 34W
San Antonio, *Belize* **87 D7** 16 15N 89 2W
San Antonio, *Chile* **94 C1** 33 40S 71 40W
San Antonio, *N. Mex., U.S.A.* **83 K10** 33 55N 106 52W
San Antonio, *Tex., U.S.A.* **81 L5** 29 25N 98 30W
San Antonio →, *U.S.A.* **81 L6** 28 30N 96 54W
San Antonio, C., *Argentina* **94 D4** 36 15S 56 40W
San Antonio, C., *Cuba* **88 B3** 21 50N 84 57W
San Antonio, Mt., *U.S.A.* **85 L9** 34 17N 117 38W
San Antonio de los Baños, *Cuba* **88 B3** 22 54N 82 31W
San Antonio de los Cobres, *Argentina* **94 A2** 24 10S 66 17W
San Antonio Oeste, *Argentina* **96 E4** 40 40S 65 0W
San Ardo, *U.S.A.* **84 J6** 36 1N 120 54W
San Augustín, *Canary Is.* **22 G4** 27 47N 15 32W
San Augustine, *U.S.A.* **81 K7** 31 30N 94 7W
San Bartolomé, *Canary Is.* **22 F6** 28 59N 13 37W
San Bartolomé de Tirajana, *Canary Is.* **22 G4** 27 54N 15 34W
San Benedetto del Tronto, *Italy* **20 C5** 42 57N 13 53 E
San Benedicto, I., *Mexico* **86 D2** 19 18N 110 49W
San Benito, *U.S.A.* **81 M6** 26 8N 97 38W
San Benito →, *U.S.A.* **84 J5** 36 53N 121 34W
San Benito Mt., *U.S.A.* **84 J6** 36 22N 120 37W
San Bernardino, *U.S.A.* **85 L9** 34 7N 117 19W
San Bernardino Mts., *U.S.A.* **85 L10** 34 10N 116 45W
San Bernardino Str., *Phil.* **37 B6** 13 0N 125 0 E
San Bernardo, *Chile* **94 C1** 33 40S 70 50W
San Bernardo, I. de, *Colombia* **92 B3** 9 45N 75 50W
San Blas, *Mexico* **86 B3** 26 4N 108 46W
San Blas, Arch. de, *Panama* **88 E4** 9 50N 78 31W
San Blas, C., *U.S.A.* **77 L3** 29 40N 85 21W
San Borja, *Bolivia* **92 F5** 14 50S 66 52W
San Buenaventura, *Mexico* **86 B4** 27 5N 101 32W
San Carlos = Sant Carles, *Spain* **22 B8** 39 3N 1 34 E
San Carlos, *Argentina* **94 C2** 33 50S 69 0W
San Carlos, *Chile* **94 D1** 36 10S 72 0W
San Carlos, *Baja Calif. S., Mexico* **86 C2** 24 47N 112 6W
San Carlos, *Coahuila, Mexico* **86 B4** 29 0N 100 54W
San Carlos, *Nic.* **88 D3** 11 12N 84 50W
San Carlos, *Phil.* **37 B6** 10 29N 123 25 E
San Carlos, *Uruguay* **95 C5** 34 46S 54 58W
San Carlos, *U.S.A.* **83 K8** 33 21N 110 27W
San Carlos, *Venezuela* **92 B5** 9 40N 68 36W
San Carlos de Bariloche, *Argentina* **96 E2** 41 10S 71 25W
San Carlos de Bolívar, *Argentina* **96 D4** 36 15S 61 6W
San Carlos del Zulia, *Venezuela* **92 B4** 9 1N 71 55W
San Carlos L., *U.S.A.* **83 K8** 33 11N 110 32W
San Clemente, *Chile* **94 D1** 35 30S 71 29W
San Clemente, *U.S.A.* **85 M9** 33 26N 117 37W
San Clemente I., *U.S.A.* **85 N8** 32 53N 118 29W
San Cristóbal = Es Migjorn Gran, *Spain* **22 B11** 39 57N 4 3 E
San Cristóbal, *Argentina* **94 C3** 30 20S 61 10W
San Cristóbal, *Dom. Rep.* **89 C5** 18 25N 70 6W
San Cristóbal, *Venezuela* **92 B4** 7 46N 72 14W
San Cristóbal de la Casas, *Mexico* **87 D6** 16 50N 92 33W
San Diego, *Calif., U.S.A.* **85 N9** 32 43N 117 9W
San Diego, *Tex., U.S.A.* **81 M5** 27 46N 98 14W
San Diego, C., *Argentina* **96 G3** 54 40S 65 10W
San Diego de la Unión, *Mexico* **86 C4** 21 28N 100 52W
San Dimitri, Ras, *Malta* **23 C1** 36 4N 14 11 E
San Dimitri Point = San Dimitri, Ras, *Malta* **23 C1** 36 4N 14 11 E
San Estanislao, *Paraguay* **94 A4** 24 39S 56 26W
San Felipe, *Chile* **94 C1** 32 43S 70 42W
San Felipe, *Mexico* **86 A2** 31 0N 114 52W
San Felipe, *Venezuela* **92 A5** 10 20N 68 44W
San Felipe →, *U.S.A.* **85 M11** 33 12N 115 49W
San Félix, *Chile* **94 B1** 28 56S 70 28W
San Félix, *Pac. Oc.* **90 F2** 26 23S 80 0W
San Fernando = Sant Ferran, *Spain* **22 C7** 38 42N 1 28 E
San Fernando, *Chile* **94 C1** 34 30S 71 0W
San Fernando, *Baja Calif., Mexico* **86 B1** 29 55N 115 10W
San Fernando, *Tamaulipas, Mexico* **87 C5** 24 51N 98 10W
San Fernando, *La Union, Phil.* **37 A6** 16 40N 120 23 E
San Fernando, *Pampanga, Phil.* **37 A6** 15 5N 120 37 E
San Fernando, *Spain* **19 D2** 36 28N 6 17W
San Fernando, *Trin. & Tob.* **89 D7** 10 20N 61 30W
San Fernando, *U.S.A.* **85 L8** 34 17N 118 26W
San Fernando de Apure, *Venezuela* **92 B5** 7 54N 67 15W
San Fernando de Atabapo, *Venezuela* **92 C5** 4 3N 67 42W
San Francisco, *Argentina* **94 C3** 31 30S 62 5W
San Francisco, *U.S.A.* **84 H4** 37 47N 122 25W
San Francisco →, *U.S.A.* **83 K9** 32 59N 109 22W
San Francisco, Paso de, *S. Amer.* **94 B2** 27 0S 68 0W
San Francisco de Macorís, *Dom. Rep.* **89 C5** 19 19N 70 15W
San Francisco del Monte de Oro, *Argentina* **94 C2** 32 36S 66 8W
San Francisco del Oro, *Mexico* **86 B3** 26 52N 105 50W
San Francisco Javier = Sant Francesc de Formentera, *Spain* **22 C7** 38 42N 1 26 E
San Francisco Solano, Pta., *Colombia* **90 C3** 6 18N 77 29W
San Gabriel, *Chile* **94 C1** 33 47S 70 15W
San Gabriel Mts., *U.S.A.* **85 L9** 34 20N 118 0W
San Gorgonio Mt., *U.S.A.* **85 L10** 34 7N 116 51W
San Gottardo, P. del, *Switz.* **18 C8** 46 33N 8 33 E
San Gregorio, *Uruguay* **95 C4** 32 37S 55 40W
San Gregorio, *U.S.A.* **84 H4** 37 20N 122 23W
San Ignacio, *Belize* **87 D7** 17 10N 89 0W
San Ignacio, *Bolivia* **92 G6** 16 20S 60 55W
San Ignacio, *Mexico* **86 B2** 27 27N 113 0W
San Ignacio, *Paraguay* **88 C2** 26 52S 57 3W
San Ignacio, L., *Mexico* **86 B2** 26 50N 113 11W
San Ildefonso, C., *Phil.* **37 A6** 16 0N 122 1 E
San Isidro, *Argentina* **94 C4** 34 29S 58 31W
San Jacinto, *U.S.A.* **85 M10** 33 47N 116 57W
San Jaime = Sant Jaume, *Spain* **22 B11** 39 54N 4 4 E
San Javier, *Misiones, Argentina* **95 B4** 27 55S 55 5W
San Javier, *Santa Fe, Argentina* **94 C4** 30 40S 59 55W
San Javier, *Bolivia* **92 G6** 16 18S 62 30W
San Javier, *Chile* **94 D1** 35 40S 71 45W
San Jeronimo Taviche, *Mexico* **87 D5** 16 38N 96 32W
San Joaquin, *U.S.A.* **84 J6** 36 36N 120 11W
San Joaquin →, *U.S.A.* **84 G5** 38 4N 121 51W
San Joaquin Valley, *U.S.A.* **84 J6** 37 20N 121 0W
San Jon, *U.S.A.* **81 H3** 35 6N 103 20W
San Jordi = Sant Jordi, *Spain* **22 B9** 39 33N 2 46 E
San Jorge, *Argentina* **94 C3** 31 54S 61 50W
San Jorge, B. de, *Mexico* **86 A2** 31 20N 113 20W
San Jorge, G., *Argentina* **96 F3** 46 0S 66 0W
San José = San Josep, *Spain* **22 C7** 38 55N 1 18 E
San José, *Costa Rica* **88 E3** 9 55N 84 2W
San José, *Guatemala* **88 D1** 14 0N 90 50W
San José, *Mexico* **86 C2** 25 0N 110 50W
San Jose, *Mind. Occ., Phil.* **37 B6** 12 27N 121 4 E
San Jose, *Nueva Ecija, Phil.* **37 A6** 15 45N 120 55 E
San Jose, *U.S.A.* **84 H5** 37 20N 121 53W
San Jose →, *U.S.A.* **83 J10** 34 25N 106 45W
San Jose de Buenavista, *Phil.* **37 B6** 10 45N 121 56 E
San José de Chiquitos, *Bolivia* **92 G6** 17 53S 60 50W
San José de Feliciano, *Argentina* **94 C4** 30 26S 58 46W
San José de Jáchal, *Argentina* **94 C2** 30 15S 68 46W
San José de Mayo, *Uruguay* **94 C4** 34 27S 56 40W
San José del Cabo, *Mexico* **86 C3** 23 0N 109 40W
San José del Guaviare, *Colombia* **92 C4** 2 35N 72 38W
San Josep, *Spain* **22 C7** 38 55N 1 18 E
San Juan, *Argentina* **94 C2** 31 30S 68 30W
San Juan, *Mexico* **86 C4** 21 20N 102 50W
San Juan, *Puerto Rico* **89 C6** 18 28N 66 7W
San Juan □, *Argentina* **94 C2** 31 9S 69 0W
San Juan →, *Argentina* **94 C2** 32 20S 67 25W
San Juan →, *Nic.* **88 D3** 10 56N 83 42W
San Juan →, *U.S.A.* **83 H8** 37 16N 110 26W
San Juan Bautista = Sant Joan Baptista, *Spain* **22 B8** 39 5N 1 31 E
San Juan Bautista, *Paraguay* **94 B4** 26 37S 57 6W
San Juan Bautista, *U.S.A.* **84 J5** 36 51N 121 32W
San Juan Bautista Valle Nacional, *Mexico* **87 D5** 17 47N 96 19W
San Juan Capistrano, *U.S.A.* **85 M9** 33 30N 117 40W
San Juan Cr. →, *U.S.A.* **84 J5** 35 40N 120 22W
San Juan de Guadalupe, *Mexico* **86 C4** 24 38N 102 44W
San Juan de la Costa, *Mexico* **86 C2** 24 23N 110 45W
San Juan de los Morros, *Venezuela* **92 B5** 9 55N 67 21W
San Juan del Norte, *Nic.* **88 D3** 10 58N 83 40W
San Juan del Norte, B. de, *Nic.* **88 D3** 11 0N 83 40W
San Juan del Río, *Mexico* **87 C5** 20 25N 100 0W
San Juan del Sur, *Nic.* **88 D2** 11 20N 85 51W
San Juan I., *U.S.A.* **84 B3** 48 32N 123 5W
San Juan Mts., *U.S.A.* **83 H10** 37 30N 107 0W
San Justo, *Argentina* **94 C3** 30 47S 60 30W
San Kamphaeng, *Thailand* **38 C2** 18 45N 99 8 E
San Lázaro, C., *Mexico* **86 C2** 24 50N 112 18W
San Lázaro, Sa., *Mexico* **86 C3** 23 25N 110 0W
San Leandro, *U.S.A.* **84 H4** 37 44N 122 9W
San Lorenzo = Sant Llorenç des Cardassar, *Spain* **22 B10** 39 37N 3 17 E
San Lorenzo, *Argentina* **94 C3** 32 45S 60 45W
San Lorenzo, *Ecuador* **92 C3** 1 15N 78 50W
San Lorenzo, *Paraguay* **94 B4** 25 20S 57 32W
San Lorenzo →, *Mexico* **86 C3** 24 15N 107 24W
San Lorenzo, I., *Mexico* **86 B2** 28 35N 112 50W
San Lorenzo, Mte., *Argentina* **96 F2** 47 40S 72 20W
San Lucas, *Bolivia* **92 H5** 20 5S 65 7W
San Lucas, *Baja Calif. S., Mexico* **86 C3** 22 53N 109 54W
San Lucas, *Baja Calif. S., Mexico* **86 B2** 27 10N 112 14W
San Lucas, *U.S.A.* **84 J5** 36 8N 121 1W
San Lucas, C., *Mexico* **86 C3** 22 50N 110 0W
San Luis, *Argentina* **94 C2** 33 20S 66 20W
San Luis, *Cuba* **88 B3** 22 17N 83 46W
San Luis, *Guatemala* **88 C2** 16 14N 89 27W
San Luis, *Ariz., U.S.A.* **83 K6** 32 29N 114 47W
San Luis, *Colo., U.S.A.* **83 H11** 37 12N 105 25W
San Luis □, *Argentina* **94 C2** 34 0S 66 0W
San Luis, I., *Mexico* **86 B2** 29 58N 114 26W
San Luis, Sierra de, *Argentina* **94 C2** 32 30S 66 10W
San Luis de la Paz, *Mexico* **86 C4** 21 19N 100 32W
San Luis Obispo, *U.S.A.* **85 K6** 35 17N 120 40W
San Luis Potosí, *Mexico* **86 C4** 22 9N 100 59W
San Luis Potosí □, *Mexico* **86 C4** 22 10N 101 0W
San Luis Reservoir, *U.S.A.* **84 H5** 37 4N 121 5W
San Luis Río Colorado, *Mexico* **86 A2** 32 29N 114 58W
San Manuel, *U.S.A.* **83 K8** 32 36N 110 38W
San Marcos, *Guatemala* **88 D1** 14 59N 91 52W
San Marcos, *Mexico* **86 B2** 27 13N 112 6W
San Marcos, *Calif., U.S.A.* **85 M9** 33 9N 117 10W
San Marcos, *Tex., U.S.A.* **81 L6** 29 53N 97 56W
San Marino, *San Marino* **16 G7** 43 55N 12 30 E
San Marino ■, *Europe* **20 C5** 43 56N 12 25 E
San Martín, *Argentina* **94 C2** 33 5S 68 28W
San Martín →, *Bolivia* **92 F6** 13 8S 63 43W
San Martín, L., *Argentina* **96 F2** 48 50S 72 50W
San Martín de los Andes, *Argentina* **96 E2** 40 10S 71 20W
San Mateo = Sant Mateu, *Spain* **22 B7** 39 3N 1 23 E
San Mateo, *U.S.A.* **84 H4** 37 34N 122 19W
San Matías, *Bolivia* **92 G7** 16 25S 58 20W
San Matías, G., *Argentina* **96 E4** 41 30S 64 0W
San Miguel = Sant Miguel, *Spain* **22 B7** 39 3N 1 26 E
San Miguel, *El Salv.* **88 D2** 13 30N 88 12W
San Miguel, *Panama* **88 E4** 8 27N 78 55W
San Miguel, *U.S.A.* **84 K6** 35 45N 120 42W
San Miguel →, *Bolivia* **92 F6** 13 52S 63 56W
San Miguel de Tucumán, *Argentina* **94 B2** 26 50S 65 20W
San Miguel del Monte, *Argentina* **94 D4** 35 23S 58 50W
San Miguel I., *U.S.A.* **85 L6** 34 2N 120 23W
San Nicolás, *Canary Is.* **22 G4** 27 58N 15 47W
San Nicolás de los Arroyas, *Argentina* **94 C3** 33 25S 60 10W
San Nicolas I., *U.S.A.* **85 M7** 33 15N 119 30W
San Onofre, *U.S.A.* **85 M9** 33 22N 117 34W
San Pablo, *Bolivia* **94 A2** 21 43S 66 38W
San Pablo, *U.S.A.* **84 H4** 37 58N 122 21W
San Pedro, *Buenos Aires, Argentina* **94 C4** 33 40S 59 40W
San Pedro, *Misiones, Argentina* **95 B5** 26 30S 54 10W
San Pedro, *Chile* **94 C1** 33 54S 71 28W
San Pédro, *Ivory C.* **50 H4** 4 50N 6 33W
San Pedro, *Mexico* **86 C2** 23 55N 110 17W
San Pedro □, *Paraguay* **94 A4** 24 0S 57 0W
San Pedro →, *Chihuahua, Mexico* **86 B3** 28 20N 106 10W
San Pedro →, *Nayarit, Mexico* **86 C3** 21 45N 105 30W
San Pedro →, *U.S.A.* **83 K8** 32 59N 110 47W
San Pedro, Pta., *Chile* **94 B1** 25 30S 70 38W
San Pedro Channel, *U.S.A.* **85 M8** 33 30N 118 25W
San Pedro de Atacama, *Chile* **94 A2** 22 55S 68 15W
San Pedro de Jujuy, *Argentina* **94 A3** 24 12S 64 55W
San Pedro de las Colonias, *Mexico* **86 B4** 25 50N 102 59W
San Pedro de Macorís, *Dom. Rep.* **89 C6** 18 30N 69 18W
San Pedro del Norte, *Nic.* **88 D3** 13 4N 84 33W
San Pedro del Paraná, *Paraguay* **94 B4** 26 43S 56 13W
San Pedro Mártir, Sierra, *Mexico* **86 A1** 31 0N 115 30W
San Pedro Mixtepec, *Mexico* **87 D5** 16 2N 97 7W
San Pedro Ocampo = Melchor Ocampo, *Mexico* **86 C4** 24 52N 101 40W

San Pedro Sula, *Honduras* .. 88 C2 15 30N 88 0W
San Pietro, *Italy* .... 20 E3 39 8N 8 17 E
San Quintín, *Mexico* 86 A1 30 29N 115 57W
San Rafael, *Argentina* 94 C2 34 40S 68 21W
San Rafael, *Calif., U.S.A.* ... 84 H4 37 58N 122 32W
San Rafael, *N. Mex., U.S.A.* . 83 J10 35 7N 107 53W
San Rafael Mt., *U.S.A.* 85 L7 34 41N 119 52W
San Rafael Mts., *U.S.A.* 85 L7 34 40N 119 50W
San Ramón de la Nueva
Orán, *Argentina* 94 A3 23 10S 64 20W
San Remo, *Italy* .... 18 E7 43 49N 7 46 E
San Roque, *Argentina* 94 B4 28 25S 58 45W
San Roque, *Spain* 19 D3 36 17N 5 21W
San Rosendo, *Chile* 94 D1 37 16S 72 43W
San Saba, *U.S.A.* 81 K5 31 12N 98 43W
San Salvador, *El Salv.* 88 D2 13 40N 89 10W
San Salvador, *Spain* .... 22 B10 39 27N 3 11 E
San Salvador de Jujuy,
Argentina 94 A3 24 10S 64 48W
San Salvador I., *Bahamas* .. 89 B5 24 0N 74 40W
San Sebastián = Donostia-
San Sebastián, *Spain* 19 A5 43 17N 1 58W
San Sebastián, *Argentina* ... 96 G3 53 10S 68 30W
San Sebastián de la Gomera,
Canary Is. 22 F2 28 5N 17 7W
San Serra = Son Serra, *Spain* 22 B10 39 43N 3 13 E
San Severo, *Italy* .... 20 D6 41 41N 15 23 E
San Simeon, *U.S.A.* 84 K5 35 39N 121 11W
San Simon, *U.S.A.* 83 K9 32 16N 109 14W
San Telmo = Sant Telm,
Spain .... 22 B9 39 35N 2 21 E
San Telmo, *Mexico* 86 A1 30 58N 116 6W
San Tiburcio, *Mexico* 86 C4 24 8N 101 32W
San Valentin, Mte., *Chile* ... 96 F2 46 30S 73 30W
San Vicente de la Barquera,
Spain 19 A3 43 23N 4 29W
San Vito, *Costa Rica* 88 E3 8 50N 82 58W
Sana', *Yemen* .... 46 D3 15 27N 44 12 E
Sana →, *Bos.-H.* .... 16 F9 45 3N 16 23 E
Sanaga →, *Cameroon* ...... 52 D1 3 35N 9 38 E
Sanaloa, Presa, *Mexico* 86 C3 24 50N 107 20W
Sanana, *Indonesia* .... 37 E7 2 4S 125 58 E
Sanand, *India* .... 42 H5 22 59N 72 25 E
Sanandaj, *Iran* .... 44 C5 35 18N 47 1 E
Sanandita, *Bolivia* 94 A3 21 40S 63 45W
Sanawad, *India* .... 42 H7 22 11N 76 5 E
Sancellas = Sencelles, *Spain* 22 B9 39 39N 2 54 E
Sanchahe, *China* .... 35 B14 44 50N 126 2 E
Sánchez, *Dom. Rep.* 89 C6 19 15N 69 36W
Sanchor, *India* .... 42 G4 24 45N 71 55 E
Sancti Spíritus, *Cuba* 88 B4 21 52N 79 33W
Sancy, Puy de, *France* ..... 18 D5 45 32N 2 50 E
Sand →, *S. Africa* .... 57 C5 22 25S 30 5 E
Sand Hills, *U.S.A.* 80 D4 42 10N 101 30W
Sand Springs, *U.S.A.* 81 G6 36 9N 96 7W
Sanda, *Japan* .... 31 G7 34 53N 135 14 E
Sandakan, *Malaysia* .... 36 C5 5 53N 118 4 E
Sandan = Sambor, *Cambodia* 38 F6 12 46N 106 0 E
Sandanski, *Bulgaria* .... 21 D10 41 35N 23 16 E
Sanday, *U.K.* 12 B6 59 16N 2 31W
Sandefjord, *Norway* .... 9 G14 59 10N 10 15 E
Sanders, *U.S.A.* 83 J9 35 13N 109 20W
Sanderson, *U.S.A.* 81 K3 30 9N 102 24W
Sandersville, *U.S.A.* 77 J4 32 59N 82 48W
Sandfire Roadhouse,
Australia .... 60 C3 19 45S 121 15 E
Sandfly L., *Canada* 73 B7 55 43N 106 6W
Sandfontein, *Namibia* ...... 56 C2 23 48S 29 1 E
Sandía, *Peru* 92 F5 14 10S 69 30W
Sandila, *India* .... 43 F9 27 5N 80 31 E
Sandnes, *Norway* .... 9 G11 58 50N 5 45 E
Sandnessjøen, *Norway* ..... 8 C15 66 2N 12 38 E
Sandoa, *Dem. Rep. of
the Congo* .... 52 F4 9 41S 23 0 E
Sandomierz, *Poland* .... 17 C11 50 40N 21 43 E
Sandover →, *Australia* ..... 62 C2 21 43S 136 32 E
Sandoway, *Burma* .... 41 K19 18 20N 94 30 E
Sandoy, *Færoe Is.* 8 F9 61 52N 6 46W
Sandpoint, *U.S.A.* 82 B5 48 17N 116 33W
Sandray, *U.K.* 12 E1 56 53N 7 31W
Sandringham, *U.K.* .... 10 E8 52 51N 0 31 E
Sandstone, *Australia* ...... 61 E2 27 59S 119 16 E
Sandusky, *Mich., U.S.A.* 78 C2 43 25N 82 50W
Sandusky, *Ohio, U.S.A.* 78 E2 41 27N 82 42W
Sandviken, *Sweden* .... 9 F17 60 38N 16 46 E
Sandwich, C., *Australia* .... 62 B4 18 14S 146 18 E
Sandwich B., *Canada* 71 B8 53 40N 57 15W
Sandwich B., *Namibia* ..... 56 C1 23 25S 14 20 E
Sandy, *Oreg., U.S.A.* 84 E4 45 24N 122 16W
Sandy, *Pa., U.S.A.* 78 E6 41 6N 78 46W
Sandy, *Utah, U.S.A.* 82 F8 40 35N 111 50W
Sandy Bay, *Canada* 73 B8 55 31N 102 19W
Sandy Bight, *Australia* ..... 61 F3 33 50S 123 20 E
Sandy C., *Queens., Australia* 62 C5 24 42S 153 15 E
Sandy C., *Tas., Australia* ... 62 G3 41 25S 144 45 E
Sandy Cay, *Bahamas* 89 B4 23 13N 75 18W
Sandy Cr. →, *U.S.A.* 82 F9 41 51N 109 47W
Sandy L., *Canada* 70 B1 53 2N 93 0W
Sandy Lake, *Canada* 70 B1 53 0N 93 15W
Sandy Valley, *U.S.A.* 85 K11 35 49N 115 36W
Sanford, *Fla., U.S.A.* 77 L5 28 48N 81 16W
Sanford, *Maine, U.S.A.* 77 D10 43 27N 70 47W
Sanford, *N.C., U.S.A.* 77 H6 35 29N 79 10W
Sanford →, *Australia* ...... 61 E2 27 22S 115 53 E
Sanford, Mt., *U.S.A.* 68 B5 62 13N 144 8W
Sang-i-Masha, *Afghan.* ..... 42 C2 33 8N 67 27 E
Sanga, *Mozam.* .... 55 E4 12 22S 35 21 E
Sanga →, *Congo* .... 52 E3 1 5S 17 0 E
Sangamner, *India* .... 40 K9 19 37N 74 15 E
Sangar, *Afghan.* .... 42 C1 32 56N 65 30 E
Sangar, *Russia* .... 27 C13 64 2N 127 31 E
Sangar Sarai, *Afghan.* ..... 42 B4 34 27N 70 35 E
Sangarh →, *Pakistan* ...... 42 D4 30 43N 70 44 E
Sangay, *Ecuador* 92 D3 2 0S 78 20W
Sange, *Dem. Rep. of
the Congo* .... 54 D2 6 58S 28 21 E
Sangeang, *Indonesia* ...... 37 F5 8 12S 119 6 E
Sanger, *U.S.A.* 84 J7 36 42N 119 33W
Sangerhausen, *Germany* .... 16 C6 51 28N 11 18 E
Sanggan He →, *China* ...... 34 E9 38 12N 117 15 E
Sanggau, *Indonesia* .... 36 D4 0 5N 110 30 E
Sanghar, *Pakistan* .... 42 F3 26 2N 68 57 E
Sangihe, Kepulauan,
Indonesia .... 37 D7 3 0N 125 30 E
Sangihe, Pulau, *Indonesia* .. 37 D7 3 35N 125 30 E
Sangju, *S. Korea* .... 35 F15 36 25N 128 10 E
Sangkapura, *Indonesia* ..... 36 F4 5 52S 112 40 E
Sangkhla, *Thailand* .... 38 E2 14 57N 98 28 E
Sangkulirang, *Indonesia* .... 36 D5 0 59N 117 58 E
Sangla, *Pakistan* .... 42 D5 31 43N 73 23 E
Sangli, *India* .... 40 L9 16 55N 74 33 E
Sangmélima, *Cameroon* .... 52 D2 2 57N 12 1 E
Sangod, *India* .... 42 G7 24 55N 76 17 E
Sangre de Cristo Mts., *U.S.A.* 81 G2 37 30N 105 20W
Sangrur, *India* .... 42 D6 30 14N 75 50 E
Sangudo, *Canada* 72 C6 53 50N 114 54W
Sangue →, *Brazil* 92 F7 11 1S 58 39W
Sanibel, *U.S.A.* 77 M4 26 26N 82 1W
Sanirajak, *Canada* 69 B11 68 46N 81 12W
Sanjawi, *Pakistan* .... 42 D3 30 17N 68 21 E
Sanje, *Uganda* .... 54 C3 0 49S 31 30 E
Sanjo, *Japan* .... 30 F9 37 37N 138 57 E
Sankh →, *India* .... 43 H11 22 15N 84 48 E
Sankt Gallen, *Switz.* .... 18 C8 47 26N 9 22 E
Sankt Moritz, *Switz.* .... 18 C8 46 30N 9 50 E
Sankt-Peterburg, *Russia* .... 24 C5 59 55N 30 20 E
Sankt Pölten, *Austria* ...... 16 D8 48 12N 15 38 E
Sankuru →, *Dem. Rep. of
the Congo* .... 52 E4 4 17S 20 25 E
Sanliurfa, *Turkey* .... 25 G6 37 12N 38 50 E
Sanlúcar de Barrameda,
Spain 19 D2 36 46N 6 21W
Sanmenxia, *China* .... 34 G6 34 47N 111 12 E
Sanming, *China* .... 33 D6 26 15N 117 40 E
Sannaspos, *S. Africa* ...... 56 D4 29 6S 26 34 E
Sannicandro Gargánico, *Italy* 20 D6 41 50N 15 34 E
Sânnicolau Mare, *Romania* . 17 E11 46 5N 20 39 E
Sannieshof, *S. Africa* ...... 56 D4 26 30S 25 47 E
Sannin, J., *Lebanon* .... 47 B4 33 57N 35 52 E
Sanniquellie, *Liberia* 50 G4 7 19N 8 38W
Sanok, *Poland* .... 17 D12 49 35N 22 10 E
Sanquhar, *U.K.* 12 F5 55 22N 3 54W
Sant Antoni Abat, *Spain* .... 22 C7 38 59N 1 19 E
Sant Carles, *Spain* .... 22 B8 39 3N 1 34 E
Sant Feliu de Guíxols, *Spain* 19 B7 41 45N 3 1 E
Sant Ferran, *Spain* .... 22 C7 38 42N 1 28 E
Sant Francesc de Formentera,
Spain .... 22 C7 38 42N 1 26 E
Sant Jaume, *Spain* .... 22 B11 39 54N 4 4 E
Sant Joan Baptista, *Spain* .. 22 B8 39 5N 1 31 E
Sant Jordi, *Ibiza, Spain* .... 22 C7 38 53N 1 24 E
Sant Jordi, *Mallorca, Spain* . 22 B9 39 33N 2 46 E
Sant Jordi, G. de, *Spain* .... 19 B6 40 53N 1 2 E
Sant Llorenç des Cardassar,
Spain .... 22 B10 39 37N 3 17 E
Sant Mateu, *Spain* .... 22 B7 39 3N 1 23 E
Sant Miquel, *Spain* .... 22 B7 39 3N 1 26 E
Sant Telm, *Spain* .... 22 B9 39 35N 2 21 E
Santa Agnés, *Spain* .... 22 B7 39 3N 1 21 E
Santa Ana, *Bolivia* 92 F5 13 50S 65 40W
Santa Ana, *El Salv.* 88 D2 14 0N 89 31W
Santa Ana, *Mexico* 86 A2 30 31N 111 8W
Santa Ana, *U.S.A.* 85 M9 33 46N 117 52W
Sant' Antioco, *Italy* .... 20 E3 39 4N 8 27 E
Santa Bárbara, *Chile* 94 D1 37 40S 72 1W
Santa Bárbara, *Honduras* ... 88 D2 14 53N 88 14W
Santa Bárbara, *Mexico* 86 B3 26 48N 105 50W
Santa Barbara, *U.S.A.* 85 L7 34 25N 119 42W
Santa Barbara Channel,
U.S.A. 85 L7 34 15N 120 0W
Santa Barbara I., *U.S.A.* 85 M7 33 29N 119 2W
Santa Catalina, Gulf of, *U.S.A.* 85 N9 33 10N 117 50W
Santa Catalina, I., *Mexico* ... 86 B2 25 40N 110 50W
Santa Catalina I., *U.S.A.* 85 M8 33 23N 118 25W
Santa Catarina □, *Brazil* 95 B6 27 25S 48 30W
Santa Catarina, I. de, *Brazil* . 95 B6 27 30S 48 40W
Santa Cecília, *Brazil* 95 B5 26 56S 50 18W
Santa Clara, *Cuba* 88 B4 22 20N 80 0W
Santa Clara, *Calif., U.S.A.* ... 84 H5 37 21N 121 57W
Santa Clara, *Utah, U.S.A.* ... 83 H7 37 8N 113 39W
Santa Clara, El Golfo de,
Mexico 86 A2 31 42N 114 30W
Santa Clara de Olimar,
Uruguay 95 C5 32 50S 54 54W
Santa Clarita, *U.S.A.* 85 L8 34 24N 118 30W
Santa Clotilde, *Peru* 92 D4 2 33S 73 45W
Santa Coloma de Gramenet,
Spain .... 19 B7 41 27N 2 13 E
Santa Cruz, *Argentina* 96 G3 50 0S 68 32W
Santa Cruz, *Bolivia* 92 G6 17 43S 63 10W
Santa Cruz, *Chile* 94 C1 34 38S 71 27W
Santa Cruz, *Costa Rica* 88 D2 10 15N 85 35W
Santa Cruz, *Madeira* 22 D3 32 42N 16 46W
Santa Cruz, *Phil.* .... 37 B6 14 20N 121 24 E
Santa Cruz, *U.S.A.* 84 J4 36 58N 122 1W
Santa Cruz →, *Argentina* ... 96 G3 50 10S 68 20W
Santa Cruz de la Palma,
Canary Is. 22 F2 28 41N 17 46W
Santa Cruz de Tenerife,
Canary Is. 22 F3 28 28N 16 15W
Santa Cruz del Norte, *Cuba* . 88 B3 23 9N 81 55W
Santa Cruz del Sur, *Cuba* ... 88 B4 20 44N 78 0W
Santa Cruz do Rio Pardo,
Brazil 95 A6 22 54S 49 37W
Santa Cruz do Sul, *Brazil* ... 95 B5 29 42S 52 25W
Santa Cruz I., *U.S.A.* 85 M7 34 1N 119 43W
Santa Cruz Is., *Solomon Is.* . 64 J8 10 30S 166 0 E
Santa Domingo, Cay,
Bahamas 88 B4 21 25N 75 15W
Santa Elena, *Argentina* 94 C4 30 58S 59 47W
Santa Elena, C., *Costa Rica* . 88 D2 10 54N 85 56W
Santa Eulària des Riu, *Spain* 22 C8 38 59N 1 32 E
Santa Fe, *Argentina* 94 C3 31 35S 60 41W
Santa Fe, *U.S.A.* 83 J11 35 41N 105 57W
Santa Fé □, *Argentina* 94 C3 31 50S 60 55W
Santa Fé do Sul, *Brazil* 93 H8 20 13S 50 56W
Santa Filomena, *Brazil* 93 E9 9 6S 45 50W
Santa Gertrudis, *Spain* ..... 22 C7 39 0N 1 26 E
Santa Inês, *Brazil* 93 F11 13 17S 39 48W
Santa Inés, I., *Chile* 96 G2 54 0S 73 0W
Santa Isabel = Rey Malabo,
Eq. Guin. .... 52 D1 3 45N 8 50 E
Santa Isabel, *Argentina* 94 D2 36 10S 66 54W
Santa Isabel do Morro, *Brazil* 93 F8 11 34S 50 40W
Santa Lucía, *Corrientes,
Argentina* 94 B4 28 58S 59 5W
Santa Lucía, *San Juan,
Argentina* 94 C2 31 30S 68 30W
Santa Lucía, *Uruguay* 94 C4 34 27S 56 24W
Santa Lucia Range, *U.S.A.* .. 84 K5 36 0N 121 20W
Santa Magdalena, I., *Mexico* 86 C2 24 40N 112 15W
Santa Margarita, *Argentina* . 94 D3 38 28S 61 35W
Santa Margarita, *Spain* ..... 22 B10 39 42N 3 6 E
Santa Margarita, *U.S.A.* 84 K6 35 23N 120 37W
Santa Margarita →, *U.S.A.* . 85 M9 33 13N 117 23W
Santa Margarita, I., *Mexico* . 86 C2 24 30N 111 50W
Santa María, *Argentina* 94 B2 26 40S 66 0W
Santa Maria, *Brazil* 95 B5 29 40S 53 48W
Santa Maria, *U.S.A.* 85 L6 34 57N 120 26W
Santa María →, *Mexico* 86 A3 31 0N 107 14W
Santa María, B. de, *Mexico* . 86 B3 25 10N 108 40W
Santa Maria da Vitória, *Brazil* 93 F10 13 24S 44 12W
Santa Maria del Camí, *Spain* 22 B9 39 38N 2 47 E
Santa Maria di Léuca, C., *Italy* 21 E8 39 47N 18 22 E
Santa Marta, *Colombia* 92 A4 11 15N 74 13W
Santa Marta, Sierra Nevada
de, *Colombia* 92 A4 10 55N 73 50W
Santa Marta Grande, C., *Brazil* 95 B6 28 43S 48 50W
Santa Maura = Levkás,
Greece .... 21 E9 38 40N 20 43 E
Santa Monica, *U.S.A.* 85 M8 34 1N 118 29W
Santa Paula, *U.S.A.* 85 L7 34 21N 119 4W
Santa Ponça, *Spain* .... 22 B9 39 30N 2 28 E
Santa Rita, *U.S.A.* 83 K10 32 48N 108 4W
Santa Rosa, *La Pampa,
Argentina* 94 D3 36 40S 64 17W
Santa Rosa, *San Luis,
Argentina* 94 C2 32 21S 65 10W
Santa Rosa, *Brazil* 95 B5 27 52S 54 29W
Santa Rosa, *Calif., U.S.A.* ... 84 G4 38 26N 122 43W
Santa Rosa, *N. Mex., U.S.A.* . 81 H2 34 57N 104 41W
Santa Rosa de Copán,
Honduras 88 D2 14 47N 88 46W
Santa Rosa de Río Primero,
Argentina 94 C3 31 8S 63 20W
Santa Rosa del Sara, *Bolivia* 92 G6 17 7S 63 35W
Santa Rosa I., *Calif., U.S.A.* . 85 M6 33 58N 120 6W
Santa Rosa I., *Fla., U.S.A.* ... 77 K2 30 20N 86 50W
Santa Rosa Range, *U.S.A.* .. 82 F5 41 45N 117 40W
Santa Rosalía, *Mexico* 86 B2 27 20N 112 20W
Santa Sylvina, *Argentina* ... 94 B3 27 50S 61 10W
Santa Tecla = Nueva San
Salvador, *El Salv.* 88 D2 13 40N 89 18W
Santa Teresa, *Argentina* 94 C3 33 25S 60 47W
Santa Teresa, *Australia* .... 62 C1 24 8S 134 22 E
Santa Teresa, *Mexico* 87 B5 25 17N 97 51W
Santa Vitória do Palmar,
Brazil 95 C5 33 32S 53 25W
Santa Ynez →, *U.S.A.* 85 L6 35 41N 120 36W
Santa Ynez Mts., *U.S.A.* 85 L6 34 30N 120 0W
Santa Ysabel, *U.S.A.* 85 M10 33 7N 116 40W
Santai, *China* .... 32 C5 31 5N 104 58 E
Santana, *Madeira* 22 D3 32 48N 16 52W
Santana, Coxilha de, *Brazil* . 95 C4 30 50S 55 35W
Santana do Livramento, *Brazil* 95 C4 30 55S 55 30W
Santander, *Spain* 19 A4 43 27N 3 51W
Santander Jiménez, *Mexico* . 87 C5 24 11N 98 29W
Santanilla, Is., *Honduras* ... 88 C3 17 22N 83 57W
Santanyí, *Spain* .... 22 B10 39 20N 3 5 E
Santaquin, *U.S.A.* 82 G8 39 59N 111 47W
Santarém, *Brazil* 93 D8 2 25S 54 42W
Santarém, *Portugal* 19 C1 39 12N 8 42W
Santaren Channel, *W. Indies* 88 B4 24 0N 79 30W
Santee, *U.S.A.* 85 N10 32 50N 116 58W
Santee →, *U.S.A.* 77 J6 33 7N 79 17W
Santiago, *Brazil* 95 B5 29 11S 54 52W
Santiago, *Chile* 94 C1 33 24S 70 40W
Santiago, *Panama* 88 E3 8 0N 81 0W
Santiago □, *Chile* 94 C1 33 30S 70 50W
Santiago →, *Mexico* 66 G9 25 11N 105 26W
Santiago →, *Peru* 92 D3 4 27S 77 38W
Santiago de Compostela,
Spain 19 A1 42 52N 8 37W
Santiago de Cuba, *Cuba* 88 C4 20 0N 75 49W
Santiago de los Cabelleros,
Dom. Rep. 89 C5 19 30N 70 40W
Santiago del Estero,
Argentina 94 B3 27 50S 64 15W
Santiago del Estero □,
Argentina 94 B3 27 40S 63 15W
Santiago del Teide, *Canary Is.* 22 F3 28 17N 16 48W
Santiago Ixcuintla, *Mexico* .. 86 C3 21 50N 105 11W
Santiago Papasquiaro,
Mexico 86 C3 25 0N 105 20W
Santiaguillo, L. de, *Mexico* .. 86 C4 24 50N 104 50W
Santo Amaro, *Brazil* 93 F11 12 30S 38 43W
Santo Anastácio, *Brazil* 95 A5 21 58S 51 39W
Santo André, *Brazil* 95 A6 23 39S 46 29W
Santo Ângelo, *Brazil* 95 B5 28 15S 54 15W
Santo Antônio do Içá, *Brazil* . 92 D5 3 5S 67 57W
Santo Antônio do Leverger,
Brazil 93 G7 15 52S 56 5W
Santo Domingo, *Dom. Rep.* . 89 C6 18 30N 69 59W
Santo Domingo, *Baja Calif.,
Mexico* 86 A1 30 43N 116 2W
Santo Domingo, *Baja Calif. S.,
Mexico* 86 B2 25 32N 112 2W
Santo Domingo, *Nic.* 88 D3 12 14N 84 59W
Santo Domingo de los
Colorados, *Ecuador* 92 D3 0 15S 79 9W
Santo Domingo Pueblo,
U.S.A. 83 J10 35 31N 106 22W
Santo Tomás, *Mexico* 86 A1 31 33N 116 24W
Santo Tomás, *Peru* 92 F4 14 26S 72 8W
Santo Tomé, *Argentina* 95 B4 28 40S 56 5W
Santo Tomé de Guayana =
Ciudad Guayana, *Venezuela* 92 B6 8 0N 62 30W
Santoña, *Spain* 19 A4 43 29N 3 27W
Santoríni = Thíra, *Greece* ... 21 F11 36 23N 25 27 E
Santos, *Brazil* 95 A6 24 0S 46 20W
Santos Dumont, *Brazil* 95 A7 22 55S 43 10W
Sanwer, *India* .... 42 H6 22 59N 75 50 E
Sanyuan, *China* .... 34 G5 34 35N 108 58 E
São Bernardo do Campo,
Brazil 95 A6 23 45S 46 34W
São Borja, *Brazil* 95 B4 28 39S 56 0W
São Carlos, *Brazil* 95 A6 22 0S 47 50W
São Cristóvão, *Brazil* 93 F11 11 1S 37 15W
São Domingos, *Brazil* 93 F9 13 25S 46 19W
São Francisco, *Brazil* 93 G10 16 0S 44 50W
São Francisco →, *Brazil* 93 F11 10 30S 36 24W
São Francisco do Sul, *Brazil* . 95 B6 26 15S 48 36W
São Gabriel, *Brazil* 95 C5 30 20S 54 20W
São Gonçalo, *Brazil* 95 A7 22 48S 43 5W
Sao Hill, *Tanzania* .... 55 D4 8 20S 35 12 E
São João da Boa Vista, *Brazil* 95 A6 22 0S 46 52W
São João da Madeira,
Portugal 19 B1 40 54N 8 30W
São João del Rei, *Brazil* 95 A7 21 8S 44 15W
São João do Araguaia, *Brazil* 93 E9 5 23S 48 46W
São João do Piauí, *Brazil* ... 93 E10 8 21S 42 15W
São Joaquim, *Brazil* 95 B6 28 18S 49 56W
São Jorge, Pta. de, *Madeira* . 22 D3 32 50N 16 53W
São José, *Brazil* 95 B5 27 38S 48 39W
São José do Norte, *Brazil* ... 95 C5 32 1S 52 3W
São José do Rio Prêto, *Brazil* 95 A6 20 50S 49 20W
São José dos Campos, *Brazil* 95 A6 23 7S 45 52W
São Leopoldo, *Brazil* 95 B5 29 50S 51 10W
São Lourenço, *Brazil* 95 A6 22 7S 45 3W
São Lourenço →, *Brazil* 93 G7 17 53S 57 27W
São Lourenço, Pta. de,
Madeira 22 D3 32 44N 16 39W
São Lourenço do Sul, *Brazil* . 95 C5 31 22S 51 58W
São Luís, *Brazil* 93 D10 2 39S 44 15W
São Luís Gonzaga, *Brazil* ... 95 B5 28 25S 55 0W
São Marcos →, *Brazil* 93 G9 18 15S 47 37W
São Marcos, B. de, *Brazil* ... 93 D10 2 0S 44 0W
São Mateus, *Brazil* 93 G11 18 44S 39 50W
São Mateus do Sul, *Brazil* .. 95 B5 25 52S 50 23W
São Miguel do Oeste, *Brazil* . 95 B5 26 45S 53 34W
São Paulo, *Brazil* 95 A6 23 32S 46 37W
São Paulo □, *Brazil* 95 A6 22 0S 49 0W
São Paulo, I., *Atl. Oc.* 2 D8 0 50N 31 40W
São Paulo de Olivença, *Brazil* 92 D5 3 27S 68 48W
São Roque, *Madeira* 22 D3 32 46N 16 48W
São Roque, C. de, *Brazil* 93 E11 5 30S 35 16W
São Sebastião, I. de, *Brazil* .. 95 A6 23 50S 45 18W
São Sebastião do Paraíso,
Brazil 95 A6 20 54S 46 59W
São Tomé,
São Tomé & Principe .... 48 F4 0 10N 6 39 E
São Tomé, C. de, *Brazil* 95 A7 22 0S 40 59W
São Tomé & Principe ■,
Africa .... 49 F4 0 12N 6 39 E
São Vicente, *Brazil* 95 A6 23 57S 46 23W
São Vicente, *Madeira* 22 D2 32 48N 17 3W
São Vicente, C. de, *Portugal* . 19 D1 37 0N 9 0W
Saona, I., *Dom. Rep.* 89 C6 18 10N 68 40W
Saône →, *France* .... 18 D6 45 44N 4 50 E
Saonek, *Indonesia* .... 37 E8 0 22S 130 55 E
Saparua, *Indonesia* .... 37 E7 3 33S 128 40 E
Sapele, *Nigeria* .... 50 G7 5 50N 5 40 E
Sapelo I., *U.S.A.* 77 K5 31 25N 81 12W
Saposoa, *Peru* 92 E3 6 55S 76 45W
Sapphire, *Australia* .... 62 C4 23 28S 147 43 E
Sappho, *U.S.A.* 84 B2 48 4N 124 16W
Sapporo, *Japan* .... 30 C10 43 0N 141 21 E
Sapulpa, *U.S.A.* 81 H6 35 59N 96 5W
Saqqez, *Iran* .... 44 B5 36 15N 46 20 E
Sar Dasht, *Iran* .... 45 C6 32 32N 48 52 E
Sar-e Pol □, *Afghan.* ...... 40 B4 36 20N 65 50 E
Sar Gachineh = Yāsūj, *Iran* .. 45 D6 30 31N 51 31 E
Sar Planina, *Macedonia* .... 21 C9 42 0N 21 0 E
Sara Buri = Saraburi, *Thailand* 38 E3 14 30N 100 55 E
Sarāb, *Iran* .... 44 B5 37 55N 47 40 E
Sarabadi, *Iraq* .... 44 C5 33 1N 44 48 E
Saraburi, *Thailand* .... 38 E3 14 30N 100 55 E
Saradiya, *India* .... 42 J4 21 34N 70 2 E
Saragossa = Zaragoza, *Spain* 19 B5 41 39N 0 53W
Saraguro, *Ecuador* 92 D3 3 35S 79 16W
Sarai Naurang, *Pakistan* .... 42 C4 32 50N 70 47 E
Saraikela, *India* .... 43 H11 22 42N 85 56 E
Sarajevo, *Bos.-H.* .... 21 C8 43 52N 18 26 E
Sarakhs, *Turkmenistan* ..... 45 B9 36 32N 61 13 E
Saran, Gunung, *Indonesia* ... 36 E4 0 30S 111 25 E
Saranac L., *U.S.A.* 79 B10 44 20N 74 10W
Saranac Lake, *U.S.A.* 79 B10 44 20N 74 8W
Saranda, *Tanzania* .... 54 D3 5 45S 34 59 E
Sarandí del Yi, *Uruguay* 95 C4 33 18S 55 38W
Sarandí Grande, *Uruguay* ... 94 C4 33 44S 56 20W
Sarangani B., *Phil.* .... 37 C7 6 0N 125 13 E
Sarangani Is., *Phil.* .... 37 C7 5 25N 125 25 E
Sarangarh, *India* .... 41 J13 21 30N 83 5 E
Saransk, *Russia* .... 24 D8 54 10N 45 10 E
Sarapul, *Russia* .... 24 C9 56 28N 53 48 E
Sarasota, *U.S.A.* 77 M4 27 20N 82 32W
Saratoga, *Calif., U.S.A.* 84 H4 37 16N 122 2W
Saratoga, *Wyo., U.S.A.* 82 F10 41 27N 106 49W
Saratoga Springs, *U.S.A.* ... 79 C11 43 5N 73 47W
Saratok, *Malaysia* .... 36 D4 1 55N 111 17 E
Saratov, *Russia* .... 25 D8 51 30N 46 2 E
Saravane, *Laos* .... 38 E6 15 43N 106 25 E
Sarawak □, *Malaysia* ...... 36 D4 2 0N 113 0 E
Saray, *Turkey* .... 21 D12 41 26N 27 55 E
Sarayköy, *Turkey* .... 21 F13 37 55N 28 54 E
Sarbāz, *Iran* .... 45 E9 26 38N 61 19 E
Sarbīsheh, *Iran* .... 45 C8 32 30N 59 40 E
Sarda →, *India* .... 41 F12 27 21N 81 23 E
Sardarshahr, *India* .... 42 E6 28 30N 74 29 E
Sardegna □, *Italy* .... 20 D3 40 0N 9 0 E
Sardhana, *India* .... 42 E7 29 9N 77 39 E
Sardina, Pta., *Canary Is.* ... 22 F4 28 9N 15 44W
Sardinia = Sardegna □, *Italy* 20 D3 40 0N 9 0 E
Sardis, *Turkey* .... 21 E12 38 28N 28 2 E
Sardūīyeh = Dar Mazār, *Iran* 45 D8 29 14N 57 20 E
S'Arenal, *Spain* .... 22 B9 39 30N 2 45 E
Sargasso Sea, *Atl. Oc.* 66 G13 27 0N 72 0W
Sargodha, *Pakistan* .... 42 C5 32 10N 72 40 E
Sarh, *Chad* .... 51 G9 9 5N 18 23 E
Sārī, *Iran* .... 45 B7 36 30N 53 4 E
Saria, *India* .... 43 J10 21 38N 83 22 E
Sariab, *Pakistan* .... 42 D2 30 6N 66 59 E
Sarıgöl, *Turkey* .... 21 E13 38 14N 28 41 E
Sarikei, *Malaysia* .... 36 D4 2 8N 111 30 E
Sarila, *India* .... 43 G8 25 46N 79 41 E
Sarina, *Australia* .... 62 C4 21 22S 149 13 E
Sarita, *U.S.A.* 81 M6 27 13N 97 47W
Sariwŏn, *N. Korea* .... 35 E13 38 31N 125 46 E
Sarju →, *India* .... 43 F9 27 21N 81 23 E
Sark, *U.K.* 11 H5 49 25N 2 22W
Sarkari Tala, *India* .... 42 F4 27 39N 70 52 E
Şarköy, *Turkey* .... 21 D12 40 36N 27 6 E
Sarlat-la-Canéda, *France* ... 18 D4 44 54N 1 13 E
Sarmi, *Indonesia* .... 37 E9 1 49S 138 44 E
Sarmiento, *Argentina* 96 F3 45 35S 69 5W
Särna, *Sweden* .... 9 F15 61 41N 13 8 E
Sarnia, *Canada* 78 D2 42 58N 82 23W
Sarolangun, *Indonesia* ..... 36 E2 2 19S 102 42 E
Saronikós Kólpos, *Greece* ... 21 F10 37 45N 23 45 E
Saros Körfezi, *Turkey* ...... 21 D12 40 30N 26 15 E
Sarpsborg, *Norway* .... 9 G14 59 16N 11 7 E
Sarre = Saar →, *Europe* .... 18 B7 49 41N 6 32 E
Sarreguemines, *France* .... 18 B7 49 5N 7 4 E
Sarthe →, *France* 18 C3 47 33N 0 31W
Saruna →, *Pakistan* .... 42 F2 26 31N 67 7 E

Sierra Blanca, U.S.A. 83 L11 31 11N 105 22W
Sierra Blanca Peak, U.S.A. 83 K11 33 23N 105 49W
Sierra City, U.S.A. 84 F6 39 34N 120 38W
Sierra Colorada, Argentina 96 E3 40 35S 67 50W
Sierra Gorda, Chile 94 A2 22 50S 69 15W
Sierra Leone ■, W. Afr. 50 G3 9 0N 12 0W
Sierra Madre, Mexico 87 D6 16 0N 93 0W
Sierra Mojada, Mexico 86 B4 27 19N 103 42W
Sierra Nevada, Spain 19 D4 37 3N 3 15W
Sierra Nevada, U.S.A. 84 H8 39 0N 120 30W
Sierra Vista, U.S.A. 83 L8 31 33N 110 18W
Sierraville, U.S.A. 84 F6 39 36N 120 22W
Sífnos, Greece 21 F11 37 0N 24 45 E
Sifton, Canada 73 C8 51 21N 100 8W
Sifton Pass, Canada 72 B3 57 52N 126 15W
Sighetu-Marmaţiei, Romania 17 E12 47 57N 23 52 E
Sighişoara, Romania 17 E13 46 12N 24 50 E
Sigli, Indonesia 36 C1 5 25N 96 0 E
Siglufjörður, Iceland 8 C4 66 12N 18 55W
Signal, U.S.A. 85 L13 34 30N 113 38W
Signal Pk., U.S.A. 85 M12 33 20N 114 2W
Sigsig, Ecuador 92 D3 3 0S 78 50W
Sigüenza, Spain 19 B4 41 3N 2 40W
Siguiri, Guinea 50 F4 11 31N 9 10W
Sigulda, Latvia 9 H21 57 10N 24 55 E
Sihanoukville = Kampong Saom, Cambodia 39 G4 10 38N 103 30 E
Sihora, India 43 H9 23 29N 80 6 E
Siikajoki →, Finland 8 D21 64 50N 24 43 E
Siilinjärvi, Finland 8 E22 63 4N 27 39 E
Sijarira Ra. = Chizarira, Zimbabwe 55 F2 17 36S 27 45 E
Sika, India 42 H3 22 26N 69 47 E
Sikao, Thailand 39 J2 7 34N 99 21 E
Sikar, India 42 F6 27 33N 75 10 E
Sikasso, Mali 50 F4 11 18N 5 35W
Sikeston, U.S.A. 81 G10 36 53N 89 35W
Sikhote Alin, Khrebet, Russia 27 E14 45 0N 136 0 E
Sikhote Alin Ra. = Sikhote Alin, Khrebet, Russia 27 E14 45 0N 136 0 E
Síkinos, Greece 21 F11 36 40N 25 8 E
Sikkani Chief →, Canada 72 B4 57 47N 122 15W
Sikkim □, India 41 F16 27 50N 88 30 E
Sikotu-Ko, Japan 30 C10 42 45N 141 25 E
Sil →, Spain 19 A2 42 27N 7 43W
Silacayoapan, Mexico 87 D5 17 30N 98 9W
Silawad, India 42 J6 21 54N 74 54 E
Silchar, India 41 G18 24 49N 92 48 E
Siler City, U.S.A. 77 H6 35 44N 79 28W
Silesia = Śląsk, Poland 16 C9 51 0N 16 30 E
Silgarhi Doti, Nepal 43 E9 29 15N 81 0 E
Silghat, India 41 F18 26 35N 93 0 E
Silifke, Turkey 25 G5 36 22N 33 58 E
Siliguri = Shiliguri, India 41 F16 26 45N 88 25 E
Siling Co, China 32 C3 31 50N 89 20 E
Silistra, Bulgaria 21 B12 44 6N 27 19 E
Silivri, Turkey 21 D13 41 4N 28 14 E
Siljan, Sweden 9 F16 60 55N 14 45 E
Silkeborg, Denmark 9 H13 56 10N 9 32 E
Silkwood, Australia 62 B4 17 45S 146 2 E
Sillajhuay, Cordillera, Chile 92 G5 19 46S 68 40W
Sillamäe, Estonia 9 G22 59 24N 27 45 E
Silloth, U.K. 10 C4 54 52N 3 23W
Siloam Springs, U.S.A. 81 G7 36 11N 94 32W
Silsbee, U.S.A. 81 K7 30 21N 94 11W
Šilutė, Lithuania 9 J19 55 21N 21 33 E
Silva Porto = Kuito, Angola 53 G3 12 22S 16 55 E
Silvani, India 43 H8 23 18N 78 25 E
Silver City, U.S.A. 83 K9 32 46N 108 17W
Silver Cr. →, U.S.A. 82 E4 43 16N 119 13W
Silver Creek, U.S.A. 78 D5 42 33N 79 10W
Silver L., U.S.A. 84 G6 38 39N 120 6W
Silver Lake, Calif., U.S.A. 85 K10 35 21N 116 7W
Silver Lake, Oreg., U.S.A. 82 E3 43 8N 121 3W
Silverton, Colo., U.S.A. 83 H10 37 49N 107 40W
Silverton, Tex., U.S.A. 81 H4 34 28N 101 19W
Silvies →, U.S.A. 82 E4 43 34N 119 2W
Simaltala, India 43 G12 24 43N 86 33 E
Simanggang = Bandar Sri Aman, Malaysia 36 D4 1 15N 111 32 E
Simard, L., Canada 70 C4 47 40N 78 40W
Simav, Turkey 21 E13 39 4N 28 58 E
Simba, Tanzania 54 C4 2 10S 37 36 E
Simbirsk, Russia 24 D8 54 20N 48 25 E
Simbo, Tanzania 54 C2 4 51S 29 41 E
Simcoe, Canada 78 D4 42 50N 80 20W
Simcoe, L., Canada 78 B5 44 25N 79 20W
Simdega, India 43 H11 22 37N 84 31 E
Simeria, Romania 17 F12 45 51N 23 1 E
Simeulue, Indonesia 36 D1 2 45N 95 45 E
Simferopol, Ukraine 25 F5 44 55N 34 3 E
Sími, Greece 21 F12 36 35N 27 50 E
Simi Valley, U.S.A. 85 L8 34 16N 118 47W
Simikot, Nepal 43 E9 30 0N 81 50 E
Simla, India 42 D7 31 2N 77 9 E
Simmie, Canada 73 D7 49 56N 108 6W
Simmler, U.S.A. 85 K7 35 21N 119 59W
Simojoki →, Finland 8 D21 65 35N 25 1 E
Simojovel, Mexico 87 D6 17 12N 92 38W
Simonette →, Canada 72 B5 55 9N 118 15W
Simonstown, S. Africa 56 E2 34 14S 18 26 E
Simplonpass, Switz. 18 C8 46 15N 8 3 E
Simpson Desert, Australia 62 D2 25 0S 137 0 E
Simpson Pen., Canada 69 B11 68 34N 88 45W
Simpungdong, N. Korea 35 D15 40 56N 129 29 E
Simrishamn, Sweden 9 J16 55 33N 14 22 E
Simsbury, U.S.A. 79 E12 41 53N 72 48W
Simushir, Ostrov, Russia 27 E16 46 50N 152 30 E
Sin Cowe I., S. China Sea 36 C4 9 53N 114 19 E
Sinabang, Indonesia 36 D1 2 30N 96 24 E
Sinadogo, Somali Rep. 46 F4 5 50N 47 0 E
Sinai = Es Sînâ', Egypt 47 F3 29 0N 34 0 E
Sinai, Mt. = Mûsa, Gebel, Egypt 44 D2 28 33N 33 59 E
Sinai Peninsula, Egypt 47 F3 29 30N 34 0 E
Sinaloa □, Mexico 86 C3 25 0N 107 30W
Sinaloa de Leyva, Mexico 86 B3 25 50N 108 20W
Sinarádhes, Greece 23 A3 39 34N 19 51 E
Sincelejo, Colombia 92 B3 9 18N 75 24W
Sinch'ang, N. Korea 35 D15 40 7N 128 28 E
Sinchang-ni, N. Korea 35 E14 39 24N 126 8 E
Sinclair, U.S.A. 82 F10 41 47N 107 7W
Sinclair Mills, Canada 72 C4 54 5N 121 40W
Sinclair's B., U.K. 12 C5 58 31N 3 5W
Sinclairville, U.S.A. 78 D5 42 16N 79 16W
Sincorá, Serra do, Brazil 93 F10 13 30S 41 0W
Sind, Pakistan 42 G3 26 0N 68 30 E
Sind □, Pakistan 42 G3 26 0N 69 0 E
Sind →, Jammu & Kashmir, India 43 B6 34 18N 74 45 E
Sind →, Mad. P., India 43 F8 26 26N 79 13 E
Sind Sagar Doab, Pakistan 42 D4 32 0N 71 30 E
Sindangan, Phil. 37 C6 8 10N 123 5 E
Sindangbarang, Indonesia 37 G12 7 27S 107 1 E
Sinde, Zambia 55 F2 17 28S 25 51 E
Sindh = Sind □, Pakistan 42 G3 26 0N 69 0 E
Sindri, India 43 H12 23 45N 86 42 E
Sines, Portugal 19 D1 37 56N 8 51W
Sines, C. de, Portugal 19 D1 37 58N 8 53W
Sineu, Spain 22 B10 39 38N 3 1 E
Sing Buri, Thailand 38 E3 14 53N 100 25 E
Singa, Sudan 51 F12 13 10N 33 57 E
Singapore ■, Asia 39 M4 1 17N 103 51 E
Singapore, Straits of, Asia 39 M5 1 15N 104 0 E
Singaraja, Indonesia 36 F5 8 7S 115 6 E
Singida, Tanzania 54 C3 4 49S 34 48 E
Singida □, Tanzania 54 D3 6 0S 34 30 E
Singitikós Kólpos, Greece 21 D11 40 6N 24 0 E
Singkaling Hkamti, Burma 41 G19 26 0N 95 39 E
Singkang, Indonesia 37 E6 4 8S 120 1 E
Singkawang, Indonesia 36 D3 1 0N 108 57 E
Singkep, Indonesia 36 E2 0 30S 104 25 E
Singleton, Australia 63 E5 32 33S 151 0 E
Singleton, Mt., N. Terr., Australia 60 D5 22 0S 130 46 E
Singleton, Mt., W. Austral., Australia 61 E2 29 27S 117 15 E
Singoli, India 42 G6 25 0N 75 22 E
Singora = Songkhla, Thailand 39 J3 7 13N 100 37 E
Singosan, N. Korea 35 E14 38 52N 127 25 E
Sinhung, N. Korea 35 D14 40 11N 127 34 E
Sinjai, Indonesia 37 F6 5 7S 120 20 E
Sinjār, Iraq 44 B4 36 19N 41 52 E
Sinkat, Sudan 51 E13 18 55N 36 49 E
Sinkiang Uighur = Xinjiang Uygur Zizhiqu □, China 32 C3 42 0N 86 0 E
Sinmak, N. Korea 35 E14 38 25N 126 14 E
Sinnamary, Fr. Guiana 93 B8 5 25N 53 0W
Sinni →, Italy 20 D7 40 8N 16 41 E
Sinop, Turkey 25 F6 42 1N 35 11 E
Sinor, India 42 J5 21 55N 73 20 E
Sinp'o, N. Korea 35 E15 40 0N 128 13 E
Sinsk, Russia 27 C13 61 8N 126 48 E
Sintang, Indonesia 36 D4 0 5N 111 35 E
Sinton, U.S.A. 81 L6 28 2N 97 31W
Sintra, Portugal 19 C1 38 47N 9 25W
Sinŭiju, N. Korea 35 D13 40 5N 124 24 E
Siocon, Phil. 37 C6 7 40N 122 10 E
Siófok, Hungary 17 E10 46 54N 18 3 E
Sion, Switz. 18 C7 46 14N 7 20 E
Sion Mills, U.K. 13 B4 54 48N 7 29W
Sioux City, U.S.A. 80 D6 42 30N 96 24W
Sioux Falls, U.S.A. 80 D6 43 33N 96 44W
Sioux Lookout, Canada 70 B1 50 10N 91 50W
Sioux Narrows, Canada 73 D10 49 25N 94 10W
Siping, China 35 C13 43 8N 124 21 E
Sipiwesk L., Canada 73 B9 55 5N 97 35W
Sipra →, India 42 H6 23 55N 75 28 E
Sipura, Indonesia 36 E1 2 18S 99 40 E
Siquia →, Nic. 88 D3 12 10N 84 20W
Siquijor, Phil. 37 C6 9 12N 123 35 E
Siquirres, Costa Rica 88 D3 10 6N 83 30W
Şīr Banī Yās, U.A.E. 45 E7 24 19N 52 37 E
Sir Edward Pellew Group, Australia 62 B2 15 40S 137 10 E
Sir Graham Moore Is., Australia 60 B4 13 53S 126 34 E
Sir James MacBrien, Mt., Canada 68 B7 62 8N 127 40W
Sira →, Norway 9 G12 58 23N 6 34 E
Siracusa, Italy 20 F6 37 4N 15 17 E
Sirajganj, Bangla. 43 G13 24 25N 89 47 E
Sirathu, India 43 G9 25 39N 81 19 E
Sīrdān, Iran 45 B6 36 39N 49 12 E
Sirdaryo = Syrdarya →, Kazakstan 26 E7 46 3N 61 0 E
Siren, U.S.A. 80 C8 45 47N 92 24W
Sirer, Spain 22 C7 38 56N 1 22 E
Siret →, Romania 17 F14 45 24N 28 1 E
Sirghāyā, Syria 47 B5 33 51N 36 8 E
Sirmaur, India 43 G9 24 51N 81 23 E
Sirohi, India 42 G5 24 52N 72 53 E
Sironj, India 42 G7 24 5N 77 39 E
Síros, Greece 21 F11 37 28N 24 57 E
Sirretta Pk., U.S.A. 85 K8 35 56N 118 19W
Sirrī, Iran 45 E7 25 55N 54 32 E
Sirsa, India 42 E6 29 33N 75 4 E
Sirsa →, India 43 F8 26 51N 79 4 E
Sisak, Croatia 16 F9 45 30N 16 21 E
Sisaket, Thailand 38 E5 15 8N 104 23 E
Sishen, S. Africa 56 D3 27 47S 22 59 E
Sishui, Henan, China 34 G7 34 48N 113 15 E
Sishui, Shandong, China 35 G9 35 42N 117 18 E
Sisipuk L., Canada 73 B8 55 45N 101 50W
Sisophon, Cambodia 38 F4 13 38N 102 59 E
Sisseton, U.S.A. 80 C6 45 40N 97 3W
Sīstān, Asia 45 D9 30 50N 61 0 E
Sīstān, Daryācheh-ye, Iran 45 D9 31 0N 61 0 E
Sīstān va Balūchestān □, Iran 45 E9 27 0N 62 0 E
Sisters, U.S.A. 82 D3 44 18N 121 33W
Siswa Bazar, India 43 F10 27 9N 83 46 E
Sitamarhi, India 43 F11 26 37N 85 30 E
Sitampiky, Madag. 57 B8 16 41S 46 6 E
Sitapur, India 43 F9 27 38N 80 45 E
Siteki, Swaziland 57 D5 26 32S 31 58 E
Sitges, Spain 19 B6 41 17N 1 47 E
Sitía, Greece 23 D8 35 13N 26 6 E
Sitka, U.S.A. 72 B1 57 3N 135 20W
Sitoti, Botswana 56 C3 23 15S 23 40 E
Sittang Myit →, Burma 41 L20 17 20N 96 45 E
Sittard, Neths. 15 C5 51 0N 5 52 E
Sittingbourne, U.K. 11 F8 51 21N 0 45 E
Sittoung = Sittang Myit →, Burma 41 L20 17 20N 96 45 E
Sittwe, Burma 41 J18 20 18N 92 45 E
Situbondo, Indonesia 37 G16 7 42S 114 0 E
Siuna, Nic. 88 D3 13 37N 84 45W
Siuri, India 43 H12 23 50N 87 34 E
Sivand, Iran 45 D7 30 5N 52 55 E
Sivas, Turkey 25 G6 39 43N 36 58 E
Siverek, Turkey 44 B3 37 50N 39 19 E
Sivomaskinskiy, Russia 24 A11 66 40N 62 35 E
Sivrihisar, Turkey 25 G5 39 30N 31 35 E
Sîwa, Egypt 51 C11 29 11N 25 31 E
Sîwa, El Wâhât es, Egypt 48 D6 29 10N 25 30 E
Siwa Oasis = Sîwa, El Wâhât es, Egypt 48 D6 29 10N 25 30 E
Siwalik Range, Nepal 43 F10 28 0N 83 0 E
Siwan, India 43 F11 26 13N 84 21 E
Siwana, India 42 G5 25 38N 72 25 E
Sixmilebridge, Ireland 13 D3 52 44N 8 46W
Sixth Cataract, Sudan 51 E12 16 20N 32 42 E
Siziwang Qi, China 34 D6 41 25N 111 40 E
Sjælland, Denmark 9 J14 55 30N 11 30 E
Sjumen = Shumen, Bulgaria 21 C12 43 18N 26 55 E
Skadarsko Jezero, Montenegro, Yug. 21 C8 42 10N 19 20 E
Skaftafell, Iceland 8 D5 64 1N 17 0W
Skagafjörður, Iceland 8 D4 65 54N 19 35W
Skagastølstindane, Norway 9 F12 61 28N 7 52 E
Skagaströnd, Iceland 8 D3 65 50N 20 19W
Skagen, Denmark 9 H14 57 43N 10 35 E
Skagerrak, Denmark 9 H13 57 30N 9 0 E
Skagit →, U.S.A. 84 B4 48 23N 122 22W
Skagway, U.S.A. 68 C6 59 28N 135 19W
Skala-Podilska, Ukraine 17 D14 48 50N 26 15 E
Skala Podolskaya = Skala-Podilska, Ukraine 17 D14 48 50N 26 15 E
Skalat, Ukraine 17 D13 49 23N 25 55 E
Skåne, Sweden 9 J15 55 59N 13 30 E
Skaneateles, U.S.A. 79 D8 42 57N 76 26W
Skaneateles L., U.S.A. 79 D8 42 51N 76 22W
Skara, Sweden 9 G15 58 25N 13 30 E
Skardu, Pakistan 43 B6 35 20N 75 44 E
Skarżysko-Kamienna, Poland 17 C11 51 7N 20 52 E
Skeena →, Canada 72 C2 54 9N 130 5W
Skeena Mts., Canada 72 B3 56 40N 128 30W
Skegness, U.K. 10 D8 53 9N 0 20 E
Skeldon, Guyana 92 B7 5 55N 57 20W
Skellefte älv →, Sweden 8 D19 64 45N 21 10 E
Skellefteå, Sweden 8 D19 64 45N 20 50 E
Skelleftehamn, Sweden 8 D19 64 40N 21 9 E
Skerries, The, U.K. 10 D3 53 25N 4 36W
Ski, Norway 9 G14 59 43N 10 52 E
Skiathos, Greece 21 E10 39 12N 23 30 E
Skibbereen, Ireland 13 E2 51 33N 9 16W
Skiddaw, U.K. 10 C4 54 39N 3 9W
Skidegate, Canada 72 C2 53 15N 132 1W
Skien, Norway 9 G13 59 12N 9 35 E
Skierniewice, Poland 17 C11 51 58N 20 10 E
Skikda, Algeria 50 A7 36 50N 6 58 E
Skilloura, Cyprus 23 D12 35 14N 33 10 E
Skipton, U.K. 10 D5 53 58N 2 3W
Skirmish Pt., Australia 62 A1 11 59S 134 17 E
Skíros, Greece 21 E11 38 55N 24 34 E
Skive, Denmark 9 H13 56 33N 9 2 E
Skjálfandafljót →, Iceland 8 D5 65 59N 17 25W
Skjálfandi, Iceland 8 C5 66 5N 17 30W
Skoghall, Sweden 9 G15 59 20N 13 30 E
Skole, Ukraine 17 D12 49 3N 23 30 E
Skópelos, Greece 21 E10 39 9N 23 47 E
Skopi, Greece 23 D8 35 11N 26 2 E
Skopje, Macedonia 21 C9 42 1N 21 26 E
Skövde, Sweden 9 G15 58 24N 13 50 E
Skovorodino, Russia 27 D13 54 0N 124 0 E
Skowhegan, U.S.A. 77 C11 44 46N 69 43W
Skull, Ireland 13 E2 51 32N 9 34W
Skunk →, U.S.A. 80 E9 40 42N 91 7W
Skuodas, Lithuania 9 H19 56 16N 21 33 E
Skvyra, Ukraine 17 D15 49 44N 29 40 E
Skye, U.K. 12 D2 57 15N 6 10W
Skykomish, U.S.A. 82 C3 47 42N 121 22W
Skyros = Skíros, Greece 21 E11 38 55N 24 34 E
Slættaratindur, Færoe Is. 8 E9 62 18N 7 1W
Slagelse, Denmark 9 J14 55 23N 11 19 E
Slamet, Indonesia 37 G13 7 16S 109 8 E
Slaney →, Ireland 13 D5 52 26N 6 33W
Slangberge, S. Africa 56 E3 31 32S 20 48 E
Śląsk, Poland 16 C9 51 0N 16 30 E
Slate Is., Canada 70 C2 48 40N 87 0W
Slatina, Romania 17 F13 44 28N 24 22 E
Slatington, U.S.A. 79 F9 40 45N 75 37W
Slaton, U.S.A. 81 J4 33 26N 101 39W
Slave →, Canada 72 A6 61 18N 113 39W
Slave Coast, W. Afr. 50 G6 6 0N 2 30 E
Slave Lake, Canada 72 B6 55 17N 114 43W
Slave Pt., Canada 72 A5 61 11N 115 56W
Slavgorod, Russia 26 D8 53 1N 78 37 E
Slavonski Brod, Croatia 21 B8 45 11N 18 1 E
Slavuta, Ukraine 17 C14 50 15N 27 2 E
Slavyanka, Russia 30 C5 42 53N 131 21 E
Slavyansk = Slovyansk, Ukraine 25 E6 48 55N 37 36 E
Slawharad, Belarus 17 B16 53 27N 31 0 E
Sleaford, U.K. 10 D7 53 0N 0 24W
Sleaford B., Australia 63 E2 34 55S 135 45 E
Sleat, Sd. of, U.K. 12 D3 57 5N 5 47W
Sleeper Is., Canada 69 C11 58 30N 81 0W
Sleepy Eye, U.S.A. 80 C7 44 18N 94 43W
Slemon L., Canada 72 A5 63 13N 116 4W
Slide Mt., U.S.A. 79 E10 42 0N 74 25W
Slidell, U.S.A. 81 K10 30 17N 89 47W
Sliema, Malta 23 D2 35 55N 14 30 E
Slieve Aughty, Ireland 13 C3 53 4N 8 30W
Slieve Bloom, Ireland 13 C4 53 4N 7 40W
Slieve Donard, U.K. 13 B6 54 11N 5 55W
Slieve Gamph, Ireland 13 B3 54 6N 9 0W
Slieve Gullion, U.K. 13 B5 54 7N 6 26W
Slieve Mish, Ireland 13 D2 52 12N 9 50W
Slievenamon, Ireland 13 D4 52 25N 7 34W
Sligeach = Sligo, Ireland 13 B3 54 16N 8 28W
Sligo, Ireland 13 B3 54 16N 8 28W
Sligo, U.S.A. 78 E5 41 6N 79 29W
Sligo □, Ireland 13 B3 54 8N 8 42W
Sligo B., Ireland 13 B3 54 18N 8 40W
Slippery Rock, U.S.A. 78 E4 41 3N 80 3W
Slite, Sweden 9 H18 57 42N 18 48 E
Sliven, Bulgaria 21 C12 42 42N 26 19 E
Sloan, U.S.A. 85 K11 35 57N 115 13W
Sloansville, U.S.A. 79 D10 42 45N 74 22W
Slobodskoy, Russia 24 C9 58 40N 50 6 E
Slobozia, Romania 17 F14 44 34N 27 23 E
Slocan, Canada 72 D5 49 48N 117 28W
Slonim, Belarus 17 B13 53 4N 25 19 E
Slough, U.K. 11 F7 51 30N 0 36W
Slough □, U.K. 11 F7 51 30N 0 36W
Sloughhouse, U.S.A. 84 G5 38 26N 121 12W
Slovak Rep. ■, Europe 17 D10 48 30N 20 0 E
Slovakia = Slovak Rep. ■, Europe 17 D10 48 30N 20 0 E
Slovakian Ore Mts. = Slovenské Rudohorie, Slovak Rep. 17 D10 48 45N 20 0 E
Slovenia ■, Europe 16 F8 45 58N 14 30 E
Slovenija = Slovenia ■, Europe 16 F8 45 58N 14 30 E
Slovenské Rudohorie, Slovak Rep. 17 D10 48 45N 20 0 E
Slovyansk, Ukraine 25 E6 48 55N 37 36 E
Sluch →, Ukraine 17 C14 51 37N 26 38 E
Sluis, Neths. 15 C3 51 18N 3 23 E
Słupsk, Poland 17 A9 54 30N 17 3 E
Slurry, S. Africa 56 D4 25 49S 25 42 E
Slutsk, Belarus 17 B14 53 2N 27 31 E
Slyne Hd., Ireland 13 C1 53 25N 10 10W
Slyudyanka, Russia 27 D11 51 40N 103 40 E
Småland, Sweden 9 H16 57 15N 15 25 E
Smalltree L., Canada 73 A8 61 0N 105 0W
Smallwood Res., Canada 71 B7 54 0N 64 0W
Smarhon, Belarus 17 A14 54 20N 26 24 E
Smartt Syndicate Dam, S. Africa 56 E3 30 45S 23 10 E
Smartville, U.S.A. 84 F5 39 13N 121 18W
Smeaton, Canada 73 C8 53 30N 104 49W
Smederevo, Serbia, Yug. 21 B9 44 40N 20 57 E
Smerwick Harbour, Ireland 13 D1 52 12N 10 23W
Smethport, U.S.A. 78 E6 41 49N 78 27W
Smidovich, Russia 27 E14 48 36N 133 49 E
Smith, Canada 72 B6 55 10N 114 0W
Smith Center, U.S.A. 80 F5 39 47N 98 47W
Smith Sund, Greenland 4 B4 78 30N 74 0W
Smithburne →, Australia 62 B3 17 3S 140 57 E
Smithers, Canada 72 C3 54 45N 127 10W
Smithfield, S. Africa 57 E4 30 9S 26 30 E
Smithfield, N.C., U.S.A. 77 H6 35 31N 78 21W
Smithfield, Utah, U.S.A. 82 F8 41 50N 111 50W
Smiths Falls, Canada 79 B9 44 55N 76 0W
Smithton, Australia 62 G4 40 53S 145 6 E
Smithville, Canada 78 C5 43 6N 79 33W
Smithville, U.S.A. 81 K6 30 1N 97 10W
Smoky →, Canada 72 B5 56 10N 117 21W
Smoky Bay, Australia 63 E1 32 22S 134 13 E
Smoky Hill →, U.S.A. 80 F6 39 4N 96 48W
Smoky Hills, U.S.A. 80 F5 39 15N 99 30W
Smoky Lake, Canada 72 C6 54 10N 112 30W
Smøla, Norway 8 E13 63 23N 8 3 E
Smolensk, Russia 24 D5 54 45N 32 5 E
Smolikas, Óros, Greece 21 D9 40 9N 20 58 E
Smolyan, Bulgaria 21 D11 41 36N 24 38 E
Smooth Rock Falls, Canada 70 C3 49 17N 81 37W
Smoothstone L., Canada 73 C7 54 40N 106 50W
Smorgon = Smarhon, Belarus 17 A14 54 20N 26 24 E
Smyrna = İzmir, Turkey 21 E12 38 25N 27 8 E
Smyrna, U.S.A. 76 F8 39 18N 75 36W
Snæfell, Iceland 8 D6 64 48N 15 34W
Snaefell, U.K. 10 C3 54 16N 4 27W
Snæfellsjökull, Iceland 8 D2 64 49N 23 46W
Snake →, U.S.A. 82 C4 46 12N 119 2W
Snake I., Australia 63 F4 38 47S 146 33 E
Snake Range, U.S.A. 82 G6 39 0N 114 20W
Snake River Plain, U.S.A. 82 E7 42 50N 114 0W
Snåsavatnet, Norway 8 D14 64 12N 12 0 E
Sneek, Neths. 15 A5 53 2N 5 40 E
Sneeuberge, S. Africa 56 E3 31 46S 24 20 E
Snelling, U.S.A. 84 H6 37 31N 120 26W
Sněžka, Europe 16 C8 50 41N 15 50 E
Snizort, L., U.K. 12 D2 57 33N 6 28W
Snøhetta, Norway 9 E13 62 19N 9 16 E
Snohomish, U.S.A. 84 C4 47 55N 122 6W
Snoul, Cambodia 39 F6 12 4N 106 26 E
Snow Hill, U.S.A. 76 F8 38 11N 75 24W
Snow Lake, Canada 73 C8 54 52N 100 3W
Snow Mt., Calif., U.S.A. 84 F4 39 23N 122 45W
Snow Mt., Maine, U.S.A. 79 A14 45 18N 70 48W
Snow Shoe, U.S.A. 78 E7 41 2N 77 57W
Snowbird L., Canada 73 A8 60 45N 103 0W
Snowdon, U.K. 10 D3 53 4N 4 5W
Snowdrift →, Canada 73 A6 62 24N 110 44W
Snowflake, U.S.A. 83 J8 34 30N 110 5W
Snowshoe Pk., U.S.A. 82 B6 48 13N 115 41W
Snowtown, Australia 63 E2 33 46S 138 14 E
Snowville, U.S.A. 82 F7 41 58N 112 43W
Snowy →, Australia 63 F4 37 46S 148 30 E
Snowy Mt., U.S.A. 79 C10 43 42N 74 23W
Snowy Mts., Australia 63 F4 36 30S 148 20 E
Snug Corner, Bahamas 89 B5 22 33N 73 52W
Snyatyn, Ukraine 17 D13 48 27N 25 38 E
Snyder, Okla., U.S.A. 81 H5 34 40N 98 57W
Snyder, Tex., U.S.A. 81 J4 32 44N 100 55W
Soahanina, Madag. 57 B7 18 42S 44 13 E
Soalala, Madag. 57 B8 16 6S 45 20 E
Soaloka, Madag. 57 B8 18 32S 45 15 E
Soamanonga, Madag. 57 C7 23 52S 44 47 E
Soan →, Pakistan 42 C4 33 1N 71 44 E
Soanierana-Ivongo, Madag. 57 B8 16 55S 49 35 E
Soanindraniny, Madag. 57 B8 19 54S 47 14 E
Soavina, Madag. 57 C8 20 23S 46 56 E
Soavinandriana, Madag. 57 B8 19 9S 46 45 E
Sobat, Nahr →, Sudan 51 G12 9 22N 31 33 E
Sobhapur, India 42 H8 22 47N 78 17 E
Sobradinho, Reprêsa de, Brazil 93 E10 9 30S 42 0 E
Sobral, Brazil 93 D10 3 50S 40 20W
Soc Giang, Vietnam 38 A6 22 54N 106 1 E
Soc Trang, Vietnam 39 H5 9 37N 105 50 E
Socastee, U.S.A. 77 J6 33 41N 79 1W
Soch'e = Shache, China 32 C2 38 20N 77 10 E
Sochi, Russia 25 F6 43 35N 39 40 E
Société, Is. de la, Pac. Oc. 65 J12 17 0S 151 0W
Society Is. = Société, Is. de la, Pac. Oc. 65 J12 17 0S 151 0W
Socompa, Portezuelo de, Chile 94 A2 24 27S 68 18W
Socorro, N. Mex., U.S.A. 83 J10 34 4N 106 54W
Socorro, Tex., U.S.A. 83 L10 31 39N 106 18W
Socorro, I., Mexico 86 D2 18 45N 110 58W
Socotra, Yemen 46 E5 12 30N 54 0 E
Soda L., U.S.A. 83 J5 35 10N 116 4W
Soda Plains, India 43 B8 35 30N 79 0 E
Soda Springs, U.S.A. 82 E8 42 39N 111 36W
Sodankylä, Finland 8 C22 67 29N 26 40 E
Soddy-Daisy, U.S.A. 77 H3 35 17N 85 10W
Söderhamn, Sweden 9 F17 61 18N 17 10 E

Stanislav = Ivano-Frankivsk, *Ukraine* **17 D13** 48 40N 24 40 E
Stanke Dimitrov, *Bulgaria* **21 C10** 42 17N 23 9 E
Stanley, *Australia* **62 G4** 40 46S 145 19 E
Stanley, *Canada* **73 B8** 55 24N 104 22W
Stanley, *Falk. Is.* **96 G5** 51 40S 59 51W
Stanley, *U.K.* **10 C6** 54 53N 1 41W
Stanley, *Idaho, U.S.A.* **82 D6** 44 13N 114 56W
Stanley, *N. Dak., U.S.A.* **80 A3** 48 19N 102 23W
Stanley, *N.Y., U.S.A.* **78 D7** 42 48N 77 6W
Stanovoy Khrebet, *Russia* **27 D13** 55 0N 130 0 E
Stanovoy Ra. = Stanovoy Khrebet, *Russia* **27 D13** 55 0N 130 0 E
Stansmore Ra., *Australia* **60 D4** 21 23S 128 33 E
Stanthorpe, *Australia* **63 D5** 28 36S 151 59 E
Stanton, *U.S.A.* **81 J4** 32 8N 101 48W
Stanwood, *U.S.A.* **84 B4** 48 15N 122 23W
Staples, *U.S.A.* **80 B7** 46 21N 94 48W
Star City, *Canada* **73 C8** 52 50N 104 20W
Star Lake, *U.S.A.* **79 B9** 44 10N 75 2W
Stara Planina, *Bulgaria* **21 C10** 43 15N 23 0 E
Stara Zagora, *Bulgaria* **21 C11** 42 26N 25 39 E
Starachowice, *Poland* **17 C11** 51 3N 21 2 E
Staraya Russa, *Russia* **24 C5** 57 58N 31 23 E
Starbuck I., *Kiribati* **65 H12** 5 37S 155 55W
Stargard Szczeciński, *Poland* **16 B8** 53 20N 15 0 E
Staritsa, *Russia* **24 C5** 56 33N 34 55 E
Starke, *U.S.A.* **77 L4** 29 57N 82 7W
Starogard Gdański, *Poland* **17 B10** 53 59N 18 30 E
Starokonstantinov = Starokonstyantyniv, *Ukraine* **17 D14** 49 48N 27 10 E
Starokonstyantyniv, *Ukraine* **17 D14** 49 48N 27 10 E
Start Pt., *U.K.* **11 G4** 50 13N 3 39W
Staryy Chartoriysk, *Ukraine* **17 C13** 51 15N 25 54 E
Staryy Oskol, *Russia* **25 D6** 51 19N 37 55 E
State College, *U.S.A.* **78 F7** 40 48N 77 52W
Stateline, *U.S.A.* **84 G7** 38 57N 119 56W
Staten, I. = Estados, I. de Los, *Argentina* **96 G4** 54 40S 64 30W
Staten I., *U.S.A.* **79 F10** 40 35N 74 9W
Statesboro, *U.S.A.* **77 J5** 32 27N 81 47W
Statesville, *U.S.A.* **77 H5** 35 47N 80 53W
Stauffer, *U.S.A.* **85 L7** 34 45N 119 3W
Staunton, *Ill., U.S.A.* **80 F10** 39 1N 89 47W
Staunton, *Va., U.S.A.* **76 F6** 38 9N 79 4W
Stavanger, *Norway* **9 G11** 58 57N 5 40 E
Staveley, *N.Z.* **59 K3** 43 40S 171 32 E
Stavelot, *Belgium* **15 D5** 50 23N 5 55 E
Stavern, *Norway* **9 G14** 59 0N 10 1 E
Stavoren, *Neths.* **15 B5** 52 53N 5 22 E
Stavropol, *Russia* **25 E7** 45 5N 42 0 E
Stavros, *Cyprus* **23 D11** 35 1N 32 38 E
Stavrós, *Greece* **23 D6** 35 12N 24 45 E
Stavrós, Ákra, *Greece* **23 D6** 35 26N 24 58 E
Stawell, *Australia* **63 F3** 37 5S 142 47 E
Stawell →, *Australia* **62 C3** 20 20S 142 55 E
Stayner, *Canada* **78 B4** 44 25N 80 5W
Stayton, *U.S.A.* **82 D2** 44 48N 122 48W
Steamboat Springs, *U.S.A.* **82 F10** 40 29N 106 50W
Steele, *U.S.A.* **80 B5** 46 51N 99 55W
Steelton, *U.S.A.* **78 F8** 40 14N 76 50W
Steen River, *Canada* **72 B5** 59 40N 117 12W
Steenkool = Bintuni, *Indonesia* **37 E8** 2 7S 133 32 E
Steens Mt., *U.S.A.* **82 E4** 42 35N 118 40W
Steenwijk, *Neths.* **15 B6** 52 47N 6 7 E
Steep Pt., *Australia* **61 E1** 26 8S 113 8 E
Steep Rock, *Canada* **73 C9** 51 30N 98 48W
Stefanie L. = Chew Bahir, *Ethiopia* **46 G2** 4 40N 36 50 E
Stefansson Bay, *Antarctica* **5 C5** 67 20S 59 8 E
Steiermark □, *Austria* **16 E8** 47 26N 15 0 E
Steilacoom, *U.S.A.* **84 C4** 47 10N 122 36W
Steilrandberge, *Namibia* **56 B1** 17 45S 13 20 E
Steinbach, *Canada* **73 D9** 49 32N 96 40W
Steinhausen, *Namibia* **56 C2** 21 49S 18 20 E
Steinkjer, *Norway* **8 D14** 64 1N 11 31 E
Steinkopf, *S. Africa* **56 D2** 29 18S 17 43 E
Stellarton, *Canada* **71 C7** 45 32N 62 30W
Stellenbosch, *S. Africa* **56 E2** 33 58S 18 50 E
Stendal, *Germany* **16 B6** 52 36N 11 53 E
Steornabhaigh = Stornoway, *U.K.* **12 C2** 58 13N 6 23W
Stepanakert = Xankändi, *Azerbaijan* **25 G8** 39 52N 46 49 E
Stephens Creek, *Australia* **63 E3** 31 50S 141 30 E
Stephens I., *Canada* **72 C2** 54 10N 130 45W
Stephens L., *Canada* **73 B9** 56 32N 95 0W
Stephenville, *Canada* **71 C8** 48 31N 58 35W
Stephenville, *U.S.A.* **81 J5** 32 13N 98 12W
Stepnoi = Elista, *Russia* **25 E7** 46 16N 44 14 E
Steppe, *Asia* **28 D9** 50 0N 50 0 E
Sterkstroom, *S. Africa* **56 E4** 31 32S 26 32 E
Sterling, *Colo., U.S.A.* **80 E3** 40 37N 103 13W
Sterling, *Ill., U.S.A.* **80 E10** 41 48N 89 42W
Sterling, *Kans., U.S.A.* **80 F5** 38 13N 98 12W
Sterling City, *U.S.A.* **81 K4** 31 51N 101 0W
Sterling Heights, *U.S.A.* **76 D4** 42 35N 83 0W
Sterling Run, *U.S.A.* **78 E6** 41 25N 78 12W
Sterlitamak, *Russia* **24 D10** 53 40N 56 0 E
Stérnes, *Greece* **23 D6** 35 30N 24 9 E
Stettin = Szczecin, *Poland* **16 B8** 53 27N 14 27 E
Stettiner Haff, *Germany* **16 B8** 53 47N 14 15 E
Stettler, *Canada* **72 C6** 52 19N 112 40W
Steubenville, *U.S.A.* **78 F4** 40 22N 80 37W
Stevenage, *U.K.* **11 F7** 51 55N 0 13W
Stevens Point, *U.S.A.* **80 C10** 44 31N 89 34W
Stevenson, *U.S.A.* **84 E5** 45 42N 121 53W
Stevenson L., *Canada* **73 C9** 53 55N 96 0W
Stevensville, *U.S.A.* **82 C6** 46 30N 114 5W
Stewart, *Canada* **72 B3** 55 56N 129 57W
Stewart, *U.S.A.* **84 F7** 39 5N 119 46W
Stewart →, *Canada* **68 B6** 63 19N 139 26W
Stewart, C., *Australia* **62 A1** 11 57S 134 56 E
Stewart, I., *Chile* **96 G2** 54 50S 71 15W
Stewart I., *N.Z.* **59 M1** 46 58S 167 54 E
Stewarts Point, *U.S.A.* **84 G3** 38 39N 123 24W
Stewartville, *U.S.A.* **80 D8** 43 51N 92 29W
Stewiacke, *Canada* **71 C7** 45 9N 63 22W
Steynsburg, *S. Africa* **56 E4** 31 15S 25 49 E
Steyr, *Austria* **16 D8** 48 3N 14 25 E
Steytlerville, *S. Africa* **56 E3** 33 17S 24 19 E
Stigler, *U.S.A.* **81 H7** 35 15N 95 8W
Stikine →, *Canada* **72 B2** 56 40N 132 30W
Stilfontein, *S. Africa* **56 D4** 26 51S 26 50 E
Stillwater, *N.Z.* **59 K3** 42 27S 171 20 E
Stillwater, *Minn., U.S.A.* **80 C8** 45 3N 92 49W
Stillwater, *N.Y., U.S.A.* **79 D11** 42 55N 73 41W
Stillwater, *Okla., U.S.A.* **81 G6** 36 7N 97 4W
Stillwater Range, *U.S.A.* **82 G4** 39 50N 118 5W
Stillwater Reservoir, *U.S.A.* **79 C9** 43 54N 75 3W
Stilwell, *U.S.A.* **81 H7** 35 49N 94 38W
Štip, *Macedonia* **21 D10** 41 42N 22 10 E
Stirling, *Canada* **78 B7** 44 18N 77 33W
Stirling, *U.K.* **12 E5** 56 8N 3 57W
Stirling □, *U.K.* **12 E4** 56 12N 4 18W
Stirling Ra., *Australia* **61 F2** 34 23S 118 0 E
Stittsville, *Canada* **79 A9** 45 15N 75 55W
Stjernøya, *Norway* **8 A20** 70 20N 22 40 E
Stjørdalshalsen, *Norway* **8 E14** 63 29N 10 51 E
Stockerau, *Austria* **16 D9** 48 24N 16 12 E
Stockholm, *Sweden* **9 G18** 59 20N 18 3 E
Stockport, *U.K.* **10 D5** 53 25N 2 9W
Stocksbridge, *U.K.* **10 D6** 53 29N 1 35W
Stockton, *Calif., U.S.A.* **84 H5** 37 58N 121 17W
Stockton, *Kans., U.S.A.* **80 F5** 39 26N 99 16W
Stockton, *Mo., U.S.A.* **81 G8** 37 42N 93 48W
Stockton-on-Tees, *U.K.* **10 C6** 54 35N 1 19W
Stockton-on-Tees □, *U.K.* **10 C6** 54 35N 1 19W
Stockton Plateau, *U.S.A.* **81 K3** 30 30N 102 30W
Stoeng Treng, *Cambodia* **38 F5** 13 31N 105 58 E
Stoer, Pt. of, *U.K.* **12 C3** 58 16N 5 23W
Stoke-on-Trent, *U.K.* **10 D5** 53 1N 2 11W
Stoke-on-Trent □, *U.K.* **10 D5** 53 1N 2 11W
Stokes Pt., *Australia* **62 G3** 40 10S 143 56 E
Stokes Ra., *Australia* **60 C5** 15 50S 130 50 E
Stokksnes, *Iceland* **8 D6** 64 14N 14 58W
Stokmarknes, *Norway* **8 B16** 68 34N 14 54 E
Stolac, *Bos.-H.* **21 C7** 43 5N 17 59 E
Stolbovoy, Ostrov, *Russia* **27 B14** 74 44N 135 14 E
Stolbtsy = Stowbtsy, *Belarus* **17 B14** 53 30N 26 43 E
Stolin, *Belarus* **17 C14** 51 53N 26 50 E
Stomion, *Greece* **23 D5** 35 21N 23 32 E
Stone, *U.K.* **10 E5** 52 55N 2 9W
Stoneboro, *U.S.A.* **78 E4** 41 20N 80 7W
Stonehaven, *U.K.* **12 E6** 56 59N 2 12W
Stonehenge, *Australia* **62 C3** 24 22S 143 17 E
Stonehenge, *U.K.* **11 F6** 51 9N 1 45W
Stonewall, *Canada* **73 C9** 50 10N 97 19W
Stony L., *Man., Canada* **73 B9** 58 51N 98 40W
Stony L., *Ont., Canada* **78 B6** 44 30N 78 5W
Stony Point, *U.S.A.* **79 E11** 41 14N 73 59W
Stony Pt., *U.S.A.* **79 C8** 43 50N 76 18W
Stony Rapids, *Canada* **73 B7** 59 16N 105 50W
Stony Tunguska = Tunguska, Podkamennaya →, *Russia* **27 C10** 61 50N 90 13 E
Stonyford, *U.S.A.* **84 F4** 39 23N 122 33W
Stora Lulevatten, *Sweden* **8 C18** 67 10N 19 30 E
Storavan, *Sweden* **8 D18** 65 45N 18 10 E
Stord, *Norway* **9 G11** 59 52N 5 23 E
Store Bælt, *Denmark* **9 J14** 55 20N 11 0 E
Storm B., *Australia* **62 G4** 43 10S 147 30 E
Storm Lake, *U.S.A.* **80 D7** 42 39N 95 13W
Stormberge, *S. Africa* **56 E4** 31 16S 26 17 E
Stormsrivier, *S. Africa* **56 E3** 33 59S 23 52 E
Stornoway, *U.K.* **12 C2** 58 13N 6 23W
Storozhinets = Storozhynets, *Ukraine* **17 D13** 48 14N 25 45 E
Storozhynets, *Ukraine* **17 D13** 48 14N 25 45 E
Storrs, *U.S.A.* **79 E12** 41 49N 72 15W
Storsjön, *Sweden* **8 E16** 63 9N 14 30 E
Storuman, *Sweden* **8 D17** 65 5N 17 10 E
Storuman, sjö, *Sweden* **8 D17** 65 13N 16 50 E
Stouffville, *Canada* **78 C5** 43 58N 79 15W
Stoughton, *Canada* **73 D8** 49 40N 103 0W
Stour →, *Dorset, U.K.* **11 G6** 50 43N 1 47W
Stour →, *Kent, U.K.* **11 F9** 51 18N 1 22 E
Stour →, *Suffolk, U.K.* **11 F9** 51 57N 1 4 E
Stourbridge, *U.K.* **11 E5** 52 28N 2 8W
Stout L., *Canada* **73 C10** 52 0N 94 40W
Stove Pipe Wells Village, *U.S.A.* **85 J9** 36 35N 117 11W
Stow, *U.S.A.* **78 E3** 41 10N 81 27W
Stowbtsy, *Belarus* **17 B14** 53 30N 26 43 E
Stowmarket, *U.K.* **11 E9** 52 12N 1 0 E
Strabane, *U.K.* **13 B4** 54 50N 7 27W
Strahan, *Australia* **62 G4** 42 9S 145 20 E
Stralsund, *Germany* **16 A7** 54 18N 13 4 E
Strand, *S. Africa* **56 E2** 34 9S 18 48 E
Stranda, *Møre og Romsdal, Norway* **9 E12** 62 19N 6 58 E
Stranda, *Nord-Trøndelag, Norway* **8 E14** 63 33N 10 14 E
Strangford L., *U.K.* **13 B6** 54 30N 5 37W
Stranraer, *U.K.* **12 G3** 54 54N 5 1W
Strasbourg, *Canada* **73 C8** 51 4N 104 55W
Strasbourg, *France* **18 B7** 48 35N 7 42 E
Stratford, *Canada* **78 C4** 43 23N 81 0W
Stratford, *N.Z.* **59 H5** 39 20S 174 19 E
Stratford, *Calif., U.S.A.* **84 J7** 36 11N 119 49W
Stratford, *Conn., U.S.A.* **79 E11** 41 12N 73 8W
Stratford, *Tex., U.S.A.* **81 G3** 36 20N 102 4W
Stratford-upon-Avon, *U.K.* **11 E6** 52 12N 1 42W
Strath Spey, *U.K.* **12 D5** 57 9N 3 49W
Strathalbyn, *Australia* **63 F2** 35 13S 138 53 E
Strathaven, *U.K.* **12 F4** 55 40N 4 5W
Strathcona Prov. Park, *Canada* **72 D3** 49 38N 125 40W
Strathmore, *Canada* **72 C6** 51 5N 113 18W
Strathmore, *U.K.* **12 E5** 56 37N 3 7W
Strathmore, *U.S.A.* **84 J7** 36 9N 119 4W
Strathnaver, *Canada* **72 C4** 53 20N 122 33W
Strathpeffer, *U.K.* **12 D4** 57 35N 4 32W
Strathroy, *Canada* **78 D3** 42 58N 81 38W
Strathy Pt., *U.K.* **12 C4** 58 36N 4 1W
Strattanville, *U.S.A.* **78 E5** 41 12N 79 19W
Stratton, *U.S.A.* **79 A14** 45 8N 70 26W
Stratton Mt., *U.S.A.* **79 C12** 43 4N 72 55W
Straubing, *Germany* **16 D7** 48 52N 12 34 E
Straumnes, *Iceland* **8 C2** 66 26N 23 8W
Strawberry →, *U.S.A.* **82 F8** 40 10N 110 24W
Streaky B., *Australia* **63 E1** 32 48S 134 13 E
Streaky Bay, *Australia* **63 E1** 32 51S 134 18 E
Streator, *U.S.A.* **80 E10** 41 8N 88 50W
Streetsboro, *U.S.A.* **78 E3** 41 14N 81 21W
Streetsville, *Canada* **78 C5** 43 35N 79 42W
Strelka, *Russia* **27 D10** 58 5N 93 3 E
Streng →, *Cambodia* **38 F4** 13 12N 103 37 E
Streymoy, *Færoe Is.* **8 E9** 62 8N 7 5W
Strezhevoy, *Russia* **26 C8** 60 42N 77 34 E
Strimón →, *Greece* **21 D10** 40 46N 23 51 E
Strimonikós Kólpos, *Greece* **21 D11** 40 33N 24 0 E
Stroma, *U.K.* **12 C5** 58 41N 3 7W
Strómboli, *Italy* **20 E6** 38 47N 15 13 E
Stromeferry, *U.K.* **12 D3** 57 21N 5 33W
Stromness, *U.K.* **12 C5** 58 58N 3 17W
Stromsburg, *U.S.A.* **80 E6** 41 7N 97 36W
Strömstad, *Sweden* **9 G14** 58 56N 11 10 E
Strömsund, *Sweden* **8 E16** 63 51N 15 33 E
Strongsville, *U.S.A.* **78 E3** 41 19N 81 50W
Stronsay, *U.K.* **12 B6** 59 7N 2 35W
Stroud, *U.K.* **11 F5** 51 45N 2 13W
Stroud Road, *Australia* **63 E5** 32 18S 151 57 E
Stroudsburg, *U.S.A.* **79 F9** 40 59N 75 12W
Stroumbi, *Cyprus* **23 E11** 34 53N 32 29 E
Struer, *Denmark* **9 H13** 56 30N 8 35 E
Strumica, *Macedonia* **21 D10** 41 28N 22 41 E
Struthers, *Canada* **70 C2** 48 41N 85 51W
Struthers, *U.S.A.* **78 E4** 41 4N 80 39W
Stryker, *U.S.A.* **82 B6** 48 41N 114 46W
Stryy, *Ukraine* **17 D12** 49 16N 23 48 E
Strzelecki Cr. →, *Australia* **63 D2** 29 37S 139 59 E
Stuart, *Fla., U.S.A.* **77 M5** 27 12N 80 15W
Stuart, *Nebr., U.S.A.* **80 D5** 42 36N 99 8W
Stuart →, *Canada* **72 C4** 54 0N 123 35W
Stuart Bluff Ra., *Australia* **60 D5** 22 50S 131 52 E
Stuart L., *Canada* **72 C4** 54 30N 124 30W
Stuart Ra., *Australia* **63 D1** 29 10S 134 56 E
Stull L., *Canada* **70 B1** 54 24N 92 34W
Stung Treng = Stoeng Treng, *Cambodia* **38 F5** 13 31N 105 58 E
Stupart →, *Canada* **70 A1** 56 0N 93 25W
Sturgeon B., *Canada* **73 C9** 52 0N 97 50W
Sturgeon Bay, *U.S.A.* **76 C2** 44 50N 87 23W
Sturgeon Falls, *Canada* **70 C4** 46 25N 79 57W
Sturgeon L., *Alta., Canada* **72 B5** 55 6N 117 32W
Sturgeon L., *Ont., Canada* **70 C1** 50 0N 90 45W
Sturgeon L., *Ont., Canada* **78 B6** 44 28N 78 43W
Sturgis, *Canada* **73 C8** 51 56N 102 36W
Sturgis, *Mich., U.S.A.* **76 E3** 41 48N 85 25W
Sturgis, *S. Dak., U.S.A.* **80 C3** 44 25N 103 31W
Sturt Cr. →, *Australia* **60 C4** 19 8S 127 50 E
Stutterheim, *S. Africa* **56 E4** 32 33S 27 28 E
Stuttgart, *Germany* **16 D5** 48 48N 9 11 E
Stuttgart, *U.S.A.* **81 H9** 34 30N 91 33W
Stuyvesant, *U.S.A.* **79 D11** 42 23N 73 45W
Stykkishólmur, *Iceland* **8 D2** 65 2N 22 40W
Styria = Steiermark □, *Austria* **16 E8** 47 26N 15 0 E
Su Xian = Suzhou, *China* **34 H9** 33 41N 116 59 E
Suakin, *Sudan* **51 E13** 19 8N 37 20 E
Suan, *N. Korea* **35 E14** 38 42N 126 22 E
Suaqui, *Mexico* **86 B3** 29 12N 109 41W
Suar, *India* **43 E8** 29 2N 79 3 E
Subang, *Indonesia* **37 G12** 6 34S 107 45 E
Subansiri →, *India* **41 F18** 26 48N 93 50 E
Subarnarekha →, *India* **43 H12** 22 34N 87 24 E
Subayhah, *Si. Arabia* **44 D3** 30 2N 38 50 E
Subi, *Indonesia* **39 L7** 2 58N 108 50 E
Subotica, *Serbia, Yug.* **21 A8** 46 6N 19 39 E
Suceava, *Romania* **17 E14** 47 38N 26 16 E
Suchan, *Russia* **30 C6** 43 8N 133 9 E
Suchitoto, *El Salv.* **88 D2** 13 56N 89 0W
Suchou = Suzhou, *China* **33 C7** 31 19N 120 38 E
Süchow = Xuzhou, *China* **35 G9** 34 18N 117 10 E
Suck →, *Ireland* **13 C3** 53 17N 8 3W
Sucre, *Bolivia* **92 G5** 19 0S 65 15W
Sucuriú →, *Brazil* **93 H8** 20 47S 51 38W
Sud, Pte. du, *Canada* **71 C7** 49 3N 62 14W
Sud-Kivu □, *Dem. Rep. of the Congo* **54 C2** 3 0S 28 30 E
Sud-Ouest, Pte. du, *Canada* **71 C7** 49 23N 63 36W
Sudan, *U.S.A.* **81 H3** 34 4N 102 32W
Sudan ■, *Africa* **51 E11** 15 0N 30 0 E
Sudbury, *Canada* **70 C3** 46 30N 81 0W
Sudbury, *U.K.* **11 E8** 52 2N 0 45 E
Sûdd, *Sudan* **51 G12** 8 20N 30 0 E
Sudeten Mts. = Sudety, *Europe* **17 C9** 50 20N 16 45 E
Sudety, *Europe* **17 C9** 50 20N 16 45 E
Suðuroy, *Færoe Is.* **8 F9** 61 32N 6 50W
Sudi, *Tanzania* **55 E4** 10 11S 39 57 E
Sudirman, Pegunungan, *Indonesia* **37 E9** 4 30S 137 0 E
Sueca, *Spain* **19 C5** 39 12N 0 21W
Suemez I., *U.S.A.* **72 B2** 55 15N 133 20W
Suez = El Suweis, *Egypt* **51 C12** 29 58N 32 31 E
Suez, G. of = Suweis, Khalîg el, *Egypt* **51 C12** 28 40N 33 0 E
Suez Canal = Suweis, Qanâ es, *Egypt* **51 B12** 31 0N 32 20 E
Suffield, *Canada* **72 C6** 50 12N 111 10W
Suffolk, *U.S.A.* **76 G7** 36 44N 76 35W
Suffolk □, *U.K.* **11 E9** 52 16N 1 0 E
Sugargrove, *U.S.A.* **78 E5** 41 59N 79 21W
Sugarive →, *India* **43 F12** 26 16N 86 24 E
Sugluk = Salluit, *Canada* **69 B12** 62 14N 75 38W
Şuḥār, *Oman* **46 C6** 24 20N 56 40 E
Sühbaatar □, *Mongolia* **34 B8** 45 30N 114 0 E
Suhl, *Germany* **16 C6** 50 36N 10 42 E
Sui, *Pakistan* **42 E3** 28 37N 69 19 E
Sui Xian, *China* **34 G8** 34 25N 115 2 E
Suide, *China* **34 F6** 37 30N 110 12 E
Suifenhe, *China* **35 B16** 44 25N 131 10 E
Suihua, *China* **33 B7** 46 32N 126 55 E
Suining, *China* **35 H9** 33 56N 117 58 E
Suiping, *China* **34 H7** 33 10N 113 59 E
Suir →, *Ireland* **13 D4** 52 16N 7 9W
Suisun City, *U.S.A.* **84 G4** 38 15N 122 2W
Suiyang, *China* **35 B16** 44 30N 130 56 E
Suizhong, *China* **35 D11** 40 21N 120 20 E
Sujangarh, *India* **42 F6** 27 42N 74 31 E
Sukabumi, *Indonesia* **37 G12** 6 56S 106 50 E
Sukadana, *Indonesia* **36 E3** 1 10S 110 0 E
Sukagawa, *Japan* **31 F10** 37 17N 140 23 E
Sukaraja, *Indonesia* **36 E4** 2 28S 110 25 E
Sukarnapura = Jayapura, *Indonesia* **37 E10** 2 28S 140 38 E
Sukch'ŏn, *N. Korea* **35 E13** 39 22N 125 35 E
Sukhona →, *Russia* **24 C6** 61 15N 46 39 E
Sukhothai, *Thailand* **38 D2** 17 1N 99 49 E
Sukhumi = Sokhumi, *Georgia* **25 F7** 43 0N 41 0 E
Sukkur, *Pakistan* **42 F3** 27 42N 68 54 E
Sukkur Barrage, *Pakistan* **42 F3** 27 40N 68 50 E
Sukri →, *India* **42 G4** 25 4N 71 43 E
Sukumo, *Japan* **31 H6** 32 56N 132 44 E
Sukunka →, *Canada* **72 B4** 55 45N 121 15W
Sula, Kepulauan, *Indonesia* **37 E7** 1 45S 125 0 E
Sulaco →, *Honduras* **88 C2** 15 2N 87 44W
Sulaiman Range, *Pakistan* **42 D3** 30 30N 69 50 E
Sūlār, *Iran* **45 D6** 31 53N 51 54 E
Sulawesi Sea = Celebes Sea, *Indonesia* **37 D6** 3 0N 123 0 E
Sulawesi Selatan □, *Indonesia* **37 E6** 2 30S 120 0 E
Sulawesi Utara □, *Indonesia* **37 D6** 1 0N 122 30 E
Sulima, *S. Leone* **50 G3** 6 58N 11 32W
Sulina, *Romania* **17 F15** 45 10N 29 40 E
Sulitjelma, *Norway* **8 C17** 67 9N 16 3 E
Sullana, *Peru* **92 D2** 4 52S 80 39W
Sullivan, *Ill., U.S.A.* **80 F10** 39 36N 88 37W
Sullivan, *Ind., U.S.A.* **76 F2** 39 6N 87 24W
Sullivan, *Mo., U.S.A.* **80 F9** 38 13N 91 10W
Sullivan Bay, *Canada* **72 C3** 50 55N 126 50W
Sullivan I. = Lanbi Kyun, *Burma* **39 G2** 10 50N 98 20 E
Sulphur, *La., U.S.A.* **81 K8** 30 14N 93 23W
Sulphur, *Okla., U.S.A.* **81 H6** 34 31N 96 58W
Sulphur Pt., *Canada* **72 A6** 60 56N 114 48W
Sulphur Springs, *U.S.A.* **81 J7** 33 8N 95 36W
Sultan, *Canada* **70 C3** 47 36N 82 47W
Sultan, *U.S.A.* **84 C5** 47 52N 121 49W
Sultanpur, *Mad. P., India* **42 H8** 23 9N 77 56 E
Sultanpur, *Punjab, India* **42 D6** 31 13N 75 11 E
Sultanpur, *Ut. P., India* **43 F10** 26 18N 82 4 E
Sulu Arch., *Phil.* **37 C6** 6 0N 121 0 E
Sulu Sea, *E. Indies* **37 C6** 8 0N 120 0 E
Suluq, *Libya* **51 B10** 31 44N 20 14 E
Sulzberger Ice Shelf, *Antarctica* **5 D10** 78 0S 150 0 E
Sumalata, *Indonesia* **37 D6** 1 0N 122 31 E
Sumampa, *Argentina* **94 B3** 29 25S 63 29W
Sumatera □, *Indonesia* **36 D2** 0 40N 100 20 E
Sumatera Barat □, *Indonesia* **36 E2** 1 0S 101 0 E
Sumatera Utara □, *Indonesia* **36 D1** 2 30N 98 0 E
Sumatra = Sumatera □, *Indonesia* **36 D2** 0 40N 100 20 E
Sumba, *Indonesia* **37 F5** 9 45S 119 35 E
Sumba, Selat, *Indonesia* **37 F5** 9 0S 118 40 E
Sumbawa, *Indonesia* **36 F5** 8 26S 117 30 E
Sumbawa Besar, *Indonesia* **36 F5** 8 30S 117 26 E
Sumbawanga □, *Tanzania* **52 F6** 8 0S 31 30 E
Sumbe, *Angola* **52 G2** 11 10S 13 48 E
Sumburgh Hd., *U.K.* **12 B7** 59 52N 1 17W
Sumdeo, *India* **43 D8** 31 26N 78 44 E
Sumdo, *China* **43 B8** 35 6N 78 41 E
Sumedang, *Indonesia* **37 G12** 6 52S 107 55 E
Šumen = Shumen, *Bulgaria* **21 C12** 43 18N 26 55 E
Sumenep, *Indonesia* **37 G15** 7 1S 113 52 E
Sumgait = Sumqayıt, *Azerbaijan* **25 F8** 40 34N 49 38 E
Summer L., *U.S.A.* **82 E3** 42 50N 120 45W
Summerland, *Canada* **72 D5** 49 32N 119 41W
Summerside, *Canada* **71 C7** 46 24N 63 47W
Summersville, *U.S.A.* **76 F5** 38 17N 80 51W
Summerville, *Ga., U.S.A.* **77 H3** 34 29N 85 21W
Summerville, *S.C., U.S.A.* **77 J5** 33 1N 80 11W
Summit Lake, *Canada* **72 C4** 54 20N 122 40W
Summit Peak, *U.S.A.* **83 H10** 37 21N 106 42W
Sumner, *Iowa, U.S.A.* **80 D8** 42 51N 92 6W
Sumner, *Wash., U.S.A.* **84 C4** 47 12N 122 14W
Sumoto, *Japan* **31 G7** 34 21N 134 54 E
Šumperk, *Czech Rep.* **17 D9** 49 59N 16 59 E
Sumqayıt, *Azerbaijan* **25 F8** 40 34N 49 38 E
Sumter, *U.S.A.* **77 J5** 33 55N 80 21W
Sumy, *Ukraine* **25 D5** 50 57N 34 50 E
Sun City, *S. Africa* **56 D4** 25 17S 27 3 E
Sun City, *Ariz., U.S.A.* **83 K7** 33 36N 112 17W
Sun City, *Calif., U.S.A.* **85 M9** 33 42N 117 11W
Sun City Center, *U.S.A.* **77 M4** 27 43N 82 18W
Sun Lakes, *U.S.A.* **83 K8** 33 10N 111 52W
Sun Valley, *U.S.A.* **82 E6** 43 42N 114 21W
Sunagawa, *Japan* **30 C10** 43 29N 141 55 E
Sunan, *N. Korea* **35 E13** 39 15N 125 40 E
Sunart, L., *U.K.* **12 E3** 56 42N 5 43W
Sunburst, *U.S.A.* **82 B8** 48 53N 111 55W
Sunbury, *Australia* **63 F3** 37 35S 144 44 E
Sunbury, *U.S.A.* **79 F8** 40 52N 76 48W
Sunchales, *Argentina* **94 C3** 30 58S 61 35W
Suncho Corral, *Argentina* **94 B3** 27 55S 63 27W
Sunch'ŏn, *S. Korea* **35 G14** 34 52N 127 31 E
Suncook, *U.S.A.* **79 C13** 43 8N 71 27W
Sunda, Selat, *Indonesia* **36 F3** 6 20S 105 30 E
Sunda Is., *Indonesia* **28 K14** 5 0S 105 0 E
Sunda Str. = Sunda, Selat, *Indonesia* **36 F3** 6 20S 105 30 E
Sundance, *Canada* **73 B10** 56 32N 94 4W
Sundance, *U.S.A.* **80 C2** 44 24N 104 23W
Sundar Nagar, *India* **42 D7** 31 32N 76 53 E
Sundarbans, *Asia* **41 J16** 22 0N 89 0 E
Sundargarh, *India* **41 H14** 22 4N 84 5 E
Sundays = Sondags →, *S. Africa* **56 E4** 33 44S 25 51 E
Sunderland, *Canada* **78 B5** 44 16N 79 4W
Sunderland, *U.K.* **10 C6** 54 55N 1 23W
Sundre, *Canada* **72 C6** 51 49N 114 38W
Sundsvall, *Sweden* **9 E17** 62 23N 17 17 E
Sung Hei, *Vietnam* **39 G6** 10 20N 106 2 E
Sungai Kolok, *Thailand* **39 J3** 6 2N 101 58 E
Sungai Lembing, *Malaysia* **39 L4** 3 55N 103 3 E
Sungai Petani, *Malaysia* **39 K3** 5 37N 100 30 E
Sungaigerong, *Indonesia* **36 E2** 2 59S 104 52 E
Sungailiat, *Indonesia* **36 E3** 1 51S 106 8 E
Sungaipenuh, *Indonesia* **36 E2** 2 1S 101 20 E
Sungari = Songhua Jiang →, *China* **33 B8** 47 45N 132 30 E
Sunghua Chiang = Songhua Jiang →, *China* **33 B8** 47 45N 132 30 E
Sunland Park, *U.S.A.* **83 L10** 31 50N 106 40W
Sunndalsøra, *Norway* **9 E13** 62 40N 8 33 E
Sunnyside, *U.S.A.* **82 C3** 46 20N 120 0W
Sunnyvale, *U.S.A.* **84 H4** 37 23N 122 2W
Suntar, *Russia* **27 C12** 62 15N 117 30 E
Suomenselkä, *Finland* **8 E21** 62 52N 24 0 E
Suomussalmi, *Finland* **8 D23** 64 54N 29 10 E
Suoyarvi, *Russia* **24 B5** 62 3N 32 20 E
Supai, *U.S.A.* **83 H7** 36 15N 112 41W
Supaul, *India* **43 F12** 26 10N 86 40 E
Superior, *Ariz., U.S.A.* **83 K8** 33 18N 111 6W
Superior, *Mont., U.S.A.* **82 C6** 47 12N 114 53W
Superior, *Nebr., U.S.A.* **80 E5** 40 1N 98 4W
Superior, *Wis., U.S.A.* **80 B8** 46 44N 92 6W
Superior, L., *N. Amer.* **70 C2** 47 0N 87 0W
Suphan Buri, *Thailand* **38 E3** 14 14N 100 10 E

T

Toliara, Madag. 57 C7 23 21S 43 40 E
Toliara □, Madag. 57 C8 21 0S 45 0 E
Tolima, Colombia 92 C3 4 40N 75 19W
Tolitoli, Indonesia 37 D6 1 5N 120 50 E
Tollhouse, U.S.A. 84 H7 37 1N 119 24W
Tolo, Teluk, Indonesia 37 E6 2 20S 122 10 E
Toluca, Mexico 87 D5 19 20N 99 40W
Tom Burke, S. Africa 57 C4 23 5S 28 0 E
Tom Price, Australia 60 D2 22 40S 117 48 E
Tomah, U.S.A. 80 D9 43 59N 90 30W
Tomahawk, U.S.A. 80 C10 45 28N 89 44W
Tomakomai, Japan 30 C10 42 38N 141 36 E
Tomales, U.S.A. 84 G4 38 15N 122 53W
Tomales B., U.S.A. 84 G3 38 15N 123 58W
Tomar, Portugal 19 C1 39 36N 8 25W
Tomaszów Mazowiecki, Poland 17 C10 51 30N 20 2 E
Tomatlán, Mexico 86 D3 19 56N 105 15W
Tombador, Serra do, Brazil 92 F7 12 0S 58 0W
Tombigbee →, U.S.A. 77 K2 31 8N 87 57W
Tombouctou, Mali 50 E5 16 50N 3 0W
Tombstone, U.S.A. 83 L8 31 43N 110 4W
Tombua, Angola 56 B1 15 55S 11 55 E
Tomé, Chile 94 D1 36 36S 72 57W
Tomelloso, Spain 19 C4 39 10N 3 2W
Tomini, Indonesia 37 D6 0 30N 120 30 E
Tomini, Teluk, Indonesia 37 E6 0 10S 121 0 E
Tomintoul, U.K. 12 D5 57 15N 3 23W
Tomkinson Ranges, Australia 61 E4 26 11S 129 5 E
Tommot, Russia 27 D13 59 4N 126 20 E
Tomnop Ta Suos, Cambodia 39 G5 11 20N 104 15 E
Tomo →, Colombia 92 B5 5 20N 67 48W
Toms Place, U.S.A. 84 H8 37 34N 118 41W
Toms River, U.S.A. 79 G10 39 58N 74 12W
Tomsk, Russia 26 D9 56 30N 85 5 E
Tonalá, Mexico 87 D6 16 8N 93 41W
Tonantins, Brazil 92 D5 2 45S 67 45W
Tonasket, U.S.A. 82 B4 48 42N 119 26W
Tonawanda, U.S.A. 78 D6 43 1N 78 53W
Tonbridge, U.K. 11 F8 51 11N 0 17 E
Tondano, Indonesia 37 D6 1 35N 124 54 E
Tondoro, Namibia 56 B2 17 45S 18 50 E
Tone →, Australia 61 F2 34 25S 116 25 E
Tone-Gawa →, Japan 31 F9 35 44N 140 51 E
Tonekābon, Iran 45 B6 36 45N 51 12 E
Tong Xian, China 34 E9 39 55N 116 35 E
Tonga ■, Pac. Oc. 59 D11 19 50S 174 30W
Tonga Trench, Pac. Oc. 64 J10 18 0S 173 0W
Tongaat, S. Africa 57 D5 29 33S 31 9 E
Tongareva, Cook Is. 65 H12 9 0S 158 0W
Tongatapu Group, Tonga 59 E12 21 0S 175 0W
Tongchŏn-ni, N. Korea 35 E14 39 50N 127 25 E
Tongchuan, China 34 G5 35 6N 109 3 E
Tongeren, Belgium 15 D5 50 47N 5 28 E
Tongguan, China 34 G6 34 40N 110 25 E
Tonghua, China 35 D13 41 42N 125 58 E
Tongjosŏn Man, N. Korea 35 E15 39 30N 128 0 E
Tongking, G. of = Tonkin, G. of, Asia 32 E5 20 0N 108 0 E
Tongliao, China 35 C12 43 38N 122 18 E
Tongling, China 33 C6 30 55N 117 48 E
Tongnae, S. Korea 35 G15 35 12N 129 5 E
Tongobory, Madag. 57 C7 23 32S 44 20 E
Tongoy, Chile 94 C1 30 16S 71 31W
Tongres = Tongeren, Belgium 15 D5 50 47N 5 28 E
Tongsa Dzong, Bhutan 41 F17 27 31N 90 31 E
Tongue, U.K. 12 C4 58 29N 4 25W
Tongue →, U.S.A. 80 B2 46 25N 105 52W
Tongwei, China 34 G3 35 0N 105 5 E
Tongxin, China 34 F3 36 59N 105 58 E
Tongyang, N. Korea 35 E14 39 9N 126 53 E
Tongyu, China 35 B12 44 45N 123 4 E
Tonj, Sudan 51 G11 7 20N 28 44 E
Tonk, India 42 F6 26 6N 75 54 E
Tonkawa, U.S.A. 81 G6 36 41N 97 18W
Tonkin = Bac Phan, Vietnam 38 B5 22 0N 105 0 E
Tonkin, G. of, Asia 32 E5 20 0N 108 0 E
Tonle Sap, Cambodia 38 F4 13 0N 104 0 E
Tono, Japan 30 E10 39 19N 141 32 E
Tonopah, U.S.A. 83 G5 38 4N 117 14W
Tonosí, Panama 88 E3 7 20N 80 20W
Tons →, Haryana, India 42 D7 30 30N 77 39 E
Tons →, Ut. P., India 43 F10 26 1N 83 33 E
Tønsberg, Norway 9 G14 59 19N 10 25 E
Toobanna, Australia 62 B4 18 42S 146 9 E
Toodyay, Australia 61 F2 31 34S 116 28 E
Tooele, U.S.A. 82 F7 40 32N 112 18W
Toompine, Australia 63 D3 27 15S 144 19 E
Toora, Australia 63 F4 38 39S 146 23 E
Toora-Khem, Russia 27 D10 52 28N 96 17 E
Toowoomba, Australia 63 D5 27 32S 151 56 E
Top-ozero, Russia 24 A5 65 35N 32 0 E
Top Springs, Australia 60 C5 16 37S 131 51 E
Topaz, U.S.A. 84 G7 38 41N 119 30W
Topeka, U.S.A. 80 F7 39 3N 95 40W
Topley, Canada 72 C3 54 49N 126 18W
Topocalma, Pta., Chile 94 C1 34 10S 72 2W
Topock, U.S.A. 85 L12 34 46N 114 29W
Topoľčany, Slovak Rep. 17 D10 48 35N 18 12 E
Topolobampo, Mexico 86 B3 25 40N 109 4W
Toppenish, U.S.A. 82 C3 46 23N 120 19W
Toraka Vestale, Madag. 57 B7 16 20S 43 58 E
Torata, Peru 92 G4 17 23S 70 1W
Torbalı, Turkey 21 E12 38 10N 27 21 E
Torbat-e Heydārīyeh, Iran 45 C8 35 15N 59 12 E
Torbat-e Jām, Iran 45 C9 35 16N 60 35 E
Torbay, Canada 71 C9 47 40N 52 42W
Torbay □, U.K. 11 G4 50 26N 3 31W
Tordesillas, Spain 19 B3 41 30N 5 0W
Torfaen □, U.K. 11 F4 51 43N 3 3W
Torgau, Germany 16 C7 51 34N 13 0 E
Torhout, Belgium 15 C3 51 5N 3 7 E
Tori-Shima, Japan 31 J10 30 29N 140 19 E
Torin, Mexico 86 B2 27 33N 110 15W
Torino, Italy 18 D7 45 3N 7 40 E
Torit, Sudan 51 H12 4 27N 32 31 E
Torkamān, Iran 44 B5 37 35N 47 23 E
Tormes →, Spain 19 B2 41 18N 6 29W
Tornado Mt., Canada 72 D6 49 55N 114 40W
Torne älv →, Sweden 8 D21 65 50N 24 12 E
Torneå = Tornio, Finland 8 D21 65 50N 24 12 E
Torneträsk, Sweden 8 B18 68 24N 19 15 E
Tornio, Finland 8 D21 65 50N 24 12 E
Tornionjoki →, Finland 8 D21 65 50N 24 12 E
Tornquist, Argentina 94 D3 38 8S 62 15W
Toro, Spain 22 B11 39 59N 4 8 E
Toro, Cerro del, Chile 94 B2 29 10S 69 50W
Toro Pk., U.S.A. 85 M10 33 34N 116 24W
Toroníios Kólpos, Greece 21 D10 40 5N 23 30 E
Toronto, Canada 78 C5 43 39N 79 20W
Toronto, U.S.A. 78 F4 40 28N 80 36W
Toropets, Russia 24 C5 56 30N 31 40 E
Tororo, Uganda 54 B3 0 45N 34 12 E
Toros Dağları, Turkey 25 G5 37 0N 32 30 E
Torpa, India 43 H11 22 57N 85 6 E
Torquay, U.K. 11 G4 50 27N 3 32W
Torrance, U.S.A. 85 M8 33 50N 118 19W
Torre de Moncorvo, Portugal 19 B2 41 12N 7 8W
Torre del Greco, Italy 20 D6 40 47N 14 22 E
Torrejón de Ardoz, Spain 19 B4 40 27N 3 29W
Torrelavega, Spain 19 A3 43 20N 4 5W
Torremolinos, Spain 19 D3 36 38N 4 30W
Torrens, L., Australia 63 E2 31 0S 137 50 E
Torrens Cr. →, Australia 62 C4 22 23S 145 9 E
Torrens Creek, Australia 62 C4 20 48S 145 3 E
Torrent, Spain 19 C5 39 27N 0 28W
Torreón, Mexico 86 B4 25 33N 103 26W
Torres, Brazil 95 B5 29 21S 49 44W
Torres, Mexico 86 B2 28 46N 110 47W
Torres Strait, Australia 64 H6 9 50S 142 20 E
Torres Vedras, Portugal 19 C1 39 5N 9 15W
Torrevieja, Spain 19 D5 37 59N 0 42W
Torrey, U.S.A. 83 G8 38 18N 111 25W
Torridge →, U.K. 11 G3 51 0N 4 13W
Torridon, L., U.K. 12 D3 57 35N 5 50W
Torrington, Conn., U.S.A. 79 E11 41 48N 73 7W
Torrington, Wyo., U.S.A. 80 D2 42 4N 104 11W
Tórshavn, Færoe Is. 8 E9 62 5N 6 56W
Tortola, Br. Virgin Is. 89 C7 18 19N 64 45W
Tortosa, Spain 19 B6 40 49N 0 31 E
Tortosa, C., Spain 19 B6 40 41N 0 52 E
Tortue, I. de la, Haiti 89 B5 20 5N 72 57W
Torūd, Iran 45 C7 35 25N 55 5 E
Toruń, Poland 17 B10 53 2N 18 39 E
Tory I., Ireland 13 A3 55 16N 8 14W
Tosa, Japan 31 H6 33 24N 133 23 E
Tosa-Shimizu, Japan 31 H6 32 52N 132 58 E
Tosa-Wan, Japan 31 H6 33 15N 133 30 E
Toscana □, Italy 20 C4 43 25N 11 0 E
Toshkent, Uzbekistan 26 E7 41 20N 69 10 E
Tostado, Argentina 94 B3 29 15S 61 50W
Tostón, Pta. de, Canary Is. 22 F5 28 42N 14 2W
Tosu, Japan 31 H5 33 22N 130 31 E
Toteng, Botswana 56 C3 20 22S 22 58 E
Totma, Russia 24 C7 60 0N 42 40 E
Totnes, U.K. 11 G4 50 26N 3 42W
Totness, Surinam 93 B7 5 53N 56 19W
Totonicapán, Guatemala 88 D1 14 58N 91 12W
Totten Glacier, Antarctica 5 C8 66 45S 116 10 E
Tottenham, Australia 63 E4 32 14S 147 21 E
Tottenham, Canada 78 B5 44 1N 79 49W
Tottori, Japan 31 G7 35 30N 134 15 E
Tottori □, Japan 31 G7 35 30N 134 12 E
Toubkal, Djebel, Morocco 50 B4 31 0N 8 0W
Tougan, Burkina Faso 50 F5 13 11N 2 58W
Touggourt, Algeria 50 B7 33 6N 6 4 E
Toul, France 18 B6 48 40N 5 53 E
Toulon, France 18 E6 43 10N 5 55 E
Toulouse, France 18 E4 43 37N 1 27 E
Toummo, Niger 51 D8 22 45N 14 8 E
Toungoo, Burma 41 K20 19 0N 96 30 E
Touraine, France 18 C4 47 20N 0 30 E
Tourane = Da Nang, Vietnam 38 D7 16 4N 108 13 E
Tourcoing, France 18 A5 50 42N 3 10 E
Touriñán, C., Spain 19 A1 43 3N 9 18W
Tournai, Belgium 15 D3 50 35N 3 25 E
Tournon-sur-Rhône, France 18 D6 45 4N 4 50 E
Tours, France 18 C4 47 22N 0 40 E
Toussora, Mt., C.A.R. 52 C4 9 7N 23 14 E
Touws →, S. Africa 56 E3 33 45S 21 11 E
Touwsrivier, S. Africa 56 E3 33 20S 20 2 E
Towada, Japan 30 D10 40 37N 141 13 E
Towada-Ko, Japan 30 D10 40 28N 140 55 E
Towanda, U.S.A. 79 E8 41 46N 76 27W
Towang, India 41 F17 27 37N 91 50 E
Tower, U.S.A. 80 B8 47 48N 92 17W
Towerhill Cr. →, Australia 62 C3 22 28S 144 35 E
Towner, U.S.A. 80 A4 48 21N 100 25W
Townsend, U.S.A. 82 C8 46 19N 111 31W
Townshend I., Australia 62 C5 22 10S 150 31 E
Townsville, Australia 62 B4 19 15S 146 45 E
Towraghondi, Afghan. 40 B3 35 13N 62 16 E
Towson, U.S.A. 76 F7 39 24N 76 36W
Towuti, Danau, Indonesia 37 E6 2 45S 121 32 E
Toya-Ko, Japan 30 C10 42 35N 140 51 E
Toyama, Japan 31 F8 36 40N 137 15 E
Toyama □, Japan 31 F8 36 45N 137 30 E
Toyama-Wan, Japan 31 F8 37 0N 137 30 E
Toyohashi, Japan 31 G8 34 45N 137 25 E
Toyokawa, Japan 31 G8 34 48N 137 27 E
Toyonaka, Japan 31 G7 34 50N 135 28 E
Toyooka, Japan 31 G7 35 35N 134 48 E
Toyota, Japan 31 G8 35 3N 137 7 E
Tozeur, Tunisia 50 B7 33 56N 8 8 E
Trá Li = Tralee, Ireland 13 D2 52 16N 9 42W
Tra On, Vietnam 39 H5 9 58N 105 55 E
Trabzon, Turkey 25 F6 41 0N 39 45 E
Tracadie, Canada 71 C7 47 30N 64 55W
Tracy, Calif., U.S.A. 84 H5 37 44N 121 26W
Tracy, Minn., U.S.A. 80 C7 44 14N 95 37W
Trafalgar, C., Spain 19 D2 36 10N 6 2W
Trail, Canada 72 D5 49 5N 117 40W
Trainor L., Canada 72 A4 60 24N 120 17W
Trákhonas, Cyprus 23 D12 35 12N 33 21 E
Tralee, Ireland 13 D2 52 16N 9 42W
Tralee B., Ireland 13 D2 52 17N 9 55W
Tramore, Ireland 13 D4 52 10N 7 10W
Tramore B., Ireland 13 D4 52 9N 7 10W
Tran Ninh, Cao Nguyen, Laos 38 C4 19 30N 103 10 E
Tranås, Sweden 9 G16 58 3N 14 59 E
Trancas, Argentina 94 B2 26 11S 65 20W
Trang, Thailand 39 J2 7 33N 99 38 E
Trangahy, Madag. 57 B7 19 7S 44 31 E
Trangan, Indonesia 37 F8 6 40S 134 20 E
Trangie, Australia 63 E4 32 4S 148 0 E
Trani, Italy 20 D7 41 17N 16 25 E
Tranoroa, Madag. 57 C8 24 42S 45 4 E
Tranqueras, Uruguay 95 C4 31 13S 55 45W
Transantarctic Mts., Antarctica 5 E12 85 0S 170 0W
Transilvania, Romania 17 E12 46 30N 24 0 E
Transilvanian Alps = Carpaţii Meridionali, Romania 17 F13 45 30N 25 0 E
Transvaal, S. Africa 53 K5 25 0S 29 0 E
Transylvania = Transilvania, Romania 17 E12 46 30N 24 0 E
Trápani, Italy 20 E5 38 1N 12 29 E
Trapper Pk., U.S.A. 82 D6 45 54N 114 18W
Traralgon, Australia 63 F4 38 12S 146 34 E
Trasimeno, L., Italy 20 C5 43 8N 12 6 E
Trat, Thailand 39 F4 12 14N 102 33 E
Tratani →, Pakistan 42 E3 29 19N 68 20 E
Traun, Austria 16 D8 48 14N 14 15 E
Traveller's L., Australia 63 E3 33 20S 142 0 E
Travemünde, Germany 16 B6 53 57N 10 52 E
Travers, Mt., N.Z. 59 K4 42 1S 172 45 E
Traverse City, U.S.A. 76 C3 44 46N 85 38W
Travis, L., U.S.A. 81 K5 30 24N 97 55W
Travnik, Bos.-H. 21 B7 44 17N 17 39 E
Trébbia →, Italy 18 D8 45 4N 9 41 E
Třebíč, Czech Rep. 16 D8 49 14N 15 55 E
Trebinje, Bos.-H. 21 C8 42 44N 18 22 E
Trebonne, Australia 62 B4 18 37S 146 5 E
Tregaron, U.K. 11 E4 52 14N 3 56W
Tregrosse Is., Australia 62 B5 17 41S 150 43 E
Treherne, Canada 73 D9 49 38N 98 42W
Treinta y Tres, Uruguay 95 C5 33 16S 54 17W
Trelawney, Zimbabwe 57 B5 17 30S 30 30 E
Trelew, Argentina 96 E3 43 10S 65 20W
Trelleborg, Sweden 9 J15 55 20N 13 10 E
Tremadog Bay, U.K. 10 E3 52 51N 4 18W
Tremonton, U.S.A. 82 F7 41 43N 112 10W
Tremp, Spain 19 A6 42 10N 0 52 E
Trenche →, Canada 70 C5 47 46N 72 53W
Trenčín, Slovak Rep. 17 D10 48 52N 18 4 E
Trenggalek, Indonesia 37 H14 8 3S 111 43 E
Trenque Lauquen, Argentina 94 D3 36 5S 62 45W
Trent →, Canada 78 B7 44 6N 77 34W
Trent →, U.K. 10 D7 53 41N 0 42W
Trento, Italy 20 A4 46 4N 11 8 E
Trenton, Canada 78 B7 44 10N 77 34W
Trenton, Mo., U.S.A. 80 E8 40 5N 93 37W
Trenton, N.J., U.S.A. 79 F10 40 14N 74 46W
Trenton, Nebr., U.S.A. 80 E4 40 11N 101 1W
Trepassey, Canada 71 C9 46 43N 53 25W
Tres Arroyos, Argentina 94 D3 38 26S 60 20W
Três Corações, Brazil 95 A6 21 44S 45 15W
Três Lagoas, Brazil 93 H8 20 50S 51 43W
Tres Lomas, Argentina 94 D3 36 27S 62 51W
Tres Marías, Islas, Mexico 86 C3 21 25N 106 28W
Tres Montes, C., Chile 96 F1 46 50S 75 30W
Tres Pinos, U.S.A. 84 J5 36 48N 121 19W
Três Pontas, Brazil 95 A6 21 23S 45 29W
Tres Puentes, Chile 94 B1 27 50S 70 15W
Tres Puntas, C., Argentina 96 F3 47 0S 66 0W
Três Rios, Brazil 95 A7 22 6S 43 15W
Tres Valles, Mexico 87 D5 18 15N 96 8W
Tresco, U.K. 11 H1 49 57N 6 20W
Treviso, Italy 20 B5 45 40N 12 15 E
Triabunna, Australia 62 G4 42 30S 147 55 E
Triánda, Greece 23 C10 36 25N 28 10 E
Triangle, Zimbabwe 57 C5 21 2S 31 28 E
Tribal Areas □, Pakistan 42 C4 33 0N 70 0 E
Tribulation, C., Australia 62 B4 16 5S 145 29 E
Tribune, U.S.A. 80 F4 38 28N 101 45W
Trichinopoly = Tiruchchirappalli, India 40 P11 10 45N 78 45 E
Trichur, India 40 P10 10 30N 76 18 E
Trida, Australia 63 E4 33 1S 145 1 E
Trier, Germany 16 D4 49 45N 6 38 E
Trieste, Italy 20 B5 45 40N 13 46 E
Triglav, Slovenia 16 E7 46 21N 13 50 E
Tríkkala, Greece 21 E9 39 34N 21 47 E
Trikomo, Cyprus 23 D12 35 17N 33 52 E
Trikora, Puncak, Indonesia 37 E9 4 15S 138 45 E
Trim, Ireland 13 C5 53 33N 6 48W
Trincomalee, Sri Lanka 40 Q12 8 38N 81 15 E
Trindade, Brazil 93 G9 16 40S 49 30W
Trindade, I., Atl. Oc. 2 F8 20 20S 29 50W
Trinidad, Bolivia 92 F6 14 46S 64 50W
Trinidad, Cuba 88 B4 21 48N 80 0W
Trinidad, Trin. & Tob. 89 D7 10 30N 61 15W
Trinidad, Uruguay 94 C4 33 30S 56 50W
Trinidad, U.S.A. 81 G2 37 10N 104 31W
Trinidad →, Mexico 87 D5 17 49N 95 9W
Trinidad & Tobago ■, W. Indies 89 D7 10 30N 61 20W
Trinity, Canada 71 C9 48 59N 53 55W
Trinity, U.S.A. 81 K7 30 57N 95 22W
Trinity →, Calif., U.S.A. 82 F2 41 11N 123 42W
Trinity →, Tex., U.S.A. 81 L7 29 45N 94 43W
Trinity B., Canada 71 C9 48 20N 53 10W
Trinity Is., U.S.A. 68 C4 56 33N 154 25W
Trinity Range, U.S.A. 82 F4 40 15N 118 45W
Trinkitat, Sudan 51 E13 18 45N 37 51 E
Trinway, U.S.A. 78 F2 40 9N 82 1W
Tripoli = Tarābulus, Lebanon 47 A4 34 31N 35 50 E
Tripoli = Tarābulus, Libya 51 B8 32 49N 13 7 E
Trípolis, Greece 21 F10 37 31N 22 25 E
Tripolitania, N. Afr. 51 B8 31 0N 13 0 E
Tripura □, India 41 H18 24 0N 92 0 E
Tripylos, Cyprus 23 E11 34 59N 32 41 E
Tristan da Cunha, Atl. Oc. 49 K2 37 6S 12 20W
Trisul, India 43 D8 30 19N 79 47 E
Trivandrum, India 40 Q10 8 41N 77 0 E
Trnava, Slovak Rep. 17 D9 48 23N 17 35 E
Trochu, Canada 72 C6 51 50N 113 13W
Trodely I., Canada 70 B4 52 15N 79 26W
Troglav, Croatia 20 C7 43 56N 16 36 E
Troilus, L., Canada 70 B5 50 50N 74 35W
Trois-Pistoles, Canada 71 C6 48 5N 69 10W
Trois-Rivières, Canada 70 C5 46 25N 72 34W
Troitsk, Russia 26 D7 54 10N 61 35 E
Troitsko Pechorsk, Russia 24 B10 62 40N 56 10 E
Trölladyngja, Iceland 8 D5 64 54N 17 16W
Trollhättan, Sweden 9 G15 58 17N 12 20 E
Trollheimen, Norway 8 E13 62 46N 9 1 E
Trombetas →, Brazil 93 D7 1 55S 55 35W
Tromsø, Norway 8 B18 69 40N 18 56 E
Trona, U.S.A. 85 K9 35 46N 117 23W
Tronador, Mte., Argentina 96 E2 41 10S 71 50W
Trøndelag, Norway 8 D14 64 17N 11 50 E
Trondheim, Norway 8 E14 63 36N 10 25 E
Trondheimsfjorden, Norway 8 E14 63 35N 10 30 E
Troodos, Cyprus 23 E11 34 55N 32 52 E
Troon, U.K. 12 F4 55 33N 4 39W
Tropic, U.S.A. 83 H7 37 37N 112 5W
Trostan, U.K. 13 A5 55 3N 6 10W
Trout →, Canada 72 A5 61 19N 119 51W
Trout L., N.W.T., Canada 72 A4 60 40N 121 14W
Trout L., Ont., Canada 73 C10 51 20N 93 15W
Trout Lake, Canada 72 B6 56 30N 114 32W
Trout Lake, U.S.A. 84 E5 46 0N 121 32W
Trout River, Canada 71 C8 49 29N 58 8W
Trout Run, U.S.A. 78 E7 41 23N 77 3W
Trouville-sur-Mer, France 18 B4 49 21N 0 5 E
Trowbridge, U.K. 11 F5 51 18N 2 12W
Troy, Turkey 21 E12 39 57N 26 12 E
Troy, Ala., U.S.A. 77 K3 31 48N 85 58W
Troy, Kans., U.S.A. 80 F7 39 47N 95 5W
Troy, Mo., U.S.A. 80 F9 38 59N 90 59W
Troy, Mont., U.S.A. 82 B6 48 28N 115 53W
Troy, N.Y., U.S.A. 79 D11 42 44N 73 41W
Troy, Ohio, U.S.A. 76 E3 40 2N 84 12W
Troy, Pa., U.S.A. 79 E8 41 47N 76 47W
Troyes, France 18 B6 48 19N 4 3 E
Truchas Peak, U.S.A. 81 H2 35 58N 105 39W
Trucial States = United Arab Emirates ■, Asia 46 C5 23 50N 54 0 E
Truckee, U.S.A. 84 F6 39 20N 120 11W
Trudovoye, Russia 30 C6 43 17N 132 5 E
Trujillo, Honduras 88 C2 16 0N 86 0W
Trujillo, Peru 92 E3 8 6S 79 0W
Trujillo, Spain 19 C3 39 28N 5 55W
Trujillo, U.S.A. 81 H2 35 32N 104 42W
Trujillo, Venezuela 92 B4 9 22N 70 38W
Truk, Micronesia 64 G7 7 25N 151 46 E
Trumann, U.S.A. 81 H9 35 41N 90 31W
Trumansburg, U.S.A. 79 D8 42 33N 76 40W
Trumbull, Mt., U.S.A. 83 H7 36 25N 113 8W
Trundle, Australia 63 E4 32 53S 147 35 E
Trung-Phan = Annam, Vietnam 38 E7 16 0N 108 0 E
Truro, Canada 71 C7 45 21N 63 14W
Truro, U.K. 11 G2 50 16N 5 4W
Truskavets, Ukraine 17 D12 49 17N 23 30 E
Trutch, Canada 72 B4 57 44N 122 57W
Truth or Consequences, U.S.A. 83 K10 33 8N 107 15W
Trutnov, Czech Rep. 16 C8 50 37N 15 54 E
Truxton, U.S.A. 79 D8 42 45N 76 2W
Tryonville, U.S.A. 78 E5 41 42N 79 48W
Tsandi, Namibia 56 B1 17 42S 14 50 E
Tsaratanana, Madag. 57 B8 16 47S 47 39 E
Tsaratanana, Mt. de, Madag. 57 A8 14 0S 49 0 E
Tsarevo = Michurin, Bulgaria 21 C12 42 9N 27 51 E
Tsau, Botswana 56 C3 20 8S 22 22 E
Tselinograd = Astana, Kazakstan 26 D8 51 10N 71 30 E
Tses, Namibia 56 D2 25 58S 18 8 E
Tsetserleg, Mongolia 32 B5 47 36N 101 32 E
Tshabong, Botswana 56 D3 26 2S 22 29 E
Tshane, Botswana 56 C3 24 5S 21 54 E
Tshela, Dem. Rep. of the Congo 52 E2 4 57S 13 4 E
Tshesebe, Botswana 57 C4 21 51S 27 32 E
Tshibeke, Dem. Rep. of the Congo 54 C2 2 40S 28 35 E
Tshibinda, Dem. Rep. of the Congo 54 C2 2 23S 28 43 E
Tshikapa, Dem. Rep. of the Congo 52 F4 6 28S 20 48 E
Tshilenge, Dem. Rep. of the Congo 54 D1 6 17S 23 48 E
Tshinsenda, Dem. Rep. of the Congo 55 E2 12 20S 28 0 E
Tshofa, Dem. Rep. of the Congo 54 D2 5 13S 25 16 E
Tshwane, Botswana 56 C3 22 24S 22 1 E
Tsigara, Botswana 56 C4 20 22S 25 54 E
Tsihombe, Madag. 57 D8 25 10S 45 41 E
Tsiigehtchic, Canada 68 B6 67 15N 134 0W
Tsimlyansk Res. = Tsimlyanskoye Vdkhr., Russia 25 E7 48 0N 43 0 E
Tsimlyanskoye Vdkhr., Russia 25 E7 48 0N 43 0 E
Tsinan = Jinan, China 34 F9 36 38N 117 1 E
Tsineng, S. Africa 56 D3 27 5S 23 5 E
Tsinghai = Qinghai □, China 32 C4 36 0N 98 0 E
Tsingtao = Qingdao, China 35 F11 36 5N 120 20 E
Tsinjoarivo, Madag. 57 B8 19 37S 47 40 E
Tsinjomitondraka, Madag. 57 B8 15 40S 47 8 E
Tsiroanomandidy, Madag. 57 B8 18 46S 46 2 E
Tsitondroina, Madag. 57 C8 21 19S 46 0 E
Tsivory, Madag. 57 C8 24 4S 46 5 E
Tskhinvali, Georgia 25 F7 42 14N 44 1 E
Tsna →, Russia 24 D7 54 55N 41 58 E
Tso Moriri, L., India 43 C8 32 50N 78 20 E
Tsobis, Namibia 56 B2 19 27S 17 30 E
Tsodilo Hill, Botswana 56 B3 18 49S 21 43 E
Tsogttsetsiy = Baruunsuu, Mongolia 34 C3 43 43N 105 35 E
Tsolo, S. Africa 57 E4 31 18S 28 37 E
Tsomo, S. Africa 57 E4 32 0S 27 42 E
Tsu, Japan 31 G8 34 45N 136 25 E
Tsu L., Canada 72 A6 60 40N 111 52W
Tsuchiura, Japan 31 F10 36 5N 140 15 E
Tsugaru-Kaikyō, Japan 30 D10 41 35N 141 0 E
Tsumeb, Namibia 56 B2 19 9S 17 44 E
Tsumis, Namibia 56 C2 23 39S 17 29 E
Tsuruga, Japan 31 G8 35 45N 136 2 E
Tsurugi-San, Japan 31 H7 33 51N 134 6 E
Tsuruoka, Japan 30 E9 38 44N 139 50 E
Tsushima, Gifu, Japan 31 G8 35 10N 136 43 E
Tsushima, Nagasaki, Japan 31 G4 34 20N 129 20 E
Tsuyama, Japan 31 G7 35 3N 134 0 E
Tsyelyakhany, Belarus 17 B13 52 30N 25 46 E
Tual, Indonesia 37 F8 5 38S 132 44 E
Tuam, Ireland 13 C3 53 31N 8 51W
Tuamotu Arch. = Tuamotu Is., Pac. Oc. 65 J13 17 0S 144 0W
Tuamotu Is., Pac. Oc. 65 J13 17 0S 144 0W
Tuamotu Ridge, Pac. Oc. 65 K14 20 0S 138 0W
Tuao, Phil. 37 A6 17 55N 121 22 E
Tuapse, Russia 25 F6 44 5N 39 10 E
Tuatapere, N.Z. 59 M1 46 8S 167 41 E
Tuba City, U.S.A. 83 H8 36 8N 111 14W
Tuban, Indonesia 37 G15 6 54S 112 3 E
Tubani, Botswana 56 C3 24 46S 24 18 E
Tubarão, Brazil 95 B6 28 30S 49 0W
Tūbās, West Bank 47 C4 32 20N 35 22 E
Tubas →, Namibia 56 C2 22 54S 14 35 E
Tübingen, Germany 16 D5 48 31N 9 4 E
Tubruq, Libya 51 B10 32 7N 23 55 E

U

W

X

Y

KEY TO WORLD MAP PAGES

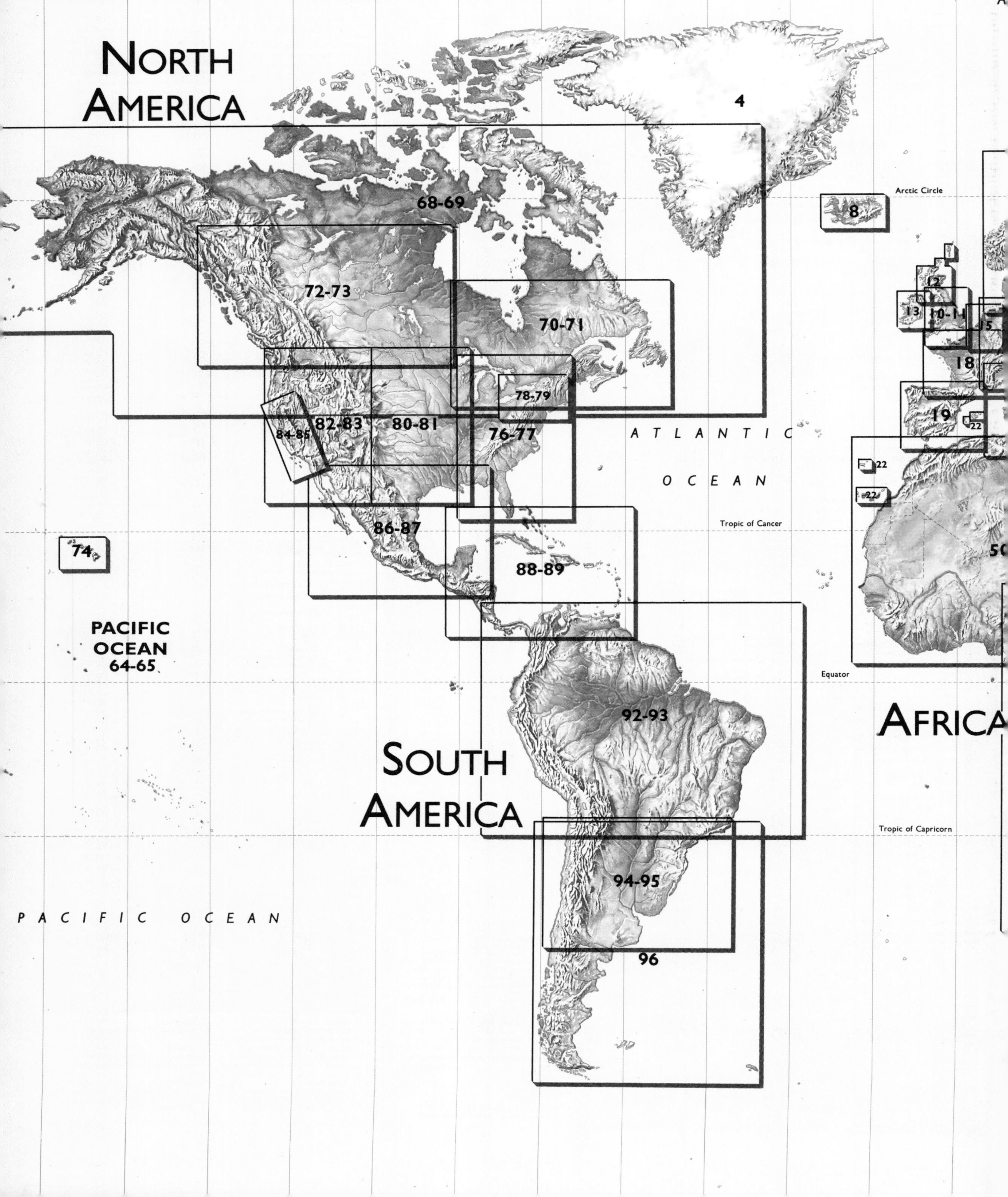

NORTH AMERICA
4
68-69
8
Arctic Circle
72-73
70-71
12
13
10-11
15
18
78-79
19
22
84-85
82-83
80-81
76-77
ATLANTIC OCEAN
22
22
86-87
Tropic of Cancer
74
88-89
PACIFIC OCEAN 64-65
Equator
92-93
AFRICA
SOUTH AMERICA
Tropic of Capricorn
94-95
PACIFIC OCEAN
96